access to plants"

Our greatest desire in producing this book was to reveal the treasures of THIS GARDEN EARTH, and make it simpler for our readers and fellow gardeners to gain access to plants and the skills necessary to grow them.

THE GARDENER'S CATALOGUE is a profusely illustrated compendium of sources and information for indoor and outdoor gardening.

Never before has this much "How To Do It, Where To Find It" information for plant lovers been compiled between the covers of a single book.

The Catalogue contains real information culled from generally untapped sources that amateurs, old timers and professionals alike will find new and exciting. Many of our illustrations were retrieved from collections of antique manuscripts and books rarely seen by the gardening public. They are placed among some of the most up-to-date bits of gardening data available, to create a texture of old and new.

Walk down a city street after dark. The blue glow of plant lights in many a window testifies to the boom in popularity of indoor gardening.

Turn the corner and you're likely to come upon a formal garden laid out on a once-vacant lot. An active community has replaced litter and broken bottles with beautiful flowers and shrubs.

Small plant shops appear in vacant store-fronts overnight, springing up like mushrooms. On tenement rooftops, in cramped suburban backyards, down back-country roads, people who never planted anything before are growing their own fruit, vegetables, herbs and ornamentals.

These are the new gardeners. They are generally curious people who want to learn the hows and whys of gardening. Most are too impatient to spend a lifetime of trial and error learning the skills for successful gardening. They want answers to important questions, now.

"My plants cost so much. Why are they dying? Can I feed three people from a third-of-an-acre plot?

"What's the best way to deal with crabgrass? Bugs? Who's the best source for tools? Fertilizers?

"Does gardening organically really affect the quantity and quality of my yield? Can I make any money from my garden?"

Whether you are an old timer or beginner, cultist or generalist, there is always a need for good information. The search for it is something all serious gardeners have in common—whether indoor gardeners, outdoor gardeners, fruit and vegetable gardeners, ornamental horticulturists, growers of great trees, growers of microscopic plant life, those that spray and those that ladybug, them that mulch with spoiled hay, them as swears by plastic mulch, the ones that can quote a hundred orchid pedigrees but still have crabgrass on their own lawns.

At first many people turn to the garden-center operators with questions. These operators like to be helpful, but most are tired of correcting the same misconceptions over and over again, and in any case are necessarily preoccupied with the salable materials on their shelves, especially the perishables. They are apt to throw up their hands in disgust and say: "Go on down the street to so-and-so. That guy'll tell you whatever you want to believe is true."

Then there are the gardening books. Even those with real information are apt to have it in thin and fragmented form. And many of the books contain merely a lot of pop wisdom or even outright misinformation.

Don't despair. Accurate information is available.

So far, about 250,000 different species of plants have been described. The government, universities and industry produce overwhelming amounts of material relating to almost any question you might ask about any plant and the plot it's planted in.

The gardening information produced by the government is under-promoted. Yet for the cost of postage, all the scientists working for the United States Department of Agriculture, the state extension services, and the various forestry and conservation agencies can become your own private think tank. These scientists work for the government. We pay their salaries. It's their job to answer our questions.

The universities develop a good deal of important new information. But professors can be a clubby bunch, publishing primarily for each other and for their academic reputations, refusing, for the most part, to be persuaded that they are responsible for public dispersion of their ideas. This is not entirely their fault. Most university presses make no effort at all to promote even the most significant of their writers' work. Yet the academics are a valuable source of good gardening information that can be exploited.

Turning to the horticultural industry, we find a small group of multi-million dollar corporations whose combined gross is billions of dollars annually. These large companies sell to a variety of jobbers, wholesalers and retailers. The horticultural giants spend huge amounts on basic research. The results, unfortunately, seem to filter down no further than the major commercial growers. Though the industry also prints and distributes lots of literature for consumers, great care must be taken to separate real information from product promotion.

Many communities are lucky enough to have botanical gardens, arboretums, horticultural or plant societies. These often have splendid libraries. Some offer very fine courses and how-to literature for beginners as well as specialists. For example, the Brooklyn Botanic Garden in New York gives many courses each year and publishes perhaps the most economical set of gardening pamphlets available. Plant societies also generally publish information magazines and bulletins for their members. And the library at the New York Botanical Gardens in the Bronx is exceptional.

However, in order to do their work all these groups depend on contributions from members. Many are staffed almost entirely by volunteers directed by a few professionals. The booming new interest in gardening has overwhelmed their ability to answer all the inquiries addressed to them. Since the main problem here is funding, we suggest you become a contributing member of the organizations you exploit for their information potential.

TABLE OF CONTENTS

The complete inversion of the furrow-slice.

The Most Important New Gardening Tool Since The Watering Can

We don't mean to suggest that a book can replace what you learn grubbing around in the soil. But good gardening sources are tools you will find very useful if you want good results. The Catalogue is the most extensive central listing of sources available to the gardening public today. Once you learn how to make use of the two pounds of data contained in this volume it will become an important gardening tool for you, too.

THE GARDENER'S CATALOGUE was not designed to be our personal statement on all aspects of gardening. It was designed to fill the gardening information gap. Therefore we have written very few of the articles ourselves. These of course do express our own viewpoints and carry our Ladybug Sigil. But the bulk of the material in The Catalogue was extracted from the sources we have mentioned above.

They are all sources you can explore yourself. Keep in mind that the material we have published in The Catalogue is only a fraction of what is available, if you know where to look. It's just a matter of having the right name, the right title, and the right address. That's primarily what THE GARDENER'S CATALOGUE is all about.

HOW TO USE THE GARDENER'S CATALOGUE

You may have guessed from our cover that The Catalogue is not necessarily the sort of book meant to be read by starting on the first page and ending on the last. As a matter of fact, this book was not designed to be read in any special order at all, though the meat of its matter is hung on the skeleton of botanical science.

The articles and illustrations it contains represent only the top of the proverbial iceberg as far as available gardening information is concerned. The words and graphics are meant to be entertaining as well as informative. However, the most important strata of this book is buried in the source lists and bibliographies.

Gardening is definitely a do-it-yourself pastime—unless you can afford to orchestrate a crew of gardeners and groundskeepers. So, now it is up to you. You can start digging by checking the Table of Contents, The Index, and the Lists. Or just flip through the pages until something catches your eye.

We have designed THE GARDENER'S CATALOGUE with a hypnogogic/catalogic density that will allow you to painlessly absorb hundreds, perhaps even thousands, of gardening tidbits by just continuing to browse through the pages, looking at the pictures, reading only what piques your curiosity at the moment.

But you may also delve deeper—find a book, join a society, send for a magazine or catalogue, take a course, and so on. The deeper you dig, the more you will learn.

Wherever possible, we have stressed good mail-order sources. Be patient when you use them. Some may be small companies, unprepared to handle the volume about to descend on them. Others are large wholesalers whose minimum order may exceed your needs by many levels of magnitude. Don't be peeved if you are referred to a local dealer and must pay the going retail price for the items you want. That's business.

Try to find the best deal possible. Get together with friends and neighbors to buy cooperatively. Not only will this give you more muscle in the market, but it also will put you in touch with others who work THIS GARDEN EARTH.

ARE YOU IN THE GARDENER'S CATALOGUE?

While THE GARDENER'S CATALOGUE maintains a strong consumer-protection stand, we also help the gardening industry by making the public aware of the many fine goods and services it makes available. Though many companies were not included in our listings, due to time and space requirements, The Catalogue is perhaps the greatest free public-relations job ever done for any single industry.

All we ask in return is that you in the industry treat your customers fairly and openly. Keep on sending catalogues, press releases and evaluation samples to THE GARDENER'S CATALOGUE, Evaluation Dept., P.O. Box 3202, New York, N.Y. 10001. If we missed you this time around maybe we'll catch you in our next volume.

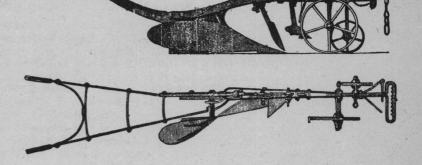

FEEDBACK: SHARPENING THE GARDENER'S CATALOGUE

Even as this volume is being put to bed, thousands of new bits and pieces of gardening information are flowing into our studio offices at THE GARDENER'S CATALOGUE. If this flow continues to come in at the same rate, we could go on clipping and compiling forever.

But first we'd like to hear from our readers. Feedback is very important to us. If The Catalogue is to be a useful tool in the future, it must be kept sharp. Your contributions and comments will help us keep our edge.

While this first volume has been entirely made from our efforts and the contributions of professionals, the next Catalogue should be built largely from your responses. Your letters and our new research, together, will make The Catalogue a backyard fence we can all gossip over to exchange gardening news and ideas.

Gathering and presenting THE GARDENER'S CATALOGUE was an enormous task. We have not had the opportunity to do business with every company listed. Nor have we completely read every book, pamphlet and magazine included in The Catalogue.

It is very important that you let us know how the dealers treat you and what you think of the literature we mention.

Let us hear about any gardening goodies, books, or sources of information and product you feel we have left out.

Remember to include the title, author, publisher and date of publication of any pieces of literature you send along to us. When recommending a gardening product, try to let us know not only the brand name, but the name and address of the manufacturer or distributor.

The best how-to information for gardeners is in the heads and hands of other gardeners. So write us about your garden, big or small, indoors or outdoors. Let's hear about your problems and your successes. If you have an anecdote or a bit of secret gardening lore you would care to see in The Catalogue, send it along.

Even if you don't feel like contributing, but would like to see more GARDENER'S CATALOGUES, send us a letter or postcard with just the word MORE.

Our address is:
THE GARDENER'S CATALOGUE
P.O. Box 3202
New York, N.Y. 10001

If you send something our way, please remember to include your name and address. Let us know if you move. Then, maybe someday soon, you'll see your name and material in THE GARDENER'S CATALOGUE.

Keep us sharp. Stay in touch!

THERE IS NOTHING FOR SALE BUT GOOD DEALS MAY BE COMING

At this point you can buy nothing directly through THE GARDENER'S CATALOGUE. Most of the ads in this book are antiques meant to show how little things have changed. All the where-to-buy-it information is contained in the source lists.

Many of our friends in the gardening industry have expressed amazement at this state of affairs. After all, they say, if you are publishing a catalogue you should sell something in it.

We explained that we were compiling an information catalogue. They still insisted that catalogues should sell something, and tempted us with some very good deals if we could buy in quantity. Maybe we might be involved in some things like that in the future. But if so, they largely would be dependent on you. Write and let us know if you would like to hear about these special offers from time to time. Also tell us if you would like to become involved in a seed- and book-buying cooperative. As we say elsewhere, buying cooperatively gives muscle in the market.

Let's hear from you. If the response is great enough we will put it all together.

As a reminder, our address is THE GARDENER'S CATALOGUE, P.O. Box 3202, New York, N.Y. 10001.

Always remember to include your name and address and zip number when you write to us.

MULTIPLICATION MEANS PROPAGATION

VIEW OF SEEDHOUSE AND WINDMILL,

WITH GLIMPSE OF PROPAGATING HOUSE AND ASTER AND DAHLIA BEDS.

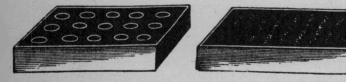

POTS OF SEED SUNK IN MOSS. SEEDS STARTED IN A BOX. SEEDS GROWING IN POTS.

PETUNIA.

As the young seedlings develop transplant to give them
room. Strong growth in youth means vigor in maturity

GUIDE TO PLANT PROPAGATION

When a gardener speaks of propagation, he is talking about the reproduction and multiplication of plants.

In flowering plants, seeds are the commonest means of reproduction. This is basically a sexual process—the union of sperm (pollen) and eggs (ova) to produce seeds. Seed production is practically universal among all plants grown in cultivation. It is, perhaps, the simplest method of propagation.

Given the right temperature and moisture conditions, any seed placed in the correct medium will germinate. Again, given the right diet, light and weather conditions, the help of wind, insects or the hand of man, cross-pollination will occur and give forth more seed, and so on, and so on, and . . .

By this means, it is possible to achieve enormous yields very quickly. For example, a commercial grower may start with five seeds of a species of bean plant. In six successive harvests he can produce 10,000 pounds of these particular beans.

However, from the grower and gardener's point of view, propagation by seed, in many instances, leaves something to be desired.

Some extremely valuable plants, especially certain hybrid varieties, are sterile and do not produce vital seed. For example, think of seedless navel oranges.

Other hybrids may set ample quantities of seed, but their offspring do not always breed true to the desirable hybrid characteristics the breeder has achieved. In order to preserve the valuable hybrid traits of the parent plant, another method of propagation must be found.

Finally, other methods of propagation yield mature plants in far less time than by planting seed.

These other methods do not involve sex cells. They are called vegetative propagation.

Some of these methods of propagation occur in nature. Strawberry plants, for example, multiply by extending runners and certain lillies form bulblets at the base of their leaves.

Other methods have been invented or improved upon by gardeners and farmers throughout the centuries. The most widely used of these methods of propagation are budding, grafting, layering, root cuttings, leaf and leaf bud cuttings, stem cuttings, and division.

Vegetative propagation works because every plant is made up of millions of living cells. Each of these cells contains the potentialities of the entire plant. So, as the salamander is able to regenerate a new leg or the lobster can grow a new claw to replace the lost or damaged member, entire plants may be grown from a piece of root or part of a leaf severed from the parent plant and then placed in the correct medium.

Recent experiments suggest that it is possible to grow entire plants from a single cell. This method, known as cloning, implies that from any given plant we might be able to propagate millions of offspring exactly like their parent plant. Think of what a breakthrough this would be in terms of preserving endangered species!

Generally, we suggest sterilized soil or a soil-less medium for starting indoor plants. The soil-less medium usually consists of vermiculite, sand and/or perlite. Its use eliminates the problem of damping off among young seedlings due to fungus or other plant diseases potentially present in unsterilized soil.

Try to germinate seeds in "Jiffy" type pots, using sterilized soil in order to avoid damage to new root systems and shock, resulting from cutting out plants for transplant. These mosspots disintegrate in the soil within a few weeks.

Out-of-doors, the ground should be loose before planting so the root section has a better chance to develop. Mix a soil conditioner like peatmoss or dehydrated cow manure into the soil to give plants a good start.

Refer to "Indoor," "Outdoor" and "Gardening Structure" sections for more specific information. Also, look at the charts and material throughout this chapter and experiment with all the methods. We have included our suggested reading list and some books offered by THE AMERICAN NURSERYMAN for professional growers. Most of these have not been reviewed by us, so let us know if you find them valuable.

Reprinted from pages 191–195 of the
1972 Yearbook of Agriculture

good seeds for plant propagation
and how they get that way

TO MOST PEOPLE, propagating plants from seeds seems a rather simple matter. You buy seeds at the hardware store or garden center, take them home, and put them in the soil. If conditions are right, in a few days you'll have some seedlings.

Many people do this year after year, blissfully unaware of the vast amount of work that has gone into making sure that the seeds they buy will yield disease-free plants, good wholesome vegetables, or beautiful flowers.

Seeds are the product of the labor of many men. Research scientists, geneticists, plant breeders, and seedsmen all had a hand in improving the seed that you buy.

They maintain the seed's heredity, and see that the seeds are free of diseases, are not contaminated with the unwanted seeds of weed pests, have good vitality and germination ability, and are protected against fungi and insects in the soil.

Heredity of a seed is as important to a plant breeder as it is to a breeder of thoroughbred racehorses. And, with seeds, heredity is more difficulty to protect. Many of the seeds we use today are from varieties developed for certain valuable characteristics. Once a particularly valuable strain is developed, care must be taken to maintain it. Cross-pollination from other strains must be prevented.

Another important characteristic of good seed is freedom from seedborne diseases. Some diseases such as halo blight and anthracnose of beans may be carried from one season to the next or from one field to another on the seed. One of the best methods of preventing this perpetuation and spread of certain diseases is to produce the seed in dry regions of the Western United States where these diseases rarely occur. Also, seed crops must be inspected for presence of those diseases.

Certain field and turf seeds are often contaminated with seeds of serious weed pests. One method of avoiding such contamination in crops grown for seed is to plant clean seed in fields that are free of the more objectionable weeds. Ingenious seed cleaning machines are used to remove contaminants. They work on the basis of weight, size, shape, or even the roughness of the seed coat.

Another significant seed quality characteristic is the ability to germinate. Because seeds cannot always be planted under ideal conditions, the ability to germinate over a wide range of conditions is especially desirable. That ability is often related to the seed's vitality.

The development and maintenance of good germinating ability and vitality in seeds require not only good production procedures but also careful harvesting, processing, and storage. Too much moisture on mature seed prior to harvest, mechanical injury during harvesting or processing, or storage at too high a seed moisture content or too high a relative humidity may be injurious to both germinability and vitality.

Seeds planted in soil often find themselves in a hostile environment. Nonsterilized soil contains fungi that can attack unprotected seeds. Some insects may also attack seeds before they can germinate. The seed corn maggot is an example. For these reasons, the proper treatment of seeds with seed protectants makes them more valuable.

Author B. E. CLARK is Professor of Seed Investigations, New York State Agricultural Experiment Station, Cornell University, Geneva, N.Y.

Coauthor A. A. KHAN is Associate Professor of Seed Physiology at the experiment station.

Fortunately, we have laboratories for testing seed quality. Some of these are maintained by seed companies for their own use. Some are private laboratories that provide services for various clients. Others are governmental (State or Federal) laboratories which are usually maintained at least partially to enforce laws requiring the labeling of seed quality. Most State laboratories will conduct tests for State residents for an established fee.

Seed testing laboratories can't measure all aspects of seed quality. Varietal purity is difficult to measure in a laboratory except for a few kinds of seeds. Freedom from seedborne diseases is also difficult to ascertain in laboratory tests. But the presence of objectionable weed seeds, seeds of other kinds of crops, and chaff or other nonseed contaminants can readily be detected by examination of the seed.

Ability to germinate can be determined by placing the seeds on moist material in controlled temperature chambers and also by chemical means. There are some tests of seed vitality that are now being used to a limited extent, but the science of testing seeds for vitality is still in the early stages of development.

All States have laws covering field seeds (corn, for example), turf seeds (such as lawn-seeding mixtures), and vegetable seeds. The laws of some States cover flower seeds, and in certain States tree and shrub seeds are also covered. The State laws regulate seeds distributed within each State and there is a Federal Seed Act which regulates interstate distribution of seeds. At present, the Federal Seed Act covers field, turf, and vegetable seeds but does not cover flower or tree and shrub seeds.

When you buy seeds, you can select them on the basis of required labeling information. If you are purchasing a lawn-seeding mixture, for instance, you can determine from the label the kinds of seeds that are in it, the percentage germination of each kind, and the date that the seeds are tested. After you have determined from a reliable source the kinds of lawn seeds that are best suited to your situation, you can use the required label information to select a mixture containing those kinds.

Anyone buying seeds from a commercial source is taking advantage of many services provided for him, varying all the way from the knowledge and skill of professional plant breeders to the protection of seed laws. In spite of this, there is sometimes a temptation to save one's own seed. If you are tempted to do so you should recognize that many of the safeguards of purchasing seed at a commercial outlet are lacking. Thus, your risk of failure in propagating plants from the seed you save is increased.

There are times when a gardener finds he has seeds left over from a previous season and he may wonder whether to use them or buy new ones. Some seeds are now being packaged

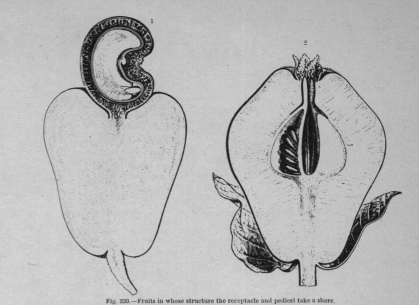

Fig. 330.—Fruits in whose structure the receptacle and pedicel take a share.

¹ Longitudinal section of the fruit of the Cashew-nut Tree (*Anacardium occidentale*). ² Longitudinal ... ough a Quince (*Cydonia*). (After Baillon.)

SEEDS

LAWN SEED MIXTURE			
Fine - Textured Grasses:		Germination	Tested
Kentucky bluegrass	30.00%	75%	1 - 72
Red fescue	20.00%	80%	2 - 72
Coarse Kinds:			
Annual Ryegrass	20.00%	90%	11 - 71
Ky 31 Tall fescue	24.00%	90%	12 - 71
Other Ingredients:			
Inert matter	5.55%		
Other crop seeds	0.20%		
Weed seeds	0.25%		
Noxious - weed seeds-None			
Lot No. B - 256			
ABC Seed Company			
Philadelphia, Pa.			

A sample seed label.

commercially in hermetically sealed containers. Such seeds are specially dried before they are packaged and, if the package is kept sealed without being opened, the seeds can be expected to stay germinable as long as 3 years.

The storage life of seeds that are not put in hermetically sealed containers will vary with their environment. They may die completely after a few weeks of storage under moist conditions, or they may live for several years under dry conditions. If you store any seeds from one year to the next you should have them retested for germination before you use them. You can test small quantities of seeds which would not justify the cost of a laboratory germination test by planting a few of them in a flower pot or other container filled with soil, sand, or peat moss.

Germination of a seed is one of the dramatic phenomena of nature. How efficiently a seed can be transformed to a seedling not only preoccupies seed growers and gardeners, but also offers a challenge to the seed technologist who is constantly experimenting to learn more about germination.

The biochemical revolution of the past decade has left an indelible mark on seed technology. We now understand more clearly some of the mechanisms governing germination. Recent studies have enabled us to predict and control germination to a greater extent.

Seed germination is a result of an interplay of environmental factors such as light, temperature, and moisture with a vast array of chemicals inside the seed. That these factors would have different effects on different seeds is only to be expected as no two seeds (even seeds of the same lot belonging to a species) are chemically identical.

Scientists have known for a long time that during germination of a seed there is a mobilization of storage chemicals followed with their breakdown into smaller molecules. Recent discoveries have shown that the plant hormones—promoters as well as inhibitors—play a decisive role in initiating or stopping these changes.

The hormones primarily responsible for controlling germinations are the gibberellins, cytokinins, and inhibitors. Each of these hormones has a different function in seeds.

Gibberellins play a central role in germination. The actions of cytokinins and inhibitors are secondary, and are essentially permissive and preventive respectively. The cytokinins will permit the completion of a gibberellin-induced germination when it is blocked by the inhibitors.

Based on the presence or absence of these three hormones, there are several hormonal situations or combinations likely to occur in nature in various seeds. Thus, depending on a particular hormonal combination, a seed could remain dormant or germinate. Dormancy in a seed can result not only from the presence of an inhibitor, but also from the absence of a gibberellin (primary stimulus) or a cytokinin (permits gibberellin action by opposing the effect of an inhibitor).

If all this seems too complicated, think of dormancy as a jailbreak that didn't happen, for one of several reasons. Either there was a guard on the wall to prevent it (the presence of an inhibitor); or the convict didn't want to break out because there was snow on the ground and he had holes in his shoes (absence of a primary stimulus or gibberellin); or he couldn't persuade a friend (a cytokinin) to restrain the guard while he escaped. So he stays in prison.

Gibberellins appear to be a must for germination of all seeds. In the absence of these hormones, germinative processes such as production of certain key enzymes are not initiated. Post-harvest dormancy of many grasses and grains of cereals is released by a treatment with gibberellins alone. A short moist prechilling treatment (5 days at 50° F.) or prolonged dry storage will also break the dormancy of these seeds. Both treatments increase the level of gibberellin in the seed, an example of changes in hormone level resulting from environmental changes.

The bur of the cocklebur contains two seeds, one of which is smaller than the other. The larger seed will germinate at maturity but the smaller seed is usually dormant. Gibberellin is ineffective in releasing the dormancy of the smaller seed. This seed contains an inhibitor which appears to block the action of gibberellin, thereby causing the dormancy. Dormancy in this or other seeds when clearly resulting from such a block can be released by treatment with a cytokinin. Cytokinins, thus, permit the action of gibberellin by opposing the action of inhibitors.

Some seeds, among them apple and pear, are dormant and have to be moist prechilled at 35° to 40° F. for extended periods of time to break their dormancy. Such prechilling occurs naturally in moist soil during fall, winter, and spring or it can be provided artificially by storing seeds in moist sphagnum moss in a refrigerator. The content of inhibitors is decreased by such treatment. Dormancy of the seeds can also be released to some extent by gibberellins as well as by cytokinins. A combination of these hormones is more effective than either one alone.

Another instance of a direct relationship between an environmental factor and a hormone is provided by Grand Rapids lettuce seeds. These seeds will germinate in light, but are dormant in darkness. If treated with gibberellin, however, they will germinate in the dark as well.

Some seeds with impermeable or semipermeable seedcoats fail to germinate even with the right complement of hormones. Seeds of geranium, okra, morning-glory, and various other kinds contain anywhere from a few to a large percentage of seeds in this "hard-seeded" category. To speed up germination, these seeds require abrasion of the seedcoat by mechanical or chemical means. Rubbing them against sandpaper or soaking them in sulphuric acid for a short time will bring about their immediate germination.

In nature, the impermeable seedcoats are eventually made permeable through the action of bacteria or by physical or chemical means as they lie in the soil.

Certain seeds have still more elaborate systems of dormancy and of germination. Instances are the so-called "two-year seeds," "double dormancy," "root dormancy," and "epicotyl dormancy," and combinations of two or more of these. In the case of the tree peony, the root develops normally when the seed germinates, but the epicotyl, from which the above-ground portion of the seedling develops, requires a low temperature treatment for 2 to 3 months before a complete plant can be produced.

In the case of freshly harvested Indian rice grass, seed scarification alone is not enough to promote germination. A moist cold treatment or gibberellin treatment after scarification is also essential for maximum germination. For *Trillium*, a common wild flower, roots as well as shoots must undergo low-temperature treatment interspersed with warm temperatures for development of normal seedlings.

In nature, self-preservation sometimes requires that a seed remain dormant when conditions are not suitable for survival of a young seedling. The seed finally becomes germinable with the advent of a new growing season. This environment-sensing capability of a seed is a highly evolved trait and appears to work principally through changes in hormonal balance.

For example, depending upon its

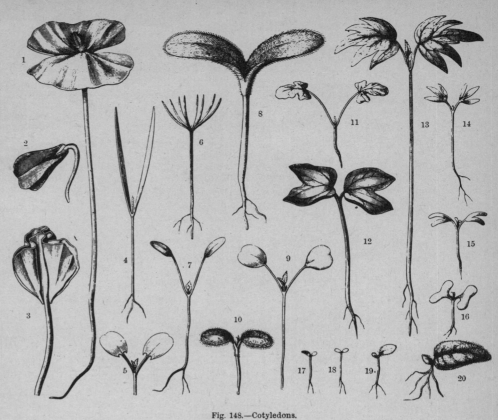

Fig. 148.—Cotyledons.

1, 2, 3 *Fagus sylvatica.* 4 *Fumaria officinalis.* 5 *Galeopsis pubescens.* 6 *Abies orientalis.* 7 *Convolvulus arvensis.* 8 *Borago officinalis.* 9 *Senecio erucifolius.* 10 *Rosa canina.* 11 *Erodium Cicutarium.* 12 *Quamoclit coccinea.* 13 *Tilia grandifolia.* 14 *Lepidium sativum.* 15 *Eucalyptus orientalis.* 16 *Eucalyptus coriaceus.* 17-20 *Streptocarpus Rexii.*

—Liberation of the Cotyledons from the cavity of the seed or fruit husk.

1

physiological state, a seed can be induced to germinate with no hormonal treatment (if essential hormones are present in the proper balance and concentrations), or by treatments with gibberellin (if gibberellin is lacking and there is no inhibitor), cytokinin (if gibberellin and an inhibitor are both present), or a combination of gibberellin and cytokinin (if gibberellin is lacking and an inhibitor is present).

Although propagators of certain trees and shrubs and a few kinds of grasses and flowers will encounter seed dormancy that has to be overcome before they can obtain germination, most gardeners will be using kinds of seeds that are not ordinarily dormant at planting time.

Even nondormant seeds, however, have relatively precise requirements for germination.

All seeds, of course, need the proper amount of moisture for germination, and that moisture is supplied from the medium in which they are planted. Satisfactory transfer of moisture from the medium to the seed requires good contact between the two. It is usually necessary to compact the germination medium over the seed to provide a good contact.

Germinating seeds also require oxygen. The amount of water applied to the germination medium affects the amount of oxygen available. If you use too much water the air is driven out of the medium and not enough oxygen is available to the seed. Therefore, the medium should be kept moist but not too wet.

Each kind of seed has its own temperature requirements for germination. Some germinate best at a temperature as low as 40° F. while others germinate best at temperatures above 70°. Still others germinate better when the temperature is alternated daily between a low and high temperature than at any constant temperature.

Most seed packets and various garden books and Extension publications provide instructions for planting individual kinds of seeds to meet their water, oxygen, and temperature requirements. For the successful propagation of plants from the different kinds of seeds, those instructions should be followed very carefully.

For further reading:
U.S. Department of Agriculture, *How to Buy Lawn Seed.* Home and Garden Bulletin 169, Washington, D.C. 20250, 1969.

SPECIAL SEEDS

John Brudy's Rare Plant House,
 Box 84, Cocoa Beach, Fla. 32931

Chesco,
 Box 10362, Santa Ana,
 Calif. 10362

Deedee's,
 Box 416,
 Menlo Park, Calif. 94025

De Sylva Seeds,
 29114 Tanager St.,
 Colton, Calif. 92324

Glecklers Seedmen,
 Metamora, Ohio 43540

J. L. Hudson, Seedsman,
 Box 1058
 Redwood City, Calif. 94064

Illinois Foundation Seeds,
 Box 722,
 Champaign, Ill. 61820

Kitazawa Seed Co.,
 356 W. Taylor St.,
 San Jose, Calif. 95110

Le Jardin Du Gourmet,
 Box 119
 Ramsey, N. J. 07446

Mail Box Seeds,
 2042 Encinal Ave.,
 Alameda, Calif. 94501

Metro Myster Farms,
 R. 1, Box 285.
 Northampton, Penna. 18067

Nichols Garden Nursery,
 1190 N. Pacific Hwy.,
 Albany, Oregon 97321

Clyde Robin,
 Box 2091,
 Castro Valley, Calif 94546

F. W. Schumacher Co.,
 Sandwich, Maine 02563

SEEDS

Burgess Seed and Plant Co.,
 Galesburg, Mich. 49053

Burnett Bros., 92 Chambers St.,
 New York, NY 10007

W. Atlee Burpee,
 Philadelphia, Penna. 19121

Burrell Seed Co.,
 Rocky Ford, Colo. 81067

Comstock, Ferre & Co.,
 Wethersfield, Conn. 06109

DeGiorgi Co., 1411 3rd St.,
 Council Bluffs, Iowa 51501

Farmer Seed & Nursery Co.,
 Fairbault, Minn. 55021

Henry Field Seed & Nursery Co.,
 Shenandoah, Iowa 51601

Charles C. Hart Seed Co.,
 Wethersfield, Conn. 06109

Herbst Bros. Seedsmen,
 1000 N. Main St.,
 Brewster NY 10905

Gurney Seed and Nursery Co.,
 Yankton, S.D. 57078

Joseph Harris Co.,
 Moreton Farm, Rochester,
 NY 14624

J. W. Jung Seed Co.,
 Randolph, Wisconsin 53956

D. Landreth Seed Co.,
 2700 Wilmarco Ave.,
 Baltimore, MD 21223

Earl May Seed & Nursery Co.,
 Shenandoah, Iowa 51601

Natural Development Co.,
 Box 215, Bainbridge,
 Penna 17502

L. L. Olds Seed Co., Box 1068.
 2901 Packers Ave.,
 Madison, Wisconsin 53701

Geo. W. Park Seed Co.,
 Greenwood, SC 29646

Evans Plant Co.,
 Ty Ty, Ga. 31795

Piedmont Plant Co.,
 Albany, Ga. 31702

Fred Stoker,
 Box 107, R. 1
 Dresden, Tenn. 38225

Seedway, Inc.,
 Hall, NY 14463

R. H. Shumway Seedsman,
 628 Cedar St.,
 Rockford, Ill. 61101

Stokes Seeds,
 Box 548
 Buffalo, NY

Otis S. Twilley,
 Salisbury, Md. 21801

SEEDLINGS AND TRANSPLANTS

Carino Nurseries,
 Box 538,
 Indiana, Penna. 15701

Flickingers' Nursery,
 Sagamore, Penna. 16250

Musser Forests,
 Indiana, Penna 15701

Raymond Nelson Tree Nursery,
 DuBois, Penna. 15801

Pikes Peak Nurseries,
 Box 670,
 Indiana, Penna. 15701

Silver Falls Nursery,
 Star Route, Box 5,
 Silverton, Ore. 97381

Suter Nursery,
 3220 Silverado Trail N.,
 St. Helena, Calif. 94574

Vans Pines,
 West Olive, Mich. 49460

Western Maine Forest Nursery,
 Fryeburg, Maine 04037

1 Gourd (*Cucurbita Pepo*). **2** Asafœtida (*Scorodosma Asa fœtida*). **3** Immortelle (*Helichrysum annuum*).
4 Cross-section through the cotyledons, showing them curled up in the pericarp of the Immortelle.
5 *Cardopatium corymbosum* Fig. 1–3, natural size; fig. 4–5, somewhat enlarged.

Annuals that often self-sow and that can be planted directly in the garden in fall

Calendula
Calliopsis
Centaurea cyanus (Bachelor's Button)
Cleome (Spider Flower)
Cosmos
Cynoglossum
Dianthus
Eschscholzia (California poppy)
Gaillardia

Iberis (Candytuft)
Larkspur
Lathyrus (Sweet pea)
Lobularia (Sweet alyssum)
Nicotiana
Nigella
Poppies
Salvia farinacea (Mealy cup sage)
Snapdragon

Perennials that grow easily from seed[3]

Achillea
Aethionema
Ajuga
Alyssum
Althaea
Anchusa
Anthemis
Arabis
Armeria
Artemisia
Aquilegia
Asphodelus
Aster
Asclepias
Aubrieta
Bellis
Boltonia
Campanula
Centaurea
Cerastium
Chelone
Chrysanthemum
Coreopsis
Delphinium
Dianthus
Digitalis

Doronicum
Echinops
Epilobium
Erigeron
Erinus
Eryngium
Eupatorium
Euphorbia
Gaillardia
Geum
Gypsophila
Helenium
Helianthus
Heliopsis
Hesperis
Hibiscus
Hypericum
Iberis
Incarvillea
Inula
Kniphofia
Lamium
Lathyrus
Lavandula
Liatris

Limonium
Linaria
Linum
Lobelia
Lotus
Lupinus
Lychnis
Lysimachia
Lythrum
Maclaeya
Malva
Mentha
Mimulus
Myosotis
Nepeta
Oenothera
Onopordum
Papaver
Penstemon
Polemonium
Polygonum
Potentilla
Pyrethrum
Physostegia
Platycodon

Primula
(common species)
Rudbeckia
Salvia
Saponaria
Scabiosa
Sedum
(common species)
Sidalcea
Stokesia
Tradescantia
Tunica
Valeriana
Verbascum
Veronica
Viola
(common species)
Sempervivum
Silene
Solidago
Stachys
Teucrium
Thymus
Trifolium
Yucca

[3] Applies to the more common cultivated species and assumes fresh seed.

SELECTED REFERENCES — PROPAGATION

Hartman, Hudson T. and Kester, Dale E.
PROPAGATION: PRINCIPLES AND PRACTICES
Prentice-Hall, Englewood Cliffs 1959

Hottes, Alfred C.
PLANT PROPAGATION: 999 QUESTIONS ANSWERED
DeLaMare, New York 1934

Kains, M.G. and McQuesten, L.M.
PROPAGATION OF PLANTS
Orange Judd, New York 1945

SEEDS
The Yearbook of Agriculture 1961
U.S. Govt. Printing Office, Washington 1961

Wells, James S.
PLANT PROPAGATION PRACTICES
Macmillan, New York 1957

A. Filling bottom of flat with coarse soil   B. Sifting soil on top of flat

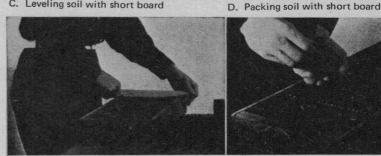

C. Leveling soil with short board   D. Packing soil with short board

E. Making furrows with thin strip of wood   F. Sowing seeds

G. Sifting soil over seeds to cover them   H. Covering flat with burlap

Flowers from Seed

USDA

TIME TO SOW SEEDS AND TO TRANSPLANT ANNUALS TO HAVE PLANTS READY TO SET IN THE GARDEN THE LAST WEEK IN MAY

Plant	Sow seed in	Transplant seedlings in:
Ageratum	March, third week	April, third week
Amaranthus	April, third week	May, first week
Anagallis	April, first week	April, fourth week
Babysbreath	May, first week	May, first week
Balsam	April, second week	May, first week
Bachelor's button	April, third week	May, first week
Calendula	April, third week	May, first week
California poppy	April, third week	May, first week
Calliopsis	April, first week	April, fourth week
Candytuft	April, third week	May, first week
China aster	April, second week	April, fourth week
Chrysanthemum	April, third week	May, first week
Clarkia	April, fourth week	May, second week
Cleome	April, third week	May, second week
Cockscomb	April, second week	April, fourth week
Cosmos	April, fourth week	May, second week
Cynoglossum	April, first week	April, fourth week
Dahlia	March, first week	March, fourth week
Dianthus	April, first week	April, fourth week
Dimorphotheca	April, first week	April, fourth week
Gaillardia	April, third week	May, first week
Godetia	April, second week	April, fourth week
Gomphrena	April, third week	May, second week
Hunnemannia	April, first week	April, fourth week
Kochia	April, second week	May, first week
Larkspur	April, first week	April, fourth week
Lavatera	April, second week	May, first week
Lobelia	March, third week	April, third week
Marigold	April, second week	April, fourth week
Mignonette	April, third week	May, first week
Mimulus	April, third week	May, first week
Morning glory	April, third week	May, first week
Nasturtium	April, third week	May, first week
Nicotiana	April, second week	May, first week
Nierembergia	March, third week	April, first week
Nigella	April, first week	April, third week
Petunia	March, first week	April, first week
Phlox	April, second week	April, fourth week
Poppy	April, fourth week	May, second week
Salpiglossis	April, first week	April, third week
Salvia	April, first week	May, first week
Scabiosa	April, third week	May, second week
Schizanthus	April, third week	May, first week
Snapdragon	March, second week	April, fourth week
Statice	April, first week	April, third week
Straw flower	April, first week	April, third week
Sunflower	May, first week	May, second week
Sweet alyssum	April, second week	April, fourth week
Verbena	March, second week	April, second week
Vinca	April, first week	April, third week
Zinnia	April, fourth week	May, second week

COURTESY OF ORGANIC GARDENING AND FARMING MAGAZINE

Some Words About Seeds

I have come to the conclusion that there is more ritual than facts in some methods of seed sowing and a lot of hokus pokus that passes for scientific "truth."
RICHARD ROE
Steubenville, Ohio

SINCE WE ALL WORK so much with seeds, but seem to take them pretty much for granted, it might be a good thing here to define what a seed is and what goes on when it germinates and takes root. A seed consists of the embryo, which is the dormant but almost complete plant in miniature; and the endosperm, which is the stored food the embryo needs in order to develop. The vital embryo is made up of a "growing point" or plumule, and a short, descending axis or caulicle. From this stemlet, the radicle or elementary root will develop. Again, the embryo is a complete but minute dormant plant which also is provided with seed leaves or cotyledons and a hypocotyl or stem which connects them to the embryonic root system.

The embryo can vary greatly in size and form in different seeds. Many of the so-called seeds are really fruits that contain one or two seeds. Among these are the seeds of beets, lettuce and sea-kale. Acorns, walnuts, butternuts and chestnuts are also fruit, so are grains of corn and wheat and also the seeds of the strawberry. Beans and peas are true seeds; the fruit part is the pod in which they are contained. Apples and pears are also true seeds; the fruit is the fleshy part that surrounds them.

The correct soil temperature is of the utmost importance. It varies with different seeds and can be controlled if you plant indoors where you can regulate temperature with a soil heating cable. But outdoors, you must depend upon the sun to heat the soil, and the following planting tables, suggested by Burgess Seed, should be an effective guide:

Varieties that can be planted early while the ground is still cool: asparagus, broad beans, broccoli, Brussels sprouts, carrots, cress, celery, cabbage, cauliflower, collards, endive, kale, kohlrabi, lettuce, leek, mustard, onion, parsley, parsnip, peas, radish, rutabaga, salsify, spinach, turnip.

Varieties that should be planted only when the ground is warm: lima and snap beans, corn, cucumber, melons, okra, peanuts, pumpkin, squash.

Varieties you can plant every two weeks for a continuous supply include: beets (greens), cress, mustard, kohlrabi, radishes, lettuce (*Oakleaf, Matchless, Salad* Bowl), spinach, tampala.

Finally, these varieties can be planted in midsummer for a fall crop: bush beans, beets, broccoli, Brussels sprouts, cabbage and cauliflower (all plants), collards, cress, endive, kale, kohlrabi, lettuce, mustard, onions (green), radish, spinach, tampala, turnip.

Another chart — supplied by W. Atlee Burpee — should be of interest and practical help to you as the time approaches to move your seeds and seedlings from the house to the garden. Note that seed germination temperatures are definitely higher than growing temperatures. Germination time in days is also given, which should enable you to check your pots and flats with some confidence.

GERMINATION AND GROWING TEMPERATURES

Crop	Germination Temp. °F.	Germination Time in Days	Growing Temp. °F.	Approximate Plants per One Oz. of Seed
Broccoli	70°		55-65°	
Cabbage		5		4,000
early crop	70°	4-5		
late crop	70°	4-5	50-65°	4,000
Cauliflower	70°	5-6	50-65°	4,000
Celery	70-75°	10-20	55-65°	4,000
Cucurbits	80-85°	3-5	55-65°	10,000
Eggplant	75-80°	6-8	65-75°	500
Lettuce	70°	3-4	65-75°	2,000
Onion	75-80°	4-5	55-65°	10,000
Pepper	75-80°	7-8	60-70°	5,000
Tomato			60-70°	2,000
early crop	75-85°	6	60-70°	5,000
main crop	75-85°	6	60-70°	5,000

Many methods have been used to speed and assure the germination of seeds. Rosa James has reported that bathing seeds in a weak solution of liquid manure brings quicker reactions. Francis Bacon did the same thing, using wine, while soaking the seeds of bramble fruits in vinegar is supposed to help germination. In Italy whole ripe olives are fed to turkeys. They germinate quickly after they have passed through the birds' digestive tracts. Thousands of seedlings appear as if by magic after a forest fire. The seeds have been brought there by animals and birds, and the heat of the fire has weakened or broken their hard, thick coats.

Richard Roe has reported that "gentle bottom heat is the single most important factor in the speed of germination." He cites snapdragon seed

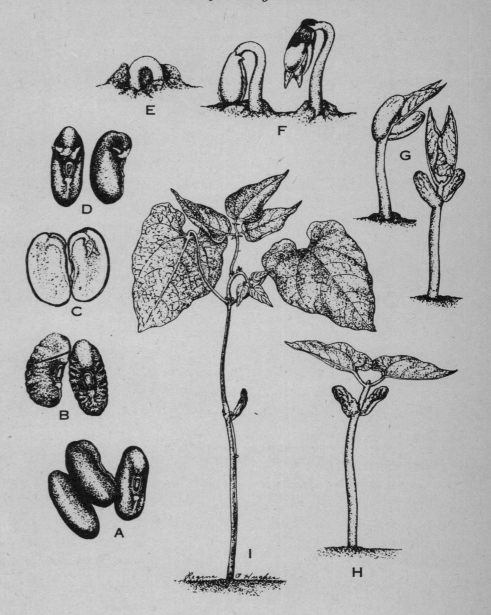

Development of a Bean

A, *dry seeds of beans;* B, *the seeds have imbibed water, the seedcoats are wrinkled;* C, *the seed opened to show the embryo;* D, *the radicle appears;* E, *the seedling is pushing up through the soil;* F, *the seedlings are up, part of the seedcoat still adheres to the one on the right;* G, *the seedlings are straightening up, the primary leaves are unfolding, and the seedling on the right shows how the two leaves are fitted together;* H, *the primary leaves are open and the stem has elongated;* I, *the trifoliate leaves have appeared.*

Yearbook of Agriculture, 1961

which requires 15 to 20 days to germinate in cool soil. "But in a warm room or with bottom heat, there is no problem in getting a high percentage to sprout in less than 10 days," he stresses. However, for best results, the heat should not be constant. Most seeds, he noted, "respond more rapidly to an alternating temperature, varying about 15 to 20 degrees during each day."

Out of his experience, gardener Roe has distilled a six-point program "for getting the highest percentage of germination from all seeds with a minimum of time and effort." Here they are.

1 — Don't sow seeds outdoors in the garden until the soil has warmed up enough for the type of seed you're working with. When in doubt check the "Germination and Growing Temperatures" chart that appears here. Bear in mind that all seeds will sprout more promptly in summer than in spring. This holds true even for peas and lettuce.

2 — Try to have the top inch of soil particularly rich in humus. This means you'll have plenty of moisture without rain or using the hose. The loose soil structure is also easier on the emerging seedlings.

3 — Don't cover the seeds any deeper than necessary. They need light and oxygen as well as moisture.

4 — When the seeds are covered, firm the soil to give them immediate contact with the moist — *but not wet* — soil. This practice is more important than any amount of future watering.

5 — If the soil is moist when the seeds are sown, no future watering is needed except for the rare seeds that take 20 or more days to sprout. The recommended procedure is to make drills for the seeds, soak them with water, press the seeds into the soil and then cover them with barely moist soil. A single watering is enough to insure germination — more may do more harm than good, Roe cautions.

6 — However, while seeds do not require a lot of moisture for sprouting, the seedlings that emerge do need water. Once sprouting has begun, give the seedbed or garden a thorough soaking. The ideal is to have the root zone moist while the surface is dry. This encourages deep rooting and subsequent resistance to drought.
M.F.F.

Producing better transplants

The variety of crops grown commercially in North America is very wide. They would include the various ornamental plants such as bedding plants, cut flowers, pot plants, shrubs, evergreens and ornamental trees. Another major section would be the food crops, including both the vegetables grown outside and those grown in greenhouses. Crops are grown for other uses also: tobacco, cotton, trees for lumber and for pulp, etc. Some of the plants that produce these crops are started from seed sown directly into the field, but many of them come from transplants, and it is that group with which we are concerned.

One fact is common to all these fields: in order to produce the best crop obtainable, *the best possible transplant should be used.* The more closely we can approach the growing of the "best" transplant, the better the possibility for maximum production from the crop we are growing. This is true whether it be tomatoes, petunias, junipers, chrysanthemums, tobacco, or what you may.

The basic characteristics of a "better transplant," however, are about the same for each and every crop grown. A sturdy plant with a well-developed root system is certainly essential. In appearance, the top growth should be bushy and stocky with full-bodied leaves of good color and sturdy, well-shaped stems—not a thin, spindly, weak appearance; nor yet an overly-lush, soft growth. The roots would be active, disease-free and extensively fibrous in order that the plant may absorb water and nutrients as freely as possible. Also, the better transplant would be young and actively growing—vigorous by comparison with others of a similar variety grown in the same climate.

Further, as the word "transplant" implies, this plant is one t̶ will be moved to another location to finish its growth. ̶ be transplanted to a field, garden, greenhouse bench, ̶ pot. Transplants may either be bare-root as they ̶ n the field or from flats, or they may be grown in ̶, such as a pot or plant band. Bare-root trans- ̶ e least expensive but they also have the poor- ̶ ate and almost inevitably suffer a checking of ̶ following transplanting. To grow the better

̶ *oot system should be disturbed as little as* ̶ s basically the most important part of the ̶ e anchor and the means through which ̶ ements are taken in for food. The roots ̶ carefully at all times in order to pro- ̶ lant."

̶ pot or peat pellet does this job as no ot̶ can. It contains the major portion of the ro̶ , and the plant suffers no setback or checking of ̶ owth when moved. Plants appear to make remarkably fast and vigorous growth in peat pots for reasons that have not been fully determined as yet. Whether it is the *excellent moisture control* that is obtained, the *superior aeration,* or the *nutrients in the pot walls,* one cannot say, but many experienced growers all over the world agree that peat pots and peat pellets grow **better** plants **faster.**

A suitable medium in which to grow is also essential to producing a "better transplant." For centuries, soil has been the accepted medium for this purpose, but good soil is becoming scarce and often expensive, and in some areas of the country is simply not to be found. For these reasons, we believe that a manufactured soil substitute may be the most satisfactory solution to these problems. An artificial growing medium provides the nice loose structure of good soil, together with the nutrients essential to good plant growth. Most of all, it is uniform from one year to the next, and makes it easy for the grower to establish a fertilizer program that will react in the same way at all times.

Of course we all know that plants must have nutrients available for proper growth from the time seeds first germinate or cuttings are planted until maturity of the crop. Even the best of soils or artificial growing media cannot supply all the nutrients required for most plants. In our experience we have found that a fertilizer that releases the major elements constantly, and as the plants require them for the whole growing period of the plant, is most satisfactory, both for producing the "better transplant" and for growing on the plants until maturity. A controlled-release fertilizer. such as MagAmp, is proving most satisfactory for this purpose.

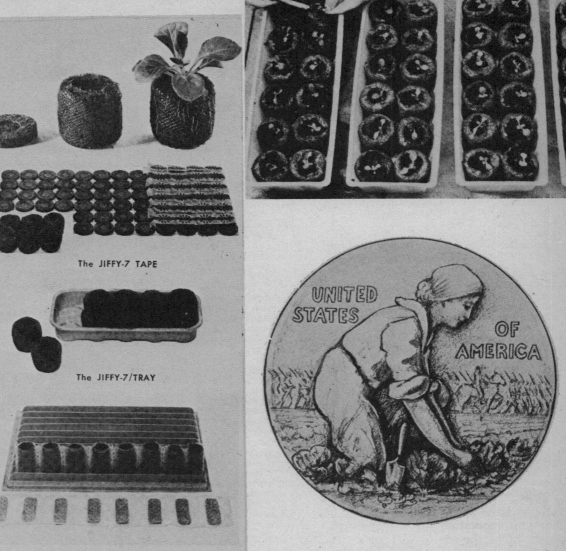

The JIFFY-7 TAPE

The JIFFY-7/TRAY

The JIFFY BELT

UNITED STATES OF AMERICA

Producing Better Transplants

HOUSE PLANTS AND HOW TO GROW THEM

SCIENTIFIC NAME	COMMON NAME	HOW TO PROPAGATE
Abutilon spp.	flowering maple	stem tip cuttings, seeds
Acorus gramineus variegatus		division
Adiantum spp.	maiden-hair fern	division, spores
Aechmea spp.	airpine	offsets, suckers
Aeonium spp.		leaf cuttings, offsets
Agapanthus spp.		seeds, division
Aglaonema modestum	Chinese evergreen	stem tip cuttings, air layer
Aloe Variegata	Kanniedood aloe	offsets
Amaryllis spp.		seeds (slow), bulbs
Anthericum spp.		offsets
Anthurium spp.		division
Araucaria excelsa	Norfolk Island pine	stem tip cuttings, shoot cuttings
Ardisia crenata	coral berry	step tip cuttings, seeds
Asparagus plumosus	asparagus fern	seeds, division
Asparagus sprengeri		seeds, division
Aspidistra elatior	cast-iron plant	division
Asplenium nidus	birds-nest fern	spores
Azalea spp.		stem tip cuttings, seeds
Begonia rex		stem tip cuttings, leaf cuttings
Begonia semperflorens		stem tip cuttings, seeds
Beloperone guttata	shrimp plant	stem tip cuttings
Billbergia spp.		division
Caladium bicolor		bulbs
Calathea sanderiana	Sanders calathea	division
Camellia japonica		stem tip cuttings
Capsicum frutescens var. conoides	tabasco redpepper	seeds
Ceropegia woodi	rosary vine	stem tip cuttings, aerial tubers
Chlorophytum capense	spider plant	offsets, runners
Cissus antarctica	kangaroo vine	stem tip cuttings
Clivia miniata	Kafir-lily	division
Coleus spp.		stem tip cuttings
Crassula arborescens	jade plant	stem tip cuttings, leaf cuttings
Cryptanthus sonatus var. zebrinus		offsets
Cyanotis somaliensis	pussy ears	stem tip cuttings
Cyclamen persicum	florists' cyclamen	seeds
Cyperus alternifolius	umbrella plant	leaf cuttings, division
Dieffenbachia spp.	dumb ane	stem tip cuttings, air layer
Dracaena fragrans		air layer
Dracaena godseffiana		stem tip cuttings, air layer
Echeveria spp.		leaf cuttings, offsets
Epiphyllum spp.		stem tip cuttings
Episcia cupreata		leaf cuttings, runners
Euphorbia pulcherrima	poinsettia	stem tip cuttings
Euphorbia splendens	crown-of-thorns	stem tip cuttings
Fatshedera lizei		stem tip cuttings
Ficus elastica	rubber plant	leaf cuttings, air layer
Ficus lyrata	fiddle-leaf fig	stem tip cuttings, air layer
Ficus pumila	climbing fig	stem tip cuttings
Ficus radicans var. variegata	variegated rooting fig	stem tip cuttings
Fittonia verschaffelti	tall fittonia	stem tip cuttings
Fuchsia spp.		stem tip cuttings
Gardenia spp.		stem tip cuttings
Gasteria hybrida		offsets
Gynura aurantiaca	velvet plant	stem tip cuttings
Haworthia spp.		offsets
Hedera helix	English ivy	stem tip cuttings
Helxine soleiroli	baby's tears	division
Hoya carnosa	wax plant	stem tip cuttings
Impatiens sultani	touch-me-not	stem tip cuttings
Kalanchoe blossfeldiana		leaf cuttings, seeds
Kalanchoe daigremontana		small plants form on leaves
Kalanchoe pinnata	air plant	small plants form on leaves
Kalanchoe tomentosa		leaf cuttings
Lachenalia tricolor	Cape cowslip	offsets
Lantana spp.		stem tip cuttings
Malpighia coccigers		stem tip cuttings
Mammillaria microcarpa	fish-hook mammillaria	seeds, offsets
Maranta Leuconeura var. kerchoveana	prayer plant	stem tip cuttings, division
Monstera deliciosa	ceriman	stem tip cuttings, air layer
Neomarica gracilis	apostle plant	division, new plants from flower shoots
Nephrolepis exaltata var. bostoniensis	Boston fern	division, offsets, runners
Notocactus leninghausi		seeds, offsets
Oxalis rubra		division
Pandanus veitchi	screw-pine	stem tip cuttings, offsets, suckers
Pelargonium hortorum	zonal or fish geranium	stem tip cuttings
Pelargonium peltatum	ivy-leaved geranium	stem tip cuttings
Peperomia obtusifolia		stem tip cuttings, leaf cuttings
Peperomia sandersi var. argyreia		leaf cuttings, division
Primula malacoides	fairy primrose	seeds
Saintpaulia ionantha	African-violet	leaf cuttings, division
Sansevieria zeylanica	snake plant	leaf cuttings, division
Saxifraga sarmentosa	strawberry-geranium	division, runners
Schlumbergera bridgesi	Christmas cactus	stem tip cuttings
Scindapsus aureus	Solomon Island ivy-arum	stem tip cuttings
Selaginella uncinata	blue selaginella	stem tip cuttings
Sempervivum spp.	house-leek	offsets
Senecio cruentus	cineraria	seeds
Sinningia speciosa	gloxinia	leaf cuttings, seeds
Solanum pseudo-capsicum	Jerusalem cherry	seeds
Stapelia grandiflora	carrion flower	seeds, division
Syngonium podophyllum		stemp tip cuttings
Tolmiea menziesi	pick-a-back-plant	leaf cuttings, offsets
Tradescantia spp.	wandering jew	stem tip cuttings
Veltheimia viridifolia		bulbs
Zantedeschia elliottiana	golden calla	seeds, division, bulbs

BOSTON FERN.

THE BOSTON FERN.
(Nephrolepis Bostoniensis.)

FANCY-LEAVED CALADIUM.

SINGLE FUCHSIA.

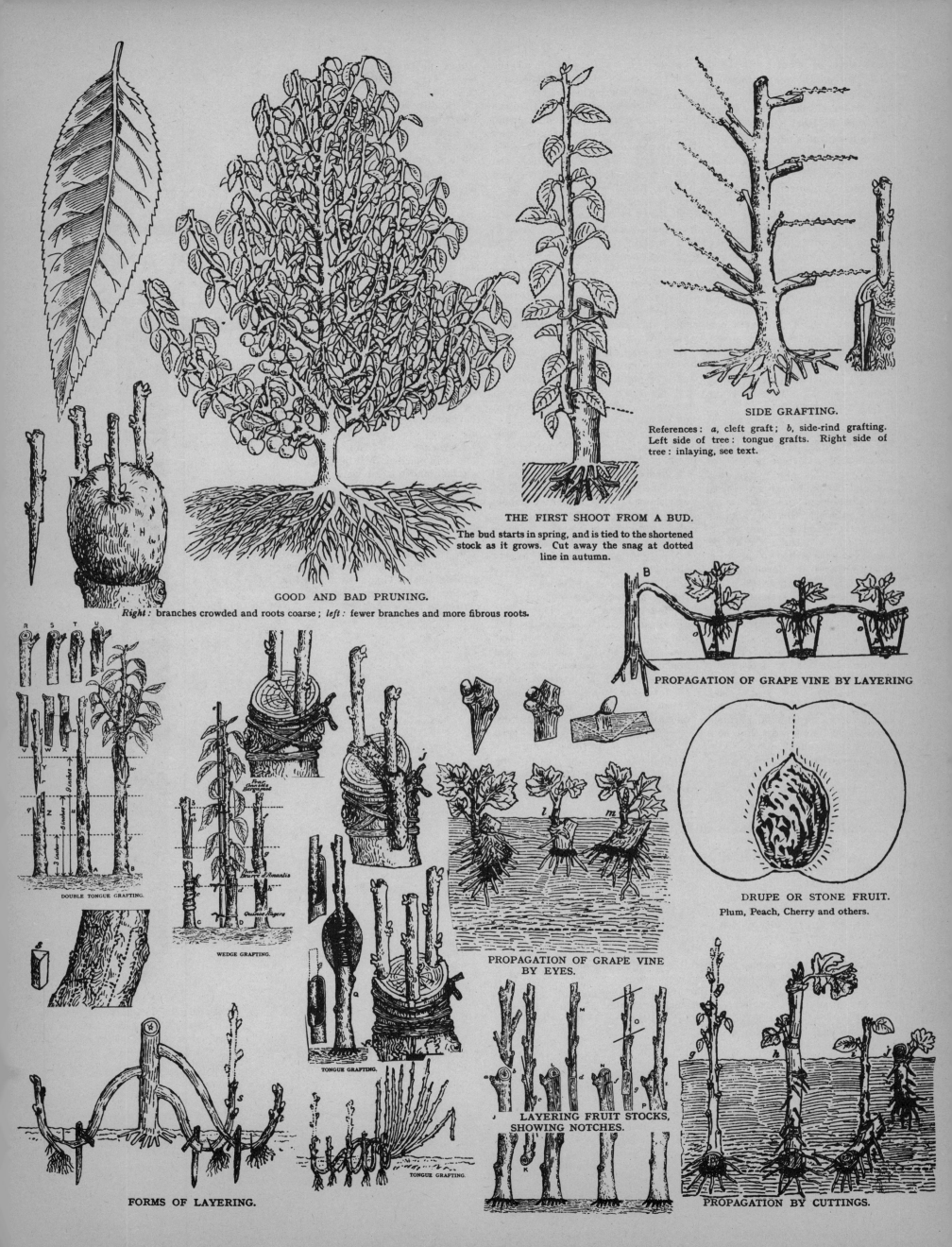

SIDE GRAFTING.

References: *a*, cleft graft; *b*, side-rind grafting. Left side of tree: tongue grafts. Right side of tree: inlaying, see text.

THE FIRST SHOOT FROM A BUD.

The bud starts in spring, and is tied to the shortened stock as it grows. Cut away the snag at dotted line in autumn.

GOOD AND BAD PRUNING.

Right: branches crowded and roots coarse; *left*: fewer branches and more fibrous roots.

PROPAGATION OF GRAPE VINE BY LAYERING

DOUBLE TONGUE GRAFTING.

WEDGE GRAFTING.

TONGUE GRAFTING.

PROPAGATION OF GRAPE VINE BY EYES.

DRUPE OR STONE FRUIT.

Plum, Peach, Cherry and others.

FORMS OF LAYERING.

TONGUE GRAFTING.

LAYERING FRUIT STOCKS, SHOWING NOTCHES.

PROPAGATION BY CUTTINGS.

Identification of plants with labels makes your garden more informative and complete. Visitors can readily learn names of plants they do not know, and the label helps your own memory if a plant is new to you.

The kind of label you choose will be influenced by the purpose. In seed starting projects, indoors or out, labels are essential to mark the space where seeds lie, and identify the seedlings when they come up. For this purpose, the label is temporary. You need not use materials that last a long time. The writing surface need not be large. Labels for vegetable gardens and gardens of annual flowers are also in this category. Label when you plant or sow seeds (indoors or outdoors) so you will have identification right from the start. This is especially important when you have several varieties of the same plant, such as tomatoes.

In perennial and rock gardens, labels may also serve to guard the places of plants during their disappearance in the dormant season, as well as identify them while they grow and bloom. For this you need a label durable enough to last many seasons outdoors, through hot sun and freezes, wind and rain, and to withstand even perhaps the knocks of the gardener's hoe or his misplaced foot upon it. Moreover, here you want labels that do their job without detracting from the garden's beauty and serenity. The aim is neatness and performance without being conspicuous.

In shrub gardens and for trees you need labels even more long lasting, thinking in terms of decades instead of just years. Such labels need to be of a durable material such as metal, and permanently attached in a way that does not damage the shrub or tree.

For container plants you have a choice of putting the label in the pot soil or on the outside of the pot. Since such plants are grown for their decorative effect, it is more important than ever that the labels be neat and not detracting, just large enough to carry the necessary words.

Write on the label enough of the plant's name to identify it for you. In an entire bed of daylilies, there is no need for every label to say "daylily." If it is an already-familiar plant such as monarda, there is no need to repeat "monarda." The variety names are enough. You may want to list the botanical names on new specimen plantings, or plants in a mixed bed. Many gardeners are interested in botanical names. A label may save you the embarrassment of a lapse of memory when a visitor asks what something is.

Some gardeners like to add the date of planting and the source of the plant. This information can go into a garden notebook if there is no room on the label.

Labels may be written with pencils, wax markers, or weatherproof pens made for the purpose and sold by label suppliers, stationery counters and stores. Use lead pencil or wax marker on temporary labels you plan to re-use. These marks are easy to clean off with scouring powder. Indelible inks are harder and sometimes impossible to remove.

Plastic embossed tapes (made with a label making tool) may be applied to plant labels. They make a neat appearance, and are good if you need something that will last just one season. Usually, unless under protective covering, they begin peeling off a plastic or metal label base within several months. Label makers come in ¼- and ⅜-inch sizes. The wider size naturally is more legible. This is a good type of label to affix to flower pots.

Plant labels of many descriptions can be bought in garden supply stores, garden counters and catalogs. Many gardeners also make their own, cost-free, from metal or plastic discards—perfectly satisfactory for temporary purposes but perhaps not handsome or uniform enough to install in the permanent garden display.

Here are some rules to help you have a well labeled garden:

1. Select a label appropriate to the intended use in durability, size and appearance, and a writing medium (pencil, ink, etc.) that will last as long as needed.

2. List enough information on the label to tell you what you will want to know about that plant.

3. Place labels uniformly in relation to plants in the garden. Most gardeners put them in front or at one (always the same) side. This way you can find labels even after the plants are overgrown.

4. Anchor label firmly enough to hold it in place against buffeting by weather and garden work.

5. Keep the labels neat in all respects, and as inconspicuous as possible.

6. When plants or plantings are finished, collect and remove the pertaining labels. This saves them for another season, and prevents a clutter in the garden.

by Bill Davidson

Chat-huant.

PLANT LABELS

Courtesy of
Flower and Garden Magazine
July 1974

Galvanized steel 15″ display marker with label frame holds aluminum card that fits through slots and folds back to stay in position. Makes permanent marker for trees and shrubs.

DIFFERENT TYPES OF LABELS COMPARED

Small wood labels are economical and good for temporary use with seedlings and pot plants. Unless treated, wood takes up moisture and writing becomes illegible in a few months. For longer term, dip these in paint or shellac before use.

Redwood in one-inch thickness cut to 2 x 24-inch size makes a good tree label driven into ground at the base. Write on it with waterproof marker; or rout name into wood with routing tool. Lasts many years.

Plastic comes in many grades, colors and sizes. White is the most readable, but conspicuous in garden. Good for one-season use on flowers and vegetables. Smallest sizes useful for seed starting and pot plants. Easy to write on with pencil or wax marker; may be scoured off for re-use. Also acceptable for labeling perennials and bulbs if marked with special waterproof ink pens. Most plastic is rather brittle, breaks easily with age or cold weather; cannot stand impacts. Tie-on or wire-on kinds that swing from wire stakes last longer, but the fluttering effect is distracting in the garden.

Aluminum foil—with name scribed into the foil with a sharp point. While relatively permanent, it wrinkles, darkens, and becomes hard to read unless marked over with metallic (weatherproof) ink. Some labels of this type have glass or clear plastic covers over the foil.

Zinc makes about as permanent as a label can be. Writing with weatherproof pencil soon becomes indelible as weather affects the surrounding metal. Inconspicuous, almost indestructible. Excellent for perennial or rock gardens; bulb plantings. May be pushed in to ground lebel. In time, zinc strips may work loose from wire stakes.

Galvanized steel is usually used for larger than average labels, and intended for permanent marking for high readability. Label area is replaceable (foil or plastic). Will last indefinitely.

HOME MADE LABELS

For temporary marking of seed flats or pots, cuttings, vegetable gardens and similar short-term uses, labels may be made from:
  Aluminum pie plates cut into ¾ x 4″ strips. Mark with a nail point or ball-point pen. Cut with scissors.
  Plastic milk, bleach or cider jugs. Cut the flat sides into ¾ x 4″ strips. Mark with waterproof felt marking pen.
  Wood tongue depressors, purchased at pharmacy. Mark with pencil.
  Plastic meat trays (from self-service meat counter) cut into convenient size strips. Mark with waterproof felt marking pen.

A GOOD SOIL is one that encourages good plant root and top growth by providing the right amount of nutrients, water, and air throughout the growing season. You may not have this kind of soil around your home, but with some knowledge and effort you can develop it.

The average homeowner has little control over the quality of the soil on which his house is built. The soil around your home may be very different from the soil of the general area. Extensive grading or filling may have removed or buried the fertile topsoil. Also, the heavy construction equipment may have compacted the soil so that water infiltration and movement in the soil is restricted.

Thus, poor soil conditions may be limiting plant growth in your garden or lawn.

What is soil? In simple terms, it is the thin covering of a mixture of weathered rock and organic matter on the earth's surface that supports all land plants. It is continually changing.

Mechanical disintegration of rock is brought about by frost action, plant roots, temperature changes, and erosion. Water, oxygen, and carbon dioxide produce chemical changes. The soil is alive with untold millions of microorganisms which decompose organic residues and convert them into humus.

When the remains of plants and animals are deposited under water, organic soils called peats and mucks are formed.

Chemical and physical properties of the entire soil profile must be considered in assessing the potential use of soils. This is extremely important in plantings around a home or in a small garden because the normal profile may have been destroyed by construction.

Roots of many plants grow several feet into the soil. If rock, cement, or other construction debris have been buried, they may interfere with normal root development. If these materials are abundant, they should be removed. Also, compacted subsoil should be loosened to permit water movement.

A soil contains different sizes of particles. The particles are classified as sand, silt, or clay—clay being the smallest and sand the largest. Soil texture is determined by the relative amounts of the sand, silt, and clay fractions.

A loamy soil is an ideal balance of these. It is a mixture containing from 7 to 27 percent clay, 28 to 50 percent silt, and less than 52 percent sand. As the composition changes we may move into a silt loam, clay loam, or sandy loam, all of which are good garden soils.

making the most of soil and water; sound practices for the garden

CLOSELY-MASSED ROCKS ON FINISHED STEEP BANK.

ROUGH UNGRADED BANK.

Author W. E. LARSON is a Soil Scientist in the Corn Belt Branch, Soil and Water Conservation Research Division, Agricultural Research Service (ARS), St. Paul, Minn.

Coauthor H. L. BARROWS is Chief of the Northeast Branch, Soil and Water Conservation Research Division, ARS, at Beltsville, Md.

The key to good soil texture rests in the word "balance". If there is too much clay, the size and connections among the pores are insufficient for adequate water movement and aeration. With too much sand, the soil loses the ability to store adequate water and nutrients.

Although a laboratory analysis is required to determine accurately the textural class, the homeowner can estimate the texture by feeling the moist soil. A soil with considerable sand feels gritty. A moist clay soil has a smooth plastic feel and will hold its shape. Intermediate mixtures of sand, silt, and clay will be less gritty or less plastic.

On small areas where soil conditions are not desirable they can be changed by adding sand, clay, or synthetic materials. For flowerbeds it may be desirable to remove the existing soil and replace it with a mixture of two parts loam, one part sand or perlite, and one part peat.

Structure of a soil is directly related to its texture. Moist soil materials will bond together to form porous aggregates. A desirable structure is one that contains aggregates of about one-eighth to one-fourth inch. The larger pores between aggregates provide for the drainage of excess water, while the many fine pores within the aggregates retain water for plant use.

A good structured soil will contain about 50 percent solid material, 25 percent water, and 25 percent air by volume. Most plants will not grow in very compacted soils.

Roots may not be able to penetrate the compacted zone, and because of the reduced air volume, those that do enter may not survive. Plant roots give off carbon dioxide and absorb oxygen during respiration. Either too little oxygen or too much carbon dioxide in the soil can slow or kill plant growth. Since oxygen moves into the soil and carbon dioxide moves out by diffusion, the rate of diffusion is critical and is reduced in compacted zones.

Clay and organic matter are the two most common soil constituents that bind particles. Too much clay favors large, hard clods when dry; too little clay results in a single-grained structure that cannot retain adequate amounts of nutrients and water. The clay content cannot be changed easily, but the homeowner may improve the soil structure by adding organic matter.

Presence of organic matter in a soil is the essential difference between a productive surface soil and a mass of rock fragments.

—A section through soil permeated by the protonemal threads of the Moss *Pottia intermedia*. (Magnified.)

A good garden soil contains 4 to 5 percent of organic matter which is intimately associated with the mineral particles. To maintain this, fresh organic materials—either plant residues or manure—must be added to the soil periodically. The added organic material not only serves as an energy source for soil micro-organisms and soil fauna (such as earthworms) but also furnishes nutrients that become available to plants as the organic material decays.

Soluble nutrients added to a soil would leach or wash below the root zone if there were not some mechanism for retaining them. Fortunately, both organic matter and clay retain most nutrients and release them to the plant roots as needed. This process is called cation exchange.

Since clay particles are negatively charged, they attract and hold positively charged ions (cations) such as calcium, magnesium, potassium, and ammonium. As these cations are removed from clay by plant roots, they are exchanged with hydrogen.

If most of the exchange sites are occupied by hydrogen, the soil is acid or sour. On the other hand, when most of the sites are occupied by bases (calcium, magnesium, potassium, or sodium) the soil will be neutral or basic. Generally speaking, soils in the Eastern United States must be amended periodically with lime to bring the pH (the measure of acidity) up to the neutral range.

Many plants can grow in the range pH 4 (highly acidic) to pH 9 (highly alkaline), but most plants grow best when the pH is between 6.0 to 7.5. Soil pH can be tested easily with test kits or indicator solutions. The pH can be raised by adding lime, and lowered by adding either elemental sulfur, iron sulfate, or aluminum sulfate.

Earlier in this chapter we referred to the water-holding capacity of soils. All soil water is not available to plant roots. During a soaking rain or irrigation, water moves into the soil pores by gravity and capillary attraction. By the end of the day following the rain, water has drained from the larger pores. The soil is then at field capacity.

When plants have removed water until they permanently wilt, the soil is said to be at the wilting point. The amount of water in the soil between field capacity and the wilting point is the available water holding capacity.

The soil structure, texture, and organic matter content determine the available water holding capacity of a soil. Sandy soils hold the least total water, and clays hold the most. However, the intermediate textures (loams) retain the most available water. Most garden soils can store from 1 to 2 inches of available soil water per foot of depth.

Gardens and lawns, when actively growing, usually require about 1 inch of water per week. If rainfall does not furnish this, supplemental watering is needed. Watering should be started when about a third to half of the available water has been removed by plants, and should be continued until the soil in the root zone is thoroughly wet. One good soaking per week is much better than more frequent light sprinkles.

Most lawn and garden sprinklers apply about a quarter of an inch per hour. This can easily be checked. Place one or more tin cans or other containers with straight sides in the area to be sprinkled and measure the amount collected.

Drainage of excess water from the root zone is just as important for gardens and lawns as is too little water. Inadequate drainage occurs in clay soils, soils with compacted subsoils, and soils with other impeding layers.

Where necessary, drainage may be increased by sloping the surface toward a drainageway, by providing furrows, by tiling, by deep loosening, or by a combination of these.

Soil will often settle around a house so that excess water will flow toward the foundation. If so, the area should be filled so that the slope is away from the house.

Furrows to prevent excess surface water from running onto a garden or lawn or to lead excess water off are often helpful.

If subsoils have been compacted during construction, loosening of the soil to several feet is desirable. For special plantings in high clay soils, it is best to replace the subsoil with a sandy or loamy soil.

A hole much larger than the initial root system should be made when planting shrubs or trees.

Some plantings are extremely sensitive to excess water during establishment. On larger areas, tiling may be desirable. Usually the design of a tile system requires technical assistance. For help contact your county agricultural extension office, soil conservation office, or a drainage contractor.

Although the practice of no-tillage on farms is becoming more prevalent, some tilling of the home garden is desirable. This is usually done in late fall or early spring with a motorized tiller or by spading. Tilling incorporates organic residues into the soil, loosens up compacted areas, and provides the home gardener with the nostalgic odor of freshly turned earth.

The desirable depth of tillage varies. Soils high in organic matter and with good structure need only shallow tilling, perhaps only enough to cover the plant residues. Soils that have infertile subsoils and compacted layers should be tilled as deep as practical while incorporating ample amounts of plant residues, manure, and fertilizer. This insures a deep root zone for storage of water and nutrients, and it will probably pay in reduced costs of watering.

Where wind and water erosion is a hazard, soils should not be fall-tilled unless the surface is protected with a cover crop or mulch.

Tilling for weed control should always be shallow. Deep tillage, especially close to the rows, damages plant roots. On many soils a shallow tillage to break soil crusts may be desirable even if weeds are not present. Breaking the crust will enhance water intake.

In this short discussion we have not gone into all of the soil and water problems facing the home gardener. We have mentioned those that probably have the greatest influence on the success or failure of the garden.

Fertilizers and mulches are also very important but are covered in the next two chapters.

For specific information about managing garden and lawn soils in your locality, contact your local county extension office, Soil Conservation Service office, State university, or a local garden or landscape dealer.

When establishing a new lawn or garden, the soil should be tested for lime and fertilizer needs. On soils needing lime and phosphate, ample quantities should be worked in as deep as practical. Working ample phosphate

YEARBOOK SEPARATE NO. 3808

Reprinted from pages 227–232 of the 1972 Yearbook of Agriculture

WEEPING BEECH

into the soil will meet the needs of plants for several years and will insure that the phosphate does not enrich run-off waters.

Moisture content of the soil at tillage is critical, particularly on soils with relatively large amounts of clay. Tilling a clay loam or finer textured soil when too wet or too dry often results in large clods.

At an intermediate water content the soil can usually be broken without destroying the natural aggregate structure. The proper moisture content can be determined very easily. Dig up a handful of the soil. Squeeze it. If it crumbles, the moisture is right for tillage. If it remains in a tight ball, it is too wet.

Fall tillage is usually desirable in areas where the soil freezes. Exposure of the clods to freezing and thawing helps to promote natural granulation. By leaving the surface rough, water can enter more freely and the soil will warm more quickly in the spring.

WEEPING BEECH IN WINTER.

fertilizer

Prepared by National Program Staff,
Agricultural Research Service

Soil in its natural state rarely is fertile enough for best growth of plants. Usually it is necessary to supplement the earth's store of plant nutrients before we can obtain the most vigorous lawn, the most abundant flowers, or the greatest yield of tasty and nutritious vegetables. The easiest way to furnish these added nutrients is through application of mixed fertilizers.

Fertilizer Recommendations

What fertilizer should you use? And how much should you apply? These questions are best answered by specialists at your State agricultural experiment station. These specialists will test a sample of your soil and recommend a program of liming and fertilizing for your plants.

Some States perform this service free of charge for State residents; others charge a small fee. For information regarding soil tests—how much they cost, how to take samples, and where to send them—consult your county agricultural agent. His office generally is located at the county seat.

Publications of your State extension service and the U.S. Department of Agriculture also are sources of information regarding kinds and amounts of fertilizer to use. Fertilizer manufacturers, too, generally supply guides for the use of their products.

Even after you have obtained recommendations for a program of fertilizer application, you may have difficulty in selecting a fertilizer from the many kinds that are available.

Fertilizer Materials

Garden-supply stores offer for sale a wide variety of materials for fertilizing lawns and gardens. Some of these products are considerably more expensive than others. They vary in price because of—

Nutrient content. Products containing a high percentage of plant nutrients—nitrogen, phosphoric oxide, and potash—cost more per pound than those containing a small percentage of nutrients.

Ingredients. Products containing slowly available forms of nitrogen cost more per pound than those containing quickly available forms.

Form. Granular, pelleted, or soluble fertilizers cost more than powdered fertilizers.

Added materials. Products containing added trace elements or pesticides cost more than plain fertilizers.

Package size. Fertilizer in a small container costs more per pound than the same product in a large container.

Are the expensive products worth the extra price? After considering their advantages over the less expensive fertilizers, you may decide that they are. Or you may decide that the least expensive fertilizer is satisfactory for your needs.

Package Size

As with most other products, fertilizers cost more per pound in small packages than they do in large packages. Packaging costs account for much of the expense of fertilizer merchandizing.

Paying the higher rate for small packages of fertilizer may be justified if you need only a small amount, if the ease of handling smaller packages is sufficiently advantageous, or if storage of large packages is a problem.

For greatest economy, determine the total amount of each kind of fertilizer that you need for one season, then buy this amount in the largest available packages.

MANAGING YOUR SOIL

Fertilizer application is only one step in effective soil management. For best growth of lawns, vegetables, and ornamentals, you should also provide the proper soil acidity, soil structure, and soil moisture.

You can adjust soil acidity by applying liming or acidifying materials. You can improve or maintain soil structure by working the soil properly and by incorporating organic matter into the soil. You can control soil moisture by improving drainage, by irrigating, and, where practical, by applying mulches.

For information on these essential steps, consult your county agricultural agent or refer to State extension or USDA publications dealing with the crops or ornamentals that you wish to grow.

Added Materials

Fertilizer mixtures containing added materials—trace elements, insecticides, or weed killers—are offered for sale by many garden-supply stores. These added materials usually cost more when bought as components of combination products than they do when bought separately.

Trace Elements.—Trace elements—more properly, micronutrients—are essential to the growth of plants but are needed only in very small amounts. Known micronutrients are iron, manganese, zinc, copper, cobalt, molybdenum, sodium, boron, sulfur, and chlorine. There may be others.

Do not apply trace elements routinely. Plants need tiny amounts of these elements, but an over-abundance of them may be toxic to plants. Apply trace elements only if they are recommended by your county agricultural agent or your State agricultural experiment station.

Insecticides and Weed Killers.—Fertilizer-insecticide combinations and fertilizer-weed killer combinations generally are designed for use on lawns.

One problem with such combinations is that chemicals are being applied that would normally be used less frequently or not at all. In some instances, fertilizers containing preemergence crabgrass herbicides are applied in the fall when, in fact, the herbicide should be applied in the spring. Some fertilizer-herbicide combinations injure or kill trees or shrubs when applied to grass under them. Pushing a fertilizer spreader back and forth under a tree or shrub often results in applying much more than the recommended rate of material.

Another problem is the concentration of the ingredients. There is no way of adjusting the rate of application for different uses.

Combination fertilizer and broadleaf weed herbicides are often applied when broadleaf weeds are not present in the lawn. Also, there is a tendency to apply fertilizer with a broadleaf weed killer in the summer when cool-season grasses should not be fertilized.

Homeowners should be aware of these problems and considerations when purchasing and applying fertilizer-insecticide or herbicide combinations.

Usually, fertilizers and pesticides are best applied separately.

CAUTION: Combinations of materials may be ineffective or even harmful. Their misuse can kill desirable plants or make the soil unproductive. Apply combinations of fertilizer and insecticides or herbicides only on the recommendation of your State agricultural experiment station. Never apply them on a windy day. Be sure your spreader is correctly set to avoid overapplication.

Ingredients

Nitrogen is the most expensive component of a fertilizer mixture. Slowly available forms of nitrogen—urea-form and other organic sources—are more expensive than quickly available forms. Therefore, the more nitrogen a mixture contains—especially slowly available forms of nitrogen—the more expensive the mixture is.

Before plants can utilize nitrogen from a fertilizer mixture, the nitrogen-source material must be soluble. The more expensive forms of nitrogen must break down into soluble forms—nitrates, or, in some cases, ammonium—before they can be used by plants. They break down slowly and release nitrogen to the plants over a long period of time. Less expensive forms of fertilizer nitrogen are already in available form; they can be used by plants immediately.

Fruits and vegetables properly fertilized with quickly available nitrogen are as healthful and tasty as those fertilized with slowly available forms. Because of their slow rate of breakdown, however, urea-form and other organic sources of nitrogen may be more convenient to use than the quickly available forms. One application of the slow-release forms of nitrogen may nourish the plants throughout the growing season, whereas several applications of quickly available forms may be necessary.

Form

Most ordinary farm fertilizers are granulated or pelleted materials. Fertilizer mixtures also are available in the powdered form but the granulated fertilizers are more convenient for you to use.

Pelleted fertilizers are not as dusty and they do not cake as readily as powdered fertilizers. They flow readily through fertilizer spreaders, and they roll off the plant foliage, reducing danger of fertilizer burn. Farmers prefer this form rather than the powdered form.

Fertilizer concentrates, mixed with water, can be applied by garden hose through use of a relatively inexpensive mixing device. Being liquid, these fertilizers are readily available to the plants; some nutrients are absorbed by the leaves of the plants. Because the materials are diluted considerably in application, there is little danger of damage to the foliage.

Nutrient Content

Manufacturers of mixed fertilizers are required by law to state on the container the guaranteed content of primary nutrients. These primary nutrients are nitrogen, phosphoric oxide, and potash.

The primary-nutrient content of a fertilizer mixture is indicated by its grade—a series of three numbers separated by dashes. The numbers show the percentage of nitrogen, phosphoric oxide, and potash, in that order, contained in the mixture. For example, a mixture with the grade 5-10-5 contains 5 percent of total nitrogen, 10 percent of available phosphoric oxide, and 5 percent of soluble potash.

These nutrients are commonly known as nitrogen, phosphorus, and potassium. They are used by plants in large amounts and are likely to be deficient in the soil. When you buy a fertilizer, you generally buy it for its content of these materials.

The relative proportions of primary nutrients in a fertilizer mixture determine the suitability of the mixture for specific soils and plants. Lawn fertilizers, for example, usually are highest in their proportion of nitrogen. Fertilizers for use on vegetables may be highest in their proportion of phosphoric oxide. It usually is wasteful, and may even be harmful, to use the wrong type of fertilizer. Follow recommendations closely.

Specialty fertilizers—manufactured in grades usually suitable for use on a specific kind of plant—are available for most garden applications. These specialty fertilizers include products for lawns, tomatoes, and azaleas and other acid-soil plants. Usually they are satisfactory for use according to directions on their labels, but they usually cost more than ordinary farm fertilizers of the same grades.

Fertilizers of several grades may contain the same proportions of primary nutrients. For example, 5-10-5 and 6-12-6 are both composed of one part of nitrogen, two parts of phosphoric oxide, and one part of potash, though 6-12-6 contains the higher percentage of these nutrients.

Fertilizers having the same proportions of primary nutrients generally can be used interchangeably. It usually is only necessary to alter the rate of application so the desired amounts of primary nutrients are applied to the area being fertilized.

Frequently the price per pound of the nutrients in fertilizer mixtures containing a high percentage of nutrients may be lower than the price per pound of nutrients in fertilizer mixtures containing a lower percentage. For example, 1 pound of 10-20-10 contains the same amount of nutrients as 2 pounds of 5-10-5, yet an 80-pound bag of 10-20-10 may cost only one-third more than an 80-pound bag of 5-10-5.

For greatest economy, buy fertilizer for its weight of nutrients, not for its total weight.

Lord & Burnham Irvington on Hudson
New York, N.Y.

HORTICULTURAL STRUCTURES

Generally, horticultural structures are used to expedite plant growth in northern climates during the winter season. However, control is the key here, and closed systems the ideal for commercial growers regardless of location.

In ancient Rome, aristocrats built cold-frames, hotbeds and greenhouses glazed with sheets of mica so they could enjoy expensive, out-of-season fruits and vegetables and grow collections of exotic ornamentals all year round.

Today, commercial growers talk in terms of putting thousands of acres under glass. The possibilities approach the realm of science fiction, conjuring images of totally enclosed, computer-controlled ecosystems, growing produce immune from the seasons and the weather.

Cold frames are the simplest form of structure for forcing. They can be knocked together from old window frames and scrap lumber. But, for a more permanent structure, consider building the frame of masonry or concrete.

Frames should be situated in well drained areas. They should face south for growing seedlings but, east or west exposures may also be used. For propagating cuttings, the frame may face north.

While cold frames are used primarily to aid propagation in warmer climates, they are also used for hardening off tender perennials and annuals started inside and intended for transplant outdoors in colder areas.

Hotbeds are similar in structure to cold frames, except they are heated. North of New York City in the east, or St. Louis in the midwest, a hot frame is a useful addition to any garden. They may be heated with decaying manure, hot water, steam, or electricity. The heat encourages more active growth, so be prepared to pay more attention to a hotbed than a simple cold frame.

Greenhouses are used to create an artificial envelope of climate by balancing moisture, temperature, light and gases in order to obtain more perfectly controlled plant growth than outside conditions allow.

In addition, these days, commercial produce is picked green, then shipped for several weeks before reaching your table. So, a family greenhouse may be the only way to get really fresh lettuce for salad.

The kind of greenhouse you may build is determined by how much land is available and how much time and money you want to spend.

Inexpensive, do-it-yourself greenhouses built of wood and polyethelene sheets are available. For example, plans are available from the Virginia Polytechnic Institute and State University. Companies like Lord and Burnham make several varieties of small prefab greenhouses. But, if you are considering a greenhouse for commercial applications or large scale serious gardening and do not want to invest huge sums for a glass house, the best bet is the 30' x 90' Criterion Polyethylene Greenhouse by X. S. Smith, available complete with heating, ventilating and inflating systems from the George Ball Corporation for under $4,000.

If you've built or designed your own greenhouse, send us some pictures. Let us know how you're doing.

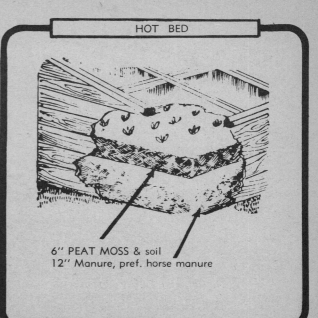

HOT BED

6" PEAT MOSS & soil
12" Manure, pref. horse manure

Lord & Burnham

CUTTINGS

Keep cuttings buried in moist PEAT MOSS over the winter

USE SOIL MIXTURE of equal parts PEAT MOSS & coarse sand

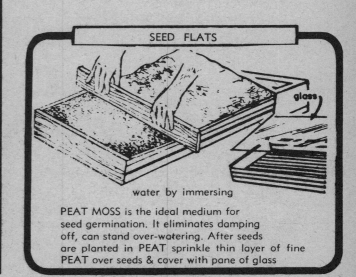

SEED FLATS

water by immersing

PEAT MOSS is the ideal medium for seed germination. It eliminates damping off, can stand over-watering. After seeds are planted in PEAT sprinkle thin layer of fine PEAT over seeds & cover with pane of glass

Annapolis Valley Peat Moss Co., Ltd.
Berwick, Nova Scotia
Canada

LIGHT GARDEN EQUIPMENT

Environment One,
   2773 Balltown Rd.,
   Schenectady, N.Y. 12309

Floralite Co.,
   4124 E. Oakwood Rd.,
   Oak Cree, Wisc. 53154

The Green House,
   9915 Flower,
   Bellflower, Calif. 90706

Grower's Supply Co.,
   Box 1132, 33 N. Staebler Rd.,
   Ann Arbor, Mich. 48106

Hall Industries,
   2323 Commonwealth Ave.,
   North Chicago, Ill. 60064

H. P. Supplies,
   16337 Wayne Rd.,
   Livonia, Mich. 48154

Lifelite,
   1036 Ashby Ave.,
   Berkeley, Calif. 94710

Lord & Burnham,
   Irvington, N.Y. 10533

Shoplite Co.,
   566 Franklin Ave.,
   Nutley, N.J. 07110

Tube Craft,
   1311 W. 80th St.,
   Cleveland, Ohio 44102

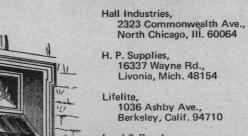

LATH-ROLLER BLIND.

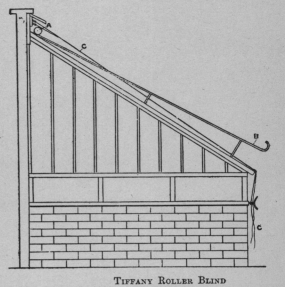

Lord & Burnham
Irvington on Hudson
New York, N.Y.

TIFFANY ROLLER BLIND
(Sectional View).

References: — *a*, roller blind ; *b*, light iron rod to elevate the blind ; *c*, draw cord.

Urbana, Illinois   Revised, April, 1972

Issued in furtherance of Cooperative Extension Work, Acts of May 8 and June 30, 1914, in cooperation with the U.S. Department of Agriculture. JOHN B. CLAAR, *Director*, Cooperative Extension Service, University of Illinois at Urbana-Champaign.

This circular describes a rigid frame greenhouse for home use which is attractive and can be constructed at low cost. It can be built with common tools, and the frames can be prefabricated indoors during inclement weather.

Covering. This greenhouse is designed for covering with rigid fiberglass panels or with film plastics such as weatherable vinyl, or inexpensive polyethylene. Construction of the framing is slightly different for corrugated fiberglass than for flat fiberglass and the film plastics (see plan in the center fold). For descriptions and recommended thicknesses of different plastic materials suitable for greenhouses, refer to University of Illinois Circular 879, *Home Greenhouses.*

Building the frames. The rigid frames are made of 2″ x 4″ construction grade fir lumber (or other grades and species having equal strength). A jig or pattern forming the dimensions given in the plan (center fold) can be made by nailing boards to a wooden floor, plywood sheets, or to other boards. The 2″ x 4″ members are then cut and fitted in the jig. The frames are made rigid by gluing and nailing ⅜″ AC exterior-grade plywood gussets over the joints (Fig. 1). Resorcinol-resin glue, which is waterproof and which sets under low pressure at normal air temperatures, is recommended for greenhouse construction. The frames should be stored level for 24 hours after nailing and gluing the gussets. A complete frame can be made from two 10-foot 2″ x 4″ members.

Size of greenhouse. The frames should be spaced according to the width and kind of the plastic to be used, but not wider than 36″ on center. Frames can be spaced 32 inches on center for 34-inch wide corrugated fiberglass, or 36 inches on center for polyethylene, vinyl, or flat fiberglass. Convenient greenhouse sizes for these frame spacings are 10′ x 10′8″ (5 frames) or 10 x 15 (6 frames), respectively. The techniques described in this circular can be used to build frames for a lean-to greenhouse (half frames) or for a greenhouse of larger dimensions.

Foundation. Two solid and inexpensive foundations are shown in the plan (center fold). The concrete foundation is recommended for a permanent, trouble-free installation (Fig. 2). Framing anchors or angle-iron braces attach the frames to the sill plate and foundation. Pieces cut 2½ inches wide from 2½- or 3-inch angle-iron and drilled for ⅜-inch bolts make excellent anchors.

Floor. A center walk can be made of concrete, flagstones, stepping stones, or pea-gravel and should be raised and sloped for run-off of water.

Crushed rock or stones can be placed under the benches for neat appearance and to catch excess water.

Installation of plastic. The frames must be notched at the peak and eaves of the roof to receive continuous 1″ x 4″ members for film plastics or flat fiberglass (Fig. 3). One edge of the eave and peak members must be beveled to form a smooth corner surface for application of the plastic. This additional cutting and fitting is not necessary for installation of corrugated fiberglass (Fig. 4).

Film plastics (vinyl or polyethylene) are attached with painted 1″ x 2″ fir or redwood strips nailed to the frames (Fig. 3). Flat fiberglass can be attached with round-head screws backed with neoprene washers.

The roof can be easily covered with corrugated fiberglass by cutting 10-foot panels in half. This will allow a 3- to 4-inch overhang at the eave. Two 34-inch wide corrugated panels, installed horizontally with proper overlap, exactly covers one side. Special rubber or redwood closure strips are used to seal along the edges of the wall and roof (Fig. 4). Detailed installation instructions, available from fiberglass manufacturers and suppliers, should be obtained before construction. Flat, rather than corrugated fiberglass, may be used for easier covering of the ends.

Benches. The greenhouse is designed for two 30- to 36-inch wide benches. The plan shows how to construct supports for the bench shown in Fig. 5. A permanent bench to rest on the pipe supports can be made of cypress or redwood boards. Prefabricated benches made of asbestos cement (Fig. 5) or redwood are available from greenhouse supply companies.

Paint. All wooden framing members should be painted with a good white paint. Special greenhouse paint, which usually contains a fungicide, is preferable. Paints which give off toxic vapors, especially those containing mercury compounds, should be avoided.

Benches and wood members in or near the ground can be treated with a good wood preservative such as 2 percent copper naphthenate. Never use creosote or pentachlorophenol preservatives in a greenhouse.

Heating and ventilation. The greenhouse must be properly heated and ventilated for year-round enjoyment. Thermostatically controlled exhaust fans, rather than manual vents, are recommended for positive ventilation of this rigid frame home greenhouse. Refer to University of Illinois Circular 879, *Home Greenhouses,* for information on heaters for small greenhouses, amount of heat required, and ventilation.

Approximate Material Costs for a 10′ x 10′8″ Rigid Frame Home Greenhouse

Framing (lumber, glue, nails)	$ 50-60
Plastic (including necessary fasteners)	
Fiberglass	125–175
Vinyl	25–35
Polyethylene	15–20
Foundation	
Post	15–25
Concrete	30–50
Heater	75–125
Ventilation fan (shutters, wall box, guard, thermostat)	75–100
Benches (two 3′ x 10′, redwood or asbestos)	50–75

Gray's Conservatory.

DO IT YOURSELF

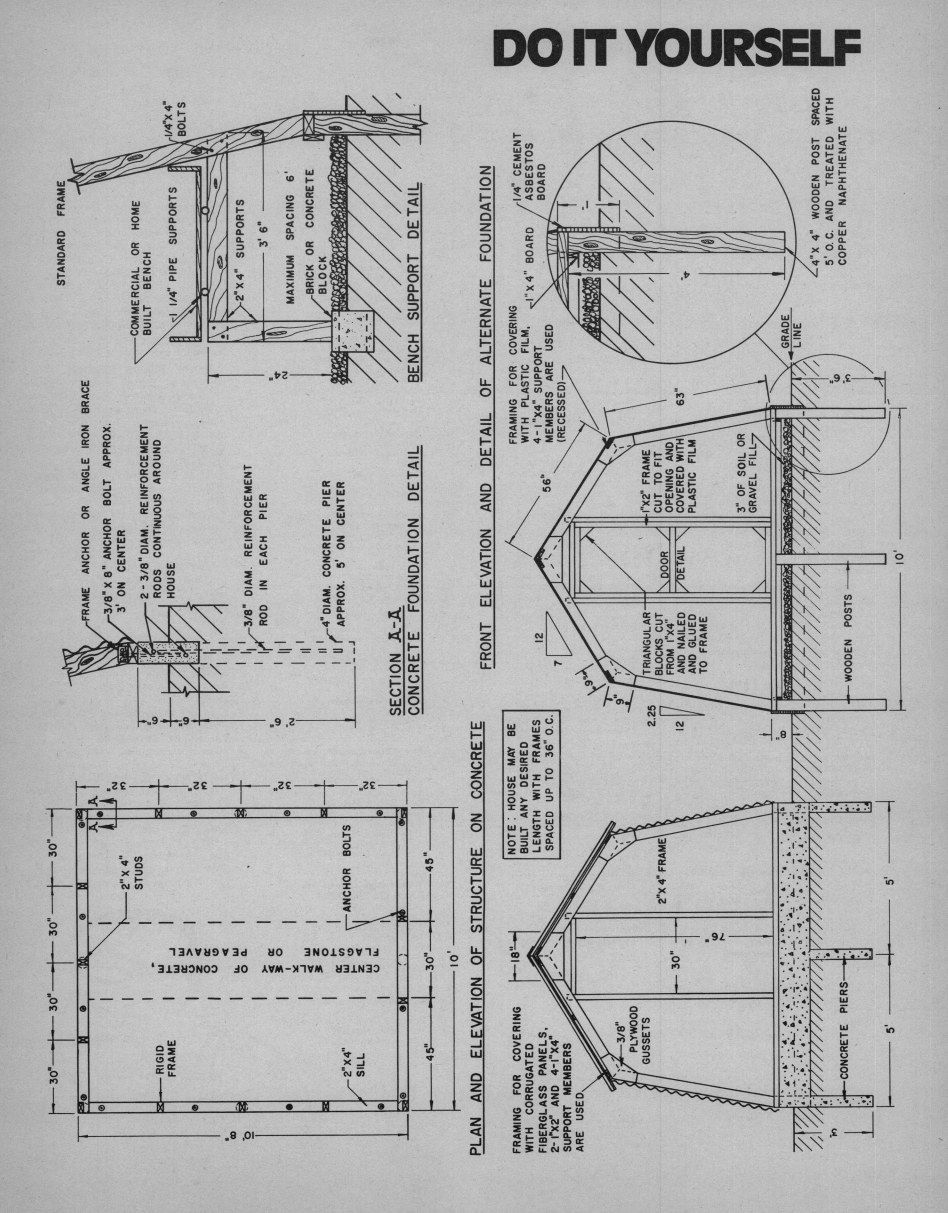

STANDARD FRAME

1/4"x 4" BOLTS

COMMERCIAL OR HOME BUILT BENCH

1 1/4" PIPE SUPPORTS

2"x 4" SUPPORTS

3' 6"

MAXIMUM SPACING 6'

BRICK OR CONCRETE BLOCK

24"

BENCH SUPPORT DETAIL

FRAME ANCHOR OR ANGLE IRON BRACE

3/8" X 8" ANCHOR BOLT APPROX. 3' ON CENTER

2 - 3/8" DIAM. REINFORCEMENT RODS CONTINUOUS AROUND HOUSE

3/8" DIAM. REINFORCEMENT ROD IN EACH PIER

4" DIAM. CONCRETE PIER APPROX. 5' ON CENTER

6" 6" 2' 6"

SECTION A-A
CONCRETE FOUNDATION DETAIL

FRAMING FOR COVERING WITH PLASTIC FILM, 4 - 1"x4" SUPPORT MEMBERS ARE USED (RECESSED)

1/4" CEMENT ASBESTOS BOARD

1"X 4" BOARD

4"X 4" WOODEN POST SPACED 5' O.C. AND TREATED WITH COPPER NAPHTHENATE

4'

1'

63"

56"

1"x2" FRAME CUT TO FIT OPENING AND COVERED WITH PLASTIC FILM

DOOR DETAIL

3" OF SOIL OR GRAVEL FILL

GRADE LINE

3' 6"

10'

WOODEN POSTS

12 7

TRIANGULAR BLOCKS CUT FROM 1"x4" AND NAILED AND GLUED TO FRAME

9" 9"

2.25 12

8"

FRONT ELEVATION AND DETAIL OF ALTERNATE FOUNDATION

32" 32" 32" 32"

30"

30"

2"x 4" STUDS

30"

ANCHOR BOLTS

30"

CENTER WALK-WAY OF CONCRETE, FLAGSTONE OR PEAGRAVEL

45"

30"

30"

45"

10'

RIGID FRAME

2"x 4" SILL

10' 8"

PLAN AND ELEVATION OF STRUCTURE ON CONCRETE

NOTE: HOUSE MAY BE BUILT ANY DESIRED LENGTH WITH FRAMES SPACED UP TO 36" O.C.

18"

2"X 4" FRAME

76"

30"

3/8" PLYWOOD GUSSETS

5'

5'

CONCRETE PIERS

3"

FRAMING FOR COVERING WITH CORRUGATED FIBERGLASS PANELS, 2-1"X2" AND 4-1"X4" SUPPORT MEMBERS ARE USED

Prepared by J. W. Courter, Associate Professor of Horticulture, and J. O. Curtis, Professor of Agricultural Engineering.

BOOKS

Ball, Vic., ed. 1965.
THE BALL RED BOOK. 11th ed. 368 pp.
Geo. J. Ball, Inc., West Chicago, Ill.

Berry, A. K. 1965.
BUILDING A GREENHOUSE AND POTTING
SHED. 104 pp.
Pergamon Press, Inc., 4401 21st St., Long
Island City, N. Y. 11101.

Bewley, W. F. 1963.
COMMERCIAL GLASSHOUSE CROPS.
Revised ed. 523 pp.
Transatlantic Arts, Inc., 105 Blue
Spruce Rd., Levittown, N. Y. 11756

Dulles, Marion. 1956.
GREENHOUSE GARDENING AROUND
THE YEAR. 195 pp.
MacMillan Co., 60 5th Ave., New York,
N.Y. 10011.

Jackson, P. G. 1965.
GLASSHOUSES. 122 pp.
Longmans, Green and Co., Ltd.,
48 Grosvenor St., London W. 1,
England.

Langfield, Paul. 1964.
A TO Z OF GREENHOUSE PLANTS;
A GUIDE FOR BEGINNERS. 107 pp.
Max Parrish and Co., Ltd., 6
Chandoes St., London, W. 1,
England.

Laurie, Alex, Kiplinger, D. C., and
Nelson, K. S. 1958.
COMMERCIAL FLOWER FORCING.
6th ed.
McGraw-Hill Book Co., 330 West
42nd St., New York, N. Y. 10036.

Laurie, Alex, and Ries, V. H. 1950.
FLORICULTURE, FUNDAMENTALS
AND PRACTICES. 2d ed.
McGraw-Hill Book Co., 330 West
42nd St., New York, N. Y. 10036.

Lewis, C. C. 1965.
THE GREENHOUSE. 222 pp.
Pergamon Press, Inc., 4401 21st St.,
Long Island City, N. Y. 11101.

Menage, R. H. 1964.
INTRODUCTION TO GREENHOUSE
GARDENING. 201 pp.
Phoenix House, Ltd., Aldine House,
10-13 Bedford St., Strand,
London, W. C. 2, England.

Nelson, K. S. 1967.
FLOWER AND PLANT PRODUCTION
IN THE GREENHOUSE. 2d ed.
335 pp.
Interstate Printers and Publishers, Inc.,
19 N. Jackson St., Danville, Ill.
61832.

Noble, Mary, and Merkel, J. L. 1956.
GARDENING IN A SMALL GREEN-
HOUSE. 236 pp.
D. Van Nostrand Co., 120 Alexander St.,
Princeton, N. J. 08540.

Northen, H. T., and Northen, R. T.
1956.
COMPLETE BOOK OF GREENHOUSE
GARDENING. 353 pp.
Ronald Press Co., 15 E. 26th St.,
New York, N. Y. 10010.

Potter, C. H. 1967.
GREENHOUSE: PLACE OF MAGIC.
255 pp.
E. P. Dutton and Co., Inc., 201 Park
Ave. S., New York, N.Y. 10003.

Preston, F. G. 1958.
GREENHOUSE; A COMPLETE GUIDE
TO THE CONSTRUCTION AND
MANAGEMENT OF GREENHOUSES
OF ALL KINDS. 640 pp.
Taplinger Publishing Co., Inc., 29
East 10th St., New York, N.Y.
10003.

Taylor, Kathryn S., and Gregg,
Edith W. 1969.
WINTER FLOWERS IN GREENHOUSE
AND SUN HEATED PIT.
Charles Scribner and Sons, New York,
N. Y. 10017.

Sources for Greenhouse Accessories

George J. Ball, Inc.
West Chicago, Illinois 60185
seeds, plants, rooted cuttings,
greenhouse supplies

Dillon Industries, Inc.
P. O. Box 224
Melrose, Massachusetts 02176
soil pasteurizers

Florist Products
1843 E. Oakton
Des Plaines, Illinois 60018
greenhouse supplies

H. P. Supplies
Box 18101
Cleveland, Ohio 44118
lighting and watering devices

Humex, Ltd.
5 High Road
Byfleet, Weybridge, Surrey
England
or
E. and W. International
290 Sandringham Road
Rochester, New York 14610
automatic nonelectric watering devices, automatic capillary watering
devices, nonelectric automatic
ventilators, shading devices, ten-
siometers (devices for measuring
need of watering)

Walter F. Nicke
P. O. Box 71
Hudson, New York 12534
general supplies

Al Saffer and Co., Inc.
130 West 28th St.
New York, New York 10001
chemicals, greenhouse accessories

Shoplite Co., Inc.
566 Franklin Ave.
Nutley, New Jersey 07110
fluorescent lighting supplies

X. S. Smith Company
Box 272
Red Bank, New Jersey 07701
black cloth for shading chrysanthemums

Sudbury Laboratory, Inc.
Box 1028
Sudbury, Massachusetts 01776
soil testing equipment

The House Plant Corner
P. O. Box 810
Oxford, Maryland 21654
general plant aids

The Modern Greenhouse
Manufacturing Co.
2511 Jackson St. N. E.
Minneapolis, Minn. 55418

National Greenhouse Co.
Pana, Ill. 62557

J. A. Nearing Co., Inc.
10788 Tucker St.
Beltsville, Md. 20705

Noordlan Greenhouse
1059 Bellmore Rd.
North Bellmore, N. Y. 11710

Pacific Coast Greenhouse
Manufacturing Co.
525 East Bayshore Highway
Redwood City, Calif. 94063

Pan American Hydroponics, Inc.
Post Office Box 470
Grapevine, Tex. 76051

Patio Greenhouses
Department PP
Opelika, Ala. 36801

Plant Products Corp.
Blue Point
Hicksville, N. Y. 11715

Redfern's Prefab Greenhouse
Manufacturing Co.
3482 Scotts Valley Dr.
Santa Cruz, Calif. 95060

Peter Reimulle
Greenhouseman
Box 5276-F1
Riverside, Calif. 92507

Rough Bros.
4229 Spring Grove Ave.
Cincinnati, Ohio 45223

W. S. Rough Sales Co.
Post Office Box 98
Bloomington, Ill. 61701

Stearns Greenhouses
98 Taylor St.
Neponset
Boston, Mass. 02122

Sturdi-Built Manufacturing Co.
11304 Southwest Boones Ferry Rd.
Portland, Oreg. 97219

Texas Greenhouse Co.
2717 Saint Louis Ave.
Fort Worth, Tex. 76110

Tiger Enclosures Inc.
3826 Raleigh St.
Post Office Box 5484 (28205)
Charlotte, N. C. 28206

Trans-Sphere Trading Corp.
Post Office Box 1564
Mobile, Ala. 36601

Trox Manufacturing Co.
18 Angell St.
Battle Creek, Mich. 49017

Turner Greenhouses
Turner Equipment Co., Inc.
Post Office Box 1260
Goldsboro, N. C. 27530

Winandy Greenhouse Construction
Post Office Box 597
Richmond, Ind. 47374

For further reference:

Acme Engineering and Manufactur-
Corp., *The Greenhouse Climate Con-
trol Handbook: Principles and Design
Procedures.* Acme Engineering and
Manufacturing Corp., Muskogee, Okla.,
1970. $2.00.

Biles, Roy E., *The Complete Book of
Garden Magic,* J. G. Ferguson Publisher, Chicago, 1953.

Blake, Claire L., *Greenhouse Gardening for Fun.* M. Barrow and Company, Inc., New York, 1967.

Coutier, J. W., and Curtis J. O., *A
Simple Rigid Frame Greenhouse for
Home Gardeners.* Cooperative Extension Service, Circular 880, University
of Illinois, College of Agriculture, Urbana 1964. Out of State, 10¢.

Coutier, J. W., and Curtis, J. O.,
*Home Greenhouses for Year-round
Gardening Pleasure.* Cooperative Ex-
tension Service, Circular 879, Univer-
sity of Illinois, College of Agriculture,
Urbana, 1964. Out of State, 10¢.

Edison Electric Institute, *Electric
Gardening.* Edison Electric Institute,
90 Park Avenue, New York, 1970.
(Available from your local electric
power supplier.)

Liu, R. C., Bailey, W. A., Klueter,
H. H., and Krizek, D. T. *New Shapes
of Hobby Greenhouses,* U.S. Department of Agriculture, ASAE Paper 68-
925. Phyto-Engineering Laboratory,
Beltsville, Md. 20705, 1968.

Lord and Burnham, *Your Gateway to
Year-round Gardening Pleasure.* Burn-
ham Corporation, Irvington, N.J., 1971
(Free).

Lord and Burnham, *Greenhouse
Gardens that Take Care of Themselves.* Burnham Corporation, Irvington, N.J., 1971 (Free)

Potter, Charles H., *Greenhouse:
Place of Magic.* E. P. Dutton and Co.,
Inc., New York, 1967.

Sunset Book, *Garden and Patio
Building Book.* Lane Magazine and
Book Co., Menlo Park, Calif., 1971.
$1.95.

Sunset Book, *Garden Work Centers.*
Lane Magazine and Book Co., Menlo
Park, Calif., 1970. $1.95.

U.S. Department of Agriculture,
Electric Heating of Hotbeds, Leaflet
445, Washington, D.C. 20250, 1969.

U.S. Department of Agriculture,
Plastic Covered Greenhouse Coldframe.
Miscellaneous Publication 1111, Wash-
ington, D.C. 20250, 1969.

U.S. Department of Agriculture,
List of Sources of Information on
Greenhouses, Correspondence Aid 34-
134, Washington, D.C. 20250, 1970.

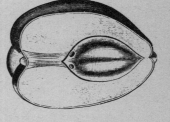

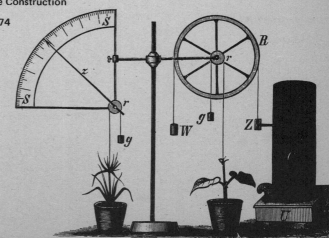

Comparisons of Different Plastic Materials for Covering Greenhouses

Plastic and approximate cost per square foot	Available thickness[a]	Available width	Recommended thickness[b]	Durability[c]	Notes
Polyethylene Regular (0.4 to 2.0¢)	1.5 to 10 mil	3 to 40 feet	4 or 6 mil, outside layer; 2 or 4 mil, inside layer	3–10 months	Polyethylene covered greenhouses are not suitable for continuous year-round use. Polyethylene breaks down rapidly during the summer, deteriorating first where folded. Unfolded rolls are available up to 14 feet wide. Application of an inside lining to form a 2- to 4-inch air space can reduce heating costs by 20 percent or more.
UV-treated and copolymer films (1.2 to 2.1¢)	4 or 6 mil	10 to 40 feet	4 or 6 mil	8–24 months	Ultra violet resistant (UV-treated) polyethylene is recommended over regular polyethylene for covering during late summer or fall. New extra-strength copolymer films are the most durable.
Vinyl (PVC) Film (3 to 10¢)	3 to 12 mil	4 to 6 feet (seamed to larger widths)	8 to 12 mil	2–4 years	Use only weatherable vinyl. Clear or translucent grades are available. Vinyl is pliable and contracts and expands with temperature. Vinyl becomes dirty easily.
Fiberglass (20 to 50¢)	.03 to .09 inch or 4 to 12 ounces per square foot	2 to 4 feet	Use greenhouse grade 5 oz. or heavier with durability guarantee. Tedlar-coated panels are preferred.	5–15 years or longer	Corrugated or flat available in panels 6 to 12 feet long, rolls, and glass-sized panes. Light is diffused, but clear grades generally transmit 80 percent or more of visible light. Shading often is not needed. Will burn.

[a] 1 mil = 0.001 inch.
[b] Thinner, less expensive grades can be used but they will probably be less durable.
[c] Properly installed for greenhouse use.

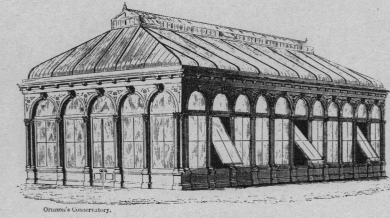

Ormson's Conservatory.

Manufacturers

Aluminex Incorporated
2408 Forney St.
Los Angeles, Calif. 90031

Aluminum Greenhouses
R. J. Nolan and Associates
1309 Center St.
Des Plaines, Ill. 60018

American-Moniger Greenhouse
Manufacturing Co.
1820 Flushing Ave.
Brooklyn, N . Y. 11237

Columbus Porta-Green Co.
41 Fornof Road
Columbus, Ohio 43207

Durapane Corp.
78 Ewing St.
Kansas City, Kans. 66118

Emerson Industries, Inc.
132 Adams Ave.
Hempstead, Long Island
N. Y. 11550

Ethyl Corporation
Visqueen Division
Post Office Box 2242
Baton Rouge, La. 70821

Florida Industries Inc.
Post Office Box 15175
Tampa, Fla. 33614

Foley Greenhouse Manufacturing Co.
7711 Van Buren St.
Forest Park, Ill. 60130

E. C. Geiger
Harleysville, Pa. 19438

Greenhouse Specialties Co.
9849 Kimker Lane
Saint Louis, Mo. 63127

Hill Greenhouse Mfg. Corp.
Shelby Center
Medina, N. Y. 14103

Ickes-Braun Greenhouse
Manufacturing Co.
2320-2342 Wabansia Ave.
Chicago, Ill. 60647

Albert J. Lauer Co.
16700 Highway 3
R. F. D. 1
Rosemount, Minn. 55068

Lord & Burnham
Irvington, N . Y. 10533

Ludy Greenhouse Manufacturing
Corp.
Railroad St. Box 85
New Madison, Ohio 45346

Maco Products
434 Cottage St. S. E.
Salem, Oreg. 97301

Mankato Greenhouses
Mankato, Kans. 66956

Dome East
325 Duffy Ave.
Hicksville, New York 11801

Humex, Ltd.
5 High Road
Byfleet, Weybridge, Surrey
England
or
E. and W. International
290 Sandringham Road
Rochester, New York 14610

Lord and Burnham
Irvington, New York 10533
or
Des Plaines, Illinois 60018

J. A. Nearing Co., Inc.
10788 Tucker St.
Beltsville, Maryland 20705

Redfern's Prefab Greenhouses
55 Mt. Hermon Road
Scotts Valley, California 95060

Peter Reumuller, Greenhouseman
P. O. Box 2666
Santa Cruz, California 95060

Stearns Greenhouses
98 Taylor St.
Neponset, Massachusetts, 02122

Sturdi-Built Manufacturing Co.
11304 S. W. Boones Ferry Road
Portland, Oregon 97219

Texas Greenhouse Co., Inc.
2710 St. Louis Ave.
Fort Worth, Texas 76110

Turner Greenhouses
P. O. Box 1260
Goldsboro, North Carolina 27530
(also fiberglass greenhouses)

Sources for Seeds and Plants

Abbey Garden
Box 167
Reseda, California 91335
succulents

Alberts & Merkel Bros., Inc.
Boynton Beach, Florida 33435
orchids and tropical foliage plants

Antonelli Bros.
2545 Capitola Road
Santa Cruz, California 95010
tuberous begonias

Armacost & Royston
2005 Armacost Ave.
West Los Angeles, California 90025
orchids

Buell's Greenhouses
Eastford, Connecticut 06242
African violets, gloxinia, and
other gesneriads

Burgess Seed and Plant Co.
P. O. Box 218
Galesburg, Michigan 49053
seeds and plants

W. Atlee Burpee Co.
Philadelphia, Pennsylvania 19132
seeds of annuals, biennials, and
perennials

Butchart Gardens, Ltd.
P. O. Box 4010, Station "A"
Victoria, British Columbia
seeds

Edelweiss Gardens
Robbinsville, New Jersey 08691
general plants

Fennell Orchid Co.
26715 S. W. 157th Ave.
Homestead, Florida 33030
orchids

Fischer Greenhouse
Linwood, New Jersey 08221
African violets

J. Howard French
Box 37
Lima, Pennsylvania 19060
bulbs

Joseph Harris Co., Inc.
Moreton Farm, Buffalo Road
Rochester, New York 14624
vegetable seeds

Alexander I. Heimlich
71 Burlington St.
Woburn, Massachusetts 01801
miniature bulbs, corms, and tubers

Margaret Ilgenfritz
P. O. Box 665
Monroe, Michigan 48161
orchids

Jones and Scully, Inc.
2200 N. W. 33rd Ave.
Miami, Florida 33142
orchids

Michael Kartuz
92 Chestnut St.
Wilmington, Massachusetts 01887
general plants

Magazines

Anonymous. "Handbook on Greenhouses" in PLANTS AND GARDENS, Vol. 19, 97 pp. Summer 1963. (The entire issue is devoted to the subject.)

THE FLORISTS EXCHANGE AND HORTICULTURAL TRADE WORLD, published by The A. T. De La Mare Co., Inc., 448 W. 37th St., New York, N. Y. 10018.

THE FLORISTS REVIEW, published by the Florists Publishing Co., 343 South Dearborn St., Chicago, Ill. 60604.

THE MARKET GROWERS JOURNAL, published by Market Growers Journal, Inc., 11 S. Forge St., Akron, Ohio 44304.

THE SOUTHERN FLORIST AND NURSERYMEN, published by Southern Florist Publishing Co., 120th St. Louis St., Fort Worth, Tex. 76101.

UNDER GLASS, published by Lord & Burnham, P. O. Box 114, Irvington, N. Y. 10533.

Logee's Greenhouses
Danielson, Connecticut 06239
general plants

Lyndon Lyon
Dolgeville, New York 13329
African violets

Merry Gardens
Camden, Maine 04843
general plants

George W. Park Seed Co.
Greenwood, South Carolina 29646
seeds

J. A. Peterson
3132 McHenry Ave.
Cincinnati, Ohio 45211
African violets

John Scheepers, Inc.
37 Wall Street
New York, New York 10005
bulbs

Sunnyslope Gardens
8638 Huntington Drive
San Gabriel, California 91775
rooted chrysanthemum cuttings

Thompson & Morgan, Ltd.
London Road
Ipswich IP2 OBA
Suffolk, England
seeds of annuals, biennials, perennials, and shrubs; wide variety of species

Vetterle Bros.
P. O. Box 1246
Watsonville, California 95076
tuberous begonias

TROPICAL AND SUBTROPICAL RAIN FOREST PLANTS
24

GARDENS FOR INDOOR LIVING

There is no reason to forego the pleasures of gardening just because you lack a piece of land to call your own.

Bring the beauty of the outdoors in. Build a garden for indoor living. A living, growing decor can change the way you feel about your home and maybe even improve the way you feel about yourself.

Generally, people are very timid when decorating their homes. They see a wall and say to themselves, "What a nice place to hang a picture." They look at the floor and say, "Oh, a rug will go there." Windows are for curtains, of course. And, hardly anyone, these days, decorates a ceiling.

The same is true, unfortunately, when people begin to bring plants into their homes. At first, timid potted plants appear on the windowsill. Then, perhaps a dull little five and dime store terrarium is put on the coffee table where it dies from lack of light.

These collections of horticultural knic-knacs are a far cry from what we consider Gardens for Indoor Living. What we have in mind begins on a somewhat grander scale and proceeds immediately to the grandiose.

Whether indoors or out, the elements required for plant growth are light, moisture, soil and air. Indoors, there is the additional requisite that these elements do not damage the building's structure or furnishings.

But, all of these requirements were met by Victorian Gardeners, and are easy to satisfy today with modern materials and technology.

You can start by looking over the material we have gathered on plant lights, container gardening, and the particular plants you decide to grow.

Don't be afraid to innovate. If you wish to become an indoor gardener, you must forget for a moment that you are surrounded by walls, ceilings, and a floor. Stand in each area of your home and say, "This can be a garden, a forest, a veritable jungle, if I so choose."

Perhaps a few examples of indoor gardens we have seen will stimulate your imagination.

For instance, an apartment dweller we know of has turned a dull 8 x 10 dining room into a spectacular hanging garden. Her first step was to install three eight-foot fluorescent grow lights on the ceiling. Below, she hung a trellis made of painted strips of one-inch lath spaced, to create a grid of 12-inch squares below the ceiling. She filled hanging baskets with fast growing vines and suspended these from the trellis-work. In a short time, she was dining in a leafy arbor, made and planted with her own two hands.

Trelliage and plant lights may also be used to create indoor wall gardens. One couple we know of, set a large mirror behind a very plain sofa bracketed by two simple side tables. The trellis was erected beside and behind each coffee table and another decorative trellis was arched over the entire arrangement. Grow lights were installed above, climbing vines planted at the base and hanging baskets were suspended in front of the mirror to suggest more depth in the setting.

Windows are perhaps the simplest area to start indoor gardens. But, even there you should use grow lamps to ensure your plants are getting enough light.

Easily created green screens can replace curtains or blinds on windows. In one home we know of, pieces of antique stained glass were attached to the existing windows. A wide variety of ceramic hanging baskets were suspended from above, and potted plants were placed on the windowsill and floor. This arrangement not only provided privacy, but improved the view through what was otherwise a very ordinary city window.

Then, there are those who have gone far beyond container gardening, indoors. One such person filled an entire room—floor, wall and ceiling with plants, pools, bridges, trellises, gold fish, lizards and birds.

He started simply by covering the floor with a sheet of polyethelene, which he tacked to the walls about twelve inches up. Prefabricated figerglass pools were set in earth and stone. Ceiling and wall-mounted grow lights were concealed behind trees and trellises. Immersible pumps sent water gurgling up through cracks in the rocks and the holes of inverted red clay pots, piled on atop the other to resemble pagodas.

It was an altogether charming place until a neighbor complained about the birds. This led to a visit from a building inspector with no sense of humor and little love for plants. So, this secret garden is no more.

This little story, though, illustrates two points. First, that total outdoor settings for indoor gardens are possible if you want them. Second, if you are working inside a structure built to stand certain stresses, be sure your floors, walls and ceilings are built to take the weight.

Also, it is especially important to make arrangements for adequate drainage and at the same time, prevent leakage outside your indoor garden area. This is a difficulty you'll share with many penthouse gardeners. But, with modern plastics, light-weight waterproof cement, tile, and so forth, it should be easy to overcome.

So, fill your home with plants until you can call it a garden. Sit back. Inhale the sweet aroma of earth and greenery. Enjoy the beneficence of nature's own air conditioners.

Don't forget, send us pictures if you have a spectacular garden for indoor living.

—Ornamental Screen of Ivy.

Flower Stand for Parlor Window.

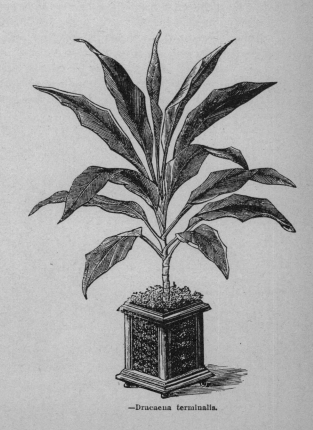

—Dracaena terminalis.

Plant Department.

EXHIBITING FLOWERS

One great pleasure derived from the cultivation of flowers is the evident delight they afford our friends; and the amateur, or even the true professional florist, is almost as proud of his choice flowers as is the mother of her children. Then, there is great satisfaction in knowing that your flowers are exerting an influence for good on all who behold them, some of whom are sure to become imitators and successful cultivators. It is for this reason I desire all my customers to become imitators and successful cultivators. It is for this reason I desire all my customers to exhibit their flowers at their State and County Fairs as far as practicable, so that these exhibitions may be made productive of good. One fine floral exhibition will do more for taste and morals than a million horse races, or "trials of speed," if you please. It is strange that the officers of Agricultural societies should offer such insignificant premiums for flowers, and still more strange that, as a general rule, no adequate preparation is made for their exhibition. We have often taken flowers to County Fairs, and had to lay them on a dry board to wither and die.

Officers of Agricultural Societies, who design to treat every exhibitor fairly, often fail from want of knowledge. They do not know what exhibitors of flowers require, and, of course, cannot provide for their wants. The exhibitor arrives on the ground, but he finds no vials in which to put his cut flowers, no vases or glasses for his boquets. The President and Secretary both feel sorry, but it is too late to remedy the evil. To all such honorable officers, who design to do their whole duty and accommodate every exhibitor, I wish to show a way in which they can please their floral friends, and secure a fine exhibition of flowers, and with very little labor and expense, and avoid all trouble of buying or borrowing crockery. Make a common rough board table, about three and a half feet in width, and as long as necessary to accommodate all exhibitors. In front of this table nail a board four inches wide, and at the back a board five inches in width, projecting upward, and a similar board at each end, as seen in the engraving. The space thus formed, fill with moist sand, and make it smooth on the top. The exhibitors place their flowers in this sand, and it keeps them as fresh as if in water. The taller flowers or boquets can be placed at the back part of the table, where the sand is the deepest. For a dividing line between different collections, tack a piece of red tape, or an evergreen wreath.

To keep the crowd from pressing upon the table and injuring the flowers, place a guard around, and about eighteen inches from the table, as shown in the engraving. This space furnishes a place for the committees and for exhibitors, where they can stand and answer any questions the people may ask, or give any information they may desire. If it is desired to make the exhibition somewhat elegant in appearance, the sand can be covered with moss, and the table and guard ornamented with evergreens or wreaths. Place a barrel of water near the entrance or some other convenient place, and also obtain two pails and two sprinkling pots for the use of Floral Hall, with a hammer and a few nails, and your exhibition will pass off pleasantly, and every one will be satisfied. We commend these suggestions to every one interested in Floral exhibitions.

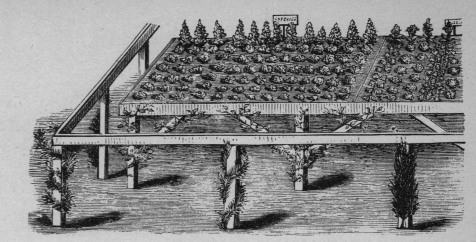

TABLE FOR EXHIBITING FLOWERS.

CYPERUS ALTERNIFOLIUS (Umbrella Plant).

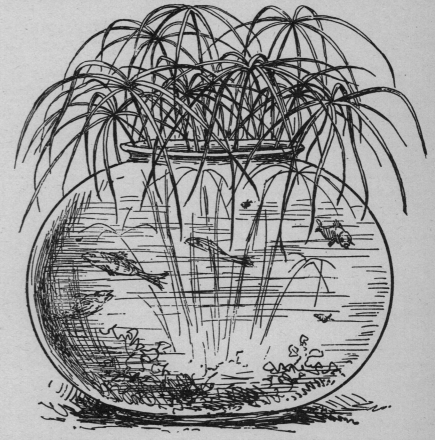

A beautiful, easy growing plant that is admirably adapted to many different modes of culture, in fact it seems to thrive in almost any situation and under all circumstances. It makes a very showy plant for pot culture, is one of the best for ferneries, while for the aquarium it is without an equal. Plants, each, 25 cents.

—An Ivied Picture Frame.

A Saucer Garden.

Decorated Bee Hive Crocus Pot.
Price, 80c. (Requires 36 Crocus.)

Decorated Hedgehog Crocus Pot.

Roman Hyacinth Pot.

REVOLVING ADJUSTABLE STAND.

Selecting and growing
HOUSE PLANTS

By Henry M. Cathey, *Plant Genetics and Germplasm Institute, Northeastern Region, Agricultural Research Service*

Bromeliads. Left, Aechmea chantinii; center top, Vriesia carinata; center bottom, Cryptanthus zonatus; right, Neoregelia hybrid.

Success in growing decorative plants in the home probably depends as much on good judgment in selecting the plants as on skill in caring for them.

First, decide why you want house plants. Do you want them only for use as decorative accessories? Or are you interested in growing and tending the plants as well as in displaying them?

If you want plants only as decorative accessories, buy them for their appearance. Get healthy, well-formed plants that are near the size that you need for decorative effect. Water the plants regularly until their appearance becomes unsatisfactory, then replace them with new plants.

If you are interested in growing house plants and keeping them in good condition year after year, you must next decide how much attention you can give them. Are you able, or willing, to adapt some part of your home to the needs of the house plants? Or would you rather restrict your choice of plants to those that tolerate an environment that is comfortable to human inhabitants? This last course of action is probably the wisest.

Many house plants will survive under adverse household conditions. For best results, however, supply the environment—light, temperature, and humidity—that is recommended for each plant.

FOLIAGE PLANTS

AGLAONEMA

Description.—Chinese evergreen, the commonest member of this group that is used as a house plant, has dark-green leaves growing at the end of canelike stems. This plant will flourish for years in the dark part of a room and requires a minimum of care.

Culture.—Grow in water (see "Water Culture," p. 26) or in humus soil. If grown in humus soil, keep the soil moist. Grow in warm atmosphere with low humidity and subdued daylight.

Special requirements.—When stems of Chinese evergreen become too long, cut off the tops and reroot them (see "Propagation," p. 28).

ANTHURIUM

Description.—Some anthuriums are grown for their long-lasting cut flowers, others for their foliage. *A.*

andreanum has brilliant red, white, coral, or pink flowers that look like patent leather. *A. crystalinum* has leaves that are velvety green with silver veins; its flowers are inconspicuous.

Culture.—Pot in humus soil; keep the soil moist. Keep the plant warm—60° minimum temperature at night. Grow in indirect sunlight or subdued daylight. Provide high humidity.

Special requirements.—Add fertilizer to water only once a month.

Anthuriums produce aerial roots below the base of each leaf. Wrap these aerial roots with sphagnum moss and keep the moss damp.

APHELANDRA

Description.—*Aphelandra squarrosa* is a small shrub with large, elliptic leaves. It tolerates dim light but grows best in indirect sunlight.

Culture.—Plant in humus soil; keep the soil moist. Grow in indirect sunlight, warm temperatures, and low humidity.

ARAUCARIA

Description.—Branches of the Norfolk Island Pine (*Araucaria excelsa*) are borne in symmetrical tiers. This formal symmetry makes Norfolk Island pine valuable as a decorative plant.

Culture.—Plant in humus soil; keep the soil moist. Grow in indirect sunlight, moderate temperatures, and low humidity.

Special requirements.—This plant needs sufficient light to prevent irregular growth. If the plant grows too tall, air-layer the top (see p. 28).

ASPIDISTRA

Description.—Aspidistra will endure heat, dust, darkness, and lack of water better than most other house plants. When it is well cared for, it produces a mass of broad, glossy green leaves and bears flowers close to the ground.

Culture.—Plant in potting soil; keep the soil moist. Grow in shade or subdued daylight, moderate temperature, and medium humidity.

BEGONIA

Description.—*Begonia rex*, grown for its foliage, has large, thick leaves that are shaped and marked irregularly.

Anthuriums. Left, A. andreanum; right, A. crystalinum.

Culture.—Plant in humus soil; keep the soil moist. Grow in indirect sunlight, warm temperatures, and medium to high humidity.

Special requirements. — During the summer, grow begonia plants in a bright window out of direct sun, or on a shady porch, or bury the pots up to the rims in the ground in partial shade.

For information on flowering begonias, see p. 18.

BROMELIADS

Description. — The bromeliads (*Bromelia, Aechmea, Cryptanthus, Neoregelia,* and *Vriesia*) are the most adaptable of all foliage plants. Their leaves hold water and the plants grow well under dry indoor conditions in light or shade.

When the plants are mature, a brilliantly colored flower spike

grows from beneath the pool of water in the center of the plant. The flower spike lasts for several months.

Culture.—Plant in humus soil; keep the soil moist. Grow in full sun, warm temperatures, and medium humidity.

Special requirements.—Keep the center of the plants filled with water. Occasionally spray the leaves with water to remove the dust. Propagate from lateral shoots that grow from the main plant after the flower withers.

Left to right: Rhoeo discolor, Araucaria excelsa, and Pilea caderei.

27

African violet (Saintpaulia ionantha), Streptocarpus (S. Kewensis), and Episcia (F. coccinea).

AFRICAN VIOLETS

Description.—African violets are the most commonly grown house plants. They produce single or double flowers colored white, or blue, or a combination of red and blue.

Culture.—Pot in regular soil mixture; keep the soil moist. Grow in indirect sunlight and warm temperatures with high humidity, moderate temperatures with medium humidity, or cool temperatures with low humidity.

Special requirements.—Plant African violets in subirrigating pots (see p. 23), so the plants can be watered and fertilized from the bottom; if leaves are wetted with water that is cooler or warmer than the air, light-colored spots will develop on them.

If the petioles (leaf stems) lie across the wet clay rim of a flower pot, they may rot. To prevent this, cover the rim with parafilm or aluminum foil.

Wash the leaves regularly with soapy water at room temperature. Allow the leaves to dry in a shady place before returning the plants to the growing area.

African violet

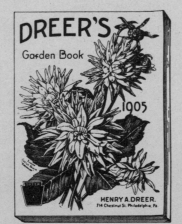

GLOXINIA

Description.—Gloxinias are grown from tubers. The plants, which are almost stemless, have broad velvety leaves and deep, bell-like flowers that are brilliantly colored.

Culture.—Pot in humus soil; keep the soil moist. Grow in indirect sunlight, moderate temperatures, and high humidity.

AMARYLLIS

Description.—Amaryllis are tropical bulbs that can be kept growing continuously. A flower stem with three to six flowers appears 6 to 8 weeks after the bulb is planted. After the plant flowers, its leaves appear.

Many other plants of the same type—*Nerine* and *Chlidathus*, for example—can be grown in the same way.

Culture.—Pot in humus soil; keep the soil moist. Grow in full sun or shade with moderate temperatures and medium humidity.

Special requirements.—Pot the bulbs with two-thirds of the bulb above soil level. Place in full sun and keep the soil moist. After the flower has passed, let the leaves grow for good development of the bulb. As soon as the leaves begin to yellow, stop watering; the plant will become dormant. Store the dormant plant in a cool place—38° to 45°. You can keep the bulb dormant as long as you want. When you wish it to grow again, resume watering.

CROSSANDRA

Description.—Crossandra leaves are large and glossy with a waxy texture. The plant produces large, bright-salmon flowers through most of the year.

Culture.—Plant in humus soil; keep the soil moist. Grow in full sunlight, warm temperatures, and high humidity.

Special requirements.—Seed can be sown at any time. If the plant is grown at 65° to 70°, it will begin to bloom 6 to 7 months after planting.

DUTCH BULBS

Description.—Hyacinths, tulips, and various kinds of narcissus can be forced into flower for window-garden use. The Chinese sacredlily, paperwhite narcissus, and hyacinths can be forced in water.

Culture.—Store narcissus bulbs dry for 12 weeks at 50°, and tulip bulbs for the same period at 45°. Then pot the bulbs and place the pots in the light at 60°. The bulbs bloom in about 1 month.

Store hyacinths at 63° for 4 weeks. Then pot and keep the potted bulb at 55° until the tip of the shoot is 1½ inches above the bulb. Then place the pot in the light at 65°. The bulbs bloom in about 1 month.

Formerly it was recommended that bulbs be kept in a cool place until a root system developed. Growth of roots is not a reliable sign that the bulbs are ready for potting; irregular flowering often results from following the old recommendation.

To force bulbs in water, place the bulbs in a wide-mouth jar or shallow dish and support them with stones. Add charcoal to keep the water from souring. Keep the bulbs cool and dark until the tops begin to expand. Then move the containers to a cool, sunny room for forcing. Usually, bulbs are forced at too high a temperature and the leaves and flowers grow too long.

After bulbs have flowered, they may be planted in the garden when danger of frost is past. Few bulbs flower again the first year; some are so depleted from forcing that they never again flower well.

EPISCIA

Description.—Episcias are noted for their decorative foliage and vividly colored flowers. They often are potted in hanging baskets. They require care similar to that for African violets.

Culture.—Plant in humus soil; keep the soil moist. Grow in indirect sunlight, warm temperatures, and high humidity.

FUCHSIA

Descriptions.—Fuchsias, grown for their brilliantly colored flowers, need a well-drained soil and a night temperature of 60° to grow best. High night temperatures and low light intensities inhibit their flowering.

Culture.—Plant in regular potting soil; keep the soil moist. Grow in subdued daylight, moderate to warm temperatures, and medium humidity.

Special requirements.—Remove ends of stems frequently to promote branching. Propagate by cuttings or seeds.

GARDENIA

Description.—Gardenias seldom do well as house plants. They are exacting in their temperature requirements; if night temperature is above 65°, the flower buds drop. If it is below 60° to 62°, the leaves turn yellow. In spite of these exacting requirements, many people grow gardenias as house plants, and occasionally a gardenia plant produces a few flowers in late spring.

Culture.—Pot in humus soil; keep the soil moist. Grow in full sun, warm temperatures, and medium humidity.

GERANIUM

Description.—The most commonly grown geranium, *Pelargonium hortorum*, produces single or double flowers throughout the year. It can be distinguished by the dark zone on its soft leaves.

Pelargonium domesticum produces flowers marked with blotches of contrasting colors. It usually flowers for 4 to 6 weeks in late spring or early summer. Its leaves are deep green.

Culture.—Pot in regular soil mixture; allow the soil to dry moderately between waterings. Grow in full sun, cool temperatures, and low to medium humidity.

Special requirements.—Geraniums need full sun and cool temperatures for best blooming. Ideal temperatures at night are 55° to 60°. Night temperatures above 60° inhibit flowering.

Do not let water stand on leaves or stems of geraniums; these parts rot easily.

Propagate by cuttings.

CALADIUM

Description.—Caladiums grow during the spring and summer and are dormant during the winter. The leaves of caladium are large and arrow shaped. Some kinds have pink leaves, some have red leaves, some have variegated leaves.

Culture.—Plant in humus soil; keep the soil moist. Grow in indirect sunlight and normal summer temperatures and humidities.

Special requirements.—Pot tubers in the spring, At the end of summer, gradually prolong the periods between waterings until the plants become dormant. Then store the tubers, without removing them from the soil, in a cool place (about 60°). The next spring, repot the tubers and resume watering. Avoid overwatering; caladiums rot easily.

CALATHEA

Culture.—Pot in humus soil; keep the soil moist. Grow in indirect sunlight or shade, warm temperatures, and high humidity.

CHINESE EVERGREEN

See Aglaonema.

CODIAEUM (Croton)

Description.—Crotons are gaudy tropical shrubs with tough, evergreen leaves. The leaves are variously shaped and marked with patterns of yellow, scarlet, green, white, and pink.

COLEUS

Culture.—Plant in potting soil; keep the soil moist. Grow in bright sun, warm temperatures, and medium humidity.

Special requirements.—As croton plants grow old, the lower leaves fall leaving the trunk bare. The top can be air layered to form new roots, then cut from the old trunk and potted as a new plant.

COLEUS

Description.—Coleus plants are available having a wide range of foliage colors and patterns. Coleus thrives in a warm atmosphere. It needs plenty of sunshine and moisture, but will survive chilling or overwatering.

Culture.—Plant in regular potting soil; keep the soil moist. Grow in full sun, warm temperatures, and medium humidity.

Special requirements.—Remove tips of the plants frequently to induce branching. Propagate from seeds or from cuttings rooted in water (see p. 28).

DIEFFENBACHIA
(Dumb Cane)

Description.—Dieffenbachia, one of the most spectacular of the house plants, is grown for its large, variegated foliage. *Diffenbachia amoena* has dark green leaves with white markings along the veins. *D. picta* variety Rudolph Roehrs has yellow-green leaf blades that are blotched with ivory and edged in green. *D. amoena* withstands lower temperatures than *D. picta*.

Culture.—Plant in regular potting soil; allow the soil to dry moderately between waterings. Grow in indirect sunlight, warm temperatures, and low humidity.

Special requirements.—Though dieffenbachia tolerates dim light, it grows best in bright light. It often is overwatered; overwatering causes the roots and base of the canes to rot quickly. Keep the soil on the dry side.

Eventually the lower leaves turn yellow. When this happens, remove the yellowed leaves. If the stem becomes bare and objectionable, cut off the top of the plant and root it in sand or water. Keep the canes; they eventually grow lateral shoots.

Caution: Dieffenbachia sap is toxic in open cuts. Be careful when removing leaves or cutting the cane.

This plant is double potted, with sphagnum moss between the inside pot and the outside container. Soil in the pot dries more slowly and needs watering less frequently than soil in pots that are exposed to the air.

MARANTA (CALATHEA) MASSANGEANA.

JONQUIL
RUGULOSUS.

❦❧

KALANCHOE

Description.—Kalanchoe *bloss-feldiana* bears clusters of scarlet flowers in late winter and early spring.

Culture.—Pot in regular soil mixture; keep the soil moist. Grow in full sun, moderate temperatures, and medium humidity.

FUCHSIA.

Special requirements.—Kalanchoe needs at least 3 weeks of long nights to bloom successfully. Beginning in the middle of October, keep the plant in total darkness for 15 hours a night.

LANTANA

Description.—Lantana flowers continuously. It can be used as a bedding plant as well as a house plant.

Culture.—Pot in regular soil mixture; keep the soil moist. Grow in full sunlight, moderate to warm temperatures, and medium humidity.

Special requirements.—Sow seed in early spring or grow plants from cuttings.

OLEANDER

Description.—*Nerium oleander* bears upright clusters of pink or white flowers. It blooms in early summer and sometimes throughout the year. If oleander is kept fairly dry during the winter, it can withstand temperatures near freezing.

WARNING: All parts of this plant are poisonous when eaten; one leaf can kill a man. Avoid handling fresh or dry leaves or inhaling smoke from burning plants.

Culture.—Pot in regular soil mixture; keep the soil moist. Grow in full sun, moderate temperatures, and medium humidity.

IMPATIENS

Description.—Impatiens grows easily from seed. It begins to bloom about 3 months after seed is planted and blooms continuously thereafter.

Culture.—Plant in regular potting soil; keep the soil moist. Grow in full sun, warm temperatures, and medium humidity.

Special requirements.—Pinch off the tips of the plants to make them branch. Keep the plants warm; leaf drop occurs at temperatures below 65°.

Grow the plants in a sunny window during the winter. Move them to a porch box during the summer.

JERUSALEM CHERRY

Description.—Jerusalem cherry (*Solanum pseudo-capsicum*) produces round orange or scarlet fruit the size of a cherry. The fruits persist for a long time. **Warning:** The fruits may cause a rash by coming in contact with the skin. Avoid handling them.

Culture.—Pot in regular soil mixture; allow the soil to dry moderately between waterings. Grow in direct sunlight, cool temperatures, and medium humidity.

Special requirements.—Grow plants for a year, then discard them. Plants more than a year old do not fruit well. Grow new plants from seed.

If growth of the plant is checked, it drops its leaves, develops bare stems, and becomes unsightly. This is a common problem; it usually is caused by low humidity.

ORCHIDS

Description.—Best orchids for home culture are *Cattleya bowringiana*, *Cattleya mossiae* (florist orchid), *Dendrobium nobile* (cane orchid), and *Paphiopedilum insigne* (ladyslipper orchid).

Culture.—Plant in pure humus; water weekly. Grow in subdued daylight, moderate temperature, and high humidity.

Special requirements.—Orchids need humidity that is maintained between 40 and 80 percent with temperatures from 65° to 80°. They are often grown in glass cases over a moisture stage of wet gravel or sphagnum moss.

Moisten the leaves every day. Water the pots once a week.

STREPTOCARPUS

Description.—Streptocarpus produces trumpet-shaped flowers that are about 2 inches long and have expanded frilled edges.

Culture.—Plant in humus soil; keep the soil moist in summer, allow to dry moderately between waterings in winter. Grow in subdued daylight, cool temperatures, and high humidity.

Dieffenbachia picta "Rudolph Roehrs," Dieffenbachia amoena, and Ficus pandurata.

DOUBLE FUCHSIA.

DRACAENA

Description.—Dracaenas grow slowly and retain their foliage for long periods. *Dracaena godseffi-ana,* the most common and most rugged form, has dark-green leaves spotted with pale yellow. The leaves of *D. fragrans* are broad and strap shaped; they are green with a gold band down the middle. *D. sanderiana* is smaller than the other dracaenas; it has gray-green leaves that are bordered with a white band.

Culture.—Plant in regular potting soil; keep the soil wet. Grow in indirect sunlight, warm temperatures, and low humidity.

Special requirements. — W a s h foliage once a month with soapy water. When the bare stem beneath the foliage gets too long, air-layer the top.

FATSHEDERA

Description. — Fatshederas are evergreen shrubs. They produce leathery five-lobed leaves that are lustrous dark green.

Culture.—Plant in regular potting soil; keep the soil moist. Grow on support in full sun, cool temperature, and low to medium humidity.

FERNS

Description.—Ferns are among the most satisfactory house plants. They have many forms of fronds. Among the best ferns for growing as pot plants are maidenhair fern (*Adiantum wrightii*), swordferns (*Nephrolepsis*), birdsnest fern (*Asplenium midus*), spider ferns (*Pteris*), and house hollyfern (*Cyrtomium falcatum*).

Culture.—Plant in humus soil; keep the soil moist. Grow in subdued daylight, warm temperatures, and high humidity.

Special requirements. — Protect ferns from extreme chilling. Watch for special seasons of growth and provide additional water at this time. During the rest of the year, give less water.

FICUS

Description.—Rubber plant (*Ficus elastica*) has large oval leaves that are leathery and dark green. Fiddleleaf (*F. pandurata*) has thick, shiny leaves shaped, as is described by its common name, like a fiddle. Creeping fig (*F. pumila*) has small leaves. It forms a close mat of clinging stems and can be used to cover a brick or masonry wall or the bottom of a planter.

These plants all are adaptable to a wide range of growing conditions. While they grow best in a warm, moist atmosphere, they do fairly well under normal household conditions of temperature and humidity.

They can be grown in full sun or shade.

Left to right: Dracaena sanderiana, Dracaena fragrans, and Aphelandra squarrosa

Alsophila Leichardtiana.

—*Ficus* with girdle-like clasping roots, at Darjeeling in the Sikkim Himalayas. (From a photograph.)

Culture.—Plant in regular potting soil; keep the soil moist. Grow in diffused sun, warm temperatures, and medium humidity.

Special requirements. — When grown in pots, these plants tend to develop a single stem. The leaves drop if the plant is chilled or if it is moved from one place to another. If the leaves drop and leave a bare stem, the top can be air layered (see p. 28).

Wipe the leaves with wet cloth at frequent intervals.

GEORGENANTHUS (Seersucker Plant)

Description.—Georgenanthus is a low-growing, suckering plant. It has fleshy, quilted leaves that are dark, metallic green with several bands of pale gray. The underside of the leaf is red.

Culture.—Pot in regular soil; keep the soil moist. Grow in indirect sunlight, warm temperatures, and low humidity.

IRESINE (Blood Leaf)

Culture.—Plant in regular potting soil; keep the soil moist. Grow in full sun, moderate temperature, and medium humidity.

IVY

Description.—Even in its common form, ivy makes an excellent house plant. Some of the smaller-leaved forms of ivy make even better house plants than the common form. These plants have leaves that not only are smaller, but also are shaped differently than the common three-lobed variety.

Various other plants are called ivy though they are not related to the real ivy plant. They also make good house plants and are grown in the same way that ivy is. German ivy, or ivy groundsel, is a trailing or climbing vine with maplelike leaves and dull, orange-yellow flowers. Kenilworth ivy is a trailing vine with flowers that look like tiny lavendar snapdragons. Grape ivy is a climbing vine with coiling tendrils on its branches. Its leaves are composed of three sharp-toothed oval leaflets.

Culture.—Plant in regular potting soil; keep the soil moist. Grow in full sun, cool temperatures, and low to medium humidity.

Special requirements. — Begin training ivy when it is small. Pinch off the ends of the shoots frequently to produce a mass of laterals. Train the laterals against a trellis or bamboo rod placed in the pot.

MARANTA (Prayer Plant)

Description.—P r a y e r plant (*Maranta leuconeura kerchoveana*) folds up its leaves at night. The leaves are light green above and purple beneath; the leaf veins are fine and have a silken sheen.

Culture.—Plant in regular potting soil; keep the soil moist. Grow in diffused sun, warm temperatures, and high humidity.

Special requirements. — Do not allow water to stand on the crowns; the stems rot easily.

NEPHTHYTIS

See Syngonium.

PALMS

Description.—Most palms are too large for use as house plants. Two species — the pygmy Roebelin phoenix (*Phoenix roebelini*) and parlor palm (*Collinia elegans*) — are small enough to use as pot plants. Roebelin phoenix eventually grows to a 12-foot tree, but it normally grows for a long time before it begins to form a trunk. The parlor palm grows rapidly to about 8 feet. It is very tolerant of dim light.

Culture.—Plant in regular potting mixture; keep the soil wet. Grow in diffused sun, warm temperature, and low to moderate humidity.

PANDANUS (Screwpine)

Description.—The screwpines develop fine clumps of leaves that are arranged spirally along the trunk. The long, arching leaves are shaped like sword blades.

Culture.—Plant in regular potting mixture; allow the soil to dry moderately between waterings. Grow in indirect sunlight and warm dry atmosphere.

PEPEROMIA

Description. — Peperomias will tolerate neglect but will rot if overwatered. Though they tolerate dim light, they grow best in bright light.

Peperomia obtusifolia in its typical form has fleshy green leaves; the variegated form has leaves that are predominantly golden yellow with green markings. *Peperomia sandersi* (watermelon peperomia) bears leaves in rosettes. The leaf stems are deep red; the fleshy, heart-shaped leaves are deep green to bluish and have bands of silver radiating from their upper centers.

Culture.—Plant in regular potting soil mixture; allow the soil to dry moderately between waterings. Grow in indirect sunlight, warm temperatures, and low humidity.

PILEA

Description.—*Pilea carderii* (aluminum plant) has thin, fleshy, quilted foilage with unusual silver markings. The flowers of *P. microphylla* (artillery plant) discharge a cloud of pollen when shaken.

Culture.—Plant in humus soil; keep the soil moist. Grow in indirect sunlight, warm temperatures, and low humidity.

Special requirements.—Artillery plant requires clipping to promote branching.

PHILODENDRON

Description.—Philodendrons grow better than most other house plants under the adverse conditions found inside modern houses. They do well as long as they are kept warm—65° minimum—moderately moist, and out of direct sunlight.

Many forms of philodendron are available. *Philodendron oxycardum*, the most commonly grown form, has heart-shaped leaves. It

Philodendrons. Left to right: P. dubium, P. pertusum, and P. panduraeforme.

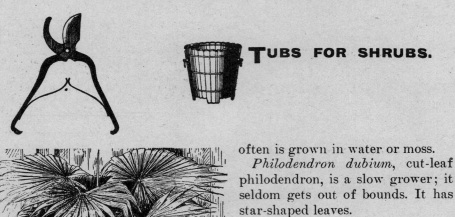

TUBS FOR SHRUBS.

Chinese Fan Palm (Livistonia chinensis) *a garden plant in Florida and California, is also a favorite Northern house plant*

often is grown in water or moss.

Philodendron dubium, cut-leaf philodendron, is a slow grower; it seldom gets out of bounds. It has star-shaped leaves.

Philodendron panduraeforme, fiddleleaf philodendron, has irregularly shaped, olive-green leaves.

Philodendron pertusum, which is really the juvenile form of *Monstera deliciosa*, has perforated leaves that are irregularly shaped. The adult form of *M. deliciosa* has broad, thick leaves that contain many perforations.

Philodendron squamiferum, anchorleaf philodendron, has leaves and petioles that are covered by red hairs. The leaves are shaped like daggers.

Philodendrons often are grown on trellises or moss-covered poles. When one of these plants grows to the end of the supporting pole, its stems sometimes begin to grow rapidly and the plant produces widely spaced small leaves.

Some forms of philodendron do not need support from a pole or trellis. These forms require a minimum of care. Among these forms are *Philodendron bipinnatifidum*, *P. selloum*, and *P. wendlandi*.

Philodendron bipinnatifidum, twice-cut philodendron, has leaves that resemble those of *P. dubium*, but are twice as large and more deeply notched.

P. selloum produces leaves that are almost solid when the plant is small. As the plant grows larger, it produces cut leaves. This species is resistant to cold; it can withstand temperatures down to freezing.

P. wendlandi has long, narrow leaves that can withstand extremes of temperatures and humidity.

Culture.—Plant in regular potting mixture; keep the soil moist. Grow in indirect sunlight, warm temperatures, and low humidity.

Special requirements.—Wash philodendron leaves once a month with soap and water. Do not get soapy water on the soil. If leaves are cleaned regularly this way, special foliage waxes are unnecessary.

When plants grow to the end of their supporting trellis or pole, cut back the stems to force new branches to develop. Pin the stem back to the support. Increase the light intensity on the plant and decrease the amount of water given it.

ADIANTUM BAUSEI.

MOSES IN THE CRADLE
(Rhoeo discolor)

Description.—Moses in the cradle produces a cluster of stiff, lance-shaped leaves that are dark, metallic green on top and glossy purple on the lower surface. Small white flowers are borne in boat-shaped bracts.

Culture.—Pot in regular soil mixture; keep the soil moist. Grow in indirect sunlight, moderate temperatures, and medium humidity.

PODOCARPUS

Description.—Yew podocarpus (*Podocarpus macrophylla*) is an evergreen shrub that can grow to a height of 50 feet. It grows well as a pot plant under household conditions and can be kept small by shearing.

Culture.—Plant in regular potting soil; keep the soil moist. Grow in indirect sunlight, cool temperatures, and low humidity.

POTHOS

See Scindapsus.

SANSEVIERIA (Snake Plant)

Description.—Snake plants develop clumps of erect, strap-shaped leaves. The leaves of *Sansevieria zeylanica* are dark green banded with lighter green. The leaves of *S. laurentii* normally are longitudinally striped with golden yellow. These plants grow in almost any environment.

Culture.—Plant in regular soil mixture; allow the soil to dry moderately between waterings. Grow in any light intensity from dim interior to full sunlight. Keep in moderate to warm atmosphere with low humidity.

SCHEFFLERA
(Umbrella Tree)

Description.—*Schefflera actinophylla* is a rapid grower. It produces large compound leaves. The leaflets are slender, fleshy, and glossy green.

Special requirements.—Propagate by division or leaf cuttings. When propagated by division of the clump, *S. laurentii* continues to produce striped leaves. But when it is propagated by leaf cuttings, it produces plain-green leaves.

Culture.—Plant in regular potting soil; allow soil to dry moderately between waterings. Grow in indirect sunlight, warm temperatures, and low to medium humidity.

— An Epiphytic Fern (*Platycerium*) on a Tree Trunk.
The more upright leaves next the trunk of the tree serve to collect water and to accumulate a deposit of decaying vegetable matter, while the outer leaves serve as foliage and bear spores.

Sansevieria trifaciata   Codiaeum varigatum   Ficus elastica

SCINDAPSUS

Description.—*Scindapsus aureus* looks like a smooth-stemmed philodendron but can be distinguished from philodendron by its ridged stems. It can be grown and trained like philodendron but should be watered less frequently. Silver Marble, a variegated form, must be grown in temperatures above 70°; the green forms may be grown at 65°.

Culture.—Plant in humus soil; allow soil to dry moderately between waterings. Grow in indirect sunlight, warm temperatures, and low humidity.

SYNGONIUM (Nephtythis)

Description.— Syngonium has heart-shaped leaves with silver-white or green centers. It thrives under household conditions.

Culture.—Plant in regular potting soil; keep the soil moist. Grow in indirect sunlight, warm temperatures, and low humidity.

Special requirements.—Provide with a pole or totem for support. Prune occasionally to keep in bounds.

WANDERING-JEW

Description.—Three species of plants belonging to the spiderwort family are called wandering-jew—*Zebrina pendula*, *Tradescantia fluminensis*, and *Commelina nudiflora*. Their foliage is so similar that they cannot easily be distinguished from one another until they bloom. All of these plants are easy to grow

Culture.—Pot in regular soil mixture; keep the soil moist. Grow in indirect sunlight, moderate temperatures, and medium humidity.

Special requirements.—Propagate wandering-jew from tip cuttings

SUCCULENTS

Succulents are plants having thick, jucy stems or leaves. They are found in many plant families. Succulents are good house plants because they do not require much care and they grow well under household conditions.

Kinds of Succulents

Cactus is a favorite among the succulents that are used as house plants. Some of the kinds of cactus are *Echinocactus, Espostoa, Echinocereus, Opuntia, Ferocactus,* and *Trichocereus.*

Aloes also are available in many forms. Two of the favorite aloes are Barbados aloe, *A. vera,* and *Aloe variegata.*

One of the best species of Euphorbia for pot culture in *Euphorbia lactea,* which grows erect like a tree and has a spiny, three-sided trunk. Its leaves are small and they drop off soon after they are formed.

Haworthia, which come from South Africa, belong to the lily family. They are grown primarily for their foliage. One group of plants, of which *Haworthia fasciata* is an example, has leaves that are semitranslucent. Another group, of which *H. tesselata* is an example, has thick, leathery leaves.

Other well-known succulents are *Crassula, Sempervivum, Sedum, Bryophyllum,* and *Kalanchoe.*

Culture

Culture of all of the succulents is similar: Plant in regular potting soil; allow the soil to dry moderately between waterings. Grow in full sun, moderate temperatures, and medium to low humidity.

FLOWERING PLANTS

ACHIMENES

Description.—Achimenes leaves are finely cut and are tinted red or green. The flowers, shaped like those of petunias, may be red or blue. Achimenes plants are grown from rhizomes planted during March, April, or May and kept in a sunny window or in a hanging basket that is exposed to full or partial sun. The plant blooms during the summer.

Culture.—Plant in humus soil; keep the soil wet. Grow in indirect sunlight and normal summer temperatures and humidities.

Special requirements.—In late summer after the flowers have passed, allow the soil to dry gradually. When the plant withers, dig up the rhizome and store it through the winter in dry sand at a temperature of 45° to 50°.

CALLA FLOWERS AND FOLIAGE.

CITRUS

Description.—Otaheite orange, ponderosa lemon, and Meyer lemon are the kinds of citrus most likely to flower and fruit indoors. Grapefruit seeds, planted in a low bowl, form a mass of foliage from the crowded seedlings.

Culture.—Plant in regular potting soil; keep the soil moist. Grow in subdued daylight, cool temperatures, and medium humidity.

Special requirements.—Propagate flowering citrus plants from seeds or cuttings.

BEGONIA

Description.—Fiberous-rooted begonia has succulent stems and shiny leaves. It produces flowers continuously. The flowers may be white, pink, or scarlet.

Tuberous-rooted begonias bear large white, yellow, orange, or red flowers and have watery stems and brittle, pointed leaves. These plants may be grown in pots or may be used outdoors as bedding plants in partial shade.

The showiest of the begonias is the semituberous begonia (*B. socotrana*), which is available as a Christmas-gift plant. It also is the most difficult to grow. It is best to keep this plant in full sun until the flowers pass, then discard it.

Culture.—Plant in humus soil; keep the soil moist. Grow in full sun or bright, diffused sunlight, warm temperatures, and medium to high humidity.

Special requirements.—Plant tuberous-rooted begonia in March. Keep the soil moist. Grow it in full sun until May, then move it to bright, indirect sunlight. Using fluorescent tubes or a 75-watt incandescent bulb 3 feet above the plant, light the plant from 10 p.m. to 2 a.m. each night during the winter. With this supplementary illumination the plant will bloom throughout the year.

Fiberous-rooted begonia needs full sunlight during the winter. It can be propagated from seeds or terminal cuttings.

CALLA

Description.—Calla leaves are large and arrow shaped. The showy part of the plant is not a true flower, but an envelope surrounding the member on which the true flowers are borne. Callas will grow continuously when permitted to do so, but their flowers get smaller and smaller. This can be prevented if the plants are allowed to become dormant during the summer.

Culture.—Pot in regular soil mixture; keep the soil wet. Grow in full sun, cool temperatures, and medium humidity.

Special requirements.—Pot calla rhizomes in late summer or early fall. Start the plants at temperatures of 60° to 65°. When growth starts, move the plants to an area where the temperature is 55° to 60° and the plants have full sunlight. Withhold water in summer to bring on dormancy. Repot the rhizomes after the summer-dormancy period.

CHRISTMAS CACTUS

Description.—Christmas cactus produces many flat-stemmed fleshy branches that serve as leaves. Brilliant pink pendant flowers grow from the edges of the younger parts of the plant. Christmas cactus often fails to bloom because of nighttime exposure to high temperatures or artificial light.

Culture.—Pot in humus soil. Keep the soil moist in winter, spring, and summer; allow it to dry moderately between waterings in fall. Grow in full sunlight, cool temperatures, and medium humidity.

Special requirements. — Beginning September 1, keep the plant in total darkness—with no artificial light—for at least 12 hours a night. Maintain a night temperature of no more than 70°. During summer, grow the plant in a cool, shaded area.

Propagate Christmas cactus from pieces of branches two or three segments long.

INDOOR AND TROPICAL PLANTS

Edelweiss Gardens,
54 Robbinsville-Allentown Rd.,
Robbinsville, N.J. 08691

Greenland Flower Shop,
R. 1,
Port Matilda, Penna. 16870

International Growers Exchange,
Box 397,
Farmington, Mich. 48024

Lehua Anthurium Nursery,
80 Kokea St.,
Hilo, Hawaii 96720

Logee's Greenhouses,
Danielson, Conn. 06239

Paul F. Lowe,
23045 S.W. 123 Rd.,
Goulds, Fla. 33170

Loyce's Flowers,
R. 2, Box 11,
Granbury, Tex. 76048

McComb Greenhouses,
R. 1,
New Straitsville, Ohio 43766

House Plant Corner,
Box 810,
Oxford, Md. 21654

Merry Gardens,
Camden, Maine 04843

Trader Horn,
Box 1675,
Miami, Fla. 31138

MASDEVALLIA ARMINI.

Terms Used in Descriptions of House-Plant Culture

Cool temperatures.—Temperature range during winter on a window sill in an unheated room—40 to 45 deg. at night, 55 to 60 deg. on sunny days, and 50 deg. on cloudy days.

Dimlight.—Lighting intensity of room interior away from windows.

Full sun.—Sunlight unbroken by curtains or frosted glass. South windows have full sun for the longest period during the day.

High humidity.—Atmosphere saturated with moisture. Attainable only in a greenhouse or terrarium.

Humus.—Pure sphagnum moss, firbark, or osmunda fiber.

Humus soil.—Mixture of 3 parts humus and 1 part coarse sand.

Indirect sunlight.—Sunlight diffused by a lightweight curtain placed between the sun and the plant.

Low humidity.—Normal humidity in a heated or air-conditioned house—40 to 50 percent relative humidity.

Medium humidity.—Relative humidity of about 70 percent.

Moderate temperatures.—Winter range of temperatures on the window sill of a normally heated room—50 to 55 deg. at night, 70 deg. on sunny days, and 60 deg. on cloudy days.

Potting mixture.—Equal parts of garden soil and organic matter—peat moss or shredded sphagnum moss—with 1 level teaspoon of 20-percent superphosphate added per quart of mixture.

Subdued daylight.—Daylight with no direct sun; light from a north window.

Warm temperatures.—65 deg. at night and 80 to 85 deg. during the day. Supplemental heaters usually are needed to provide warm temperatures.

GROWING PLANTS IN DIM LIGHT

If house plants have the proper amount of water and heat for good growth but do not have enough light, they tend to grow long and spindling. Often, planters are used as decorating accessories in locations that are not lighted well enough for good growth of plants. However, foliage plants can be acclimated to low light intensities.

To grow house plants successfully where they get little or no daylight—

Water the plants only often enough to prevent wilting.

Reduce the amount of fertilizer that you apply to the plants.

Keep the air temperature as cool as you can tolerate.

Provide supplementary lighting with fluorescent tubes.

Double pot plants that are to be grown under artificial light. This makes soil-moisture control easier than leaving the pot exposed to the air.

Begin watering as frequently as you would if the plant had sufficient light. Then gradually lengthen the intervals between waterings.

A few of the oldest leaves may die while you are adapting the plant to dry-soil conditions; this is part of the readjustment to the new environment.

Do not let the plant wilt at any time.

Fertilize the plants more sparingly than normal. Use only about one-third as much fertilizer as is recommended for plants growing vigorously. Continue to fertilize frequently.

Maintain an air temperature that is as low as human occupants can comfortably tolerate. Most plants thrive at temperatures of 60 to 75 degrees. In general, weakly lighted plants do best in the lower limits of this range, while brightly lighted plants do best in the upper limits.

If you can add moisture to the air, do so. Plants will grow under conditions of low humidity, but they need more attention to watering than they do under moderate humidity.

Fluorescent tubes are best for supplying supplementary lighting. Regular incandescent lights or reflector floods can be used for spot lighting, but they are too hot when used in numbers large enough to provide the relatively high lighting intensities required by the plants.

The required lighting intensity for a plant varies according to the time the plant is lighted; the dimmer the light, the longer the plant must be lighted.

If you use a fixture containing two 40-watt fluorescent tubes and light the plants for 16 hours a day, the minimum lighting intensity for growing foliage plants can be supplied by placing the fixture the following height above the plants:

54 to 66 inches:
Aglaonema commutatum
Dieffenbachia picta
Dracaena sanderiana
Philodendron cordatum

36 to 54 inches:
Anthurium hybrids
Bromeliads
Peperomia obtusifolia
Scindapsus aureus

Closer than 36 inches:
Fatshedera lizei
Ficus pandurata
Hedera helix
Ciccus rhombifolia

These are maximum distances for satisfactory plant growth. All the plants grow best if they are no farther than 36 inches from the lighting fixture.

BAMBOO

Pacific Bamboo Gardens,
Box 16145,
San Diego, Calif. 92116

GUIDE TO INDOOR GARDEN LIGHTING

The GRO-LUX lamp is most beneficial for plant propagation, and enhances vegetative and reproductive growth of many plants for the home and commercial use.

Courtesy of Sylvania, Inc.

Reg. Trade Mark

DURATION OF LIGHT

Duration of light each day is known as a photoperiod. It defines the hours of light exposure per day on the growth of the plant. Plants are grouped into short day, long day and indeterminant with respect to the effect of the length of day on flowering.

In general, short day plants need 10 to 13 hours of light per day to flower when the balance of the day is a continuous dark period. Some common short day plants are chrysanthemums, gardenias, Christmas begonia and poinsettias.

Long day plants need 14 to 18 hours of light to flower. In this group are included China asters, calceolaria, coreopsis, dahlias, nasturtiums and many of the annuals grown for spring flowering.

Indeterminant plants will produce flowers at all seasons of the year. This group includes roses, carnations, and many household plants such as the African violets, gloxinias, begonias, geraniums and coleus. They will blossom in varying degrees of abundance, whether they are exposed to 12, 14, 16 or 18 hours of light.

It is a good practice to group the plants according to their photoperiod for flowering. By installing an inexpensive automatic timer the plants will receive the required light period from day to day.

For the germination of seeds and rooting cuttings: A light period of 16 hours produces satisfactory results. With newly germinated seedlings and rooted cuttings, prior to transplanting, a longer light period of up to 20 hours may be used with good results.

LIGHT INTENSITIES

In contrast to the photoperiod, light intensity is the amount or quantity of light energy needed for photosynthesis and plant growth. Different plant types and growth phases require different light intensities as described below. The light intensity can be simply determined from the number of lamp watts per square foot of growing area. If, for example, two-20 watt Gro-Lux

may be used is to cover the seeds lightly with soil, vermiculite or perlite and then comb or scrape the surface lightly after soaking the cover medium. This allows for better penetration of light as well as incorporating air in the seed areas.

For low energy growing plants: 15 lamp watts per square foot of growing area. The light source should be 12" to 15" above plant tops. Many household plants fall in this classification.

For high energy growing plants: 20 lamp watts or more per square foot of growing area. The light source should be 12" to 15" above plant tops. Plants such as chrysanthemums, carnations, roses, tomatoes, beans, and most vegetable crops fall in this classification. When these crops are grown in enclosed areas where there is no available sunlight 10 to 20 per cent of the total wattage should be provided by incandescent lamps, or the Standard Gro-Lux lamps should be substituted with Wide Spectrum Gro-Lux lamps. These lamps provide the far red radiation which is important for normal growth development with high energy plants.

For germinating seeds and rooting cuttings: 10 lamp watts per square foot of growing area. The light source should be 6" to 8" above the soil or planting media. Recent studies indicate that if some seeds are exposed rather than being lightly covered, a higher germination percentage is obtained. Another system that lamps (40 lamp watts) are used to uniformly light two square feet of growing area, then the light intensity can be described as 20 lamp watts per square foot. Light intensities described in this manner for different applications are shown below.

THE STANDARD GRO-LUX FLUORESCENT LAMP IS USED BY THE HOBBYIST:

To accelerate germination of most seeds.

To produce stockier seedlings.

To reduce susceptibility to damping-off infection.

To stimulate the rooting of cuttings.

To produce fibrous root systems.

To display flowering plants.

To light aquariums.

Examples of plants that have been successfully grown under Standard Gro-Lux Fluorescent Lamps are listed below:

Copper leaf	Pineapple	Orchids
Blue African lily	Lily of the field	Flamingo flower
Flowering maple	Variegated Japanese	Star begonia
Christmas tree plant	laurel	Wax begonia
Rex begonia	Christmas pepper	Coffee plant
Camellia	Dracaena	Crotons
Butterfly coleus	Holly fern	Irish ivy
Christmas cyclamen	English ivy	Paradise palm
Variegated rubber plant	Garden geranium	Split-leaf
Glossy privet	Spadeleaf philodendron	philodendron
American rubber plant	Variegated	Heart-leaved
African violets	philodendron	philodendron
Pansy	Dumb cane	Wandering Jew
Chinese evergreen	Flamingo lily	Variegated pothos
Giant glocasia	Crystal anthurium	Coleus

THE WIDE SPECTRUM GRO-LUX FLUORESCENT LAMP

combines the far-red energy of incandescent lamps that certain high-energy crops require. The lamp can be used for starting and growing to maturity: Florists Crops - Herbs - Vegetable Crops.

Examples of a few of the many plants grown successfully under Wide Spectrum Gro-Lux Fluorescent Lamps:

Geraniums	Leaf Lettuce	Other Herbs
Asters	Soft-headed Lettuce	Chrysanthemums
Dahlias	Dill	Some Orchids
Cherry Tomatoes	Sweet Basil	Tomatoes

Annuals to be germinated and grown in the seedling stage (to be moved out-of-doors) should be started under Standard Gro-Lux Fluorescent Lamps.

LIGHT QUALITY

Light quality refers to the wavelengths or color of light energy most effective in photosynthesis and plant growth. Studies have shown that the blue and red light rays are most effective, and the balanced spectrum of Gro-Lux lamps has already been described.

TEMPERATURE

Proper regulation of the temperature is essential for developing the quality of the plants. The optimum night temperatures should be between 60° and 65°F., and when the lights are on temperatures should be in the range of 70° to 75°F.

Temperature influences the various metabolic processes of plant growth — the rate of absorption by the roots, transpiration (giving off of water vapor through the leaves), respiration, the rate of assimilation of carbon dioxide, and the production of chlorophyll.

Night temperatures are far more important than most people realize. Plants manufacture their food during the light hours, but they can assimilate or use it during the dark period, and this process is aided by cool temperatures.

To maintain optimum temperatures, accurate thermometers should be employed. It is essential to pay attention to this important factor.

VENTILATION

Ventilation provides circulation of air, which is important in preventing the development of disease organisms. All plants continuously lose water vapor through small pores or stomates found on the leaf surface. This process is known as transpiration. Poor ventilation causes this water vapor to condense in a film on the leaf surface, and offers ideal germinating conditions for the spores of disease producing organisms. Ventilation also allows for the entrance of carbon dioxide necessary for photosynthesis, as well as to provide a good supply of oxygen for respiration.

RELATIVE HUMIDITY

Humidity is the amount of water held by the air in vapor form. Increasing the amount of water in the air greatly reduces the amount of water lost by the plant through the leaves. The water that is absorbed by the roots is used in keeping the plant firm, and unless the plant has a sufficient supply of water, it fails to grow.

The importance of humidity in propagation cannot be overemphasized. It plays a key role in successful rooting. The failure of many plants to root from cuttings can be traced to a lack of proper humidity. The recommended humidity for most plants is between 50% to 60% for normal growth. This also is the range of humidity that is generally considered as comfortable for humans. 100% relative humidity would mean the air was saturated as with dense fog. 50% relative humidity means the air actually contains 50% of the total water vapor possible if it were saturated.

PLANT SPACING

Adequate distance between plants prevents legginess. Crowding results in the development of long, weak petioles (leaf stems) which cannot support the leaves; provides ideal conditions for development of foliage diseases due to insufficient aeration. No definite rules can be given regarding exact distance, but in general, plants should not be allowed to touch each other.

SOIL TYPES

There are two types of soil from the standpoint of use by the grower, inorganic and organic. Inorganic soils are composed largely of gravel, sand, silt and clay, proceeding from the largest particle size to the smallest. Sandy soils are gritty and small grains of sand may be noticed in them. Organic soils are muck and peat. Muck is well decomposed peat possessing little or no fibrous structure.

Mixtures of clay, silt and sand are called loams, such as silty clay loam, sandy loam, etc. Usually, loam has organic matter in the form of decayed plant and animal materials.

Clay soils are heavy and retain moisture for a long time. They must be loosened, to permit air to enter and improve drainage, by the addition of sand and organic matter.

A good soil mixture for most

A spectral activity curve of the chlorophyll synthesis process is shown in Figure 1, together with the spectral energy distribution curve of the Standard Gro-Lux® lamp.

The spectral energy distribution curves in Figure 2 give the relative energy outputs of Standard Gro-Lux and Gro-Lux/WS lamps. An S.E.D. curve is a curve of relative energy output versus wavelength of light. Note that the Gro-Lux/WS lamp has much more output in the far red, that is, beyond 700 nanometers. See Table 1 which compares the total energy emission in various spectral bands of the Gro-Lux/WS, Standard Gro-Lux, Cool White, and Warm White fluorescent lamps.

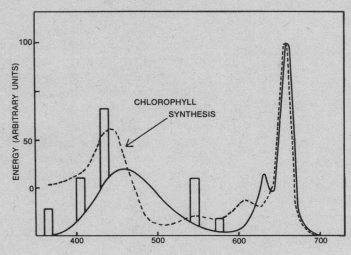

Figure 1 — Spectral energy distribution for standard GRO-LUX fluorescent lamps, designed especially to enhance vegetative plant growth, compared to energy used in chlorophyll synthesis.

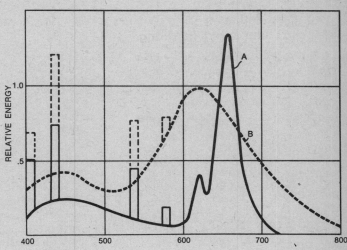

Figure 2 — Comparison of the SED Curves of the two Gro-Lux Lamps. (A) Standard Gro-Lux and (B) Gro-Lux/WS.

TABLE 1: ENERGY EMISSION IN ARBITRARY COLOR BANDS
40 WATT FLUORESCENT LAMPS In Watts and Percent of Total Emission

Ultra Violet	< 380	0.13	1.52	0.16	1.68	0.10	1.42	0.27	3.16
Violet	380-430	0.46	5.15	0.72	7.57	0.70	9.67	1.07	12.48
Blue	430-490	1.15	12.91	1.98	20.78	1.96	27.07	1.22	14.29
Green	490-560	1.80	20.24	2.35	24.67	1.02	14.02	1.24	14.49
Yellow	560-590	2.06	23.17	1.74	18.27	0.10	1.42	0.83	9.77
Orange	590-630	2.13	23.95	1.69	17.75	0.44	6.05	1.36	15.93
Red	630-700	1.03	11.53	0.81	8.47	2.86	39.55	1.86	21.78
Far-Red	700-780	0.13	1.53	0.07	0.81	0.06	0.80	0.69	8.10
TOTAL		8.89	100.00	9.52	100.00	7.24	100.00	8.54	100.00

plants is as follows: Three parts of loam, one part of leaf mold or peat moss, and one part of coarse sand. Your soil mixture will need sterilizing to kill harmful diseases, insects and weed seeds. The easiest way is to bake the soil in an oven for a half an hour at 212°F. When sterilizing the soil keep it thoroughly wet all the way through with some water standing on top. The conversion of this water into steam is what does so effective a job of sterilizing.

Prepared, sterile soil substitutes are commercially available for use in potting and starting seedlings or cuttings.

FERTILIZERS

Fertilizers are necessary for the production of high quality plants. The most important mineral nutrients concerned in the culture of plants are nitrogen, phosphorus, potassium and calcium. These major nutrients play an important function in plant growth.

There are many kinds of complete fertilizers in the market — tablet, dry powder, and liquid types. Complete fertilizer usually means having the three primary or major elements — nitrogen, phosphorus and potassium. A more complete fertilizer also contains minor elements such as magnesium and iron which are important in photosynthesis and metabolism.

Follow the directions of the manufacturer and remember that too little fertilizer is better than too much. A fairly safe rule when fertilizing the plants is as follows:

With a liquid fertilizer, feed plants about once every two weeks, taking the place of watering for that day. With a dry fertilizer, feed plants about once a month. Dry fertilization should be followed by a moderate watering in order to make the minerals available to the plant.

THE IMPORTANCE OF pH MEASUREMENTS

The pH measurement is a convenient expression of the acidity or alkalinity of the soil. In simple terms the pH measurements indicate whether the soil is sour (acid) or sweet (alkaline).

The pH scale runs from 0 to 14 with 7 being neutral; values below 7 being acid and those above being alkaline.

Temperature and pH are not directly related but the Fahrenheit scale may serve to illustrate the concept of pH measurement and its relationship to proper plant growth. See Chart 1.

Most plants prefer a slightly

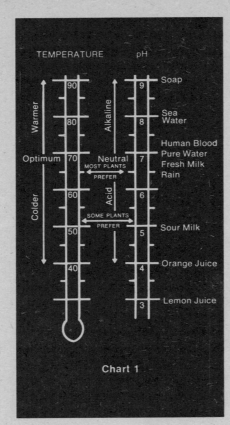

Chart 1

acid soil which falls in the pH range of 6.2 to 6.8 with the optimum pH of 6.5. Generally ground limestone is used to correct acid soil, sulphur to correct alkaline soil conditions. To make sure that the soil is at the proper pH level, at the time of mixing the soil, add a 4-inch pot of ground limestone for every 2½ bushels of potting soil, or 6 teaspoons of ground limestone to every 3 quarts of soil.

On the other hand to correct alkaline soils, add a 2-inch pot of sulphur for every 2½ bushels of soil or 3 teaspoons of sulphur to every 3 quarts of soil.

The only sure way to ascertain whether a soil has the proper pH

NITROGEN
1 Gives dark green color to foliage.
2 Promotes leaf, stem and fruit growth.
3 Improves the quality of the leaf.
4 Produces rapid growth.
5 Increases the protein content of plants.

PHOSPHORUS
1 Stimulates early root formation and growth.
2 Gives rapid and vigorous start to plants.
3 Hastens maturity.
4 Stimulates blooming and aids in fruit formation.

POTASSIUM
1 Imparts increased vigor and decisive resistance to plants.
2 Improves seed quality.
3 Essential to formation and transfer of starches, sugar and oils in plant system.

CALCIUM
1 Influences absorption of plant nutrients.
2 Neutralizes acid conditions in soil.
3 Promotes early root formation and growth.
4 Neutralizes toxic compounds produced in the plant.

and nutrient level is to have a soil analysis made of the soil. This analysis can be obtained, free of charge, from all the State Agricultural experiment stations in the country.

PROPAGATION METHODS

Plants are propagated by seeds, bulbs, and cuttings depending on the type of plant to be grown.

SEEDS

Even the best light sources and cultural operations cannot produce good plants unless good seeds are used. Buy tested seeds grown by reliable seed companies. Specially prepared mediums for germination are more satisfactory than using ordinary soil because the requirements for successful seed germination are more exacting than for growth of the plant. The following mediums are suggested:

1. A mixture of equal volumes of clean sand and fine grade of peatmoss.

2. Vermiculite or expanded mica is useful. It retains moisture yet permits air circulation, provided it is not firmed or packed. The finer grades are more suitable. This medium provides sanitary conditions for germination.

To insure against seed-borne, disease organisms, one may buy seeds that are treated with seed disinfectants. Treated seeds are marked on the outside of the package with the material used.

SOWING THE SEEDS

When small quantities are to be sown, a 4"x8"x3" seed tray flat, or a pot, makes a convenient container; larger quantities are handled in flats 12"x18"x3".

Sow a small amount of seeds in rows or bands 1 inch apart for small seeds; 1½ to 2 inches apart for medium seeds; and 2½ to 3 inches apart for large seeds. Do not crowd the seeds. Give them room to grow. For small seed, sow 3 per inch; medium seed, 2 per inch; and large seed, 4 per foot. See Figure 2.

The depth to plant depends on the size of the seed. See Figure 3. A general rule to follow is twice the diameter of the seed. The seeds should be covered lightly, with the same medium in which they are sown and firmed except when using the vermiculite medium. The tray, flat or pot should be watered with a fine spray and covered with paper, clear plastic or glass. The covering is applied to maintain the

moisture of the medium. Mark each row or band of seeds for proper variety identification. The germination processes are dependent upon the factors of temperature, moisture, oxygen, and light.

The temperature for seed germination should be about 10°F. higher than required for normal growth of the plant. For most plants a temperature range of 75° to 85°F. is necessary for optimum germination results.

The presence of water softens the seed coat, permitting water, accompanied by oxygen, to enter the seed. Enzyme reaction and the necessary life processes are hastened, respiration increases, stored food in the seed is translocated; all resulting in growth of the embryo and the initial formation of the primary root.

Light requirements are definite for many seeds. Gro-Lux lamps supply the quality light necessary for rapid germination.

Gro-Lux lamps are particularly useful for germinating seeds for outdoor spring planting. When the Gro-Lux seedlings are to be transplanted to the outdoor environment, proper steps must be taken to harden the seedlings. This is accomplished by gradually reducing the temperature and keeping the plants somewhat drier than usual until they are acclimated to the outside conditions. A common procedure is to expose the seedlings to the out of doors during the day and take them in for the night until they are firm enough to leave outside permanently. It may take about one and a half weeks to fully harden the seedlings. During the first few days, however, the young plants need protection from the sunlight by providing some type of shade. An important factor to remember when hardening plants is to have air circulation, especially if they are in protected areas. This will prevent the buildup of high temperatures, and thereby reduce the wilting of the young seedlings.

CUTTINGS

A cutting may be defined as any part which has been cut from a plant and is capable of regeneration. Cuttings may be classified on the basis of the plant part from which they are taken — leaf and leaf-bud cuttings. This Method of propagation is important because many plants do not come true from seed.

The rooting medium used may be clean sand, vermiculite, perlite or peat moss (fine grain). The same type of containers can be used as were used for the seeds.

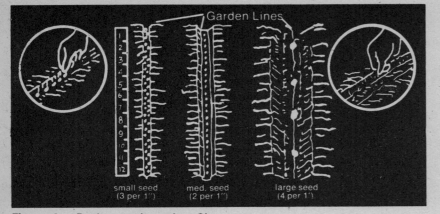

Figure 2 — Don't crowd seeds. Give them room to grow.

LEAF CUTTING

The leaf petiole (leaf stem) should be at least ½ inch long to help anchor the leaf in the rooting medium. Mature leaves should be used for propagation since they produce better plants than young leaves. Plants with thick fleshy leaves, such as African violets and begonias, are used for this type of cutting.

LEAF BUD CUTTING

To make leaf bud cutting, place the knife about one-half inch above a bud on the stem and cut in and down so the knife leaves the stem about three quarters of an inch below the bud. The cutting consists of the leaf blade, its petiole and a small section of the main stem.

PLANTING THE CUTTINGS

Proper insertion requires that one-third to one-half of the length of the cutting be covered with the rooting medium, which should be firmed tightly about its base. As previously stated the vermiculite should not be firmed. The cuttings are stuck in loose vermiculite and watered in.

Enough space should be left between the rows to provide good circulation. The temperature of the cutting should be around 70° to 75°F. to hasten rooting. Not only should the rooting medium be kept moist but a high humidity of 50% in the air surrounding the cuttings is most beneficial. Moisture is important in keeping the cuttings turgid, as well as maintaining optimum absorption, translocation and photosynthetic activity. Light quality plays an important role in photosynthesis which is the manufacture of food.

TRANSPLANTING

The seedlings or rooted cuttings should be planted into pots, as

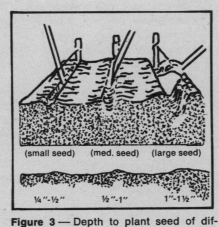

Figure 3 — Depth to plant seed of different sizes.

soon as they are ready. Preferably, they should be planted as soon as the cotyledon leaves of seedings (first leaves coming up through the soil) are fully developed or when the roots of cutting are ¼ inch long. To keep root injury to a minimum, the medium should be thoroughly wet before the plants are removed. The standard clay pot is most universally used for transplanting which measures between 2½ to 3 inches across the top.

Before transplanting, first cover the drainage hole of the pot with a piece of broken pot, called a "crock." This keeps the soil from washing out at the bottom. Cover the crock with coarse gravel, then add soil up to the rim of the pot, leaving a half-inch space at the top of the pot for watering. See Figure 4.

A hole is made large enough to hold the roots of the plant. Next, using a fork or spoon, dig up the seedling from the rooting medium, being careful to leave as much as possible of the rooting medium clinging to the root system. Place the roots in the hole, being careful not to bury any of the leaves. Give the pot a thump to settle the soil, then press with your fingers to pack the soil all around the roots.

Planting rooted cuttings is done in a different manner. Since cuttings have more roots, they cannot be pushed into a hole in the soil. After the crock is placed in

the pot, a little soil is added, then hold the cutting in the pot. Sift the soil all around the roots and fill the pot to the top leaving about a half-inch space at the top for watering. Jar the pot to shake down the soil, then press with your fingers to make the soil firm around the roots. Water the transplants with enough water to thoroughly soak the root area. This helps to bring the soil in contact with the roots and prevents drying of plant.

POT INFORMATION

The clay pot is porous, relatively light and nests well. The porosity of the pot promotes aeration of the soil which is essential for healthy root systems.

The plastic or painted clay pots are not porous. However, when using plastic pots make sure to use dark colored ones. The reason for this is that the light colored pots reflect heat and maintain a lower soil temperature, while the darker pots absorb heat, producing a slightly higher soil temperature which enhances root growth.

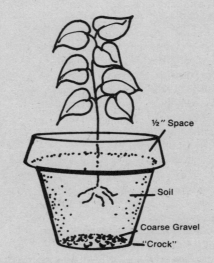

Figure 4 — Leave half-inch watering space at top of pot after potting.

WATERING

Water plants in the morning when the temperature is rising and there is a greater need for water. It is not a good practice to water plants or to have the soil wet when the temperature is falling because diseases may get started this way.

Put enough water to soak all the soil in the pot. Watering a little bit and often is not a good practice. At least once a week the pot should be put in the kitchen sink and left there to soak 5 to 15 minutes. Take it out and let it drain before returning to its place

A general rule to follow is to water plants approximately three times a week or more frequently if the plants show signs of wilting.

Some plants are sensitive to the chlorine in the water (ferns, African violets). For these plants,

use water that has stood overnight in an open container.

Wick watering is a method that draws water up by a wick from a saucer full of water

The wick is made of spun glass or fiber glass. Cut the wick large enough to flatten it out on the bottom of the pot and also so it reaches the water in the saucer. Do not use any crock when you use a wick. The pot should sit on a metal dish that is resting on the saucer. This raises the pot above the water level in the saucer. Plants do not like to have "wet root." The saucer should have water in it all of the time. Wick watering works best on plants whose leaves must be kept dry, such as African violets or gloxinias.

PLANT PESTS AND THEIR CONTROL

Insects are controlled by the knowledge of their feeding habits. Classified according to their mouth parts, insects may be placed into chewing and sucking types.

Chewing insects eat holes in the leaves, chew stems or cut them off. Others burrow into stems and eat their way along until the plant breaks off or dies. Sucking insects suck the juice from the leaves or stem of the plant. This causes the leaves to curl and turn brown or the plant to wilt or die.

A plant disease is defined as "any variation from the normal structure of/or function of plants." Diseases are primarily caused by fungi and bacteria. The rapid advance in development of agricultural chemicals for control of plant pests makes it impractical to give specific recommendations since they would soon be out-of-date.

Generally speaking, the fungus and bacterial diseases of the leaves are not too common to many household plants. Many of the foliage diseases are developed from long periods of moisture on the leaves.

A good control against such infections is to avoid constant wetting of the leaves. Most diseases of the household plants affect the roots and lower stems. They develop most frequently in heavy, poorly drained soils. A good control measure is to avoid overwatering.

A good control policy to follow is to apply combination dusts or sprays. They contain both insecticides for the insects and fungicides or bacteriacides for the diseases, and one application can control most of the pests. It is very important that the directions on the package be carefully followed.

LIGHT & CHEMICALS

ESCALATING GROWTH OF PLANTS— LIGHT AND CHEMICALS

By Henry M. Cathey

Plant Science Research Division, Agriculture
Research Service
United States Department of Agriculture,
Beltsville, Maryland 20705

The first cultural step in the growing of many plants is to select the proper combinations of temperature, light, chemicals, moisture, and protection system. Plants grown out-of-doors, however, can have only a minimum of regulation exerted on them as uncontrollable occurrences in nature may nullify manipulations made by man. Yet the grower once decides to grow plants in an enclosed environment, to attain maximum growth rates with minimum of hazards, he must immediately make many arbitrary decisions.

This paper presents current progress in environmental and chemical methods which can be used by growers to accelerate growth, thus producing salable or flowering plants in a minimum time. It suggests that the enhancement of one environmental aspect slightly boosts the growth rate whereas several aspects, simultaneously enhanced, rapidly accelerate growth rates: less time is needed to initiate a node, increase the number of lateral branches and form flowers. The simultaneous enhancement of many environmental factors which results in great acceleration of growth is called "escalated growth."

To review the recent research, one must examine the parts and then integrate them into "escalated growth" techniques.

Photoperiod-Temperature

Prior to studying the enhancement of environmental factors, certain basic growth requirements must be fulfilled. The conversion of protochlorophyll to chlorophyll and the maximum functioning of chlorophyll are dependent on visible light at carefully defined ranges of temperature. Light systems are an intertwining of photosynthesis, various high energy reactions, and phytochrome, low-energy mediated reactions each of which utilizes different parts of the visible light. Some may require several thousands of foot candles of light, others can be manipulated with several foot candles of light. Light systems are generally separated into two parts, the main light period and the photoperiod extension or interruption.

Main Light Period

Light for growing many kinds of plants can be provided by using 1500MA (milliamperes) fluorescent lamps with an addition of 10% of the wattage from incandescent-filament lamps. Plants grown with 2500-3000 foot candles of light above them respond much like those grown out-of-doors. Levels of light higher than 4000 foot candles often create problems of excessive heat and rapid drying of the plants and growing media which compromise their positive effects. The search for alternative light sources to circumvent these problems has led to the development of color-improved fluorescent lamps which emit more light in the far red region (about 700 nm), and thus boost leaf temperatures than does the standard cool white fluorescent lamp. Such lamps usually give lower foot candle readings than the cool white lamps since foot candle readings are based on maximum sensitivity of the light meter in the yellow-green region.

Other light sources have been developed which have greater efficiency than fluorescent lamps. The High-pressure sodium lamps emit high levels of light, but primarily in the yellow region, and by themselves, are relatively ineffective in regulating growth. Metal-halide lamps, mercury lamps with selected metal iodides added to the discharge are, emit light throughout the visible spectrum and also radiate vast amounts of heat. Both of these lamps are pinpoint sources of light and require special devices to reflect and distribute the light uniformly over a growing area. The mercury-type lamps (metal-halide lamps), and high-pressure sodium lamps in combination offer the opportunity for the development of facilities with great efficient operation and useful life. Several experimental facilities have been built but many air flow and heat distribution problems are yet to be solved.

The main light period for most plants is still obtained by growing them in greenhouses exposed to sunlight. Substitution or supplementation of sunlight is the most expensive modification in the traditional green-house. Although research supports the possibility of using high out-put lamps in greenhouses the high cost of installation maintainance and operation inhibits their utilization for routine culture procedures. The increased productivity of the plants is not offset by the cost of the lamps and electricity.

Photoperiod Manipulation

Once the main light period is satisfied, photoperiod manipulation is obtained through the use of relatively low levels of light. The patterns of using light to create long day effects on plants have changed through the years: from extension of the photoperiod to produce an artificial long day; to interruption of the long dark period to create two short dark periods; to cyclic lighting when lamps are turned on for a given percentage of a cycle (cycles of light and dark ranging from 1 to 30 minutes) and induce the same effects as continuous illumination for a similar duration of time. As cyclic lighting requires less electricity lighting may be expanded to several growing areas rather than one. Equipment to manipulate light circuits, effectiveness of various light levels, cycle durations, and light percentages of cycle are well known to many ornamental plant growers.

Selection of the kind of lamp to create the long day effects has remained unchanged for many years. The incandescent-filament lamp is efficient because it emits lamp in equal parts of red (660 nm) and and far red (730 nm), it operates on ordinary line voltage and amperage, and it requires simple pie-pan reflectors to redistribute light. Some growers realize maximum efficiency from clear-bottom, silver-coated neck, 250 watt 230-250 volt incandescent lamps. Originally developed for use in the lighting of chicken houses, and called brooder lamps, they permit the use of a few rather than many lamps to create long day effects and are easily installed. Most long day effects are obtained with 2 to 20 foot candles, rarely exceeding 40 foot candles.

The literature is filled with conflicting information on other light sources for producing long day effects. Fluorescent lamps, effective in delaying the flowering of short day plants when used as an interruption of the dark period are relatively ineffective when used for photoperiod extension. Fluorescent lamps produce a deeper green on plant foliage than do incandescent-filament lamps. Photographic safety lamps—BCJ lamps—are incandescent-filament lamps with a deep red glass covering. They emit much less red light than frosted lamps, but often are as effective as ordinary incandescent-filament lamps in controlling flowering. However, they promote excessive stem extension, the development of pale green leaves and poorly-colored flowers. The light levels required to obtain effects with light sources are several times those obtained with incandescent-filament lamps.

Incandescent-filament lamps, available with a ceramic coating of various colors, yellow, orange, or red, filter out the blue light but transmit all the red (660 nm) and far red (730 nm) light. These lamps are thus interchangeable with the ordinary frosted ones for controlling photoperiod, but neither attract nor repel night-flying moths. At night moths are attracted to blue light (440 nm), and apparently do not see other radiation, the grower can light plants out-of-doors without increasing the moth population in the growing area. Ceramic-coated lamps are made only in wattages of 100 or less; higher wattage lamps will not retain the ceramic coating.

ERANTHIS HYEMALIS.

Carbon Dioxide

Information on the responses of plants to elevated levels of carbon dioxide, available in the literature, parallels the development of light systems. Carbon dioxide, however, is a gas and must either be generated in large volumes to boost the ambient levels or must be released in gas-tight chambers. Many scientists suggest that high levels of carbon dioxide will partially compensate for the reduced levels of sunlight available during the winter months. Coupled with higher levels of temperature and fertilizers than those traditionally used, CO_2 increases plant quality as measured by stem strength, foliage color and size, flower size, and rate of development. Simple CO_2 generators, using propane, kerosene, or natural gas, are available for installation in greenhouses. They can be used only when outside temperatures are low and the ventilators can be kept closed. System controls are relatively inaccurate since individual greenhouses vary in structure and insulation. These limitations inhibit the development of absolute standards for using carbon dioxide in greenhouses.

CONTROLLED ENVIRONMENTS

As long as the sun is the major source of light, plants must be exposed to it through some transparent barrier. A uniform, consistent, and reproducible environment is always difficult to create.

The alternative approach is to create, in an enclosed area, a totally controlled environment through established engineering principles. This approach allows for the development of standards for size, heat load, air movement, lamp placement, and light distribution. Once these aspects are regulated, copies of the original growth chamber can be built. Prefabricated chambers are generally preferred to custom-installed facilities as their engineering aspects have already been worked out prior to installation. Moreover being modular they can be easily replicated, moved or serviced without affecting the operation of the other chambers.

The environmental control varies greatly from one commercially-built chamber to another. Most provide light, tempeature, and airflow control but few are capable of regulating the atmospheric composition of gases and moisture or of automatically watering and fertilizing the plants. Most chambers are not gas-tight; thus the plants are subjected to some influences from the surrounding environment.

The experimental system developed in the Phyto-Engineering Laboratory of the U.S. Department of Agriculture, Beltsville, Maryland, USA, is unique in the degree of environmental control achieved. The basic system consists of a large cold room in which a number of small (2' x 2' x 2') experimental growth chambers are placed and which air and moisture from environmental controllers (called Aminco-Aire units—designed to create environments to test electrical equipment). Carbon dioxide, from bottled gas, is metered into the chamber by means of an infra-red analyzer and a series of solenoids and pumps. The chambers are placed under lamp banks which provide 2000-2500 foot candles of light from fluorescent and incandescent-filament lamps. Watering and fertilizers are automatically applied through individual plastic tubes, to separate pots, every 4 to 6 hours. The standard growth chamber environment growing consists of the following: 2000-2500 foot candles of light; 16-hour day; day temperature of 24 degrees C, night temperature of 18 degrees C; 65% relative humidity; air velocity of 35-40 feet per minute; and carbon dioxide content of 400 PPM. The equipment has the potential of manipulating these factors individually or in any combination to study the maximum benefits of controlled environments. Phenomenal growth rates have been obtained with flowering annuals, vegetables, forage, and woody plants. To attain maximum growth rates treatments were initiated at seedling emergence or at the start of regrowth of a rooted cutting. Plants treated in this manner, for only two weeks of growth, weighed 20 to 50 times those grown in a traditional greenhouse environment, even though daylength and temperatures were similar for the two environments. Coupled with the great increase in fresh and dry weight of the plants were the production of more and larger leaves, heavier stems, more lateral shoots, and earlier and more abundant flowers than those grown under normal greenhouse conditions. Plants started in an escalating environment continue to show favorable influences of the "head start" treatments after transfer to traditional greenhouses or out-of-doors.

Some day these techniques, when refined for specific plants, will be utilized by commercial growers—starting with seed, growing tip, or callus from tissue culture—to schedule plant production, characteristics, flowering and maturity, during early growth stages, and so allow these exceptional plants to develop literally under greenhouse, field or garden conditions.

Other environmental factors are yet to be identified as integral parts of the design and functioning of growth chambers. All chambers in operation are limited in their ability to control, or even monitor atmospheric pressure or pollution, gravity, magnetism, or cosmic radiation. Many systems which try to recirculate the same air so alter the gaseous balance that normal-functioning plants cannot be grown.

ESCALATING GROWTH WITH CHEMICAL GROWTH REGULATORS

Chemical growth regulators boost, retard or shift the patterns of the growth of plants already being regulated through light, temperature, gaseous composition and mineral nutrition. Although dramatic changes occur in the visible growth of plants treated with chemicals, the order of magnitude is low in comparison with environmental manipulations. Chemicals can be used to alter germination, rooting, elongation, branching, color, flowering, fruiting, and senescence. The various regulators will be discussed under these topics.

Seed Germination

Gibberellins substitute for the light requirements of many kinds of seed. They also reduce the amount of chilling required for many perennial seeds.

Rooting

Auxins have been used for many years to stimulate the formation of roots on the base of cuttings. The techniques of application, dosage and selective action are well-known by most growers. Even so many kinds of plants require careful handling and failure to root is a common occurrence. The chemical growth retardant, 2, 2-dimethyl hydrazide succinic acid (B-9, Alar), has recently been shown to stimulate the rooting of cuttings; when applied as a 15 to 60 second dip of the basal end of the cutting root number and length increased several fold over those of untreated cuttings. Over-treatment depressed rooting by damaging the exposed surfaces of the cuttings.

Elongation

Gibberellins, applied at the proper dosage and frequency can greatly stimulate stem elongation and promote accumulation of dry weight of plant. The net result, however, is a redistribution without materially enhancing the plant's appearance or usefulness.

Abscisic acid, also a naturally occurring chemical, but now synthesized by man, counteracts the long day effects on many plants, promotes prompt cessation of growth and imposes a momentary dormancy. When the daily or weekly spray applications are discontinued, the plants resume growth and respond to the new photoenvironment. There are apparently many naturally occurring growth inhibitors present in plants still to be discovered and applied in horticulture.

Branching

Fatty acid esters, derived from palm oil or the tallow of soybeans selectively kill only the growing tip of many plants without damaging the leaves or stems. The most active compounds are the methyl, ethyl, and propyl esters of the C_8 to C_{12} fatty acids. They are insoluble in water and must be emulsified with a suitable surfactant to form collodial emulsions which are applied as a thin film over the entire surfaces of the plant, but penetrate only the growing tips. The auxillary meristems begin to develop and the plants develop as many, or more, lateral shoots than those pruned manually. Millions of evergreen azaleas were chemically pruned during the summer growing season of 1969. Chemical pruning allows for programming time of branching, produces more sites for the formation of cuttings since less plant material is removed, and makes it unnecessary for the operator to touch the plants—thus reducing the chances of transferring viruses from one plant to another.

Flowering and Fruiting

Plants vary in their flowering requirements. Some never flower in response to chemical treatments while others are easily triggered with exposure to ethylene. Bromeliads, the pineapple family, flower in response to unsaturated gases in the air. Ethylene or ethylene releasing chemicals, are the most effective and allow one to program the flowering of bromeliads. Ethylene on most plants cause immediately leaf drop and eventual senescence. Most long day plants flower on short days when sprayed with gibberellins. Rapid stem elongation usually precedes flower initiation; the flowers often produce no viable pollen. As growth retardants limit stem elongation of many woody plants, plant initiate flower buds earlier and in greater numbers than untreated plants. Flower buds develop only after exposure to weeks of chilling, or to drops of concentrated solutions of gibberllin applied in a wound at the base of the flower bud.

Senescence

Cytokinins applied to the maturing or harvested leaves of plants mobilize the nutrients in the plant and delay the degreening of tissues. Research with various cytokinin analogs, method of formulation and application, and the responses of various kinds of plants is currently at a standstill.

CONCLUSIONS

Multiplication of plants can be planned and paced by the careful selection of growing environment and chemical growth regulators. A very low order of increase can be obtained with a simple photoenvironment which primarily controls temperature and daylength. A much higher order of proliferation can be obtained if sunlight can be supplemented or substituted. We then can boost the levels of temperature, carbon dioxide, humidity, and mineral nutrients in the enclosed growing environment. Each facet of the accumulating knowledge suggests that ever-increasing growth rates of plants will be attained. It awaits the technology and creativity of man.

HOW TO GROW
African Violets

ANYONE can grow beautiful African Violets ANYWHERE if they will provide the simple conditions required for healthy growth.

ADEQUATE LIGHT IS MOST IMPORTANT for abundant bloom. Any window that has strong bright light is good. Avoid windows covered by porches or heavy shade trees. Mild direct sunshine is beneficial. Shield from hot mid-day sun with sheer curtains. Remember, the more light, the more bloom. Turn pots 1/4 turn each day. Light intensity decreases sharply as you move away from light source, so do keep the plants as near the window as possible. If you do not have good natural light, use fluorescent lights 12 to 14 hours a day. Cool white, daylight or tubes designed specifically for growing plants may be used alone or in combination. Distance from light depends upon intensity and type of tube as well as variety of plant. A general rule is 8 to 12 inches from top of pot to bottom of light tube. Light fixtures should be adjustable to raise or lower to attain desired height. If plants grow upright with long leaf stems, move closer to lights. If they grow too compactly or become hard and brittle, move further from light. At proper distance and with proper feeding, plants will be flat uniform rosettes with many blooms.

PROPER WATERING is the most important single factor of good African Violet culture. Use any water that is fit for drinking. Never use water that has been through a water softener. Collected rain water is ideal.

WHEN TO WATER — Only when top of the soil is dry to the touch. **Always** use **tepid** water.

HOW TO WATER — from top, bottom or by wicks. At least every third watering should be from the top to wash down accumulating salts. A gentle wash with tepid water of all foliage is helpful to keep plants clean. Do not expose to direct sun or drafts while foliage is wet. Never allow plants to stand in water after the soil has taken up what it can hold. Violets do not like cold wet feet. Check to see that the plants are ready for water. The use of water by each plant is related to temperature, humidity, type of soil, size and vigor of the plant. Remember, plants get air not only through foliage but also through the roots, so **don't** over-water! **Don't** drown the plant.

HUMIDITY is ideal at 40% to 50% — some homes have it and others do not. Many humidifiers are available and the increased humidity will benefit you as well as your plants. Some simple ways to increase humidity include: elevate plants on pebbles, overturned pots or wire so that pots do not contact the water. You may mist or fog the plants **but not while exposed to direct sun.** Freshly transplanted plants can be given a high-humidity start by totally enclosing plant and pot in a clear polyethylene bag, placed in good light, but out of direct sun.

SOIL formulas are as many as there are violet growers! In general, soil should be light and easily penetrated by the soft roots. It should allow for free passage of air and of water. It should always be sterilized. No plant is any better than its root system. The plant will develop good roots if the roots can readily penetrate the growing medium and proper watering is done. When available, it is best to buy one of the many fine soils especially prepared and sterilized for African Violets.

FEEDING — Some growers use a fairly rich soil with minimum supplemental feeding. Others prefer a inert growing medium devoid of plant food and depend entirely on mild feeding with each watering. For supplemental feeding of plants grown in soil, use good water-soluable fertilizer as recommended by the manufacturer; every 4 to 8 weeks is usually adequate. For constant feeding with every watering, use about 1/16 strength fertilizer.

DO NOT OVERFEED — Always be sure soil is damp before feeding. Remember that the water evaporates and unused fertilizer accumulates in the soil. Excess fertilizer will burn roots and may cause hard, brittle foliage. Too little will give poor, light colored foliage and few small flowers. Your plants will tell you much if you observe carefully. African Violets are slow growers and the effects of any change in culture cannot be observed immediately.

FRESH CIRCULATING AIR should reach your plants at all times. Avoid cold drafts directly on plants. They dislike a stale atmosphere and it is an invitation to mildew. The principal food of all plants is carbon dioxide from the air and hydrogen from the water. Fresh air is as invigorating to your violets as it is to you.

TEMPERATURE is ideal at 65° to 70° at night with a 5 to 10 degree rise during the day. Temperatures below 60° for any extended period will slow the growth. If too high, plants will grow sappy and spindly, with too few blooms which drop before gaining good size. Better a bit cool than too hot, especially if humidity is low.

PROPAGATION AND CULTURE of African Violets is easy. Remove all extra sprouts from your plant and grow it with a single crown. Pot it on into a larger shallow pot as its size or your desire dictates. More plants may be formed from leaf cuttings, offset sprouts or seeds.

More about all aspects of happy growing appears in each issue of The African Violet Magazine, illustrated in full color, published 5 times a year by the nonprofit membership of the African Violet Society of America.

PESTS AND DISEASES are usually not common unless brought in from the garden on hands or clothing, cut flowers, or on new plants. Isolate all new plants from healthy collections for at least two months. Use only sterilized African Violet soil for repotting.

MITES are the worst pest, invisible to the naked eye. Their presence is indicated by hardening and graying of the center foliage and shortening and twisting of the flower stems. Use a systemic such as Cygon 2E in your soil or spray with Kelthane to clean out and prevent.

THRIPS are very tiny, fast moving insects. They can cause streaked leaves and blossoms, blasted buds and premature dropping of blossoms. Spray with Malathion.

MEALY BUGS (white, cotton-like, do not move) can be eradicated by dipping entire foliage in Malathion solution. Add soap or detergent to the solution to penetrate their wax-like coating.

SOIL MEALY BUG is controlled by a systemic such as Cygon 2E.

ROOT KNOT NEMATODES are best controlled by good sanitation, discarding of all infected plants and not allowing pots to set in damp sand or vermiculite.

MILDEW is best prevented by warm, fresh circulating air. A pinch of Flowers of Sulphur in your hand, blown over your plant, or Mildex, or Fermate will usually clear it up.

CROWN ROT is avoided by the use of sterilized soil and by **not** over watering.

REMEMBER — All pesticides are **Poison!**

Follow manufacturer's directions with care and store pesticides in a locked closet or container.

The AVSA or distributors of this pamphlet will not be responsible for any injury caused by the use of any product mentioned in this pamphlet.

The African Violet Magazine tries to keep its readers informed of current pesticide information from the United States Department of Agriculture.

WHAT IS THE MAGAZINE LIKE? It is a wonderful blending of the writings of the pro-

Violet colour'd African

fessional and amateur grower. In each issue are articles written by the nation's leading growers and hybridizers, recognized experts in their fields, and articles written by someone whose growing conditions will resemble yours — African Violets grown in the home under less-than-perfect conditions. You learn by sharing these experiences. Each issue contains full color pictures of breathtaking new varieties just introduced, magnificent specimens of older varieties, scenes from shows all around the country, articles on arrangements and artistic plantings.

If you are looking for anything that pertains to African Violets, you will find an ad in the magazine to answer your wants. The leading growers and suppliers advertise in the African Violet Magazine.

WE INVITE YOU TO JOIN AVSA —
A Nonprofit Member Organization.

WHAT ARE ITS SERVICES TO MEMBERS?

1. Five issues of the African Violet Magazine yearly — June, Sept., Nov., Jan. and March.
2. Boyce Edens Research Fund sponsors research to improve varieties and culture of African Violets.
3. The Booster Fund helps meet needs through special services to membership.
4. Official Registration Authority for genus Saintpaulia (African Violet). Registers variety names. Compiles best-variety list.
5. Annual convention and show with awards. Make new AV friends, exhibit your plants, win prizes, learn and have fun at workshops, programs and tours. Join State and local affiliated groups.
6. The AVSA Library has books and color slide programs for your enjoyment which cover all phases of growing and showing African Violets. The June magazine lists programs and special packets.
7. Responsible for qualified judges through established judging standards and rules.
8. Gives special awards for shows sponsored by AVSA affiliates.

AFRICAN VIOLET SOCIETY OF AMERICA, INC.
P. O. Box 1326, Knoxville, Tennessee 37901
I submit my application for regular membership in the AVSA. I enclose payment of $6.00 to cover annual dues from March 1 through February 28 of each year. Membership includes the African Violet Magazine published five (5) times a year.

African Violet Society of America, Inc.

A Non-Profit Corporation   Founded 1946

AFRICAN VIOLETS

Judy's Violets & Greenhouses
Route 1, Box 111
Silverhill, Ala. 36576
On Highway 104
AC: 205 928-9932
African Violets and Gesneriads
Closed on Sunday

Norma and Russell Butler
260 El Valle (Fairway II)
Green Valley, Ariz. 85614
Phone: 625-3266
Postal address is P. O. Box 810

The House of Violets
(Ralph & Charlyne Reed)
936 Garland
Camden, Ark. 71701
AC: 501 Temple 6-3016

Mrs. Fred Fore
1711 South Y Street
Fort Smith, Ark. 72901
Phone: 783-0609

Mrs. Ralph Denney
4625 South 24th St.
Ft. Smith, Ark. 72901

C. F. Van Valkenberg
1236 Mansanita St.
Los Angeles, Calif. 90029

John E. Wilson
702 Grissom Street
San Diego, Calif. 92154
Phone: 424-6973

The Green House
Carol Green Anderson
9515 Flower St.
Bellflower, Calif. 90706
Phone: 925-0870

Flora Greenhouses (Mrs. Robert Flora)
African Violets and Ferns
2712 Trousdale Dr.
Mailing address: Box 1191
Burlingame, Calif. 94010
AC: 415 697-2299
Please write or phone in advance.

Beth Millett
3452 Fuchsia Street
Costa Mesa, Calif. 92626
AC: 714 557-7592

C & I Orchids & African Violets
Irene Hazeltine
365 South Henry Ave.
San Jose, Calif. 95117
AC: 408 247-1412
Phone first.

Mrs. Adeline Barta
500 Hawthorne Ave.
San Bruno, Calif. 94066
AC: 415 583-7850

Mrs. Hazel Schilke
2060 E Third St., # 2
Long Beach, Calif. 90814
AC: 213 439-4986
Please call first.

Violets by Constantinov
(Victor Constantinov)
3321 - 21st St., Apt. 7
San Francisco, Calif. 94110
Phone: 648-9135
Please write or phone in advance.

Tropical Nursery (J. P. Mills)
10343 No. 99 Hwy.
Stockton, Calif. 95205
Phone: 931-1228

The Violet House
(Mrs. Frances Williams)
1480 S. Jersey Way
Denver, Colo. 80222

Powder Hill Violets "at Zavisza's"
100 Abbe Road, Off Route 191
Enfield, Conn. 06082
Phone: 749-4394

Dorothea Wagner, DBA
Violet Nook-kery
364 Kelseytown Road
Clinton, Conn. 06413
AC: 203 669-2341

Louray of Salisbury (Judith S. Becker)
Undermountain Road
Salisbury, Conn. 06068
AC: 203 435-2263

Mary V. Boose
9 Turney Place
Trumbull, Conn. 06611
AC: 203 268-4368
By appointment only.

Violets by Suzy (Mrs. H. Steven Johnson)
741 West Colonial Drive
Orlando, Florida 32804
AC: 305 422-6437

The Orchid Jungle
Fennell Orchid Co., Inc.
26715 S. W. 157 Ave.
Homestead, Fla. 33030
AC: 305 247-4824

African Violets Inc.
"Mimi's" African Violets
1100 Stevens Avenue
Deland, Florida 32720
AC: 904 734-1675

Mrs. R. V. Rudd
Route 2, Box 117
Quincy, Fla. 32351
AC: 904 627-3613
5 mi. from Quincy on Hwy. 65.

Nell's African Violets
Mrs. Nell D. Ransone
17 Hazard St., Golfview
West Palm Beach, Fla. 33406
Phone: 683-6310

Mrs. Myrtle Warman
11711 North Armenia Avenue
Tampa, Florida 33612
Phone: 935-9134

Lake City Greenhouses (A. T. Vaughan)
2899 W. Leon St.
Lake City, Florida 32055
Phone: 752-3309

McFarland's Violetry
2256 Sunnyside Place
Sarasota, Fla. 33579
AC: 813 366-4488

Benke's Greenhouse
Box 235 Bilter Rd., R.R. 1
Aurora, Illinois 60504
AC: 312 892-3480

Rose Knoll Gardens
(Mr. and Mrs. Jeff Rhoades)
Assumption, Illinois 62510
AC: 217 226-3249

Mrs. Mary Boatright
724 West Poplar
Harrisburg, Illinois 62946
AC: 618 252-3094

Mary-Ray African Violets
5007 Terry Drive
Alton, Illinois 62002
AC: 618 466-0146
Mon. thru Fri. 1-5 p.m.
Weekends, holidays by appointment

Dates Violetry
1 Orlando Place and U.S. Hwy. 50
1 block East of Rt. 159
Fairview Heights, Illinois 62208
AC: 618 ME 2-6409

Glass House of Violets (Mrs. E. T. Glass)
1213 Pine Valley Dr., Greenvale Addition
Fort Wayne, Ind. 46805
Phone: 422-7707

Tropical Gardens (Betty Stoehr)
Route 1, Box 143
Greenwood, Indiana 46142
AC: 317 862-4698

Quality Violet House (Susan Feece)
Route 3, Box 947
Walkerton, Ind. 46574
AC: 219 586-2456

Mrs. Fred Schumacher
314 S. Sixth St.
Clinton, Iowa 52732
Antiques and African Violets

Tropical Paradise Greenhouse
(Mrs. H. E. Dillard)
8825 West 79th St.
Overland Park, Kan. 66204

Payne's Violets & Gesneriads
6612 Leavenworth Road
Kansas City, Kansas 66104
Phone: 299-2541

McKinney's Glassehouse
(James B. McKinney)
89 Mission Rd., Eastborough
Wichita, Kan. 67207
AC: 316 686-9438
African Violets, Gesneriads, Exotic Plants

Rev. Blade's Violetry
308 N. Long Street
London, Ky. 40741

Poynor's Greenhouse
Route 2, Box 107-J
Hammond, La. 70401
Phone: 345-5558 and 345-7961

Mr. and Mrs. George F. Vincent
96 Paul Molbert Rd., Judice
Duson, La. 70529
AC: 318 873-8437
African Violets and Supplies

Mrs. James M. Harris
618 Creole Lane
Lake Charles, La. 70601
Phone: 477-3685

The House Plant Corner
100 W. Division St.
Oxford, Md. 21654
Open daily 9-4 and on Saturdays 9-2.
Phone: Oxford 5471

Mary's African Violets (Mary Hofer)
19788 San Juan
Detroit, Michigan 48221
AC: 313 341-7474

O. K. Violets
The Rainsbergers
8220 Secor Road
Lambertville, Mich. 48144
AC: 313 856-3048

Verna's African Violets
4122 Costa Dr., N. E.
Grand Rapids, Mich. 49505
Phone: EM 3-2084
No Sunday calls.

Mackglentheo Gardens (Mrs. Manvell Jensen)
4090 West Barnes Road
Millington, Mich. 48746
AC: 517 871-3308

Kramer Violet and Gift Boutique
2923 Portugal Drive
St. Louis, Mo. 63125
Phone: 892-1715

White Cloud Farm
Grand Avenue Rd.
Highway 71 South
Carthage, Mo. 64836

Wilson's Greenhouse
Ozark, Missouri 65721
Monday - Friday from 8 to 6 p.m.

Roger Drury
Route 1
St. Genevieve, Mo. 63670

Krouse's African Violets
(Lucille Krouse)
14200 East 39th Terrace
Independence, Mo. 64055
Phone: 254-7164

Mrs. Bert E. Routh
African Violets and Begonias
Louisburg, Missouri 65684
½ mile south on Highway 65
AC: 417 752-2252

Robert D. Wagner
511 West Hudson
Wellsville, Mo. 63384
Missouri Highway No. 19
AC: 314 684-2776
A.V., Gesneriads, Begonias, Cacti

—Seeds with a Reserve-tissue.

Mrs. Leonard Volkart
R.F.D. #1
Russellville, Mo. 65074
Phone: California, Mo., AC: 314 796-4949

Engardt's Violet House
(Mrs. R. H. Engardt)
7457 Schuyler Drive
Omaha, Nebraska 68114
Phone: 391-6362

Mrs. R. E. Good
4 miles NW Oconto on Hwy. 40
Oconto, Nebraska 68860
Phone: 858-4802

"Cellar of Violets"
Mrs. Paul Steckowych
1235 Island Pond Rd.
Manchester, N. H. 03103
Phone: 623-7564

High Hat Violets
Carol Morrissette
RFD 4, Box 270 D
Manchester, N. H. 03102
AC: 603 774-4886
Please phone for directions.

Kolb's Greenhouses
725 Belvidere Rd.
Phillipsburg, N. J. 08865
AC: 201 859-3369
By appointment only

Fischer Greenhouses
Oak Avenue
Linwood, New Jersey 08221
AC: 609 641-3525

Edelweiss Gardens
Robbinsville, N. J.

Roehrs Exotic Nurseries
R. D. 2, Box 144, Route 33
Farmingdale, N. J. 07727
AC: 201 938-5111

Lucile Loughlin
105 Pompton Road
Haledon, N. J. 07508
Phone: 279-3533

McIntosh's (Mary McIntosh)
Page Brook Road
Chenango Forks, New York 13746
AC: 607 648-9731

Schmelling's African Violets
5133 Peck Hill Road
Jamesville, N. Y. 13078
AC: 315 446-1539

Pat Nowell
12 Grove Street
Cambridge, N. Y. 12816
If not home try Scott's Florist.

Turner's Greenhouses
101 East Duquesne St.
Celeron, N. Y. 14720

Champion's African Violets
8848 Van Hoesen Road
Clay, New York 13041

Lyndon Lyon
14 Mutchler Street
Dolgeville, New York 13329
Phone: 429-3591

Electric Farm
Gesneriad Specialists
104B Lee Road
Oak Hill, N. Y. 12460
AC: 518 239-4030

Manelta Lanigan
330 List Avenue
Rochester, New York 14617
AC: 716 266-8607

Everson's House Plants
4328 S. Salina St.
Syracuse, N. Y. 13205
Phone: 469-5653

Wayne E. Hiatt
125 Woodcrest Dr., Off Hwy. 97 West
Rocky Mount, N. C. 27801
AC: 919 442-7300

L. Easterbrook Greenhouses
10 Craig Street
Butler, Ohio 44822
AC: 419 883-3931
Daily after 3 p.m., all day Sat. and Sun.

Mrs. Sylvia Wells
566 Cherry Hill Place
Fairborn, Ohio 45324

Nature's Way Products (Fred A. Veith)
3505 Mozart Avenue
Cincinnati, Ohio 45211
Supplies only — no plants

Mrs. John Slivka
403 E. George St.
Fayette, Ohio 43521
AC: 419 237-2124

Granger Gardens (Hugh & Dale Eyerdom)
1060 Wilbur Rd.
Medina, Ohio 44256
AC: 216 239-9300
Monday-Saturday from 8 to 5 p.m. Closed
Sundays and holidays.

Mrs. Elsie A. Kellerman
4109 So. Harvey St.
Oklahoma City, Okla. 73109
Phone: ME 4-5530

Mrs. Robert J. Rowan
105 Crestmont
Norman, Okla. 73069

Betty's Violetry (Betty Mestrovich)
9282 S.E. Yamhill
Portland, Ore. 97216

Arndt's Floral Garden
20454 N.E. Sandy Blvd.
Mailing address: Rt. 2, Box 336
Troutdale, Oregon 97060
Closed Wednesdays

Sim T. Holmes
100 Tuscarawas Road
Beaver, Pennsylvania 15009
AC: 412 774-5208

Mary Lou's Violet Closet
902 Neuhoff Lane
Nashville, Tenn. 37205
AC: 615 352-4944
Please write or phone in advance.

Betty's African Violets
R.R. 3, Box 14A
Westmoreland, Tenn. 37186
Phone: 644-2895

Mrs. G. E. Thayer
131 Renner Drive
San Antonio, Texas 78201
AC: 512 732-7760

Mrs. J. S. Berry
1832 Turner Drive
Houston, Texas 77016
Phone: 695-5020

Gwen Williams
1063 North Ollie
Stephenville, Texas 76401
Phone: 968-2377

Mrs. Hardy Young
Route 1, Box 10
Rockdale, Texas 76567
AC: 512 446-3179

Volkmann Brothers
2714 Minert Street
Dallas, Texas 75219
AC: 214 LA 6-3484

Swift's Violets (Mr. and Mrs. John A. Swift)
P. O. Box 28012
10645 Ferguson Rd.
Dallas, Texas 75228   AC: 214 279-2932

Klinkel's Floral
Lucille Klinkel
1553 Harding
Enumclaw, Wash. 98022
Phone: TA 5-4442

Sue Lasswell
4815 - 148th, S.W.
Edmonds, Wash. 98020
Phone: 743-2482

Bernard D. Greeson
3548 N. Cramer St.
Milwaukee, Wis. 53211
Supplies only — no plants.
Closed during August.

Sue's Violetry
2169 N. Sherman Blvd.
Milwaukee, Wisc. 53208
Phone: 445-8941
By appointment.

Mrs. William E. Lau
1503 North 47 Street
Milwaukee, Wisc. 53208
AC: 414 453-1048

CANADA

Fisher's Quality African Violets
32 Downsview Avenue
Downsview, Ont., Can. M3M 1C9
AC: 416 241-3977
Closed Sunday. When visiting, please notify
us a week before so that we can have necessary certificate ready.

Harborcrest Nurseries
1425 Benvenuto Avenue
Brentwood Bay
Victoria, British Columbia, Canada
AC: 604 652-2021

Wood's African Violets
330 Dixon Rd., Unit 2105
Weston, Ontario, Can.
Phone: 247-8471

African Violets by Mrs. Hawkins
505 - 30th Avenue, N.W.
Calgary, Alberta, Canada T2M 2N7
Phone: 289-5480

MEXICO

Alys Honey (Mrs. T. Patrick Honey)
Rio Escondido 27
Mexico City 10, DF, Mexico

EXOTIC PLANTS

Alberts & Merkel Bros., Inc.
2210 South Federal Hwy.
Boynton Beach, Fla. 33435
AC: 305 732-2071

Fischer Greenhouses
Oak Avenue
Linwood, New Jersey 08221

Roehr's Exotic Nurseries
R. D. 2, Box 144, Route 33
Farmingdale, N. J. 07727

FOR LASTING SPLENDOUR BEGONIAS
INDOORS AND OUTDOORS FROM JUNE TO NOVEMBER

Modern trends in home gardening are using more begonias every year. Take advantage of the merits of this delightful range of Begonias. They are remarkably easy to grow. Be assured of success by following these simple instructions. Select firm plump tubers from your Garden Shop in January, February, or March. Remember to keep them away from frost.

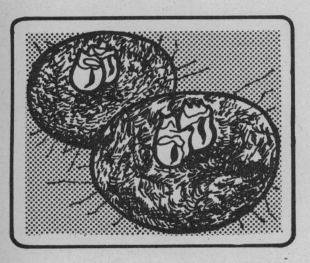

Once the shoots are showing, development becomes more rapid. Give maximum light but shade from strong direct midday sun. Water regularly never allowing the soil to become dry. An application of a good liquid plant food will improve growth.

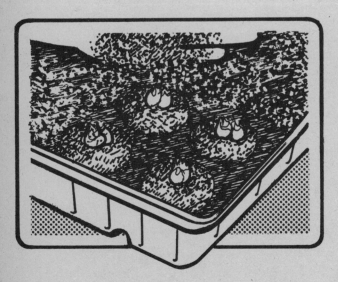

In March plant the tubers, hollow side up, just below soil level in moist peat compost, using seed trays or small pots. Place on a window sill where the temperature does not fall below 60 °F, 16/17 °C. Cover with paper or polythene to promote growth but remove as soon as this appears. Water sparingly until growth commences. This may take up to 5/6 weeks ; root growth will begin earlier.

There are few summer flowering plants that can claim the merits for which Begonias have a justifiable reputation. They have a flowering period from late June to November. Suitable for outside culture in Tubs, Window Boxes, Hanging Baskets and Borders and as pot plants, they provide a delightful show of colour throughout the summer, in the greenhouse or sun room. They do not mind a situation in partial shade or constant shade. They like a fair amount of water. They are not particular

about the soil being acid or alkaline as long as the drainage is good. The range of types is certainly unique, qualifying successfully for a place in every garden or greenhouse, and in colours ranging from the deepest velvet crimson through the reds, salmon, pink, yellow and pastel shades to the purest white. There are the large double camellia flowered and frilled petal varieties for pots and bedding. The medium sized Multiflora Maxima for window boxes and tubs and the Pendulas for Hanging Baskets.

In May, or when growth reaches 3 inches, plants are ready to be moved. They can be transplanted either into pots, window boxes, hanging baskets or to the garden border. Use a 6 or 7 inch pot, in window boxes plant 6 inches apart and in the garden 10 inches apart. The recommended soil mixture for pot grown plants is equal parts of good topsoil, leafmold or peatcompost. Good drainage is essential. Begonias thrive in semi-shade and must not be subjected to the midday sun. Begonias dislike dry conditions, so water generously, especially during periods of hot weather. Every two or three weeks a well balanced plant food should be given. Remove all wilted leaves and flowers to encourage flowering throughout the summer months.

Your begonias will now flower continuously for 4 to 5 months. Immediately after the first frost, lift the tubers, shake off most of the soil, dry in sun for a few hours and store the tubers in dry peat moss in cool place 46 to 50 °F.

SINGLE AND DOUBLE TUBEROUS BEGONIAS.

— Sink watering.

The Genus Gloxinia was founded in 1785 by l'Heritier of Brazil. Few flowers can surpass the large soft velvety textured trumpetshaped blooms. Following are some recommended varieties, especially beautiful for their richness and vividly colored blooms : Emperor Frederick, Emperor Wilhelm, Crispa Meteor, Etoile De Feu and the interesting spotted Tigrinas. Leaves grow close to the base of the plant in a rosette formation and may produce as many as fifty to hundred buds with ten to twenty flowers open at the same time.

Select firm plump tubers from your Garden Shop in December to March. Be assured these are healthy as they are particularly subject to cold conditions. Remember to keep them away from frost.

From December to March plant the tuber, smooth side down, just below soil level in moist rich soil, using a 5'' to 6'' pot. Cover with paper or polythene to promote growth but remove as soon as this appears. Water sparingly until growth commences. Once the growth is showing, development becomes more rapid. Water regularly never allowing the soil to become dry. Gloxinias like a warm, humid atmosphere, in the summer they should be shaded from strong sunlight. Keep away from draughts. Gloxinias, like African Violets, do not like to get their leaves wet, so give water on the saucer. An application, every 2 or 3 weeks, of a good liquid plant food will improve growth and blooming.

After blooming, Gloxinias need a rest, giving no water. Remove the dried growth. When completely dried remove from pot, snip off dead roots from the tuber and store in dry peat moss in cool place 46° to 50° F. Replant in January.

Scaly Rhizomes

Another group of gesneriads grows from *scaly rhizomes*. A rhizome resembles a thick scaly root. These rhizomes and the plants that develop from them are grown in the same way as gloxinias, including the rest period. Smithianthas are aptly described by their common name of Temple Bells. If you are growing under fluorescent lights be sure you have selected a compact variety as some grow quite tall. Kohlerias and Achimenes also grow from rhizomes. These plants are pictured and described in the Cultural Handbook mailed to all new Society members.

Fibrous Roots

Another large group of gesneriads consists of those with *fibrous roots*. These grow all year long, without a rest period. The familiar African violet belongs in this group. The Streptocarpus, or cape primrose, has many varieties and species. The commonest are the Rexii Hybrids with large trumpet-shaped blooms. The Episcia, also known as the flame violet, is a vine with runners like a strawberry plant. There are many varieties with beautifully patterned foliage and tubular-shaped flowers of various colors. The Columneas are also generally vining, with spectacular flowers and are rapidly growing in popularity. Since some of the newer hybrids are much easier to bloom than the species, the beginner should start with these. The Lipstick Vine, a species of Aeschynanthus, is also a rewarding plant to grow in the home.

This information sheet has been prepared by the

American Gloxinia and Gesneriad Society

Special Offer

If you want to know more about these plants and the Society, use the form below. Send 50¢ and get a packet of mixed gesneriad seeds and a copy of THE GLOXINIAN magazine, which is published six times a year by the American Gloxinia and Gesneriad Society.

- -

WINDOW WITH BRACKET AND SHELF.

You can grow gloxinias — the easy way

The spectacularly beautiful gloxinia with its huge, velvety bell-shaped blooms is not difficult to grow in your home. The gloxinia is a member of a large family of plants called gesneriads. (Pronounce these names any way you like — you will be in good company.) Men and women in all walks of life, young and old, grow gesneriads as a hobby. These plants propagate easily and thus are moderate in cost. The method described here is by no means the only way these plants can be grown, but it is advisable for the beginner to follow a proven procedure. At first glance there seems to be a lot to read and a lot to know, but all procedures are simple.

Gloxinia tubers can be purchased at many variety stores and garden centers, as well as through the mail from dealers who specialize in them and can offer a greater variety. To get started use a five-inch diameter squatty flower pot and put one inch of clean pebbles in the bottom. Fill the pot to about three inches from the top with African violet soil which you should be able to buy in the same place where you obtained your tuber. Pour the soil into the pot but do not press it down. Place the tuber in the center of the pot with the rounded side down. Gently cover the tuber with about one inch of soil. If the tuber has already sprouted be careful not to break off the sprout. Water so that some water runs out the bottom of the pot and place in a well-lighted window. Water sparingly until growth shows above the ground. If more than one sprout appears, break off all but the strongest one.

Once your plant has started you will need to satisfy its basic requirements. WATER: Do not water until the soil is dry on the surface—it will lighten in color as it dries out or you can feel it. Too frequent watering is harmful. Use luke-warm water, applied until it starts to run out the bottom. LIGHT: If your plant grows tall and spindly it is not getting enough light. Leaves should spread out flat and nearly horizontally from a short main stem. Place the plant close to your sunniest window and rotate it slightly every few days to produce symmetrical growth. Gloxinias require stronger light than African violets, but in the summertime full sunlight may be too strong, causing leaves to hug the pot. If this happens, move your plant back slightly from the window on a small table or use a sheer curtain to break the direct sunlight. HUMIDITY: The air in most homes is too dry for gloxinias during the heating season. Spraying the plant with water from a Windex bottle twice a day will improve humidity. Don't spray while sunlight is on plants. Several plants grouped together will maintain a higher humidity. A larger group of plants can be placed on a tray of moist pebbles or gravel. TEMPERATURE: Normal house temperatures are suitable for gloxinias. However, less than 60° is harmful and plants should be taken off windowsills on cold nights. FERTILIZER: A soluble African violet fertilizer should be mixed ¼ teaspoon per gallon and applied with every watering. The solution may be stored between waterings. Concentrations recommended on fertilizer labels are generally too strong for gloxinias. INSECTS: These are not a serious problem with gloxinias, and can be controlled with a regular push-button houseplant spray. BUD BLAST: Buds that turn brown or fail to open into flowers may be caused by low humidity, overwatering or too much fertilizer.

Your plant should bloom in three to four months. Once your plant has finished blooming, cut off the stem above the lowest two good leaves. Continue to water the plant sparingly for another month. If no new growth is seen, stop watering until the leaves wither. If new growth does appear, let it develop into a second cycle of bloom and stop watering when blooming ceases. Store the pot in a cool, not cold, place (50°-60°). Water just enough — about once a month — to keep the tuber from shriveling. Overwatering will rot a dormant tuber. Its rest period may vary from several weeks to several months. When a new sprout appears, your plant is ready for a new cycle of growth and should be repotted in fresh soil. If the tuber has increased in size it would be best to replant it in a pot one size larger. If your plant begins new growth during the short days of winter it may become "leggy." If this happens, you can encourage more compact growth by cutting back to the lowest pair of leaves in early spring.

Gloxinias can be grown outdoors in the summertime, provided they are placed in the dappled shade, in a sheltered place so that heavy rains will not damage the foliage.

Growing from Seed

It is very easy to grow gloxinias from seed. The seed can be started in a covered clear plastic box a few inches deep. Drill some holes in the bottom of the box for drainage and a few in the cover for ventilation. Fill the box to a one-inch depth with damp — not wet — milled sphagnum moss or Vermiculite, or a mixture of the two. You can buy the materials where you obtained your tuber. This starting medium should be leveled off and compacted slightly. As the seeds are very tiny, the trick is to sow them evenly and sparingly over the surface and not all in a bunch. Do this by using a folded piece of paper with the seed in the fold. Tap the paper so that a few seeds fall off while the hand holding the paper moves over the medium. Do not bury the seeds. Do not use soil of any kind to start seeds, as the risk of loss from damp-off, a fungus disease, is too great. The starting medium must be kept moist at all times and not allowed to dry out. Watering is done by placing the plastic box in a shallow pan of water until enough is drawn up through the bottom holes to dampen the surface of the medium. Place the box in a warm, well-lighted place, but not on top of a radiator or exposed to direct sunlight. In one or two weeks the tiny green specks of sprouted seed should appear on the top of the medium but do not be impatient if it takes a longer time. Begin using the weak fertilizer solution recommended above. When the plants have four leaves, transplant them to another covered box of starting medium, placing them one inch apart. After a week gradually increase ventilation by gradually raising the cover, removing it entirely in about another week. When they are big enough for the leaves to touch, transplant to 2½" pots of African violet soil. If your plants are spindly or "leggy" bury the bottom two leaves and cover the stem up to the next set of leaves in transplanting. When plants are 4 to 5 inches across transplant once more to 4-inch pots where they can stay until blooming. You should have flowers in from four to nine months, depending on the time of year and your growing conditions. You can have a lot of fun with mixed hybrid seed as there is enormous variety and you never know what a flower will look like until it opens.

You can also produce more plants by planting the extra sprouts that come from your tuber or by planting a leaf with its stem in the seed starting medium. Be sure to cover with a clear plastic bag and avoid direct sunlight while the new roots are forming. The sprout will form roots and can then be planted in soil. The leaf will root and then send up tiny plantlets which can be taken off and treated as seedlings, or it may first form a tuber which will sprout later. These two methods are called vegetative propagation and will give you plants and bloom exactly like the parent plant.

Fluorescent Lights

Fluorescent lighting frees you from dependence on the sun for light in growing plants and will help you to make them bloom in the wintertime. A basement or dark corner can be transformed into an indoor garden. The usual set-up is a fixture with three 4-ft. or 8-ft. tubes placed 12 inches above a bench 24 to 30 inches wide. Young plants and seedlings are placed closer to the lights on top of inverted flower pots. Lights should be on approximately 14 hours per day. An automatic timer, costing about ten dollars, will take over the job of turning the lights off and on each day. Plant-Gro and Gro-Lux tubes are especially made for growing plants. If you buy Gro-Lux, the ones marked "W/S" (wide spectrum) are better.

The Tuberous Gesneriads

The florist's gloxinia, whose proper name is *Sinningia speciosa*, comes in a wide range of solid flower colors as well as speckled and banded patterns. There are varieties with two rows of petals called doubles, as well as slipper types with nodding blossoms.

There are many other tuberous plants in this family worth growing in the home, among them the thimble-sized *Sinningia pusilla*, which is generally grown in a closed jar to provide humidity. Other miniatures have been hybridized recently — 'Bright Eyes', 'Connecticut Hybrids', 'Dollbaby', 'Pink Petite', and 'Wood Nymph'. Closely related to the Sinningias are the Rechsteinerias, which also grow from tubers. The one most often seen is *R. cardinalis*, which has large heart-shaped soft green leaves and brilliant scarlet firecracker-shaped flowers. Rechsteinerias and Sinningias have been intercrossed to produce hybrids called Gloxineras. These are handsome plants and profuse and dependable bloomers.

Courtesy of The American Gloxinia and Gesneriad Society
P.O. Box 174, New Milford, Connecticut

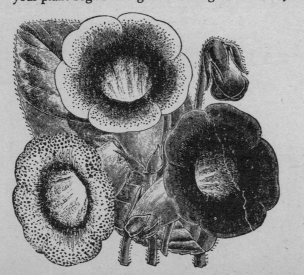

HYBRID GLOXINIAS.

HANGING

—Trailing Morning Glory—Convolvulus Mauritanicus.

Climbing Aroids (*Philodendron pertusum* and *P. Imbe*) with cord-like aërial roots.

BASKETS

47

HAPPY HOUSE PLANTS

By Dr. Henry M. Cathey

Decorative Flower Stand for Parlor, Window, or in front of Looking Glass.

Reprint From
Plants Alive
Indoor Growing and Greenhouse Journal
319 NE 45th Street
Seattle, Washington 98105

Decoration of Dinner Table with Palms.

At a time when a great many people are trying to give plants emotions, some of the old-line horticulturists, with a knowing smile, are saying that they have known this bit for many years.

The "emotions" that plants show, however, haven't a thing to do with Freud, psychoanalysis, hostility, or love, or, for that matter, violence or nonviolence.

Plants communicate their "emotions" without attachments of wires, flaming matches, language, or movement. They show their state of being in a way that can be recognized by those trained to use their sense of vision, touch, and smell.

For example, you can see leaf color, growth rate, and angle of leaves; with your sense of touch, you can determine texture of leaves and their thickness; and with smell, odor of the soil, leaves, and flowers. However, house plants are not for eating. Nor can you use sound as any criteria of plant health. The sound of leaves moving as the air circulates may be pleasant, but not significant.

Most people don't know how to detect the health or "happiness" of house plants, although anyone can learn, and more people are learning every day.

Why bother? For one thing, bothering means the difference between plants just hanging on or really thriving. It changes the way we live with plants, shifting the emphasis from those that are for display only, to those that perform. Plants for display are those grown by someone other than the owner, which all too frequently die in the hands of the purchasers (the so-called "black-thumb" people, who unfortunately seem to comprise the majority of the population). Plants that perform are those that respond to the care given them and become a part of the environment and the lives of their owners (the "green-thumb" people who constitute a minority of the population, but who are rapidly increasing in number).

Knowing what constitutes an adjusted or conditioned plant enables you to exert maximum control over its growth. Your plant has no native ability to live in the surroundings you have picked for it—whether home, office, or public area. It needs to be trained to adjust to its alien environment. To get your plant to do its best for you, you must slow down its growth, permit leaves to get accustomed to dark, dry conditions in the area where it is to be placed, and permit it to accumulate mineral ions and carbohydrates to help maintain itself during periods of stress. Then, and only then, will you have an adjusted plant. This takes a great deal of patience on your part, but it's well worth the effort.

How to tell

Can you pick the "happy" plant as contrasted with those showing signs of fear, hostility, anger, and hate? Here's what a conditioned plant will look like:

(1) All the foliage is dark green, thick, and plush looking.

(2) The foliage is green all the way to the soil line.

(3) Growth is slowed and consequently, few or no new leaves are showing. The little growth that shows is dark green in color. The stem is thick in diameter at the top of the plant.

(4) The net of roots is well established and fills most of the pot, covering the whole surface of the soil ball.

(5) The plant appears to be slightly larger than it should be for the soil ball and container.

There are certain things you can do at the beginning that will make for well-adjusted plants such as these. Here are the steps to follow:

Step 1 - Selecting plants. The attached list gives some of my selections. What you pick depends on taste, space, and use. Every plant should be potted individually. It's almost impossible to train plants when they are potted together.

Step 2 - Washing and cleaning plants. All plants except those with hairy-surfaced leaves (African violets and begonias) should be washed in warm soapy water of bath temperature, about 90 to 100 degrees, using real soap. Wash all leaves, stems, and buds with a soft sponge, holding your hand under each individual leaf. Clean both sides. Rinse with water, shake and allow to dry overnight in the sink or on a newspaper. This procedure removes dirt, insect eggs, and insecticides. Do it at frequent intervals to bring out the natural shine of the foliage.

Step 3 - Locating training area. Pick the spot with the brightest light, but where direct sunlight won't fall on the leaves. Keep plants away from drafts, heating ducts, or open doors. Put them on a waterproof area; this may be a wooden frame, covered with polyethylene, which is then covered with a layer of coarse gravel or sand. Or use colorful inexpensive plastic trays, tubs, pans, and basins. Don't scar the underside of these containers; it ruins the waterproofing.

Step 4 - Buying fertilizer. Buy a complete fertilizer. Plants need at least twelve elements for growth. The label should list the major ingredients—nitrogen, potassium and phosphorus—and a mixture of trace elements. I personally prefer a liquid fertilizer that's easy to mix and can be adjusted for concentration; one whose elements are immediately available to the plant. Gardeners use many other fertilizer sources and this is fine, with reservations. Some fertilizers may smell, some have varying nutrient content, and some may be in a form not easily taken up by the plant. Be sure you know what you are getting. Incidentally, low but more frequent applications help sustain growth better than high rates. Luxury levels of fertilizers promote soft growth.

Step 5 - Determining amount of water to use. All right, so now you have light, a waterproof area, and fertilizer. Now you have to determine how much water the container, soil and root system will hold. It's essential for you to know how many ounces or cups of water the plant medium will require. The soil and roots are a mass filled with pore spaces; you want to add the water until the area is filled and everything is moist. But leave no excess water standing. Mark on a label the amount used. If you want to really know, buy a large plastic or metal funnel and mark the 1, 2, and 3-cup lines inside. Plunge the funnel into the soil and till with a measured amount of water. Leave the funnel in place overnight. Continue to add water until no additional water enters the growing medium. The soil medium will hold water by gravity, but will not hold any excess. Note the amount each container needs. From then on you can automatically add the correct amount.

Step 6 - Training the plant. Plant leaves begin to change from dark to light green and become flaccid or limp when watering is required. Start to train your plant by watering it every third day to saturation as described in step 5, then begin to delay the time that you would normally water it. I use a calendar on which I mark the dates of watering—every third, fourth, fifth, seventh, ninth, twelfth, or fourteenth day—according to the moisture requirements from the table. With this procedure, you permit the medium to become a little dryer and slow down top growth, while maintaining an active root system. It takes at least 3 months for most plants to adjust their growth in this way. Not all plants can be managed this way, however. Some, like the violets, must be watered daily and never permitted to dry.

Step 7 - Adjusting light levels. Move the plant away from the window to a darker part of the room. After 3 to 6 months, move it to the desired location, to light levels as listed on the attached table. You can determine how much light you have with an inexpensive foot-candle meter costing less than $24. Chances are you can borrow one, though, by asking around at a garden center, garden club meeting, or at your local power company. If a foot-candle meter isn't available, try a regular photographic light meter.

In using the light meter, set the ASA exposure index to 75, the lens opening to f/8, and use an exposure time of 1/60th of a second. This gives the approximate equivalent of 1,000 foot-candles. Thus, for 500 foot-candles, use one f-stop larger, or double the ASA index or the exposure time. For 2,000 foot-candles, use one f-stop less, or half the ASA index or exposure time.

Step 8 - Keeping plants in shape. Go over your plants every 3 months to keep them in shape. Maintain a definite water and fertilizer schedule for best growth. Keep a regular schedule for pruning, removing dead leaves, and for staking.

Step 9 - Checking for communication. After all this busy work, see if the plants are communicating their needs. Checking the feel of the leaves and their color and development should give you an idea of what to do. In a sense, the plants have used their body language—the non-verbal language—to let you know what they need and how well they feel.

Step 10 - Planning for replacements. Remember, plan for replacements. In time, all plants become pot bound and overgrown in size. The medium becomes filled with roots and depleted in organic matter. Plants can reach the roof to the point where there's simply no room for them. So here's a chance to try new plants and new combinations.

—Design for Plant Stand.

Plants for the beginner

If you want only one plant to experiment with, try the Peperomia obtusifolia, or the peperomia plant, available in a solid green, or in various green and white combinations. This plant can be trained to go into a cabinet, a dark corner in a hallway, or into a hanging waterproof basket. It requires minimum care. It will die rapidly, however, if over-watered and over-fertilized. It must be trained. The peperomia is from tropical South and Central America. Its fleshy leaves are about 4-inches long and 2½-inches wide. It branches rapidly and the stems fall over the surface of the container.

If you are interested in experimenting further, you may wish to try the Spathiphyllum Mauna Loa. This plant, originally from Columbia, has long green, lance-shaped foliage that forms spathes (like an anthurium), 2½-inches long. The spadix is greenish-yellow to white. The plant throws interesting shadows around it, giving the impression of wide open spaces. It is almost an art form. The plant must be kept moist at all times to survive.

Or you might wish to try a tree, the Ficus retusa nitida. This is a small-leaf rubber tree plant that actually grows on the streets in the Indian and Malayan tropics, and can be trained to any form by pruning. Its dark green foliage is 2- to 4-inches long and it gives the distinct effect of a tree. I have a 12-foot one in my living room with nests and make-believe cardinals to give it the look of a living environment. It is available on the market as a 6-foot tree in poodle, screen, or fan forms. It rapidly loses its leaves unless trained. It prefers watering about once a week.

For more information on indoor gardens for growing and showing plants, you may obtain Home and Garden Bulletin No. 187, Indoor Gardens with Controlled Lighting, for 15 cents from the Superintendent of Documents, U.S. Government Printing Office, Washington, D.C. 20402.

Name	Light level	Water requirements
Aechmea fasciata (Bromeliad)	medium	moist
Aglaonema roebelinii (Pewter plant)	low	moist
Brassaia actinophylla (Schefflera)	medium	dry
Chamaedorea elegans (Neanthe bella palm)	low	moist
Dieffenbachia amoena (Dumb cane)	medium	dry
Dracaena fragrans (Corn plant)	low	wet
Fatsia japonica (Japanese aralia)	medium	moist
Ficus elastica 'Decora' (Rubber plant)	medium	moist
Hoya carnosa (Wax plant)	medium	dry
Maranta Leuconeura (Prayer plant)	medium	moist
Nephrolepis exaltata bostoniensis (Boston fern)	medium	moist
Podocarpus Macrophyllus 'Maki' (Podocarpus)	high	moist

Flower Stand for a Hall.

FERNS

POLYPODIUM SCHNEIDERI.

The figures are elucidatory of the interesting subject.

1. The prothallium or first growth from the spore. 2. The first frond appearing and roots extending. 3. Spore case bursting and dispersing spores.

4. Spore germinating and cellular growth forming the prothallium (1) which bears reproductive organs analogous to flowers. 5. Antheridium, containing male spores and emerging antherozoids. 6. Archegonium, or female organ. 7. Spore cases magnified, as taken from the plant A at 7, the back of the frond, on which they form as the result of fertilisation, as shown and explained.

A Spray of a Common Asparagus (not the edible species)

The fern fancier will also find it well worth while to join a fern study group. The Los Angeles International Fern Society, c/o Wilbur Olson, 13715 Cordary Avenue, Hawthorne, California 90250 provides monthly lesson sheets with emphasis on tropical ferns. The dues are minimal and much of the information cannot be obtained from any other source. The American Fern Society, c/o LeRoy K. Henry, Division of Plants, Carnegie Museum, Pittsburgh, Pa. 15213, Treasurer, has a publication which appears quarterly. This Society also conducts a spore exchange for its members. ◆

FERTILISATION AND GROWTH OF FERNS.

FERNS

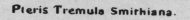

Pteris Tremula Smithiana.

GYMNOGRAMMA SCHIZOPHYLLA.

A Parlor Fernery

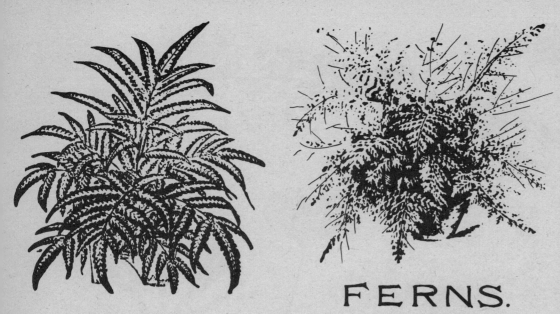

FERNS.

STAGHORN

FERNCASES

—Ornamental Fern Case and Stand.

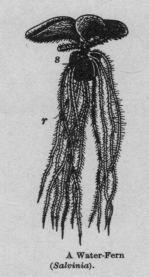

A Water-Fern
(*Salvinia*).

CASE FOR FERNS.

The American Fern Society, Inc.

The American Fern Society is composed of individuals who are interested in ferns. Membership is on a calendar year basis, running from January 1st through December 31st ($5.00 per year for annual membership, $10.00 or more for sustaining membership, $100.00 for life membership). Dues notices are sent to members late in November and are payable upon receipt. Membership entitles each annual or sustaining member to the American Fern Journal and the newsletter (both issued as quarterlies) for each year for which dues are paid.

Any person joining the Society during the first nine months of the calendar year is considered to be a member as of that year, and all issues of the Journal published in the year of his application will be sent to him. One joining after September may elect, by so stating in writing, to have the membership begin with January 1st of the coming year instead of applying his dues for the nearly spent year.

Members should receive their initial issues of the Journal and newsletter within 60-90 days after joining the Society, unless applying at the end of the year, in which case the publications will arrive about March 1 of the following year.

Please allow at least *two months* for a change of address.

Dean P. Whittier, Dept. of Biology, Vanderbilt Univ., Nashville, Tenn. 37235

—Interior of Fernery.

FERNERIES

Ferns.

ADIANTUM FARLEYENSE.

—Fern Case.

—Formation of Buds on the apices of the Fronds of Ferns: *Asplenium Edgeworthii.*

Fig. 45.—Ferns in a Window Garden.

PELLÆA TERNIFOLIA.

1 *Nephrolepis Duffi.*   2 *Trichomanes Lyelli.*   3 Sorus of the same Fern with cup-shaped investment seen in longitudinal section. 4 *Rhipidopteris peltata.*   5 *Polypodium serpens.*   6 Pinna of *Gleichenia alpina.*   7 *Schizœa fistulosa.*   8 *Botrychium lanceolatum.*   9 Under side of a pinna of *Gleichenia alpina*; in the two upper cavities the sporangia are covered by leaflets, in the under ones they are exposed.   10, 11 Pinna of *Cyathea elegans.*   12 Longitudinal section through a Sorus and Cup of *Cyathea.*   13 Sporangium of *Cyathea.*   14 Sporangium of *Polypodium.*   15 Sporangium of *Schizœa.*   16 Under side of the Prothallium of Spleenwort.   1, 2, 4, 5, 6, 7, 8 natural size ; 3, 9, 10, 11, 12, 13, 14, 15, 16 magnified from 5 to 20 times.

EXOTIC ORCHIDS

—*Angræcum eburneum* epiphytic on a tree-trunk (Madagascar).

ORCHIDS

Alberts & Merkel Bros.,
Boynton Beach, Fla. 33435

Armacost & Royston,
11920 La Grange Ave., Box 25576,
W. Los Angeles, Calif. 90069

John Ewing Orchids,
Box 613, Chatsworth, Calif. 91311

Fennell Orchid Co.,
26715 S.W. 157th Ave.,
Homestead, Fla. 33030

Finck Floral Co.,
9849 Kimker Ln.
St. Louis, Mo. 63127

Fox Orchids,
6615 W. Markham,
Little Rock, Ark. 72205

Herb Haber Orchids,
Box 544,
Santa Cruz, Calif. 95060

Hausermann,
Box 353,
Elmhurst, Ill. 60126

Margaret Ilgenfritz Orchids,
Box 665,
Monroe, Mich. 48161

Jones and Scully,
2200 N.W. 33rd Ave.,
Miami, Fla. 33142

Wm. Kirch, Ltd.,
2630 Waiomo Rd.,
Honolulu, Hawaii 96816

Lager & Hurrell,
426 Morris Ave.,
Summit, N.J. 07901

Rod McLellan Co.,
1450 El Camino Real,
So. San Francisco, Calif. 94080

Orchidglen,
1540 Truro Ave.,
Reynoldsburg, Ohio 43068

Penn Valley Orchids,
239 Old Gulph Rd.,
Wynnewood, Penna. 19096

Shaffer's Orchids,
1220 41st Ave.,
Santa Cruz, Calif. 95060

Fred A. Stewart,
1212 E. Las Tunas Dr.,
San Gabriel, Calif. 91778

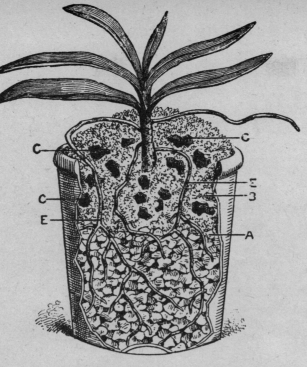

POTTING DISTICHOUS ORCHID (AEBIDES).

References :—a, crocks for drainage ; *b*, moss ; *c*,
charcoal ; *e*, roots passing through drainage.

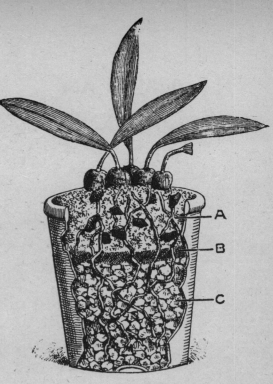

POTTING PSEUDO-BULBOUS ORCHID
(CŒLOGYNE).

References :—b, compost ; *b*, layer of moss to
protect drainage (*c*).

RARE HOUSE PLANT SOURCE LIST

ALL-GROVE
Box 459H
Wilmington, Mass. 01887
Terrariums, bonsai, insect-
ivorous plants, ferns, sakei

BART'S BONSAI NURSERY
522 5th St.
Fullerton, Whitehall
Pennsylvania 18052
Bonsai

PAUL BRECHT ORCHID COMPANY
1989 Harbor Blvd.
Costa Mesa, Calif.
Bromeliads, ferns, orchids,
bonsai insectivorous plants

ORCHID BASKET.

W. J. BRUDY
113 Aucila Road
Cocoa Beach, Fla. 32931
Seeds of tropical woody
plants

CACTUSLAND
Rt. 3, Box 44
Edinburg, Texas 78539
Cacti

CENTRAL NURSERY COMPANY
2675 Johnson Ave.
San Luis Obispo, Calif. 93401
Seeds of palms, confiers
and other woody plants

COOK'S GERANIUM NURSERY
712 North Grand
Lyons, Kansas 67554
Geraniums

CORNELISON'S BROMELIADS
225 San Bernardino St.
North Fort Myers, Fla. 33903
Bromeliads

L. EASTERBROOK
10 Craig St.
Butler, Ohio 44822
African violets, gesneriads,
begonias, house plants

EDELWEISS GARDENS
Robinsville, New Jersey 08691
Unusual house plants

FENNELL ORCHID COMPANY
157 Avenue
Homestead, Fla. 33030
Orchids

FISCHER GREENHOUSES
Linwood, New Jersey 08221
African violets

GREENLAND FLOWER SHOP
Route 1, Stormstown
Port Matilda, Penna. 16871
Rare house plants

THE HOUSE PLANT CORNER
P. O. Box 810
Oxford, Maryland 21654
House plant supplies,
African violets

MARGARET ILGENFRITZ
Department H
Monroe, Michigan 48161
Orchids

KARTUZ GREENHOUSES
92 Chestnut St.
Wilmington, Mass. 01887
Gesneriads, begonias,
geraniums

LOGEE'S GREENHOUSES
Danielson, Conn. 06239
Begonias, rare plants,
geraniums

ROD McLELLAN COMPANY
1455 El Camino Real
South San Francisco, Calif. 94080
Bonsai

MERRY GARDENS
Camden, Maine 04843
Flowering & foliage house
plants, geraniums, begonias

OAKHILL GARDENS
Route 3, Box 87-F
Dallas, Oregon 97338
Orchids

OAKHURST GARDENS
P. O. Box 444
Arcadia, California
Orchids, unusual bulbs, and
house plants

PARADISE GARDENS
Route 18
Whitman, Mass. 02382
Aquatic plants, goldfish,
pools

PLAZA NURSERY & FLOWER SHOP
7430 Crescent Ave.
Buena vista, Calif. 90620
Bromeliads

THE JULIUS ROEHRS COMPANY
Rutherford, N. J. 07073
Rare house plants

HARRY SAIER
Dimondale, Michigan 48821
Seeds

SLOCUM WATER GARDENS
Department H-4
1101 Cypress Gardens Road
Winter Haven, Fla. 33880
Waterlilies, lotus,
goldfish, tubs, pools

TALNADGE'S FERNS
354 "G" Street
Chula Vista, Calif. 92010
Ferns

THREE SPRINGS FISHERIES
1640 Main Road
Lilypons, Maryland 21717
Hardy waterlilies,
aquatic plants

WILLIAM TRICKER, INC.
1963 Allendale Ave.
Saddle River, New Jersey
Waterlilies

VAN NESS WATER GARDENS
2460 North Euclid Ave.
Upland, Calif. 91786
Waterlilies

JOHN VERMEULEN & SONS, INC.
Neshanic Station, New Jersey 08853
Bonsai

ZINK'S GREENHOUSES
P. O. Box 1676
Vista, Calif. 92083
Cacti, succulents

ZYGOPETALUM MACKAYI.

POTTING ONCIDIUM (correct).
Basal roots within the compost.

AMERICAN ORCHID SOCIETY

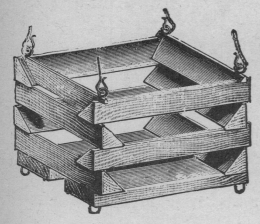

WEST'S PATENT BASKET.

SAY THEIR NAMES OUT LOUD

It all started as a form of madness that infected aristocrats of the English variety in the latter half of the nineteenth century. In particular, it seized those with a penchant for scientific collecting, who commissioned costly expeditions to scour the earth with fanatic zeal to bring back specimens of the rare and beautiful orchid.

The good gentlemen who shared this mania that has been said to lie somewhere between collecting rare, small bottles and carving animals out of peach pits, also shared a penchant for secrecy. When they did publish their results in the journals of the day, these upstanding citizens contrived to lie about the locations of their discoveries and to omit crucial details concerning the care and propagation of these lovely plants.

Thus, the mistaken idea that orchids can only be grown by fanatic experts.

Thus, the loss of some of the species and the near extinction of others.

It is the same sort of pillage for profit, and pillage in the name of science, that is currently destroying not only isolated species of plant life, but whole rain forests. Will we save the planet in the nick of time, the way Professor Lewis Knudson rescued many varieties of orchids from extinction during the 1920's?

Strangely, the problem then was that this vast family of plants of about 25,000 species, some producing over one million seeds per pod, appeared impossible to propagate by seed. The tiny seeds contain insufficient nutrients for germination. Professor Knudson cleverly achieved germination by placing the seeds in a glass flask containing agar jelly, chemical nutrients and sugar. Thanks to this breakthrough, the work of horticultural groups like The Orchid Society, and the appearance of many publications on the subject, orchid growing has become a hobby that you may now begin to enjoy in your home.

Wild orchids grow in almost every region of the earth, except the extremely arid desert areas and the cold belts. Most wild orchids live in tropical zones at altitudes of between 3,000 and 9,000 feet. However, there are many that thrive at higher and lower altitudes.

Cattleya, Cymbidium and Phalaenopsis are the names of the orchids you generally see used for corsages. Many growers also specialize in Dendrobian, Vanda and Epidendron. It should be simple to obtain any of these varieties.

There is an enormous variety of orchids with varied habits available to the consumer. With study and work, it is now possible to keep a constant flow of amazingly formed, remarkably hued blossoms in your home year round.

Habenaria carnea

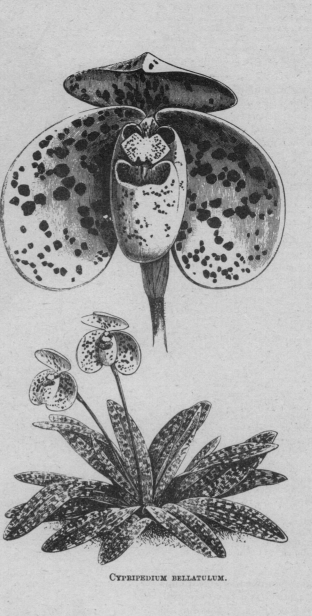

Cypripedium bellatulum.

Spot in Orchids.

But first, start with a good stock plant. Watch it go through its cycles of development. Then, try your hand at working with large groupings.

Orchids are not grown in ordinary soil. They require a special mix, such as Cornell Mix For Tropical Plants. However, most reputable gardening centers package their own mix and they should suggest appropriate mixes for orchids that need special care. Information in this field is plentiful, so find out the right way and do it that way. It's well worth it.

After you watch your first flower open, we think you'll know why many grow these fantastic blooms with cultish devotion. The spectacular results will make it well worth the work and the wait.

Odontoglossum Pescatorei Duchess of Westminster.

Vanda Sanderiana.

by Russell C. Mott, L. H. Bailey Hortorium

Editor's Note: The following was prepared for presentation at the Hudson Valley Foliage Plant Conference sponsored by Cooperative Extension of Dutchess, Orange, Putnam, Rockland, Ulster, and Westchester Counties on Thursday, October 26th at the Holiday Inn, Mt. Kisco, New York. It is reproduced here to assist in providing information for use in growing foliage plants in interior environments, such as public buildings.

The Cornell Tropical Mixes are formulated for growing tropical plants. The Foliage Plant Mix and the Epiphytic Mix are especially adapted for their respective plant types. They are modifications of the original peat-lite mixes. Their formulae are given in Table I and Table II.

The *Cornell Foliage Plant Mix* is recommended for those plants which need a growing medium with high moisture-retention characteristics. Plants having a fine root system or possessing many fine root hairs are included in this group.

Table 1.   Cornell Plant Mix

Material	1 Cubic Yard	1 Bushel
Sphagnum peat moss (screened ½" mesh)	½ cu yd	½ bu
Horticultural vermiculite (No. 2)	¼ cu yd	¼ bu
Perlite (medium grade)	¼ cu yd	¼ bu
Ground dolomitic limestone	8¼ lbs	8 Tbs*
20% superphosphate (powdered)	2 lbs	2 Tbs
10-10-10 fertilizer	2¾ lbs	3 Tbs
Iron sulfate	¾ lb	1 Tbs
Potassium nitrate (14-0-44)	1 lb	1 Tbs
Fritted Trace Element Mix, *e.g.* Peter's FTE, etc.	2 oz	omit
Granular wetting agent *e.g.* Aqua-Gro, etc.	1½ lbs	3 Tbs

* Level Tablespoon

The Cornell Foliage Plant Mix in Table 1 is recommended for the following plants, and others which require similar culture.

Amaryllis
Aphelandra squarrosa
Begonias
Beloperone guttata
Buxus
Caladiums
Cissus
Citrus
Coleus blumei
Ferns
Pelargoniums
Hedera Helix cultivars
Helxine soleirolii
Marantas
Oxalis
Palms
Pileas
Sansevierias
Tolmiea menziesii
Ficus

The *Cornell Epiphytic Mix* is recommended for plants which require good drainage, aeration and have the ability to withstand drying between waterings. Plants having coarse, tuberous or rhyzomatous roots are in this category.

AQUA-GRO GRANULAR

TREATED MIX — Reduces the surface and interfacial tensions of water. When the tension of water is reduced there is an increase in the penetration and availability of both water and nutrient solutions. This promotes better rooted, denser, and more uniform healthy plants.

Premix 1½ to 3 pts. in every cubic yeard of soil mix. Mixes wet instantly! No soaking of peat-Lite Mixes needed. Mixes rewet instantly if allowed to dry. Aqua-GRO granular available in 3, 15, 30 or 55 gallon containers.

Reprinted by Aquatrols Corp. of America
1400 Suckle Hwy., Pennsauken, N.J. 08110

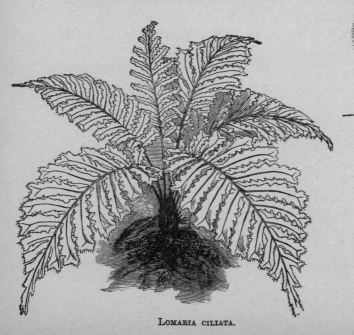

LOMARIA CILIATA.

Aërial Roots of an Orchid epiphytic upon the bark of the branch of a tree.

TRICHOCENTRUM ALBO-PURPUREUM.

SUPPLIES

Reinfrank and Associates, 5414 Sierra Vista Ave., Los Angeles, Calif. 90038
South Shore Floral Co., Woodmere, Long Island, New York 11598
Wrightwood Floral Co., 1420 Wrightwood Ave., Houston, Tex. 77009

AGAR AND AGAR-NUTRIENT MIXTURES

Difco Laboratories, Detroit, Mich. 48201
Daniel M. Hill, P.O. Box 1184, Ontario, Calif. 91762
Julius O. Leuschner, 1050 W. 6th St., Los Angeles, Calif. 90017

FLASKING, MERISTEM SERVICE

Armacost and Royston, Inc., 2005 Armacost Ave., West Los Angeles, Calif. 90025
Gallup and Stribling Laboratories, 645 Stoddard Lane, Santa Barbara, Calif. 93103
Hauserman's Orchids, Inc., P.O. Box 363, Elmhurst, Ill. 60126
Iwanage & Taba Laboratories, 2614 Waiomao Rd., Honolulu, Hawaii 96816
Jones and Scully, 2154 N.W. 33rd Ave., Miami, Fla. 33142
Marion Ryerson, 18320 S.W. 294th St., Homestead, Fla. 33030

VIRUS TESTING SERVICE

Florida West Coast Scientific Labs., P.O. Box 11914, Tampa, Fla. 33610

GREENHOUSES

Aluminum Greenhouses, Inc., 14615 Lorrain Ave., Cleveland, Ohio 44111
Janco Greenhouses, 10788 Tucker St., Beltsville, Md. 20705
Lord and Burnham, Irvington, N. Y. 10533
Mid-America Greenhouse Co., 10907 Manchester, St. Louis, Mo. 63122
National Greenhouse Co., P.O. Box 100, Pana, Ill. 62557
Pacific Coast Greenhouse Mfg. Co., 525 East Bayshore Rd., Redwood City, Calif. 94063
Redfern's Prefab Greenhouses, 55 Mt. Hermon Rd., Scotts Valley, Calif. 95060
Southern Calif. Greenhouse Mfrs., 3266 N. Rosemead Blvd., Rosemead, Calif. 91770
Stearns Greenhouses, 98 Taylor St., Meponset, Boston, Mass. 02122
Sturdi-Built Manufacturing Co., 11304 S.W. Boones Ferry Rd., Portland, Ore.
Texas Greenhouse Co., Inc., 2711 St. Louis Ave., Fort Worth, Tex. 76110
Turner Greenhouses, Box 1260, Goldsboro, N.C. 27530

Cornell Tropical Plant Mixes

Table 2.   Cornell Epiphytic Mix

Material	1 Cubic Yard	1 Bushel
Sphagnum peat moss (screened ½″ mesh)	⅓ cu yd	⅓ bu
**Douglas, red or white fir bark (⅛—¼ inch size)	⅓ cu yd	⅓ bu
Perlite (medium grade)	⅓ cu yd	⅓ bu
Ground dolomitic limestone	7 lbs	8 Tbs*
20% superphosphate (powdered)	4½ lbs	6 Tbs
10-10-10 fertilizer	2½ lbs	3 Tbs
Iron sulphate	½ lb	1 Tbs
Potassium nitrate (14-0-44)	1 lb	1 Tbs
Fritted Trace Element Mix, e.g. Peter's FTE, etc.	2 oz	omit
Granular wetting agent e.g. Aqua-Gro, etc. ✓	1½ lbs	3 Tbs

*Level Tablespoon
**Fir bark comes from Douglas, fir white or red fir or redwood, ground & screened to a definite size. Finely ground bark (⅛-¼″) has a dry weight of 11.5 pound per cubic foot. Fresh bark has a pH of about 5.0 Upon weathering it becomes slightly more alkaline. The bark contains some nutrients, but these will not adequately meet the requirements of growing plants.

The Cornell Epiphytic Mix in Table 2 is recommended for the following plants and others which require good drainage, aeration and have the ability to withstand drying between irrigation.

African violets	Gloxinias
Aglaonemas	Hoyas
Aloes	Monsteras
Bromeliads	Nephthytis
Cacti	Philodendrons
Crassulas	Pothos
Diffenbachias	Peperomias
Episcias	Syngoniums

Fertilizers:

Long lasting or slow-release forms of fertilizers are used with soilless mixes. Osmocote 14-14-14 and Peters 14-7-7 have been used with the tropical plant mixes with good results. Other nutrient fertilizers are omitted with the exception of dolomitic limestone and 20% superphosphate which are added to adjust the pH and to maintain adequate phosphorus levels. Peter's Fritted Trace Element Mix is added to assure a balance of minor elements.

Table 3.   Slow-release Fertilizers

Material	1 Cubic Yard	2 Bushels
Osmocote 14-14-14	5 lbs	3.8 -4.0 oz
Peters 14-7-7	5 lbs	3.8 oz
Mag Amp 7-40-6 (medium particle size)	5-10 lbs	7.5 oz
Scotts 23-7-7	3 lbs	2. 3oz

Sources of Supply:

Fir bark (⅛ - ¼″ size) is available from orchid-supply houses such as Thomas Flynn Orchids, Div. Vaughans Seed Company, Chimney Rock Road, Bound Brook, New Jersey 08805.

Aqua-Gro is manufactured by Aquatrols Corporation of America, Box 385, Delair, New Jersey 08110 and available from florist-nursery supply houses. Other wetting agents available. ✓

Peter's Fritted Trace Element Mix is manufactured by Robert B. Peters Company, Inc., Allentown, Pennsylvania 18104, and is available from florist-nursery supply houses.

(NOTE: To help avoid confusion, tradenames are used as they appear on the label. No endorsement of named products is intended nor is criticism of unnamed products implied.)

For further information on peat-lite mixes, see Cornell Information Bulletin No. 43, "Cornell Peat-Lite Mixes for Commercial Plant Growing".

BRASSIA BRACHEATA.

MAXILLARIA SANDERIANA XANTHOGLOSSA.

SELAGINELLA GRANDIS.

THE AMERICAN ORCHID SOCIETY INC.
BOTANICAL MUSEUM OF HARVARD
UNIVERSITY, CAMBRIDGE, MASS. 02138

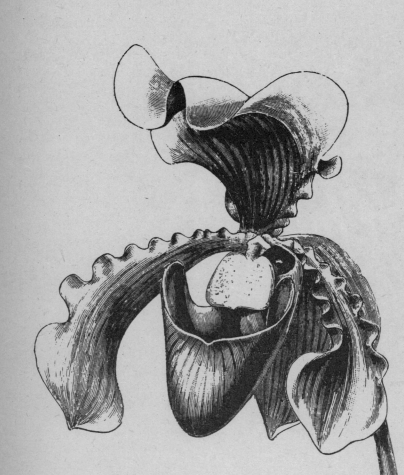

CYPRIPEDIUM INSIGNE SANDERÆ.

ORCHID PLANTS (In addition to these there may be local growers who can furnish plants.)

Alberts and Merkel Bros., Inc., P.O. Box 537 AO, Boynton Beach, Fla. 33435

Armacost and Royston, Inc., 2005 Armacost Ave., West Los Angeles, Calif. 90025

Armstrong and Brown, J. L. Humphreys, Tunbridge Wells, Kent, England

Ashcroft Orchids, 19062 Ballinger Way, Seattle, Wash. 98155

The Bangkrabue Nursery, 15 Klahom's Lane, Bangkrabue, Bangkok, Thailand

M. J. Bates—Orchids, 7911 U. S. 301, Ellenton, Fla. 33532

Black and Flory, Ltd., Slough, Bucks, England

James Bloom, 1329 N.E. 7th Ave., Fort Lauderdale, Fla. 33304

Blue Grass Orchids, Winchester Rd., R.F.D. 4, Lexington, Kentucky

Braemar Orchids, 3139 Braemar Rd., Santa Barbara, Calif. 93105

Paul Brecht Orchids, Costa Mesa, Calif.

Casa Luna Orchids, Star Rte. 1, Box 219A, Beaufort, S.C. 29902

Charlesworth and Co., Ltd., Haywards Heath, Sussex, England

Chow Cheng Orchids, 194 Litoh St., Taichung, Taiwan

Cobb's Orchids, Inc., 780 La Buena Tierra, Santa Barbara, Calif. 93105

Creve Coeur Orchids, 12 Graeser Acres, Creve Coeur, Mo. 63141

Clark Day, Jr., 19311 Bloomfield Ave., Artesia, Calif.

Walter R. Diggleman, 2356 Tiffin Rd., Oakland, Calif.

Dos Pueblos Orchid Co., P.O. Box 158, Goleta, Calif. 93017

Everglades Orchids, P.O. Box 401, Belle Glade, Fla. 33430

Fennell Orchid Co., Homestead, Fla. 33030

Field's Orchids, 196 N.W. 91st St., Miami, Fla. 33150

Fink Floral Co., 9849 Kimker Lane, St. Louis, Mo. 63127

Fred-Ken Orchids, P.O. Box 660, Homestead, Fla. 33030

Fort Caroline Orchids, 13142 Fort Caroline Rd., Jacksonville, Fla. 32225

Arthur Freed Orchids, Inc., 5731 So. Bonsall Dr., Malibu, Calif. 90265

Fricker Orchids and Greenhouse Mfrs., 5248 Sereno Dr., Temple City, Calif.

Franklin W. Gamble, 62 Shell Rd., Mill Valley, Calif.

G. Ghose and Co., Orchids, Town-End, Darjeeling, West Bengal, India

R. H. Gore Orchids, Box 211, Fort Lauderdale, Fla. 33315

Etta Gray Orchids, 1653 Barnard Rd., Claremont, Calif. 91711

Greenhouse Hawaii, John K. Noa, P.O. Box 180, Waimanalo, Hawaii 96795

Gubler Orchids, 9441 E. Broadway, Temple City, Calif.

Herb Hager Orchids, P. O. Box 544, Santa Cruz, Calif. 95060

Hauserman's Orchids, Inc., P. O. Box 363, Elmhurst, Ill. 60126

Hilo Vanda Nursery, Dr. H. Nishimra, 10-11 Young Bldg., Hilo, Hawaii

S. M. Howard Orchid Imports, 11802 Houston St., N. Hollywood, Calif. 91607

Gordon M. Hoyt, Orchids, Seattle Heights, Wash. 98063

Margaret Ilgenfritz, Orchids, P.O. Box 665, Monroe, Mich. 48161

H. Iwanaga, 5398 Papae St., Honolulu, Hawaii 96816

J. and L. Orchids, Chestnut Hill Rd., R.D. 2. ¼ptts≠ town, Pa. 19464

Jones and Scully, Inc., 2200 N.W. 33rd Ave., Miami, Fla. 33142

Patrick O. Kawamoto, 3142 E. Manoa Rd., Honolulu, Hawaii 96822

T. Kazumura Orchid Nursery, 145 N. Judd St., Honolulu, Hawaii 96817

A. J. Keeling and Sons, Westgate Hill, Nr. Bradford, Yorks, England

Kensington Orchids, Inc., 3301 Plyers Mill Rd., Kensington Md. 20795

Wm. Kirch Orchids, Ltd., 2630 Waiomao Rd., Honolulu, Hawaii 96816

Oscar M. Kirsch, 2869 Oahu Ave., Honolulu, Hawaii 96822

Kodama Orchid Nursery, Ltd., 1039 Kamehameha Rd., Honolulu, Hawaii 96819

Lager and Hurrell, 426 Morris Ave., Summit, N.J. 07901

Landamar Orchids, P.O. Box 698, Tarzana, Calif. 91356

Marcel Lecoufle, 5 Rue de Paris, 94 Boissy-St. Leger, France

Lines Orchids, Taft Highway, Signal Mountain, Tenn. 37377

Stuart Low Co., Jarvisbrook (Crowborough), Sussex, England

Manor Orchids, 970 East Social Row Rd., Dayton, Ohio 45459

Mansell and Hatcher, Ltd., Rawdon, Leeds, Yorks, England

Marcy Orchids, Inc., 6901 S.W. 97th Ave., Miami, Fla. 33143

McBean's Cymbidium Orchids, Cooksbridge, Lewes, Sussex, England

Mrs. Lester McCoy Orchids, 3735 Diamond Head Rd., Honolulu, Hawaii 96803

McKee Jungle Garden, Vero Beach, Fla.

McKeral's Orchid Range, 1801 Hypoluxo Rd., Lantana, Fla. 33460

Rod McLellan Co., 1450 El Camino Real, S. San Francisco, Calif. 94080

Mid-Florida Orchid Center, Inc., S. 9th St., P.O. Box 1031, Winter Garden, Fla. 32787

M. Miyamoto Orchids, 617 Libby St., Honolulu, Hawaii 96792

Moore's Orchids, P.O. Box 2366, Hialeah, Fla. 33012

Muse's Orchids, 3187 S.W. 26th St., Miami, Fla. 33133

Dr. and Mrs. Yoshio Magano, 261 Eifukucho, Suginami, Tokyo, Japan

Nelson Nurseries, 1975 Opa Locka Blvd., Miami, Fla.

T. Ogawa Orchids, 1454 Kilauea Ave., Hilo, Hawaii

The Orchid House, 699 Sage Ave., Los Osos, San Luis Obispo, Calif. 93401

Orchid Oaks Nursery, 9440 S.W. 107th Ave., Miami, Fla. 33143

Orquideario Catarinense, P.O. Box 1, Corupa, Santa Catarina, Brazil

Orchids by Turner, Inc., 226 Park St., North Attleboro, Mass. 01760

Orchids of Africa, Helen Cockburn and Frank Piers, F.L.S., Box 2041, Nairobi, Kenya, East Africa

Orchids International, P.O. Box 66560, Burien, Wash. 98166

Osment Orchids, 2435 Cleveland St., Hollywood, Fla.

H. Otake Orchid Nursery, 45-270-A Puaae Rd., Kaneohe, Oahu, Hawaii

Pacific Coast Orchid Estate, P.O. Box 281, Moss Beach, Calif. 94038

H. Patterson and Sons, Bergenfield, N. J. 07621

Penn Valley Orchids, 239 Gulph Rd., Wynnewood, Pa. 19096

Joseph R. Redlinger, Orchids, 9236 S.W. 57th Ave., Miami, Fla. 33156

Research Breeders, William West, 753 Kansas Ave., Lovell, Wyo. 82431

Rivermont Orchids, Signal Mountain, Tenn. 37377

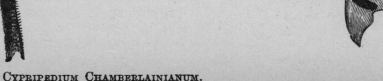

CYPRIPEDIUM CHAMBERLAINIANUM.

MILTONIA JOICEYANA.

Your Guide to Orchids

Orchids come in many sizes, shapes and colors. There are approximately 50,000 different orchids in the world. Each is a jewel of a flower.

You can recognize the major cultivated types from the nearby sketches. Compare these drawings with blooms in orchid shows and nurseries.

Some orchid flowers are as big as plates. Some are as tiny as pinheads. Most are sizes in between. Some spray orchids have dozens of blooms on a stem. Some orchid blooms stay fresh for several weeks.

All the colors of the rainbow are found in orchids. Purple, white, red, yellow, green, pink, alone or in combinations.

Look for the "lip" which distinguishes orchids. On every orchid flower the lip is different in shape, color or size from the other five segments of the flower.

How to Grow Orchids

Grow orchids in sunlight, fresh warm air and high humidity. Place plants in east or south windowsills, glassed porches, or swimming pool enclosures. Small greenhouses are even better and prefab models are inexpensive.

Some people grow orchids under artificial lights in basements or apartments in cold climates, or outdoors under trees in warm climates.

Cattleyas, Vandas and Phalaenopsis need to be warm, 55 degrees is the preferable night minimum. Cymbidiums and some Dendrobiums prefer cooler, but not freezing, temperatures. Grow Cymbidiums and Vandas in strong sunlight, Phalaenopsis and Cypripediums in shadier places.

Nurserymen from whom you buy plants will give you specific instructions.

Ruben in Orchids, Golden Hours, Inc., 12500 S.W. 46th St., Miami, Fla. 33165
Rapee Sagarick, G.P.O. Box 953, Bangkok, Thailand
David Sanders Orchids, Ltd., Selsfield, East Grinstead, Sussex, England
T. M. Sanders, 12502 Prospect Ave., Santa Ana, Calif. 92705
Santa Barbara Orchid Estate, 1250 Orchid Dr., Goleta, Calif. 93105
Walter Scheeren Orchids, Poestenkill, N. Y. 12140
Shaffer's Tropical Gardens, Inc., 1220 41st Ave., Santa Cruz, Calif. 95060
Sherman Orchid Gardens, Glendora, Calif. 91740
Shimamoto Orchid Nursery, 271 Momi Lane, Wailuku Maui, Hawaii 96793
Sign of the Coon, Powderville, Mont.
Earl J. Small Orchids, Inc., 6901 49th St., Pinellas, Park, Fla. 33565
Ralph Smathers Orchids, P.O. Box 477, Coral Gables, Fla. 33134
Sterling Orchids, Inc., 5502 Sterling Rd., Knoxville, Tenn. 37918
Fred A. Stewart, Inc., 1212 E. las Tunas Dr., San Gabriel, Calif. 91778
Thornton's Orchids, 3200 N. Military Trail, W. Palm Beach, Fla. 33401
Tradewinds Orchids, Inc., 12800 S.W. 77th Ave., Miami, Fla. 33156
Maurice Vacherot, 31 Rue de Valenton, Boissy-St. Leger (V. de M.) France
Vacherot and Lecoufle, "La Tuilerie," 94 Boissy-St. Leger (V. de M.), France
Voo Doo Orchids, 1340 Jewel Box Lane, Naples, Fla.
J. Milton Warne, 260 Jack Lane, Honolulu, Hawaii 96817
Weeki Wachee Orchids, Rte. 4, Box 65, Brooksville, Fla. 33512
Westenberger Orchid Co., 10150 Foothill Blvd., San Fernando, Calif. 91342
E. C. Wilcox, 1336 N. Michillinda Ave., Arcadia, Calif. 91006
Wilcox's Orchids, 490 Beverly Ave., San Leandro, Calif.
Wilkins Orchid Nursery, 21905 S.W. 157 Ave., Goulds, Fla.

HEALTHY CATTLEYA GROWTH

SWOLLEN CATTLEYA GROWTH.

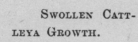

PLANTLET ON DENDROBIUM STEM.

ZYGOCOLAX VEITCHI.

ODONTOGLOSSUM WILCKEANUM PITTÆ.

ONCIDIUM ORNITHORHYNCHUM ALBUM.

GROWING BONSAI

Bonsai are miniature trees grown in pots. The aim of bonsai culture is to develop a tiny tree that has all the elements of a large tree growing in a natural setting. This look is achieved, principally, by branch and root pruning and shaping, but other factors are also important. The texture of the trunk, its look of age, the moss and underplantings in the container—all contribute to the illusion of a minature tree as it is seen in nature.

A presentable bonsai can be created in a few seasons. Cultivating these miniature potted trees is both an intriguing hobby, and a means of adapting a wide range of plants to specialized and decorative uses. Bonsai require daily watering during their growing season, and, because the plants are rooted in shallow pots, careful pruning.

Bonsai are kept outdoors most of the year, but—from time to time—these miniaturized versions of nature are brought indoors for display. Only certain tropical trees, shrubs, and vines can be continuously kept indoors full time as bonsai.

Bonsai, as an art form, stems from ancient oriental culture. It originated in China and was developed by the Japanese. In the 13th century, the Japanese collected and potted wild trees that had been dwarfed by nature. These naturally formed miniatures were the first bonsai.

When demand for the small trees outgrew the supply, Japanese gardeners began to train bonsai from native trees. They shaped the trees to give them the illusion of age and naturalness. Over the years, the Japanese devised standards of shape and form which gradually became the classic bonsai styles.

American bonsai are much freer in concept and style than Japanese bonsai. American bonsai growers have recognized that the horticultural and aesthetic rules are important, but are specifically aimed at Japanese culture. Because of this, Americans have taken oriental styles and applied them to plants never grown by the Japanese. Therefore, the rigid procedures and names used by the Japanese are not used in this bulletin.

PRINCIPLES OF BONSAI

Not all plants are equally effective as bonsai. To produce a realistic illusion of a mature tree, look for plants with the following characteristics—

- Small leaves or needles.
- Short internodes, or distances between leaves.
- Attractive bark or roots.
- Branching characteristics for good twig forms.

All parts of the ideal bonsai—trunk, branches, twigs, leaves, flowers, fruits, buds, roots—should be in perfect scale with the size of the tree. Plants used for bonsai should have small leaves, or leaves that become small under bonsai culture. Plants with overly large leaves, such as the avocado, will look out of proportion if chosen for bonsai. Sycamores also develop leaves that are too large. Certain species of both maple and oak trees usually respond well to bonsai culture and develop leaves that are in proportion.

Among the plants with small leaves and needles are: spruce, pine, zelkova, pomegranate, and certain oaks and maples.

Plants chosen for bonsai should have attractive bark, and the trunk must give the illusion of maturity. The trunk should have girth, but must remain in proportion to the entire tree. The trunk should taper gradually toward the top of the tree. Sometimes one or two of the main branches must be shortened to emphasize the vertical line of the trunk and give the trunk a balanced appearance.

To give the appearance of age, the upper one-third of the root structure of a mature bonsai is often exposed. This is especially effective if the roots have good girth and form. Twisted and tangled roots should be straightened before potting or repotting a tree to achieve an aged appearance.

Bonsai from nursery stock, and trees collected from the wild, should have a root system that will—when exposed—add to the appearance of the finished bonsai.

Plants have a "best profile" just as people do. Decide on the front of the tree at the very beginning, because planting and shaping are done with the front of the tree in mind. However, you may change your ideas about the plant's ultimate shape as you clip and prune.

The front of a bonsai should offer a good view of the main trunk which must be clearly visible from the base to the first branch, typically about one-third the way up. Everywhere on the tree, but mostly from the front, the branches should look balanced and appear to be floating in space; they should not appear lopsided or top heavy. The branches should not be opposite one another with their lines cutting horizontally across the trunk. The branches give the bonsai dimension and establish the tree's basic form.

A bonsai should have a harmonious arrangement of branches without unsightly gaps. Flaws can be spotted by looking down on a bonsai. Upper branches should not overshadow lower branches.

Before deciding on the shape of your bonsai, study the tree carefully, and take into account the natural form of the species. Observe the way mature trees of the same kind grow in their natural setting to achieve an impression of age and reality.

Decide on the final shape and size of your bonsai before starting. Make a rough sketch of what you wish to create and use it as a guide.

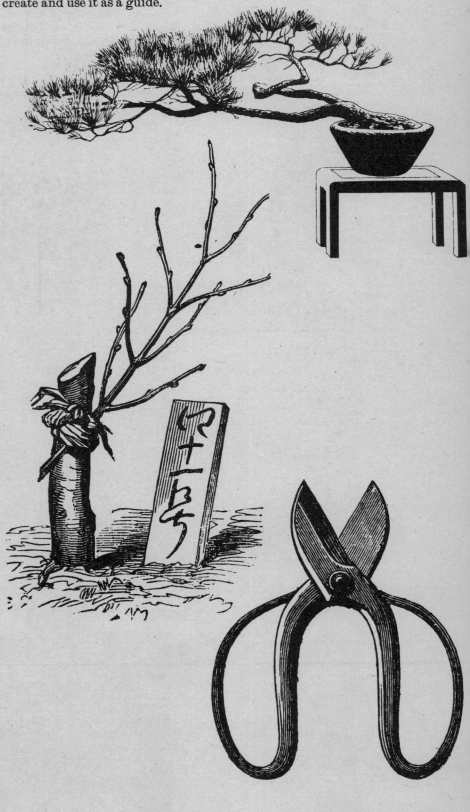

Prepared by HENRY M. CATHEY, PLANT GENETICS AND GERMPLASM INSTITUTE, NORTH-EASTERN REGION, AGRICULTURAL RESEARCH SERVICE

BONSAI GUIDE

Trees and shrubs.—The following alphabetical list of plants includes trees and shrubs suitable for traditional bonsai. This is not intended to be a complete list. Specialty nurseries often have a wide selection of dwarf and semi-dwarf varieties of many of these species. Dwarf plants, however, do not always convey the same impression as their full size counterparts because their growth habit is quite different.

APRICOT:
  Prunus species
ARBORVITAE:
  American, *Thuja occidentalis*
  Oriental, *Thuja orientalis*
AZALEA:
  Hiryu, *Rhododendron obtusum*
  Indica azalea, *Rhododendron indicum*
  Kurume, *Rhododendron hybrids*
BEECH:
  American, *Fagus grandifolia*
  European, *Fagus sylvatica*
BIRCH:
  White, *Betula alba*
BOX:
  Buxus species
BURNINGBUSH:
  Euonymus nana
CEDAR:
  Atlas, *Cedrus atlantica*
  Deodar, *Cedrus deodara*
CHERRY:
  Prunus species
COTONEASTER:
  Cotoneaster species
CRABAPPLE:
  Malus species
CRYPTOMERIA:
  Cryptomeria japonica and cultivars
CYPRESS:
  Bald, *Taxodium distichum*
  Dwarf hinoki, *Chamaecyparis obtusa var. compacta*
ELM:
  American, *Ulmus americana*
  Chinese, *Ulmus parvifolia*
  Siberian, *Ulmus pumila*
FIR:
  Abies species
FIRETHORN:
  Pyracantha species
GINKGO:
  Ginkgo biloba
GOLDENRAIN:
  Koelreuteria paniculata
GUM:
  Sweet, *Liquidambar styraciflua*
HAWTHORN:
  English, *Crataegus oxyacantha*
  Washington, *crataegus phaenopyrum*
HEATHER:
  Calluna vulgaris
HEMLOCK:
  Canadian, *Tsuga canadensis* and cultivars
HORNBEAM:
  American, *Carpinus caroliniana*
  Japanese, *Carpinus japonica*

IVY:
  Hedera helix and cultivars
JASMINE:
  Winter, *Jasminum nudiflorum*
JUNIPER:
  Juniperus species and cultivars
LOCUST:
  Black, *Robinia pseudoacacia*
MAPLE:
  Amur, *Acer ginnala*
  Hedge, *Acer campestre*
  Trident, *Acer buergerianum*
OAK:
  English, *Quercus robur*
  Pin, *Quercus palustris*
  Scarlet, *Quercus coccinea*
  White, *Quercus alba*
PEACH:
  Prunus species
PINE:
  Bristlecone, *Pinus aristata*
  Japanese white, *Pinus parviflora*
  Japanese black, *Pinus thunbergi*
  Mugo, *Pinus mugo mughus*
  Swiss stone, *Pinus cembra*
  White, *Pinus strobus*
PLUM:
  Prunus species
POMEGRANATE:
  Dwarf, *Punica granatum nana*
QUINCE:
  Japanese, *Chaenomeles japonica*
SNOWBELL:
  Japanese, *Styrax japonica*
SPRUCE:
  Picea species and cultivars
WILLOW:
  Weeping, *Salix blanda*
WISTERIA:
  Japanese, *Wisteria floribunda*
YEW:
  Taxus species and cultivars
ZELKOVA:
  Graybark elm, *Zelkova serrata*

House plants.—American gardeners have taken bonsai concepts and have applied them to house plants. By combining traditional procedures for handling house plants with bonsai concepts of design, growers have created different bonsai styles. The following alphabetical list consists of woody plants (native to the tropics and subtropics of the world) that have been grown as indoor bonsai. These plants can be obtained from either local or specialized nurseries.
ACACIA:
  Acacia baileyana
ARALIA:
  Polyscias balfouriana
  Polyscias fruticosa
  Polyscias guilfoylei
BIRD'S EYE BUSH:
  Ochna multiflora
CAMELLIA:
  Camellia japonica
  Camellia sasanqua
CAPE-JASMINE:
  Gardenia jasminoides radicans
  Gardenia jasminoides
CITRUS:
  Citrus species (calamondin, kumquat, lemon, lime, orange, and tangerine)

CHERRY:
  Surinam, *Eugenia uniflora*
CYPRESS:
  Arizona, *Cupressus arizonica*
  Monterey, *Cupressus macrocarpa*
FIG:
  Mistletoe, *Ficus diversifolia*
HERB:
  Elfin, *Cuphea hypssopifolia*
HIBISCUS:
  Hibiscus rosa-sinensis Cooperi
HOLLY:
  Miniature, *Malpighia coccigera*
JACARANDA:
  Jacaranda acutifolia
JADE:
  Crassula species
JASMINE:
  Jasminum parkeri
  Orange, *Murraea exotica*
  Star, *Trachelospermum jasminoides*
LAUREL:
  Indian, *Ficus retusa*
MYRTLE:
  Classic, *Myrtus communis*
OAK:
  Cork, *Quercus suber*
  Indoor, *Nicodemia diversifolia*
  Silk, *Grevillea robusta*
ORCHID TREE:
  Bauhinia variegata
OLIVE:
  Common, *Olea europaea*
OXERA PULCHELLA
PEPPER TREE:
  California, *Schinus molle*
PISTACHIO:
  Chinese, *Pistacia chinensis*
PLUM:
  Natal, *Carissa grandiflora*
POINCIANA:
  Royal, *Delonix regia*
POMEGRANATE:
  Dwarf, *Punica granatum nana*
POPINAC:
  White, *Leucaena glauca*
POWDERPUFF TREE:
  Calliandra surinamensis
SERISS FOETIDA
SHOWER TREE:
  Cassia eremophila

For more information on house plants and their care, see Home and Garden Bulletin 82, "Selecting and Growing House Plants." Single copies are available free from the U.S. Department of Agriculture, Washington, D.C. 20250. Send your request on a post card. Include your ZIP code in your return address.

You can also obtain books that supply information about growing plants indoors from your local library.

Some publications aimed at American bonsai growers include:
Bonsai Bulletin, Post Office Box E, Bronx, N.Y. 10466.
Bonsai Journal, American Bonsai Society, 229 North Shore Dr., Lake Waukomis, Kansas City, Mo. 64151.
Bonsai Magazine, Bonsai Clubs International, Post Office Box 1032, Los Altos, Calif. 94022.
Texas Bonsai, Post Office Box 11054, Dallas, Tex. 75223.

SEASONAL CARE

Bonsai from miniature forest trees must live outdoors all the time. They are brought into the house for short periods on special occasions. Bonsai from forest trees will die if kept too long indoors, particularly in overheated rooms. These bonsai may be brought inside once or twice a week for 2 or 3 hours—during winter, spring, and autumn. They should not be brought inside in summer unless the room is well ventilated.

Summer care.—Bonsai are very sensitive and thrive best in localities that offer cool nights, sunny days, and mist or rain almost daily. Most of the United States does not have this climate, so special provisions must be made to compensate for the lack of desired climatic conditions. Extremes in temperature, light, rain, and wind are to be avoided.

Place your bonsai on a platform or table in your garden where the plants can receive 3 to 5 hours of direct sunlight a day. The site should be shaded, preferably in the afternoon. If the area is subject to drying winds, put up screening around the plants to protect them. Screening also serves to provide the plants with shade.

Water the entire bonsai—plant and soil—daily. If you skip even 1 day you can permanently damage the plant. Make sure your plants are located where rain can fall on them. However, plants should not remain wet or water-logged for long periods.

Fertilizer.—To maintain plant growth use fertilizer to supply nutrients. Maintain the nutrient level in the soil mix throughout active growth with monthly applications of a diluted liquid fertilizer. Apply fertilizer only before and during active growth. For liquid fertilizer you can use a typical house-plant fertilizer (20–20–20 or its equivalent) diluted to one-quarter to one-half the strength on the label.

Fall care.—During this period bonsai must be prepared to endure the approaching cold. Plant growth must be slowed. Water plants less frequently to slow growth, and, when growth slows, reduce applications of fertilizers.

Do not prune or cut any branches after mid-August. Do not use artificial night lighting (incandescent filament lamps) on plants after August 1. To reduce winter dieback of flowering trees and maples make light applications of 0–10–10 fertilizer.

Winter care.—A major problem in winter is to protect bonsai against low temperatures and drying winds. Bonsai can only be left outdoors in Climates where temperatures drop no lower than 28° F. This is not the case throughout most of the United States, so a greenhouse, pit, or coldframe is necessary.

Winter frosts will seldom bother bonsai that are sheltered under the foliage of a spreading tree. Watch out, however, during the frost period for drying soil.

Coldframes.—It is easy to construct a simple coldframe for bonsai. Before the ground is frozen, dig a hole at least 1½ feet in the soil. Make the hole as long and as wide as you need for all your plants. Line the sides of this hole with exterior grade plywood which extends 6 inches above the surface. Put 4 to 6 inches of gravel in the bottom of the hole, set your plant containers on this gravel, and spread straw around and over them. Put a loose-fitting cover on the frame made of polyethylene sheeting or any similar material.

Be sure the top of your coldframe is strong enough to withstand a heavy load of snow. Ventilate on days when the air temperature is above 40° F. to keep the plants cool and dormant.

To purchase a cold frame kit, check your local nurseries or see catalogs of mail-order garden supply houses.

Spring care.—Spring is the time when new bonsai are started. It is the time for any pruning and training of last season's bonsai. The plants then have a whole growing season to readjust to these changes.

Watering.—In the summer, during hot weather when the temperatures are over 90°, water the bonsai plants one or more times a day. If the plants are in an unusually sandy soil they will require watering three or more times a day.

In early autumn, follow the watering directions for late spring. In late autumn, follow the watering directions for early spring.

In winter, keep the trees in a coldframe and ventilate the plants on one or more sides to keep them dormant. Check for dryness every 2 weeks. Water the plants every second day, or less, as required. Keep in mind that far more bonsai are killed by overwatering than by a lack of water.

BONSAI

PROPAGATING YOUR OWN BONSAI

Seedlings. — Growing bonsai from seed is a slow process, unless you intend to grow plants whose maximum height will be 6 inches. A more nearly perfect tree can be grown from seed because the trunk can be shaped from the beginning to suit the grower.

To develop the trunk rapidly, plant seedlings in the ground outdoors; seedlings are kept outside from 2 to 5 years, depending on the type of material planted and its rate of growth.

Each spring dig up the plant and prune its roots just as if it were in a pot.

Grafting is usually done in the winter or early spring when the buds are dormant. There are numerous methods of grafting, but the most popular among bonsai enthusiasts are "cleft" and "whip" grafting.

Plants that propagate easily from cuttings are olive, willow, cotoneaster, firethorn, azaleas, and boxwood.

Grafting.—Grafting is complex and requires patience and practice, especially by the novice bonsai grower. It is not as successful as the other methods of propagation. One of the drawbacks for bonsai is that even after a graft has taken, an ugly scar remains. The "side" or "notch" grafting methods have the advantage of hiding the scar.

When you choose a seedling, select one that has small leaves to begin with. For example, silk oak and *cherimoya* seedlings have been successfully grown indoors.

Cuttings.—Starting bonsai from cuttings is faster than starting them from seed.

Make cuttings in the late spring and early summer, just before the buds open or after the new growth has hardened.

SUCCESSFUL TERRARIUMS

Introduction to Terrariums was written by Ken Kayatta and Steven Schmidt, authors of SUCCESSFUL TERRARIUMS, (A STEP BY STEP GUIDE), published by Houghton Mifflin, Boston, Massachusetts. Anyone interested in terrarium gardening will find this profusely illustrated book a worthwhile investment—humorous, interesting and botanically correct.

If you'd like a great looking collection of indoor greenery, but don't want to be tied down caring for it, terrariums are for you. Terrariums provide ideal growing conditions for many plants, some of which are otherwise demanding.

You'll find that they always bring admiring comments and questions from your friends. But, by all means, enjoy a creative experience and save money by making your own. Storebought terrariums are often badly designed, poorly planted, and full of pagodas, bunnies, bilious blue gravel, and other "additions" that have no place in a re-created scene from nature.

Strictly speaking, a terrarium is a group of plants growing in a moisture balanced environment inside a closed, clear container. The key, here, is "moisture balanced," which means that a water cycle is established so that moisture condenses on the sides and top of the container, provides high humidity, and eliminates the need for watering.

But, we don't feel you have to stick to that form alone; you can also have an open container (which means some watering and misting) or a terrarium with desert plants (which must not be covered).

If you add small lizards, frogs, salamanders or other animals, you will have made a vivarium. This means you've got to consider the special needs of the animals and be willing to give them regular food and care.

A real showpiece is the bottle garden, which calls for special tools and procedures, plus loads of patience and a steady hand.

We don't think you can assemble a successful terrarium from just a few paragraphs of instruction. A neighbor recently brought us a dying bottle garden constructed according to four paragraphs of instruction. It had no drainage, insufficient soil depth, and incompatible plants. The instructions said: "if your plants need water, add some," which is no help at all. If you really want to succeed, invest in a book that gives you full information—soil mixes, plants, containers, planting steps, what to do if problems arise.

The basic elements of a terrarium are a container, drainage, charcoal, soil mix, and plants. We add a fiberglass "soil separator" between the drainage elements and the soil mix. We're convinced that ceramic elves eat plants and purple sand causes mold. Leave them out and use surface elements such as pebbles, acorns, and twigs to complete the look of nature. We want the reaction to a finished terrarium to be "How great!" not "How cute!"

Be sure to use compatible groups of plants in a terrarium. The three most basic are tropical, woodland, and desert. You can also create a bog garden, and for more advanced terrarium gardeners, there are carnivorous plants, flowering plants, and the use of artificial lights to grow terrariums in such locations as dim city apartments or basement recreation rooms.

The first decisions you must make when planning a terrarium are: where it will go and what size it should be. Terrariums can range in size from a tiny jar holding only one plant, up to giant size aquariums. Light conditions are equally important. Closed tropical and woodland terrariums should receive the brightest light possible, but no direct sun. Desert terrariums, however, should receive at least four hours of sun a day. Normal living temperatures will be fine with terrarium plants.

Your terrarium should establish an ideal environment for your plants. Only simple maintenance is needed.

There is, however, one catch. Diseases, insects, and other plant problems will also thrive in this environment if you allow them to get started. For this reason you should observe your terrariums carefully, especially in the first few weeks when trouble is most likely to occur. Your goal should be to maintain the status quo. Terrariums are meant to be viewed, and as you look at yours, be sure to notice any changes that occur. Anything other than slight plant growth should immediately be analyzed and corrected.

A question that always comes up when your friends see your closed terrarium is, "Don't the plants need air to live?" Of course they do, specifically the carbon dioxide found in the air. But, don't worry, even a closed container isn't airtight. The moisture is trapped inside, but a little air is always seeping in and out. It's a good idea to open the lid or remove the cork once a week and say "Hello" to the plants inside. This will give them a change of air and some carbon dioxide. But, be sure to close the terrarium after a few minutes to preserve the moisture balance.

Terrariums are great projects for kids. They really get a kick out of seeing their plants grow and prosper, while learning about botany, nature study, and indoor gardening at the same time. With simple instructions and a little help, even very young children can plant a simple terrarium. Teenagers will find them a snap, but make sure they don't get over-enthusiastic and miss a step in the planting procedure.

Terrarium building can become a great hobby. You may find yourself looking for locations all over your home. Terrariums also make terrific presents, but be sure to plant them a couple of weeks ahead to establish the moisture cycle and make sure that all is well. We know that plastic plants aren't the solution to carefree indoor greenery, but, for us, terrariums are. Happy planting.

SUCCESSFUL TERRARIUMS
A STEP-BY-STEP GUIDE

KEN KAYATTA and STEVEN SCHMIDT

TERRARIUMS

Arthur Eames Allgrove,
North Wilmington, Maine 01887

Armstrong Associates,
Box 127,
Basking Ridge, N.J. 07920

Bolduc's Greenhill Nursery,
2131 Vallejo St.,
St. Helena, Calif. 94572

Peter Pauls Nurseries,
R. 4,
Canandiagua, N.Y. 14424

monstrous flowers.

DESERT TERRARIUMS

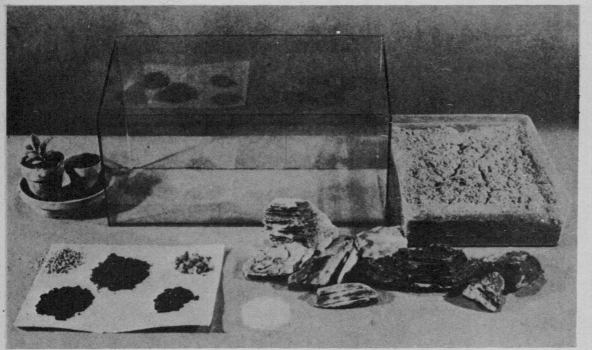

Desert terrariums courtesy of:
F. A. Giles
College of Agriculture
University of Illinois
Urbana, Illinois

After all the plants are in place, firm the soil and prepare to place the final stone that is seen tilted forward in the lower center

MAKING CACTUS GRAFTS

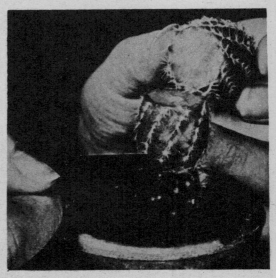

Here the final stone has been pressed into place. Covering the soil with stone, gravel, or sand helps contain moisture in the soil core

Plants for Desert Terrariums

Tiger Jaws (Aloe brevifolia)
Dwarf Century Plant (Agave filifera compacta)
Old Man Cactus (Cephalocereus senilis)
Peanut Cactus (Chamaecereus silvestri)

Mexican Firecracker (Echeveria setosa)
Barrel Cactus (Echinocactus)
Knobby Euphorbia (Euphorbia)
Gasteria (Gasteria hybrida)
Clustering Cactus (Gymnocalycium bruchi)
Chin Cactus (Gymnocalycium mihanovichi)
Windowed Haworthia (Haworthia cymbiformis)

Curiosity Cactus (Cereus peruvianus)
Cone Plant (Conophytum aureum)
Columnar Crassula (Crassula columnaris)
Pyramid Crassula (Crassula imperialis)
Club Moss Crassula (Crassula lycopodioides)
Propeller Plant (Crassula perfossa)
Large Pyramidal Crassula (Crassula pyramidalis)
Rattlesnake Crassula (Crassula teres)

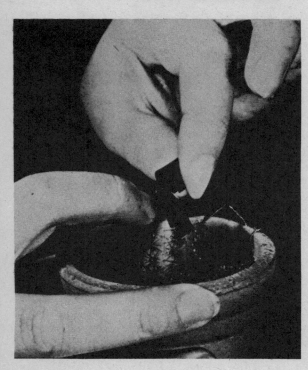

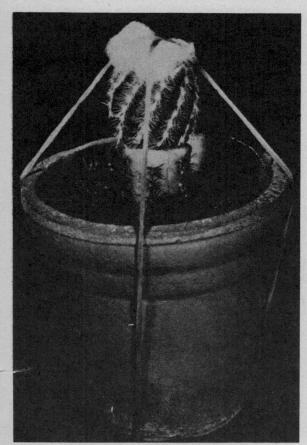

Next pack soil into all cracks and chink holes with a small blunt stick

With all plants in place, it becomes much harder to place soil and not get it on plants or on the container. A plastic spoon is very handy for this job

Zebra Haworthia (*Haworthia fasciata*)
Needle Haworthia (*Haworthia radula*)
Wart Plant (*Haworthia 'Margaritifera'*)
Whorled Haworthia (*Haworthia limifolia*)
Panda Plant (*Kalanchoe tomentosa*)
Stone Face (*Lithops*)
Pincushion Cactus (*Mammillaria*)
Golden Star Cactus (*Mammillaria elongata*)

Feather Cactus (*Mammillaria plumosa*)
Lemon Ball (*Notocactus leninghausi*)
Bunny-Ears (*Opuntia microdasys*)
Choya Cactus (*Opuntia cylindrica*)
Gray Crown (*Pachyveria haagei*)
Crown Cactus (*Rebutia kupperiana*)

Crest Cactus (*Rebutia senilis crestata*)
Coral Beads Plant (*Sedum stahli*)
Green Burro Tail (*Sedum rubrotinctum*)
Hen and Chicks (*Sempervivum*)

CARNIVOROUS PLANTS

Legends about man-eating plants have persisted throughout history. But, no one has managed to bring on back alive. So, we must content ourselves collecting plants that merely devour insects.

This in itself is truly marvelous. Just consider, for a moment, how you might solve the problem of catching food on the wing if you were rooted to one spot all your life.

To solve this problem and survive, plants like the venus flytrap, the fly-catcher and the pitcher plant became expert trappers, in a sense, and evolved digestive systems capable of extracting nutrients from their prey.

These plants may attract insects with the perfumes they exude, or with brightly colored flowers and foliage. Some capture the insects on specially adapted, sticky appendages. Or, as in the case of the venus flytrap, a bit of nectar lures the unsuspecting victim into the trap which quickly snaps shut.

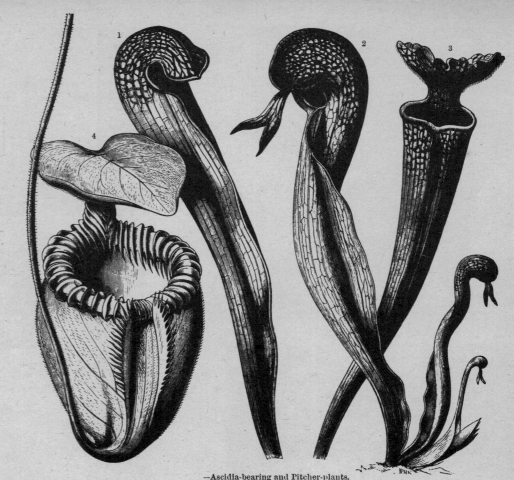

—Ascidia-bearing and Pitcher-plants.

1 *Sarracenia variolaris.* 2 *Darlingtonia Californica.* 3 *Sarracenia laciniata.* 4 *Nepenthes villosa*, reduced to one-half natural size.

—Venus's Fly-trap (*Dionæa muscipula*).

CARNIVOROUS PLANT CULTURE
(Save these culturing instructions as none are shipped with order)
All of these carnivorous plants require a high humidity for best results. This may be provided by growing them in greenhouses, terrariums, aquariums, fish bowls, wide mouth gallon containers, etc. The containers should be partially covered with some transparent material to prevent loss of moisture. Lack of adequate ventilation could result in mold growth which may be harmful to the plants. During sunny weather the lid may have to be removed in order to prevent a build up of high temperatures. When selecting a container keep in mind that some of the pitcher plants may reach heights of 3 feet or more.

—Common Pitcher-Plant.
At the right one of the pitcher-like leaves is shown in cross-section.

VENUS FLY TRAP PLANTS (Dionaea muscipula)

This almost "animal" plant has traps at the end of its leaves. The traps are two opposite segments "hinged" at the center and edged with cilia (bristles). On the inside surface of the traps there are usually 3 trigger hairs, which when touched or stimulated cause closing of the traps. It takes traps from several seconds to less than ½ second to close depending on temperature and age of trap. During closure the segments of the trap move toward each other until they touch and their cilia interlock just as your fingers do when you fold your hands. This prevents the escape of most insects. The stimulation of the trap by insects causes the trap to secrete digestive juices which digest the soft parts of the insect's body. Traps will reopen in 4 to 20 days depending on the nature of the meal. If the trigger hairs are stimulated by something not digestible, the traps will usually reopen within a day. The leaves and traps turn black with age. This is normal, simply snip them off and new ones will grow. In plenty of light the traps will become a deep crimson color whereas in limited light the color will be green. In the spring delicate flowers are produced.

Venus Flytrap.

Sundew (*Drosera rotundifolia*).

—The Fly-catcher (*Drosophyllum lusitanicum*).

WATER: Carnivorous plants must be kept moist and in a humid atmosphere. The pitcher plants cannot be over-watered. They do well if their root endings are continually in water. The Sundews, Butterworts and Venus Fly Traps need plenty of moisture but their roots should not be in water continually. The Nepenthes should be planted in soil which has good drainage. Distilled water, rain water and melted snow are best. If treated tap water is used, it should be left in an open container for a few days before used for watering the plants.

SOIL: The soil should be acidic. Peat moss or sphagnum moss may be used individually or mixed together.

LIGHT: All the carnivorous plants require plenty of sunlight. During the summer it is best to have filtered sunlight, that is, provide some shading for the plants. In any case care must be taken to prevent temperatures inside the container from getting too high.

TEMPERATURES: We have found that plants thrive well at temperatures of about 80 degrees. They will grow at lower temperatures, but growth will be slower. The Nepenthes MUST have a soil temperature of from 75 to 90 degrees. The temperature for the Nepenthes must be kept fairly constant. When temperatures drop near the freezing point the carnivorous plants will become dormant with the exception of the Nepenthes which will be killed. When it warms up the dormant plants will start new growth.

PLANTING TERRARIUM SETS OR COMBINATIONS OF CARNIVOROUS PLANTS: When making such plantings it is wise to slope the soil in the container. The Pitcher Plants and Cobra Lily should be planted at the bottom of the slope. The Sundews, Butterworts and Venus Fly Traps should be planted on the upper end of the slope. Starting with the Pitcher Plants and Cobra Lily at the bottom of the slope, the Venus Fly Trap plants should be next, then the Butterworts with the Sundews on the highest part of the slope. Thus when the terrarium is watered, the water collects at the bottom of the soil and the plants on the lower slope will have their roots in water, which they enjoy and the others can be kept moist without having their roots in water continuously. Newly planted plants should be kept a bit damper than normal and out of bright sunlight for about 12 days. This will help them adjust more easily to their new environment.

All seeds of carnivorous plants may be sown on the surface of peat or sphagnum moss. They should be maintained at a high humidity. Nepenthes seeds will benefit from bottom heat.

PETER PAULS NURSERIES, Canandaigua, N.Y. 14424

CARNIVOROUS PLANTS
Armstrong Associates, Inc., Box 127, Basking Ridge, N.J. 07920. Venus flytrap.
Clinton Nurseries, Clinton, Conn. 06413. Venus flytrap.
Cupboard, Box 61-0, Terre Haute, Ind. 47801. Cobra lily.
Peter Pauls Nurseries, Building 2, Canandaigua, N.Y. 14424. Insect-eating plants.
Spencer Gifts, Spencer Bldg., Atlantic City, N.J. 08400. Venus flytrap.

Cactus

5 *Mamillary Cactus*

Warted Coral Aloe

ARIZONA CACTUS CURIOS CO.
Cactus Gardens
2528 E. Madison
Phoenix, Arizona 85034

ARTHUR EAMES ALLGROVE
No. Wilmington, Mass. 01887
Pots, Supplies, L

BOB'S CACTUS NOOK
1311 N. 45th St.
Birmingham, Alabama 35212
592-6542

BOOL CACTUS NURSERY
2735 E. Camelback Rd.
Phoenix, Arizona 85016
(Herb Bool)
C, S, Seed, MO, P, W, R

CACTUS EXPORTS
1409 Likens Dr.
El Paso, Texas 79925
(Mr. Garress)
C, S, MO, L

THE CACTUS GARDENS
Rt. 3, Box 44
Edinburg, Texas 78539
C, S, Seed, MO, L, W, R

CACTUS LAND
5740 S. 6th Ave.
Tucson, Arizona
(Hugo C. Johnston)
294-1992
C, Native Plants, MO, R, P

CACTUS RANCH
P. O. Box 90
Wittman, Arizona 85361
C, S, MO

CARSCALLEN NURSERY LABEL CO.
P. O. Box 18092
Dallas, Texas 75218
Labels

DAVIS CACTUS GARDEN
1522 Jefferson St.
Kerrville, Texas 78028
C, S, MO, L, R
Daily from 3:30 p.m.
All day Sat. & Sun.

DESERT PLANT COMPANY
Box 880
Marfa, Texas
C, MO, W, R

EL PASO CACTUS GARDENS
P. O. Box 133
Anthony, New Mexico - Texas
(Clark Champie)

JAPAN CACTUS TRADING CO.
No. 48 Aza-Takeda, Oaza-Oguchi
Oguchi-cho, Niew-gun, Aichi Pref.
Japan
C, S, MO, L

THE MARTIN BROTHERS
Box 70, Mayaguez
Puerto Rico 00708
C (native), MO, L

MRS. DOROTHEA MUHR
El Aguilar, Prov. de Ju Juy
Republic of Argentina
C, MO, L

J. NIEDERLE
209 Emerson Ave.
London, Ontario, Canada
C, MO, L

QUINTA FO. SCHMOLL
(Willi Wagner B.)
Cadereyta de Montes
Queretaro, Mexico
C, S, L (Send U.S. Permit tag)

ROSELLA PARK NURSERIES LTD.
Chaplin St., Mangeie East
Auckland, New Zealand
C, MO, L, R
Mon thru Fri 8-4:30
Sat 8-12

SAN MARINA CACTUS GARDENS
P. O. 214, Somerset West
Cape Province
Rep. of So. Africa
(Mr. Jac Swanepoll)
S, MO, L

SHEILAM NURSERY
P. O. Box 157
Robertson, Cape Province
South Africa
C, Seed, S, W, MO

CACTUS AND SUCCULENTS

SEABORN DEL DIOS NURSERY
Rt. 3 Box 455
Escondido, Calif. 92025
(714) 745-6945
C, S, MO, L, R

SHARP, P. R.
104 N. Chapel Ave. Apt. 3
Alhambra, Calif. 91801
(213) 284-4149

TAYLORS CACTUS GARDEN
1640 E. Main
El Cajon, Calif.
(Bob Taylor)
   (Crests & Grafts are
   specialties) C, S, R
Closed Sunday Morning

TEGELBERG'S CACTUS GARDENS
Star Rt. Box 456
So. Camp Rock Rd.
Lucerne Valley, Calif.
(714) 248-7482
C, S, W, R by appt.

WHIORA CACTUS & SUCCULENT GARDENS
Tennyson Via Prairie
Phone: 3572
Victoria, Australia
C, S, Seed, MO, L, W, R

ZINKS GREENHOUSE
P. O. Box 1676
Visiting Address:
3550 Gopher Canyon Road
Vista, Calif. 92083
C, S, MO, L (send .20)

MOSTLY BROMELIADS

Bennett's Bromeliads,
   Box 1532,
   Winter Park, Fla. 32789

Cornelison Bromeliads,
   225 San Bernardino,
   North Fort Myers, Fla. 33903

Marz Bromeliads,
   10782 Citrus Dr.,
   Moorpart, Calif. 93021

Plaza Nursery and Flower Shop,
   7430 Crescent Ave.,
   Buena Park, Calif. 90620

Seaborn Del Dios Nursery,
   R. 3, Box 455,
   Escondido, Calif. 92025

Pine Apple

Short thick leav'd Aloe

CACTUS AND SUCCULENTS

Abbey Gardens,
   Box 167,
   Reseda, Calif. 91335

Beahm Gardens,
   2686 Paloma St.,
   Pasadena, Calif. 91107

Cactus by Mueller,
   10411 Rosedale Hwy.,
   Bakersfield, Calif. 93308

Cactus Gem Nursery,
   Box 327,
   Aromas, Calif. 95004

Cox's Epiphyllum Nursery,
   90 McNeill St.,
   Encintas, Calif. 92024

Davis Cactus Garden,
   1522 Jefferson St.,
   Kerrville, Tex. 78028

Desert Plant Co.,
   Box 880,
   Marfa, Tex. 79843

Grigsby Cactus Gardens,
   2354 Bella Vista Dr.,
   Vista, Calif. 92083

Henrietta's Nursery,
   1345 N. Brawley,
   Fresno, Calif. 93705

Jack's Cactus Garden,
   1707 W. Robindale St.,
   West Covina, Calif. 91790

New Mexico Cactus Research,
   Box 787,
   Belen, N.M. 87002

Dick Wright,
   11011 Tarawa Dr.,
   Los Alamitos, Calif. 90720

—Agaves of the Mexican uplands (from a photograph).

Senecio scaposus

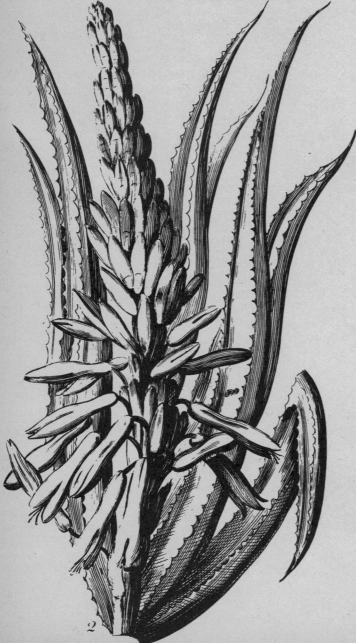

2

Purple Socotrine Aloe

CACTUS AND SUCCULENTS

Exotic, spectacular, beautiful, stately, unbelievable, tough, substantial—these are some of the terms that occur to me when I think of cacti and other succulents.

Since childhood, I have loved and been interested in plants. But, I have zeroed in on cacti and other succulents in the last few years. No other group of plants has the variety of shape and form, or the exotic flowers that some of these bear.

Let me explain the term "cacti and other succulents." All cacti—about 1500 species—belong to the family Cactaceae, a botanical plant family. They are all succulents to varying degrees.

The other succulents belong to families that contain many non-succulent species. In the lily family, for example, Aloes and Haworthia. In the same family as the lovely poinsettia, Euphor biacrae are extremely succulent in nature. Many closely resemble cacti. Some South African succulents are related to the common marigolds and zinnias.

Cacti are native only to North and South America. Other succulents come from all parts of the world. Their one common trait is the ability to withstand long periods of drought. This ability to survive is accomplished in several ways, the primary one being succulence, the ability to store water in plant tissues.

There are essentially two types, stem succulents and leaf succulents. The difference being, as their names indicate, that the first type has very succulent stems and either no leaves at all, or deciduous leaves only during periods of moisture. Leaf succulents have very fleshy, succulent leaves and normally come from areas of heavier rainfall than stem succulents.

Aside from being able to store water, these plants are able to conserve water much more efficiently than any other group of plants. There is much less surface area exposed to light and air, in proportion to the total mass of the plant. Thus, there is less surface to transpire and lose water. Other methods of conserving water include very heavy "spination", which shades the body of the plant by forming a waxy coating on the plant body, lowering the intensity of the light hitting the body of the plant. Another characteristic the waxy cacti or succulents have is that the stomato (plant pores), are closed by day and open at night.

A characteristic that I find very interesting is that of the so-called window succulents. These plants live buried in the soil with just their tips exposed to the light. The tips have lenses in them to permit a limited amount of light to enter the plant's body.

I often say that these plants thrive on neglect. This is not really the case, of course. They do thrive with much less watering than any other group of plants though, and are very tolerant of the dry conditions we find in many homes.

Knowledge and understanding of individual plants will be necessary if you intend to collect cacti and succulents seriously and successfully. Identifying the plant and knowing where it comes from will enable you to water in the proper season and let the plants go dormant when you should. Also, know whether the plant likes full sun, or if by nature prefers shade or something in between. Most important of all, learn to observe your plants and be knowledgeable enough to respond to their needs according to your observation.

The collecting and culture of cacti and succulents is a study. But, it is a pleasure not a chore. The more you learn about them, the more you will find there is to learn. It is a fascinating area.

If you do get involved with these plants, I would suggest you locate the Cactus and Succulent Society in your area. Attend a few meetings. Talking to the experts can really improve your knowledge.

The author of this article is David Remnek, one of the two owners of Farm and Garden Nursery in Manhattan. Aside from operating one of the most complete inner city garden centers around, he was show chairman of the New York Cactus and Succulent Society and is a fanatic in his love for these plants.

—*Æchmea paniculata* (after Baillon).

Short-thick leav'd Aloe

Notocactus haselbergii

EVERMAN GARDEN CENTER
208 E. Trammell
Everman, Texas 76140
    C, S, R

GOLDEN BARREL CACTUS NURSERY
318 W. Jackson St.
Harlingen, Texas 78550
423-9685
(Fred Tijerina Salinas)
    C, Seed, MO, P

BEN HAINES
1902 Lane
Topeka, Kansas 66604
    C, S, MO, L

HEINLEIN NURSERY
19395 S. 248th St.
Homestead, Florida 33030
    C, S, MO, L

HORTA-CRAFT CORP.
311 W. Cass St.
Albion, Michigan 49224
(517) 629-4862
    Labels

KARR KACTUS
P. O. Box 190
Canon City, Colo. 81212
    C, L

FRANK LEWIS
P. O. Box 517
Alamo, Texas 78516
    C, MO, L

MAC PHERSON GARDENS
2920 Starr Ave.
Oregon, Ohio 43616
    S, Seed, R, MO, W, P

MC LEAN BULB FARMS INC.
Puyallup, Washington 98571
(206) 845-8131
    Pots & Supplies

MERRY GARDENS
Camden, Maine 04843
    C, S, MO, L, P
    (House plants)

CACTUSLAND
502 Gleneagles
Killarney, Johannesburg
So. Africa
(Arthur R. Rebson)
Phone: 41-8979
    C, S, MO, L

LEO CADY
Box 88 P, O.
Kiama NSW
Australia 2533
    8 a.m. to 5 p.m.
    Closed Tues. & Fri.
    C, S, MO, L

CHUO COMMERCIAL CO., LTD.
P.O. Box No. 2 Komaki
Komaki, Komaki City
Aichi Prefecture, Japan
    C, S, Seed, MO, L

H. FECHSER
E. Ramseyer 835
Olives F.C.B.M.
Prov. Buenos Aires
Argentina
    C (native), MO, P

MRS. W. HARLAND
'BOOALBYN'
Blackburn Road
Wedderburn N.S.W. 2560
Phone: Campbelltown 341266
Australia
    C, S, MO, L, Visitors by appt.

74

FOREIGN NURSERIES
ENGLAND

GORDON FOSTER
Oak Dene, 10 Back Lane West
Royston, nr. Barnsley
Yorkshire, England
  C, S, Seed, no MO, L

E. & J. FOWELL
101 Spencer Road
Rushden, Northhamptonshire
England
Phone: Rushden 3292
  C, S

ERNEST HEPWORTH
Mira Mar, 133 Ambleside Ave.
Telscombe Cliff, Sussex, England
  C, S, MO, L, P

HOLLY GATE NURSERY
Spear Hill Ashington
Sussex, England
Phone: Ashington 439
(Clive F. Innes)
  C, S, Seed, MO, L, R, W

W. T. NEALE & CO., LTD.
The Exotic Collection
16 Franklin Road
Worthin, Sussex, England
  C, S, Seed, MO, L, P

THE SPINES
174 Avenue Road
Rushden, Northants, England
NN10-OSW
Phone: Rushden 3456
  C, S, MO, L
  Visitors Sat. & Sun.

SPRING GARDENS "Garfield"
Ventnor, Isle of Wight, England
(D. Sargent)
Phone: Ventnor 699
C, S, MO, L, Seed
  Visitors by appt.

UPLANDS NURSERY
Blackhorse Lane
Downend, Bristol, England
Phone: 653657
  9 a.m. - 6 p.m. Mon thru Sat
  10 a.m. - 2 p.m. Sun
  C, S, MO, Seed, R, W, P

WARFIELD GARDENS
Bridgnorth, Shrophire
England
(Sir Oliver Leese)
  Open Easter to end
  of September
  C, S, MO, L

EUROPEAN (other than England)

ROBERT BLOSSFELD
D24 Liibeck-Postfach 1550
Germany
  C, S, MO, L, Seed

H. E. BORN
D5810 Witten
P. O. Box 1207
Germany
  C, S, Seeds, Supplies, MO, L

A. N. BULTHUIS & CO. CV
Provinciale Weg Oost 8
Cothen, Holland
Phone: 03436-267
  7 a.m. to 7 p.m.
  Monday thru Saturday
  C, S

C. DE HERDT
Kaphaanlei 80
B-2510 Mortsel, Belgium
Phone: 55.41.08
  C, S, Seed, MO, L, P

H. VAN DONKELAAR
Cactus-Kivekerij
Multiflora
Laantje la
Werkendam, Holland
Phone: 01835-430
  C, S, Seed, MO, L

SU-KA-FLOR
5610 Wohlen
Wilerzelgstrasse 18
Switzerland
(W. Uebelmann)
  C, MO

PETER THIELE
Samenstelle
6451 Froschhausen
Germany (Bamburg 2)
  C, Seed, MO, L

KARLHEINZ UHLIG
7053 Rommelshausen bel Stuttgart
Lilienstrasse 5, Germany
  C, S, MO, L

H. WINTER
Frankfutham Main-Fechenheim
Fachfeldstrasse 51
Germany
  C, Seed only, MO, L

CARTERS
Tewksbury, Mass
  C, S

BEN VELDHUS LTD.
154 King St.
Dundas, Ontario, Canada
  C, S

ALBERT SCHENKEL
2 Hamburg-Blankeness
W. Germany
  Seeds only

D. BOUWMAN
Dijkweg 56B
Naaldwijk, Holland
  C, S, L

Cereus—Ritter's Black Spined

Mammillaria elegans schmollii

Pearl Aloe

Pachphytum "Blue Haze"

HOW TO PLANT COLD CLIMATE CACTI AND SUCCULENTS

Since these plants are to be left to winter outside, it is essential that they be given excellent drainage so they can survive the wet and cold periods of spring, fall and winter. This must be done even if it causes you to water some in the hot dry periods of summer.

A cold frame is useful in some areas of high moisture and-or low temperature. A sand box type of bed with a depth of 6 to 18 inches is a good method. Fill this with river gravel which has a slight amount of sand in it. Such a mixture is called a scree. A very small amount of topsoil or peat moss may be added to this gravel mix. However, in Topeka I find that some of my plants do best in a clay pot filled with gravel which is set in a sunny, well drained spot and not artificially watered unless the plants begin to yellow.

I propagate my cactus from cuttings or small plants. The cut surface must be allowed to heal until dry and hard. This may take several days or weeks. Heal cuttings in part shade. The sedums, and sempervivums, etc. usually like a layer of ¼ to ½ inch of dirt on top of the gravel so they can have direct contact with dirt. Some sedums like a moist humus in semi-shade.

I have failed several seasons with some plants until I found a successful method. It might be wise to persist in your attempts.

DISEASES AND PESTS

The greatest enemy of succulent plants is rot. If it starts at the root it will spread through the plant before you notice it. Dryness and good drainage is the best protection. Rot caused by above ground damage can often be cut out, dusted with sulfur, and let dry in the sun.

Fungi is a disease which is aided by moisture and darkness. Fungicides, dryness, and sun are the best preventatives.

Pests are numerous. There are boring, suching and chewing bugs. Some such as scale and mealy bugs try to attach themselves permanently to the plant. Nematodes attack the roots and produce lumps.

Ordinary bug sprays are useful. However, consult the technical books I have listed. "Cactus Guide" by Cutak is very good on this.

THE ENVIRONMENT AND STRUCTURE OF SUCCULENT PLANTS

Some cacti and succulents are epiphytic, some are bog-dwelling, some rock-inhabiting, and many live in deserts and grass lands. All live where water storage is necessary. These plants have succulent leaves, stems, or roots or combinations of these. Many of these plants open their pores (stomata) only at night in order to conserve moisture. I understand that only those plants with above ground succulent parts are considered succulents. However, I will list a few which have only succulent roots and are very cold hardy: Asclepias tuberosa, has typical milk weed seed pod, orange flower occasionally primrose-yellow. To 3 ft. (Asclepiadaceae); Helianthus tuberosus, a sun flower with yellow disk, the roots are edible potato like tubers often called Jerusalem Artichokes, to 12 ft. (Compositae); Impomoea leptophylla, bush morning-glory with purple flower, large root over 4 ft. deep sometimes weighing 70 lbs. to 4 ft. (Convolvulaceae); Cucurbita foetidissima, has large underground tap root, found as far north as Nebraska. (Cucurbitaceae). The cold climate cacti and succulents which I will describe in the following pages are able to stand the cold of Topeka, Kansas which usually has a touch of minus 15 to 20 F. with no cover and averages 35 inches of rain per year. However, some of these plants can take minus 40 F. with no cover if dry and of course a cold frame or snow cover aids winter survival without artificial heat.

The above group of plants includes about 30 cacti, over 100 sempervivums, about 100 sedums, and some others. I also mention Sage (Artemisia) and Yuccas which are not succulents.

Fig. 457.—Distribution of detached sprout-like offshoots by means of animals.

1 *Mamillaria placostigma*. 2 *Mamillaria gracilis*.

IDENTIFICATION OF PLANTS

The identification of cacti and succulents is especially controversial. The Opuntia and Echinocereus are quite variable and intergrade as you travel across the country. The Sedums and Sempervivums have many hybrids and there is much controversy about the species. The types I list are almost certainly distinct from each other.

Of course I am not saying that the genera (Opuntia, Echinocereus, Sedum & Sempervivum) intergrade.

The succulent plants, including the cactus family, involve approximately 45 plant families, 400 genera, and 8,500 species.

However, only about 300 types (species?) are cold climate plants.

The following are the plant groups which have succulent cold climate members.

CACTACEAE (ROSALES)

The cactus are related to the rose family (Rosaceae). The cacti listed in this article are divided into several groups.

OPUNTIEAE

CYLINDROPUNTIA (Joints cylindrical)
Opuntia arborescens (inbricata), O. davisii, O. Clavata

PLATYOPUNTIA (Joints, all or some flattened)
All other opuntias listed.

ECHINOCEREANAE
Only the Echinocereus are listed as cold climate.

ECHINOCACTANAE
Sclerocactus, Coloradoa, Pediocactus are all that are cold climate plants.

CORYPHANTHANAE
Coryphantha, Neobesseya are all that are cold climate.

PORTULACACEAE
These are members of the rose moss family. Lewisia, Talinum.

CRASSULACEAE
Sedum, Sempervivum

EUPHORBIACEAE
Euphorbia

YUCCA

ARTEMISIA
Sage Brush

Ben M. Haines
Cactus Catalog
1902 Lane, Topeka, Kansas

A Melon-Cactus

TO THE AMATEUR COLLECTOR OF COLD CLIMATE CACTI AND SUCCULENTS

I have become aware that there are a number of persons who live in the temperate parts of the world who are interested in succulent plants for rock garden, border and bed. They want plants which are hardy in winters which have touches of cold to minus 20 to 40 F. This article lists and pictures such plants in a non-technical way.

For a more technical description I refer you to the following:

"Colorado Cacti" by Bossevain & Davidson, Abbey Garden Press, Box 167, Reseda, Calif. 91335 (1940).

"Hortus Second" by Bailey & Bailey, The Macmillan Company, New York (1941).

"A Handbook of Succulent Plants" by Herman Jacobsen, Blandford Press, London, 3 vols., (1960) sold by Abbey Garden Press, Box 167, Reseda, California 91335.

"The Cactaceae" by Britton and Rose (Reprint) sold by Abbey Garden Press. The original sets sell for $300. This set sells for $26. An exceptional buy!

"Cactaceae" by Marshall & Bock, Abbey Garden Press (1941) 220 pp. Good identification charts. Lists new things since Britton & Rose.

"Cactus Guide" by Ladislaus Cutak, D. Van Nostrand Co., Inc., New York (1956). Has excellent bibliography.

"The Book of Cacti and Other Succulents" by Chidamian (1958) sold by Abbey Garden Press. A popular book with good bibliography.

"Handbook on Succulent Plants" by Brooklyn Botanic Garden, 1000 Washington Avenue, Brooklyn 10025, New York. Lists many societies and suppliers.

Bromeliads Growing in Natural Condition

Flowers of Cacti

Groupings of Cacti

Flowers of Cacti

CACTUS AND SUCCULENT JOURNAL

CHARLES GLASS, Editor

Cactus and Succulent Society of America
Box 167, Reseda, California 91335

IF you're just a novice, loving Cactuses because they're strange and unusual —

IF you're a fancier, making the possession and cultivation of Cacti and other Xerophytes a hobby —

IF you're a botanist, engaged in the life work of scientific research and study of plants, including the Cactaceae or other Succulent plants —

IF you're a professional gardener or nurseryman who maintains a stock of Cactus and other Succulents —

IF you're a collector, making excursions into the desert in search of specimens, and making exchanges of your treasures with other collectors —

THEN YOU SHOULD BE A SUBSCRIBER TO THE CACTUS JOURNAL, a bi-monthly magazine devoted to Cacti and other Succulents, for botanists and amateurs. The JOURNAL is owned by the Cactus & Succulent Society of America, and published in Reseda, California by Abbey Garden. Your subscription of _____ carries with it an active membership in the Society.

Our Society has members from all parts of the world. The JOURNAL goes into every state and all foreign countries. In 1929 Scott Haselton began the JOURNAL and published and edited it until his recent retirement without missing a single issue in 37 years, nor changing its policy or format. This is a world's record for a specialized magazine and its stability is assured. It has weathered all storms including wars and depressions; The JOURNAL is a unique achievement for consistently presenting material of interest to the foremost botanists throughout the world, as well as to the enthusiast who has just bought his first Cactus plants. Subscribers share the editorship by sending in material for publication.

Through the columns of the JOURNAL all lovers of Cacti and Succulents will be apprised of what species are rare and exceptional, and where they may be found or how obtained. There are articles on the care and propagation of cuttings and seedlings, and abundant illustrations, both half tones and color, for identification of plants commonly found in collections. The JOURNAL regularly contains a travelogue relating the experiences of collectors through the land of cacti, into the most remote deserts of the world, describing as well the conditions under which the plants grow in the wild, and listing the various plants found in specific areas. In addition the JOURNAL introduces its subscribers to the famous public and private gardens and collections of succulents in all parts of the world. Advertising in the JOURNAL is limited to suppliers of Cactus and Succulent plants and related equipment. The Journal remains the single, most valuable source of information on Cacti and Succulents.

The JOURNAL publishes many articles describing and illustrating various genera of Cacti and Succulents, describing new species, etc. The JOURNAL is considered by many to be the finest publication of its kind, and its list of contributors reads like a Who's Who of world-renowned botanists and authorities. The articles, which are of great value to students of botany, are painstakingly scientific in their text and yet are not couched in phraseology intended to baffle the amateur.

The Volume starts with January, and you may start your subscription with that issue, or the current issue. JOURNALS are mailed on or about the 20th of every other month.

Join the Cactus and Succulent Society of America now and receive the JOURNAL. Attend local meetings and the biennial conventions, shows, etc.; enjoy desert trips, visit collections, enjoy good fellowship — all for _____ per year. Foreign _____ by International Post Office Money Order.

Correspondence and questions are invited, and the many letters testify to the responsiveness of the members to the editorial plan and to the Society's aims.

BRANCH OF PINUS THUNBERGII
WITH SEVENTY-FOUR CONES

CACTI AND OTHER SUCCULENTS

ABBEY GARDEN
Box 167
Reseda, Calif. 91107

BEAHM GARDENS
2686 Paloma St.
Pasadena, Calif 91107

CACTUS BY MUELLER
10411 Rosedale Hwy.
Bakersfield, Calif 93308
    Send stamp.

COX'S SPIPHYLLUM NURSERY
90 McNeill St.
Encinitas, Calif. 92024
    Fifteen cents.

DAVIS' CACTUS GARDEN
1522 Jefferson St.
Kerrville, Texas 78028

A' HUGH DIAL
7685 Deer Trail
Yucca Valley, Calif. 92284

GRIGSBY CACTUS GARDENS
2354 Bella Vista Dr.
Vista, Calif. 92083
    Twenty cents.

HELEN'S CACTUS
2205 Mirasol
Brownsville, Texas 78520
    Send stamp.

KIRKPATRICK'S
27785 DeAnza St.
Barstow, Calif. 93xxx

MODLIN'S CACTUS GARDENS
Rt. 4, Box 3034
Vista, Calif. 92083

NEW MEXICO CACTUS RESEARCH
Box 787
Belen, New Mexico 87002
    Fifty cents.

HEINZ PLASTIC LABELS
1840 17th Ave.
Santa Cruz, Calif. 95060
    Labels, L, MO

HEINZE GARDEN SUPPLY
100 Oak Ave. S.E.
Mountain View, Calif. 94040
    Labels, L, MO

ALCO LABEL CO.
612 S. Del Mar Ave.
San Gabriel, Calif. 91776
    Labels, L, MO

DICKISON'S CACTUS
1008 W. Wllace
San Saba, Texas 76877
    C, S, crests

HELEN'S CACTUS
2205 Mirasol
Brownsville, Texas
    C, S

HUMMEL'S EXOTIC GARDENS
3926 Park Drive
Carlsbad, Calif. 92008

HUGO C. JOHNSTON'S
5740 & 5730 S. Sixth Ave.
Tucson, Ariz. 85706
    C

ABBEY BROOK CACTUS NURSERY
Prop. B & R Fearn
Rock House, Greenfield Main Rd.
Sheffield 8, England
    Rare plants, C,
    S, L, MO

OAKHILL GARDENS
Rt. 3, Box 87
Dallas, Oregon 97338
(Slim & Helen Payne)
(503) 623-4612
    S, MO, L

PRAIRIE GEM RANCH
Smithwick, South Dakota 57782
(Claude H. Barr)
    C, Seeds, L

TEXAS CACTUS RANCH
4830 Moravian Dr.
Corpus Christi, Texas 78415
853-5847
C, S   cS

SOUTHWEST CACTUS CO.
P. O. Box 851
Alpine, Texas 79880
(Homer A. Jones)
    C, S, MO, L

TANQUE VERDE GREENHOUSES
10810 Tanque Verde Road
Tucson, Arizona 85715
    C

ECHEVERIAS
Dick Wright
11011 Tarawa Dr.
Los Alamitos, Calif. 90720
    S, L, R, W

MODLIN'S CACTUS GARDENS
Rt. 4, Box 3034
2416 El Corto
Vista, Calif. 92083
    C, Seed, L, R

JOE E. GRANGER
612 E. Ave. E
Alpine, Texas
69830
    C, L, MO, W, R

CORONA CACTUS AND
SUCCULENT NURSERY
    20091 Winton St.
    C, S, MO

CACTUS GEM NURSERY
10092 Mann Dr.
Cupertino, Calif. 95014
    C, L, R
    Sat. and Sun.

K. KNEIZ JR.
Chota 827 O.P.
No. 702
Lima, Peru
    C, MO

MARGARETE
P. O. Box 10248
Colmena, Peru
    Seed only

BROMELIADS

BENNETT'S BROMELIADS & BONSAI
Box 1532
Winter Park, Florida 32789
    Send stamped envelope.

CORNELISON'S BROMELIAD NURSERY
225 San Bernardino St.
North Fort Myers, Florida 33903
    Send stamped envelope.

FUCHSIA LAND
4629 Centinela
Los Angeles, Calif. 90066

JENKINS NURSERY
Box 702
320 E. 33rd Ave.
Covington, Louisiana 70433

MARZ BROMELIADS
10782 Citrus Dr.
Moorpark, Calif. 93021
    Sixteen cents.

PLAZA NURSERY & FLOWER SHOP
7430 Crescent Ave.
Buena Park, Calif. 90620

SEABORN DEL RIOS NURSERY
Rt. 3, Box 455
Escondido, Calif. 92025
    $1.00.

WILLIFORD'S NURSERY
Box 511, Rt. 3
Smithfield, North Carolina 27577
    Sixteen cents.

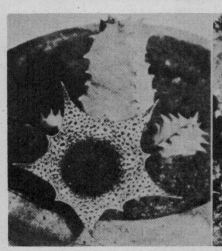

Prickly Spotted leav'd Aloe

LITHOPS
A genus of small South African mimicry plants in the Mesembryanthema.

A. disceptata hybr. :   Agave cernua
A. Ghiesbreghti: A. Ferdinandi—
A. potatorum var. Verschaffelti

ALOE ARISTATA

ALOE BREVIFOLIA VAR. SERRA

ALOE MIFRIFORMIS

ALOE STRIATA

ALOE COMMUTATA

AGAVE

A genus of plants of the Amaryllis family; including the so-called "Century Plant."

ALOE

A genus of succulent plants of the family Lilliaceae, tribe Aloineae.

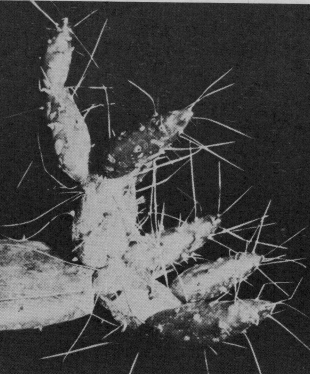

OPUNTIA ANDICOLA

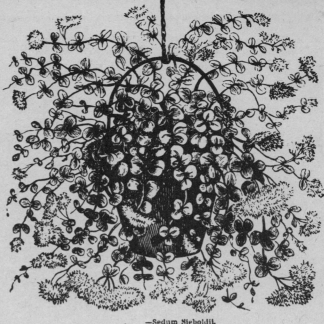

SEMPERVIVUMS AND SEDUMS
(Hen and Chicks)   (Stonecrop)

Oakhill Gardens

Phone 1-503-623-4612

R. N. (Slim) and Helen E. Payne   Rt. 3. Box 87   Dallas, Oregon 97338   1974

—Sedum Sieboldii.

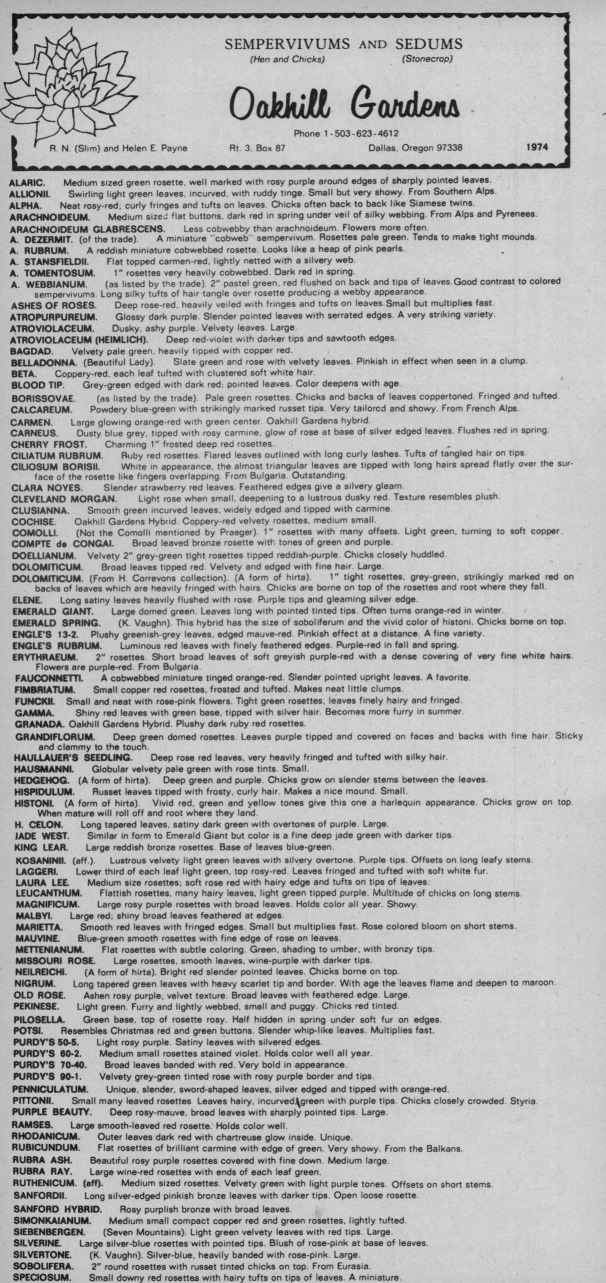

ALARIC. Medium sized green rosette, well marked with rosy purple around edges of sharply pointed leaves.

ALLIONII. Swirling light green leaves, incurved, with ruddy tinge. Small but very showy. From Southern Alps.

ALPHA. Neat rosy-red; curly fringes and tufts on leaves. Chicks often back to back like Siamese twins.

ARACHNOIDEUM. Medium sized flat buttons, dark red in spring under veil of silky webbing. From Alps and Pyrenees.

ARACHNOIDEUM GLABRESCENS. Less cobwebby than arachnoideum. Flowers more often.

A. DEZERMIT. (of the trade). A miniature "cobweb" sempervivum. Rosettes pale green. Tends to make tight mounds.

A. RUBRUM. A reddish miniature cobwebbed rosette. Looks like a heap of pink pearls.

A. STANSFIELDII. Flat topped carmen-red, lightly netted with a silvery web.

A. TOMENTOSUM. 1" rosettes very heavily cobwebbed. Dark red in spring.

A. WEBBIANUM. (as listed by the trade). 2" pastel green, red flushed on back and tips of leaves. Good contrast to colored sempervivums. Long silky tufts of hair tangle over rosette producing a webby appearance.

ASHES OF ROSES. Deep rose-red, heavily veiled with fringes and tufts on leaves. Small but multiplies fast.

ATROPURPUREUM. Glossy dark purple. Slender pointed leaves with serrated edges. A very striking variety.

ATROVIOLACEUM. Dusky, ashy purple. Velvety leaves. Large.

ATROVIOLACEUM (HEIMLICH). Deep red-violet with darker tips and sawtooth edges.

BAGDAD. Velvety pale green, heavily tipped with copper red.

BELLADONNA. (Beautiful Lady). Slate green and rose with velvety leaves. Pinkish in effect when seen in a clump.

BETA. Coppery-red, each leaf tufted with clustered soft white hair.

BLOOD TIP. Grey-green edged with dark red; pointed leaves. Color deepens with age.

BORISSOVAE. (as listed by the trade). Pale green rosettes. Chicks and backs of leaves coppertoned. Fringed and tufted.

CALCAREUM. Powdery blue-green with strikingly marked russet tips. Very tailored and showy. From French Alps.

CARMEN. Large glowing orange-red with green center. Oakhill Gardens hybrid.

CARNEUS. Dusty blue grey, tipped with rosy carmine, glow of rose at base of silver edged leaves. Flushes red in spring.

CHERRY FROST. Charming 1" frosted deep red rosettes.

CILIATUM RUBRUM. Ruby red rosettes. Flared leaves outlined with long curly lashes. Tufts of tangled hair on tips.

CILIOSUM BORISII. White in appearance, the almost triangular leaves are tipped with long hairs spread flatly over the surface of the rosette like fingers overlapping. From Bulgaria. Outstanding.

CLARA NOYES. Slender strawberry red leaves. Feathered edges give a silvery gleam.

CLEVELAND MORGAN. Light rose when small, deepening to a lustrous dusky red. Texture resembles plush.

CLUSIANNA. Smooth green incurved leaves, widely edged and tipped with carmine.

COCHISE. Oakhill Gardens Hybrid. Coppery-red velvety rosettes, medium small.

COMOLLI. (Not the Comolli mentioned by Praeger). 1" rosettes with many offsets. Light green, turning to soft copper.

COMPTE de CONGAI. Broad leaved bronze rosette with tones of green and purple.

DOELLIANUM. Velvety 2" grey-green tight rosettes tipped reddish-purple. Chicks closely huddled.

DOLOMITICUM. Broad leaves tipped red. Velvety and edged with fine hair. Large.

DOLOMITICUM. (From H. Correvons collection). (A form of hirta). 1" tight rosettes, grey-green, strikingly marked red on backs of leaves which are heavily fringed with hairs. Chicks are borne on top of the rosettes and root where they fall.

ELENE. Long satiny leaves heavily flushed with rose. Purple tips and gleaming silver edge.

EMERALD GIANT. Large domed green. Leaves long with pointed tinted tips. Often turns orange-red in winter.

EMERALD SPRING. (K. Vaughn). This hybrid has the size of soboliferum and the vivid color of histoni. Chicks borne on top.

ENGLE'S 13-2. Plushy greenish-grey leaves, edged mauve-red. Pinkish effect at a distance. A fine variety.

ENGLE'S RUBRUM. Luminous red leaves with finely feathered edges. Purple-red in fall and spring.

ERYTHRAEUM. 2" rosettes. Short broad leaves of soft greyish purple-red with a dense covering of very fine white hairs. Flowers are purple-red. From Bulgaria.

FAUCONNETTI. A cobwebbed miniature tinged orange-red. Slender pointed upright leaves. A favorite.

FIMBRIATUM. Small copper red rosettes, frosted and tufted. Makes neat little clumps.

FUNCKII. Small and neat with rose-pink flowers. Tight green rosettes, leaves finely hairy and fringed.

GAMMA. Shiny red leaves with green base, tipped with silver hair. Becomes more furry in summer.

GRANADA. Oakhill Gardens Hybrid. Plushy dark ruby red rosettes.

GRANDIFLORUM. Deep green domed rosettes. Leaves purple tipped and covered on faces and backs with fine hair. Sticky and clammy to the touch.

HAULLAUER'S SEEDLING. Deep rose red leaves, very heavily fringed and tufted with silky hair.

HAUSMANNI. Globular velvety pale green with rose tints. Small.

HEDGEHOG. (A form of hirta). Deep green and purple. Chicks grow on slender stems between the leaves.

HISPIDULUM. Russet leaves tipped with frosty, curly hair. Makes a nice mound. Small.

HISTONI. (A form of hirta). Vivid red, green and yellow tones give this one a harlequin appearance. Chicks grow on top. When mature will roll off and root where they land.

H. CELON. Long tapered leaves, satiny dark green with overtones of purple. Large.

JADE WEST. Similar in form to Emerald Giant but color is a fine deep jade green with darker tips.

KING LEAR. Large reddish bronze rosettes. Base of leaves blue-green.

KOSANINII. (aff.). Lustrous velvety light green leaves with silvery overtone. Purple tips. Offsets on long leafy stems.

LAGGERI. Lower third of each leaf light green, top rosy-red. Leaves fringed and tufted with soft white fur.

LAURA LEE. Medium size rosettes; soft rose red with hairy edge and tufts on tips of leaves.

LEUCANTHUM. Flattish rosettes, many hairy leaves, light green tipped purple. Multitude of chicks on long stems.

MAGNIFICUM. Large rosy purple rosettes with broad leaves. Holds color all year. Showy.

MALBYI. Large red; shiny broad leaves feathered at edges.

MARIETTA. Smooth red leaves with fringed edges. Small but multiplies fast. Rose colored bloom on short stems.

MAUVINE. Blue-green smooth rosettes with fine edge of rose on leaves.

METTENIANUM. Flat rosettes with subtle coloring. Green, shading to umber, with bronzy tips.

MISSOURI ROSE. Large rosettes, smooth leaves, wine-purple with darker tips.

NEILREICHI. (A form of hirta). Bright red slender pointed leaves. Chicks borne on top.

NIGRUM. Long tapered green leaves with heavy scarlet tip and border. With age the leaves flame and deepen to maroon.

OLD ROSE. Ashen rosy purple, velvet texture. Broad leaves with feathered edge. Large.

PEKINESE. Light green. Furry and lightly webbed, small and puggy. Chicks red tinted.

PILOSELLA. Green base, top of rosette rosy. Half hidden in spring under soft fur on edges.

POTSI. Resembles Christmas red and green buttons. Slender whip-like leaves. Multiplies fast.

PURDY'S 50-5. Light rosy purple. Satiny leaves with silvered edges.

PURDY'S 60-2. Medium small rosettes stained violet. Holds color well all year.

PURDY'S 70-40. Broad leaves banded with red. Very bold in appearance.

PURDY'S 90-1. Velvety grey-green tinted rose with rosy purple border and tips.

PENNICULATUM. Unique, slender, sword-shaped leaves, silver edged and tipped with orange-red.

PITTONII. Small many leaved rosettes. Leaves hairy, incurved, green with purple tips. Chicks closely crowded. Styria.

PURPLE BEAUTY. Deep rosy-mauve, broad leaves with sharply pointed tips. Large.

RAMSES. Large smooth-leaved red rosette. Holds color well.

RHODANICUM. Outer leaves dark red with chartreuse glow inside. Unique.

RUBICUNDUM. Flat rosettes of brilliant carmine with edge of green. Very showy. From the Balkans.

RUBRA ASH. Beautiful rosy purple rosettes covered with fine down. Medium large.

RUBRA RAY. Large wine-red rosettes with ends of each leaf green.

RUTHENICUM. (aff). Medium sized rosettes. Velvety green with light purple tones. Offsets on short stems.

SANFORDII. Long silver-edged pinkish bronze leaves with darker tips. Open loose rosette.

SANFORD HYBRID. Rosy purplish bronze with broad leaves.

SIMONKAIANUM. Medium small compact copper red and green rosettes, lightly tufted.

SIEBENBERGEN. (Seven Mountains): Light green velvety leaves with red tips. Large.

SILVERINE. Large silver-blue rosettes with pointed tips. Blush of rose-pink at base of leaves.

SILVERTONE. (K. Vaughn). Silver-blue, heavily banded with rose-pink. Large.

SOBOLIFERA. 2" round rosettes with russet tinted chicks on top. From Eurasia.

SPECIOSUM. Small downy red rosettes with hairy tufts on tips of leaves. A miniature.

TECTORUM.   Large green rosettes, heavily marked with reddish purple at edges and tips. Grown on roofs in Europe in other times as a guard against lightning or a charm against the devil.
THAYNE.   Large rosettes, blue-green leaves with maroon tips. Good contrast to red or purple Sempervivums.
TRISTE.   Slender pointed leaves, lavender-violet shading to red-bronze.
VIOLESCENS.   Large blue-green rosette heavily flushed with violet.
WARDS No. 2.   Sharp tapered light green leaves stained with wine-red.
WOLCOTT'S VARIETY.   Light green slender leaves with rose-pink center.
ZENOBIA.   Medium sized green, strikingly marked with deep purple.
No. 10.   (Ginnie's Delight). Deep rose-red leaves heavily tufted and fringed with curly hair. 2″ rosettes.

SEDUMS

Please Indicate Substitutions

ALBUM.   Small fat leaves turn cherry red when grown in poor soil or on driftwood. Flowers pinkish in starlike sprays.
ALBUM MICRANTHUM.   Miniature shiny bright green beady leaves in tufts. Tiny white flowers.
ALBUM MURALE.   Miniature form of album with purplish leaves and pinker flowers.
ANACAMPSEROS.   Brownish serpentine stems closely packed with shingled blue-green leaves. Purplish flowers. Spain.
ANOPETALUM.   Dark olive green linear leaves tinged red. Yellow flowers on tall slender stems. From Asia Minor.
CONFUSUM.   4-5″ mounds of beautiful waxy light green leaves with tints of orange red. Hardy to 10°
CAUTICOLUM.   (Purple carpet). Blue-grey leaves with purplish cast. Large rose-red flowers. Deciduous. Japan.
CHRYSANTHUM.   Light green rosettes that pile one on top of another. Creamy yellow flowers.
CYANEUM.   (Pluricaule, Rose Carpet). Fleshy, almost opalescent, blue-gray leaves with overtones of pinkish-purple. Showy rose colored flowers. Deciduous.
DIVERGENS.   Fat egg shaped leaves with copper tones. New form from Chrystal Mt.
EWERSII.   Blue-gray leaves with purple bloom. Semi-trailing habit. Deciduous. From western Himalayas.
EWERSII HOMOPHYLLUM.   Blue-grey leaves form 2-4″ mounds with purplish-pink flowers. A miniature of the above.
HISPANICUM.   Tiny pointed leaves in tufts, blue-green shading to pink. Pale pink flowers. Persia.
KAMTSCHATICUM VARIEGATUM.   Toothed green leaves splashed with white, pink and orange. Arching form and showy orange flowers.
LANCEOLATUM.   (formerly S. stenopetalum; name changed by Dr. Clausen). A small sedum from the Rocky Mountains. Blue-green leaves in short tight tufts. Yellow flowers.
LYDIUM.   Tightly packed linear leaves that take on crimson tints in summer. Forms nice mats. White flowers. Asia Minor.
MIDDENDORFIANUM.   Upright growth habit to 3″. Narrow bronze tinted leaves turn brilliant scarlet in fall. Yellow flowers with dark brown centers and orange anthers. Neat clumps. Manchuria.
MIDDENDORFIANUM VAR. DIFFUSUM.   A prostrate creeping form with long, slender notched leaves. Flowers 2-3″ across, golden yellow. After the flowers fade the star-shaped fruit turns bright red creating a brilliant effect.
MORANENSE.   A bushy little plant with wiry reddish stems. 3-4″ high. Triangular fleshy leaves. From Real de Moran, Mexico.
NEVII.   A fine N. American native. Pale green rosettes form creeping tufts. Looks like little green roses.
NEVII VAR. BEYRICHIANUM.   A larger, looser form with larger flowers. From Blue Ridge Mts., Virginia.
OREGANUM.   Shiny green fleshy rosettes on red stems. Leaves turn coral in summer. Oregon native.
OREGONENSE.   Thick bluish green leaves in rosette form. Coral tints in summer. Cream colored bloom. Oregon native.
PULCHELLUM.   Large recurved branched flowers of rosy lilac. Foliage finely cut, a fresh green with orange tints. Midwest U.S.
REFLEXUM CRISTATUM.   (Cock's Comb). A creeping crested form. Keep unfasciate branches pinched off.
RUBY GLOW.   Beautiful purplish-grey foliage covered with glowing ruby-red flowers. Upright growth habit to 8″. Deciduous.
SEXANGULARE.   Tightly crowded leaves arranged in six parallel rows spiraling around stem, copper colored with a bright yellow display of flowers covering the plant.
SIEBOLDII.   Large light blue leaves rimmed with rose. Stems spray out. Large rose-pink flowers. From Japan. Deciduous.
SPATHULIFOLIUM.   Grey green leaves in rosette form make spreading mats. Sun or shade. Oregon native. Yellow flowers.
SPATH PRUINOSUM.   Larger, very powdery form. Often turns beautiful rose-pink in summer. If this effect is desired do not plant in rich soil. Best in shade.
SPATH. CAPE BLANCO.   A miniature form of Spath. Pruinosum. Silver-grey leaves and pink stems. Grows on cliffs at Cape Blanco, Oregon.
SPATH PURPUREUM.   Rosettes red-purple becoming more red when planted in poor soil. When wet with rain it is shiny blood red.
SPATH. ROSEUM.   A new one from Germany. Soft rose color with same rosette form as the other spathulifoliums. Longer leaves and slightly different growth habit.
SPURIUM DRAGON'S BLOOD.   Shiny reddish green leaves with glowing dark red flowers.

SANDY'S SILVER CREST.   A cream tipped sport of Reflexum. This is not a variegated form, but has a definite cream colored tip, often turning pink in bright sun. New and rare.
KAMTSCHATICUM FROM TEKARI DAKI.   This beautiful sedum has been much admired at our nursery. Upright growth habit to 6″. Red stems and shining deep green leaves with red tints, notched in upper third. Large golden flowers.
LINEARE VARIEGATUM.   Semi-trailer. Light green leaves with a margin of white stems pink. Color often depends on exposure. In shade the plant will look almost silver — in sun the variegated foliage is very distinct. Yellow flowers. Can be used in hanging baskets. May need winter protection in cold climates. From Japan and China.
MAKINOI.   Light green spoon shaped leaves in rosette form. When grown in full sun and poor but porous soil the plant has a luminous quality. Resembles S. oreganum but it is more delicate in appearance. Yellow flowers. From Japan.

RARE WESTERN NATIVES

Please Indicate Substitutions

LAXUM SSP. HECKNERI.   A bluish form with heart shaped leaves. The bloom is a beautiful pink globular cluster flowering stem is crowded with leaves that clasp it. From the region near the Trinity Alps.
LAXUM SSP. LATIFOLIUM.   Very broad, very thick heart-shaped blue-green leaves. Flowers are white suffused with pale pink. From south side of the Siskiyous.
LAXUM FROM COAST AND KLAMATH MTS.   Thick blue-green lance-shaped leaves, (pointed at tips rather than indented). Flowers are deep rose-pink with wine centers on a branched stem.
LAXUM 'CROCKER'S BLUE'.   Metallic blue rosettes with fleshy pointed oblong leaves. Pale pink flowers. In short supply, please indicate substitution.
LAXUM 'MINA'.   This unusual laxum is a miniature (half the size of any of the others). Shining green heart-shaped leaves and pale pink flowers. In short supply.
PURDYI.   Emerald green flattened, domed rosettes. Offsets on bright red runners. Burst of golden bloom at top of red stalk clothed with red leaves. We suggest growing this in shade or filtered shade for the first year to see how it does.
SPATHULIFOLIUM SUBSP. ANOMALUM.   Luminous green leaves red tinted on backs. Offsets on bright red runners. Yellow flowers. So named because it is the only spathulifolium that is not powdery. From the Sierra Nevadas.
MORANII.   (Formerly listed as GLANDULIFERUM. The name has been changed by Dr. Clausen.) This rare Oregon sedum is known to grow in only one place: the cliffs of the Rogue River. The grey-blue leaves of the rosette are long and lance-shaped. Flowers are a very pleasing soft yellow.

....

    SILVERMOON.   A very rare, hitherto unknown natural hybrid of S. laxum and S. spathulifolium. Determined by Dr. Robert T. Clausen. Perfectly rounded mounds of silvery pale green rosettes with tones of pink and red. The tightly closed rosettes open in the late fall. Collected from the Trinity Alps region in N. Calif. A real jewel for the rock garden.

....

The following Sempervivums are from a collection that came from the University at Budapest Hungary.

FONTANAE.   1″ rosettes, finely haired, fringed, with red-brown tips. Offsets on smooth brown stolens.
GREENII.   Resembles a small Calcareum, except leaves more slender. Steel blue-green with maroon tips.
GRIMMERI.   Very downy, large, medium green rosettes.
HIRTUM var. GLABRESCENS.   Large grey and purple form of Hirta.

Collections of sempervivums and sedums may be seen at the following:
Arnold Arboretum of Harvard University, Jamaica Plain, Mass.
Alfred L. Boerner Botanical Gardens, Hales Corners, Wisc.
Botanic Garden of the Chicago Horticultural Society, Glencoe, Ill.
The Golden Gate Park, Strybing Arboretum, San Francisco, Calif.
Milton Hershey School, Hershey, Penn.
Tennessee Botanical Gardens, Cheekwood, Nashville, Tenn.
University of Idaho Arboretum, Moscow, Idaho
Longwood Gardens, Kennett Square, Penn.
University of California, Berkeley, Calif.
Lousiana State University, Baton Rouge, La.
Denver Botanic Gardens, Denver, Colo.
The Dawes Arboretum, Newark, Ohio
Queens Botanical Gardens, Flushing, N.Y.
Schenley Park, Pittsburgh, Pa.
Ohme Gardens, Wenatchee, Wash.
Hood River County Park, Hood River, Ore.

Note: No two authorities whether they be English, American, German or French, agree completely on sempervivums. All agree that there is great confusion in the names.

SEMPERVIVUMS AND SEDUMS

Arcady Gardens,
2646 Calhoun Rd.,
Medford, Ore. 97501

MacPherson Gardens,
2920 Starr Ave.,
Oregon, Ohio 42616

Oakhill Gardens,
R. 3, Box 87,
Dallas, Ore. 97338

Palette Gardens,
26 W. Zion Hill Rd.,
Quakertown, Penna. 18951

—Sempervivum soboliferum. On the lower step of the rock lie five ball-shaped offshoots which have become detached from the upper rocky platform and have rolled down. The butterfly and snail are introduced into the picture to show the true proportions of the offshoots.

Hybrids by E. Skrocki.

BEDIVERE.   Neat clumps. Reddish. Different.

CAMELOT.   (#100). Large velvety rose pink.

COLLAGE.   Smooth grey-green and pink leaves. Unusual form.

CLIPPER.   Burnished dark red-purple rosettes with fringed leaves.

GRAPETONE.   Purple grape color, smooth leaves.

OHIO BURGUNDY.   Deep burgundy with hairy leaves. Firm, compact grower. Merit award entry in England.

OLIVETTE.   Unusual chubby rosettes. Polished olive green leaves.

PATRICIAN.   Bright smooth red and green leaves with fringed edges. Tight, medium sized, resembling a full rose.

ROYAL RUBY.   Dark red shading to glowing purple. Smooth pointed leaves. Holds color well. Large.

RUBICON.   Very fine deep ruby red with smooth waxy leaves. 2" rosettes. Merit award entry in England.

SERENA.   Smooth light pinkish lavender rosettes with silvery edges.

TRACY SUE.   Velvety green with tawny overtone.

TRISTAM.   Slender, pointed, smooth leaves flushed pinkish-magenta, silvery fringed edges.

PACKARDIAN.   Very large bronzy purple with copper overtone.

LAVENDER AND OLD LACE.   (Oakhill Gardens hybrid). Base of rosette green, the rest is a beautiful rosy lavender with silvered edges. Choice and unusual.

HEUFFELII No. 1.   (Formerly listed as Reginae Amaliae). Plushy textured rosette with upper third of leaves heavily marked red-purple. Propagated by division of rosette and root. Soft yellow flowers. From S. E. Europe to Greece.

HEUFFELII No. 2.   Bright reddish-purple velvety leaves, light green at base. Flowers are yellow but are different in form from Heuffelii No. 1.

HEUFFELII No. 3.   Leaves light green with purple flush on end and backs of leaves. Leaves appear smooth but when touched feel like a cat's tongue.

OROSTACHYS SPINOSA.   Most unusual luminous grey green rosettes with spiny tips that look sharp but aren't. Goes dormant in winter and looks grey and dead. Protect from too much moisture. Resembles a sempervivum.

GREENWICH TIME.   Medium purple in spring with deeper purple margin and tip. (K. Vaughn).

JUNGLE SHADOWS.   Dark purplish-grey, smooth leaves with bright purple edges and tips. Large. (K. Vaughn).

LIPSTICK.   Downy brick-red leaves, with darker edges. (K. Vaughn).

RUBY HEART.   Silver-blue rosettes with bright red at base of leaves. (K. Vaughn).

SILVER SONG.   Smooth steel blue leaves flushed violet in spring. (K. Vaughn).

ARENARIA.   Species from Austria. Very small bright green rosettes, heavily marked dark red.

GUISEPPI.   Species from Spain. Very hairy tapered bright green leaves. Rose colored flowers.

DEGENIANUM.   2" light purple covered with fine down.

MONTANUM var. BRAUNII.   Large velvety pale green. Many long slender leaves.

PILIFERUM.   Medium small, red flushed, with fringed and tufted leaves.

PITTONII.   Small, many leaved, hairy rosettes. A better form of this species.

PYRENAICUM.   Light green with purple tips, beautifully hazed by fine down. Small.

WEBBIANUM.   Medium sized red. Leaves heavily tufted and fringed. In spring looks like a ruby goblet full of snow.

Recommended Books on Sedums and Sempervivums.

THE SEMPERVIVUM & JOVISBARBA HANDBOOK   P. J. MITCHELL
11 Wingle Tye Rd., Burgess Hill, Sussex, England
AN ACCOUNT OF THE SEMPERVIVUM GROUP   PRAEGER
AN ACCOUNT OF THE GENUS SEDUM, (as found in cultivation)   PRAEGER
A GARDENER'S GUIDE TO SEDUMS BY R. L. Evans. Published by Alpine Garden Society, 58
Denison House, 296 Vauxhall Bridge Rd., London, S.W.1, England.
DR. ROBERT CLAUSEN'S BOOK ON SEDUMS   WHEN PRINTED
ALPINES IN COLOUR AND CULTIVATION   MANSFIELD

LIVE INNOCENTLY

Karl Linnaeus, (1707-1778) spent the better part of his life compiling long accurate tables noting the minute structural details of plants and animals in an effort to construct a workable system to classify all the living species known in his era.

Before his time, botanists had only given one name to each set of plants. All roses were called Rosa, for example. Then, a long-winded description was appended to describe just which Rosa they had in mind. For the Romanas rose, a botanist might be obliged to say Rosa, Sylvestri vulgaris, flore odorato incarnato—common woodland rose with a flesh-colored, sweet-scented flower. Under the new system, this rose is simply Rosa rugosa (botanical name).

The beauty of the Linnaean system, is that it allows anyone to examine any unknown plant and discover its correct name by checking its characteristics against previously catalogued species.

To accomplish this, Linnaeus classified all plants chiefly according to the number and arrangements of their stamens and pistils—the seed producing parts. Then, he subdivided them according to the character and position of their leaves, stems and so forth.

When describing the geranium, for example, he first mentions the sepals (little green leaves under the flower). There are five of these and they are very pointed he says. Then he mentions the petals. There are five of these also. They grow on the sepal and are heart-shaped.

There are ten stamens, he goes on to explain. They grow separately. The anthers—pollen vessels—are oblong and contain yellow dust. The pistil—seed vessel—is formed of five parts. These are joined together into one long beak which ends in five points.

The seeds are kidney shaped and covered with a skin. Often, he notes, they have a long spiral tip.

That is the basic classification of the characteristics of genus Geranium. But, many geraniums fit that description. So, he goes on with his description.

The sepals, he says, are joined into one piece. The stem is woody. The joints are fleshy. The leaves are slightly feathered at the edge. These additional characteristics are peculiar to the geranium to which he gave the specific name, Geranium gibbosum.

Above his door, Linnaeus placed the motto, "Live innocently, God is present."

But controversy followed this humble scientist's death. His mother and sisters sold his collections to an Englishman. When the news arrived at court, the King of Sweden dispatched a man-of-war to intercept the naturalist's treasure trove. An historic sea chase, under full sail followed. But, the collection was lost to the Swedes forever.

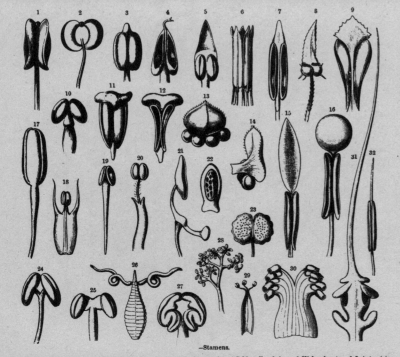

—Stamens.

¹ Empleurum serrulatum. ² Hypericum olympicum. ³ Juglans regia. ⁴ Soldanella alpina. ⁵ Viola odorata. ⁶,⁷ Artemisia Absynthium. ⁸ Haminia (after Baillon). ⁹ Abies excelsa. ¹⁰ Euphorbia canariensis. ¹¹,¹² Platanus orientalis. ¹³,¹⁴ Juniperus Sabina. ¹⁵ Haliemonemis gibbosa. ¹⁶ Halantium Kulpianum. ¹⁷ Sanguinaria canadensis. ¹⁸ Allium sphærocephalum. ¹⁹ Actæa spicata. ²⁰ Aconitum Napellus. ²¹ Salvia officinalis. ²² Viscum album. ²³ Mirabilis Jalapa. ²⁴ Tilia ulmifolia. ²⁵ Thymus serpyllum. ²⁶ Acalypha (after Baillon). ²⁷ Bryonia dioica. ²⁸ Ricinus communis. ²⁹ Corydalis capnoides. ³⁰ Polygala amara. ³¹ Doryphora (after Baillon). ³² Paris quadrifolia. (All figures somewhat enlarged.)

CHRISTMAS ROSE.
(HELLEBORUS NIGER.)

THE DEVELOPMENT OF HORTICULTURE IN AMERICA

by John M. Fogg, Jr.

Director, The Arboretum of the Barnes Foundation

Based on a talk given April 3, 1973, on the occasion of the Hundredth Anniversary of the Germantown Horticultural Society.

Any comprehensive treatment of the development of horticulture in America must take us back nearly three centuries and should give due consideration to the importance of Philadelphia as a botanical and horticultural center.

It was in 1694 that a sect of German Pietists, presided over by Kelpuis, established on the banks of the lower Wissahickon Creek a garden where medicinal plants were raised for use and study. Although no longer in existence and its exact location unknown, it may be considered the first botanical garden in America.

Francis Daniel Pastorius, the Founder of Germantown, who died in 1719, was botanist, gardener, linguist and poet. He was the author of "Medicus Dilectus," a discussion of the medicinal herbs of Pennsylvania and elsewhere, and of "Hortensis Deliciae," written in English, German, French, Latin and Dutch, which contains rhymes about the rare plants grown in his garden.

James Logan, whose homestead was close to Germantown Avenue at Stenton, had come to this country with William Penn, and later became Lieutenant-Governor of the colony of Pennsylvania. Experiments which he carried on in his garden with maize clearly demonstrated the role of sexuality in plants.

Christopher de Witt, an Englishman by birth, came to this country in 1704 and settled in Germantown. His garden was on the site now occupied by Germantown High School, as is proclaimed by a bronze plaque at the corner of Germantown Avenue and High Street. In addition to being a botanist, de Witt was a theosophist, mystic, Rosicrucian and physician. It is stated by the late Charles Jenkins that he sent a specimen of our eastern hemlock (*Tsuga canadensis*) to Peter Collinson in London prior to 1730. This was one of the first introductions of an American tree into Europe.

Although Stenton mansion still stands, all of these early gardens are gone. There is, however, one notable exception and this is the garden that Philadelphia's own John Bartram established on the banks of the Schuylkill River in 1731. Although Bartram was primarily a farmer, and apparently a very good one, he possessed many of the attributes of a naturalist. Among his early friends were Christopher de Witt, James Logan and Benjamin Franklin. Thanks to another friend, Joseph Breitnall, Bartram was put in touch with Peter Collinson, a London wool merchant, who commissioned him to collect seeds of American plants and it was through Collinson that Bartram also became a collector of American plants for Dr. John Fothergill.

Later Bartram came to know Peter Kalm, a student of Linnaeus, who visited Philadelphia in the 1740's, as well as Cadwalader Colden (Governor of New York), Alexander Garden (for whom *Gardenia* is named) and many others. His foreign correspondents included Sir Hans Sloane (who wrote the first account of the flora of the West Indies), Philip Miller (the director of the Chelsea Physic Garden in London), J.F. Gronovius (a distinguished Dutch botanist), and, above all, Carl Linnaeus of Sweden, the father of modern botany.

In 1765 John Bartram was appointed Botanist to King George III at an annual stipend of 50 pounds. He was then 66 years of age. It was in October of this same year that he and his son Billy discovered the Franklin tree on the banks of the Altamaha River near Fort Bennington, Georgia.

This is not the place to recount the details of John Bartram's journeys, which took him from upper New York state down through the Carolinas and Georgia to Florida. Suffice it to say that as a result of some forty years of traveling through largely uncharted wilderness this simple Philadelphia farmer sent between 150 and 200 species of American plants to his friends across the Atlantic.

At the same time that Bartram was dispatching plants to Europe he was growing them in his own garden and making them available to American horticulture. Had he done nothing more than introduce *Franklinia* into cultivation, he would certainly be entitled to a niche in Horticulture's "Hall of Fame." But there were others—many, many others—far too numerous to enumerate here in full. They included the star anise (*Illicium floridanum*), the silver-bell (*Halesia*), the Carolina allspice (*Calycanthus*), the fringe-tree (*Chionanthus virginicus*) and the beautiful southern evergreen rhododendron (*R. catawbiense*). Bartram's garden was the first repository of its kind in the New World and the debt which both European and American horticulture owe to it is incalculable.

Another Philadelphia collector and seedsman, whose birth-date is unknown but who died in 1785, was William Young, Jr. who sold American plants and seeds to dealers in the Old World. His "Catalogue," published in Paris in 1783, was one of the first listings of American plants available to horticulturists.

Humphrey Marshall, who was a cousin of John Bartram, established in 1773 what was probably the first arboretum in the New World at Marshallton, in Chester County, Pa. In it he sought to grow all trees and shrubs, both native and exotic, hardy in this area and from it in 1785 he wrote his "American Grove" (Arbustum Americanum), probably the first indigenous treatise on botany published by an American.

One might well wish that Adam Kuhn, who was born in Germantown in 1741, and who studied under the illustrious Linnaeus in Uppsala, might have made a significant contribution to botany and horticulture. Alas, although apparently the first Professor of Botany in America (at the University of Pennsylvania, then the College of Philadelphia) Kuhn failed completely to fulfill the promise entertained for him by his preceptor.

Among those who contributed greatly to the advancement of horticulture in the New World were the Michaux's, Andre the father, and Francois Andre, the son.

It was the father who is said to have sent back to France some 60,000 specimens of American trees, only a few of which arrived in a living state. He is best known for his studies of the oaks of America, many of which he described for the first time.

The son traveled widely in the eastern United States, from Maine to Georgia and in 1817-19 there appeared his three volume "North American Sylva," a work which exerted considerable influence on the study of arboriculture in eastern North America.

In the meantime, William Hamilton had become the owner of a large estate known as "The Woodlands" in West Philadelphia. He is credited with having introduced the first Lombardy poplar (*Populus nigra italica*) to this country in 1784. His grounds were reputed to contain one of the finest collections of native and exotic plants to be found outside the gardens of Europe.

Even more significant was the patronage which he extended to two young botanists from abroad. John Lyon, a Scotsman, was employed by Hamilton in 1796 or 1797. Upon leaving "The Woodlands" he traveled widely through the southeastern states and in 1803 his journal records that he found six or eight plants of *Franklinia* on the spot where Bartram had discovered it nearly forty years before. Lyon was therefore apparently the last person to see the Franklin tree in its native state.

The plants which Lyon collected were established in several nurseries preparatory to their shipment abroad. One of these was the firm of David Landreth which had established a nursery in Philadelphia in 1784. The catalog which Lyon prepared of his offerings consisted of thirty-four pages.

Hamilton also assisted Frederick Pursh, the author of the first comprehensive "Flora of North America", published in 1814. It was Pursh whom Thomas Jefferson wished to appoint as botanist to the Lewis and Clark expedition in 1804, but the young explorer was off in the Country of the Five Nations and could not be reached.

It will be apparent from all of this that American botany had its roots very largely in horticulture. The demand for novelties from the New World for European gardens not only stimulated the activities of the collectors we have mentioned (and many more), but led to the establishment of nurseries and seed houses. In addition to Landreth's there were in the Philadelphia area the famous firms of Bernard M'Mahon, Thomas Meehan, Robert Buist and Anthony Waterer. Prince's Nursery was perhaps the first on Long Island and was followed by Parmentiers, Parsons and Hicks.

The Musk Hibiscus

Luther Burbank
and Friends

It will be noted, also, that up until the early years of the nineteenth century the flow of plant materials across the Atlantic was mostly from west to east. Naturally, some of the early settlers brought with them plants with which they were familiar, either as fruits, medicinals or ornamentals. And with the opening up of great estates there was a demand for material from Europe. This was largely supplied by English nurseries which specialized in native species or were in a position to propagate and offer plants from the Orient. Kaempfer, Thunberg and Siebold had visited Japan and sent home plants collected largely in gardens. Cunningham, D'Incarville, Osbeck, John Reeves, William Kerr and Robert Fortune had traveled sparingly in China and had enriched European gardens with their finds.

The invention in 1834 of the Wardian Case had greatly facilitated the shipment of living plants, which were no longer at the mercy of sailors who treated them with neglect, if not contempt.

In 1853 the United States dispatched an expedition to Japan under Commodore Perry. The naturalist on this mission was James Morrow, who had taken his degree in medicine at the University of Pennsylvania. Morrow took with him a shipment of plants from Buist's nursery and in return was instructed to bring back seeds and plants for experimentation from China and Japan. Although he encountered hostility from the natives, who on several occasions boiled seeds before delivering them to him, he succeeded in introducing seeds of such economic plants as melons, rice and wheat, as well as a few ornamental species.

It remained, however, for George Hall, an American physician, to introduce any appreciable number of ornamental plants from the Far East directly into the United States. Hall visited Japan in 1861 and 1862 and spent almost fifteen years in China. Many of his finds were deposited at Parson's nursery on Long Island, others were sent to Francis Parkman in Boston. Some of them, however, found their way into one or more of the Philadelphia nurseries mentioned above. Among his introductions were *Magnolia stellata* and *M. Kobus* (both from Japan), *Malus Halliana*, *Wisteria floribunda*, *Hydrangea paniculata* and *Lilium auratum*.

Although Philadelphia was no longer at dead center, it was still very much in the inner circle of horticultural activities in the United States.

In 1872, a year prior to the founding of the Germantown Horticultural Society, there occurred an event of great significance to those who were concerned with the growing of trees and shrubs. This was the establishment of the Arnold Arboretum of Harvard University, made possible by a bequest in the estate of James Arnold. Charles Sprague Sargent was appointed Director in 1873 and retained this position until his death in 1927.

In 1874 Dr. Sargent went abroad to investigate sources of supply for plant material and, according to Dr. Donald Wyman, within a year the Arnold Arboretum received 56 plants and 264 packets of seeds from Great Britain and 307 plants and 1620 packets of seeds from Europe.

During the slightly more than one hundred years of its existence the Arnold Arboretum has not only supported plant collecting expeditions in distant lands, but has been extremely generous in distributing material to other arboreta as well as to nurseries.

Sargent had encouraged the Russian botanist, E.V. Bretschneider, to send plants from China to the Arboretum and in 1892 he himself journeyed to Japan and brought home seeds of many interesting plants from the northern portion of Honshu (Nippon) and the north island of Hokkaido.

However, the brightest jewel in the Arboretum's crown was E.H. Wilson, who had begun his career as a collector for the distinguished English firm of Veitch & Son, but in 1909 had joined the staff of the Arnold. On its behalf he explored and collected plants in China, Japan, Korea and Taiwan. It has been estimated that the number of species which he introduced into cultivation was approximately one thousand. This number contained, among many prized ornamentals, the renowned dove-tree, *Davidia involucrata*, the beauty bush (*Kolkwitzia*) and the regal lily (*Lilium regale*).

In the meantime, events had been taking place in other sections of the country, among them the Philadelphia area.

As early as 1800 the Peirce Arboretum, which was later to become Longwood Gardens, was established at Kennett Square, Pa. Sometime between 1825 and 1830 two Quaker brothers by the name of Painter had begun to assemble a collection of hardy native and exotic trees and shrubs on the grounds of their property at Lima, Pa. Today this is known as the Tyler Arboretum.

In 1887 Mr. John T. Morris acquired a parcel of land in Chestnut Hill, Philadelphia. Mr. Morris became friendly with Dr. Sargent and made contributions to the work of the Arnold Arboretum. As a result he became the recipient of many of the novelties acquired from the explorations of Wilson and others. Mr. Morris

died in 1915, but was survived by his sister, Miss Lydia T. Morris. Upon her death in 1932 the property was left to the University of Pennsylvania and has since been known as the Morris Arboretum.

When the late Albert C. Barnes purchased a 13-acre property in Merion, Pa. in the early 1920's, for the purpose of constructing a building to house his art collection, he turned the development of the grounds over to his wife, Laura L. Barnes. The result of her imaginative planning and planting is the institution that is now the Arboretum of The Barnes Foundation.

On the campus of Swarthmore College, in the suburb of that name, there came into being, in 1929, the Arthur Hoyt Scott Arboretum, presided over for many years by its first director, Dr. John C. Wister.

Add to this the Taylor Arboretum at Chester, Swiss Pines Park, and the Bowman's Hill Wild Flower Preserve, and it will readily be apparent that the Philadelphia area must still be considered a mecca for everyone interested in horticulture.

Certainly no account, however sketchy, of the development of horticulture in the New World would be complete without reference to Liberty Hyde Bailey, who was born in 1858, and lived to be ninety-one, almost a century in one man. Dr. Bailey was the author not only of our standard "Cyclopedia of Horticulture," but also of the very useful "Manual of Cultivated Plants," the second edition of which appeared in 1949. A keen student not only of palms, but of such difficult genera as Carex and Rubus, L.H. Bailey stood head and shoulders above his contemporaries.

If I have failed to describe the achievements of such explorers and collectors as J.G. Jack, J.F. Rock, Frank Meyer and David Fairchield, it is simply because time permits only the briefest mention of those who have contributed so many of the plants which we take for granted in our gardens.

The Pennsylvania Horticultural Society was founded in 1827 and shortly thereafter sponsored the first Philadelphia Flower Show. It was at this event that the Poinsettia, collected in Mexico by Joel Poinsett of Greensboro, South Carolina, made its debut.

Perhaps the full dimension of present-day horticulture can best be appreciated by considering its international character. The First International Horticultural Congress was held in Brussels in 1864. Ninety-eight years later, in 1962, the Sixteenth Congress took place in the same city, and four years after that the Seventeenth convened at the University of Maryland in College Park.

The Maryland Congress, the first one to take place in the United States, was sponsored by the American Horticultural Society, the American Society for Horticultural Science, and the International Society for Horticultural Science, in cooperation with the American Institute of Biological Sciences. I mention these agencies merely to indicate the tremendous scope of modern horticulture.

At this Congress there were registrants from fifty countries including Finland, Ghana, Indonesia, Sudan and Tunisia. More than 700 papers were presented, necessitating the fractionating of the program into a score or more of sectional sessions with such headings as Fruit Breeding, Vegetable Breeding, Woody Plant Hardiness, Ornamental Plant Hardiness, Nutrition, Viruses, Flower Crops, Growth Regulators, Photoperiodism, Weeds and Weed Control, Water Relations, Seeds and Seedage, Mechanical Harvesting, Tropical Plants, Sub-arctic Horticulture and so on.

As Philadelphia considers its role in the forthcoming celebration of this nation's two hundredth anniversary it is to be hoped that appropriate emphasis will be devoted to this city's vitally important contribution to the origins and growth of botany and horticulture in America.

The home of John Bartram.

FOUR GOOD CLEMATISES.

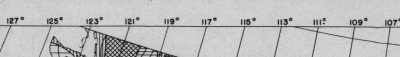

PODZOLS

1 Rough stony land.

2 Loams and silt loams, developed from sandstones and shales. (Leetonia, De Kalb.)

3 Sands and loamy sands, developed on glacial drift. (Roselawn, Kalkaska.)

4 Loams and clay loams, developed on glacial drift. (Hermon, Ontonagon.)

GRAY-BROWN PODZOLIC SOILS

5 Loams and silt loams, developed on calcareous glacial drift. (Miami, Crosby and Honeoye Ontario.)

6 Silty loams or stony loams, developed on sandstones and shales. (Muskingum, Westmoreland.)

7 Loams and silt loams, developed on acid glacial drift, sandstone and shale material. (Canfield, Volusia, Lordstown, Wooster.)

8 Stony and gravelly loams, developed on glacial drift. (Gloucester, Troy.)

9 Loams and silt loams, developed on the crystalline rocks of the northern Piedmont. (Chester, Manor.)

10 Sandy loams developed on northern Coastal Plain sands and clays. (Sassafrass, Collington.)

11 Brown silt loams, developed on limestone. (Hagerstown, Maury, Frederick.)

12 Shallow soils developed on interbedded limestone and calcareous shales. (Fairmont, Lowell.)

13 Loams and stony loams from granitic material with hilly to mountainous relief. (Ashe, Porters.)

14 Silt loams with heavy clay subsoils, developed on Illinoian glacial till. (Gibson, Cory, Clermont, Rossmoyne.)

15 Silt loams, developed largely from loess. (Clinton, Fayétte.)

16 Imperfectly drained grayish silt loams developed from acid glacial drift. (Spencer.)

17 Loams and silt loams developed from sandstones and shales. (Melbourne.)

18 Grayish-yellow to reddish silt loams, developed from cherty limestones. (Clarksville, Dickson, Baxter.)

RED AND YELLOW SOILS

19 Brownish-red clay loams and gray sandy loams, developed from crystalline rocks of the southern Piedmont. (Cecil, Durham, Appling, Georgeville, Davidson.)

20 Yellow to light brown silt loams, developed on loess. (Memphis, Grenada.)

21 Gray to yellow sandy, fine sandy loams, developed from Coastal Plain materials. (Norfolk, Ruston, Orangeburg.)

22 Brownish-red to red silt loams and clay loams, developed from limestone. (Dewey, Decatur, Fullerton.)

23 Grayish-yellow to light brown sands and fine sands of the Coastal Plain. (Norfolk sands.)

24 Grayish fine sandy loams with some gray or black loams, in the Flatwoods area of the Coastal Plain. (Coxville, Leon, Portsmouth.)

25 Grayish-yellow to reddish fine sandy loams and silt loams, developed from sandstones and shales. (Hartsells, Hanceville, Conway.)

26 Red soils of the Pacific slopes. (Aiken, Sierra, Sites.)

PRAIRIE SOILS

27 Reddish-brown soils, developed on sandstones, shales clays and sands. (Zaneis, Renfrew.)

LEGEND FOR PLANT

1 North Pacific Coast.

2 Willamette Valley -- Puget Sound.

3 Central California Valleys.

4 Cascade - Sierra Nevada.

5 Southern California.

6 Columbia River Valley.

7 Palouse - Bitterroot Valley.

8 Snake River Plain Utah Valley.

9 Great Basin - Intermontane.

10 Southwestern Desert.

11 Southern Plateau.

12 Northern Rocky Mountains.

13 Central Rocky Mountains.

14 Southern Rocky Mountains.

15 Northern Great Plains.

16 Central Great Plains.

17 Southern Plains.

HORTICULTURAL

CALIFORNIA

CALIFORNIA ACADEMY OF SCIENCES LIBRARY
Golden Gate Park
San Francisco, CA 94118

CALIFORNIA STATE POLYTECHNIC
COLLEGE LIBRARY
3801 West Temple Avenue
Pomona, CA 91768

FOREST HISTORY SOCIETY
Box 1581
Santa Cruz, CA 95061

LOS ANGELES STATE AND COUNTY ARBORETUM
PLANT SCIENCE LIBRARY
301 North Baldwin Avenue
Arcadia, CA 91006

RANCHO SANTA ANA BOTANIC GARDEN LIBRARY
1500 North College Avenue
Claremont, CA 91711

COLORADO

DENVER BOTANIC GARDENS
HELEN K. FOWLER LIBRARY
1005 York Street
Denver, CO 80206
Solange Huggins, Librarian
303-297-2547

DISTRICT OF COLUMBIA

DUMBARTON OAKS GARDEN LIBRARY
1703 32nd Street, N.W.
Washington, D.C. 20007
Professor E. MacDougall, Dir.
202-232-3101

SMITHSONIAN INSTITUTION LIBRARIES
Natural History Building
Washington, DC 20560
Dr. Russell Shank, Librarian
Mrs. Ruth Schallert, Botany Librarian
202-381-5382

U.S. NATIONAL ARBORETUM
U.S. NATIONAL ARBORETUM LIBRARY
Washington, D.C. 20002
Mrs. Jane MacLean, Librarian
202-399-5400

FLORIDA

FAIRCHILD TROPICAL GARDEN
MONTGOMERY LIBRARY
10901 Old Cutler Road
Miami, FL 33156
Director
305-667-1651

UNIVERSITY OF FLORIDA INSTITUTE OF FOOD
AND AGRICULTURAL SCIENCES
HUME LIBRARY
Gainesville, FL 32611

GEORGIA

CALLAWAY GARDENS
Pine Mountain, GA 31822
Fred C. Galle

ILLINOIS

CHICAGO HORTICULTURAL SOCIETY LIBRARY
Botanic Garden
P.O. Box 90
Glencoe, IL 60022
Mrs. Beverly Cartwright
312-835-5360

FIELD MUSEUM OF NATURAL HISTORY LIBRARY
Roosevelt Road and Lake Shore Drive
Chicago, IL 60605
312-922-9410

MORTON ARBORETUM
STERLING MORTON LIBRARY
Lisle, IL 60532
Mr. Ian MacPhail
312-968-0074

KENTUCKY

UNIVERSITY OF KENTUCKY AGRICULTURE LIBRARY
Agricultural Science Center North
Lexington, KY 40506

LOUISIANA

AMERICAN ROSE SOCIETY LENDING LIBRARY
P.O. Box 30,000
Shreveport, LA 71130
H. S. Goldstein, Exec. Dir.
318-938-5403

MASSACHUSETTS

ARNOLD ARBORETUM, HARVARD UNIVERSITY
22 Divinity Avenue
Cambridge, MA 02318
Patricia Hall, Librarian
617-495-2366

LIBRARY OF THE GRAY HERBARIUM
HARVARD UNIVERSITY
22 Divinity Avenue
Cambridge, MA 02138
Patricia Hall, Librarian
617-495-2366

MASSACHUSETTS HORTICULTURAL SOCIETY
300 Massachusetts Ave.
Boston, MA 02115
Mrs. Frances Dowd, Librarian
617-536-9280

OAKES AMES ORCHID LIBRARY
22 Divinity Ave., Rm. 109
Cambridge, MA 02138
Herman R. Sweet, Librarian

OLD STURBRIDGE VILLAGE RESEARCH LIBRARY
Sturbridge, MA 01566
Etta Falkner, Librarian

UNIVERSITY OF MASSACHUSETTS, AMHERST
MORRILL LIBRARY
Amherst, MA 01002

WELLESLEY COLLEGE LIBRARY
Biological Sciences
Sage Hall
Wellesley College
Wellesley, MA 02181

WORCESTER COUNTY HORTICULTURAL SOCIETY
30 Elm Street
Worcester, MA 01608
Fayre L. Nason, Librarian
617-752-4274

MICHIGAN

MICHIGAN HORTICULTURAL SOCIETY
The White House, Belle Isle
Detroit, MI 48207
James McMillan, Treasurer
313-824-3155

MINNESOTA

UNIVERSITY OF MINNESOTA LANDSCAPE
ARBORETUM
ANDERSON HORTICULTURAL LIBRARY
Route 1, Box 132-1
Chaska, MN 55318

UNIVERSITY OF MINNESOTA
ST. PAUL CAMPUS LIBRARY
St. Paul, MN 55101

GROWTH REGIONS OF THE UNITED STATES
SOIL CONSERVATION SERVICE

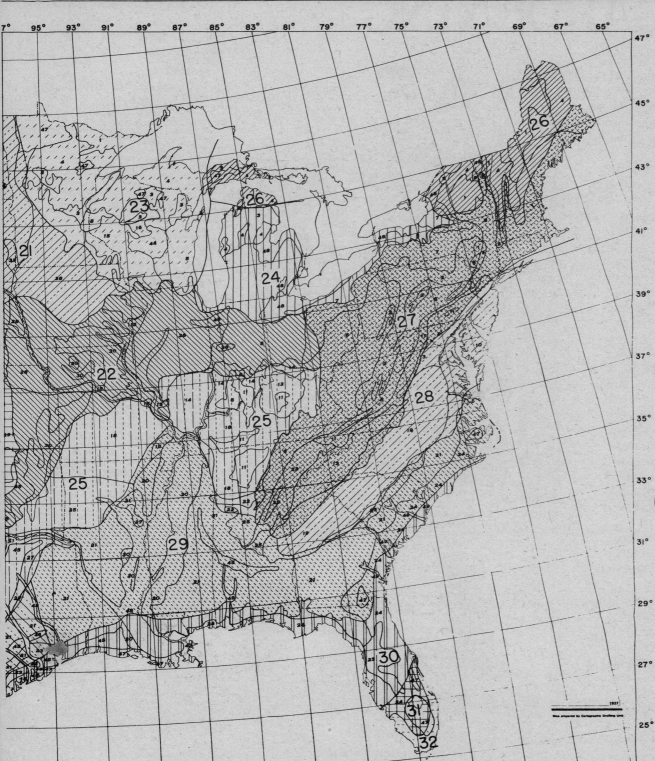

28 Dark brown silt loams with yellowish-brown subsoils, developed on glacial drift and loess. (Carrington, Tama, Clarion, Marshall.)

29 Dark brown to reddish-brown silt loams and clay loams, developed from limestone and calcareous shales. (Summit, Crawford.)

30 Dark brown or grayish-brown silt loams, having heavy subsoils or claypans. (Cherokee, Parsons, Grundy, Putnam.)

NORTHERN CHERNOZEM

31 Black loams, silt loams and clay loams, developed on calcareous glacial drift or lacustrine deposits. (Barnes, Bearden, Fargo.)

32 Dark grayish-brown loams and silt loams, developed from loess. (Moody, Holdrege.)

33 Dark grayish-brown silt loams with claypans, developed from loess. (Crete, Hastings.)

SOUTHERN CHERNOZEM -- DARK BROWN SOILS

34 Heavy or moderately heavy dark brown soils, developed from calcareous materials. (Pullman, Abilene, Victoria.)

35 Predominantly red and brown sandy loams and sands, developed largely from unconsolidated calcareous materials. (Amarillo, Miles, Duval.)

NORTHERN DARK BROWN (CHESTNUT) SOILS

36 Dark brown soils developed on unconsolidated, calcareous sands, silts, and clays. (Scobey, Rosebud, Keith, Walla Walla.)

37 Dark brown soils, developed on heterogeneous material.

BROWN SOILS

38 (Northern) brown loams, developed on unconsolidated sands, silts and clays. (Joplin, Weld.)

39 (Southern) light brown to gray fine sandy loams to silty clay loams, developed on limestone or unconsolidated sands, silts, and clays. (Uvalde, Reagan.)

SIEROZEM AND DESERT SOILS

40 (Northern) gray and grayish-brown soils, developed on loess and alluvial fans. (Ritzville, Portneuf,)

41 (Southern) gray, brown, and reddish soils, developed on alluvial fans. (Reeves, Mohave.)

SOILS OF THE PACIFIC VALLEYS

42 Soils too intimately associated to separate on a schematic map. (San-Joaquin, Fresno, Hanford.)

INTRAZONAL AND AZONAL SOILS

43 Rough and mountainous.

44 Largely sands, some of which are associated with bogs. (Valentine sand, Dune sand, etc.)

45 Black (or brown) friable soil underlain by chalky materials. These soils develop under a prairie vegetation and are known as Rendzinas (Houston, Sumter,)

46 Shallow stony soils from limestone. (Valera, Ector.)

47 Marsh, Swamp and Bog. (Carlisle, Pamlico, Rifle.)

48 Soils developed upon lake plains. (Brookston, Maumee, Vergennes.)

49 Alluvial soils. (Huntington, Sharkey, Columbia, Cass.)

50 Rough broken land, including Pierre soils.

GROWTH REGIONS

- 18 Northern Black Soils.
- 19 Central Black Soils.
- 20 Southern Black Soils.
- 21 Northern Prairies.
- 22 Central Prairies.
- 23 Western Great Lakes.
- 24 Central Great Lakes.
- 25 Ozark - Ohio - Tennessee River Valleys.
- 26 Northern Great Lakes - St. Lawrence.
- 27 Appalachian.
- 28 Piedmont.
- 29 Upper Coastal Plain.
- 30 Swampy Coastal Plain.
- 31 South - Central Florida.
- 32 Subtropical Florida.

LIBRARIES

MISSOURI

NATIONAL COUNCIL OF STATE GARDEN CLUBS, INC.
4401 Magnolia Ave.
St. Louis, MO 63110
Mrs. C. E. Fitzwater, Chairman
314-776-7574

MISSOURI BOTANICAL GARDEN LIBRARY
2315 Tower Grove Avenue
St. Louis, MO 63108
James R. Reed, Librarian
314-865-0440

NEBRASKA

UNIVERSITY OF NEBRASKA, EAST CAMPUS
C. Y. THOMPSON LIBRARY
Lincoln, NE 68503

NEW HAMPSHIRE

UNIVERSITY OF NEW HAMPSHIRE
BIOLOGICAL SCIENCES LIBRARY
Kendall Hall
Durham, NH 03824
Lloyd Heidgerd, Librarian

NEW JERSEY

RUTGERS UNIVERSITY
COOK COLLEGE
Box 231
New Brunswick, NJ 08903

NEW YORK

BROOKLYN BOTANIC GARDEN LIBRARY
1000 Washington Avenue
Brooklyn, NY 11225

CORNELL UNIVERSITY
ALBERT R. MANN LIBRARY
Ithaca, NY 14850

MONROE COUNTY PARK DEPARTMENT
HERBARIUM LIBRARY
County Park Office
375 Westfall Road
Rochester, NY 14620
Alvan R. Grant, Director
716-244-4640

NEW YORK BOTANICAL GARDEN LIBRARY
Bronx, NY 10458

NEW YORK STATE AGRICULTURAL EXPERIMENT
STATION LIBRARY
Geneva, NY 14456
P. Jennings, Librarian

OHIO

FRED W. GREEN MEMORIAL GARDEN
CENTER LIBRARY
123 McKinley Avenue
Youngstown, OH 44509

KINGWOOD CENTER LIBRARY
Box 966
Mansfield, OH 44901
Mrs. Marjorie Dickinson
419-522-0211

OHIO AGRICULTURAL RESEARCH AND
DEVELOPMENT CENTER LIBRARY
Wooster, OH 44691

THE GARDEN CENTER OF GREATER CLEVELAND
ELEANOR SQUIRE LIBRARY
11030 East Blvd.
Cleveland, OH 44106
Mr. R. T. Isaacson, Librarian
216-721-1600

THE HOLDEN ARBORETUM LIBRARY
9500 Sperry Road
Kirtland, P.O.
Mentor, OH 44060
Mrs. R. H. Norweb, Jr., Librn.
216-946-4400

OREGON

OREGON STATE UNIVERSITY LIBRARY
Corvallis, OR 97331

PENNSYLVANIA

HUNT BOTANICAL LIBRARY
Carnegie-Mellon University
Pittsburgh, PA 15213

LONGWOOD GARDENS LIBRARY
Kennett Square, PA 19348
Librarian
215-388-6741

THE MORRIS ARBORETUM
UNIVERSITY OF PENNSYLVANIA
9414 Meadowbrook Avenue
Philadelphia, PA 19118
Dr. H. L. Li, Sci. Director
215-CH7-5777

PENNSYLVANIA STATE UNIVERSITY
AGRICULTURAL AND BIOLOGICAL SCIENCES
LIBRARY
University Park, PA 16802

THE PENNSYLVANIA HORTICULTURAL SOCIETY,
INC.
325 Walnut St.
Philadelphia, PA 19106
Julie Morris, Librarian
215-922-4801

SOUTH DAKOTA

SOUTH DAKOTA STATE UNIVERSITY
LINCOLN MEMORIAL LIBRARY
Brookings, SD 57006

TENNESSEE

TENNESSEE BOTANICAL GARDENS AND
FINE ARTS CENTER
Cheekwood
Cheek Road
Nashville, TN 37205
Eleanor Steinke, Ed. Director
615-356-3306

STATE UNIVERSITY OF NEW YORK
AGRICULTURAL & TECHNICAL COLL.
W. C. HINKLE MEMORIAL LIBRARY
Alfred, NY 14802

THE HORTICULTURAL SOCIETY OF NEW YORK
128 West 58th Street
New York, NY 10019
Charles D. Webster, President
212-757-0915

TEXAS

TEXAS A & I UNIVERSITY
CITRUS CENTER LIBRARY
P.O. Box 2000
Weslaco, TX 78596

TEXAS

VIRGINIA

THE AMERICAN HORTICULTURAL SOCIETY
HAROLD B. TUKEY MEMORIAL LIBRARY
Mount Vernon, VA 22121

VIRGINIA

THE AMERICAN HORTICULTURAL SOCIETY

WASHINGTON

UNIVERSITY OF WASHINGTON ARBORETUM
Seattle, WA 98105

ONTARIO, CANADA

CIVIC GARDEN CENTRE LIBRARY
Metro Toronto Edwards Gardens
777 Lawrence Ave., East
Don Mills, Ontario, Canada M3C 1P2
416-445-1552

ROYAL BOTANICAL GARDENS
Box 399
Hamilton, Ontario, Canada L8N 3H8
Librarian
416-527-1158

OUTDOOR GARDENING

Whether they grow vegetables in the East or ornamentals on the Coast, all outdoor gardeners share an eye for the weather and a determination to work their piece of earth no matter what little tricks nature may play. They are at the mercy of storm and drought, insects, disease and pollution. But year after year the number of gardeners plowing up lawns and breaking new ground for cultivation continues to grow.

Most of the material in THE GARDENER'S CATALOGUE relates directly to gardening out-of-doors. So, here we are only going to comment in the most general way.

Selecting a site is important. It is easier to culture plants in rich humus than in stoney hard scrabble soils. There should be water nearby—it weighs about eight pounds a gallon and is no fun to carry on hot summer days. If there are trees nearby, try to locate the portions of the garden that need full sunlight beyond the moving shadows cast by the trees.

If your place is small, or conditions are poor, plan your garden within the limits of these conditions and gradually work to improve them. We have seen flower gardens blooming in the desert and vegetable patches cut from dense forests. It just takes work, perseverance, and acquired know-how. The first two steps you must generate yourself. The Catalogue should help with the third. At the very least, it should help you to formulate the questions and steer you to the kinds of people in your region who can help you. Generally, your State Extension Service will have more information relevant to your particular locale than the national organizations can provide. However, both tend to suggest the use of pesticides and chemical fertilizers to promote high yields in commercial applications. If you prefer to garden organically, extract the information you want from these sources and supplement it from specialized organic-gardening publications.

The best information by far, though, still comes from concerned local gardeners with the same dirt under their fingernails that you have under yours. Give it a few years and you'll find yourself becoming an expert on local weather, insects and soil.

There is great joy being in tune with the subtle, ever-changing relationships of nature. If enough people would coax the soil and nurture plants, it would be possible to reverse the dramatic deterioration in our environment. Together a mass of gardeners in one area could potentially create a new mini-micro-climate where the stench of industry would be replaced by the clean fragrance of greenery and man will feel at home on his own ground again.

So, cultivate your own garden, organize locally and stay in touch.

Professional, Semi-professional and Trade Associations

There are many organizations of people whose primary occupation relates to horticulture. These groups are diverse and differ widely in their orientation. Some are membership organizations welcoming participation of individuals, clubs and other appropriate groups. Some publish periodicals of interest to horticulturists, and these major publications are listed. Frequently, these horticultural organizations, institutions and centers offer services and/or programs to the horticultural community. They are either national or broadly regional in scope and have a substantial influence on American horticulture.

ALL-AMERICA GLADIOLUS SELECTIONS
3008 Centralia Court
Jeffersonville, IN 47130
George W. Lasch, Dir. Publ. Inf.
812-944-1487

ALL-AMERICA ROSE SELECTIONS, INC.
Box 218
Shenandoah, IA 51601
George E. Rose, Dir., Pub. Rel.
712-246-2884

ALL-AMERICA SELECTIONS
Box 1
Gardenville, PA 18926
Derek Fell, Director
215-794-8187

AMERICAN ASSOCIATION OF BOTANICAL
GARDENS AND ARBORETA
Department of Horticulture
New Mexico State University
Las Cruces, NM 88003
Dr. Fred B. Widmoyer, Sec-Trs.
505-646-1521
AMERICAN ASSN. OF BOTANICAL GARDENS
& ARBORETA BULLETIN (quarterly)

AMERICAN ASSOCIATION OF NURSERYMEN, INC.
230 Southern Building
Washington, D.C. 20005
Robert F. Lederer, Exec. V.P.
202-737-4060

AMERICAN INSTITUTE OF BIOLOGICAL
SCIENCES
3900 Wisconsin Avenue, N.W.
Washington, D.C. 20016
Dr. John R. Olive, Director
202-244-5581
BIO-SCIENCE (monthly)

AMERICAN POMOLOGICAL SOCIETY
103 Tyson Building
University Park, PA 16802
Dr. Loren D. Tukey, Sec-Treas
814-805-2572
$8.00 yr. includes
FRUIT VARIETIES JOURNAL (quarterly)

AMERICAN SEED TRADE ASSN.
Executive Building
Suite 964
1030 15th Street, Northwest
Washington, D.C. 20005
Harold D. Loden, Exec. V.P.
202-223-4080
YEARBOOK AND PROCEEDINGS (annually)

AMERICAN SOCIETY OF CONSULTING ARBORISTS
12 Lakeview Avenue
Milltown, NJ 08850
201-821-8948
THE CONSULTING ARBORIST (bimonthly)
Specializing in answers to botanical and
legal tree problems.

AMERICAN SOCIETY OF LANDSCAPE
ARCHITECTS
1750 Old Meadow Road
McLean, VA 22101
Robert Bennett, Administrator
LANDSCAPE ARCHITECTURE (quarterly)

AMERICAN SOCIETY OF PLANT PHYSIOLOGISTS
9650 Rockville Pike
Bethesda, MD 20014
Dr. Houston Baker, Bus. Exec.
301-530-2745
PLANT PHYSIOLOGY (monthly)

SOCIETY OF AMERICAN FORESTERS
1010 16th Street, Northwest
Washington, D.C. 20036
H. R. Glascock, Jr., Exec. V.P.
JOURNAL OF FORESTRY (monthly)
FOREST SCIENCE (quarterly)

SOIL SCIENCE SOCIETY OF AMERICA
677 South Segoe Street
Madison, WI 53711
Dr. Matthias Stelly, Exec. V.P.
608-274-1212
SOIL SCIENCE SOCIETY OF AMERICA
PROCEEDINGS (bimonthly)

SOUTHERN NURSERYMEN'S ASSOCIATION
3813 Hillsboro Road
Nashville, TN 37215
Thomas L. Henegar, Exec. Sec.
615-383-5674

SWEET POTATO COUNCIL OF THE
UNITED STATES, INC.
Dept. of Agric. Economics
University of Maryland
College Park, MD 20742
Harold H. Hoecker
301-454-3805

THE AMERICAN INSTITUE OF CROP ECOLOGY
809 Dale Drive
Silver Spring, MD 20910
Dr. M. Y. Nuttonson
301-589-4185

VEGETABLE GROWERS ASSOCIATION
OF AMERICA
1616 H Street, Northwest
Washington, D.C. 20006
A. E. Mercker, Exec. Sec.
202-638-0656
VGAA NEWS (monthly)

WEED SCIENCE SOCIETY OF AMERICA
113 North Neil Street
425 Illinois Building
Champaign, IL 61820
C.J. Cruse, Business Manager
217-356-3182
WEED SCIENCE (bimonthly)

WESTERN ASSOCIATION OF NURSERYMEN
9305 Vaughn Street
Raytown, MO 64133
Mrs. Pat Klapis, Exec. Sec.
816-353-1203

WHOLESALE NURSERY GROWERS OF
AMERICA, INC.
230 Southern Building
Washington, D.C. 20005

INTERNATIONAL SHADE TREE CONFERENCE, INC.
Box 71
3 Lincoln Square
Urbana, IL 61801
E. C. Bundy, Exec. Sec.
217-328-2032
ARBORIST'S NEWS (monthly)

MAIL ORDER ASSOCIATION OF NURSERYMEN
Roachdale, IN 46172
Wm. H. Wilson, Sec.-Treas.
317-596-3455

NATIONAL AGRICULTURAL CHEMICALS
ASSOCIATION
1155 15th Street, Northwest
Washington, D.C. 20005
Parke C. Brinkley, President
202-296-1585

NATIONAL ARBORIST ASSOCIATION
1750 Old Meadow Road
McLean, VA 22101
Robert C. LaGasse, Exec. Sec.

NATIONAL ASSN. OF PLANT PATENT
OWNERS, INC.
230 Southern Building
Washington, D.C. 20005

NATIONAL CHRISTMAS TREE ASSOC.
225 East Michigan Street
Milwaukee, WI 53202
Donald McNeil, Exec. Sec.
414-276-6410
AMERICAN CHRISTMAS TREE JOURNAL
(quarterly)

NATIONAL GARDEN BUREAU
Box 1
Gardenville, PA 18926
Derek Fell
215-794-8187

NATIONAL LANDSCAPE ASSOCIATION, INC.
230 Southern Building
Washington, D.C. 20005

NATIONAL PEACH COUNCIL
231 N. Tennessee Ave.
Martinsburg, WV 25401
Robert K. Phillips
304-267-6024
Mailing Address:
P.O. Box 1085
Martinsburg, WV 25401

NATIONAL RECREATION AND PARK ASSOCIATION
1601 North Kent Street
Arlington, VA 22209
Dwight F. Rettie, Exec. Sec.
703-525-0606
PARKS AND RECREATION MAGAZINE (monthly)

NEW ENGLAND NURSERYMEN'S ASSOCIATION
50 New Street
West Haven, CT 06516
Charles Barr, Exec. Sec.
203-934-2653

POTATO ASSOCIATION OF AMERICA
University of Maine
Orono, ME 04473
Hugh Murphy, Secretary
AMERICAN POTATO JOURNAL (monthly)

PROFESSIONAL GROUNDS MANAGEMENT
SOCIETY
1750 Old Meadow Road
McLean, VA 22101
703-893-7787

SOCIETY OF AMERICAN FLORISTS
901 North Washington Street
Alexandria, VA 22314
John H. Walker, Exec. V.P.
703-836-8700

AMERICAN SOCIETY OF PLANT TAXONOMISTS
Department of Botany
Duke University
Durham, NC 27706
D. E. Stone
919-684-2019
BRITTONIA (quarterly)

ASSOC. LANDSCAPE CONTRACTORS OF
AMERICA, INC.
1750 Old Meadow Road
McLean, VA 22101
Thomas Hal Stewart, Exec. Dir.
703-893-5440

BETTER LAWN AND TURF INSTITUTE
Route 4
Kimberdale
Maryville, OH 43040
Dr. Robert W. Schery, Dir.
513-642-1777

BOTANICAL SOCIETY OF AMERICA
Rutgers University
New Brunswick, NJ 08903
Barbara F. Palser, Secretary
201-932-2847
AMERICAN JOURNAL OF BOTANY (monthly,
except bi-monthly May/June, Nov/Dec.)
PLANT SCIENCE BULLETIN (quarterly)

DEL-MAR-VA ASSOCIATION OF NURSERYMEN
Bunting's Nurseries, Inc.
Selbyville, DE 19110
Harold Timmons, Sec.-Treas.
302-436-8231

EASTERN REGIONAL NURSERYMEN'S
ASSOCIATION
101 Executive Boulevard
Elmsford, NY 10523
John A. Richards, Exec. Dir.

ECOLOGICAL SOCIETY OF AMERICA
Department of Botany
University of North Carolina
Chapel Hill, NC 27514
Dr. Frank McCormick

ENTOMOLOGICAL SOCIETY OF AMERICA
4603 Calvert Road
College Park, MD 20740
Wallace P. Murdoch, Exec. Sec.
301-864-1334
JOURNAL OF ECONOMIC ENTOMOLOGY
(bimonthly);
ANNALS OF THE ESA (bimonthly)
ENVIRONMENTAL ENTOMOLOGY (bimonthly)

FEDERATED PECAN GROWERS ASSOCIATION
OF THE U.S.
Box AX
Louisiana State Univ. Station
Baton Rouge, LA 70803
Dr. W. A. Meadows, Sec.-Treas.
504-388-2222

GARDEN CENTERS OF AMERICA, INC.
230 Southern Building
Washington, D.C. 20005

GARDEN WRITERS ASSOCIATION OF AMERICA
101 Park Avenue
Room 607
New York, NY 10017
Margaret Herbst, Exec. Sec.
212-685-5917
GWAA BULLETIN (quarterly)

HORTICULTURAL RESEARCH INSTITUTE, INC.
230 Southern Building
Washington, D.C. 20005

INTERNATION PLANT PROPAGATORS' SOCIETY
P.O. Box 209
Milltown, NJ 08850
Wm. E. Snyder, Sec.-Treas.
THE PLANT PROPAGATOR (quarterly)

Garden Tools

GARDEN ROLLER.

Tools include Landside Plow, 3-tooth Cultivator, 1-tooth Cultivator, Furrow-maker, Scuffle Hoe.

GARDEN TOOLS, EQUIPMENT AND OTHER SUPPLIES

American Honda Motor Co.,
Power Products Div.,
Box 50,
Gardena, Calif. 90247

Amerind-MacKissic,
Box 111,
Parker Ford, Penna. 19457

AMF Lawn & Garden Div.,
3811 McDonald Ave.,
Des Moines, Iowa 50302

Ariens Co.,
655 W. Ryan St.,
Brillion, Wisc. 54110

Atlas Tool & Mfg. Co.,
5151 Natural Bridge Ave.,
St. Louis, Mo. 63115

Auto-Hoe,
South 3rd St.,
De Pere Wisc., 54115

Billy Goat,
Box 229,
Grandview, Mo. 64030

J. I. Case Co.,
Outdoor Power Equip. Div.,
Winneconne, Wisc. 54986

Columbia,
Box 2741,
Cleveland, Ohio 44111

Deere & Co.,
John Deere Rd.,
Moline, Ill. 61265

Edko Mfg.,
2725 2nd Ave.,
Des Moines, Iowa 50313

Engineering Products Co.,
1525 Ellis St.,
Waukesha, Wisc., 53186

FMC Corp.,
Outdoor Power Equip. Div.,
Box 249,
Port Washington, Wisc. 53074

Feldmann Engineering Co.,
639 Monroe St.,
Sheboygan Falls, Wisc. 53084

Ford Motor Co.,
Tractor & Implement Opns.,
2500 E. Maple Rd.,
Troy, Mich. 48084

Formway Co.,
224 Ahwanee,
Sunnyvale, Calif. 94086

Geiger Corp.,
Box 385,
Harleysville, Penna. 19438

General Electric Co.,
Outdoor Power Equipment,
Corporation Park, Bldg. 702,
Schenectady, N.Y. 12345

Gilson Bros.,
Box 152,
Plymouth, Wisc. 53073

Graveley Div.,
1 Graveley Ln.,
Clemmons, N.C. 27012

Hahn, Inc.,
1625 N. Garvin St.,
Evansville, Ind. 47717

Heald, Inc.,
Box 1148,
Benton Harbor, Mich. 49022

Hesston Lawn Equipment Div.,
8640 Brookville Rd.,
Indianapolis, Ind. 46239

Homelite Div.,
70 Riverdale Ave.,
Port Chester, N.Y. 10476

Howard Rotavator Co.,
Box 100,
Harvard, Ill. 60033

Huffman Mfg. Co.,
Box 1204,
Dayton, Ohio 45401

International Harvester Co.,
401 N. Michigan Ave.,
Chicago, Ill. 60611

Jacobsen Mfg. Co.
1721 Packard Ave.,
Racine, Wisc. 53403

Kees Mfg. Co.,
Box 8,
Beatrice, Nebr. 68310

Kemp Shredder Co.,
Box 6275,
Erie, Penna. 16512

Kubota Tractor Corp.,
300 W. Carole St.,
Compton, Calif. 90220

Lickity Div.,
Box 605,
Piqua, Ohio 45403

Lindig Mfg. Corp.,
1875 W. County Rd.,
St. Paul, Minn. 55113

Little Wonder Div.,
1028 Street Rd.,
Southampton, Penna. 18966

Magna American Corp.,
Box 90,
Raymond, Miss. 39154

Massey-Ferguson,
1901 Bell Ave.,
Des Moines, Iowa 50315

M-B Company,
1609-23 Wisconsin Ave.,
New Holstein, Wisc. 53061

McDonough Power Equipment,
McDonough, Ga. 30253

McGraw-Edison Co.,
Portable Electric Tools Div.,
1200 E. State St.,
Geneva, Ill. 60134

Merry Mfg. Co.,
Box 370,
Edmonds, Wash. 98020

Mitts & Merrill,
109 McCoskry St.,
Saginaw, Mich. 48601

Mono Mfg. Co.,
Box 2787,
Springfield, Mo. 65802

Mtd Products,
5389 W. 130th St.,
Box 2741,
Cleveland, Ohio 44111

Ohio Steel Fabricators,
2575 Ferris Rd.,
Columbus, Ohio 43224

Oregon Mfg. Co.,
6920 SW 111th,
Beaverton, Ore. 97005

Osborne Mfg. Co.,
Box 29,
Osborne, Kans. 67473

Planet Jr. Div.,
4910 S. Boyle,
Los Angeles, Calif. 90058

Red Cross Mfg.,
Box 317,
Bluffton, Ind. 45714

Roof Mfg. Co.,
1011 W. Howard St.,
Pontiac, Ill. 61764

Root Mfg. Co.,
Box 191,
Baxter Springs, Kans. 66713

Roper Sales Corp.,
1905 W. Court St.,
Kankakee, Ill. 60901

Roto-Hoe Co.,
Box 10,
Newbury, Ohio 44065

Rowe Mfg. Co.,
614 W. 3rd St.,
Galesburg, Ill. 61401

Royer Foundry & Machine Co.,
158 Pringle St.,
Kingston, Penna 18704

Rysdyk Associates,
1 W. Red Oak Ln.,
White Plains, N.Y. 10604

The Sensation Corp.,
7577 Burlington St.,
Ralston, Nebr. 68127

Speedex Tractor Co.,
367 N. Freedom St.,
Ravenna, Ohio 44266

Solo Motors, Inc.,
Box 5030,
Newport News, Va. 23605

Simplicity Mfg. Co.,
500 N. Spring St.,
Port Washington, Wisc. 53074

Sunbeam Outdoor Co.,
Box 430,
Manning, S. C.

Toro Co.,
8111 Lyndale Ave. S.,
Bloomington, Minn. 55420

Tradewinds, Inc.,
2331 S. Tacoma Ave.,
Tacoma, Wash. 98402

Vandermolen Corp.,
119 Dorsa Ave.,
Livingston, N.J. 07039

Village Blacksmith Div.
1200 E. State St.,
Geneva, Ill. 60134

Wheel-Horse Products,
515 W. Ireland Rd.,
South Bend, Ind. 46614

Winona Attrition Mill,
1009 W. 5th St.,
Winona, Minn. 55987

W-W Grinder Corp.,
2957 N. Market,
Wichita, Kans. 67219

Yard-Man,
1410 W. Ganson St.,
Jackson, Mich. 49202

Alsto Co.,
11052 Peal Rd.,
Cleveland, Ohio 44136

American Science Center,
5700 Northwest Hwy.,
Chicago, Ill. 60644

Aqua-Pots,
7602 30th St. W.,
Tacoma, Wash. 98466

Ward Brook,
East Candia, N.H. 03040

Chapin Watermatics,
368 N. Colorado Ave.,
Watertown, N.Y. 13601

B. Courtman,
Cambridge Springs, Penna. 16403

Jorge Epstein,
487 Norfolk St.,
Mattapn, Maine 02126

Garden Way,
Charlotte, Vt. 05445

Bernard D. Greeson,
3548 N. Cramer St.,
Milwaukee, Wisc. 53211

Havahart,
Box 551
Ossining, N.Y. 10562

A. H. Hummert Co.,
2746 Chouteau Ave.,
St. Louis, Mo. 63103

Hydroponic Chemical Co.,
Box 4300,
Copley, Ohio 44321

Jupiter Mfg. Co.,
Box 297,
Kearney, N.J. 07032

A. M. Leonard & Son,
Piqua, Ohio, 45356

Lilly's Garden,
510 S. Fulton Ave.,
Mount Vernon, N.Y. 10550

R. McKinney,
Box 553,
Concord, Maine 01742

TREES AND SHRUBS

When the hordes of European settlers washed ashore, the American landscape was lush with trees. Verdant forests stretched from the Atlantic shore, over the mountains, towards the Great Plains.

Trees were revered in an almost mystical fashion, appearing as symbols on many revolutionary flags. It was only natural. Trees have provided food, shelter and beauty for man wherever they could sink their roots together.

But, trees also provided the fuel and raw material for the Age of Wood—a time when craftsmen were so sophisticated in its use that a tool as simple as a rake might be made of three or four different kinds of wood.

As the settlers flooded across the continent, forests were ravaged at an ever-increasing rate. By the 1880's, when New England paper barons were in the process of defoliating Michigan, an eminent visiting historian felt obliged to comment that there is something in Americans that hated trees.

Flying across the United States today, looking down at the landscape below, seems to confirm that opinion. The vast forests have vanished. Farms and housing developments have mushroomed up where trees once stood.

Recent developments are gouged from the earth by bulldozers. They are devoid of trees. Trees that replenish the oxygen, purify the ground water, screen us from wind, provide shade from the sun, and act as buffers to reduce noise, like silent natural air conditioners.

Indeed, the lawns and flowerbeds of annuals that surround these homes, however beautiful, symbolize the temporary nature of our lives.

Maybe it's the initial cost, or maybe the pressures that drive Americans to move so frequently from place to place that leads them to ignore the value of permanent woody material when planning their gardens. But, by planting trees and shrubs which in most cases should outlive them, gardeners demonstrate their generous nature—leaving great gifts for the future. So . . .

PLANT A TREE COME SPRING

Trees are nature's strongest plants. Growing and maintaining them is relatively easy. Whether you plant a coy dwarf fruit tree in the center of your lawn, or decide to reforest that vacant lot across the road, the basic steps are the same.

Handy tools for the job can include a wheelbarrow, a shovel or spade, a bucket or garden-hose, wire, mesh, tin snips and a tree wrap. You should also have peatmoss and fertilizer on hand.

Trees generally come from the nursery in three forms: bare root, container grown or, B & B (balled and burlaped). It is best to get them in the ground as soon as possible. But, if you are forced to hold them for a while, soak the roots overnight in thick muddy water. This is especially important with bare root stock.

The hardest job when planting a tree is digging the hole. It should be large enough to allow the roots to spread into a natural position. For B & B or container stock, dig the hole so that it is about two feet wider than the rootball.

It is very important to set the trees in the soil at the same depth they grew to in the nursery. You will find a clear soil or separation mark on the tree trunk. It should remain at ground level.

Dig a hole about 18 inches deep and fill it with water to test drainage. If, after 36 hours, water is still in the hole, the drainage is not good enough.

In clay or hardpan soil add a foot to the dimensions of the hole and line it with stone or shards of broken pots to help drainage.

Backfill with topsoil or a mixture of loam, peatmoss and compost. Remember to use enough fill to bring the plant up to the same level it grew to at the nursery. Soak the soil with water and cover the rootball leaving a slightly dished bed extending as far from the trunk as possible. Water again to settle the soil. Mulch the dish. Where sunscald could be a danger, wrap the trunk of the tree with burlap strips in an overlapping spiral. Tie it at approximately 18-inch intervals.

To avoid wind damage to your freshly transplanted trees, drive a strong post into the ground six to ten inches from the trunk. Fasten the tree to the post with a length of wire wrapped in old gardening hose. Larger trees of over 3-inch diameters should be supported by guy-wires. Drive one stake in the direction of the prevailing winds, drive two more stakes to form a triangle and tie wire wrapped in gardenhose to the tree forming a pyramid. Guy-wires should remain from one to four years depending on the size of the transplant.

—Disciflorae.

REFOREST AMERICA

Where animals are a problem, wrap wire mesh around saplings to protect them. But, be sure to leave them enough room to grow. Some claim a layer of aluminum strips also works. Others favor a coating of lard and cayenne pepper. While still others use commercial chemical preparations.

Water every two or three days when rainfall is limited. Avoid over watering or your new tree will stagnate. Fertilize according to the needs of each particular plant.

The same rules apply generally to shrubs. Though most are not as long lived as trees, they must be thought of as permanent garden residents.

Select your trees and shrubs, kekeping this in mind. Try to visualize what they will look like all year round. They will be with you for many seasons.

But, now we're getting into the topic of landscaping. That's a whole other chapter.

FREE TREES

IF YOU ARE REALLY INTERESTED IN LARGE-SCALE TREE PLANTING, SEEDLINGS ARE GENERALLY AVAILABLE AT NO COST FROM STATE CONSERVATION BUREAUS.

1 Dig the hole a foot deeper than the height of the roots, and twice as wide as the root span, or the rootball. Loosen several inches of soil at the bottom of the hole to facilitate drainage.

2 Add soil to the hole and build it up in a mound beneath the plant, so that the plant sits at the same level as before it was moved.

1 Before you start to dig, go out 1 foot for each inch of trunk diameter.

2 Dig with the back of the spade toward the plant to avoid prying up uncut roots. After the rootball is cut, trim and shape the ball, and undercut the roots.

3 Fill three-fourths of the hole with soil, then water.

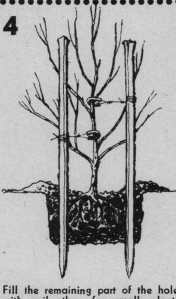

4 Fill the remaining part of the hole with soil, then for small plants drive in stakes to secure them. For securing large plants, use guy wires, see page 11.

3 Tip the ball and tuck a roll of burlap under it. Tip the ball in the opposite direction; unroll and pull the burlap under the ball.

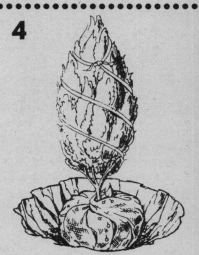

4 Pin the burlap together with nails. If the soil is especially dry and crumbling, further secure the burlap with a nylon cord or small rope. Do not lift the plant by its trunk or branches. Lift small plants by the rootball and larger ones by prying up with 2 spades.

To assist in the identification of trees, a simplified key, based chiefly upon leaves and twigs, has been inserted in the text. This key is an outline in which trees with certain characteristics in common are grouped together. The name of a tree specimen is found by elimination through successive selection of one from a pair of groups, with descriptive characters that fit the specimen. The paired groups are designated by the same letter, single and double, beginning with "A" and "AA," at the left of the page. Under the group fitting the specimen, the elimination continues with the next paired groups indented below, such as from "AA" to "N" or "NN" and from "NN" to "O" or "OO," the pair next indented to the right, until the name is reached. Some descriptive notes applying to a genus have been inserted in the key and not repeated in the notes under each species. The key is limited to the tree species represented here and will not serve to identify other trees. Identifications, of course, may be made directly from the drawings, maps, and descriptive notes, without use of the key.

The arrangement of species in the lists of eastern and western trees is artificial, to fit the key, rather than botanical. In each list the conifers are placed first, sorted into those with needlelike leaves and those with scale-like leaves, followed by broadleaf trees. The latter are grouped into trees with paired (opposite) simple leaves, trees with paired (opposite) compound leaves, trees with single (alternate) compound leaves, and trees with single (alternate) simple leaves, with the oaks placed last. (A compound leaf is divided into leaflets, which usually are smaller than leaves and are attached on a common leafstalk that sheds with them. Also, the leaf has a developing bud at its base, while the leaflets of a compound leaf do not.)

Various handbooks, manuals, and other publications may be consulted for the identification of the trees of the United States, especially those not found here, and for additional information. A list of 30 references for identification of trees, both popular and technical, including the illustrated books on the commoner trees of the United States and books on the trees of geographic regions, will be found in the bibliography. Trees are described also in the various botanical floras and manuals, usually technical and without illustrations, which have been prepared for geographical regions, single States, or smaller areas.

The State forester can furnish information about publications on the trees of your State and how to obtain them.

To identify with certainty the numerous kinds of native trees, some of which differ but slightly, some knowledge of systematic botany or dendrology as well as of the technical terminology is desirable. Properly prepared dried and pressed botanical specimens of twigs with leaves and flowers or fruits may be submitted for identification to specialists, such as to departments of botany and schools of forestry in universities and colleges, to botanical gardens, herbaria, and museums, or to the United States Department of Agriculture. Specimens should be accompanied by notes, such as locality where found, collector's name, date, size, whether wild or planted, and other data of interest. Material for the Department of Agriculture may be sent to either of the following: Forest Service, Washington 25, D. C.; or Bureau of Plant Industry, Soils, and Agricultural Engineering, Plant Industry Station, Beltsville, Md.

On the next two pages are indexes of common and scientific names of the species discussed on pages 768-814. Thus, a reader who wishes to look up pecan finds that it has the number 41 in the index of common names. By going through the list, he finds pecan described on page 780.

Or, if he encounters the scientific name *Carya illinoensis*, he will learn from the index of scientific names that it is number 41 and described (as pecan) on page 780.

INDEX OF COMMON NAMES BY NUMBER

In addition to these accepted common names for the 165 species, lumber names and other common names in use are listed in the text.

INDEX OF SCIENTIFIC NAMES BY NUMBER

Widely used synonyms of these accepted scientific names for the 165 species are mentioned in the text. The numbers refer to the entries on pages 768-814.

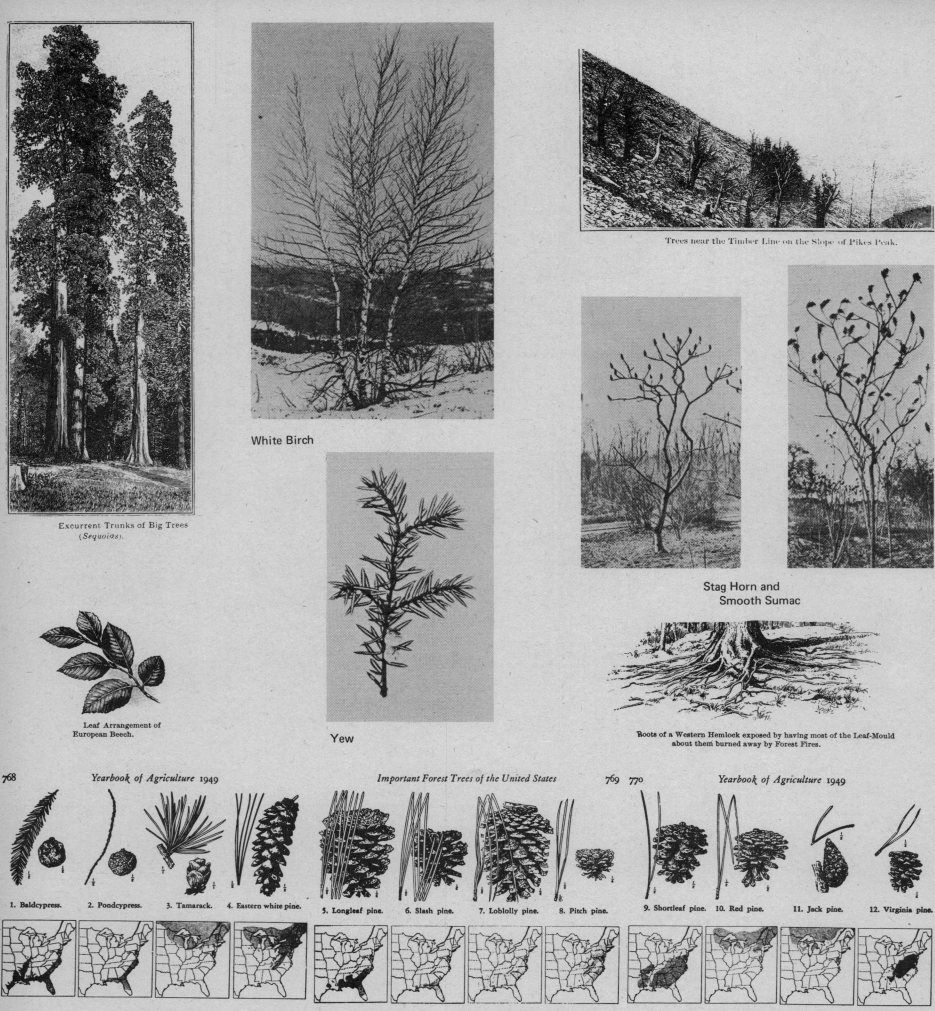

Excurrent Trunks of Big Trees (*Sequoias*).

White Birch

Trees near the Timber Line on the Slope of Pikes Peak.

Stag Horn and Smooth Sumac

Leaf Arrangement of European Beech.

Yew

Roots of a Western Hemlock exposed by having most of the Leaf-Mould about them burned away by Forest Fires.

1. Baldcypress.   2. Pondcypress.   3. Tamarack.   4. Eastern white pine.   5. Longleaf pine.   6. Slash pine.   7. Loblolly pine.   8. Pitch pine.   9. Shortleaf pine.   10. Red pine.   11. Jack pine.   12. Virginia pine.

EASTERN TREES

Tree species Nos. 1 to 100 are native wholly or mainly in the eastern half of the United States, west to the prairie-plains. In addition, species No. 150 in the list of western trees occurs also in the eastern United States.

GYMNOSPERMS (CONIFERS OR SOFTWOODS)

A (AA on p. 774). Trees resinous, with leaves needlelike or scalelike, evergreen (except Nos. 1–3); seeds borne on scales of a cone (berrylike in juniper, Nos. 22, 23)— GYMNOSPERMS (conifers or softwoods, such as pines, spruces, firs).
   B. Leaves shedding in fall, on slender twigs mostly shedding in fall also or on short spur branches.
     C. Leaves needlelike or scalelike, on slender twigs mostly shedding in fall—BALD-CYPRESS (*Taxodium*).

1. BALDCYPRESS, *Taxodium distichum* (L.) Rich. (common baldcypress, southern cypress, red cypress [lumber], yellow cypress [lumber], white cypress [lumber], tidewater red cypress, gulf cypress).
   Large tree with swollen base and "knees," swamps and river banks, South Atlantic and Gulf Coastal Plains and Mississippi Valley. Bark reddish brown or gray, with long fibrous or scaly ridges. Leaves crowded featherlike in two rows on slender horizontal twigs, flat, ⅜ to ¾ inch long, light yellow green, or whitish beneath, shedding in fall. Cones ¾ to 1 inch in diameter, of hard scales.
   Principal uses: Chiefly for building construction and heavy construction. Boxes and crates, caskets, general millwork, and tanks. Also ships and boats, greenhouses, and railroad-car construction. Railroad ties. Ornamental.

2. PONDCYPRESS, *Taxodium ascendens* Brongn. (pond baldcypress, cypress).
   Large tree with swollen base, ponds, swamps, and river banks, South Atlantic and Gulf Coastal Plains. Bark reddish brown or gray, with long fibrous or scaly ridges. Leaves nearly flat against the slender erect twigs, scalelike or needlelike, ⅛ to ⅜ inch long, light yellow green, shedding in fall. Cones ¾ to 1 inch in diameter, of hard scales. (Perhaps only a variety of No. 1.)
   Principal uses: Same as No. 1.

CC. Leaves needlelike, many in cluster on short spur branches—LARCH (or tamarack, *Larix*).

3. TAMARACK, *Larix laricina* (Du Roi) K. Koch (eastern larch, American larch, hackmatack; *L. americana* Michx.).
   Medium-sized tree of wet soils in northeastern United States, and across Canada to Alaska. Bark reddish brown, scaly. Needles many in cluster on short spur branches (or single on leading twigs), 3-angled, ¾ to 1 inch long, blue green, shedding in fall. Cones upright, ½ inch long.
   Principal uses: Lumber (largely framing for houses), and railroad ties. Also ship knees in shipbuilding.

BB. Leaves evergreen, on normal twigs.
   D. Leaves needlelike, more than ½ inch long (usually shorter in No. 17).
     E. Needles in clusters of 2 to 5 with a sheath at base—PINE (*Pinus*).

4. EASTERN WHITE PINE, *Pinus strobus* L. (northern white pine [lumber], white pine, northern pine, soft pine, Weymouth pine).
   Large tree (the largest northeastern conifer) of northeastern United States, adjacent Canada, and Appalachian Mountain region. Bark gray or purplish, deeply fissured into broad ridges. Needles 5 in cluster, slender, 2½ to 5 inches long, blue green. Cones long-stalked, long and narrow, 4 to 8 inches long, yellow brown, with thin, rounded scales.
   Principal uses: Important timber species. Chiefly for boxes, formerly mostly for building construction. Also patterns for castings, millwork, caskets, and many other uses. Shade tree and ornamental. (State tree of Maine and Minnesota.)

FF. Needles 2 or 3 in a cluster—YELLOW (HARD, OR PITCH) PINES.
   G. Needles 3 in cluster.
     H. Needles more than 8 inches long.

5. LONGLEAF PINE, *Pinus palustris* Mill. (southern pine [lumber], longleaf yellow pine, southern yellow pine, pitch pine, hard pine, heart pine; *P. australis* Michx. f.).
   Large tree of South Atlantic and Gulf Coastal Plains. Bark orange brown, coarsely scaly. Needles 3 in cluster, slender, very long, 10 to 15 inches long, dark green. Cones large, 5 to 10 inches long, dull brown, prickly.
   Principal uses: A leading world producer of naval stores. Lumber for miscellaneous factory and construction purposes, flooring, railroad-car construction, shipbuilding.

6. SLASH PINE, *Pinus caribaea* Morelet (southern pine [lumber], Cuban pine, yellow slash pine, swamp pine, pitch pine).
   Large tree of South Atlantic and Gulf Coastal Plains; also in West Indies and Central America. Bark purplish brown, with large thin scales. Needles 3 (or 2 and 3) in cluster, stout, 8 to 12 inches long, dark green. Cones 3 to 6 inches long, shiny brown, with minute prickles.
   Principal uses: Same as No. 5. (State tree of Alabama.)

HH. Needles mostly less than 8 inches long.

7. LOBLOLLY PINE, *Pinus taeda* L. (southern pine [lumber], North Carolina pine [lumber], Arkansas pine [lumber], oldfield pine, shortleaf pine).
   Large tree of Atlantic and Gulf Coastal Plains. Bark reddish brown, deeply fissured into broad scaly plates. Needles 3 in cluster, slender, 6 to 9 inches long, pale green. Cones 3 to 5 inches long, reddish brown, with stiff, sharp prickles.
   Principal uses: Important timber species. Same as No. 9.

8. PITCH PINE, *Pinus rigida* Mill. (southern pine [lumber], southern yellow pine; variety: pond pine, *P. rigida* var. *serotina* (Michx.) Loud.).
   Medium-sized tree of Atlantic coast and Appalachian Mountain regions and in adjacent Canada. Needles 3 in cluster, stout, 3 to 6 inches long (6 to 8 inches in a variety, pond pine), dark yellow green. Cones short and broad, 1½ to 3 inches long, light brown, shiny, with small prickles, remaining on branches several years after opening.
   Principal uses: Fuel and lumber.

GG. Needles 2 in cluster (or partly 3 in No. 9).
   I. Needles more than 3 inches long.

9. SHORTLEAF PINE, *Pinus echinata* Mill. (southern pine [lumber], North Carolina pine [lumber], Arkansas pine [lumber], shortleaf yellow pine, yellow pine, southern yellow pine).
   Large tree of southeastern quarter of United States north to New York. Bark reddish brown, with large, irregular, flat, scaly plates. Needles 2 or 3 in cluster, slender, 2½ to 5 inches long, dark blue green. Cones small, 1½ to 2½ inches long, dull brown, with small prickles.
   Principal uses: Important timber species. Lumber chiefly for building material including millwork, also for boxes and crates, agricultural implements, motor vehicles, low-grade furniture. Veneer for containers. This and other southern pines are the leading native pulpwoods and leading woods in production of slack cooperage. Also

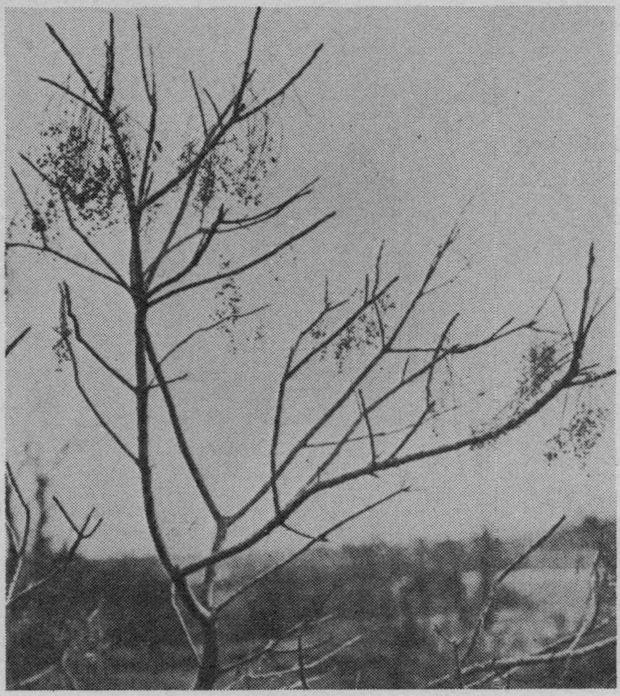

SUMAC

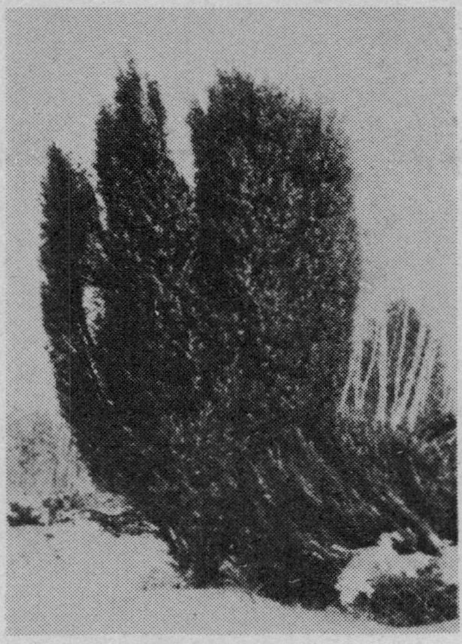

COMMON JUNIPER

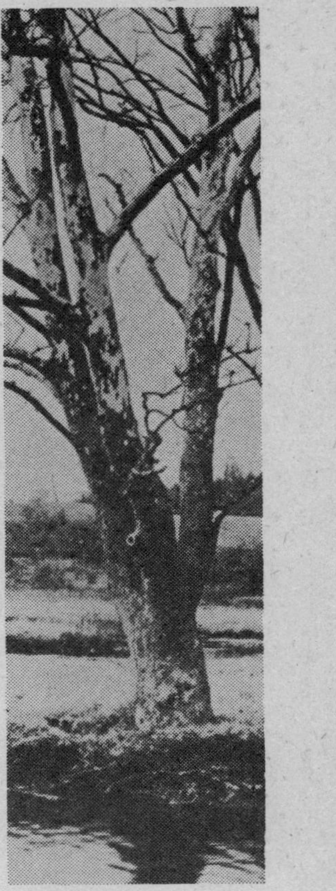

SYCAMORE

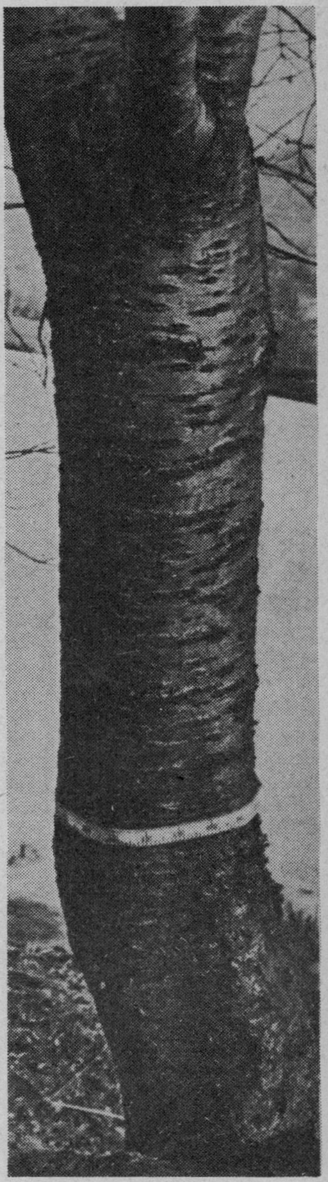

SOUR CHERRY

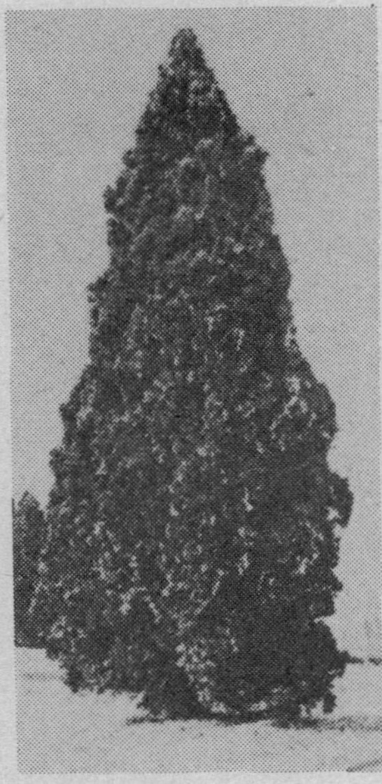

ARBOR UTAH

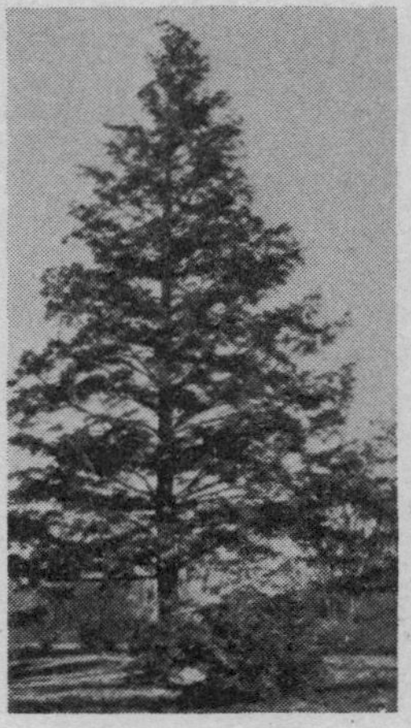

HEMLOCK

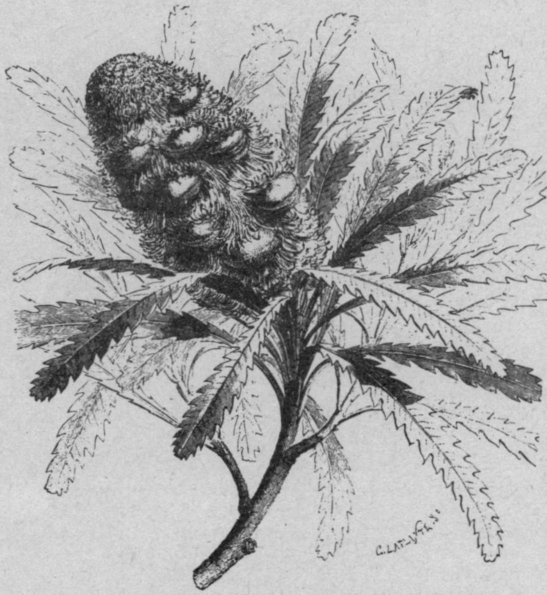

-Flowering branch of *Banksia serrata* with thick-walled dehiscent capsules.

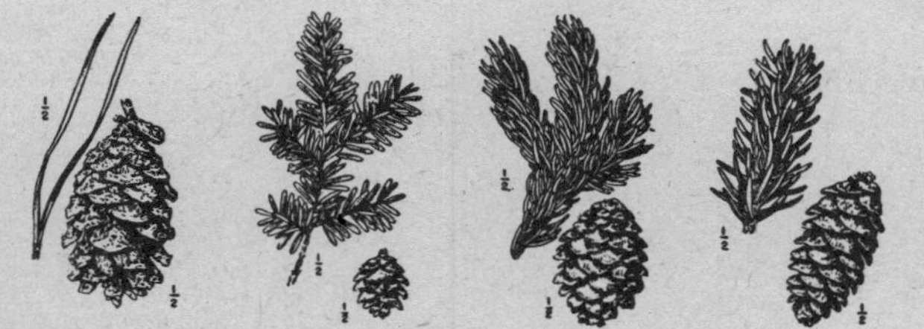

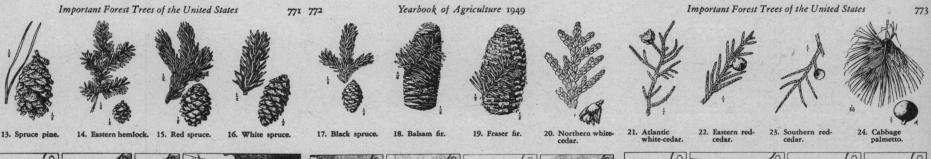

13. Spruce pine. 14. Eastern hemlock. 15. Red spruce. 16. White spruce.

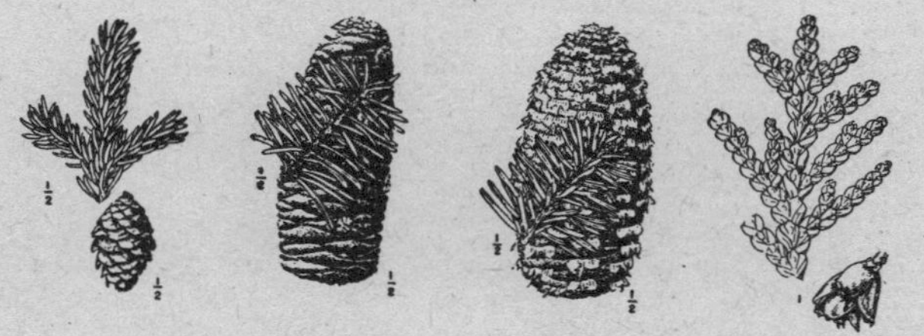

17. Black spruce. 18. Balsam fir. 19. Fraser fir. 20. Northern white-cedar.

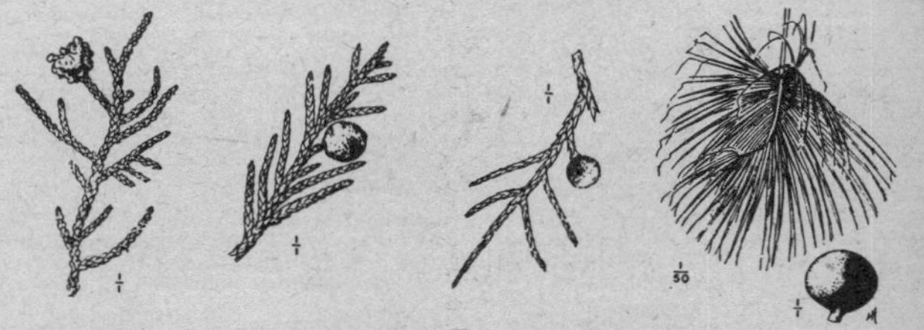

21. Atlantic white-cedar. 22. Eastern red-cedar. 23. Southern red-cedar. 24. Cabbage palmetto.

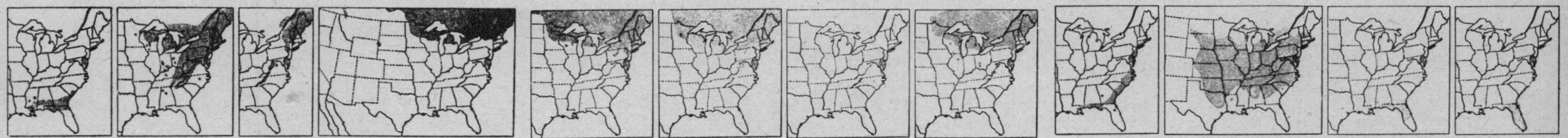

railroad ties, poles, piling, mine timbers, excelsior, and veneer. Ornamental. (Pine (*Pinus* spp.) is the State tree of Arkansas.)

10. RED PINE, *Pinus resinosa* Ait. (Norway pine [lumber]).

Medium-sized to large tree of northeastern United States and adjacent Canada. Bark reddish brown, with broad, flat, scaly plates. Needles 2 in cluster, slender, 5 to 6 inches long, dark green. Cones 2 inches long, light brown, without prickles.

Principal uses: General building construction, planing-mill products, general millwork, and boxes and crates. Pulpwood. Ornamental and shade tree.

II. Needles less than 3 inches long.

11. JACK PINE, *Pinus banksiana* Lamb. (scrub pine, gray pine, black pine).

Usually small (or medium-sized) tree of northeastern United States and nearly across Canada. Bark dark brown, with narrow scaly ridges. Needles 2 in cluster, stout, twisted, $\frac{3}{4}$ to $1\frac{1}{2}$ inches long, dark green. Cones one-sided, much curved, small, 1 to 2 inches long, light yellow, without prickles, remaining closed at maturity.

Principal uses: Pulpwood, lumber for boxes and crates and rough construction, and fuel. Ornamental.

12. VIRGINIA PINE, *Pinus virginiana* Mill. (North Carolina pine [lumber], Jersey pine, scrub pine).

Usually small tree (sometimes large) of Atlantic Coastal Plain, Appalachian Mountain, and Ohio Valley regions. Bark dark brown, thin, with scaly plates. Needles 2 in cluster, stout, twisted, 2 to 3 inches long, gray green. Cones 2 inches long, reddish brown, shiny, very prickly.

Principal uses: Lumber and fuel.

13. SPRUCE PINE, *Pinus glabra* Walt. (cedar pine, southern white pine).

Medium-sized to large tree of Gulf and South Atlantic Coastal Plains. Bark on small trunks and limbs gray and smooth; bark on large trunks with flat scaly ridges. Needles 2 in cluster, slender, $1\frac{1}{2}$ to 3 inches long, dark green. Cones 1 to 2 inches long, reddish brown, shiny, with minute prickles.

Principal uses: Lumber and fuel.

EE. Needles borne singly and not in clusters.

J. Twigs roughened by projecting bases of old needles; cones hanging down.

K. Needles flat, soft, blunt-pointed, with short leafstalks, appearing in 2 rows—HEMLOCK (*Tsuga*).

14. EASTERN HEMLOCK, *Tsuga canadensis* (L.) Carr. (Canada hemlock, hemlock spruce).

Medium-sized to large tree of northeastern United States, adjacent Canada, and Appalachian Mountain region. Bark brown or purplish, deeply furrowed into broad scaly ridges. Needles short-stalked, flat, soft, blunt-pointed, $\frac{3}{8}$ to $\frac{5}{8}$ inches long, shiny dark green, lighter beneath, appearing in two rows. Cones $\frac{5}{8}$ to $\frac{3}{4}$ inches long, brownish.

Principal uses: Building construction and boxes and crates. Pulpwood. The bark is a source of tannin. Ornamental and shade tree. (State tree of Pennsylvania.)

KK. Needles 4-angled, stiff, sharp-pointed, without leafstalk, extending out on all sides of twig—SPRUCE (*Picea*).

15. RED SPRUCE, *Picea rubens* Sarg. (eastern spruce [lumber], Canadian spruce, yellow spruce, West Virginia spruce; *P. rubra* (Du Roi) Link, not A. Dietr.).

Medium-sized to large tree of northeastern United States, adjacent Canada, and Appalachian Mountain region. Bark reddish brown, thin, scaly. Twigs hairy. Needles 4-angled, $\frac{1}{2}$ inch long, dark green, shiny. Cones $1\frac{1}{4}$ to $1\frac{1}{2}$ inches long, light reddish brown, shiny, with scales rigid, rounded, and with edges smooth or slightly toothed.

Principal uses: Pulpwood. Boxes and crates, construction. Also furniture, millwork, ladder rails. Christmas trees. Ornamental and shade tree.

16. WHITE SPRUCE, *Picea glauca* (Moench) Voss (eastern spruce [lumber], Canadian spruce, skunk spruce, single spruce; *P. canadensis* (Mill.) B. S. P., not (Michx.) Link); variety: western white spruce, *P. glauca* var. *albertiana* (S. Brown) Sarg., Alberta white spruce).

Medium-sized tree of northeastern United States, Black Hills, and across Canada to Alaska. Bark gray or brown, thin, scaly. Twigs without hairs. Needles 4-angled, $\frac{1}{2}$ to $\frac{3}{4}$ inch long, blue green, of disagreeable odor when crushed. Cones slender, $1\frac{1}{2}$ to 2 inches long, pale brown and shiny, with scales thin, flexible, rounded, and with smooth margins.

Principal uses: Same as No. 15. Important timber species of Canada.

17. BLACK SPRUCE, *Picea mariana* (Mill.) B. S. P. (eastern spruce [lumber], bog spruce, swamp spruce).

Small to medium-sized tree of bottom lands and bogs, northeastern United States and across Canada to Alaska. Bark grayish brown, thin, scaly. Twigs hairy. Needles 4-angled, $\frac{1}{4}$ to $\frac{5}{8}$ inch long, pale blue green. Cones $\frac{3}{4}$ to $1\frac{1}{2}$ inches long, dull gray brown, with scales rigid, rounded, and slightly toothed.

Principal uses: Same as No. 15.

JJ. Twigs smooth; cones upright, in top of tree—FIR (*Abies*).

18. BALSAM FIR, *Abies balsamea* (L.) Mill. (eastern fir [lumber], balsam, Canada balsam).

Medium-sized tree of northeastern United States, Appalachian Mountain region, and across Canada to Alberta. Bark gray or brown, thin, smoothish, with many resin blisters, becoming scaly. Needles flat, $\frac{1}{2}$ to $1\frac{1}{4}$ inches long, dark green, usually rounded at tip. Cones upright, 2 to 3 inches long, purple, with cone scales usually covering the bracts.

Principal uses: Pulpwood. Lumber, chiefly for boxes and crates. Canada balsam (an oleoresin). Christmas trees.

19. FRASER FIR, *Abies fraseri* (Pursh) Poir. (balsam fir [lumber], eastern fir [lumber], Fraser balsam fir, southern balsam fir, balsam).

Medium-sized tree of Appalachian Mountains in Virginia, North Carolina, and Tennessee. Bark gray or brown, thin, smoothish, with many resin blisters; bark on larger trunks with thin papery scales. Needles flat, $\frac{1}{2}$ to 1 inch long, dark green, usually rounded at tip. Cones upright, $1\frac{1}{2}$ to $2\frac{1}{2}$ inches long, purple, with yellow-green bracts partly covering the cone scales.

Principal uses: Same as No. 18.

DD. Leaves scalelike, less than $\frac{1}{4}$ inch long (or needlelike and up to $\frac{3}{8}$ inch long on leading shoots).

L. Leafy twigs more or less flattened.

M. Twigs much flattened, about $\frac{1}{8}$ inch broad including leaves—THUJA (*Thuja*).

20. NORTHERN WHITE-CEDAR, *Thuja occidentalis* L. (eastern arborvitae, white-cedar, swamp-cedar, arborvitae).

Medium-sized tree of northeastern United States, adjacent Canada, and Appalachian Mountain region. Bark reddish brown, thin, fibrous, with narrow connecting ridges. Twigs flattened and branching in one plane. Leaves appearing flattened in 2 rows, scalelike, $\frac{1}{16}$ to $\frac{1}{8}$ inch long, light yellow green, aromatic. Cones $\frac{3}{8}$ to $\frac{1}{2}$ inch long, pale brown.

Principal uses: Poles, railroad ties, and posts. Lumber for boxes, millwork, tanks, and building construction. Cedar-oil, used in medicine. Ornamental.

MM. Twigs slightly flattened, less than $\frac{1}{16}$ inch broad including leaves—WHITE-CEDAR (*Chamaecyparis*).

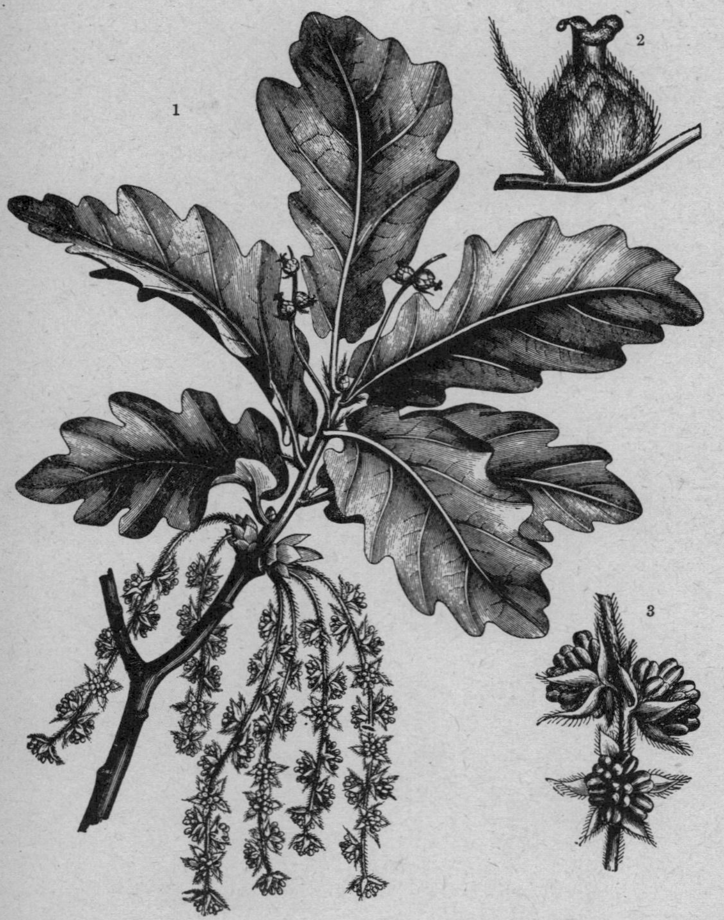

Fig. 286.—Type of a monœcious plant.

[1] Oak (*Quercus pedunculata*); pistillate flowers on the upper part of the twig, staminate flowers (in pendent catkins) below. [2] A single pistillate flower of the same plant. [3] Three staminate flowers of the same plant. [1] nat. size; [2] and [3] × 4.

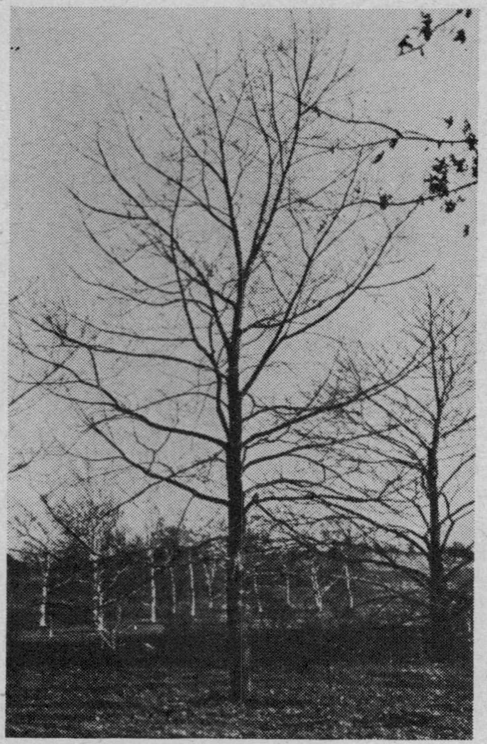

CHESTNUT OAK

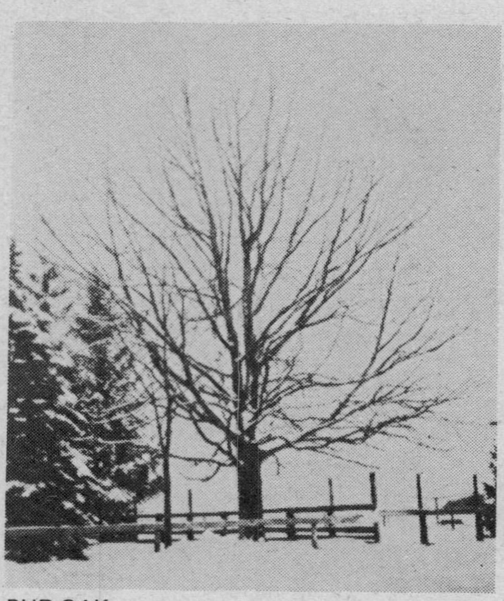

BUR OAK

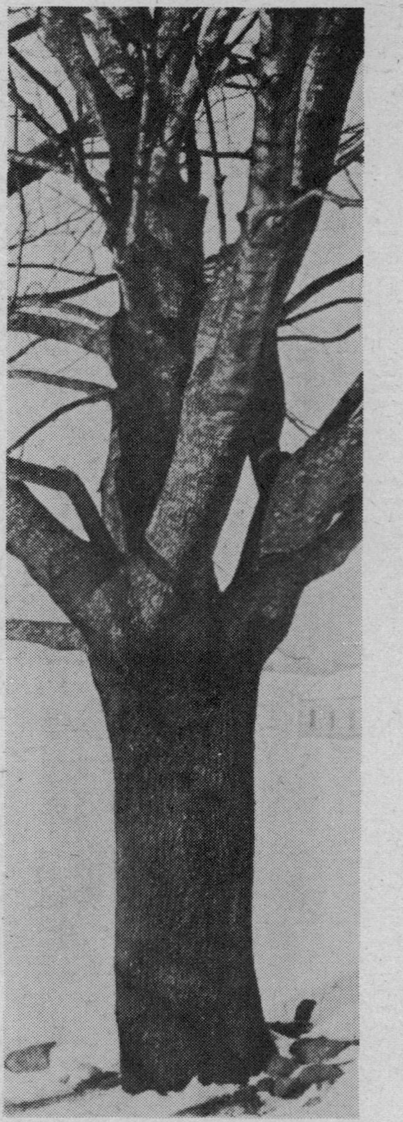

NORWAY MAPLE

21. ATLANTIC WHITE-CEDAR, *Chamaecyparis thyoides* (L.) B. S. P. (southern white-cedar [lumber], white-cedar false-cypress, white-cedar, swamp-cedar, juniper).

Medium-sized tree of swamps, Atlantic and Gulf Coastal Plains. Bark reddish brown, thin, fibrous, with narrow connecting ridges. Leafy twigs slightly flattened (or partly 4-angled). Leaves scalelike, 1/16 to 1/8 inch long, dull blue green. Cones 1/4 inch in diameter, bluish purple, with a bloom.

Principal uses: Lumber for siding, porches, boxes and crates, small boats, and tanks. Woodenware, poles, and shingles. Ornamental. (State tree of New Jersey.)

LL. Leafy twigs rounded or 4-angled—JUNIPER (*Juniperus*).

22. EASTERN REDCEDAR, *Juniperus virginiana* L. (redcedar, red juniper).

Medium-sized tree of eastern half of United States and adjacent Canada. Bark reddish brown, thin, fibrous and shreddy. Leafy twigs rounded or 4-angled, slender. Leaves scalelike, 1/16 inch long, dark blue green, or on leading shoots needlelike, up to 3/8 inch long. "Berry" 1/4 to 3/8 inch in diameter, dark blue.

Principal uses: Fence posts. Lumber for chests, wardrobes, and closet lining. Also flooring and pencils. Cedar-leaf oil is used in medicine and cedar-wood oil in medicine and perfumes. Ornamental and shelterbelts. (State tree of Tennessee.)

23. SOUTHERN REDCEDAR, *Juniperus silicicola* (Small) Bailey (eastern redcedar [lumber]; *J. lucayana* auth.).

Medium-sized tree of South Atlantic and Gulf Coastal Plains. Bark reddish brown, thin, fibrous and shreddy. Leafy twigs rounded or 4-angled, very slender, usually hanging down. Leaves scalelike, 1/16 inch or less in length, dark blue green, or leaves on leading shoots needlelike. "Berry" 3/16 inch or less in diameter, dark blue.

Principal uses: Wood used same as No. 22. Ornamental.

ANGIOSPERMS (FLOWERING PLANTS)

AA (A on p. 768). Trees nonresinous, with leaves broad, shedding in fall in most species (evergreen in palmetto, holly, magnolia, live oak, etc.); seeds enclosed in a fruit—ANGIOSPERMS (flowering plants).

MONOCOTYLEDONS

N. Leaves parallel-veined, evergreen, clustered at top of trunk or large branches; trunk with woody portions irregularly distributed, without clear distinction of bark and wood, and without annual rings—MONOCOTYLEDONS (palms, yuccas, etc.).

24. CABBAGE PALMETTO, *Sabal palmetto* (Walt.) Lodd. (palmetto, cabbage-palm).

Medium-sized palm tree of south Atlantic and Gulf coasts from North Carolina to Florida. Trunk stout and unbranched, grayish brown, roughened or ridged, with a cluster of large leaves at the top. Leaves evergreen, coarse, fan-shaped, 4 to 7 feet long, thick and leathery, much folded and divided into narrow segments with threadlike fibers hanging between. Leafstalks 5 to 8 feet long. Fruits in a much branched cluster about 7 feet long, numerous, 3/8 to 1/2 inch in diameter, black, 1-seeded.

Principal uses: Trunks are used for wharf pilings, docks, and poles. Brushes and whiskbrooms are made from the young leafstalk fibers; baskets, mats, hats, brooms and thatch are made from the leaves. Ornamental. (State tree of Florida and South Carolina.)

DICOTYLEDONS (BROADLEAF TREES OR HARDWOODS)

NN. Leaves net-veined; trunk with bark and wood distinct and with annual rings in wood—DICOTYLEDONS (broadleaf trees, or hardwoods, such as oaks, poplars, ashes, maples).

O (OO on p. 779). Leaves and usually branches in pairs (opposite; or in threes in No. 25).

P. Leaves not divided into leaflets (simple).

Q. Leaf edges smooth, not lobed.

R. Leaves heart-shaped, large, more than 6 inches long, in threes or pairs—CATALPA (*Catalpa*).

25. NORTHERN CATALPA, *Catalpa speciosa* Warder (western catalpa, hardy catalpa, cigartree).

Medium-sized to large tree of lower Ohio Valley and central Mississippi Valley, naturalized elsewhere in eastern United States. Bark reddish brown, with flat, scaly ridges. Leaves in threes or paired, large, heart-shaped, 6 to 12 inches long, long-pointed, edges smooth, thick, dark green above, hairy beneath. Leafstalk 4 to 6 inches long. Flowers large and showy, about 2 inches long, whitish and purple spotted, in few-flowered clusters in late spring. Fruiting capsule cigarlike, long and narrow, 8 to 18 inches long and 5/8 inch thick, dark brown, with many winged seeds.

Principal uses: Fence posts. Shade tree and ornamental. Shelterbelts.

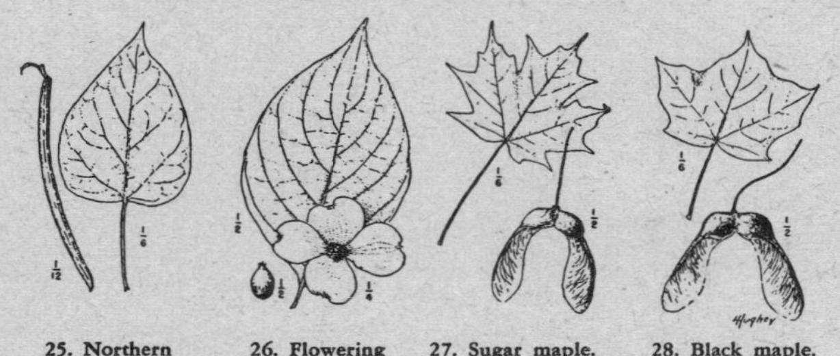

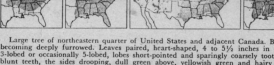

25. Northern catalpa. 26. Flowering dogwood. 27. Sugar maple. 28. Black maple.

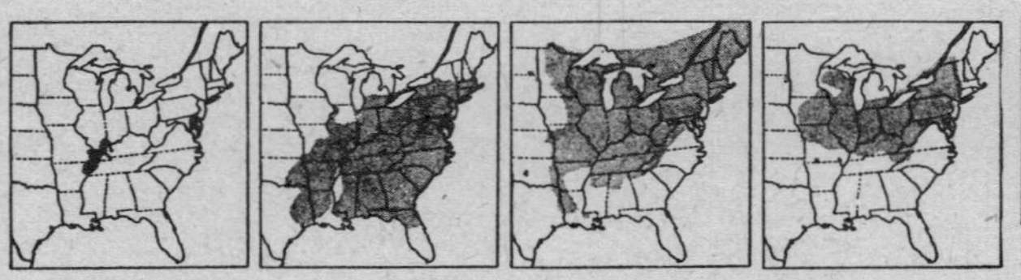

RR. Leaves elliptical, less than 6 inches long—DOGWOOD (*Cornus*).

26. FLOWERING DOGWOOD, *Cornus florida* L. (dogwood, boxwood; *Cynoxylon floridum* (L.) Raf.).

Small tree of eastern half of United States; also in southern Ontario and a variety in northeastern Mexico. Bark dark reddish brown, broken into small square or rounded blocks. Leaves paired, elliptical or oval, 3 to 6 inches long, short-pointed, edges appearing smooth but minutely toothed, lateral veins curved, bright green and nearly smooth above, whitish and slightly hairy beneath, turning bright scarlet above in fall. Flowers greenish yellow, in a dense head with 4 showy, white, petallike bracts 2 1/4 to 4 inches in diameter, in early spring. Fruits egg-shaped, 3/8 inch long, bright scarlet, shiny, fleshy, 1- or 2-seeded.

Principal uses: Important ornamental tree. The outstanding wood for shuttles (used in textile weaving). (Dogwood is the State tree of North Carolina and Virginia.)

QQ. Leaf edges toothed, deeply 3- or 5-lobed (fruit of paired, long-winged "keys")—MAPLE (*Acer*).

S. Teeth of leaves few and blunt—HARD MAPLES.

27. SUGAR MAPLE, *Acer saccharum* Marsh. (hard maple [lumber], rock maple; *A. saccharophorum* K. Koch).

Large tree of eastern half of United States and adjacent Canada. Bark gray, furrowed into irregular ridges or scales. Leaves paired, heart-shaped, 3 to 5 1/2 inches in diameter, 3- or 5-lobed with the lobes long-pointed and sparingly coarsely toothed with few blunt teeth, dark green above, light green or pale and usually smooth beneath, turning yellow, orange, or scarlet in fall. Key fruits 1 to 1 1/4 inches long, maturing in fall.

Principal uses: As a group, the maples rank third in production of hardwood lumber, next to oak and sweetgum, and are among the leading furniture woods. Sugar maple is used for flooring, furniture, boxes and crates, shoe lasts, handles, woodenware and novelties, spools and bobbins, and motor-vehicle parts. Also distillation products, veneer, railroad ties, and pulpwood. Sugar maple is the outstanding wood for flooring under heavy use and is the commercial source of maple sugar and sirup. Much planted as a shade tree. (State tree of New York and Vermont. Maple (*Acer* spp.) is the State tree of Rhode Island and Wisconsin.)

28. BLACK MAPLE, *Acer nigrum* Michx. f. (hard maple [lumber], black sugar maple, sugar maple; *A. saccharum* var. *nigrum* (Michx. f.) Britton).

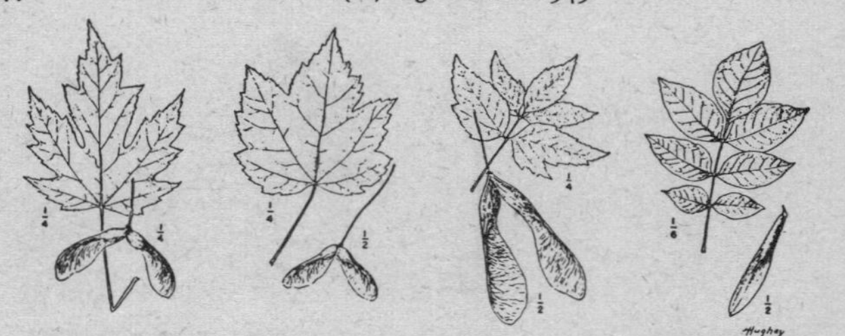

29. Silver maple. 30. Red maple. 31. Boxelder. 32. White ash.

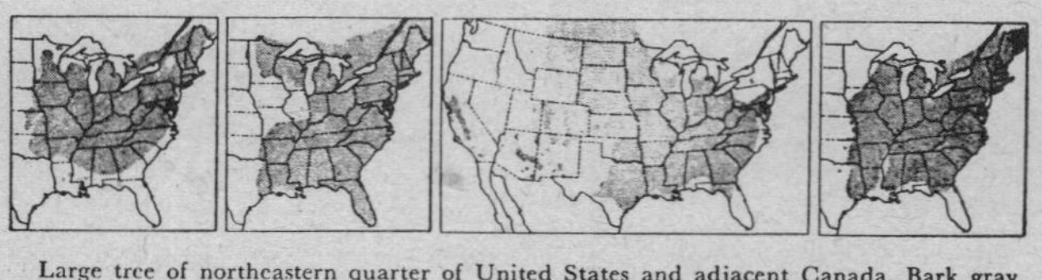

Large tree of northeastern quarter of United States and adjacent Canada. Bark gray, becoming deeply furrowed. Leaves paired, heart-shaped, 4 to 5 1/2 inches in diameter, 3-lobed or occasionally 5-lobed, lobes short-pointed and sparingly coarsely toothed with blunt teeth, the sides drooping, dull green above, yellowish green and hairy beneath, turning yellow in fall. Key fruits 1 to 1 1/4 inches long, maturing in fall. (Perhaps only a variety of No. 27.)

Principal uses: Same as No. 27.

SS. Teeth of leaves many and sharp—SOFT MAPLES.

29. SILVER MAPLE, *Acer saccharinum* L. (soft maple [lumber], white maple, river maple, water maple, swamp maple).

Large tree of eastern half of United States and adjacent Canada. Bark gray, thin, smooth, on large trunks broken into long, thin scales. Leaves paired, slight heart-shaped, 3 to 6 inches long, deeply 5-lobed, lobes long-pointed, deeply, sharply, and irregularly toothed, bright green above, silvery white beneath, turning yellow in fall. Key fruits 1 1/2 to 2 1/2 inches long, maturing in spring.

Principal uses: Furniture, boxes and crates, handles, woodenware and novelties, and spools and bobbins. Also distillation products, railroad ties, and pulpwood. Shade tree. Shelterbelts.

30. RED MAPLE, *Acer rubrum* L. (soft maple [lumber], water maple, scarlet maple, white maple, swamp maple).

Large tree of eastern half of United States and adjacent Canada. Bark gray, thin, smooth, on large trunks broken into long, thin scales. Twigs reddish. Leaves paired, heart-shaped, 2 1/2 to 4 inches long, 3- or 5-lobed, lobes short-pointed, irregularly and sharply toothed, dark green and shiny above, whitish and slightly hairy beneath, turning scarlet or yellow in fall. Key fruits 3/4 inch long, maturing in spring.

Principal uses: Same as No. 29.

PP. Leaves divided into 3 to 11 leaflets (compound).

T. Leaflets attached along the extended leafstalk (pinnate).

U. Leaflets 3 to 7, sharply toothed, with veins extending to the teeth (fruits paired, clustered, long-winged "kels")—BOXELDER (*Acer negundo*).

31. BOXELDER, *Acer negundo* L. (ash-leaf maple, three-leaf maple; *Negundo aceroides* Moench).

Medium-sized tree, including its varieties widely distributed across the United States and adjacent Canada. Bark gray or brown, thin, with narrow ridges and fissures. Twigs green. Leaves paired, compound, with usually 3 or 5, rarely 7 or 9, oval or lance-oblong

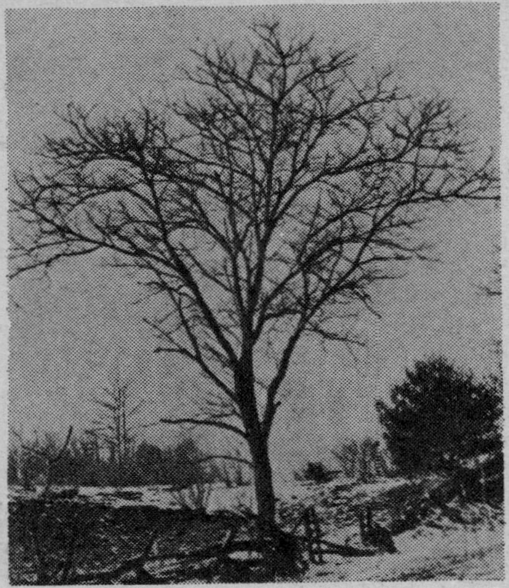

BUTTERNUT

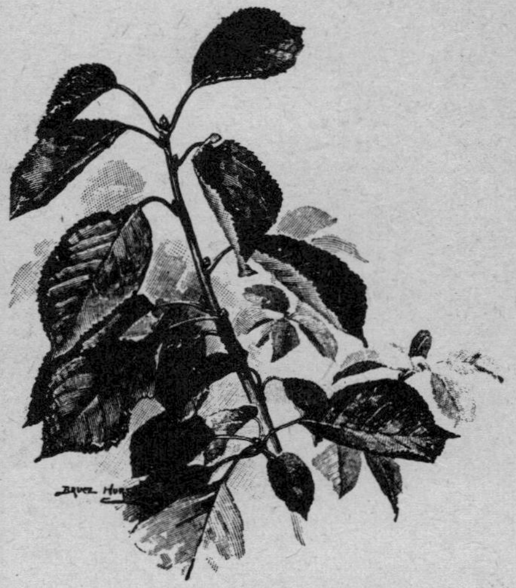

Alternate Leaves of Cultivated Cherry, with Buds in their Axils, in October.

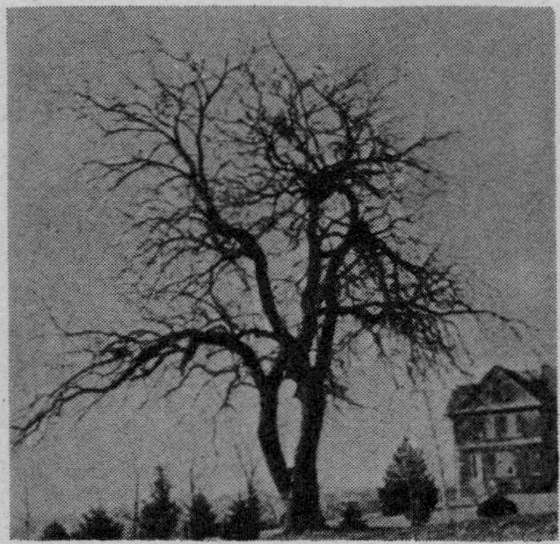

WHITE MULBERRY

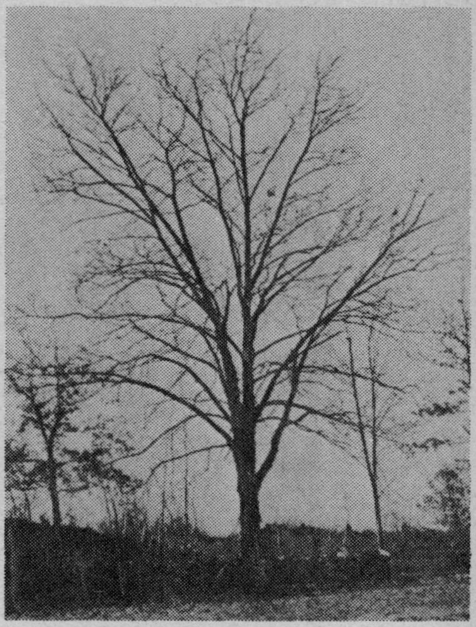

SHAGBARK HICKORY

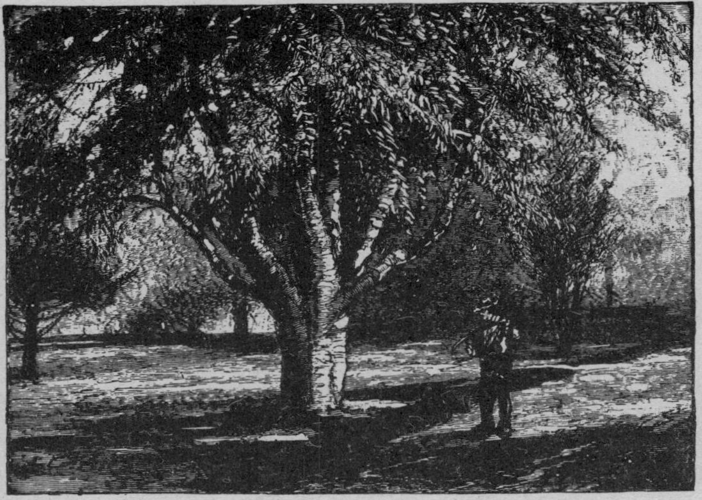

THE DOUBLE-FLOWERING CHERRY. (PRUNUS CERASUS, FL. PL.)

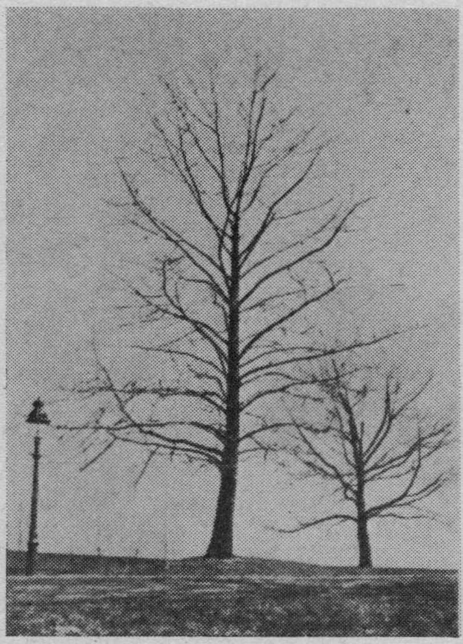

SWEET GUM

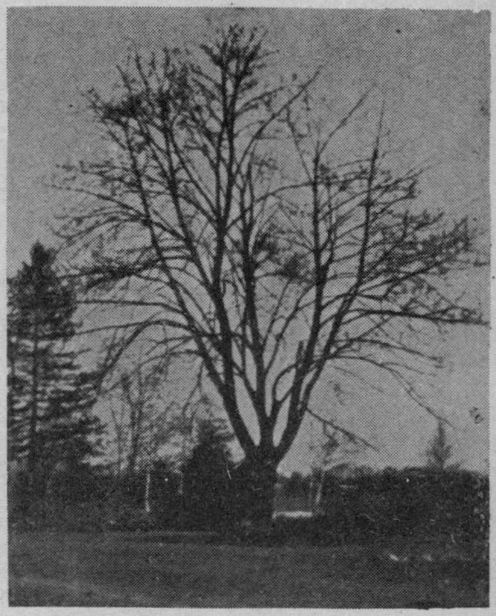

HACKBERRY

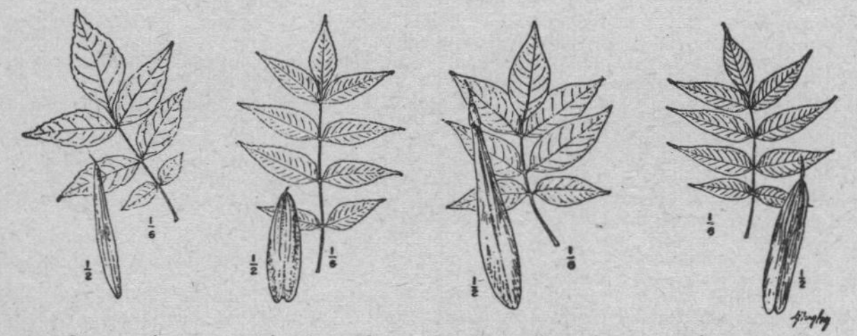

33. Green ash. 34. Blue ash. 35. Pumpkin ash. 36. Black ash.

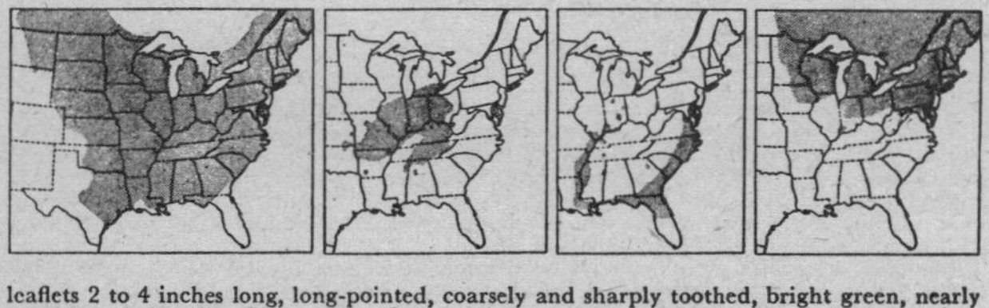

leaflets 2 to 4 inches long, long-pointed, coarsely and sharply toothed, bright green, nearly smooth or hairy. Key fruits 1 to 1½ inches long, paired and in clusters, maturing in fall.

Principal uses: Same as No. 29.

UU. Leaflets 5 to 11, bluntly toothed or without teeth, with veins curved within the edges (fruits clustered but not in pairs, long-winged "keys")—ASH (*Fraxinus*).

V. Leaflets with stalks.

32. WHITE ASH, *Fraxinus americana* L. (American ash, Biltmore ash; *F. biltmoreana* Beadle).

Large tree of eastern half of United States and adjacent Canada. Bark gray, with deep, diamond-shaped fissures and narrow, forking ridges. Leaves paired, compound, 8 to 12 inches long, with 5 to 9, usually 7, stalked, oval or broadly lance-shaped leaflets 2½ to 5 inches long, long- or short-pointed, edges usually smooth or slightly toothed, smooth or hairy beneath. Key fruits 1 to 2 inches long and ¼ inch wide, with wing at end.

Principal uses: Handles, cooperage, furniture, motor-vehicle parts, boxes, baskets, and crates, and sporting and athletic goods. Also railroad ties, veneer, and fuel. Shade tree.

33. GREEN ASH, *Fraxinus pennsylvanica* Marsh. (red ash is the typical variety; green ash is *F. pennsylvanica* var. *lanceolata* (Borkh.) Sarg., white ash, swamp ash, water ash; *F. viridis* Michx.).

Medium-sized tree of eastern half of United States and adjacent Canada west to Montana and Texas. Bark gray, fissured. Leaves paired, compound, 10 to 12 inches long, with 7 or 9, stalked, oval or lance-shaped leaflets 2 to 6 inches long, long-pointed, slightly toothed, smooth or hairy beneath. Key fruits 1¼ to 2¼ inches long, ¼ inch or more in width, with wing extending nearly to base.

Principal uses: Same as No. 32. Also shelterbelts and shade tree. (Green ash is the State tree of North Dakota.)

34. BLUE ASH, *Fraxinus quadrangulata* Michx.

Medium-sized to large tree of Central States, chiefly Ohio and Mississippi Valley regions; also in southern Ontario. Bark gray, fissured, with scaly and shaggy plates. Twigs 4-angled and more or less winged. Leaves paired, compound, 8 to 12 inches long, with 7 to 11, short-stalked, oval or lance-shaped leaflets 2½ to 5 inches long, long-pointed, toothed. Key fruits 1¼ to 2 inches long, ⅜ to ½ inch wide, oblong, with wing extending to base.

Principal uses: Same as No. 32.

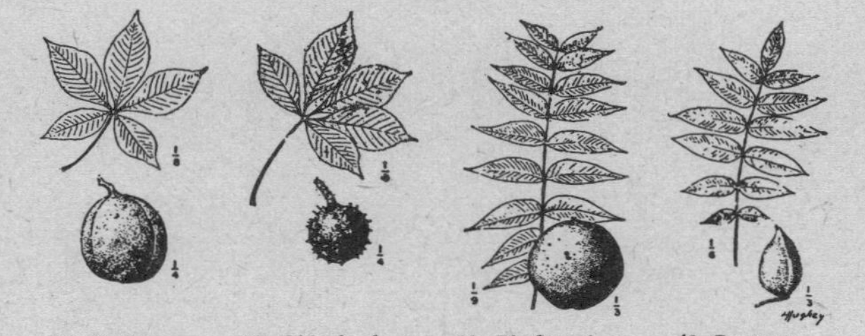

37. Yellow buckeye. 38. Ohio buckeye. 39. Black walnut. 40. Butternut.

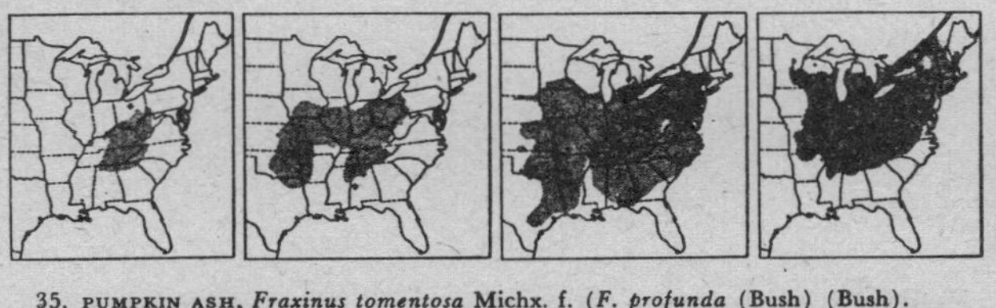

35. PUMPKIN ASH, *Fraxinus tomentosa* Michx. f. (*F. profunda* (Bush) (Bush).

Large tree with swollen base, wet soils in Mississippi Valley and coastal plain regions. Bark gray, fissured. Twigs and leafstalks hairy. Leaves paired, compound, 9 to 18 inches long, with 7 to 9, stalked, elliptical or lance-shaped leaflets 4 to 10 inches long, long-pointed, with edges smooth or slightly toothed, soft hairy beneath. Key fruits 2 to 3 inches long and ⅜ to ½ inch wide, with large broad wing.

Principal uses: Cooperage, furniture, and boxes, baskets, and crates. Also railroad ties, veneer, and fuel.

VV. Leaflets without stalks.

36. BLACK ASH, *Fraxinus nigra* Marsh. (brown ash, hoop ash, basket ash, swamp ash, water ash).

Medium-sized to large tree of wet soils in northeastern quarter of United States and adjacent Canada. Bark gray, scaly or fissured. Leaves paired, compound, 12 to 16 inches long, with 7 to 11, stalkless, oblong or broadly lance-shaped leaflets 3 to 5 inches long, long-pointed, finely toothed, with tufted hairs beneath. Key fruits 1 to 1½ inches long, ⅜ inch wide, flat, with wing extending to base.

Principal uses: Same as No. 35.

TT. Leaflets 5 (or 7), all attached at end of leafstalk and spreading fingerlike (palmate)—BUCKEYE (*Aesculus*).

37. YELLOW BUCKEYE, *Aesculus octandra* Marsh. (sweet buckeye, large buckeye).

Medium-sized tree of Central States, chiefly Ohio Valley and Appalachian regions. Bark gray, separating into thin scales. Leaves paired, compound, with leafstalks 4 to 6 inches long. Leaflets 5, oblong or elliptical, 4 to 6 inches long, long-pointed, narrowed at base, finely toothed. Flowers in branched clusters 4 to 6 inches long, showy, 1¼ inches long, yellow, with petals unequal in length. Fruiting capsule 2 to 2½ inches in diameter, smooth, with 2 poisonous seeds 1½ to 1¾ inches wide.

Principal uses: Furniture, boxes and crates, and caskets. Also artificial limbs. Ornamental.

38. OHIO BUCKEYE, *Aesculus glabra* Willd. (fetid buckeye, stinking buckeye, American horsechestnut).

Small tree (or shrubby to medium-sized) of Central States, chiefly Ohio and Mississippi Valley regions. Bark gray, much furrowed and broken into scaly plates. Leaves paired, compound, with leafstalks 4 to 6 inches long. Leaflets 5 (5 to 7 in shrubby varieties),

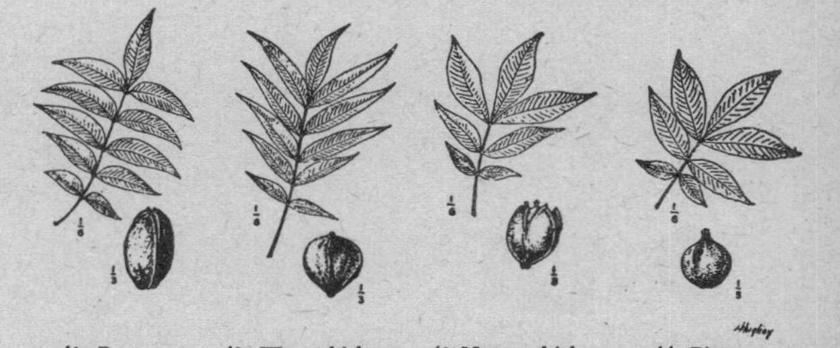

41. Pecan. 42. Water hickory. 43. Nutmeg hickory. 44. Bitternut hickory.

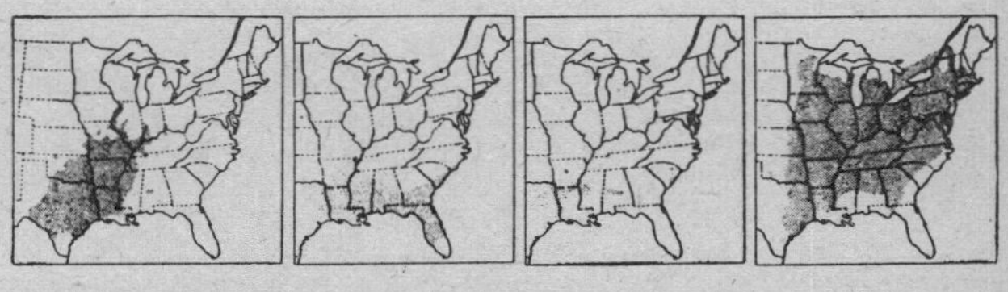

elliptical, 3 to 5 inches long, long-pointed, narrowed at base, finely toothed. Flowers in branched clusters 4 to 6 inches long, showy, ¾ to 1¼ inches long, pale greenish yellow, with petals nearly equal in length. Fruiting capsule 1¼ to 2 inches in diameter, prickly, with 1 or 2 poisonous seeds 1 to 1½ inches wide.

Principal uses: Same as No. 37. (State tree of Ohio.)

OO (O on p. 774). Leaves and usually branches borne singly (alternate).

W (WW on p. 782). Leaves divided into leaflets (compound), attached along the extended leafstalk (pinnate).

X. Leaflets long-pointed; twigs not spiny; fruit rounded or egg-shaped.

Y. Leaflets finely toothed, shedding in fall; fruit a nut with a husk.

Z. Leaflets 11 to 23; pith of twigs in plates; husk of nut not splitting off—WALNUT (*Juglans*).

39. BLACK WALNUT, *Juglans nigra* L. (eastern black walnut, American walnut, walnut).

Large tree of eastern half of United States and southern Ontario. Bark dark brown to black, thick, with deep furrows and narrow, forking ridges. Compound leaves 12 to 24 inches long. Leaflets 15 to 23, without stalks, broadly lance-shaped, 2½ to 5 inches long, long-pointed, finely toothed, nearly smooth above, soft hairy beneath. Nuts single or paired, 1½ to 2½ inches in diameter including the thick husk, nearly spherical, irregularly ridged, thick-shelled, sweet and edible, known as walnuts.

Principal uses: Valuable furniture wood, solid and as veneer. Also for radio and phonograph cabinets, sewing machines, and interior finish. The leading wood for gunstocks. Edible walnuts. Shade tree. Shelterbelts. (State tree of Iowa.)

40. BUTTERNUT, *Juglans cinerea* L. (white walnut, oilnut).

Medium-sized to large tree of northeastern quarter of United States and adjacent Canada. Bark light gray, furrowed into broad, flat ridges. Compound leaves 15 to 30 inches long. Leaflets 11 to 19, without stalks, broadly lance-shaped, 2 to 4½ inches long, long- or short-pointed, finely toothed, slightly hairy above, soft hairy beneath. Nuts 3 to 5 in drooping clusters, 1½ to 2½ inches long including the thick husk, egg-shaped, pointed, irregularly ridged, thick-shelled, sweet and oily, known as butternuts.

Principal uses: Furniture. Shade tree. Edible butternuts.

ZZ. Leaflets 5 to 11 (11 to 17 in No. 41); pith of twigs solid; husk of nut splitting off—HICKORY (*Carya;* formerly known also as *Hicoria*).

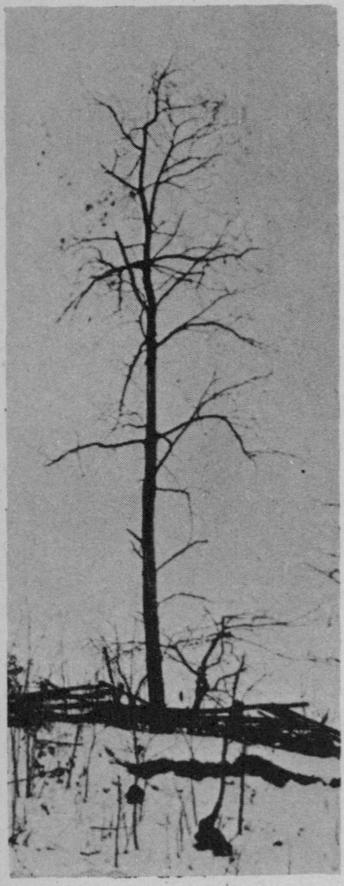

LONGTOOTH ASPEN

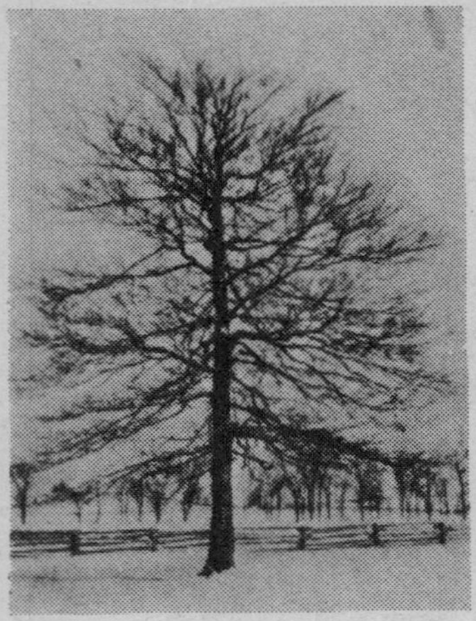

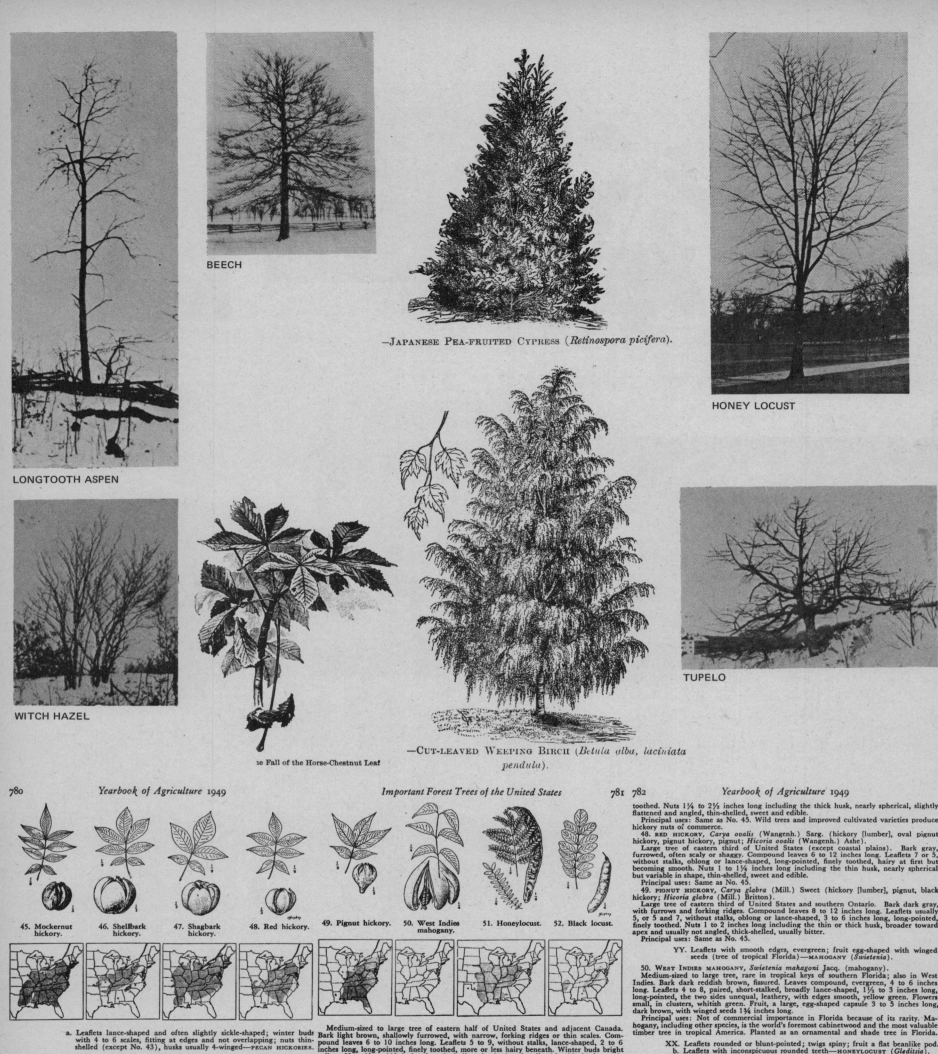

BEECH

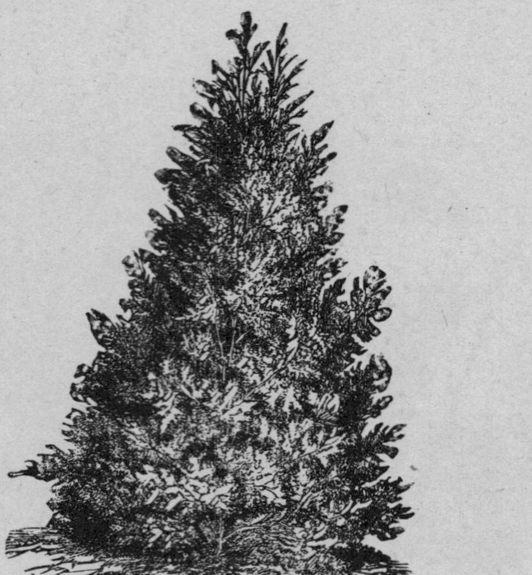

—Japanese Pea-fruited Cypress (*Retinospora picifera*).

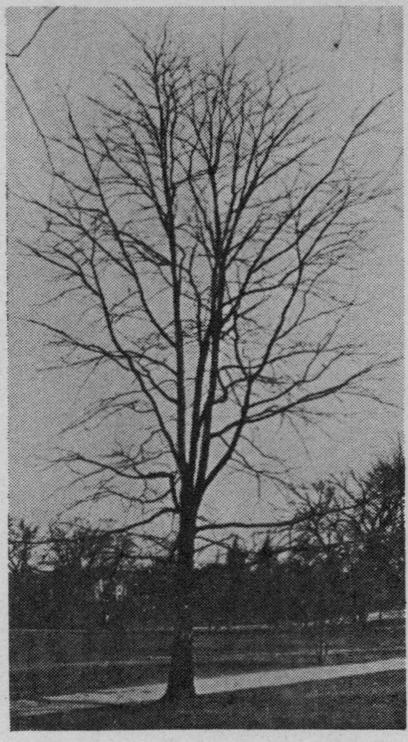

HONEY LOCUST

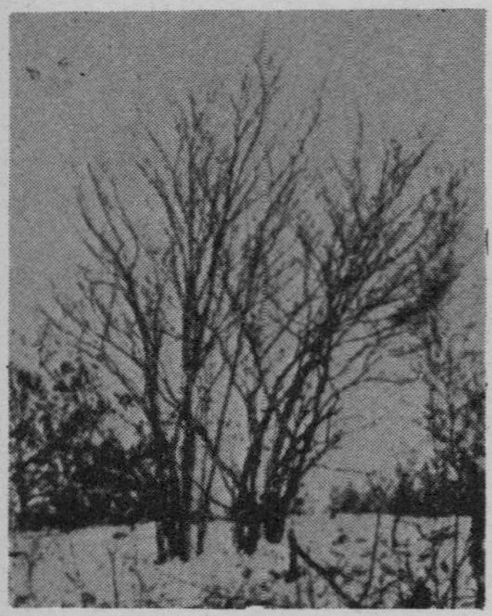

WITCH HAZEL

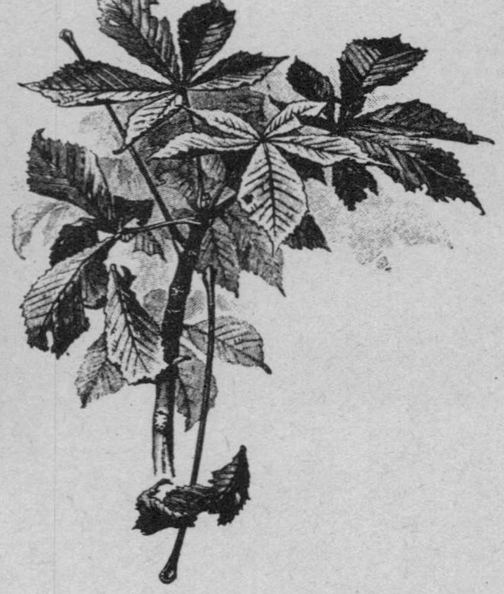

1e Fall of the Horse-Chestnut Leaf

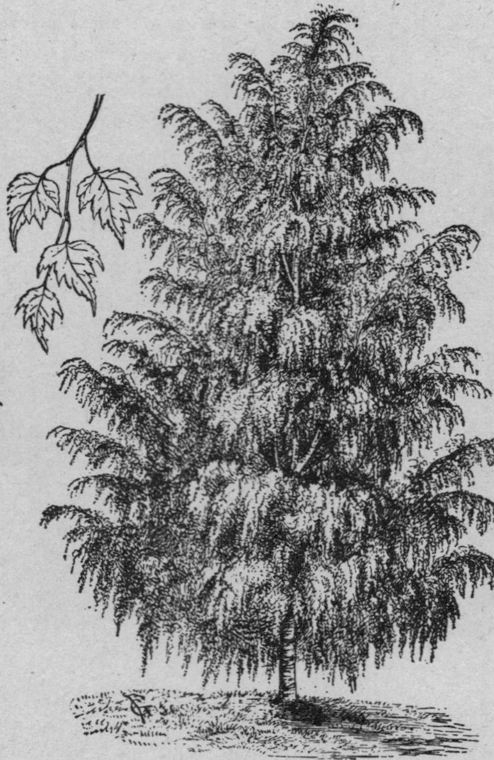

—Cut-leaved Weeping Birch (*Betula alba, laciniata pendula*).

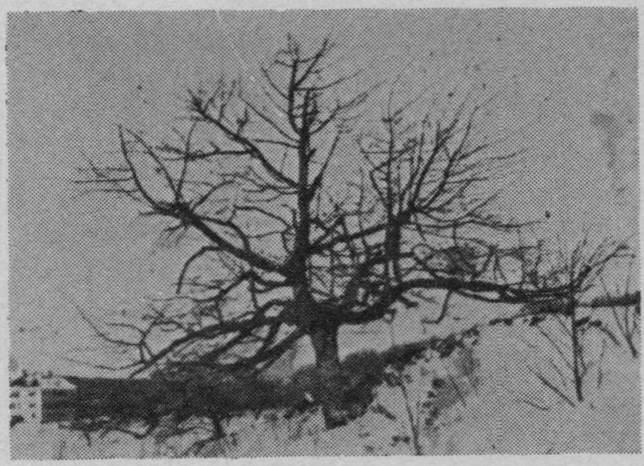

TUPELO

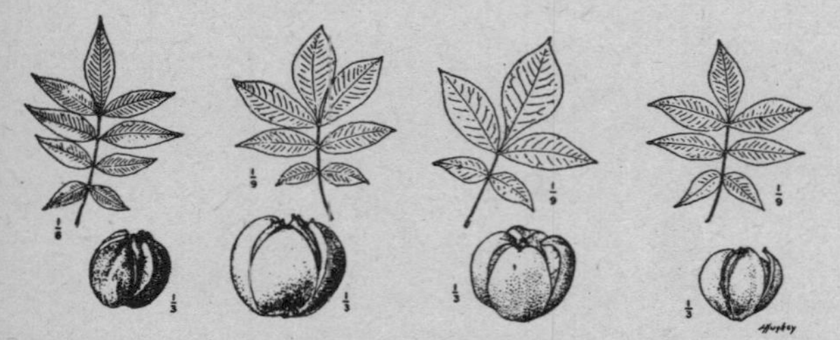

45. Mockernut hickory. 46. Shellbark hickory. 47. Shagbark hickory. 48. Red hickory.

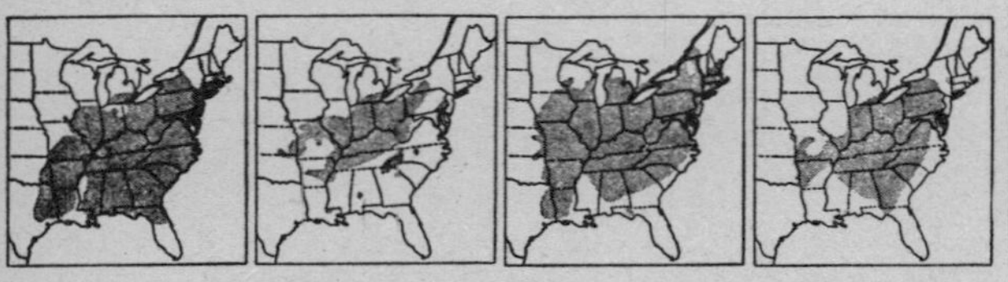

a. Leaflets lance-shaped and often slightly sickle-shaped; winter buds with 4 to 6 scales, fitting at edges and not overlapping; nuts thin-shelled (except No. 43), husks usually 4-winged—PECAN HICKORIES.

41. PECAN, *Carya illinoensis* (Wangenh.) K. Koch (sweet pecan; *C. pecan* (Marsh.) Engl. & Graebn., *Hicoria pecan* (Marsh.) Britton).

Large tree of Mississippi Valley region; also in Mexico. Bark light brown or gray, deeply and irregularly furrowed and cracked. Compound leaves 12 to 20 inches long. Leaflets 11 to 17, short-stalked, lance-shaped and slightly sickle-shaped, 2 to 7 inches long, long-pointed, finely toothed, smooth or slightly hairy. Nuts 1 to 2 inches long including the slightly 4-winged, thin husk, oblong, pointed, thin-shelled, sweet and edible, known as pecans.

Principal uses: Boxes and crates, motor vehicles, furniture, and flooring. Fuel and for smoking meats. Pecan nuts from wild and cultivated trees. Shade tree. (State tree of Texas.)

42. WATER HICKORY, *Carya aquatica* (Michx. f.) Nutt. (pecan [lumber], bitter pecan, swamp hickory; *Hicoria aquatica* (Michx. f.) Britton).

Medium-sized or large tree of wet soils in South Atlantic coast, Gulf coast, and Mississippi Valley regions. Bark light brown, fissured, with long, thin scales. Compound leaves 9 to 15 inches long. Leaflets 7 to 13, stalkless or short-stalked, lance-shaped, 2 to 5 inches long, long-pointed, finely toothed, dark green above, brownish and hairy or smooth beneath. Nuts 1 to 1½ inches long including the pointed, 4-winged, thin husk, nearly spherical, flattened, angled, and wrinkled, thin-shelled, bitter.

Principal uses: Wood used same as No. 41.

43. NUTMEG HICKORY, *Carya myristicaeformis* (Michx. f.) Nutt. (pecan [lumber], bitter water hickory, swamp hickory; *Hicoria myristicaeformis* (Michx. f.) Britton).

Large tree of South Atlantic coast and Gulf coast regions; also in Mexico. Bark dark brown, fissured, with small, thin scales. Compound leaves 7 to 14 inches long. Leaflets 5 to 9, short-stalked, broadly lance-shaped or oblong, 2 to 5 inches long, long-pointed, finely toothed, dark green above, more or less hairy or smooth and whitish beneath. Nuts 1¼ to 1½ inches long including the pointed, 4-winged, thin husk, nearly spherical but longer than broad, thick-shelled, sweet and edible.

Principal uses: Wood used same as No. 41. Edible hickory nuts.

44. BITTERNUT HICKORY, *Carya cordiformis* (Wangenh.) K. Koch (pecan [lumber], bitternut, pignut, swamp hickory; *Hicoria cordiformis* (Wangenh.) Britton).

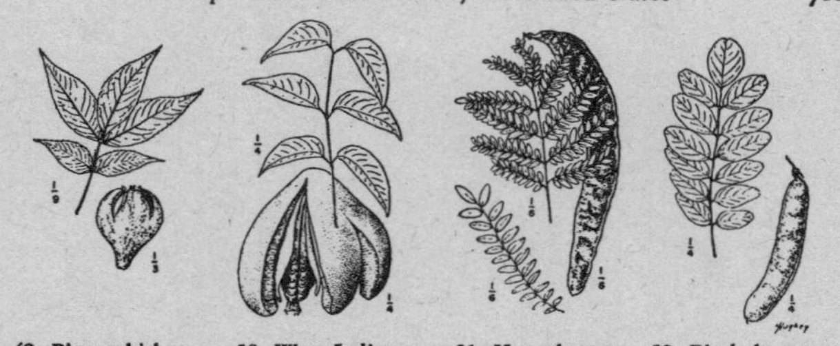

49. Pignut hickory. 50. West Indies mahogany. 51. Honeylocust. 52. Black locust.

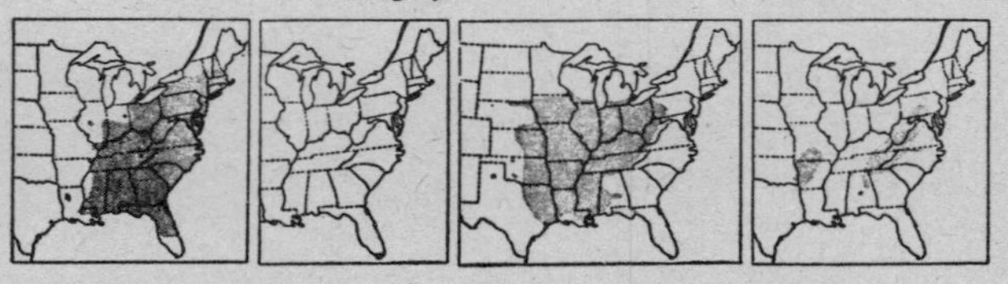

Medium-sized to large tree of eastern half of United States and adjacent Canada. Bark light brown, shallowly furrowed, with narrow, forking ridges or thin scales. Compound leaves 6 to 10 inches long. Leaflets 5 to 9, without stalks, lance-shaped, 2 to 6 inches long, long-pointed, finely toothed, more or less hairy beneath. Winter buds bright yellow. Nuts ¾ to 1¼ inches long including the 4-winged, yellowish, thin husk, nearly spherical, slightly flattened, short-pointed, thin-shelled, bitter.

Principal uses: Wood used same as No. 41.

aa. Leaflets oblong to broadly lance-shaped; winter buds with more than 6 overlapping scales; nuts thick-shelled (except Nos. 47 and 48), husks without wings—TRUE HICKORIES.

45. MOCKERNUT HICKORY, *Carya tomentosa* Nutt. (hickory [lumber], mockernut, whiteheart hickory, bullnut, hognut, white hickory; *C. alba* auth., *Hicoria alba* auth.).

Medium-sized to large tree of eastern half of United States except northern border; also in southern Ontario. Bark gray, irregularly furrowed into flat ridges. Compound leaves 8 to 20 inches long. Leaflets 7 or 9, without stalks, oblong or broadly lance-shaped, 2 to 8 inches long, long-pointed, finely toothed, dark yellow green and shiny above, pale and densely hairy beneath. Nuts 1½ to 2 inches long including the thick husk, nearly spherical, slightly flattened and angled, thick-shelled, sweet and edible.

Principal uses: Hickory, including several species, is the world's foremost wood for tool handles. Also for vehicle parts, fuel, and smoking meat. Hickory nuts.

46. SHELLBARK HICKORY, *Carya laciniosa* (Michx. f.) Loud. (hickory [lumber], bigleaf shagbark hickory, big shellbark, western shellbark, thick shellbark, bottom shellbark, kingnut; *Hicoria laciniosa* (Michx. f.) Sarg.).

Large tree of Ohio and Mississippi Valley regions. Bark gray, shaggy with long, thin, straight plates. Compound leaves 15 to 22 inches long. Leaflets usually 7, without stalks or short-stalked, broadly lance-shaped, 2 to 8 inches long, long-pointed, finely toothed, dark green and shiny above, pale and soft-hairy beneath. Nuts 1¾ to 2½ inches long including the thick husk, nearly spherical, slightly flattened and angled, pointed at ends, thick-shelled, sweet and edible.

Principal uses: Same as No. 45. Hickory nuts of commerce.

47. SHAGBARK HICKORY, *Carya ovata* (Mill.) K. Koch (hickory [lumber], shagbark, shellbark hickory, scalybark hickory, upland hickory; *Hicoria ovata* (Mill.) Britton).

Large tree of eastern half of United States and adjacent Canada. Bark gray, shaggy with long, thin, curved plates. Compound leaves 8 to 14 inches long. Leaflets usually 5, without stalks, elliptical or broadly lance-shaped, 3 to 7 inches long, long-pointed, finely

toothed. Nuts 1¼ to 2½ inches long including the thick husk, nearly spherical, slightly flattened and angled, thin-shelled, sweet and edible.

Principal uses: Same as No. 45. Wild trees and improved cultivated varieties produce hickory nuts of commerce.

48. RED HICKORY, *Carya ovalis* (Wangenh.) Sarg. (hickory [lumber], oval pignut hickory, pignut hickory, pignut; *Hicoria ovalis* (Wangenh.) Ashe).

Large tree of eastern third of United States (except coastal plains). Bark gray, furrowed, often scaly or shaggy. Compound leaves 6 to 12 inches long. Leaflets 7 or 5, without stalks, oblong or lance-shaped, long-pointed, finely toothed, hairy at first but becoming smooth. Nuts 1 to 1¼ inches long including the thin husk, nearly spherical but variable in shape, thin-shelled, sweet and edible.

Principal uses: Same as No. 45.

49. PIGNUT HICKORY, *Carya glabra* (Mill.) Sweet (hickory [lumber], pignut, black hickory; *Hicoria glabra* (Mill.) Britton).

Large tree of eastern third of United States and southern Ontario. Bark dark gray, with furrows and forking ridges. Compound leaves 8 to 12 inches long. Leaflets usually 5, or 5 and 7, without stalks, oblong or lance-shaped, 3 to 6 inches long, long-pointed, finely toothed. Nuts 1 to 2 inches long including the thin or thick husk, broader toward apex and usually not angled, thick-shelled, usually bitter.

Principal uses: Same as No. 45.

YY. Leaflets with smooth edges, evergreen; fruit egg-shaped with winged seeds (tree of tropical Florida)—MAHOGANY (*Swietenia*).

50. WEST INDIES MAHOGANY, *Swietenia mahagoni* Jacq. (mahogany).

Medium-sized to large tree, rare in tropical keys of southern Florida; also in West Indies. Bark dark reddish brown, fissured. Leaves compound, evergreen, 4 to 6 inches long. Leaflets 4 to 8, paired, short-stalked, broadly lance-shaped, 1½ to 3 inches long, long-pointed, the two sides unequal, leathery, with edges smooth, yellow green. Flowers small, in clusters, whitish green. Fruit, a large, egg-shaped capsule 3 to 5 inches long, dark brown, with winged seeds 1¾ inches long.

Principal uses: Not of commercial importance in Florida because of its rarity. Mahogany, including other species, is the world's foremost cabinetwood and the most valuable timber tree in tropical America. Planted as an ornamental and shade tree in Florida.

XX. Leaflets rounded or blunt-pointed; twigs spiny; fruit a flat beanlike pod.
b. Leaflets with inconspicuous rounded teeth—HONEYLOCUST (*Gleditsia*).

51. HONEYLOCUST, *Gleditsia triacanthos* L. (common honeylocust, sweet-locust, thorny locust).

Large tree of Appalachian Mountain and Mississippi Valley regions, naturalized elsewhere in eastern half of United States; also in southern Ontario. Bark grayish brown or black, fissured into long, narrow, scaly ridges. Trunk and branches with large, stout, usually branched spines, rarely absent. Leaves once or twice divided (compound), 4 to 8 inches long. Leaflets numerous in pairs, elliptical, ⅜ to 1¼ inches long, blunt-pointed or rounded at apex, with inconspicuous rounded teeth, shiny dark green and smooth above, yellow green and nearly smooth beneath. Flowers small, greenish or whitish, in narrow clusters 2 to 2½ inches long, in late spring. Pods 12 to 18 inches long and 1 to 1¼ inches wide, flat, dark brown, hairy, slightly curved and twisted.

Principal uses: Wood used locally for fence posts, construction, furniture, and railroad ties. Shade tree. Shelterbelts. The sweetish pods are eaten by livestock and wildlife.

bb. Leaflets not toothed—LOCUST (*Robinia*).

52. BLACK LOCUST, *Robinia pseudoacacia* L. (locust, yellow locust, shipmast locust).

Medium-sized tree, native in Appalachian Mountain and Ozark regions and widely naturalized in eastern half of United States and southern Canada. Bark brown, thick, deeply furrowed, with rough, forked ridges. Twigs with a pair of spines about ½ inch long developing at base of each leaf. Compound leaves 8 to 14 inches long. Leaflets 7 to 19, oval, 1 to 2 inches long, usually rounded at apex, with smooth edges, dark blue green and smooth above, pale and smooth or nearly so beneath. Flowers white and very fragrant, ⅝ to ¾ inch long, in clusters 4 to 8 inches long, in spring. Pods 2 to 4 inches long and ½ inch wide, flat, brown.

Principal uses: Fence posts, mine timbers, poles, railroad ties, stakes, and fuel. The principal wood for insulator pins. Also lumber for rough construction. Planted for ornament and shade, shelterbelts, and erosion control.

WW (W on p. 779). Leaves not divided into leaflets (simple).
c. Leaves aromatic when bruised, edges smooth or 2- or 3-lobed; twigs bright green—SASSAFRAS (*Sassafras*).

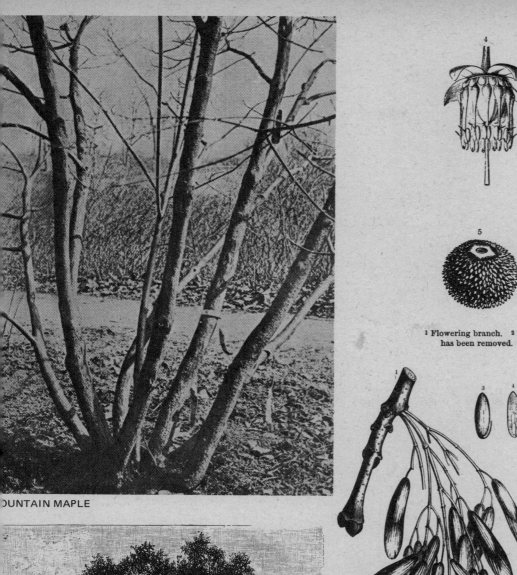

MOUNTAIN MAPLE

SOULANGE'S MAGNOLIA. (MAGNOLIA SOULANGEANA.)

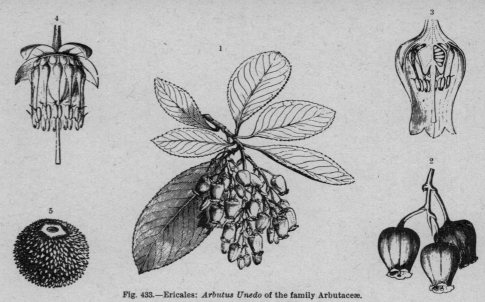

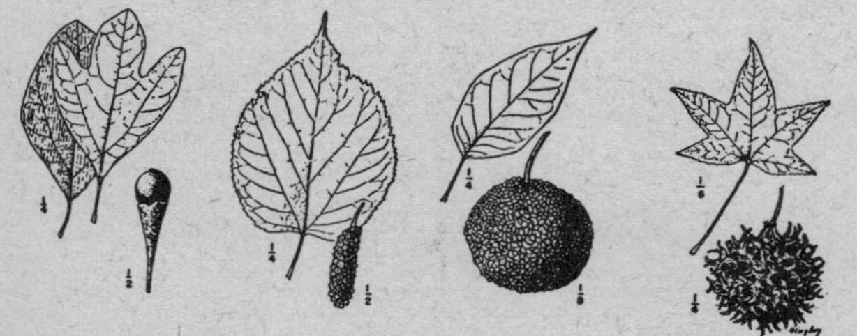

Fig. 433.—Ericales: *Arbutus Unedo* of the family Arbutaceæ.

1 Flowering branch. 2 Three flowers magnified. 3 Longitudinal section through a flower. 4 Flower from which the corolla has been removed. 5 Papillose berry. 2, 3 and 4 magnified. (After Baillon.)

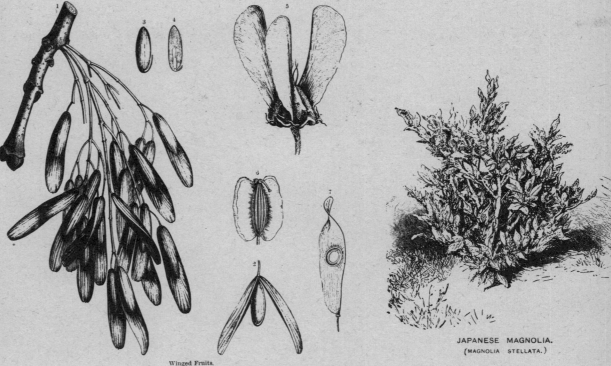

Winged Fruits.

1 Cluster of fruits of the Ash (*Fraxinus excelsior*). 2 A single fruit artificially opened. 3 Seed of *Fraxinus excelsior*. 4 The same seed in longitudinal section. 5 Fruit of *Banisteria*. 6 Fruit of *Angelica sylvestris*. 7 Fruit of *Ailanthus glandulosa*. the central, seed-containing portion seen in section. (Partly after Baillon.)

JAPANESE MAGNOLIA.
(MAGNOLIA STELLATA.)

53. Sassafras. 54. Red mulberry. 55. Osage-orange. 56. Sweetgum. 57. American sycamore. 58. Yellow-poplar. 59. Southern magnolia. 60. Sweetbay. 61. Cucumbertree. 62. Common persimmon. 63. Water tupelo. 64. Black tupelo.

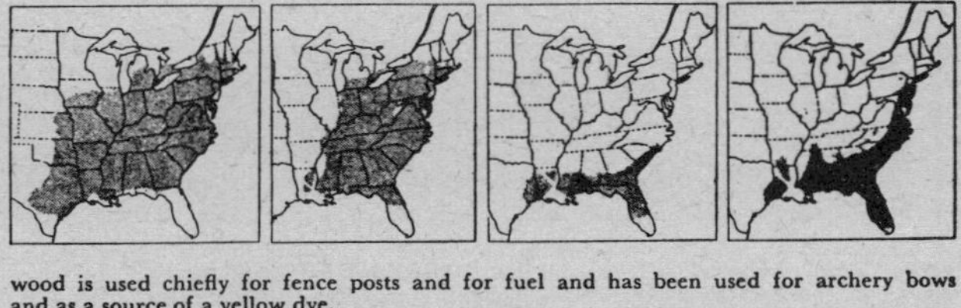

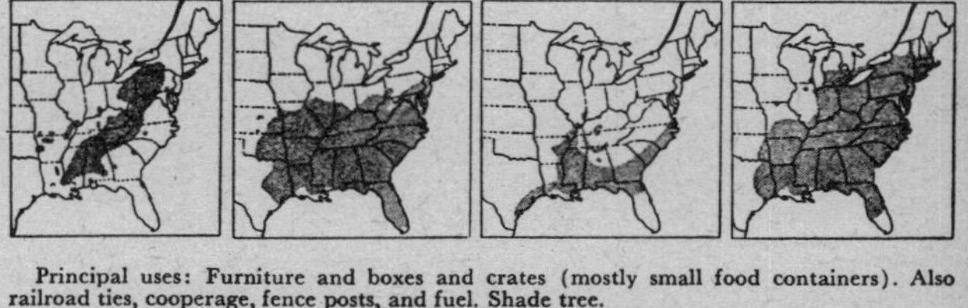

53. SASSAFRAS, *Sassafras albidum* (Nutt.) Nees (common sassafras; *S. officinale* Nees & Eberm., *S. variifolium* (Salisb.) Ktze.).

Medium-sized tree (sometimes large) with aromatic odor and taste, eastern half of United States and southern Ontario. Bark reddish brown, deeply furrowed. Leaves oval or elliptical, 3 to 5 inches long, blunt-pointed, often 2- or 3-lobed, with smooth edges, bright green above, paler and smooth or hairy beneath, turning orange or scarlet in fall. Flowers about ⅜ inch long, yellow, in small clusters in early spring. Fruits egg-shaped, ⅜ inch long, dark blue, with fleshy red stalk.

Principal uses: Fence posts. Lumber occasionally mixed with that of black ash (No. 36). Sassafras tea and oil of sassafras, used to perfume soap, are prepared from roots and root bark. Shade tree and ornamental.

cc. Leaves not aromatic, edges smooth, toothed, or lobed; twigs brown or gray.
d. Juice milky.
e. Leaves toothed, sometimes 2- or 3-lobed; twigs not spiny—MULBERRY (*Morus*).

54. RED MULBERRY, *Morus rubra* L. (mulberry).

Medium-sized tree of eastern half of United States and southern Ontario. Bark dark brown, fissured and scaly. Leaves broadly oval or heart-shaped, 3 to 7 inches long, abruptly long-pointed, coarsely toothed, sometimes 2- or 3-lobed, rough above, soft-hairy beneath. Fruits 1 inch long, dark purple or black, sweet, juicy, and edible, known as mulberries.

Principal uses: Wood used locally for fence posts, furniture, interior finish, agricultural implements, and cooperage. Shade tree. Edible mulberries, eaten also by domestic animals and wildlife.

ee. Leaves with smooth edges; twigs spiny—OSAGE-ORANGE (*Maclura*).

55. OSAGE-ORANGE, *Maclura pomifera* (Raf.) Schneid. (bodark, mockorange, bowwood, hedge; *Toxylon pomiferum* Raf.).

Medium-sized tree with milky juice, native of Arkansas, Oklahoma, Louisiana, and Texas but naturalized in eastern half of United States except northern border. Bark orange brown, deeply furrowed. Twigs with stout straight spines ⅜ to 1 inch long. Leaves oval or narrowly oval, 2 to 5 inches long, long-pointed, with smooth edges, shiny dark green above and paler beneath. Fruit a yellowish ball 4 to 5 inches in diameter.

Principal uses: Extensively planted for shelterbelts, hedges, ornament, and shade. The wood is used chiefly for fence posts and for fuel and has been used for archery bows and as a source of a yellow dye.

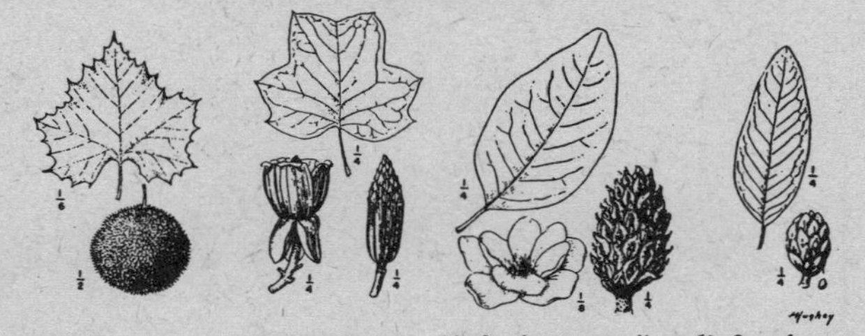

dd. Juice watery.
f (ff on p. 793). Winter buds 1 or none at tip of twig; pith of twigs round or nearly so in cross section (star-shaped in Nos. 77 to 80 and 90); fruit not an acorn.
g. Leaves with 3 to 6 lobes.
h. Leaves with pointed apex and 3 or 5 lobes.
i. Leaves star-shaped, deeply 5-lobed—SWEETGUM (*Liquidambar*).

56. SWEETGUM, *Liquidambar styraciflua* L. (redgum [lumber], sapgum [lumber], American sweetgum, starleaf-gum, bilsted).

Large tree of eastern third of United States, except northern border; also in Mexico and Central America south to Nicaragua. Bark gray, deeply furrowed. Twigs reddish brown, developing corky ridges. Leaves maplelike, star-shaped, 3 to 7 inches long and wide, with 5 long-pointed, finely toothed lobes, shiny dark green above, paler beneath, slightly aromatic, turning deep crimson in fall. Fruit a brownish, spiny ball 1 to 1¼ inches in diameter.

Principal uses: Important timber tree in United States, second in production among the hardwoods, the leading furniture wood, and second in veneer production. Also boxes and crates, radio and phonograph cabinets, interior trim and millwork, woodenware and novelties, and slack barrels. Shade tree. The gum, "sweetgum" or storax, is used in perfumes and drugs.

ii. Leaves heart-shaped, slightly 3-lobed—SYCAMORE (*Platanus*).

57. AMERICAN SYCAMORE, *Platanus occidentalis* L. (American planetree, sycamore, buttonwood, planetree, buttonball-tree).

A very large tree (the largest eastern hardwood in trunk diameter) of wet soils in eastern half of United States and southern Ontario. Bark of branches whitish, thin, smooth; bark of trunk peeling off in large flakes, smoothish, with patches of brown, green, and gray. Leaves heart-shaped, 4 to 8 inches long and wide, slightly 3- or 5-lobed, the shallow, pointed lobes coarsely toothed with long-pointed teeth, with 3 main veins from base, bright green and smooth above, paler and slightly hairy beneath. Fruit a ball 1 inch in diameter.

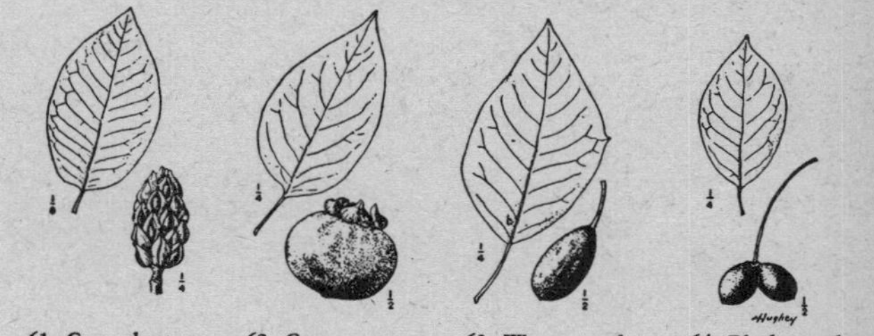

Principal uses: Furniture and boxes and crates (mostly small food containers). Also railroad ties, cooperage, fence posts, and fuel. Shade tree.

hh. Leaves with broad, slightly notched apex and 4 or 6 lobes—YELLOW-POPLAR (*Liriodendron*).

58. YELLOW-POPLAR, *Liriodendron tulipifera* L. (tuliptree, whitewood, white-poplar, tulipwood, hickory-poplar, poplar).

Large tree (the tallest eastern hardwood) of eastern third of United States and southern Ontario. Bark brown, becoming thick and deeply furrowed. Leaves of unusual squarish shape with broad, slightly notched or nearly straight apex and 2 or 3 lobes on each side, 3 to 6 inches long, long and broad, shiny dark green above and pale green beneath. Flowers large and showy, tulip-shaped, 1½ to 2 inches in diameter, greenish and orange, in spring. Fruit conelike, 2½ to 3 inches long, ½ inch thick.

Principal uses: Furniture (solid and veneer), boxes and crates, interior finish, siding, fixtures, radio cabinets, musical instruments, and caskets. Pulpwood. Ornamental and shade tree. (State tree of Indiana and Kentucky.)

gg. Leaves with edges smooth or toothed but without lobes.
j. Leaf edges smooth (see also No. 76).
k. Twigs with faint ring at base of each leaf—MAGNOLIA (*Magnolia*).

59. SOUTHERN MAGNOLIA, *Magnolia grandiflora* L. (magnolia [lumber], evergreen magnolia).

Medium-sized to large tree of South Atlantic and Gulf Coastal Plains. Bark gray or light brown, broken into small, thin scales. Leaves evergreen, oblong or elliptical, 5 to 8 inches long, short-pointed, edges smooth, leathery, shiny bright green and smooth above, rusty-hairy beneath. Flowers cup-shaped, very large, 6 to 8 inches across, white, fragrant, spring and summer. Fruit conelike, 3 to 4 inches long, 1½ to 2½ inches thick, rusty-hairy.

Principal uses: Furniture, boxes, and venetian blinds. Ornamental and shade tree. (State tree and State flower of Louisiana and Mississippi.)

60. SWEETBAY, *Magnolia virginiana* L. (magnolia [lumber], sweetbay magnolia, swampbay, swamp magnolia).

Small to medium-sized tree of Atlantic and Gulf Coastal Plains. Bark brownish gray, smoothish. Leaves shedding in winter or almost evergreen in the South, elliptical or narrowly oval, 3 to 5 inches long, short-pointed, wedge-shaped at base, edges smooth, thick, shiny bright green and smooth above, whitish and nearly smooth beneath. Flowers cup-

HORSE CHESTNUT

WHITE OAK

—Fairy Rings in a meadow near Trins in the Tyrol, formed by the ascomycetous fungus *Spathularia flavida*.

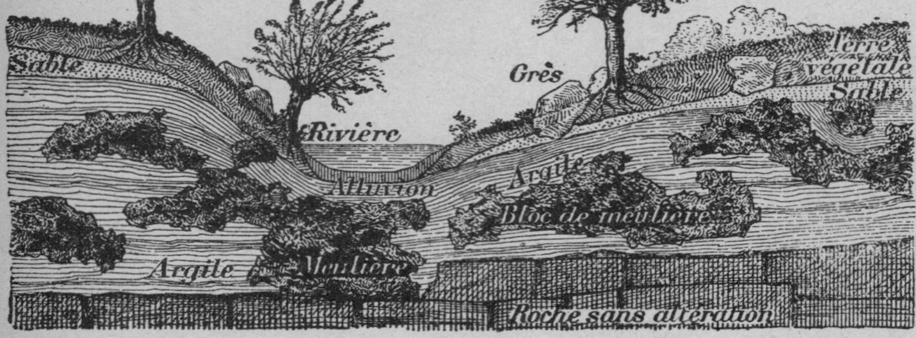

Sable — Grès — Rivière — terre végétale Sable — Argile — Alluvion — Bloc de meulière — Argile — Meulière — Roche sans alteration

NOBLE SILVER FIR.
(ABIES NOBILIS.)

—JAPANESE MAPLE (*A. polymorphum*).

65. Ogeechee tupelo. 66. American holly. 67. American basswood. 68. White basswood. 69. American elm. 70. Slippery elm. 71. Rock elm. 72. Winged elm.

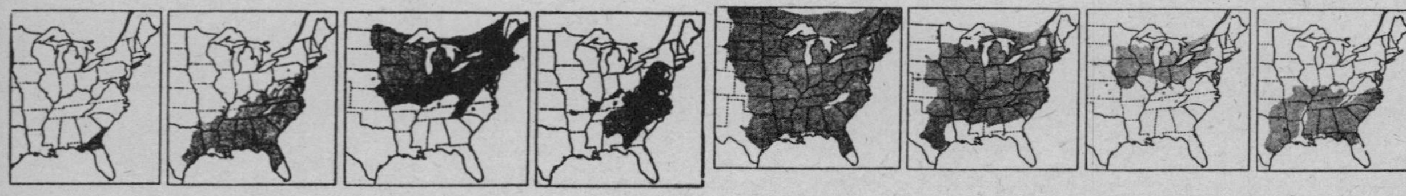

shaped, 2 to 2½ inches across, white, fragrant, spring and early summer. Fruit conelike, 1½ to 2 inches long and ½ inch thick, dark red, smooth.

Principal uses: Furniture, boxes, and venetian blinds. Ornamental.

61. CUCUMBERTREE, *Magnolia acuminata* L. (cucumbertree magnolia, mountain magnolia).

Large tree of Appalachian Mountain and Ozark regions and intervening portions of Ohio and Mississippi Valleys; also in southern Ontario. Bark dark brown, furrowed, with narrow, scaly, forking ridges. Leaves elliptical or oval, 5 to 10 inches long, short-pointed, yellow green and smooth above, light green and soft-hairy or nearly smooth beneath. Flowers bell-shaped, greenish yellow, 2½ to 3½ inches long. Fruit conelike, 2 to 3 inches long and 1 inch thick, red.

Principal uses: Wood used same as yellow-poplar, No. 58. Ornamental and shade tree.

    kk. Twigs without rings.
    l. Leaves broadest below middle—PERSIMMON (*Diospyros*).

62. COMMON PERSIMMON, *Diospyros virginiana* L. (persimmon).

Medium-sized tree of eastern half of United States except northern border. Bark dark brown, thick, deeply divided into small, square, scaly blocks. Leaves oval or elliptical, 2½ to 6 inches long, long-pointed, rounded at base, shiny dark green above, pale green and smooth or hairy beneath. Male and female flowers on different trees in spring, ⅜ to ⅝ inch long, whitish, in angles of leaves. Fruits ¾ to 1¼ inches in diameter, yellow or pale orange, maturing in fall, fleshy, sweet, and edible, known as persimmons.

Principal uses: Shuttles (used in textile weaving) and golf-club heads. Sometimes planted for the edible persimmon fruits and for ornament.

    ll. Leaves broadest above middle—TUPELO (*Nyssa*).

63. WATER TUPELO, *Nyssa aquatica* L. (tupelo, tupelo-gum, swamp tupelo, cotton-gum, sour-gum).

Large tree with swollen base, swamps of South Atlantic Coastal Plain, Gulf Coastal Plain, and lower Mississippi Valley. Bark dark brown, thin, rough, with scaly ridges. Leaves oval or oblong, 4 to 6 inches long, short- or long-pointed, edges smooth or with a few teeth, shiny dark green above, pale and soft-hairy beneath. Fruits oblong, 1 inch long, fleshy, purple, acid, 1-seeded.

Principal uses: Furniture, boxes, crates, and baskets, and pulpwood. Also railroad ties and cooperage.

64. BLACK TUPELO, *Nyssa sylvatica* Marsh. (blackgum, sour-gum, tupelo, pepperidge, tupelo-gum; variety: swamp tupelo, *N. sylvatica* var. *biflora* (Walt.) Sarg., blackgum, swamp blackgum, swamp black tupelo).

Large tree of eastern third of United States; also in southern Ontario and Mexico. Bark reddish brown, deeply fissured into irregular and block-shaped ridges. Leaves elliptical or oblong, 2 to 5 inches long, short- or blunt-pointed, wedge-shaped or rounded at base, edges smooth, shiny dark green above, pale and often hairy beneath, turning bright scarlet in fall. Fruits egg-shaped, ⅜ to ½ inch long, fleshy, blue black, bitter, 1-seeded.

Principal uses: Boxes, crates, and baskets, furniture, and pulpwood. Also railroad ties and cooperage. Ornamental and shade tree.

65. OGEECHEE TUPELO, *Nyssa ogeche* Bartr. (sour tupelo-gum, sour tupelo, Ogeechee-lime, limetree).

Small to medium-sized tree, local in swamps of Coastal Plain in South Carolina, Georgia, and Florida. Bark dark brown, thin, irregularly fissured. Leaves elliptical, 4 to 6 inches long, short- or blunt-pointed, wedge-shaped at base, edges smooth, thick, shiny dark green and slightly hairy above, pale and hairy beneath. Fruits 1 to 1½ inches long, fleshy, red, sour, 1-seeded.

Principal uses: A preserve, Ogeechee-lime, is made from the fruit. The wood is of little importance commercially.

    jj. Leaf edges toothed (see also No. 63).
    m. Leaves with few large spiny teeth, evergreen—HOLLY (*Ilex*).

66. AMERICAN HOLLY, *Ilex opaca* Ait. (holly, white holly, evergreen holly, boxwood).

Medium-sized to large tree of Atlantic coast, Gulf coast, and Mississippi Valley regions. Bark light gray, thin, smoothish, with wartlike projections. Leaves evergreen, elliptical, 2 to 4 inches long, spine-pointed and coarsely spiny-toothed, stiff and leathery, shiny dark green above and yellowish green beneath. Male and female flowers on different trees, small, greenish white. Berrylike fruit spherical, ¼ to ⅜ inch in diameter, red.

Principal uses: Christmas decorations. The wood is used for scientific and musical instruments, toy boats, furniture inlays, and sporting and athletic goods. Ornamental and shade tree. (State tree of Delaware.)

    mm. Leaves with many small teeth, shedding in fall.
    n. Leaves with the 2 sides unequal and 1 side larger at base, in 2 rows on twig.
    o. Leaves broad, heart-shaped, with leafstalks more than 1¼ inches long (the fragrant, pale yellow flowers and round,

nutlike fruits borne on a strap-shaped greenish stalk)—BASSWOOD (or linden, *Tilia*).

67. AMERICAN BASSWOOD, *Tilia americana* L. (American linden, basswood, linden, linn, beetree, limetree; *T. glabra* Vent.).

Large tree of northeastern quarter of United States and adjacent Canada. Bark gray, deeply furrowed into narrow, scaly ridges. Leaves in 2 rows, heart-shaped, 4 to 8 inches long, long-pointed, coarsely toothed with long-pointed teeth, dark green above, light green beneath with tufts of hair in angles of main veins. Fruits nutlike, ⅜ to ½ inch in diameter.

Principal uses: Boxes (especially food containers), venetian blinds, millwork, furniture, apiary supplies, and woodenware. Also veneer, excelsior, and cooperage. Shade tree and important honey plant.

68. WHITE BASSWOOD, *Tilia heterophylla* Vent. (beetree linden).

Large tree of Appalachian Mountain region west to Mississippi Valley. Bark gray, deeply furrowed. Leaves in 2 rows, heart-shaped, 3 to 6 inches long, long-pointed, the 2 sides unequal at base, finely toothed, shiny dark green and smooth above, beneath white or brownish with dense hairy coat. Fruits nutlike, ¼ to ⅜ inch in diameter.

Principal uses: Same as No. 67.

    oo. Leaves narrower, with leafstalks less than ½ inch long (flowers not on a strap-shaped stalk).
    p. Leaves with 1 main vein (midrib) and many parallel lateral veins; fruits flat, elliptical or rounded, bordered with a wing, maturing in spring (maturing in fall in Nos. 73 and 74)—ELM (*Ulmus*).
    q. Twigs round, not corky winged.

69. AMERICAN ELM, *Ulmus americana* L. (white elm [lumber], soft elm [lumber], water elm, gray elm, swamp elm).

Large spreading tree of eastern half of United States and adjacent Canada, now threatened in the Northeast by the Dutch elm disease. Bark gray, deeply furrowed, with broad, forking, scaly ridges. Twigs soft-hairy, becoming smooth, not corky winged. Leaves in 2 rows, elliptical, 3 to 6 inches long, long-pointed, the 2 sides unequal, coarsely and doubly toothed with unequal teeth, thin, dark green and smooth or slightly rough above, pale and usually soft-hairy beneath. Fruits elliptical, flat, ⅜ to ½ inch long.

Principal uses: Containers (boxes, baskets, crates, and barrels), furniture, dairy, poultry, and apiary supplies, caskets, and vehicle parts. American elm is extensively planted as a shade tree across the United States. Shelterbelts. (State tree of Massachusetts.)

70. SLIPPERY ELM, *Ulmus rubra* Muhl. (soft elm [lumber], red elm, gray elm; *U. fulva* Michx.).

Medium-sized tree of eastern half of United States and adjacent Canada. Bark dark brown, deeply furrowed; inner bark mucilaginous. Twigs hairy and rough, not corky winged. Leaves in 2 rows, elliptical, 4 to 8 inches long, long-pointed, the 2 sides unequal, coarsely and doubly toothed with unequal teeth, thick, dark green and very rough above, densely soft-hairy beneath. Fruits oval, flat, ½ to ¾ inch long.

Principal uses: Wood used same as No. 69.

    qq. Twigs usually becoming corky winged.

71. ROCK ELM, *Ulmus thomasi* Sarg. (cork elm, hickory elm; *U. racemosa* Thomas, not Borkh.).

Medium-sized to large tree of northeastern quarter of United States and adjacent Canada. Bark gray, deeply furrowed. Twigs often corky winged. Leaves in 2 rows, elliptical, 2 to 4 inches long, short-pointed, the 2 sides unequal, coarsely and doubly toothed with unequal teeth, thick, shiny dark green and smooth above, pale and soft-hairy beneath. Fruit elliptical, flat, ⅜ to ¾ inch long.

Principal uses: Wood used same as No. 69. Shade tree.

72. WINGED ELM, *Ulmus alata* Michx. (wahoo, cork elm).

Medium-sized tree of southeastern quarter of United States. Bark light brown, thin, irregularly fissured. Twigs usually becoming corky winged. Leaves in 2 rows, oblong, 1¼ to 2½ inches long, short-pointed, the 2 sides unequal, coarsely and doubly toothed with unequal teeth, thick, dark green and smooth above, pale and soft-hairy beneath. Fruit elliptical, flat, ⅜ inch long.

Principal uses: Wood used same as No. 69. Shade tree.

73. SEPTEMBER ELM, *Ulmus serotina* Sarg. (red elm).

Medium-sized tree of Mississippi Valley region from Illinois to Georgia and Oklahoma. Bark light brown, thin, fissured. Twigs often corky winged. Leaves in 2 rows, oblong, 2 to 3 inches long, long-pointed, the 2 sides unequal, coarsely and doubly toothed with

RED BIRCH

YELLOW BIRCH

BLACK BIRCH

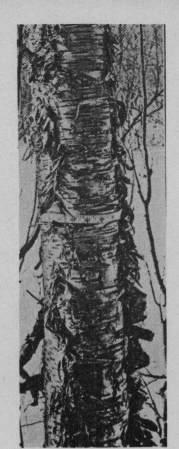

YELLOW BIRCH

EUROPEAN WHITE BIRCH

BEAR OAK

PAPER BIRCH

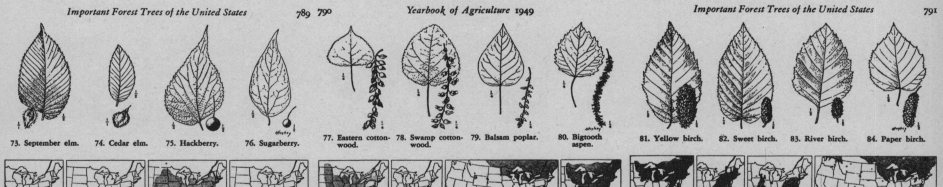

73. September elm.   74. Cedar elm.   75. Hackberry.   76. Sugarberry.   77. Eastern cottonwood.   78. Swamp cottonwood.   79. Balsam poplar.   80. Bigtooth aspen.   81. Yellow birch.   82. Sweet birch.   83. River birch.   84. Paper birch.

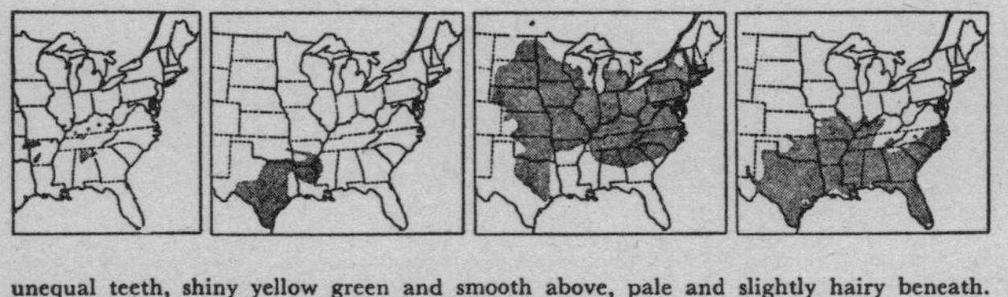

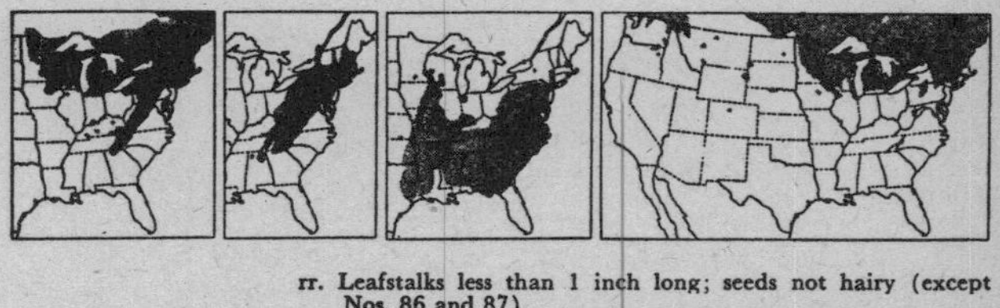

unequal teeth, shiny yellow green and smooth above, pale and slightly hairy beneath. Flowering in fall. Fruit elliptical, ½ inch long, flat.
Principal uses: Wood used same as No. 69.

74. CEDAR ELM, *Ulmus crassifolia* Nutt. (red elm, basket elm, southern rock elm).
Large tree of lower Mississippi Valley to Texas and adjacent Mexico. Bark light brown, fissured. Twigs usually becoming corky winged. Leaves in 2 rows, elliptical, 1 to 2 inches long, short-pointed or rounded, the 2 sides unequal, coarsely and doubly toothed with unequal teeth, thick, shiny dark green and rough above, soft-hairy beneath. Flowering in late summer or fall. Fruit oblong, ⅜ to ½ inch long, flat.
Principal uses: Wood used same as No. 69.

     pp. Leaves with 3 main veins from base; fruits round, wingless, maturing in fall—HACKBERRY (*Celtis*).

75. HACKBERRY, *Celtis occidentalis* L. (common hackberry, sugarberry).
Medium-sized to large tree of eastern half of United States except southern border; also in adjacent Canada. Bark light brown to gray, with corky warts or ridges becoming scaly. Leaves in 2 rows, oval 2 to 4½ inches long, usually long-pointed, the 2 sides unequal, sharply toothed except in lower part, with 3 main veins from base, bright green and smooth or sometimes rough above, paler and nearly smooth beneath. Fruits ¼ to ⅜ inch in diameter, dark purple, 1-seeded.
Principal uses: Furniture and boxes and baskets. Shelterbelts and shade tree.

76. SUGARBERRY, *Celtis laevigata* Willd. (sugar hackberry, hackberry, Mississippi hackberry, southern hackberry; *C. mississippiensis* Spach).
Medium-sized to large tree of southeastern quarter of United States, with a variety west to New Mexico and northeastern Mexico. Bark gray, smoothish, with prominent corky warts. Leaves in 2 rows, broadly lance-shaped, 1½ to 4 inches long, long-pointed, the 2 sides unequal, edges smooth or sometimes with a few teeth, with 3 main veins from base, dark green and smooth or sometimes rough above, paler and usually smooth beneath. Fruits ¼ inch in diameter, orange red, or purple, 1-seeded.
Principal uses: Furniture and boxes and baskets. Shelterbelts and shade tree.

     nn. Leaves with both sides equal, spreading around twig (in 2 rows in No. 89).
     r. Leafstalks more than 1½ inches long, slender; seeds cottony, in long-clustered capsules—POPLAR (*Populus*; see also Nos. 150 and 151).

77. EASTERN COTTONWOOD, *Populus deltoides* Bartr. (cottonwood, eastern poplar, Carolina poplar, necklace poplar; *P. balsamifera* auth.).
Large tree of eastern half of United States and adjacent Canada. Bark at first yellowish green and smooth, becoming gray and deeply furrowed. Leaves triangular, 3 to 6 inches long and wide, long-pointed, coarsely toothed with curved teeth, smooth, light green and shiny. Leafstalks flat.
Principal uses: Lumber and veneer, used principally for boxes and crates but also for furniture, dairy and poultry supplies, etc. Also pulpwood, excelsior, and fuel. Shade tree and shelterbelts. (Cottonwood (*Populus* spp.) is the State tree of Kansas, Nebraska, and South Dakota.)

78. SWAMP COTTONWOOD, *Populus heterophylla* L. (cottonwood, swamp poplar, black cottonwood, river cottonwood).
Medium-sized to large tree of Atlantic coast, Gulf coast, and Mississippi Valley regions. Bark grayish brown, furrowed into scaly ridges. Leaves heart-shaped, 4 to 7 inches long and nearly as wide, short-pointed or rounded at apex, finely toothed with small, curved teeth, hairy when unfolding but becoming smooth or remaining woolly beneath, dark green above, paler beneath. Leafstalks round.
Principal uses: Boxes and crates and pulpwood.

79. BALSAM POPLAR, *Populus tacamahaca* Mill. (tacamahac, tacamahac poplar, balm-of-Gilead, balm-of-Gilead poplar, balsam, cottonwood; *P. balsamifera* auth.).
Large tree widely distributed in northeastern border of United States, northern Rocky Mountain region, and across Canada to Alaska. Bark at first reddish brown and smooth, becoming gray, furrowed, with flat, scaly ridges. Winter buds resinous and fragrant. Leaves oval or broadly lance-shaped, 3 to 5 inches long, short-pointed, finely toothed with rounded teeth, smooth or nearly so, shiny dark green above, pale green beneath. Leafstalks round.
Principal uses: Boxes and crates and pulpwood. Balm-of-Gilead, derived from the buds, is used in cough medicine. Ornamental.

80. BIGTOOTH ASPEN, *Populus grandidentata* Michx. (largetooth aspen, aspen, poplar, popple).
Medium-sized tree of northeastern quarter of United States and adjacent Canada. Bark greenish, smooth, thin, becoming dark brown, irregularly fissured, with flat ridges. Leaves elliptical or nearly round, 2½ to 4 inches long, coarsely toothed with curved teeth. Leafstalks flat.
Principal uses: Pulpwood, boxes and crates, excelsior, and matches.

     rr. Leafstalks less than 1 inch long; seeds not hairy (except Nos. 86 and 87).
     s. Leaf edges with teeth of 2 sizes and slightly irregular; fruit a cone, upright in Nos. 81–83, hanging down in Nos. 84 and 85—BIRCH (*Betula*).

81. YELLOW BIRCH, *Betula lutea* Michx. f. (birch [lumber], gray birch, silver birch, swamp birch).
Large tree of northeastern United States and adjacent Canada and Appalachian Mountain region. Bark (aromatic on young branches) yellowish or silvery gray, shiny, separating into papery, curly strips; on old trunks reddish brown. Leaves oval, 3 to 5 inches long, long- or short-pointed, sharply and doubly toothed, mostly with 9 to 11 main veins on each side, nearly smooth, dull dark green above, yellow green below. Cones ¾ to 1¼ inches long.
Principal uses: Birches are among the leading furniture woods. Also boxes, baskets, crates, woodenware, handles, spools and bobbins, millwork, flooring, distillation products, railroad ties, and fuel. Yellow birch plywood is used in airplane construction. Shade tree. (State tree of New Hampshire.)

82. SWEET BIRCH, *Betula lenta* L. (birch [lumber], black birch, cherry birch).
Medium-sized to large tree of Appalachian Mountain region and adjacent Canada. Bark aromatic on young branches, dark reddish brown, smooth, shiny; on large trunks fissured into scaly plates. Leaves oval, 2½ to 5 inches long, long-pointed, sharply and doubly toothed, mostly with 9 to 11 main veins on each side, silky-hairy beneath when young but becoming nearly smooth, dark dull green above, light yellow green beneath. Cones ¾ to 1½ inches long.
Principal uses: Same as No. 81.

     tt. Leaves mostly with 4 to 9 main veins on each side.

83. RIVER BIRCH, *Betula nigra* L. (red birch).
Medium-sized to large tree of wet soil in eastern half of United States. Bark reddish brown or silvery gray, shiny, becoming fissured and separating into papery scales. Leaves oval, 1½ to 3 inches long, short-pointed, wedge-shaped at base, doubly toothed, mostly with 7 to 9 main veins on each side, shiny dark green above, whitish and usually hairy beneath. Cones 1 to 1½ inches long.
Principal uses: Ornamental and for erosion control.

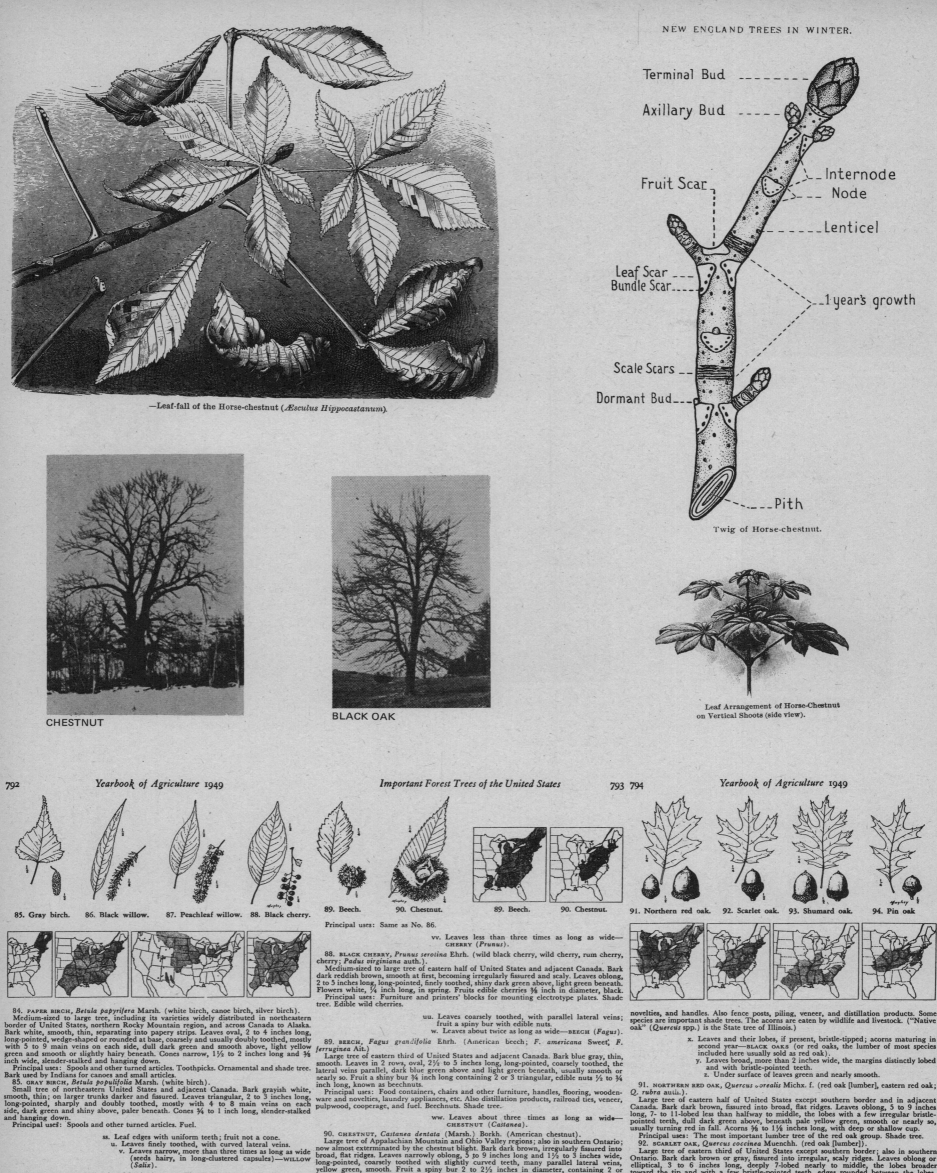

—Leaf-fall of the Horse-chestnut (*Æsculus Hippocastanum*).

Terminal Bud
Axillary Bud
Fruit Scar
Internode
Node
Lenticel
Leaf Scar
Bundle Scar
1 year's growth
Scale Scars
Dormant Bud
Pith

Twig of Horse-chestnut.

CHESTNUT

BLACK OAK

Leaf Arrangement of Horse-Chestnut on Vertical Shoots (side view).

85. Gray birch.   86. Black willow.   87. Peachleaf willow.   88. Black cherry.

89. Beech.   90. Chestnut.   89. Beech.   90. Chestnut.

91. Northern red oak.   92. Scarlet oak.   93. Shumard oak.   94. Pin oak.

84. PAPER BIRCH, *Betula papyrifera* Marsh. (white birch, canoe birch, silver birch).
Medium-sized to large tree, including its varieties widely distributed in northeastern border of United States, northern Rocky Mountain region, and across Canada to Alaska. Bark white, smooth, thin, separating into papery strips. Leaves oval, 2 to 4 inches long, long-pointed, wedge-shaped or rounded at base, coarsely and usually doubly toothed, mostly with 5 to 9 main veins on each side, dull dark green and smooth above, light yellow green and smooth or slightly hairy beneath. Cones narrow, 1½ to 2 inches long and ⅜ inch wide, slender-stalked and hanging down.
Principal uses: Spools and other turned articles. Toothpicks. Ornamental and shade tree. Bark used by Indians for canoes and small articles.
85. GRAY BIRCH, *Betula populifolia* Marsh. (white birch).
Small tree of northeastern United States and adjacent Canada. Bark grayish white, smooth, thin; on larger trunks darker and fissured. Leaves triangular, 2 to 3 inches long, long-pointed, sharply and doubly toothed, mostly with 4 to 8 main veins on each side, dark green and shiny above, paler beneath. Cones ¾ to 1 inch long, slender-stalked and hanging down.
Principal uses: Spools and other turned articles. Fuel.

ss. Leaf edges with uniform teeth; fruit not a cone.
 u. Leaves finely toothed, with curved lateral veins.
  v. Leaves narrow, more than three times as long as wide (seeds hairy, in long-clustered capsules)—WILLOW (*Salix*).

86. BLACK WILLOW, *Salix nigra* Marsh. (swamp willow, willow).
Medium-sized to large tree of wet soil, eastern half of United States and adjacent Canada. Bark dark brown or blackish, deeply furrowed, with scaly, forking ridges. Leaves lance-shaped, 2½ to 5 inches long, long-pointed, finely toothed, green on both sides, shiny above and pale beneath. Male and female flowers on different trees in early spring, minute, yellowish or greenish, many in narrow clusters 1½ to 3 inches long.
Principal uses: Boxes and baskets, furniture, and caskets. A special use is for artificial limbs. Erosion control. Shade tree.
87. PEACHLEAF WILLOW, *Salix amygdaloides* Anders. (peach willow, almond willow).
Small to medium-sized tree of wet soil, nearly across northern United States and adjacent Canada, south to Texas and Arizona. Bark brown, irregularly fissured into flat ridges. Leaves lance-shaped, 2½ to 5 inches long, long-pointed, finely toothed, shiny green above and pale beneath. Male and female flowers on different trees in early spring, minute, yellowish or greenish, many in narrow clusters 2 to 3 inches long.

Principal uses: Same as No. 86.

  vv. Leaves less than three times as long as wide—CHERRY (*Prunus*).
88. BLACK CHERRY, *Prunus serotina* Ehrh. (wild black cherry, wild cherry, rum cherry, cherry; *Padus virginiana* auth.).
Medium-sized to large tree of eastern half of United States and adjacent Canada. Bark dark reddish brown, smooth at first, becoming irregularly fissured and scaly. Leaves oblong, 2 to 5 inches long, long-pointed, finely toothed, shiny dark green above, light green beneath. Flowers white, ¼ inch long, in spring. Fruits edible cherries ⅜ inch in diameter, black.
Principal uses: Furniture and printers' blocks for mounting electrotype plates. Shade tree. Edible wild cherries.

 uu. Leaves coarsely toothed, with parallel lateral veins; fruit a spiny bur with edible nuts.
  w. Leaves about twice as long as wide—BEECH (*Fagus*).
89. BEECH, *Fagus grandifolia* Ehrh. (American beech; F. *americana* Sweet; F. *ferruginea* Ait.).
Large tree of eastern third of United States and adjacent Canada. Bark blue gray, thin, smooth. Leaves in 2 rows, oval, 2½ to 5 inches long, long-pointed, coarsely toothed, the lateral veins parallel, dark blue green above and light green beneath, usually smooth or nearly so. Fruit a shiny bur ¾ inch long containing 2 or 3 triangular, edible nuts ½ to ¾ inch long, known as beechnuts.
Principal uses: Foot containers, chairs and other furniture, handles, flooring, woodenware and novelties, laundry appliances, etc. Also distillation products, railroad ties, veneer, pulpwood, cooperage, and fuel. Beechnuts. Shade tree.

  ww. Leaves about three times as long as wide—CHESTNUT (*Castanea*).
90. CHESTNUT, *Castanea dentata* (Marsh.) Borkh. (American chestnut).
Large tree of Appalachian Mountain and Ohio Valley regions; also in southern Ontario; now almost exterminated by the chestnut blight. Bark dark brown, irregularly fissured into broad, flat ridges. Leaves narrowly oblong, 5 to 9 inches long and 1½ to 3 inches wide, long-pointed, coarsely toothed with slightly curved teeth, many parallel lateral veins, yellow green, smooth. Fruit a spiny bur 2 to 2½ inches in diameter, containing 2 or 3 broad, flattened, edible nuts ½ to 1 inch wide, known as chestnuts.
Principal uses: The wood, largely from blight-killed trees, is the main domestic source of tannin. Lumber for construction and for manufacture of furniture, caskets, and boxes and crates. Pulpwood. Chestnuts. The leaves are an official drug.

ff (f on p. 784). Winter buds 3 or more in cluster at tip of twig; pith of twigs star-shaped in cross section; fruit an acorn—OAK (*Quercus*).
Twenty species of eastern oaks included here have commercially important wood.
Principal uses: Oaks are the most important hardwood timbers of the United States. Oak is used principally for lumber, fuel (including charcoal), and cooperage (white oak group), and is the leading wood for railroad ties and mine timbers. Besides the lumber used in building construction, much is manufactured into flooring (oak is the principal flooring wood), boxes and crates, furniture, railroad-car construction, vehicle parts, general millwork, ships and boats, agricultural implements, caskets, fixtures, woodenware and novelties, and handles. Also fence posts, piling, veneer, and distillation products. Some species are important shade trees. The acorns are eaten by wildlife and livestock. ("Native oak" (*Quercus* spp.) is the State tree of Illinois.

 x. Leaves and their lobes, if present, bristle-tipped; acorns maturing in second year—BLACK OAKS (or red oaks, the lumber of most species included here usually sold as red oak).
  y. Leaves broad, more than 2 inches wide, the margins distinctly lobed and with bristle-pointed teeth.
   z. Under surface of leaves green and nearly smooth.
91. NORTHERN RED OAK, *Quercus borealis* Michx. f. (red oak [lumber], eastern red oak; Q. *rubra* auth.).
Large tree of eastern half of United States except southern border and in adjacent Canada. Bark dark brown, fissured into broad, flat ridges. Leaves oblong, 5 to 9 inches long, 7- to 11-lobed less than halfway to middle, the lobes with a few irregular bristle-pointed teeth, dull dark green above, paler beneath, smooth, usually turning red in fall. Acorns ⅝ to 1⅛ inches long, with deep or shallow cup.
Principal uses: The most important lumber tree of the red oak group. Shade tree.
92. SCARLET OAK, *Quercus coccinea* Muenchh.
Large tree of eastern third of United States except southern border; also in southern Ontario. Bark dark brown or gray, fissured into irregular, scaly ridges. Leaves oblong or elliptical, 3 to 6 inches long, deeply 7-lobed nearly to middle, the lobes broader toward the tip and with a few bristle-pointed teeth, edges rounded between the lobes, bright green, shiny, and smooth above, paler and nearly smooth beneath, turning scarlet in fall. Acorns ½ to ¾ inch long, a third to half enclosed by the deep cup.
Principal uses: Red oak lumber. Shade tree.
93. SHUMARD OAK, *Quercus shumardii* Buckl. (red oak [lumber], Shumard red oak, Schneck oak, Texas oak, southern red oak).
Large tree of eastern United States, chiefly in Atlantic coast, Gulf coast, and Mississippi Valley regions. Bark gray or reddish brown, fissured into scaly plates. Leaves oval or elliptical, 3 to 7 inches long, 5- to 9-lobed more than halfway to middle, the lobes with a few bristle-pointed teeth, edges rounded with tufts of hairs along midrib. Acorns ⅝ to 1⅛ inches long, with shallow or deep cup.
Principal uses: Important timber tree for red oak lumber. Furniture, cabinet work, and veneer. Shade tree.

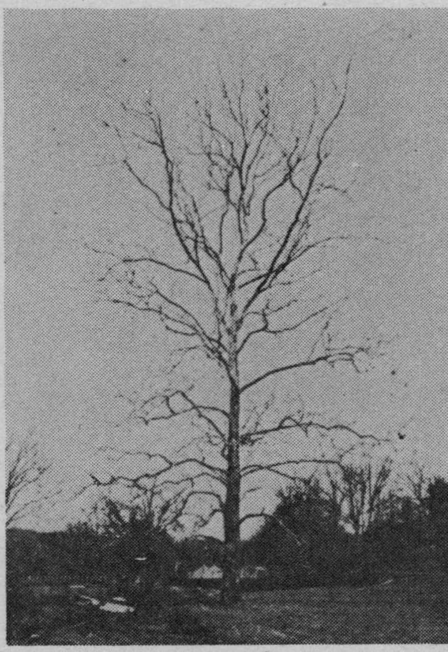

SYCAMORE MAPLE

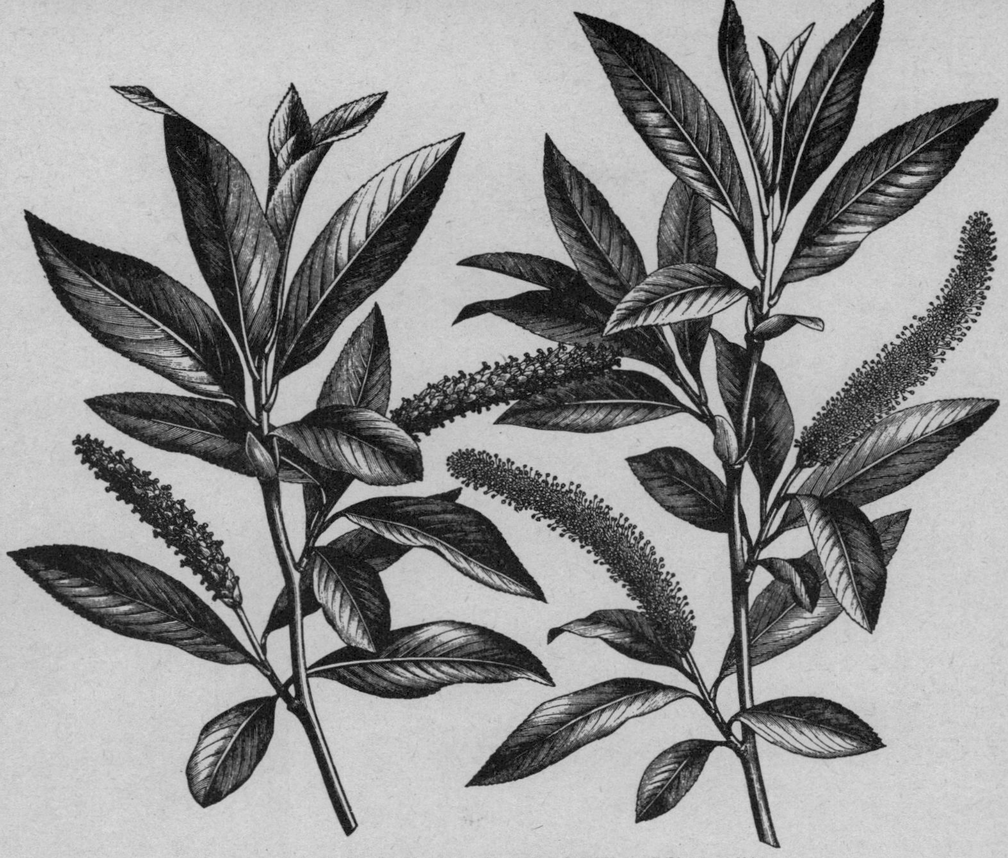

–Type of a diœcious plant: Crack Willow (*Salix fragilis*).

[1] Twig with pistillate catkins. [2] Twig with staminate catkins. Natural size.

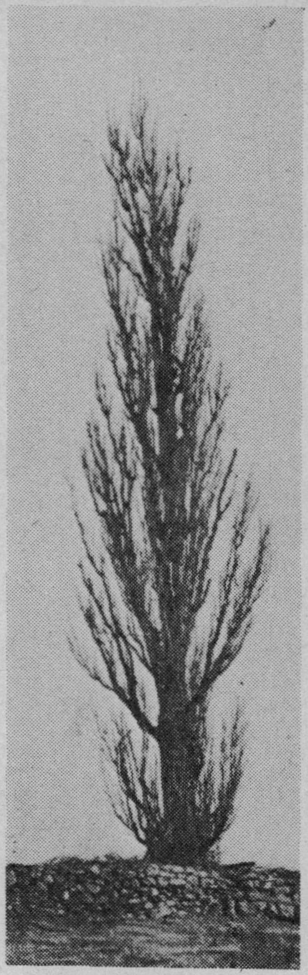

LOMBARY POPLAR

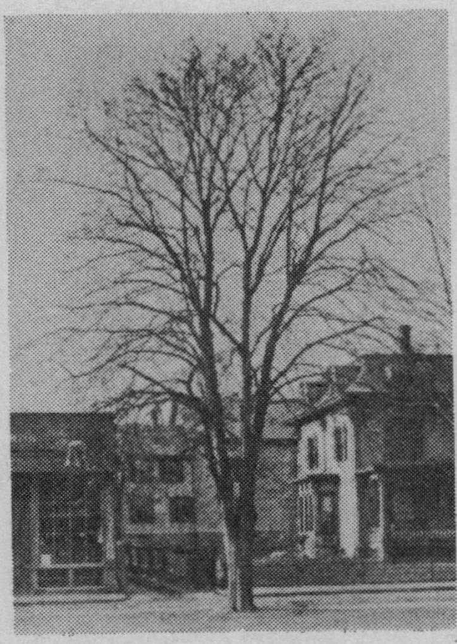

SYCAMORE

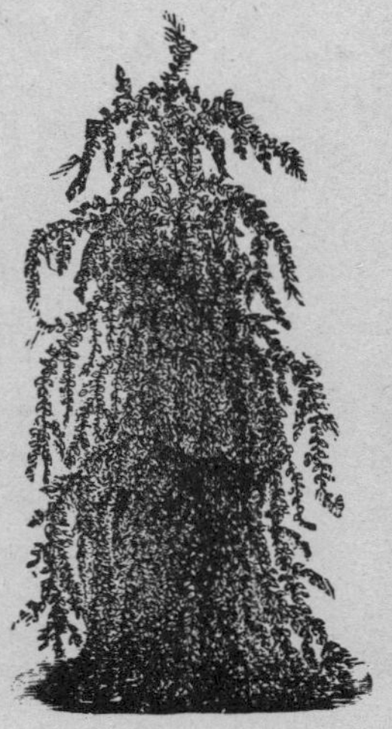

–WEEPING BEECH (*F. syl., pendula*).

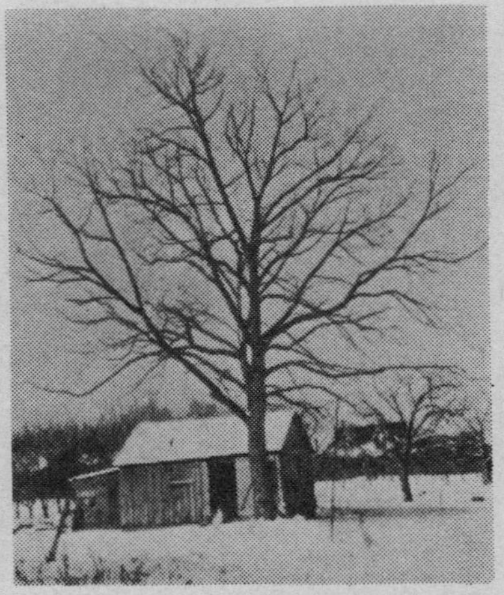

BLACK WALNUT

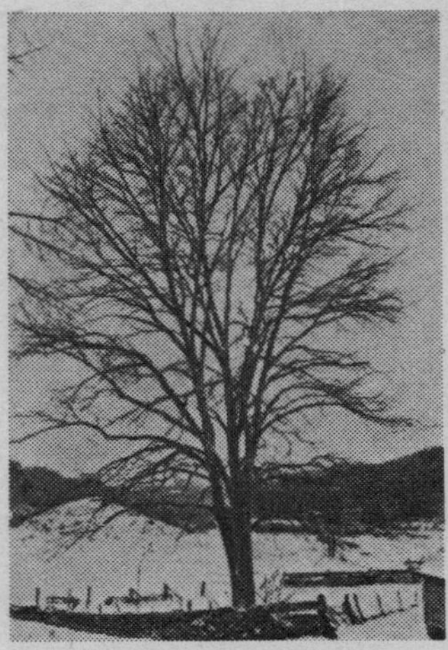

BUTTERNUT

Important Forest Trees of the United States 795 796 *Yearbook of Agriculture 1949* *Important Forest Trees of the United States* 797

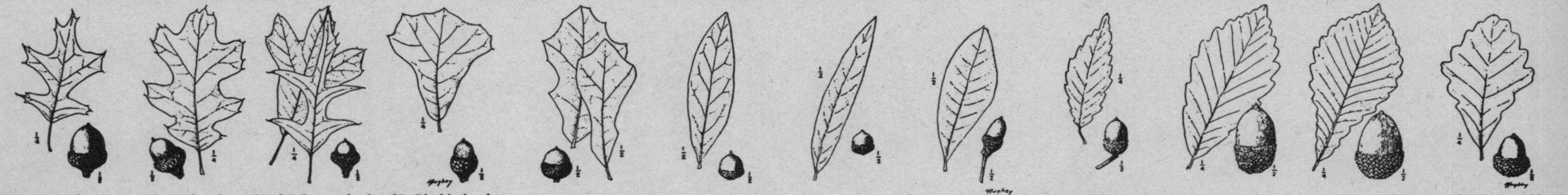

95. Nuttall oak. 96. Black oak. 97. Southern red oak. 98. Blackjack oak. 99. Water oak. 100. Laurel oak. 101. Willow oak. 102. Live oak. 103. Chinquapin oak. 104. Chestnut oak. 105. Swamp chestnut oak. 106. Swamp white oak.

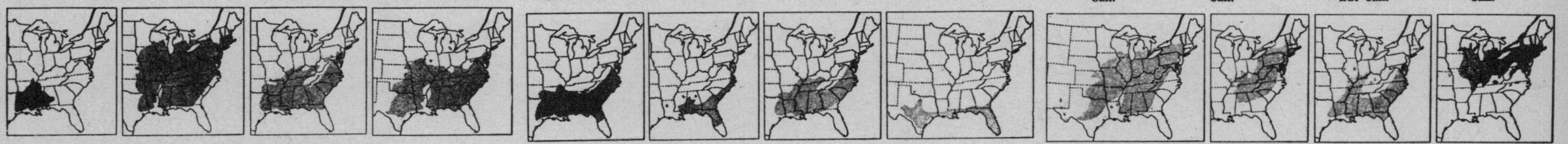

94. PIN OAK, *Quercus palustris* Muenchh. (swamp oak).

Large tree of northeastern quarter of United States except northern border; also in southern Ontario. Bark grayish brown, smooth, becoming fissured with low, scaly ridges. Leaves elliptical, 3 to 5 inches long, deeply 5- to 7-lobed nearly to middle, the lobes with a few bristle-pointed teeth, dark green and very shiny above, light green and nearly smooth beneath. Acorns rounded, about ½ inch in diameter, with shallow cup.

Principal uses: Fuel wood, charcoal, and distillation products. Shade tree.

95. NUTTALL OAK, *Quercus nuttallii* Palmer (red oak [lumber]).

Large tree of lower Mississippi Valley and Gulf Coastal Plain regions from Alabama to Missouri and Texas. Bark dark brownish gray, slightly fissured. Leaves oblong or elliptical, 4 to 8 inches long, deeply 5- or 7-lobed, the narrow lobes with a few bristle-pointed teeth, dark green above, paler and nearly smooh beneath. Acorns oblong, ¾ to 1¼ inches long, enclosed one-third to one-half by the deep cup.

Principal uses: Red oak lumber.

zz. Under surface of leaves with brownish or gray hairy coat.

96. BLACK OAK, *Quercus velutina* Lam. (red oak [lumber]), yellow oak, quercitron oak).

Large tree of eastern half of United States and southern Ontario. Bark blackish, thick, deeply furrowed, with blocklike ridges; inner bark yellow. Leaves oval or oblong, 4 to 10 inches long, 7- to 9-lobed about halfway to middle, the lobes broad and with a few bristle-pointed teeth, shiny dark green above, usually brown-hairy beneath, turning dull red or brown in fall. Acorns ⅝ to ¾ inch long, half enclosed by the deep cup.

Principal uses: Red oak lumber. The bark is a source of tannin. Fuel. Shade tree.

97. SOUTHERN RED OAK, *Quercus falcata* Michx. (red oak [lumber], Spanish oak; *Q. rubra* auth.; variety: swamp red oak, *Q. falcata* var. *pagodaefolia* Ell., cherrybark oak).

Large tree of Atlantic coast, Gulf coast, and Mississippi Valley regions. Bark dark brown, thick, fissured into narrow ridges. Leaves elliptical or oval, 3 to 8 inches long, deeply 3- to 7-lobed nearly to middle or slightly 3-lobed near broad apex (less deeply 5- to 11-lobed in the variety, swamp red oak), the lobes with 1 to 3 bristle-pointed teeth, dark green, smooth, and shiny above, rusty or grayish hairy beneath, turning brown or orange in fall. Acorns rounded, about ½ inch in diameter, with shallow cup.

Principal uses: Important timber tree for red oak lumber. Shade tree.

98. BLACKJACK OAK, *Quercus marilandica* Muenchh. (blackjack, jack oak, black oak).

Small tree of eastern half of United States except northern border. Bark blackish, thick and rough, divided into small squarish blocks. Leaves oval, 3 to 7 inches long, broadest and 3-lobed at apex, the lobes shallow and broad with 1 or few bristle-pointed teeth, dark green, smooth, and shiny above, brownish or rusty-hairy beneath, turning brown or yellow in fall. Acorns ¾ inch long, about half enclosed by the deep cup.

Principal uses: Fuel wood, charcoal, and distillation products.

yy. Leaves narrow, less than 2 inches broad, with edges smooth or slightly 3-lobed.

99. WATER OAK, *Quercus nigra* L. (red oak [lumber]).

Large tree of Atlantic coast, Gulf coast, and Mississippi Valley regions. Bark gray, fissured into irregular, scaly ridges. Leaves oval, 1½ to 5 inches long, broadest at the 3-lobed or smooth apex or sometimes with several lobes, dull blue green, paler beneath, becoming smooth except for tufts of hairs along axis, turning yellow in fall and shedding in winter. Acorns rounded, ⅜ to ⅝ inch in diameter, with shallow cup.

Principal uses: Red oak lumber. Fuel. Shade tree.

100. LAUREL OAK, *Quercus laurifolia* Michx.

Large tree of South Atlantic and Gulf Coastal Plains. Bark dark brown, smoothish, on large trunks becoming deeply furrowed, with broad ridges. Leaves oblong, 2 to 5½ inches long, short-pointed with smooth or sometimes slightly lobed edges, shiny dark green above, light green beneath, smooth, nearly evergreen but shedding in early spring. Acorns rounded, about ½ inch in diameter, with shallow cup.

Principal uses: Fuel wood, charcoal, and distillation products. Shade tree.

101. WILLOW OAK, *Quercus phellos* L. (red oak [lumber]).

Large tree of Atlantic coast, Gulf coast, and Mississippi Valley regions. Bark gray or brown, smoothish, on large trunks becoming fissured into scaly ridges. Leaves very narrowly oblong or lance-shaped, 2 to 4 inches long and ⅜ to ¾ inch broad, short-pointed with smooth or slightly wavy edges, light green and shiny above, beneath dull and slightly hairy or nearly smooth, turning pale yellow in fall. Acorns small, rounded, ⅜ inch in diameter, with shallow cup.

Principal uses: Red oak lumber. Shade tree.

xx. Leaves and their lobes not bristle-tipped; acorns maturing in first year—WHITE OAKS (the lumber of most species sold as white oak).

A. Leaves with edges usually smooth and rolled under, evergreen.

102. LIVE OAK, *Quercus virginiana* Mill.

Medium-sized, widespreading tree of South Atlantic coast and Gulf coast regions. Bark dark brown, furrowed and slightly scaly. Leaves evergreen, elliptical or oblong, 2 to 5 inches long, usually rounded at apex, edges usually smooth and rolled under, shiny dark green above, whitish hairy beneath. Acorns 1 to 5 on stalks ½ to 3 inches long, ¾ to 1 inch long, narrow, with deep cup.

Principal uses: Shade tree. Formerly used in shipbuilding. (State tree of Georgia.)

AA. Leaves with edges lobed or toothed, shedding in fall.

B. Leaf edges wavy with uniform, rounded teeth (CHESTNUT OAKS).

103. CHINQUAPIN OAK, *Quercus muehlenbergii* Engelm. (chestnut oak, yellow oak).

Large tree of eastern half of United States and local in New Mexico; also in southern Ontario. Bark light gray, thin, fissured, and flaky. Leaves oblong or broadly lance-shaped, 4 to 6 inches long, short- or long-pointed, usually rounded at base, edges wavy with coarse, slightly curved teeth, dark or yellowish green above, whitish hairy beneath, turning orange and scarlet in fall. Acorns ½ to ¾ inch long, rounded, half enclosed by the deep cup.

Principal uses: Railroad ties and construction timbers.

104. CHESTNUT OAK, *Quercus montana* Willd. (white oak [lumber], rock chestnut oak, rock oak; *Q. prinus* auth.).

Large tree of Appalachian Mountain and Ohio Valley regions; also in southern Ontario. Bark brown or blackish; on large trunks becoming deeply furrowed into broad ridges. Leaves oblong, 5 to 8 inches long, short- or long-pointed, narrowed and pointed or rounded at base, edges wavy with rounded teeth, shiny yellow green above, paler and hairy or nearly smooth beneath, turning dull orange in fall. Acorns large, 1 to 1½ inches long, one-third to one-half enclosed by the thin, deep, warty cup.

Principal uses: White oak lumber and railroad ties. The bark is a source of tannin.

105. SWAMP CHESTNUT OAK, *Quercus prinus* L. (white oak [lumber], basket oak, cow oak; *Q. michauxii* Nutt.).

Large tree of Atlantic coast, Gulf coast, and Mississippi Valley regions. Bark light gray, fissured and scaly. Leaves oblong, 4 to 8 inches long, short- or long-pointed, wedge-shaped or rounded at base, edges wavy with rounded teeth, shiny dark green above, grayish hairy beneath, turning crimson in fall. Acorns large, 1 to 1½ inches long, one-third or more enclosed by the thick, deep cup composed of many distinct scales.

Principal uses: White oak lumber.

106. SWAMP WHITE OAK, *Quercus bicolor* Willd. (white oak [lumber]).

Large tree of northeastern quarter of United States and adjacent Canada. Bark brown, scaly; on old trunks becoming furrowed into long, scaly ridges. Leaves oblong, 4 to 6 inches long, gradually narrowed toward base, broadest above middle, edges wavy with rounded teeth or lobes, dark green and shiny above, whitish hairy beneath, turning yellow

RED OAK

APPLE

POST OAK

SCARLET OAK

SMALL TOOTH ASPEN

CEDAR OF LEBANON.
(CEDRUS LIBANI.)

The original home of Cedar-of-Lebanon is Asia Minor, where centuries ago it formed extensive stands of timber. However, uncontrolled lumbering and grazing has eliminated it from many areas where it formerly grew. The tree is a rapid grower in moderately mild climates and can reach a girth of 35 feet and a height of 140 feet in 200 years. Trees only 50 or 60 years old often look quite ancient. The true cedars greatly resembly larch in the shape and attachment of their needles, but they are evergreen while the larch drops its needles each fall.

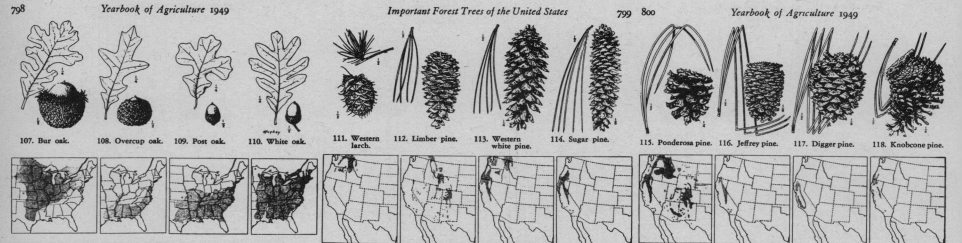

107. Bur oak.   108. Overcup oak.   109. Post oak.   110. White oak.   111. Western larch.   112. Limber pine.   113. Western white pine.   114. Sugar pine.   115. Ponderosa pine.   116. Jeffrey pine.   117. Digger pine.   118. Knobcone pine.

brown, orange, or red in fall. Acorns usually in pairs on stalks 1½ to 3 inches long, ¾ to 1¼ inches long, one-third enclosed by the deep cup.
Principal uses: White oak lumber.

BB. Leaf edges deeply lobed.

107. BUR OAK, *Quercus macrocarpa* Michx. (mossycup oak).
Large tree of eastern half of United States west to Montana and in adjacent Canada west to Saskatchewan. Bark light brown, deeply furrowed into scaly ridges. Leaves oblong, 4 to 10 inches long, wedge-shaped at base, broadest above middle, the lower part deeply lobed nearly to middle and the upper half with shallow lobes, dark green and usually shiny above, grayish or whitish hairy beneath, turning yellow or brown in fall. Acorns usually large, ¾ to 2 inches long, broad, half enclosed by the large cup with fringelike border.
Principal uses: Lumber and railroad ties. Shelterbelts. Shade tree and ornamental.

108. OVERCUP OAK, *Quercus lyrata* Walt. (swamp white oak; white oak [lumber]).
Medium-sized to large tree of Atlantic coast, Gulf coast, and Mississippi Valley regions. Bark brownish gray, fissured into large irregular, scaly ridges. Leaves oblong, 6 to 8 inches long, wedge-shaped at base, deeply lobed nearly to middle with 7 to 9 rounded or pointed lobes, the 2 lowest lobes on each side much smaller, dark green and smooth above, white hairy beneath, turning yellowish, orange, or scarlet in fall. Acorns ½ to 1 inch long, nearly enclosed by the spherical deep cup with ragged edge.
Principal uses: White oak lumber.

109. POST OAK, *Quercus stellata* Wangenh.
Small to medium-sized (rarely large) tree of eastern half of United States except northern border. Bark reddish brown, fissured into broad, scaly ridges. Leaves oblong, 4 to 8 inches long, usually wedge-shaped at base, deeply 5- to 7-lobed (3-lobed in a variety), the lobes broad and middle lobes largest, dark green and rough above, grayish hairy beneath, turning brown in fall. Acorns ½ to 1 inch long, nearly half enclosed by the deep cup.
Principal uses: Railroad ties and construction timbers.

110. WHITE OAK, *Quercus alba* L.
Large tree of eastern half of United States and adjacent Canada. Bark light gray, fissured into scaly ridges. Leaves oblong, 4 to 9 inches long, deeply or shallowly 5- to 9-lobed, smooth, bright green above, pale or whitish beneath, turning deep red in fall. Acorns ¾ to 1 inch long, with shallow cup.
Principal uses: The most important lumber tree of the white oak group and one of the best oaks with high-grade all-purpose wood. The outstanding wood for tight barrels. Shade tree. (State tree of Connecticut, Maryland, and West Virginia.)

WESTERN TREES

Tree species Nos. 111 to 165 are native in the western half of the United States, west of the prairie-plains. In addition, the following 9 species in the list of eastern trees occur also in western United States: Nos. 16, 31, 33, 76, 79, 84, 87, 103, and 107. Also, Nos. 11, 17, and 18 extend to western Canada though not to western United States. The 18 important tree species of Alaska, mostly in the list of western trees, are: Nos. 3, 16, 17, 79, 84, 119, 122, 123, 124, 127, 130, 131, 138, 140, 147, 150, 152, and 153.

GYMNOSPERMS (CONIFERS OR SOFTWOODS)

A (AA on p. 808). Trees resinous, with leaves needlelike or scalelike, evergreen (except larch, No. 111); seeds borne on scales of a cone (berrylike in juniper, Nos. 142 to 145, or seeds single in a fleshy scarlet disk in yew, No. 122)—GYMNOSPERMS (conifers or softwoods, such as pines, spruces, firs).
  B. Leaves shedding in fall, needlelike, many in cluster on short, spur branches—LARCH (*Larix*; see also No. 3).

111. WESTERN LARCH, *Larix occidentalis* Nutt. (larch, western tamarack, tamarack, mountain larch, Montana larch, hackmatack).
Large tree of mountains of northwestern United States and southeastern British Columbia. Bark reddish brown, scaly, becoming deeply furrowed into flat ridges with many overlapping plates. Needles many in cluster on short, spur branches (or single on leading twigs), 3-angled, 1 to 1¼ inches long, light pale green, shedding in fall. Cones upright, 1 to 1½ inches long, with long, pointed bracts.
Principal uses: Lumber for building construction, also interior finish, flooring, and millwork. Railroad ties, mine timbers, fuel. The gum (galactin) can be used in manufacture of baking powder. Ornamental.

BB. Leaves evergreen, needlelike or scalelike, single or not more than 5 in a cluster.
  C. Leaves with a sheath at base, in clusters of 2 to 5 (or 1 in No. 121) needlelike—PINE (*Pinus*).
    D. Needles 5 in a cluster—WHITE (SOFT) PINES.

112. LIMBER PINE, *Pinus flexilis* James (Rocky Mountain white pine, white pine; variety: *P. flexilis* var. *reflexa* Engelm., *P. strobiformis* auth.).
Medium-sized tree of Rocky Mountain region, including adjacent Canada and Mexico. Bark dark brown, furrowed into rectangular, scaly plates. Needles 5 in cluster, slender, 2 to 3½ inches long, dark green. Cones short-stalked, 3 to 6 inches long, yellow brown, with thick, rounded scales and large seeds ⅜ to ½ inch long.
Principal uses: Lumber (mostly for rough construction and occasionally for boxes), mine timbers, railroad ties, poles, and fuel.

113. WESTERN WHITE PINE, *Pinus monticola* Dougl. (Idaho white pine [lumber], white pine).
Large tree of northern Rocky Mountain and Pacific coast regions, including southern British Columbia. Bark gray, thin, smoothish, becoming fissured into rectangular, scaly plates. Needles 5 in cluster, stout, 2 to 4 inches long, blue green. Cones long-stalked, 5 to 12 inches long, yellow brown, with thin, rounded scales.
Principal uses: Important timber tree. Lumber for building construction, matches (the leading match wood), boxes, and millwork. (State tree of Idaho.)

114. SUGAR PINE, *Pinus lambertiana* Dougl. (California sugar pine).
Large tree (largest of the pines) of Pacific coast region from Oregon to Lower California. Bark brown, furrowed into irregular, scaly ridges. Needles 5 in cluster, stout, 3 to 4 inches long, blue green. Cones long-stalked, very large, 12 to 18 inches long, yellow brown, with thin, rounded scales.
Principal uses: Lumber for building construction, boxes and crates, millwork, and foundry patterns.

DD. Needles 3 or fewer in a cluster—YELLOW (HARD) PINES (Nos. 115 to 119) and PINYONS (or nut pines, Nos. 120 and 121).
  E. Needles more than 4 inches long.

115. PONDEROSA PINE, *Pinus ponderosa* Laws. (western yellow pine, pondosa pine, western soft pine, yellow pine; variety: *P. Ponderosa* var. *scopulorum* Engelm, Rocky Mountain ponderosa pine).

PROTECTING WOODY PLANTS IN WINTER

J. W. CADDICK*

The best prevention of winter damage to your shrubs starts with selecting reliably hardy plants and then growing them in the best location under the best conditions. However, this is not always possible or desirable.

Many of you may want a variety of plants and often desire to locate them, for aesthetic or other reasons, where conditions may not be entirely favorable. Some such locations might be at the corners of buildings, ends of fences or hedges, or similar spots where the wind is accentuated or funneled into bands of greater intensity.

Another area is an exposed south wall or sun pocket where it is warm. This may cause your plants to grow later in fall and start growth earlier in the spring, thus making them more susceptible to late or early frosts. Additional heat in winter may also accentuate some of the causes of injury listed below. If you recognize that some winter damage is likely to occur in these cases, you may be able to minimize the injury by taking a few simple precautions.

Causes of Injury and Preventive Practices

1. Extreme cold	No control
2. Drying or burning of evergreens	Water in fall and, if necessary, in winter. Apply anti-desiccant spray and see 3, 4, 5, 6 below
3. Temperature fluctuation of foliage and stems	Shade
4. Temperature fluctuation of roots	Mulch
5. Hot sun	Shade
6. Excessive winds	Windbreak
7. Girdling by animals	Screen or fence
8. Heaving	Mulch
9. Snow or ice breakage	Mechanical support

*Associate professor of horticulture

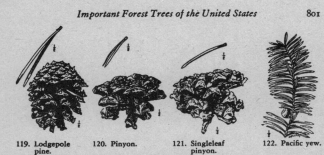

1. Extreme cold

There is no practical method you can use to prevent injury from extreme cold. However, a solid wood or weatherproof fiber board box-like structure over tender plants may provide enough protection for the survival of your borderline plants in "normal" winters.

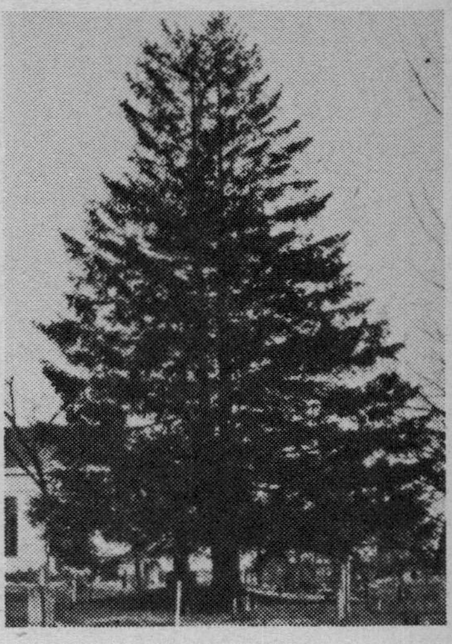
Norway Spruce

2. Drying or burning of evergreens

This will result in leaves or needles of evergreens turning tan or brown on tips, edges, spots, or overall. You may see discoloration on a few leaves, a branch, or over the entire plant (Figure 1). Damage to deciduous shrubs is generally confined to the death of tips or end portions of branches, and is not noticeable until new leaves are formed below the injured area.

This type of injury is closely associated with one or more of the following conditions which influence water loss from foliage or stems of the plant. If the ground moisture is low or frozen, normal water loss cannot be replaced and injury results.

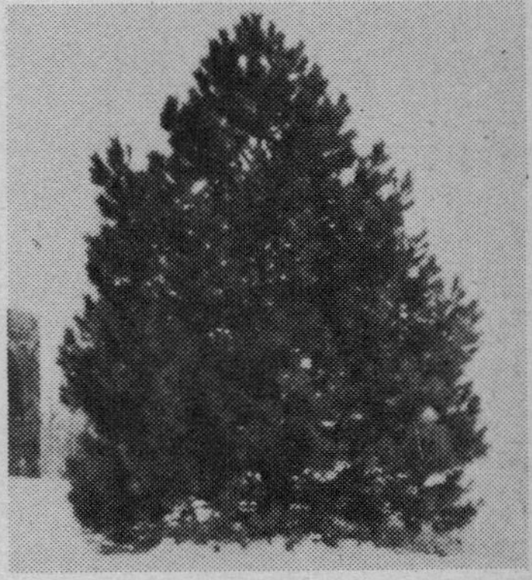
Austrian Pine

Often, thorough watering in late fall and, if the winter is dry, on warm days in winter and spring, will help to minimize the damage.

You can also take the extra precaution of coating the foliage and stems with an anti-desiccant spray in late fall. This forms a thin invisible layer of wax or plastic which slows down the water loss.

If these measures do not prevent injury or if there are extremely tender plants in more exposed locations, it may be necessary for you to supplement them with some or all of those listed under 3, 4, 5, 6 as preventive practices.

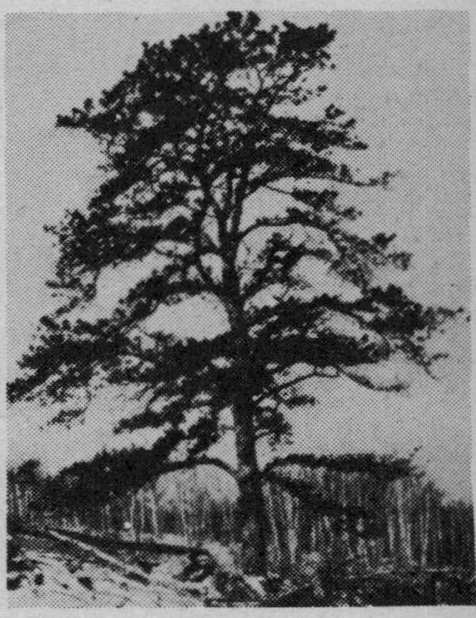
Pitch Pine

3. Temperature fluctuation

Rapid change of temperature in the foliage and stems of a plant causes rapid freezing and thawing of the sap. This may result in rupturing of tissues and chemical changes. While you can do little to prevent low temperatures, shading the plants will

Important Forest Trees of the United States 801

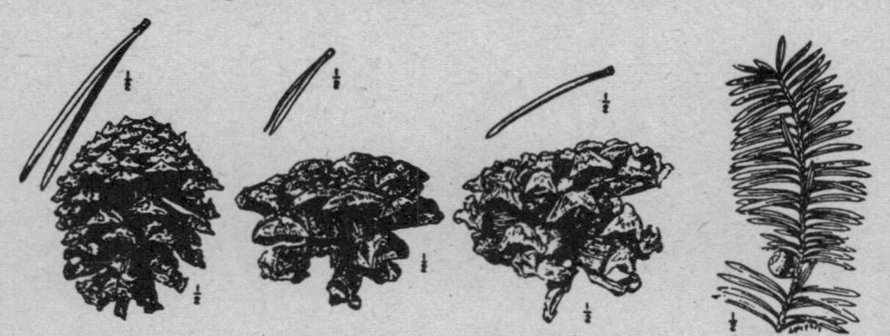

119. Lodgepole pine. 120. Pinyon. 121. Singleleaf pinyon. 122. Pacific yew.

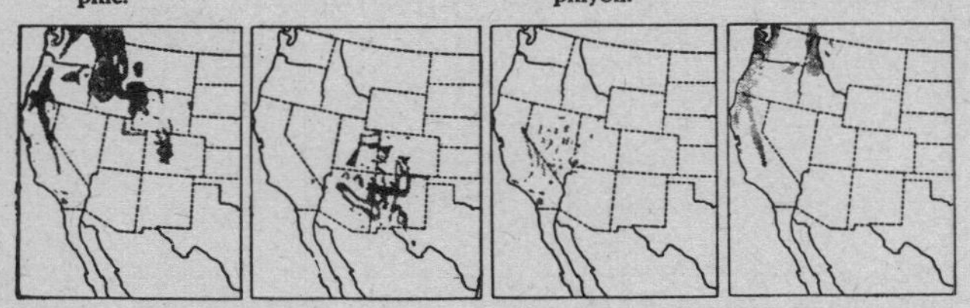

Large tree of Rocky Mountain and Pacific coast regions, including adjacent Canada. Bark brown or blackish, furrowed into ridges; on older trunks becoming yellow brown and irregularly fissured into large, flat, scaly plates. Needles 3 or 2 and 3 in cluster, stout, 4 to 7 inches long, dark green. Cones short-stalked, 3 to 6 inches long, light reddish brown, the scales with prickles.

Principal uses: Important timber tree, the most important western pine, and second to Douglas-fir in total stand in United States. Lumber for many uses, such as building construction, boxes and crates, and millwork; also caskets, furniture, toys. Piling, poles, posts, mine timbers, veneer, railroad ties, and fuel. Shelterbelts and ornamental. (State tree of Montana.)

116. JEFFREY PINE, *Pinus jeffreyi* Grev. & Balf. (western yellow pine).

Large tree of Pacific coast region from Oregon to Lower California. Bark purplish brown, becoming fissured into large plates. Needles 3 in cluster, stout, 5 to 10 inches long, blue green. Cones short-stalked, 5 to 10 inches long, light brown, the scales with prickles.

Principal uses: Lumber sold as ponderosa pine (No. 115) and has similar uses.

117. DIGGER PINE, *Pinus sabiniana* Dougl. (gray pine, bull pine).

Medium-sized tree of California foothills. Bark dark brown, irregularly furrowed into broad, irregular, scaly ridges. Needles 3 in cluster, slender and drooping, 8 to 12 inches long, pale blue green. Cones long-stalked, 6 to 10 inches long, red brown, with stout scales ending in curved spines. Seeds ¾ to ⅞ inch long, edible.

Principal uses; Fuel. Shelterbelts.

118. KNOBCONE PINE, *Pinus attenuata* Lemm.

Small to medium-sized tree of southwestern Oregon and California. Bark brown, thin, fissured into large, scaly ridges. Needles 3 in cluster, slender, 3 to 7 inches long, yellowish green. Cones usually clustered and abundant, 1-sided, 3 to 6 inches long, light yellow brown, with prickly scales, remaining closed on the tree indefinitely.

Principal uses: Fuel. Shelterbelts.

EE. Needles less than 3 inches long.

119. LODGEPOLE PINE, *Pinus contorta* Dougl. (shore pine, knotty pine, black pine, spruce pine, jack pine; *P. contorta* var. *latifolia* Engelm.).

Medium-sized to large tree of Rocky Mountain and Pacific coast regions including adjacent Canada and Lower California; the typical variety shore pine, a small tree of

802 *Yearbook of Agriculture* 1949

Pacific coast north to Alaska. Bark brown, thin, with many loose scales. Needles 2 in cluster, stout, often twisted, 1 to 3 inches long, yellow green. Cones egg-shaped, 1-sided, ¾ to 2 inches long, light yellow brown, with prickly scales, remaining closed on the tree many years.

Principal uses: Mine timbers, railroad ties, poles, posts, fuel, lumber, and pulpwood. (Lodgepole pine is the State tree of Wyoming.)

120. PINYON, *Pinus edulis* Engelm. (nut pine, pinyon pine, Colorado pinyon pine; *Pinus cembroides* var. *edulis* (Engelm.) Voss).

Small tree of southern Rocky Mountain region, including adjacent Mexico. Bark reddish brown, furrowed into scaly ridges. Needles 2 (sometimes 3) in cluster, stout, ¾ to 1½ inches long, dark green. Cones egg-shaped, 1½ to 2 inches long, light brown, with stout, blunt scales and large, wingless, edible seeds ½ inch long, known as pinyon nuts.

Principal uses: The edible seeds are a wild, commercial nut crop, sold as pinyon nuts and Indian nuts. Mine timbers and fuel. Ornamental. (State tree of New Mexico.)

121. SINGLELEAF PINYON, *Pinus monophylla* Torr. & Frém. (nut pine, pinyon; singleleaf pinyon pine; *Pinus cembroides* var. *monophylla* (Torr. & Frém.) Voss).

Small tree of Great Basin region to California and Lower California. Bark dark brown, furrowed into scaly ridges. Needles 1 in a sheath, stout, 1 to 2 inches long, gray green. Cones egg-shaped, 2 to 2½ inches long, light brown, with stout, blunt scales, and large, wingless, edible seeds ¾ inch long, known as pinyon nuts.

Principal uses: The edible seeds are sold locally as pinyon nuts and pine nuts. (Pinyon is the State tree of Nevada.)

CC. Leaves without sheath at base, not in clusters, needlelike or scalelike.
F (*FF* on page 805), Leaves needlelike, mostly more than ½ inch long.
G. Twigs roughened by projecting bases of old needles.
H. Needles with leafstalks, flattened (rounded in No. 124), appearing in 2 rows.
I. Needles stiff, sharp-pointed, extending down the twig—YEW (*Taxus*).

122. PACIFIC YEW, *Taxus brevifolia* Nutt. (western yew, yew).

Small to medium-sized tree of Pacific Coast and northern Rocky Mountain regions north to Canada and Alaska. Bark purplish brown, very thin, smoothish, with papery scales. Needles in 2 rows, flat, slightly curved, paler beneath, stiff, sharp-pointed, ½ to 1 inch long, dark yellow green, the leafstalks extending down the twigs. Seeds single, ⅜ inch long, exposed at apex but partly surrounded by a thick, fleshy, scarlet, cuplike disk.

Principal uses: Of limited use because of its scarcity. Poles, canoe paddles, bows, and small cabinet work. Ornamental.

II. Needles soft, blunt-pointed, not extending down the twig—HEMLOCK (*Tsuga*).

123. WESTERN HEMLOCK, *Tsuga heterophylla* (Raf.) Sarg. (west coast hemlock [lumber], Pacific hemlock, hemlock; formerly *Tsuga mertensiana* auth.).

Large tree of Pacific coast and northern Rocky Mountain regions north to Canada and Alaska. Bark reddish brown, deeply furrowed into broad, flat ridges. Needles short-stalked, flat, ¼ to ¾ inch long, shiny dark green, lighter beneath. Cones ¾ to 1 inch long, brownish.

Principal uses: Important timber tree. Pulpwood, and lumber for building material, boxes and crates, and flooring. The bark is a potential source of tannin. Ornamental. (State tree of Washington.)

124. MOUNTAIN HEMLOCK, *Tsuga mertensiana* (Bong.) Carr. (black hemlock, alpine hemlock).

Large tree of timber line, Pacific coast and northern Rocky Mountain regions north to Canada and Alaska. Bark reddish brown, deeply furrowed into narrow ridges. Needles short-stalked, rounded or angled, ¼ to 1 inch long, blue green. Cones long, 1 to 3 inches long, usually purplish but turning brown.

Principal uses: Ornamental.

HH. Needles without leafstalks, 4-angled (flat in No. 127), sharp-pointed, extending out on all sides of twig—SPRUCE (*Picea;* see also Nos. 16 and 17).

125. ENGELMANN SPRUCE, *Picea engelmanni* Parry (white spruce, mountain spruce, silver spruce).

Large tree of high altitudes, Rocky Mountain and Pacific coast regions, including adjacent Canada. Bark grayish or purplish brown, thin, with loosely attached scales. Needles 4-angled, ⅝ to 1⅛ inches long, dark or pale blue green, of disagreeable odor

Important Forest Trees of the United States 803

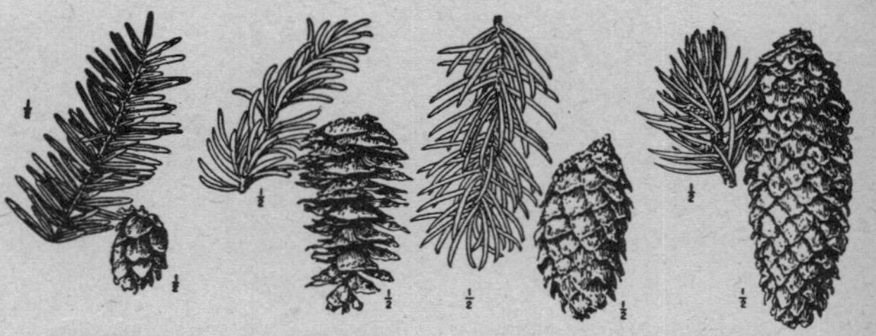

123. Western hemlock. 124. Mountain hemlock. 125. Engelmann spruce. 126. Blue spruce.

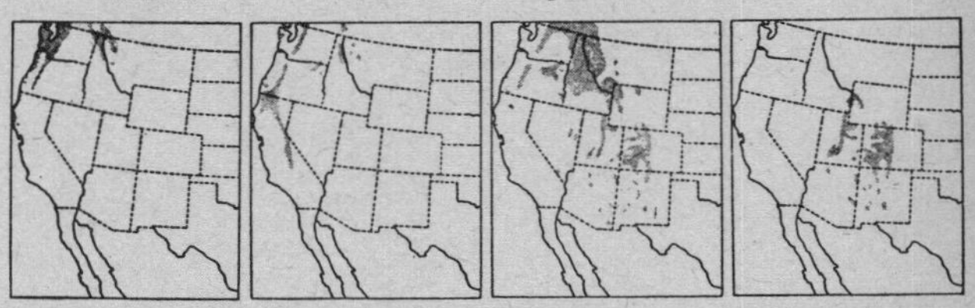

when crushed. Cones 1½ to 2½ inches long, light brown, with long, thin, flexible scales irregularly toothed and more or less pointed.

Principal uses: Lumber for building construction and boxes. Also mine timbers, railroad ties, and poles. Ornamental.

126. BLUE SPRUCE, *Picea pungens* Engelm. (Colorado blue spruce, Colorado spruce, silver spruce).

Large tree of Rocky Mountain region. Bark gray or brown, furrowed into scaly ridges. Needles 4-angled, ¾ to 1⅛ inch long, dull blue green. Cones 2½ to 4 inches long, light brown, with long, thin, flexible scales irregularly toothed and more or less pointed.

Principal uses: Ornamental and shelterbelts. Posts, poles, and fuel. (State tree of Colorado and Utah.)

127. SITKA SPRUCE, *Picea sitchensis* (Bong.) Carr. (yellow spruce, tideland spruce, western spruce, silver spruce, coast spruce).

Large to very large tree of Pacific coast region north to Canada and Alaska. Bark reddish brown, thin, with loosely attached scales. Needles flat, ⅝ to 1 inch long, dark green. Cones 2 to 3½ inches long, light orange brown, with long, stiff scales, rounded and irregularly toothed.

Principal uses: Lumber for boxes and crates, furniture, planing-mill products, millwork, ladders, and construction. Pulpwood and cooperage. The most important wood for aircraft construction. Ornamental.

GG. Twigs smooth or nearly so.
J. Needles with short leafstalks; cones hanging down—DOUGLAS-FIR (*Pseudotsuga*).

128. DOUGLAS-FIR, *Pseudotsuga taxifolia* (Poir.) Britton (Douglas-spruce, red fir, yellow fir, Oregon pine, common Douglas-fir; *Ps. douglasii* (Sabine) Carr., *Ps. mucronata* (Raf.) Sudw.; variety: *Ps. taxifolia* var. *glauca* (Mayr) Sudw.).

Large tree (next to giant sequoia and redwood in size) of Pacific coast and Rocky Mountain regions, including Canada and Mexico. Bark reddish brown, thick, deeply furrowed into broad ridges. Needles short-stalked, flat, ¾ to 1¼ inches long, dark yellow green or blue green. Cones 2 to 4 inches long, light brown, with thin, rounded scales and long, 3-toothed bracts.

Principal uses: Important timber tree, first in United States in total stand, lumber production, and production of veneer for plywood. Used principally for building construc-

prevent rapid warming and cooling during sunny periods. (If materials such as cord, snowfence, boxes, baskets which are used for protecting plants are dyed green, they may be less objectionable in appearance

4. Temperature fluctuation of roots

This causes much the same type of injury as occurs above ground. In addition, low temperature freezes the soil moisture, making it unavailable to the plant. A mulch of several inches of loose fluffy material over the plant's root zone will do much to minimize root injury. This also slows down the freezing rate and reduces the depth of freezing of the soil moisture.

Many materials have been used, depending upon availability, cost, and personal preference for their appearance. Some suggestions are peat moss, clean straw, corn stalks or ground corncobs, marsh hay, cranberry clippings, cut evergreen branches, glass wool, sawdust, wood chips, oak leaves, sugar cane pulp buckwheat hulls, and rock wool. In windy spots it may be necessary for you to use chicken wire or other restraining material to hold some of these in place.

A "living mulch" of evergreen ground cover plants such as myrtle, pachysandra, evergreen wintercreeper, or hardy English ivy may be the best way to permanently solve this problem.

5. Hot sun

The absorption of heat from the sun causes rapid evaporation of moisture from foliage and stems. During periods of slow water replacement, the rate and amount of water loss may be such that the tissues collapse and die. In addition, the rapid changes in tissue temperature may cause internal changes which are harmful.

Preventive measures are the same as those listed under number 3.

6. Excessive winds

These cause rapid evaporation of water from the above-ground parts of the plant and from the soil by literally blowing moisture away. To help slow down these wind currents you can erect windbreaks, use a mulch over the ground surface, and use an anti-desiccant spray. Watering in late fall, winter, and spring may be necessary to replenish the soil moisture which is lost.

7. Girdling by animals

Mice, rats, rabbits, or woodchucks strip or gnaw lower stems or branches of a plant when other food is unavailable. Some materials such as dried blood, resin and alcohol; or various commercial preparations which you can spray on and about the bases of plants, may discourage the animals. But a mechanical barrier of wire or expanded metal is the most effective device you can use. Care should be taken to install the barrier from below ground line to well above snow line.

8. Heaving

Soil disturbance is the result of freezing and thawing of the ground. This action breaks small roots which are needed to absorb the moisture needed in the plant. Small plants may be forced out of the ground sufficiently to expose the crown and roots or even to topple the plant. A mulch, as discussed above, is the best way you can minimize this damage.

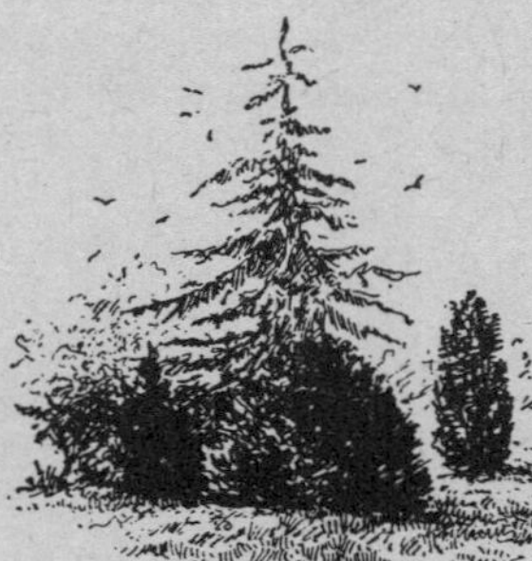

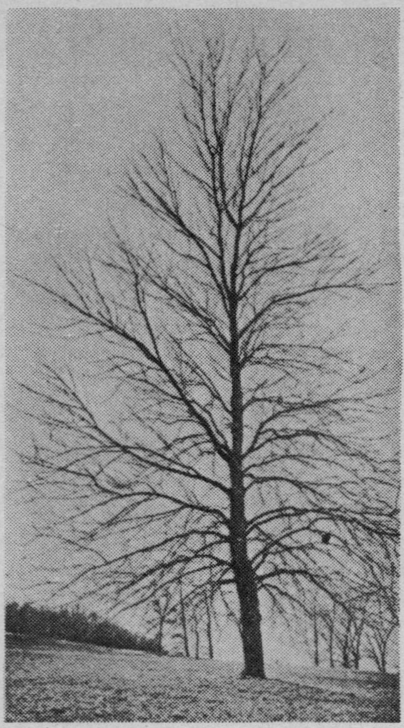

Red Ash

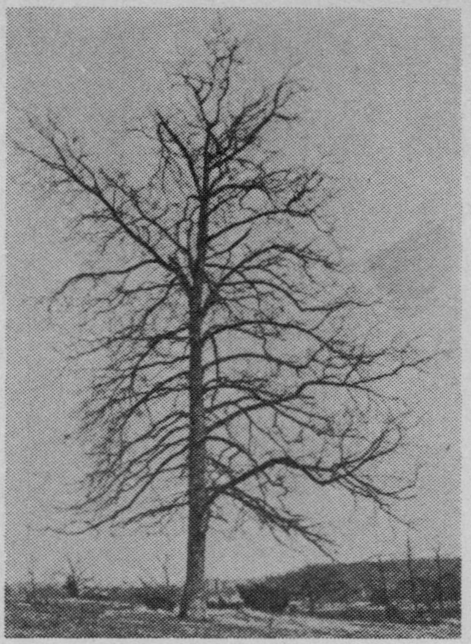

Mocknut

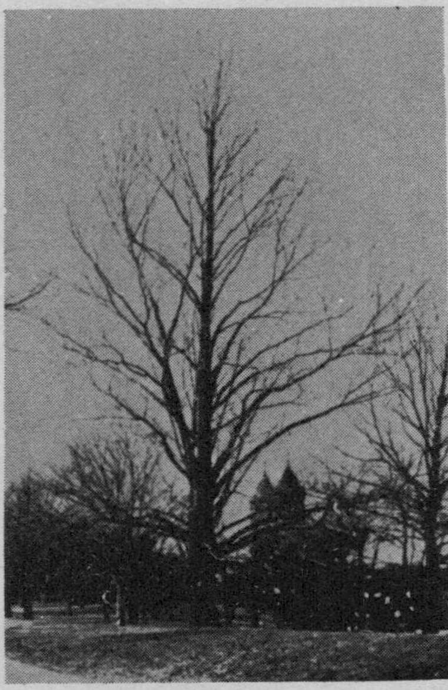

Cucumber

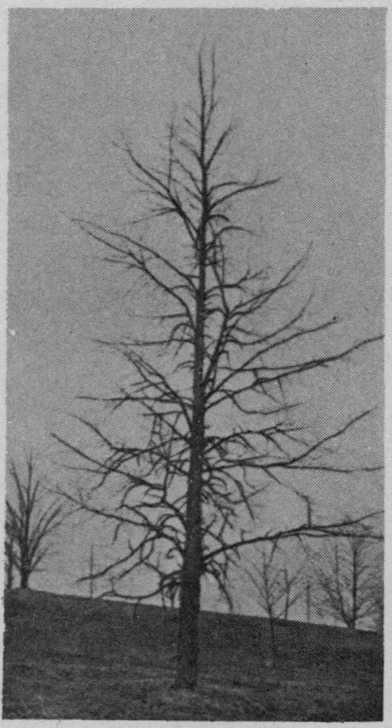

Cork Elm

804 *Yearbook of Agriculture 1949* — *Important Forest Trees of the United States* 805 — 806 *Yearbook of Agriculture 1949*

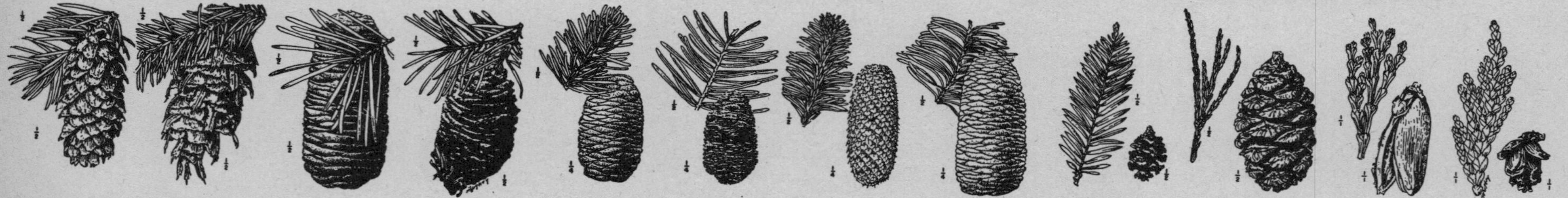

127. Sitka spruce. 128. Douglas-fir. 129. White fir. 130. Alpine fir. 131. Pacific silver fir. 132. Grand fir. 133. Noble fir. 134. California red fir. 135. Redwood. 136. Giant sequoia. 137. Incense-cedar. 138. Western redcedar.

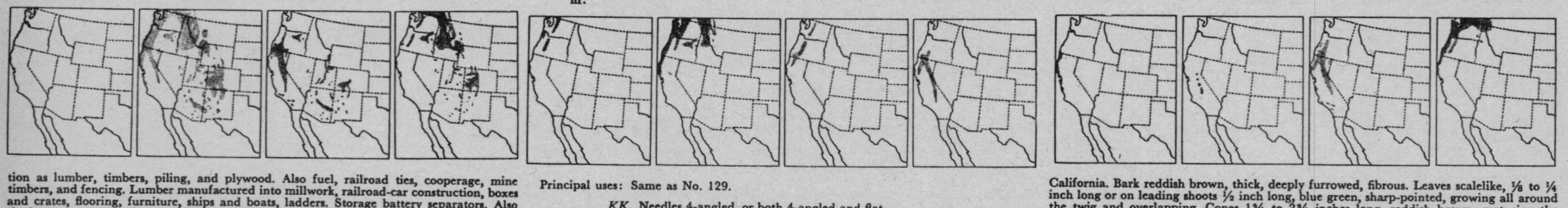

tion as lumber, timbers, piling, and plywood. Also fuel, railroad ties, cooperage, mine timbers, and fencing. Lumber manufactured into millwork, railroad-car construction, boxes and crates, flooring, furniture, ships and boats, ladders. Storage battery separators. Also shade tree, ornamental, and shelterbelts. (State tree of Oregon.)

JJ. Needles without leafstalks; cones upright, in top of tree—FIR (*Abies;* see also No. 18).
K. Needles flat.

129. WHITE FIR, *Abies concolor* (Gord. & Glend.) Hoopes (balsam fir, silver fir, white balsam).

Large tree of Rocky Mountain and Pacific coast regions, south to Lower California. Bark gray, smoothish, becoming thick, deeply furrowed into scaly ridges. Needles flat, $1\frac{1}{2}$ to $2\frac{1}{2}$ inches long, pale blue green. Cones upright, 3 to 5 inches long, greenish, purple, or yellow.

Principal uses: Lumber for building construction, chiefly in houses, boxes and crates, planing-mill products, and general millwork. Pulpwood. Ornamental and shade tree.

130. ALPINE FIR, *Abies lasiocarpa* (Hook.) Nutt. (white fir [lumber], balsam, white balsam).

Large tree of high altitudes, Rocky Mountain region north to Canada and Alaska. Bark gray, smoothish, becoming fissured. Needles flat, 1 to $1\frac{3}{4}$ inches long, blue green. Cones upright, $2\frac{1}{2}$ to 4 inches long, purple.

Principal uses: Same as No. 129.

131. PACIFIC SILVER FIR, *Abies amabilis* (Dougl.) Forb. (silver fir [lumber], white fir [lumber], Cascades fir, red fir, lovely fir).

Large tree of Pacific coast region from Oregon north to Canada and Alaska. Bark gray, smoothish. Needles flat, $\frac{3}{4}$ to $1\frac{1}{4}$ inches long, dark green and shiny, silvery white beneath. Cones upright, 3 to 6 inches long, purple.

Principal uses: Same as No. 129.

132. GRAND FIR, *Abies grandis* (Dougl.) Lindl. (white fir [lumber], lowland white fir, balsam fir, lowland fir, silver fir, yellow fir).

Large tree of northern Rocky Mountain and Pacific coast regions, including southern British Columbia. Bark reddish brown, becoming deeply furrowed into narrow ridges. Needles flat, 1 to 2 inches long, dark green and shiny, silvery white beneath. Cones upright, 2 to 4 inches long, green.

Principal uses: Same as No. 129.

KK. Needles 4-angled, or both 4-angled and flat.

133. NOBLE FIR, *Abies procera* Rehd. (white fir [lumber], red fir; *A. nobilis* (Dougl.) Lindl., not A. Dietr.).

Large tree of Northwest Pacific coast region. Bark gray brown, smoothish, becoming furrowed and broken into irregular scaly plates. Needles of lower branches flat and of top branches 4-angled, 1 to $1\frac{1}{2}$ inches long, blue green. Cones upright, 4 to 6 inches long, purplish brown, with long greenish bracts covering the cone scales.

Principal uses: Lumber for interior finish, moldings, sidings, and millwork, aircraft construction, venetian blinds, ladder rails, and boxes. Pulpwood. Ornamental.

134. CALIFORNIA RED FIR, *Abies magnifica* A. Murr. (golden fir [lumber], white fir [lumber], red fir).

Large tree (the largest native true fir) of Oregon and California. Bark reddish brown, thick, deeply furrowed into narrow ridges. Needles 4-angled, $\frac{3}{4}$ to $1\frac{1}{2}$ inches long, blue green. Cones upright, 6 to 9 inches long, purplish brown.

Principal uses: Same as No. 129.

FF (*F* on p. 802). Leaves scalelike, less than $\frac{1}{4}$ inch long, or both scalelike and needlelike (to $\frac{3}{4}$ inch long).
L. Leaves single—SEQUOIA (*Sequoia*).

135. REDWOOD, *Sequoia sempervirens* (D. Don) Endl. (coast redwood, California redwood).

Large tree (the world's tallest tree species) of Pacific coast in California and southwestern Oregon. Bark reddish brown, thick, deeply furrowed, fibrous. Leaves both scalelike and needlelike, flat, slightly curved, unequal in length, $\frac{1}{4}$ to $\frac{3}{4}$ inch long, dark green, spreading in 2 rows. Cones $\frac{3}{4}$ to 1 inch long, reddish brown, maturing the first year.

Principal uses: Important timber tree. Largely for building construction and bridges and other heavy construction. Also boxes and crates, planing-mill products, general millwork, paneling, tanks, caskets, greenhouse construction. Insulating material is made from the bark. Ornamental. (State tree of California.)

136. GIANT SEQUOIA, *Sequoia gigantea* (Lindl.) Decne. (bigtree, Sierra redwood; *S. wellingtonia* Seem.).

Large tree (including the world's largest and oldest) with swollen base, Sierra Nevada, California. Bark reddish brown, thick, deeply furrowed, fibrous. Leaves scalelike, $\frac{1}{8}$ to $\frac{1}{4}$ inch long or on leading shoots $\frac{1}{2}$ inch long, blue green, sharp-pointed, growing all around the twig and overlapping. Cones $1\frac{3}{4}$ to $2\frac{3}{4}$ inches long, reddish brown, maturing the second year.

Principal uses: The largest trees are preserved in national parks and national forests. Formerly lumbered for the same uses as No. 135.

LL. Leaves in pairs, threes, or fours, scalelike.
M. Leafy twigs more or less flattened.
N. Twigs much flattened, more than $\frac{1}{16}$ inch broad including leaves.
O. Joints of leafy twigs distinctly longer than broad—INCENSE-CEDAR (*Libocedrus*).

137. INCENSE-CEDAR, *Libocedrus decurrens* Torr. (California incense-cedar).

Large tree of Pacific coast region from Oregon to Lower California. Bark reddish brown, thick, deeply and irregularly furrowed into shreddy ridges. Twigs flattened, the internodes wedge-shaped, $\frac{1}{8}$ to $\frac{1}{2}$ inch long, bright green, with scale leaves $\frac{1}{16}$ to $\frac{1}{8}$ inch long, their bases extending down the twigs. Cones $\frac{3}{4}$ to 1 inch long, reddish brown.

Principal uses: The leading wood for pencils. Venetian blinds, lumber for rough construction, fence posts, and railroad ties. Ornamental and shade tree.

OO. Joints of leafy twigs about as long as broad—THUJA (*Thuja*).

138. WESTERN REDCEDAR, *Thuja plicata* Donn (giant arborvitae, canoe cedar, arbovitae, shinglewood, gigantic cedar, Pacific redcedar).

Large to very large tree of Pacific coast and northern Rocky Mountain regions north to Canada and Alaska. Bark reddish brown, thin, fibrous. Twigs flattened and branching in one plane. Leaves scalelike, $\frac{1}{16}$ to $\frac{1}{8}$ inch long, shiny, dark green. Cones $\frac{1}{2}$ inch long, pale brown, with leathery scales.

Principal uses: The chief wood for shingles. Lumber used largely in construction such as siding. Also a leading wood for poles and widely used for posts.

NN. Twigs slightly flattened, less than $\frac{1}{16}$ inch broad including leaves—WHITE-CEDAR (*Chamaecyparis*).

139. PORT-ORFORD-CEDAR, *Chamaecyparis lawsoniana* (A. Murr.) Parl. (Port-Orford white-cedar, Lawson falsecypress, Oregon cedar, Lawson cypress).

9. Snow or ice breakage

Mechanical supports, ties or breakers will help to minimize this damage. To help support bushy or spreading types of plants, you can use supports made of stakes driven into the ground around the plant and interlaced with heavy soft cord. Tying and wrapping with the same type of cord will normally prevent upright types with several stems from splitting apart. A wrapping of coarse green-dyed fishnet might be satisfactory for some plants (Figure 8).

For those plants near buildings from which there may be falling chunks of snow or ice, teepees of boards or poles which break the force of the falling material often prevent damage to plants (Figure 6).

Selection of plants with single stems or strong stems rather than weak flexible ones, plants with strong crotches instead of narrow weak ones, and plants with strong flexible wood rather than brittle wood may prevent trouble and the necessity of protecting susceptible plants. Proper pruning, cabling, and bracing practices will do much to prevent this type of injury.

There are a few types of plants which can be grown successfully if they are laid on the ground and mounded with soil or tipped over into a trench and buried during the winter. Some examples of these are figs, tree roses, tender berries, and tender grapes.

All of these protective measures are most important for the first winter after planting.

Though much of the injury to plants occurs during the "winter," it is true that fall and spring are often as critical periods. An early cold snap may kill plants or portions of plants which are actively growing or have not "hardened off." The injury may not be apparent until the following spring. A great deal of injury may occur during early spring. Keep all shades, screens, and temporary mulches in place at least until *all* frost is out of the ground.

If Damage Occurs

If, in spite of preventive measures, damage occurs during an "unusual" winter:

- Be patient. Occasionally, some plants such as holly will appear to be dead for a year before showing signs of recovery.
- Any week in spring or summer during which there is not at least one inch of rainfall, soak the ground thoroughly around any injured plants.
- Prune any obviously dead or injured branches, but do not prune below any area where green inner bark is found.
- When plants show signs of recovery, apply one-half cup of lawn-type fertilizer per square yard and water heavily.

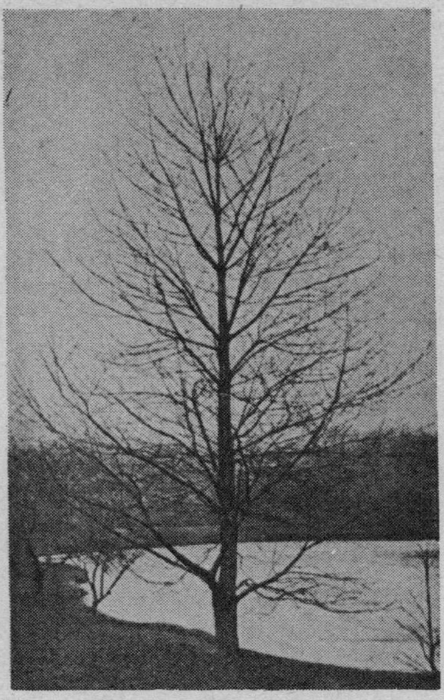
Sweet Cherry

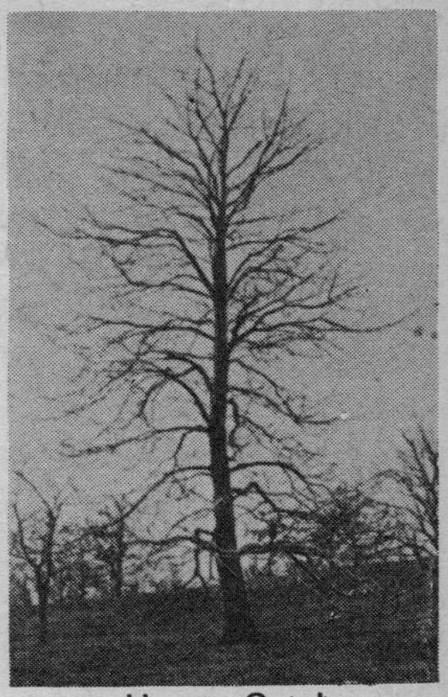
Hearty Catalpa

Some Plants Often Injured

Some plants often injured include:

Abelia
Andromeda
Blue or Pink Hydrangea
Drooping Leucothoe
English Ivy
Evergreen Barberry
Evergreen or Semi-Evergreen Azaleas
Firethorn
Hemlock
Holly
Kerria
Mountain Laurel
Oregon Hollygrape
Rhododendron

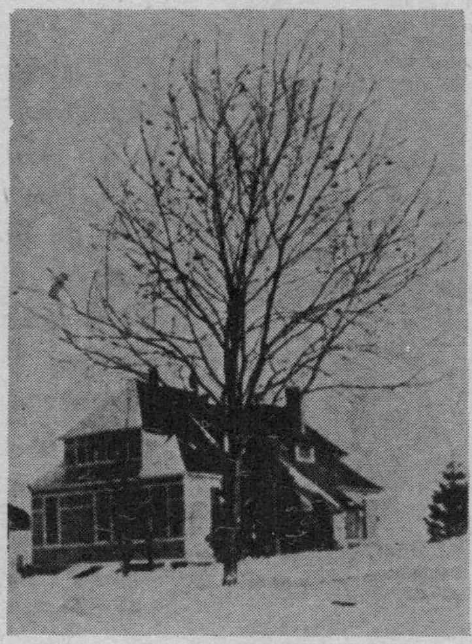
Mountain Ash

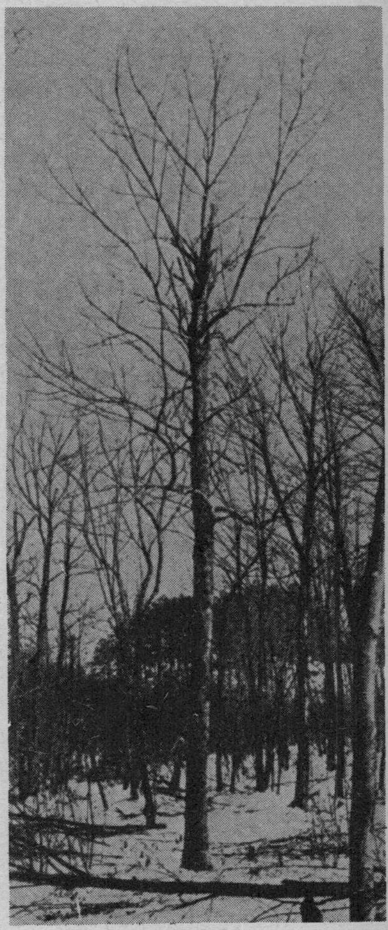
Black Ash

Cooperative Extension Work in Agriculture and Home Economics, University of Rhode Island and U. S. Department of Agriculture cooperating. Issued in furtherance of Acts of May 8 and June 30, 1914. David F. Shontz, acting director.

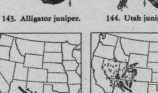

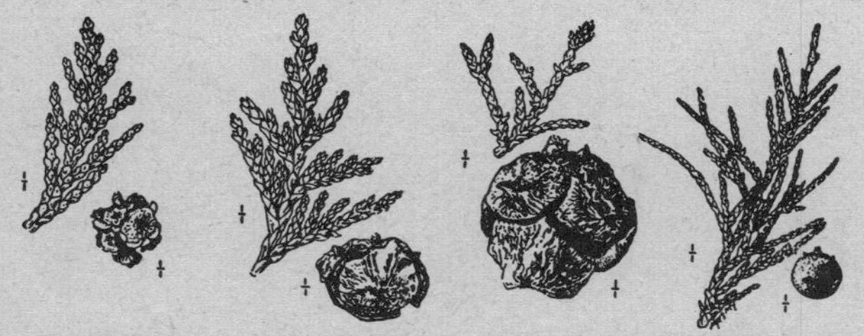
139. Port-Orford-cedar. 140. Alaska-cedar. 141. Arizona cypress. 142. Rocky Mountain juniper.

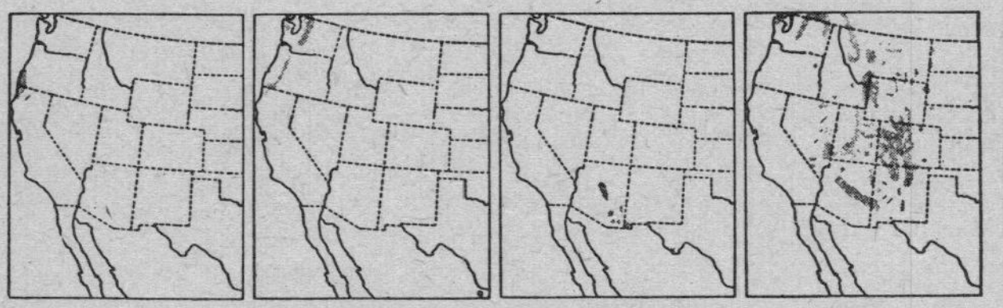

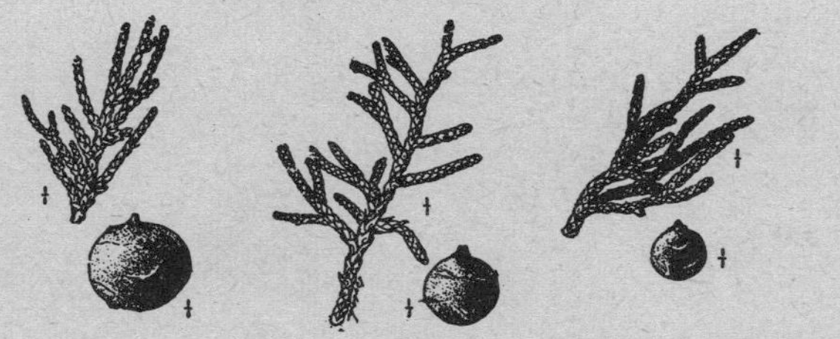
143. Alligator juniper. 144. Utah juniper. 145. Western juniper.

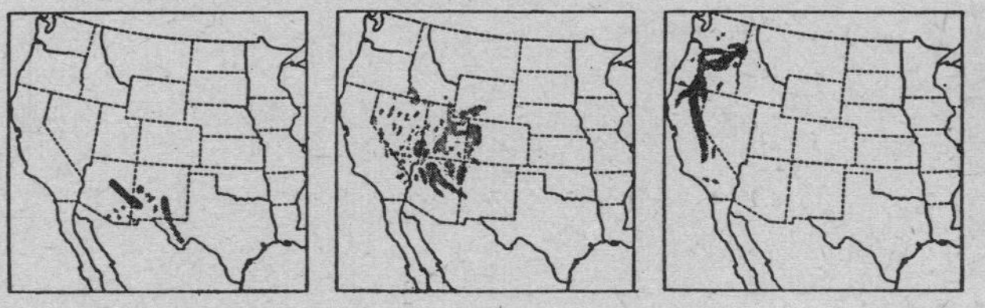

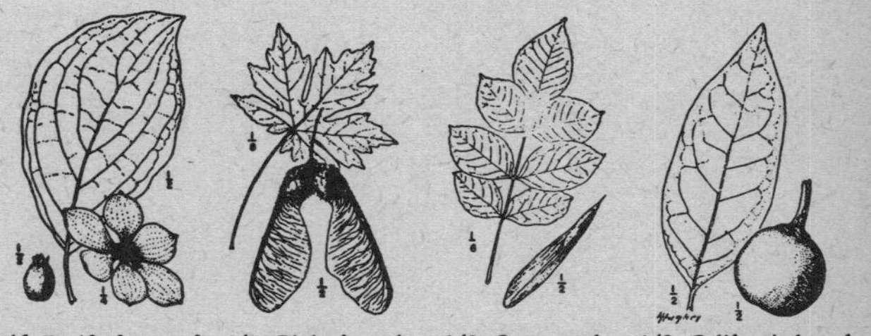
146. Pacific dogwood. 147. Bigleaf maple. 148. Oregon ash. 149. California-laurel.

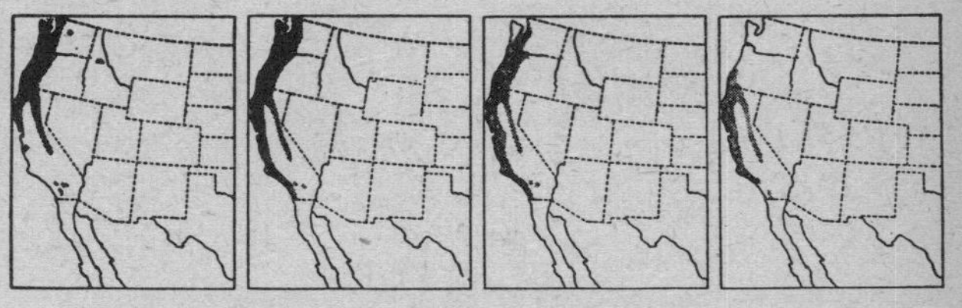

Large to very large tree of Pacific coast in southwestern Oregon and northwestern California. Bark reddish brown, very thick, deeply furrowed into large, fibrous ridges. Twigs slender, flattened. Leaves 1/16 inch long, or 1/8 to 1/4 inch long on leading shoots, bright green or pale beneath, glandular on the back. Cones about 3/8 inch in diameter.

Principal uses: The principal wood for storage battery separators. Venetian blinds. Lumber for construction and other uses. Shade tree, ornamental, and shelterbelts.

140. ALASKA-CEDAR, *Chamaecyparis nootkatensis* (D. Don) Spach (Alaska yellow-cedar, Nootka falsecypress, yellow-cedar, Sitka cypress, yellow cypress).

Large tree of Northwest Pacific coast region north to Canada and Alaska. Bark grayish brown, thin, irregularly fissured, fibrous and scaly. Twigs stout, 4-angled or slightly flattened. Leaves 1/8 inch long, or 1/4 inch long on leading shoots, dark green, usually without glands. Cones nearly 1/2 inch in diameter.

Principal uses: Interior finish, cabinet work, small boats, furniture, and novelties. Ornamental.

MM. Leafy twigs rounded or 4-angled.
P. Leafy twigs regularly branched almost at right angles; seeds in a hard cone—CYPRESS (*Cupressus*).

141. ARIZONA CYPRESS, *Cupressus arizonica* Greene (smooth cypress; *C. glabra* Sudw.).

Medium-sized tree of southwestern United States and adjacent Mexico. Bark gray, rough, furrowed and fibrous, or checkered, or smoothish and shedding in thin scales. Leaves scalelike, 1/16 inch long, pale blue green. Cones 3/4 to 1 1/4 inches in diameter, on stout stalks 1/4 to 1/2 inch long and remaining attached several years.

Principal uses: Fence posts, ornamental, and shelterbelts.

PP. Leafy twigs irregularly branched at small angles; seeds in a "berry"—JUNIPER (*Juniperus*).

142. ROCKY MOUNTAIN JUNIPER, *Juniperus scopulorum* Sarg. (western juniper [lumber], Rocky Mountain redcedar, redcedar).

Small to medium-sized tree of Rocky Mountain region, including adjacent Canada. Bark reddish brown, thin, fibrous and shreddy. Leafy twigs slender, about 1/32 inch in diameter. Leaves scalelike, 1/16 inch long, usually gray green, or on leading shoots needlelike, up to 1/4 inch long. "Berry" 1/4 inch in diameter, bright blue, bloomy, usually 2-seeded, maturing the second year.

Principal uses: Fence posts, fuel, lumber. Shelterbelts and ornamental.

143. ALLIGATOR JUNIPER, *Juniperus deppeana* Steud. (western juniper [lumber]; *J. pachyphloea* Torr.).

Medium-sized tree of southwestern United States and Mexico. Bark gray, thick, deeply furrowed into checkered or square plates. Leafy twigs 1/32 to 1/16 inch in diameter. Leaves scalelike, 1/16 inch long, blue green, glandular, often with whitish drops of resin, or on leading shoots needlelike, up to 1/4 inch long, pale or whitish. "Berry" 1/2 inch in diameter, bluish or brownish, bloomy, 4-seeded, maturing the second year.

Principal uses: Fuel and fence posts.

144. UTAH JUNIPER, *Juniperus osteosperma* (Torr.) Little (western juniper [lumber]; *J. utahensis* (Engelm.) Lemm.).

Small tree of Great Basin and Rocky Mountain regions. Bark gray, fibrous and shreddy. Leafy twigs stout, about 1/16 inch or less in diameter. Leaves 1/16 inch or more in length, yellow green. "Berry" 1/4 to 1/2 inch in diameter, brownish, bloomy, with 1 or 2 seeds.

Principal uses: Fence posts, fuel, and interior finish.

145. WESTERN JUNIPER, *Juniperus occidentalis* Hook. (western juniper [lumber], Sierra juniper).

Small to medium-sized tree of Pacific coast region. Bark reddish brown, furrowed and shreddy. Leafy twigs stout, 1/16 inch or more in diameter. Leaves scalelike, 1/16 inch or more in length, glandular. "Berry" 1/4 inch in diameter, bluish black, with 2 or 3 seeds.

Principal uses: Fence posts, fuel, pencils.

ANGIOSPERMS (FLOWERING PLANTS)

AA (*A* on p. 799). Trees nonresinous, with leaves broad, shedding in fall in most species (evergreen in some oaks, tanoak, golden chinquapin, California-laurel, palms, etc.); seeds enclosed in a fruit—ANGIOSPERMS (flowering plants).
Q. Leaves parallel-veined, evergreen, clustered at top of trunk or large branches; trunk with woody portions irregularly distributed, without clear distinction of bark and wood, and without annual rings—MONOCOTYLEDONS (palms, yuccas, etc.; omitted here).

DICOTYLEDONS (BROADLEAF TREES OR HARDWOODS)

QQ. Leaves net-veined; trunk with bark and wood distinct and with annual rings in wood—DICOTYLEDONS (broadleaf trees, or hardwoods, such as oaks, poplars, ashes, maples).
R. Leaves and usually branches in pairs (opposite).
S. Leaves not divided into leaflets (simple).
T. Leaf edges smooth, not lobed—DOGWOOD (*Cornus*).

146. PACIFIC DOGWOOD, *Cornus nuttalli* Audubon (western dogwood, dogwood).

Small to medium-sized tree of Pacific coast region north to British Columbia. Bark reddish brown, thin, smoothish. Leaves paired, oval, 3 to 5 inches long, short-pointed, edges appearing smooth but minutely toothed, lateral veins curved, bright green and nearly smooth above, whitish and hairy beneath, turning orange and scarlet in fall. Flowers greenish yellow, in a dense head with 4 to 6 (usually 6) showy, white, petallike bracts 3 to 5 inches in diameter, in early spring. Fruits egg-shaped, 3/8 to 1/2 inch long, bright red or orange.

Principal uses: Shuttles (used in textile weaving). Ornamental.

TT. Leaf edges toothed, deeply 3- or 5-lobed—MAPLE (*Acer*).

147. BIGLEAF MAPLE, *Acer macrophyllum* Pursh (Oregon maple, broadleaf maple).

Large tree of Pacific coast region north to Canada and Alaska. Bark gray brown, thin, smoothish, becoming deeply furrowed. Leaves paired, heart-shaped, very large, 6 to 12 inches in diameter, deeply 3- or 5-lobed with additional smaller lobes, dark green and shiny above, pale green below, turning bright orange in fall. Leafstalks long and stout, 10 to 12 inches long. Key fruits 1 1/4 to 2 inches long, long-winged, paired and in clusters.

Principal uses: Veneer, furniture, handles and fixtures, and woodenware and novelties. Shade tree.

SS. Leaves subdivided into 5 to 9 leaflets (compound)—ASH (*Fraxinus*; see also Nos. 31 and 33).

148. OREGON ASH, *Fraxinus oregona* Nutt.

Medium-sized to large tree of Pacific coast region, including British Columbia. Bark dark gray or brown, with diamond-shaped fissures and forking ridges. Leaves paired, compound, 5 to 14 inches long. Leaflets usually 7 or 5, usually without stalks, elliptical, 2 to 5 inches long, short-pointed, edges smooth or slightly toothed, light green, nearly

GINKGO

The Ginkgo or Maidenhair tree has been planted so long that one tends to forget that it is a link with the geological past. If the Dawnredwood is a living fossil, the Ginkgo is even more so. Ginkgo was an ancient tree before there was a Dawnredwood, going back into the distant past some 200 million years. Fossilized leaves of this tree are often found in coal seams.

The tree was first recognized in 1690 in Japan and China, growing in gardens and around temple grounds. The tree was brought to Europe in 1730 and was first planted in the United States in 1784. As the Maidenhair tree is quite tolerant to smoke and city growing conditions, it has been planted for many years as a city tree both in Europe and in this country.

For many years it was believed that this tree existed only as a planted ornamental and that it no longer existed in the wild. It was believed that it had been saved from extinction by being in cultivation. However, in 1914 Ginkgo was found growing wild over some 10 square miles in Chekiang Province, China.

Ginkgo is quite different from many trees we now have. It resembles the ferns by having swimming sperms. It resembles pines and firs by having wood in which the structure and details are quite similar. It resembles many hardwoods by having flat leaves which drop off each fall.

Ginkgo is also one of the earliest of the seed plants. There are male and female plants. The flowers are wind pollinated, as the tree developed before many pollinating insects were around. The fruit resembles a plum, with a hard pit surrounded by a yellow flesh which has quite an offensive odor when it ripens—it smells like rancid butter. In the Orient the pits are roasted and the kernel inside is eaten. It is interesting to speculate whether the vile smell attracted some Pterodactyl or dinosaur to eat this fruit as the Ginkgos were part of the landscape when dinosaurs were still quite numerous.

The wood is quite hard but is easily worked. At one time it was much sought after by wealthy Chinese to make coffins.

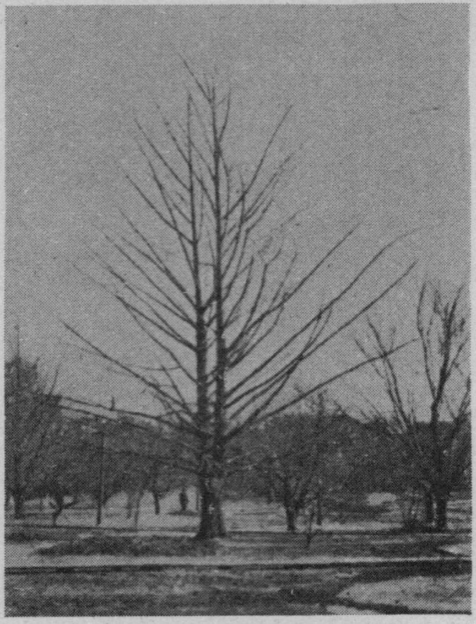
Ginkgo

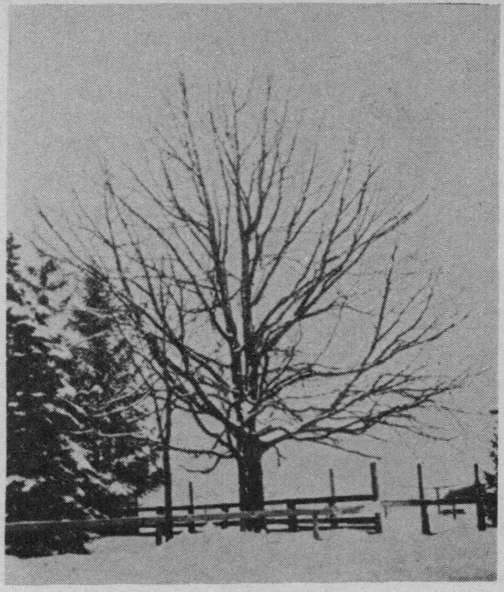
Bur Oak

HOPHORNBEAM

A small tree seldom planted but often found hiding in the woods under the shelter of larger trees is the Hophornbeam. These trees are seldom very numerous but are usually found as single scattered trees in local woodlands. The name comes from the clusters of seed pods resembling hops and from the wood which is hard as horn. The tree grows slowly, making the wood very close-grained. Ironwood is another name for this tree as the wood is very strong and quite difficult to work. In the old days this wood was used for levers, rake teeth, mallets, and household utensils which "lasted forever." A unique use for this wood 100 years ago was the fashioning of the beams of ox yokes.

The leaves resemble those of birch, to which this tree is related. In the fall they turn a bright yellow color and focus attention on this tree growing in the understory of the woods. The unusual bark of the Hophornbeam is quite different from that of its cousin, the birch, in that it is quite shreddy or shaggy and cannot be mistaken for any other tree.

The tree is usually quite small, seldom growing more than 18 inches in diameter and 30 feet tall.

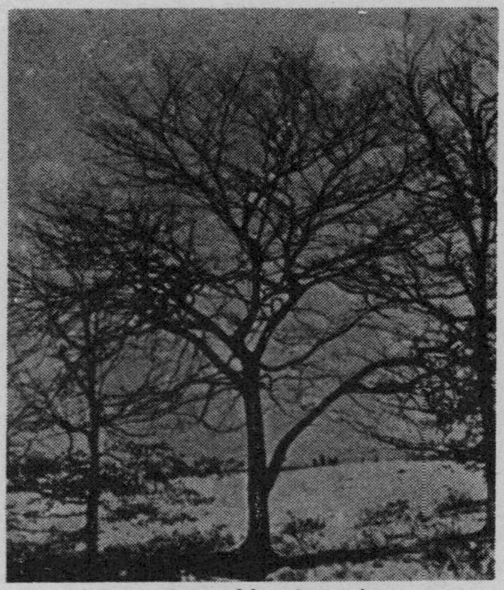
American Hophornbeam

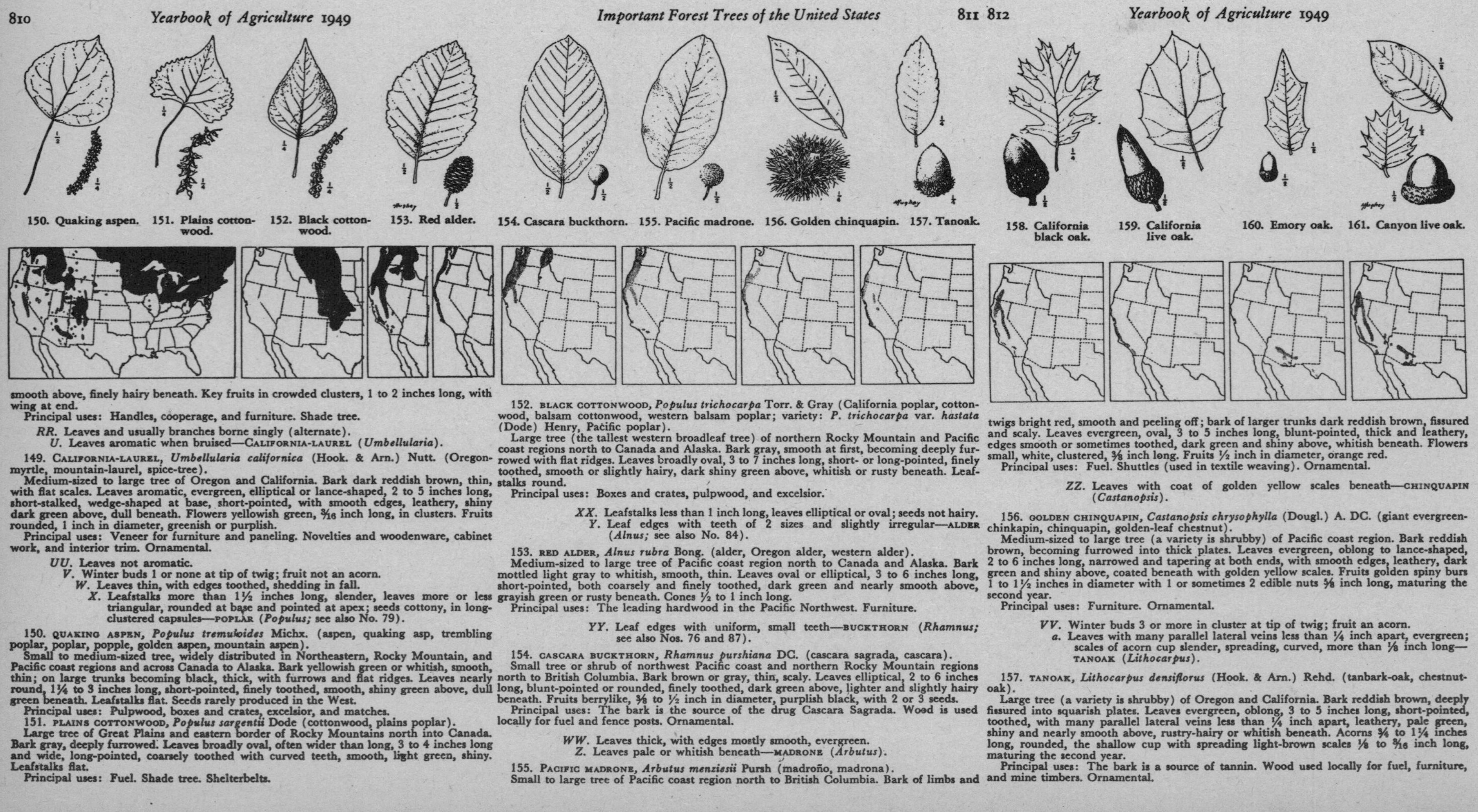
810 Yearbook of Agriculture 1949 Important Forest Trees of the United States 811 812 Yearbook of Agriculture 1949

150. Quaking aspen. 151. Plains cottonwood. 152. Black cottonwood. 153. Red alder. 154. Cascara buckthorn. 155. Pacific madrone. 156. Golden chinquapin. 157. Tanoak. 158. California black oak. 159. California live oak. 160. Emory oak. 161. Canyon live oak.

smooth above, finely hairy beneath. Key fruits in crowded clusters, 1 to 2 inches long, with wing at end.

Principal uses: Handles, cooperage, and furniture. Shade tree.

RR. Leaves and usually branches borne singly (alternate).

U. Leaves aromatic when bruised—CALIFORNIA-LAUREL (*Umbellularia*).

149. CALIFORNIA-LAUREL, *Umbellularia californica* (Hook. & Arn.) Nutt. (Oregon-myrtle, mountain-laurel, spice-tree).

Medium-sized to large tree of Oregon and California. Bark dark reddish brown, thin, with flat scales. Leaves aromatic, evergreen, elliptical or lance-shaped, 2 to 5 inches long, short-stalked, wedge-shaped at base, short-pointed, with smooth edges, leathery, shiny dark green above, dull beneath. Flowers yellowish green, 3/16 inch long, in clusters. Fruits rounded, 1 inch in diameter, greenish or purplish.

Principal uses: Veneer for furniture and paneling. Novelties and woodenware, cabinet work, and interior trim. Ornamental.

UU. Leaves not aromatic.

V. Winter buds 1 or none at tip of twig; fruit not an acorn.

W. Leaves thin, with edges toothed, shedding in fall.

X. Leafstalks more than 1½ inches long, slender, leaves more or less triangular, rounded at base and pointed at apex; seeds cottony, in long-clustered capsules—POPLAR (*Populus;* see also No. 79).

150. QUAKING ASPEN, *Populus tremuloides* Michx. (aspen, quaking asp, trembling poplar, poplar, popple, golden aspen, mountain aspen).

Small to medium-sized tree, widely distributed in Northeastern, Rocky Mountain, and Pacific coast regions and across Canada to Alaska. Bark yellowish green or whitish, smooth, thin; on large trunks becoming black, thick, with furrows and flat ridges. Leaves nearly round, 1¼ to 3 inches long, short-pointed, finely toothed, smooth, shiny green above, dull green beneath. Leafstalks flat. Seeds rarely produced in the West.

Principal uses: Pulpwood, boxes and crates, excelsior, and matches.

151. PLAINS COTTONWOOD, *Populus sargentii* Dode (cottonwood, plains poplar).

Large tree of Great Plains and eastern border of Rocky Mountains north into Canada. Bark gray, deeply furrowed. Leaves broadly oval, often wider than long, 3 to 4 inches long and wide, long-pointed, coarsely toothed with curved teeth, smooth, light green, shiny. Leafstalks flat.

Principal uses: Fuel. Shade tree. Shelterbelts.

152. BLACK COTTONWOOD, *Populus trichocarpa* Torr. & Gray (California poplar, cottonwood, balsam cottonwood, western balsam poplar; variety: *P. trichocarpa* var. *hastata* (Dode) Henry, Pacific poplar).

Large tree (the tallest western broadleaf tree) of northern Rocky Mountain and Pacific coast regions north to Canada and Alaska. Bark gray, smooth at first, becoming deeply furrowed with flat ridges. Leaves broadly oval, 3 to 7 inches long, short- or long-pointed, finely toothed, smooth or slightly hairy, dark shiny green above, whitish or rusty beneath. Leafstalks round.

Principal uses: Boxes and crates, pulpwood, and excelsior.

XX. Leafstalks less than 1 inch long, leaves elliptical or oval; seeds not hairy.

Y. Leaf edges with teeth of 2 sizes and slightly irregular—ALDER (*Alnus;* see also No. 84).

153. RED ALDER, *Alnus rubra* Bong. (alder, Oregon alder, western alder).

Medium-sized to large tree of Pacific coast region north to Canada and Alaska. Bark mottled light gray to whitish, smooth, thin. Leaves oval or elliptical, 3 to 6 inches long, short-pointed, both coarsely and finely toothed, dark green and nearly smooth above, grayish green or rusty beneath. Cones ½ to 1 inch long.

Principal uses: The leading hardwood in the Pacific Northwest. Furniture.

YY. Leaf edges with uniform, small teeth—BUCKTHORN (*Rhamnus;* see also Nos. 76 and 87).

154. CASCARA BUCKTHORN, *Rhamnus purshiana* DC. (cascara sagrada, cascara).

Small tree or shrub of northwest Pacific coast and northern Rocky Mountain regions north to British Columbia. Bark brown or gray, thin, scaly. Leaves elliptical, 2 to 6 inches long, blunt-pointed or rounded, finely toothed, dark green above, lighter and slightly hairy beneath. Fruits berrylike, 3/8 to ½ inch in diameter, purplish black, with 2 or 3 seeds.

Principal uses: The bark is the source of the drug Cascara Sagrada. Wood is used locally for fuel and fence posts. Ornamental.

WW. Leaves thick, with edges mostly smooth, evergreen.

Z. Leaves pale or whitish beneath—MADRONE (*Arbutus*).

155. PACIFIC MADRONE, *Arbutus menziesii* Pursh (madroño, madrona).

Small to large tree of Pacific coast region north to British Columbia. Bark of limbs and twigs bright red, smooth and peeling off; bark of larger trunks dark reddish brown, fissured and scaly. Leaves evergreen, oval, 3 to 5 inches long, blunt-pointed, thick and leathery, edges smooth or sometimes toothed, dark green and shiny above, whitish beneath. Flowers small, white, clustered, 3/8 inch long. Fruits ½ inch in diameter, orange red.

Principal uses: Fuel. Shuttles (used in textile weaving). Ornamental.

ZZ. Leaves with coat of golden yellow scales beneath—CHINQUAPIN (*Castanopsis*).

156. GOLDEN CHINQUAPIN, *Castanopsis chrysophylla* (Dougl.) A. DC. (giant evergreen-chinkapin, chinquapin, golden-leaf chestnut).

Medium-sized to large tree (a variety is shrubby) of Pacific coast region. Bark reddish brown, becoming furrowed into thick plates. Leaves evergreen, oblong to lance-shaped, 2 to 6 inches long, narrowed and tapering at both ends, with smooth edges, leathery, dark green and shiny above, coated beneath with golden yellow scales. Fruits golden spiny burs 1 to 1½ inches in diameter with 1 or sometimes 2 edible nuts 5/8 inch long, maturing the second year.

Principal uses: Furniture. Ornamental.

VV. Winter buds 3 or more in cluster at tip of twig; fruit an acorn.

a. Leaves with many parallel lateral veins less than ¼ inch apart, evergreen; scales of acorn cup slender, spreading, curved, more than 1/8 inch long—TANOAK (*Lithocarpus*).

157. TANOAK, *Lithocarpus densiflorus* (Hook. & Arn.) Rehd. (tanbark-oak, chestnut-oak).

Large tree (a variety is shrubby) of Oregon and California. Bark reddish brown, deeply fissured into squarish plates. Leaves evergreen, oblong, 3 to 5 inches long, short-pointed, toothed, with many parallel lateral veins less than ¼ inch apart, leathery, pale green, shiny and nearly smooth above, rustry-hairy or whitish beneath. Acorns ¾ to 1¼ inches long, rounded, the shallow cup with spreading light-brown scales 1/8 to 5/16 inch long, maturing the second year.

Principal uses: The bark is a source of tannin. Wood used locally for fuel, furniture, and mine timbers. Ornamental.

ANGIOSPERMÆ, DICOTYLEDONES.

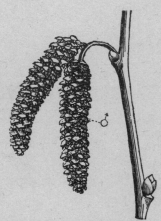

Hazel Nut—Monœcious
Flower.

YELLOW WILLOW

RED MAPLE

—Amentales.

¹ Birch (*Betula alba*) shoot with male and female catkins (the former at the apex). ² Ripe female catkin of same. ³ Winged nut of same. ⁴ Subtending scale of fruit of same. ⁵ Shoot of Hornbeam (*Carpinus Betulus*) with male and female catkins (latter to right). ⁶ Scale of female catkin with flowers of same. ⁷ Scale from male catkin with stamens. ⁸ Scale of female catkin with ripe fruit. ³, ⁴, ⁶, ⁷ enlarged; the rest nat. size.

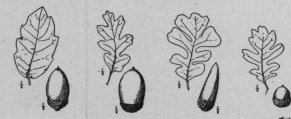

162. Blue oak.   163. Oregon white oak.   164. California white oak.   165. Gambel oak.

aa. Leaves with lateral veins not parallel (except in No. 161), falling in autumn or evergreen; scales of acorn cup small and inconspicuous—OAK (*Quercus*).
  b. Leaves with bristle-tipped teeth; acorns maturing the second year (first year in No. 159)—BLACK OAKS.

158. CALIFORNIA BLACK OAK, *Quercus kelloggii* Newb. (black oak; *Q. californica* (Torr.) Coop.).
  Large tree of Oregon and California. Bark dark brown, furrowed into irregular plates and ridges. Leaves falling in autumn, oblong, 4 to 10 inches long, usually 7-lobed about halfway to middle, each lobe with a few bristle-pointed teeth, thick, dark yellow green and smooth above, light yellow green and smooth or hairy beneath. Acorns 1 to 1½ inches long, rounded, with deep cup.
  Principal uses: Fuel.

159. CALIFORNIA LIVE OAK, *Quercus agrifolia* Née (coast live oak).
  Large tree of California and Lower California. Bark dark brown, thick, deeply furrowed. Leaves evergreen, elliptical to oblong, ¾ to 3 inches long, short-pointed or rounded at tip, spiny-toothed, thick and stiff, dark green above, beneath paler, shiny, and smooth or hairy. Acorns long, ¾ to 1½ inches long, pointed, with deep cup.
  Principal uses: Fuel. Shade tree and ornamental.

  bb. Leaves lobed, toothed, or entire but not bristle-tipped; acorns maturing the first year (second year in No. 161)—WHITE OAK (see also Nos. 105 and 107).
    c. Leaves not lobed or only shallowly lobed.

160. EMORY OAK, *Quercus emoryi* Torr. (black oak).
  Medium-sized tree of Southwestern region and adjacent Mexico. Bark blackish, divided into thin plates. Leaves evergreen, broadly lance-shaped, 1 to 2½ inches long, short-pointed, with a few short teeth, thick, stiff, leathery, flat, shiny dark green on both sides, nearly smooth. Acorns ½ to ¾ inch long, rounded, edible.
  Principal uses: Fuel.

161. CANYON LIVE OAK, *Quercus chrysolepis* Liebm. (live oak, maul oak); variety: Palmer oak, *Q. chrysolepis* var. *palmeri* (Engelm.) Sarg.).
  Medium-sized to large tree (a variety is shrubby) of Pacific coast and Southwestern regions and adjacent Mexico. Bark gray brown, scaly and flaky. Leaves evergreen, elliptical or oval, 1 to 3 inches long, with edges spiny-toothed or smooth, thick and leathery, bright green and smooth above, yellow-hairy or whitish beneath. Acorns 1 to 2 inches long, broad, with thick yellowish cup.
  Principal uses: Parts of vehicles and agricultural implements. Ornamental. Fuel.
162. BLUE OAK, *Quercus douglasii* Hook. & Arn. (California blue oak, mountain white oak).

Medium-sized tree of California. Bark gray, scaly. Leaves shedding in fall, oblong, 1 to 3 inches long, short-pointed or rounded at apex, with edges coarsely toothed, shallowly 4- or 5-lobed, or smooth, rigid, pale blue green above, pale and slightly hairy beneath. Acorns ¾ to 1½ inches long, broad, with shallow cup.
  Principal uses: Fuel.

    cc. Leaves deeply lobed halfway or more to middle.

163. OREGON WHITE OAK, *Quercus garryana* Dougl. (Garry oak, Oregon oak).
  Medium-sized to large tree of Pacific coast region from California to British Columbia. Bark light gray or brown, thin, with narrow fissures, broken into scaly ridges. Leaves shedding in fall, oblong, 3 to 6 inches long, deeply 5- to 9-lobed halfway or more to middle with blunt-pointed or slightly toothed lobes, dark green above, light green and usually hairy beneath. Acorns 1 to 1½ inches long, broad and rounded, with shallow cup.
  Principal uses: Furniture, shipbuilding, construction, agricultural implements, cooperage, cabinet work, interior finish, and fuel. Shade tree.
164. CALIFORNIA WHITE OAK, *Quercus lobata* Née (valley white oak, white oak, valley oak).
  Large tree of California. Bark gray or brown, thick, deeply furrowed and broken horizontally into thick plates. Leaves shedding in fall, oblong, 2½ to 4 inches long, broad, deeply 7- to 11-lobed more than halfway to middle, dark green above, gray-hairy beneath. Acorns long, 1¼ to 2¼ inches long, slender and pointed, with deep cup.
  Principal uses: Shade tree. Fuel.
165. GAMBEL OAK, *Quercus gambelii* Nutt. (Rocky Mountain white oak, Utah white oak; *Q. utahensis* (A. DC.) Rydb.).
  Small tree or shrub of Rocky Mountain region, including adjacent Mexico. Bark gray brown, scaly. Leaves shedding in fall, oblong, 4 to 8 inches long, deeply 7- to 11-lobed halfway or more to middle, dark green above, light green and soft-hairy beneath. Acorns ⅜ to ¾ inch long, broad and rounded, with deep cup.
  Principal uses: Fence posts and fuel.

ELBERT L. LITTLE, JR., *dendrologist in the Division of Dendrology and Range Forage Investigations, Forest Service, in Washington, D. C., has been in research work with the Forest Service since 1934. He has published papers on names of trees of the United States and various botanical subjects. During the Second World War he made forestry and botanical surveys in Latin American countries. Dr. Little holds degrees from the Universities of Oklahoma and Chicago.*

Small Deciduous Trees for the Home Landscape

TREES GENERALLY NOT EXCEEDING 30′ IN HEIGHT

PEAR OAK

Small trees planted in patios, dooryards, or within view of windows are especially suited to close association with people. Some do provide shade, but they are usually selected for other reasons: showy flowers or fruits, interesting foliage or buds, attractive bark, or structural trunk and branching patterns—features which give them continuous interest from season to season. Some of them have fruits which persist into winter or which attract birds.

Many small trees can be grown with multiple as well as single trunks, offering a variety of picturesque forms. In naturalistic groupings they can be used to create intimate spaces, form screens for privacy, frame a view, serve as a background, or soften the static forms of houses and fences. They are useful along driveways, in and around patios, in walled city gardens, in shrub borders, and as individual lawn specimens. They combine well with underplantings of low shrubs and ground covers, creating plantings that are in good scale with most suburban houses and yards. In large-scale landscape compositions, they provide ideal transitional scale between tall trees and the surrounding spaces.

Small trees are especially appropriate for locations where their branches can be trained to arch over entrance gates or doorways, creating inviting overhead canopies and providing pleasing human scale relationships. In the training process, interesting sculptural features can be further empha-

RED BUD

sized by carefully studied pruning. Small trees are also desirable for plantings beneath power lines, where the maximum tree height at maturity should not exceed twenty to twenty-five feet. The pruning required to keep larger trees from interfering with the overhead wires is often severely disfiguring. It is always better to select trees which at maturity will not be too tall, than to attempt to keep them in bounds by pruning.

The trees in this list generally do not reach more than thirty feet in height in the Chicago area, approximately the height of an average two-story house. They are recommended for northeastern Illinois on the basis of ornamental value, proven hardiness, reasonable availability, and freedom from serious problems.

BOOKS USEFUL IN SELECTING TREES

Ornamental Growers Association of Northern Illinois, Planting Guide for Northern Illinois. *Wheeling, Illinois, 1970.*

Crockett, James Underwood, ed., Trees. *New York, Time-Life Encyclopedia of Gardening, 1972.*

Wyman, Donald, Trees for American Gardens. *New York, Macmillan, 1965.*

Nelson, William R., Jr., Landscaping Your Home. *Urbana, U. of Illinois College of Agriculture Cooperative Extension Service, 1963.*

Zion, Robert L., Trees for Architecture and the Landscape. *New York, Reinhold Book Corporation, 1968.*

QUINCE

| BEECH, BLUE | Height: 25-30′ |
| *Carpinus caroliniana* | Spread: 15-25′ |

A rounded, compact tree with multiple trunks. Smooth, blue-gray, sinewy bark. Dense foliage. Can be sheared. Slow growing.

Texture: medium   *Fall color:* yellow-orange
Fruits: decorative bracts in late summer
Soil: Prefers rich, moist soils
Site: Prefers partial shade but tolerates full shade and sun

| CHESTNUT, CHINESE | Height: 25-40′ |
| *Castanea mollissima* | Spread: 30-40′ |

A rounded, irregular tree with coarse glossy leaves. Moderate to fast growth rate.

Texture: coarse   *Fall color:* russet-tan to yellow
Flowers: creamy-white, ill-scented
Fruits: edible nuts in prickly husks, August to September (requires cross-pollination)
Soil: well-drained   *Site:* prefers full sun

FLOWERING DOGWOOD.
(CORNUS FLORIDA.)

| CRAB, FLOWERING | Height: 15-20′ |
| *Malus floribunda* | Spread: 15-20′ |

Rounded, spreading, low-branching tree with short trunk. Moderate to fast growth rate.

Texture: medium   *Fall color:* dull yellow-orange
Flowers: pale pink fading to white, profuse, in May
Fruits: persistent red, berry-like pomes, ¼″
Soil: tolerant   *Site:* sunny open areas

| CRAB, ZUMI | Height: 20-30′ |
| *Malus × zumi calocarpa* | Spread: 20-30′ |

Rounded, spreading, irregular. Low-branched, dense foliage. Can be trained. Moderate to fast growth rate.

Texture: medium   *Fall color:* yellow to brown
Flowers: profuse, pink turning to white, in May
Fruits: red berry-like pomes in August; persistent; ½″
Soil: tolerant   *Site:* sunny open areas

| DOGWOOD, PAGODA | Height: 20-25′ |
| *Cornus alternifolia* | Spread: 15-20′ |

Rounded tree with layered branching effect, multiple trunks, red to greenish twigs. Moderate growth rate.

Texture: medium   *Fall color:* russet-red
Flowers: creamy-white in mid-May to early June
Fruits: bluish-black berries on red pedicels
Soil: moist but well-drained; does not tolerate drouth
Site: does best in cool lightly shaded site

DOGWOOD

Texture: medium   *Fall color:* yellow-orange
Flowers: yellow-green catkins as leaves emerge
Fruits: nutlets enclosed in bladder-like pods; persistent
Soil: moist loam, well-drained
Site: full sun to moderate shade

MAGNOLIA, SAUCER   *Height:* 20-25'
Magnolia × soulangiana   *Spread:* 20-25'

Oval irregular tree, often with multiple trunks. Smooth gray bark. Large, dark gray-green leaves. Moderate growth rate.

Texture: coarse   *Fall color:* dull yellow
Flowers: large, creamy; outside of petals rose-pink; bloom in April and early May before leaves emerge
Fruits: upright cone-like husks, splitting to expose red seed clusters; sparse
Soil: moist, well-drained; avoid heavy clay
Site: full sun or light shade; shelter from severe wind

MAGNOLIA, STAR   *Height:* 15-20'
Magnolia stellata   *Spread:* 10-15'

Rounded shrub-like tree with multiple trunks and smooth gray bark. Dark foliage. Slow to moderate growth rate.

Texture: medium   *Fall color:* dull yellow
Flowers: white, profuse in April
Fruits: orange-red seeds enclosed in irregular cone-like husks; sparse
Soil: moist, well-drained; avoid heavy clay
Site: full sun or light shade; shelter from early spring wind

MAPLE, AMUR   *Height:* 15-20'
Acer ginnala   *Spread:* 20-25'

Rounded, irregular spreading tree usually with multiple trunks. Dense dark green foliage. Moderate growth rate.

Texture: medium   *Fall color:* orange-red to pink
Fruits: attractive pink-to-red samaras in late summer; persistent
Soil: well-drained
Site: full sun or light shade; tolerates urban conditions

MAPLE, HEDGE   *Height:* 20-25'
Acer campestre   *Spread:* 20-25'

A rounded, short-trunked tree, low-branching and often with multiple trunks. Handsome, dense, dark foliage. Can be sheared. Slow-growing.

Texture: fine to medium   *Fall color:* dull yellow
Soil: well-drained, preferably rich loam; tolerates dryness
Site: full sun to light shade; tolerates urban conditions

Texture: fine   *Fall color:* bronze-orange
Flowers: white, delicate, late April and May
Fruits: bluish-purple, berry-like, edible; attract birds
Soil: rich, moist, well-drained
Site: full sun to partial shade

SILVER BELL   *Height:* 25-30'
Halesia monticola   *Spread:* 20-25'

A rounded irregular tree with large, dark, gray-green leaves. Multiple trunks, striped gray bark. Hardier than, but sometimes sold as, *H. carolina.* Slow to moderate growth rate.

Texture: coarse   *Fall color:* yellow
Flowers: delicate white bell-like flowers in May, 1"

Fruits: brown, four-winged; persistent
Soil: rich, well-drained
Site: full sun or light shade; needs some protection

TREE-LILAC, JAPANESE   *Height:* 20-30'
Syringa amurensis japonica   *Spread:* 20-30'

Rounded to broadly open irregular tree, usually with multiple trunks. Dark cherry-like bark. Moderate growth rate.

Texture: medium   *Fall color:* yellow-brown
Flowers: creamy white in mid-June, fragrant
Fruits: brown clusters, persistent
Soil: rich, moist, well-drained
Site: full sun; tolerates light shade but does not flower well there

JAPANESE PLUM

SLIPPERY ELM

RED MULBERRY

KENT COFFEE TREE

FRINGETREE   *Height:* 15-25'
Chionanthus virginicus   *Spread:* 15-20'

A rounded upright tree with single or multiple trunks. Leafs out late. Slow growing

Texture: coarse   *Fall color:* yellow
Flowers: profuse, white, feathery, in early June
Fruits: dark blue, grape-like, in late summer
Soil: prefers moist, well-drained
Site: full sun or light shade; tolerates urban conditions

HAWTHORN, COCKSPUR   *Height:* 25-30'
Crataegus crus-galli   *Spread:* 30-35'

Rounded, spreading tree with irregular horizontal branching and dark glossy leaves. Gnarled trunks and long shiny thorns. Thornless variety available. Slow to moderate growth rate.

Texture: medium   *Fall color:* red-bronze
Flowers: white, in May; ill-scented
Fruits: persistent dull red berry-like pomes, ⅜"
Soil: well-drained, otherwise tolerant
Site: full sun; tolerates urban conditions

HAWTHORN, LAVALLE   *Height:* 25-30'
Crataegus × lavallei   *Spread:* 25-30'

Compact vase-shaped tree with dense glossy foliage. Low branching and single or multiple trunks. Moderate growth rate.

Texture: medium   *Fall color:* red-bronze
Flowers: white in May: ill-scented
Fruits: persistent red-to-orange berry-like pomes, ⅝"
Soil: well-drained, otherwise tolerant
Site: full sun; tolerates urban conditions

HAWTHORN, WASHINGTON   *Height:* 25-30'
Crataegus phaenopyrum   *Spread:* 20-25'

Rounded, open tree with low branching and multiple trunks. Dark, glossy foliage. Upright when young. Moderate to fast growth rate. Excellent all-around tree.

Texture: medium   *Fall color:* bronze to scarlet
Flowers: white in late May or June; ill-scented
Fruits: persistent clusters of bright red berry-like pomes, ¼"
Soil: well-drained, otherwise tolerant
Site: full sun; tolerates urban conditions

IRONWOOD   *Height:* 30-40'
Ostrya virginiana   *Spread:* 20-30'

Rounded narrow tree, becoming irregular with age. Single trunk with light bark shredding in narrow vertical strips. Slow growing. Good small shade tree.

MAPLE, PAPERBARK   *Height:* 20-25'
Acer griseum   *Spread:* 20-25'

A rounded, rather open tree with attractive cinnamon-brown, peeling bark. Slow growing. May be difficult to obtain in some areas.

Texture: medium   *Fall color:* red-bronze to burnt orange
Soil: relatively tolerant; prefers average or better drainage
Site: full sun to partial shade; shelter from winds is helpful

YELLOW WOOD

PEAR, BRADFORD
Pyrus calleryana 'Bradford'   Height: 25-30'   Spread: 20-30'

A rounded tree becoming irregular with age. Dense, dark, glossy foliage. Moderate growth rate. Mildly susceptible to fire blight.

Texture: medium   Fall color: red to scarlet
Flowers: white in May
Fruits: tiny russet-brown pears, inedible; persistent
Soil: tolerant
Site: full sun; tolerates air pollution

PLUM, WILD
Prunus americana   Height: 15-20'   Spread: 15-20'

Rounded irregular tree that suckers freely and may create naturalistic thickets; may be single trunked. Moderate growth rate. May suffer from black knot on twigs.

Texture: medium   Fall color: yellow-orange
Flowers: white, in May, profuse; fragrance delicate
Fruits: yellow-pink edible plums
Soil: avoid heavy clay   Site: tolerant

REDBUD
Cercis canadensis   Height: 15-30'   Spread: 15-25'

Irregular flat-topped tree with large heart-shaped leaves. Interesting brown bark, sloughing off with age to expose light red inner bark. Slow to moderate growth rate. Select known northern-grown stock.

Texture: coarse   Fall color: yellow
Flowers: magenta pea-like flowers in late April and May before the leaves emerge
Fruits: persistent brown pods
Soil: rich, moist, well-drained
Site: prefers partial shade; tolerates sun

SHADBLOW, DOWNY
Amelanchier arborea   Height: 20-30'   Spread: 15-20'

A rounded narrow tree, usually multiple-trunked, with attractive smooth gray bark. Delicate, airy effect. Moderate to fast growth rate. Often sold as *A. canadensis*.

JAPANESE MAPLE.

JAPANESE MAPLES

Acer palmatum (Japanese maple)
Acer palmatum 'Atropurpureum' (Bloodleaf Japanese maple)

These attractive small trees are not reliable in our climate, but sometimes succeed when planted in well protected sites such as among loose conifers, in sheltered corners, or shaded by lath structures. They require protection from rapid temperature changes, especially in spring and late fall, and for this reason should not be planted on the south or west side of a house.

WHITE BIRCHES

Betula verrucosa (European white birch)
Betula papyrifera (Canoe or paper birch)

Birches in this area are highly susceptible to the bronze birch borer, for which no effective control has been approved. Hot summers and heavy soils further prevent paper birch from thriving here as it does farther north. Birches other than river birch, *Betula nigra*, are not recommended for planting in the Chicago region.

White birches can be enjoyed here as "temporary" features in the garden if the homeowner is willing to replace them from time to time. Although there are exceptions, white birches do not usually live more than eight to ten years in this area.

—OAK-LEAVED MOUNTAIN ASH (*Pyrus aucuparia quercifolia*).

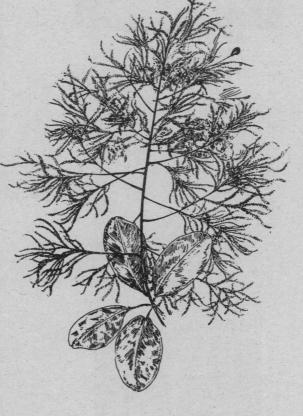

— Fruit of Smoke-Tree (*Rhus Cotinus*).
Only one pedicel bears a fruit, all the others are sterile, branched, and covered with plumy hairs.

—SILVER MAPLE (*Acer dasycarpum*).

MOUNTAIN ASHES

Sorbus americana (American mountain ash)
Sorbus aucuparia (European mountain ash)

These attractive trees are also short-lived in northeastern Illinois. They are subject to serious attack by the round-headed borer and also suffer from sunscald, fire blight, and apple scab. Like white birches, they do not usually live more than eight to ten years here and should be considered a "temporary" feature if used at all.

RUSSIAN OLIVE

Elaeagnus angustifolia

This fast-growing gray-green tree is frequently planted in the landscape as a screen. However, it is subject to severe *Verticillium* wilt in this region, causing unsightly die-back and premature death. Its short life offsets any benefits of its rapid growth, and it is not recommended.

CRAB APPLES

Malus species

Many crab apple species are susceptible to apple scab and cedar-apple rust, which cause the leaves to discolor and drop off early in the season. Fortunately there are a number of species that are resistant to these diseases, and a list of those recommended for our region is available.

Disease-Resistant Trees

Asiatic Elms *Ulmus parvifolia* and *U. pumila:* Resistant to Dutch elm disease.

Chinese and Japanese Chestnuts *Castanea mollissima* and *C. japonica:* Resistant to chestnut blight but susceptible to twig blight and canker.

Chinese Hackberry *Celtis sinensis:* Resistant to witches' broom.

Cockspur, Washington, and **Toba Hawthorns** *Crataegus crus-galli, C. phaenopyrum,* and *C. mordenensis* cv. Toba: Resistant to the *Diplocarpon* leaf blight which is so serious on Paul's scarlet hawthorn.

Crabapple, Flowering
Malus cv. Abundance
M. cv. Adams
M. cv. Albright
M. baccata var. *himalaica*
M. baccata cv. Jackii
M. cv. Beauty
M. cv. Beverly
M. cv. Burton
M. cv. Cardinal King
M. cv. Caramel
M. cv. David
M. cv. Donald Wyman
M. cv. Dorothy Rowe
M. cv. Gibbs' Golden Gage
M. cv. Gwendolyn
M. cv. Henry Kohankie
M. cv. Inglis
M. cv. Honeywood #7
M. cv. Honeywood #14
M. kansuensis
M. cv. Kibele
M. cv. Lee Trio
M. cv. Margaret
M. cv. Mount Arbor Special
M. cv. Ormiston Roy
M. cv. Peachblow
M. cv. Professor Sprenger
M. cv. Robert Nairn
M. cv. Robinson
M. cv. Toschprince. All resistant to cedar apple rust, fire blight, powdery mildew, and scab.

Horse Chestnut
Aesculus arguta
A. glabra var. *monticola*
A. glabra var. *sargentii*
A. parviflora
A. parviflora var. *serotina:* Resistant to leaf blotch caused by *Guignardia aesculi.*

Japan Poplar *Populus maximowiczii:* Resistant to Cryptodiaporthe canker.

Junipers
Juniperus chinensis cv. Femina
Iowa
Keteleeri
Pfitzeriana Aurea
Robusta
var. *sargentii*
sargentii cv. Glauca
cv. Shoosmith
J. communis cv. Ashfordii
Aureo-spica
var. *depressa*
cv. Hulkjaerhus
Prostrata Aurea
Repanda
var. *saxatilis*
cv. Suecica
J. horizontalis cv. *Depressa*
cv. Depressa Aurea
Procumbens

BRANCH OF SWEET, OR SPANISH CHESTNUT.

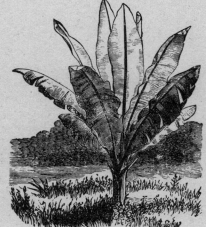

—Abyssinian Banana (*Musa ensete*).

J. sabina cv. Broadmoor
Knap Hill
Skandia
J. scopulorum cv. Silver King
J. squamata cv. Campbellii
var. *fargesii*
cv. Prostrata
Pumila
J. virginiana cv. Tripartita

All resistant to twig blight caused by *Phomopsis juniperovora.*

White Cedar (*Chamaecyparis*) The following cultivars, all of *C. pisifera* Filifera Aureovariegata, Plumosa Aurea, Plumosa Argentea, Plumosa Lutescens, Squarrosa Sulfurea: Resistant to twig blight caused by *Phomopsis juniperovora.*

Weeping and Bay-Leaved Willows *Salix babylonica* and *S. pentandra:* Resistant to leaf blight and black canker caused by *Pollacia saliciperda* and *Physalospora miyabeana.*

Trees Relatively Free of Disease

*__**Atlas Cedar** *Cedrus atlantica*__
Amur Cork-Tree *Phellodendron amurense*
Bald Cypress *Taxodium distichum*
Beech *Fagus grandiflora* and *F. sylvatica*
Cedar of Lebanon *Cedrus libani*
Cedrela *Cedrela sinensis*
*__**China-Fir** *Cunninghamia lanceolata*__
Cork-Tree *Phellodendron* sp.
Cucumber-Tree *Magnolia acuminata*
*__**Dove-Tree** *Davidia involucrata*__
Eucommia *Eucommia ulmoides*
Franklinia *Franklinia altamaha*
Ginkgo *Ginkgo biloba*
*__**Glossy Privet** *Ligustrum lucidum*__
Golden Larch *Pseudolarix amabilis*
Honey-Locust *Gleditsia triacanthos*
Hop Hornbeam *Ostrya virginiana*
Hornbeam *Carpinus caroliniana*
Japanese Plum Yew *Cephalotaxus drupacea*
Japanese Rasin-Tree *Hovenia dulcis*
Japanese Torreya *Torreya nucifera*
Japanese Yew *Taxus cuspidata*
Kalopanax *Kalopanix pictus*
Katsura-Tree *Cercidiphyllum japonicum*

*Trees generally hardy only as far north as southeastern Pennsylvania.

Kentucky Coffee-Tree *Gymnocladus dioicus*
Larch *Larix decidua* and *L. eurolepis*
Magnolia *Magnolia* sp.
Parrotia *Parrotia persica*
Pawpaw *Asimina triloba*
Persimmon *Diospyros virginiana*
*__**Phoenix or Chinese Parasol-Tree** *Firmiana simplex*__
Sassafrass *Sassafrass albidum*
Silverbell-Tree *Halesia monticola*
Snowbell, *Styrax japonica, S. Obassia,* and *S. dayantha*
Sorrel-Tree or Sour Wood *Oxydendrum arboreum*
Stewartia *Stewartia pseudo-camellia* and *S. korena*
Sweet Gum *Liquidamber styraciflua*
Tree-of-Heaven *Ailanthus altissima*
Tupelo *Nyssa sylvatica*
Turkish Hazelnut *Corylus colurna*
Umbrella-Pine *Sciadopitys verticillata*
Yellow-Wood *Celastrus lutea*
Yew *Taxus* sp.

113

Catalpa—Verticillium wilt

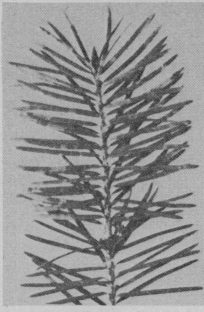

Douglas fir— needle cast

Pine—needle rust

TREE DISEASES

Dogwood—crown or trunk canker

Hawthorn—rust on leaves and fruit

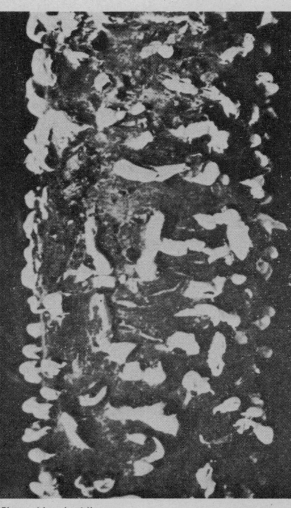

Pine—white pine blister rust

Mountain Ash—leaf spot

Maple—tar spot

Elm—black leaf spot

Crab, flowering—scab on leaves

Horse Chestnut—leaf blotch

Oak, white-anthracnose

Juniper-twig blight. Spores oozing out of fruiting bodies of the causal fungus on an affected twig.

Chestnut—blight canker

Hawthorn—rust on leaves and fruit

Pine—needle cast

Dutch Elm Disease — Dutch elm disease was first observed in the United States in Ohio in 1930. Since then it has spread throughout the east and as far west as Idaho. All American elm species are susceptible. This disease has eliminated elms from many eastern and midwestern communities.

Dutch elm disease is caused by the fungus, *Ceratocystis ulmi*, which invades and plugs the water-conducting system of the tree. The foliage wilts and turns yellow, usually first on one or more individual branches, but soon the whole tree is involved (Figure 11). Leaves may curl and turn yellow before falling or may wither and fall suddenly while still green. Infected trees may die within a few weeks or may decline slowly over a 1- to 2-year period or longer. Affected branches develop a brown discoloration in the outer layers of sapwood just under the bark. On the ends of cut twigs the discoloration may appear as a complete browning of one or more of the outermost annual rings (Figure 12).

The causal fungus is carried from tree to tree by two species of elm bark beetles—the smaller European elm bark beetle and the native elm bark beetle.

The infection cycle begins in the spring during May when adult bark beetles emerge from infected trees. If overwintering took place in trees killed by Dutch elm disease, then many of the emerging beetles will have sticky spores of the Dutch elm fungus on their bodies. The emerging beetles seek living, healthy elms where they feed in crotches of small twigs. Fungus spores are deposited in water-conducting tubes opened by the feeding injury. Elms so inoculated usually develop the disease during that summer. The majority of the beetles feed 600 feet or less from the dead wood in which they are overwintered. Where elms are scarce, beetles may fly several miles in search of feeding sites.

After feeding for a few days, the beetles seek a suitable egg-laying site. They require dying or recently dead elm wood with the bark still tightly attached. This may be a standing dead tree, a log, a weakened tree, or a weakened branch on a healthy tree. Wood also may be inoculated during the egg-laying activities of beetles carrying the fungus. Thus, elms weakened or killed by any means may become infected with the fungus and become a source of a new brood of infectious beetles.

Beetles will not infest wood without bark or with loose, cracked bark such as occurs on old logs or trees dead more than a year. Beetles reproduce in all species of elm.

Although broods of bark beetles may occur every 35 to 40 days during the summer, much of the spread of the disease is associated with feeding injuries of the first spring brood. At this season the long water-conducting tubes in the wood of elms are near the surface and are easily opened by the beetle's feeding.

An important factor in the spread of the disease is the egg-laying site of the last brood of beetles of the season. If these adults lay eggs in Dutch elm disease-killed trees, then it is likely that beetles emerging next spring will be coated with fungus spores. If such trees are removed during the winter, the threat of infection is greatly reduced.

Control: All trees infected with Dutch elm disease should be cut and peeled as soon as possible. All stumps should be peeled to below ground level. Any unpeeled branches larger than 1/2-inch in diameter may harbor beetles. Limbs or trunks saved for firewood should be completely peeled and all remaining branches chipped or buried under at least 2 feet of soil. The beetle population and the threat of spread may be reduced by pruning all dead or weakened branches on non-diseased trees. This sanitation program is especially helpful in areas where the Dutch elm disease is just beginning to be a problem.

Where elms are closely planted (50 feet or less between trees) the fungus may spread through root grafts between trees. To prevent such spread, as soon as possible after the disease appears, a narrow trench should be dug or a root-cutting blade should be passed through the soil at the midpoint between the trees. A trench or cut 2 feet deep and extending beyond the spread of the branches will sever most tree-to-tree connections. Another means of preventing spread of the disease by root graft is to treat the soil half-way between the diseased and healthy trees with Vapam, a liquid soil fumigant. This will result in a section of dead roots through which the Dutch elm disease fungus will not pass. A line of holes 6 to 8 inches apart and from 15 to 24 inches deep is made with an electric drill and 2-inch auger. The line of holes should pass halfway between the trees and extend beyond the spread of

DUTCH ELM DISEASE

the branches. Vapam is diluted 1 part to 4 parts water, and 1 cup of the mixture is poured into each hole. As soon as each hole is filled, the top of the hole should be sealed with a sod plug or by tamping it closed with the heel. For best results, the soil temperature should be at least 50°F. The grass may be killed for a short distance around each hole. This area may be reseeded about one month after treatment.

Beetle Control by Spraying — Under most circumstances, it is impractical and uneconomical to try to prevent Dutch elm disease by spraying the trees to kill elm bark beetles. The difficulty of obtaining complete spray coverage in the tops of tall trees renders the spray programs only partially effective. The amount of protection provided by such a program is not sufficient to compensate for the cost.

Spraying elm trees for bark beetle control to protect against Dutch elm disease can be justified only for a few, very high-valued trees. No spray program should be undertaken unless sanitation and removal of beetle breeding sites also are being done. To date, systemic insecticides have not satisfactorily protected trees from the disease.

Curative or Preventive Chemicals — At present, there is no research-proven chemotheraputant available that will prevent or cure Dutch elm disease.

Elms Resistant to Dutch Elm Disease — Although none of the species of elms is immune to Dutch elm disease, some are highly resistant. However, these species are smaller and lack the desirable vase-shaped form of the American elm. Resistant species are *Ulmus pumila*, the Siberian elm, and *Ulmus parvafolia*, the Chinese elm. A Netherlands elm selection, the Christine Buisman elm, is also resistant. However, this selection is susceptible to the elm leaf beetle and is not winter hardy in the northernmost range of the American elm.

Diseased American elm

Maple-anthracnose of Norway maple

Maple-anthracnose of sugar maple

Oak-leaf blister

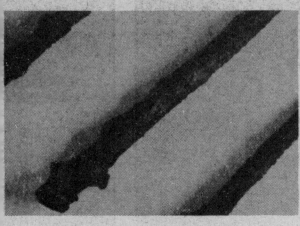

Oak-twig blight

TRUNK ROT

Prepared by Lester P. Nichols, Plant Pathology Extension
University of Rhode Island, Cooperative Extension Service
Kingston, R. I.

Tablespoons of Fungicides
for use in Gallon Lots of Spray

Small Amounts of Liquid Fungicides

Amount of Fungicide Recommended for 100 Gallons of Spray	Amount of Fungicide to Use in 1 Gallon of Spray
12 gallons	32 tablespoons or 1 pint
10 gallons	26 3/4 tablespoons or 4/5 pint
1 gallon	2 1/2 tablespoons
1 quart	5/8 tablespoon

When using fungicides in the wettable-powder form, it is much more accurate to weigh the material than it is to measure it by volume. Wettable powders tend to settle in the container, and will fluff up when the container is moved. In either case, the amount of material in a measuring cup or spoon will vary, contributing to inaccuracy. Variations in the amount measured out for a 100-gallon batch may amount to as much as 5 ounces.

An accurate scale or balance should be part of the equipment of all commercial arborists, and all personnel doing the mixing should know how to use the equipment. Cleaning after each use is important, dirt on the scales leads to inaccurate weighing and can contribute to contamination.

Homeowners who do not have access to a balance or scale must, of course, use a volume measurement. One level tablespoon of material in 1 gallon of water is roughly the same concentration as 1 pound of material in 100 gallons of liquid. This is of use to the homeowner only in very small quantities; however, commercial growers must weigh to achieve the accuracy necessary for effective control at minimum cost.

117

1 Branch of the Walnut-tree (*Juglans regia*) with hanging male catkins, and a small cluster of female flowers; natural size
2 The tip of a male catkin; enlarged.

—The Elm (*Ulmus campestris*).

1 With flowers.   2 With fruits.

SIX IDEAS TO MAKE ORNAMENTALS MORE USEFUL

There's far more to flowering plants and shrubs than just a pretty face. True, they *are* attractive and colorful, lending varied, natural charm to our yards, paths or doorways. But they fill other roles, too — and fill them well. While dressing up the garden, ornamentals do a fistful of practical jobs that make them about the most versatile things you can grow.

Let's take a close look at six basic ways any gardener can put ornamentals to work for him:

1. Use flowering plants to help control pests. Companion planting should be a steady part of the organic backyarder's defense against insect troubles. Start with marigolds, for instance. The strong-smelling, golden blossoms have a reputation for discouraging Mexican bean beetles from vegetable rows. Also, the root system of marigolds exudes a natural substance into the soil which suppresses harmful organisms, such as damaging nematodes. Marigolds may clear an area of wireworms, while their presence discourages nematodes (microscopic eelworms) attacking potatoes, strawberries, various bulb plants. Mexican marigold, planted as a cover crop in Georgia and Alabama, cut nematode populations to such an extent that highly susceptible crops could then be grown successfully.

Other flowers that help foil pests include cosmos, asters, chrysanthemums, pyrethrum or painted daisies — all of which have strong aromas. Nasturtiums benefit the whole garden, including fruit trees. They keep plant lice (aphids) from vegetation, deter squash bugs and striped pumpkin beetles. Besides being effective planted under fruit trees, nasturtiums make good companions to radishes, cabbage, melons and the rest of the cucurbit family.

And many of the attractive ornamental herbs chase bugs from the surrounding area as fast as they put in an appearance. "Plants that repel pests tend to have a common characteristic — a strong scent," writes Ruth Tirrell, who has used them for over 20 years to control insects in her garden. "That doesn't mean a scent disagreeable to humans," she adds. "Not at all — though if we were as tiny as insects, or if these plants were a jungle of tall trees, we too might find the smells rank and overpowering."

Which of the herbs deter pests? The mints are especially helpful with cabbage and broccoli. Tansy, a tall, hardy perennial with handsome jagged leaves and clusters of button-size yellow-orange flowers, does the best job of discouraging ants (which bring aphids). Planted at the back door, it helps keep both them and flies out of the house. Japanese beetles also stay clear of berries and cane fruits with a clump of tansy planted nearby. Rue, basil and oregano — another trio of aromatic herbs — repel flies and other bugs in borders close to buildings. Bush basil, which grows about a foot tall, is suitable for potting on a sunny kitchen shelf to drive out flies already inside. In the garden, basil teams with tomato plants to provide protection, enhancing growth and flavor as well. Other herbal helpers include savory, rosemary and sage (carrot fly, cabbage moth, bean beetles); borage (tomato worm); and both chives and garlic, the strongest-scented pest-chasers that deliver a wallop around grapevines, fruit trees, roses, raspberries.

2. Select some ornamental plants that encourage birds. While you don't need to set up a full-scale wildlife shelter, sharing room and board with birds pays off in scores of ways. Winged friends make rapid work of bugs galore, cheering the scene with action, color and song while they're at it. A single chickadee, reported one bird authority, will destroy more than 138,000 cankerworm eggs; a quail taken in Texas had 127 boll weevils in its craw; another in Pennsylvania had eaten over 100 potato bugs; a tree swallow's stomach revealed 40 chinch bugs; and that of a killdeer contained 300 mosquito larvae. As part of the overall setting, birds represent an essential ingredient in the environmental-balance recipe.

Good choices for attracting birds — all of them plants which look good in anyone's yard — include the choke-cherry shrub, Tatarian honeysuckle, dogwood, mulberry, red and black raspberries, Hansen bush cherry, elderberry, Russian olive, hawthorn and of course sunflowers. Birds like lots of other flowering plants, bushes and trees, too. The thing to remember is that aside from pesticide spraying, nothing dispels these benefactors faster than bare expanses of yard, fields or neighborhoods lacking a clump or two of protective shrubs and other plants.

3. Let ornamentals be your fence. Where there's a boundary, there's a plant choice that fits right in as a "living fence" — far more appealing than any other sort. Hardy shrubs make friendly border choices along neighboring lines, patios and the road. They also serve a dual purpose as ecological aids, curbing noise, improving the air, even spreading some nose-delighting aromas. Choose something like a mock orange, spirea, deutzia, or an old-fashioned lilac, now back in style with improved varieties. A windswept yard would do well with a miniature "shelter belt" of evergreen shrubs, planted several rows thick along the gusty side. And don't think evergreens are only green — holly has big red berries; rhododendrons bear bell-shaped blossoms in every hue from white through deep purple; and abelia carries delicate shell-pink flowers all summer, to mention just a few.

Boxwood is an old standby for hedges, too. Forsythia makes a good fence, spreads easily, and shows off bright brassy-yellow flowers. Multiflora rose develops a dense, thorny barrier, grows very fast, and produces clusters of cheerful white blooms plus an abundance of Chinesered fruits. It's a valuable fence or hedge choice for wildlife shelter and birds.

4. Include ornamentals that produce food. Lots of plants play this dual role — serving as attractive parts of the garden and also serving up good things to eat. Make your selections among ornamentals for eye-appeal; include several that bring appetizing bonuses to the table. American elderberry, for instance, a fast-growing deciduous type, has a profusion of early-spring bloom, then produces loads of sweet purplishblack berries rich in vitamin C as well as flavor. Flowering quince, including a dwarf variety that stands city conditions well, blooms in many shades of pink, white and coral. Its yellow fruit goes into an excellent preserve. Beach plum, a 6-foot deciduous type, is best for dry soil or along the seashore. Plenty of pretty white flowers are followed by purplish fruits for jams and jellies.

One choice not to be overlooked is the unique rugosa rose. It's not only a prolific-blossoming shrub, but a source of berries (or hips) remarkably rich in vitamin C and usable for teas, jams, soups and other dishes. A bush-type nut tree, the chinquipin — found mostly from southern Pennsylvania to Florida and Texas — is easy to grow, produces nuts which taste like a sweet chestnut. Several dwarf fruits, such as low-growing apples, can be trained as yard-dividers or fruiting hedges.

Many of the herbs already mentioned double-up as useful spices and flavorings — and are nice-looking garden occupants. To borage, thyme,

basil, sage, etc., add flowering herbs like marjoram, parsley, lavender, lemon balm, oregano and tarragon. Edgings or borders of perky plants such as these decorate the yard while enhancing the kitchen's production.

5. Select some ornamentals to provide shade or support for other plants. Mixed plantings can be multiplied blessings -- when they are planned carefully. Certain vegetable crops do best in cooling shade, particularly green-growers like lettuce, kale, Brussels sprouts, cauliflower and cabbage. Spot-plant a few taller-growing ornamentals to lend their shade. The combined effect will also help draw bees for better pollination among vegetables and fruits in the garden.

Another intercropping idea calls for letting vegetables that grow on tendrils, such as pole beans, squash, cucumbers, etc., use other plants for support. Usually this supporting role is played by another vegetable — as with beans climbing asparagus stalks after harvest, or cornstalks holding up a vine or bean plant. But some ornamentals will do the job too. Sunflowers — which add a super-food in their tasty seeds — have sturdy stalks for the task. So do a number of the taller growing cactus family, along with shrub types like highbush cranberry, which also rewards the gardener with fine red berries.

6. Pick ornamentals for effective landscaping. Whether it's to soften lines of the foundation around the house, break up a wide expanse of lawn, or accent any section of the garden, ornamentals make the first choice. As with the fences, landscape plants can help feed the family, too. Fruit trees, especially dwarf varieties, make one obvious selection. But how about bush cherries for foundation plantings? Blueberries as property dividers? Strawberries as flower borders? Oregon grape, currants, gooseberries are some others.

Front yards usually need an "eye-catcher," a single flowering, berrying or unusual-foliage-type shrub. Make it your own favorite. Often used are white or pink dogwood, weeping Japanese cherry, hibiscus, flowering crab, butterfly bush, spirea, etc. Dwarf, semi-dwarf or slowgrowing types are generally best for spotlighting. For the backyard, try blossoming choices to put in splashes of color and shade or to break up all-low settings. Azaleas, lilacs, crape myrtle and forsythia are some good ones.

Useful as well as ornamental? That's certainly the case with a happy lot of flowers and shrubs. This spring, get them started for more mileage in *your* garden!

M. C. GOLDMAN

— Hazel (*Corylus Avellana*) with flowers and fruits.

Organic Gardening
and Farming ®

HOW TO PRUNE COMMON SHRUBS[1]

ABELIA, GLOSSY (Abelia grandiflora). Zones 2–3. Medium rate of growth. Dense plant, excellent foliage, and small flowers appearing during most of the summer. Responds well to rejuvenation type of pruning done every 2 or 3 years in early spring. Height: 5 feet. Spread: 4–5 feet.

ALMOND, FLOWERING (Prunus glandulosa). Zones 1–3. Slow to medium growth. Upright. Single- or double-flowering varieties available. Prune in early spring to remove old or diseased wood at ground level by using the renewal method. Height: 4 feet. Spread: 4 feet.

AZALEA, DECIDUOUS (Azalea mallis and Exberry hybrids). Zones 1–3. Slow-growing, low, well-shaped, symmetrical plant. Attractive foliage, showy flowers. Many varieties available in numerous flower colors. Prune as little as possible. Maintenance prune by cutting out old flower stems. Corrective cuts or severe pruning should be done early in spring. Use the heading-back method. Height: 3–6 feet. Spread: 3–5 feet.

AZALEA, EVERGREEN (Azalea Kurume). Zones 2–3. Slow-growing evergreen. Attractive foliage and flowers. Prune as little as possible and use the heading-back method. Remove old flower heads for better flowers the next year. Height: 4–5 feet. Spread: 4–5 feet.

BARBERRY, JAPANESE (Berberis thunbergi). Zones 2–3. Slow-growing, dense, round plant, good in all seasons. Red-foliage variety also available. Bar-

berry used other than in hedges should be pruned in early spring as a single-stem plant. Height: 5–7 feet. Spread: 4–7 feet.

BARBERRY, MENTOR (Berberis mentorensis). Zones 2–3. Slow-growing, upright, semi-evergreen plant. Withstands dry summers and low winter temperature. Good substitute for wintergreen barberry. Old plants can be pruned by the rejuvenation method in early spring. If plants are in a hedge, use the shearing method described for hedges (Figs. 19 to 21). Height: 5–6 feet. Spread: 4–5 feet.

BAYBERRY, NORTHERN (Myrica pensylvanica). Zones 1–3. Slow to medium growing. Compact, rounded, with excellent semi-evergreen foliage and fruit. Sexes separated. Combines well with junipers. Prune as needed in early spring to protect berry crop. Can be severely pruned because it recovers rapidly. Use the heading-back or rejuvenation method. Height: 5 feet. Spread: 3–5 feet.

BEAUTYBUSH (Kolkwitzia amabilis). Zones 1–3. Slow growing, broad, vase-shaped. Old large limbs should be removed to ground. Prune hard and regularly in spring. This plant becomes too large for most home grounds. Use the renewal method and the heading-back method in combination when working with old woody plants. Height: 6–10 feet. Spread: 6–9 feet.

BLUEBEARD (Caryopteris clandonensis.) Zones 1–3. Fast growing, round, and spreading. Valued for late flowers. In Zones 1 and 2, top of plant will die back to ground and plant will require heavy pruning in early spring. Rejuvenate in early spring. Height: 3–4 feet. Spread: 4 feet.

BUCKTHORN, COMMON (Rhamnus cathartica). Zones 1–3. Medium rate of growth, round and dense, handsome foliage. Tolerates pruning with the heading-back method in late spring. Height: 12 feet. Spread: 10–12 feet.

BUCKTHORN, TALLHEDGE (Rhamnus frangula "Columnaris"). Zones 1–3. Fast-growing hedge plant that does not do well when sheared. The plant can be maintained in the narrow hedge form by selective cutting of side branches and using the heading-back method of pruning. Make as few cuts as possible. Height: 18 feet. Spread: 3–5 feet.

CHERRY, MANCHU (Prunus tomentosa). Zones 1–3. Fast growing, broad, spreading, rounded. Showy when in flower. Prune with the renewal method and head back slightly. Height: 8–10 feet. Spread: 10–15 feet.

CINQUEFOIL, BUSH (Potentilla fruticosa). Zones 1–3. Slow growing, bushy, dense. Can be pruned heavily. Chief value lies in its long period of flowering. Tolerates rejuvenation pruning. Remove only diseased or damaged wood; prune in early spring. Height: 3 feet. Spread: 3 feet.

CORALBERRY, CHENAULT (Symphoricarpos chenaulti). Zones 2–3. Fast growing; low, loose growth. Larger fruit than Indiancurrant Coralberry. Prune with the renewal method unless the plant is old and woody, then rejuvenate. Height: 3–4 feet. Spread: 4 feet.

CORALBERRY, INDIANCURRANT (Symphoricarpos orbiculatus). Zones 1–3. Fast growing, round, dense. Good in shade but tolerates sun. Clustered fruit persists. Rejuvenates well when needed; prune in early spring. Prune with the renewal method unless the plant is old and woody,

then rejuvenate. Height: 3–4 feet. Spread: 3–4 feet.

COTONEASTER, BEARBERRY (Cotoneaster dammeri). Zones 2–3. Slow-growing, prostrate, evergreen plant. To shape this plant, head back. Usually needs little pruning. Height: 12 inches. Spread: 6–12 inches.

COTONEASTER, PEKING (Cotoneaster acutifolia). Zones 1–3. Slow growing, erect, and spreading. Requires little care. Tolerates pruning. Withstands wind. Prune with the heading-back method. Height: 8–10 feet. Spread: 8–10 feet.

COTONEASTER, ROCK (Cotoneaster horizontalis). Zones 2–3. Slow-growing, low, dense, horizontally spreading plant, with excellent foliage and persistent fruit. Difficult to transplant. Prune with the heading-back method. Height: 2–3 feet. Spread: 4–6 feet.

COTONEASTER, SPREADING (Cotoneaster divaricata). Zones 2–3. Medium rate of growth. Arching and spreading. Withstands wind. Difficult to transplant. Excellent fruiting habit. Prune with the heading-back method. Height: 6 feet. Spread: 5–6 feet.

CURRANT, ALPINE (Ribes alpinum). Zones 1–2. Medium rate of growth. Compact and dense, attractive foliage. Does well in shade. Tolerates pruning. Usually sheared as a hedge; prune in late spring after new growth matures. If plant becomes old and woody rejuvenate in early spring. Height: 4–6 feet. Spread: 4–5 feet.

DEUTZIA, COMPACT LEMOINE (Deutzia lemoinei compacta). Zones 1–3. Medium growth rate, dense, compact; abundant flowers. Remove old limbs to the ground by the renewal method to avoid a woody, trashy plant. Prune after flower. Height: 4 feet. Spread: 3–4 feet. Exposure: either sun

—JAPANESE AZALEA (*Azalea mollis*).

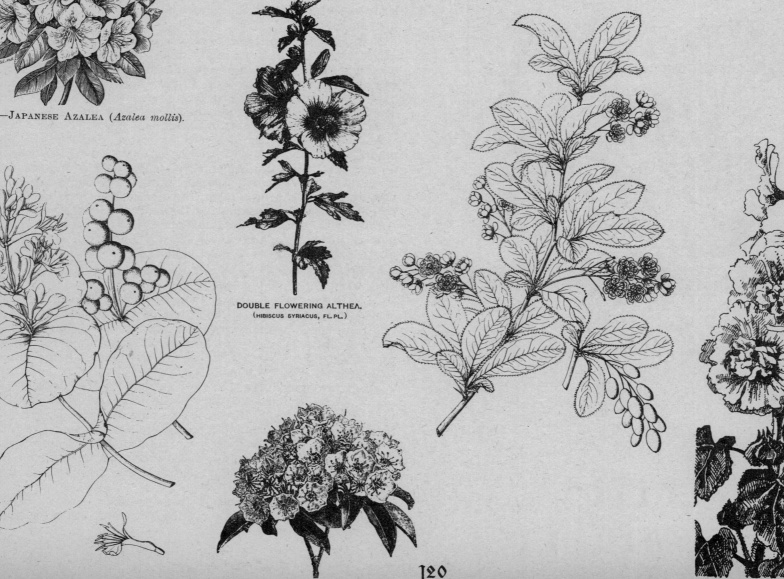

DOUBLE FLOWERING ALTHEA.
(HIBISCUS SYRIACUS, FL. PL.)

or partial shade. Texture: medium fine. Flower effects: white in June. Fruit effects: not showy. Use: doorway, facer, group.

DEUTZIA, SLENDER (Deutzia gracilis). Zones 1–3. Slow growing, low, compact, abundantly flowering, reliable. Easy to transplant. Rejuvenate when needed. Head back and renew if plant is too tall or out of balance. Height: 3–4 feet. Spread: 3 feet.

DOGWOOD, GRAY (Cornus racemosa). Zones 1–3. Erect and spreading, medium in rate of growth. Tolerates pruning. Head back and use renewal pruning if needed. Prune in late fall or early spring. Height: 8–15 feet. Spread: 8–12 feet.

DOGWOOD, REDOSIER (Cornus stolonifera). Zones 1–3. Slow-growing, broad, spreading shrub valued for its winter color. Bloodtwig Dogwood (C. sanguinea) is similar to this variety. Remove dark stem to the ground each year to preserve the bright-colored stem for which these plants are grown. Prune in early spring. Prune with the renewal method. Some heading-back may be needed if the plant is too large. Height: 8 feet. Spread: 8–10 feet.

DOGWOOD, YELLOWTWIG REDOSIER (Cornus stolonifera flaviramea). Zones 1–2. Medium to slow growth rate. Spreading shrub valued for yellow twigs during winter. Remove dark stem to the ground each year to preserve the bright-colored stem for which these plants are grown. Prune in early spring with the renewal method. This plant will require some thinning of the current year's growth to avoid excess growth. Height: 8 feet. Spread: 6–8 feet.

EUONYMUS, BIGLEAF WINTERCREEPER (Euonymus fortunei vegetus). Zones 2–3. Slow-growing evergreen shrub. Thick, leathery, glossy leaves. Grows upright with support, but otherwise forms a mounded mass. Subject to scale infestations. Rejuvenate when plant becomes old, diseased, or woody. Prune any time from February to mid-summer. Use the renewal method of pruning. When woody or scale infested, rejuvenate and treat. Height: 2–4 feet.

EUONYMUS, DWARF WINGED (Euonymus alatus compactus). Zones 1–3. Slow growing, dense, compact, outstanding fall color. Transplants easily. In early spring, prune with the heading-back method. Height: 6 feet. Spread: 4 feet.

EUONYMUS, EASTERN WAHOO (Euonymus atropurpureus). Zones 1–3. Slow growing, treelike, spreading, with outstanding foliage and fruit color. Prune in early spring the same as flowering dogwood, unless a multistem plant is desired; use a combination of renewal pruning and heading back. Height: 15–20 feet. Spread: 8–15 feet.

EUONYMUS, LONGWOOD (Euonymus fortunei radicans). Zones 1–3. Excellent, fast-growing ground cover. Can be sheared close to ground level or rejuvenated if infested with scale.

EUONYMUS, SARACOXIE (Euonymus fortunei Saracoxie). Zones 1–3. Slow-growing, handsome, upright broadleafed evergreen. Tolerates pruning. Rejuvenate when plant becomes old, diseased, or woody. Prune anytime from February to mid-summer. Height: 6 feet. Spread: 3–4 feet.

EUONYMUS, SPREADING (Euonymus kiautschovicus). Zones 2(?), 3. Slow-growing, bushy, round semi-evergreen. Flowers attract flies. Head back and rejuvenate when plant becomes old, diseased, or woody. Prune anytime from February to mid-summer. Height: 5–6 feet. Spread: 6 feet.

EUONYMUS, WINGED (Euonymus alatus). Zones 1–3. Slow-growing, dense, broad, horizontally branched; outstanding fall color. Reliable and transplants easily. In early spring, prune with the heading-back method. Height: 8–10 feet. Spread: 6–8 feet.

FIRETHORN, SCARLET (Pyracantha coccinea). Zones 2(?),3. Medium rate of growth. Broad, spreading, deciduous in north, evergreen in south. Fruit adds vivid color to winter scene. Prominent thorns. Tolerates pruning. Subject to fireblight. This plant is grown for its fruit, which is borne on two-year wood. To further complicate pruning, the plant is a rampant grower and new growth covers the fruit. Remove approximately ⅓ of the new growth back to the main frame or ground level if the plant is multi-stemmed by using the renewal method. To make the plant more attractive, head back lightly. Prune in early spring. Height: 6 feet. Spread: 6–10 feet.

FORSYTHIA (Forsythia varieties). Zones 1–3. Fast growing; erect, arching, and trailing varieties available. Reliable shrub, easily transplanted. Showy flowers and good foliage. Prune in late spring after flower. Use the renewal method. Head back if the remaining plant is too stringy. Height: 8–10 feet. Spread: 10–15 feet.

FOTHERGILLA (Fothergilla gardenii) (Fothergilla major). Zones 1–3. Fast-growing shrub, flowers in spring. Both dwarf and standard forms can be pruned the same way. Use the heading-back method after flower. The standard form, major, has a height of 8 to 10 feet and a spread of 10 feet. The dwarf form, gardenii, has a height of 5 feet and a spread of 4 to 5 feet.

FRINGETREE, WHITE (Chionanthus virginicus). Zones 1–3. Slow growing, round, spreading, treelike. Particularly tolerant to city conditions. Leaves appear late in spring. Subject to scale insects. Sexes usually separate. When used as a multi-stemmed shrub, thin by removing old or unwanted stems to the ground. When used as a tree, prune in early spring as illustrated for dogwood. Height: 10–20 feet. Spread: 8–20 feet.

HOLLY, AMERICAN (Ilex Opaca). Zones 1–3. Slow-growing, tree-type holly with red fruit. Prune by lightly heading back. The plant grows with one to four upright stems with lateral branches. Some plants will grow to one side or the other, so head back to regain the conical shape. Prune in late spring after flowering. Height: 35 feet. Spread: 15 feet.

HOLLY, CONVEXLEAF JAPANESE (Ilex crenata convexa). Zones 1(?),2,3. Slow-growing, broader than it is high; good substitute for boxwood. Broadleafed evergreen. Tolerates pruning — can be held to any size preferred. Prune with the heading-back method. When used as a hedge, shear as described for evergreen hedges on page 13. Height: 4–20 feet. Spread 4–15 feet.

HOLLY, ENGLISH (Ilex aquifolium Fosterii). Zones 2–3. Slow-growing, tree-type holly with red fruit. Prune by lightly heading back. The plant grows with one to four upright stems with lateral branches. Some plants will grow to one side or the other, so head back to regain the conical shape. Prune in late spring after flowering. Height: 15 feet. Spread: 8 feet.

HOLLY, WINTERBERRY (Ilex verticillata). Zones 1–3. Slow growing, spreading; excellent foliage; fruit persists to midwinter. Interesting the year around. Easily transplanted.

DEUTZIA GRACILIS.

—PURPLE-FRINGE (Rhus cotinus)

VARIEGATED DOGWOOD (Cornus Siberica, variegatus).

—GOLDEN-BELL (Forsythia riridissima).

Prune by heading back in late spring. Height: 6–8 feet. Spread: 3–5 feet.

HOLLYGRAPE, OREGON (Mahoala aquifolium). Zones 2–3. Medium rate of growth. Round, upright evergreen. Interesting holly-shaped, lustrous foliage and grapelike clusters of fruit. This plant gets tall and woody. To keep new bright green foliage abundant, prune old wood out to the ground with the renewal method to force new, lush foliage from the ground up. Prune in early spring before new growth starts. Height: 3–5 feet. Spread: 2–3 feet.

HONEYSUCKLE, BUSH (Lonicera tatarica). Zones 1–3. Medium-fast growing. Varieties broad, spreading, rounded. Vigorous shrubs with an abundance of small flowers and small bright-colored fruit. All honeysuckle responds well to all types of pruning in early spring or after flower. Height: 5–12 feet. Spread: 5–12 feet.

HONEYSUCKLE, HALLS (Lonicera japonica Halliana). Zones 1–3. Fast-growing vine with yellow flowers. Prune with the rejuvenation method. Height: 3 feet. Spread: 20 feet.

HONEYSUCKLE, WINTER (Lonicera fragrantissima). Zones 2–3. Medium rate of growth. Round spreading, with handsome foliage. Flowers are fragrant and appear in very early spring. Tolerates pruning. All honeysuckle responds well to all types of pruning in early spring. Height: 6 feet. Spread: 6 feet.

HYDRANGES, FLORIST'S HYDRANGEA (Hydranges Macrophylla). Zone 3 and southern half of Zone 2. Florist's hydrangeas produces flower buds on terminals of previous year's growth. Severe weather or fall pruning removes flower buds and prevents flowering. Prune after bloom

(early August) to 6- to 8-inch stubs. Space stems to prevent crowding. Mulch entire plant with leaves for consistent flowering. Height: 3 feet. Spread: 3–4 feet.

HYDRANGEA, HILLS-OF-SNOW (Hydrangea arborescens grandiflora). Zones 1–3. Fast-growing, broad, upright plant that gives a good texture accent. Showy flowers. Requires severe pruning in spring. Cut all dead stems in spring just after growth begins. Stub back live twigs to shape a low, more compact plant that will flower more heavily. Height: 4–8 feet. Spread: 5–8 feet.

HYDRANGEA, OAKLEAF (Hydrangea quercifolia). Zones 1–3. Fast-growing, upright plant with large flower heads. Prune by heading back in early spring.

JETBEAD, BLACK (Rhodotypos scandens). Zones 2–3. Medium rate of growth. Spreading and open growth. Excellent flower and foliage. Prune hard after flowering by the renewal method. Height: 5–6 feet. Spread: 4–5 feet.

JUNIPER, ANDORRA (Juniperus horizontalis plumosa). Zones 1–3. Fast-growing, low, spreading, somewhat mounding evergreen. Feathery foliage turns from silver green to lavender during winter. Very difficult to prune because of creeping growth habit. Start pruning early and prune as described for Pfitzer junipers. Prune in June or July. Height: 1½ feet. Spread: 4–5 feet.

JUNIPER, COMPACT PFITZER (Juniperus chinensis Pfitzer Compact). Zones 1–3. Fast to medium growing, dwarf, spreading evergreen with plumelike foliage. Very difficult to prune because of creeping growth habit. Start pruning early and prune

—Viburnum pubescens.—

CHINESE WISTARIA (Wistaria sinensis).

—MOCK-ORANGE, LARGE-FLOWERED (Philadelphus grandiflorus).

as described for Pfitzer junipers. Prune in June or July. Height: 5 feet. Spread: 5 feet.

JUNIPER, PFITZER (Juniperus chinensis Pfitzer). Zones 1–3. Fast-growing, large, spreading evergreen with plumelike blue-green foliage. In June or July prune hard as described and prune often. Height: 8–10 feet. Spread: 8–10 feet.

JUNIPER, SARGENTS OR WAUKEGAN (Juniperus horizontalis varieties). Zones 1–3. Medium rate of growth. Flat, spreading, somewhat trailing evergreens. Blue-green foliage. Very difficult to prune because of creeping growth habit. Start pruning early and prune as described for Pfitzer junipers. Prune in June or July. Height: ½–1 foot. Spread: 5 feet.

JUNIPER, SHORE (Juniperus conferta). Zones 2 and 3. Medium rate of growth. Flat, spreading evergreen with a very soft texture. Difficult to prune because of its creeping growth habit. Prune in June or July as described for Pfitzer junipers on page 5.

KERRIA, JAPANESE (Kerria japonica). Zones 1–3. Medium growing, broad, loose habit with year-round interest in flowers, foliage, and twigs. Requires annual pruning. Prune two-year-old wood to the ground each year. Some new wood should also be removed to improve flower show. Prune after flowering by using the renewal method. Height: 4–6 feet. Spread: 6–8 feet.

LILAC (Syringa varieties). Zones 1–3. Medium rate of growth. Reliable upright round shrub. Handsome, showy flowers in both single and double varieties. This is the classic plant for renewal pruning as is described in this circular. Prune after flowering. Height: 6–15 feet. Spread: 6–12 feet.

LILAC, PERSIAN (Syringa persica). Zones 2–3. Medium rate of growth. Dense and shapely, valued for flowers. This is the classic plant for renewal pruning as is described in this circular. Prune after flowering. Height: 4–8 feet. Spread: 5–10 feet.

MAGNOLIA, SAUCER (Magnolia soulangeana). Zones 2–3. Medium rate of growth. Shrubby tree with showy flowers effective in front of evergreens. Because of fleshy roots, plants should always be moved with a ball of earth. Numerous varieties and flower colors available. The type of plant you desire determines how to prune. If you want a tree, then prune to a main frame. If a large multi-stemmed shrub is desired, then promote and protect new shoots that occur at the base. As older trunks get too large or too tall, remove them at their base. Prune in early spring before buds begin to swell. Height: 25 feet. Spread: 30 feet.

MAGNOLIA, STAR (Magnolia stellata). Zones 2–3. Slow growing; dense, broad, round, treelike. Showy flowers effective in front of evergreens. Will not tolerate competition with other tree roots. Because of fleshy roots, plants should always be moved with a ball of earth. The type of plant you desire determines how to prune. If you want a tree, then prune to a main frame. If a large multi-stemmed shrub is desired, then promote and protect new shoots that occur at the base. As older trunks get too large or too tall, remove them at their base. Prune in early spring before buds begin to swell. Height: 8–10 feet. Spread: 10–15 feet.

MOCKORANGE (Philadelphus varieties). Zones 1–3. Slow growing; varieties compact, rounded, or erect. Valued for flowers, which are usually fragrant. Prune two-year-old wood to the ground each year. Some new wood

J. PAGE

—JAPANESE ROSE (*Rosa rugosa*).

—Rosa lutea

should also be removed to improve flower show. Prune after flowering by the renewal method in early spring. Height: 4–12 feet. Spread: 4–12 feet.

NINEBARK, COMMON (*Physocarpus opulifolius*). Zones 1–3. Fast-growing, loose, spreading shrub, resembling spirea. Because of coarseness not recommended in refined small gardens. This plant can be pruned into a formal hedge. To do this, prune in late spring after new growth matures. Height: 10 feet. Spread: 10 feet.

PEARL BUSH (*Exochorda var.*). Zones 1–3. Fast-growing shrub, flowers in spring. Works well in mass plantings. Prune with renewal method and some heading back. Height: 8–10 feet. Spread: 8–10 feet.

PEASHRUB, SIBERIAN (*Caragana arborescens*). Zones 1–3. Fast growing, oval, erect and thin with age. Useful in sandy areas; good foliage mass. Prune old wood by the renewal method in early spring. Height: 15–18 feet. Spread: 12 feet.

PINE, DWARF MUGHO (*Pinus mugho mughus Dwarf*). Zones 1–3. Slow-growing, round evergreen. Easily confined to small size by pruning. Prune as described for pine, every other year in late June. On intermittent years remove all buds but two or three that formed at last year's cut. This will help keep the plant foliage from getting too dense. Height: 4–8 feet. Spread: 12–20 feet.

PLUM, FLOWERING (*Prunus triloba*). Zones 2–3. Fast growing, rounded, spreading. Prune in early spring the same as illustrated for flowering trees. Cuts larger than one-inch should be treated with a prepared wound paint. Height: 8–10 feet. Spread: 8 feet.

PLUM, PURPLELEAF (*Prunus var. Thundercloud*). Zones 1–3. Fast growing, round. Prune in early spring the same as illustrated for flowering trees. Cuts larger than one-inch should be treated with a prepared wound paint. Height: 15–20 feet. Spread: 10 feet.

PRIET, AMUR (*Ligustrum amurense*). Zones 1–3. Fast growing; dense upright branches with round top. Tolerates pruning. Prune in early spring the same as illustrated for flowering trees. Cuts larger than one-inch should be treated with a prepared wound paint. If this plant is used as a hedge, shear it as described for deciduous hedges on page 20. If used as a single plant, head back in early spring or after flower. Height: 10–15 feet. Spread: 6–10 feet.

PRIVET, GOLD LEAF (*Ligustrum amurense*). Zones 1–3. Fast growing; dense upright branches with round top. Can be used as a specimen plant or an unclipped hedge. Prune by the renewal method. Height: 10–15 feet. Spread: 6–10 feet.

PRIVET, REGELS BORDER (*Ligustrum obtusifolium regelianum*). Zones 1–3. Medium rate of growth. Hortizontally branching, dense foliage. Reliable, excellent form. Do not shear; prune by the renewal method to maintain good leaf and fruit color. Prune after fruit is gone or in early spring. Height: 6 feet. Spread: 6 feet.

PURPLE-FLOWERED LOCUST (*Robinia Idaho*). Zones 1–3. Fast-growing shrub that becomes erect and thin with age. Useful in sandy areas. Prune old wood with the renewal method if the plant is multi-stemmed. Head back if it is single-stemmed. Height: 15–20 feet. Spread: 10 feet.

QUINCE, FLOWERING (*Chaenomeles lagenaria*). Zones 1–3. Fast-growing, spreading plant. Good foliage, showy flowers, winter color. Prune the same as common lilac after flower-

ing or in early spring. It is important to keep the plant thinned to avoid trashy centers that are very unattractive in winter. Height: 6–8 feet. Spread: 6 feet.

REDCEDAR, CANAERT EASTERN (*Juniperus virginiana Canaert*). Zones 1–3. Medium rate of growth. Loose and open yet slender pyramidal form of evergreen. Prune as little as possible. If absolutely necessary, use the procedure described for the upright junipers. These plants are trees and should be grown as such. Sheared plants cannot be reduced in size because of the very thin shell of green foliage left to work with. If you prune back past this green material, there will be a permanent dead hole in the plant. Height: 20 feet. Spread: 8–10 feet.

ROSA (CLIMBERS AND RAMBLERS). Zones 1–3. Bloom in early summer on old canes. Prune immediately after blooming. Remove the old canes (two and three years old) to the crown or to a strong shoot. Spread: 6–15 inches as arching and vining shoots.

ROSA (EVERBLOOMING CLIMBERS). Zone 1–3. Bloom heavily in early summer and light to moderate rebloom throughout the summer and fall season. Lightly prune throughout the season to remove old flower clusters and weak wood on old stems. Remove 2- to 4-year-old canes in the fall when new canes occur for replacements.

ROSE (FLORIBUNDA TYPE) (*Rosa varieties*). Zones 1–3. Medium rate of growth. Rounded, upright, small-growing rose that flowers all season. Many varieties and flower colors from which to select. Prune out old, diseased, or unwanted canes in fall. In spring, before growth starts, reduce in size as illustrated in the section

on roses. Height: 3–5 feet. Spread: 3–4 feet.

ROSE, FATHER HUGO (*Rosa hugonis*). Zones 2–3. Fast growing, dense, rounded. Excellent, showy flowers. Prune out old, diseased, or unwanted canes in fall. In spring, before growth starts, reduce in size as illustrated in the section on roses. Height: 6–10 feet. Spread: 10 feet.

ROSE OF SHARON (SHRUB-ALTHEA) (*Hibiscus syriacus* varieties). Zones 2–3. Slow to medium growing; upright, somewhat vase-shaped; tolerates city conditions. Showy flowers in late summer. Young plants are less winter-hardy than older plants. This plant has the most unsightly base of all the ornamentals. Keep the old diseased wood cut to ground level with the renewal method to reduce the amount of shade on the base and stimulate new growth. Height: 10–15 feet. Spread: 6–10 feet.

ST. JOHNSWORT, SUNGOLD (*Hypericum var.* Sungold). Zones 2–3. Medium growth rate, dense, rounded. Showy flowers in summer. Prune by using the rejuvenation method only when needed, not more often than every 2 years after flowering. Height: 3–4 feet. Spread: 3 feet.

SERVICEBERRY, SHADBLOW (*Amelanchier canadensis*). Zones 1–3. Fast growing, loosely round to oval, tree-like. Good combined with broadleafed evergreens. Prune in early spring by thinning out and heading back. Height: 25 feet. Spread: 12 feet.

SPIREA, ANTHONY WATERER (*Spiraea bumalda Anthony Waterer*). Zones 2–3. Fast growing, low, broad, flat on top. Attractive foliage, tinged pink when it first appears. Prune once every 2 to 3 years by the rejuvenation method after flowering, and this plant will bloom twice. Height: 2–3 feet. Spread: 3 feet.

SPIREA, BRIDALWREATH (Spiraea prunifolia). Zones 1–3. Fast growing, graceful, upright. Reliable, showy flowers, excellent fall color. Double variety available. Prune by the renewal method. Some heading back may be needed to shape the plant. Never shear off tops. That makes a very unattractive plant with a green tuft on top and a stemmy, dead base. This plant can be sheared into a formal hedge, but will have no flowers and a shortened useful life. Prune in early spring; if the plant is in a hedge, shear in late spring and mid-summer. Height: 6 feet. Spread: 6 feet.

SPIREA, VAN HOUTTE (Spiraea vanhouttei). Zones 1–3. Fast growing, vase-shaped, round top. Showy when in bloom. Prune two-year and older stems to the ground by the renewal method. Never shear off tops. That makes a very unattractive plant with a green tuft on top and a stemmy, dead base. This plant can be sheared into a formal hedge, but will have no flowers and a shortened useful life. Prune in early spring; if the plant is in a hedge, shear in late spring and mid-summer. Height: 8–10 feet. Spread: 8 feet.

SUMAC, STAGHORN (Rhus typhina). Zones 1–3. Fast growing, irregular, picturesque. Cutleaf variety available. Interesting fuzzy twigs which hold dust so avoid use in dusty areas. This is grown for its stems, so be very careful only to remove limbs that may make the plant unbalanced or weak. Prune in early spring by lightly heading back. Height: 20–25 feet. Spread: 20 feet.

VIBURNUM, AMERICAN CRANBERRYBUSH (Viburnum trilobum). Zones 1–3. Fast growing, dense, broad, round. Fruit showy in color and mass. This plant must be pruned differently from any of the other flowering shrubs. Usually it is a shrub with one to four main stems so it must be pruned by

the renewal method, but thinned to keep good foliage to the base of the plant. It is often pruned into a small tree shape with a single stem. That is easily done, as described for flowering trees, but to do it, the plant must be pruned to a single stem when it is planted. If all stems but one are removed on older plants, the remaining stem will be badly misshapen. Prune after flower or in early spring. Height: 6–12 feet. Spread: 8–12 feet.

VIBURNUM, ARROWWOOD (Viburnum dentatum). Zones 1–3. Fast growing, upright, dense, with handsome foliage. Prune by the renewal method and head back to shorten the plant. Prune after flower or in early spring. Height: 15 feet. Spread: 6–12 feet.

VIBURNUM, BURKWOOD (Viburnum burkwoodi). Zones 2–3. Medium rate of growth, upright, with fragrant flowers and attractive foliage. This shrub is much like a tree and for best results should be handled as such. Even if the plant is multi-stemmed, prune as illustrated for multi-stem flowering trees. Prune in early spring or after flowering by thinning and heading back. Height: 4–8 feet. Spread: 6–8 feet.

VIBURNUM, DOUBLEFILE (Viburnum tomentosum). Zones 1–3. Medium rate of growth. Broad spreading, interesting horizontal branching. Outstanding in flowers. This plant must be pruned differently from any of the other flowering shrubs. Usually it is a shrub with one to four main stems so it must be pruned by heading back, but thinned to keep good foliage to the base of the plant. It is often pruned into a small tree shape with a single stem. That is easily done, as described for flowering trees, but to do it, the plant must be pruned to a single stem when it is planted. If all stems but one are removed on older plants, the remaining stem will be badly misshapen. Prune after flower

or in early spring. Height: 8–10 feet. Spread: 8–10 feet.

VIBURNUM, DWARF EUROPEAN CRANBERRYBUSH (Viburnum opulus nanum). Zones 1–3. Medium rate of growth. Dense, dwarf irregular, picturesque. Tolerates pruning. If it is a multi-stemmed plant, use renewal pruning. If it is single-stemmed, prune by heading back.

VIBURNUM, KOREANSPICE (Viburnum carlesi). Zones 1–3. Medium rate of growth. Upright, with fragrant flowers and attractive foliage. This plant must be pruned differently from any of the other flowering shrubs. Usually it is a shrub with one to four main stems so it must be pruned by the renewal method, but thinned to keep good foliage to the base of the plant. Prune after flower or in early spring. Height: 4–8 feet. Spread: 6–8 feet.

VIBURNUM, LEATHERLEAF (Viburnum rhytidophyllum). Zones 2–3. Medium rate of growth. Upright evergreen, with lustrous, dark-green, puckered foliage. This is an evergreen in zones 2 and 3 and a semi-evergreen in zone 1. Prune with the renewal method. If the plant is old, some heading back will also be needed. This plant must be pruned in late spring after the new growth matures in June. Height: 9 feet. Spread: 8–9 feet.

WEIGELA (Weigela varieties). Zones 2–3. Fast growing, round, spreading, with showy flowers. Requires annual pruning because of general die-back of branches. Often suffers winter injury in north. Many varieties available. This is one of the most rapidly growing plants used in the home landscape. It can be rejuvenated. Older plants that require a great deal of pruning should be pruned after flowering or in February. Renewal prune and then do some light heading back to keep the plant in balance. Height: 4–6 feet. Spread: 5–6 feet.

WITCHHAZEL, CHINESE (Hamamelis vernalis). Zones 2–3. Slow-growing, upright to spreading plant, valued for early flowering and dense foliage. Root-prune before transplanting. Prune in early spring the same as flowering trees by heading back. Height: 6 feet, Spread: 6–8 feet.

WITCHHAZEL, COMMON (Hamamelis virginiana). Zones 1–3. Slow growing; loose irregular habit of growth; tolerates city conditions. Root-prune before transplanting. Attractive flower appearing after foliage drops in fall. Prune in early spring the same as flowering trees by heading back. Height: 12–20 feet. Spread: 12–20 feet.

YEW, DWARF SPREADING JAPANESE (Taxus cuspidata nana). Zones 1–3. Slow-growing, compact, spreading evergreen. Deep color. Sexes separate. This plant is easy to prune because new growth will form anywhere up and down the stem. Follow instructions given in this circular, and if a mistake is made the plant will recover in time. Height: 3–4 feet. Spread: 4–5 feet.

YEW, HATFIELD OR HICKS (Taxus media varieties). Zones 1–3. Slow-growing, dense, slender, conical evergreen. Tolerates pruning. Deep color. Sexes separate. This plant is most commonly used in hedges because of its columnar form of growth. Prune as illustrated for hedges. Hicks yew is sometimes used singly. In these cases, prune as described for dense yew. Height: 8 feet. Spread: 4–5 feet.

YEW, SPREADING (Taxus media var.). Zones 1–3. Varieties in this category are T. Densiformis, T. Wardi, T. Nigra, and T. Tauntoni. Slow-growing, dense, upright evergreen. Deep color. Sexes separate. This plant is easy to prune because new growth will form anywhere up and down the stem. Follow instructions given in this circular, and if a mistake is made the plant will recover in time. Height: 4–5 feet. Spread: 4 feet.

YEW, SPREADING JAPANESE (Taxus cuspidata). Zones 1–3. Slow-growing, spreading evergreen. Deep color. Sexes are separate. This plant is easy to prune because new growth will form anywhere up and down the stem. Follow instructions given in this circular, and if a mistake is made the plant will recover in time. Height: 8–10 feet. Spread: 8–12 feet.

YEW, UPRIGHT JAPANESE (Taxus cuspidata capitata). Zones 1–3. Slow-growing, erect, broad, pyramidal evergreen. Deep color. Sexes separate. This is the tree form of the yew and should be planted and used as such. It can be sheared or pruned as illustrated for upright junipers, but this will only work for a short period of time. The plant will soon outgrow your efforts to keep it in bounds. Height: 10–40 feet. Spread: 15–20 feet.

YUCCA (ADAMSNEEDLE) (Yucca filamentosa). Zones 1–3. Fast-growing, stiff, upright, dramatic evergreen. This plant dies after flowering. Remove the stock that produces the flower. Encourage the growth of the side suckers to produce a new plant. Remove some of the suckers to prevent the plant from becoming too bushy. Height: 3 feet. Spread: 3–4 feet.

—JAPANESE SNOWBALL (Viburnum plicatum).

—VAN HOUTT'S SPIRÆA (Spiræa Van Houttii).

—WEIGELA (Diervilla rosea).

—BRIDAL-WREATH (Spiræa prunifolia).

HOLLY

WHY HOLLIES FAIL TO FRUIT

Most hollies must be pollinated before they will set an effective display of berries. Some hollies, through a process known as parthenocarpy, will produce berries without being pollinated. *Ilex cornuta* and its variety 'Burford', however, are the only hollies common to our gardens that will set an effective display of berries by this process. If your holly plants do not set berries, the reason may be that—

● The plant is male. Male and female flowers are borne on separate plants and male plants do not form berries.

● The plant is too young to flower. Hollies do not flower freely until they are 6 to 8 years old.

● A male plant of the same species is not close enough for effective pollination. Bees can bring pollen from male plants that are up to 2 miles away. But the shorter the distance between male and female plants, the better the chances for effective pollen transfer and heavy fruit set. A male plant of the same species as the female makes the best pollinator.

● Cold weather at flowering time reduces activity of bees, thus reducing chances for pollination. In addition, cold weather may kill the female flowers.

● CHINESE HOLLY. A number of Chinese hollies are in cultivation, but the group name usually refers to the species *Ilex cornuta*. This species typically has glossy foliage, large red berries, and viciously spined leaves; however, it is best known by its spineless-leaved form *Ilex cornuta* 'Burford'.

● JAPANESE HOLLY. The Japanese hollies (*Ilex crenata*) are the most widely grown of all hollies. Because of their small spineless leaves, resembling those of the box plant, and their black fruit, Japanese hollies are not recognized by most people as being hollies. The dwarf form *Ilex crenata* 'Helleri' is widely grown.

● MISCELLANEOUS EVERGREEN HOLLIES. Among the most readily available miscellaneous evergreen hollies are *Ilex glabra*, the native black-fruited Inkberry, which is the hardiest of all evergreen hollies; two Chinese species, *Ilex pedunculosa*, having red fruits suspended on long stalks, and *Ilex pernyi*, a slow-growing species with spiny leaves; and *Ilex aquipernyi*, a hybrid of *Ilex pernyi* with *Ilex aquifolium*. *Ilex* 'Foster', a recent hybrid between *Ilex opaca* and *Ilex cassine*, shows great promise for use as a hedge.

● DECIDUOUS HOLLIES. Several kinds of deciduous hollies are growing in the Arboretum; however, the only deciduous holly usually available from nurseries is our native Winterberry (*Ilex verticillata*), also called Black Alder. Though it normally is a plant of swamplands, it will adapt itself to garden conditions and produce an abundance of red berries that are plump and firm at Christmas time. Its Asiatic counterpart, *Ilex serrata*, is usually covered with masses of red berries in early autumn.

CULTURAL SUGGESTIONS

The cultural needs of hollies are not great. A liberal quantity of organic matter added to the soil at planting time usually assures a good start for the plants, even in heavy clay soils. A 2- to 3-inch mulch of decayed sawdust, leaves, or wood chips should be applied annually under the spread of the branches. Failure to maintain the mulch at its original depth, however, can be detrimental because of the extensive rooting that occurs in the mulch.

ILEX FRUCTU LUTEO WITH ITS EFFECTIVE YELLOW BERRIES

A HANDSOME GREEN-LEAVED HOLLY, ILEX WILSONI

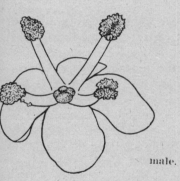

male.

Holly flowers: female;

Box Trees

Boxwoods have been cultivated in the Middle Atlantic States from colonial times. The center of climatic adaptation for boxwoods is the Chesapeake Bay region and the foothills of the Blue Ridge in Virginia and North Carolina. Fine specimens are also found in the Piedmont of South Carolina, in Tennessee and Kentucky, in the vicinity of Delaware Bay, on Long Island, N.Y., and on the Pacific coast.

SPECIES AND VARIETIES

The two most widely cultivated boxwood varieties are the English box and the common box. Both are members of the botanical species *Buxus sempervirens*. The English box, or *B.s. suffruticosa*, is a dwarf shrub, often less than 3 feet tall at maturity. The common box, or *B.s. arborescens*, is larger, usually attaining the height of a small tree. Both have standard boxwood characteristics: Dense foliage and full, rounded shapes.

Some other forms of the species *B. sempervirens* are—

• Weeping box—a tall boxwood with drooping branches and wispy foliage. Example: *B.s. pendula.*

• Fastigiate box—a narrow, upright type particularly suitable for hedges. Example: *B.s. fastigiata.*

• Variegated box—a shrub that has leaves mottled or bordered with white or light yellow. Example: *B.s. argenteo-variegata.*

Other species of boxwood, in addition to *B. sempervirens,* include *B. balearica, B. harlandii,* and *B. microphylla.* Two hardy plants, the Japanese box and the Korean box, are members of the species *B. microphylla.* *B. balearica* plants are somewhat scarce, but the other species are available from nurserymen.

HARDINESS

Boxwood varieties differ in their ability to resist cold weather (see plant hardiness zone map, p. 3). Boxwood culture is almost impossible in areas where temperatures drop to —10° F. or lower. The dry, cold winters of the Midwest are unsuitable for boxwood growth.

PRUNING

Boxwood foliage is very dense. Outer shoots should be pruned so that inner shoots can get light and air.

Small shoots should be pruned at their juncture with larger branches. If large branches must be removed, standard precautions should be observed: The cut should be close and clean; the bark should be bruised as little as possible; and cut surfaces of a square inch or more should be promptly coated with shellac followed by tree paint.

At least once a year, remove debris (leaves, twigs, etc.) that has accumulated in your boxwoods. Much of it will come out if you shake the bushes vigorously. Pick out the rest. If debris is not removed, it may promote fungus growth.

TRANSPLANTING

Boxwoods can be transplanted at any time except when they are in active growth or when the ground is frozen.

Rootballs should be large and solid. Dwarf boxwoods require a rootball with a diameter at least half the diameter of the top of the plant. Tree boxwoods should have a rootball with a diameter at least one-third the height of the top.

Plants 2 to 3 feet high or broad should be shaded for a year after transplanting. A lattice that cuts off about half the light should be used. Shading is especially important if the plants are moved from a partly shaded to an exposed site. The lattice should clear the foliage by 10 to 18 inches and should protect at least the sunny sides as well as the top of the plant.

Newly transplanted boxwoods must be watered thoroughly and regularly. Direct a slow flow of water underneath the crown to the trunk.

Boxwoods may need winter covers. In mild climates, pine branches placed along the north side of hedges will provide adequate protection.

BOXWOOD

RHODODENDRON.

Care of Rhododendrons

AFTER PLANTING

1. **WATERING** — Base of plant should be watered every few days for a month after planting. Once established, the roots should be kept slightly moist. In colder climates it is well to soak the ground heavily before it freezes.

2. **FERTILIZING** — A balanced acid fertilizer should be applied in April or May. In alkaline areas sulphur should be added to maintain acid condition. An application of superphosphate in February will increase the bud set for the following season. Iron chelates will improve foliage color.

3. **PEST CONTROL** — Every three weeks from May to October spray with a mixture of two level tablespoons of 25% Malathion W.P., two level tablespoons of 50% Captan W.P., and six drops of Dupont Spreader and Sticker, to one gallon of water. If root rot is a problem Dexon and Terraclor may be used as shown on product label.

4. **WEEDING** — As Rhododendron roots are surface-feeding, no hoeing or spading should be done. Pull weeds by hand. The herbicide "Caseron" may be used safely with Rhododendrons, but it will harm some Azaleas and other plant materials.

5. **REMOVING OLD BLOOMS** — After blooming, snap off and destroy flower clusters being careful not to injure the leaf axils.

6. **SHAPING** — To encourage branching in younger plants, pinch out the single new leaf bud as it starts to push out in the spring. Larger plants may be shaped by pruning but the cut should always be made just above a fan of leaves.

7. **WINTER PROTECTION** — An antidesiccant such as Wilt Pruf may be used safely on Rhododendrons.

Rhododendron Society Garden
Box 14773
Portland, Ore 98214

PLANTING INSTRUCTIONS
Rhododendrons

1. Rhododendrons require a porous, acid soil. It is best to plant in raised beds and add an acid-type fertilizer if a heavy or alkaline soil condition exists.

2. Select a site protected from wind and under partial shade. Some sun is required for buds to form.

3. Avoid planting close to masonry walls, exposed to direct sun, shallow rooting trees, or fences and buildings which will reflect heat.

4. Soak rootball in a tub of water for 30 minutes.

5. Remove ties and burlap.

6. Expose root ends by washing with a forceful stream from a hose.

7. Dig a hole twice the diameter of the rootball and about five inches deeper. Mix soil removed with 50% course peat moss and a light application of chlordane dust.

8. Place six inches of mixture at bottom of hole. Set Rhododendron so that the top of the rootball is at the surface. Fill in remaining soil.

9. Settle the plant by watering in lightly, not by tramping it in.

10. Mulch with two to three inches of oak leaves, pine needles, wood chips or barkdust.

AZALEA MOLLIS

MOUNTAIN LAUREL.—*K. latifolia.*

ACID LOVING PLANTS

AZALEAS	RHODODENDRONS
DOGWOOD	LILY
HEATHER	PRIMROSE
MOUNTAIN HOLLY	PHLOX
LILY of the VALLEY	TRAILING ARBUTUS
IRIS	COLUMBINE
LADY SLIPPER	GENTIAN
PAINTED TRILLIUM	WILD INDIGO
WHITE ELDER	MARSH MARIGOLD
MAGNOLIA	BEGONIAS
BLACKBERRY	RASPBERRY

ALL THESE DO ESPECIALLY WELL
IN SOILS CONSISTING OF 50%
OR MORE PEAT MOSS

Annapolis Valley
Peat Moss Co., Ltd.

THE FUNDAMENTALS OF RHODODENDRON AND AZALEA CULTURE

J. Harold Clarke

Botanical Classification—Rhododendrons and azaleas belong to the genus Rhododendron of the family Ericaceae. This is sometimes called the heath family and does include the heaths and heathers, besides blueberries, pernettya, kalmia, andromeda and several other ornamental plants. Most of this group require a rather acid soil and good drainage.

More than a thousand species have been described within the genus Rhododendron. Because of the extreme complexity of the genus, the species have been grouped into some forty or more series, each including a number of species which have points of similarity. All of the species of Rhododendron known as azaleas are included in one group, the Azaleas Series, which includes some seventy or more different species. These are distinguished by botanical characters but it is not easy to give a simple distinction separating all those rhododendrons which belong to the Azalea Series from those which belong to the other Series. There are evergreen rhododendrons and azaleas and also deciduous rhododendrons and azaleas.

Used botanically, therefore, the word Rhododendron includes azaleas. Horticulturally we usually speak of rhododendrons and azaleas, the former including all the non-azalea members of the genus, and that is the way the terms are used in the following pages.

The many rhododendron species have come from a wide range of native habitats. A large number of our cultivated rhododendrons are derived from species coming from Asia, especially the foothills of the Himalaya Mountains, western China, northern India, Burma and Assam. Others come from Japan, some from Europe and some from North America, including R. catawbiense, the source of hardiness of most of the hardy hybrids grown in the eastern United States. At present a rather large group of species is being studied and named in the East Indies, especially New Guinea.

Up to the present time some 10,000 rhododendron and azalea horticultural varieties have been named, although not all of them are still in existence; but many new varieties are being named each year.

Membership Information

To: Mrs. William Curtis, Executive Secretary
The American Rhododendron Society
24450 S.W. Grahams Ferry Road
Sherwood, Oregon 97140

HISTORY OF CAMELLIAS

Camellias are native from the Indo-China mainland to Korea and the islands that lie offshore. Early merchant seamen trading in these waters took some of the beautiful Japanese camellia plants home to England with them. Later on, between 1783 and 1797, camellias were brought from England to the United States. The first camellia imported was a red-flowering japonica variety.

Botanical Description

Camellias are members of the botanical family Theaceae, which includes the common tea plant, C. sinensis, as well as the genera Franklinia, Gordonia, and Stewartia. There are approximately 45 species of the genus Camellia native to tropical and subtropical Asia. Noted for their conspicuous flowers, camellias are considered by botanists to be evergreen shrubs or small trees.

Kinds of Camellias

Three species of camellias are in general cultivation in the United States: Camellia japonica, Camellia sasanqua, and Camellia reticulata. These are the species of particular interest here at the Arboretum along with a fourth species, Camellia oleifera.

You will also see some plantings of Camellia rusticana and Camellia hiemalis.

Camellia japonica is the most hardy camellia in the Washington, D.C., area. It is the best species for planting along the Atlantic Coast north of Washington, D.C. C. japonica generally blooms in the spring.

Camellia sasanqua is almost as hardy as C. japonica; its northern limit of hardiness along the Atlantic Coast is Washington, D.C. C. sasanqua blooms in October and November. Both japonica and sasanqua camellias have been grown in China and Japan for centuries for use as ornamental plants.

Camellia reticulata is the tenderest of the camellias commonly grown in the United States. It blooms in the spring and has very large flowers. It can be grown outdoors in Southern California, but in other areas it needs indoor protection during the winter.

Although Camellia oleifera is not in general cultivation throughout the United States, there is a mass planting of oleifera seedlings here at the Arboretum. C. oleifera, with single white flowers, is known as the oil-bearing camellia. The seeds contain a very high percentage of oil, which is extracted by oriental peoples and used for hair tonic.

GROUNDCOVERS

— Aerial Adventitious Roots of the Ivy.

By F.A. Giles, R.L. Courson
Vocational Agriculture Service
University of Illinois
Urbana, Illinois 61801

Fig. 113.—Leaf-mosaic.

VINES

GROUND COVERS AND THEIR USES

Embankments and Steep Slopes:

Embankments present a special problem. Steep areas are usually dry and constructed of clay fill. If such areas are sunny, not too extensive, and will be maintained, there are several good choices. Winter creeper, lilyturf, tall fescue and snow-in-summer all have a wide range of soil and moisture requirements and will hold up well with minimal maintenance. Creeping juniper may be used if embankment is not too steep.

No matter what plant is used, establishment, the time between planting and cover to prevent erosion, is a problem. A soil net can be useful in stopping erosion over this period. Plant closer than normal for flat areas and plant horizontally, not vertically.

Fertilizer is the best and least expensive aid to establishing ground cover on slopes. It should be applied prior to planting, to soil test, and/or plant requirements. Applying a low analysis fertilizer often throughout the growing season is also desirable since water carries off much of the surface-applied fertility. Mulch can also be useful and well worth the expense of application to hold moisture near the surface while the ground cover becomes established.

Shady embankments present a different problem. If the area is shady and protected from the wind, periwinkle (heavily mulched), ajuga, hosta, and English ivy are good choices. Japanese spurge could also be considered if the area is in deep shade and has winter wind protection. All other procedures should be the same as described for sunny embankments.

Enclosed Areas:

Enclosed areas, such as between entrance sidewalks and the house, islands in patios, or circle drives, allow use of ground covers that should be used nowhere else. Ground covers, such as polygonum, creeping phlox, and goutweed, should be trapped so they will not escape into lawn areas. Plants do well in such enclosed areas and can be kept homogeneous, which is good from a design standpoint.

The reverse is true of plants like Longwood's euonymus, St. Johnswort, thyme, wild ginger, bunchberry, and pachistima. These should be enclosed to protect them from encroachment of grass.

High Competition Areas:

Inhospitable areas unsuited to turf, such as under large old trees, may best be handled with one of the ground covers discussed below. If water can be supplied, or if the area is naturally moist, periwinkle, ajuga, English and hosta make good cover. In areas that will remain dry due to dense root growth and little water, winter creeper, purple leaf winter creeper, goutweed, wineleaf cinquefoil, English ivy, and creeping potentilla are good. Remember, goutweed will escape, however.

Good Combinations of Ground Covers, Shrubs, and Other Materials:

When combining plants, environmental requirements such as soil pH, moisture, and sunlight should be considered first. Then, consider plant color, flower color, texture, and growth habit.

Some of the best combinations are potentilla fruiticosa as a shrub and potentilla verna as a ground cover; azaleas and wineleaf cinquefoil; rhododendrons and periwinkle; white birch and English ivy; weeping willows and daylilies or yellowroot; Japanese limber pine or contorted pine and pathistima; abelia and purple leaf winter creeper; magnolia and wild ginger; flowering dogwood and bunchberry; tall hedge buckthorn and winter creeper; large boulders and a sedum collection; thyme and flagstone walks; Anthony waters spirea and creeping spirea; English ivy and wrought iron; ivy and oak trees; stonecrop and flagstone retaining walls; bulbs in almost all ground covers that remain under 12 inches in height; and forsythia and dwarf forsythia.

Special Soil and Climate Conditions:

1. Shady, wet: Yellowroot, daylilies, plantain lily
2. Shady, dry: English ivy, winter creeper, pachistima
3. Hot, sandy: Dwarf forsythia, creeping potentilla, creeping spirea, creeping juniper
4. Shady, sandy soil: Hosta, English ivy, barren strawberries
5. Sunny, acid soil: Sedum, creeping spirea
6. Shady, acid soil: Polygonum in an enclosure, winter creeper, bunchberry, English ivy, wineleaf cinquefoil
7. Shady, alkaline soil: Daylilies, Japanese spurge, ajuga

These ground covers are some of the best when used as described. They will flourish when grown in their own hardiness zones and preferred environmental settings. After each of the ground covers described you will find the capital letter D which stands for deciduous, or E which stands for evergreen. The two numbers preceding the letter H refer to the average height range in inches. The zone numbers listed refer to areas of the state where these plants are hardy.

In groves of smaller trees or flowering trees, barren strawberries, daylilies, wild ginger and bunchberry will do well, especially in good soil or soil that has been improved with fertilizer and mulch.

In areas where the soil has a low pH, such as in rhododendron or azalea beds, the wineleaf cinquefoil is a good choice. Periwinkle and English ivy are two ground covers that blend well with broadleaf evergreens and will tolerate acid soils.

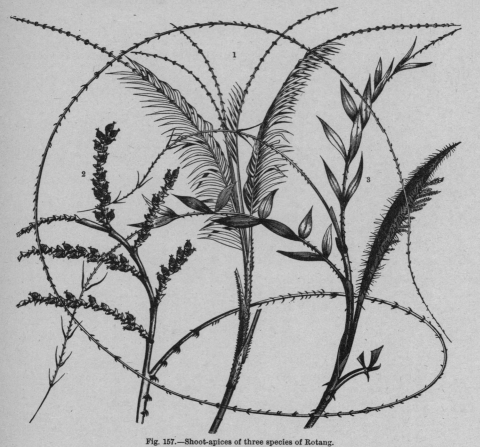

Fig. 157.—Shoot-apices of three species of Rotang.

¹ *Dæmonorops hygrophilus*. ² *Calamus extensus*; with inflorescence. ³ *Desmoncus polyacanthus*; much reduced.

Large, Rough Areas:

Areas that will be seldom viewed, road and pond banks for example, can be covered with crownvetch, tall fescue, or lilyturf. All three will resist encroachment by other plants and easily maintain themselves. Occasionally, honeysuckle is used for such an area, but it invites seedlings, such as poison ivy and tree of heaven (Ailanthus), especially in rural areas.

More visible rough areas are best covered with a combination of the shrubby and the creeping ground covers. To enable leveling of an area, plant covers like creeping spirea, St. Johnswort bigleaf winter creeper and dwarf forsythia in the low area and in higher areas use barren strawberries, bugleweed, creeping potentilla and wineleaf cinquefoil. Yellowroot can be used near water or in wet areas. The combination of types both relieves monotony and covers ground more economically.

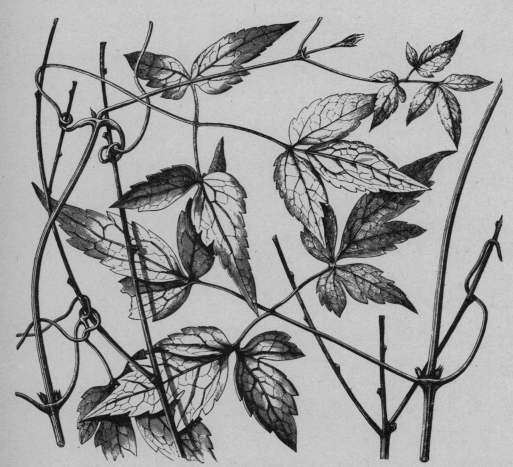

Fig. 163.—Leaf-stalk tendrils of *Atragene alpina*.

Natural Areas:

Planting these areas takes planning and good execution to properly develop. Rock gardens, wooded paths, Japanese gardens, and streams can be made attractive and useful if done properly, or they can quickly become weedy.

Ground covers used in these areas should not compete too strongly with flowering perennials, ferns, bulbs, and small shrubs. They should preferably be self-renewing each spring and not be too viny, since vines hold leaves and become trashy. Plants, such as ajuga, wild ginger, daylilies, bunchberry, hosta and barren strawberry are excellent in the natural setting. If a vining-type plant is desired, the periwinkle would be the best choice since it can be cleaned in the spring and is not too woody. Creeping juniper, creeping potentilla, and wineleaf cinquefoil are excellent choices for the Japanese garden, because their growth habit and appearance are oriental.

Water Areas:

Yellowroot and daylilies are good near streams and ponds and will effectively control weeds. Polygonum is also good in wet areas, but it must be enclosed on an island or between a sidewalk and the water's edge. If it escapes, it can become a problem. Tall fescue is a good cover for pond banks and larger rough areas.

Aegopodium podagraria 'Variegatum' - Goutweed - Zones 1-4

Good in shade, wet or dry; has a pH range of 4.5-7.5; will escape and must be enclosed. Goutweed will grow in any soil type, but prefers sandy conditions, spreads rapidly. Is used for its brightly variegated white and yellow-green foliage; flowers are white and not very showy. Plant 14-18" apart. This plant can become a lawn weed and should not be allowed to escape.

Ajuga reptans - Bugleweed - D 6-8" H - Zones 2, 3 & 4

Will grow in sun or shade (better in some shade) in soil with a pH range of 4.5-7.0, preferably moist. This plant needs winter wind protection. Flowers are deep blue in early spring on 4-6" spikes. Plants spread rapidly, so plant 14-16" apart. Ajuga is an excellent ground cover where it is hardy. Always buy nemotode-free plants. There are three major foliage colors: solid green, purplish green, and a white and red variegated. The latter is not winter hardy north of zone 3.

Asarum canadense - Wild Ginger - D 7-10" H - Zones 1-4

Needs deep shade and moist, rich soil with a pH of 4.5-5.5; excellent for use in wooded areas. Flowers not showy; plant 10-15" apart. This is an excellent plant for entryways and protected areas to add a very interesting texture. Ginger blends well with earth-tone colored stone or low statuary.

Coronilla varia - Crownvetch - D 18" H - Zones 1, 2 & 3

Should be used primarily for large areas not near residences. Tolerates a wide range of soil types and has a pH range of 5.0-7.5; should be planted on 12-14" centers; flowers pink in early summer. Crownvetch is good for large, rough areas away from residences. In many areas it draws rodents. It also dries very early and is unsightly. Best use is for road cuts that are not too steep. It is not as effective an erosion stopper as once thought.

Cerastium tomentosum - Snow-in-Summer - D 12-14" H - Zones 1-4

Tolerates a hot dry soil, needs good drainage. Does well in soil pH of 5-7.5. Good quick cover for hot areas. Spreads rapidly, so plant 18-24" apart. Covered with small white flowers in late spring.

Convallaria majalis - Lily-of-the-Valley - D 12-14" H - Zones 1-4

Grows in any soil type or pH. Will grow in full shade or sun. This plant spreads rapidly, plant 14-18" apart. Lily-of-the-Valley will become a weed in lawn or flower bed, and it is difficult to eradicate. Each root will produce a new plant. Has 12" spike of small white flowers in late spring.

Cornus canadensis - Bunchberry - D 6-8" H - Zones 2 & 3

A very delicate plant that needs a moist, acid soil (pH 4.5) in 50% or greater shade. Should be used for special areas; spreads slowly and should be planted 6" apart. Plant has a beautiful white flower identical to the flowering dogwood (cornus Florida). Beautiful in entryways and in wooded settings.

Fig. 164.—Branch-tendrils of *Serjania gramatophora*.

Cotoneaster dammeri - Bearberry Cotoneaster - D 2-3' H - Zones 1-4

Prefers a well-drained, sandy soil that is slightly acid. This plant needs full sun and good growth. Spreads rapidly, plant 2' apart. Flowers and orange fruit, not showy.

Cotoneaster horizontalis - Rock Spray Cotoneaster - D 10-18" H - Zones 1-4

Prefers a well-drained soil that is slightly acid. This plant will tolerate 25% shade. Spreads rapidly, plant 2' apart. Flowers are not showy, but fruit is outstanding.

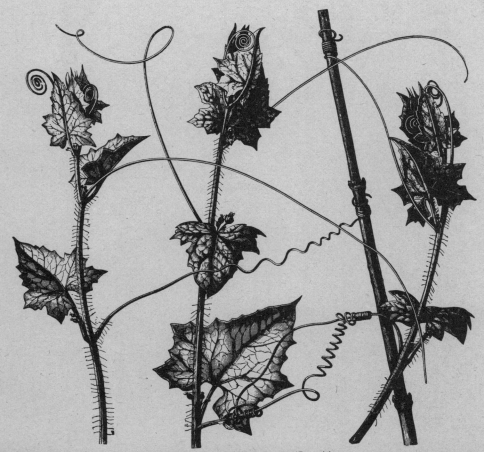

Fig. 165.—Tendrils of the Bryony (*Bryonia*).

Euonymus fortunei 'Vegetus' - Bigleaf Winter Creeper - E 18-24" H - Zones 1-4

The culture is the same as for Winter Creeper. This plant will cover larger areas faster and in some cases the coarser texture is desirable. All of the larger Euonymus are outstanding ground covers for use in large areas. They are very hardy and dependable.

Euonymus fortunei radicans - Winter Creeper - E 12-18" H - Zones 1-4

Very versatile as to soil types, pH levels, and growing conditions; plant 2' apart. Will survive sun, shade, or competition. Very hardy and good in Zone 1; euonymus scale is a major problem. No flowers.

Euonymus fortunei radicans 'Variegata' - Variegated Winter Creeper - E 18-24" H - Zones 3 & 4

The culture and use is the same as Winter Creeper, except it is not nearly as hardy.

Euonymus fortunei 'Coloratus' - Purple Leaf Winter Creeper - E 12-18" H - Zones 1-4

Versatile as to soil type, pH, and growing conditions; plant 2' apart. Will survive sun, shade, or competition; very hardy and is good in Zone 1. One major problem is euonymus scale. No flowers.

Euonymus fortunei 'Longwood' - Longwood's Euonymus - E 4-6" H - Zones 1-4

Longwood's will tolerate a soil pH of 5.5-7.0; plant 12-14" apart. Requires some protection from grass and other plants; a slow grower, but very good for enclosed areas that will be viewed closely. Tolerates soil of all types; requires more moisture than Winter Creeper. Flowers are not showy.

Forsythia 'Arnold Dwarf' - Arnold's Dwarf Forsythia - D 24-36" H - Zones 1-4

Has a soil pH requirement of 5.5-7.0 and needs full sun. Plant 2' on centers. Will tolerate dry conditions after it is established. Does not flower. Good for covering large areas that are rough and will only be viewed from a distance or infrequently.

Forsythia viridissima 'Bronxensis' - Dwarf Flowering Forsythia - D 18-24" H - Zones 1-4

Culture and use the same as for Arnold Dwarf. The advantage of 'Bronxensis' is that it flowers (after 2 or 3 years) and is somewhat smaller.

Festuca arundinacea - Tall Fescue - D 10-14" H - Zones 2, 3 & 4

Tolerates a wide range of soil types and pH levels. Grows well in full sun or 50% shade. Has been used as turfgrass, but when used as the more conventional ground covers, it excels. Fescue discourages encroachment by other plants, is inexpensive, and easy to establish, especially in large, rough areas, Excellent for erosion control. Seed at rate of 100 lbs. per acre.

Festuca ovina glauca - Sheep's Fescue - E 10" H - Zones 2 & 4

Cultural requirements for this Fescue is the same as Tall Fescue. The use is much different. This plant is used in a design, pattern, or accent plant. The tight, ball-shape habit of growth makes it very interesting. Use it on mounds or in protected areas such as courtyards.

Hedera helix 'Rochester' - Fine Leaf English Ivy - E 6" H - Zones 3 & 4

Culture is the same as the Thorndale Ivy, except it is not quite as hardy. Rochester is slow to spread, so plant on 12-14" centers. This compact-growing ivy is excellent near a structure or an area where the coarse stems of the Thorndale are objectionable. Excellent used where it is viewed closely.

Fig. 182.—Undulations of old ribbon-shaped liane stems (*Bauhinia anguina*) from an Indian jungle.

Juniperus horizontalis 'Wiltoni' - <u>Blue Rug</u> - D 2-6" H - Zones 1-4

Requires full sun, a pH of 5.0-7.0, and well-drained soil. Junipers will survive drought periods in good condition. This variety is resistant to juniper blight; plant 4' apart on steep slopes 20% and above and 4½' on slopes below 20%. Do not plant Blue Rug in or near grass. The grass will smother and cause die-back to occur. Waukegan 'Douglasii' is a larger, similarly-colored juniper that can be used near grass or in competition with other plants.

Juniper chinensis 'Sargenti' - <u>Sargents Juniper</u> - E 18-30" H - Zones 1-4

Culture requirements the same as Blue Rug. This is the juniper that is used for ground cover in large open areas. They do cover rapidly, but junipers should not be used to control erosion. Junipers will not tie down the soil under their wide limb spread, so the area is left subject to undercutting. The entire planting can be washed away on steep areas.

Juniperus procumbens - <u>Japanese Garden Juniper</u> - E 18-24" H -

Cultural requirements are the same as for the Blue Rug. The best use of this plant is in rock gardens.

Liriope spicata - <u>Lilyturf</u> - D 8-12" H - Zones 1-4

Does well in a wide range of soil types and has a pH range of 5.0-7.5. Plant 12" apart. Full sun is best, but lilyturf will grow in 50% shade. Does well in moist soil but will tolerate dry conditions for long periods. Will resist encroachment by other plants, yet will not escape or spread too rapidly. Flowers are lilac on spikes that just show through the foliage. Lilyturf is good used in combination with other ground covers. Makes an excellent contrast to Sheep's Fescue. Interesting patterns can be worked with these two plants.

Lonicera japonica 'Halliana' - <u>Hall's Honeysuckle</u> - D 18-24" H - Zones 1-4

Tolerates and does well in all soil types and has a pH range of 4.0-7.5. Plant 2' apart. It climbs and should be used in open areas without trees or other objects to climb. Will grow rapidly in sun or up to 75% shade. Flowers are yellow or white. Good cover for large steep area. This plant blends well in wooded area or near water. Caution; this plant will climb and smother young trees.

Lysimachia nummularia - <u>Moneywort</u> - D 1" H - Zones 1-4

Prefers sun but will tolerate shade. Grows in any type of soil as long as moisture levels are high. Plant 18" apart. Will become a lawn weed if it escapes. Spreads rapidly. Flowers are deep yellow in spring and bloom for a long period. Good in rock gardens or enclosed area such as entryways. Moneywort is an excellent hanging plant.

Hedera helix 'Thorndale' - <u>English Ivy</u> - E 8-10" H - Zones 1, 2 & 3

Has the broadest range of uses of all the ground covers; will tolerate a soil pH of 4.5-7.5, sandy to clay, sun or shade, cool and moist, and will survive in hot, dry conditions after it is established. Ivy is slow to establish so plant on 12-14" centers. Does not flower; will climb walls of brick, wood, or stone. This is the most frequently used of all the ground covers.

Hemerocallis - <u>Daylily</u> - D 24" H - Zones 1, 2 & 3

Requires moisture and a soil with a pH range of 5.0-7.0; plant every 18". Thrives in sun or shade and is grown for flowers, which are of numerous colors and shades. This plant is rather unattractive in winter.

Hosta decorata - <u>Plantain Lily</u> or <u>Funkia</u> - D 6-24" H - Zones 1-4

Excellent in shady or wooded areas; prefers a moist soil with a pH of 5.0-6.5. Plant 14-18" apart. Will survive under dry conditions as well if they are shaded and allowed to become established. Flowers on spikes, white or purple in July and August. Beautiful in large wooded areas.

Hosta undulata - <u>Variegated-Leaved Plantain Lily</u> - D 2-3' H - Zones 1-4

Culture and use the same as Hosta Decorata. This plant is a little more susceptible to sunburn. Good for narrow borders.

Heuchera sanguinea - <u>Coral-bells</u> - D 10-14" H - Zones 1-4

Tolerates almost any soil type and pH of 4.5-7.5; will grow in 50% shade but prefers sun. This plant spreads slowly so should be planted 12-14" apart. Has a flower of coral red, pink, or white on a 2' spike in June and July. Coral-bells will hold their leaves quite late in Zones 3 and 4 and until December in Zone 2.

Iberis sempervirens - <u>Evergreen Candy Tuft</u> - E 10-14" H - Zones 3 & 4

This plant prefers an acid soil with a pH range of 4.5-6.0, well-drained. Plant 12-14" apart. Needs some shade--afternoon is best. Candy Tuft does not compete well with other plants because of its slow growth. The flowers are very showy in early spring. This makes this plant very useful to add color to large area of some other ground cover.

Fig 31. *Lonicera ciliosa* in South Carolina

Phlox subulata - Creeping Phlox - D 4-6" H - Zones 1-4

Has soil pH range of 5.0-7.0; needs full sun and should be enclosed to prevent escape into lawn. Phlox are rampant growers and should be planted 12-14" apart. The plant is used primarily for its spring flowers, which come in many colors. In some areas it becomes a lawn weed. Does best where it can be controlled, such as a planter box or between side walk and buildings.

Potentilla verna - Creeping Potentilla - D 4" H - Zones 1-4

Is one of the best low-matting types of ground cover and requires a soil pH from 4.5 to 6.5. It thrives in full sun; plant 12" apart. The flowers are deep yellow and good for mass flower effect in spring. This is a very neat, compact plant.

Potentilla tridentata - Wineleaf Cinquefoil - E 4-6" H - Zones 1-4

Will grow in any soil type, but the pH should be slightly acid, 4.0-6.0. Will tolerate dry conditions after established. Spreads slowly and must be planted 6-8" apart. White flowers in May. Grows best in sun, but will do well in 50% shade. Excellent in combination with azaleas and other plants that require a low pH.

Pachysandra terminalis - Japanese Spurge - E 12-18" H - Zones 2, 3 & 4

Needs complete winter shade and moist, rich soil with a pH of 6.5-7.0 for best results. Plant 12" apart. Will not do well in exposed, dry areas. Has inconspicuous flowers. This plant is best managed in smaller beds unless it is used in deep wooded areas.

Pachysandra terminalis 'Variegata' - Variegated Japanese Spurge - E 12-14" H - Zones 3 & 4

Culture and use the same as the green Japanese Spurge. The only difference is winter hardiness. Only good in Zones 3 and 4.

Pachistima canbyi - Pachistima - E 10-18" H - Zones 1-4

Does not tolerate over-watering, especially in periods of slow growth as fall and winter. Soil should be sandy and well-drained above and below the surface. Soil pH of 5.0-6.0 is best; will grow in higher pH, but this causes discoloration and slower growth. Spreads slowly so plant 12-14" apart. This plant will not control erosion. Flowers are not showy. Does well in areas of root competition with large old trees.

Polygonum affine - Fleece-flower - D 4-6" H - Zones 1-4

Soil pH is not important, 4.0-7.5. Plant 2' apart. Grows best with plenty of moisture. Must be enclosed; it will escape and become a problem due to its rapid growth. Grows in a wide range of soil types; tolerates sun or shade. Will compete with any plant for growing space, so is best used alone in an enclosed area; flowers are pink.

Spiraea japonica 'Alpina' - Creeping Spirea - D 10-18" H - Zones 1-4

Is excellent on dry or sandy soil with a pH range of 5.5 to 7.5; needs 50% sun for best flower. Plant 18-24" apart. Flowers are pink in late spring. This plant combines well with the larger spirea, such as Anthony Waters, which is itself used as a ground cover in large, rough areas.

Sedum acre - Goldmoss Stonecrop - D 6-8" H - Zones 1-4

Good in wide range of soil and pH types; grows well in sun and 50% shade. Plant 10-12" apart. Works well in retaining walls and under large trees. Bright yellow flower in early summer.

Sedum acre serangulare - Large Leaf Stonecrop - D 6-8" H - Zones 1-4

Culture and use is the same as Dragon's Blood. This sedum has a beautiful yellow flower in late spring. Best yellow-flowered sedum of all.

Sedum pruinatum - Blue Spruce Sedum - D 6-8" H - Zones 1-4

This plant will tolerate a wide range of soil but prefers well-drained sandy condition. Soil pH does not seem to be important (pH 4-7.5). Spreads well so plant 12' apart. Small yellow flowers on spikes in the fall.

Sedum spurium - Dragon's Blood - D 6-8" H - Zones 1-4

Will tolerate dry, sunny conditions after established; soil should have a pH range of 5.0-7.0 and be well drained. This sedum has a deep red flower in summer. Plant every 12"; sedums do not compete well for space with other plants. In hot dry areas, the sedums all perform well. The Dragon's Blood under these conditions forms a low, dense mat that is quite attractive. Under shade the plant stretches and becomes soft and open.

Groundcover Test Plots

1. Arnold Arboretum, Case Estates
   Weston, Mass.

2. Los Angeles State & County Arboretum
   Arcadia, Calif.

3. University of Minnesota Arboretum
   Wayzata, Minn.

4. Morton Arboretum
   Lisle, Ill.

5. Fairchild Tropical Garden
   Coconut Grove, Fla.

6. Nassau County Park (Salisbury)
   near Bowling Green, Long Island, New York

7. North Willamette Experiment Sta.
   Aurora, Oregon.

Stephanandra incisa - Stephanandra - D 18-24" H - Zones 1-4

Requires a very acid soil pH of 4.0-5.0. Plant 18-24" apart. In most areas iron should be supplied as well. Needs sun but will tolerate 50% shade. Spreads slowly. Small, pinkish-white flowers in fall.

Thymus serpyllum - Mother of Thyme - D 1-2" H - Zones 1-4

Will grow in almost any soil as long as there is good drainage. Prefers a pH of 6.5-7.5. Plant 6" apart. Used primarily for fill in brick or flagstone walks and retaining walls. Flowers are purple on spikes from June through September.

Thymus vulgaris - Common Thyme - D 6" H - Zones 1-4

This is a sun plant that will tolerate a wide range of pH 5.5-7.5 and soil types. Grows slowly, plant 12" apart. It prefers a dry, well-drained sandy soil. This plant is excellent in rock gardens or dry, hot areas. Flowers are pale lavendar on small 1½" spikes.

Vinca minor - Periwinkle - E 6-10" H - Zones 2, 3 & 4

Should be planted in a protected area, especially away from winter wind. Tolerates a wide range of soil types and pH of 4.5-7.5. Plant 12-14" apart. Soil fertility levels should be high in all cases. Where planted in open, unprotected areas, develops disease problems. Flowers are blue in early spring. Blends well with broad leaf evergreens.

Viola papilionacea - Violets - D 6-8" H - Zones 1-4

This plant is a shade plant but will tolerate full sun. Will grow in any type soil. Plant 10" apart. Likes moisture and spreads rapidly by seed and crown enlargement. Flowers in spring are outstanding and come in a wide range of colors--violet, deep purple, blue, white. Yellow violets do not make good ground cover. This plant can become a serious lawn weed in shady areas.

Waldsteinia fragarioides - Barren Strawberry - D 6-8" H - Zones 1-4

Prefers moist-average to rich soil in a pH range of 5.5-7.0. Medium grower. The plant has a small yellow flower in spring. Makes a good cover for wooded or partially shaded locations. Excellent for planting under shrub masses.

Xanthorhiza simplicissima - Yellowroot - D 24" H - Zones 1-4

Good for use in wet areas and near water. Tolerates a wide range of soil types and pH levels and will grow in sun or shade. Plant 2' apart. Flowers not showy. Very good water edge plant to control shore weeds and mud.

GROUNDCOVER SOURCES

Perry's Plants
19362 Walnut Drive
LaPuente, Calif. 91745
(wholesale only) — All groundcovers

Monrovia Nursery Co.
18331 E. Foothill Blvd.
Azusa, Calif. 91702
(wholesale only) — Low and prostrate shrubs and conifers and perennials

Select Nurseries, Inc.
12831 E. Central
Brea, Calif. 92621 — Low and prostrate shrubs and conifers and perennials

Oda Nursery
9381 Bolsea Ave.
Westminster, Calif. 92683
(wholesale only) — Low and prostrate shrubs and conifers and perennials

Deigaard Nurseries, Inc.
More Mesa Rd.
Goleta, Calif.
(wholesale only) — Low and prostrate shrubs and conifers and perennials

Gardena Valley Nursery Growers
16420 So. Avalon Blvd.
Gardena, Calif. 90247 — Low and prostrate shrubs and conifers and perennials

Leatherman's Gardens
2637 N. Lee Ave.
South El Monte, Calif. 91733 — Ferns

Johnson Cactus Gardens
Box 207
Bonsall, Calif. — Succulents

Brimfield Gardens Nursery
245 Brimfield Rd.
Wetherfield, Conn. 06109 — Rock garden plants, alpines, dwarf conifers

Reynolds Farms
Richards Ave., RFD 30
South Norwalk, Conn. 06856 — Perennials

Hemlock Hill Herb Farm
Litchfield, Conn. 06759 — Herbs

White Flower Farm
Litchfield, Conn. 06759 — Herbs

Caprilands Herb Farm
Silver St.
Coventry, Conn. 06238 — Herbs

Mrs. E. Reed Brelsford
1816 Cherry St.
Jacksonville, Fla. 32205 — Ferns

Haverfield's Herbs
1959 Kimberly Rd.
Atlanta, Georgia 30331 — Herbs

Henderson's Botanical Gardens
Rte. 6
Greensburg, Ind. 47240 — Herbs

House of Wesley
Bloomington, Ill. 61701 — Perennials

Merry Gardens
Camden, Maine 04843 — Ferns and herbs

Burgess Seed & Plant Co.
Galesburg, Michigan 49053 — Perennials

The Rock Garden
Litchfield, Maine 04350 — Rock garden plants and alpines

Rakestraw's Gardens
3094 S Term.
Flint, Mich. 48507 — Rock garden plants and alpines

American Perennial Gardens
P.O. Box 37
Garden City, Mich. 48135 — Rock garden plants and alpines

Mincemoyers
R.D. 5 Box 379
Jackson, New Jersey 08527 — Ferns

Edelweiss Gardens
Robbinsville, New Jersey 08691 — Ferns

Mayfair Nurseries
Nichols, New York 13812 — Hardy heathers and rock garden plants, alpines

Oak Park Nurseries
East Patchogue, New York 11772 — Low and prostrate shrubs, conifers and perennials

Sterns Nurseries
Geneva, New York 14456 — Perennials, popular groundcovers

E. C. Robbins
Ashford, McDowell County
North Carolina 28603 — Rock garden plants and alpines

The Three Laurels
Marshall, North Carolina 28753 — Rock garden plants and alpines and ferns

Gardens of the Blue Ridge
Ashford, North Carolina 28603 — Ferns and herbs

Sunnybrook Farm
9448 Mayfield Rd.
Chesterland, Ohio 44026 — Herbs

MacPherson Gardens
2920 Starr Ave.
Oregon, Ohio 43616 — Sempervivums

Wayside Gardens
Mentor, Ohio 44060 — Low and prostrate shrubs and conifers, perennials and herbs

Horton Nurseries, Inc.
Painesville, Ohio 44077 — Low and prostrate shrubs and conifers, perennials

Rocknoll Nursery
Morrow, Ohio 45152 — Perennials, moss phlox

Spring Hill Nurseries
311 Elm St.
Tipp City, Ohio 45371 — Perennials

Edsal Wood
Wood Nursery Co.
Portland, Oregon — All groundcovers

OxBow Botanical Gardens
Gresham, Oregon 97030 — Succulents, sedums, sempervivums and other groundcovers

Oakhill Gardens
Rte. 3, Box 87A
Dallas, Oregon 97338 — Succulents

Mitsch Nursery Co.
Aurora, Oregon 97002
(wholesale only) — Low and prostrate shrubs and conifers, perennials

Carl Starker Gardens
Jennings Lodge, Oregon 97267 — Rock garden plants and alpines

Musser Forests
Indiana, Pa. 15701 — Low and prostrate shrubs and conifers, perennial groundcovers

Lakeland Nurseries
Hanover, Pa. 17331 — Perennials

Greene Herb Gardens
Greene, R.I. 02826 — Herbs

Charles Thurman
Rte. 2, Box 259
Spokane, Washington 99207 — Rock garden plants, alpines

Lamb Nurseries
E. 101 Sharp Ave.
Spokane, Washington 99202 — Low and prostrate shrubs and conifers, perennial groundrovers and herbs

The Wild Garden
8423 NE 119th
Kirkland, Wash. 98033 — Ferns

Woodland Acres Nursery
Crivitz, Wisc. 54114 — Ferns

Alpenglow Gardens
13328 Trans-Canada Hwy
North Surrey P.O.
New Westminster, B.C., Canada — Dwarf conifers, rock garden plants and alpines

PAMPAS GRASS.
(GYNERIUM ARGENTEUM.)

ROCK GARDENING ALPINES

—Arrangement of Rocks

Arrangement of Rocks.

PRIMROSES

Far North Gardens,
15621 Auburndale Ave.,
Livonia, Mich. 48154

Skyhook Farm,
Johnson, Vt. 05656

HOSTAS

Minks Fairway Gardens,
114 The Fairway,
Albert Lea, Minn. 46007

Savory's Greenhouses,
5300 Whiting Ave.,
Minneapolis, u inn. 55435

Alex J. Summers,
14 I. U. Willets Rd., W.,
Roslyn, N.Y. 11576

HEATHS AND HEATHERS

Spring Hill Farm,
Box 42,
Gig Harbor, Wash. 98335

Sylvan Nursery,
1028 Horseneck Rd.,
South Westport, Maine 02790

DWARF WOODY PLANTS

Carroll Gardens,
Westminster, Md. 21157

Girard Nurseries,
Box 428,
Geneva, Ohio 44041

Mayfair Nurseries
R. 2, Box 68,
Nichols, N.Y. 13812

Raraflora, 1195 Stump Rd.,
Feasterville, Penna. 19047

Joel Spingarn,
1535 Forest Ave.,
Baldwin, N.Y. 11510

Alpine Willows with stems and branches clinging to the ground in the Tyrol.

ROCK GARDENING

During the 1930's, a rock gardening craze swept the country. As such crazes will, it blew aside many sound designs and gardening practices, leaving in its wake a hodge-podge of misinformation and new product unsuited for this type of gardening.

Originally, rock gardens were developed as an attempt to create natural settings for Alpine plant collections. They required a great amount of work to create and maintain, but were especially rewarding, as they offered gardeners a wide range of textures and forms other plant groups do not possess.

As the rock gardening craze spread, the emphasis shifted from plants to rocks. So, today what many people think of as rock gardens are merely heaps of stone decorated with plants that would do better elsewhere.

While this may still be pleasing to some, we favor traditional, naturalistic rock gardens, planted with carefully selected Alpines. This, we feel, is a more challenging and therefore more satisfying approach to gardening.

Anyone who has hiked up beyond the tree line of a mountain has seen that true Alpines rarely grow more than a foot tall. Wind and weather bend and mold shrubs and stone into tortured shapes and spectacular forms. In selecting plants and stone, not only shape, but scale is very important. Balance must be achieved. These are the key things to remember when planning your rock garden.

Appropriate soil and drainage conditions must also be considered. Rock gardens planted with dwarf perennials do well in any good gardening soil. However, many true Alpines are native to granite and other non-calcareous rock formations. For these, an equal mixture of loam, sand and humus in the form of moss or leaf mold is preferred by many aficionados. If sand and stone free of lime is not available locally, add a few drops of hydrochloric acid to balance soil ph.

Super-drainage is essential for keeping the gnarled, dwarfed appearance of rock garden plants. For the same reason, these plants should be starved, and no fertilizer should be used.

We're interested in hearing your experiences with rock GARDENING. Reserve the dope on ROCK gardening for your friendly neighborhood geologist.

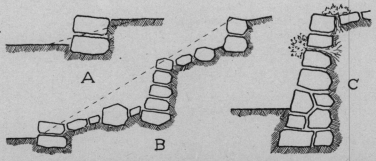

Some Notes on the Cultivation of the Plants in this Catalogue

INITIAL TREATMENT

Unpacking. Unpack the plants carefully immediately they arrive. If planting cannot be undertaken immediately, remove the wrapping-paper completely from each plant, together with any packing material around the foliage, and keep the plants upright in a shady place (during frost keep in a cold greenhouse, frame or light porch, etc.). Moisten the rootball if it becomes dry.

Planting. Most plants are sent in waxed paper pots or black polythene bag-pots, and these should be removed before planting. Those in red whalehide pots, (the roots can usually be seen piercing the sides and base of these), should be planted intact, but the top half-inch of the whalehide should be torn off first. The ground should be well prepared before planting (see p. 4).

Ensure that the rootball is thoroughly moist, and lightly squeeze it to loosen the roots at the base and remove any crust of hard compost etc. from around the neck or "collar" of the plant. Plant deep enough just to cover the roots and firm the plant in well with the fingers. Water in well, especially during dry weather in the spring and summer months. Complete the operation by levelling the soil around the plants and top-dress with a good layer of chippings or coarse grit.

Every plant is sent with its own indelibly printed, green plastic label, designed especially for the rock-garden, where it will last as long as the plant, be unobtrusive and yet easily read.

AFTERCARE

Watering. All newly-planted alpines are susceptible to drought for the first few weeks after planting, especially in spring and early summer. Regular watering is therefore most important, and dwarf conifers, heathers and other evergreens benefit from an overhead spray in summer evenings.

Feeding. All alpines benefit from a top-dressing and light feed each spring. Coarse grit or chippings, mixed with peat and a little bone-meal or general organic fertilizer, is ideal to spread over the rock garden, raised beds, etc., and even ordinary boarders.

Pruning. The timing of pruning, cutting-back, etc. varies according to variety, but generally is best done immediately after flowering—this applies mainly to vigorous spreading plants such as Aubrieta, Alyssum, Phlox, etc. which require cutting back each season to maintain a tight cushion-like habit. The majority of smaller alpines need no treatment at all except for the cutting out of any dead patches and over-spreading growth.

Maintenance. Ensure that small plants are not crowded by more vigorous neighbours—in the growing season, strong-growing plants can easily smother more delicate cushion plants and ruin them in a week or less. Autumn removal of leaves and debris is also vital in this respect. Remove annual weeds regularly and re-mulch with chippings whenever necessary.

GARDENING WITH ALPINES

Adaptability. One of the advantages of growing aplines is that a large and varied collection can be grown in a very limited space. It should not be thought that these plants must be kept within the confines of a rock garden, for rocks are by no means essential to their well-being. Most alpines can be grown in ordinary well-drained garden soil, with little extra preparation, in the front of a mixed border, in raised or island beds, in retaining walls, by driveway or patio, or in freestanding double walls (see below), and will flourish in these situations as well as in the traditional rock garden. The beginner is well advised to start with some of the easier alpines, however, and we have prepared special collections for just this purpose (see p. 8).

The Rock Garden.

Most people who become interested in alpines will, sooner or later, wish to build a rock garden, and the following notes are designed to help the beginner.

Site. Choose a site, if possible, well away from buildings or large trees to avoid draughts and drips, in an open position sloping slightly towards the south, with free drainage. These are ideal conditions, but a lot can be done by choosing plants carefully, if any or all of these conditions are wanting.

Soil Preparation and Landscaping. The site must be thoroughly dug and weeded beforehand, and particular attention must be paid to deep-rooted and perennial weeds. If the soil is heavy, dig in plenty of peat and sand or grit; if light, incorporate peat, leafmould and organic matter. Shape the soil into the contours of hill and valley required. A flat site requires more consideration than one on a natural slope, but much can be done by excavating from one part to form mounds elsewhere. Be careful not to mix topsoil and subsoil.

Stone in the Rock Garden. Stone is used to give some semblance of the plants' natural habitat and to provide a cool root-run and crevices in which many plants thrive. Local stone is usually cheaper and more in keeping with soil and surroundings; it may be used to build a series of informal terraces, with irregular lines of rock holding back the soil, or in 'outcrops' with wider expanses of soil between. The latter gives a more natural appearance, but is more difficult to build successfully; the former method can provide a wider range of planting positions and is more suited to the smaller garden.

The correct placing of rock is an art which can only be learned by experience; it is particularly important to ensure that the lines of strata, if apparent, should be roughly parallel—they need not be horizontal, and might for example tip back somewhat into a slope. Make the rocks firm, but do not bury them unduly; firm the soil behind them to eliminate air pockets but do not ram it into a compacted mass. Do not slope soil surfaces too steeply or erosion will occur before plants become established.

Planting. If it has been possible to make the entire soil suitable, planting may proceed after the soil has settled; it is best otherwise to dig in peat, sand and chippings where each plant is to go. The entire soil surface should be covered with 1-2 ins. of coarse grit or chippings after planting; this keeps the soil moist in summer, prevents plants from becoming plastered with mud in winter, helps with surface drainage and, to some extent, keeps down weeds and slugs.

Pot-grown plants can be planted at any time except during severe frost, drought or prolonged wet weather. Do not overcrowd when planting—any gaps which occur can always be filled later. Please refer back (p. 3) for detailed planting instructions.

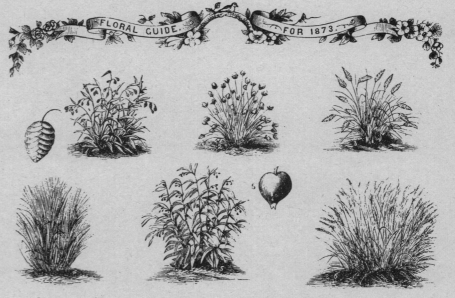

CHRYSURUS CYNOSUROIDES.

FLORAL GUIDE FOR 1873.

1, BRIZA.   2, LAGURUS.   3, PENNISETUM.   4, AGROSTIS.   5, JOB'S TEARS.   6, STIPA.

ORNAMENTAL GRASSES

LILY OF THE VALLEY.

Alpine Gardening.

The above notes refer mainly to the more vigorous rock plants, and these are often grown separately from the smaller, slower-growing and sometimes more delicate plants which are often termed 'alpines' (the distinction between the two is blurred and sometimes not made at all, but is helpful when considering their cultivation). Certain refinements have been evolved for the growing of such alpines, and these are often referred to in the plant descriptions; a few explanatory notes might help those who are unfamiliar with these methods and terms.

Scree. An artificial scree is a bed of special compost which provides perfect drainage allied to adequate moisture and an unrestricted root-run. This bed should be raised above the general soil level (i.e. in the higher parts of the rock garden or in a raised bed—see below). If sunk in an excavation at ground level, drainage material consisting of stones, bricks, etc. should be used to prevent the formation of a pond particulary in heavy soil.

The scree should be between 12 and 18 ins. deep; the compost can be varied to suit the plants grown, but normally ranges from a rich mixture at the base—equal parts of good loam and coarse grit—to a 6 in. surface layer of peat, sand and chippings in equal parts, with a little good loam and a sprinkling of bone-meal. Rocks may be used as described above, and an entire alpine garden may be made in this way.

The Peat Garden or Peat Bed. This is the ideal way to grow the smaller Primulas, other shade and moisture lovers, and lime-hating plants, including many members of the Ericaceae. The site should preferably face west or north-west, very lightly shaded by distant trees or background shrubs such as Rhododendrons. The compost normally consists of equal parts of lime-free loam and peat, with coarse sand or grit for extra drainage. On heavy soils, the bed should be raised, and on limy or chalky soils, a layer of drainage material will discourage the roots from penetrating into the limy soil.

The retaining walls should be of sandstone or peat-blocks; the latter are frequently used nowadays, but to be most effective they should be of top-spit peat, containing heather or sedge roots to bind the peat together, as large as can be conveniently handled, and should not have been allowed to dry out. They should be built into 12 in. walls retaining ledges and beds of the peaty compost. This compost should be well firmed behind and between the blocks, and planting can be carried out at the same time. A top-dressing of peat or lime-free leafmould should be given each spring.

The Alpine House. Many of the smaller, more difficult or early-flowering alpines are seen to their best advantage and to our greater comfort when grown either in pots or planted out in a greenhouse. Many plants are particularly well adapted to pan culture, and make superb alpine house specimens. Such a house must admit the maximum amount of light and fresh air, and should therefore have a low span, continuous ventilation at the ridge and sides, and be set north-south to ensure that both sides receive an equal amount of light. Specially built structures can be obtained, but most ordinary greenhouses are capable of being adapted to the purpose.

Heat is not necessary unless some tender plants are to be grown, but if it is required, an electrically-run fan heater is excellent, as the air is continuously circulated, thus eliminating damping-off in winter and keeping the plants cool in summer.

Deep pots or half-pots (dwarf pots) are preferable to shallow pans, except for such plants as Sempervivums, Pleiones, etc. Plastic and clay pots are equally effective, but they do require different management and should not be mixed if possible. Clay pots should always be plunged in sand unless continual removal and replacement is envisaged. A simple compost of loam, peat and sand is suitable for most plants, and top-dressings of chippings should always be used.

Watering should be reduced to a minimum during November-February, and if the pots are plunged it will only be necessary to moisten the plunging material occasionally during this period. Shading is best done with lath roller blinds, but muslin, etc. can also be used; a colour wash on the glass is not recommended.

Wherever possible, all plants not in flower should be removed to a cold frame during the summer months. Full ventilation should be given at all times, except during damp, foggy weather, severe frost and high winds.

Certain plants are difficult to grow out of doors, and yet do not take kindly to pot-culture, and for these a rock garden under glass is suitable. This may take the form of a scree, peatbed, etc. made up in the usual way, or raised up to waist level, but particular attention must be paid to watering in summer.

Raised Beds. The raised bed is a very popular method of growing alpines, being cheaper and easier to build than a conventional rock garden, more in keeping with a small garden, and easier to maintain without stooping. These beds may be formal or informal in shape to suit their position, normally between 3 and 6 ft. wide, and about 2 ft.-2 ft. 6 ins. high. The walls may be of stone or brick or any material which is to hand, providing it does not look unsightly or unsympathetic to plant growth. Such beds can be filled with any desired soil mixture, and can therefore be used to grow almost any kind of plant. The narrow 'double-wall' type of bed is liable to dry out in summer, and is best reserved for the more vigorous and tolerant rock plants.

Troughs and Sinks. One of the most fascinating ways of growing the smaller alpines is the miniature garden, preferably constructed in an old stone trough. There must be at least one drainage hole, which should be covered with crocks and coarse drainage material. The compost used should be as described for alpine house plants, but can of course be varied to suit any particular plants. A few pieces of rock can be used to construct a small landscape, and if a shallow sink is being used, rocks should be built up to increase the depth of soil. The compost should always be covered with a top dressing of chippings. Many troughs, especially the shallower types, look more effective if raised up slightly on stone pillars.

VAUGHAN'S "LONDON MARKET" BRAND.

THE PLANT NOVELTY OF THE AGE.

OLD STONE TROUGHS AND SINK GARDENS

There is great interest and pleasure to be found in constructing miniature gardens in stone sinks and troughs. For such gardens as these the smaller alpine plants and pygmy shrubs and conifers in which we specialise are ideal.

Genuine old stone sinks and troughs are becoming scarce and are difficult to obtain. We have access to all possible sources of supply throughout the country and we carry here a large stock of old stone sinks and troughs in a wide variety of sizes and shapes. These can be seen at the Nursery and prices quoted after inspection.

We also have a large selection of such sinks and troughs made up, planted and established and these, too, can be seen and quoted for as complete gardens, Delivery can usually be arranged within a reasonable distance from the Nursery. Smaller empty sinks and troughs can usually be conveyed in customer's own cars. We can supply all plants and materials required for sink gardens.

These little landscapes are not difficult to construct and offer wide scope in their arrangement and planting. A good standard soil mixture to use is composed of two parts loam, or good top-spit garden soil, one part leafsoil or fine-grade granulated moss peat, and one part sharp sand or fine grit, all parts by bulk. A good dusting of bonemeal or hoof and horn added to the ingredients as they are mixed provides all the additional fertiliser that is needed.

Small, shapely pieces of weathered stone can be arranged in little outcrops and the plants and shrubs set among them. Before filling the container with soil, drainage must be provided by placing a piece of perforated zinc, or a large piece of broken clay-pot over the hole or holes in the base. Over this spread a layer of coarse material, such as broken potsherds, small stones or coarse ash. Over this spread a further thin layer of semi-decayed leaves, loam fibre or sphagnum moss. This will prevent the finer soil above from filtering into and spoiling the drainage.

After-care consists largely of careful attention to watering. With the exception of gardens which are designed to contain shade-loving plants, they should be placed in open, sunny positions. During dry, sunny weather, they will appreciate at least one good soaking daily applied in the early morning or in the evening. It is important that the water should be applied gently and slowly so that it penetrates thoroughly.

Short absences from home can be catered for by placing a tin, in the base of which a minute hole has been bored, on a high point, and filling it with water. The hole should be so small that the water does not "run" out, but drips very slowly. A pint of water in such a container will deal with the moisture requirements of a stone trough of average size for several days. If the whole surface area between the stones and plants is surfaced with fine grit, this will also conserve moisture and reduce the amount of water required.

To meet the scarcity we construct sinks in concrete which are excellent substitutes for the genuine article. They quickly weather to the appearance of old stone, as we use a measure of peat in the mixture from which they are cast. They have the advantage of extra good drainage from the several holes in the base. These concrete sinks are made in two standard sizes, details and prices of which may be discovered on page 68.

We have always deprecated the use of glazed sinks, but "needs must when the Devil drives" and we have adapted the use of a "Hypertufa" compound to apply a covering to the outer surface of glazed sinks which, as it weathers – a speedy process – renders them indistinguishable from genuine stone. The advantages of these sinks consists of a greater depth, and cheapness, but the real thing is preferable if availability and economics permit.

ORDER FORM

To:

C. G. HOLLETT
GREENBANK NURSERY,
NEW STREET, SEDBERGH, YORKS. LA10 5AG
TEL. SEDBERGH 20286 (STD CODE 0587)

Plants for special purposes

The following lists are an indication of the types of plants which are particularly suitable for certain uses. They are by no means exhaustive, nor should they be taken as anything but a rough guide, for plants will often thrive in what may seem to be the most unlikely position. In such surprises lies some of the fascination of gardening, so do not be afraid to experiment.

Plants for Troughs and Sinks

Abies balsamea 'Hudsonia'	Papaver miyabeanum
Androsace sempervivoides	Penstemon campanulatus pulchellus
Antennaria dioica 'Minima'	Phlox douglasi 'Rose Cushion'
Arabis bryoides 'Olympica'	Picea mariana 'Nana'
A. ferdinandi-coburgi 'Variegata'	Potentilla dwarf vars.
Bellium minutum	Primula 'Blairside Yellow'
Campanula arvatica	P. pubescens 'Freedom'
C. planiflora alba	Rhododendron keleticum
Celsia acaulis	Rhodohypoxis baurii
Chamaecyparis pisifera 'Nana'	Saponaria 'Bressingham X'
C. p. 'Nana Variegata'	Saxifraga—all smaller Kabschia Sec.
Cotoneaster congestus nanus	Saxifraga—smaller Euaizoon Sec.
Dianthus alpinus	S. retusa
D. 'Arvernensis'	Scleranthus biflorus
D. 'La Bourbrille'	Sedum acre 'Minimum'
D. neglectus	S. dasyphyllum 'Glanduliferum'
D. 'Mars'	S. ewersii 'Hayesii'
D. 'Whitehills'	S. hispanicum 'Aureum'
Draba rigida	S. farinosum
D. zapateri	S. leibergii
Erodium in var.	S. oreogonum
Genista delphinensis	Sempervivella alba
Gentiana saxosa	Sempervivum fimbriatum
Hypericum—small vars.	S. arachnoideum 'Rubrum'
Iberis saxatilis	S. soboliferum
Ilex crenata	Silene acaulis 'Pedunculata'
Junoperus communis 'Compressa'	Teucrium aroanium
Lychnis alpina	T. subspinosum
Micromeria varia	Thymus drucei 'Elfin'
Minuartia in var.	T. d. 'Minor'
Morisia monanthos	Veronica selleri
Myosotis rupicola	Edraianthus pumilio
Oxalis enneaphylla	Thlaspi in var.

Plants for Sunny Retaining Walls and Banks

Acaena 'Blue Haze'	Haelinthemum in var.
Achillea in var.	Hypericum olympicum in var.
Aethionema in var.	Iberis in var.
Alyssum in var.	Juniperus communis 'Depressa Aurea'
Arabis alpina in var.	J. conferta
Arenaria montana 'Grandiflora'	J. procumbens 'Nana'
Armeria in var.	J. horizontalis 'Glauca'
Asarina	J. sabina 'Tamariscifolia'
Aubrieta in var.	Lewisia in var.
Campanula 'Birch X'	Linaria alpina
C. carpatica	Linum arboreum
C. cochlearifolia	Lithospermum 'Heavenly Blue'
C. poscharskyana	Oenothera missouriensis
Cheiranthus in var.	Penstemon in var.
Chiastophyllum	Phlox in var.
Cytisus kewensis	Pinus mugho 'Mughus'
Dianthus arenarius	Polygonum in var.
D. 'Brilliancy'	Pterocephalus
D. 'Dubarry'	Ramonda myconi (shade)
D. gratianopolitanus	Rosmarinus lavandulaceus
D. 'Waithmans Beauty'	Saponaria ocymoides
Dryas sundermanii	Saxifraga—Euaizoon Sec.
Erinus in var.	Sedum hybridum
Erysimum in var.	S. spathulifolium in var.
Euphorbia myrsinites	S. spurium in var.
Genista lydia	Sempervivum in var.
Gypsophila in var.	Silene maritima in var.
Halimiocistus in var.	Thymus in var.
Haplopappus	Veronica in var.

RARE PLANTS

We are always pleased to purchase or exchange plants, seeds, cuttings, etc. of rare and choice plants of which we currently have no stock, with a view to propagation and eventual dissemination amongst our customers.

We believe that not only is it in our own and our customers best interests that we offer as wide a range of good plants as possible, but it is also the best means of ensuring that little-known and sometimes difficult plants do not become lost to cultivation.

With this in mind, we shall be delighted to receive details of plants which you have to spare and consider may be of interest. We would mention, however, that we already have stocks of many thousands of varieties which we are currently engaged in propagating; please, therefore, let us know what you can offer before sending any plant material!

Plants Suitable for Alpine House Culture

Alopecurus lanatus
Anacyclus
Anchusa caespitosa
Asperula suberosa
Campanula vidalii
Carduncellus
Convolvulus cneorum
Cordyalis wilsoni
Draba polytricha
Crassula sarcocaulis
Erodium in var.
Fuchsia procumbens
Hypericum dwarf vars.
Leptospermum nichollsii 'Prostratum'
Lewisia in var.

Linaria tristis lurida
Lithospermum oleifolium
Plantago nivalis
Pleione in var.
Primula bellidifolia
P. macrophylla H78
P. Group 3
Saxifraga—Kabschia Sec.
Teucrium subspinosum
Thymus cilicicus
T. membranaceus
Verbascum dumulosum
V. 'Letitia'
Veronica bombycina
Viola hederacea

Plants for Groundcover between Shrubs, and in Shady Places

Acaena in var.
Acorus in var.
Alchemilla in var.
Ajuga in var.
Arisarum
Arum in var.
Asarum europeum
Campanula poscharskyana
Chiastophyllum
Cornus
Cotoneaster dammeri radicans
Euonymus fortunei in var.
Genista sagittalis
Geranium dalmaticum

Gunnera magellanica
Heuchera villosa
Lysimachia
Maianthemum
Ourisia coccinea
Parochetus
Polygonum affine 'Lowndes Var.'
Salix x moorei
Saxifraga—"mossy kinds"
Sedum spurium in var.
Tellima
Tolmiea
Vinca
Erica carnea in var.

Plants for Hot, Dry Positions, in Full Sun

Acaena in var.
Alyssum in var.
Aubrieta in var.
Cheiranthus in var.
Dianthus in var.
Erysimum in var.
Genista in var.
Halimiocistus
Helianthemum in var.
Helichrysum splendidum
Hieraceum in var.

Hypericum in var.
Lavandula 'Munstead'
Paronychia
Salvia in var.
Sedum in var.
Sempervivum in var.
Tanacetum in var.
Thymus in var.
Tuberaria lignosa
Veronica prostrata in var.

Dwarf Shrubs for the Rock Garden

Acer in var.
Andromeda in var.
Berberis in var.
Betula
Bruckenthalia
Buxus in var.
Caragana
Cassiope in var.
Chamaedaphne
Convolvulus cneorum
Corylopsis
Cotoneaster in var.
Cytisus in var.
Daphne in var.
Euryops
Escallonia in var.
Euonymus in var.
Fuchsia in var.
Gaulnettya
Gaultheria
Genista in var.
Halimiocistus

Hebe in var.
Hedera in var.
Ilex in var.
Hypericum shrubby vars.
Kalmia
Jasminum parkeri
Leucothoe
Lonicera
Margyricarpus
Olearia
Pernettya in var.
Phyllodoce in var.
Pieris
Potentilla—shrubby vars.
Rhododendron in var.
Evergreen Azalea in var.
Salix in var.
Senecio leucostachys
Spiraea in var.
Syringa
Vaccinium in var.
Viburnum in var.

Plants for Growing in Paving, Paths, Alpine Lawns, etc.

Acaena in var.
Ajuga in var.
Antennaria in var.
Arenaria balearica
Armeria in var.
Azorella in var.
Campanula cochlearifolia
Cotoneaster in var.
Cotula in var.
Cymbalaria in var.
Dianthus deltoides in var.
D. neglectus
Draba aizoides
Dryas in var.
Erinus in var.
Erysimum in var.
Frankenia
Goodenia
Gypsophila in var.
Haplocarpha
Helxine in var.
Herniaria
Houttuynia
Hypericum reptans
Hypsela

Iberis saxatilis
Juniperus communis 'Depressa Aurea'
J. procumbens 'Nana'
J. horizontalis 'Glauca'
Leptospermum humifusum
Mazus in var.
Mentha
Minuartia imbricata
Montia
Paronychia in var.
Phlox in var.
Pinus mugho 'Mughus'
Potentilla cinerea
P. tabernaemontana nana
Pratia
Prunella in var.
Raoulia
Saxifraga "mossy" types
Scleranthus in var.
Sedum—low-growing kinds
Selaginella
Sempervivum in var.
Thymus—creeping kinds
Veronica in var.
Vinca

Choice Plants for a Sunny Scree

Aethionema in var.
Allium amabile
Anacyclus
Anchusa caespitosa
Androsace sempervivoides
Aquilegia japonica
Arabis breweri
Asperula suberosa
Artemisia schmidtiana nana
Aster natalense
Campanula arvatica
Carduncellus
Dianthus alpinus
D. erythrocoleus
D. microlepis
Douglasia
Draba in var.
Edraianthus in var.
Epilobium crassum
Geranium napuligerum

Lewisia nevadensis
Linaria tristis lurida
Lithospermum oleifolium
Minuartia graminifolia
Myosotis
Papaver miyabeanum
Plantago nivalis
Rhodohypoxis
Rosularia
Saponaria 'Bressingham X'
Saxifraga—Kabschia Sec.
Saxifraga—smaller Euaizoon Sec.
Sedum—small kinds
Sempervivella
Silene acaulis 'Pedunculata'
Teucrium aroanium
T. subspinosum
Thymus membranaceus
Veronica bombycina
V. kellereri

Choice Plants for a Peat Bed, and for Growing in Peat-block Walls

Adonis in var.
Andromeda in var.
Arisaema
Arisarum
Arum in var.
Asarum in var.
Astilbe glaberrima saxatilis
Calceolaria tenella
Cassiope in var.
Chamaedaphne
Chamaelirium
Codonopsis in var.
Coprosma
Cyclamen
Cypripedium
Dicentra
Disporum
Dodecatheon
Empetrum
Epigaea
Erythronium in var.
Galax
Gaultheria
Gentiana in var.
Haberlea
Hepatica in var.
Hylomecon
Kalmia
Leucothoe
Meconopsis quintuplinervia

Mentha
Mitchella
Ophiopogon
Orchis
Ourisia
Patrinia
Pernettya in var.
Phyllodoce
Pieris
Polygala
Pimelia in var.
Polygonatum
Polygonum tenuicaule
Primula—Group 2
Ramonda
Rhododendron in var.
Evergreen Azalea in var.
Salix reticulata
Sanguinaria
Saxifraga fortunei 'Wadas Form'
S. strigosa
S. veitchiana
Shortia
Soldanella
Thalictrum
Tricyrtis in var.
Trillium in var.
Uvularia in var.
Vaccinium in var.
Viola hederacea

PLANT LIST

Achillea

argentea. *Eastern Alps.* An easy, useful and charming plant for any sunny soil. It forms close mats of silvery grey leaves and in summer has a long succession of white flowers borne in flat heads on 6 inch stems ..

Actaea

spicata alba. *N. America.* The Baneberry has short, blunt spikes of creamy white flowers, appearing above the handsome aruncus-like foliage in spring, and by late summer develop heads of snowy white berries — which are poisonous. Likes good soil in shade .. ..

Aethionema

grandiflora. *Lebanon.* A sun lover, never happier than when cascading from a dry wall where in early summer it flaunts its 3 inch spikes of bloom – deep pink at their tips and paler below. 6–8 inches .. ..

pulchellum. *Asia Minor.* Rounded shell-pink flower-heads lavishly produced in early summer above heath-like steel-blue leaves. For any sunny position, but specially good on dry walls. 9 inches ..

Warley Rose. Deservedly a most popular plant with neat bushy habit, small glaucous-grey leaves and many heads of bright rosy blooms in spring and summer. For walls or any sunny spot. 6 inches .. ..

Ajuga

reptans Delightful. This and the two which follow are gay strong-growing ground-cover plants for the front of the border or any part of the garden that needs to be brightened up with little trouble. The 6 inch blue flower spikes are pretty but not very important; Ajugas are primarily foliage plants. *A. r. Delightful* is a new variety with bronze and gold leaves washed over with pink to give a most original effect. .

reptans metallica. A striking form whose crinkled prostrate leaves are highly glossed and beetroot-red .. ..

reptans Rainbow. The glossy bronze-purple leaves are splashed at various times of the year with gold, pink and green .. ..

Alchemilla

mollis. *Asia Minor.* Beautiful and adaptable herbaceous plant growing in almost any soil in sun or shade. Forms a 2 foot mound of rounded, scolloped and toothed leaves of softest grey-green, which hold raindrops like a handful of diamonds. The feathery plumes of lime-green flowers appear in summer. Invaluable as ground cover and indispensable to flower arrangers. 12–15 inches ..

Allium

beesianum. *Yunnan, etc.* Towards the end of summer, 6 inch stems carry pendent heads of soft wedgwood-blue flowers just above the narrow upright foliage. An easy, charming plant for any sunny position ..

cernuum. *East U.S.A.* A specially good form of this easy and attractive plant which gained an R.H.S. Award of Merit. The pendent heads of rosy purple bells are carried gracefully amongst the flattened rush-like leaves. Any sunny soil. 8–10 inches .. ..

ALLIUM—continued

flavum. *S. Eur. Caucasus.* A useful summer flowerer, with slender 8–10 inch stems, bearing umbels of many primrose-yellow bells. Adaptable to any sunny soil

narcissiflora. *Caucasus, etc.* Perhaps the most beautiful of the family with elegant pendant 1 inch-long bells of rosy red, carried on 6 inch stems. Likes a sunny well-drained soil and may take a year or two to get into full production

pulchellum. *Mediterranean.* The long-persisting crimson-maroon flowers are carried on wiry 18 inch stems in mid and late summer. Easily grown, unusual and attractive

pulchellum nanum. A new charmer, only 4–5 inches high, with small clustered heads of blooms of an unusual soft amethyst colour

sikkimense. *N. India.* The little nodding heads of sky-blue flowers swing just above the small tufts of narrow tubular leaves. Small enough and very attractive in a trough garden. 5–6 inches

Alstroemeria

ligtu Hybrids. Do not fail to turn to page 2 for description of these lovely plants. £2·00 for 10, £9·00 for 50, £17·00 for 100.
Carriage and packing extra.

Alyssum

montanum. *Europe.* An easy-going sun lover which forms rounded foot-wide mounds of very small ash-grey leaves, and in early spring bears heads of bright yellow flowers. 6–8 inches

serpyllifolia. *Mt. Cenis, etc.* The tiny thyme-like leaves form a miniature silver carpet, less than an inch high; the little rounded heads of golden flowers appear in spring. For a sunny scree or trough garden

troodii. A rare endemic from the screes and crevices in the highest parts of the Troodos Mountains of Cyprus. Forms a low rounded bushlet covered in tiny silver leaves and rounded yellow flower heads in spring. For a sunny scree or trough. 4–5 inches .. .. ..

Anacyclus

depressus. *Morocco.* From the central tuft of greyish, finely cut ferny leaves many prostrate stems radiate in early summer, each bearing several inch-wide daisy flowers. Wide open they are snowy white, closed at dusk the crimson reverse is shown. It likes full sun and good drainage

Anchusa

caespitosa. *Endemic to Crete,* where it inhabits rocky parts of the high White Mountains. Forms a flat rosette of narrow bristly leaves in the centre of which nestle the stemless flowers of brilliant deep blue. Grow in a gritty soil in the alpine house, or outdoors in a sunny scree

Androsace

arachnoidea superba. The neat half-inch rosettes, greyish and furry, are hidden in spring under the clustered heads of snowy flowers on inch-high stems. Each bloom opens with a small yellow eye which turns to crimson after a few days. A bewitching plant that, given sun and good drainage, grows and flowers willingly in scree, trough garden or alpine house. 1–2 inches ..

jacquemontii. *Himalayas.* A recent introduction which is rather like a dwarf *A. sarmentosa,* with grey woolly leaf-rosettes and heads of bloom of an unusual lavender-pink. A valuable and distinct addition to the family, which has proved hardy and free flowering in a well-drained sunny scree. An excellent alpine house plant also. 2–3 inches

jacquemontii Pink Form. An exact counterpart of the type but with flowers of deep rose-pink. Award of Merit R.H.S. .. .. ..

ANDROSACE—continued

lanuginosa. *Himalayas.* Trailing stems with brilliantly silvery leaves and heads of pink, crimson-eyed flowers over a long period of summer and autumn. A splendid plant of easy culture if given a sunny raised position where it can indulge its trailing habit. 6 inches

lanuginosa Wisley. A distinct new form whose flowers show a decided lavender flush

sarmentosa sherriffii. *Himalayas* A newcomer, less hairy in the leaf than most of the *sarmentosa* group, hence less vulnerable to winter damp. A vigorous grower and free flowerer it enjoys a sunny, well-drained ledge or scree. 3–4 inches

sarmentosa yunnanensis. *Yunnan.* The finest of this group, which likes very sharp drainage in a sunny place. The heads of deep rose-coloured flowers are carried in 3 inch stems above the intensely woolly leaf rosettes

sempervivoides. *Himalayas.* Small, neat, emerald leaf rosettes and compact little heads of bright pink blooms in early summer. Attractive and accommodating in scree or trough garden. 2–3 inches .. ..

villosa. *Alps of Europe and Asia.* A miniature charmer for sunny scree, well-drained trough or alpine house. Close tufts of downy leaves and 1 inch-high stems, each bearing six to eight snow-white flowers in April–May

villosa taurica. A distinct form from the garden of that most generous of gardeners, the late E. B. Anderson. Each leaf is noticeably needle-pointed and a week or so after opening the central ring of crimson on each flower spreads into the whites of the petals. 1–2 inches .. ..

Anemone

magellanica major. *S. America.* An easy and useful plant for almost any sunny soil. The basal leaves are slightly hairy and much divided. From early summer on, upright 1 foot-high stems carry creamy white flowers 1 inch or more across

narcissiflora. *Europe, Asia, and N. America.* From the basal clump of lobed leaves arise 15 inch stems, each bearing a many-flowered cluster of white, pink-flushed flowers, backed by a ruff of smaller leaves. A pretty plant of wide alpine distribution; as a garden plant it enjoys a well-drained loam in full sun .. ..

Antennaria

dioica rubra. A neat non-invasive carpeter to fill a sunny pocket with a close mat of small silvery grey leaves. The bunched heads of reddish flowers appear in late spring on 3–4 inch stems .. ..

Anthemis

rudolphiana. Brilliantly silver leaves of filigree fineness and 1 inch-wide rayed flowers of rich gold. A most attractive plant, which is easy and hardy in any sunny position. 6–8 inches .. .. ..

Anthyllis

montana rubra. Forms mats of small grey fern-like leaves and in summer has many deep crimson clover-like flower-heads. Enjoys life in any sunny spot. 2–3 inches .. ..

Aquilegia

einseliana. *Italy, France.* An unusual plant with darkish greyish leaves, contrasting nicely with the deep blue, almost dusky, flowers. Any good sunny soil suits it. 8 inches

bertolonii. *European Alps.* An engaging miniature whose rich sapphire blooms are borne, singly or in pairs, on 3 inch stems in early summer. For a sunny pocket in the rock garden or enchanting in a trough garden

Alpine Windflower.

Arabis

albida variegata. A gay flamboyant plant whose light green leaves are vigorously splashed with gold. A strong grower for use as a border edging, on a dry wall or anywhere else that needs year-round brightening

ferdinandi-coburgi variegata. Recently introduced plant of great charm which slowly forms a neat 1 foot-wide hummock of close-packed rosettes, each inch-long leaf being irregularly bordered with creamy gold to give a most striking effect. The 4 inch stems of white flowers are of little beauty and no importance. In 1972 it received the unusual distinction of being given an Award of Merit by the R.H.S. as a foliage plant for the rock garden . . . .

Arenaria

purpurascens Elliott's Var. A distinct form my father and I discovered in the Canatabrian Mountains of Spain, whose small starry flowers are a clear clean pink. It likes full sun and good drainage and is never invasive, but slowly forms a close carpet of small heath-like leaves. Excellent in troughs . . . .

Armeria

caespitosa. Spain. A very dwarf Thrift, making small dense pincushions of narrow, glossy, dark green leaves and bearing rounded heads of soft pink flowers on 1 inch stems. Well suited in a sunny scree or trough, or in the alpine house. 2–3 inches . . . . . .

Artemisia

lanata. Mts. of S. and Cent. Europe. The small leaves cut to needle fineness form a 1 inch-high carpet of brilliant silver. Quite outstanding if given full sun and sharp drainage. Given time it will spread to a couple of feet across . . . .

Arum

italicum pictum. The arrow-shaped leaves of deep glossy green are exquisitely marbled over their entire surface with yellowish white. They die down during summer, to reappear in autumn and remain uniquely handsome throughout winter and spring. Prefers a moist soil and is tolerant of shade. A flower arranger's 'must'. 9 inches . .

Aster

alpinus Elliott's Var. A fine form of this typical alpine pasture plant, which my father collected many years ago at Mont Cenis. Each 6 inch stem carries a full-petalled 2 inch daisy flower of deep lavender, enriched by a central disc of intense orange. Grows happily in any good sunny loam . . . .

Astrantia

Margery Fish. It seems appropriate to give this good plant the name of the great gardener and dear person (now, sadly, no longer with us) from whom it originally came to me. Each 1 inch-wide creamy flower cluster is cupped in applegreen bracts, to give the effect of a miniature Victorian posy. Many of these flowers are borne on branching 18–24 inch stems. An easy plant in any soil, sun or shade . . . . . .

Berberis

corallina compacta. An enchanting miniature, seldom reaching more than 12 inches. The small glossy leaves are spiny and evergreen, and the whole plant smothers itself in early summer with a mass of glowing orange flowers, often producing a second smaller crop of blooms in autumn . . . .

Carduncellus

mitissimus. France, Spain. Of mildly running habit, it will fill a sunny pocket of well-drained soil with its 3 inch rosettes of dark cut leaves, and produce its stemless lavender-blue, thistle-like flowers in June. 3–4 inches . . . .

Carex

firma variegata. A most original and intruiging miniature grass, forming tightly packed tufts of 1 inch-long leaves, firm, rigid and tapering, each one bordered with a gold line. The whole effect is most striking. So far it has thrived here in a gritty soil that is not too dry and is in half shade. Probably best divided up every other year or so. R.H.S. Award of Merit, 1972, as a foliage plant for the rock garden . .

Chamaecyparis

pisifera 'Boulevard'. A beautiful slow-growing conifer forming an irregularly rounded plant of the most intense silvery blue-grey. It colours best in semi-shade with the lime content of the soil reduced to a minimum. Young pot-grown plants . . . . . .

Chrysanthemum

haradjanii. A new introduction, previously listed under the name Achilea P.D. 16366, which is invaluable as a foliage plant. Each leaf is like a silvery white, finely cut miniature fern, and might be the exquisite work of a silversmith. It will spread to a 1 foot-wide clump and is perfectly hardy on a well-drained ledge in full sun. The few yellow flowers are of little account. 3–4 inches. . . . .

Cortusa

matthiolii. Mts. of Europe and Asia. A natural woodlander for a shady peaty spot where the new leaves appear in spring, rounded, lobed and softly hairy. The umbels of pendent reddish purple flowers are carried on 6–10 inch stems in early summer . . . .

Cotoneaster

congesta nana. This name may not be valid but describes well this very dwarf plant, which forms congested and absolutely prostrate mats of twigs covered with tiny rounded evergreen leaves. It is an excellent miniature ground cover or will hug every contour of any rock it is planted near . . . .

Cotyledon

simplicifolia. Caucasus. An easy and attractive plant anywhere; particularly effective on a dry wall and tolerant of both sun and shade. The 3 inch catkins of golden flowers swing above the fleshy leaves – which are apple-green all summer, turning to bronze in autumn . .

Crepis

pygmaea foliis-purpureis. A plant I discovered in a stony river-bed scree in the Pyrenees; so far its identity has not positively established. The spoon-shaped leaves form flat 4 inch rosettes, their colour an unusual purplish-bronze, bloomed like a grape. The flowers are crimson in bud, primrose-yellow when opened, and are carried singly on 2 inch stems. The plant must have the poorest stony scree; in anything richer it tends to lose its character . . . .

Cyananthus

integer. N. India. (syn. C. microphyllus). An autumn-flowering charmer for a leafy, gritty soil. The radiating prostrate stems, clothed in bronzy wedge-shaped leaves, each end in an upturned starry flower of clear periwinkle-blue. 2–3 inches . . . . .

Brachycome

rigidula. Australia. A newcomer of some charm which forms a low, foot-wide mat of distinct, glossy, pale green, much divided leaves and carries a summer-and-autumn-long succession of little lavender-coloured daisy flowers on 3–4 inch stems. It seems perfectly hardy here in a sunny well-drained soil . . . . . .

Buxus

microphylla. Japan. A dwarf Box said to reach 3–4 feet in time, though my oldest plant, now more than ten years old and in fairly good soil, is still no more than 12 inches high and about as much through. The small glossy evergreen leaves take on varying tints with the seasons

Calceolaria

darwinii. Str. of Magellan. Growing wild in such a wind- and rain-swept region this little plant needs a soil with plenty of humus that is constantly moist but well drained, and sheltered from the full sun. Here with care it will make an inch-high mat of its glossy leaves and carry its absurdly large flowers on stems just long enough to clear them of the ground. The baggy blooms are of deep mahogany and gold, with a curious snow-white waxy lip across the mouth. An unusual and engaging plant with a keen sense of the ridiculous . . . . .

Campanula

arvatica. N. Spain. A charming miniature making a carpet of tiny ivy-shaped leaves in a scree or crevice and carrying its many star-shaped flowers of violet-blue on frail 1 inch-high stems in June and July. Perfect in a trough . .

carpatica Bressingham White. A beautiful and dependable plant, producing its massive show of 2 inch snow-white saucer-shaped flowers in mid and late summer. 6–8 inches.

garganica. Italy, etc. Ideal plant for a wall garden or any sunny pocket, where the prostrate stems are wreathed in light blue star-shaped flowers in June and July. 3–4 inches

Mist Maiden. An unusual and beautiful plant; from the basal mass of finely cut ash-grey leaves a forest of 8–10 inch stems arise, bearing many fairy bells of purest white. Happy and vigorous, though not invasive, in almost any sunny spot . . . .

Molly Pinsent. Of tufted habit, forming a rounded plant 6–8 inches high; the leaves slightly bronzed and the open bell-shaped flowers 1 inch across of soft lavender. Vigorous and free flowering . . . .

morettiana. E. European Alps. I have a limited stock only of this rare and challenging beauty. It is essentially a plant for the alpine house, where in a gritty, limy soil it forms tufts of small hairy leaves, from which radiate the prostrate stems, each bearing a single upturned bell of glowing violet-blue in late summer and autumn . . . . .

muralis major (syn C. portenschlagiana major). A most accommodating and beautiful plant, which produces a summer-long succession of upturned violet bells in almost any soil or situation. 6–8 inches . .

nitida alba. The leaves are of deepest glossy green, curiously crimped at their edges and gathered into flat 2 inch rosettes. Each 6 inch flower spike bears four or more 1 inch-wide saucer-shaped blooms of an intense white in June. Unlike any other . . . .

pilosa superba. Japan. Two-inch rosettes of distinct glossy leaves and upright funnel-shaped blooms of violet-blue from June onwards. Excellent in scree, trough or alpine house. It has a running, but by no means invasive, habit. 2 inches . . . . . .

BRIZOPYRUM SICULUM.

STIPA PENNATA.

—Alpine plants established on old fort wall.

Cytisus

ardoinii. *Maritime Alps.* A gay miniature Broom, forming a 6 inch forest of greyish stems and leaves, smothered in spring in a glowing mass of golden blooms. Will spread to 1 foot or 2 feet across, in any light, sunny soil

decumbens. Forms a 1 foot-wide tangle of deep green stems flat on the ground; the tiny leaves are barely noticeable but not so the deep gold Broom flowers, which cover the plant in early summer. Likes full sun. 1–2 inches

Dianthus

alpinus. *Austrian Alps.* Close packed glistening green leaves and inch-wide bright rose blooms with speckled centres; for sunny limestone scree or trough. 3 inches

alpinus Joan's Blood. An astonishing form with flowers of deepest blood-red.

Ariel. Tufts of needle-like grey-green leaves and singly richly scented flowers of bright crimson-cerise. 4–5 inches

× arvenensis. Arching 3 inch stems carry the little, single, scented, pink blooms above a flat carpet of small, close-packed, grey leaves. Excellent for any small sunny pocket or spilling over the edge of a trough

caesius plenus. Dwarf and compact mats of silvery grey leaves and a profusion of well-scented, semi-double flowers of clear pink. Excellent for walls, paving, or anywhere else in the garden. 6 inches

deltoides Wisley Var. A striking form of the Maiden Pink, with deep bronze leaves and a thousand tiny blooms of deepest crimson. For walls, paving, etc. 6 inches

Hidcote. A first-rate dwarf which spreads into dense, foot-wide mats of intense silver-grey leaves and carries its small crimson flowers on 4–5 inch stems

Janet Walker. A grand little hybrid of *D. caesius* which I first introduced some years ago, forming close mats of silvery grey leaves and producing an almost continuous summer succession of single, scented, deep pink blooms on 2–3 inch stems

La Bourbille. Forms a tight slow-growing mat of silvery grey leaves. The freely produced pink flowers are scented and carried on 2–3 inch stems in summer. Restrained enough to spill discreetly over the side of a trough garden or happy in a sunny pocket or scree

microlepis (syn. *D. musalae*). *Bulgaria.* A choice rare species making tight round buns of needle leaves, hidden in late spring by the almost stemless pink blooms. Ideal in habit and size for the trough garden, though happy elsewhere in a very gritty limy soil. 1–2 inches high; 3–4 inches across – in time

Oakington Hybrid. A fine dwarf variety with freely produced double blooms of deep warm rose and good grey 'grass'. Enjoys life in any sunny position. 6–8 inches

Pike's Pink. A very neat little job, with large double scented blooms of warm pink. on 3 inch stems

Waithman's Beauty. A most distinct variety with single scented flowers of deep ruby-crimson, each petal having a white 'snow flake' in its centre. 6–8 inches

Diascia

cordata. *Basutoland.* An invaluable newcomer, which in spite of its native habitat has proved completely hardy here in a sunny well-drained soil. It forms a 1 inch-high mat of rounded glossy leaves and for most of the summer throws up a succession of 6 inch stems, each bearing five or six rounded twin-spurred flowers of an unusual tangerine-pink

Ruby Field. A fine new hybrid (*D. cordata × D. barberae*) akin to *cordata* in general habit, but with larger flowers of a deeper colour. It has proved hardy here without protection for the past three years, and has flowered even more freely and for longer than its parent

Dimorphotheca

barbariae compacta. *S. Africa.* The dark centred, rich pink daisy flowers are borne in continuous succession from summer to late autumn, above the dark green aromatic leaves. For the larger rock garden or border front. Hardy. 10–15 inches

Douglasia

laevigata ciliata. A form of this Western American high alpine, as yet unflowered here, said to have large flowers of the deepest, richest pink. Grow in the alpine house or in a selected pocket outdoors in a peaty gritty soil. 2–3 inches

vitaliana praetutiana. The free-flowering form of this tufted silvery leaved ally of the Androsaces, with a mass of small golden flowers in spring. Enjoys life best in a sunny scree or trough. 1–2 inches

Draba

aizoides. *Eur. Alps.* Forms 1 inch-wide rosettes of deep green, bristle-tipped leaves and bears 3 inch stems of golden flowers in April. Easy and adaptable in any sunny soil in the rock garden or trough

bryoides imbricata. *Caucasus.* In earliest spring the tiny close-packed rosettes turn the most vivid emerald; the little golden blooms are held on 1 inch-long threads. A compliant jewel for screen, trough, or alpine-house

Dryas

octopetala. *Mts. of Eur. and N. America.* An invaluable evergreen carpeting or trailing plant, eventually forming a yard-wide mat of 1 inch-long oval glossy leaves. The creamy white anemone-like flowers are followed by attractive fluffy seed-heads. For a sunny position almost anywhere. 4–5 inches

octopetala minor. An exact counterpart of the type plant with all its parts reduced in size by half. Specially useful draping itself in a curtain over the side of a trough garden but equally suitable elsewhere when space is limited. 2–3 inches

× sundermannii major. A splendid hybrid with much the same habit as *D. octopetala* but with freely produced flowers matching the richest Jersey cream in colour

---

Epilobium

Broadwell Hybrid. This occurred here as a spontaneous hybrid between *E. glabellum* and *E. kai-koense* and is intermediate between the two in almost all respects. The glossy leaves show signs of bronzing with age; the 6–7 inch stems bear a summer-long succession of creamy funnel-shaped flowers flushed with pink. An easy and long-flowering plant

glabellum. *New Zealand.* Upright stems 1 foot or so high, clothed in glossy leaves varying from green to bronze, and a summer-long succession of milky white flowers. Pretty, easy and non-invasive

glabellum sulphureum. An excellent form with greener leaves and flowers of soft sulphur-yellow

Erinus

alpinus Dr. Hanele. Surely amongst the dozen best alpines, with its little spikes of brilliant crimson. Will sow itself about on mossy rocks and in crevices without ever becoming a nuisance. 3 inches

alpinus Mrs. Boyle. A very pretty form with flowers of deep pink. 3 inches

Eriophyllum

lanatum (syn. *E. caespitosum*). *N.W. America.* A vigorous plant for any sunny well-drained soil, quickly forming a foot-wide patch of low, much divided, silvery leaves. The deep gold daisy flowers remain for several weeks in the spring

Erodium

chamaedryoides album. Exactly similar to *roseum* except that the flowers are white, delicately criss-crossed with crimson veins

chamaedryoides roseum. From spring to autumn this charming little plant gives an almost continuous succession of its rosy blooms over the tufts of small scalloped leaves. Enjoys life in any sunny corner of the rock garden or trough. 1–2 inches

Erysimum

Sprite. A charming dwarf Wallflower that came to me unnamed; its diminutive size and cheerful gaiety suggested *Sprite* as an appropriate name. Its narrow deep green leaves make a carpet only 2 inches high and for several weeks in spring comes a succession of 3 inch soft primrose flower spikes. It has proved itself hardy, perennial and quite captivating in a sunny limey soil

Euryops

acraeus. *Basutoland.* Previously known, and offered here, as *E. evansii*. An invaluable dwarf shrub which has now proved itself indisputably hardy in all parts of the country. It forms a low rounded bush 12 or 18 inches across, covered in narrow evergreen leaves of brilliant silver. Though primarily a foliage plant, the freely produced golden flowers in early summer are most attractive. It thrives on almost any sunny spot

Festuca

glauca. A tufted non-invasive grass forming a 9 inch fountain of narrow leaves of intense blue-grey. Most decorative

Genista

tinctoria fl. pl. The double form of our native Dyer's Green Weed. It forms a neat wiry stemmed 1 foot-high bush and is smothered in early summer with 2 inch spikes of the gayest golden blooms. Give it full sun

TRYCHOLÆNA ROSEA.

BRIZA MAXIMA.

Gentiana

acaulis. *Europe.* The immortal Gentianella of gardens. Huge deep sapphire trumpets, freckled and striped with emerald in the throat. This glorious Gentian is *not* a lime hater and should be tried in every garden. 2–3 inches

asclepiadea. *Europe.* The Willow Gentian, which is happiest with some shade in a soil that is not too dry. The leaves are borne in pairs up the gently arching 18–24 inch stems; the deep blue trumpet flowers come in August in the axils of the leaves on the upper half of the stem

clusii. The form of *G. acaulis* usually found on limestone formations in the East European Alps. The leaves are more pointed than 'garden *acaulis*' and the trumpet flowers shorter and of deep sky-blue, spotted with green inside. It may well grow and bloom where garden *acaulis*' fails

farreri. *N.W. China.* Quite one of the most beautiful members in a family of famous beauties and with the very great advantage amongst the Asiatic Gentians of being tolerant of lime. Here in the limy Cotswolds it grows in the ordinary garden loam perfectly happily if some peat is added at planting time. All it asks is moisture during the growing season, good drainage — and a year to establish itself. In early spring the central winter rosettes begin to lengthen and form a mass of narrow bright green leaves; then in August and on into autumn come the trumpet blooms of intense cambridge-blue shading to white inside the throat and pencilled on the outside with delicate lines of olive-green. 3–4 inches

lutea. *Alps of Eur. and Asia.* The giant of the family, with extremely handsome deeply ribbed leaves up to 1 foot in length. It takes several years to reach maturity, the flower spikes, when they appear, reach 4–5 feet, with yellow blooms carried in whorls up their length. It likes a good deep soil in full sun

saxosa. *New Zealand.* Quite untypical of the family, this intriguing plant has narrow bronzy leaves which are almost fleshy, and rounded veined flowers of creamy white carried on 1–3 inch stems. It likes an open gritty soil in sun, and always attracts attention when it flowers in mid to late summer

septemfida. *Asia Minor.* A plant with the greatest anxiety to please, thriving in almost any soil or situation, and always giving abundantly of its handsome heads of bright blue trumpets in August. 8–10 inches

verna angulosa. *Europe and Asia.* A particular speciality of this nursery and surely one of the most exquisite and satisfying of all alpines, with its brilliant stars of almost unbelievably vivid deep blue. It is not a difficult plant provided it is given a few essentials: an open sunny position, sharp drainage without ever being dry, and a rich diet, including a good portion of leafmould or peat and some well-rotted cow manure. If you start with vigorous *young* plants — which I supply — and give them these conditions, they will thrive and give immense joy. 2 inches

Geranium

cinereum. *Pyrenees.* A beautiful and rare species with rounded, soft grey, deeply indented leaves and with inch-wide blooms of pink, strikingly veined with crimson. For a sunny scree or the alpine house. 4–6 inches

dalmaticum. *Dalmatia.* An easy and beautiful plant, quickly forming tufts of round glossy leaves, which often take on brilliant autumn tints. In late spring starts a succession of beautifully formed flowers of rich glowing pink. Apparently quite without fads, it thrives in any open sunny situation. 4–5 inches

subcaulescens splendens. Of low tufted habit, smothered for most of the summer with inch-wide blooms of bright crimson-magenta. Pays vivid rent in any sunny, well-drained soil

Glaucium

phoeniceum. *Asia Minor.* An extremely handsome foliage plant, which has proved itself both hardy and perennial here. The 1 foot-wide starfish rosettes are made up of long narrow leaves curiously cut and indented, and covered with a thick felty hairyness of brilliant silvery whiteness. The sparsely branched flower stems bear poppy-like blooms of orange-scarlet during the summer. It seems to enjoy all the sun it can be given

Globularia

cordifolia. *Eur. and W. Asia.* Forms a network of fine woody stems, matted over with 1 inch-long spoon-shaped, deep green, glossy leaves. The little rounded balls of blue flowers are carried on 2 inch stems in early summer. An easy useful carpeter of any sunny well-drained soil

Gypsophila

dubia. Forms an attractive prostrate mat of bronzy grey leaves and has a long succession of small pink flowers in summer and autumn. An easy accommodating plant, equally well suited on the flat or in a wall. It enjoys sun

Haberlea

rhodopensis. *Greece.* A handsome plant that must have deep shade and sufficient moisture, where it will form a mound of its deep green leathery leaf rosettes. The many sprays of flowers — like small lavender yellow-throated Gloxinias, come in early summer. 5–6 inches

Haplopappus

coronopifolius. *S. America.* A useful and handsome summer bloomer, forming a low mound of small, dark green indented leaves. The deep gold daisy flowers 1 inch across are carried on 6 inch stems from midsummer onwards. Enjoys full sun and resists drought

Hebe

Carl Teschner. A valuable new dwarf shrub which received an R.H.S. Award of Merit in 1965. Growing only 5 or 6 inches high, its wiry stems are clothed in small, oval glossy leaves, and each stem produces in summer a tapered spike of soft lavender flowers. Its compact habit and freedom of flower make it ideal rock garden shrub

darwiniana variegata. An airy and elegant dwarf evergreen shrub whose myriad of small pointed leaves are brightly variegated. 2–3 feet

pimelioides glauca. Another excellent dwarf shrub with slender deep brown stems, clothed in little oval strikingly blue-grey leaves. The tapered spikes of densely packed lavender-blue flowers appear freely from midsummer on. 8–10 inches

Hedera

conglomerata. An intriguing non-climbing dwarf Ivy, which forms gnarled congested hummocks of glossy deep green leaves attractively veined. 6–8 inches

conglomerata erecta. A form in which the stems grow rigidly upright to a height of 12–15 inches, with the close-packed leaves arranged in two planes with uncanny symmetry

Helianthemum

alpestre serpyllifolium. *S. Europe.* A miniature Rock Rose, hugging the ground with a close mat of small, oval greyish leaves, and giving a long succession of golden blooms. 1 inch

lunulatum. *Italy.* Forms a neat grey-leaved shrub 6 or 8 inches high, and covers itself all summer with little round yellow blooms the size of a ½p. Enjoys a sunny position

oblongatum. The miniature of the family, with short red-brown creeping stems clothed in glossy ¼ inch leaves and many small flowers of rich gold, the whole plant rising barely 1 inch above the ground. Ideal spilling over the side of a trough or in a sunny pocket

---

The following are better known as Rock Roses or Sun Roses:

Alice Howorth. A newcomer, first offered from this nursery a few years ago and already established as a favourite. The long succession of blooms are large, fully double and of a most unusual and attractive mulberry-crimson. The leaves are dark green and glossy

Amy Baring. A more prostrate grower with flowers of rich eggyolk-gold. 3–4 inches

Ben Mohr. Fine variety with flowers of burnished copper colour

Gaiety. A sport from *H. Mrs. Earle*, which cropped up here. The flowers are the same but the leaves are paler and edged with gold. The effect is pleasing throughout the year

Jubilee. Glossy leaves and fully double flowers of rich gold

Mrs. Earle. Companion of *Jubilee* with double brick-crimson flowers

Sudbury Gem. Neat grey leaves and nice rose flame-centred flowers

The Bride. Grey leaves and snow-white golden-centred flowers

Watergate Rose. Inaptly named for the blooms are rich deep crimson. Recommended

Wisley Pink. Greyish leaves and soft pink flowers; vigorous and free flowering

Wisley Primrose. A lovely combination of soft grey leafage and gentle primrose flowers

Helichrysum

coralloides. *New Zealand.* A unique and intriguing plants whose tiny, glossy, evergreen, scale-like leaves are pressed close to the stems to give a snake-skin effect. It forms a dense much-branched bushlet, eventually 8–10 inches high and through, and has proved absolutely hardy here in a variety of sunny situations

milfordiae. *Basutoland.* This is the plant that has been known and grown as *H. marginatum* — wrongly, it now appears — since its introduction just before the war. In a light well-drained soil and full sun it is perfectly hardy and spreads into a wide mat of brilliantly silver rosettes, on which dew and raindrops glisten like diamonds. The crimson and white everlasting flowers come more freely when the plant is starved. 2 inches

Helleborus

corsicus. *Corsica, etc.* A plant of truly noble stature to be grown in a deep rich loam in a sheltered position. The blue-green leathery leaves, down-curved and spiny edged, rise to a height 18–24 inches, and are handsome throughout the year. The massive twenty to thirty flowered panicles of greenish yellow flowers unfold in late winter or earliest spring, according to the season and position. Young plants from pots

foetidus. Wonderfully handsome winter-flowering plant, forming a pyramid whose base is formed by the narrow leaves of darkest green, the apex by the gradually expanding flower spike of palest citron; the contrast is most striking. It likes to be out of the sun and when happy will seed itself quite freely. 24 inches

niger Potter's Wheel. This astonishing form of the Christmas Rose created a stir when it was first publicly shown in 1958 and was given an immediate Award of Merit by the R.H.S. Discovered in a garden in the Potteries district, its name is doubly apt, for the blooms are of immense size, often up to 4 inches across. They are of showy whiteness and borne on stout stems 6 or more inches long. Like the rest of the family it likes a deep well-nourished soil, shaded from the hot sun. Young pot-grown plants are offered for growing on

orientalis. A mixed race of the handsome Lenten Lily, whose colours embrace whites, creams and lime-greens to pinks and deep crimson. As they are sold as well-established plants before their first flowering, no guarantee can be given as to the colours you will receive, but they are all decorative and free flowering, and will tolerate a shady corner if asked. The old leaves are best cut to ground level as soon as the buds can be seen emerging in the spring. 1–2 feet

Granite tor.

Hieraceum

waldsteinii. A beautiful foliage plant of easy culture, whose oval pointed leaves are heavily felted in brilliant silvery grey. The 1 foot-high stems carry flowers of little importance and may be removed .. .. ..

Hypericum

coris. *S. Europe.* Forms a miniature shrub 6 inches high, clothed in small heath-like leaves and covered for most of the summer with 1 inch-wide golden flowers. Enjoys life in full sun .. ..

moserianum tricolor. A gaily attractive shrub of 2–3 feet, showily dressed in leaves of pink, gold and green. Can be badly cut in a really severe winter – so protect or propagate .. ..

olympicum. *S.E. Europe, etc.* Handsome and indispensable plant for summer bloom. Small glaucous-grey foliage and open 2 inch flowers of rich gold, filled with a mass of stamens. Easy and long flowering in any sunny position, and excellent on walls. 6–8 inches

olympicum aurantiaca. An engaging form in which the unopened buds are a rich bronzy orange colour .. ..

olympicum citrinum. A beautiful variant with flowers of soft primrose-yellow .. ..

Iberis

Little Gem. A neat dwarf perennial Candytuft forming a small rounded bushlet of dark glossy leaves and smothering itself in early summer with snowy white flowers. 6 inches .. ..

Incarvillea

delavayi Bee's Pink. Extremely handsome leaves, dark green glossy and divided; stout stems bearing great 3 inch trumpets of clear rose-pink. An unusual plant of great beauty for a deep, rich, well-drained soil. 8–10 inches .. ..

Iris

foetidissima variegata. This form of our native Gladwin is one of the handsomest of foliage plants, with its congested clumps of 2 feet leaves striped longitudinally in green and silver. Being evergreen it is just as striking – and even more welcome – in winter as it is in the summer. Will tolerate quite deep shade and moisture if asked, but is quite content in the front of a sunny border. Specially appreciated by flower arrangers. Open ground plants .. .. ..

Juniperus

communis compressa. The Noah's Ark Tree, growing an inch or less each year, to form a beautifully upright little column of evergreen blue-grey leaves .. ..

communis depressa aurea. Of low, slow-growing, spreading habit, the young twigs are richly gold-tinted in early summer. 10–12 inches by 3–4 feet eventually .. .. ..

Lavandula

Baby Blue. The smallest of all Lavenders, forming little grey-green bushes, authentically scented, 6–8 inches high, topped in summer by 3 inch spikes of flowers. It is happy in any sunny position suitable to its size

Leontopodium

alpinum. *Europe.* The inimitable Edelweiss of the Alps, with star-shaped flowers of white 'felt'. An amusing and perfectly easy plant to grow in any sunny well-drained soil. 6 inches .. ..

× **Mountain Song.** A new hybrid with very large flowers of immaculate whiteness, borne on 4–5 inch stems. The plants show some variation but all are good and easily grown in a sunny scree or crevice ..

Lewisia

nevadensis. *Western N. America.* Forms small rosettes of thick fleshy leaves and has wide-open, snow-white green-veined flowers – the whole plant no more than 1 inch high and 2–3 inches across. Probably safest in the alpine-house or frame, where it can be kept dry in winter .. ..

Pinkie. A charming hybrid with 3–4 inch rosettes of narrow fleshy leaves and an almost continuous succession of clear pink flowers, enhanced by crimson anthers, on short stems. For a gritty soil in the alpine house or a selected shady crevice outdoors. 3–4 inches

Trevosia. Believed to be a hybrid between *L. howellii* and *L. columbiana.* The 3–4 inch rosettes of narrow fleshy leaves and 6 inch stems bear many flowers in a subtle mixture of mulberry-orange and pinkish purple. An unusual plant happiest in the alpine-house or a carefully selected crevice facing north. Award of Merit, R.H.S., 1964 .. ..

Linum

flavum. For several weeks bears branched heads of sunshine-gold flowers above its neat mound of narrow grey-green leaves. Sun. 8–10 inches

Gemmell's Hybrid. Charming child of *L. elegans* and *L. flavum,* with trim rosettes of glaucous grey leaves and a succession of deep gold flowers in early summer. Likes a well-drained soil in full sun. 3–4 inches

narbonense. *S. Europe.* The lovely perennial Flax, giving a summer-long succession of shimmering blue. Full sun. 18–24 inches .. ..

salsaloides nanum. A charming miniature with thread-like stems hugging the ground and clothed in tiny greyish needle-shaped leaves. The funnel-shaped flowers of pearly opalescence appear on 1 inch-high stems in early summer. For scree or trough garden .. ..

Lithospermum

intermedium. An excellent dwarf, sun-loving, evergreen shrub, forming a rounded dome of narrow, 2 inch, grey-green leaves and producing many pendent clustered heads of deep rich blue flowers in summer. A lime lover which is happy in any position where maximum sun can strike it. 8–10 inches × 12–24 inches .. ..

oleifolium. *Pyrenees.* Another dwarf, sun and lime lover of low twiggy habit, with broad silver-grey leaves. The clusters of soft china-blue flowers come over a long summer period. When established it will increase by underground runners. 4–6 inches .. ..

Mertensia

pterocarpa. A plant of character and great beauty, native of the mountain woodlands of Japan. From the basal clump of elegant glaucous leaves arise a long succession of arching, foot-high stems bearing many pendent bells of sky-blue. It likes a fairly moist and leafy or peaty soil in semi-shade .. ..

Mimulus

Plymtree. In a moist or lightly shaded position few plants flower for a longer summer period. The trumpet-shaped flowers are an unusual and pleasing plum-crimson. 6–7 inches .. ..

Whitecroft Scarlet. A gay flamboyant plant which will romp away in a really moist soil, and grow in any soil that is not too dry. The trumpet-shaped flowers of burnished copper-scarlet appear over a long summer period on 6 inch stems .. .. ..

Nerine

bowdenii Fenwick's Var. An improved form of the loveliest of all hardy autumn-flowering bulbs, with deep pink, wavy petalled blooms on stout 18 inch stems in September and October. It enjoys life best with its back to a south or west wall, where it can roast in full sun all summer. The bulbs should be planted shallow with their necks barely covered. If frost threatens, buds cut and brought indoors will open fully in a few days. First Class Certificate, R.H.S.

× **Hera.** A magnificent hybrid of *N. bowdenii* with broader petalled flowers of rich, deep glowing pink. Raised between the wars it received an R.H.S. First Class Certificate, but has seldom been offered. It has inherited all *N. bowdenii's* hardiness and dependability and should by given the same treatment .. ..

Oenothera

glaber. A striking and distinct plant with erect 1 foot-high stems clothed in oval mahogany-red leaves. The flowers, which appear in early summer, in clustered heads, are rich golden yellow and before they open are enclosed in scarlet buds. The contrast of mahogany, scarlet and gold is most effective. Prefers a sunny soil that is not too dry

Origanum

laevigatum. *Asia Minor.* An exciting newcomer content for most of the year to remain a pleasant green carpet of small glossy leaves, and then erupting in late summer into a mass of wiry, much-branched stems 1 foot or so high, bearing many hundreds of tiny crimson-purple flowers. It is perfectly hardy and seems happy in any reasonably good soil .. ..

Oxalis

enneaphylla rosea. This attractive plant from the Falkland Isles thrives in a well-drained but not too poor soil, in an open sunny position. The curious grey leaves are folded and pleated like a miniature Toby ruff; the 1inch-wide funnel-shaped flowers of glowing pink nestle amongst them in early summer. 2 inches .. .. ..

Paeonia

mlokosewitschii. *Caucasus.* A strikingly beautiful and unusual plant, with broad-lobed leaves of fresh apple-green and delicately scented flowers fully 5 inches across, of clear primrose-yellow. The handsome seed heads split open in autumn to reveal the blueblack seeds resting in a bed of rich crimson. The plant enjoys life in any deep well-manured loam and will tolerate or even enjoy partial shade. 2–3 feet. Open ground plants, which will be sent out in autumn or early spring

Pentstemon

Garnet. A grand plant for the front or middle of the border, giving an endless succession of tapering spires or rich garnet-crimson flowers. Completely hardy. 2–2½ ft. .. .. ..

pinifolius. *Western U.S.A.* Bright green heath-like foliage and many narrow tubular flowers of brilliant orange-scarlet. Of recent introduction and great merit, it grows happily in any reasonably light soil. 6–8 inches .. ..

Pink Dragon. A new free-flowering hybrid of really good value, forming a low spreading bush, 4–5 inches high, clothed in darkish inch-long leaves and carrying many tubular flowers of light pink in early summer

roezlii. *Western U.S.A.* A most attractive dwarf, compact evergreen shrub, with small rounded leaves and a mass of brilliant red tubular flowers in May. Enjoys the sun and will eventually reach 9 inches by 12 inches, or thereabouts .. ..

scouleri. *N.W. America.* Forms a loose, 1 foot-high bush and has a long summer succession of quite large heads of soft lavender-pink flowers. A very lovely and too little grown species which is happy in any reasonably drained soil in full sun .. ..

What to Avoid.
Sketched in the Botanic Gardens, Regent's Park, 1872.

Phlox

douglasii Boothman's Var. Excellent variety smothered in cheeky lilac blooms with violet eyes. 3–4 inches ..

kelseyi Rosette. The unusual lilac-pink flowers are carried just above a dense and absolutely prostrate mat of leaves. Quite distinct. 2–3 inches

Norah Leigh. A very old herbaceous plant which, since its re-introduction to our gardens a few years ago, has created a great stir. The leaves are green in their centres and broadly and irregularly margined with silver to give an effect in the border which is quite outstanding. It gained an R.H.S. Award of Merit as a foliage plant. The pinkish flowers are of little importance. 3–3½ feet. Young pot-grown plants

subulata G. F. Wilson. An old variety and still a good one; of loose cascading growth, the flowers are of cool steely blue, with small dark centres. 5–6 inches

subulata Marjory. A good strong grower with flowers of good strong pink. 3–4 inches

subulata Oakington Blue Eyes. Makes a low mat of needle leaves and bears many late spring flowers of gentle sky-blue. 3–4 inches

Violet Seedling. A fine new free-flowering form with exceptionally deep coloured flowers. 3–4 inches.. .. ..

Phyteuma

comosum. *L. Garda, Dolomites, etc.* A rare limestone cliff dweller of strange and compelling beauty. Over the short-stemmed jagged-edged leaves are carried clustered heads of pale lilac flask-shaped blooms, each tapering to a deep purple tip through which the forked stigma protrudes. Grow in a gritty, limy soil in the alpine house or cold-frame, or in a sunny hole bored into tufa rock .. ..

Platycodon

apoyensis. *Japan.* A new introduction of great individuality; in effect a dwarf form of the better-known *P. grandiflora.* The erect stems, no more than 6 inches high and clothed in 1 inch-long, pointed glaucous leaves, each carry six or more balloon-like buds which open into large, open, five-pointed bowls of deep lavender-blue veined with purple, 2 inches across. It thrives here in good, well-drained loam in full sun. Care must be taken that slugs do not attack the fleshy roots during winter and early spring .. ..

Polygonum

tenuicaule. *Japan.* The carpet of pointed dark green leaves arises from the ground to form a striking background for the many 4 inch spikes of white flowers. A charming gently spreading plant for a semi-shady place, flowering in spring and early summer..

vaccinifolium. *Himalayas.* An invaluable late summer and autumn bloomer, producing a forest of 6 inch spikes of tightly packed pink flowers. Of spreading habit it is never happier than when cascading down a sunny wall .. ..

Potentilla

nitida rubra. A free-flowering form of this lovely high alpine cliff dweller, whose deep rose flowers are carried just above the brilliantly silver foliage. Must have a sunny crevice or scree, where winter moisture is quickly discharged. 1 inch

roxana. Strawberry-like leaves and trailing stems 1 foot or more long, bearing a long succession of flowers of great beauty in fiery orange-scarlet, shaded on the edges and enhanced by a central boss of black and yellow stamens ..

verna nana. This nice little plant forms concise mats of small palmate leaves and has a long succession of gay golden flowers on 1 inch-high stems. For a sunny pocket or trough..

Prunella

Loveliness. A distinct form of the handsome old *Prunella grandiflora,* which I collected in Spain. The large heads of hooded lavender-coloured flowers remain for a long summer period. Planted as a ground cover on the outskirts of the rock garden or as a border edging, it forms a mat of dark green leaves through which few weeds will penetrate. A mixed planting of this and the two varieties that follow is most effective

Pink Loveliness. Deep pink counterpart of *P. Loveliness*..

White Loveliness. Pure white form of *P. Pink Loveliness.* ..

Ptilotrichum

spinosum roseum (syn. *Alyssum spinosum roseum*). *France, Spain.* A rabid sun lover which forms a dense spiny dome, with small silvery grey leaves and inch-wide heads of pinky flowers in early summer. Ideal in or on a dry wall or planted in a sunny scree. 4–6 inches

Pulsatilla

vulgaris (syn. *Anemone pulsatilla*). *Europe.* The large goblet flowers emerge around Easter time, the inside purple, with a central boss of golden stamens, the outside paler and covered in golden down. The finely cut, ferny leaves appear just after the blooms ..

vulgaris Native Form. Seedlings (*not* collected plants, heaven forbid!) of our beautiful rare native Pasque Flower. It is dwarfer than most other forms with deep purple flowers. It likes a well-drained limey soil in full sun .. ..

vulgaris rubra. A distinct form with flowers of deep blood-red ..

Ramonda

myconii (syn *R. pyrenaica*). *Pyrenees.* An intriguing plant that needs a north-facing crevice filled with moisture-holding peat, where it will make a flat rosette, up to 6–8 inches across, of spoon-shaped leaves, deeply crinkled and ruggedly hairy. The leafless 4-inch flower stems appear in late spring and each bears three or more rounded reflexed blooms of crystaline lavender, with a central beak of orange stamens

Roscoea

cautlioides Kew Form. The magnificent Award of Merit form of this beautiful plant for a semi-shaded position in good soil. From the 1 foot-high fans of channelled glossy leaves come the spikes bearing several large hooded blooms, like some exotic orchid in soft primrose-yellow. Perfectly hardy but a late starter, often not appearing above ground till mid or late May ..

Salix

repens argentea. A small Willow, making a forest of 18 inch whippy stems on which small yellow catkins appear in spring, followed by ½ inch leaves of glistening silver

reticulata. An extremely slow-growing plant forming a prostrate network of angled glossy stems which bear 1 inch-long oval leaves, felted when young but later becoming polished and showing a fascinating mesh of veins. Red catkins stand 1 inch or so above the leaves in spring ..

retusa. *Cent. and E. Eur.* Slowly forms a much-branched, prostrate, self-rooting bushlet 6 inches or so high, with tiny pointed glossy leaves. The small catkins are mahogany-red before the yellow stamens appear

species Nepal. An unusual, new and as yet un-named plant which makes a useful ground cover. The prostrate trailing stems are clothed in inch-long, highly glossed, parallel-sided leaves. It is a rapid grower, rising only 2 or 3 inches above ground, and seems content with almost any soil

wehrhahnii. Spectacular shrub whose bare polished brown stems are wreathed with white catkins in early spring. May grow in time to 5 feet

SHRUBBY POTENTILLAS

The Shrubby Potentillas which follow are some of the dwarfer forms of a large group. They are invaluable plants for the larger rock garden, border front or anywhere else in the garden. Their nomenclature has been muddled, to say the least; the names that follow I believe to be correct at the present date.

arbuscula Kingdon Ward's Form. Of lax open habit with many summer flowers an inch or more across, of deep rich gold. Distinct by virtue of the large papery brown stipules which enclose the new growths and remain attached to the stems for several years

Elizabeth. Formerly known, and offered here, as *P. fruticosa arbuscula.* Probably the best garden value offered in this catalogue; no dwarf shrub could possibly offer a longer succession of beauty. In a couple of years it will spread into an open twiggy bush a foot or so high and maybe twice as much across. From spring till late autumn it will be covered — yes, *covered* — with large strawberry-like flowers of soft cool primrose. It seems able to adapt itself to almost any soil or situation

fruticosa algarvensis. The whippy upright stems reach 3 feet or so and are clothed in small shiny green leaves. For most of the summer there is a succession of pretty primrose-coloured flowers. A useful and accommodating small shrub where something a little taller than the other *fruticosa* varieties offered here is needed

fruticosa mandschurica. A pretty dwarf, usually less than a foot high, with greyish silver leaves and a long succession of white flowers ..

fruticosa nana argentea (syn. *P. f. beesii*). Another dwarf with striking silvery leaves and a generous number of deep gold flowers ..

fruticosa Sunset. With *P. f. Tangerine,* this plant constitutes a new colour break in the group. The freely produced flowers are fiery orange; the habit dwarfish and twiggy. 15–18 inches ..

fruticosa Tangerine. Of rather more spreading habit (2–3 feet by maybe 24 inches high), with many blooms of intriguing tawny orange. The plant grows quite happily in light shade and appears to hold its colour better in such a position .. ..

Primula

allionii Avalanche. A fine white form of this rare plant, which I raised here. The flowers are beautifully rounded and of good substance. *P. allionii* and its many forms can, as a rule, only be grown successfully in an alpine house or cold-frame, where overhead moisture can be controlled. It should be given a very sharply drained, limy soil with ½ inch of sharp grit round its vulnerable collar. Water amply but carefully during the growing season and minimally from October to February. A limited stock only ..

auricula. *Alps of Europe.* One of the original parents of a million hybrids and a captivating plant in its own right. The one-sided umbels of clear yellow, fragrant flowers are borne four to ten to each 2 inch stem over the 3 inch rosettes of rounded leathery leaves. Flowers, stems and leaves are lightly dusted with golden farina. Grow in a crevice or a peaty well-drained soil ..

auricula Alpine Triumph. A fine race of mixed seedlings with flowers in a subtle range of crimson, yellow, buff, etc., like shaded Victorian velvet

auricula Yellow Dusty Miller. A fine old plant whose leaves are dusted with golden meal. The nodding golden flowers brighten spring and are deliciously scented. Give it a cool well-nourished soil ..

clarkei. *Kashmir.* A diminutive jewel which brightens March with its cheeky flowers of brightest pink. It likes a moist but well-drained soil in half shade and is best lifted and divided every second or third year. 2 inches

suffrutescens. *California.* Makes trailing, almost woody stems clothed in glossy, blunt-tipped leaves and in early summer bears umbels of yellow-centred, deep rose coloured flowers. An unusual member of the family, which likes a gritty soil with plenty of peat. 3–4 inches ..

warshenewskiana. *Afghanistan.* A diminutive and still fairly new species which, given some shade and a light leafy or peaty soil, will produce its brilliant pink flowers in early spring at almost the same time as its small, oval, glossy leaves. It is unusual in the family in its habit of increasing by underground stolons, and is best lifted and divided every few years. 1–2 inches ..

What to Avoid.
Rustic Arch (after Loudon)

—Frontispiece of a book on alpine plants.

Santolina

chamaecyparissus Weston. A valuable dwarf form of Cotton Lavender which forms a densely packed dome of brilliant silver-white leaves no more than 5–6 inches high. Enjoys all the sun it can get and very sharp drainage. Award of Merit, R.H.S.. 1966 . . . . . .

Satureia

subspicata. An intriguing dwarf deciduous shrub, forming a rounded bush 6–8 inches high and 1 foot or so across, with narrow aromatic leaves. The mauve flowers borne on the tips of each stem are most welcome – opening as they do in late autumn . . . . . .

Saxifraga

KABSCHIA SECTION

This section of the family are dwarf slow-growing creatures, building themselves slowly into small dense hummocks of grey or green leaves and flowering with complete abandon in early spring. They are perfect plants for trough or miniature gardens; they are charming and at home in a scree or selected crevice in the rock garden, where they should be shielded from the hottest sun; and above all they are ideal plants for growing in pans in the alpine-house of cold-frame. They all like gritty limey soil.

apiculata. The easiest and strongest-growing of the group, forming close dense mounds of apple-green, with loose heads of primrose-yellow blooms. 4–5 inches . . . . . .

apiculata alba. White counterpart of its parent. Just as easy and useful

arco-valleyi alba. Forms a dense hard dome of close-packed leaves, on which the round white flowers sit almost stemlessly. 1–2 inches . .

boydii. Deep yellow, well rounded flowers and dark green leaf rosettes. Interesting as the first yellow hybrid *Kabschia* produced

burseriana crenata. On their inch-high red stems, the snowy white flowers have a beautifully waved and scolloped edge to their petals

burseriana major lutea. Very fine new form with large soft yellow blooms on crimson stems, produced with great freedom. The grey needle-leaves make a firm hard cushion. 2–3 inches . .

burseriana sulphurea. Rather smaller in all its parts with clear sulphur-yellow flowers. 2–3 inches . . . . . .

Cranbourne. One of the most satisfactory and beautiful with olive-green foliage and almost stemless deep pink blooms in great profusion. 1–2 inches . . . . . .

diapensioides lutea. Forms very slow-growing buns of grey-green, and bears several primrose-coloured flowers on each 2 inch stem. It is always the last of this group to flower – in April or early May . .

erythrantha. *Greece.* Another rare and distinct species with large firm rosettes of pale leaves, whose margins are beautifully encrusted with lime. The flowers, borne in heads, open white and turn to rose-pink. 4–5 inches . . . . . .

Faldonside. The finest yellow with large beautifully shaped blooms of a rich butter-yellow, carried singly on crimson stems. Neat and compact cushions of pearl-grey leaves. 2–3 inches . .

Grace Farwell. Firm hard cushions and short-stemmed flowers of an unusual cherry-red. 2 inches . .

Iris Prichard. Rather looser rosettes and several flowers of creamy apricot, borne on each 2 inch stem . . . . . .

jenkinsii. One of the very best; a good grower and prodigiously free flowerer, hiding its hard grey hummock of pointed leaves under a mass of clear shell-pink blooms. 2–3 inches . . . . . .

kellereri. One of the earliest of this group to flower, often starting to send up branched pink-brown stems in January. Small pink graceful flowers

lilacina. *W. Himalayas.* The little rounded flowers, carried singly ½ inch above the flattish domes of pale green leaves, are of a colour unique in the family, and best described as amethyst. This plant is often quoted as a lime hater, but it seems very content with my limey soil and water . . . . . .

Marie Louise. A lovely newcomer and the first of the section to flower; with the protection of an alpine-house the buds can often be seen forming by Christmas and the well-formed showy white blooms will uncurl from their red buds in January and February; outdoors they will come a week or two later. The leaf-rosettes are in handsome silvery grey. 3 inches

tombeanensis. Very choice slow-growing species; hard steel-grey domes and snow-white flowers of good texture. Rare. 2–3 inches . .

'SILVER' SECTION

The Silvers' are an essential part of every rock garden and most trough and wall gardens. They are happiest filling the crevices between rocks, where their gay plumes of flowers can spray outwards in spring and early summer. The squat masses of silver-frosted leaves give colour and beauty throughout the year.

aizoon baldensis. *Mt. Baldo.* The smallest of the group, with tiny frosted leaves forming flat carpets, and sprays of creamy flowers. 3–4 inches

aizoon rosea. Inch-wide rosettes of grey leaves and heads of pink flowers. Useful and dependable. 6 inches . .

burnatii. *Maritime Alps.* A natural hybrid between *S. aizoon* and *S. cochlearis.* Striking, silvery lime-beaded leaves, and loose sprays of white flowers on crimson stems. 4–5 inches . .

canis dalmatica. Grey-green incurved rosettes and 10 inch sprays of white flowers, heavily spotted with minute purple dots. A most original plant . .

cochlearis major. Humped domes of heavily encrusted silvery leaves, and white flowers on reddish stems. 6 inches . .

cochlearis minor. One of the most charming. Hard tight domes of small brilliantly silver leaves and milky white flowers on crimson stems. 4 inches . . . . . .

cotyledon norvegica. Green, broad-leaved rosettes up to 6 inches across and noble arching panicles of white blooms as much as 18 inches long

Dr. Ramsey. Beautifully symmetrical rosettes of silvery leaves and arching 8 inch sprays of clear white flowers

Esther. Grey-green rosettes and fine heads of primrose-yellow flowers. Free flowering, free growing and an unusual colour. 6–7 inches

lingulata albertii. Striking rosettes of strap-shaped leaves in silver and green, and 1 foot-long arching sprays of white flowers. A fine plant with an iron constitution . . . . . .

lingulata superba. A distinct and beautiful collected form with very narrow silvery leaves and 8 inch curving sprays of snowy white flowers . . . . . .

Whitehill. Blunt-leaved rosettes of curious and attractive ash-grey, and dense spikes of creamy flowers. 4–5 inches . . . .

MISCELLANEOUS SAXIFRAGES

Cloth of Gold. A remarkable 'mossy' which forms dense domes of bright gold leaves. The white flowers are quite unremarkable and may be removed without loss. For the best effect it should be grown in partial shade, shielded from the fiercest sun. 3–4 inches . .

grisebachii Wisley Var. One of the most intriguing and beautiful of the whole family. The 1 inch-wide rosettes of symmetrically arranged silvery leaves are themselves of great merit, but the arching stems clothed in bracts of crimson 'velvet' are quite outstanding. For a sunny limestone scree or crevice, or in the alpine-house. 4–6 inches. . . .

moschata variegata. A vigorous 'mossy', forming wide mats of filigree leaves which are distinctly variegated; the general effect is an intriguing mistiness, quite unlike any other plant . . . . . .

oppositifolia splendens. The large clear pink blooms sit almost stemlessly in earliest spring on the pad of moss-like leaves. A slow-growing jewel well suited in a trough or any sunny pocket. 1 inch . .

Peter Pan. A most attractive dwarf mossy variety, making low mats of fresh green leaves with deep red flowers on crimson stems. 3–4 inches

primuloides Elliott's Var. Surely one of the ten best alpines. Like a small neat London Pride, it grows with perfect ease in any soil or situation, making concise clumps of glossy emerald foliage, and throwing out each spring a rosy veil of a myriad tiny blooms. 4–8 inches according to soil . . . . . .

retusa. *S. Eur. Alps.* Choice and charming miniature, creeping very slowly, pressed close to the ground, with dark green moss-like leaves, and carrying little corymbs of rosy crimson blooms on 1 inch-high stems in late spring. For scree or sunny trough . . . . . .

Tumbling Waters. I am pleased to be able to offer the true plant, propagated from cuttings, and not one of the many seedlings often sold under this magic name. A well-grown plant in the alpine house (though it is perfectly hardy outdoors too) can make a rosette nearly a foot across with a cascading flower spike up to 2 feet long, containing hundreds of pure white flowers. A unique plant . . . . . .

Scabiosa

alpina nana. A new introduction of great charm, making low tufts of dark indented leaves, and having a long succession of small scabious flowers of rosy lavender on 4 inch stems, in late spring and early summer. Perfectly easy in any sunny well-drained soil . . . . . .

Sedum

cauticolum. *Japan.* An absolutely first-rate introduction of the greatest value and beauty. The fleshy leaves of soft lavender-grey are a great adornment during spring and summer, and make a perfect background for the numerous flat heads of crimson flowers which come in late autumn when little else is in bloom. Hardy and perfectly easy in any sunny position; retires below ground in winter. 3–4 inches . .

kamtschaticum variegatum. An extremely handsome plant with leaves gaily variegated in gold and green; in summer and early autumn the flat heads of rich orange-yellow flowers are an added attraction. In winter it retires to ground level, resting buds. Easily suited in almost any soil . . . . . .

Ruby Glow. Invaluable for late colour, giving many flat heads of rich ruby flowers in autumn. The fleshy purple-grey leaves are a pleasing bonus. 8–10 inches . . . . . .

spathulifolium cappa blanca. A splendid variety with rosettes of fleshy leaves densely coated with white meal. Flat heads of deep yellow flowers. 3 inches

spathulifolium purpureum. One of the best. The rich plum-purple leaves give year-round colour, and the flat heads of golden flowers are attractive in early summer. 3 inches

spurium Dragon's Blood. An attractive and most accommodating plant whose creeping stems bear bronzed scolloped leaves and 2 inch flat dense heads of brilliant carmine-crimson flowers in late summer. 2–3 inches

telephium roseo-variegatum. A most unusual plant whose fleshy leaves, as they emerge from the ground in spring, are bright rose-pink. After some weeks, as growth proceeds, they revert to normal grey-green and are topped by heads of purple-red flowers in late summer. 10–12 inches

Vera Jameson. A really exciting new plant which I regard as probably the most interesting, beautiful and worth while that it has been my good fortune to introduce. It cropped up as a seedling in the garden of a friend whose name it bears, and is probably a cross between *S. maximum purpureum* and *S. Ruby Glow.* It has inherited the deep bronzy purple leaves of the former with the dwarfer habit of the latter. In spring the resting buds grow out to form arching stems 8–10 inches long densely clothed with opposite pairs of fleshy, rounded purple leaves, which are strikingly spectacular throughout summer and autumn – specially if placed near a silver- or grey-leaved neighbour. The flat heads of dusky-pink flowers come in late summer and are a nice bonus, but this is essentially a foliage plant. My faith in this plant has been well justified by the R.H.S. Award of Merit granted to it in 1972 . . . . . .

Site for natural rock-garden.

Sempervivum

calcaratum. One of the larger Houseleeks, with handsome fleshy rosettes of purplish leaves up to 6 or more inches across. An easily-grown plant in almost any soil, no matter how dry and sunny .. ..

Silene

maritima plena. From the central tuft of crinkled grey-green leaves the prostrate stems radiate all summer, each bearing a large fully double white flower. The plant is happy in any sunny soil, particularly when able to hang down a wall or over a rock. 2–3 inches ..

schafta Abbotswood Var. Useful, and easy late bloomer, producing a mass of deep rosy blooms from August on, in almost any soil of situation. 4–6 inches .. ..

Sisyrinchium

douglasii. *N. America.* Slender rush-like leaves and two or three pendant purple bells on each flower stem. Likes a soil with ample humus and moisture in spring, and dies down soon after flowering in spring. 6 inches

filifolium. *Falkland Isles.* A rare plant and one with a unique and delicate charm. Nodding, scented white bells of gossamer fineness, lightly traced with faint red lines. It flowers in May and is best suited in a gritty, peaty soil. 5–6 inches

odoratissimum. *Southern S. America.* A rare and exquisite beauty that has had a variety of names given to it in recent years; I am sticking to the best known until the botanists make up their minds. From among the slender rush-like leaves appear in June delicate trumpet-shaped blooms, hanging gracefully, of white or straw colour, often pencilled on the outside with maroon, and powerfully scented. It likes best a fairly well-drained and nourishing soil. 10–12 inches .. ..

Soldanella

carpatica. *Carpathian Mts.* A geographical form of *S. montana* which here, at any rate, has flowered with a regular freedom not shown by any other member of the family. The fringed amethyst bells, two or three to each stem, are pure enchantment. Likes a sunny, moist, but well-drained soil. 5–6 inches .. ..

Spiraea

bullata. *Japan.* This charming dwarf shrub, seldom more than 12 inches high, forms a dense rounded bushlet, covered in small rounded and crisply crinkled dark green leaves; bears congested heads of deep crimson flowers in summer .. ..

bumalda Nyewood. Charming and useful pygmy shrub for late colour in the rock garden. Makes a forest of wiry stems 6–8 inches high and carries many heads of rosy crimson flowers from midsummer till autumn

Strawberry

Baron Solemacher Improved. A great wave of popularity has overtaken the so-called Alpine Strawberries in recent years, and not without reason, for they have many advantages over their larger cousins. They need no netting or strawing for their fruit is carried aloft on wiry stems and birds seem unaware of their juicy delicacy; they are easily grown and immune to all the devastating disease which so often cripple the larger varieties; and above all they fruit almost continuously from June to late autumn. *Baron Solemacher Improved* is established as the leading variety for free-fruiting capacity and delicacy of flavour — and has fruit about the size of a cob nut. It also has the great advantage of being a non-running variety. Each plant forms a compact clump 1 foot or so across and about as high. The plants should be put into well-dug and well-manured ground in full sun. They make an excellent edging in the kitchen garden and are more easily picked when planted thus in a single line. Pot-grown plants are offered which can be transplanted at almost any time. £1·40 per 10, £6·50 per 50, and £12·00 per 100

Syringa

palibiniana. *Korea.* A charming dwarf Lilac, which seldom exceeds 3 feet even in maturity. The dense 3 inch spikes of lilac-pink blooms are produced with the greatest freedom each spring and are authentically-scented. Easily grown in almost any soil in a position in which it will not be over-shadowed in its early years .. ..

Tellima

grandiflora purpurea. A useful border-front and ground-cover plant, forming dense clumps of rounded 2 inch leaves which are green all summer but turn brilliant beetroot-red in autumn and winter

Teucrium

aroanum. *Greece.* An attractive dwarf creeping sub-shrub for a sunny and sheltered scree. The curious dusky-lavender purple-veined blooms lie about carelessly on the mat of grey-green silver-edged leaves. 2–3 inches .. ..

Thalictrum

diffusiforme. *Himalayas.* A beautiful rarity, liking a cool, shady, leafy soil. The leaves are like a delicate grey Maidenhair Fern and each branched foot-high stem bears several exquisitely poised, inch-wide blooms of soft amethyst-blue .. ..

Thymus

citrodorus aureus. Forms a low creeping mass, with gay golden leaves throughout the year. Highly aromatic and excellent in paving — and for cooking. 3–4 inches .. ..

citrodorus E. B. Anderson. Given me un-named by the great gardener whose name it bears. It is much dwarfer and more compact than *T. c. aureus* and through autumn, winter and spring its leaves are brilliant gold. 2 inches .. ..

citrodorus Golden King. The leaves have golden margins .. ..

citrodorus Silver Queen. In this form the leaves are gaily variegated silver and green. 5–6 inches .. ..

leucotrichos. A newly introduced species which makes a low, aromatic, grey-leaved bush and smothers itself in early summer with small blunt heads of pink flowers. Give it gritty soil in a hot sunny pocket. 3–4 inches .. ..

Tiarella

wherryi. *S.E. U.S.A.* A species which was only discovered just before the war and which I had the pleasure of introducing to this country. It forms 1 foot-high clumps of handsome fresh green vine-shaped leaves, many of which take on rich autumn hues. The compact 2 inch spikes of flower, on 9 inch stems, are creamy white, tapering to a pink blush of unopened buds. They are produced with astonishing freedom in April and May, after which the plant is seldom without a few blooms until late autumn. The plant is a natural woodlander and prefers shade in the garden; given this, it is any easy hardy plant, whose quiet beauty and extraordinary long flowering period make it a most valuable addition to the garden. It received an R.H.S. Award of Merit in 1948 .. ..

Verbascum

× Letitia. This exciting newcomer gained an R.H.S. Award of Merit, quickly followed by a well-deserved First Class Certificate. It makes a 1 foot-wide, low, rounded bushlet of oval pointed soft grey leaves, and throughout the summer bears a succession of 3 inch spikes of clear primrose-yellow mullein flowers. It has survived ten winters here, unprotected in a sunny and stony soil — and has given lasting pleasure in my alpine-house .. ..

Veronica

rupestris (syn. *V. prostrata*). *Europe, etc.* An easy and most satisfying plant, producing a mass of upright tapered spires of deep blue flowers above the prostrate mat of stems and leaves. 4–5 inches .. ..

rupestris Blue Pearl. A new form in which the flowers are of soft china-blue .. ..

rupestris nana. A form of real charm, the leaves close packed and glossy green. The tapered flower spikes of deep blue are a mere 2–3 inches high .. ..

rupestris rosea. In this variety the flowers are clear rose-pink .. ..

saturioides. *Dalmatia.* Makes a small dense mass of wiry stems bearing tiny highly glossed leaves. The deep blue flowers each with a little crimson eye, are crowded on to 2 inch stems; they appear in spring and early summer .. ..

teucrium bastardii. Showy and rewarding plant, paying high dividends for a minimum of trouble, with a long summer display of blunt spikes of clear china-blue flowers. Grows happily almost anywhere except in deep shade. 5–6 inches .. ..

teucrium Bluetit. An excellent dwarf collected form of a useful plant which varies greatly in nature. From the gently creeping mat of leaves come 3–4 inch stems bearing tapered spikes of deep sky-blue flowers. Easy in any sunny soil

Viola

Ardross Gem. Dwarf, vigorous and free flowering with blooms of dusky gold and blue — an original and intriguing combination. 6 inches. Recommended .. ..

Connie. A seedling raised here and named after a dear friend whose pert and cheerful optimism the plant seems to epitomize. It is a dwarf and willing grower and yields an endless succession of small lavender flowers from spring to autumn. 6 inches .. .. ..

cornuta. A useful and easy plant with crisp leaves and small butterfly flowers of lavender. Useful in the front of the border and will grow happily in tree-shade that is not too dense. 8–12 inches according to situation .. ..

Martin. A grand plant I raised here some years ago, which has become a firm and invaluable favourite. It forms a dense low cushion of leaves above which the 1 inch-wide rounded blooms of velvety deep purple appear in continuous succession from spring to late autumn. Few plants can offer such sustained value for so little trouble.

zoysii. Often regarded as the eastern European form of the beautiful and ubiquitous lavender-coloured *V. calcarata* that graces so many high alpine pastures. Over dense tufts of glossy, deep green leaves it carries wavy, inch-wide, rounded blooms of rich butter-yellow, deliciously scented. It has proved an excellent alpine house plant in a rich gritty soil and seems to enjoy the same diet outdoors. 2–3 inches. ..

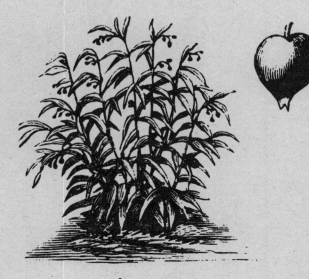

JOB'S TEARS.

ALPINE FLOWERS

The right way, after preparing the ground, is to make it firm and level, and then make a little cut or trench. The side of this trench should be firm and

1. Right. 2. Wrong.

smooth, and the plant placed against it, the roots spread out, and the neck of the plant set just at the proper level, as in fig. 1. Then the fine earth of the little trench is to be thrown against the roots, and as much *side* pressure applied as may be necessary to make the whole quite firm. In this way not a fibre of the most fragile plant need be injured.

BOTANICAL TERMS

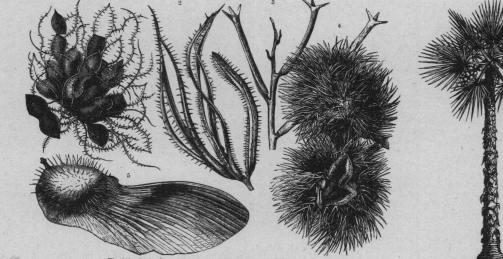

Fig. 339.—Protection of ripening seeds against the attack of animals.
¹ *Mimosa hispidula.* ² *Schrankia.* ³ *Matthiola tricuspidata.* ⁴ *Castanea vulgaris.* ⁵ *Centrolobium robustum.*

Abnormal—Differing from the usual structure.

Abortion—Imperfect development or non-development of an organ.

Abortive—Imperfectly developed or rudimentary.

Acuminate—Tapering at the end.

Acute—Forming a sharp angle.

Adhesion—The union of members of different floral whorls.

Adnate—Grown together.

Adventitious—Occurring out of the regular order.

Aestivation—The arrangement of floral organs in the bud.

Akene—A small, dry, hard, one-celled, one-seeded, indehiscent fruit.

Albumen—A name applied to the food store laid up outside the embryo in many seeds; also nitrogenous organic matter found in animals and plants.

Alburnum—Sapwood.

Alternate—Applied to that form of leaf arrangement in which only one leaf occurs at a node.

Ament—A scaly spike or catkin.

Angiosperms—Those plants which bear their seeds within a pericarp.

Anther—That part of the stamen which bears the pollen.

Apetalous—Having no petals.

Appressed—Lying close and flat against.

Arborescent—A tree in size and habit of growth.

Aril—The exterior coat of some seeds.

Awl-shaped—Narrowed upward from the base to a slender or rigid point.

Axil—The upper one of the two angles formed by the juncture of the leaf with the stem.

Axillary—Situated in an axil.

Bast—A name applied to the inner layer of the bark.

Beaked—Ending in a prolonged tip.

Berry—A fruit whose entire pericarp is succulent.

Bi-pinnate—Applied to a leaf which is twice compounded on the pinnate plan.

Bractlets—The smaller bracts borne on pedicels.

Bracts—The modified leaves borne on flower peduncles or at the base of flower stems.

Caducous—Applied to the calyx of a flower when it falls off before the flower expands; also to the stipules of a leaf if they fall as the leaf appears.

Calyx—The outer whorl of floral envelopes.

Campanulate—Bell-shaped.

Capsule—A dry, usually dehiscent fruit, made up of two or more carpels.

Carpel—A simple pistil, or one member of a compound pistil.

Catkin—An ament.

Cellulose—A primary cell-wall substance.

Chlorophyll—The green grains in the cells of plants.

Claw—The stalk or contracted base of a petal.

Cohesion—The union of members of the same floral whorl.

Conduplicate—Doubled together. The vernation of a leaf is conduplicate when the two sides are folded together lengthwise, face to face.

Connate—Grown together.

Connective—That portion of the anther which connects the two lobes.

Contorted—Twisted together.

Convolute—Rolled up; applied to leaves that are rolled from one edge.

Cordate—Heart-shaped; applied to a leaf which has a deeply indented base.

Coriaceous—Thickish and leathery in texture.

Corolla—The inner whorl of floral envelopes.

Corymb—A flower cluster in which the axis is shortened and the pedicels of the lower flowers lengthened, so as to form a flat-topped cluster.

Corymbose—Like a corymb.

Cotyledon—One of the parts of the embryo performing in part the functions of a leaf, but usually serving as a storehouse of food for the developing plant.

Crenate—Scalloped.

Crenulate—Finely crenate.

Cross-Fertilization—When the stigma of one flower receives the pollen of a different flower.

Cruciform—Applied to corollas of four distinct petals arranged in form of a cross.

Cuspidate—Tipped with a sharp and rigid point.

Cyme—A broad and flattish inflorescence with the central or terminal flowers blooming earliest.

Deciduous—Not persistent; applied to leaves that fall in autumn and to calyx and corolla when they fall off before the fruit develops.

Decurrent—Applied to leaves which are prolonged down the side of the petiole.

Definite—Limited or defined.

Dehiscence—The act of splitting open.

Deltoid—Triangular, somewhat like the Greek letter delta.

Dentate—Applied to leaves that have their margins toothed, with the teeth directed outward.

Diadelphous—In two brotherhoods. Applied to stamens when cohering by their filaments into two sets.

Dichotomous—Forking; dividing into two equal branches.

Dicotyledon—A plant whose embryo has two opposite cotyledons.

Diffuse—Widely spreading.

Digitate—Applied to a compound leaf in which all the leaflets radiate from the top of the petiole.

Dioecious—In two households. With staminate and pistillate flowers separate and on separate plants.

Discoid—Having the form of a disc. Descriptive of the shapes of certain stigmas, glands, etc.

Disk—A development of the receptacle at or around the base of the pistil.

Dissepiment—A partition in a fruit.

Drupe—A fleshy or pulpy fruit with the inner portion of the pericarp hard or stony. A stone fruit.

Duramen—Heartwood.

Echinate—Beset with prikles.

Emarginate—Notched. Applied to a leaf which is notched at the apex.

Embryo—Applied in botany to the tiny plant within the seed.

Endocarp—The inner layer of the pericarp.

Epigynous—Growing on the summit of the ovary, or apparently so.

Erose—Irregularly toothed, as if gnawed.

Etaerio—A fruit, the product of a single flower, which consists of small aggregated drupes.

Exocarp—The outer layer of the pericarp.

Exserted—Protruding; as stamens extending beyond the throat of a corolla.

Extrorse—Facing outward. Applied to anthers which face away from the pistil.

Falcate—Curved or sickle-shaped.

Fascicle—A bundle. Applied to a compact cyme or a compact cluster of leaves.

Fertilization—The union which takes place when the contents of the pollen cell enters the ovule.

Fibro-vascular bundles—the bundles of vascular tissues of plants.

Filament—The stalk which supports the anther.

Filiform—Thread-like.

Foliaceous—Leaf-like.

Fugacious—Soon falling off.

Galbulus—A berry-like cone, as the fruit of the Juniper.

Gamopetalous—Having the petals more or less united.

Gamosepalous—Having the sepals more or less united.

Germination—The sprouting of a seed.

Gibbous—Swollen on one side.

Glabrous—Smooth; destitute of hairs.

Glands—A secreting surface or structure; a protuberance having the appearance of such an organ.

Glans—A nut.

Glaucous—Covered or whitened with a bloom.

Globose—Spherical or nearly so.

Gymnosperms—Plants bearing naked seeds; without an ovary.

Gynoecium—The pistils of a flower taken as a whole.

Habitat—The geographical range of a plant.

Head—A compact cluster of nearly sessile flowers.

Hilum—The point of attachment of an ovule or seed.

Hispid—Bristly.

Hybrid—A cross between two species.

Hypogynous—Situated on the receptacle, beneath the ovary and free from it and from the calyx. Applied to petals and stamens.

Imbricate—Overlapping.

Incised—Cut sharply and deeply.

Included—Applied to stamens or pistils that do not project beyond the corolla.

Indefinite—Applied to petals or other organs when too numerous to be conveniently counted.

Indehiscent—Not splitting open.

Indigenous—Native to the country.

Inferior—Applied to an ovary which has an adherent calyx.

Inflorescence—The flowering part of a plant.

Innate—Applied to anthers which are attached by their base to the apex of the filament.

Inserted—Attached to or growing out of.

Internode—The portion of a stem between two nodes.

Introrse—Facing inward; applied to stamens that face toward the pistil.

Involucel—A secondary involucre.

Involucre—A collection of bracts at the base of a flower cluster or of a single flower.

Involute—A form of vernation in which the leaf is rolled inward from its edges.

Lanceolate—Applied to leaves which are slender, broadest near the base and narrowed to the apex.

Leaflet—A single division of a compound leaf.

Legume—A fruit formed of a simple pistil and usually splitting open by both sutures.

Lenticels—Small oval dots which appear upon the branches.

Liber—The inner layer of the bark.

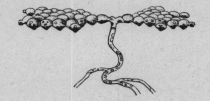

Ligneous—Woody.

Limb—The spreading portion of a gamophyllus calyx or corolla.

Linear—Applied to an organ with parallel margins that is many times longer than broad.

Lobe—Any segment of an organ.

Loculicidally—Dehiscent through the back of a cell of a capsule.

Medulla—The pith.

Medullary Rays—Rays of fundamental tissue which connect the pith with the bark.

Membranous, Membranaceous—Thin and rather soft, more or less translucent.

Mesocarp—The middle layer of the pericarp.

Metabolism—The oxydizing processes that go on in the living plant.

Midrib—The central or main rib of a leaf.

Monadelphous—In one brotherhood. Applied to stamens which are united by their filaments into one set.

Monocotyledonous—Possessing but one cotyledon or seed leaf.

Monoecious—In one household. Applied to plants which have separate staminate and pistillate flowers, but both borne on the same plant.

Mucronate—Tipped with a small soft point.

Multiple fruit—A fruit composed of numerous small fruits, each the product of a separate flower; ex. mulberry.

Nectary—The honey gland or honey repository of a flower.

Nerved—Veined.

Node—The point on a stem of a plant from which the leaf develops.

Obconic—Conic with the point of attachment at the apex.

Obcordate—Inversely heart-shaped.

Oblanceolate—Inversely lanceolate.

Oblong—Considerably longer than broad, with flowing outline.

Obtuse—Blunt, rounded.

Oval—Broadly elliptical.

Ovary—The part of the pistil that contains the ovaries.

Ovoid—Egg-shaped. Applied to solid bodies.

Ovule—The rudimentary seed.

Panicle—A compound raceme.

Papilionaceous—A term descriptive of such flowers as those of the Pea.

Parted—Cleft nearly but not quite to the base or midrib.

Pedicel—The stem of an individual flower of a cluster.

Peduncle—A flower stalk.

Perfect—Applied to a flower which has both pistil and stamens.

Perianth—A term applied to the floral envelopes taken as a whole.

Pericarp—The walls of the ripened ovary, the part of the fruit that encloses the seeds.

Perigynous—Borne around the pistil instead of at its base. Applied to stamens and petals borne on the throat of the calyx.

Persistent—Long continuous, applied to leaves that remain on the tree over winter and to a calyx that remains until the fruit ripens.

Petal—One of the leaves of the corolla.

Petiole—The stem of a leaf.

Pinna (pl. pinnae)—One of the primary divisions of a pinnately compound leaf.

Pinnate—Applied to compound leaves where the leaflets are arranged on each side of a common petiole.

Pistil—The modified leaf or leaves which bear the ovules; usually consisting of ovary, style and stigma.

Pistillate—Applied to flowers that possess pistils but not stamens.

Plicate—Folded like a fan.

Plumule—The primary bud of the embryo.

Pollen—The fertilizing powder produced by the anther.

Polygamous—Applied to plants which produce staminate, pistillate, and perfect flowers all on the same plant.

Protoplasm—The living matter of the cell.

Pubescent—Downy, covered with soft hairs.

Raceme—A simple inflorescence of pedicelled flowers upon a common, more or less, elongated axis.

Rachis—The axis of inflorescence.

Radicle—The primary root of the embryo.

Receptacle—The shortened stem on which the floral organs are inserted.

Reduplicate—Doubled back.

Reflexed—Bent outward.

Repand—Leaf margin toothed like the margin of an umbrella.

Revolute—Rolled backward.

Rotate—Flat circular disk; applied to corollas.

Samara—An indehiscent dry fruit provided with a wing-like appendage.

Secund—Flowers arranged along one side of a lengthened axis.

Sepal—One of the leaves of the outer whorl of floral organs.

Serrate—Toothed, with sharp teeth projecting forward.

Sinuate—Wavy.

Sinus—The cleft between two lobes.

Spatulate—Resembling a spatula in outline.

Spike—A form of simple inflorescence in which the flowers are sessile or nearly so, borne upon a lengthened axis. The lower flowers bloom first.

Spray—The ultimate division of a branch.

Stamen—The pollen-bearing organ of the flower, usually consisting of filament and anther.

Staminate—Applied to flowers which have stamens but not pistils.

Sterigma (pl. sterigmata)—The woody base upon which the leaves of many of the evergreens are borne.

Stigma—That part of the pistil which receives the pollen.

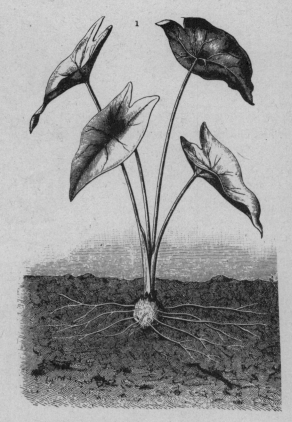

Stipe—The stalk possessed by some pistils.

Stipule—One of the blade-like bodies at the base of the petiole of leaves.

Stoma (pl. stomata)—A breathing pore found in the epidermis of the higher plants.

Strobile—A compact flower cluster with large scales concealing the flowers. When this cluster matures and contains seeds it is still called a strobile.

Style—That part of the pistil which connects the ovary with the stigma.

Superior—Applied to an ovary that is not at all adherent to the calyx.

Syncarp—A multiple fruit.

Taproot—The main root or downward continuation of the plant axis.

Terete—Nearly cylindrical.

Terminal—Placed at the end.

Thyrse or Thyrsus—A compact panicle.

Tomentose—Applied to surfaces which are covered with matted hairs.

Tomentum—Matted hairs.

Torus—Another name for receptacle.

Truncate—Ending abruptly as if cut off.

Tryma—A drupe-like fruit which is commonly two-celled, has a bony nucleus and thick, fibrous epicarp.

Turbinate—Top-shaped.

Umbel—A flower cluster in which the axis is very short and the pedicels radiate from it.

Undulate—Wavy.

Valvate—Meeting by the edges without overlapping.

Vascular—Possessing vessels or ducts.

Vein—Thread of fibro-vascular tissue in a leaf.

Veinlet—Small vein.

Venation—The system of veins as that of a leaf.

Vernation—The arrangement of the leaves in the bud.

Versatile—Applied to an anther that turns freely on its support.

Villous—Covered with long, soft, shaggy hairs.

Whorl—An arrangement of organs in a circle about a central axis.

Fig. 478.—Fruits with hooks.

¹ *Marrubium vulgare.* ² *Medicago agrestis.* ³ *Rumex nepalensis.* ⁴ *Scorpiurus sulcata.* ⁵ *Agrimonia odorata.* ⁶ *Orlaya grandiflora.* ⁷ *Pteranthus echinatus.* ⁸ *Rochelia Persica.* ⁹ *Onobrychis æquidentata.* ¹⁰ *Triumfetta Plumieri.* ¹¹ Hooked bristles on the fruit of *Triumfetta Plumieri* magnified. ¹² *Medicago radiata.* ¹³ *Xanthium spinosum.* ¹⁴ *Ceratocephalus falcatus.* ¹⁵ *Geum urbanum.* ¹⁶ A single fallen fruit of *Geum urbanum.* ¹⁷ *Lappa major.*

2, PORTULACA.　　3, PLATYSTEMON.　　1, POPPY.

INDEX OF COMMON AND BOTANICAL NAMES

COMMON NAMES

Many garden plants are known by common or English names. These are often confusing and irrelevant, but may be the only indication of their true identity.

Following is a list of over 300 common names with their botanical equivalents.

CHINESE PEONY — FLOWER, PLANT AND ROOT.

GERANIUM SANGUINEUM.

DIANTHUS LACINIATUS FLORE-PLENO.　　DIANTHUS DIADEMATUS FLORE-PLENO.

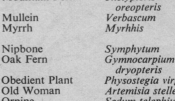

COMMON NAME	BOTANICAL NAME
African Lily	Agapanthus
Alkanet	Anchusa
Alum Root	Heuchera
Alum Root, False	Tellima grandiflora
Apple Mint	Mentha rotundifolia
Asphodel, Giant	Eremurus
Asphodel, White	Asphodelus cerasiferus
Asphodel, Yellow	Asphodeline lutea
Aster, Stokes'	Stokesia
Avens	Geum
Avens, Mountain	Dryas
Barrenwort	Epimedium
Batchelors' Buttons	Ranunculus acris 'Flore Pleno'
Beach Wormwood	Artemisia stellerana
Bear's Breeches	Acanthus
Bedstraw	Galium
Bee Palm	Monarda didyma
Beech Fern	Thelypteris phegopteris
Bell-flower	Campanula
Bergamot	Monarda
Bethlehem Sage	Pulmonaria saccharata
Betony	Stachys macrantha
Birth-root	Trillium erectum
Bishop's Hat	Epimedium
Bistort	Polygonum bistorta
Black-eyed Susan	Rudbeckia fulgida speciosa
Bladder Fern	Cystopteris
Bleeding Heart	Dicentra spectabilis
Blood Root	Sanguinaria canadensis
Blue-eyed Grass	Sisyrinchium angustifolium
Blue Oxalis	Parochetus communis
Buckler Fern	Dryopteris
Bugbane	Cimicifuga
Bugle	Ajuga
Burnet	Sanguisorba
Burning Bush	Dictamnus albus
Butterburr, Giant	Petasites japonicus giganteus
Buttercup	Ranunculus
Butterfly-weed	Asclepias tuberosa
Caffre Lily	Schizostylis
Calamint	Calamintha
Californian Fuchsia	Zauschneria californica
Campion	Lychnis; Silene
Candytuft	Iberis
Candytuft, Persian	Aethionema grandiflorum
Cape Fig Wort	Phygelius capensis
Cape Gooseberry	Physalis
Cape Marigold	Dimorphotheca
Carnation	Dianthus
Cartwheel Flower	Heracleum mantegazzianum
Catchfly	Lychnis; Silene
Catmint	Nepeta
Cat's Ear	Antennaria dioica
Chamomile	Anthemis
Chinese Bellflower	Platycodon
Chinese Lantern	Physalis
Chinese Ragwort	Senecio tanguticus
Christmas Rose	Helleborus niger
Cinquefoil	Potentilla
Cocksfoot Grass	Dactylis
Columbine	Aquilegia
Comfrey	Symphytum
Cone Flower	Rudbeckia
Coral Berry	Margyricarpus setosus
Cornflower	Centaurea
Corsican Mint	Mentha requienii
Corsican Nettle-moss	Helxine soleirolii
Cow Parsnip	Heracleum
Crane's Bill	Geranium
Creeping Dogwood	Cornus canadensis
Creeping Forget-me-not	Omphalodes verna
Creeping Jenny	Lysimachia nummularia
Crosswort	Phuopsis stylosa
Daisy	Bellis
Dame's Violet	Hesperis
Day Lily	Hemerocallis
Dead Nettle	Lamium
Dittany	Origanum
Dragon's Head	Dracocephalum
Dragon Plant	Dracunculus vulgaris
Drum-stick Primula	Primula denticulata
Dusty Miller	Artemisia stellerana
Dutchman's Breeches	Dicentra
Edelweiss	Leontopodium alpinum
Elecampane	Inula helenium
Evening Primrose	Oenothera
Everlasting Flower	Helichrysum and Anaphalis
Everlasting Pea	Lathyrus latifolius

COMMON NAME	BOTANICAL NAME
False Alum Root	Tellima grandiflora
Feather Grass	Stipa pennata
Fennel, Common	Foeniculum vulgare
Flag	Iris
Flax	Linum
Fleabane	Erigeron
Foam Flower	Tiarella
Forget-me-not	Myosotis
Foxglove	Digitalis
Foxglove, Fairy	Erinus
Gardener's Gaiters	Phalaris arundinacea 'Picta'
Gentian	Gentiana
Germander	Teucrium
Giant Hogweed	Heracleum mantegazzianum
Globe Artichoke	Cynara scolymus
Globe Daisy	Globularia
Globe Flower	Trollius
Globe Thistle	Echinops
Goat's Beard	Aruncus dioicus
Goat's Rue	Galega
Gold Drop	Onosma tauricum
Gold Dust	Alyssum saxatile
Golden Rod	Solidago
Goldilocks	Crinitaria linosyris
Gromwell	Lithospermum
Hair-grass	Deschampsia
Hardhead	Centaurea
Hard Fern	Blechnum spicant
Hart's Tongue Fern	Phyllitis scolopendrium
Hawkweed	Hieraceum
Hemp Agrimony	Eupatorium
Heron's Bill	Erodium
Himalayan Parsley	Selinum tenuifolium
Hogweed	Heracleum
Holly Fern	Polystichum lonchitis
Horseshoe Vetch	Hippocrepis comosa
Hottentot Fig	Carpobrotus edulis
Hound's Tongue	Cynoglossum
Houseleek	Sempervivum
Hyssop	Hyssopus
Indian Physic	Gillenia trifoliata
Iodine Plant	Macleaya
Jacob's Ladder	Polemonium
Japanese Anemone	Anemone × hybrida
Japanese Bellflower	Platycodon
Kansas Gay Feather	Liatris
Kidney Vetch	Anthyllis
Knapweed	Centaurea
Ladies' Slipper Orchid	Cypripedium calceolus
Ladslove	Artemisia abrotanum
Lady Fern	Athyrium filix-femina
Lady's Mantle	Alchemilla
Lamb's Tongue	Stachys lanata
Larkspur	Delphinium
Lavender	Lavandula
Lavender Cotton	Santolina
Leadwort	Ceratostigma plumbaginoides
Lemon-scented Fern	Thelypteris oreopteris
Lenten Rose	Helleborus orientalis
Leopard's Bane	Doronicum
Lily-of-the-Valley	Convallaria majalis
Live-long	Sedum telephium
London Pride	Saxifraga × urbium
Loosestrife	Lysimachia
Loosestrife, Purple	Lythrum
Lungwort	Pulmonaria
Lungwort, Smooth	Mertensia
Lupin	Lupinus
Lyme Grass	Elymus arenarius
Madwort	Alyssum
Maidenhair Fern	Adiantum
Male Fern	Dryopteris filix-mas
Mallow	Malva
Mallow, Greek	Sidalcea
Mallow, Tree	Lavatera
Marjoram	Origanum
Masterwort	Astrantia
Meadow Rue	Thalictrum
Meadow Sweet	Filipendula ulmaria
Michaelmas Daisy	Aster
Mint	Mentha
Mind-Your-Own-Business	Helxine soleirolii
Monk's Hood	Aconitum
Moon Daisy	Chrysanthemum uliginosum
Mountain Avens	Dryas
Mountain Everlasting	Antennaria dioica
Mountain Fern	Thelypteris oreopteris
Mullein	Verbascum
Myrrh	Myrrhis
Nipbone	Symphytum
Oak Fern	Gymnocarpium dryopteris
Obedient Plant	Physostegia virginana
Old Woman	Artemisia stellerana
Orpine	Sedum telephium
Ostrich Fern	Matteuccia struthiopteris
Oswego Tea	Monarda didyma
Pampas Grass	Cortaderia
Parsley Fern	Cryptogramma crispa

COMMON NAME	BOTANICAL NAME
Pasque Flower	Pulsatilla vulgaris
Pendulous Sedge	Carex pendula
Penny Cress	Thlaspi
Pennyroyal	Mentha pulegium
Peony	Paeonia
Peppermint	Mentha piperita
Periwinkle	Vinca
Peruvian Lily	Alstromeria
Pincushion Flower	Scabiosa
Pink	Dianthus
Plantain	Plantago
Plantain Lily	Hosta
Pleurisy Root	Asclepias tuberosa
Plumbago, Hardy	Ceratostigma
Plume Poppy	Macleaya
Pokeberry	Phytolacca
Poke Weed, Virginian	Phytolacca americana
Polypody	Polypodium
Poppy	Papaver
Poppy, Blue	Meconopsis betonicifolia
Poppy, Iceland	Papaver nudicaule
Poppy, Oriental	Papaver orientale
Poppy, Plume	Macleaya
Poppy, Tree	Romneya
Prickly Thrift	Acantholimon glumaceum
Primrose	Primula vulgaris
Prophet Flower	Arnebia echioides
Provence Reed	Arundo

Red Hot Poker	Kniphofia
Red Ink Plant	Phytolacca americana
Rhubarb, Ornamental	Rheum palmatum
Ribbon Grass	Phalaris arundinacea 'Picta'
Rock Cress	Arabis
Rocket	Hesperis
Rock Jessamine	Androsace
Rock Purslane	Calandrina umbellata
Rock Rose	Helianthemum
Rose Campion	Lychnis coronaria
Rosemary	Rosmarinus
Rosette Mullein	Ramonda
Royal Fern	Osmunda regalis
Rue	Ruta graveolens
Rupture Wort	Herniaria
Rush Lily	Sisyrinchium
Rustyback Fern	Ceterach officinarum

Sage	Salvia
St. Bernard's Lily	Anthericum liliago
St. John's Wort	Hypericum
Sandwort	Arenaria
Satin Flower	Sisyrinchium
Savory	Satureia
Sawwort	Serratula
Scabious	Scabiosa
Scabious, Giant	Cephalaria
Scabious, Yellow	Cephalaria
Scotch Creeper	Tropaeolum speciosum
Scotch Thistle	Onopordon acanthium
Sea Heath	Frankenia laevis
Sea Holly	Eryngium
Sea Pink	Armeria maritima
Seakale	Crambe
Sea Lavender	Limonium
Sedge	Carex
Self-heal	Prunella
Sensitive Fern	Onoclea sensibilis
Shamrock	Oxalis
Shamrock Pea	Parochetus communis
Shasta Daisy	Chrysanthemum maximum
Sheep's-bit Scabious	Jasione
Shield Fern	Polystichum
Shooting Stars	Dodecatheon
Skull Cap	Scutellaria
Snow-in-Summer	Cerastium tomentosum
Soap Wort	Saponaria
Solomon's Seal	Polygonatum
Southernwood	Artemisia abrotanum
Sow's Ear	Stachys lanata
Speedwell	Veronica
Spiderwort	Tradescantia
Spleenwort	Asplenium
Spring Bitter Vetch	Lathyrus vernus
Spurge	Euphorbia
Stonecrop	Sedum
Stork's Bill	Erodium
Sunflower, Orange	Heliopsis
Sunflower, Perennial	Helianthus
Sun Rose	Helianthemum
Sweet Cicely	Myrrhis odorata

Tansy	Chrysanthemum vulgare
Thrift	Armeria
Thyme	Thymus
Toad Flax	Linaria
Toad Flax Ivy-leaved	Cymbalaria muralis
Torch Lily	Kniphofia
Turtle Head	Penstemon barbatus
Umbrella Plant	Peltiphyllum peltatum
Valerian, Red	Centranthus
Vervain	Verbena
Violet, Sweet	Viola odorata
Virginian Cowslip	Mertensia virginica

COMMON NAME	BOTANICAL NAME
Wake Robin	Trillium grandiflorum
Wallflower Perennial	Cheiranthus
Wall Rue	Asplenium ruta-muraria
Wand Flower	Dierama
Wild Aniseed	Myrrhis
White Rock	Arabis caucasica
White Sage	Artemisia ludoviciana
Whitlow Grass	Draba
Willow Gentian	Gentiana asclepiadea
Willow Herb	Epilobium
Windflower	Anemone
Wire Plant	Muehlenbeckia
Wood Lily	Trillium
Woodruff	Galium odoratum
Wood Rush	Luzula
Wood Sorrel	Oxalis
Wormwood	Artemisia
Woundwort	Stachys
Yarrow	Achillea
Yorkshire Fog	Holcus mollis

FLORAL GUIDE. FOR 1873.

SWEET ALYSSUM. AMARANTHUS SALICIFOLIUS. ALONSOA.

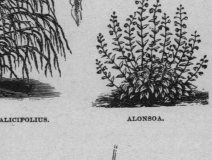

CHRYSANTHEME à carene

PURPLE LOOSESTRIPE.
(LYTHRUM SALICARIA.)

PENTSTEMON BARBATUS.
(VAR. TORREYI.)

RESTREPIA STRIATA.

White Shrub Aster

JAMES VICK ROCHESTER, N.Y.

DOUBLE ZINNIA.

151

VICK'S FLORAL GUIDE

ORDER ROOM.

Another season of buds and blossoms, and balmy breezes, freighted with the odor of a thousand flowers, is gone, never to return. We no longer tread the velvety lawn, no more indulge in moonlight rambles among the shrubs, sparkling with thousands of brilliant dew-drops. The voice of the singing bird is hushed, and the insect chorus is silent. The once merry croquet ground is deserted, while here and there a bent arch stands as a sad memorial of departed pleasures. The happy voices of the children no longer keep time with the click of the mallets, nor their joyous spirits run over in the merry laugh. The beds and borders recently so beautiful, bear scarcely a trace of former loveliness. The vases that appeared so chaste in the spring, so brilliant in the summer, and gorgeous in the autumn, are robbed of their glory, and stored away ignominiously in barn or cellar. The hanging-baskets are dismantled, or removed from the balcony to the house. The graveled walks no more echo the pleasant foot-fall. All nature is at rest. The sleep—may we not say, the death—of winter is upon us. No; nature is not dead, but sleepeth. In a little while there will be, if not a new creation, a resurrection. Spring, with all her light and life and loveliness will appear; for we have the promise that "seed-time and harvest shall never fail." The season—the year—however, is gone, never to return. Nature does not repeat herself. No two leaves, or flowers, or seasons, are alike. The pleasures and toils, the successes and failures, of the dead year can live again only in memory. We may, indeed we must, learn wisdom from the lessons of the past; and I have no doubt my readers are better prepared for the duties and responsibilities of life—more fitted now than ever before to conquer its evils and enjoy its pleasures. I think, next season, they will plant more carefully and skillfully, and reap a richer harvest of pleasure and profit. I flatter myself that I can furnish a better Catalogue than any previously issued; if not, I have studied and labored the past year in vain. I have certainly made the attempt; of its success my readers must judge.

To my two hundred thousand customers I return my best thanks for continued and increased confidence during a long series of years. I have endeavored to merit your regard, and have never in any case sent out a package of seed that I had not good reason to believe was right in every respect—not a single paper that I would not have been willing to sow in my own grounds. My earnest desire is that all may enjoy a happy and prosperous year, that no thorns may beset your way, but that all your paths be strewn with flowers, and that you may live to enjoy their beauty and fragrance for many long and happy years, until fully ready to be transplanted to a better clime.

To all my customers, and those who design to become so, I say, please study the Guide during the leisure of winter, and make plans for the future with care. Do not undertake more than you can do well, nor invest more money than you can afford. We garden for pleasure, and there is no pleasure in half-done work, or unwise expenditures. The true lover of flowers can obtain a heart-full of pleasure from a few small beds or plants, if this is all that circumstances will allow. I have visited palace gardens, and the magnificent grounds of the most devoted lovers of rural art, and witnessed the pleasure

and pride with which they viewed the beautiful landscape, in a measure the creation of their own genius; yet I never saw so much joy in any of these as was expressed in the countenances of three little girls, not long since, who had clubbed their pennies together to buy a single pot plant and were permitted to carry it off in triumph by the good gardener, although their united purse lacked a few pennies of the required sum. After the plans are completed, and you ascertain what seeds and bulbs will be needed, order them early. Do not neglect to send for seeds until the hot-bed is made, and when a few days delay will cause inconvenience and loss. Order early, even if you have to send for a second time.

I present my Eleventh Floral Guide and Catalogue, for 1873, to all customers of the previous year, as a New Year's gift. This annual presentation of a Catalogue has been my custom for several years. I do so this season with unusual pleasure, because I think it will be found in some respects, at least, superior to any previous issue. Increased experience, observation and travel, have enabled me to gather a mass of facts, which I have endeavored to present in such a form as to be attractive and easily remembered. Its appearance, too, is quite respectable, and by many, even experienced bookmakers, considered unusually genteel—quite superb. I have certainly spared neither labor nor expense to make it entirely worthy the attention and perusal of my numerous customers. My labors in this respect have always been more than appreciated. Two hundred and twenty-five thousand were printed last year, and judging from the past I shall need about three hundred thousand to supply the demand

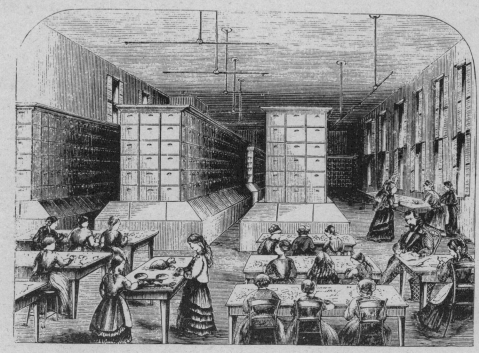

this eason. This I can meet without embarrassment, having strengthened almost every department—artists, engravers, printers and binders; and these being connected with my own establishment, and solely under my control, I am prepared to meet the public demand, no matter how large it may become. Here, I will say, that as my establishment is, no doubt, the largest and best arranged retail Seed House in the world, and as it is visited by thousands every year as a matter of curiosity and interest, for the benefit of distant customers, I will give in these introductory pages a brief sketch of my Seed Rooms, manner of doing business, etc. Although I furnish Catalogues to those who are not customers at cost, or even less, and to my customers free, so that there is no profit in the transaction, yet there is great pleasure in knowing that my efforts to instruct and please the lovers of flowers are appreciated, and that I send out more Catalogues than any four houses either in Europe or America, while for beauty and true value it is acknowledged to be unequaled.

My Floral Guide, I observed, is sent free to customers of the previous year, and if it fails to arrive, the fact must be charged to some accident or miscarriage, which I shall be pleased to correct by sending another copy as soon as informed of the delay or loss. Thousands of persons who live in cities and villages where they have no ground, or who, from other causes, have no opportunity to grow flowers, desire to possess my Guide, and yet are reluctant to send for it as it has been furnished at a merely nominal price, and for the benefit of those designing to purchase. I have, therefore, determined to supply the Guide to all who wish it at just the cost to me, or a little less, twenty-five cents each. If any person purchasing the Guide shall afterward conclude to order seeds to the amount of One Dollar or more, the money sent for the book may be deducted from the amount forwarded for seeds. Every member of a club ordering seeds to the amount of One Dollar or more shall be entitled to a copy without charge. Persons ordering less than a dollar's worth of seeds must pay for the Floral Guide if they desire one. This rule is necessary because my Guide has become so costly that all can see that I cannot afford to supply it free to those who order only a few pennies' worth of seed.

BINDERY.

Occasionally a person writes to know if I have certain articles advertised in the Catalogue. I do not design to offer anything of which I have not a fully supply—enough for all demands. To get from Europe as large a stock of seeds as I need, I have to order very early, and also to published my Catalogue before I get full returns. Occasionally the crop of a certain variety partially fails, and I only get a small quantity, and sometimes the crop is entirely destroyed, so that I can obtain none, or, in testing, a variety proves worthless, with no time to obtain a new stock. These are the only cases in which I cannot supply everything advertised, and they are very few indeed. Some years nothing of the kind occurs.

OUR SEED HOUSE

It is acknowledged that I have the largest and best regulated retail Seed House in the world. It is visited by thousands every year from all parts of this country, and by many from Europe, and I take pleasure in exhibiting everything of interest or profit to visitors. As hundreds of thousands of my customers will probably never have the opportunity of making a personal visit, I thought a few facts and illustrations would be interesting to this large class whom I am anxious to please, and be, at least, an acknowledgement of a debt of gratitude for long continued confidence, which I can feel, but not repay.

OUR SEED HOUSE.

Two Catalogues are issued each year, one of Bulbs in August, and on the first of December a beautiful Floral Guide, of 130 pages, finely illustrated with hundreds of engravings of Flowers and plants and colored plates. Last year, the number printed was three hundred thousand, at a cost of over sixty thousand dollars. In addition to the ordinary conveniences of a well regulated Seed House, there is connected with this establishment a Printing Office, Bindery, Box Making Establishment, and Artists' and Engravers' Rooms. Everything but the paper being made in the establishment.

To do this work fully occupies a building four stories in height (besides basement,) sixty feet in width, and one hundred and fifty feet in length, with an addition in the upper story of a large room over an entire adjoining block.

Basement.—The large basement is arranged with immense quantities of drawers, etc., for storing Bulbs. Here, too, are stored the heavier kinds of Seeds, in sacks, etc., piled to the ceiling. The heavier packing is also done here.

Seed box for starting plants indoors.

First Floor.—The first floor is used entirely as a sales-shop, or "store," for the sale of Seeds, Flowers, Plants and all Garden requisites and adornments, such as baskets, vases, lawn mowers, lawn tents, aquariums, seats, etc., etc. It is arranged with taste, and the songs of the birds, the fragrance and beauty of the flowers, make it a most delightful spot in which to spend an hour.

Second Floor.—on the second floor is the Business and Private Offices, and also the Mail Room, in which all letters are opened. The opening of letters occupies the entire time of two persons, and they perform the work with astonishing rapidity—practice making perfect— often opening three thousand in a day. After these letters are opened they are passed into what is called the Registering Room, on the same floor, where they are divided into States, and the name of the person ordering, and the date of the receipt of the order registered. They are then ready to be filled, and are passed into a large room, called the Order Room, where over seventy-five hands are employed, divided into gangs, each set, or gang, to a State, half-a-dozen or more being employed on each of the larger States. After the orders are filled, packed and directed, they are sent to what is known as the Post Office, also on the same floor, where the packages are weighed, the necessary stamps put upon them, and stamps cancelled, when they are packed in Post Office Bags, furnished us by Government, properly labelled for the different routes, and sent to the Postal Cars. Tons of Seeds are thus dispatched every day during the business season.

Third Floor.—Here is the German Department, where all orders written in the German language are filled by German clerks; a Catalogue in this language being published. On this floor, also, all seeds are packed, that is, weighed and measured and placed in paper bags and stored ready for sale. About fifty persons are employed in this room, surrounded by thousands of nicely labelled drawers.

Fourth Floor.—On this floor are rooms for Artists and Engravers, several of whom are kept constantly employed in designing and engraving for Catalogues and Chromos. Here, also, the lighter seeds are stored. In a large room adjoining, is the Printing Office, where the Catalogue is prepared, and other printing done, and also the Bindery, often employing forty or fifty hands, and turning out more than ten thousand Catalogues in a day. Here is in use the most improved machinery for covering, trimming, etc., propelled by steam.

Miscellaneous.—The immense amount of business done may be understood by a few facts: Nearly one hundred acres are employed, near the city, in growing flower seeds mainly, while large importations are made from Germany, France, Holland, Australia and Japan. Over three thousand reams of printing paper are used each year for Catalogues, weighing two hundred thousand pounds, and the simple postage for sending these Catalogues by mail is thirteen thousand dollars. Over fifty thousand dollars have been paid the Government for postage stamps last year. Millions of bags and boxes are also manufactured in the establishment, requiring hundreds of reams of paper, and scores of tons of paste-board. The business is so arranged that the wrappers are prepared for each State, with the name of the State conspicuously printed, thus saving a great deal of writing, as well as preventing errors.

INTERIOR OF STORE.

I had prepared several other engravings of German Room, Printing Office, Artists' Room, Counting Room, Mail Room, Post Office, etc., but have already occupied quite enough space to give readers somewhat of an idea of the character of my establishment. Another year I may give further particulars.

FLOWERS

FLORAL GUIDE. FOR 1873.

PORTULACA. PLATYSTEMON. POPPY.

SOLANUM.

PERENNIALS AND ANNUALS

SILENE.

THE MAIDEN'S PINK (DIANTHUS DELTOIDES), AND THE NIEREMBERGIA
RIVULARIS.

TEN-WEEKS STOCK.

155

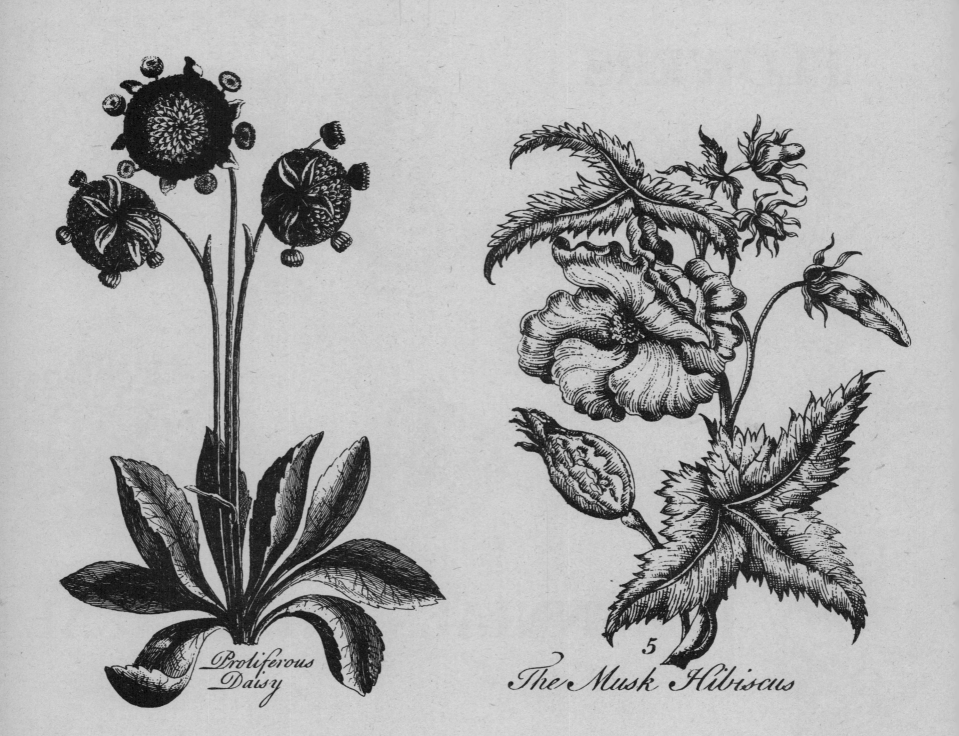

Proliferous Daisy

5

The Musk Hibiscus

HARDY, ALL-PURPOSE PERENNIALS

The following plants are field grown in rows 21 inches apart and spaced properly to make nice plants.

ACHILLEA

Angel's Breath. Green Foliage. A new double variety. White. 15 to 18 inches. July

Coronation Gold. Large golden yellow flowers. Fernlike foliage 4 to 5 inch flowering heads on sturdy 30-inch stems from July until September

Millefolium Roseum. Large heads of soft rose-red blossoms on 20" stems. June, July and August

Moonshine. Sulphur yellow flowers with silver-grey foliage. 18 to 24 inches. June to September

AGROSTEMA

Bright crimson florets nicely arranged on 18-inch bushy plants in June and July. Soft silver tinted foliage

AJUGA
(Bugle — Ground Cover)

Burgundy Glow. A new introduction valued for its attractive foliage. Purple flowers on 6-inch stems in May and June

Genevensis. Deep blue flowers. Light green foliage. 6 inches. May

Pyramidalis. Solid clumps with deep blue flowers in early Spring. 10 inches tall.

Reptans Rubra. Dense mats of reddish bronze foliage, deep purple flowers on 6-inch stems

Variegated. For borders, edging and ground covers. Pale green foliage with attractive white veins or markings in the leaves. 5 inches. May

ALLUIM
(Chives, belongs to the Herb family)

Schoenophrasum. Mauve flowers on 15 inch stems used as a cut flower, is not pungent. Indifferent to soil. Sun or light shade. Chop leaves for seasoning, also used as an ornamental or edging plant.

VARIETY

ALYSSUM
(Basket of Gold)

Saxatile Compactum (Gold Dust). 10 inches. May

Saxatile Citrinium. A lovely pale yellow. 10 inches. May

ANCHUSA

Myosotiflora. Sky blue forget-me-not flowers on 12-inch stems. Large green leaves. Does best in partial shade. Begins blooming about May 15th

ANEMONE PULSATILLA
(Pasque Flower)

One of the most fascinating dwarf perennials in existence, hardy as an oak and easily grown anywhere. This delightful harbinger of Spring will increase in size and beauty in your garden many years. A cluster of furry buds of silky texture arise a few inches above the ground and burst open into large lavender or soft violet cups with golden central tassels. Dozens of these charming blooms are produced over a period of several weeks on established plants. Tidy, ornamental, fernlike leaves follow the blooms which are replaced by seeds in the form of globular masses of silvery down on 8 to 12 inch stems in May and June

ANTHEMIS

Tinctoria Kelwayi. Clear yellow daisy. 18 inches

ARABIS
(Ground Cover)

Snow Cap (Rock Cress). Pure white flowers from April to June, excellent for rock border. 6 inches

Spring Charm. Soft rose-tinted flowers with similar characteristics as the white variety above. 6 inches.

ARTEMISIA

Dracunulus (Tarragon). A herb used to flavor vinegar, fish dishes, soups, salads, and jellied molds.

Silver King. A striking white leaved contrast plant. A "must" for setting off bouquets and combinations. A frosted silver color. 18 inches

Silver Mound (Ground Cover). A compact mound-like plant, 10 inches in diameter. Foliage is fern-like and silvery grey for rockery or for edging beds and walks.

VARIETY

AQUILEGIA
(Columbine) June, 18 inches

Crimson Star. A most striking crimson with a white corolla

Dragon Fly Hybrids. Dwarf, full color range mixture of rose, blue, yellow, white, pink and crimson on a plant that grows only 18 inches high as compared with the 2½ to 3½ foot height of present strains

Longissima. Yellow shades. 18 inches. May-June

Long Spurred Blue. Large flowers in all shades of blue, sturdy grower

Long Spurred White. White

McKana Giant Hybrids. Large showy flowers with long spurs more widely flared than any other Aquilegia

Rose Queen. Pink Shades

ARMERIA

Glory of Holland. Rich pink pin cushion type crowns on 12-inch stems in June and July

ASCLEPIAS TUBEROSA

Butterfly Flower. Bright orange. July and August, 15-inch

HARDY ASTERS
(September)

Blue Bouquet. Lovely blue, 15 inch mounds in August and September

Bonnie Blue. Beautiful, clear soft blue flowers on low mounds about 10 inches high and 15 inches across

Countess of Dudley. An excellent Dwarf Pink variety, forms 12-inch mounds

Eventide. A true English aristocrat. Almost fully double deep purple flowers of gigantic size. When fully developed, the plants are known to reach a height of 3 feet

Fellowship. The finest pink Aster. Lovely 30 inch plants

Freida Ballard. Makes a perfect mound of bright red flowers in early fall. 24 inches

Gold Flake. Gold-yellow flowers from July to September. 15 inches

Goliath. 15-inch mounds of soft blue flowers in August and September

Continued On Next Page

VARIETY

HARDY ASTERS — Continued

Lassie. Delicate pink flowers artistically arranged on sturdy stems that often attain the height of 36 inches

Lilac Time. One of the newer dwarf varieties. 10 to 12 inches.

Madam Henry Maddox. 15 inch mounds of soft pink flowers in August and September

Melba. Showy semi-double, rose pink flowers form a tight blanket over 12-inch bushy plants

Party Pink. Lovely 12 inch mounds of shell pink flowers in late July and August.

Patricia Ballard. Thick double flowers of delightful rose pink sprays on 3-foot plants. Early fall

Pink Bouquet. Lovely soft pink flowers completely cover low 12-inch mounds

Red Rover. Showy rose-red flowers on 24-inch stems in August and September. Good green foliage. Exceptionally vigorous

Rose Serenade. Soft rose florets — low-growing 12 inches

Schneekissen. White with yellow center. 12-15 inches

Snowball (new dwarf). A compact growing plant, 8-inch mounds of pure white

Snow Cushion. A sheet of sparkling snow-white blooms completely cover low 10-inch plants

Starlight. Wine red flowers covering 15 to 18 inch mounds in August and September.

Violet Carpet. Deep violet blue flowers on compact 10-inch plants that literally hug the ground

Wartberg Star (Subcoerulens). Bright lavender blue with yellow center, fine for cutting. July and August, 24 inches

White Fairy. Pure white, 15 inch mounds in August and September

ASTILBE (Spirea)

One of our most beautiful perennials that does well in that shady spot. Elegant, lacy foliage above which are borne the many spire-like clusters of flowers in lovely shades of pink, red and white. Stems are about 2 feet high and bloom in June. A wonderful cut flower and always in demand by flower arrangement devotees.

Labeled as to color — Pure White, Carmine Pink and Brilliant Red Divisions

Double Indian Nasturtium

Scarlet Lantana

CHRYSANTHEMUMS

One-year-old field-grown clumps with all the stolens left intact. We trim off most of the top growth just prior to shipping. Excellent for stock plants from which to take your own cuttings, etc. Your choice of varieties listed below

Height	Color	Variety	Bloom Period Begins	Kind
Tall	Algonquin	Bright Yellow	Oct. 10	Large Double
Medium	Bright	Clear Yellow	Oct. 1	Double
Medium	Bronze Cushion	Bronze	Oct. 10	Double
Short	Browni	Soft Bronze	Sept. 25	Double
Short	Carnation Rose	Rose Pink	Oct. 1	Double
Medium	Evelyn Garrison	Rose Pink	Oct. 10	Double
Dwarf	Golden Mound	Bright Yellow	Oct. 10	Double
Medium	Golden Queen	Golden Yellow	Oct. 1	Double
Medium	Golden Surprise	Gold	Sept. 25	Double
Medium	Lipstick	Bright Red	Oct. 1	Double
Dwarf	New Paper White	White	Oct. 1	Semi-Double
Dwarf	Orange Cushion	Bright Orange	Oct. 1	Double
Medium	Orchid Helen	Orchid Pink	Oct. 1	Double
Medium	Prairie Dawn	Deep Pink	Oct. 1	Double
Medium	Purple Cloud	Purple	Oct. 1	Double
Medium	Purple Waters	Lavender-Purple	Oct. 1	Double
Medium	Red Dessert	Rich Crimson	Oct. 1	Double
Dwarf	Red Gleam	Cerise Red	Oct. 10	Double
Medium	Salute	Purple	Oct. 10	Semi-Double
Dwarf	Snowball	Pure White	Sept. 25	Double
Medium	Superior	Orange Bronze	Sept. 20	Double
Medium	Winchell's Gold	Gold	Oct. 10	Double
Medium	Yellow Cushion	Bright Yellow	Oct. 1	Double

FALL LARKSPUR.
(DELPHINIUM ELATUM.)

SWEET-WILLIAM.
(DIANTHUS BARBATUS.)

Tree Mint

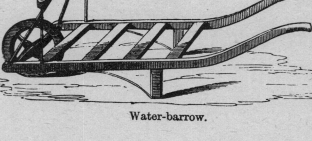

Water-barrow.

VARIETY

CENTAUREA
(June - July)

Dealbata Rose. Soft rose-pink flowers on 2 foot stems

Montana Blue. Blue flowers, 2 feet tall

CERASTIUM TOMENTOSUM
(Ground Cover)

Columnoe Snow in Summer. Gives a heavy cover of white leaves and white flowers on 8-inch stems. Full sun

CHEIRANTHUS ALLIONII
(May)

Siberian Wallflower. Bright orange, 15 inch

DORONICUM
(Leopardbane)

Caucasicum. Bright yellow daisy-like flowers on 15-inch stems during late April and May. Excellent for cutting

ECHINOPS
(July)

Globe Thistle. Ornamental thistle, blue flowers, 2-3 feet

ERIGERON
(July-August)

Red Beauty. Lovely ruby red flowers with yellow centers on 15 to 18 inch stems

Speciosus. Large blue, violet-tinted flowers, yellow centers. 15 to 18 inches

EUPATORIUM
(Mist flower; Hardy Ageratum)

Prized Cut flower. Lovely fall border plant. Sun or light shade. Blooms August until frost on 24-inch stems

EUPHORBIA

Polychroma. A beautiful plant growing 1 foot high, forming a hemispherical clump covered with yellow flowers in May and June, changing to a rosy bronze

FESTUCA GLAUCA

Here we have an ornamental grass that is in demand by landscapers for contrast. Imagine a hardy perennial grass with a silver-grey appearance that seldom grows taller than 8 inches. The blades of this silver-color grass are gracefully arched to give an effect of about 5 inches in overall height. Can be transplanted almost any time of the year. This is a neat grass for edging or to plant en masse on a bank or anywhere as a ground cover

FOUNTAIN GRASS

Eulalia Gracillima. A beautiful fine-leaved hardy ornamental grass of rather dwarf habit 4 to 5 feet. Flower heads of rich mahogany tipped white, becoming feathery white in late fall. Field-grown 1-year-old plants

FUNKIA
(Ground Cover)

Variegated. Lilac flowers, green and white veined leaves. Shade or partial shade. One-eye divisions

VARIETY

GAILLARDIA
(Blanket Flower — June, July and August)

Baby Cole. Dwarf compact plant. Less than 8 inches tall. Red flowers with yellow edges from June until frost

Burgundy. Rich wine-red, 16 inches

Dazzler. Golden-yellow with rich maroon center, 16 inches

Goblin. Are you looking for a compact variety that grows less than 14 inches tall? This may be your answer. Full size red and yellow bi-color flowers on erect sturdy stems

Portola Hybrids. Varied metallic reds, gold-tipped, 16 inches

The Sun. Golden-yellow, 12 inches

GERANIUM (Cranesbill)

True hardy perennial with lovely foliage for rock gardens or borders.

Alpinum. It makes a neat compact plant less than 12 inches tall and 12 to 14 inches across. Ideal for borders and rock gardens. The purple blue flowers are produced almost all summer long. Thrives in full sun or partial shade. It is not particular to soil, but like most perennials, requires good drainage.

GEUM

Lady Stratheden. Deep golden-yellow flowers, 2 feet

Mrs. Bradshaw. Large double fiery orange-red, 2 feet

GYPSOPHILA (Baby's Breath — July)

Bristol Fairy. Fine for cutting or border exhibition, 36 inches

Paniculata. Double white, 24 inches

Pink Fairy. Clear bright double flowers on 18-inch stems

Repens. Pink (from seeds) dwarf light rose flowers

HARDY BALTIC IVY
(Hedera Helix — Ground Cover)

Beautiful trailing ground cover for both sunny and shady locations. Ready for landscape planting.

Rooted Cuttings (100 Per Flat)

Peat Pots

VARIETY

HEMEROCALLIS — Continued

Halls Pink. Low-growing light pink.
Hawthorne Rose. Rose and yellow.
Hearts Afire. Early red.
Jewell Russell. Huge soft yellow.
Lemon Frost. Very late chartreuse.
Madrigal. Orange and red.
Magic Dawn. Light large pink.
Miss Jessie. Red and gold two-tone.
Moon Ruffles. Light yellow ruffled edge.
Pleasant Hours. Bright yellow.
President Marcue. Very light yellow almost white.
Prima Donna. Yellow with pink overtone heavy texture.
Purple Finch. French purple.
Red Magic. Large non-fading red.
Scrambled Eggs. Gold and chartreuse.
September Gold. Very late deep gold.
Sitting Bull. Deep red.
Summer Love. Giant yellow.
Tick Tock. Small flowered gold.
Velvet Fire. Blended red.
Yellow Stone. Giant gold.

HEMEROCALLIS
(Newer Varieties)

Beloved Country. Pastel Blend of orchid and pink

Channel Island. Creamy yellow with white ribs and green heart

Empire. Chrome Yellow

Frosted Beauty. Orchid Pink with gold throat

Tiny Toy. Bright yellow with gold green throat

HEUCHERA
(Coral Bells)

Chatterbox (Bristol Pink). A variety originated by Rod Cummings. Deep rose-pink flowers on 18-inch quite-erect stems, long-blooming season

Coral Cloud. Vivid coral-pink flowers

Sanguinea. Bright crimson. The tiny flowers are borne on 15-inch stems

HIBISCUS (July)

*Grandiflora Albus. Large white flowers

Continued on Next Page

VARIETY

HELENIUM
(Helen's Flower)

Cut flower and for borders. Full Sun. Plant singly or in masses for that first hint of fall effect.

Bruno. A glowing mahogany-red from late July until frost. 3 to 4 feet

Butter Pat. Golden yellow flowers

HELIANTHEMUM

Sun Rose. Low-growing evergreen plants forming large clumps covered with blooms in July and August, 10 inches

HELIANTHUS
(Perennial Sunflower)

A cut flower that resembles Dahlias. 3 to 4 feet. Blooms in July and August. Full Sun. Excellent for borders and background material.

Multiflorous Fl. Pl. Large Double Yellow

HELIOPSIS
(False Sunflower)

Patula. Golden flowers up to 3 inches across on 3-foot stems from July to September. Fine for cutting

Summer Sun. Soft yellow 2-inch flowers on 30-inch stems from July to September

HEMEROCALLIS
(Day Lily)

Very hardy garden flower of clean fragrance. Heat and drought resistant. Sun or semi-shade. July-August

Autumn Red.
Black Friar. Black red.
Cibola. Orange yellow.
Cloe. Late butter yellow.
Display. Intense red.
Dorothea. Gold and lavender.
Ebony Prince. Purple red.
Fairy East. Bright rose.
Fond Caress. Ruffled yellow.
Georgia. Orange red.
Golden Gate. Huge gold.
Goliath. Large clear yellow.

Continued on Next Page

Double Crimson Hollyhock

Great Snapdragon

Canary Bell flower.

VARIETY	VARIETY	VARIETY	VARIETY

HIBISCUS — Continued

*Grandiflora Roseus. Large rose-pink flowers

*Grandiflora Rubra. Large red flowers

Mallow Marvels. Mixed. Colors of red, pink, white florets 8 inches across on 42-inch stalks

*These seeds were supplied by a seed company in West Germany.

HOLLYHOCK
(June-July)

Charter's Double. Available in separate colors: Scarlet, Lilac Beauty, Newport Pink, White Virgin Queen, Yellow, Chamois - Salmon Rose, Maroon, 42 inches

IBERIS
(Candytuft — Late April and May)

Sempervirens. Covered with a sheet of white flowers in early spring, completely covering its rich dark green foliage

Snow Mantel. Dark green foliage, 8-inch mounds of large pure white flowers in early spring

INCARVILLEA
(Late April and May)

Brevipes. Deep rose trumpets on 12-inch stems

Delavayi. Pink trumpets on 12-inch stems

IRIS KAEMPFERI
(Japanese Iris)

Blooming season begins in mid-June. Gorgeously colored and giant in size, this Iris is perhaps the most striking of all. It has crepe-like blooms that may measure nearly 12 inches across. Stately, 36-inch stems are surrounded with lovely green foliage.

Unlike most Bearded Irises, the Japanese Iris is a flat bloom, the leaves are narrower, and the rhizomes are smaller and more compact. They delight in water while in bloom, but not at other times of the year.

Per 100 (Mixed colors)

IRIS SIBIRICA
(Siberian Iris)

Caesar's Brother. Rich deep blue flowers on 2½-foot stems during May and June

LAMIUM
(Lay'-Mi-Um — Ground Cover)

False Salvia-Maculatum. A really fine plant with heavily-marbled evergreen foliage. Will grow in full sun or dense shade if given reasonable moisture. Forms broad mats of dark red tinted foliage heavily-marbled with silver veins. Rose-pink Salvia-like flowers beginning in April, 8 inches

Galeobdolon Variegatum. One of the choicest ground covers for shady or semi-shaded spots. Attractive green and silver foliage on long, ground-hugging stems. Bright yellow flowers in the spring

LATHYRUS
(Sweet Pea — Ground Cover)

Latifolius. Vigorous climber, fine for cutting. Colors: red, pink, white, or mixed. July-August

LAVENDULA VERA

Sweet Lavender. 12 to 18 inch, used as borders around evergreens, also can be dried and used in bureau or dresser drawers for their delightful fragrance

LIATRIS
(Kansas Gay Feather — July-September)

Kobalt Blue. Violet-rose flowers on 24-inch spikes. Earliest to bloom in the Liatris family

Pychnostachya Alba. Large white spikes, 3 to 4 feet.

Pychnostachya. Large spikes of rich purple, 3 to 4 ft.

Scariosa Purple. A very sturdy and hardy plant which will thrive in almost any type of soil with reasonable drainage. Excellent cut flower material, 42 inches

LILY-OF-THE-VALLEY
(Ground Cover — available after Feb. 1, 1974)

Pure white, 6-8 inches. May and June (3 to 5 eyes bundled)

LINUM

Flavum. Transparent yellow flowers, June, 10 inches

Perennial Flax. Heavenly blue, 18 inches

LIRIOPE

Muscaria Majestic. Does well in sun or shade. Grass-like foliage. Deep Purple flowers in spikes. Chop leaves for seasoning, also used as an ornamental or edging plant

LUNARIA
(Money Plant — May)

Biennis. Dark crimson flowers, silver pod, 16 inches

LUPINES
(June-July)

Russell's Hybrids. Solid spires of closely-set Sweet Pea type blossoms. Require moist location in sun or partial shade, 24 inches

LYCHNIS

Chalcedonica. Bright scarlet heads on 24-inch stems in June and July

Viscaria Flore-Pleno Rose Champion. One of our favorite dwarf perennials. It is absolutely fool-proof and easily grown in any kind of soil with sunny exposure. Large double-clusters of brilliant rose-red make a showy display during midsummer. Wonderful low-border plant about 1 foot high

LYTHRUM
(July and August)

Mordens Gleam. Full-flowering spikes of carmine-rose, 36 inches

Mordens Pink. The plant grows to a height of 3-4 feet, and bears dozens of spikes covered with deep Phlox-like florets

Purple Spires. Showy, 42-inch spikes of Fuchsia purple flowers

Robert. A clear fuchsia-pink with sparkling reddish glow, about 18 inches tall

MATRICARIA
(Feverfew)

Golden Ball. Double butter-yellow flowers on bushy 12-inch plants in June and July

Ultra-Double White. (Grown from seeds). Stately 24-inch plants with flowers so double it closely resembles the quality usually obtained from top cuttings

White Star. Extra dwarf, only 6 inches tall. An abundance of unusual flowers with broad guard petals around button-type centers

MENTHA (Belongs to the Herb Family; Spearmint)

Emerald "N" Gold. An unusual form of Mint. Dark green foliage, liberally flecked with yellow. 14 inches

MONARDA (Bee-Balm — Bergamot)

Cut flower with aromatic leaves, moist soil, light shade. June-July, 2 feet.

Cambridge Scarlet. Billiant crimson flowers from June to August. A good shady border plant

Croftway Pink. Delicate rose pink

MYOSOTIS ALPESTRIS

Victoria Dark Blue. Dwarf compact bushy globular plants 6 to 8 inches, May and June

NEPETA

Blue Wonder. Improved compact growing and longer-blooming variety. 12 to 15 inch plants with lavender-blue flowers in May and June

OENOTHERA
(Evening Primrose)

Missouriensis. A low-growing profuse bloomer from June until September. Large yellow flowers

Youngi (Fruiticosa). Bright yellow flowers neatly arranged on 24-inch stems. July and August

OPUNTIA
(Prickly Pear)

Humifusa. Flat, spiny thickened leaves. Yellow flowers. Useful in rock gardens. Sun. Requires a well-drained soil

ORIENTAL POPPY

Beauty of Livermore. Deep oxblood-red on 30-inch stems late May and June

Orange Scarlet. Grown from seeds

Queen Alexander. Bright salmon-pink flowers on 30-inch stems late May and June

PACHYSANDRA (Terminalis — Ground Cover)

Excellent ground cover around evergreens, etc. Rich shiny green foliage. Loves shade. 2¼" pots only

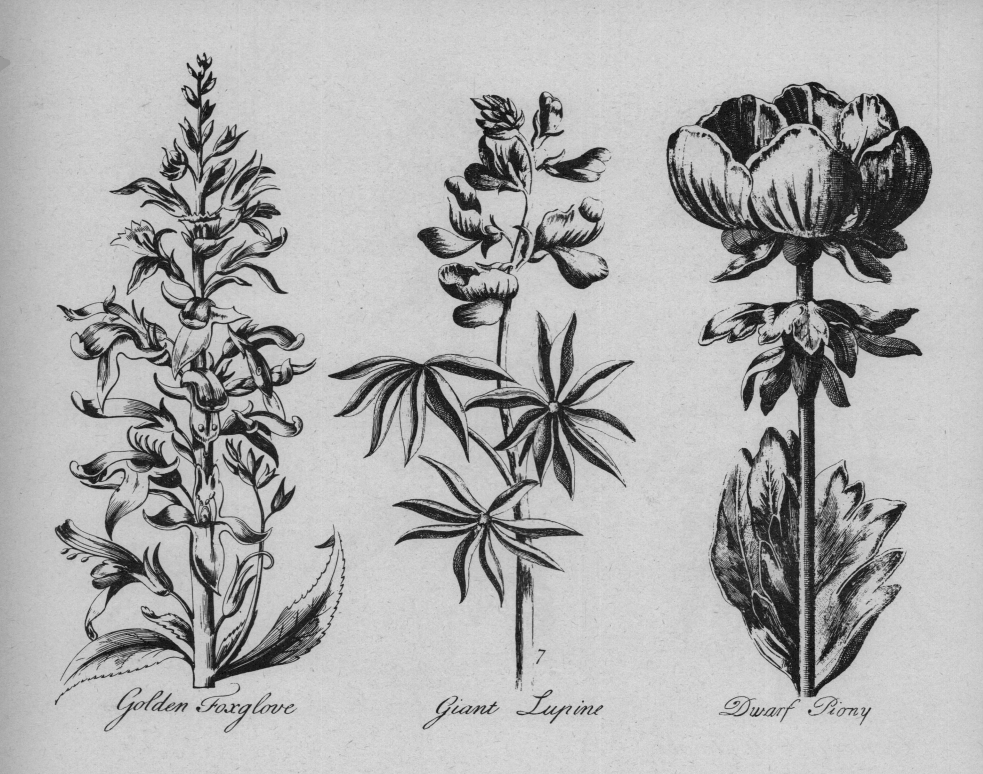

Golden Foxglove   *Giant Lupine*   *Dwarf Piony*

VARIETY

PACHYSTIMA

Canbyi. Spreading little evergreen with glossy foliage.

PENSTEMON
(Beard Tongue)

Barbartus, Elfin Pink. Clear pink. Dwarf. Hardy. 12 inches high

Pinifolius. A dwarf 8-inch bushy plant with Pine-like foliage, orange-scarlet flowers

Prairie Dusk. Sturdy rose-purple spikes during June and July, 20 inches

Prairie Fire. Showy fire-red miniature trumpet-shaped florets on 20-inch stems during June and July

PEONY

Peony. Double-flowering — available by color — red, pink, or white. Strong 3 to 5 eye divisions for potting

HARDY FIELD GROWN PHLOX

For that splash of color during July and August
(No. 1 Transplants)
American Beauty. Clear rose-pink.
Apollo. White, large grower.
August Fackel. Cherry red — late-blooming variety.
Blue Moon. Soft bluish mauve with white glow.
Border Queen. Pure pink.
Boulvardier. Large violet with darker eye.
Bridesmaid. White with crimson eye.
B. Symens Jeune. Truly an outstanding variety. Soft pink with sparkling crimson eye.
Caroline Vanden Berg. Lavender-blue.
Chieftain. Intense deep crimson.
Dodo Hanbury Forbes. (new) Pink with red eye.
Dresden China. Very large soft-pink strong grower.
E. I. Farrington. Soft salmon-pink with lighter eye.
Elizabeth Arden. Heavy trusses of soft pastel pink with pale pink ring around the eye.
Eva Forster. Bright salmon-rose.
Eventide. A good blue Phlox.
Everest. Purest white — pink eye.
Fairest One. Lovely shell pink florets on exceptionally large well-formed heads. Sturdy 24-inch stems.
Continued on Next Page

VARIETY

HARDY FIELD PHLOX — Continued

Fairy's Petticoat. Very light pink with deeper eye.
Flash. Bright carmine crimson.
Frauenlob. Soft chamois-pink florets with carmine centers. An outstanding variety in this color class.
Fuchia. A purplish blue.
Harvest Fire. Fiery crimson.
Hauptmann Koehl. Dark crimson.
Leo Schlageter. Bright crimson scarlet with large clusters filled with big florets.
Marlborough. New orchid purple.
Mary Louise. Waxy white.
Mrs. R. P. Struthers. Orange-red.
Orange. Orange.
Otley Choice. Large flowering carmine.
Prime Minister. Vigorous grower, white with red eye.
Prince George. Stately red heads on 30-inch stems.
Princess. Dazzling snow-white.
Progress. Pastel blue with purple-blue eye.
Purple Sweethear. Reddish purple with darker eye.
Royal Purple. Dark violet-blue.
Salmon Beauty. Delicate salmon-pink.
San Antonio. Outstanding blood-red.
Sandra. Enormous showy scarlet heads on rather short stems, about 18 inches overall.
Sir John Falstaff. Enormous trusses of rich salmon-pink
Snowstorm. Lovely pure white.
Starfire. Considered one of the best red varieties.
Starlight. Purplish-violet with white star.
Sunray. Salmon-rose with orange sheen.
Tenor. A bright red only 2 feet tall. Blooms very early.
Thunderbolt. Bright tangerine scarlet overlaid. Large florets, eyes of rouge.
Von Lassburg. Pure white.
White Admiral. New, produces beautiful snow mounds of pure white flowers on enormous heads. Excellent late blooms.
Windsor. Bright salmon pink, large trusses.

Trial order — 6 plants each of 10 named varieties — shippers selection for $15.00.

For those who have a problem with the lower leaves on
Continued on Next Page

VARIETY

HARDY FIELD PHLOX — Continued

Phlox, we suggest a spray formula: 3T 25% Malathion, 2T 50% Captan. All in the form of wettable powder mixed thoroughly in 1 gallon of water and repeated every 8 to 10 days during warm weather.

HARDY PHLOX SUFFRUITICOSA
(Early Phlox)

Miss Lingard. June-flowering white Phlox on 24-inch stems
Take advantage of our best crop we have ever grown. Imagine stately 24-inch stems crowned with 6-inch heads of fragrant white florets in June, for weddings, etc.

WALTERS' PHLOX SUBULATA
(Ground Cover — Spring-Flowering — April and May)

Atropurpurea. Rich wine-red
Blue Emerald. A blue sport of Emerald Pink
Blue Hills. Showy sky-blue
Crimson Beauty. Large flowers of brilliant red covering and dense soft mats of foliage
Elaire. Large showy bright pink florets covering 8 to 10-inch mounds of soft green foliage
Emerald Pink. A close, compact evergreen foliage, florets of unusual size, color a pure unbleached pink
May Snow. Pure snow-white florets on compact type plants
Pink Perfection. A very nice pink with a deeper red eye
Red Wing. It begins blooming after most other varieties have faded out. Immense jumbo-sized florets of striking crimson with dark eyes
Rosea. Bright rose
Scarlet Flame. Fiery bright crimson florets on light green foliage. Vigorous growing habits
White Delight. Probably the largest pure white in existence today. Bright green foliage

PHYSALIS
(Chinese Lanterns — July-August)

Franchetti. Bright orange-scarlet, 20 inches

VARIETY

PHYSOSTEGIA
(False Dragonhead) — (August and September)
(Also Called Obedient Plant)

Bouquet. Bright pink, excellent cut flower, attractive and effective, 3 ft.

White Virginia. Pure white, 2 ft.

PLATYCODON
(Balloon Flower — July-August)

Mariesi Blue. Deep violet-blue bell-shaped flowers on 12-inch plants

Shell Pink. 15 inches

White. Pure white, 15 inches

PLUMBAGO LARPENTAE
(For ground cover or borders)

Rich dark green foliage mounds covered with intense blue flowers from late July to September. Leaves take on reddish hues in the fall

POLEMONIUM

Jacobs Ladder. Clear light blue flowers in early Spring, excellent for borders. 16 inches

POLYGONUM
(Dwarf Lace Plant — Ground Cover)

Border Jewel. A true creeping ground cover only 4 inches high, dark green foliage, small light pink flowers in May

Reynouti. Excellent ground cover for unshaded areas where Vinca and Pachysandra are not satisfactory. Light green foliage turns crimson-red in late August. Red buds — coral-pink flowers

POTENTILLA
(Cinquefoil, Five Finger)

Nepalensis Miss Willmott. 12-inch plants covered with bright carmine-scarlet flowers in June and July

Double Violet

Double French Marygold

Aethiopian Marygold

VARIETY	VARIETY	VARIETY	VARIETY

PRIMULA
(Hardy Primrose)

Pacific Giant Strain. Very large flowers in a wide color range and longer stems. The finest strain available. Seed is produced by hand Hybridization under glass. For best result plant in partial shade. 2¼" pots

PYRETHRUM
(Painted Daisy — June and July)

James Kelway. Deep scarlet, 18 inches

Robinson Hybrids. Exceptionally large, 18 inches

RUDBECKIA (Coneflower)

Purpurea. Reddish-purple flowers on 2½ to 3 ft. stems formed from July to September

SALVIA
(June and July)

Superba Compacta. Spires of rich purple covering the entire plant for many weeks. 24 to 30 inches

SANTOLINA
(Ground Cover)

Incana. Grey feathery foliage forms into 12-inch mounds

SAPONARIA
(Rock Soapwart — Ground Cover)

Ocymoides. Broad spreading leafy plants studded with bright pink flowers. A rampant plant giving color to the rock garden in the summer, 8 inches tall

SCABIOSA
(July-August)

Caucasica Houses Hybrids. A lovely mixture of color shades ranging from soft lavender to pure white. 15 to 18 inches

Caucasica White. Pure white form of above, 15 inches

SEDUM
(Ground Cover)

Interesting fleshy-leaved plants ideal for rockery or dry banks as well as low borders because of mat-forming habit and distinctive foliage which change with the seasons. Perfectly hardy, will grow in any soil. Full sun.

Ellacombianum. Excellent ground cover for sunny, dry slopes and banks. Lovely 8-inch mounds of lemon-yellow flowers during June month. Attractive green foliage during summer and fall.

Autumn Joy. Bronze flowers on 10-inch stems from July until September

Bronze Carpet. Dwarf prostrate mats of bronze colored foliage

Dragon's Blood. Grows only 3 to 4 inches tall and is covered with brilliant red flowers from June until August

Glauca. Prostrate mats of tiny blue-grey rosettes covered with white flowers in May and June

Globosum (Old Man Bones). Many intertwining branches with interesting globular puffed-up leaves. Rich bronze color effect. Very unusual tufted carpet effect

Continued on Next Page

SEDUM — Continued

Golden Carpet. Compact mats of golden yellow flowers formed in June

Kamtschaticum. Orange-yellow flowers, dark green leaves, July-September. 3-4 inches

Oregonum Glaucum. Fat little globular leaves of brilliant emerald on 2-inch twigs that hug the ground, soft yellow flowers

Pruinatum Forsterianum. Masses of silvery-blue spruce-like branches on low 3-inch mats. Yellow flowers

Reflexum. Bluish green spruce-like foliage sends out attractive 8-inch ornamental flowering stems during the month of June. Soft yellow flowers

Rosy Glow. A cross between Sieboldi and Spectabile Atropurpurea. Excellent blue-green foliage and large pink flowers

Spathulifolium. Fat globular leaves on silver-green stems with yellow flowers in June and July

Spectabile Brilliant. Erect-growing mass of rose-colored flower heads, 18 inches tall, blooming in August and September. Ideal for shady area.

Stoloniferium. Fine evergreen blue spruce creeper. Soft pink flowers form during the month of June on ornamental-like 8-inch stems

Stoloniferium Album. New soft white form of above

Supurium Coccineum (Bronze Carpet). Bright rose flowers on reddish stems and leaves

Worm Grass (Album). White flowers on dainty compact foliage

SEDUM MAXIMUM
(Mahogany Plant)

Atropurpurea. Novelty. 18-inch stems with mahogany red-tinted foliage topped with cream-colored flowers in August and September

SEMPERVIVUM
(Hens and Chicks — Houseleek — Ground Cover)
(sim-per-vy'-vum. From Sempervivo, to live forever)

The majority of Sempervivums that are cultivated are used as rockery or rock wall plants. They are also used in the perennial border and in miniature gardens, in porch boxes, in garden vases, and for edging.

Continued on Next Page

SEMPERVIVUM — Continued

They will grow well in a wide variety of soils, even pure sand. They should have a good drainage. (A fine mixture of various sorts)

1 year old clumps
Single Rosettes
10 each of 5 named varieties
10 each of 10 named varieties

STATICE
(Sea Lavender)

Airy sprays of miniature flowers form immense heads. Leathery leaves spread out at base of plant. Excellent subjects to cut and dry for year-around filler

Latifolia. Small lavender-blue flowers.

STOKESIA
(Stokes Aster)

Blue Danube. 5 to 6 inch flowers on a 12 to 18 inch stem. Dark blue flowers. Blooms all summer

TEUCRIUM
(Germander)

Canadensis. An unusually attractive and useful ground cover or edging plant that we recommend highly. 6 inches. Ground-hugging evergreen, spreads slowly. Thick shiny green foliage that springs up after walking on it. Rose-colored flowers. June-July. More colorful than chamaedrys and winters much better. Does well in shade or sun.

Chamaedrys. Glossy green foliage, resembling dwarf Boxwood, can be clipped to suit any height up to 12 inches

THERMOPSIS
(June and July)

Caroliniana. Yellow pea-shaped flowers on long stems 2-3 feet tall

THYMUS
(Creeping Thymus — Ground Cover)

Citriodorus. Lemon-flavored, light green foliage with tiny pink flowers blooming in June and July, 12 inches

Coccineum. Brilliant scarlet flowers in June and July, 6 inches

Blue Pyrenaan

Double Primrose

VARIETY	VARIETY	VARIETY	VARIETY

TRADESCANTIA
(Spider Wort)

Cut flower with ornamental purple-veined foliage. Prolific bloomer from late June to September. 18-inch stems, border plant.

Red Cloud. Bright, rosy red. 10-12 inches

Pauline. Orchid pink. 10 to 12 inches

TREE PEONIES

One-year-old grafted Tree Peonies imported from Japan well-developed and carefully graded. These plants will bloom one year after they are planted.

Available after January 1, 1974.

Red Varieties. Jitsugetsu, Nishiki and Higurashi

Pink Varieties: Yachyatsubaki and Tamafuyo

Purple Varieties: Hanadaijan, Kamata and Fuji

White Varieties. Godaishu and Hakuoishu

TRITOMAS
(Poker Plant — July, August and September)

Early Hybrids. Red and orange shades, 30 inches

Pfitzeri. Deep orange flower spikes on 18-24 inch stems. Excellent cut flowers

Primrose Beauty. Real primrose yellow. Height 30 inches

VERBENA
(Ground Cover)

Canadensis. A hardy creeping plant covered with bright reddish-purple flowers from June until September, 8 inches

VERONICA
(July-September)

Barcarole. A choice new Veronica, with deep rose-pink flowers. It grows compact to about 10 inches.

Blue Giant. A new introduction from our friends in Europe. This is a new improved variety which blooms earlier, June to September, with large spikes of deep blue. It grows 18 to 24 inches tall, lovely in the garden and excellent for cutting

Crater Lake Blue. Gentian-blue flowers. June until August. 15 inches
Continued on Next Page

VERONICA — Continued

Icicle. Unusual 18 to 20 inch snow-white spikes. Good foliage

Incana. Silvery-grey foliage with deep blue 12-inch flower spikes

Minuet. Soft rose-pink flowers on erect 15-inch stems

Pavane. A fine shade of clear pink, 18 inches high. As many as 20 spikes on one plant

Rupestris Heavenly Blue. Sapphire blue flowers. Prostrate growth, evergreen foliage. May to June. Only 3 to 4 inches tall

Spicata Blue. Violet-blue, 18-24 inches

VINCA MINOR
(Ground Cover)

Bowles Variety. Ground cover for slopes, banks and under trees and shrubbery. Loves shade

VIOLA ODORATA

Sweet Violet, Royal Robe. Giant sweet-scented violets in a lustrous shade of deep violet-blue. Long stems makes this the best variety for cutting. Early spring and late fall

YUCCA FILAMENTOSA
(Adams' Needle)

Strong stately spikes rise 5 to 6 feet tall, and are covered with creamy white bell-shaped flowers. The broad bright green sword-like foliage is unusual and attractive for sunny and well-drained locations

YUCCA GLAUCA BLUE

Narrow stiff blades edged white, excellent for use in rock-covered area. Flowers on shorter stems and earlier than others. One-year plants for potting or growing on

ASPARAGUS

Martha Washington, 1-year-old
2-year-old

BEGONIAS

Tuberous Rooted: (Double Camellia-Flowered) Red, pink, scarlet, salmon, orange, yellow, copper and white.
2 inch and up diameter
1½-2 inch diameter

Pendula Begonias (Hanging) Red, pink, yellow, white and orange.
2 inch and up diameter
1½-2 inch diameter

ISMENE CALATHINA
(Peruvian Daffodils)
2-inch and up

MADEIRA VINES
(Boussingaultia baselloides)

Quick-growing vine for indoor as well as outdoor planting
3-inch and up
2-3 inch

OXALIS, PINK-FLOWERING
Clover-like

TUBEROSES
4/6-inch

GLADIOLUS COLLECTION

1,000 Gladiolus, 1½'' and up, in 10 varieties with pictures

500 Gladiolus, 1½'' and up, in 10 varieties with pictures

CANNAS
(Strong healthy 2 to 5 eye divisions)

Ambassador, deep red, red foliage, medium height

City of Portland, pink, green foliage, medium height

Florence Vaughan, deep yellow, green foliage, medium height

Red King Humbert, red, bronze foliage, tall

Richard Wallace, yellow-green foliage, dwarf

The President, large bright red, green foliage, dwarf

Wyoming, deep orange, bronze foliage, medium height

Yellow King Humburt, yellow variegated with red spots, medium green foliage

HORSERADISH
Whole plants

LILIUM
(Hardy Lilies)

Auratum, gold banded Lily 8/9 inch
Henryi, orange-yellow 8/9 inch
Regal, white shading cream 8/9 inch
Rubrum, rose-pink spotted red 8/9 inch

RHUBARB

Victoria, 1 year seedlings
Canada Red, divisions

Typical list from:
Walters Gardens, Inc.
P.O. Box 137
96th Ave, at M-21
Zeeland, Mich. 49464

162

Evergreen

Aethionema
Alchemilla
Ajuga
Alyssum
Arabis
Arenaria
Armeria
Aubrieta
Baptisia
Dianthus Caesius
Festuca
Heath
Heather
Helleborus
Helianthemum
Heuchera
Iberis
Lewisia
Liriope
Linum Narbonense
Nepeta
Pachistima
Pachysandra
Phlox Subulata
Potentilla
Rosemarinus Officinalis
Sedum Acre
Sedum Alba
Sedum Album Magnificum
Sedum Bronze Carpet
Sedum Lydium
Sedum Reflexum
Sedum Spurium Dragons Blood
Sedum Sexangulare
Sedum Spurium Coccineum
Sempervivum
Senecio
teucrium
Thymus
Tunica
Vinca
Yucca

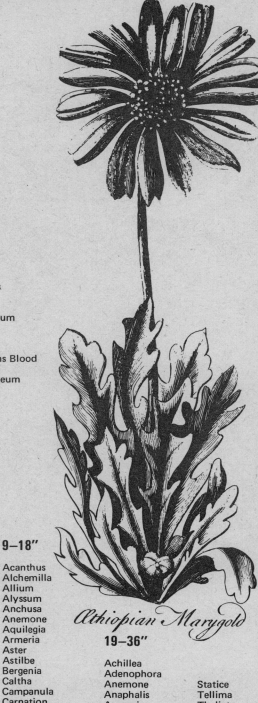

Æthiopian Marygold

9–18"

Acanthus
Alchemilla
Allium
Alyssum
Anchusa
Anemone
Aquilegia
Armeria
Aster
Astilbe
Bergenia
Caltha
Campanula
Carnation
Catananche
Chrysanthemum
Coreopsis
Corydalis
Dianthus
Dicentra
Erigeron
Euphorbia
Festuca
Filipendula
Geranium
Geum
Gypsophila
Heath
Heather
Helianthemum
Hypericum
Iberis
Incarvillea
Lamium
Lavandula
Leontopodium
Linum
Lychnis
Liriope
Lysimachia
Mertensia
Molinia
Nepeta
Oenothera
Penstemon
Platycodon
Phlox
Plumbago
Polemonium
Polygonum
Potentilla
Primula
Pulmonaria
Ranunculus
Ruta
Salvia
Santolina
Saxifraga
Scabiosa
Sedum
Statice
Stokesia
Symphytum
Teucrium
Thermopsis
Tradescantia
Veronica

19–36"

Achillea
Adenophora
Anemone
Anaphalis
Amsonia
Anthemis
Aquilegia
Artemisia
Asclepias
Aster
Bergenia
Campanula
Centaurea
Chrysanthemum
Clematis
Crocosmia
Delphinium
Dianthus
Dicentra
Dictamnus
Digitalis
Doronicum
Echinops
Erigeron
Eryngium
Eupatorium
Funkia
Gaura
Geum
Gillenia
Heathers
Heliopsis
Helleborus
Heuchera
Inula
Iris Siberica
Liatris
Ligularia
Lychnis
Lythrum
Malva
Monarda
Oenothera
Pardanthus
Penstemon
Pol
Peony
Phlox
Physostegia
Physalis
Poppy
Pyrethrum
Rudbeckia
Salvia
Santolina
Sedum
Solidag
Sidalc

Statice
Tellima
Thalictrum
Tritoma
Trollius
Valeriana
Veronica

36" and over

Aconitum
Anchusa
Artemisia
Aster
Baptisia
Bocconia
Boltonia
Clematis
Delphinium
Digitalis
Filipendula
Gypsophila
Helenium
Helianthus
Hemerocallis
Hibiscus
Hollyhocks
Iris Spuria
Iris Japanese
Iris Marhigo
Lathyrus
Liatris
Lobelia
Lythrum
Miscanthus
Phlox
Rudbeckia
Salvia
Thermopsis
Verbascum
Yucca

HEIGHT GUIDE

2–8"

Achillea
Aethionema
Ajuga
Antennaria
Anthemis
Arabis
Arenaria
Artemisia
Aubrieta
Campanula
Cerastium
Chrysanthemum
Chrysogonum
Convallaria
Dianthus
Draba
Euphorbia
Gaillardia
Geranium
Geum
Heather
Hypericum
Hylomecon
Iberis
Leontopodium
Lewisia
Linum
Lotus
Mazus
Myosotis
Nierembergia
Pachistima
Pachysandra
Phlox Subulata
Phlox Divaricata
Platycodon
Polygonum
Potentilla
Primula
Pycnanthemum
Scabiosa
Sedum
Sempervivum
Senecio
Silene
Stachys
Eucrium
Thymus
Tunica
Veronica
Vinca
Viola

SINGLE GERANIUM.

The Bee Flower

DOUBLE GERANIUM.

LIVER LEAF.
(HEPATICA TRILOBA.)

COMPASS PLANT.
(SILPHIUM LACINIATUM.)

COLOR GUIDE

White

Achillea
Aconitum
Ajuga
Anaphalis
Anthemis
Aquilegia
Arabis
Arenaria
Aster
Astilbe
Aubrieta
Bergenia
Bocconia
Boltonia
Carnation
Cerastium
Chrysanthemum
Convallaria
Clematis
Delphinium
Dianthus
Dictamnus
Digitalis
Euphoriba
Filipendula
Funkia
Gypsophila
Heaths
Heather
Helleborus
Helianthemum
Heuchera
Hibiscus
Hollyhock
Iberis
Iris
Lathyrus
Leontopodium
Liatris
Linum
Lychnis
Monarda
Nierembergia
Peony
Phlox
Pimelia
Physostegia
Platycodon
Poppy
Polygonatum
Potentilla
Pyrethrum
Rudbeckia
Scabiosa
Saxifrage
Sedum
Sidalcea
Silene
Stokesia
Thymus
Tritoma
Tradescantia
Verbascum
Veronica
Vinca
Viola
Yucca

BLUE

Aconitum
Adenophora
Ajuga
Amsonia
Anchusa
Aquilegia
Aster
Baptisia
Campanula
Catananche
Centaurea
Clematis
Delphinium
Eryngium
Erigeron
Eupatorium
Funkia
Geranium
Iris
Linum
Mazus
Mertensia
Monarda
Myosotis
Nepeta
Penstemon
Perovskia
Phlox
Platycodon
Plumbago
Polemonium
Pulmonaria
Salvia
Scabiosa
Statice
Stokesia
Tradescantia
Veronica
Vinca
Viola

Red

Achillea
Allium
Anemone
Armeria
Aster
Astilbe
Aubrieta
Bergenia
Carnation
Dianthus
Gaillardia
Geum
Heather
Helianthemum
Heuchera
Hibiscus
Hollyhock
Incarvillea
Iris
Lathyrus
Linum
Lychnis
Lythrum
Malva
Monarda
Penstemon
Peony
Phlox
Poppy
Polygonum
Primula
Pulmonaria
Pyrethrum
Rudbeckia
Sedum
Sempervivum
Symphytum
Teucrium
Thymus
Tradescantia
Tritoma
Viola

PINK

Aethionema
Ajuga
Anemone Japonica
Antennaria
Aquilegia
Arabis
Armeria
Aster
Astilbe
Aubrieta
Carnation
Chrysanthemum
Clematis
Dianthus
Dicentra
Dictamnus
Erigeron
Gaura
Geranium
Gillenia
Gypsophila
Heaths
Heather
Helleborus
Helianthemum
Heuchera
Hibiscus
Hollyhock
Iberis
Iris
Lamium
Lathyrus
Lavandula
Liatris
Lewisia
Lythrum
Monarda
Penstemon
Peony
Phlox
Physostegia
Platycodon
Polygonum
Poppy
Primula
Pyrethrum
Pulmonaria
Rudbeckia
Saponaria
Scabiosa
Sedum
Sidalcea
Stachys
Teucrium
Thymus
Tradescantia
Tunica
Valeriana
Verbascum
Veronica
Viola

Purple and Lavender

Ajuga
Allium
Anemone
Aster
Aubrieta
Campanula
Delphinium
Echinops
Funkia
Geranium
Heaths
Heather
Incarvillea
Iris
Lavandula
Liatris
Liriope
Lythrum
Nepeta
Penstemon
Platycodon
Poppy
Phlox
Salvia
Sidalcea
Statice
Thalictrum
Tradescantia
Veronica
Vinca
Viola

Orange

Asclepias
Crocosmia
Erigeron
Geum
Helenium
Heliopsis
Hemerocallis
Ligularia
Pardanthus
Penstemon
Poppy
Phlox
Physalis
Potentilla
Tritoma
Trollius

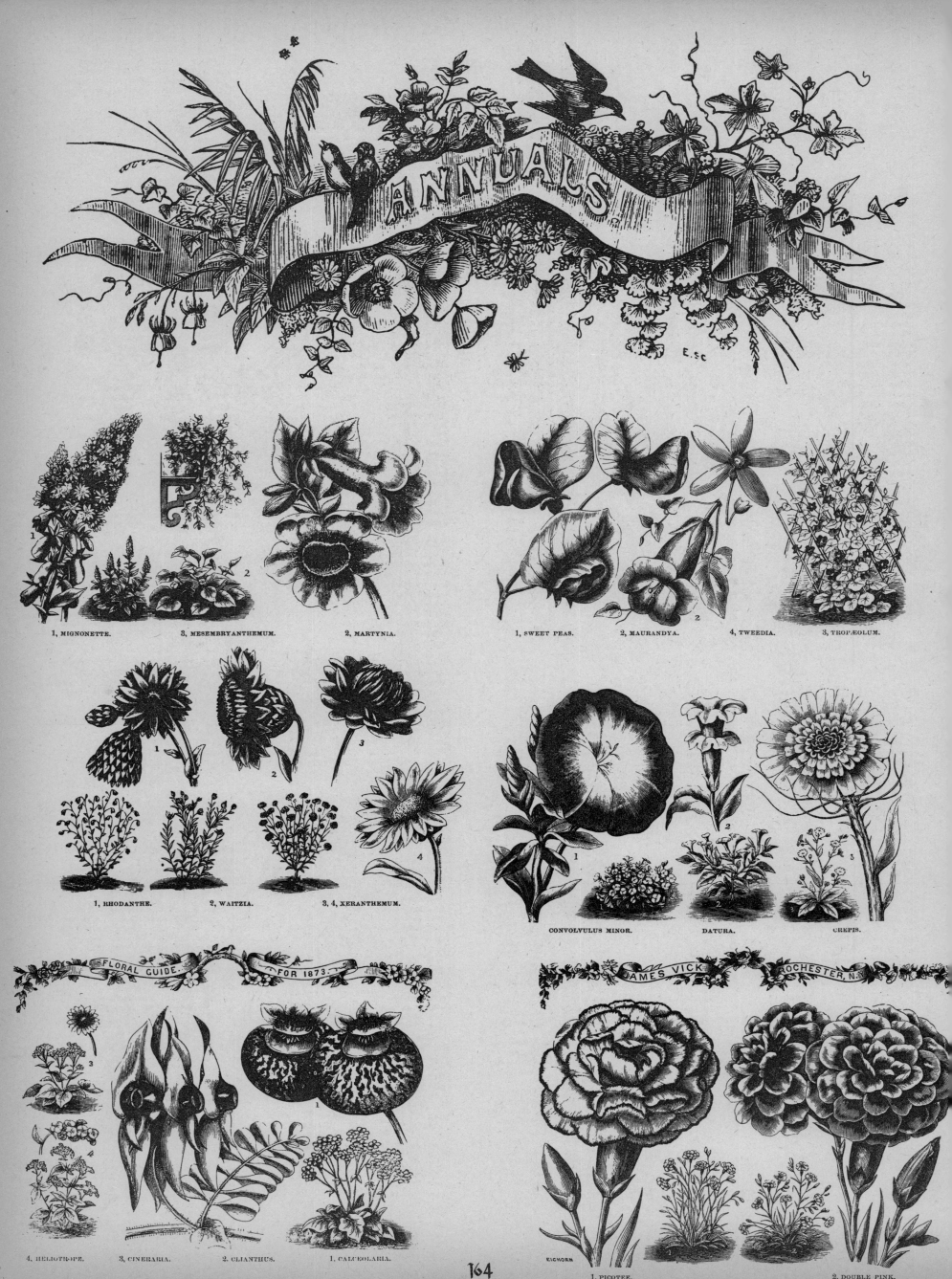

ANNUALS

E.SC

1, MIGNONETTE. 3, MESEMBRYANTHEMUM. 2, MARTYNIA.

1, SWEET PEAS. 2, MAURANDYA. 4, TWEEDIA. 3, TROPÆOLUM.

1, RHODANTHE. 2, WAITZIA. 3, 4, XERANTHEMUM.

CONVOLVULUS MINOR. DATURA. CREPIS.

FLORAL GUIDE. FOR 1873. JAMES VICK ROCHESTER, N.

4, HELIOTROPE. 3, CINERARIA. 2, CLIANTHUS. 1, CALCEOLARIA.

EICHORN

1. PICOTEE, 2, DOUBLE PINK.

164

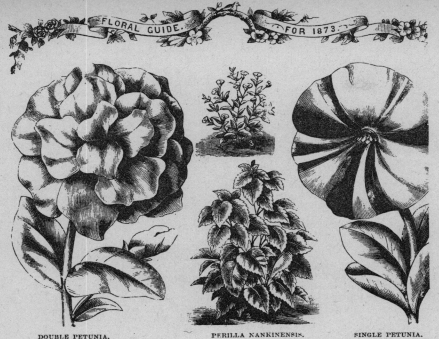

FLORAL GUIDE FOR 1873.

DOUBLE PETUNIA.   PERILLA NANKINENSIS.   SINGLE PETUNIA.

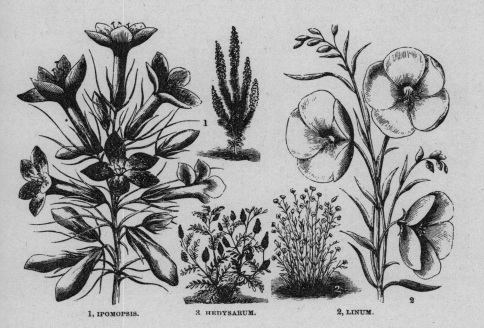

1, IPOMOPSIS.   3. HEDYSARUM.   2, LINUM.

2. PERENNIAL PEA.   1, PENTSTEMON.

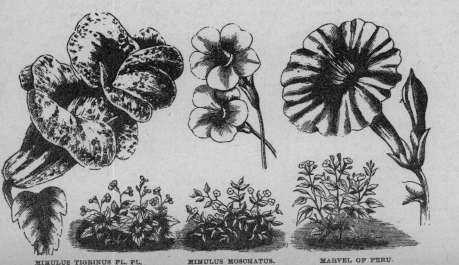

MIMULUS TIGRINUS FL. PL.   MIMULUS MOSCHATUS.   MARVEL OF PERU.

MAIL-ORDER RETAIL NURSERIES

Ackerman Nurseries, Lake St., Bridgman, Michigan 49106. (616) 465-3422. Retail and wholesale. Fruit and nut trees, berry plants, ornamental trees and shrubs. Mail-order catalog.

Adams Nursery, Box 525, Rte. 20, Westfield, Massachusetts 01085. (413) 562-3644, 736-0443. Retail and wholesale. General nursery stock. Catalog.

Alberta Nurseries & Seeds, Ltd., Bowden, Manitoba, Canada. (403) 224-3362. Mostly retail. Ornamental and fruit trees. Vegetable and flower seed. Mail-order catalog.

J. Herbert Alexander, 1224 Wareham St., Middleboro, Massachusetts 02346. (617) 947-3397. Lilacs, Flowering quince, blueberries, phlox. Descriptive mail-order list.

Alley Pond Nurseries, 323-10 Horace Harding Blvd., Bayside, New York 11364. (212) 225-8700. Local retail. General nursery stock.

Alpenglow Gardens (Michaud & Company), 13328 King George Highway, North Surrey, British Columbia, Canada. (604) 581-8733. Rock garden plants, dwarf conifers. Mail-order catalog and periodic supplements.

Armstrong Nurseries, 830 W. Phillips, Ontario, California 91764. (714) 984-1211. Retail and wholesale. Hybrid tea and other roses. Mail-order catalog.

Arnold's Clematis Nursery, 2005 S. E. Park Ave., Milwaukie, Oregon 97222. (503) 654-1347. Retail. Extensive clematis listing. Mail-order catalog

Arrowhead Gardens, 115 Boston Post Rd., Wayland, Massachusetts 01778. (617) 358-7333. Retail and wholesale. General nursery stock.

Avalon Mountain Gardens, Dana, North Carolina 38724. (704) 692-9898. Retail. Azaleas, heathers and perennials. List. Ships.

Bachman's, Inc., 6010 Lyndale Ave. South, Minneapolis, Minnesota 55423. (612) 827-3561. Retail and wholesale. Garden centers. General nursery stock. Retail catalog. Ships.

Boething Treeland Farms, 23475 Ventura Blvd., Woodland Hills, Calif 91364. (213) 347-8822. Eight nurseries and garden centers in Los Angeles, Riverside and Ventura counties. Container-grown plants. Service charge on truck deliveries more than 100 miles from Woodland Hills. Retail catalog.

Warren Baldsiefen, Box 88, Bellvale, New York 10912. Retail. Rhododendrons. Mail-order catalog $1.50, refundable on first purchase. Nursery not open to visitors.

Patsy Bello Nurseries, 5600 Flatlands Ave., Brooklyn, New York 11234. (212) 743-0815, 444-3800. Retail and wholesale. General nursery stock. Does not ship.

Bountiful Ridge Nurseries, Princess Anne, Maryland 21853. (301) 651-0400. Fruit and nut trees, berry plants and ornamentals. Retail and wholesale. Garden center. Mail-order catalog.

The Bovees, 1735 S. W. Coronado, Portland, Oregon 97219. (503) 244-9341. Retail only. Uncommon rhododendron species and hybrids, Exbury azaleas. Visitors by appointment. Mail-order catalog 25 cents.

Breck's of Boston, 200 Breck Building, Boston, Massachusetts 02210. Standard nursery stock plus a wide listing of annual and vegetable seeds. Gardening supplies. Mail-order catalog.

Bunting's Nurseries, Selbyville, Delaware 19975. (302) 436-8231. Separate retail and wholesale catalogs. Strawberries, fruit and nut trees, ornamentals. Mail-order catalog.

Burgess Seed and Plant Co., Box 218 Galesburg, Michigan 49053. (616) 665-7079. Retail. Fruit and nut trees, berry plants, ornamentals. Vegetable and flower seed. House plants, garden supplies. Mail-order catalog.

W. Atlee Burpee Co., Hunting Park Ave. at 18th St., Philadelphia, Pennsylvania 19132. (215) 228-8800. Branches in Clinton, Iowa and Riverside, California. Vegetable and flower seeds, general nursery stock. Trees and shrubs sold retail. Mail-order catalog.

California Nursery Co., 36501 Niles Blvd., Fremont (Niles District), California 94536. (415) 797-3311. Roses, fruit and ornamental trees. Berry plants, nut trees. General catalog Ships retail.

Carroll Gardens, E. Main St., Ext., Westminster, Maryland 21157. (301) 848-5422. Retail and wholesale. Dwarf evergreens, trees and shrubs, roses, perennials, herbs and ground covers. Mail-order catalog.

City of Glass, Melville Rd., Farmingdale, New York 11735. (516) 249-1700. Garden center. Local retail. General nursery stock.

Comerford's, Box 100, Marion, Oregon 97359. (503) 769-5278. Retail and wholesale. Rhododendrons, Exbury and other azaleas. Hard-to-find cultivars. Mail-order catalog.

John Connon Nurseries, Waterdown, Ontario, Canada (416) 689-4631. Retail and wholesale. General nursery stock. Mail-order catalog.

Corliss Bros. Garden Center, Ipswich, Massachusetts. See No. 6 in wholesale list.

Dauber's Nurseries, 1705 N. George St., Box 1746, York, Pennsylvania 17405. (717) 764-4553. Retail and wholesale. Uncommon trees and shrubs, often of landscape size. Hollies. Retail catalog.

Devon Nurseries, 1408 Royal Bank Building, Edmonton, Alberta, Canada. (403) 424-9696. Retail (catalog) and wholesale (list). General nursery stock and perennials. Ships.

Sam Dible Nursery, R.F.D. 3, Shelocta, Pennsylvania 15774. (412) 726-5377. Retail and wholesale. Evergreens for Christmas tree plants, reforestation. Ships.

Bill Dodd Nurseries, Box 235, Semmes, Alabama 36575. (205) 649-2398. Retail. Price list of uncommon magnolias. Ships. Outlet for hard-to-find native rhododendrons and azaleas.

Dutch Mountain Nursery, Augusta, Michigan 49012. (616) 731-4550. Retail. Trees and shrubs for wildlife plantings. Price list. Ships.

Eastern Shore Nurseries, Box 743, Rte. 331, Easton, Maryland 21601. (301) 822-1320. Retail and wholesale. General nursery stock, often of landscape size. Catalog. Ships.

H. M. Eddie & Sons, 4100 S. W. Marine Dr., Vancouver, British Columbia, Canada. (604) 261-3188. Retail and wholesale. General nursery stock, roses. Mail-order catalog.

Eisler Nurseries, Box 70, 219 E. Pearl St., Butler, Pennsylvania 16001. (412) 287-3703. General nursery stock with emphasis on landscape sizes. Retail catalog, with price adjustment for trade customers.

Emlong Nurseries, Stevensville, Michigan 49127. (616) 429-3431. Retail and wholesale. Garden centers in Stevensville and Niles, Mich. General nursery stock. Fruit trees. Mail-order catalog.

Farmer Seed and Nursery Co., Rte. 60, Faribault, Minnesota 55021. (507) 334-6421. Seven Minn. stores. General nursery stock, vegetable and flower seeds, and garden supplies. Mail-order catalog.

Earl Ferris Nursery, 811 Fourth St. N.E., Hampton, Iowa 50441. (515) 456-2563. Retail. Wholesale mainly for evergreens and shrubs. Garden Center. General nursery stock. Mail-order catalog.

Henry Field Seed and Nursery Co., 407 Sycamore St., Shenandoah, Iowa 51601. (712) 246-2110. Retail and wholesale. General nursery stock. Mail-order catalog.

Fiore Enterprises, Rte. 22, Prairie View, Illinois 60069. (312) 634-3400. Retail? also wholesale (as Charles Fiore Nurseries). Trees and shrubs, mainly of landscape size. Separate retail and wholesale catalogs. Ships.

Flickingers' Nursery, Sagamore, Pennsylvania 16250. (412) 783-6528. Retail and wholesale. Evergreen seedlings for Christmas trees and reforestation. Mail-order price list.

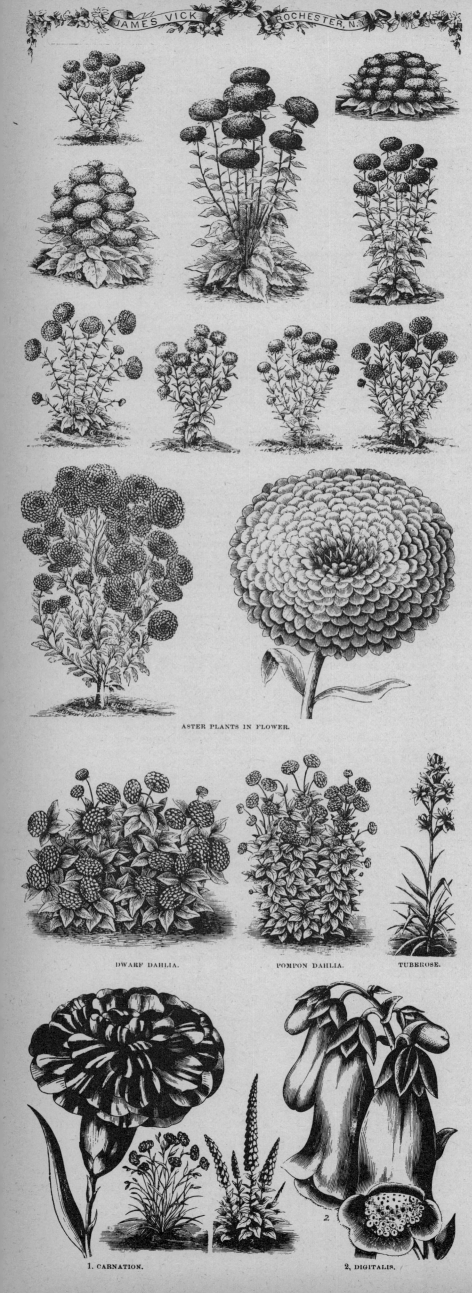

JAMES VICK ROCHESTER, N.Y.

ASTER PLANTS IN FLOWER.

DWARF DAHLIA.   POMPON DAHLIA.   TUBEROSE.

1. CARNATION.   2. DIGITALIS.

H. L. Larson, 3656 Bridgeport Way, Tacoma, Washington 98466 (206) 564-1488. Seeds of uncommon rhododendron species. No plants shipped. List.

A. M. Leonard & Son, Box 816, Piqua, Ohio 45356. (513) 773-2694. Gardening and pruning tools. Extensive catalog.

Henry Leuthardt Nurseries, Montauk Highway, East Moriches, New York 11940. (516) 878-1387. Dwarf and espaliered fruit trees. Mail-order list.

Light's Landscape Nurserymen, 9153 East D Ave., Richland, Michigan 49083. (616) 629-9761. Retail and limited wholesale. Unusually wide range of trees and shrubs. Large specimens at nursery. Delivery arranged to various points. Catalog. Ships.

Linn County Nurseries, 520 Franklin, Center Point, Iowa 52213. (319(849-1423. Retail and wholesale. General nursery stock for the Plains. Specimen-size trees and shrubs. Garden Center. Catalog.

Littlefield-Wyman Nurseries, 227 Centre Ave. (Rte. 123), Abington, Massachusetts 02351. (617) 878-1800 (from Boston area call 472-1195.) General nursery and garden center. Landscape-size trees and shrubs, evergreens. Delivery within 20 miles of Abington, beyond by special arrangement. Catalog.

May Nursery Co., Box 1312, 212 N. 3rd Ave., Yakima, Washington 98901. (509) 453-8219. Retail and wholesale. Fruit trees, berry plants and other nursery stock. Mail-order catalog.

Earl May Seed & Nursery Co., 100 N. Elm St., Shenandoah, Iowa 51601. (712) 246-1020. Primarily retail. 42 garden centers in Iowa, Nebraska, Missouri and South Dakota. General nursery stock, fruit trees, flower and vegetable seed. Mail-order catalog.

Medford Nursery, Eayrestown - Red Lion Rd., R. D. 1, Medford, New Jersey 08055. (609) 267-8100. Retail and wholesale. General nursery stock, container grown plants and pot grown liners. Hollies. Ships retail.

Mayfair Nurseries, R. D. 2, Nichols, New York 13812 (nursery at Windham, Pa.). (717) 395-3154. Retail and wholesale. Dwarf conifers, heaths, heathers, dwarf rhododendrons and other rock garden plants. Mail-order catalog .25.

McKay Nursery Co., 254 Jefferson St., Waterloo, Wisconsin 53594. (414) 478-2121. (Sales offices in Milwaukee and Madison). Retail and wholesale. General nursery stock, specimen-size trees and shrubs. Landscape catalog.

Mellinger's, Inc., 2310 W. S. Range Rd., North Lima, Ohio 44452. (216) 549-2027. Retail. Extensive variety of trees and shrubs in small sizes. Pre-bonsai. Tree seeds. Unusually large list of garden supplies, grafting tools, pruning shears, etc. Reference books. Mail-order catalog.

Musser Forests, Inc., Box 340, Rte. 119, Indiana, Pennsylvania 15701. (412) 465-5686. Conifers in quantity units for Christmas tree plantings and reforestation. Deciduous trees, flowering shrubs. Mail-order catalog.

Raymond Nelson Nursery, R. D. 3, Dubois, Pennsylvania 15801. (814) 371-3983. Retail and wholesale. Serviceberry trees (Amelanchier), evergreens for Christmas tree plantings. Ships.

Neosho Nurseries, Box 550, Neosho, Missouri 64850. (417) 451-1212. Retail and wholesale. General nursery stock, fruit trees, roses and perennials. Gardening supplies. The firm issues a mail-order catalog.

Nuccio's Nurseries, 3555 Chaney Trail, Altadena, California 91001. (213) 794-3383. Retail. Extensive camellia listing. Azaleas. Nursery closed Wednesdays. Mail-order catalog.

Oliver Nurseries, 1159 Bronson Rd., Fairfield, Connecticut 06430. (203) 259-5609. Retail. Dwarf conifers and rock garden evergrens. Dwarf rhododendrons. Uncommon trees. Pre-bonsai plants. Catalog. Does not ship.

Palette Gardens, 26 W. Zion Hill Rd., Quakertown, Pennsylvania 18951. (215) 536-4027. Dwarf conifers (no catalog), uncommon rock garden perennials (price lists). Will ship conifers and perennials. Best call for appointment, since hours vary.

Panfield Nurseries, 322 Southdown Rd., Huntington, New York 11743. (516) 427-0112. Retail and wholesale. Extensive selection of trees and shrubs, many in specimen size. Heathers, conifers, broad-leaf evergreens. Separate retail and wholesale lists.

Park Gardens, 1435 Huntington Tpke., Trumbull, Connecticut 06611. (203) 374-3103. Retail and wholesale. Dwarf conifers and rock garden shrubs. List available. Ships.

George W. Park Seed Co., Greenwood, South Carolina 29646, *803) 451-3341. Retail and wholesale for vegetable and flower seed, exclusively retail for nursery stock. Small sizes. Mail-order catalog.

Patmore Nurseries, Brandon, Manitoba, Canada (204) 727-1371. Retail nursery stock for the Northern Plains. Mail-order catalog.

Pellett Gardens, Atlantic, Iowa 50022. (712) 243-1917. Honey plants. Mail-order list.

Peters & Wilson Nursery, E. Millbrae Ave. & Rollins Rd., Millbrae, California 94030. (415) 697-5373. Retail and wholesale. Garden center. Closed Wednesdays. Wide selection of ornamental trees and shrubs for southern California. Fruit trees. Catalog $1.00.

Pikes Peak Nurseries, Box 670, Indiana, Pennsylvania 15701. (412) 473-7747. Retail and wholesale. Evergreens for Christmas tree plantations and reforestation. General nursery stock. Mail-order catalog.

Pioneer Nursery, Box 665, Rte. 1, Ridgefield, Washington 98642. (206) 887-3420. Retail outlet of Viewcrest Nurseries.

Plumfield Nurseries, Box 410, 2105 N. Nye Ave., Fremont, Nebraska 68025. (402) 721-3622. Garden center, 735 W. 23rd St. (Rte. 30) (721-3520). Retail orders handled through garden center, wholesale orders through the nursery. General nursery stock. Separate retail and trade lists.

Orlando S. Pride, 523 Fifth St., Butler, Pennsylvania 16001. (412) 285-4242. Retail and wholesale. Azaleas, hollies, rhododendrons, others. Catalog. Ships.

Primex Garden Center, 435 W. Glenside (Montgomery County), Pennsylvania 29038. (215) 887-7500. Local Retail. General nursery stock.

Putney Nursery, Putney, Vermont 05346. (802) 387-5577. Retail. Wildflowers, ferns, perennials, ornamental trees and shrubs. Woody plants available only at the nursery. Mail-order catalog.

Perry's Plants, Inc., 19362 Walnut Dr., La Puente, California 91745. (213) 964-1285. Retail and wholesale. Ground covers in quantity units. Catalog.

Rainier Mt. Alpine Gardens, 2007 S. 126th, Seattle, Washington 98168. (206) 242-4090. Retail (wholesale only at nursery). Dwarf conifers, uncommon rhododendrons, rock garden shrubs. Mail-order catalog.

Raraflora, Fred W. Bergman, 1195 Stump Rd., Feasterville, Pennsylvania 19047. (215) 357-3791. Retail. Extensive selection of dwarf conifers. Japanese maples, uncommon trees and shrubs. List available. Will ship, but encourages pick-up at nursery. Visitors by appointment only.

Rayner Bros., Box 348, Salisbury, Maryland 21801. (301) 742-1594. Retail. Fruit and nut trees, strawberries, other berry plants. Mail-order catalog.

Herbert Read, Dwarf & Bonsai Plants, 2713 N. Myers St., Burbank, California 91504.

Clyde Robin, Box 2091, Castro Valley, California 94546. (415) 581-3467. Retail. Unusual conifers, ornamental trees and shrubs in small sizes. Pre-bonsai. California native plants. Tree and wildflower seeds. Mail-order catalog .50.

Rocknoll Nursery, Box 301, Morrow, Ohio 45152. (513) 899-3861. Retail and wholesale. General Nursery stock in small sizes. Mail-order catalog.

Fig. 14.—Irrigation of Rain-water.

1 In *Alfredia cernua.* 2 In a Mullein (*Verbascum phlomoides*).

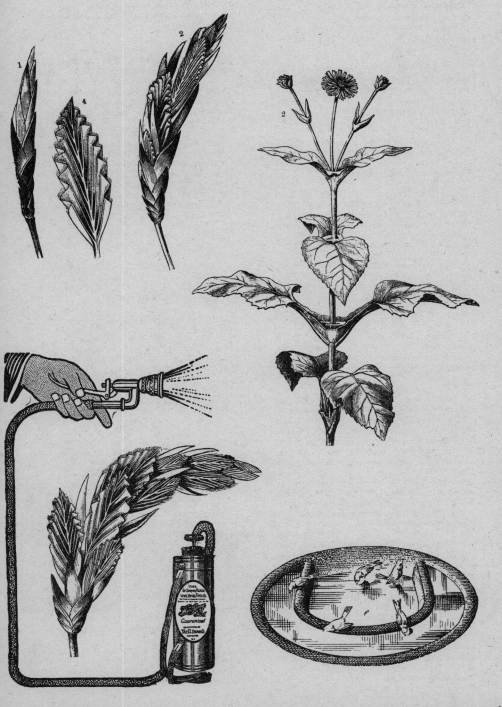

Mabel Franklin, 9225 S. Penn Ave., Minneapolis, Minnesota 55431. (612) 881-7870. Lilacs. Mail-order price list.

French's Garden Center, 1215 W. Baltimore Pike (rte. a), Lima (Delaware) County, Pennsylvania 19060. (215) 566-4270. Local retail. General nursery stock.

Game Food Nurseries, Box 371, Oshkosh, Wisconsin 54901. (414) 235-8160. Wild rice; other marsh and upland plants for gamebirds. Seeds. Catalog 25 cents. Ships.

The Garden Spot, 4032 Rosewood Dr., Columbia, South Carolina 39205. Cuttings of 100 kinds of English ivy (hedera helix). Euonymus, liriope and vinca forms. Cross vine ((Bignonia capreolata). List. Ships.

Gardens of the Blue Ridge, Ashford (McDowell County), North Carolina 28602. (704) 756-4339. Nursery on Rte. 221 in Pineola. Retail, limited wholesale. Native trees and shrubs, wide selection of wildflowers. Mail-order catalog.

Gardenside Nurseries, Shelburne, Vermont 05482. (802) 985-2735. Retail. General nursery stock, landscape size. Price list. Does not ship.

D. S. George Nurseries, 2491 Penfield Rd., Fairport, New York 14450. (716) 377-0731. Retail and wholesale. Clematis. List ten cents. Ships.

Gilmore Plant & Bulb Co., Box 8, Rte. 421, Julian, North Carolina 27283. (919) 685-4451. Retail and wholesale. General nursery stock, evergeens, fruit trees. Catalog.

Girared Nurseries, R. D. No. 4, North Ridg East, Geneva, Ohio 44041. (216) 466-2881. Retail and wholesale. Dwarf and unusual evergreens, azaleas, uncommon trees. Pre-bonsai conifers. Conifer seeds. Mail-order catalog.

Gossler Farms Nursery, 1200 Weaver Rd., Springfield, Oregon 97477. (503) 746-3922. Retail. Rare magnolias. Flowering cherries. Trees chosen for bar character. Eucryphia. Unusually refined selection. Price list. Ships.

Gurney Seed & Nursery Co., Yankton, South Dakota 57078. (605) 665-7481. Retail. Vegetable and flower seeds. Trees and shrubs for the Plains. Garden psupplies. Mail-order catalog.

Handleman's Garden Center, 16 Reservoir Rd., White Plains, New York 10603 . (914) 949-3613. Local retail. General nursery stock.

H. G. Hastings Co., Box 4088, Atlanta, Georgia 30302. (404) 522-9464. Three garden centers in Atlanta, one each in Birmingham and Charlotte. Retail and wholesale. Camellias, azaleas and other broad-leaf evergreens for the South. Roses, vegetable and flower seed. Fruit trees. Ornamental trees and shrubs. Mail-order catalog.

Heard Gardens, 5355 Merle Hay Rd. (Rte. No. a, Box 134), Des Moines, Iowa 50323. (515) 276-4533. Retail and wholesale. Trees and shrubs of landscape size. Large selection of lilacs and crab apples. No catalog, but willing to ship particular items retail.

Alexander I. Heimlich Nursery & Garden Center, 71 Burlington St., Woburn, Massachusetts 01801. (617) 933-7053. Local retail. Dwarf evergreens.

Thomas Henny Nursery, 78aa Stratford Drive, N.E., Brooks, Oregon 97305. (503) 792-3376. Retail, with quantity discount. Gable and Glenn Dale azaleas, also a good selection of rhododendrons. Pieris. Mail-order catalog.

Heronwood Nursery, Rear Admiral Neill Phillips, Rte. 50, Upperville, Virginia 22176. (703) 592-3788. Topiary.

Hillier & Sons, Winchester, England. Probably the largest selection of trees and shrubs grown anywhere by a commercial firm. Import permits needed.

C. M. Hobbs & Sons, 9300 W. Washington St., Bridgeport, Indiana 46231. (317) 241-9253. Retail and wholesale. Trees and shrubs, often of landscape size. Limited retail shipment.

Holly Heath Nursery, Rte. 25A, Wading River, New York (mailing address: Box 55A, Calverton, New York 11933). (516) 727-0859. Retail. Holly, heather, Glenn Dale and other azaleas, dwarf plants. Does not ship.

Huttar's Garden Center, 3662 Richmond Rd., Staten Island, New York 10306. (212) 351-5100. Retail. General nursery stock. Does not ship.

Indian Run Nursery, Allentown Rd., Robbinsville, New Jersey 08691. (609) 259-2600. Retail. Rhododendrons. Catalog. Does not ship. Closed Mondays.

Inter-State Nurseries, Hamburg, Iowa 51640. (712) 382-2411. Retail and wholesale. General nursery stock, fruit trees, perennials. Mail-order catalog.

Island Gardens, 701 Goodpasture Rd., Eugene, Oregon 97401. (503) 343-4711. Retail and wholesale. Exbury azaleas, rhododendrons. Mail-order catalog.

Jackson & Perkins Co., Box 1028, Medford, Oregon 97501. (503) 779-4521. Retail and wholesale. Roses, spring bulbs. Mail-order catalog.

Kansas Landscape & Nursery Co., 1416 E. Iron Ave., Salina, Kansas 67401. (913) 827-0051. Retail and wholesale. General nursery stock. Mail-order catalog.

Kelly Bros. Nurseries, 23 Maple St., Dansville, New York 14437. (716) 987-2211. Retail and wholesale. General nursery stock, fruit and nut trees, bulbs. Mail-order catalog.

Kingsville Nurseries, H. J. Hohman, Kingsville, Maryland 21087. (301) 592-2931. Retail and wholesale. Rare trees and shrubs, probably the most extensive nursery collection in the country. Especially wide variety of azaleas, maples, flowering cherries, viburnums and conifers. No current catalog. The common practice is to send Mr. Hohman a "want" list, since some plants are in short supply and may take a year or two before available. Visitors by appointment only.

Rudolph Kluis Nursery, Box 116, Ryan Rd., Marlboro, New Jersey 07746. (201) 462-4694. Retail. Dwarf conifers, hard-to-find shrubs. Catalog 25 cents. Does not ship. No deliveries. Visitors by appointment only. Closed on Sunday.

Joseph J. Kern Rose Nursery, Box 33, Jackson St. & Heisley Rd., Mentor, Ohio 44060. (216) 255-8627. Retail and wholesale. Old and new roses. Rare kinds. Custom budding. Visitors June-October by appointment only. Mail-order catalog.

Kimberly Barn Floral & Garden Center, 1221 E. Kimberly Rd., Davenport, Iowa 52807. (319) 324-1955. Local retail. General nursery stock.

Krider Nurseries, Middlebury, Indiana 46540. (219(835-2181. Retail and wholesale. Fruit trees, ornamental trees and shrubs. Mail-order catalog.

Kroh Nurseries, Box 536, Rte. 287, Loveland, Colorado 80537. (303) 667-4223. Retail and wholesale. Ornamental trees and shrubs for the Rocky Mountains. Fruit trees. Larger specimens at nursery. Mail-order catalog.

LaBars' Rhododendron Nursery, Box 111, Bryant St., Stroudsburg, Pennsylvania 18360. (717) 421-5880. Retail and wholesale. Landscape-size trees and shrubs available at the nursery. Mail-order catalog for rhododendrons and other ericaceous plants.

LaFayette Home Nursery, Box 148, Rte. 17, LaFayette, Illinois 61449. (309) 995-3311. Retail and wholesale. Extensive selection of trees and shrubs, many in large specimen size. Lengthy retail price list. Nursery ships wholesale to other firms; also rhips retail if customer so desires.

Lafkins Garden Center, Mamaroneck Ave. at Rosedale, White Plains, New York, 10603. (914) 946-2300. Local retail. General nursery stock.

Lamb Nurseries, E 101 Sharp Ave., Spokane, Washington 99202. (509) 328-7956. Dwarf shrubs, rock garden plants, perennials, ground overs, herbs, hardy succulents. Mail-order catalog.

ADONIS 2 ALYSSUM 3 WALLFL'R 4 HOLLYHOCK 5 POTENTILLA 6 HONESTY 7 ADLUMIA 8 DELPHINIUM 9 POPPY

AQUILEGIA—SINGLE AND DOUBLE.   CAMPANULA.

DAHLIAS—FLOWER AND PLANT.

Rosedale Nurseries, Saw Mill River Parkway, Hawthorne, New York 10532. (914) 769-1300; also, Rosedale - in - Dutchess, Rte. 44, Mill brook, New York 12545, (914) 677-3938. Retail. Large selection of general nursery stock. Shade trees of landscape size. Many plants not in catalog (50 cents) are stocked. Does not ship.

Rose Hill Nursery, 2380 W. Larpenteur Ave., St. Paul, Minnesota 55113. (612) 646-7541; also at E. Hennepin & Fulham, Minneapolis. Retail. General stock, fruit trees, berry plants. Catalog. Ships.

Scarff's Nursery, Rte. 1, New Carlisle, Ohio 45344. (513) 845-2551. Retail and wholesale. General nursery stock.

Seven Dees Nursery, 6025 S. E. Powell, Portland, Oregon 97206. (503) 777-1412. Retail outlet of Sherwood Nursery Co.

A. Shammarello & Son Nursery, 4590 Monticello Blvd., South Euclid, Ohio 44143. (216) 381-2510. Retail and wholesale. Rhododendrons and other broadleaf evergreens. Mail-order catalogl

Sheridan Nurseries, 100 Sherway Dr., Etobicoke, Ontario, Canada. (416) 259-5095. Sales stations also at Greenhedges, 650 Montee de Liesse, Montreal 377, P. Q. (514-744-2451); Glenpark, 2827 Yonge St., Toronto 317, Ontario; others in Clarkson and Unionville, Ontario. Retail and wholesale. Wide selection of general nursery stock, perennials, roses. Deliveries in Toronto-Hamilton and Metropolitan Montreal. Catalog. Ships.

The Shop in the Sierra, Carl Stephens. Box 1, Midpines, California 95345. Western native trees and shrubs. Mail-order catalog 25 cents.

Silver Falls Nursery & Christmas Tree Farm, Silver Falls Highway, Star Route, Box 55, Silverton, Oregon 97381. (503) 873-4945. Retail. Large selection of unusual conifers, shrubs and trees, western native plants. Small sizes, many plants suited for bonsai initiation. Mail-order catalog.

Francis M. Sinclair, R. F. D. 1, Newmarket Rd., Exeter, New Hampshire 03833. (603) 772-2362. Quantity dealer in wildflowers, native trees and shrubs. Material collected from the wild. Price list. Ships.

Siskiyou Rare Plant Nursery, 522 Franquette St., Medford, Oregon 97501. Retail. Dwarf shrubs, rare alpine plants. Mail-order catalog 50 cents.

Joel W. Spingarn, 1535 Forest Ave., Baldwin, New York 11510. (516) 623-7810. Retail. Extensive selection of dwarf conifers. Japanese maples, rock garden rhododendrons. List 25 cents. Ships. Visitors by appointment only.

Squirrel Hill Nursery, 2945 Beechwood Blvd., Pittsburgh, Pennsylvania 15217. (412) 421-1900. Retail and wholesale. General nursery stock. Catalog. Does not ship. Delivery arranged in greater Pittsburgh area.

Spring Hill Nurseries, Elm St., Tipp City, Ohio 45371. (513) 667-2491. Retail and wholesale. General stock, perennials, ground covers, vines. Mail-order catalog.

Star Roses (Conard-Pyle Co.), West Grove, Pennsylvania 19390. (215) 869-2426. Retail mail order catalog limited to roses. Garden centers in West Grove and Lancaster offer a wide range of shrubs and trees, besides roses. Wholesale catalog for roses and general stock.

Stark Bros. Nurseries & Orchards Co., Louisiana, Missouri 63353. (314) 754-5511. Retail. Large selection of fruit trees. Ornamental shrubs and trees. Mail-order catalog.

Stern's Nurseries, Geneva, New York 14456. General nursery stock, including fruit plants, roses and perennials. Mail-order catalog 50 cents.

Sylvan Nursery, 1028 Horseneck Rd., South Westport, Massachusetts 02790. (617) 636-4573. Retail. Heaths, heathers, seashore plants. List. Ships.

Tennessee Nursery Co., Box 1299, Cleveland, Tennessee 37311. (615) 476-4142. Retail. General nursery stock. Mail-order catalog.

Thomasville Nurseries, Box 7, 1842 Smith Ave., Thomasville, Georgia 31792. (912) 226-5568. Retail. Camellias, roses, daylilies, liriopes. Mail-order catalog.

Tillotson's Roses, 992 Brown's Valley Rd., Watsonville, California 95076. (408) 724-3537. Retail, with discount for quantity purchase. Extensive selection of old-fashioned and modern roses. Catalog $1, deductible on first order.

Tomlinson's Nursery, 11758 E. Whittier Blvd., Whittier, California 90601. (213) 693-9234. Retail outlet of Select Nurseries. Se

William Tricker, Inc., 174 Allendale Ave., Saddle River, New Jersey 07458. (201) 327-0721; also, 7125 Tanglewood Dr., Independence, Ohio 44131, (216) 524-2430. Water Lilies and bog plants. Mail-order catalog.

Valley Nursery, Box 845, 2801 N. Montana, Helena, Montana 59601. (406) 442-8460. Retail and wholesale. Uncommon trees and shrubs for cold climates. Seedlings in quantity units. Price list. Ships.

Marinus Vander Pol, 776 Washington St. Fairhaven, Massachusetts 02719. (617) 992-0330. Retail and wholesale. General nursery stock. Mail-order clematis catalog 35 cents.

Martin Viette Nurseries, Rte. 25A (Northern Blvd.), East Norwich, New York 11732. (516) 922-5530. Retail and wholesale. Extensive nursery stock, including an unusually wide range of perennials and wildflowers. Catalog 50 cents. Does not ship.

Watnong Nursery, The Don Smiths, Morris Plains, New Jersey 07950. (201) 539-0312. Retail. Extensive selection of dwarf evergreens, rare shrubs and trees. Container-grown. Availability lists. Does not ship. Open by appointment only.

Waynesboro Nurseries, Box 987; Lyndhurst-Sherando Lake Rd., Waynesboro, Virginia 22980. (703) 942-4141. Retail and wholesale. General nursery stock, fruit trees, berry plants. Smaller trees and shrubs shipped, larger ones at the nursery. Mail-order catalog.

Weall and Cullen Nurseries, 784 Sheppard Ave. E., Willowdale, Ontario, Canada (416) 225-7705. Other Metropolitan Toronto garden centers at 1774 Ellesmere Rd., Scarborough, Ont. (416-291-1931) and Highway 27, R. R. 3, Woodbridge, Onto. (416-851-2281). General nursery stock, garden supplies. Mail-order catalog.

NEW SCHILLER ASTER.   ASPERULA.

HARDY BULBS AND PLANTS

Illustration of a garden scene with house, pathway, and plants labeled:
- AMPELOPSIS VEITCHII
- ANEMONE JAPONICA ALBA
- CLEMATIS JACKMANNI

"I know not which I love the most,
Nor which the comeliest shows,
The timid bashful violet,
Or the royal-hearted rose."

FLORAL GUIDE. FOR 1873.

GLADIOLUS

The Gladiolus is the most beautiful of our Summer Bulbs, with tall spikes of flowers, some two feet or more in height, and often several from the same Bulb. The flowers are of almost every desirable color—brilliant scarlet, crimson, creamy white, striped, blotched and spotted in the most curious and interesting manner. The culture is very simple. Set the Bulbs from six to nine inches apart and cover about three inches. If set in rows they may be set six inches apart in the rows, and the rows one foot apart. The planting may be done at different times, from the middle of April to the first of June, to secure a long succession of bloom. Keep the earth mellow, and place a neat stake to support the spikes in storms. I have never known a case where the Gladiolus failed to give the most perfect satisfaction, opening a new field of beauty to those unacquainted with its merits. For in-door decoration, such as ornamenting the dining table, schools, churches, etc., it is unsurpassed, making a magnificent display with little trouble. In the fall, take up the Bulbs, let them dry in the air for a few days, then cut off the tops and store the Bulbs out of the way of frost, for next season's planting. Look at them occasionally. If kept in a place too moist, they will show signs of moisture and perhaps mildew. If this appears, remove them to a dryer position. If the Bulbs shrivel, it shows they are getting too dry; but they do not usually suffer from a dry atmosphere. In all foreign and American Catalogues several varieties are described as white. I have made descriptions as found true in my own grounds, but to prevent disappointment, will say I know of no reliable pure white Gladiolus.

TIGRIDIA

A beautiful and curious shell-like flower, giving abundance of bloom for a long season. A small bed of these bulbs is scarcely ever without flowers. About eighteen inches in height.

CANNA

The Canna is a fine foliage plant, making a good bed alone, but particularly desirable as the center of a group of foliage plants, of which it is one of the very best. Growing from three to four feet. The leaves are sometimes two feet in length, of a beautiful green, some varieties tinted with red. The flowers are on spikes, pretty but not conspicuous. Roots can be taken up and placed in the cellar. They flourish and are vigorous in the dryest and hottest weather.

Amaryllis.   Hippeastrum.   Zephyranthes.   Sprekelia

PROMINENT TYPES OF AMARYLLIS.

DAHLIA.

TYPES OF DOUBLE DAHLIAS.

GROWING DAHLIAS

Dahlias are popular additions to many gardens because they display a variety of sizes, shapes, and colors. They are also an excellent source of cut flowers for indoor arrangements.

Dahlias are native to the Western Hemisphere, and grow with relatively little care in all parts of the United States. They do well even in dry areas, if sufficient water is provided. They are hardy plants and, depending on the length of the growing season in your locale, will provide colorful blooms from July until they are killed by frost in autumn.

Fully grown dahlia plants range from less than 1 to more than 6 feet in height. They may be bushy and filled with clusters of miniature or medium-sized flowers, or they may have two to four stalks bearing one to several very large blooms on each.

The flowers measure from less than 2 to more than 8 inches in diameter. Colors range from pure white to pastel tints; to brighter shades of yellow, red, and orange; and to deeper hues of red and purple.

You may decide to raise dahlias for show or simply to beautify your yard. In either case you can choose from thousands of named varieties.

CLASSES OF DAHLIAS

Dahlias are primarily classified according to the shape and arrangement of their petals. Single-flowering dahlias have no more than a few rows of petals and show a central disk. Double-flowering dahlias have multiple rows of petals and display no central disk. Dahlias of any variety that grow on a low, bush-type plant are referred to as dwarf dahlias.

Single-flowering dahlia plants are generally about 3 feet tall with flowers 4 inches or less in diameter. Double-flowering plants are usually taller and have larger blooms. But, because dahlias vary so in height and blossom size, be sure to select varieties that will suit your purposes. Height and flower size are given in most garden catalogs, or you can ask your nurseryman.

You Are Invited to *JOIN* **THE AMERICAN DAHLIA SOCIETY**

DAHLIAS

Ackman's Dahlia Gardens,
9114 Oakview,
Plymouth, Mich. 48170

Douglas Dahlias,
R. 1, Box 91,
Myrtle Creek, Ore. 97457

Legg Dahlia Gardens,
R. 2, Hastings Rd.,
Geneva, N.Y. 14456

E. Ray Miller's Dahlia Gardens,
167 N.W. 12th Ave.,
Hillsboro, Ore. 97123

Pennypack,
Cheltenham, Penna. 19012

Rocky River Dahlia Gardens,
13089 E. River Rd.,
Columbia Station, Ohio 44028

Ruschmohr Dahlia Gardens,
38 Vincent, Box 236,
Rockville Centre, N.Y. 11571

S & K Gardens,
401 Quick Srd.,
Castle Rock, Wash. 98611

Swan Island Dahlias,
Box 800,
Canby, Ore. 97013

Todd's Farm,
Suches, Ga. 30572

White Dahlia Gardens,
2480 S.E. Creighton Ave.,
Milwaukie, Ore. 97222

UNDIVIDED CLUMP OF DAHLIA TUBERS.

KINDS OF PANSIES

We read about pansies in the poetry of 16th and 17th Century England, but the flowers described are hardly like the ones we know today. In many cases they were the Viola tricolor, known since ancient Greek times, a relatively small and simple ancestor of the large and fancy blooms we grow now.

The Viola tricolor, so named because it is generally a combination of three colors—white, yellow, and either blue or purple—is still grown in some gardens, but with decreasing frequency.

The modern pansy probably represents crosses among the Viola tricolor and other members of the Viola family. Shortly after 1800, British growers began to breed the now familiar "faces" into pansy flowers, and to improve color and markings generally. Later, French, Belgian, Swiss, and American breeders developed the larger, brighter-colored, fancier varieties that are now available.

Pansies come in named varieties of pure colors and mixtures, as well as first-generation hybrids that are becoming increasingly popular because of plant vigor, uniform color and a wider color range, increased flower size, and greater heat resistance.

Pansies nowadays display scores of hues. They range in color from white and pastel shades, rich gold and burnished orange, to deep rose, violet and blue, and even deeper maroons and browns. They may be single-colored, streaked, or blotched.

Certain types have petals with crinkled fluffy edges; others do not. Flower size may range from about 1 to 3 inches in diameter, depending on culture.

PANSY.

GROWING PANSIES

Pansies are among the most popular garden flowers today. They exhibit a wide range of colors, markings, and sizes.

Although pansies are hardy biennials, they are also grown as annuals. The ideal temperature range for growing pansies is from about 40 degrees F. at night to 60 degrees F. during the day. They will grow in all parts of the United States. They produce best flowers in the spring when the weather is mild, then fade and are usually discarded when really hot weather arrives. In areas where long periods without frost are common, strong pansy plants will bloom in the fall and even in the winter.

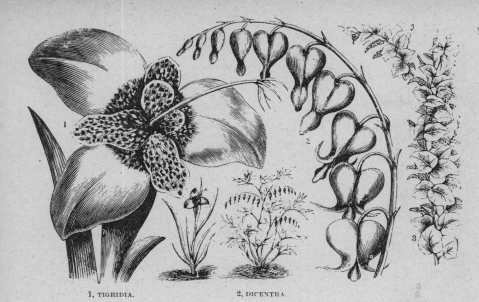

1, TIGRIDIA. 2, DICENTRA.

GLADIOLUS.

FLOWERING BULBS

It is rare, these days, to find gardeners who use bulbs to their full potential. For, if bulbs are massed and marshalled with some forethought and imagination, gardens can be orchestrated with wave after wave of colorful blooms that carpet the ground from March through September.

When speaking of bulbs, we are referring not only to true bulbs with fleshy scales such as the lily, but, also corms like the crocus, roots like the dahlia and rhizomes like canna. All of these are treated in a relatively dormant state and are lumped together in the bulb category.

Bulbs that remain in the ground through winter, are classified as hardy bulbs. Half-hardy bulbs can winter in the ground in mild climates but require protection and good drainage to survive in colder climates. Tender bulbs must be brought in except in very cold climates.

As a rule of thumb, bulbs should be planted at a depth of about three times their length, or at least two inches deep.

Hardy bulbs should be planted as early in the fall as possible. Anemone, for example tends to dry out. They should be planted in September. Lily bulbs should be planted immediately upon receipt. Mid-December, just before the ground freezes, is the limit for planting narcissus, tulips and hyacinths. But, earlier planting is generally preferable. Crocus and other small bulbs are usually planted from mid-October to mid-November.

Keep in mind that your bulbs may be storing food even after the blooms are gone. So, it's a good idea not to cut back foliage until it yellows and begins to wilt.

If you want to find out just how far the mania for bulb-planting can go, visit a Dutch travel agent. Their posters will illustrate the possibilities bulb beds offer. Have fun. Try a floral mosaic designed with bulbs.

Amaze or offend your neighbors! Plant any design you can imagine. Spell out THE GARDENER'S CATALOGUE in tulips. If it's a spectacular success—send pix!

Fig. 30.

NARCISSUS.

POTTS' MONTBRETIA OR TRITONIA.

DAHLIAS—FLOWER AND PLANT.

DAFFODIL.

(NARCISSUS PSEUDO-NARCISSUS.)

GROUP OF NARCISSUS.

GLADIOLUS BULB BUYER'S GUIDE

Baldridge Glads,
Sidney L. Baldridge,
1729 19th Ave.,
Greeley, Colorado 80631

Bevington Greenacres,
R. R. 1,
Galveston, Indiana 46932

Leonard W. Butt,
Huttonville, Ontario, Canada

Champlain View Gardens,
Peter DeJager and Sons,
South Hamilton, Massachusetts 01982

Lynn Coon,
Route 1, Box 9,
Paul, Idaho 83347

Dickman Bulb Farms,
Buce L. Dickman,
Box 9117,
Salem, Oregon 97305

Eden Glad Gardens,
William Herborn,
Box 7,
Mount Eden, California 94557

Ed—Lor Glads,
H. Edward Frederick,
234 South Street,
South Elgin, Illinois 60177

Harbor Acres,
John Eppig,
Port Washington, New York 11050

Flad's Glads,
Stan Skolaski,
2109 Cliff Court,
Madison, Wisconsin 53713

TYPES OF GLADIOLUS.

Gladside Gardens,
Corys M. Heselton,
61 Main St.,
Northfield, Massachusetts 01360

Robert A. Griesbach,
404 South Cumberland Ave.,
Park Ridge, Illinois 60068

A. M. Grootendorst, Inc.,
P. O. Box 123,
Benton Harbor, Michigan 49022

Gruber Glad Gardens,
Albert Gruber,
2910 West Locust Street,
Davenport, Iowa 52804

Gurney Seed and Nursery Co.,
Bert Carlson,
2nd and Capitol,
Yankton, South Dakota 57078

Harmony Hill Glads,
Don and Audrey Walker,
323 Aqueton Road,
New Hope, Pennsylvania 18938

Henry Field Seed and Nursery Co.,
John W. Knapp,
407 Sycamore, Shenandoah, Iowa 51601

House of Spic and Span,
P.O. Box 63,
Newfield, New Jersey 08344

Idaho Ruffled Gladiolus Garden,
Oscar W. Johnson,
612 East Main St.,
Jerome, Idaho 83338

Interstate Nurseries, Inc.,
Lawrence E. Sjulin,
Hamburg, Iowa 51640

Jenkins Foundation for Research,
B. Charles Jenkins,
330 Maple St.,
Salinas, California 93901

J. J. K. Flower Bulbs Inc.,
P.O. Box 734,
Upper Montclair, New Jersey 07043

J. W. Jung Seed Co.,
335 South High St.,
Randolph, Wisconsin 53956

Knisley's Gladiolus Farms,
Elwood and Ken Miedema,
Rt. 1,
Saint Anne, Illinois 60964

George Melk and Sons,
Rt. 2,
Plainfield, Wisconsin 54966

Moran's Glad Gardens,
Erle Moran,
Rt. 3, Box 480,
Chehalis, Washington 98532

Nagel Bulb Farm,
Henry Nagel,
1630 East E Avenue,
Kalamazoo, Michigan 49004

Noweta Gardens,
Carl Fischer,
949 Saint Charles Ave.,
Saint Charles, Minnesota 55972

Pleasant Valley Glads,
163 Senator Ave.,
Agawan, Massachusetts 01001

Allen Poest,
245 South Wall St.,
Zeeland, Michigan 49464

Quality Gladiolus Gardens,
Chester Sirois,
P.O. Box 458,
Jonesboro, Arkansas 72401

Rich Glads,
Marion C. Rich,
P.O. Box 84,
Marion, New York 14505

Thomas Rogers,
225 East Ave.,
Greenville, Pennsylvania 16125

Winston Roberts,
Box 3123,
Boise, Idaho 83703

Selected Glads Inc.,
P.O. Box 26,
New Albany, Indiana 47150

Squires Bulb Farm,
Edward Squires,
3419 Eccles Ave.,
Ogden, Utah 84403

Alex Summerville,
Rt. 1,
Box 449,
Glassboro, New Jersey 08028

Timberland Gardens,
Mirl Vawter,
2324 Fuller Lane,
Lebanon, Oregon 97355

Thayer's Glads,
J.E. Thayer,
423 Franklin St.,
Fort Collins, Colorado 80521

Turk Bulb Farm,
Henry W. Turk,
P.O. Box 694,
Grants Pass, Oregon 97526

Valley Stream Farm,
D. R. Woudstra,
Orono, Ontario, Canada

Van Bourgondien and Sons, Inc.,
P. O. Box A,
Babylon, New York 11702

Peter J. Vandenberg,
P.O. Box 514,
Ruskin, Florida 33570

Warner Gladiolus Gardens,
Gordon Warner,
P.O. Box 695,
Medford, Oregon 97501

Woodworth Bros. Nurseries,
David Woodworth,
Rt. 2,
West Hamilton St.,
Geneva, New York 14456

Mrs. John Zeller,
Java, South Dakota 57452

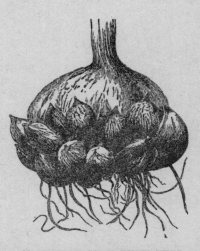

GLADIOLUS CORM WITH FULL
GROWN OFFSETS.

BULBS

AND

Tuberous-Rooted Plants

THEIR

HISTORY, DESCRIPTION, METHODS OF
PROPAGATION

AND

COMPLETE DIRECTIONS FOR THEIR SUCCESSFUL CULTURE

IN THE

Garden, Dwelling and Greenhouse

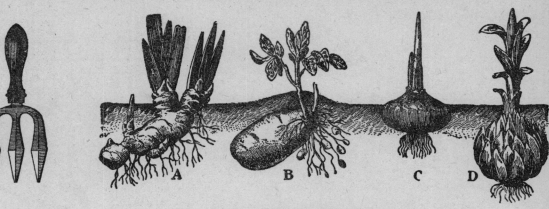

Tiges souterraines.

A. Rhizome (*Iris*). — B. Tubercule (*Pomme de terre*). — C. Bulbe tuniqué
(*Oignon*). — D. Bulbe écailleux (*Lis blanc*).

How to Plant Fall Bulbs
For Spring Flowers

Spring blooming bulbs such as tulips, narcissi and hyacinths must be planted in fall — narcissi and the small bulbs like crocus — in early fall (September): Tulips and lilies as late as the ground is workable. Fall planted bulbs should be planted in specially prepared beds which possess good natural drainage. The most satisfactory soil for growing bulbs is a fibrous loam well supplied with sharp sand. See planting chart below.

Tulips may be planted deeper than indicated (to 1') if soil is not too heavy and their location is permanent. Deep planting prolongs the effectiveness of the tulip bulb. Narcissus may be naturalized in grass or woodland. Foliage must be allowed to yellow before cutting.

How to Plant Lilies

The most desirable soil for lilies is a loose sandy loam which should be enriched by top dressing of manure and should be well drained. Plant lilies in groups about 4 to 6 inches deep for base rooting types, 5 to 8 inches for stem rooting. Tip bulbs on sides slightly and surround with a few handfuls of sand to assure sharp drainage around each bulb. They may be left in the ground from year to year.

How to Plant Summer Flowering Bulbs and Tubers

Most summer flowering bulbs are warm weather plants. Don't plant too soon. Cannas, Tuberous Begonias and Dahlias may be started in flats indoors and set out after danger of frost. Tritomas should be planted in early spring. Gladioli can be planted at 10 day intervals for a succession of bloom allowing 70 to 90 days for maturity.

SEEDLING GLADIOLUS. Page 88.

JAMES VICK 85 ROCHESTER, N.Y.

POET'S NARCISSUS.

(NARCISSUS POETICUS.)

GLADIOLUS.

FRAGRANT JONQUIL.

(NARCISSUS ODORUS.)

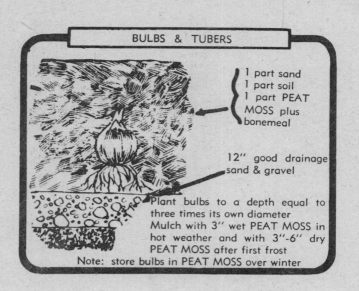

TYPES OF IMPROVED ACHIMENES.

FLOWERS AND BULB OF
NEAPOLITAN ALLIUM.

ROYAL DUTCH AMARYLLIS
Cultural Directions

POTTING & GROWING INSTRUCTIONS

You will have success with Royal Dutch Amaryllis if you follow a few simple rules.

Amaryllis can be potted from November until April. Use a fairly deep flower pot which is about an inch larger in circumference than the bulb, and place a small stone or similar object on the hole in the bottom of the pot. Plant the bulb about half its depth above the top of the soil. Place your amaryllis in a warm shaded place, preferably where it has gentle bottom heat (70-75°). Even temperature day and night will give the best results. Very little water should be given until the bud is formed.

Once the flower bud is well developed, the pot could be placed in a cooler and lighter atmosphere (not direct sunlight). At this stage the roots can stand more moisture and regular watering is required.

When the amaryllis is in full bloom, cool night temperature (50°) will lengthen your flower's life.

HOW TO PRESERVE BULBS FOR THE FOLLOWING YEAR

After flowering, the bulb should be kept growing indoors by keeping the soil moist. Add a little plant food from time to time. When chance of frost outside is past, take pot with plant and plunge this in the garden, preferably in semi-shade. Top of the pot should be about 2 inches below soil level. Dehydrated manure can be placed on top of the soil around the pot. This treatment will enable the bulb to regain strength and firmness which it has lost while producing flowers. Before any frost occurs, possibly the latter part of September or early October, take the pot and the plant out of the soil. Store in a dry place about 65° and stop watering completely. The foliage will gradually turn yellow and when it has done so, you may cut off the foliage 2 inches above the top of the bulb. Leave the pot dry and undisturbed for a month or two and then repeat the potting and growing instructions mentioned above.

ADDITIONAL HINTS

An earthen pot is better when plunging the pot outside than using a plastic pot.

This bulb can be kept growing indoors if you have no place for planting outside. Just keep watering it and give it some plant food every few weeks. You may cut the foliage off the latter part of October — then follow the above instructions.

HAPPY GARDENING

ANEMONE FULGENS.   TYPES OF ANEMONE CORONARIA.   ROMAN HYACINTH.

174

ALLIUM SCHUBERTI

The flowers are of a dull purple in colour, and not particularly showy. The plant is remarkable for flowering first on short stalks, and when these are in the fruiting stage, others are in full bloom on peduncles six to eight inches in length, giving the umbel some semblance to a porcupine. Many of the flowers have to be cut away to enable the head to be placed on a herbarium sheet.

ALLIUM TRIQUETRUM

To most of us, I think, the odor of the majority of the Allium species is so objectionable that they require to posess a considerable degree of floral charm to ensure their cultivation. This a considerable number of the species do possess and, if proof were needed for those who do not know the genus well, the authority of the late Reginald Farrer may be cited, as he devotes rather more than three pages of his ENGLISH ROCK GARDEN, to a consideration and running commentary upon the Alliums.

It is a capital subject for shrubberies and for naturalizing in grass, and may even be utilised in corners of the rock garden, where its seedlings cannot harm choice subjects. Farrer stated that it is "a plant of great attraction," with its triangular stalks and heads of clear white flowers which droop gracefully from these stems. Incidentally, it may be mentioned that these triangular stems, which attain a foot in height, serve the purpose of depositing the seeds away from the parent, as they fall over and the heads, with the precious seeds, lie about a foot or so from the parent.

This species comes from Spain, where it inhabits shady banks and moist places, but it will grow almost anywhere. Its odor is only apparent when the plant is touched or bruised. It flowers in June, and should be planted two inches deep in good loam.

GIANT SNOWDROPS!

GLORY OF THE SNOW

BULBS & PLANTS.

E.SC

DAYLILIES

Blackburn's Olinda Gardens,
R. 4, Box 441,
Rocky Mount, N.C. 27801

Jack Caldwell,
Box 39051,
Birmingham, Ala. 35208

Frank Child's Nursery,
Jenkinsburg, Ga. 30234

Davidson Gardens,
1215 Church St.,
Decatur, Ga. 30030

Englerth Gardens,
R. 1,
Hopkins, Minn. 49328

The Hancock Gardens,
210 2nd Ave., S.E.,
Steele, N.D. 58482

Howard J. Hite,
270 Waddington Rd.,
Birmingham, Mich. 48009

Howell Gardens,
q587 Letitia St.,
Baton Rouge, La. 70808

Hughes Garden,
R. 3, Box 127,
Mansfield, Texas 76063

Iron Gate Gardens,
R. 3, Box 101,
Kings Mountain, N.C. 28086

Lenington Gardens,
7007 Manchester Ave.,
Kansas City, Mo. 64133

Louisiana Nursery,
R. 1, Box 43,
Opelousas, La. 70570

Maxwell's Garden,
R. 1, Box 155,
Olla La. 71465

Parry Nurseries,
Signal Mountain, Tenn. 37377

C. G. Simon Nursery,
Box 2873,
Lafayette, La. 70501

Starmont Daylily Farm,
16415 Shady Gove Rd.,
Gaithersburg, Md. 20760

Tanner's Garden,
Box 385,
Chenneyville, La. 71325

Tranquil Lake Nursery,
45 River St.,
Rehoboth, Maine 02769

Wheeler's Daylily Farm,
10024 Shady Lane,
Houston, Texas 77016

Gilbert H. Wild and Son,
Sarcoxie, Mo. 64862

Double Scarlet Lilly.

—DISPORUM OREGANUI

176

LILIUM AURATUM

The decorative value of this handsome Lily, whether grown as a pot plant or in the open border, is so well-known and acknowledged that it is not necessary to recommend it; but the object of this note is to record an extra-ordinary result from a system of cultivation in pots which is not universally practised. The system is that of growing these plants in pots from year to year without shaking out the bulbs and repotting, simply removing the top soil and top-dressing with new compost, and relying on intensive feeding to maintain vigour in the plant.

Three bulbs are grown in each ten-inch pot, and the plants showed remarkable vigour and flowered with great freedom. One bulb of L. auratum, however, carried an extra-ordinary inflorescence. Throwing a single, but fasciated stem, this divided at a height of five feet into several short umbels, the whole producing a monstrous head with a total of forty-eight flowers. The individual flowers, although relatively small, were perfect in every way.

It is recorded that a single plant grown in a pot was shown at a meeting of the Royal Horticultural Society in September, 1884, carrying twenty-five flowers, the stem being fasciated and the flowers borne in two distinct umbels; it would be interesting to know if there are other records of such a large number of flowers.

CROCUS PULCHELLUS

Crocus pulchellus is one of the most delightful of the autumn-flowering Crocuses, of which far too few are grown in gardens where the conditions are suitable. Like most of the family, C. pulchellus calls for a light soil and a sunny situation in our climate. Given these and a sheltered spot, it is likely to give unbounded delight to all who love the flowers of autumn and who seek to brighten their gardens with such gems as this Crocus. Its flowers are not large, it is true, but they are charming in every way. That this praise is justified may be learned from what Farrer wrote in his ENGLISH ROCK GARDEN, where he calls it "one of the darlings of the family," and adds that it is good enough for the "choicest slopes and beds of the choicest plot." It is of a delightful delicate lavender, beautifully lined and with orange spots at the base.

There is also a lovely white form, and the type varies from seeds. These plants seeded, and the seedlings were allowed to remain where they sprung up. Like other autumn-flowering Crocus species, C. pulchellus should be planted in July or early August, in sandy soil, in a sunny place, at a depth of an inch. C. pulchellus is lovely on a sunny rockwork, or in a border, and is a delightful subject for the alpine house.

DISPORUM OREGANUM

Considerable confusion seems to exist with regard to this Liliaceous plant. At one time it was known as Prosartis oregana, and several authorities have included it in the genus Uvularia.

It is a dwarf, rather attractive, herbaceous plant, suitable for planting in woodland in conjunction with Fritillarias and Uvularias. Its branching, wiry stems, about eighteen inches in height, are clothed with ovate or oblong-lanceolate, acutely-pointed leaves. The campanulate flowers are produced either singly or in drooping racemes of three or four, on slender pedicels arising from the axils of the leaves. They are dull purplish-brown in colour.

Disporum oreganum grows freely and increases rapidly by rhizomatous growths when once established.

A I S MEMBERSHIP BRINGS YOU MANY PLEASURES AND PRIVILEGES

What Every Iris Grower Should Know—An illustrated booklet free to new members, filled with information on all types of irises and how to grow them, together with details of AIS programs providing the many services and activities its members enjoy.

The quarterly AIS Bulletin—Issues average more than 100 pages of interesting feature articles, helpful reports on iris varieties, culture, exhibiting, hybridizing, plus many other iris subjects.

A Round Robin Program—Correspondence groups which you may join to discuss your iris interests and problems with members in your Region, across the country, or around the world.

Regional and national activities—annual meetings and conventions, combining garden tours, visits to test gardens, programs and panel discussions.

A scientific committee and other assistance with technical and scientific problems of culture, hybridizing, etc.

A species committee for acquiring rare species and varieties.

A judges training committee for special training for judging and exhibiting.

The chance to vote for your favorite varieties in the annual iris popularity poll taken by AIS.

As an AIS member you may join the Sections of the Society specializing in median, Siberian, spuria, Japanese and reblooming irises, and receive additional publications in these fields. Many members also belong to local societies affiliated with the AIS and are welcome in special societies for dwarf, aril, Louisiana and other kinds of irises.

WHO BELONGS TO THE AMERICAN IRIS SOCIETY?

The rolls of AIS include outstanding iris specialists, gardening experts and horticulturists with interests in many kinds of ornamentals, but the Society is primarily for the amateur gardener who enjoys growing irises. There are no other special qualifications for membership.

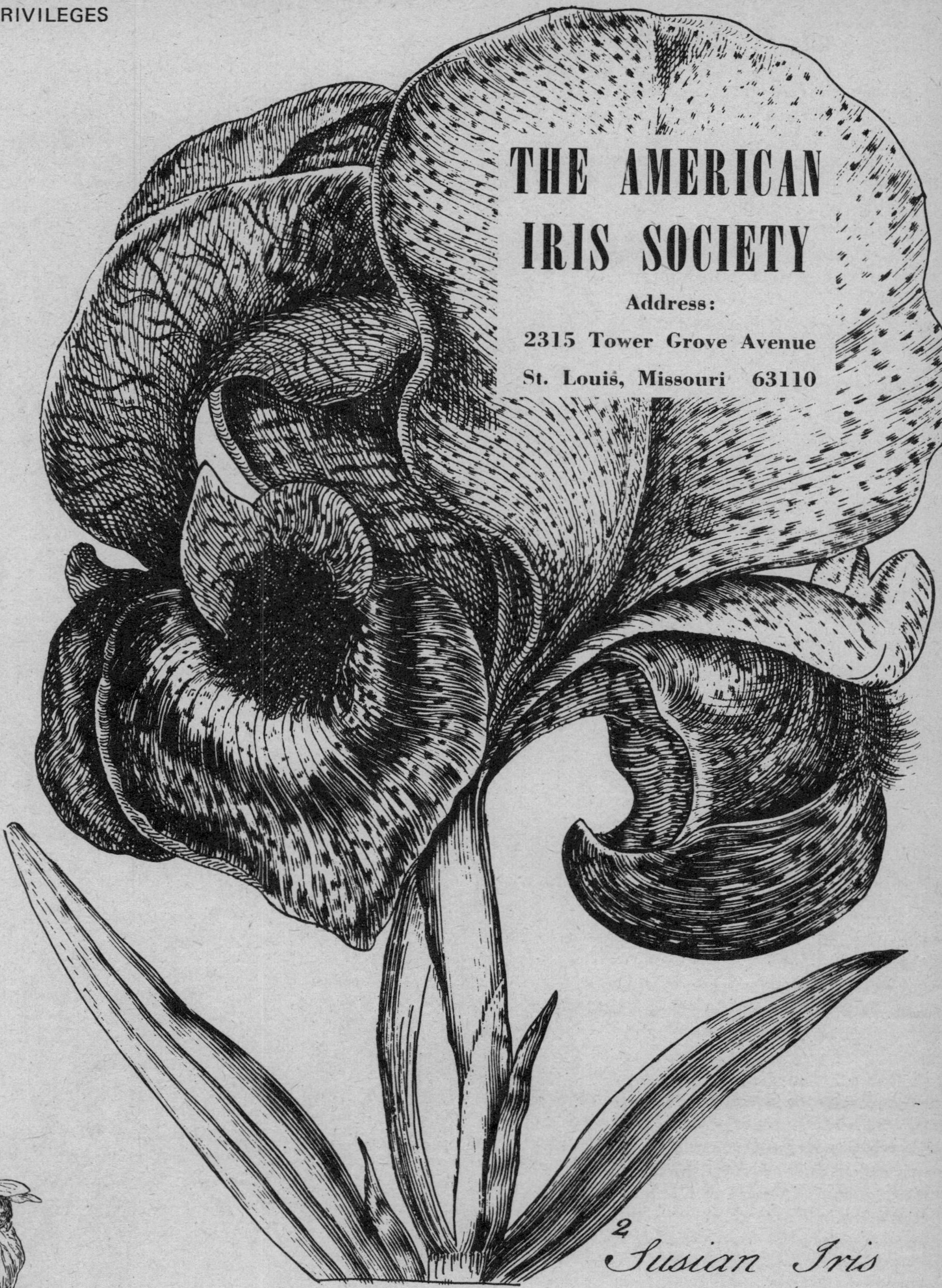

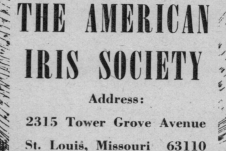

THE AMERICAN IRIS SOCIETY

Address:

2315 Tower Grove Avenue
St. Louis, Missouri 63110

Susian Iris

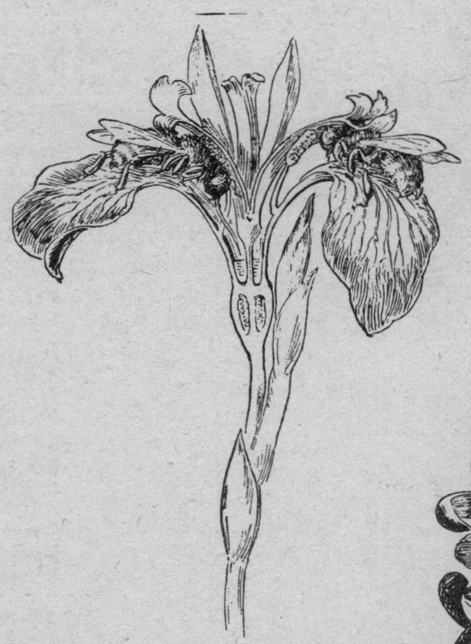

WILD IRIS

CHRYSANTHEMUMS.

MUMS

Dooley Gardens,
Hutchinson, Minn. 55350

Fleming's Flower Fields,
Box 4607,
3100 Leighton Ave.,
Lincoln, Nebr. 68504

Flowerland,
816 English St.,
Racine, Wisc. 53402

Gable's Nursery,
Haralson, Ga. 30229

Huff's Gardens,
Box 267,
Burlington, Kans. 66839

Jernigan's Gardens,
R. 5,
Dunn, N.C. 28334

King's Mums,
3723 E. Castro Valley Blvd.,
Castro Valley, Calif. 84546

The Lehman Gardens,
Faribault, Minn. 55021

Spafford Greenhouses,
Barker, N.Y. 14012

Star Mums,
West Grove, Penna. 19390

Sunnyslope Gardens,
8638 Huntington Dr.,
San Gabriel, Calif. 91775

Thon's Garden Mums,
4815 Oak St.,
Crystal Lake, Ill. 60014

Tom's Garden Mums,
Box 87,
Ashton, Nebr. 68814

CHRYSANTHEMUMS

GROWING IRIS IN THE HOME GARDEN

Garden irises are hardy, long-lived perennials that need a minimum of care. They are an established "backbone" of home gardens because they bloom when few other plants do—after spring-flowering bulbs and before peonies, delphinium, and phlox.

Easy-to-grow iris varieties adapted to every region of the United States are available. They produce graceful flowers in a wide range of shapes, sizes, and colors.

DESCRIPTION

Iris flowers have 6 petals. The 3 upright petals are called standards; the 3 that hang down are called falls. Flowers may be white, yellow, pink, purple, blue, reddish, or bicolored.

Principal types of irises are bearded, beardless, crested, and bulb.

Bearded irises have a fuzzy line, or beard, that runs down the middle of the falls. They are called German iris or pogoniris. Iris germanica is the most commonly grown bearded species.

Bearded irises live through severe droughts and cold. The sword-shaped leaves are evergreen in warm climates and remain green until late fall in cold climates.

Most bearded iris plants grow 2 to 3 feet tall. Because they are easy to grow, tall bearded irises are recommended for beginning gardeners.

Usually, tall bearded irises bloom in May and June. Several varieties bloom in both spring and fall.

A group of bearded irises that naturally grow 4 to 9 inches tall is called dwarf iris. The two most common species are I. pumila and I. chamaeiris. Both are well adapted to rock gardens because they spread quickly and form dense mats of foliage. They bloom in March, April, and May.

Beardless irises are called apogoniris or apogons. They have smooth fall petals and thin, grasslike leaves. Plants grow 1 to 4 feet tall. Most varieties bloom in June.

Japanese (I. kaempferi) and Siberian (I. sibirica) irises are the most commonly grown beardless species.

Japanese irises have soft, drooping standards and wide falls. Plants grow 2 to 4 feet tall. Flowers are borne on long stems.

Siberian irises have stiff, narrow falls and narrow, upright standards. Stems grow 18 inches to 2 feet tall. Beardless types, which thrive in moist soil, frequently are planted on stream and lake banks.

Crested irises have a small raised area, or crest, on the middle of each fall. Often, the color of these crests contrasts with petal colors. One of the more popular crested irises is a dwarf species, I. cristata.

For information on bulb irises, see Home and Garden Bulletin 136, "Spring Flowering Bulbs." You may obtain a copy from Office of Communication, U.S. Department of Agriculture, Washington, D.C. 20250; send your request on a post card and include your zip code.

TYPES OF THE JAPANESE IRIS.

Iris—Rhizome.

PEONY

Mons Jules Elie: Light rose pink. Very early.
Mons. Martin Cahuzac: Dark maroon-red. Early-midseason.
Philip Revoire: Dark crimson. Mid-season.
Primevere: Cream yellow, gold center. Mid-season.
Reine Hortense: Blush pink, deeper flecked center. Early.
Sarah Bernhardt: Apple blossom pink. Late.
Venus: Shell pink.

SINGLE PEONY

Mikado: Brilliant red, large center crown of rose stamens, tipped with gold. Mid-season.
Isani-Gidui: Large, white flowers with rich buff centers.
Jacques Doriat: Silvery red pink, yellow petaloids
Snow Cloud: Snow white, slightly tinged rose, large dome-shaped flowers.
The Pearl: Bright clear pink with a full center of stamens, cream edged with white.

Typical Nursery List

SPRINGBROOK GARDENS, INC., 6776 HEISLEY ROAD, MENTOR, OHIO 44060

IRIS

Bay View Gardens,
1201 Bay St.,
Santa Cruz, Calif. 95060

Brown's Sunnyhill Gardens,
R. 3, Box 102,
Milton-Freewater, Ore. 97862

Burge's Iris Garden,
1414 Amhurst,
Denton, Texas 76201

Charjoy Gardens,
Box 511,
117 Acadia Dr.
Lafayette, La. 70501

Cooley's Gardens,
Silverton, Ore. 97381

Cordon Bleu Farms,
418 Buena Creek Rd.,
San Marcos, Calif. 92069

CRAMER'S IRIS GARDENS
Payson, Ill. 62360

Crooked Creek Gardens,
Star Route,
Marquand, Mo. 63655

Eden Road Iris Garden,
Box 117,
Wenatchee, Wash. 98801

Fleur de Lis Gardens,
Box 670,
Canby, Ore. 97013

N. Freudenburg Gardens,
310 E. Maple,
Norfolk, Neb. 68701

Gable Iris Gardens,
2543 28th Ave., S.,
Minneapolis, Minn. 55406

Hammer's Iris Garden,
1040 Perris Blvd.
Perris, Calif. 92370

Hildenbrandt's Iris Garden,
Star R. 4,
Lexington, Neb. 68850

Imperial Flower Garden,
Box 255,
Ornell, Ill. 61319

J and J Iris Garden,
R. 1, Box 329,
Cashmere, Wash. 89915

Walter Marx Gardens,
Boring, Ore. 97009

Mathews Iris Gardens,
201 Sunny Dr.,
College Place, Wash. 99324

Melrose Gardens,
309 Best Rd. South,
Stockton, Calif. 95206

Mission Bell Gardens,
2778 W. 5600 South,
Roy, Utah 87067

Mount-Clare Iris Gardens,
3036 N. Narragansett Ave.,
Chicago, Ill. 60634

Pilley's Gardens,
Box 396,
San Marcos, Calif 92069

Riverdale Iris Gardens,
7124 Riverdale Rd.,
Minneapolis, Minn. 55430

Schoonover Gardens,
404 S. 5th St., Box 7,
Humboldt, Kansas 66748

Schreiner's Gardens,
3625 Quinaby Rd., N.E.,
Salem, Ore. 97303

Southern Meadows Garden,
1424 S. Perrine, Box 230,
Centralia, Ill. 62801

Summerlong Iris Gardens,
R. 2, Box 163,
Perrysville, Ohio 44864

Top O' The Ridge,
100 N.E. 81st St.,
Kansas City, Mo. 64118

GROWING PEONIES
By HENRY M. CATHEY
Plant Science Research Div., Agricultural Research Service

Peonies are hardy perennial plants. They need little care and live through severe winters. After they become established in a garden, peonies bloom each spring for many years. They are the backbone of the perennial border and make good cut flowers.

Plant peonies in clumps of three, in masses, or among other plants. Planted singly, they contribute little to good landscaping. Like iris, daylily, and chrysanthemum, their leaves make an excellent background for small plants; grow them in beds at least 4 feet wide. Group them with phlox and plantain lily for contrast of foliage and time of blooming.

Most peonies are grown in States north of South Carolina and Texas. Some varieties will grow farther south, but they seldom bloom because winter temperatures are not low enough for flower buds to develop properly.

Great Crimson Piony.

Dwarf Piony

PEONIES

Atha Gardens,
   West Liberty, Ohio 43357

Brand Peony Farms,
   Box 36,
   Faribault, Minn. 55021

Lienau Peony Gardens,
   9135 Beech Daly Rd.,
   Detroit, Mich. 48239

Louis Smirnow,
   85 Linden Ln.,
   Brookville, P.O.
   Glen Head, N.Y. 11545

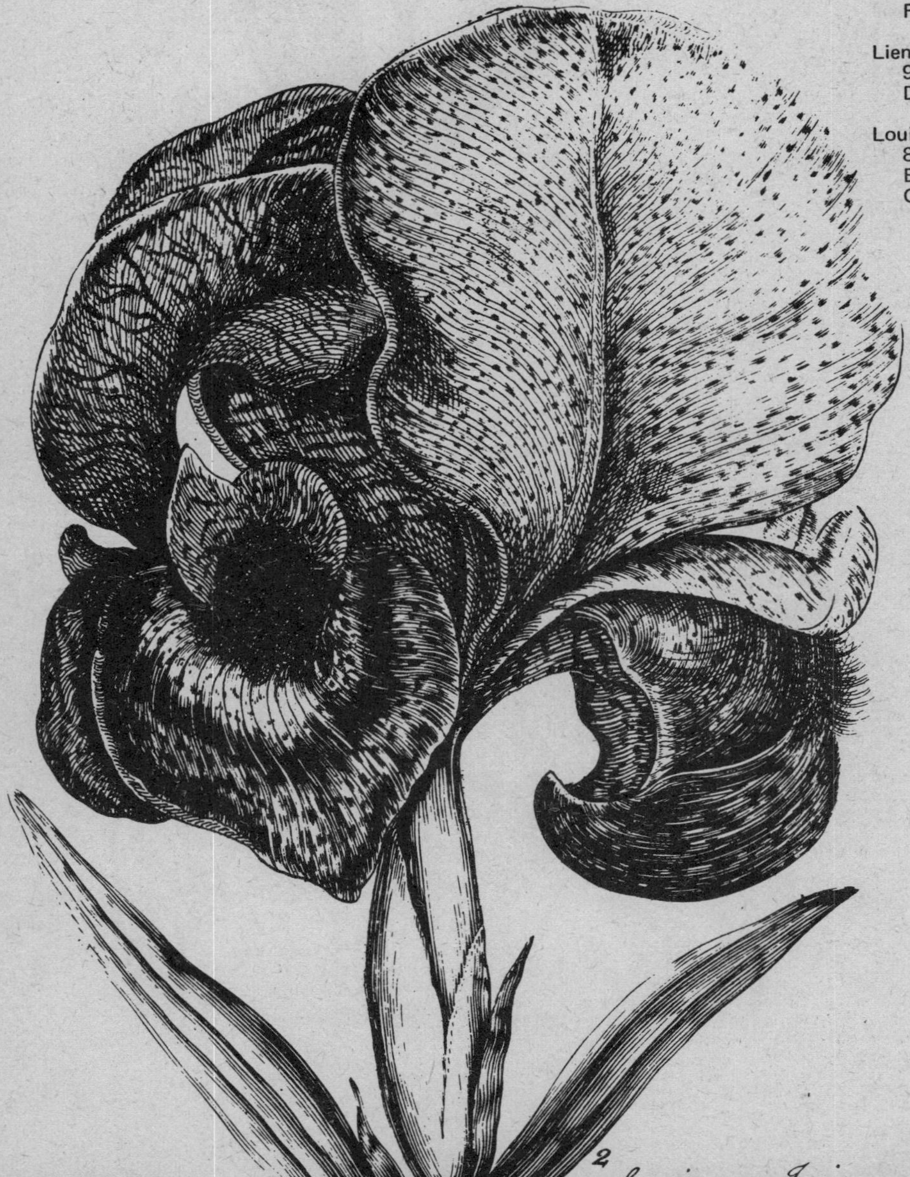

Susian Iris

IRIS KAEMPFERI (Japanese Iris)
Excellent cut flower, with crepe-like blooms. Requires abundant moisture; acid soil. June—July. 3'
   Eleanor Parry: Double. Caret-red.
   Fascination: Light powder blue veined white.
   Kagari Bi: Rose pink, silver veins.
   Kumchii Gumii: A rich dark blue variety with yellow markings in the center.
   Mount Hood: Double dark blue, orange center.
   Mahogany: Double dark mahogany.
   Rose Anna: Double wine red, heavily veined purple, golden throat.
   Seacrest: Double white, deep purple tufted center, yellow at base of petal.
   Shadow: Rich dark purple, almost black.
   Sigo No Urinus: Large, double rich violet with a tufted center.
   Wake Musha: Double purple tufted center, light veins, yellow at base of petal.

IRIS MARHIGO (Japanese Iris)
Large beautiful iris. Blooms early to mid-season.
   Summer Storm: Dark velvety purple with big black tufted center. Blooms late. 3½'
   Worlds Delight: True orchid-pink. Double. 40"

IRIS SIBERICA (Siberian Iris)
Finest cut flower. Beardless variety. All season. Good in border or large rockery.
   Caesar's Brother: Dark pansy purple.
   Snow Queen: Pure white.

IRIS SPURIA (Yellow-Banded Iris)
Exquisite cut flower. Lasts a week in water. June. 4'
   Ochroleuca Gigantea: White standards, yellow falls.

LILIES.

Corsages of Jan de Graaff lilies

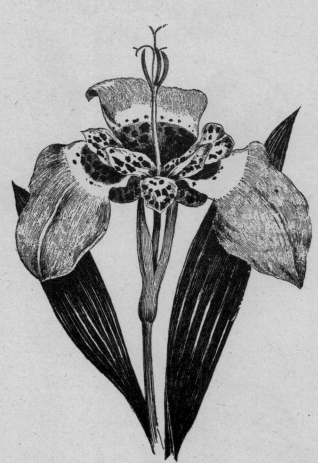

TIGRIDIA FLOWER

THE NORTH AMERICAN LILY SOCIETY, Inc.

Can help you with lilies by:

1. Informing you of the proper cultural procedures,
2. Sharing the latest information on diseases and their prevention,
3. Providing low-cost seed thru the seed exchange,
4. Advising on successful methods for growing lilies from seed,
5. Having informed persons to contact for some of your problems,
6. Furnishing means of communication with other persons interested in lilies thru the Round Robins,
7. Maintaining a valuable library and slide collection,
8. Publishing interesting Quarterly Bulletins and a Yearbook,
9. Giving you an opportunity to show lilies at local and international shows and compete for awards, and
10. Enabling you to help develop, preserve and register hybrid lilies throughout the world.

1, TIGRIDIA.   2, DICENTRA.

BULBS & PLANTS.

180

WHY GROW LILIES

Lilies are the most diverse of plants:

  they have many types of forms from trumpets, to bowls, to turks cap

  they have a diversity of flower position from upfacing, to out-facing, to hanging

  they are almost every color except blue

  they have a varied bloom period from late spring to frost

  they have many possible uses from borders, to rock garden, to beds, to patio pots

Lilies are also among the most beautiful of all flowers and excite the interest of all who see them.

THE NORTH AMERICAN LILY SOCIETY, Inc.

MRS. BETTY CLIFFORD, Executive Secretary
Route 1, Box 395
Colby, Wisconsin 54421

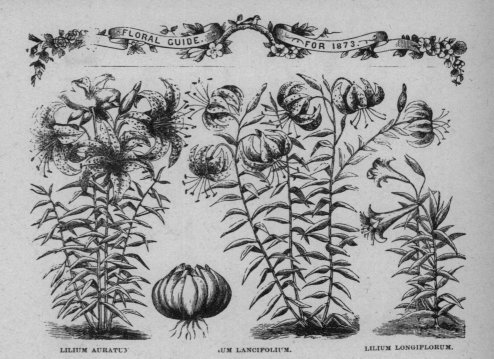

FLORAL GUIDE FOR 1873.

LILIUM AURATUM.   ..UM LANCIFOLIUM.   LILIUM LONGIFLORUM.

BATEMAN'S, AND THE CHALCEDONIAN LILY.

ANNUAL MEETING and SHOW

Each year the Society and a Regional sponsors the Annual Meeting and Show in various places throughout the United States and Canada, usually during early July. These are excellent means of learning more about lilies, and more importantly, meeting and making friends.

The N.A.L.S. began in Boston in 1946 as an outgrowth of the Lily Committee of the American Horticultural Society. It now has members from almost every state and province in North America, with members in many countries of Europe, Asia, Africa, South America, and Australia - New Zealand.

Your area is included in a regional lily society. Regionals are an important part of the lily fellowship. Most regionals publish a bulletin and offer several meetings a year with sharing and fellowship. You may contact the Executive Secretary for regional information.

Turk's Cap Lily.   Lilium superbum.

BELLINGHAM HYBRIDS

The Persian   Lilly.

GREENHOUSE BARROW.

THE VAUGHAN GREENHOUSE BARROW

BLACKBERRY LILY OR LEOPARD FLOWER.

Photos courtesy of
Rex Lilies
Newburg, Ore.

fig. 32.—Tye's Single Hyacinth Glass.

NARCISSI (DAFFODILS)

A daffodil is probably one of the easiest and least demanding of plants to grow. Normally when a bulb is planted it will come up and flower, provided that an unbalanced fertilizer is not put on. Fertilizers containing an excess of nitrogen should be avoided, as should manure. However, the species do need more understanding and care and must be treated with the respect accorded to most plants in the garden. If they are happy they will become established and multiply.

The varieties we offer vary from 3'' to 18'' in height. Only a few are species and are clearly marked as such. The remainder are hybrids, being crosses between small species and larger-flowered varieties and, as normally happens, the hybrids have more vigour and adaptability. The hybrid daffodils which we list will grow almost anywhere, but this only applies to a very few of the species, many of which are alpines and need treatment, especially drainage, suitable for these subjects. Species daffodils may be seen all over the high ground in Spain and Portugal, where *N. asturiensis*, *bulbocodium*, *rupicola* and *triandrus* are found growing through the melting snow like Crocus in the Alps.

The *jonquils* however seem to like places where the soil is often heavy and where they get a thorough baking in summer. Few of the *tazetta* group are hardy in this country and then only in unusually warm spots — in other words their growth is restricted to south of a line from the Severn to the Wash. However, together with the North African species, they will grow well if brought in to a cold house by the middle of November but *not forced*.

The *bulbocodiums* grow almost all over the Iberian peninsula in varying conditions from marshland to dry road verges. When grown in this country it is found that those which increase by seed flower well but those whose bulbs split are likely to be flowerless after a few years. These trends can only be found out by experience as they seem to vary from garden to garden. Many of the *triandrus* family, all of which need good drainage, flower in partial shade, often on northern slopes.

Many people like to grow *daffodils* in grass. However it should be remembered for this form of naturalising that the bulbs should be planted 6'' deep — in other words rather deeper than usual — and the grass should not be mown until after the leaves have died down. Many of the hybrids we list are suitable for this purpose, especially *February Silver*, *Peeping Tom*, *February Gold*, *Beryl* and the *poeticus* varieties. Also of course the wild daffodil of Northern Europe, now called *pseudo narcissus*. Many of the smaller hybrids are better grown in the border and rock garden where their daintiness can be appreciated to the full.

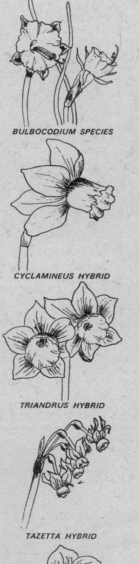

BULBOCODIUM SPECIES

CYCLAMINEUS HYBRID

TRIANDRUS HYBRID

TAZETTA HYBRID

JONQUIL HYBRID

CHINESE SACRED LILY

HYACINTHS IN POTS.

SMALL BULBS FOR FORCING

The forcing of such bulbs as Hyacinths, Narcissi and Tulips for conservatory and room decoration during the early months of the year, is sure to receive attention, but sufficient importance is not always given to the possibilities of the smaller bulbs grown in little pots for the decoration of the front of the plant stages or for standing on small tables in living rooms.

Cultural details do not differ from those employed in the growing of larger bulbs, except that, on the whole, they will not submit to quite so much forcing, but as their natural season of flowering is fairly early, there is no need for this, and under quite cool treatment they are sure to flower early if the bulbs have been potted in good time and have made plenty of roots.

Crocuses are excellent subjects for small pots, and the old variety Cloth of Gold may be had in flower at mid-winter with very little trouble. Some of the larger and more showy Dutch varieties will easily follow this under similar treatment and will make a charming display of colour during the early part of the year.

Iris reticulata is a delightful early flowering plant for growing in small pots. Its natural flowering season out-of-doors is February, and very little encouragement is necessary to anticipate this by a few weeks. The common blue and white Grape Hyacinths, Muscari botryoides coeruleum and album follow these in season, and are highly attractive when grown in small pots together with Chionodoxa Luciliae var. sardensis and Scilla sibirica as companions.

The Babianas with their deep green, compact foliage and blue, rose and crimson flowers, are excellent little pot plants if grown in a cold frame and not introduced to even gentle warmth until March.

The dwarf Star Tulip, Calochortus Benthamii, with its charming, cup-like flowers, vivid yellow with dark blotch at the base, is also a delightful little pot plant, but should be kept in a cold house, when it flowers at about the end of April. Similarly, the Sparaxis is a gem for small pots, and it is difficult to imagine anything more striking than the combination of scarlet and orange.

Milla uniflora and its variety violacea are particularly valuable for forcing in small pots, and as the flowers open in succession they remain in beauty over a considerable period. These small bulbous plants are an asset to the spring-flowering scheme in the conservatory, and give an added interest by their simple gracefulness.

FOUR STEPS FOR FORCING TULIPS:

(1) Position bulbs so they nearly touch.

(2) Cover with soil; water well.

(3) Place in dark, cool place.

(4) After roots form and leaf tips show, forcing may begin.

Single Hyacinth.

Narcissus and Hyacinths for Winter Window Gardening

HYACINTHS IN GLASSES.

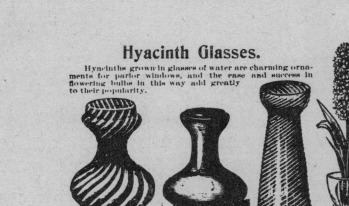

Hyacinth Glasses.

Hyacinths grown in glasses of water are charming ornaments for parlor windows, and the ease and success in flowering bulbs in this way add greatly to their popularity.

Hyacinth in glass.

JAMES VICK   ROCHESTER, N.Y.

The Summer Bulbs are a most useful and brilliant class of flowers, and becoming every year more popular, both among florists and amateurs everywhere. The Gladiolus now takes rank at the very head of the list, and the Dahlia still retains a good share of its old popularity. The Summer Bulbs are tender, and therefore destroyed by freezing, and must not be planted until frost is over in the spring. In the autumn they must be taken up before very hard frosts, and kept in the cellar or some other safe place until spring. They are easily preserved in good condition, and will richly repay for the little care required in their treatment. These Bulbs will not be forwarded until severe frosts are over, so that there will be no danger of injury on the way. Where Bulbs are ordered with Seeds, the Seeds will be forwarded at once and the Bulbs sent as soon as the weather will permit. Customers must not, therefore, feel disappointed because they do not find the Bulbs in the first package. To the Pacific coast only do we forward Summer Bulbs in the early winter, except where particularly desired for special purposes. Usually we can commence sending out Bulbs by the middle of March, filling orders from the Southern States first; but as we then have a large quantity of orders on hand, it is usually the middle of April before all are shipped, which is quite early enough for the Northern States.

EARLY ROMAN HYACINTHS WHITE-YELLOW-PINK-BLUE

DOUBLE MIXED TULIPS.

PARROT-TULIPS.

—Pot of Tulips.

TULIPS

In addition to their decorative value in the formal beds of the flower garden, Tulips are invaluable when grown in the less-frequented parts of the garden. It is essential to secure good bulbs; the so-called cheap mixtures obtainable late in the season cannot be relied upon to produce really good blooms.

Narrow borders at the foot of new walls may be made attractive by planting Tulips such as Bleu Celeste (syn. Blue Flag), a late-flowering, double, purple-mauve variety, with large flowers of good substance. Excellent Darwin Tulips for the same positions are Bleu Aimable, dark heliotrope, and Dream, mauve. Borders containing late-flowering herbaceous subjects may be made attractive during the early season by planting scarlet Tulips , such as Couleur Cardinal and Prince of Austria (perhaps not true scarlets), but excellent for the purpose suggested; also many others.

Tulip Artus, scarlet, flowering over a carpet of the Munstead strain of Polyanthus is very effective, and forms one of the few instances where lemon, yellow and scarlet flowers may be associated. Garden vases may be planted with suitable varieties of Tulips. It is generally safe to plant the bulbs direct into the vases, but where the position is very exposed or an effect is required on a certain date, the bulbs may be planted in pots and transferred to the vases as desired.

Yellow varieties are very charming when growing old, moss-covered vases or shallow bowls.

Bold groups of the Cottage Tulips are attractive between dwarf shrubs. These Tulips are particularly adapted for the supply of cut flowers. The Darwin varieties are most useful during the latter part of May, at a time when many early-flowering bulbous subjects have passed out of bloom.

Yellow Tulips and blue Forget-me-nots are most attractive in beds and borders, whilst pink Tulips, springing from a carpet of white Arabis, are always admired.

It is wise to thoroughly prepare the ground by deep digging, and heavy soils should be improved by adding leaf-mould, or road grit, and decayed manure. Plant all the bulbs at an even depth to ensure the simultaneous production of the flowers. On light, dry soils, plant the Tulips three inches deep, but on heavy or wet soils, a depth of two inches will suffice. Do not plant where Tulips were grown the year before unless new soil has been prepared.

When bulbs are planted year after year in the same beds or borders, the ground should be dug two feet, or more, in depth, bringing the bottom soil to the surface. By this means thorough drainage is secured and fresh soil made available for the plants.

BULBS FOR CUT BLOOMS

As Daffodils and Tulips are in demand during the early spring for floral decorations indoors, it will save spoiling the beds in the flower garden, when they are in their full beauty, if special plantings are made for the purpose in the kitchen and vegetable quarters, where odd places may be found for them.

Some of the less expensive varieties of both flowers are admirably suited for supplying cut blooms, and they may be set along the borders of the kitchen garden and under fruit trees.

The bulbs serve a double purpose; they not only provide valuable material for cut blooms, but they make the kitchen garden interesting at a time of the year when bright flowers are doubly appreciated. In addition to its freedom of blooming, and as the flowers are produced on long stalks, it is charming for furnishing vases in dwelling rooms. Other Narcissi suited to the purpose are Emperor, Barrii conspicuus, Mrs. Langtry, Golden Spur, Pheasant's Eye, ornatus, Horace, Sir Watkin, princeps, Waterwitch, Lucifer, Whitewell and Horsfieldii.

Of Tulips, there is a wealth of beautiful varieties that are reasonable in price, such as Clara Butt, Pride of Haarlem, Harry Veitch, Farncombe Sanders, Safrano, Vermilion Brilliant, Couleur Cardinal, White Swan, Loveliness and Vuurbaak.

BLUMENZWIEBELN
GARTENBAUBETRIEB „ZWANENBURG"
VAN · TUBERGEN
HAARLEM

New York Botanical Garden

AMORPHOPHALLUS TITANUM

HARDY WATER LILLIES

Their Culture in Tubs, Tanks and Ponds

In many gardens there are naturally-formed ponds in which collections of Water Lilies are grown. These Lilies are general favorites, and nearly every owner of a garden who sees them wishes to have a few. There need, of course, be no difficulty in growing the plants in ponds fed with a regular stream of water. Where such are not available, then artificial ponds or tanks must be substituted; and, on a much smaller scale, tubs partly sunk in the ground.

The round pond may be made to look very charming with Water Lilies, but one with curving outlines and, perhaps, gently undulating edges and banks may be made still more effective. In the case of the first named especially, a judicious use should be made of suitable Water Rushes to break up the formal outline.

The first operation should be to make soundings near the edges and to mark, by inserting sticks in the mud, the best positions—those where the water varies in depth from 2ft. to 4ft. or so. If the mud is very soft and easily moved, drive in, about 1ft. apart, five stakes for each plant, leaving the ends 1ft. or so above the mud. These stakes will retain the loam for the roots of the plants, which should be sunk in large pieces until the latter are well established.

The plants must be gently sunk and placed in the center of the prepared bed of loam, having first made them secure in suitable baskets filled with the following compost: Turfy loam, rotted leaves —oak or beech for preference—and coarse grit or sand. Of course, the compost must be placed round the roots of the plants firmly, but with care and, to prevent displacement, tie down both plants and soil to the basket itself. In due course these baskets will decay, but that matters not at all, as by that time the roots will be well established in the bed of prepared loam placed among the driven-in stakes.

Small, artificially constructed ponds must have a lining at least 9ins. thick of puddled clay. Such ponds are not at all expensive to make, and still less so where the surrounding soil is clayey, as then only the bottom need be of puddled clay.

A brick and cement tank is expensive to construct, but if the work be well done will last for many years.

If possible, the tanks should be built in a place where there is a natural supply of water or where water-pipes can be laid.

In connection with the tank, I also refer to the sunk tub shown at No. 1, loam No. 2, basket containing the plant, No. 3. Two brick and cement tanks are shown. One may be built, or a series with water running through from the first to the last. No. 4 tanks; No. 5, cement linings on the brick walls (No. 6). No. 7 shows how the water should pass from one tank to the other. No. 8, water entering in and running out at the opposite end.

On a concrete base lay in cement a course of bricks on edge, No. 9. At No. 10 the inner cement lining is shown thickened and rounded off at the bottom on both sides. No. 11 shows the baskets firmly embedded in the layer of loam. To hold these baskets in position use a few loose bricks and whole turves at the sides. The brick walls are shown at No. 12, and should be 9ins. thick, so that there will be no risk of cracking the cement lining, as might occur in case of a wall of a single brick thickness.

The depths may vary in the different tanks, being 2ft. in one, 3ft. in another and 4ft. in a third. This last depth is generally found sufficient for even the strongest growers. Both tubs and tanks should be, mainly, below the normal level of the surrounding ground. If the edge is 9ins. above, it will look well, and to do away with the bare and artificial appearance of such tanks, borders of suitable width may be formed round them and planted with moisture-loving plants or, indeed, with other kinds so that they may be furnished, leaving spaces so that one may approach near enough to inspect and enjoy the beauties of the Water Lilies. Hardy Ferns judiciously used make a feathery edging.

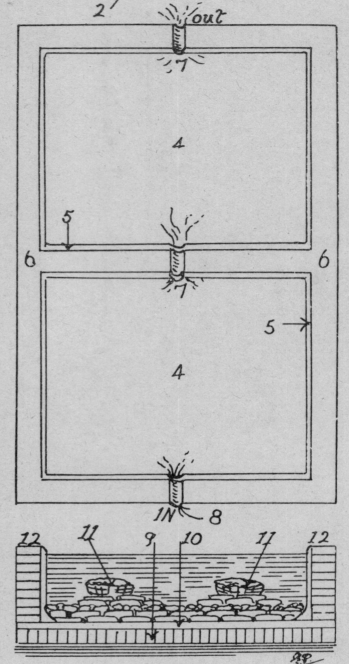

WATER LILY TANKS IN PLAN AND SECTION

Alba.

Odorata.

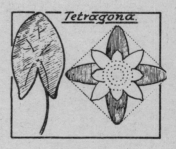
Tetragona.

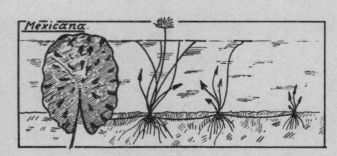
Mexicana.

Tuberosa.

—Transitions from Petals to Stamens in White Water-Lily.
E, F, G, H, various steps between petal and stamen.

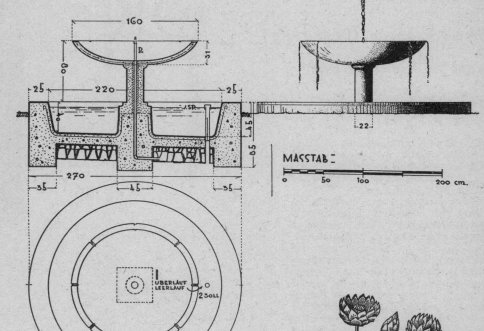

—East India Lotus (*Nelumbium roseum*).

-Purple African Water-lily (*Nymphæa Zanzibarensis*).

—Water-poppy (*Lymnocharis Humboldtii*)

AQUATIC PLANTS, POOLS AND FOUNTAINS

Hermitage Gardens,
R. 5,
Canastota, N.Y. 13032

Nelson Mfg. Co.,
Box 974,
Luling, Texas 78648

Paradise Gardens,
14 May St.,
Whitman, Maine 02382

Slocum Water Gardens,
1101 Cypress Gardens Rd.,
Winter Haven, Fla. 33880

Three Springs Fisheries,
Lilypond, Md. 21717

William Tricker,
174 Allendale Ave.,
Saddle River, N.J. 07458

Van Ness Water Gardens,
2460 N. Euclid Ave.,
Upland, Calif. 71986

THREE SPRINGS FISHERIES

Lilypons, Maryland

There's Gold in These Hills
Lodes of Goldfish and
Exotic Water Plants

LESS than ten miles south of Frederick, Maryland, is a vast area of torn earth, spotted with hundreds of shallow ponds and interlaced with miles of bare clay banks.

As the motorist enters the area, on a good road, his first impression is that of visiting a valley in which a rich lode of gold has just been struck.

In a manner of speaking, gold *has* been struck in the area, for this rough setting is the site of the Three Springs Fisheries, the world's largest center for goldfish and exotic water plants.

No one motorist has yet seen all there is to see at Lilypons, the community into which "Bloom Town" has developed, because the installation covers 1800 acres. More than 700 ponds are plotted into this acreage.

From the inception of this "gold strike" more than 30 years ago, however, procedure has been reversed a bit. Principally this reversed order has called for the pouring of gold into the place instead of taking it out. The bottom of every pond, for example, is ribbed with a network of pipelines, valves and other controls. These enable research and production workers at the fisheries to drain, refill and isolate any pond at will for carefully controlled cultivation of fish and water plants, and for the study of experimental strains, foods, disease control and the like.

It required many years of investment for the fisheries to attain their

present million-dollar installation and world-wide reputation. Currently the fisheries ship out some 80,000,000 fish and hundreds of thousands of aquatic plants annually.

During this development period every addition to the estate has been made with an eye to preserving as much natural beauty as possible. Thus far the program has succeeded. Strolling visitors still can choose practically any path winding through the area and enjoy a series of thrilling surprises along the way.

The climbing of almost any dike will reward the visitor with a breathtaking view of hundreds of lotus flowers or water lilies—pinks, reds, whites, yellows, changeable combinations—all of a beauty that can never be possessed by man, but only borrowed for the life span of his flowers.

320 pages

Here is a handsome new book that tells everything you want to know about placing, building and installing a garden pool, stocking a natural pond, choosing and planting water-lilies, lotus, and other beautiful aquatics, and selecting and caring for goldfish in pools, and also in aquariums.

POOLS, WATER-LILIES,. AND GOLDFISH is truly unique work, a product of the author's years of professional experience in lily and goldfish cultivation for amateur water gardeners, goldfish enthusiasts, landscape architects, and nurserymen throughout the country.

How to Do It!
POOLS, WATER LILIES, AND GOLDFISH

By Dr. G. L. THOMAS, JR.

- Foolproof directions and diagrams for building all kinds of pools, or installing readymade types, with information on pool edgings, planting depths, and border groupings.

- Complete lists of both hardy and tropical water-lilies, to be consulted by backyard gardeners and specialists alike.

- Exact descriptions of goldfish species and varieties essential information on their care and feeding.

- Important suggestions on how to develop a balance of life in the pool, and so keep it clean.

- 16 Pages of Striking Color Illustrations.

- 28 Pages of Black and White Photographs.

- 29 Pages of How-to-do-it Drawings.

American Nelumbo or Lotus

SHIROMAN LOTUS: Very, very double huge white flowers; each bloom is a perfect symbol of purity and chasity. Will live over winter in outside pool if protected the same as hardy water lilies.

History of the Lotus

Arrowleaved Pond Lily

The lotus is one of our oldest living links with the pre-historic days when the world was new. Along with other members of the water-lily family, it must have been one of the first flowering plants to take form on this earth. Not long ago the fossil of a lotus leaf was unearthed in eastern Asia. Age of the plant was estimated, from the geological strata in which the fossil was found, at 70,000,000 years.

Also within recent years scientists found, buried deeply in the bed of a long dead lake in southern Manchuria, lotus seeds purportedly 50,000 years old. The seeds were babied along by different scientists. Some of them germinated, they were nurtured, and today they thrive—pink Manchurian Lotus—in the Kenilworth Aquatic Gardens in Washington, D. C. Their form is the same as that of many popular commercial varieties today.

Certainly the lotus has been the most revered of flowers in Man's recorded history. Lotus blooms, leaves and pods appeared in his first crude drawings. The lotus was sacred to the ancient Hindus. The Hindu regarded the bloom as a thing of beauty representing his own country, and the lotus leaves represented surrounding countries and cultures. To the early Buddhists it was a most exalted symbol of Man—head held high, pure and undefiled in the sun, feet rooted in the world of experience. It was a basic motif for much ancient Assyrian and Persian art, and the Egyptians looked upon the lotus as the "parent of ornamentation."

The cornucopia, symbol of abundance and fertility is thought by some students to be a stylized drawing of the full-to-bursting seed pod of the lotus. The lotus may even have its place in architecture, for it has been suggested that the furled petals of the blossom inspired the design of the Ionic capital.

Just as the lotus has retained its age-old form of flower and leaf, so it has kept the atmosphere of mystery which caused the early civilizations to love and revere it. The sweetness and far-reaching qualities of its powerful fragrance, the near-miracle of its tremendous bursting bloom assured it of a prominent place in and around the temples of ancient priests. It apparently has never lost these old and aesthetic associations, for few water gardeners speak of the flower today merely as the lotus. Most of them invariably refer to it as "the sacred lotus."

Ornamental lotus listed in this catalog originated in India. In ancient times, and probably still today, natives cooked and ate the roots. They are not to be confused with the memory-killing fruits eaten by Ulysses' companions in the Homeric classic. Those fruits which grew along the north shores of Africa, according to the old Greek legends, induced such a feeling of happy languor that those who ate them forgot their native land and ceased to desire to return to it. That particular species of lotus, as well as the Lotus Eaters, exists only in the Never-Never Land of fiction.

Lotus will grow above ground if situated in a sunny patio corner and given proper care but it does best in a pool or pond. Give it a good start by holding up the planting until warm weather has come to stay.

The lotus rootstock resembles a thin, elongated banana, 12 to 18 inches long, with a tapered end which is the growing point. If the growing point is bruised or broken, the root becomes worthless.

Fill a half-barrel, wooden tub or planting box or pail to within 4 or 5 inches of its rim with a mixture of 1 part well-rotted cow manure and 3 parts good garden soil. For exceptionally fine results, put an additional 2 or 3 inches of the full-strength manure in the bottom of the container.

If natural fertilizer is not available, use any of the commercial all-purpose fertilizers at the rate of a generous double-handful to a planting box or pail full of soil, twice that much for a tub or half-barrel.

Scoop a depression in the top of the soil and lay in the rootstock. Cover it with an inch or two of soil, in such a manner as to leave half an inch of the growing point sticking out. Being careful not to touch the growing point, lay a flat rock atop the planted rootstock to hold it in place.

Place the receptacle into the pool, propping it at a level where 3 to 4 inches of water cover the growing point.

If the lotus is to be planted above ground, the bigger the container the better. Keep the container filled almost to the brim with water.

Once established in a wild state, the lotus is hard to remove. From the body of the root it grows another banana-shaped rootstock, and from the body of this another, and so on until it may form a chain-like series of roots 20 to 30 feet long in an ideal season. With the advent of frost, they grow downward. By the time freezing weather arrives they are well below the frost line. When warm weather returns, they surprise the water gardener by sending up plants at some amazing distances from where they quit blooming the previous season.

So if the plant is to be set out in a pond, remember that it has vigorous spreading habits and will soon take over a whole section of the landscape. Many estate owners plant it to do just that. If you don't want it to spread, confine its roots to a planting receptacle.

Established in a wild state, lotus reproduce generously, and quickly transform a section of farm pond into an expanse rivaling the tropics for lush growth. The species at right is Roseum Plenum.

This Mysterious Flower Which Took Shape When the World Was New, Influenced Man and His Civilizations

—Frogbit (*Hydrocharis Morsus-ranæ*). [1] Winter buds rising to the surface in spring. [2] Young floating plants which have developed from such buds. [3] Older floating plants.

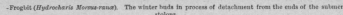

—Frogbit (*Hydrocharis Morsus-ranæ*). The winter buds in process of detachment from the ends of the submerged stolons.

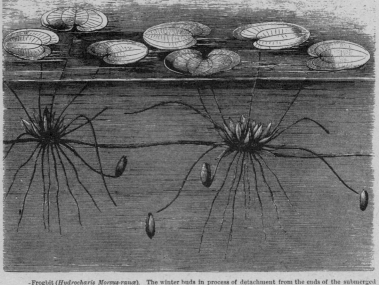

Aquatic Plants : Pond-Lilies with Floating Leaves and Sedges with Aërial Leaves.

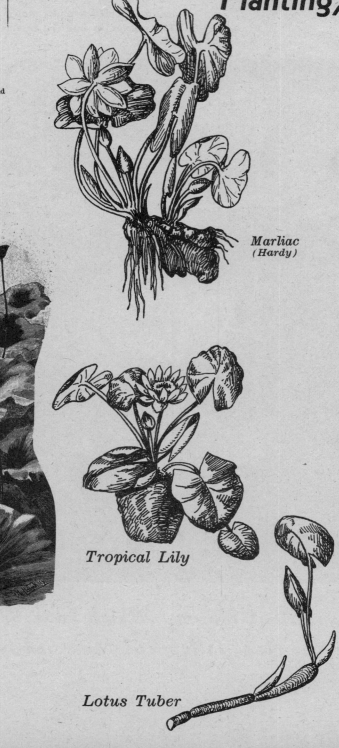

Marliac
(Hardy)

Tropical Lily

Lotus Tuber

—The Lotus Lily (*Nelumbium speciosum*). (From a photograph.)

Planting, Winter Care

Water-Lilies Are Easy to Grow, Inexpensive to Buy, Require Very Little Care

There is no addition which can be made to any home that will fit in more harmoniously than a water-lily pool.

In an undeveloped front or back lawn it quickly gives the landscape an established, finished look. On an estate already well plotted, water-lilies complement other flowers. Even the old and loved flower garden has a place for it—the water surface becomes a mirror for its own and other flowers. Water-lilies are "family" flowers, for the blooms and their culture can be enjoyed by children and adults alike.

Water-lilies are rewarding. They start blooming—several blooms to each root—in early summer and continue to first frost. Hardy lilies unfold with the morning, remain open until afternoon. Tropical day-bloomers—many quite fragrant—follow same pattern. Tropical night-bloomers open in the evening, and remain so until the following forenoon.

Water-lilies were once considered expensive, back in the days when they were grown principally on large estates, in expensive surroundings. Today they lie within easy grasp of everyone. A glance at some of the water-lily collections elsewhere in this catalog, and at their prices, will illustrate the point.

They are easy to obtain and plant. Select what you want. If you like, we'll pick a representative variety for you—1 or 2, 100 or 200.

Plant in a wooden box about 12 inches square, 10 or 12 inches deep. Fill the box with soil mixed with well-rotted cow manure—1 part manure, 3 parts soil, or 1 double handful commercial all-purpose fertilizer per planting container of soil—and plant the lily root 2 or 3 inches down in it. When you get our tropical lily roots they will have been in pots a few weeks and will have several leaves. Plant without disturbing the earth ball.

Allow a 2½ or 3-foot square of water surface for each plant. Set box into pool or quiet section of stream so crown of root is 3 inches below water surface. As plant grows, lower box another inch or so from time to time.

In winter, set planting boxes on the pool floor, so root crowns will be safely below ice line. If pool is too shallow for this carry boxes into a cool cellar for the winter, and keep soil moist. Keep boxes where mice cannot get to them.

Protect the pool in winter by sticking a log into the water to absorb ice expansion.

ROSE BUD

Long treasured for its beauty and fragrance, the rose is probably the most widely cultivated ornamental flowering plant of all times.

Even today, tens of thousands of rose fanciers wait to grow the new Rose of the Year in gardens all around the world. And, thousands read THE AMERICAN ROSE, distributed monthly by The American Rose Society.

It would take a whole book to describe all the varie-

ties of roses available. So, we will just briefly say that the most popular roses are the hybrid teas. Each of these has a single flower on one stem. Floribunda roses, on the other hand, have many flowers on each stem. There are also climbing roses. And, these may be either teas or floribundas.

The grandiflora is a tall tea. And, the multiflora is a cross between the hybrid teas, perpetuals and others.

If you have not yet tried to grow roses, perhaps you should start next season. You will find the smell of success truly sweet.

But, whether it will be your first attempt, or an annual delight you have long cultivated, we are interested in pictures. Let's hear from you.

THE GRAND NEW HYBRID TEA ROSE, PRINCESS OF NAPLES.

ROSES.

ORGANIC ROSES

For over 50 years, Mrs. George Carlin has been succeeding with roses. A consulting rosarian for the American Rose Society, she's ready and raring to take on any critic. "Roses prove the value of organic gardening," she exclaims from her home in Fair Oaks, California. And if the luxuriant foliage and colors provided by some 500 mature bushes on her hillside garden in Sacramento County aren't enough to convince the skeptic that organic gardening works, Eunice Carlin has a large drawer stuffed full of ribbons won at various rose shows in the past seven years, in addition to a showcase laden with silver trophies.

An advocate of companion planting, mulching and non-chemical controls, Mrs. Carlin's roses are widely respected for their quality. In last season's Sacramento Rose Show, reports OGF-writer Richard L. Tracy, her roses won awards for Queen of the Show (best rose in the show), Master's Trophy (best among experienced exhibitors), Show Sweepstakes (most blue ribbons), Floribunda sweepstakes (for the smaller, cluster-type roses), Queen of Floribundas (the best of that type), Queen of Grandifloras (large cluster type) and Best Three Hybrid Teas (large cutting roses).

How does she do it? For one thing, by relying on mulch. "In the Quaker community where I was raised, nothing was wasted," Mrs. Carlin recalls, "so when I watched rose growers raking off old mulch to discard it, I was shocked. We just add clean new mulch over the old and let it decay and feed the plants."

Which mulch is best depends on the type of materials readily available, she says, as well as the individual planting situation. "I've found sawdust and shavings easy to get and inexpensive. A lumber company delivers it for about $1 a cubic yard. You just have to remember to add cottonseed meal to replace the nitrogen it uses to decay. Rice hulls are cheap and plentiful in the Sacramento area, too, but the winds here on our hilltop blow them all away. Weed-free manure is hard to come by, and hay seems to have weed seed in it."

The mulch serves many purposes, Mrs. Carlin explains. "It makes water more available to my roses, insulates them from sudden heat, cold and drying winds, protects the earthworms that fertilize and aerate the roots, and feeds them, too."

Walking down weed-free rows between Eunice Carlin's roses, visitors are impressed with the soft, carpetlike feel of the soil beneath their feet, and surprised when they learn Eunice Carlin is 70 years of age and legally blind. "I let my driver's license expire because of my poor eyesight, but I can still see weeds out in my garden," she laughs. "It's not impossible to pick them, though, because the mulch keeps the soil moist and makes weeding easy.

To keep her roses in top form, Mrs. Carlin also relies on feeding them liquified seaweed, applied directly to the foliage. And she interplants garlic and tomatoes with both the mature plants and some 600 seedling roses growing in the garden. "I've found that black spot doesn't often appear on roses interplanted with tomatoes," she observes. "Something the tomatoes exude from their roots acts as a natural fungicide. The garlic helps repel aphids and keeps cats out of the rose beds." A fringe benefit of this companion planting, of course, is an abundance of healthy organic tomatoes and garlic.

To curb mildew and any aphids not dispersed by the garlic, she sprinkles diatomaceous earth over the foliage; and combats moles and gophers by putting sand in the ground around valuable plantings — or stuffing fiberglass insulation in their runs. "They dislike digging in sand because their tunnels collapse behind them, and they hate to get sticky fiberglass in their paws. I pick up the insulation free from projects where they are tearing down a building. I'm just a natural scrounger at heart, I guess, but I can't see usable material going to waste."

The Carlins' hillside also had a problem of water draining off too quickly. Eunice, who manages time to be active with two local rose societies and the Sacramento Organic Gardening Club (the Down-to-Earthers), smiles: "I have to laugh when people say it's no wonder I have such fine roses with the beautiful soil and good drainage here. It wasn't always that way. We put down broken roofing tiles, salvaged from a mission, to form a water barrier so the water didn't just flush through, but stayed long enough to encourage good root growth."

IT TAKES KNOWING YOUR ONIONS

Another rose-growing enthusiast who discovered some knacks to the trade is Anna K. Bowser of Pittsburgh, Pa. Four years ago she set about having a rose garden — in complete ignorance, as she writes. "With much care and great toil, I prepared the ground for three beds in accordance with the directions. I chose my roses carefully from catalogs and planted them with loving care. The following spring, we had many beautiful roses but, as the summer progressed, we had a succession of pests and blights — aphids, mildew, etc., and even a few Japanese beetles, so that roses blooming later in the season were often malformed and the foliage on most of the bushes was eaten or browned."

Again consulting the books, Mrs. Bowser tried the recommended sprays — "but with rather dim success for the bushes and much discomfort to my respiratory system." Soon after, she started an OGF subscription and read about a natural fertilizer formula. "I also read a letter telling of the efficacy of onions planted near roses to discourage aphids. And in another issue of the magazine, I learned that geraniums have the same effect. And so I planted *both* among the rose bushes. The fertilizer, the chives, the geraniums all served the purpose well and we had beautiful roses and very, very few pests the next season.

"This past year," she continues, "I followed the same plan and the results are astounding. The bushes and the leaves are strong and healthy; the blooms are gorgeous and profuse; the aphids and other pests are almost non-existent. The roses, the geraniums and the chives all appear to be happy — and, of course, their happiness makes Mr. Bowser and me happy."

At Schenectady, N.Y., Mrs. Frank E. Earing has been collecting and growing roses that produce those tangy, healthful seedpods or hips. "The birds enjoy the seeds along with the others we provide," writes Mrs. Earing, who is a judge and consulting rosarian of the American Rose Society. "I encourage the birds by providing food they like and water, and they help, in return, by keeping down the insect population." In addition, she notes, "I plant garlic, chives and marigolds among my roses to keep down the insect pests. I don't spray, except with a concoction of garlic and a safe detergent." For this, she uses about a half cup or so of boiled cloves and husks and one tablespoon biodegradable detergent in a gallon of water.

TAKE A ROSE TO DINNER

Feeding roses well is naturally an important factor in having them grow and look the way we'd like. Like other plants, roses need balanced feeding — nitrogen to produce vegetative growth of canes, stems and leaves, potash for deep bloom color, plus phosphorus and trace minerals for the strong roots, disease and pest resistance. To get that balance — and not the overstimulation of chemical fertilizers which force plant growth and reduce blossom development — the gradual nitrogen availability of organic matter is invaluable.

Among the ways to deliver needed organic matter: use compost, peat moss, rotted manure, cover crops, clippings. Mix 2 inches or more to a shovel depth of well-stirred soil as you plant. Bone meal also rates as a number-one fertilizer among organic rose-growers at planting time. Usual application is 2 or 3 handfuls mixed with soil for each plant. One prize-winning grower, Louis Ver of Allentown, Pa., pokes chicken bones — intact — down 2 to 3 inches away from the base of plants around his 32 rose varieties, helping to channel moisture to root level, as well as provide the bone-fertilizing benefits. For drainage, Ver layers his stony clay soil with an inch or two of wood ashes and sand, then weed-free topsoil.

Maybe you know a barber or two well enough to salvage the hair they cut for you. Experimenting with over 30 varieties of roses in his Austin, Texas, garden, William Stafford found that human hair (a rich natural source of nitrogen) produces longer stems, larger buds and deeper color tones.

M. C. GOLDMAN

Organic Gardening and Farming

INTRODUCTION TO ROSES

This article, which originally appeared in ORGANIC GARDENING AND FARMING, is an excellent introduction to the subject of rose gardening. Though the methods may be foreign to those accustomed to using chemical fertilizers and sprays, they apparently yield prize winning blooms.

If you are hesitant about committing yourself to a totally organic regimen, there is an enormous body of literature and an active National Rose Society that you may write to for other growing instructions. However, we have used the article in this context to demonstrate that organic methods, which many assume are only useful in vegetable gardening may also be applied in ornamental beds. Why not try them in yours?

CRIMSON RAMBLER ROSE.

ROSES

Armstrong Nurseries,
Ontario, Canada 91761

Jackson & Perkins Co.,
Medford, Ore. 97501

Joseph J. Kern Rose Nursery,
Box 33,
Mentor, Ohio 44060

Miniature Plant Kingdom,
4488 Stoetz Ln.,
Sebastopol, Calif. 95472

Mini-Roses,
Box 4255, Sta. A,
Dallas, Texas 75208

Moore Miniature Roses,
Box 853,
Gloucester, Maine 01930

Pixie Treasures,
Miniature Rose Nursery,
Box 11611,
Santa Ana, Calif. 92711

Roses by Fred Edmunds,
Box 68,
Wilsonville, Ore. 97070

Star Roses,
West Grove, Penna. 19390

Stern's Nurseries,
Geneva, N.Y. 14456

P. O. Tate Nursery,
R. 3,
Tyler, Texas 75701

Thomasville Nurseries,
Box 7,
Thomasville, Ga. 31792

Tillotson's Roses,
Brown's Valley Rd.,
Watsonville, Calif. 95076

Melvin E. Wyant,
Johnny Cake Ridge,
Mentor, Ohio 44060

Violet Simon, who grows her roses successfully in Villa Park, Ill., says she buries a couple of handfuls of tree seed-pods next to each plant to give them the benefit of the concentrated food energy they contain. She also grows cover crops to keep her soil in shape, cultivating lightly in the spring and sowing clover around each plant, so that the little green legume can "help prevent soil erosion and bring leached nutrients back to the surface to be available for either new or established plantings. And Phyllis Holloway, whose New Orleans, La., garden has lots of happy roses, swears by cottonseed meal (for nitrogen) and banana skins (for potash).

Other top growers who've offered their rose-feeding preferences include Melvin E. Wyant, a nurseryman who has headed Wyant Roses in Ohio for half a century, and is partial to a combination of bone meal, guano, blood meal and other organic materials, which he applies once a month during the growing season, about a handful per plant. Mrs. Dorothy Stemler of Tillotson's Roses in California, who says she uses steer manure and spent mushroom compost — both readily available in her area — spread as a 3-inch top-dressing just ahead of early spring rains. Fred S. Glaes of Reading, Pa., a former director of the American Rose Society, likes a mixture of compost, ground rock minerals, dried blood and manures, used at a rate of one pound per plant, half in April, half at the end of June or in early July. Still other successful growers favor cottonseed or soybean meal, different animal manures. Nearly all recommend bone meal.

When it comes to water, roses are heavy drinkers. With good drainage you can't give them too much although some gardeners say they seldom need to irrigate well-mulched plants. Depending on rainfall and temperatures, water enough to keep some moisture showing in your soil. Soak thoroughly to a depth of 8 to 10 inches, directing a small, slow-moving stream from a garden hose around the base of plants. One prize-winning rose-lover says a mixture of stable manure and water (manure "tea") does a better job than water alone, lasting longer and feeding soil as it supplies moisture.

Mulches help feed rose-bed soil and plants, too, of course. Besides Mrs. Carlin's sawdust-wood-chips-cottonseed-meal mixture, materials that make good mulch run from shredded bark to sugarcane, cocoa-bean hulls and coffee grounds. "It's foolhardy to attempt to grow roses without mulching," says Glaes. He uses shredded pine bark or cocoa-bean hulls, applied at approximately a 2-inch level after spring pruning and feeding. "I haven't had to cultivate my rose beds in 25 years," he adds. For weed control, moisture conservation and added fertility, a layer of organic matter — peat, ground corncobs, hay shredded leaves, cottonseed hulls, redwood sawdust are all effective. Apply mulch about a month before plants bloom, first pulling any weeds (carefully, since rose roots may grow close to surface) and raking soil lightly. Spread material evenly around plants to a depth of 2 to 3 inches or more

(some gardeners like mulches up to 4 or 5 inches deep, especially of loose, porous types such as hay), adding to it as the material decays into the topsoil.

START RIGHT AND STAY SMILING

It's safe to plant roses fall or spring where winter temperatures drop no more than to 10 degrees below zero. Under that mark, stick to springtime. The roots of roses planted in late fall start at once to take possession of their new home. They repair their "sap-pumping apparatus" and recuperate from the shock of being transplanted or out of the ground for some time. By spring they recover and are ready to get growing. Late fall means November or early December, or as long as the ground remains workable. Planting earlier risks coinciding with warm weather, which induces newly-set roses to sprout and then be caught in a sappy and soft condition by a sudden plunge of mercury.

Roses grow best where they have full sunshine all day — although they'll do quite well if they get at least 5 to 6 hours sun in a warm climate. If you must plant where shaded part of the day, try keeping them in morning sun. Leaves remain wet with overnight dew longer in the shade, and this moisture favors development of leaf diseases. Also, don't choose a site already well-occupied by tree or shrub roots, which are often too much competition for water, air and just space.

Look under the surface, too. Make sure your rose-location soil is well-drained and slightly on the acid side — preferably with a pH of about 6.0 to 6.5. Keep puddles after rain or watering somewhere else for little boys with sailboats. In a cross-country poll of rose experts by OGF, each of them called good soil drainage the most important thing for the gardener to provide. Along with it, of course, go good aeration and rich, porous organic matter for vigorous root growth. The more organic matter turned in, the less concern about the pH, since plenty of humus helps buffer any extreme — as well as improve drainage. Where soil tests too alkaline, use peat moss, leaf mold, sawdust or any of a number of acid materials to bring the reading down.

Dig planting holes wide and deep enough to avoid cramping roots when spread out. In warm areas, set the bud union at the soil surface. In colder regions, put it one inch below ground level. Firm soil over roots so no air pockets remain, then soak well and prune to 6 inches.

Give your roses enough room. Sunlight, air and "breathing space" are factors in successful growing. Hybrid teas and their cousins the floribundas and grandifloras should be kept 2½ to 3 feet apart, a little more where temperatures stay mild. In all areas, space bush or shrub types 3 to 5 feet apart, climbers at 8- to 10-foot distances.

What else contributes to rose-growing success? Things like pruning — which should be kept simple and direct—insect control and a good choice of varieties.

Most rose types should be pruned in the spring, except for climbers which need cutting right after flow-

ering. Here are 3 steps suggested to replace uncertainty about pruning: 1.) Remove any damaged canes caused by winter injury or insects and disease of the previous year. 2.) Take out any canes which rub or cross another. 3.) Remove those canes which are smaller than the diameter of a pencil.

As for pests or disease, remember that healthy, vigorous plants are their own best defense. Explains Mrs. Stemler: "I'm convinced that if the soil preparation is good and the plants are given a healthy start, they are bound to be far less susceptible to troubles. I've also found that attractant plants, those which draw insects away from roses (such as marigolds and nasturtiums), can be helpful. And I think a lot depends on variety. Older shrub types are often more disease-resistant. The hybrid Musk rose, for instance, is practically mildew-proof, and the lovely white ICEBERG floribunda has no difficulty at all with red spider."

Milky spore disease is very effective in stopping the Japanese beetle, and introducing some ladybugs or green lacewings will do a fast job of cleaning out aphids, mites and scale insects. Dorothy Schroeder, who gardens in Lyons, Colorado, describes her results with interplanting: "The bugs that most rose-growers complain about so bitterly were in a minority on my bushes. I have found that a well-mulched bush doesn't invite predators. I kept my bushes deeply mulched with a mixture of compost and peat moss." Don't forget the garlic or chives, of course.

LOTS OF KINDS TO TRY

What kind of rose to plant? For many gardeners, this means the floribundas and hybrid teas. Both are ever-blooming, produce attractive flowers, and grow on moderate-sized plants. The major difference is that the hybrid teas are more inclined to produce single, specimen blooms, whereas the other group is more likely to be cluster-flowered. Polyanthas, a third type, are still more cluster-flowered.

Then, of course, there are the climbers. Today nearly all are ever-blooming or nearly so. For connoisseurs there are the shrub roses most of which are old-fashioned types of iron-clad hardiness. These include the hybrid perpetuals which bloom intermittently throughout the season, plus the species and old historical types. Excellent "fence" and "divider" type plants, shrub roses are also less trouble, include Rugosa varieties that provide tasty rose hips. Lastly are the miniatures — little everblooming beauties usually 6 to 10 inches tall, used for edgings, pot plants, low beds, etc.

So you can put aside all those romantic songs, poems and historical anecdotes about roses. When it comes to down-to-earth gardeners, roses are strictly for growing. Oh sure, they love to talk about their rose-growing adventures, discuss techniques and varieties, and boast over exhibit ribbons. But first and foremost, they love to grow that queen of flowers they're so fond of.

Given organic care, roses really respond. Grow them naturally yourself and enjoy discovering how true it is!

The New Guide To Rose Culture

The Dingee and Conard Co. Rose Growers West Grove Chester Co Penna Roses By Mail A Specialty 1879

GLOSSARY OF TERMS FOR ROSE GROWERS

(Courtesy Minnesota Rose Society)

BALANCED (COMPLETE) FERTILIZER - A plant food containing the 3 essential nutrients: nitrogen (N), phosphorus (P), potassium (K); amounts of each indicated by percentages in NPK order; for example - 10-6-4 formula means 10% nitrogen, 6% phosphorus, 4% potassium.

BASAL BREAK - New cane arising from budhead tissue or from bud at base of old cane.

BREAKS - Any new stem or cane growth from the buds.

BUDHEAD - The enlarged growth just above the crown where hybrid variety of rose was grafted.

BUD UNION - The suture line where the hybrid budhead joins the root stock.

BUDS - So-called "eyes" on cane at nodes, base of cane or budhead; the origin of all new replacement growth. Basal bud is at base of cane or budhead. If new rose cane does not terminate in a blossom, it is called a "blind" bud.

CANES - The stem on a rose plant; has buds, nodes, hollow or pithy center, bears leaves, flowers, fruits (hips). New canes arise from buds on crown, stem, etc., & have skin for outside covering, green, brown or red in color. Old canes, usually 1 year or more in age, are brown or grey in color, show corky streaks & thickened nodes.

CANE HEAD - Enlarged growth from a single thickened node on a stem, resulting in growth pattern above the budhead.

CANKER - Disease causing purplish spots on canes, spreading & girdling cane so it dies.

CHELATING AGENT - Special chemical releasing iron & other minor elements; corrects chlorosis.

CHLOROSIS - Yellowing of normally green tissue; often due to unavailability of iron.

COMPOST - Vegetation that has decomposed.

CORKY LAYER - Tissue, extends beyond skin of cane, forms thick spongy layer over outside stem.

CROWN - Where roots & stem join, more stem in character than root.

CROWN GALL - Disease attacking crown or budhead, causing masses of bulbous growth somewhat corky & with small, thin roots attached.

CULTIVAR - A synonym for variety.

DIEBACK - A dying back of the cane or shoot from the tip; a symptom of a disease (cane blight, canker, etc.) or damage from frost or incorrect pruning.

DISBUD - To remove side flower buds to improve size & quality of those permitted to remain.

DOG-LEG - A replacement cane or stem growing outward then upward from bud, below a hat-rack.

DORMANT SPRAY - Spray (usually lime sulfur) applied in spring BEFORE new growth is 1/4-in. long, or in late fall, just before winter cover is applied. Uses a higher dosage than usual.

HARDEN OFF - Expose gradually to more difficult conditions, such as cold, dry air.

HAT-RACK - The dead end or stub of a cane cut between buds (nodes) or above stem joints.

HEEL-IN - Cover plant roots temporarily with soil in a trench, awaiting permanent planting.

HIP - The seed fruit of roses.

HUMUS - Partly or thoroughly decomposed vegetable matter in soil.

INORGANIC FERTILIZER - One derived from mineral or chemical substances.

INTERNODE - Stem space between 2 nodes or buds; it has no regenerative tissue.

MULCH - Soil covering intended to give winter protection, to conserve moisture, to prevent overheating or to keep down weeds. Also acts as sponge for soluble fertilizer.

NODE - Thickened areas on canes at which buds appear & from which all replacement growth comes.

ORGANIC FERTILIZER - One derived from organic materials - plant or animal substances. Add humus as well as nutrients to soil.

ORGANIC MATTER - Term usually applied to decomposed plant or animal refuse in the soil.

PINCH - To remove soft growth tips by twisting out with thumb and forefinger.

REPLACEMENT - Cane growth from a bud which takes the place of a removed, old or lower cane.

ROOT STOCK - The seedling or "wild" (species) plant which was rooted from a cutting and on which the hybrid was budded.

SPORT - A sudden change in some part of the plant; a mutation.

SINGLE BUD - One which develops into a single thrifty cane. (There are also double and triple buds which develop into two or three-way "break" of canes.)

STRIATIONS - Streaks or lines of corky tissue on older, mature canes; indicate blooming capacity is at or nearly ended.

STUB - Remains of a removed cane, leaving its basal attachment & a short part of original cane.

SUCKERS - Shoots or stems which arise from below the budhead, from the root stock-crown or from secondary crown on root surfaces below soil surface.

SYSTEMIC - With insecticides, one that is absorbed into internal system of plant.

194

The hundred leav'd Rose

8

How to Plant ROSES

Select a site that receives at least 6 hours of sunlight each day and drains well. Don't plant roses too close to trees or shrubs whose roots will compete for soil nutrients. A site with good air circulation helps prevent disease.

When the soil is poor, dig out the beds to a depth of 18 inches to 2 feet. Mix the soil with 25% peat moss and about 10% compost or well rotted manure.

Rose plants purchased in containers should be removed — following procedure recommended by grower for type of container used — and set in ample holes to proper depth. Fill in with soil and water generously to eliminate air pockets.

NOTE Ⓐ
SEVERE CLIMATE PLANTING LINE
MILD CLIMATE PLANTING LINE
Ⓑ

To plant dormant bare root roses, dig holes large enough to accommodate roots without crowding and deep enough to set them at the proper height. The lower part of the bud union or crown of the plant should be level with the surface of the ground in mild climates — 1 to 3" below in severe climates.

Spread the roots so they point downward at a forty-five degree angle. A mound or cone of soil built up in the hole under the base of the bush as one plants is helpful in spreading the roots. (See cut, "B") Cover the roots with loose soil, working it well underneath.

Fill the hole ¾ full and tamp soil down firmly; water well. Fill hole and mound over top 6" until growth starts, to prevent drying out of canes.

Winter protection of roses in severe climates should consist of an 8" earth mound (See cut, "A") over the base of the bush. In milder climates a 3" earth protection is sufficient.

Rose foliage is a vital part of the rose plant. Do not cut it lavishly through the growing season. Spray or dust regularly.

Roses like cool roots. A 3" mulch of peat moss or other suitable material keeps soil cool, conserves moisture and prevents weed growth.

Spacing Roses

Planting Distance	Close	Normal
Shrub Roses	4 feet	6 feet
Hybrid Teas	1½ feet	2½ feet
Hybrid Perpetuals	2 feet	3 feet
Climbers, on banks	2½ feet	3 to 4 feet
Climbers, on fences	8 feet	10 to 15 feet

In dry weather give roses plenty of water.

1974 HANDBOOK FOR SELECTING ROSES

This handbook offers you a wealth of helpful information on most roses currently available in the United States and Canada. More than 1000 rose cultivars (varieties) are described with such pertinent information as height of plant, color, horticultural classification and the valuable American Rose Society ratings. Each rose is assigned a national rating based on a 10 point scale. These ratings are obtained through an annual survey of some 18,000 American Rose Society members who report on roses they are currently growing. A score of 10 is perfect, but so far has been unobtained. Other features of this booklet include separate listings by color of the highest rated roses, a complete description of the 1974 All-America Rose Selection winners, invaluable information on the American Rose Society and some of its many important services to amateur gardeners.

Enjoy this booklet, use it often, learn to rely on it for descriptions and accurate evaluation of roses with which you are likely to come in contact.

HOW TO READ THIS BOOKLET

Use this page as your key for tracing all roses.

EXAMPLE: Akebono* yb 7.1

m — The small letter at the left of a name indicates relative height. (l-low, m-medium, t-tall)

* — Indicates new cultivars (varieties) whose rating will change with future reports.

yb — Color classification to which the rose belongs.

† — At left of a name denotes new cultivars which have not yet been given a national rating.

7.1 — National rating compiled from thousands of reports of the members of the American Rose Society.

Following are the color classification abbreviations used:

ab - apricot blend	my - medium yellow
dr - dark red	ob - orange & orange blend
dy - deep yellow	o-r - orange red
lp - light pink	pb - pink blend
dp - deep pink	r - russet
m - mauve	rb - red blend
mp - medium pink	w - white or near white
mr - medium red	yb - yellow blend

National rating

10.0 –	Perfect Rose
9.9 – 9.0	Outstanding
8.9 – 8.0	Excellent
7.9 – 7.0	Good
6.9 – 6.0	Fair
5.9 and lower	Questionable Value

Most gardeners are interested in seeing the roses classified according to popular type designations such as hybrid tea, floribunda, etc. For the benefit of skilled horticulturists and rosarians, the American Rose Society has identified all bush type roses with a digital code that indicates a more specific description of the rose. A more detailed description of each numerical classification is available from the American Rose Society upon request. The numerical designations used in this booklet are as follows:

IIIA - Large-flowered, minimal-clustering (Hybrid Tea).
IIIB - Medium-large flowers, small clusters (Grandiflora).
IIIC - Medium size flowers, medium size flat-topped clusters (Floribunda).
IIID - Small flowers, large pyramidal (cone-shaped) clusters (Polyantha).
IIIE - Miniature roses (Miniature).
IC - Miscellaneous shrub roses (Shrubs).

HYBRID TEA

Relative height letter means: l, low, under 30"; m, medium, 30" to 48"; t, tall, 48" and over.

Ht	Name	Rating
	†Adolf Horstmann	
m	Agena* mp	7.3
	Aida mr	8.9
	Akebono* yb	7.1
	Alabaster w	5.9
	†Alec's Red mr	
	Altesse dp	5.0
m	Amarillo dy	7.0
	Amatsu-Otome my	6.4
	Amelia Earhart yb	5.7
m	Americana mr	7.3
m	American Heritage yb	7.9
	American Home dr	7.3
	Ami Quinard dr	5.1
	Amoureuse yb	6.2
m	Angels Mateu ab	6.0
m	Angel Wings pb	7.5
m	Anne Letts pb	7.5
	Anne Marie*	6.3
m	Anne Watkins yb	6.0
	Anvil Sparks (Ambossfunken) ob	6.0
	Apogee* pb	6.8
	Apollo* my	6.7
	Applause dp	7.8
	Apricot Queen pb	5.5
	Apricot Silk* ab	6.4
l	Arctic Flame mr	6.5
m	Ardelle w	5.1
	Arianna* pb	6.3
m	Arlene Francis my	6.3
m	Aruba-Caribe pb	6.6
l	Astree lp	6.6
	Astrorose* mr	6.5
	Autumn	6.0
	Aventure o-r	6.1
m	Avon dr	8.0
m	Aztec o-r	7.6
	Baccara o-r	6.8
t	Bacchus dp	6.9
m	Bajazzo rb	6.0
m	Ballet dp	7.2
	Banner rb	7.5
	Battle of Britain* yb	4.4
m	Beaute' yb	7.1
m	Bel Ange mp	7.9
	Belle Blonde my	6.9
	Belle Epoque (Royale)* pb	7.7
	Benjamin Franklin* pb	5.9
	Bermudiana mp	6.4
	Better Times mr	5.9
m	Bettina ob	7.0
	Betty Uprichard pb	6.2
	Bewitched mp	7.7
	Big Ben dr	8.1
	Big Red dr	6.8
m	Bingo dr	6.8
m	Blanche Mallerin w	6.4
	Blue Moon m	8.0
	Bob Hope mr	7.2
	Bonne Nuit dr	5.1
	Bonsoir* mp	7.0
	Bon Voyage* pb	7.6
	Brandenburg o-r	7.1
	Brasilia* rb	6.4
	Bravo mr	6.5
	Briarcliff pb	6.2
	Bristol mr	6.8
m	Bronze Masterpiece ab	6.6
m	Burnaby w	7.6
	Butterscotch yb	6.1
	Caledonia w	5.1
	California ob	6.1
	Canasta mr	6.7
m	Candy Stripe pb	7.3
m	Capistrano mp	7.3
	Captain Christy	7.6
	Caramba* rb	6.5
m	Careless Love rb	5.5
	Carina mp	8.0
	Carla lp	7.8
	Casanova my	
m	Century Two* mp	8.3
m	Champagne yb	7.9
m	Chantre ob	6.8
	Charles Mallerin dr	6.0
t	Charlotte Armstrong dp	8.4
	Charm of Paris* mp	6.2
	Cherry Brandy* o-r	6.2
m	Chicago Peace pb	8.4
m	Chief Seattle yb	6.0
m	Christian Dior mr	7.7
	Christopher Stone mr	6.7
m	Chrysler Imperial dr	8.9
	Chryzia* dp	6.2
	City of Hereford* mp	7.6
l	Cleopatra rb	6.9
	Colorama* rb	6.7
	Colour Wonder* ob	7.2
	Columbia mr	6.4
t	Columbus Queen mp	7.6
	Command Performance* o-r	7.5
	Comtesse Vandal pb	6.8
	Condesa de Sastago ob	6.5
	Confederation mp	5.4
m	Confidence pb	6.8
	Constanza* o-r	5.6
	Contrast pb	4.8
	Coral Bay* ob	5.5
t	Coronado rb	7.5
t	Crimson Duke mr	7.0
m	Crimson Glory dr	8.3
	Curly Pink mp	7.4
m	Dainty Bess lp	8.3
t	Dame de Coeur mr	7.3
t	Dave Davis mr	6.8
	Day Dream* mp	6.6
	Day of Triumph mp	7.3

Ht	Name	Rating
m	Der Krad dr	6.9
m	Diamond Jubilee yb	7.0
	Dicksons Red dr	6.3
m	Diorama yb	
	Dixie Holliday* mr	6.6
m	Dorothy Anderson lp	6.3
l	Dorothy Peach yb	6.4
m	Dr. Brownell my	7.3
m	Dr. Debat pb	6.4
	Dresden w	7.5
	Duet mp	7.9
	Duke of Windsor* o-r	6.9
m	Duquesa de Penaranda ob	6.1
t	Ebb Tide ab	7.0
m	Eclipse my	7.5
m	Eden Rose dp	6.4
	Edith Nellie Perkins pb	6.7
m	Editor McFarland mp	6.2
t	Eiffel Tower mp	7.7
	El Cid* o-r	6.8
	†El Dorado yb	
	Electron (Mullard Jubilee)* dp	8.4
	Elida* o-r	7.5
	Elise* w	5.2
	Elizabeth Harkness* my	6.9
m	Emily lp	7.0
m	Ena Harkness mr	6.2
	Ernest H. Morse* mr	7.6
	Ernie Pyle mp	5.5
	Eternal Youth lp	6.5
m	Ethel Sanday yb	7.0
m	Etoile de Hollande mr	7.1
	Eve ob	5.1
	Fantastique pb	6.2
	Farny Wurlitzer* mr	7.0
	Fascinating yb	6.7
m	Favorita ob	6.3
m	Femina pb	7.2
	Festival mr	5.0
	Festival Queen lp	6.5
	Fiesta rb	6.5
	Firelight* o-r	7.5
	First Federal Gold dy	7.3
	First Lady dp	6.8
m	First Love lp	8.0
	First Prize* pb	9.0
	Flaming Peace rb	6.7
m	Flaming Sunset ob	6.8
m	Fort Vancouver mp	5.3
m	Forty-Niner rb	6.1
m	Fragrance dp	7.5
	Fragrant Charm* mr	7.3
	Fragrant Cloud o-r	8.6
	Frances Ashton mp	7.6
m	Francine rb	6.8
	Fred Edmunds ob	6.3
	Frederica mr	4.0
t	Fred Howard yb	6.9
	Fred Streeter my	7.7
	Freiburg II mr	6.7
m	Frisky mr	6.4
l	Fritz Thiedemann o-r	6.5
	Gail Borden pb	7.2
m	Garden Party w	7.9
	Gavotte lp	6.6
	George Dickson mr	7.9
	Ginger Rogers*	7.2
	Girona pb	6.6
m	Gold Crown my	6.4
	Golden Charm dy	5.7
	Golden Gate* my	6.9
m	Golden Giant my	6.8
m	Golden Masterpiece my	6.1
	Golden Prince* dy	5.7
	Golden Rapture	5.2
m	Golden Salute dy	6.7
	Golden Scepter dy	6.5
m	Golden Splendor dy	7.3
l	Golden Sun my	7.1
m	Golden Wave (Dr. A. J. Verhage) dy	6.6
m	Gold Glow dy	7.6
m	Good News pb	6.9
m	Grace de Monaco lp	7.4
	Gracious Lady pb	7.0
	Granada rb	8.4
t	Grande Duchesse Charlotte mr	7.0
m	Grand Gala rb	7.1
m	Grand'mere Jenny yb	6.4
	Grand Opera pb	7.1
	Grand Prix* mp	6.6
m	Grand Slam mr	7.5
	Grenoble mr	6.0
	Grey Pearl m	4.5
	Gruss an Berlin mr	7.5
	Gruss an Teplitz mr	6.7
	Guinevere* pb	6.5
	†Gypsy o-r	
	Haisha yb	
	Halloween* yb	5.6
l	Handsom Red mr	5.7
m	Happiness mr	6.1
	Happy Wedding Bells* w	5.8
	†Harriet Miller pb	
m	Hawaii o-r	7.5
	Heart's Desire mr	6.0
	Hector Deane rb	6.7
	Heirloom* m	7.1
t	Helene Schoen mr	7.4
m	Helen Hayes yb	7.1
t	Helen Traubel pb	8.3
	Henkell Royal* mr	6.9
	Henry Field mp	5.6
m	High Esteem pb	6.7

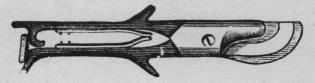
Harison's Yellow HFt
dy 8.0
Heinrich Munch HP lp 8.5
Heinrich Schultheis HP 7.6
Henry Nevard HP dr 7.6
Hermosa Ch mp 7.8
Hofgartner Kalb HCh
dp 7.5
Hon. Ina Bingham HP
mp 7.5
Honorine de Brabant B
pb 7.3
Hugh Dickson HP mr 7.0
Hugh Watson HP 7.7
Jeanne de Montfort M
mp 9.9
Jules Margottin HP mp 6.5
Julie de Mersent M mp 9.0
Juliet HP pb 6.3
Koenigin Von Daenemarck
A mp 8.8
Laneii M dp 7.8
La Reine Victoria B 7.8
Leda D lp 8.1
Leverkusen HSpn 6.6
Louise Crette HP 7.5
Louise Odier B 9.1
Mabel Morrison HP w 8.2
Magna Charta HP 6.6
Maman Cochet T mp 6.8
Marchioness of
Londonderry
HP lp 7.5
Marchioness of Lorne
HP 7.3
Marechal Niel N my 6.6
Margaret Dickson HP 7.9
Marie Louis D mp 7.3
Marshall P. Wilder HP 8.0
Mermaid HBc my 7.7
Merry England HP 6.2
Merveille de Lyon HP
lp 7.7
Mlle. Franziska Kruger T
yb 5.7
Mme. Alfred de Rouge-
mont N lp 9.0
Mme. Ernst Cabrat B
mp 7.7

Mme. Gabriel Luizet HP
lp 8.5
Mme. Hardy D w 8.7
Mme. Isaac Pereire B 8.0
Mme. Louis Leveque M
mp 7.1
Mme. Pierre Oger B pb 8.0
Mme. Scipion Cochet T
lp 7.3
Mme. Victor Verdier HP
mp 7.2
Mrs. F. W. Sanford HP 9.0
Mrs. John Laing HP mp 7.7
Nuits de Young M dr 7.7
Old Blush Ch mp 8.2
Omar Khayyam D 6.3
Oskar Cordel HP mp 8.4
Parkjuwel C dp 7.5
Paul Neyron HP mp 7.4
Paul's Early Blush HP 7.8
Persian Yellow* HFt dy 7.8
Petite de Hollande C
mp 8.2
President de Seze G m 6.6
Prince Camille de Rohan
HP dr 7.0
Reichsprasident von Hin-
denburg HP mp 6.4
Reine des Violettes HP
m 7.1
River's George IV Ch m 7.6
Robert Duncan HP dr 9.0
Robert Leopold M pb 8.8
Roger Lambelin HP rb 7.1
Rose de Peintres C mp 8.2
Rose du Roi D mr 7.3
Rosette Delizy T yb 7.3
Safrano T ab 5.9
Salet M mp 7.9
Soleil d'Or HFt yb 8.1
Souv. de la Malmaison
B lp 7.1
Souv. de Mme. H. Thuret
HP mp 7.0
Stanwell Perpetual HSpn
lp 7.7
St. Ingebert HP 7.9
Suzanne-Marie Rodocran-
achi HP mp 7.0

Symphony HP lp 6.0
Tuscany G 8.8
Tuscany Superb G dr 7.1
Ulrich Brunner Fils HP
dp 7.0
Variegata di Bologna B
rb 7.8

Violacee M m 8.2
White Bath M w 7.2
York and Lancaster D
pb 7.0
Zephirine Drouhin B
mp 7.9

HIGH RATED ROSES BY COLOR

HYBRID TEAS

RED
Chrysler Imperial dr 8.9
Tropicana o-r 8.8
Fragrant Cloud o-r 8.6
Mister Lincoln dr 8.5
Crimson Glory dr 8.3
Big Ben dr 8.1
Avon dr 8.0
Oriental Charm mr 8.0
PINK
Royal Highness lp 8.6
Pink Favorite mp 8.5
Electron (Mullard
Jubilee) dp 8.4
Charlotte Armstrong dp 8.4
Dainty Bess lp 8.3
Century Two mp 8.3
Carina mp 8.0
First Love lp 8.0
MAUVE
Lady X m 8.1
Blue Moon m 8.0
WHITE
Pascali w 8.3
Garden Party w 7.9
BLENDS
Peace yb 9.4
Tiffany pb 9.1
First Prize pb 9.0
Chicago Peace pb 8.4
Confidence pb 8.4
Manuel Pinto d'Azevedo
pb 8.4
Swarthmore pb 8.4
Helen-Traubel pb 8.3
Isabel de Ortiz ab 8.2
FLORIBUNDAS
RED
Red Glory mr 8.7
Europeana dr 8.5
Cocorico o-r 8.4

Orangeade o-r 8.4
Spartan o-r 8.4
City of Belfast o-r 8.3
Orange Sensation o-r 8.3
Anna Wheatcroft o-r 8.2
Frensham dr 8.2
Ginger o-r 8.2
PINK
Betty Prior mp 9.0
Pink Gruss an
Aachen lp 9.0
Gene Boerner mp 8.5
Gertrude Raffel dp 8.3
Tom Tom dp 8.2
Pink Rosette lp 8.1
Vera Dalton mp 8.0
MAUVE
Angel Face m 8.0
WHITE
Iceberg (Schneewittchen)
w 8.7
Ice White w 8.1
Ivory Fashion w 8.0
BLENDS
Little Darling yb 8.6
Dearest pb 8.5
Sea Pearl pb 8.5
Sweet Vivien pb 8.5
Cupids Charm pb 8.4
Vogue pb 8.2
Faberge pb 8.1
Zorina ob 8.1
Circus yb 8.0
City of Leeds pb 8.0
Fashion pb 8.0
Redgold yb 8.0
Sir Lancelot ab 8.0
Apricot Nectar ab 8.0

GRANDIFLORAS
Queen Elizabeth mp 9.3

Montezuma o-r 8.6
Carrousel dr 8.4
Camelot mp 8.2
Ole' o-r 8.1
El Capitan mr 8.0
John S. Armstrong dr 8.0
Roundelay dr 8.0
Scarlet Knight dr 8.0
Bienvenu o-r 8.0
Starfire mr 8.0
Mount Shasta w 8.0
CLIMBERS
Iceland Queen 8.7

City of York w 8.6
Handel rb 8.5
May Queen mp 8.4
New Dawn lp 8.4
Casa Blanca* w 8.3
Paul's Scarlet Climber
mr 8.3
Cl. Mrs. Sam McGredy
ob 8.2
Cl. Dainty Bess lp 8.2
Don Juan dr 8.1
Dr. W. Van Fleet lp 8.1
Cl. Tropicana o-r 8.1

1974 ALL-AMERICA ROSE SELECTIONS

BAHIA (Patent Applied For) - An eye-catching orange tinged pink Floribunda with lots of blooms borne profusely and constantly throughout the flowering season. The roses appear in clusters of three to several 2½" blooms which maintain their attractive coloration throughout the life of the flowers and until the petals fall. 'Bahia' has double flowers of 20 to 30 petals, plus 10 to 18 petaloids, which provide a massive show of color for both the rose garden and general landscape use. Added to the beauty and brilliance of this Floribunda is its very pleasing, spicy fragrance. The plant is vigorous, bushy, compact and upright-spreading with an abundance of medium-sized, semi-glossy, dark green leaves. 'Bahia' is a product of the famous American hybridizer, Walter E. Lammerts, and came from a cross between 'Rumba' and 'Tropicana'.

BON-BON (Plant Patent Applied For) - This ideal landscape Floribunda is densely covered with dozens of delightful pink and white bi-color blooms, set in a wealth of bright green foliage. The flowers are borne in heavy clusters, opening continuously and repeating the show over and over again from early spring until frost. Both its medium height (2½') and neat, compact habit make this new Floribunda especially desirable for landscaping. Its ancestors include such famous roses as 'Spartan' and 'Fashion'. The breeder of this fine new Floribunda is William Warriner of Tustin, California. The bloom pops open quickly to a round, flat flower which, with its clusters festooning the plant, puts on a most attractive showing for four or five days, followed immediately by a new set of blooms and so on through the flowering season.

PERFUME DELIGHT (Plant Patent Applied For) - A richly fragrant rose fittingly named 'Perfume Delight' is the only Hybrid Tea to win an AARS award for 1974. Another origination from O. L. Weeks of Ontario, California, this brilliant pink definitely contradicts the often heard comment that "modern roses don't have fragrance anymore." One bloom of 'Perfume Delight' will fill a room with fragrance, while three plants in a garden will add a delightful perfume to a wide area - you won't miss it as you walk by. The uses of the rose are many - the strong, long stems for cutting, the firm flower petals of heavy texture, produce a cut flower that holds well, single blooms per stem, fine for flower arrangements or single bud display. Perfume is not the only asset of this new variety. First appearing as long, pointed, classic tea rose buds, the true, clear, deep pink blooms gradually unfold to high-centered beauties with every petal clear, brilliant pink.

CATALOGUE OF ROSES,

CULTIVATED FOR SALE BY

WM. PAUL & SON,

(Successors to the late A. PAUL & Son. Established 1806),

WHO ARE HONOURED BY COMMANDS FROM

HER MAJESTY THE QUEEN
HIS ROYAL HIGHNESS THE PRINCE OF WALES.
HIS IMPERIAL MAJESTY THE EMPEROR OF AUSTRIA.
HER MAJESTY THE QUEEN DOWAGER OF DENMARK.
HIS MAJESTY THE KING DOM FERNANDO OF PORTUGAL.
HIS ROYAL HIGHNESS THE DUKE MAXIMILIAN OF BAVARIA.

The greater part of the Nobility and County Families of the United Kingdom, and the Governing Bodies of a large number of Botanic Gardens and Public Parks and Gardens in all parts of the World.

PAULS' NURSERIES & SEED WAREHOUSE,

WALTHAM CROSS, HERTS.

Trains from London (Liverpool Street and St. Pancras Stations) to Waltham in about half an hour. Visitors by Railway can enter the Nurseries from the Platform WALTHAM Station.

Robt. Edmd. Taylor, Horticultural Steam Printer, 19, Old Street, Goswell, Road, London, E.C

t High Time pb 7.6
Hinrich Gaede ob 6.3
m Honey Favorite pb 7.8
Horace McFarland ob 6.3
Imperial Gold my 7.5
Incense* w 6.5
Indianapolis* mp 5.3
Indian Chief* dp 7.1
Inge Horstman rb
m Innocence w 7.5
l Intermezzo m 5.4
t Invitation ab 7.6
Irish Fireflame ob 6.5
Irish Gold (Grandpa Dickson)* my 7.2
m Isabel de Ortiz pb 8.2
Isobel pb 7.7
m Isobel Harkness dy 6.6
Jackman's White w 6.5
Jacques Carteau w 7.7
m Jamaica mr 7.7
†Jay Jay pb
m Jeanie w 7.0
m Joanna Hill yb 7.0
m John F. Kennedy w 7.1
John Waterer* dr 7.5
Jolie Madame o-r 6.9
m Josephine Bruce dr 7.6
J. Otto Thilow mp 6.7
Jubilee pb 5.9
†Julie dr
June Park dp 7.2
Juno mp 6.8
Kaiserin Auguste Viktoria w 6.4
Kalahari* o-r 6.6
m Karl Herbst mr 7.7
m Katherine T. Marshall mp 6.8
Kathleen Mills mp 7.6
†Kentucky Derby dr
King of Hearts* mr 7.4
t King's Ransom dy 7.8
m Klaus Stortebecker mr 6.6
Kolner Karneval (Cologne Carnival) m 7.4
Konigin Luise w 5.9

m Konrad Adenauer dr 6.5
m Kordes' Perfecta pb 7.6
Kordes' Perfecta Superior mp 7.5
Lady Bird Johnson* o-r 7.0
La Canadienne ob 5.4
m Lady Elgin yb 7.4
m Lady Maysie Robinson pb 6.3
Lady Seton mp 7.1
Lady X m 8.2
La France lp 6.7
m La Jolla pb 7.0
Lamplighter* yb 5.2
Laura* lp 6.8
l Lavender Charm m 6.7
Lemon Chiffon my 4.5
m Lemon Glow my 5.9
Lemon Ice my 6.4
Lemon Spice my 7.7
Leonard Barron pb 5.5
Liberty Bell rb 6.0
Lilac Time m 5.9
Lily Pons w 7.2
Lissy Horstmann mr 6.1
Lively dp 6.9
Living rb 7.1
m Lotte Gunthart mr 7.5
m Louisiana Purchase dp 7.5
l Love Song pb 5.7
m Lowell Thomas dy 6.6
Lucky Beauty* pb 5.0
m Lucky Piece pb 7.8
Lucy Cramphorn o-r 7.8
m Lulu mp 6.7
Mahagona pb 5.5
†Mainauperle® dr
Majorette* 5.5
Mandalay my 6.4
Manitou rb
Manuela* mp 6.2
Manuel Pinto d' Azevedo pb 8.4
m Marcelle Gret my 6.2
Margaret Ann Baxter w 6.7
Marcia Stanhope w 6.3

m Margaret mp 7.7
Margaret Chase Smith* dr 6.6
Marian Anderson dp 7.6
Maria Stern* o-r 7.9
Marie Antoinette* mp 6.9
l Marjorie Le Grice ob 6.0
Mary Margaret McBride mp 6.6
Masked Ball pb 5.5
l Matterhorn w 7.5
Mauve Melody m 6.7
m McGredy's Ivory w 5.0
m McGredy's Sunset ob 6.9
m McGredy's Yellow my 6.1
†Medallion ab
l Medley lp 6.6
Melrose rb 6.4
m Memoriam lp 7.8
Metropole mp 6.9
Mexicana rb 7.7
m Michele Meilland pb 7.9
m Milord mr 7.1
m Mirandy dr 7.1
Mischief mp 7.5
Miss All-American Beauty mp 8.5
m Miss America pb 6.8
Miss Canada (Pacific Beauty) pb 7.1
Miss Hillcrest* o-r 7.9
Miss Ireland ob 7.0
Miss Windsor* o-r 8.0
m Mission Bells pb 7.1
t Mister Lincoln dr 8.5
Misty Morn w 6.1
Mme. Butterfly lp 6.8
Mme. Caroline Testout mp 6.1
Mme. Chiang Kai-shek w 6.4
t Mme. Henri Guillot rb 7.1
m Mme. Jules Bouche w 6.6
l Mme. Louis Laperriere mr 6.8
Mme. Marie Curie dy 6.5
Mme. Rene Coty 5.8

Modern Times rb 5.3
m Mojave ob 7.6
Monte Carlo ob 6.8
m Moonlight Sonata ab 6.5
Mother's Day mr 7.7
Mr. Standfast* 4.8
Mrs. Charles Bell lp 7.0
Mrs. Henry Bowles mp 6.4
Mrs. H. M. Eddie w 5.2
Mrs. Jennie Deverman pb 7.7
m Mrs. Luther Burbank mp 7.4
Mrs. Paul R. Bosley my 6.2
l Mrs. Pierre S. Du Pont yb 6.4
m Mrs. Sam McGredy ob 7.4
m My Choice pb 7.3
Nancy Reagan* o-r 6.8
Neige Parfum w 6.2
New Love* rb 6.8
m New Yorker mr 7.3
Niagara mr 7.1
Niagara Mist* pb 7.2
Night N'Day dr 7.2
Nina Marshall* dp 5.7
Nobility lp 7.0
m Nocturne dr 7.3
†Norita dr
Northern Dancer ob 5.1
†Northern Lights yb
North Star lp 6.4
t Numa Fay pb 6.4
m Oklahoma dr 7.9
Old Smoothie* mr 7.3
Oldtimer* ob 7.5
m Opera rb 6.9
Ophelia lp 7.2
Orange Delbard o-r 5.7
m Orange Flame o-r 7.1
l Orange Ruffels ob 5.9
m Orchid Masterpiece m 7.0
Oregold (Miss Harp)* dy 7.9
Oriana* rb 7.6
m Oriental Charm mr 8.0

Otto Miller* mr 7.4
†Paloma w
Pamela's Choice* 5.8
m Papa Meilland dr 7.6
m Pascali w 8.3
m Peace yb 9.4
m Peaceful pb 6.1
Peaceport pb 6.8
Peach Beauty pb 7.5
Peach Treat* pb 5.9
Peer Gynt* yb 7.3
Percy Thrower* mp 7.7
Peter Frankenfield* 8.1
Pharaoh* mr 7.4
m Piccadilly rb 7.4
m Picture lp 7.6
Pilar Landecho ob 6.2
Pilgrim* dr 7.1
Pink Champagne mp 7.6
m Pink Dawn mp 6.7
m Pink Duchess pb 7.6
m Pink Favorite mp 8.5
l Pink Fragrance mp 7.6
m Pink Masterpiece pb 7.3
m Pink Peace mp 7.7
Pink Princess lp 7.5
m Pink Spice lp 6.9
t Poinsettia mr 6.7
Portrait* pb 7.8
l Premier Bal pb 6.8
m President Eisenhower mr 5.9
t President Hoover pb 6.7
m Prima Ballerina dp 7.9
Primrose 6.6
Princesse Liliane mr 7.0
Proud Land* dr 7.8
Radar o-r 5.5
t Radiance lp 6.6
m Red American Beauty mr 6.5
Red Chief mr 7.2
Red Devil* mr 7.8
m Red Duchess mr 6.9
Red Jacket 5.6
†Red Lion mr
†Red Planet mr
Red Queen* mr 7.8
t Red Radiance dp 7.9
Red Talisman ob 7.0
Reg Willis dp 5.7
Rex Anderson w 6.2
m Rina Herholdt pb 6.7
Robert Cotton* w 4.2
Rome Glory mr 6.0
Rosaleda yb 6.7
m Rose Gaujard rb 7.3
Rose Marie mp 6.2
Rose of Freedom mr 7.7
Rouge Champion mr
Royal Canadian* mr 7.4
m Royal Highness lp 8.6
Royal Scarlet mr 6.8
Royal Tan m 5.0
m Rubaiyat dp 8.2
m Sabine dp 7.9
Sabrina rb 6.8
Saint Exupery m 5.6
Salvo mr 6.6
m Samoa o-r 7.8
San Diego* my 6.3
San Fernando mr 7.5
m San Francisco o-r 7.4
t Santa Fe mp 6.8
Santa Tereza d'Avila yb 6.9
Sarah Arnot mp 5.9
m Seneca Queen pb 5.8
Senior Prom dp 7.0
September Wedding mp 6.9
Serenade ab 5.1
†Sonoma mp
Seventh Heaven dr 7.1
Shades of Autumn rb 6.0
Shannon mp 6.4
Shot Silk pb 6.5
m Show Girl mp 7.8
Showtime* mp 7.6
Sierra Dawn pb 6.6
m Signora ob 6.8
Silva pb 5.7

m Silver Lining pb 7.6
Silver Star* m 7.0
Simon Bolivar o-r 7.7
m Simone m 6.4
m Sincera w 6.9
Smoky* rb 5.9
l Snowbird w 7.4
Snow White w 7.2
m Soeur Therese yb 6.4
Song of Paris m 6.1
Sonrisa* dr 6.6
m Soraya o-r 7.8
m South Seas mp 7.9
Souv. de Mme. Boullet yb 7.1
m Speaker Sam yb 6.8
m Starkrimson dr 5.5
Sterling Silver m 5.9
Stockton Beauty pb 7.4
Sultane rb 6.4
Summer Holiday* o-r 7.7
Summer Rainbow* pb 7.0
m Summer Sunshine dy 7.6
Sunblest* dy 6.9
Sun King my 6.1
Sunrise-Sunset* pb 7.7
†Sunset Jubilee lp
Sun Valley dy 5.9
m Suspense rb 7.6
m Sutter's Gold ob 7.8
m Suzon Lotthe pb 7.1
t Swarthmore pb 8.4
m Sweet Afton w 7.7
m Sword of Hope mr 5.6
m Symphonie pb 6.4
Syracuse mr 5.9
†Taj Mahal dp
Talisman yb 5.5
m Tallyho dp 7.5
Tanger rb 5.0
m Tanya ob 7.4
m Tapestry rb 7.3
t Texas Centennial dp 7.0
t Thanksgiving ob 7.6
The Chief dp 6.7
m The Doctor mp 6.9
Tickled Pink mp 7.3
m Tiffany pb 9.1
m Tip Toes pb 7.2
Topper mr 6.0
Touch of Venus w 6.8
Town Crier my 7.3
m Trade Wind rb 7.5
Tradition mr 6.3
m Traviata rb 6.8
Treasure Chest* my 6.1
m Tropicana o-r 8.8
l Twilight m 4.7
Tyriana* dp 7.0
m Tzigane rb 5.8
l Ulster Monarch r 6.7
†Uncle Joe dr
m Uncle Sam dp 7.9
Uncle Walter mr 6.4
Valencia ob 6.5
m Vassar Centennial pb 7.1
V for Victory my 5.6
m Vienna Charm ob 6.7
Viking dr 6.5
†Vino Delicado m
Vin Rose'* mp 5.3
Virgo w 6.8
Vision* pb 5.1
m Wendy Cussons mr 7.1
Western Sun dy 5.6
l Westminster mr 6.1
Whisky Mac* yb 6.4
m White Beauty w 7.0
White Christmas w
m White Knight w 7.2
White Masterpiece* w 7.9
m White Prince w 6.8
m White Queen w 7.4
White Swan w 6.1
m White Wings w 7.3
Williamsburg lp 6.2
Will Rogers dr 5.7
Wisbech Gold yb 5.1
m World's Fair Salute mr 7.0
m Yuletide mr 5.3
Zulu Queen dr 4.6

GRANDIFLORA

Relative height letter means: l, low, under 30", m, medium. 30" to 48", t, tall, 48" and over.

Alaska Centennial* dr 7.3
Aquarius* pb 7.6
Belle Etoille* my 6.8
m Ben-Hur mr 7.4
Bienvenu* o-r 8.0
Break O'Day ob 6.3
t Buccaneer my 7.3
Burning Love mr 6.1
m Camelot mp 8.2
Carrie Corl* mr 4.0
m Carrousel dr 8.4
m Cherry Glow mr 7.6
Comanche* o-r 7.6
m Dean Collins pb 6.7
Doctor Eldon Lyle* dr 7.5
t El Capitan mr 8.0
†Flamingo Queen dp
Floriade ob 6.8
Frank Serpa lp 7.2
t Garden State mp 7.5
Golden Fleece my 6.9
m Golden Girl my 7.4
t Governor Mark Hatfield dr 7.2
†Happy Anniversary ob
m John S. Armstrong dr 8.0

t June Bride w 6.9
Lucky Lady lp 7.4
Magic Moon* o-r 6.2
m Merry Widow dr 7.4
m Miss France o-r 7.4
m Montezuma o-r 8.6
t Mount Shasta w 8.0
l Musicale rb 6.1
m Ole' o-r 8.1
Pagliacci* yb 7.2
m Pink Parfait pb 7.8
t Polynesian Sunset o-r 7.1
t Queen Elizabeth mp 9.3
m Queen of Bermuda o-r 7.3
m Roundelay dr 8.0
San Antonio* o-r 7.6
Scarlet Knight dr 8.0
m Scarlet Queen Elizabeth o-r 7.1
Starburst* rb 7.0
m Starfire mr 8.0
m Stella pb 6.7
Strawberry Blonde o-r 7.1
The Jester yb 6.8
m War Dance o-r 6.9

PUBLIC ROSE GARDENS WELCOME YOU

The following is a list of public rose gardens to which AARS award winning roses are contributed. We suggest that all rosarians visit such gardens for a firsthand view of how the AARS winners and other roses grow in your particular area.

HARDY **DORMANT** ROSES.

SPECIMEN OF DORMANT BUDDED ROSE

Prune after planting and as shown on dotted lines.

Indiana
Fort Wayne - Lakeside Rose Garden
Richmond - Glen Miller Park
Iowa
Ames - Iowa State University Rose Garden
Bettendorf - Bettendorf Community Center Rose Garden
Cedar Rapids - Huston Park Rose Garden
Davenport - VanderVeer Park Municipal Rose Garden
Des Moines - Greenwood Park Municipal Rose Garden
Hamburg - Inter-State Nurseries Rose Garden
Muscatine - Weed Park Memorial Rose Garden

HARDY CLIMBING ROSES.

PRAIRIE QUEEN.

HARDY CLIMBING ROSES.

California
Arcadia - Arcadia County Park Rose Garden
Berkeley - Berkeley Municipal Rose Garden
Fresno - Fresno Municipal Rose Garden, Roeding Park
LaCanada - Descanso Gardens
Los Angeles - Exposition Park Rose Garden
Oakland - Morcum Amphitheatre of Roses
Riverside - Fairmont Park Rose Garden
Sacramento - Capitol Park Rose Garden
San Francisco - Golden Gate Park Rose Garden
San Jose - San Jose Municipal Rose Garden
San Marino - Huntington Botanical Gardens
Santa Barbara - Memorial Rose Garden, Armory Grounds
City Rose Garden
Visalia - Visalia Garden Club Public Rose Gardens
Westminster - Westminster Civic Center Rose Garden
Whittier - Pageant of Roses Garden, Rose Hills Memorial Park
Colorado
Longmont - Longmont Memorial Rose Garden

Connecticut
Norwich - Norwich Memorial Rose Garden
Waterbury - Hamilton Park Rose Garden
West Hartford - Elizabeth Park Rose Garden
Georgia
Atlanta - Greater Atlanta Rose Garden, Piedmont Park
Thomasville - Thomasville Rose Test Garden
Hawaii
Kula - U. of Hawaii College of Tropical Agriculture
Idaho
Lewiston - Memorial Bridge Rose Garden
Illinois
Chicago - Grant Park Rose Garden
Marquette Park Rose Garden
Highland Park - Gardener's Memorial Garden
Libertyville - Cook Memorial Rose Garden
Peoria - Peoria Park District Rose Garden
Rockford - Sinissippi Sunken Gardens
Wheaton - Robert R. McCormick Memorial Gardens

Shenandoah - Mount Arbor Demonstration Garden
State Center - Iowa Rose Society Garden
Waterloo - Byrnes Park Municipal Rose Garden
Kansas
Manhattan - Kansas State University Rose Garden
Topeka - E. F. A. Reinisch Rose & Test Gardens
Louisiana
Baton Rouge - L.S.U. Rose Test Garden
New Orleans - Pauline Worthington Memorial Rose Garden
Shreveport - The American Rose Center
Massachusetts
Westfield - The Stanley Park of Westfield
Michigan
East Lansing - Michigan State University Horticulture Gardens
Lansing - Frances Park Memorial Rose Garden

Minnesota
Duluth - Duluth Rose Garden
Minneapolis - Minneapolis Municipal Rose Garden
Missouri
Cape Girardeau - Cape Girardeau Rose Display Garden, Capaha Park
Kansas City - Jackson County Rose Society Laura Conyers Smith Memorial Rose Garden
St. Louis - Missouri Botanical Rose Garden
Montana
Missoula - Missoula Memorial Rose Garden, Sunset Park
Nebraska
Lincoln - Lincoln Municipal Rose Garden
Omaha - Omaha Memorial Park Rose Garden
Nevada
Reno - Reno Municipal Rose Garden
New Jersey
Bloomfield - Brookdale Park Rose Garden
New Mexico
Albuquerque - Prospect Park Rose Garden
Hobbs - Community Rose Garden, Lea General Hospital
New York
Brooklyn - Cranford Memorial Rose Garden, Brooklyn Botanic Garden
Buffalo - Niagara Frontier Trial Rose Garden
Newark - The National Rose Garden
New York - United Nations Rose Garden
Rochester - Maplewood Rose Garden
Schenectady - Central Park Rose Garden
Tuxedo - Sterling Forest Gardens
North Carolina
Raleigh - Raleigh Municipal Rose Garden
Ohio
Columbus - Columbus Park of Roses
Ohio State Univ. Rose Garden
Oklahoma
Muskogee - J. E. Conard Municipal Rose Garden
Oklahoma City - Municipal Rose Garden, Will Rogers Park
Tulsa - Tulsa Municipal Rose Garden
Oregon
Corvallis - Corvallis Municipal Rose Garden, Avery Park
Eugene - George E. Owen Municipal Rose Garden
Portland - International Rose Test Garden
Pennsylvania
Allentown - Malcolm W. Gross Memorial Rose Garden
Hershey - Hershey Rose Gardens & Arboretum
McKeesport - Longwood Gardens
Renziehausen Park Arboretum
Pittsburgh - Mellon Park Rose Gardens
Pottstown - Pottstown Memorial Rose Garden
Reading - Reading Municipal Rose Garden
State College - Penn State University Rose Garden
West Grove - The Robert Pyle Memorial Rose Garden
South Carolina
Orangeburg - Edisto Rose Garden
Tennessee
Chattanooga - Municipal Rose Garden, Warner Park
Memphis - Memphis Municipal Rose Garden, Audubon Park
Texas
Corpus Christi - Corpus Christi Rose Society Display Garden
Dallas - Samuell-Grand Municipal Rose Garden
El Paso - El Paso Municipal Rose Garden
Fort Worth - Fort Worth Botanic Garden
Houston - Houston Municipal Rose Garden
San Angelo - Municipal Rose Garden, Civic League Park
Tyler - Tyler Rose Garden Park
Utah
Fillmore - Territorial Statehouse Rose Gardens, Old Capitol State Park
Nephi - Municipal Memorial Rose Garden
Salt Lake City - Salt Lake Municipal Rose Garden
Virginia
Arlington - Arlington Memorial Rose Garden
Roanoke - Mountain View (Fishburn) Garden
Washington
Bellingham - Cornwall Park Rose Garden
Fairhaven Park Rose Garden
Chehalis - Chehalis Municipal Rose Garden
Seattle - Woodland Park Rose Garden
Spokane - Rose Hill-Manito Park
Tacoma - Point Defiance Park Rose Garden
West Virginia
Huntington - Ritter Park Rose Garden
Wisconsin
Hales Corners - Boerner Botanical Gardens, Whitnall Park

The American Rose Society

will help you grow better roses and enjoy the rose growing hobby

The American Rose Society is the largest special plant society in the United States. It is a non-profit organization formed in 1899 to serve the thousands of people who enjoy roses.

Some 18,000 rose enthusiasts from all parts of the country compose this congenial group. The majority of these are amateur gardeners who enjoy the rose-growing hobby and seek to expand their knowledge of rose culture.

We invite you to become a member and share the knowledge and fellowship of this national association.

ARE YOU A MEMBER OF THE AMERICAN ROSE SOCIETY?

If not, and you grow roses (no matter how few), here are some of the reasons why you should join this non-profit organization of some 18,000 amateur gardeners.

Members receive a colorful monthly magazine containing timely articles of interesting and useful information that will be helpful in your day- by-day rose growing.

Each year members receive the *American Rose Annual* – a 260-page book (valued at $6.95) with beautiful color plates, articles on all phases of rose culture and members' reports on the newest cultivars (varieties).

Members may receive advice on problems regarding roses from the ARS or from one of its committees of experts located throughout the country.

The American Rose Society is first to publish descriptions of all new roses being introduced in the United States. Further, a national rating for all roses currently grown in the United States is compiled and published through annual surveys of the Society membership.

The American Rose Society holds two national conventions and national rose shows each year. Members are eligible and encouraged to attend so they may learn more about roses and enjoy the fellowship of other growers and hobbyists.

Members may borrow books by mail from the library of over 1000 well-known titles on rose culture.

A membership card is sent to each member and is the passport to rose shows, rose gardens and rose fellowship everywhere.

A list of all public rose gardens in the United States is available upon request to each member.

The American Rose Society has more than 350 chapters and affiliated societies in the United States. Each organization offers an opportunity to learn and share rose growing experiences with rosarians in your own locale.

A Member's Handbook listing names and addresses of all ARS members is available for purchase from the Society to members only.

The cost of membership is $10.50 per calendar year (12 months). For those who wish to receive the "American Rose" magazine only, with no privileges of the American Rose Society membership, a subscription for 12 months is $6.50.

Please use coupon on page 24.

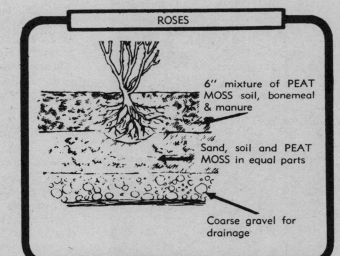

ROSIER (SPÉCIMEN DE CULTURE ANGLAISE)

Classifications Membership

REGULAR MEMBERSHIP .... $ 10.50
Memberships are concurrent with the calendar year, expiring December 31. New members joining after the first quarter may enjoy a reduced rate based on the quarter in which they join.
   Second quarter (April, May June) .... $ 9.00
   Third quarter (July, Aug., Sept.) .... $ 7.50
   Fourth quarter (Oct. Nov., Dec.) .... $ 5.00

THREE-YEAR MEMBERSHIP ... $ 28.50
ASSOCIATE MEMBERSHIP ...... $ 2.50
Available only to members of families holding at least one regular membership. Includes all benefits except copies of the **American Rose Annual** and "The American Rose" magazine.

SUSTAINING MEMBERSHIP ..... $ 25.00
For amateur rose growers who wish to make a contribution to the work of the Society.

LIFE MEMBERSHIP $225.00
For individuals who wish to enjoy the privileges of the Society and be exempt from the payment of annual dues.

ASSOCIATED CLUB MEMBERSHIP .... $ 15.00
For any organization pertaining to horticulture. Such an organization is entitled to a charter and copies of all publications upon payment of annual dues.

CHAPTER AND AFFILIATED CLUB MEMBERSHIPS .... $ 10.00
Available to organizations meeting the requirements. Write to Executive Secretary for details.

RESEARCH MEMBERSHIPS .... $ 40.00
For people dealing in roses or products related to rose culture and for individuals who wish to make a contribution of $40.00 per year, of which $30.00 is tax deductible, and is applied to the American Rose Foundation for rose research.

ROSES

6" mixture of PEAT MOSS soil, bonemeal & manure

Sand, soil and PEAT MOSS in equal parts

Coarse gravel for drainage

ROSES.

199

WHAT IS THE AMERICAN ROSE SOCIETY?

The American Rose Society is the largest special plant society in the United States. It is a non-profit, international group organized in 1899, with headquarters in Shreveport, Louisiana. The offices are located in the 118-acre park known as the American Rose Center, which is being developed into the largest private garden of its kind in the United States.

Current membership exceeds 18,000, the majority of whom are amateur gardeners who grow roses as a hobby, from every state and some 50 foreign countries. There are over 400 Chapter, Affiliated and Associated rose societies at the local level.

The American Rose Society offers the following services:

Publishes the monthly AMERICAN ROSE magazine, the only periodical devoted exclusively to information on the culture, use, and history of roses.

Publishes the American Rose Annual, a hardbound book containing up-to-date, scientific information on roses and rose growing plus other articles of general interest to rose lovers. This book has been published yearly since 1916.

Maintains an extensive mail lending library of books on roses and related horticulture.

Provides personal information on individual rose growing questions.

Maintains, through the American Rose Foundation, cooperative research programs on rose growing problems at various colleges and experimental stations.

Collects and maintains records on all matters pertaining to roses.

Sponsors two National Rose Meetings and Rose Shows each year. Also assists with District rose conferences and shows.

Cooperates with the Districts in conducting schools for training rose show judges, and accredits qualified rose judges.

Establishes the rules and regulations for conducting American Rose Society shows and sets the standards of perfection for judging.

Grants prizes and awards for outstanding achievements in rose work.

Maintains a rose registration system, and has been delegated by the International Horticultural Congress as the International Registration Authority for Roses. Publishes monthly and annual lists of all new roses registered with I.R.A.R.

Tabulates hundreds of individual reports from all over the country into an annual report of national ratings of all roses commercially available. This "Handbook For Selecting Roses" is available to anyone at ten cents per copy.

Publishes an annual tabulation of the cultivars winning awards at rose shows.

Maintains liaison with field societies and rosarians through strategically placed personnel called Consulting Rosarians. These Consulting Rosarians are available to advise and help anyone with rose problems.

Makes available to the membership rose show supplies, books, program materials and other data relative to complete operation of a rose society.

The American Rose Society extends a warm invitation to all rosarians who are interested in enjoying and taking part in this dynamic and growing association.

AMERICAN ROSE SOCIETY, P.O. Box 30,000, Shreveport, Louisiana 71130

GUIDELINES TO GOOD ROSES

prepared by

THE AMERICAN ROSE SOCIETY

POST OFFICE BOX 30,000
SHREVEPORT, LOUISIANA 71130

ROSE GROWING IS EASY

Don't think for a moment that good roses are only grown by master gardeners. In this leaflet the American Rose Society has outlined a few basic steps that will allow anyone to grow and enjoy the roses of his choice.

ROSE TYPES

In planning for a rose garden you will want to be familiar with the several different types of plants available. Modern breeding accomplishments have produced roses to fit every need ranging from miniatures used in window boxes, to climbers to cover a trellis, and shrubs and bush-type roses to meet every landscape need.

Popular rose types include:

Hybrid Tea - Buds are usually long and pointed, the flowers single, semi-double or double and are borne singly or few together. They are hardy with some winter protection.

Floribunda - Intermediate between Polyanthas and Hybrid Teas in inflorescence; hardy; free-flowering; a wide color range, and with heights and styles suited to every purpose.

Grandiflora - Free flowering habits of the Floribunda and the perfection of form of Hybrid Teas. Often taller than Hybrid Teas.

Climbers - Roses with long shoots or canes, can be trained to many forms.

Miniatures - Plants dwarfed in every respect, hardy, ever-blooming, used as potted plants grown indoors or for landscaping purposes in the garden.

Shrubs and Old Fashioned Roses - Irregular in growth habits, extremely hardy and resistant to insects and diseases, used for landscaping.

Varieties Recommended by the American Rose Society

Hybrid Teas
    Chrysler Imperial, dark red
    Fragrant Cloud, orange-red
    Tropicana, orange-red
    Charlotte Armstrong, light red and deep pink
    Mister Lincoln, medium red
    Royal Highness, light pink
    First Prize, pink blend
    Pascali, white
    Swathmore, pink blend
    Crimson Glory, dark red
    Helen Traubel, pink blend
    Chicago Peace, pink blend
    Miss All - American Beauty, medium pink
    Peace, yellow blend
    Tiffany, pink blend

Floribundas
    Spartan, orange-red
    Europeana, dark red
    Circus, yellow blend
    Redgold, yellow blend
    Gene Boerner, medium pink
    Iceberg, white
    Ivory Fashion, white
    Angel Face, mauve
    Little Darling, yellow blend
    Betty Prior, medium pink

Grandifloras
    Queen Elizabeth, medium pink
    Montezuma, orange-red
    Aquarius, pink blend
    Camelot, medium pink
    Carrousel, dark red
    Mount Shasta, white

Climbers
    Blaze, medium red
    Blossomtime, medium pink
    Don Juan, dark red
    New Dawn, light pink
    Cl. Crimson Glory, dark red
    Rhonda, medium pink
    Cl. Cecile Brunner, light pink

Shrubs and Old Fashioned Roses
    Harison's Yellow, deep yellow
    Sea Foam, white
    Nevada, white
    Dortmund, medium red
    Mrs. John Laing, medium pink

For a complete listing of all roses available in the United States with description and performance rating, order the book, "A Handbook for Selecting Roses". Send 10 cents in coin, plus a stamped, self - addressed envelope to: The American Rose Society, P. O. Box 30,000, Shreveport, Louisiana 71130.

CARE OF ROSES

On Arrival - Roses may be purchased as bare root plants or in pots. Bare root plants should be planted according to the following diagrams. Remove soil mound when new growth begins.

Potted roses may be planted any time throughout the growing season. Remove bush and soil ball from container. Dig hole large enough for entire ball. Plant at ground level; water thoroughly.

Proper Planting

Fertilizing

Plants should be fed with complete rose food at least monthly during the growing season. For specific information, write the American Rose Society for the name of an appointed Consulting Rosarian in your area. He will be glad to assist you personally.

Insect and Disease Control

Use a complete product (spray or dust) recommended for control of insects and diseases of roses. Begin operation early in the spring - prevention is the secret to healthy plants. Most gardeners prefer a preventive program with regular weekly applications throughout the growing season. Use a specific insecticide or fungicide to combat any particular enemy of the rose. American Rose Society Consulting Rosarians can be a valuable aid with specific pest problems.

Pruning

Spring pruning is important and should be done early when leaf buds first show signs of growth. First remove dead, diseased, or injured wood and weak, twiggy shoots. Cut the strong canes back to a healthy bud 18 - 24 inches above the ground (see Fig. 1). In areas where winters are severe, you must cut back to good, healthy wood (whitish green centers) which sometimes requires cutting back to near ground level.

Summer pruning is easy and can be done according to the tastes of the gardener. The plant is usually sufficiently pruned when flowers are cut. When removing flowers from a rose plant, make a clean cut far enough down the stem to leave healthy, vigorous foliage. Skilled rosarians normally cut back to a leaf that has at least 5 leaflets (see Fig. 2). The stub left will immediately develop new flowering wood.

Fall pruning is not necessary. However, in areas where winter winds may whip and damage the plants, the bushes should be topped and in some cases secured with twine or wire.

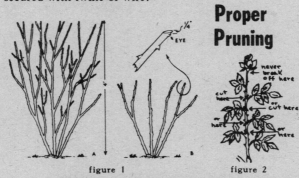

Proper Pruning

figure 1   figure 2

JOIN THE AMERICAN ROSE SOCIETY

If you have an interest in roses you will enjoy the many advantages of membership in the American Rose Society. Here are some of the reasons 18,000 American gardeners share their rose interest through membership in this non - profit association:

Members receive a *colorful monthly magazine* containing timely articles of interest and useful information that is helpful in growing and enjoying roses.

Each year members receive the *American Rose Annual* - a 260 - page book (valued at $6.95) with beautiful color plates, articles on all phases of rose culture and members' reports on the newest cultivars (varieties).

Members may receive *advice on problems* related to roses from the ARS or from one of its committees of experts located throughout the country.

The American Rose Society is first to publish *descriptions of all new roses* being introduced in the United States. Further, a *national rating for all roses* currently grown in the United States is compiled and published through annual surveys of the Society membership.

The American Rose Society holds *two national conventions and national rose shows* each year.

Members are eligible and encouraged to attend so they may learn more about roses and enjoy the fellowship of other growers and hobbyists.

Members may *borrow books* by mail from the library of over 1000 well - known titles on rose culture.

A *membership card* is sent to each member and is the passport to rose shows, rose gardens and rose fellowship everywhere including the 118 acre American Rose Center in Shreveport, Louisiana.

A *list of all public rose gardens* in the United States is available upon request to each member.

The American Rose Society has more than 350 *chapters and affiliated societies* in the United States. Each organization offers an opportunity to learn and share rose growing experiences with rosarians in a specific area.

The cost of membership is $10.50 *per calendar year* (12 months). For those who wish to receive the *American Rose* magazine only, with no privileges of the American Rose Society membership, a subscription for 12 months is $6.50.

AMERICAN ROSE SOCIETY DUES

Membership in the American Rose Society is based on the calendar year, expiring December 31. New members joining after the first quarter may enjoy a reduced rate based on the quarter in which they join. They will still receive all the remaining issues of the *American Rose* magazine plus the current *American Rose Annual.* Dues schedule is as follows:

Full year	$10.50
Second Quarter (April thru December)	$9.00
Third Quarter (July thru December)	$7.50
Fourth Quarter (October thru December)	$5.00

Members Enjoy These Useful Publications

8

The hundred leav'd Rose

American Rose Annual — a handsomely bound book of 260 pages and beautiful full-color illustrations. The many articles provide authentic information on the advances of rose culture and descriptions of the newest roses with summarized comments on their performance in different areas of the country. (Price to non-members — $6.95)

Handbook For Selecting Roses — A valuable reference for all roses available in the United States, listing height, color, hort. classification and the valuable ARS rating obtained from annual surveys of our members who report on roses they are currently growing.

Membership Card — Your passport to rose shows, rose gardens, and rose fellowship everywhere.

SPECIAL OFFER
WHAT EVERY ROSE GROWER SHOULD KNOW Completely revised by C. H. Lewis and R. C. Allen to give the beginner the essential facts about rose growing. Filled with beautiful color photographs and numerous illustrations, this handy pocket sized how-to-do-it rose book is a must for every rose grower — beginner or otherwise. $1.50 to members of the American Rose Society.

"The American Rose" magazine — a monthly full-color publication containing timely articles on every phase of the rose-growing hobby. It is the only periodical devoted exclusively to the culture, history and enjoyment of roses. (Subscription to non-members $6.50)

and there's more . . .

Rose Library — members may borrow books by mail from the largest rose library in the country. Over 1,000 titles on rose culture available and the only charge is the postage.

PROBLEMS — a committee of Consulting Rosarians strategically placed in all parts of the country to give expert advice and personal help with rose problems free of charge.

Current Leaflets — available upon request. A list of Private and Public Rose Gardens in the United States open to all American Rose Society members. A listing of Consulting Rosarians, Rose Judges and a vast assortment of specific cultural information.

Local Societies — The American Rose Society has more than 350 chapters and affiliated societies in the United States. Each organization offers an opportunity to learn and share rose growing experiences with rosarians in your own community. If you wish, the ARS will put you in touch with one of these local organizations.

How to Grow Miniature Roses in the Garden and in the Home

The A-B-C of INDOOR CULTURE

Miniature Roses make attractive and interesting house plants which will give you great enjoyment and satisfaction. The only roses which can be grown successfully indoors, they need only a little more than average care. Each flower will last for days and the plants will be a mass of bloom for weeks at a time. A more rewarding sight than these Miniature Roses blooming for you indoors would be hard to find.

It is important to keep in mind that successful indoor growing of Miniature Roses is dependent upon three things. One is sunshine. Another is humidity, and the last is moderate temperature. If you can provide these requirements, more information about which is given on other pages of this folder, you will enjoy the satisfaction of having delightful little rose blooms in your house in winter-time brought to flowering through your own care.

Such dainty beauty is always a talking point when friends come and a pleasure on its own account.

Like so many things done for the first time, growing Miniature Roses indoors might seem to you to have about it too many things to remember. Actually, they become second nature quickly.

Incidentally, the flowers may be cut if desired to make dainty, colorful miniature arrangements and boutonnieres. When spring comes (mid-May in Pennsylvania) the Miniature Roses may be planted out-of-doors, where they thrive.

Easy Steps to Successful Indoor Growing of Miniatures

POTTING

The plants you receive from the nursery are dormant, and are ready to be planted in pots or other containers. The best container is one made of clay or pottery, with plastic, metal, or china being next best. This "pot" should be about 3½ to 4 inches in diameter and about the same in depth.

The best soil mixture is 2 parts of good garden or top soil, 2 parts of peat moss or other humus and 1 part of a medium coarse sand. These should be mixed well. A small amount of this mixture should be placed in the bottom of the pot, the Miniature Rose then placed in the center, and the pot filled with soil. Firm the soil slightly so that it comes to within a half-inch of the top.

WATERING

Place the pots in a sink and water thoroughly. Soak the soil until all bubbling ceases or water seeps from the bottom of the pot.

For best growing conditions, the Miniature Roses should be placed in a tray that has a half-inch of **moist** gravel, shells or sand in it. This gravel **must be kept wet** at all times, but do not let water touch the bottom of the pot. This wet gravel keeps moisture in the air (i.e. maintains humidity) for promoting the best foliage, in a normally dry house.

Miniature Roses should be kept moist at all times. Under most conditions the roses should be watered every one or two days. Always water from the top of the pot, and apply enough at a time to **wet the soil thoroughly.**

LOCATION

The tray of wet gravel and Miniature Roses should be placed in a window that gets a maximum amount of sunlight. The roses will not do well with less than three hours of sunlight daily. An unshaded window in full sun is ideal.

A moderate room temperature of 65° to 70° is best. An even temperature away from cold drafts or heat is the most satisfactory.

FERTILIZING

When your Miniature Rose is first potted up there is no need for adding fertilizer to the soil. About three weeks after potting, when leaves have started to grow, fertilizer should be added to the soil. Any ready-made soluble fertilizer may be used, following instructions on the package. In most cases, dissolve one teaspoonful of soluble fertilizer in a quart of water and wet the soil in the pots thoroughly with the solution. Repeat this procedure every three weeks.

SPRAYING

Roses received from the nursery do not have insects or diseases. However, insects and at times diseases may eventually appear on plants in the home. A good aerosol bomb designed for house plants is an effective and easy means of keeping them under control. A weekly spraying with any house plant spray is an effective "ounce of prevention." Any spray designed for roses may also be used, following instructions given on the package.

BLOOMING

About six weeks after the Miniature Roses have been potted up, they will begin to bloom. It is at this time that these amazing little flowers will put on a dazzling show, a real reward for the weeks of waiting. The buds will not open all at once, but slowly one after another for several weeks. As soon as a flower fades, pinch it off in order to promote more blooming. When the first set of flowers has finished, keep watering and feeding and soon the Miniature Roses will bloom again. They should continue to bloom as long as growing conditions are well maintained.

Remember—the three basic needs of your Miniature Roses are:—**Sunshine - Humidity - Moderate Temperature.** With these three requirements adequately fulfilled, an indoor garden of Miniature Roses will bring untold winter-time satisfaction.

In late Spring (May north of Washington and St. Louis), your Miniature Roses may be planted out-of-doors in the garden or a window box. Read the directions for outdoor culture to know their care and uses.

—Bedding-roses.

FLORIBUNDA

Relative height letter means: l, low, under 24"; m, medium, 24" to 36"; t, tall, 36" and over.

m	Alain mr	7.9
	Albert ob	7.5
m	Allgold my	7.4
	Ama ob	6.9
m	Amy Vanderbilt m	6.3
	Angel Face* m	8.0
m	Anna Wheatcroft o-r	8.2
t	Anne Poulson mr	7.0
	Antique* rb	6.3
	Apache Tears* rb	7.3
	†Aperitif pb	
m	Apricot Nectar ab	8.0
	Arthur Bell my	7.0
	Atombombe mr	5.0
	Attraktion ob	6.7
m	Baby Blaze mr	7.6
l	Bambi mp	7.4
m	Betty Prior mp	9.0
	Bobbie Lucas* o-r	6.9
	Bonfire Night* ob	7.0
	Border Gold dy	4.6
l	Bouquet dp	7.3
	Bridal Pink* mp	6.4
l	Brownie r	6.4
	Capri o-r	7.4
	Carol Amling mp	7.4
m	Castanet o-r	7.4
	Celebration rb	7.6
	Charlie McCarthy w	6.1
l	Chatter mr	7.0
l	Cheerio mp	6.2
m	Chic pb	7.4
	Chinatown dy	6.4
	Chuckles dp	7.4
m	Circus yb	8.0
m	Circus Parade yb	7.6
	City of Belfast* o-r	8.3
	City of Leeds pb	8.0
t	Cocorico o-r	8.4
	Color Girl pb	5.6
	Columbine yb	6.1
	Contempo* ob	6.6
	Copper Pot* ob	6.9
l	Coral Glo pb	7.3
	Corsage w	7.3
	Coup de Foudre o-r	7.8
	Courvoisier* my	7.0
m	Crimson Rosette dr	8.1
m	Cupids Charm pb	8.4
	Dagmar Spaeth w	7.5
t	Daily Sketch pb	7.9
	Dearest pb	8.5
m	Diamant o-r	7.1
	Dream Waltz*	7.2
	Dr. Faust yb	7.3
m	Dusky Maiden dr	7.8
m	Elizabeth of Glamis pb	7.4
t	Else Poulsen mp	7.8
m	Elysium mp	6.8
m	Erna Grootendorst mr	6.6
	Europeana dr	8.5
m	Eutin dr	7.8
m	Evelyn Fison mr	7.7
	Faberge* pb	8.1
	Fancy Talk pb	7.8
m	Fashion pb	8.0
m	Fashionette pb	7.6
	Fee o-r	5.6
	Feurio o-r	8.0
m	Fireflame mr	7.3
t	Fire King o-r	7.8
t	Floradora o-r	7.0
	Frankfort Am Main mr	6.8
t	Frensham dr	8.2
	Fresco*	8.0
	Frolic lp	7.9
m	Fusilier o-r	7.7
m	Garnette dr	7.4
	Gay Princess lp	7.6
	Gene Boerner* mp	8.5
m	Geranium Red o-r	6.6
	Gertrude Raffel dp	8.3
m	Ginger o-r	8.2
l	Girl Scout dy	5.6
m	Gold Cup dy	5.9
	Golden Coronet* my	6.2
m	Golden Delight my	5.8
l	Golden Garnette dy	7.0
m	Golden Lace dy	5.6
m	Golden Slippers yb	7.1
l	Goldilocks my	6.5
	Goldmarie dy	5.9
	†Goldmoss my	
	Goldtopas yb	7.0
	Gruss an Aachen lp	7.6
	Gundy dp	5.3
t	Heat Wave o-r	7.8
	Heaven Scent* o-r	6.4
	Highlight ob	7.4
	Hobby mr	5.0
	Honey Chile mp	7.3
	Honeymoon my	6.6
	Hurra mr	7.3
	Iceberg (Schneewittchen) w	8.7
	Ice White w	8.1
m	Improved Lafayette dp	6.6
m	Independence o-r	7.6
m	Indian Gold yb	6.2
m	Irene of Denmark w	7.0
	Irish Mist o-r	7.5
m	Ivory Fashion w	8.0
	Jack Frost w	6.4
	Jan Spek my	6.8
	Jazz Fest* mr	7.6
	Jet Fire o-r	6.9
m	Jiminy Cricket ob	7.2
	Jingles mp	
	King Arthur* mp	6.9
	Kirsten Poulsen	7.8
t	Korona mr	7.8
	Lafayette dp	7.3
l	Lavender Girl m	7.0
	Lavender Love m	6.4
m	Lavender Pinocchio m	5.7
m	Lavender Princess m	7.1
	Lavendula m	7.2
	Leprechaun* yb	6.8
	Lichterloh mr	7.2
m	Lilac Charm m	7.8
	Lilac Dawn m	7.2
m	Lilibet lp	6.8
m	Lilli Marlene mr	7.9
t	Little Darling yb	8.6
	Magenta m	7.9
	†Magic Mountain yb	
	Malibu o-r	7.5
	Manjana* yb	7.2
t	Ma Perkins pb	7.7
	Martha Rice* dp	6.5
m	Masquerade rb	7.6
	Matador (Esther O'Farim)* ob	7.1
	Megiddo* o-r	5.0
	Merlin* mr	6.4
t	Miracle o-r	7.7
	Molly McGredy*	7.2
	Moonraker*	6.7
	Mysterium yb	6.6
	Nearly Wild mp	7.0
	Oberon ab	7.8
	Orangeade o-r	8.4
	Orange Chiffon* ob	6.1
	Orange Ice o-r	5.8
	Orange Sensation o-r	8.3
	Orange Silk* o-r	6.0
	Orion*	4.4
m	Paddy McGredy mp	7.5
	Papillon Rose mp	7.3
	Paprika o-r	8.1
	Park Royal* ob	6.8
	Parsifal*	7.0
	†Pat Nixon dr	
	People o-r	
m	Permanent Wave mr	7.9
	Pernille Poulsen*	7.4
	Picasso* pb	6.5
	Picotee rb	7.8
	Pied Piper* mr	7.6
m	Pink Bountiful mp	7.8
m	Pink Chiffon lp	7.4
	Pink Garnette	7.4
	Pink Gruss an Aachen lp	9.0
	Pink Rosette lp	8.1
m	Pinocchio pb	7.6
l	Plain Talk mr	7.8
t	Poulsen's Bedder lp	7.7
	Princess Michiko* yb	7.2
	Redcap mr	7.6
	Red Cushion dr	7.5
t	Red Glory mr	8.7
	Redgold* yb	8.0
m	Red Pinocchio dr	7.9
t	Red Ripples dr	7.0
	Rochester ab	6.8
	Roman Holiday rb	7.6
	Rosemary dp	7.1
l	Rosenelfe mp	7.9
	†Rougemoss o-r	
m	Rumba rb	7.5
	Samba yb	7.1
	Sandringham my	7.0
m	Sarabande o-r	7.9
m	Saratoga w	7.7
	Satchmo*	7.1
	Sea Pearl pb	8.5
m	Showboat yb	7.8
	Siren o-r	7.6
	Sir Lancelot* ab	8.0
m	Small Talk my	7.0
	Smiles lp	7.4
	†Sonoma mp	
	Spanish Sun* dy	7.0
t	Spartan o-r	8.4
m	Starlet my	7.4
	Sumatra o-r	7.2
m	Summer Snow w	7.7
	Sunbonnet dy	7.3
	Sunspot my	6.2
l	Sweet and Low pb	7.2
	Sweet Talk w	7.3
	Sweet Vivien pb	8.5
	Taconis*	5.0
	Tamango* dr	8.1
	Tom Tom dp	8.2
	Tony Lander ob	6.6
	Torchy* o-r	6.8
	Town Talk o-r	7.4
	Treasure Isle* pb	7.3
	†Uwe Seeler o-r	
	Vagabonde ab	7.0
l	Valentine mr	7.7
	Vera Dalton mp	8.0
	Violet Carson yb	7.8
t	Vogue pb	8.2
	Walko dr	
m	White Bouquet w	7.3
	Whitecap w	7.4
m	Wildfire mr	7.4
m	Woburn Abbey ob	7.3
m	World's Fair dr	7.5
	Yelloglo (Jean de la Lune)* dy	7.1
	Yellow Cushion my	7.1
	Yellow Holstein w	
l	Yellow Pinocchio my	6.1
m	Zambra ob	7.2
m	Zorina ob	8.1

POLYANTHA

	Baby Faurax m	6.5
	Cameo pb	7.5
	Carroll Ann	7.3
	Cecile Brunner lp	7.7
	Chatillon Rose lp	7.8
	China Doll mp	8.0
	Dopey	7.3
l	Gloria Mundi o-r	6.5
l	Golden Salmon o-r	6.3
l	Happy mr	7.3
	Ideal mr	5.8
l	Margo Koster ob	7.7
	Marie Pavic w	7.9
	Mignonette	7.0
	Milrose* lp	6.0
m	Mrs. R. M. Finch mp	8.7
l	Orange Triumph o-r	7.1
	Pinafore w	7.3
l	Pinkie mp	7.6
	Sparkler mr	6.9
m	The Fairy lp	8.5
	Yvonne Rabier w	8.5

The A-B-C of OUTDOOR CULTURE

This little folder is designed to accomplish two purposes: 1, to acquaint you with the discovery, already made by thousands of delighted gardeners, that Miniature Roses are not only the most fascinating plants in the garden, but also one of the easiest to grow; and 2, to show you how to get the most satisfaction and pleasure from them.

First, perhaps a word is in order about the background of these interesting roses. They are known to have been cultivated more than 100 years ago, not on a commercial scale, of course, but privately. Then for a long, long time, they dropped out of sight completely . . . lost to cultivation. A relatively few years ago, a real Miniature Rose was found in Switzerland, and from this discovery have come developments which now give us the varieties we have today.

In this country, Miniature Roses are now grown in quantities which permit gardeners everywhere to have and enjoy them. Each year, as the fame of these Fairy Roses, as they are sometimes called, spreads and people know how wonderful they are, the demand for them becomes increasingly greater.

Here are their general characteristics. Miniature Roses are completely hardy and very easy to grow out-of-doors. They will thrive in a good garden soil in any sunny location where they will not be overshadowed by larger plants.

They are true roses in every sense; but, are midgets, having dainty flowers and foliage that is a rich green of attractive and miniature form. The buds and open blooms are just like the big garden roses, differing only in that the open bloom is no larger than a half-dollar.

These fairies of the rose world are especially suited for borders of walks and edging of rose beds and perennial borders. They are also ideal for window or terrace planters, rock gardens, children's gardens, or a garden made with other miniature plants. No special conditions are needed for their growth other than good garden soil and sunshine, just as for most flowering plants.

The care of Miniature Roses is the same as that needed by other garden roses. When they are shipped from the nursery they are dormant plants usually without leaves, and with a small ball of soil on the roots. The growing stems are properly trimmed back to about two inches for best results in your garden.

Miniature Roses will start to bloom about the end of May, or about six weeks after planting. At this time, you will begin to enjoy the colorful, dainty flowers with their subtle fragrance.

Full enjoyment is not realized until you take some of these fairy flowers and make a miniature flower arrangement. They are very well suited for boutonnieres or nosegays, too.

For Greatest Satisfaction From Your Miniature Roses, Follow These Simple Rules

LOCATION

Select a location that gets at least half a day of sunshine; a full day's sun will be fine. Be sure that the selected spot does not collect water and stay wet after a rain. Miniature Roses like plenty of water; but, like people, they dislike "wet feet." Do not plant Miniature Roses where larger plants can grow over them, crowd them and rob them of sunshine and moisture.

PLANTING

A good garden soil that has grown other plants such as chrysanthemums, petunias, geraniums, tomatoes, lettuce or other usual garden plants, should grow good Miniature Roses. The most necessary requirement is plenty of humus or organic matter in the soil. The best sources of humus are peat moss, leaf mold, or well rotted manure. For the best results, add about one quart of humus and one tablespoonful of a rose fertilizer for each Miniature Rose. Mix this very thoroughly with the soil about eight inches deep. Plant the Miniature Roses about ten to twelve inches apart, placing the top of the soil ball about one-half inch below the surface of the ground. Press the soil firmly around the Miniature Rose and water well. Use one or two quarts of water for each plant.

WATERING

Miniature Roses like an abundance of water, but at the same time they do not like the ground constantly wet. If the location you have picked for your Miniature Roses stays covered with water for 24 hours after a rain, that location is too wet. If during the growing season there is not a good weekly rain, additional water should be provided for your Miniatures. A good soaking after a ten-day period without rain is a must. Repeat at weekly intervals until there is a soaking rain.

FERTILIZING

After the initial tablespoonful of fertilizer at planting time, an additional level tablespoonful should be worked into the soil around each plant about the middle of May, and again in early July. Use any fertilizer that is designed specifically for roses or any fertilizer composed of approximately equal percentages of nitrogen, phosphorus, and potash.

The fertilizer should be spread around the Miniature Roses about two inches away from the stems. Scratch the soil lightly to mix the fertilizer into the soil and then water the plants.

After the first year, follow the same fertilizing schedule, making applications in early April, mid-May and the final one in early July.

INSECTS AND DISEASES

Even though your Miniatures are insect and disease free when you receive them from the nursery, it will be desirable to set up a spraying or dusting schedule. Diseases are easier to prevent than to cure.

Use a spray or dust, whichever is more satisfactory to you. Use a multi-purpose material that is designed for roses. Apply the material every ten days, starting as soon as leaves begin to develop in the spring, and continue until the plants go dormant in the fall. Be sure to coat the underside of the leaves as well as the upperside.

MINIATURE

Baby Betsy McCall lp	8.2
Baby Bunting dp	6.6
Baby Cheryl lp	7.7
Baby Darling ob	8.6
Baby Gold Star dy	7.7
Baby Jayne mp	6.9
Baby Masquerade rb	8.4
Baby Ophelia pb	8.0
Baby Pinocchio pb	7.5
Beauty Secret mr	9.0
Bit o'Sunshine dy	7.3
Bobolink dp	7.5
Bo-Peep mp	8.1
Candy Cane rb	7.8
Candy Pink* lp	7.7
Chipper lp	8.8
Cinderella w	9.0
†Cl. Baby Darling ob	
Cl. Jackie w	7.1
†Coralin mr	
Coral Treasure* ob	7.6
Cricri mp	8.1
Cutie mp	7.7
Debbie yb	8.0
Dian dp	8.1
Dwarfking mr	8.8
Easter Morning w	7.9
Eleanor pb	7.8
Fairy Moss* mp	7.1
Fiesta Gold* yb	6.8
Fire Princess* mr	7.5
Fringette mp	7.4
Frostfire mr	7.1
Frosty w	7.2
Gold Coin dy	7.8
Granadina	8.1
Granate dr	8.3
Green Ice* w	7.7
Hi Ho dp	8.1
Jackie w	7.7
Janice* mp	7.7
Janna pb	8.3
Jeanie Williams rb	7.8
Jet Trail w	8.2
Jian mr	7.3
Josephine* w	6.8
Judy Fischer* mp	8.8
June Time lp	7.9
†Kara mp	
Kathy* mr	8.5
Lavender Lace m	7.9
Little Buckaroo mr	8.1
Little Chief* dp	7.2
†Little Curt dr	
Little Fireball* o-r	7.8
Little Flirt rb	7.2
†Little Juan mr	
Little Mike dr	7.4
Little Scotch my	7.6
Little Showoff yb	7.3
Little Sunset* pb	7.0
Lollipop mr	7.9
Lori Nan dp	7.5
†Magic Carrousel rb	
†Magic Dragon dr	
Magic Wand dp	7.0
Marilyn lp	8.3
Mary Adair ab	8.1
Mary Haywood mp	8.0
Mary Marshall* ob	8.7
Midget mr	7.7
Mona Ruth mp	7.8
Mon Petit dp	8.1
Mr. Bluebird m	7.2
†Nancy Hall pb	
New Penny o-r	7.6
Oakington Ruby mr	7.0
Orange Elf ob	7.3
Orange Sunshine* ob	6.7
Over the Rainbow* rb	8.4
Patty Lou pb	7.5
Peachy pb	7.5
Perky dp	7.4
Perla de Alcanada dp 7.1	
Perla de Montserrat pb	7.9
Perla Rosa mp	6.0
Persian Princess* o-r	7.8
Pink Cameo mp	8.7
Pink Frostfire* lp	6.4
Pink Heather lp	7.9
Pink Joy dp	7.9
Pink Ribbon lp	7.4
Pixie w	8.2
Pixie Gold my	7.8
Pixie Rose dp	8.5
Polka Dot w	7.5
Presumida yb	7.1
Prissy Missy mp	6.7
Pumila dp	9.0
Purple Elf m	7.1
Purple Imp* m	6.6
Red Arrow mr	7.9
Red Elf dr	7.5
Red Imp dr	8.4
Red Riding Hood dr	7.5
Red Wand dp	6.8
Rosina my	6.5
Rouletti lp	7.8
Scarlet Gem o-r	8.5
†Shooting Star yb	
Silver Tips pb	7.4
Simplex w	8.0
Starina o-r	9.2
Sweet Fairy lp	8.0
Sweet Vivid mp	8.8
†Tea Party ab	
†Temple Bells w	
Tinker Bell mp	8.5
Tiny Flame* o-r	7.0
Tiny Jack mr	7.3
Tiny Jill mp	7.1
Tom Thumb dr	7.8
Top Secret* mr	8.5
Toy Clown rb	8.6
Trinket mp	7.6
Twinkles w	7.8
Wayside Garnet dr	8.4
Westmont mr	7.5
Whipped Cream* w	7.4
†White Angel w	
White Baby Star w	7.6
White Fairy w	7.0
White King w	6.9
Willie Mae mr	7.7
Willie Winkie	8.2
Yellow Bantam w	7.6
Yellow Doll my	8.3
†Yellow Jewel my	
Yellow Magic* my	7.8
Yellow Necklace my	7.4

CLIMBERS

Aloha mp	6.8
American Pillar rb	7.4
Big Splash* rb	4.7
Blaze mr	7.9
Blossomtime mp	7.8
Cadenza dr	7.9
Casa Blanca* w	8.3
Casino my	7.5
Chevy Chase dr	8.1
Cheyenne lp	6.9
City of York w	8.6
Clair Matin mp	8.0
Cl. Bettina ob	6.8
Cl. Caledonia	5.7
Cl. Cecile Brunner lp	8.0
Cl. Charlotte Armstrong dp	7.6
Cl. Chrysler Imperial dr	7.4
Cl. Circus yb	7.4
Cl. Columbia mp	7.6
Cl. Comtesse Vandal pb	6.8
Cl. Crimson Glory dr	7.7
Cl. Dainty Bess lp	8.2
Cl. Etoile de Hollande mr	7.3
Cl. Floradora o-r	7.4
Cl. Golden Charm dy	5.8
Cl. Goldilocks my	5.7
Cl. Heart's Desire mr	6.4
Cl. Kaiserin Auguste Viktoria w	6.8
Cl. Margo Koster ob	7.8
Cl. Mirandy dr	6.5
Cl. Mme. Henri Guillot rb	7.0
Cl. Mrs. E. P. Thom my	6.6
Cl. Mrs. Henry Morse	6.5
Cl. Mrs. Pierre S. duPont my	5.8
Cl. Mrs. Sam McGredy ob	8.2
Cl. Peace yb	7.3
Cl. Picture lp	7.8
Cl. President Hoover pb	6.3
Cl. Queen Elizabeth mp	7.3
Cl. Queen O'The Lakes mr	7.7
Cl. Radiance lp	6.7
Cl. Red Talisman rb	6.2
Cl. Rose Marie mp	7.1
Cl. Shot Silk pb	7.1
Cl. Show Garden mp	7.9
Cl. Show Girl mp	7.3
Cl. Snowbird w	7.5
Cl. Spartan o-r	7.7
†Cl. Sterling Silver m	
Cl. Summer Snow w	7.6
Cl. Sutter's Gold ob	7.9
Cl. Talisman yb	6.9
Cl. The Doctor mp	6.6
Cl. Tiffany pb	7.2
Cl. Tropicana* ob	8.1
Colonial White w	7.2
†Copenhagen mr	
Coral Dawn mp	7.6
Coralita o-r	6.8
Coral Pillar mp	7.5
Coral Satin mp	7.4
Danny Boy	7.2
Delbard's Orange Climber o-r	5.6
Don Juan dr	8.1
Doubloons my	6.1
Dream Girl pb	6.7
Dr. J. H. Nicholas mp	7.3
Dr. W. VanFleet lp	8.1
Elegance my	7.6
Galway Bay mp	8.1
Gladiator mr	7.8
Glenn Dale w	8.0
Gloire de Dejon pb	7.3
Golden Showers my	7.3
Gold Rush yb	6.4
Handel rb	8.5
Heidelberg mr	8.0
High Noon my	7.0
Iceland Queen	8.7
Ilse Krohn w	5.8
Inspiration mp	7.8
Ivory Charm* w	8.0
Joseph's Coat rb	7.3
Kassel o-r	7.6
Katie mp	7.6
Kitty Kininmonth mp	7.5
Lawrence Johnston	8.0
Mary Wallace mp	7.8
May Queen mp	8.4
Meg ab	7.3
Mercedes Gallart dp	6.3
Morning Dawn lp	7.2
Mme. Gregoire Staechelin rb	8.1
Mrs. Arthur Curtiss James my	7.7
Mrs. Whitman Cross ob	7.4
New Dawn lp	8.4
Orange Beauty ob	7.0
Parade dp	7.9
Paul's Scarlet Climber mr	8.3
Pillar of Fire o-r	5.9
Raymond Chenault mr	7.8
Red Empress mr	7.6
Reviel Dijonnais rb	7.6
Rhonda* mp	8.2
Ritz mr	6.7
†Royal Flush pb	
Royal Gold my	7.4
Royal Lavender m	6.6
Swan Lake* w	7.4
Thor dr	7.3
Viking Queen mp	7.3
White Dawn w	7.0
Wind Chimes mp	7.6
Zeus my	7.3

WINTER PROTECTION

To bring your Miniature Roses through the winter place a mound of soil in the crown of the plant covering the branches about three inches up. Do this mounding in early November, after the plants have gone dormant and before the ground freezes.

In the southern states no winter protection is needed.

PREPARATION FOR INDOOR FORCING

If you should desire to bring your Miniature Roses indoors for winter forcing, it can be done easily. In late September, with the advent of cooler weather, dig up the plants with a ball of soil on the roots and plant them in pots that are about four inches in diameter and four inches deep. Place these pots in a cold frame or well protected spot in the garden. If your ground will not be frozen in early January, replant the potted Miniature, pot and all, until time to bring them indoors. If your ground will be frozen in January, place the potted Miniature Roses in a sheltered spot and when cold weather comes, cover the pots with evergreen boughs, straw, or oak leaves. For your Miniature Rose to force well in the house it is essential to allow it to go dormant out-of-doors and have a rest period in the fall and early winter. These Miniature Roses may be brought into the house for forcing any time after the first of January. Be sure to read carefully the cultural directions for indoor growing.

STEP BY STEP CARE

OUTDOORS:

1. Plant miniatures where they will receive 5 or more hours of sunlight.
2. Space plants about one foot apart.
3. Use regular garden soil for planting.
4. Water well during the growing season.
5. Feed each plant one tablespoon of fertilizer in March, June and July.
6. Cut plants back to about 5 inches in the spring.

INDOORS:

1. Keep plants on a sunny window sill.
2. Place pots in a tray filled with pebbles or sand. Keep the pebbles or sand wet at all times.
3. Water plants every two or three days—keep the soil in the pot moist but not soggy.
4. Feed with a house plant fertilizer once a month.
5. Give plants an eight week rest in the hydrator section of the refrigerator during June and July.
6. After the rest period, cut plants back to about 3 inches and resume normal care. Miniature roses need more air moisture (humidity) than modern home heating systems provide. To solve this problem the pots should be set on the tray of pebbles so that the water evaporating from the tray will raise the humidity around the plants. Yellowing leaves indicate that the air around the plants is too dry.

Under special plant lights like those used for African Violets, miniature roses should receive 18 hours of light each day. Lights should be set just above the tops of the plants.

PLANT FUMIGATOR.

FLORAL REQUISITES.

FLORAL WEEDER.

BOUQUET HOLDER.

SHRUBS

This listing also contains varieties which are not botanically listed as shrubs [most of them are suitable for landscaping needs]. Classification to which the variety belongs immediately follows the variety name. Relative height letter means: 1, low, under 30"; m, medium, 30" to 48"; t, tall, 48" and over.

E - Eglanteria	
HAlba - Hybrid Alba	HNut - Hybrid Nutkana
HBlanda - Hybrid Blanda	HRg - Hybrid Rugosa
HD - Hybrid Damask	HSet - Hybrid Setigera
HGig - Hybrid Gigantea	K - Kordesii
H Moyesii - Hybrid Moyesii	R - Rambler
HMsk - Hybrid Musk	S - Shrub

t Agnes HRg -yb	8.0	Dorothy Perkins R lp	5.9
Alberic Barbier R my	7.0	Dortmund K mr	8.2
Alchymist S	8.4	t Dr. Eckener HRg pb	7.0
Alexander von Humboldt		Eddie's Crimson	
K	6.7	HMoyesii	9.1
Amy Robsart E dp	5.5	t Elmshorn S dp	7.7
Belinda HMsk mp	7.8	Empress Josephine S	7.0
Belle Poitevine HRg		Erfurt HMsk	8.5
mp	7.9	t F. J. Grootendorst	
Berlin HMsk o-r	7.8	HRg mr	7.5
Betty Bland HBlanda	7.2	Flamingo HRg dp	7.8
Bishop Darlington HMsk		Fragrant Beauty S dp	6.6
	8.1	Francesca HMsk ob	6.8
t Blanc Double de Coubert		l Frau Dagmar Hartopp	
HRg w	7.7	HRg mp	8.3
Bloomfield Dainty HMsk		Fresh Pink S lp	8.2
my	6.0	Gartendirektor Otto	
Bonn HMsk o-r	7.6	Linne S dp	9.0
t Buff Beauty HMsk	7.7	Goldbusch E my	7.7
Canary Bird S	6.0	Golden King HRg my	6.7
Catherine Seyton E lp	7.5	mGolden Wings S my	8.2
Celestial S	8.1	t Grandmaster HMsk ab	7.3
Clytemnestra HMsk	7.4	Grootendorst Supreme	
t Conrad Ferdinand Meyer		HRg dr	7.4
HRg lp	7.4	t Hamburger Phoenix K	
Conrad O'Neal S	7.9	mr	7.3
Cornelia HMsk pb	7.9	l Hansa HRg mr	7.8
Coupe de Hebe S	7.2	Hanseat S mp	8.7
Crimson Rambler R mr	6.8	Hebe's Lip E pb	7.9
Crimson Shower R mr	6.6	Hein Muck S dr	4.8
Danae HMsk my	7.8	l Hon. Lady Lindsay S	
Daphne HMsk lp	6.7	pb	7.5
Delicata HRg lp	8.2	Illusion K mr	8.2

Ilse Haberland S mp	7.3	Poulsen's Park Rose	
Karl Forster S w	8.7	S lp	6.9
Karlsruhe K mp	7.7	Prairie Dawn S mp	7.7
Kathleen HMsk lp	7.6	Prairie Fire S mr	7.2
King's Row S yb	5.9	t Prestige S mr	7.4
Lady Curzon HRg mp	9.0	t Prosperity HMsk w	8.1
Lavender Lassie HMsk		Ritter von Barmstede	
m	7.1	K mp	6.9
Lillian Gibson HBlanda		Rose a Parfum de l'Hay	
mp	8.6	HRg mr	7.6
Lord Penzance E	7.5	Rose de Rescht S dp	7.8
Lyric S mp	6.4	Rostock HMsk lp	9.0
l Mabelle Stearns S mp	6.9	Ruskin HRg dr	7.3
Maiden's Blush HAlba		Sangerhausen HMsk	7.2
lp	8.0	Sarah Van Fleet HRg	
Maigold S	8.1	mp	7.9
Mannheim S	8.3	Schneezwerg HRg w	8.1
Marguerite Hilling		l Sea Foam S w	8.2
H Moyessi mp	6.9	t Sir Thomas Lipton	
Max Graf HRg mp	7.6	HRg w	7.2
Meg Merrilles E	7.3	t Sparrieshoop S lp	8.0
t Mentor S mp	7.2	Stadt Rosenheim S o-r	7.3
Mme. Legras de St.		Susan Louise S mp	7.4
Germain HAlba w	8.7	Sympathie K mr	7.3
Mme. Plantier HAlba		Tausendschon R pb	7.7
w	8.0	Therese Bauer HSet mp	7.3
Morgengruss K pb	9.0	Therese Bugnet HRg	
Nevada HMoyesii w	8.1	mp	7.3
Nova Zembla HRg w	9.1	Vanguard HRg ob	7.3
Nymphenburg HMsk		Vanity HMsk	6.7
pb	7.6	Veilchenblau R m	6.6
Ohio S mr	7.8	Violette R m	7.0
Oskar Scheerer S dr	7.3	Von Scharnhorst S w	7.7
t Parkdirektor Riggers		Weisse aus Sparrieshoop	
K dr	7.6	S w	8.3
Pax HMsk w	7.2	Wichmoss R lp	7.0
Pike's Peak S mp	8.6	Will Alderman HRg	7.4
Pink Grootendorst HRg		Will Scarlet HMsk mr	7.5
mp	7.7	t Zitronenfalter S my	6.5
		t Zweibrucken K dr	7.7

OLD GARDEN ROSES

This listing contains varieties which are considered to be old garden roses. Relative height letter means: 1, low, under 30"; m, medium, 30" to 48"; t, tall, 48" and over. Classification to which the variety belongs immediately follows the variety name.

A - Alba	HFt - Hybrid Foetida
B - Bourbon	HP - Hybrid Perpetual
C - Centifolia	HSpn - Hybrid Spinosissima
Ch - China	M - Moss
D - Damask	N - Noisette
G - Gallics	T - Tea

Alfred Colomb HP	5.3	†Crested Jewel M mp	
Alfred de Dalmas M lp	6.8	Desiree Parmentier G lp	6.2
American Beauty HP		Deuil De Paul Fontaine	
dp	7.1	M rb	6.5
Arrillaga HP mp	7.7	Duc de Guiche G m	7.4
Baroness Rothchild HP		Duchesse de Brabant T	
lp	7.1	mp	7.1
Baron Girod de l'Ain		Duchess of Sutherland	
HP rb	7.8	HP lp	7.4
Baronne Prevost HP mp	8.3	Everest HP w	6.4
Belle Amour lp	6.9	Fantin-Latour C lp	8.3
Belle Des Jardins G m	7.1	Felberg's Rosa Druschki	
Belle Isis G	5.6	Hp mp	7.4
Black Prince HP dr	6.0	Ferdinand Pichard HP	
Blanchefleur C	7.5	rb	7.3
Blanche Moreau M w	6.7	Frau Karl Druschki HP	
Blue Boy C m	6.3	w	7.5
Camaieux G rb	7.5	Fruhlingsduft HSpn pb	7.0
Candeur Lyonnaise HP		Fruhlingsanfang HSpn	
w	6.4	w	7.5
Captain Hayward HP		Fruhlingsgold HSpn my	8.7
dp	6.9	Fruhlingsmorgan HSpn	
Cardinal de Richelieu		mp	8.0
G m	7.3	Fruhlingszauber HSpn	8.6
Catherine Mermet T lp	7.2	Gabriel Noyelle M pb	7.7
Celsiana D lp	8.5	Geant de Batailles HP	
Charles De Mills G mr	8.0	mr	6.6
Chloris A lp	7.3	General Jacqueminot	
Clio HP lp	7.7	HP mr	6.9
Commandant Beaurepaire		General Kleber M	7.6
B pb	7.1	Georg Arends HP lp	7.3
Communis M mp	8.9	Gloire de Gullan D mr	7.7
Comtesse de Murinais M		Gloire de Mousseaux M	
lp	7.5	mp	8.1
Coquette de Alpes B w	7.9	Golden Moss M my	6.6

HOW TO GROW, PRESERVE, & SELL — EVERLASTING FLOWERS

"Everlasting Flowers" are those varieties of flowers which hold their shape and color when dried. By the easy magic of preserving flowers, all seasons are as one. The delicate color and perfect of a flower need not fade with the summer season. Nothing can bring greater joy to a heavy heart during winter than a bouquet of dried flowers. There are several varieties of flowers suitable for drying, the best being Gomphrena, Helichrysum, Statice, Xeranthemum, Acroclinum, Honesty, and Yellow Yarrow.

CULTURAL REQUIREMENTS FOR THE ABOVE VARIETIES OF EVERLASTING FLOWERS: They all need well-drained soils of average fertility. High nitrogen fertilizers must be avoided because they promote fast, soft growth. This results in weak flower stems and blooms of poor color that are slow to dry. On the other hand fertilizers that are desirable are potash and phosphates which induce plants to produce sturdy stems, and flowers with intense, bright colors. In addition, these plants should be grown in an area that is exposed to full sun; shaded areas grow plants that give blooms with inferior colors and poor conformation.

These flowers are sown and grown like any annual flower variety. The soil should be deep spaded or rototilled, then worked down into a fine seed bed. The ground is now ready to be sown with seeds. Make straight, shallow furrows spaced 18 to 20 inches apart and the seeds planted ½ inch deep, then covered. When the seedlings begin to emerge, start thinning plants so that they stand 4-inch apart in order that they have ample room to develop into large productive plants.

FLOWERS ARE READY TO CUT when they just come into full bloom, and never in an over-ripe condition. Harvesting should be done on a dry, sunny morning after the dew has dried off from the blooms. When cutting, take as much of the stem as possible. This will induce young developing stalks emerging from the base of the plant to grow rapidly and produce secondary crops of flowers. As the flowers are cut and harvested, they are gathered in small loose bunches, tied and taken indoors to process.

IN PROCESSING EVERLASTING FLOWERS FOR DRYING, place them on a table, untie each bunch, then individually take the stems and strip off their leaves. Flowers are segregated according to size and varieties, then gathered and tied into bouquets to be hung and dried. A point to note is that small flowers should be tied in tight bundles and hung head down. Flowers that produce large blooms should be hung singly, head down. Flowers dried by hanging will be ready in 10 days to two weeks. Drying is done in a room with a good circulation so that the plant moisture is removed rapidly and thus prevent molding. Bunched flowers are hung from the ceiling or rafters, well separated from each other for air circulation. While drying, flowers should be protected from direct sunlight to prevent blooms from fading.

DRIED FLOWER BOUQUETS are arranged so that the colors produce a harmonious effect. Always place the longer stemmed flowers on the outer circle of the bouquet with the shorter stems towards the center. Colors that are the same should be arranged in concentric rings around the bouquet. As each bouquet is made, wrap it in a cello-bag to protect flower heads from dust and shattering.

PRESERVING FLOWERS WITH A DRYING AGENT, such as silica gel, a commercial compound, has greatly widened the varieties of flowers that can be dried. It is light in weight, flows easily, which makes it easy to surround all parts of the flower for fast drying. In 2 or 3 days it will dry flowers that might take 10 to 15 days to dry, and what is more important, flowers not suited to air-drying can now be dried through the silica-gel compound. Hard-to-dry flowers like the rose, pansy, daisy, zinnia, violet, delphinium, etc., make good dried flowers with the use of silica-gel. Additional flower varieties adapted to drying by the use of silica-gel, are asters, Bells-of-Ireland, Marigolds, Scarlet Sage, Snapdragon, Euphorbia, Feverfew, Gerbera, Hollyhock, Lily-of-the-valley, Passionflower, tulip, Azaleas, Bayberry, Dogwood, Forsythia, Lilac, Queen Anne's Lace, Artemisia, Bee-Balm, Bachelor button, Cat-tail. As you gain experience you will find scores of other flower varieties that can be dried with good results.

In our writing to our most successful growers of dried flowers, we came to the following conclusions:

1. The best prospects for selling dried flower bouquets are gift shops, flower stores, garden stores, super-markets, and variety stores.

2. Sell for cash. Where the buyer is reluctant to buy, you can offer to place the dried flower bouquets in his store on a consignment basis. This way he pays only for those dried flowers that he sells. Where the dried flowers are sold outright for cash, they are sold at a wholesale price where the merchant makes a 40% profit. In the case of consignment selling, buyers should be willing to sell on a 25% mark-up profit. They have no money tied up in merchandise nor have they any risk involved.

3. When you go into a store to open a new account, this is your opportunity to use salesmanship which is essential in making a good impression. One of our customers who built a good business selling dried flower bouquets takes into a store two or three dozen bouquets. This not only creates an impression on the store buyer but also on the customers who see them. The "oohs" and "ahs" of exclamations from those who see all these dried flower bouquets, does much to cinch a sale.

4. In your sales presentation, point out to the buyer that you are a local grower and will be able to give him good service and stand behind whatever you sell. Always stress quality; never sell on the basis of cutting prices. Tell your customer that dried flower bouquets will keep for years, and that they are particularly welcome during winter when fresh flowers are scarce and expensive. Make regular periodic calls on stores that have bought from you. This way you will not miss out on any sales if the dried flower bouquets are sold out.

Ornamental corns and gourds make good companion items to sell right along with dried flower bouquets. If you have built up a good reputation as a reliable person, your customers will have confidence to buy other items from you.

DRYONEX - A silica-gel product that dries flowers the foolproof way. There is no mess, no trouble, no odor. The flowers come out beautiful, brilliant, and as natural as if fresh picked from the garden. Use it as often as you want. Once it has taken up its limit in moisture, by just warming it a few minutes in the oven it is as good as new. No end to the flowers you can dry.

"NEW TECHNIQUES WITH EVERLASTING FLOWERS" a good book for those interested in more detailed information.

Nichols Garden Nursery
1190 North Pacific Hwy
Albany, Oregon 97321

Double Violet

Flower DRI®
SILICA GEL FOR DRYING FLOWERS

1 Pour **FLOWER-DRI** into a cake tin or other sealable container to a depth of 2". Cut stems to length of 2" and insert flowers face up. Space them so they are not touching.

2 Sprinkle **FLOWER-DRI** over flowers until completely covered, gently working it up and around them so contact is made on all parts of the flowers.

3 Cover cake tin or other container with tight top and seal it with freezer or masking tape. Put it away for 2 to 8 days*—in a place where the contents will not be disturbed.

* See section on TIMING

4 To remove flowers, pour off mixture slowly until they are uncovered. Lift out gently and blow away any particles that adhere. **Complete removal of dust with an artist's brush is recommended.**

5 Store flowers away from light in a sealed air-tight container, to which has been added three tablespoons of **FLOWER-DRI**. This storing will keep the flowers from wilting so long as warm humid weather persists.

6 When you are ready to make your arrangement, attach to the short flower stem a length of medium weight florists' wire by spiral-wrapping it with green floral tape.

TIMING:

Flowers dry in **FLOWER-DRI** in anywhere from two to eight days, depending on the texture and maturity of the flower. For instance, the whole stalk of snapdragon is heavy and requires eight days, while zinnias do best if left in **FLOWER-DRI** two or three days. Flowers left in the mixture too long tend to fall apart; not long enough and they take on a crumpled look when exposed to air. Most importantly, if the flowers feel **crisp** they are usually dry. At this point they should be removed from the mixture but allowed to remain on **top of it** in a sealed box for another two or three days.

When blue disappears, maximum moisture content of **FLOWER-DRI** has been reached. Place mixture in heat-proof container in 250° oven. When blue color returns, **FLOWER-DRI** is ready to use again.

THINGS TO REMEMBER:

★ Pick flowers to preserve on a warm, sunny day, never just after a rain.

★ Select them at the **peak of bloom** in prime condition when rich in color—never when faded and shedding petals. For interesting variety in your arrangements, dry materials in the various stages of growth, from buds to mature blooms.

★ Dry flowers as soon as possible after cutting to preserve color. When dry, remove any adhering **FLOWER-DRI** with an artist's brush.

★ When the humidity level is high, store preserved flowers in an air-tight container as described in General Information.

★ Flowers, when dried, are crisp and should be handled with care. Should you break off a petal, apply a clear adhesive and replace.

PLANTABBS CORPORATION · TIMONIUM, MARYLAND 21093

GENERAL INFORMATION
Please Read Carefully Before Drying Flowers

The principle of drying flowers is to remove all the moisture and still retain as much of the natural color and form as possible. Since the texture of flowers varies, some will dry better than others. Flowers such as Tulips and Daffodils have an almost transparent texture when dried, whereas with flowers such as Roses and Zinnias, with more substance, the texture doesn't change appreciably. Of course, you must expect a certain amount of shrinkage to occur in the process of preserving flowers because all the moisture is removed.

As with the texture variations in flowers, so it is with color—some flowers when preserved will retain their natural color, even as vivid as when the plant was growing. White flowers when dried tend to be more cream than white, but Candytuft, Feverfew and Virburnum Maries) are excellent for drying and appear almost snow-White. You must remember, however, that all colors fade, some more quickly than others as with rugs and draperies. But the fading is so gradual you do not become aware of it. The flowers seem to "age" and the colors become more subtle and blend together. Preserved flowers will lose their color very rapidly if exposed to direct sunlight or if placed in a brightly lighted room. Experience with preserving flowers will help you appreciate these variations in texture, color and form.

Experiment with your **FLOWER-DRI** and try many kinds of flowers and foliage. You will even find that some flowers will dry in just a few days. Do not be discouraged if your first efforts fall somewhat short of expectations. Try again. Have patience and the end results should be most rewarding.

The foliage of your flowers may also be preserved. Follow directions for drying flowers, leave only a small stem, and place the leaves flat in the container, covering gently to preserve the natural form of the leaf. In preserving foliage, you will find as with flowers, some foliage is better than others. English Laurel, Elaeagnus, Butterfly Bush and Rose foliage dry extremely well. Dusty Miller is excellent material to combine with your preserved flowers and even though it can be dried by hanging upside down, you will be amazed at the difference when it is done with **FLOWER-DRI**. It will be as fresh-looking as when growing with each tiny bloom and bud in true form. Also, the lovely color of the grey-white is preserved.

Coping with humidity is an important factor to consider in any known method of drying. Some flowers are very susceptible to atmospheric conditions because of their porous nature which still exists after preserving. Flowers with a light texture such as Tulips, Daffodils and Azaleas will dry beautifully, but have a tendency to wilt in humid atmosphere. To overcome this difficulty, you should store all your flowers as soon as they are dried in an air-tight container to which has been added about three tablespoons of **FLOWER-DRI**. Wide-mouth gallon size glass jars are excellent for this purpose. Humidity will not only cause some flowers to wilt, but also will cause the color to fade. When humid weather no longer persists, remove the flowers and make a winter bouquet. You need no longer be concerned with excessive humidity because the warmth of your home should keep the flowers dry.

Italian Philadelphus

Fig. 68.—Case for preserving flowers fresh.

Fig. 63.—Fern Stand.

Many flower'd Snowdrop.

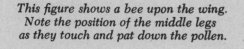

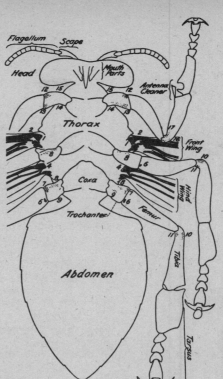

This figure shows a bee upon the wing. Note the position of the middle legs as they touch and pat down the pollen.

This diagram of the under side of a worker bee details its anatomy. The numbers refer to the location of groups of olfactory pores. Odors perceived by these organs serve as signals that motivate behavior.

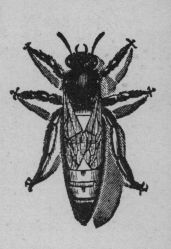

Some Facts About Bees

You'll get better production from your bees (and they'll be happier) if you know how they operate. Here are some vital facts reported by two authors from South Carolina and Texas.

CLARENCE M. LARSON AND WARD L. GOSSETT

Courtesy of Organic Gardening and Farming, Emmaus, Pa. 18049

THE BODY of an adult bee is divided into three sections — head, thorax and abdomen.

The head has a pair of "feelers" (antennae) and two large compound eyes, one on each side as well as three simple eyes, usually located on top of the head between the compound eyes. The compound eyes are composed of a very large number of distinct sections (facets) each of which is a separate lens, functioning independent of the other. The bee can see everywhere and everything at the same time.

The main mouth-parts of the bee are odified for sucking and consist of a long hollow tube, the tongue, through which the nectar is sucked and drawn back to a special storage sac (crop) in the abdominal region where it is converted into honey.

The thorax bears two pairs of wings, and serves as a point of attachment for the three pairs of legs. The wings are hooked together, but they can be unhooked by the bee and slid over each other. This makes it easier for the bee to move around inside the flowers as it collects pollen and nectar and in the cells of the hives. The legs are all covered with hairs that pick up the pollen. The front legs may have a hooklike device used to clean the antennae. The hind legs may have its middle section flattened to serve as a pollen basket. It may also have rows of bristle-like hairs, pollen combs, to gather up the pollen picked up on the bee's body and legs. There are

spurs on its legs to pull off the wax that the bee secretes. A nervous system runs through the interior of the body, as well as a muscle system which makes movement possible.

The queen carries a small internal sac (spermathaca) where she places the only supply of sperm she receives in the one mating flight of her entire life.

When the young queen leaves the hive on a mating flight, she is followed by numerous drones. The drones do nothing useful in the hive except fertilize the queen, which is accomplished by only a few — seven or eight drones who mate with the queen before she returns to the hive. All of the mating is done in mid-air. Each drone dies after mating. On this one flight, the queen receives a supply of sperm large enough to fertilize the eggs she will lay for the rest of her

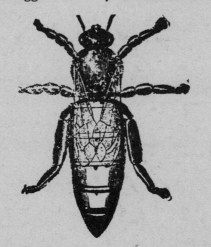

life. The queen lives for several years (ordinarily three to five years) and lays from a few hundred to several thousand eggs per day, except in late fall or winter when she will lay no eggs at all.

A bee on a foraging trip can carry one five thousandths of an ounce in its honey sac. Some 20 to 30 percent of this will evaporate. Averaging 600 to 800 trips per hour, it takes about 30,000 foraging trips and visits to countless numbers of flowers to gather and store one pound of honey.

Meanwhile, the bees have a "directional dance," reports Captain Richard Shuey of Randolph Air Force Base, Texas, "which will lead other bees to the source of pollen. When one bee finds an abundance of pollen-bearing flowers, he comes back to the hive and performs a circular dance relative to the sun's location and the distance from the hive, directing the other bees to his source."

The bee that finds the pollen will go from one fellow bee to another in order to "pass the word," says Shuey, in a real team effort.

In order to increase his knowledge about the bees, Shuey has attached a glass observation hive to his back door window where he can watch them work 24 hours a day.

In explaining the insects' habits, he notes they normally settle down during the nighttime hours. "But from sunrise to sunset there is constant movement," he said. "Also, their cleanliness is surprising. When a bee dies, it isn't long before the other members carry him away."

Shuey also pointed out that many fruit tree owners will either keep bees around or rent them to help in pollination. And he reports, some crops such as cucumbers and cantaloupes are pollinated almost exclusively by bees.

"Bees are nice in their own way," he declared. "They mind their own

business and usually won't bother you unless you kick the hive or aggravate them. In my work, I've been stung several times, even through my gloves. But I've learned how to keep the stings from affecting me."

The bee's stinger is made of a calcium-like material with the texture of a fingernail. At the end of the stinger near the body, is a poison sack which is opened when the bee stings. It's quite possible to avoid the worst part of a bee sting by brushing the bee away from your skin or clothing, whatever the case may be, instead of swatting. If you swat the insect, you only succeed in pushing the stinger

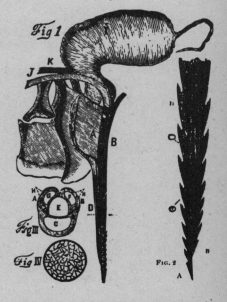

This is why a sting can really hurt.

deeper into the skin and releasing the full contents of the poison sack. If you brush the insect away, it's possible to pull the stinger out and avoid most of the poison. The stinger's average length is one-eighth of an inch, Shuey reports.

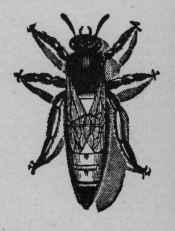

BOOKS ABOUT BEES

BEES, THEIR VISION, CHEMICAL SENSES, AND LANGUAGE
by Karl Von Frisch — Discoveries of remarkable sensory capacities and behavioral patterns in bees. Excellent.
.... $2.45

BEEKEEPING — HOW TO

FIRST LESSONS IN BEEKEEPING
by C. P. Dadant (revised edition). Reliable guide to information about bees, hives, producing honey, etc. Paper cover.
130 pages $1.00

BEEKEEPING
by J. E. Eckert and Frank Shaw. A successor to E. F. Phillips' book of the same name brought up-to-date on all phases of bees and beekeeping. Cloth cover.
540 pages $12.50

THE COMPLETE GUIDE TO BEEKEEPING
by Roger A. Morse — A very practical and complete guide to beekeeping.
.... $6.95

QUEEN REARING
by L. E. Snelgrove. Covers all phases of queen rearing. Cloth cover.
344 pages $5.00

QUEEN REARING
by H. H. Laidlaw, Jr. and J. E. Eckert. Thorough queen rearing book giving modern methods. Cloth cover.
165 pages $6.95

QUEEN INTRODUCTION
by L. E. Snelgrove. Well written and authentic. Cloth cover.
200 pages $2.50

SWARMING AND ITS CONTROL
by L. E. Snelgrove. A thorough study of the subject. Cloth cover.
100 pages $2.75

ABC & XYZ OF BEE CULTURE
by A. I. & E. R. Root. A complete encyclopedia. Arranged alphabetically. Cloth.
712 pages $6.50

THE NATURAL HEALTH FOOD

FOLK MEDICINE
by D. C. Jarvis. Includes 30 pages on healthfulness of honey. Stresses honey for health. Paper cover.
180 pages .... $ .95

ARTHRITIS AND FOLK MEDICINE
by D. C. Jarvis. Popular views of Vermont Doctor on honey and vinegar for arthritis. Paper cover.
144 pages .... $ .75

THE HIVE AND THE HONEYBEE

THE Reference Work on Bees

Used by leading Colleges and Universities as a textbook.

Has been translated into three additional languages — German, Italian and Russian.

Cloth Bound — 556 pages.
Hundreds of pictures, over 700 references
Edited by — Roy A. Grout

A collection of world famous beekeeping authorities contributed from their field of speciality to produce this excellent, complete, classic reference book of all phases of bees and beekeeping. Twenty chapters cover all the aspects of beekeeping from history of beekeeping through equipment, management, anatomy and behavior, pollination, disease, honey and honey processing, honey plants, beeswax and pesticide poisoning. This is a book no serious student of bees should be without. And, because of its wide popularity it can be sold at a very attractive price.

The Hive and the Honey Bee postpaid $6.75.

HONEY FOR HEALTH
by Cecil Tonsley. A complete guide to one of Nature's greatest life-giving foods. Paper cover.
125 pages .... $ .95

SOMETHING DIFFERENT

HONEY PLANTS MANUAL
by Harvey B. Lovell. A practical field manual for identifying honey flora.
60 pages $1.25

BEE HUNTING
by John R. Lockhard. For finding bee trees. Paper cover.
72 pages .... $ .70

IN SEARCH OF THE BEST STRAINS OF BEES
by Br. Adam. Interesting story of travels and observations by author. Paper.
128 pages $3.50

PETER AND THE BEES
by Peter Brem. Hard back. Finely illustrated story of bees for children.
60 pages, 8 by 9½ inches $2.80

INSECT POLLINATION OF CROPS
by J.B. Free — A masterful presentation of the honey bee's role in world pollination needs.
.... $24.50

BEES, WONDER STARTER SERIES
Introduces young children to the delights of the fascinating world of the honey bee.
.... $ .69

COOKING WITH HONEY

HONEY COOK BOOK
by Juliette Elkon. Excellent. 250 recipes. Cloth cover.
250 pages $5.95

HONEY RECIPES
Gems of Gold with Honey. By California Honey Advisory Board. Paper.
34 pages .... $ .35

HONEY RECIPE BOOK
By Marketing Division, Iowa Department of Agriculture. Paper cover. In color.
36 pages .... $ .50

HONEY COOKERY
by A. G. Woodman. Paper 16 pages of bee lore. Honey facts, more than 40 recipes.
Attractively priced .... $ .15

THE POOH COOK BOOK
by Virginia Ellison. Delightful children's honey recipes with quotations from Pooh Bear stories. Cloth cover.
120 pages $4.50

COOKING WITH HONEY
by Hazel Berto — Novel and exciting ways to use honey to make dishes more enticing.
.... $4.95

THE FASCINATING BEE

THE DANCING BEES
by Karl von Frisch. Detailed report by German scientist on how the bees "dance" to communicate location of nectar. Paper cover.
179 pages $3.25

A BEE IS BORN
by H. Doering. A complete study with 100 enlargements by a noted photographer and naturalist. Cloth cover.
96 pages $3.50

ANATOMY OF THE HONEY BEE
by R. E. Snodgrass. Authoritative 1956 revision. Cloth cover.
330 pages $14.50

HONEY BEE - McGraw Hill Study Prints
In full color, marvelous, suitable for framing. Twelve, 13 by 18". Includes honeycomb, food gathering and sharing. Fanning, queen, egg laying, brood, queen cells, drones, swarming, beekeeper. Brand new and fascinating!
12 prints $15.00

THE BEE LANGUAGE CONTROVERSY
by Adrian Wenner — A process of thought and design dealing with the bee language hypothesis. Paper.
109 pages $2.95

UNITED STATES DEPARTMENT OF AGRICULTURE
Agricultural Research Service

Publications dealing with HONEY BEES available from the Superintendent of Documents, U.W. Government Printing Office, Washington, D.C. 20402

Beekeeping in the United States, 1971, Agriculture Handbook 335
Instrumental Insemination of Queen Bees, 1970, Agriculture Handbook 390
Composition of American Honeys, 1962, Technical Bulletin 1261
Selecting and Operating Beekeeping Equipment, 1969, Farmers' Bulletin 2204
Controlling the Greater Wax Moth, 1972, Farmers' Bulletin 2217
Identifying Bee Diseases in the Apiary, 1967, Agriculture Information Bulletin No. 313
Protecting Honey Bees from Pesticides, 1972, Leaflet 544
A Cloth Strainer for Honey Conditioning Systems, 1966, Production Research Report 90
Beekeeping for Beginners, 1971, Home & Garden Bulletin 158
Using Honey Bees to Pollinate Crops, 1968, Leaflet 549

FIG. 252. — Bees visiting Flowers.

At the left a bumblebee on the flower of the dead nettle; below a similar bee in the flower of the horse-chestnut; above a honey-bee in the flower of a violet.

LAWNS

CULTIVATED VARIETIES (Cultivars)

BLUEGRASSES

Bluegrass is the premier sod-forming species for cool climate lawns. It is easily cared for, but 'prefers' good soil, occasional fertilization, and sun or light shade. Listed below are some outstanding Kentucky bluegrass *cultivars* which are dense and attractive, and tolerant of most diseases (or are strongly recuperative).

Adelphi (1)	*Fylking (11)*	*Nugget (7)*
Arboretum (4)	*Galaxy (12)*	*Pennstar (6)*
Arista (2)	*Glade (11)*	*Prato (5)*
Baron (3)	*Majestic (3)*	*Sodco (9)*
Bonnieblue (10)	*Merion (8)*	*Sydsport (10)*

Note: The code numbers in parentheses refer to the corresponding numbered suppliers listed at the end of this article.

FESCUES

Fine fescues are excellent companions in bluegrass mixtures, as well as proving durable in shade and on infertile or droughty soils. *Highlight, Jamestown* and *Koket* are very full and dense fescue while *Ruby* is less dense and spreading.

Highlight (2)	*Koket (10)*
Jamestown (3)	*Ruby (5)*

BENTGRASSES

The *bentgrass* clan, spreading by surface runners (stolons), provides the world's most elegantly dense and fine-textured turf. Colonial *bents* require less care than creeping or velvet ones, but all species are favored by humid climates, frequent (low) mowing, and perhaps seasonal thatch removal.

Emerald (2)	*Holfior (5)*
Exeter (3)	*Kingstown (3)*
Highland (8)	*Penncross (8)*

RYEGRASSES

The new "turf-type" perennial *ryegrasses* are the current rave among lawngrass cultivars, just as good looking as is bluegrass and with improved winter hardiness. They make cover quickly, and are great in mixtures for early establishment and cover. Given care like bluegrass, they are excellent for athletic fields and play turf; they do best where winters are mild, summers cool.

Compas (2)	*NK-200 (5)*
Manhattan (12)	*Pelo (5)*
NK-100 (1 & 5)	*Pennfine (6)*

Even now, as you look out your window at your landscape, fresh grass shoots are already forming deep in your turf, spring's annual promise for another growing season. In the far South, st. augustine and bahia . . . some zoysia, centipede and bermuda . . . will not have been really dormant all winter. And by March, bluegrasses, fescues, perennial ryegrasses and bentgrasses, those lawn dandies for the border states and northward, await just a touch of warm weather to overtop scorched winter foliage with a mantle of resplendent green. "All systems are go" come spring-time.

Some lawn-care workers, with foresight, will have anticipated this urge for spring action with preliminary autumn care that stands the lawn in good stead for spring — things like late fall fertilization, overseeding and the scratching out of thatch that impedes access of lawn-care conditioners to the soil and root-zone. If not previously tended to, lawn equipment should be serviced and put into top-notch condition because the greatest seasonal need for mowing, trimming and sprucing-up is just around the corner. Supplies of fertilizer, weed preventers, and such pest controls as may be needed, should be stockpiled ahead of necessity.

True, for the northern grasses — the bluegrasses, fescues, perennial ryegrasses and bentgrasses — some of the most healthful growing months are now behind you, during which threat of leafspot and similar disease was negligible even to highly stimulated turf; but there is still much that can be accomplished. In fact it is usually easier to find the needed supplies and new models of equipment in spring than in autumn. The lawn-care industry recognizes people's readiness, in spring, to "get busy" outdoors after a dreary winter, while in autumn they are lackadaizical about such things after the surfeit of a full season's gardening.

SPRING LAWN PREPARATION

- ● pest control
- ● booster seeding
- ● equipment needs
- ● turf construction

by Robert W. Schery, Director
THE LAWN INSTITUTE

I call attention particularly to the many new varieties of lawngrasses, seed of which is now becoming available following clean-up and packaging of the 1973 seed crop, which could not have been readied for market in time for last autumn's sowing. Listings of prominent varieties of the major lawn species, with a few comments about their use, are given at the end of this article.

FERTILIZER IS IMPORTANT

Through the bleak months of winter, biological activity in the soil has been slow, but not at a stand-still . . . and meanwhile the lawngrass has been all but inactive, absorbing nutrient supplies (released through mineralization) very little. So there should be enough "nutrient power," for initial stimulation, still available in the soil. This won't last long, however, and a feeding before spring is much advanced is certainly in order. I like the long-life fertilizers for this time of year, such as ones containing a sizable amount of ureaform nitrogen (e.g., Nitroform). Because of a rain-soaked 1973 over much of the eastern United States, soluble nutrients will doubtless have been rather thoroughly leached from the soil. The need for fertilization well may be intensified in many areas, and the long-lasting products especially appropriate this year. Fertilizers tailored to release nutrients *gradually* won't overstimulate bluegrass and its companion species. This is great, because excessive new growth draws heavily upon carbohydrate reserves that the grass accumulated during autumn, and grass forced to abundant, lush foliage (which is quickly mowed off *before* producing much food itself) drains the turf of its vitality. Northern grasses may even die out if mowed close suddenly as hot weather arrives. Almost certainly, less carbohydrate will be manufactured than consumed.

LAWN PESTS

Now is the time of year to plan for pest control, too. Many lawns have a history of troublesome crabgrass, and because of the rainy 1973, crabgrass may be a special problem this year, having flourished on last summer's moisture, producing abundant seed. This carry-over seed in the lawn will be off to a fast start once the soil warms to around 60 degrees F. (typically, from March in border states to as late as June in northern locations). A number of excellent crabgrass preventers are available — products like *Azak, Balan, Betasan, Dacthal* and *Tupersan* — which can be spread as a protective blanket over the lawn before crabgrass weather arrives.

When using such preventers, follow exactly the rates advised on the bag; formulations vary, and each must be used as directed for adequate performance. Most weed preventers have a useful life, once applied, of at least six weeks. They should be spread at least two weeks before crabgrass is likely to begin sprouting. Once crabgrass seedlings have begun growing (and you may not notice them as young plants in the lawn), it is late for a preemergence herbicide to do its job.

You may think you have safely passed the crabgrass crisis, since bluegrass looks so good in spring (and indeed, thick lawns of modern lawn varieties will of themselves do much to hold crabgrass in check) . . . but hot weather and some thinning in late summer can let even a few crabgrass plants spread into disruptive mats. Then you have to turn to arsonate (AMA, DSMA) sprays, applied at least twice, at weekly intervals, in order to check crabgrass, foxtail and other annual species.

Of course, crabgrass is a sun-loving weed, so you will not find it growing in shaded parts of the lawn. It is necessary to use a crabgrass preventer only on those sunny sections of lawn where crabgrass has been noted in previous years. One other caution — crabgrass preventers were developed mainly for northern lawns. Although they may often prove of some help in the South, *Tupersan* (siduron) at least proves very damaging to bermudagrass. Of the several preventers, only siduron will not interfere with the emergence of a new seeding. By and large, crabgrass preventers are for *established* lawns, or lawns in which young grass has already gained a good start.

BOOSTER SEEDING

Many lawns benefit from an overseeding to fill-in thin turf, or to introduce some of the new low-growing and disease-resistant varieties into turfs of ordinary grass. Formerly, this was a massive undertaking, requiring laborious tearing-up of the lawn. New seedings are still most satisfactorily made to cultivated soil — the normal way to plant a lawn on messed-up ground such as is left following construction operations.

Today, scarifying and thinning machines designed for lawn renovation can often be rented, if not used sufficiently often to merit purchase. Some of the larger units not only thin the sod and make slits into the soil, but "plant" the seed as well, and firm the ground behind the planting. These machines are more for professional use than for the homeowner, and in many areas, can be hired for custom service.

For smaller operations, powered thinning machines and dethatchers not much bigger than a lawn mower are available. These slice into the congested turf, opening it enough for bolster seeding. In most cases, it is well to set these machines (presuming they are sufficiently powered) low enough to slice shallowly into the soil, and then the turf should be gone over a second time at right angles to the first thinning so that niches, into which new seed can settle, are ample. However, if your lawn contains acceptable grass and is relatively free of weeds, you might want to thin and de-thatch

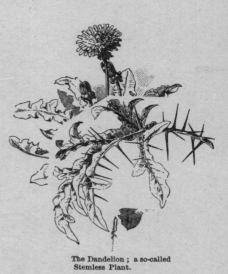

The Dandelion ; a so-called Stemless Plant.

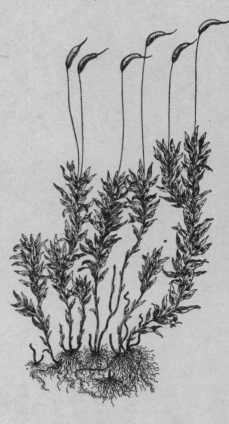

Reprint from
RESORT MANAGEMENT
Volume 28, Number 1

Lawn preparation / *continued*

only lightly. In this case, overseeding is mainly insurance that grass candidates will be at hand where weeds might otherwise arise in thinnish turf.

Normally the use of a thinning machine kicks a lot of duff (thatch) to the surface. This may impede spreading the seed, and generally "gets in the way." We suggest raking or sweeping up the detritus, and using it to mulch shrub beds or borders. In extreme cases, where the lawn contains very little satisfactory grass, a knock-down chemical treatment might well precede scarification. This will set back tough vegetation sufficiently so that it is not so likely to overwhelm the new seedlings. One hesitates to suggest what chemicals should be used for this purpose since label clearance has not been obtained for homeowner-usage with some of the better chemicals, and state laws vary in their restrictiveness. At least in farming communities, such materials are available, being used for no-tillage corn, for example. The herbicides will brown-back all green vegetation treated, but are inactivated by the soil so that seeding can proceed immediately. Paraquat, cacodylic acid, glyphosate or similar materials may or may not be available to you locally.

MAINTENANCE AIDS

Equipment for maintaining the lawn becomes better perfected each passing year. Underground sprinkling systems, for example, made of plastic and inexpensively installed (even by an inexperienced owner), are becoming more and more used, even where dryness is only brief and seasonal. Of course in arid regions, such as the Southwest and the high plains around Denver, irrigation is essential.

It is not possible to review irrigation systems at any length here, but be certain before installing an underground system that pressure and coverage are adequate to provide all parts of the lawn with the needed water. Larger installations should be engineered professionally, but sometimes it is possible to lay out a smaller home lawn system on the ground; test it for coverage, and then bury it in slit trenches that disturb the grass very little. Automatic control boxes are available for most set-ups, which can be programmed to activate sprinkling, progressively unit by unit, at any time of day or night, for a chosen span of time.

A STUDY FOR LAWN-PLANTING.

The proliferation of mowing equipment is a delight. Choice ranges from inexpensive push mowers to elaborate riding vehicles that cut a 72-inch swath (or wider, if wing units are attached). The larger machines are mainly for golf courses, but it is nice to have heavy-duty rotary machines available for swards receiving only ordinary care. These can handle both rough ground that is mowed only infrequently and normal well-kept lawns.

MOWER FEATURES

It is gratifying that modern mower design provides for a good range of cutting heights, so that the machines can be adapted to almost any type of grass or situation. By and large, reel machines are preferred for neatest cut and are especially used for low-growing turfs such as bentgrass, bermudagrass or zoysia. However reels are not so versatile, nor able to approach so closely to obstruction as most rotary machines. A good rotary mower, its blades sharpened from time to time, mows acceptably and is especially useful for higher clipping on less intensively maintained turf.

Keep in mind that as spring growth reaches a crescendo from late April into June, mower down-time can prove fatal. Have sturdy equipment in good repair ready, and with sufficient capacity to get mowing done quickly and easily. Mowing demands will lessen come summer, but during spring, you may have to cover your grounds completely each four or five days for them to remain attractive, and for the grass not to "get ahead" of the mowing (leaving stemmy clippings too lengthy to settle into the sod).

Well-built riding mowers, including garden tractors with belly-mount PTO mowers, are quite the thing nowadays for lawns of intermediate size. Most are equipped with broad, flotation-type tires that let you get out with relative impunity on soft ground so prevalent during spring. Mowers with hydrostatic drive let you go forward or backward at whatever speed you choose, under control of a single lever; this is especially advantageous for the slow trimming required around trees, and over unusually tough grass, while still permitting a "wide open" pace on the straightaway.

No mower is impervious to occasional breakdown and need for repairs. So, choose a product for which maintenance service is available and reliable in your area, and don't skimp on quality when purchasing a machine. Nothing is more frustrating at the height of the mowing season than to have to wait days for service or parts where equipment is not backed up by good service. If you are remote from service facilities, it's not a bad idea to have back-up equipment at hand in case of failure with the main unit.

SOWING NEW TURF

If you want to replant the lawn completely, nothing beats plowing under the old turf, raking up any chunks of sod or other debris which may surface. Mix fertilizer into the soilbed during cultivation. Fertilizer rich in phosphate is suggested, for phosphorus applied later at the surface is fixed by the soil and takes quite a while to work down into the root-zone. For small areas, a rotary tiller may suffice to churn the soil, although rotary tillage does not bury vegetation as well as does moldboard plowing. You are apt to find old sod clumps protruding all over the lawn. Preferably, these should be removed by raking, so that the new turf will be entirely of the type being seeded.

A seed mixture of two or three bluegrass varieties, with a little fescue (especially for shaded locations), and up to 20 percent fast-establishing perennial ryegrass, is a versatile mixture. The colonial bentgrasses are well adapted to humid regions, and seeding mixtures of them may well include a low-growing, fine-leafed bluegrass such as Fylking or Pennstar, and perhaps a mite of fine fescue as well (low-growing fescues, such as Jamestown, have proved excellent for winter seeding of southern golf courses, mowed as low as a quarter of an inch).

Of course, the soilbed should be leveled, and, if fluffy, either be rolled lightly or be settled by a soaking. Crumble the surface again into a loose overlay of soil chunks about the size of marbles. Seed will settle nicely into such a soilbed for quick and thorough sprouting. Even though spring is normally a fairly rainy season with the soil not apt to dry out rapidly, a mulch over the new seeding nonetheless helps hold the surface moisture, encouraging sprouting and seedling establishment. Both seed and a slurry of pulp mulch can be applied together by a hydraulic seeder, although so thin a mulch is not as effective as would be straw spread about a half-inch thick, or some of the manufactured mulches such as excelsior matting or woven burlap. In most instances, the mulch can be left in place to decay, and it becomes quickly invisible as the fast-growing grass overtops it.

USDA

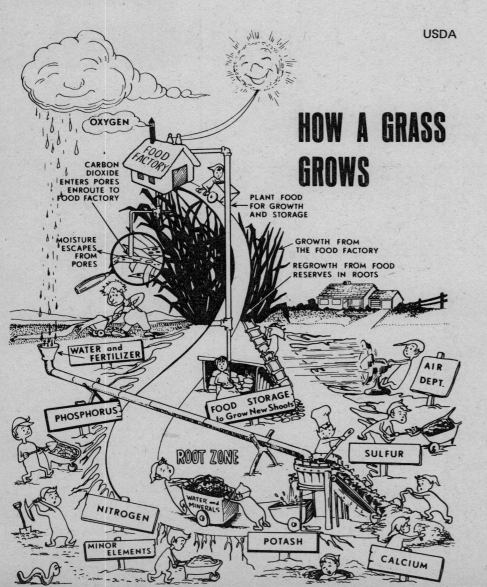

HOW A GRASS GROWS

OXYGEN

FOOD FACTORY

CARBON DIOXIDE ENTERS PORES ENROUTE TO FOOD FACTORY

MOISTURE ESCAPES FROM PORES

PLANT FOOD FOR GROWTH AND STORAGE

GROWTH FROM THE FOOD FACTORY

REGROWTH FROM FOOD RESERVES IN ROOTS

WATER and FERTILIZER

AIR DEPT.

PHOSPHORUS

FOOD STORAGE to Grow New Shoots

ROOT ZONE

SULFUR

WATER and MINERALS

NITROGEN

MINOR ELEMENTS

POTASH

CALCIUM

Lawns

Preparing a Good Seed Bed: Area should be properly sloped so water will not collect. Work in 3 to 5 pounds of Vertagreen Lawn and Garden Fertilizer per 100 sq. ft. Add limestone if needed. Rake smooth before planting seed. Spread a good grade grass seed. Water lightly and frequently to keep ground surface moist until seedlings are well established. Soils that show a pH below 5.5 should have applied to them 50 pounds of ground limestone per 100 sq. ft.

Set mower to cut grass at heights recommended in table. At no time should you remove more than one half of the grass blade. In dry weather, water lawn until soil at 6-inch depth shows moisture. Allow top 2 inches to dry before watering again. Frequent light watering encourages shallow roots, weeds and disease.

Fertilizing: For established lawns, fertilize with Vertagreen for Turf and Trees with Magnex or Vertagreen Lawn Food with Magnex. Specific instructions for applying on every bag.

Vertagreen Rotary Spreader

The spreader that's easier to load, and spreads faster and longer than others. Gives even distribution of granules. Virtually eliminates streaking

You must be completely satisfied with the results you obtain from any VERTAGREEN lawn and garden product, or your dealer will will replace it at no cost to you or refund your total purchase price, as you prefer.

USS, VERTAGREEN and MAGNEX are registered trademarks.

—Lawns

GROUP I COOL SEASON GRASSES	Relative Maintenance Requirements	Troublesome Insects	Life of Grass	Appearance of Grass	Traffic Resistance	Shade Tolerance	Mowing Height	Time required for Seeds to come up (1)
Chewings and Creeping Red Fescues	Medium	Grubs, Sod Web-worms, Leafhoppers	Permanent	Fine	Medium	Good	1½-2½"	2 to 4 weeks
Merion Bluegrass	High	"	"	Medium	Good	Fair	1½-2½"	3 to 5 weeks
Kentucky Bluegrass	Medium			Fine-Medium	Medium	Fair	1½-2½"	2 to 4 weeks
Bent Grass	Very-High	Grubs, Sod Web-worms, Leafhoppers, Chinch Bugs	"	Fine	Medium	Fair	½-3/4"	2 to 4 weeks
Rough Bluegrass	Low	Grubs, Sod Web-worms, Leafhoppers	Semi-Permanent	Fine	Poor	Very Good	1½-2½	2 to 4 weeks
Redtop	Low		Temporary	Fine-Medium	Medium	Fair	1½-2½	1 to 2 weeks
Ryegrass	Low	"		Medium	Medium	Fair	1½-2½"	1 to 2 weeks
Tall Fescue (Alta & Ky. 31)	Low	"	Permanent	Coarse	Very Good	Fair to Good	2-3"	1 to 2 weeks

(1) Times given are for average temperature and moisture conditions.

GROUP II WARM SEASON GRASSES	Relative Mainte-nance Require-ments	Troublesome Insects	Principal Diseases	Appear-ance of Grass	Frost Resist-ance	Traffic Resist-ance	Shade Toler-ance	Salt Toler-ance	Mowing Height	Rate of Estab.	Method of Estab.
Improved Bermuda Varieties	High	Sod webworms Armyworms Scale insects Mole-crickets	Brown patch Dollarspot Helminthosporium	Fine	Good	Good	Poor	Fair	½-1"	Very fast	Vegetative
St. Augustine	Moderate	Chinch bugs Sod webworms Armyworms Mole-crickets	Grey leafspot Brown patch Dollarspot	Coarse	Fair	Fair	Good	Good	1½-2½"	Medium fast	Vegetative
Zoysia	Moderate	Sod webworms Armyworms Billbugs Mole-crickets	Brown patch Dollarspot	Fine	Good	Good	Good	Good	½-1¼"	Very slow	Vegetative
Bahia	Low	Sod webworms Armyworms Mole-crickets	Brown patch Dollarspot	Interme-diate	Fair	Good	Fair	Poor	1½-2½"	Medium	Seed or vegetative
Centipede	Low	Sod webworms Armyworms Ground pearls Mole-crickets	Brown patch Dollarspot	Interme-diate	Poor	Poor	Fair	Poor	1¼-2"	Medium	Seed or vegetative
Carpet	Low	Sod webworms Armyworms Mole-crickets	Brown patch Dollarspot	Interme-diate	Poor	Poor	Fair	Poor	1¼-2"	Medium	Seed or vegetative

LAWN AND OTHER GRASS AND CLOVER SEEDS.

Northern Lawngrasses

Grass	Thumbnail Sketch	Pests And Most Used Pesticides
Bentgrass, all kinds	Outstandingly attractive for close-mowed turf, but requires care (attentive mowing, ample fertilization, usually irrigation and fungicidal protection). Will thatch. Most at home in moist, coolish locations.	Various summer diseases, winter snow mold are main affliction; use broad spectrum fungicides. Typical insect and weed troubles, controllable with insecticides, phenoxys and other northern-type herbicides (use care).
Highland	Lawns and fairways, usually mowed ½-1 inch. Represents the less demanding non-creeping varieties which also include Astoria and other Colonial types. More erect, less temperamental; high-quality seed from Oregon. Highland is from a section where summers are hot and dry; should be adequately adapted to most of East.	Usually less demanding than creepers, and often less afflicted with disease. Will tolerate most herbicides, including Banvel for clover, though temporarily scorched by Zytron (sprays) and Silvex.
Penncross	Mostly golf greens. Exquisite creeping bent, available as seed, representative of all creepers including vegetative selections. Prolific growth gives dense patches that don't mix well in other turf. Thatch is often serious. Extra and constant care needed, usually very close mowing.	Fungicides at recommended rates are safe. Be very careful or don't use phenoxy herbicides at all. Seem able to take pre-emergence treatment as with familiar crabgrass preventers.
Redtop	A coarse species used as nursegrass, seldom permanent, not a component of better seed mixtures.	Impermanent cover, not worth treating.
Bluegrasses, all kinds	Outstanding general-purpose turfgrasses, attractive, spreading, recuperative. Survive best under high mowing, and do not need elaborate care. All varieties from seed.	Weed invasion perhaps the most frequent trouble, but major weeds are easily controlled with phenoxys, preemergents and arsenicals. Sometimes sod webworm or grubs.
Kentucky, natural	A rugged performer, widely adapted, workhorse of lawn seed mixtures.	Not a prima donna; holds up well under all familiar treatments, including Zytron and Banvel sprays. Attacked by leaf spot disease (Helminthosporium), but seldom succumbs if mowed tall and not overfertilized.
Merion	An elite variety for lower growing turf. Heavy feeder and may thatch. Perhaps better adapted to northern than southern reaches of bluegrass belt.	As with other bluegrasses, except not tolerant of phenyl mercuries (PMAS) formerly much used against crabgrass. Leaf spot disease resistant.
Park	A sturdy variety, fast sprouting with seedling vigor. A combination of natural bluegrass selections.	As with natural Kentucky bluegrass.
Rough bluegrass (*Poa trivialis*)	For damp shade. A rather delicate species without wear-resistance, similar to bentgrasses.	Limited weed invasion. Treat more carefully than Kentucky bluegrass, about as considerately as bentgrass.
Fescues	Extremely rugged and drought-resistant.	About as with Kentucky bluegrass.
Fine fescues (Chewings, Creeping red, Illahee, Pennlawn, Rainier, etc.)	Fine lawngrass, good companion for Kentucky bluegrass. Well adapted to shade, dry soil and minimum fertility.	Experiencing similar pests as for Kentucky bluegrass and similarly treated. Not quite so tolerant of some pesticides as is bluegrass (viz. Zytron).
Tall and meadow fescues (Alta and Kentucky-31 varieties).	A pasture species, tough and coarse, often planted on roadsides and sometimes play areas.	Few pests, and in any event seldom worth worrying about.
Ryegrass	Mainly pasture cover, but because of low cost often main component of "cheap" seed mixtures.	Wide range of diseases and weeds, but unlike with superior, perennial grasses hardly worth expense of treatment.
Annual or Italian	May be legitimately used in small quantities as nursegrass, or as temporary cover. Quick to establish, but turns coarse.	Damping off of seedlings may sometimes be serious, but preventive measures doubtfully worth cost with this impermanent grass. Weeds come as ryegrass dies.
Perennial	Finer textured, more attractive than annual, but does not make first-rate sod. Fairly long-lasting under proper conditions.	As for group.

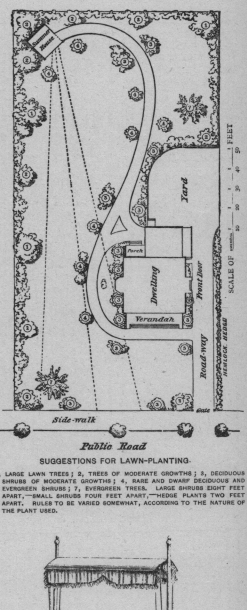

SUGGESTIONS FOR LAWN-PLANTING.

1, LARGE LAWN TREES; 2, TREES OF MODERATE GROWTHS; 3, DECIDUOUS SHRUBS OF MODERATE GROWTHS; 4, RARE AND DWARF DECIDUOUS AND EVERGREEN SHRUBS; 7, EVERGREEN TREES. LARGE SHRUBS EIGHT FEET APART,—SMALL SHRUBS FOUR FEET APART,—HEDGE PLANTS TWO FEET APART. RULES TO BE VARIED SOMEWHAT, ACCORDING TO THE NATURE OF THE PLANT USED.

NEW LAWNS

1. Remove debris and level.
2. Spread 2″ layer of **wet** PEAT MOSS over soil; add bonemeal and lawn fertilizer (4 pounds of each per 100 square feet.)
3. Mix thoroughly with top 4″ of soil, then level.
4. Rake smooth, roll, rake again.
5. Broadcast seed, roll lightly once more.
6. Cover with ¼″ layer of fine dry BLUENOSE PEAT MOSS then sprinkle.
7. Keep moist continuously.

RENOVATING OLD LAWNS

SPRING
{ Rake old grass & scratch hard crust to pierce it.
Mix a good complete garden fertilizer (4 lbs. per 100 sq. ft.)
with fine dry PEAT MOSS & top dress about ½″ thick.

AUTUMN
{ Repeat, using bonemeal. When ground heaves in winter the
fine PEAT enters cracks & keeps roots covered & alive.

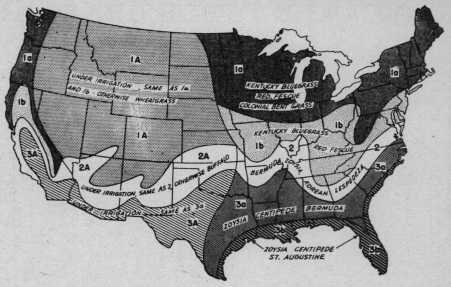

map courtesy American Potash Institute

Areas where various turfgrasses are usually most effective.

Zone 1 (1a & 1b)

Natural Kentucky Bluegrass, *Poa pratensis* (including Arboretum, Delta, Newport, Park, Troy); **Red Fescues***, *Festuca rubra* (including Chewings, Creeping Red, Illahee, Pennlawn, Rainier); Clover, *Trifolium repens*.

1a only—Merion Kentucky Bluegrass; Colonial Bent Grasses, *Agrostis tenuis* (including Astoria, Highland); occasionally Creeping Bent, *A. palustris* (including seeded Seaside and Penncross, plus golf green varieties); **Rough Bluegrass**, *Poa trivialis*.

1b only—warm, difficult sites, possibly Tall Fescue; Bermudas (annually seeded, or hardy varieties such as U-3); Redtop, *Agrostis alba*.

Zone 2

Tall Fescue*, *Festuca arundinacea* (Kentucky-31, Alta); **Zoysias***, *Z. matrella* (especially Meyer strain of "japonica" or Japanese lawngrass); **Berumda**, *Cynodon dactylon* (seeded or vegetative); Kentucky Bluegrass**; Red Fescue**; **Korean Lespedeza**, *L. stipulacea* for temporary cover.

Zone 3 (3a & 3b)

Zoysias* ("matrella" strains; Emerald); **Centipede**, *Eremochloa ophiuroides*; Carpet, *Axonopus sp.*

3a only—Bermudas (seeded, and varieties such as Tiffine, Tiflawn, Tifgreen, Texturf); **African or Uganda**, *C. transvalensis*; **Sunturf**, *C. magenesii*.

3b only—St. Augustine*, *Stenotaphrum secundatum* (including Bitter Blue, Floratine); Bahia, *Paspalum notatum* (including Pensacola); Bermuda strains.

Zones 1-A, 2-A, 3-A

These are arid versions of 1, 2, 3. The same species can be used where watering is possible, or in the higher mountains. Where irrigation is limited, some of the prairie grasses may have to be used, as:

1-A—Buffalo, *Buchloe dactyloides*; Sheep or Hard Fescue, *Festuca ovina*; **Wheat Grasses**, *Agropyron* (Crested—Fairway strain; also Intermediate, Slender, Western).

2-A—Buffalo; Gramas, *Bouteloua*; Love grasses, *Eragrostis*.

3-A—Buffalo; Love grasses (Boer, Lehman, Weeping); Meadow Fescue, *F. elatior*, in Southwest.

Ryegrass, perennial; and annual, Italian or domestic, *Lolium perenne* and *L. multiflorum*, are major ingredients of "cheap mixtures" in the North and temporary "wintergrass" in South; not good turf species.

Tall fescue (Kentucky-31 and Alta) is often an ingredient of "economy" mixtures, and may have some use in middle latitudes, which have hot, dry summers. Like ryegrass, it is not a really first-rate lawngrass, and should be avoided if possible.

* *stand shade well*
** *prefer shade*
  most-useful species are in boldface

	Pounds of seed per 1,000 square feet	Time of seeding
Bahiagrass	2-3	Spring.
Bermudagrass	2-3	Spring.
Blue gramagrass (unhulled)	1-1½	Spring.
Buffalograss (treated)	½-1	Spring.
Canada bluegrass	2-3	Fall.
Carpetgrass	3-4	Spring.
Centipedegrass	2-3	Spring.
Chewings fescue	3-5	Fall.
Colonial bentgrass (Highland, Astoria)	1-2	Fall.
Creeping bentgrass (Penncross, Seaside)	1-2	Fall.
Crested wheatgrass	1-2	Fall.
Japanese lawngrass (hulled)	1-2	Spring.
Kentucky bluegrass, common	2-3	Fall.
Kentucky bluegrass, Merion	1-2	Fall.
Red fescue	3-5	Fall.
Redtop	1-2	Fall.
Rough bluegrass	3-5	Fall.
Ryegrass (domestic and perennial)	4-6	Spring-fall.
Tall fescue (Alta, Ky. 31)	4-6	Fall.
Velvet bentgrass	1-2	Fall.
Mixture for sunny areas: 75% bluegrass, 25% red fescue	2-4	Fall.
Mixture for shady areas: 25% bluegrass, 75% red fescue	2-4	Fall.

VICK'S PORTABLE LAWN TENT

COPYRIGHT 1900 BY FINLEY LAWN RAKE CO.

FINLEY ROTARY LAWN RAKE.

LANDSCAPING AND GARDEN DESIGN

plantings for the homeowner: down to earth advice

IN 1954, when I first came to Phoenix, Ariz., a total landscape project for the average home in this area consisted of the yard being bermed, or diked, for flood irrigation (a peculiarity of desert areas), a bermuda lawn seeded and topped with steer manure, and "FHA minimum" planting. This consisted of 15 small plants, six larger plants, and three small trees.

During 1972, only the tract homes are likely to get by with this formula. Many homeowners would not be caught dead without extensive landscaping, sprinkler-irrigation systems, and even swimming pools.

Naturally many expert "designers" have shown up during this evolution of landscaping, glibly selling the homeowner all sorts of fantastic plans. The homeowner is left unhappy, dissatisfied, and uncertain as to the reason.

Dissatisfaction can usually be traced to a nerve-jarring design in the yard, or poor selection of plant material, or both.

What can you do to save yourself from winding up in the same fix?

First, remember that good landscaping is mainly applying good common sense.

If you will sit down and determine the uses to which various areas around the home will be put, these uses will not only determine the sizes of the areas involved and the traffic patterns needed to serve them, but also dictate part of the yard design.

How does this relate to plantings?

Plants are used for several things:
- To define activity areas.
- To delineate traffic patterns.
- To screen or protect.
- To shade.
- To enhance.

I will come back to these items later.

Second, familiarize yourself with the plant material that does well in your area. I did say *does well*. If you want your project to be relatively free from failure, stay away from borderline plant material and exotics. The plantings in your yard are supposed to improve each year, not die out!

Wherever you live, plant material is divided roughly into these groupings:
- Conifers (spiny evergreens with cones)
- Broadleaf evergreens
- Deciduous (lose their leaves in winter)

Next, you have to know the various uses for plants, in some detail. Let's take them up one by one.

To define activity areas. Complete screening of such areas can be done by use of tall bushes, whether conifers, broadleafs, or deciduous. Deciduous screening can be used if you want to "open up" an activity area in the winter but screen it in the summer—a badminton court, for example. In the winter when badminton is impractical,

Author F. J. MACDONALD is Executive Vice President of the American Institute of Landscape Architects, with headquarters at Phoenix, Ariz.

the yard will look much larger if all of it can be seen through the bare branches.

An optical or psychological screening of the same area can be done with the use of medium bushes—those that mature at about 3 feet in height. This will provide the feeling of a screen without obstructing vision to any extent. In addition, objects between the eye and the far boundary of a yard tend to make the yard look larger. The momentary interruption in the line of sight gives a much deeper feeling to the picture.

An even more subtle definition of activity areas can be accomplished with the use of low beds of ground cover plants, just to give an indication of a boundary.

To delineate traffic patterns. The same rules apply here as in screening activity areas except that, in many cases, you want paths, walkways, or drives to be seen: high plants would hide them. You should do much of the traffic delineation with very low plants—or none at all. Often an attractive walk or an interesting pattern of stepping stones is the most effective and attractive way to carry out the traffic pattern.

To screen or protect. Here you are primarily interested in screening the yard from the various pollutions that have become so apparent during the past few years—noise pollution, dust pollution, visual pollution. If the yard is adjacent to anything unpleasant, you can use tall shrubs or small trees to form a barrier. Shrubs effectively cut down on noise as well as dust.

One other important barrier that can be helpful is a windbreak. You can use these same tall bushes and short trees to block off the prevailing wind in order to make your yard more livable. Keep in mind, however, that only evergreen plants are effective during the entire year. In many cases a screen or hedge of plants is preferred to a wall or solid fence, since the plants allow some air movement and do not reflect the sun's glare.

To shade. Most plants produce shade in varying amounts. If you want to reduce your electric bill, heavy shade on the house during the summer will show up as substantial savings. But the more subtle use of shade is accomplished through judicious placing of deciduous and evergreen trees in the same yard.

For example, a patio on the south or west side of a house will reflect heat and sunlight toward the house and increase the cost of cooling. However, this patio planted with an umbrella of deciduous trees will remain cool and shady all summer and help keep the house cool. Comes winter when the trees shed their leaves, the opening up of the patio to the warm winter sun will brighten the house and make the patio warmer for recreational purposes.

Just one other thing about trees and shade. If you really want significant results, both from a shade standpoint and an esthetic viewpoint, plant the trees *close* to the house. This means within 6 to 8 feet. Trees have a tendency to lean away from objects nearby; so the trunks will eventually have a small curve to them and the house will give the effect of being nestled between the trees.

Not all shade is accomplished with trees. Bushes can be trained to form a canopy and vines will climb trellises and pergolas. Palm trees give much more shade than one would imagine,

but the eventual height of the trunk often puts the shade over in the neighbor's yard. This may be good public relations, but doesn't really save much on the electric bill.

One last word of caution concerning shade: Not all plants take sun and shade equally well. This applies also to grasses. So don't expect an evenly textured result from sunlight to shadow, even though you use the same plant variety throughout.

To enhance. This is the real problem, and should be attacked only after full consideration of the other four uses of plants have been thoroughly developed. Many times you see a plant of particular beauty and immediately want it in your yard, whether it belongs there or not. Also, it is difficult to believe that an exotic plant placed in your yard will not look as breathtaking as the one in *Better Homes and Gardens* or *Sunset Magazine*.

The desire for the unusual and the beautiful is probably one of the great factors causing unbalanced (even downright weird) yards. Many such yards are a collection of struggling exotics, trying for survival, and existing in spite of numerous moves from place to place. (Many ladies do not fully realize that, unlike furniture, plants cannot be rearranged whenever the mood hits one!)

If you want your yard to be comfortable, as well as beautiful, you need to carefully limit plant selection to the few varieties that accomplish your main objectives. Then if you want to make a "splash," you can group the "iffy" exotics off to one side, discreetly screened, so that their struggle will not be witnessed by the entire world. Likewise, vegetable gardens, flower gardens, and roses should be kept behind the house so that their seasonal changes will not impair one's standing with the neighbors.

To do a complete job of planting around your home, you will have to design your front yard like the rear yard: Establish use areas, traffic patterns and views—and then accent these features.

Esthetically, you may find it easier to landscape in the front of the house. You can stand back and look at bare walls and decide if you want a vine or a bush in front of it. You can determine if you want a "woodsy" or "mountain" feeling—and use boulders and coniferous evergreens. Or you can achieve a more tropical feeling with the use of the large-leafed broadleaf evergreens.

Normally you wouldn't want too much deciduous material in front of the house, since these plants are completely bare for several months during the winter.

But, to get down to specifics, you need to apply what you know about plants toward the uses that they are best suited for, and work out a planting plan.

Let's play with a yard! We will make it 70 feet by 120 feet, an arbitrary city or suburban lot somewhere. Let's crowd the backyard full of activities and direct the front yard toward friends and neighbors.

In the backyard you will have badminton, horseshoes, a barbecue, a quiet area for reading, a patio for entertaining and—why not?—a swimming pool. (If you change your mind about the pool, you can convert this area to a lawn.)

Put the patio and barbecue right off the kitchen for convenience of food service, with the pool just beyond to keep swimmers within sight of the kitchen window.

Put the badminton far over to one side to keep the players from falling

into the pool. Keep it to the rear of the lot to hold the noise level down. Horseshoes are tucked over against the fence to reduce the danger of an innocent swimmer being hit with a flying shoe.

'Way down in the corner, out of the way, put a little secluded quiet area.

These activities will generate traffic patterns which determine some of the lines and plantings.

Now the skeleton plan is taking on shape. You may want to change it later, but at least you have an idea of how things *could* be done.

In adding your plantings keep in mind that:
- The badminton court should be screened off. Since it's a small yard, a medium height screen will do the job.
- The quiet area should be screened for privacy and shaded from the sun.
- The pool should be sunny.
- The path needs more definition.
- The patio could use some summer shade, but away from the pool. You don't want to have to fish leaves out of the pool.
- The view from the family room could stand some help.

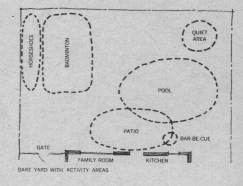

BARE YARD WITH ACTIVITY AREAS

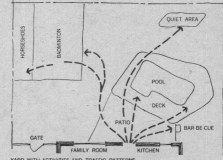

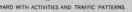

YARD WITH ACTIVITIES AND TRAFFIC PATTERNS

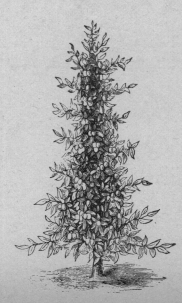

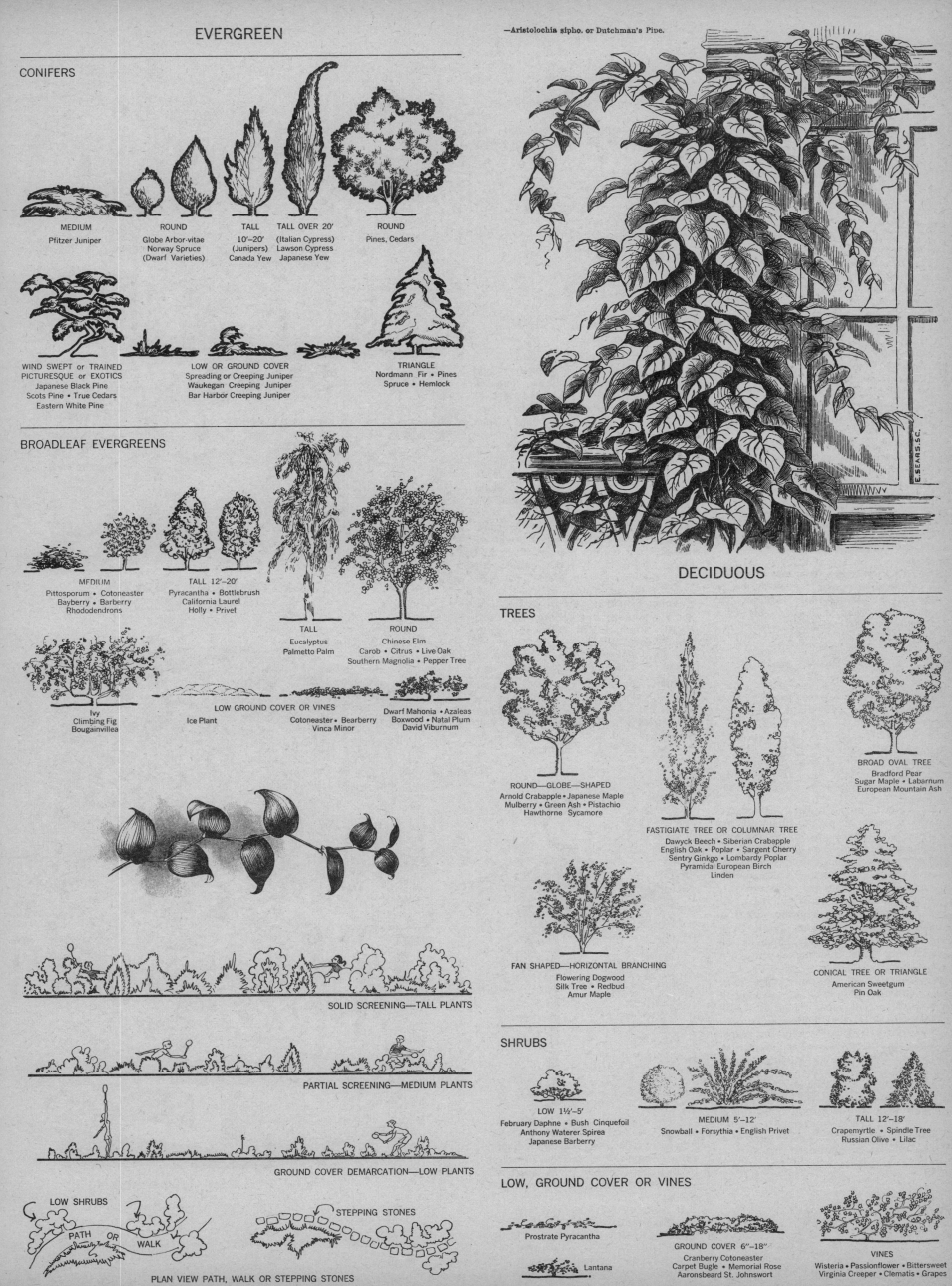

EVERGREEN

CONIFERS

MEDIUM
Pfitzer Juniper

ROUND
Globe Arbor-vitae
Norway Spruce
(Dwarf Varieties)

TALL 10'–20'
(Junipers)
Canada Yew

TALL OVER 20'
(Italian Cypress)
Lawson Cypress
Japanese Yew

ROUND
Pines, Cedars

WIND SWEPT or TRAINED PICTURESQUE or EXOTICS
Japanese Black Pine
Scots Pine • True Cedars
Eastern White Pine

LOW OR GROUND COVER
Spreading or Creeping Juniper
Waukegan Creeping Juniper
Bar Harbor Creeping Juniper

TRIANGLE
Nordmann Fir • Pines
Spruce • Hemlock

BROADLEAF EVERGREENS

MEDIUM
Pittosporum • Cotoneaster
Bayberry • Barberry
Rhododendrons

TALL 12'–20'
Pyracantha • Bottlebrush
California Laurel
Holly • Privet

TALL
Eucalyptus
Palmetto Palm

ROUND
Chinese Elm
Carob • Citrus • Live Oak
Southern Magnolia • Pepper Tree

Ivy
Climbing Fig
Bougainvillea

LOW GROUND COVER OR VINES
Ice Plant

Cotoneaster • Bearberry
Vinca Minor

Dwarf Mahonia • Azaleas
Boxwood • Natal Plum
David Viburnum

SOLID SCREENING—TALL PLANTS

PARTIAL SCREENING—MEDIUM PLANTS

GROUND COVER DEMARCATION—LOW PLANTS

LOW SHRUBS

PATH OR WALK

STEPPING STONES

PLAN VIEW PATH, WALK OR STEPPING STONES

—*Aristolochia sipho.* or Dutchman's Pipe.

E. SEARS, SC.

DECIADUOUS

TREES

ROUND—GLOBE—SHAPED
Arnold Crabapple • Japanese Maple
Mulberry • Green Ash • Pistachio
Hawthorne Sycamore

FASTIGIATE TREE OR COLUMNAR TREE
Dawyck Beech • Siberian Crabapple
English Oak • Poplar • Sargent Cherry
Sentry Ginkgo • Lombardy Poplar
Pyramidal European Birch
Linden

BROAD OVAL TREE
Bradford Pear
Sugar Maple • Labarnum
European Mountain Ash

FAN SHAPED—HORIZONTAL BRANCHING
Flowering Dogwood
Silk Tree • Redbud
Amur Maple

CONICAL TREE OR TRIANGLE
American Sweetgum
Pin Oak

SHRUBS

LOW 1½'–5'
February Daphne • Bush Cinquefoil
Anthony Waterer Spirea
Japanese Barberry

MEDIUM 5'–12'
Snowball • Forsythia • English Privet

TALL 12'–18'
Crapemyrtle • Spindle Tree
Russian Olive • Lilac

LOW, GROUND COVER OR VINES

Prostrate Pyracantha

Lantana

GROUND COVER 6"–18"
Cranberry Cotoneaster
Carpet Bugle • Memorial Rose
Aaronsbeard St. Johnswort

VINES
Wisteria • Passionflower • Bittersweet
Virginia Creeper • Clematis • Grapes

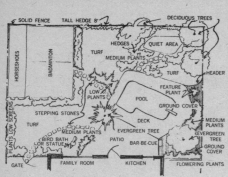

SKETCH OF BACK YARD LANDSCAPING

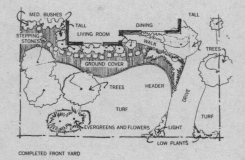

COMPLETED FRONT YARD

So let's draw up a sketch with plantings in it.

Perhaps you do not want your backyard to be this elaborate or busy. It is simple to eliminate unwanted items or make substitutions. For instance, if you don't care for badminton, you might want a vegetable and flower garden there. The pool could be eliminated and turf substituted. Stepping stones could be walks of concrete or brick.

All I am trying to do is develop a line of thought for locating your plantings, and have some sort of a reason for them being there.

How about that front yard? What will you use it for?

• An entrance to the house.
• An esthetic setting for the house.
• To complement the yards of your neighbors.

All these add up to a certain status symbol, whether you like it or not. In fact, the lack of a respectable-looking front yard may demote you to a lower status.

So let's sketch a front yard.

We will shade the front of the house, screen the dining room window, and develop a walk and some sort of a feature for the neighbors' edification.

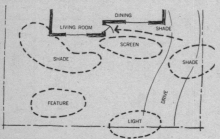

BARE FRONT YARD WITH ACTIVITY AREAS

We have used "headers" or "edgers" or "mowing strips" to delineate the lawn area. This helps in mowing as it eliminates many small corners and hard-to-mow areas, while establishing strong esthetic lines to the design. Unless a fence extends between your yard and the neighbors' yards out front, you should try not to delineate the front yard borders with plants. In this way you can utilize, visually, some of the adjoining yards and make your own yard appear larger.

Again, these are only suggestions, but it certainly didn't take too long to lay out a front yard, did it? Or backyard either, for that matter.

If you can decide where the plants are going to be, and what they are to do, you can easily decide which plants to use.

Pick out a theme—a feeling—a motif. Do you want the front of the house to be northern mountains? Then go to your list of evergreen conifers, junipers and the like, and simply put them in the design where they fit the need.

Would you rather have a tropical effect? Use the broadleaf evergreens.

Or perhaps you like drastic seasonal change and would prefer to have the branches bare and laden with snow in winter. Then deciduous material is for you.

You can mix these very nicely, too. Just remember, at the same time, that each one has a job to fulfill.

Incidentally, no one, but *no one* in the warmer sections of Arizona would landscape with deciduous material. Why man, all the friends and relatives (affectionately called "snowbirds") descend for the winter—and that's when the yard must look its best!

Then the backyard: it doesn't have to match the front, you know. All the front and back yards have to do is tie in at the sides of the house. So again you have to determine your motif for the backyard.

Just as the architecture and appearance of the front of the house will influence your choice of plants there, the decor of the family room, carried out onto the patio, will affect what you plant in the backyard.

Other than that, you are as free as a bird to establish any feeling you desire with your backyard plants. Keep in mind that each has a job to do.

I have not given you long lists of plants to work with. Geological and climatic conditions will govern plant selection wherever you live. So why try to second-guess the local nurseryman? He knows what will grow, and so will you when you look around the neighborhood and find out firsthand.

I have tried to give you general plant groups to choose from to accomplish desired results. This also gives you a very wide range from which to choose.

It really all boils down to this:

• Take your time.
• Decide what you want to do.
• Choose your material carefully.
• Use good common sense.

I should finish with this: Have fun!

CLEMATIS PANICULATA.

CLEMATIS JACKMANI.

For further reading:
U.S. Department of Agriculture, *Home Planting by Design.* Home and Garden Bulletin 164, Washington, D.C. 20250, 1969.

———, *Gardening on the Contour.* Home and Garden Bulletin 179, Washington, D.C. 20250, 1970.

Steps in the Landscape

GUNTER A. SCHOCH

Steps are obviously a means of getting from one level to another, however, in the landscape or in our garden they should do more than just fulfil this utilitarian purpose. Garden steps should be comfortable to walk on, aesthetically pleasing and, above all, should be appropriate in relationship to the architecture or landscaping around them.

For economy and convenience, steps should be built of a material that is easily obtained in the immediate locality. Their construction should be safe, durable and easily maintained. They may be constructed of brick, stone, concrete, wood, grass or a combination of these, depending on their surroundings and the material used in nearby structures.

As a general rule, outdoor steps should be much more shallow than any used indoors. If we deal with a gently sloping area, a riser of four inches with a tread of 17 - 18 inches is best. Steps with risers of more than 4 inches are not advisable for outdoor use, unless a steep slope makes this absolutely necessary. The relationship between riser and tread is based on the assumption that the average human step is 25 inches. The formula is twice the height of the riser plus the width of the tread equals 25. For instance, if the riser is 4 inches, we multiply it by 2, to equal 8. In order to arrive at 25, we add 17. Therefore, a 4-inch riser requires a 17-inch tread.

Steps are usually set into a slope or a wall. Let us first examine the slope. At least three different methods may be used to place the steps:

(a) They protrude above the face of the slope. In other words, they stand the height of one riser out of the slope, eliminating any chance of soil washing over the treads.

(b) They may be built right into the slope, having the front edge of each step level with the face of the slope. This may be quite satisfactory, if the slope is sodded.

(c) Again, built into the slope, but both sides of the steps lined with an edging material (wooden plank, a row of bricks on edge, etc.). This would also prevent soil being washed on the treads.

The variety of methods is even larger when the steps are built into a wall. The first or lowest step may be set back behind the wall line; it may be in line with the wall; it may extend in front of the wall; or even two and more steps may extend outside the wall line. In most cases, it will be necessary to continue the retaining wall around the corner along the sides of the steps which are called wing walls.

As mentioned earlier, a great variety of materials may be used to construct steps in the landscape. If they form part of a constantly used sidewalk, concrete construction with proper foundation may be necessary. However, steps used occasionally can be built quite safely on a sand or gravel foundation. As most landscape details, they are successful only when in harmony with their surroundings. Wooden steps may tie directly in with the fences, gates and arbors used in the garden or they may be combined with stones, bricks, precasted concrete blocks or asphalt that are used in walls or paving, to add variety to the composition. This is true, especially in the small garden, where all contributions, no matter how minor, are noticed and enjoyed.

THE PRAIRIE GARDEN, 1974

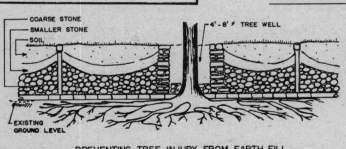

CROSS SECTION OF ROCK GARDEN, SHOWING DRAINAGE MATERIAL, SUPPORT STONES, AND PLANTING MEDIUM.

RIGHT AND WRONG PLACEMENT OF ROCKS

PREVENTING TREE INJURY FROM EARTH FILL

(Upright tiles optional if the earth fill is shallow)

The Prairie Garden

Published by

WINNIPEG HORTICULTURAL SOCIETY

Winnipeg, Manitoba 31st Annual Edition, February, 1974

THE PRAIRIE GARDEN, P.O. BOX 517, WINNIPEG, MAN. R3C 2J3

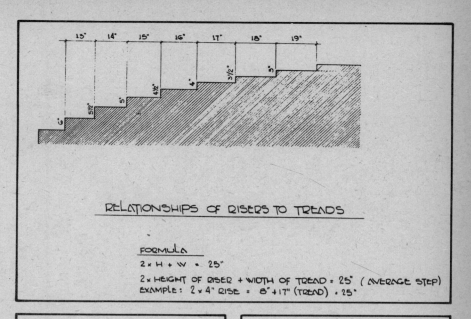

RELATIONSHIPS OF RISERS TO TREADS

FORMULA

2 x H + W = 25"

2 x HEIGHT OF RISER + WIDTH OF TREAD = 25" (AVERAGE STEP)

EXAMPLE: 2 x 4" RISE = 8" + 17" (TREAD) = 25"

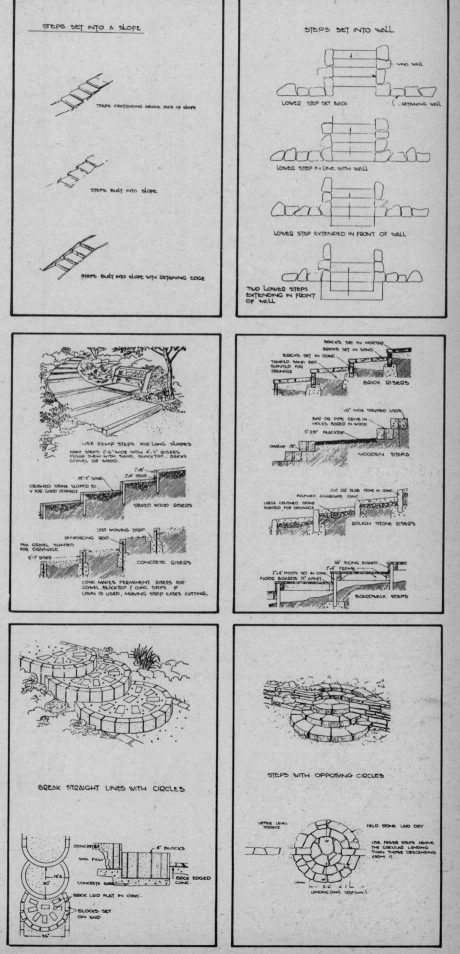

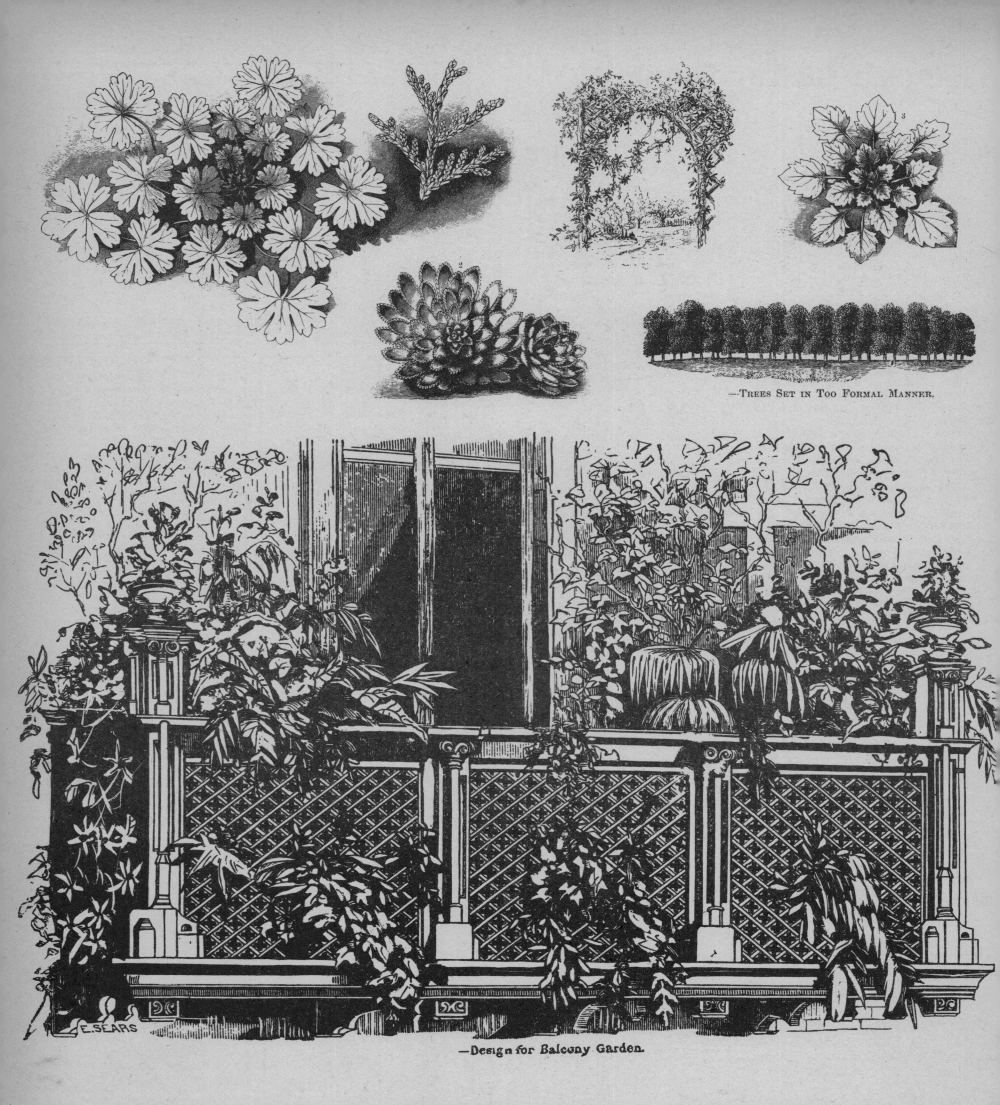

—Trees Set in Too Formal Manner.

E. SEARS

—Design for Balcony Garden.

PATIO AND TERRACE GARDENING

1. Parting Line 2. Slip Hook Block 3. To Team 4. Ring Pull Drag Plank Grab Hook 5. Plank 6. Plank

landscaping limited areas
such as terraces, patios

Author WILLIAM R. NELSON, JR., is Extension Landscape Architect, University of Illinois, Urbana-Champaign.

ORNAMENTAL GARDENS have always been an important part of our American culture. Since the time of the first settlers, the character of the home landscape has gone through many changes from the dooryard garden of herbs and flowers to the intricate fussy details of the Victorian era and finally to the garden as an extension of the indoor living environment into outdoor space.

Now urban living with its high density housing and minimal outdoor space is creating another kind of change in garden style. This change brings a greater emphasis on intensive use of limited space. This kind of gardening can be the most exciting and the most enjoyable.

Not only has the landscape changed but people too have changed as a result of this life style. Today there is less concern with traditional garden designs of heavy flower and shrub massing. Instead the design must have dramatic visual appeal. One way to achieve this visual appeal is to use natural or manmade landscape elements to complement your plants.

Before discussing the various elements available for creating a landscape, let us first consider our basic goal—to create space for people and for people's activities. Each time trees, shrubs, fences, walls are placed on the land, space has been created. The size and visual quality of this space determines its success. Therefore, as you plan your landscape, think of it as if you are creating a room outdoors. This room, like a room in your house, must have a floor, walls, and a ceiling.

The floor is the stage upon which all of your activities are organized. This ground surface might be paved, covered with gravel or other loose aggregate, planted to ground cover or grass. Which of these elements to select depends upon the intended use of the area.

Walls of the room are created by vertical elements (trees, shrubs, fences, walls). Not only do they define the space but they also provide an enclosure for privacy that is essential for outdoor living. Human nature is such that many people are not comfortable pursuing outdoor activities if they feel they can be seen or watched by others. To effectively provide a privacy screen, the material used should be above eye level.

Even in situations where privacy is not a primary concern, enclosure elements are still important to give organization to the space. In this case height is not important. In fact the effect of enclosure can be achieved through using elements only 12 to 24 inches high. This is an implied enclosure rather than the complete enclosure you would have with the privacy screen.

The final unit of your outdoor room is the ceiling. Unlike the rooms of your home it does not have to be total and complete. The ceiling may be the canopy effect of the spreading branches of a tree combined with the sky, or it may be an overhead structure over the patio or terrace. The structure may have a solid roof for complete weather protection or be partially open or louvered for filtered light and shade. Most important, there should be a partial overhead definition combined with the sky. In either case the ceiling effect should be sensed rather than seen. Therefore the design should be simple, not eye-catching or detailed.

For patios and limited space gardens, there are two primary types of space:
- Visual space—a landscape scene viewed from within or a landscape

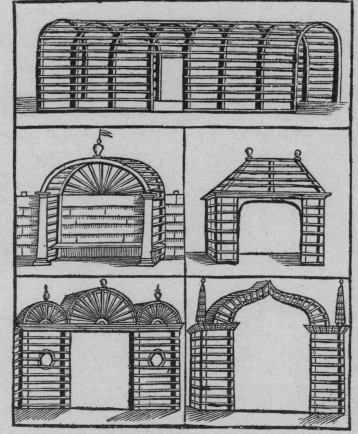

EXAMPLES OF SEVENTEENTH CENTURY DUTCH TREILLAGE

picture associated with a primary window. Visual space is created mainly through the use of plant material and it is not intended to accommodate outdoor living activities.
- Usable living space—designed for family use in entertaining, relaxation, or play. It, too, should be designed to be visually pleasing. However, it is composed of any of the landscape elements—natural or manmade—to assure that the design serves the family's interests.

Although not a part of this discussion, it should be understood that elements of both these types of space may be combined into a landscape composition. To successfully accomplish this, a larger area is required.

Both types of space are formed by using fences, walls, planting screens,

EARLY FLOWERING COSMOS.

trees, shrubs, flowers, ground covers, hard surfaced paving, loose aggregate surfacing, water features, portable or fixed planters, lighting, sculpture, and natural boulders. Not all of these elements can be used in any one design. Instead you should select those that will most effectively create the type of space and design you want.

Fences, walls, and planting screens not only define space but also provide privacy and screening where needed. For a landscape with limited space, fences and walls have greater value because they require a minimum of ground space to provide a 6-foot screen. To achieve the same effect with plants would require 4 to 6 feet of ground space to accommodate the mature spread of the plants.

Fences are easy to construct and they provide an immediate effect not possible with plants which often require 3 to 5 years to grow to the desired height. But don't feel compelled to surround your entire garden area with a fence. This is monotonous and poor design. Instead, you should identify critical areas where screening or privacy are needed and then use sections or panels of the enclosure unit. These units can easily be tied together through the skillful use of flowering trees and shrubs.

You should avoid painting fences. The first stroke of a paint brush commits you to a high maintenance program that can be avoided by staining the fence instead. It's best to select neutral colors of stain that blend well with foliage colors. In this way the fence will blend with the rest of the elements and not dominate the scene.

Trees and shrubs are the bulk of the natural materials used in the landscape. Having a permanent woody structure and being vertical elements, they too create space. For this reason they must be selected on the basis of the function they will serve in this three-dimensional composition and not just because the plant is pretty.

Trees may be divided into two groups —the large shade tree and the smaller flowering types. In situations of limited size, it is unlikely that more than one large shade tree can be introduced into the design. At this point you must decide if a shade tree or an overhead structure is going to do the best job of providing shade and the ceiling to the space. You can choose from a great variety of trees. They vary in height, soil tolerance, hardiness, and rate of growth. Your county extension agent or nurseryman can assist you in making a selection suitable for your soil and climate.

Flowering trees are generally smaller, ranging from 8 feet to 35 feet. Many varieties in this group have not only showy flowers but also interesting fruit. They may be used by themselves or as part of a shrub border. Because of their smaller size, flowering trees are often planted in containers or planters. They are valuable for patios, terraces, and other small areas. Also, when combined with a fence or wall, the crown of the flowering tree added to the height of the fence adds considerably to the vertical screening in any areas where there are elevated views into your property.

Because of the wide variety of tree flower colors, be certain to select colors that will be harmonious both with other flowers blooming at the same time and with surrounding building colors.

Since shrubs bloom for only a short time, it is important to consider foliage, fruit, branching habits, and suitability for a specific location as well as their flowers. Because shrubs are smaller than trees, you can see them in much greater detail—hence the importance of other plant qualities besides flowers. In small gardens, avoid using too many different kinds. Your design will have a strong unity and be visually more appealing if you limit the number of varieties.

One type of plant that has particular value for the small-scaled landscape is called a specimen, which is a plant that is unique in form, color, or texture, or any combination of these three elements. When used by itself, either in a planter or in the ground, it becomes a dramatic unit with great dominance and visual appeal. Only one specimen plant should be used in a composition. Using two or more is distracting and it diminishes the dramatic effect.

Flowers are not a permanent landscape element. Since they dieback to the ground during dormant seasons, they do not offer year-round structure or form to the landscape. Therefore, flowers should be considered as an accessory or embellishment. Flowers are classified as annuals and perennials. Annuals must be replanted each year whereas perennials, although they dieback to the ground each winter, do live for many seasons without replanting. In small areas, the annuals offer the most spectacular color and showiness. To be most effective they should have a background against which to be viewed.

Keep flower plantings simple. Plant flowers in masses and do not use too many different kinds or too many different colors. As a rule of thumb, small flower planting areas should include only one flower variety and all one color. When selecting your flowers, remember that most types require full sunlight. If yours is a shady situation, there are several types from which to choose. Consult your nurseryman or garden center.

Until now, consideration has been given only to the vertical landscape elements, but it is also important to consider what you will put on the floor of your landscape. In this case, the criteria for selection are based upon the intended use of the area. If the area must support heavy traffic or is an activity center such as a patio or terrace then a permanent, hard-surfaced material should be used. You may choose from concrete, brick, slate, flagstone, or wood.

Walks should be at least 4 feet wide so two people can walk side by side. The terrace or patio area should be at least 400 square feet. This will provide sufficient room for garden furniture and still leave space to move around.

Design of the terrace or patio should be carefully studied to develop a strong pattern. There are many possible shapes besides the typical square or rectangle. You may wish to consider a broad arc combined with straight (diagonal, horizontal, or vertical) lines or a straight-line design set on a 45° angle from the building. Rectangular and square areas can be made more interesting by using 2 by 4 wood divider strips to develop a modular pattern of 4- or 5-foot squares across the surface. Lawn or loose aggregates work well in areas with little or no traffic. If you use a loose aggregate for paths or walks, select a rounded rock of ¼- to ¾-inch screen size. Do not use pea gravel. It sticks to

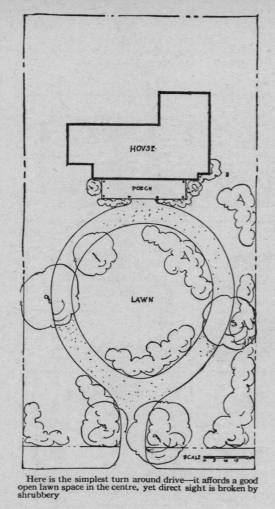

Here is the simplest turn around drive—it affords a good open lawn space in the centre, yet direct sight is broken by shrubbery

shoes and makes footing difficult. Loose aggregates such as gravel can also be used as a mulch in planting areas.

Ground cover plants do not tolerate any foot traffic, hence their use is restricted to planting bed areas. This group of plants offers a wide choice in texture and in height—from 6 inches to 18 inches. Some thrive very well in deep shade while others tolerate a hot, dry location. Be sure to select the right one for your situation. Ornamental ground covers are discussed elsewhere in this book.

In patio gardens and landscapes for limited space, special features such as water, planters, night lighting, and sculpture can enhance space whether it is visual space designed for window viewing or actually usable space.

Because the areas being discussed are assumed to be small in scale, the use of water must be controlled and obviously man designed. To try to introduce a babbling brook or a natural waterfall would be inappropriate and out of place. Your water design should have classic simplicity without superfluous decoration. The basic pattern may be straight lined or curved. In the latter case plan the design to be a "stylized" use of natural curves and not an attempt to copy nature.

The sound of water is very pleasant and has a psychological cooling effect. Sound may be achieved through the use of jets, bubblers, or sprays. If the area is breezy, the bubbler is better than the jets or sprays. Fine sprays can be carried some distance in a high breeze. Sound can also be introduced by having water fall from a higher basin into a lower one.

GREEN-LEAVED BAMBOO.
(ARUNDO DONAX.)

INDIAN BEAN.
(CATALPA BIGNONIOIDES.)

YUCCA RECURVA.

Water is also very effective for its reflective quality. To make the best use of reflection in water, paint the basin black. This will enhance the mirror-like qualities. Do not use jets or bubblers.

A great variety of planters is available for home use. Once filled with soil, a large planter is difficult to move. So study carefully where you need your planter for maximum effects, move it there, then fill it with soil.

Planters are available in concrete, fiber glass, and asbestos–concrete. Select them on the basis of their design and the soil volume in relation to the size plant you intend to use. If you have in mind a large shrub or small tree, a large volume of soil will be needed. Also keep in mind that it is important to select plants that are in good proportion and scale relationship with the planter. For example, a large, tall planter with only petunias in it lacks a good proportion and good scale relationship. It looks out of place.

In areas where cold winters may damage any permanent plantings, it's a good idea to line the inside of the planter with styrofoam sheets. This will reduce the effects of freezing and thawing.

Night lighting is no longer a costly or difficult project. New plastic insulated cable may be buried directly in the soil without using conduit. Conduit is required only where it comes out of the ground to attach to your fixture.

You can choose from a number of different light fixtures. Each is designed to achieve different effects. Consult your local power company or a local lighting store to determine which would be most appropriate.

Outdoor lighting can be used for three different purposes: to floodlight large areas; to spotlight specific features; and to illuminate areas softly by underlighting (directing the light upward into the plant or tree) to emphasize structure, form, and foliage. For small areas the last function fits best. However, there may be other features, sculpture, for example, that you may wish to spotlight.

Sculpture, murals or mosaics, and even boulders can enhance your design. These elements should be selected for form, color, texture, and interesting detail. Seldom can you ever use more than one of these elements effectively. To use more could clutter your design and result in visual confusion.

Selecting sculpture is a very personal thing. By including such an element you are creating an atmosphere expressing your tastes. For best results, you should carefully consider the scale of the piece. Small units usually need a plain, but complementary, base to elevate them to a level where the eye can appreciate the design. Usually sculpture is best set against a foliage or structural backdrop to show it to best advantage.

If you use large boulders, select specimens with unusual form, texture, and color. Place them carefully to show off their interesting qualities. This type of natural material can be most handsome. Boulders should look as if they logically belong where they are, not like they just fell out of the sky.

Successful landscape planning involves three considerations. First, consider your needs and determine how you plan to use the landscape. Second, carefully study your site for orientation, climatic factors, topography, and existing features. And finally, develop a scale drawing of the area you are going to develop.

Your family is the most important consideration in planning your landscape. Make a list of your family's needs. This will tell you which of the two types of spaces mentioned earlier will be most appropriate—a landscape scene or usable living space.

A list of family interests may help you to organize your thinking. Do you wish to extend your living activities into the outdoor area? Are there family hobbies which could be furthered by this development? Do you enjoy gardening or would you prefer a low maintenance design? How frequently do you entertain? Are the groups large or small? How often does your family cook out? Do family members enjoy sitting and relaxing outdoors? Do you wish to attract birds? Is there a need for space to store equipment?

A list, such as this, of your wants and needs will be most helpful in fashioning your final plan. It is the first and most important step to beginning your landscape, whatever the size.

Next, you need to carefully analyze your site because the character of the land, the climate, and the surrounding properties will determine the basic design and what landscape elements you should use.

Your design will be influenced by the property and its orientation to wind and sun. You should consider plantings or vertical structures that will give protection from the summer sun and also allow warmth from the winter sun, wind barriers to reduce the wind, and slopes to carry rain and melted snow from the house and the garden structures.

Identify sunny and shaded areas. You can then select plants that survive in either type of exposure. Find the average low winter temperature. Then you will know whether a plant will grow in your area. Hardiness is the word used to express a plant's tolerance to temperatures and climates. Your Cooperative Extension agent can tell you what plants are hardy in your climatic zone.

In your analysis, note the best natural resources of the site. Are there very good trees or interesting changes in grade? Carefully study good as well as bad views. Keep attractive views open. Screen out unattractive and objectionable views either by structures or by proper plantings. At the same time consider screening for privacy from your neighbors. One consideration is the height of surrounding land and buildings. You can screen by fencing and by skillful placement of shrubs and trees.

Finally, you will need to know the relative acidity or alkalinity, texture, humus content, and drainage of the soil. Soils that are extremely acid or alkaline restrict plant growth. A very heavy clay soil will drain poorly and keep needed air from the plant roots.

For easy maintenance, it is best to choose plants that will tolerate your particular soil condition.

With your list of family needs and your analysis of the site done, you are now ready to draw to scale a plan of the area. In a scaled drawing a fraction of an inch equals 1 foot. For example, ⅛ inch on paper is used to represent 1 foot on the ground; this is called a one-eighth inch scale.

To obtain the measurements for your scaled drawing you will have to make your outdoor measurements with a steel tape. First draw a rough sketch of the area and of the shape of the house on a sheet of paper. Allow enough space to jot down the measurements as you make them. Locate the position of the building in relation to the property boundaries and measure tree, walk, drive, sewer line, water line locations. Note also the location of power and telephone service, whether it's overhead or underground.

After locating all important features (don't forget windows and doors), you are ready to transfer this information to your base plan. A scale of ⅛ or ¼ inch equal to one foot will allow you to use a standard ruler. If you wish you may draw this to scale on graph paper. You can buy graph paper with various grid scales (¹⁄₁₆, ⅛, ¼) at most stationery and book stores.

You are now ready to start developing your design. The scale drawing will help you to visualize the space relationships and work out design patterns. It is amazing how mistakes and ideas will develop and show up on a plan. The more accurate you are, the more effective your plan will be. By fastening a sheet of tracing paper over your basic plan, you can try out various arrangements.

The first step in sketching out your design is to establish a basic ground pattern. There are no rules for developing a pattern. This is a personal thing. A rough guide is that lines near the building should follow the same regular pattern but as the pattern moves from the building it can become looser, more flowing and more informal.

Remember it is the shapes developed between the lines which are important —not the lines themselves.

Your final scale design will take the guesswork out of the project. And it will suggest to you additional landscape

elements to combine with those previously selected. With this approach you have the blueprint for an organized, well designed landscape whether you complete it in planned stages or all at once.

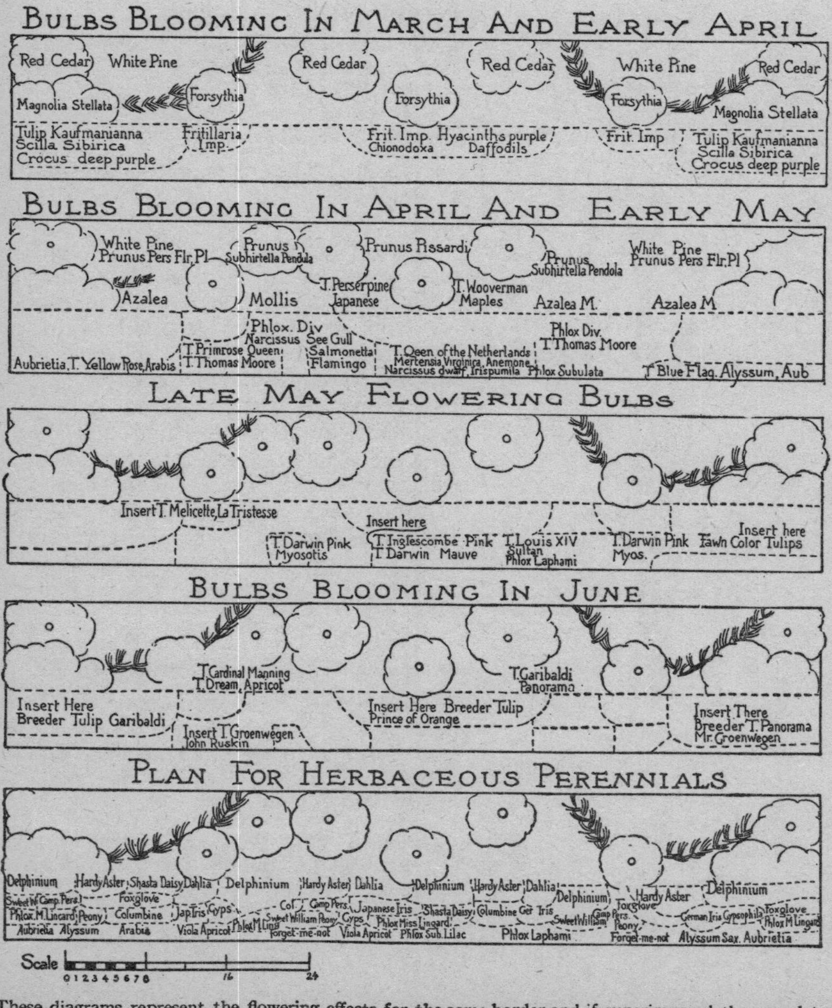

BULBS BLOOMING IN MARCH AND EARLY APRIL

Red Cedar — White Pine — Red Cedar — Red Cedar — White Pine — Red Cedar

Magnolia Stellata — Forsythia — Forsythia — Forsythia — Magnolia Stellata

Tulip Kaufmanianna — Frittillaria Imp. — Frit. Imp. Hyacinths purple — Frit. Imp — Tulip Kaufmanianna
Scilla Sibirica — Chionodoxa — Daffodils — Scilla Sibirica
Crocus deep purple — Crocus deep purple

BULBS BLOOMING IN APRIL AND EARLY MAY

White Pine — Prunus Subhirtella Pendula — Prunus Pissardi — Prunus Subhirtella Pendula — White Pine
Prunus Pers Flr. Pl. — Prunus Pers Flr.Pl

Azalea — Mollis — T. Perserpine Japanese — T. Wooverman Maples — Azalea M. — Azalea M

Phlox Div. Narcissus See Gull — Phlox Div.
T. Primrose Queen — Salmonetta — T. Thomas Moore
Aubrietia T. Yellow Rose Arabis — T. Thomas Moore — Flamingo — T. Queen of the Netherland — Phlox Subulata — T. Blue Flag. Alyssum, Aub
Mertensa Wginca Anemone
Narcissus dwarf trispumia

LATE MAY FLOWERING BULBS

Insert T. Melicette, La Tristesse — Insert here — Insert here
Insert here
T. Darwin Pink — T. Inglescombe Pink T. Louis XIV — T. Darwin Pink Tawn Color Tulips
Myosotis — T. Darwin Mauve — Sultan Myos.
Phlox Laphami

BULBS BLOOMING IN JUNE

T. Cardinal Manning — T. Garibaldi
T. Dream, Apricot — Panorama
Insert Here — Insert Here Breeder Tulip — Insert There
Breeder Tulip Garibaldi — Prince of Orange — Breeder T. Panorama
T. Groenwegen — Mr. Groenwegen
John Ruskin

PLAN FOR HERBACEOUS PERENNIALS

Delphinium — Hardy Aster Shasta Daisy Dahlia — Delphinium — Hardy Aster Dahlia — Delphinium Hardy Aster Dahlias — Delphinium
Phlox M. Lincard Peony — Foxglove — Col. Comp Pers — Japanese Iris Shasta Daisy Columbine Gp Iris — Delphinium Hardy Aster — Foxglove
Aubrietia Alyssum — Columbine — Jupiter Pers — Sweet William Pers. — Forget-me-not — German Iris Canterbury Bell Foxglove
Arabis — Viola Apricot — Viola Apricot Phlox Sub Lilac — Forget-me-not Alyssum Sax. Aubrietia

Scale
0 1 2 3 4 5 6 7 8

HYDRANGEA

These diagrams represent the flowering effects for the same border and if superimposed the complete planting plan will be produced

container gardening offers something for everyone

CONTAINER GARDENING is especially adapted to contemporary living. Plants in containers are compatible with any decor, be it the straight horizontal and vertical lines of contemporary architecture or the more comfortable lines of the early American home. Plants display great variety of form and texture. They can be used to create instant indoor gardens; they can be moved from one home to another; and they can be moved outdoors in the summer and indoors during the cooler months.

Space is not a problem. Container gardening can be conducted in a single pot on a table or windowsill, in a more elaborate room divider, or in a built-in planter.

Just as there are many kinds of plants, there are many kinds of containers. Plants can be grown in any container that will hold a growing medium. The choice ranges from the common clay pot to cans, jars, boxes, baskets, and tubs. Containers may be made of wood, plastic, glass, metal, and glazed ceramics. They can be portable or built in.

Most people select containers for both their practical and esthetic qualities. These include cost, availability, weight, strength, durability, attractiveness, and decorative and sentimental value.

When you choose a container, its size and shape should be consistent with the plant's size and shape. Tall, tapering plants are more attractive in tall, relatively narrow containers. Short, compact plants appear more at home in shallow, wide containers.

Particularly important considerations for good plant growth are the volume and depth of the container, plus some provision for drainage. Select containers that have drainage holes in the bottom for removal of excess water. Watertight containers are difficult to manage; excess water will accumulate at the bottom of the container and injure plant roots by excluding oxygen. Container volume and depth become critical in relation to the quantity of available water and nutrients.

Although the evaporation of water through the container walls is not critical, plants in porous containers will require more frequent watering to maintain moisture levels than will those in nonporous containers.

Besides the right kind of container, some fundamental requirements for plant growth must be provided if you are going to be a successful indoor gardener. Plants need light, water, nutrients, and a satisfactory temperature range.

Light is the most critical requirement. The levels of all the other requirements are adjusted in relation to the amount of light that plants receive. When plants don't have enough light, they grow slowly and become tall and spindly; it becomes difficult to avoid overwatering them. Plants are easier to maintain in good condition when their light requirements are met. You can use fluorescent lamps to supplement or replace natural light. Or you can select plants to fit the level of light that is available in a particular location.

The majority of the plants grown in containers will thrive at temperatures ranging from 60° to 75°F. In poorly

Author JOHN W. WHITE is Associate Professor of Floriculture at The Pennsylvania State University, University Park.

Coauthor JOHN W. MASTALERZ is Professor of Floriculture at the University.

lighted locations, you should keep the air temperatures as low as people will tolerate. As the amount of available light increases, higher temperatures can be used.

Plants will benefit if moisture is added to the air to increase relative humidity. Plants will grow under conditions of low humidity, but a more frequent watering will generally be necessary.

Let's say you have a location with enough light and a satisfactory temperature range, and that you've purchased a few good containers. There's not much more to indoor gardening except making sure that you have a good growing medium and keeping your plants well watered.

Growing media can be purchased at nurseries and garden centers. Special kinds are available for acid-loving plants, for orchids and for cacti, but it is fun to make your own growing medium. You can either follow another person's recipe, or you can experiment and develop your own special blend.

A good growing medium does four things. It anchors roots and provides physical support for the top; it stores nutrient elements (fertilizer); it stores water; and it is a source of oxygen for root growth.

These last two items—water and oxygen—are the cause of most problems people have with indoor gardening. Plants can very easily get too much of one and not enough of the other. Part of the job of a good growing medium is to make sure that plants have a chance to get enough of both.

For this reason, soils containing large quantities of clay and silt should not be used. Because the particles of clay and silt are very small, they clog up air pores in the soil and keep the plant's roots from obtaining enough oxygen. When this happens, the plant usually will die.

Many people have excellent results with good garden soil. But if you don't have much experience with plants, you will probably be better off using a good mixture.

In general, a mixture has three parts —soil, organic matter, and coarse aggregate.

Soil is not essential for plant growth. However, soil is usually the largest portion of most mixtures simply because it is inexpensive and readily available.

Organic matter adds air space, reduces the weight, and keeps a mixture from compacting. In other words, it has just the opposite effect of clay and silt. However, should the organic matter decompose too rapidly, these properties will be lost. Thus, if you add organic matter, use a kind that is resistant to rapid decay.

Sphagnum moss peat, peat humus, sawdust, bark, hulls, straw, cobs, compost, manure, and animal byproducts are the major types of organic matter used in mixtures for container gardening. Sphagnum moss peat is excellent because it is readily available in several grades, slow to decompose, low in mineral elements, and chemically stable when steam pasteurized.

Coarse aggregates are used primarily to improve pore space and drainage and sometimes to reduce weight. Since they are either of mineral or synthetic origin, they are generally very resistant to decomposition. Sand, gravel, vermiculite, perlite, calcined clays, cinders, and shredded plastics are examples.

When soil is placed in a shallow container, the water-holding capacity of that soil is increased and the amount of pore space occupied by air is decreased. Consequently, the soil must be amended to increase the size of the soil pores and decrease the ability of the soil to hold water. This is the reason that a mixture of ingredients is recommended as a growing medium for plants in containers.

Sometimes the medium itself plugs the drainage holes, and sometimes the roots of the plant do. To prevent this from happening, put some stones or curved pieces of broken clay pots over the drain holes. Special plastic drain pieces also may be used.

Here are some soil mixtures that will work quite well for most indoor gardening projects. The ingredients are expressed as parts by volume.

General purpose medium
  2 parts sandy loam soil
  1 part organic matter
    (medium to coarse grade)
  1 part coarse aggregate

Add superphosphate and pulverized or dolomitic limestone according to results of soil tests.

Some people add organic or complete inorganic fertilizers to their mixtures. This practice can result in root loss from excess fertilizer (soluble salts) unless you are quite knowledgeable of the correct kinds and amounts to add. If you are not sure, start out experimenting with a small batch and see how the plants do. Keep in mind that what works well for one plant species may not work at all for another. Also remember that many organic fertilizers vary greatly in chemical composition from batch to batch and from year to year.

A table has been included to give you some idea of how much fertilizer to use.

Acid lovers
(azaleas, camellias, gardenias, heathers)
1 part organic matter (preferably one with a low pH such as sphagnum moss peat)
1 part coarse aggregate

Some of these plants grow very well in only organic matter. The low pH of some peats requires the addition of limestone before growing most plants (pH indicates the intensity or strength of acidity or alkalinity in the soil. A pH of 7.0 is neutral, below 7.0 is acid, and above 7.0 is alkaline.)

Fine-rooted plants
(annual seedlings, begonias, many foliage plants, African-violets)
1 part sandy loam soil
1 part organic matter (fine grade)
1 part coarse aggregate

Cacti and succulents
(crassulas, echeverias, sedums)
2 parts sandy loam soil
1 part organic matter (fine grade)
2 parts coarse aggregate

All of the previous mixtures contained soil. Here are some soilless mix-

Slowly Soluble and Slow-Release Fertilizers With Trial Rates of Application for General Purpose or Fine-Rooted Media

Fertilizer	Ounces per bushel [1]
Nitrogen	
Urea-Formaldehyde [2] (38% N)	2 to 3.
Blood meal [2] (13% N)	1 to 2.
Fish meal [2] (11% N)	1 to 2.
Hoof and horn meal [2] (13% N)	1 to 2.
Castor pomace [2] (6% N)	2 to 3.
Osmocote 14–14–14 [2] (14% N)	3 to 6.
Osmocote 18–9–9 [2] (18% N)	4 to 8.
Mag Amp 7–40–6 (7% N) (14% Mg)	6 to 12.
Phosphorus	
Single superphosphate (20% P_2O_5)	2 to 4.
Treble superphosphate (45% P_2O_5)	1 to 2.
Potassium	
Fritted potash (Dura–K)	1 to 2.
Magnesium and calcium	
Pulverized dolomitic limestone	3 to 6.
Calcium and sulphate	
Gypsum	3 to 6.

---

[1] Use the lower rates for slow growing plants and sensitive plants like African-violets, azaleas, begonias, orchids, and ferns.
[2] Do not heat treat (steam pasteurize) soils containing these materials. They can be added safely after steaming as a 3- to 4-month source of fertilizer.

---

tures that are easy to prepare and give good results.

University of California Soil Mix
1 part fine sand (preferably around 0.5 to 0.05 mm in diameter)
1 part finely shredded peat (Canadian or German sphagnum or California hypnum)

With fertilizer formula I (given below) this mix may be stored indefinitely.

Fertilizer formula I for U.C. Soil Mix

Add to each bushel of mix 2 ounces of 20 percent superphosphate, 6 ounces dolomitic limestone, and 2 ounces pulverized limestone, 5 grams potassium nitrate, and 5 grams potassium sulfate.

Cornell Peat-Lite Mixes
1 part vermiculite (No. 2, 3, or 4 grade) or perlite (horticultural grade)
1 part shredded sphagnum moss peat

Add to each bushel of mix 3.5 ounces of pulverized dolomitic limestone, 1.5 ounces of 20 percent superphosphate, ¾ ounce potassium nitrate, and 1 gram chelated iron.

A key to success with any medium, but especially with soilless media, is thorough mixing of the fertilizers into the medium. Peat moss is often difficult to wet. Using warm water will make it easier to wet. The superphosphate and limestone are best added dry before the peat moss is wetted. But the potassium nitrate and chelated iron are easier to add in solution with a sprinkling can because of the small quantities needed.

Orchids and Bromeliads
3 parts bark (fir or redwood)
1 part sphagnum moss
1 part coarse aggregate

Camellias and Gardenias
2 parts ⅛- to ¼-inch pieces of fir bark (not tanbark)
1 part organic matter (fine grade and acid)
1 part coarse aggregate

PINXTER FLOWER.
(AZALEA NUDIFLORA.)

Grass growing in Pine Cones.

The amount of water available to a plant for growth is affected by volume and depth of the container, physical properties of the growing medium, and the amount and distribution of roots. Growing media described previously were designed to allow water to be applied frequently without danger of killing plant roots because of a lack of oxygen, assuming that adequate drainage out of and away from the container is provided. Therefore, the major concern is determining how frequently to irrigate to prevent a water deficiency.

The number and distribution of roots determines how much of the total volume of medium is being used by roots in absorbing water. A small seedling will absorb very little water because the number of roots are few and they occupy a relatively small amount of the medium. Small quantities of water must be added frequently for small plants because of their shallow root systems.

A large succulent plant, such as a geranium with foliage overlapping the sides of the container, will use as much as 20 ounces of water on a bright sunny day. Thus, on a bright day a large geranium in a 6-inch pot of general purpose growing medium would have to be watered four times a day to maintain rapid growth and development. Surface mulches will reduce these rates of water loss; this is more true for small plants in large containers than for large plants in small containers.

You can reduce the frequency of watering house plants by filling an indoor planter with peat moss and inserting the pots up to the rim in the peat. Water is applied to the peat moss and is absorbed through the walls of the containers.

Clay pots evaporate 50 percent of the water applied directly through the pot walls. In contrast, glazed clay pots and plastic pots lose no water through the pot wall. Nonporous pots will cut the frequency of watering about in half.

One inch of rainfall into a 6-inch container supplies about 15 ounces of water. If all the rainwater went into the container (most of it runs off the foliage onto the ground), 1⅓ inches of rain would be needed daily to grow the geranium. Obviously, supplemental irrigation will be necessary under these conditions.

It is usually best to apply water in excess of container capacity to be assured that the entire medium is wet. Many people double water (that is, they water twice within a half hour) to accomplish thorough wetting. Double watering also helps to expand the medium so that it seals against the container wall. This prevents water from running between the container and medium where it is lost without a chance of soaking into the medium.

Accumulation of soluble salts is another factor affecting the amount of water used. As water evaporates from the surface of the medium, salts (unused fertilizers) are left as residues. If these residues are not flushed out of the medium, they eventually accumulate to toxic amounts. Periodic additions of more water than the medium can hold are necessary to flush out these salt residues. This is called leaching. The plant symptoms of salt buildup are wilting when the medium is wet, loss of roots, and eventual drying out and necrosis (death) of the leaves.

You can apply water manually using a sprinkler can or hose with a water breaker, an attachment which reduces the force of water applied to the soil. Many people enjoy this daily task. Or, you can purchase irrigation pipe systems for use with containers. These systems are easily automated using solenoid valves and timeclocks. Such automation simplifies irrigation and removes the human factor, making it easier for you to schedule weekend trips and vacations. Also water delivered automatically can be applied more slowly, with less force, and more frequently than is convenient manually.

In some areas water quality may be a problem and may vary from season to season. As a general rule, water safe for human consumption is usually safe for container plants. One exception to this rule is that water softeners should not be used in water for irrigating plants. The reason is that water from softeners has a high sodium content which destroys soil structure. (Most water softeners are installed in homes at the point where the water line is attached to the municipal supply.)

Also, you should be wary of watering plants with a hose that has lain in the hot sun all day. It may contain water hot enough to scald both plants and root systems.

Never repot a plant into a container with more than 4-inch clearance between root ball and container wall. Excess medium in oversize containers can stay too wet and sour when out of reach of roots for very long. Toxic substances build up and damage the plants.

Some indoor gardeners have poor results with their plants despite being conscientious about using the right mixtures for the kind of plant they are growing, making sure that their containers are the right size, and seeing that the plants are properly watered and drained. What's wrong? Well, it could be that one or more essential nutrient elements may be missing from the mixture.

Sixteen elements are accepted generally as essential for plant growth. They are carbon (C), hydrogen (H), oxygen (O), phosphorus (P), potassium (K), nitrogen (N), sulfur (S), calcium (Ca), iron (Fe), magnesium (Mg), chlorine (Cl), molybdenum (Mo), boron (B), copper (Cu), manganese (Mn), and zinc (Zn). If you want to memorize these elements, here's an easy way. Learn this sentence:

The mob comes in to see Cl. Hopkins, cafe manager.

MoB CuMn Zn C Cl HOPKNS CaFe Mg

These essential elements are present in the atmosphere or growing medium most of the time. For instance, carbon and oxygen are supplied as carbon dioxide (CO_2) from the air. Hydrogen enters the plant as water (H_2O).

The other 13 elements enter the plant through the roots, although some can be absorbed through the leaves. These 13 elements can be added to the growing medium as fertilizers (salts).

CEDAR PLANT TUB.

Phosphorus, sulfur, and calcium usually are applied prior to planting as 20 percent (single) superphosphate ($CaH_4(PO_4)_2$ and $CaSO_4$), calcium and sulfur as gypsum ($CaSO_4$), calcium as pulverized limestone ($CaCO_3$) and calcium and magnesium as dolomitic limestone ($CaMgCO_3$).

Iron, chlorine, molybdenum, boron, copper, manganese, and zinc are present in sufficient quantities in most soils to supply the needs of a container-grown plant for several months. However, the soilless media do require applications of these elements. Some of these elements are added as impurities in low analysis complete fertilizers such as 5–10–5 or 10–10–10. Some must be added as separate fertilizers.

Plants use more nitrogen and potassium than they do other elements, so these must be applied at more frequent intervals. Nitrogen and potassium can be applied prior to planting in organic fertilizer forms or as slow-release inorganic chemicals, or after planting in a quickly available dry or liquid form.

To maintain good fertility, you need to take into consideration the plant species and its stage of development, plant size, season of the year, the growing medium, and irrigation practices.

Small, slow growing, reproductive plants, seedlings, and most fine-rooted plants will require less fertilizer than large, rapidly growing, highly vegetative, coarse-rooted plants.

Three basic approaches are used for fertility control. These are: a standard fertilization program; chemical analysis of the growing medium and plant tissue; and visual appearance of the plant.

Fertilization programs may range from very dilute daily applications with each irrigation to yearly top dressing with low analysis (5–10–5) slow release or organic fertilizers. For example, you can fertilize potted chrysanthemums at every irrigation with 1 level teaspoon (3.8 grams) per gallon of water using a 20–20–20 fertilizer, or once every 3 months using 1 level tablespoon per 6-inch pot of a 14–14–14 slow-release fertilizer. Additional slowly soluble fertilizers and rates of application are

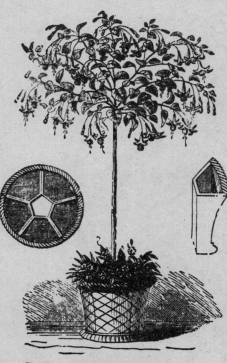

Fig. 73.—A Fuchsia trained in Umbrella form.

listed in the table on page 43. Many annuals require about one-half of these amounts; azaleas, begonias, and foliage plants need about one-fourth.

The home gardener will find that the following dry mixture is safe and easy to use on trees and shrubs grown in containers:

6 parts hoof and horn or bloodmeal
1 part ammonium nitrate
1 part treble superphosphate
1 part sulfate of potash
6 parts gypsum

Apply this mixture once monthly during the early part of the growing season at the rate of 1 level teaspoon per 4½-inch pot, 2 teaspoons per 6-inch pot, or 3 teaspoons per 7-inch pot. Narrow-leaved plants require less fertilizer than broad-leaved plants.

20-inch diameter, on 5 casters...$1.25
22 "   "   "   6 "   ... 1.50

You should avoid midsummer applications because they encourage soft growth in late fall which winterkills easily. Some nurserymen recommend applications after leaf drop. At that time the tops are dormant, but the roots are still active and capable of absorbing nutrients which may be stored until needed for growth in the spring.

Variation in fertilization levels can be used to just maintain a plant with little or no growth, or to force a plant to grow rapidly. Large and frequent applications of nitrogen and water produce the most rapid growth. Reduction in amounts of nitrogen and water slow down the rate of growth. Use a 5–10–10 for maintenance, a 10–10–10 for moderate, and a 20–10–10 fertilizer for rapid plant growth.

Soil analysis programs are available in most States either through the county extension agent's office, the State university, or commercial laboratories. Tissue analysis programs are less widely available. All growing media should be tested prior to use each year, especially for pH and total soluble salts. Most laboratories also test for phosphorus, potassium, and calcium, and some for nitrogen and magnesium. Be sure to send in a sample representative of the total contents of the container and specify on the sample that recommen-

dations should be made for container growing and not for growing in the ground.

Tissue samples are used primarily to help diagnose problems when the plants do not look healthy. Contact your local laboratories about sampling procedures.

Visual appearance of the plant can offer clues to the trained diagnostician when a plant is not healthy. However, a visual diagnosis can also be misleading since many different causes (insects, disease, air pollution) can produce similar effects.

Visual diagnosis should always be combined with soil and tissue analysis.

Many houseplants die while the owner is away from home on a vacation or business trip. The best way to prevent loss of plants while you're away is to get a friend to look in on them now and then and give them any care they need.

Watering plants during your vacation is not a difficult problem to solve. If you have time before leaving, decrease the frequency of watering for several weeks. By allowing plants to reach the wilting point several times, the need for water can be reduced. Plants will adjust to lower moisture levels without suffering permanent harm.

An alternative method is to water the plants thoroughly, seal them in clear polyethylene plastic bags, and place them in a cool location out of direct sunlight.

If your plants are in porous containers, stand them on clay bricks placed in a watertight container. Bring the water level up to the top of the bricks. Reduce the light intensity to decrease evaporation. Plants in porous containers can be taken outdoors and buried up to the rim in soil or saturated peat moss. A shady location is best.

Plants usually can get along satisfactorily by themselves for about 2 weeks. If you must be away for more than 2 weeks, reconcile yourself to loss of some of your plants. Flowering plants in particular are likely to die.

The Guelder Rose

Suggestions for Large Tubbed Specimens

Australian umbrella tree	Fiddle-leaf fig	Philodendrons
Dracaenas	India-rubber plant	Silk-oak
False-aralia	and cultivars	Tuftroot
Fatshedera	Palms	Veitch screwpine

For Special Exposures
SOUTH OR WEST WINDOWS

Amaryllis	Coleus	Oxalis
Azalea	Cyclamen	Poinsettia
Begonia (in winter)	Easter lily	Rose
Bloodleaf	Gardenia	Sweetflag
Cacti and succulents	Geranium	Tulip
Calla lily	Lily	Velvet plant

NORTH WINDOW

African-violet	Dracaena	Philodendron
(in summer)	Dumbcane	Piggyback plant
Anthericum	Fern	Pleomele
Arrowhead	Ivy	Rubber plant
Australian umbrella tree	Mother-of-thousands	Scindapsus (Pothos)
Babytears	Norfolk Island pine	Snake plant
Cast-iron plant	Peperomia	Tuftroot
Chinese evergreen		Wandering-Jew

EAST WINDOW

African-violet	Gloxinia	Serissa
Banded maranta	Ivy	Silk-oak
Caladium	Peperomia	Tuftroot
Dracaena	Philodendron	Veitch screwpine
Fatshedera	Rubber plant	Wandering-Jew
Fern	Scindapsus (Pothos)	Wax Plant

Container Plant Suggestions for Various Conditions

Plants for Low Temperature (50°–60° F. at Night)

Australian laurel	Citrus	Jerusalem-cherry
Azalea	Cyclamen	Kalanchoe
Babytears	Easter lily	Miniature holly
Black pepper	English ivy cultivars	Mother-of-thousands
Boxwood	Fatshedera	Oxalis
Bromeliads	Flowering maple	Primrose
Calceolaria	Fuchsia	Sensitive plant
Camellia	Geraniums	Spindle tree
Christmas begonia	German ivy	Vinca
Cineraria	Honeysuckle	White calla lily

Plants for Medium Temperature (60°–65° F. at Night)

Achimenes	Crown of thorns	Poinsettia
Amaryllis	Easter lily	Rose
Ardisia	English ivy cultivars	Shrimp plant
Avocado	Gardenia	Silk-oak
Bromeliads	Grape ivy	Ti Plant
Browallia	Hibiscus	Tuberous begonia
Chenille plant	Hydrangea	Velvet plant
Christmas cactus	Norfolk Island pine	Wax begonia
Chrysanthemum	Palms	Wax plant
Citrus	Peperomia	Yellow calla lily
Copperleaf	Pilea	

Plants for High Temperature (65°–75° F. at Night)

African-violet	Chinese evergreen	Golddust plant
Aphelandra	Croton	Philodendron
Arrowhead	Dracaena	Scindapsus (Pothos)
Australian umbrella tree	Episcia	Seersucker plant
Banded Maranta	Figs	Snake plant
Cacti and succulents	Gloxinia	Spathyphyllum
Caladium		Veitch screwpine

Plants That Will Withstand Abuse

Arrowhead	Fiddle-leaf fig	Pleomele
Australian umbrella tree	Grape ivy	Snake plant
Cast-iron plant	Heartleaf Philodendron	Spathyphyllum
Chinese evergreen	India-rubber plant	Trileaf Wonder
Crown of thorns	Jade plant	Tuftroot (*D. amoena*)
Devil's ivy	Ovalleaf Peperomia	Veitch screwpine
		Zebra plant

Plants for Extremely Dry Conditions

Bromeliads	Crown of thorns	Snake plant
Cacti	Ovalleaf Peperomia	Scindapsus (Pothos)
		Wandering-Jew

Vines and Trailing Plants for Totem Poles

Arrowhead	Grape ivy	Philodendron
Black pepper	Kangaroo vine	Scindapsus (Pothos)
Creeping fig	Pellionia	Syngonium
English ivy cultivars		Wax Plant

Plants for Hanging Baskets

African-violet	Fuchsia (some cultivars)	Philodendron (some species)
Anthericum	German ivy	Saxifraga
(Spider plant)	Goldfish plant	Scindapsus (pothos)
Asparagus fern	Grape ivy	Syngonium
Begonias (some types)	Honeysuckle	Trailing-coleus
Black pepper	Italian bellflower	Wandering-Jew
English ivy cultivars	Ivy geranium	Wax plant
Episcia	Peperomia (some species)	

CONTAINER MANUFACTURERS

(write for local distributor)

HEATH MANUFACTURING CO.
Coopersville, Michigan 49404

ROSENWACH, INC.
96 North 9th Street
Brooklyn, N.Y. 11211

SPAETH DISPLAYS
423 West 55th Street
New York, N.Y. 10019

—Maranta fasciata.

Standard Flower Pots

—Centaurea gymnocarpa.

Noteworthy Native Trees for Gardens

Common name	Latin name	Growth region (see the map on page 178)	Special comment
White fir	Abies concolor	4, 5, 9–14, 27, 28	Evergreen, shapely, fine foliage
Huisache	Acacia farnesiana	5, 10, 11, 17, 20, 29, 30	Grows larger with moisture. Deciduous.
Red maple	Acer rubrum	19–30	Red fall color; rapid growing
Sugar maple	Acer saccharum	2, 15, 18, 21–29	One of our most brilliantly-colored trees in autumn.
Ohio buckeye	Aesculus glabra	22, 24, 25, 27, 28, 29	Successfully planted in recent years in region 13 at lower elevations.
Madrona	Arbutus menziesii	1–3, 5, 10	Difficult to transplant, a beauty.
Hickory	Carya spp.	20–30	Usually hard to transplant.
Catalpa	Catalpa spp.	21–23, 25–30	Leaves very large, flower clusters showy.
Hackberry	Celtis occidentalis	15–30	Drought resistant. Much planted in the Great Plains.
Paloverde	Cercidium torreyanum	10–11	Excellent in desert gardens.
Port Orford cedar	Chamaecyparis lawsoniana	1, 2, 28, 29	70 or more varieties, some exceptionally pleasing.
Flowering dogwood	Cornus florida	1, 2, 20, 22–25, 27–30	Pink, white, and double flowered forms known, also a weeping form
Pacific dogwood	Cornus nuttallii	1–5, 12	Somewhat difficult to grow; forms from region 12 will probably grow in 27 and 28.
Monterey cypress	Cupressus macrocarpa	1, 5	Growth form highly picturesque, especially along the seacoast.
American beech	Fagus grandifolia	20, 22–30	Magnificent specimen tree.
White ash	Fraxinus americana	20, 22–25, 27–30	
Red ash	Fraxinus pennsylvanica	15, 18, 20; and 12 and 17 for green ash, a variety	
Honeylocust	Gleditsia triacanthos	16, 20, 22–30	There is a thornless variety. Highly resistant to drought.
American holly	Ilex opaca	20, 25, 27–30	Many varieties available, some better than the wild form.
Walnut	Juglans spp.	18–30	

Common name	Latin name	Growth region (see the map on page 178)	Special comment
Juniper (Red cedar)	Juniperus spp.	Different species occur in western mountains and in the East	Eastern red cedar is rapid growing. Western species are slower.
Larch	Larix spp.	Eastern larch 22–24, 26, 27. Western larch 4, 12	The eastern species occurs in swamps, but grows quite well on dry land. Deciduous.
Incense cedar	Calocedrus decurrens	1, 4, 5, 29, 30.	Elegant evergreen foliage.
Sweetgum	Liquidambar styraciflua	2, 20, 22, 25, 27–30	Exceptionally brilliant fall color.
Tuliptree	Liriodendron tulipifera	2, 21–29	Very rapid growing. Excellent specimen tree.
Catalina ironwood	Lyonothamnus floribundus	5	Much planted in southern California.
Magnolia	Magnolia spp.	Generally 28–30, 27 for some	The evergreen magnolia is especially beautiful; planted also in 1, 2, 3, 5. Bigleaf magnolia has the largest leaves of any American tree (25, 27–30).
Red mulberry	Morus rubra	16–25, 27–30	Highly attractive to birds.
Blackgum	Nyssa sylvatica	20, 22, 24, 25–30	Brilliant fall color.
Sourwood	Oxydendron arboreum	25, 27–30	Very attractive in flower.
Blue spruce	Picea pungens	9, 12–14, 27–29	Many cultivated varieties. Exceptional form and color. (White, black and sitka spruces are also in cultivation.)
Pines	Pinus spp.	(About 40 species, nearly all cultivated. Use any "good" pine native to your region. Big trees, except for the pinyon or nut pines of the Southwest.)	

Common name	Latin name	Growth region (see the map on page 178)	Special comment
Sycamore	Platanus spp.	Eastern S. 16, 20–22, 24–30. California S. 3, 4, 5. Arizona S. 10, 11	Majestic trees with "blotched" bark. Fine specimens. Best adapted to wet places, rich soil.
Douglas-fir	Pseudotsuga menziesii	The Rocky Mountain variety 9, 11, 13, 14, 16, 25, 27, 28, probably 29. The Pacific variety 1–6	The Rocky Mountain species is the only one successfully grown in the East.
Oaks	Quercus spp.	About 70 species, one or more in every growth region	Very slow growing, but superb trees, generally long-lived.
Black-locust	Robinia pseudoacacia	1–8, 12, 15, 16, 20–23, 25–29	
Cabbage palmetto	Sabal palmetto	30 (a related species, the Texas palm occurs in 11, 17)	
Sassafras	Sassafras albidum	2, 20, 22–30	
Redwood	Sequoia sempervirens	1	Has failed in the Eastern U.S. after many years of trial. Our tallest tree.
Sequoia	Sequoiadendron gigateum	4	Our most massive tree. Failed in the East over many years of trial.
Cypress	Taxodium spp.	17, 20, 25, 28–32	
Western red cedar	Thuja plicata	1, 2, 4, 6, 7, 12	
Basswood	Tilia spp.	Some 14 species, generally found in Eastern and Southeastern United States	Excellent shade trees.
Canadian hemlock	Tsuga canadensis	22, 25, 27–29	Excellent hedge, as well as specimen tree.
Western hemlock	Tsuga heterophylla	1, 2, 4, 6, 12	
Mountain hemlock	Tsuga mertensiana	4, 12	Slow growing. Fine specimen tree.
American elm	Ulmus americana	1, 2, 15, 16, 18–23, 25–30	Handsome, vase-shaped shade tree.
Yucca	Yucca spp.	Generally southwestern	Desert gardens.
Palms	Washingtonia spp.	Generally southwestern	The California species is much grown in 5.

USDA

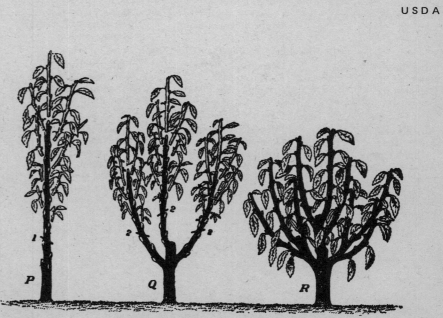

LAYING THE FOUNDATION OF A FUTURE TREE.

Common name	Latin name	Growth region (see the map on page 178)	Special comment
Flame azalea	Rhododendron calendulaceum	1, 2, 3, 20, 22, 24, 25, 27–29	Flowers yellow, orange, or red, brilliant. Rated by many as the finest native ornamental.
Flannel bush	Fremontia mexicana	5	Waxy yellow flowers. Closely-related California fremontia has golden flowers, not quite as showy, but excellent. The latter can be grown in regions 3, 4, 5, 10; if seed comes from high elevations, probably can be grown in regions 1, 2, 29, 30, 31, and possibly 28. Evergreen.
Mescalbean	Sophora secundiflora	11, 16, 17, 20, 29, 30	Wisteria-like clusters of violet-blue flowers, deliciously fragrant. Forms a little tree in favorable situations. Pods hard, seeds red or carmine.
Mountain-laurel	Kalmia latifolia	1, 2, 24–30	Pink-white flowers in clusters; highly floriferous. Evergreen.
Santa Barbara ceanothus	Ceanothus impressus	5 (possibly 29 and 30)	Foliage deep green; flowers dark blue. Prolific bloomer. "Clean, tailored" shrub, often wider than tall.
Fringe-tree	Chionanthus virginica	1, 2, 3, 20, 22, 24, 25, 27–30	Lacy, white flowers; very fragrant. A large shrub or small tree.
Mountain stewartia	Stewartia ovata var. grandiflora	1, 2, 20, 22, 24, 25, 27–30	Waxy-white flowers up to 4 inches across. Orange and scarlet fall color.

Common name	Latin name	Growth Region (see the map on page 178)	Special comment
Yaupon	Ilex vomitoria	20, 28, 29, 30 (probably 1, 2, 3 and 5)	An evergreen valuable for its profusion of red berries.
Cranberrybush	Viburnum trilobum	1, 2, 4, 12, 13, 15, 18, 21, 27	White, flat-topped flower clusters. Fruits bright red, highly attractive.
Oakleaf hydrangea	Hydrangea quercifolia	1, 2, 24, 25, 28–30 (Freezes in 27)	Large panicles of white flowers later turning copper to brown. Leaves large, oakleaf shaped. Very tolerant of shade.
Oregon-grape	Mahonia aquifolium	1, 2, 4, 6, 7, 11–16, 22, 24, 25, 27–29	Hollylike, shining green foliage. Flowers bright yellow; fruits grapelike, blue. There is a form with a dull leaf, not as good.
Creosotebush	Larrea tridentata	9, 10, 11, 16, 17	Excellent, yellow-flowered shrub for desert gardens. Foliage evergreen.
Anacahuita	Cordia boissieri	11, 17, 30; possibly 29–32	Very rare evergreen. Flowers white, with yellow centers, clustered. Fruits ivory white.
Sage brush	Artemisia tridentata	2, 4–13, 15, 27, 28	A very fine silver-white bush. Requires alkaline soil (use a little lime or crushed shells around it).

—Erect leafy Twig of the Norway Maple (*Acer platanoides*)

STREET TREE EVALUATION

In this era of environmental concern, trees are considered as positive factors both aesthetically and functionally. The impact of trees is most noticeable in an urban site, where they offer the features of softening lines of buildings, modifying the harshness of concrete and asphalt, and screening unsightly areas. In addition, they provide cooling shade, adsorb some solid pollutants, and reduce noise pollution to a limited extent. The positive psychological and economic effects of trees in commercial and residential areas are well known. Their great popularity in today's landscape industry emphasizes the importance of proper evaluation and selection for long-term effect.

Numerous new introductions from nurseries have led to confusion for people concerned with tree selection and use, such as landscape architects and contractors, utility companies, municipalities, other public agencies, and home owners. Because of the apparent need for a comprehensive evaluation of new types at one site, a research project was initiated at the Ohio Agricultural Research and Development Center in 1966.

The project is co-sponsored by eight Ohio electric utility companies, the Ohio Chapter of the International Shade Tree Conference, and the Ohio Nurserymen's Association. It is divided into two phases. One involves the planting of numerous types at a site in the Secrest Arboretum for intensive constant evaluation. The other phase includes a *performance evaluation* of existing street trees at many sites in five Ohio cities. A more complete report of the study is in Horticulture Dept. Series 376, available from the Dept. of Horticulture, OARDC, Wooster, Ohio 44691.

Secrest Arboretum
Ohio Agricultural Research
and Development Center
Wooster, Ohio 44691

CHOICE CLIMBERS

The Climbers furnish us with nature's drapery, and nothing produced by art can equal their elegant grace. As the Lilies surpass in beauty all that wealth or power can procure, or man produce, so these tender Climbers surpass all the productions of the decorator's skill. They are entirely under the control of the tasteful amateur and skillful gardener, and under their guiding hands make the unsightly building or stump bloom with beauty. The strong-growing varieties can be made in a short time to cover fences, arbors and buildings, and give both grace and shade. Those of more delicate growth are invaluable for pots and baskets.

MORNING GLORY.

COBŒA SCANDENS.

"Over canopied with lush woodbine,
With sweet musk-roses, with Eglantine."—Midsummer Night's Dream.

GINKGO TREE, IRISH YEWS, AND WEEPING SOPHORA.

RURAL HOMES

Man may be refined and happy without a garden; he may even have a home of taste, I suppose, without a tree, or shrub, or flower; yet, when the Creator wished to prepare a proper home for man, pure in all his tastes and made in His own image, He planted a garden and placed this noblest specimen of creative power in it to dress and keep it. A few suggestions on the Improving of Grounds and the Adornment of Rural Homes, I think, will be useful, and prevent a great many inquiries that I am unable to answer fully and satisfactorily by letter, especially in the business season.

In the first place, I would remark that the space in front of the house, and generally the sides exposed to view from the street, should be in grass. No arrangement of beds, or borders of box, or anything else, will look so neat and tasteful as a well kept piece of grass. It can also be kept in better order at less cost than in any other way. Mixed beds of flowers or shrubbery in the most conspicuous part of the garden is always unsatisfactory. Get a good plot of grass, and good, dry, neat walks, and all other things will soon follow with but little trouble. If the walls and the carpet of the parlor are tasteful, the room will look neat with very plain furniture, or with little of any kind. The front garden will appear well if its carpets and roads are tasteful with very little else. There is no object in making a furniture shop of the parlor, or a little nursery of the home garden.

The very first thing needed in improving ground is to secure good drainage. Have good drains made to carry off all waste water from the house and surplus water from the soil. These can be made of stone, laid in any way that will leave an open and secure place for the water to pass through, though where drain tile can be obtained they are as good as anything and usually cheaper. The drains should be from two to three feet deep. Cut a trench as wide as is needed for convenient working, and as deep as you have determine is necessary, and lay the stone or tile at the bottom, being careful that the work is well done, for this is the foundation of all improvement, and the correction of any failure is made only with a good deal of trouble and expense. This secures a dry soil at all seasons of the year, and a healthy growth of plants or trees.

The next thing is to prepare the soil and make the walks. Make no more roads than are absolutely necessary, as many walks divide the lawn too much, especially when small, and greatly disfigure it. Of course, there must be a bold walk to the front door, and one passing from this to the rear of the house, and in general no more will be necessary. These must be made in the most convenient places —in the place that one would naturally take in going from one point to the other.

Wheel hoe and hand cultivator, to be had with attachments such as plow, cultivator teeth, shovels and rake. A simple form may be made at home.

If the ground to be improved is only a small lot, it can be done best by the spade, and it is not well to endeavor to do it with the plow. In that case, mark out the walks first. Do this by setting up little sticks on the line you design for the road, as shown in the engraving, changing them until you get just the curve that seems graceful and pleasant to the eye. Put a row of sticks on each side of the road, measuring carefully so as to get the width equal. Another plan for securing the desired curve to walks is suggested in a very good work on Landscape Gardening, by J. Weidemann, and published by Orange Judd & Co. It is the use of a stout line. The idea is shown in the engraving. Next, remove the earth from the walk to about the depth of eighteen inches, using it to fill up any low places. The walks now, of course, have somewhat the appearance of ditches. The operator is prepared to pulverize the soil with the spade. Have it done thoroughly, sending the spade well down, and completely inverting the soil, but leaving about six inches on each side of the walk undisturbed for the present, so as not to break the line of the road. All stones found in digging should be thrown into the roads, and often sufficient will be obtained to fill within six or eight inches of the surface; if not, enough can be procured usually without much difficulty. The stone cutter's yards, the brick yards, and the stone piles in the roads and fields generally furnish abundant material. When the walks are filled with this rough material to within six inches of the surface of the soil, the ground being raked off nice and smooth, dig the six inches left undug on the edges of the walks, being careful to keep the

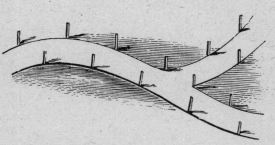

WALK STAKED OUT.

edges true and as originally staked out, and then set a turf about six inches wide for a border to the walk, as shown in the engraving, being careful to keep the turf as low as the level of the adjoining soil, or a little lower, and to do this, remove three or four inches of the soil where the turf is to set, according to its thickness.

A good deal of this rough work can be done in the autumn, so as to leave only the finishing up in the spring; but if commenced in the spring, it should be hurried up so as to get the grass sown as early as possible, for grass seed will not start well unless it has the benefit of spring showers. All being done as previously advised, sow the grass seed on the well prepared surface, raking it in, and if pretty dry, it is well to roll the soil after sowing. Sow Red-Top or Blue Grass, or a preparation of the most desirable grasses for lawns, sold as Lawn Grass, at the rate of four bushels to the acre. In our Lawn Grass we always put a little Sweet Vernal Grass, on account of its delightful fragrance. If you use Red-Top or Blue Grass, get a little Vernal and use with it, a pound or two to the acre. Most persons like also a pound or two of White Clover to the acre. I do not consider it very important what kind of grass is sown. The preparation of the soil and the after care of the lawn is of far more consequence. If the grass is sown early enough, and the weather is at all favorable, by the first of July the lawn will look pretty green, and from the middle to the last of July will need cutting, and after that must be cut as often as the little Lawn Mower can get a bite. These Lawn Mowers are a real blessing, for not one in ten thousand can cut a lawn properly with a scythe, and therefore our lawns, before the introduction of these Mowers, always looked wretched. I do not consider any of them perfect, but there are several that will do good work if a little care is had to keep them in order.

It will be strange if a great array of weeds do not appear with the grass, but do not take it for granted that these weeds came from the grass seed sown, as many have done, because if you had not sown any grass the weeds would have been just as abundant. The farmer who finds the weeds among his corn and potatoes never imagines that he planted them with his seed. As soon as the grass and weeds get high enough to be cut with a scythe or Lawn Mower, cut close and evenly, and repeat this operation as often as possible. The weeds will soon disappear. A few, perhaps, it may be necessary to remove by hand, but this will not often be the case.

After sowing the grass, finish the walks by covering the rough stones with five or six inches of gravel, as clean as can be procured. It is best to leave the finishing of the walks until the last, because, even after sowing the grass seed, at raking it in, a quantity of stones will be gathered, and you will need a place to put them and the walk will need the stones. A section of the road when done will appear as shown in the engraving, and will be always dry and free from weeds and grass. If the earth should wash from the edges of the lawn and cause weeds to start, sow salt along the edges and you will see no weeds for a season.

In very small places it would, perhaps, be as cheap to sod the whole, instead of sowing grass seed. Where this is desirable, good turf can be procured from the roadside or pasture, and it should be well and neatly laid. In large places the plow can be used instead of the spade, and with great economy of labor. In that case the whole lot should be well plowed and dragged before the walks are staked out. After this, stake the walks and remove the earth the necessary depth, using it to level off the low places. There will always be a good deal of work for the spade and rake, even when the plow and drag have been thoroughly used.

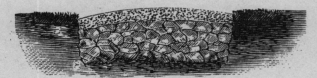

SECTION OF WALK.

Two great errors are usually made, both by gardeners and amateurs; one destroying the lawn by cutting it up with unnecessary walks and flower beds, the other producing the same result by almost literally covering it with trees and shrubbery. Grass cannot grow well among the roots and under the shadow of trees and shrubs, and no lawn can look well cut up in sections by numerous roads. Most of the little lawns we see in this country are almost entirely destroyed by one or both of these causes. The main part of the lawn should be left unbroken by any tree or shrub, as a general rule, and if any tree is admitted it should be only an occasional fine specimen, like a Purple Beech, or Magnolia, or Cut-leaved Birch. The shrubbery should be in clumps or groups, in proper places, and so thick as to cover all the ground. The soil under them should be kept cultivated and clean like a flower bed. A tree or two in certain appropriate places for shade, is, of course, desirable; but plant for the future, not for the present, and always have in view the size and form and habits of the trees when full grown, and not their present small size and perhaps delicate form. Every curve should be a sensible one; that is, have a reason for its course, either real or apparent; therefore arrange your planting so as to make an apparent necessity for every turn. The idea is shown in the little sketch accompanying, where the walk curves to accommodate the trees.

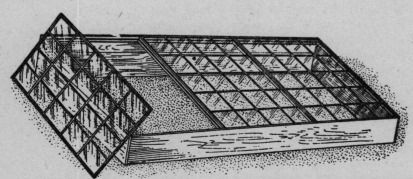

This shows the construction of an outdoor cold frame. A hotbed is built in the same way, except that for the hotbed a pit and manure are required.

LAWN TENT EXTENDED.   LAWN TENT CLOSED.

The great difficulty with American gardens is that they are too large, and not sufficiently cared for. If we gave the same amount of labor on a quarter of an acre that we now expend on an acre, the result would be much more satisfactory. No one should have more ground in garden than he can keep in the very highest state of cultivation. It is this kind of excellence that affords pleasure, while failure or partial success is a source of pain. It is not only a fault to cultivate too much ground, but even too many flowers. Some seem anxious to obtain and grow everything. This is not best, especially where there is not a good deal of time and money to be devoted to the work. A choice selection is best, and I like every cultivator of flowers to have a pet or hobby. Take, for instance, the Pansy, and make it a pet. Obtain the choicest seed, and give the plants the best of care, and you will see to what wonderful perfection it can be grown. In a few years you will tire, perhaps, of this. Then adopt the Balsam, or Stock, or Aster. Always have something choice—something grown better than any one else is growing it—something you have reason to be proud of. It will astonish you to see how flowers thrive under such petting, and what a wonderful exhibition they make of their gratitude.

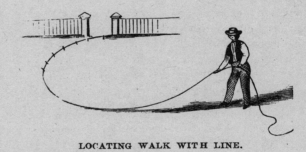

LOCATING WALK WITH LINE.

Some persons may think from what we have said in favor of grass in front of the house in preference to beds of flowers, that we are no friend of these beautiful treasures—these delightful children of the field and garden, who speak to us in every fragrant breath, and lovely tint, and graceful form, of Him who spake from naught this matchless beauty. Far from this. A home without the children of the field, and the flowers of the family, we might, perhaps, enjoy, but we have never had to endure the trial. I only wish them to be treated in a proper manner. In the center of the lawn, especially if opposite a window, it is well to make a round or oval bed, and on the borders or near the edges of the lawn, beds of various graceful forms. A few plans for these we give.

WALKS WITH TURF EDGING.

FLORAL GUIDE FOR 1873.

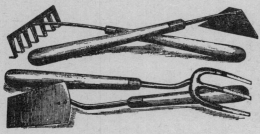

LADIES' AND CHILDREN'S GARDEN TOOLS.

A few well filled vases are a fine and appropriate decoration of any grounds if kept in good condition with healthy plants. The evaporation from baskets and vases is very great, much more than is generally supposed, as every side is exposed to air, sun, etc., and they must receive a copious supply of water every evening to keep the plants in a healthy condition. In addition to the usual forms there are very beautiful vases, of European make, representing old stumps, with openings for inserting plants.

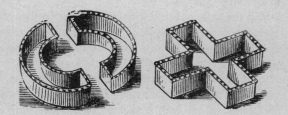

These beds should be filled with flowers that will keep in bloom during the whole season, and it is best generally to have but one kind in a bed. Phlox Drummondii, Verbena, Portulaca, and the scarlet Geraniums, are well adapted for this purpose, and occasionally it is well to introduce the ribbon style, as described on another page. These beds, it must be remembered, are for the adornment of the grounds, and they furnish no flowers for the house—no presents for friends, no boquet for the dining room, or for schools or churches, or the sick room. These we must have. So, just back of the lawn, make generous beds of flowers that you can cut freely—Asters, Balsams, Zinnias, Stocks, Mignonette, Sweet Peas, etc. In these beds you can also grow the Everlasting Flowers for winter use. It is best to make such beds oblong, about four or five feet in width, so that you can reach half way across, with alleys or paths between.

Another very pretty ornament for the garden is the Rockery, made of rough stones, tastefully laid up, with earth sufficient for the growth of the plants suitable for this work. Low growing plants with succulent and ornamental foliage are appropriate to the rockery—Portulaca is admirable. I would like my readers who have had no experience in this kind of garden ornamentation to try a specimen in some retired quarter of the garden, so that if it proves a failure no harm will be done.

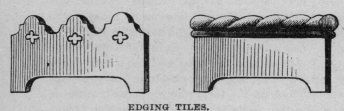

EDGING TILES.

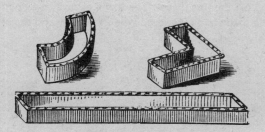

I was much pleased when in Europe to observe the great skill exhibited in giving an air of rural taste to very small city lots, that no one in America would consider capable of an exhibition of rural beauty. Many of these lots I should hardly think as much as twenty-five feet in width, and yet specimens of neatness. Some of these little gardens are attached to houses in rows, others belonging to what is known as semi-detached cottages, that is, two only joined together. I give a specimen of one of these little front gardens, or, as they are sometimes called, entrance courts.

Plants in the house afford the most pleasure in the winter season when all is dreary without, but very much can be done to make home cheerful all through the summer, especially as the garden furnishes abundance of flowers very cheaply for floral decorations; and birthdays and festivals and company will come in the summer as well as winter. There are times, too, when the garden cannot be visited by any, and very often there are members of the family who but seldom enjoy this privilege. I will therefore make a few suggestions that perhaps may be valuable to some readers.

The Ivy is one of the most tractable and useful plants we possess for adornment. Its leaves are clean, bright and glossy, it will bear heat, dust and even partial absence of light, and still grow with vigor and give evidences of health, and can be made to assume almost any form with little trouble. I give several modes of training. The first is trained to a square frame attached to a box, the space in front of the Ivy being occupied with any free-flowering plants. The next specimen is trained in umbrella form, and this is a little more difficult. It requires a good strong stem, and when young this will need support. The third example is very simple, the plant being trained on a circular frame.

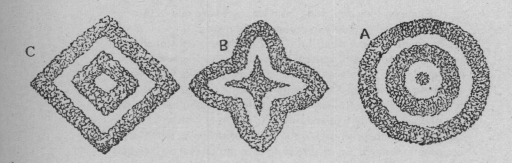

The lots are usually so narrow that the raised bed must be placed on one side of the center to allow of free passage on one side. They are generally divided by walls, as shown in the engraving, and these would be fearfully unsightly but for the fact that they are covered and usually entirely hidden with luxuriant Ivies and other climbers. The ornamental center border is made of a composition resembling stone, and is very pretty. The border for the beds on the sides is usually of common burnt clay tiles, of neat designs and quite reasonable in cost, about 12 cents per foot, and is much preferable to box, or anything of the kind, particularly in our severe climate, where plants usually suffer so much in winter. The small engravings show two very good patterns.

RUSTIC STUMP VASE.

The Window Brackets are very useful and pretty, as they can be placed almost in any position, and being jointed, can be moved near the light, or toward the interior of the room as may be desired. Each bracket is designed for one pot, which is best to have of some tasteful design. Some prefer to use the common pot and cover it with an ornamental pot cover. The Window Garden is also a very neat arrangement for the purpose.

TRAINED IVIES.

In regard to house plants, I would remark that few plants can endure the high temperature and dry atmosphere of most of our living rooms. The temperature should not be allowed to go above seventy in the day time, and not above forty-five in the night. As much air and light as possible should be given, while the leaves should be sprinkled frequently. A spare room, or parlor, or extra bed-room, is better for plants than a living room. A bay window connected with a warm room, especially if facing South or East, makes an excellent place for keeping plants in winter. It should have glass doors on the inside, which can be closed a part of the time, especially when sweeping and dusting. The main thing in keeping house plants in health is to secure an even temperature, a moist atmosphere, and freedom from dust. Sprinkle the leaves occasionally, and when water is needed use it freely. I have endeavored to show in the engraving one of these parlor gardens as described. If the green-fly, or aphis, appears, wash with soap-suds frequently, and occasionally with a little tobacco water, or a decoction of quassia chips. If the red-spider comes, it shows the plants are in too dry an atmosphere. Burn a little sulphur under the plants, the fumes of which will kill the spider, and afterward keep the stems and leaves well moistened. Occasionally, but not often, worms appear in the pots. This can be avoided in a great measure by careful potting. A little weak lime water is sometimes of benefit in such cases, also five drops of liquid ammonia to a gallon of water, though, perhaps, the better way is to re-pot, removing the earth carefully, so as not to injure the growth of the plant.

Ferneries are always agreeable, and there are many ornamental stands, etc., of wire work, both useful and quite ornamental. We can, of course, only allude to a few of the many which cost little, and yet go very far to make a home pleasant, a school of taste to the little ones, and a happy home to all.

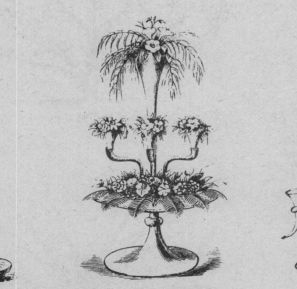

A Sitting Room Window.

DINING TABLE ORNAMENTS.

Much attention is given in Europe to Table Floral Decorations. The different Horticultural Societies offer large prizes for the best decorated Dining Table, and in some cases these exhibitions are made in rooms darkened for the occasion and lighted with gas. Nothing prettier can be imagined than some of these exhibition tables.

CANADA

LANDSCAPE
PAYSAGE

Seymour's Training.

BUYERS' GUIDE

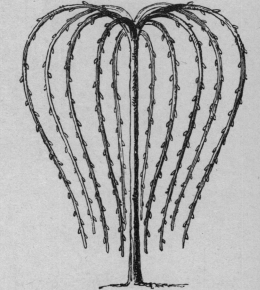

Balloon-training.

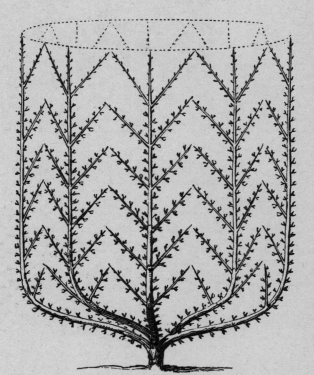

Vase with Dwarf Stem.

BEDDING PLANTS & PERENNIALS

JACK VAN KLAVEREN LTD., P.O. Box 910 (R.R. 3, 7th Street) St. Catharines, Ont. L2R 6Z4. Phone (416) 684-1103.

VAUGHAN NURSERIES LTD., 3444 Sheppard Ave. East, Agincourt, Ont. "Potted Perennials". List and prices on request.

BOOKS

POMONA BOOK EXCHANGE, 33 Beaucourt Road, Toronto, Ont. M8Y 3G1. Available: Books on all aspects of horticulture. New - Out-of-Print - Rare. Catalog available. Book search. Collections purchased.

BUDDING & GRAFTING SUPPLIES

C. FRENSCH LTD., 168 Main St. East, Grimsby, Ont. L3M 1T4. Phone (416) 945-3817.

BURLAP SQUARES

BURSTEIN BAG LTD., 500 Keele Street, Toronto, Ont. Burlap - Rolls, Bales.

CHEMICALS — GROWER OR COMMERCIAL

CHIPMAN CHEMICALS LIMITED, Hamilton, Ont. (416) 549-3023. Complete line of Insecticides, Fungicides and Herbicides. "Gramoxone".

D. & R. GARDEN SUPPLY LTD., 238 Cross Ave., Oakville, Ontario. 845-0411. "Niagara", "Green Cross" and "Chipman".

GREENLEAF GARDEN SUPPLIES, Box 82338, 4615 Dawson St., Burnaby 2, B.C. "Your Complete Garden Supply Wholesaler".

NURSERY SPECIALTY PRODUCTS, 410 Greenwich Avenue, Greenwich, Connecticut 06830. "WILT-PRUF NCF" Anti-desiccant sprays.

W. H. PERRON & CO. LTD., 515 Boul. Labelle, Chomedey (Laval), P.Q.

PLANT PRODUCTS CO. LTD., 314 Orenda Road, Bramalea, Ontario.

UNITED CO-OPERATIVES OF ONTARIO, 2549 Weston Rd., Weston, Ont. (416) 244-5604. Complete range of Horticultural Products—Fertilizers, Insecticides, Fungicides, Herbicides, Seed, Peat Moss, Hardware.

CHEMICALS — HOME AND GARDEN

CANADIAN HORTICULTURAL INDUSTRIES (Wholesale Distributors), 455 St. Peter Street, Montreal 125, Quebec. — Milorganite, So-Green, Ortho, Weedex, RX-15-20-30, Scent-Off, Ross Root Feeders, Atlas Patio Pots, String Balling Rope, Wheelbarrows, Garden Hoses, True Temper Tools, Niagara, Scott's Cure, Bracco, Vigoro, Black & Decker, Disston, Compitox, Seradix, Astro Turf, Melnor, Freunde Shears, Maytime Prods., Green Thumb Gloves, Union Plastic Pots, Ridgecraft Planters, Ball-B-Q, Folding Fences, Moto-Mowers — 84 Gardening Lines.

CANADIAN INDUSTRIES LIMITED, Lawn and Garden Products Department, P.O. Box 5201, London, Ontario N6A 4L6. Manufacturers of SLIK and WEED-ALL and other premium quality pest control products.

CHEVRON CHEMICAL (CANADA) LIMITED, Ortho Division, 1060 Industry Street, Oakville, Ontario. Write for free Ortho Booklets. "Community Action for Beauty" and "Trees for Better Neighborhoods".

CHIPMAN CHEMICALS LIMITED, Hamilton, Ont. (416) 549-3023. Complete line of Garden chemicals for the home gardener. "Weedrite", "Diazinon" Garden Spray, "Pop-in" soluble packs.

D. & R. GARDEN SUPPLY LTD., 238 Cross Avenue, Oakville, Ont. 845-0411. "Ortho", "Niagara", "Green Cross", "Chipman".

GREEN CROSS PRODUCTS, 1 Westside Drive, Etobicoke, Ont. 622-0820. Complete line of Home & Garden Herbicides, Insecticides/Fungicides and Sprayers. "Green Cross" brand.

NATIONAL GARDEN SUPPLY OF CANADA LTD., 150 Duke Street, Bowmanville, Ont. 416-623-3345 or 366-2566. Best source of quality supplies.

NURSERY SPECIALTY PRODUCTS, 410 Greenwich Ave., Greenwich, Connecticut, 06830. "WILT-PRUF NCF" Anti-desiccant sprays.

W. H. PERRON & CO. LTD., 515 Boul. Labelle, Chomedey (Laval), P.Q.

PLANT PRODUCTS CO. LTD., 314 Orenda Road, Bramalea, Ontario.

UNITED CO-OPERATIVES OF ONTARIO, 2549 Weston Road, Weston, Ont. (416) 244-5604. Complete range of Horticultural Products—Fertilizers, Insecticides, Fungicides, Herbicides, Seed, Peat Moss, Hardware.

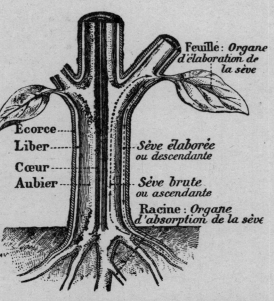

Feuille: *Organe d'élaboration de la sève*

Ecorce
Liber
Cœur
Aubier

Sève élaborée ou descendante

Sève brute ou ascendante

Racine: *Organe d'absorption de la sève*

Circulation de la sève brute ou ascendante, et de la sève élaborée ou descendante.

HORTICULTURAL SERVICES

J. W. DICKERSON & ASSOCIATES, Specialized Horticultural Services, Box 133, Troy, Ohio 45373. (513) 778-0675 or 335-4012. Horticultural Auctioneers, Appraisers, Consultants, Business Brokers and Investment Counselors.

HYDRO-SEEDERS

CHRIS-WALTER SALES LTD., R.R. 4, Salmon Arm, B.C. "SPRAY-BABY" the green machine for commercial and residential lawn making.

LABELS & TAGS

ECONOMY LABEL SALES CO. INC., P.O. Box 350, Daytona Beach, Florida 32015. Plastic, Paper, Aluminum, Pressure Sensitive and Die Cut Labels. Label Imprinter, Plant Ties. "Flag-Ty" (6 colours), 300 ft. per roll. Vinyl.

C. FRENSCH LTD., 168 Main St. East, Grimsby, Ontario L3M 1T4. Phone: (416) 945-3817.

HORTICULTURAL PRINTERS, Box 18092, Dallas, Texas 75218, U.S.A. 4 colour tags and labels on paper and plastic. Plastic identification tags. Catalogue sent free on request.

GLEN D. OGILVIE LIMITED, Box 329, Caledonia, Ontario. Hardy Plant Picture Tags.

W. H. PERRON & CO. LTD., 515 Boul. Labelle, Chomedey (Laval), Que.

WESTON NURSERY SUPPLIES, P.O. Box 398, Weston, Ontario M9N 3N1. Phone (416) 742-6921. CURLY-LOX—Labor saving label for Nurserymen —Quick as a snap of the fingers—Will not blow off—Expands with the tree—Write for Samples.

MACHINERY, EQUIPMENT & TOOLS

AGRI-TECH INC., 110 rue de Lauzon, Boucherville, Quebec J4B 1E6. Royer Soil and Compost Shredder, Power Screen, Gang Mowers, Lawn Mowers, Sweepers, Seeders, Toro Shredders, Jari Sickle S.P. Mowers, Troy Bilt Roto Tiller, Irrigation Equipment, Compact Tractors 8 to 16 h.p.

CANADIAN HORTICULTURAL INDUSTRIES (Wholesale Distributors), 455 St. Peter Street, Montreal 125, Que. Milorganite, So-Green, Ortho, Weedex, RX-15-20-30, Scent-Off, Ross Root Feeders, Atlas Patio Pots, String Balling Rope, Wheelbarrows, Garden Hoses, True Temper Tools, Niagara, Scott's Cure, Bracco, Vigoro, Black & Decker, Disston, Compitox, Seradix, Astro Turf, Melnor, Freunde Shears, Maytime Products, Green Thumb Gloves, Union Plastic Pots, Ridgecraft Planters, Ball-B-Q, Folding Fences, Moto-mowers . . . 84 gardening lines.

CANADIAN INDUSTRIES LIMITED, Lawn and Garden Products Dept., P.O. Box 5201, London, Ont. N6A 4L6. CIL Spreaders, Hydro-Seeders, Hydro-Mulchers, Sprayers.

CONSOLIDATED TURF EQUIP. (1965) LTD., 972 Powell Avenue, Winnipeg, Manitoba R3H 0H6. Distributors of powered and recreational equipment for turf maintenance and landscape construction. Jacobsen, Ryan, Parker, Yazoo, Lindig, Jari, Harley Davidson, Poraide, Standard, Mott, Bowie, Conwed, York, Olathe, Billy Goat, Foley.

FARMERS SUPPLY & EQUIPMENT LTD., 409 Main St. North, Brampton, Ont. L6X 1N7. Phone: (416) 451-4340. Tractors 8 to 25 h.p., Tillers, Landscapers, Industrial Rotary Mowers, Flail Mowers, Reel Gangs, Stump Cutters, Snow Blowers.

C. FRENSCH LTD., 168 Main St. East, Grimsby, Ont. L3M 1T4. (416) 945-3817. Manufacturers representative for Holder Tractors, Rotovators, Sprayers (motor, knapsack and hand).

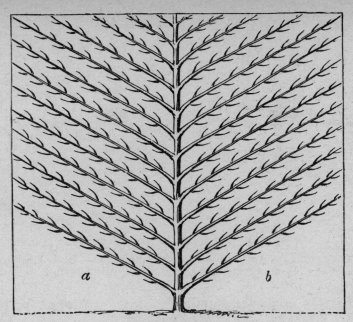

Oblique Training.

HOGLE HALLS LTD., 929 Millwood Rd., Toronto M4G 1X4. Tel. (416) 423-5625. Generac: Portable Alternators, gas, L.P., P.T.O., or pulley driven. Utility Lawn and Garden Tractors, complete line of attachments. Hotsy: High Pressure Washers & Steam Cleaners. Hot and cold water machines. Oil or L.P. fired burners. 3 point mounting units, powered by tractor hyd. Blackhawk: Mechanics Hand Tools and Torque Wrenches.

ICKES-BRAUN GLASSHOUSES OF CANADA, LIMITED, P.O. Box 2000, 90 Bartlett Rd., Beamsville, Ont. L0R 1B0. "SIMAR" tractors and "LEYATT" pruners.

IRRIGATION ST. THOMAS INC., St. Thomas, Cte. Joliette, P.Q. Irrigation systems; Pumps; Tubing; Sprinklers; Holland Transplanters; Sprayers.

LINDIG MANUFACTURING CORPORATION, 1875 West County Rd. C, St. Paul, Minnesota 55113. Mfr. of Soil Shredders and Screeners; Soil Treating Equipment. (Aerators and Carts.)

NATIONAL GARDEN SUPPLY OF CANADA LTD., 150 Duke St., Bowmanville, Ont. (416) 623-3345 or 366-2566. Best source of quality supplies.

W. H. PERRON & CO. LTD., 515 Boul. Labelle, Chomedey (Laval), P.Q.

PLANT PRODUCTS CO. LTD., 314 Orenda Road, Bramalea, Ontario.

TRUE TEMPER CANADA LIMITED, Box 3018, Station B, Hamilton, Ont. "Brands" — True Temper, Excelsior, Comet, Bulldog, Fox, Badger, Black Cat. "Products" — Hand farm and garden tools, shears, pruners, loppers, shovels, spades, scoops, cultivators and saws.

UNITED CO-OPERATIVES OF ONTARIO, 2549 Weston Rd., Weston Ontario. (416) 244-5604. Complete range of Horticultural Products—Fertilizers, Insecticides, Fungicides, Herbicides, Seed, Peat Moss, Hardware.

WILTON EQUIPMENT, 2989 Bathurst Street, Toronto M6B 3B3. Phone: 783-6161. Dealer for the famous Gravely Line of Tractors from 8 to 16 h.p. 30" to 50" Rotary Mowers. 26" to 44" Snow Blowers and a host of other attachments.

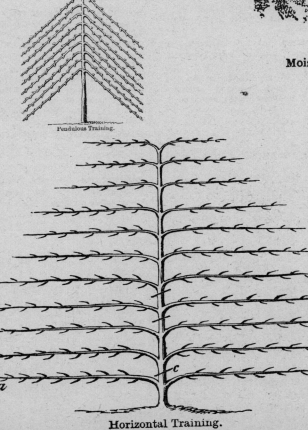

Pendulous Training.

Horizontal Training.

MANURES, SOIL, BARK, STONE

BROCKVILLE CHEMICAL INDUSTRIES LIMITED, 1232 Aerowood Drive, Mississauga, Ontario L4W 1B7. (416) 625-9030.

CANADIAN INDUSTRIES LIMITED, Lawn and Garden Products Dept., P.O. Box 5201, London, Ont. N6A 4L6. CIL Manures.

D. & R. GARDEN SUPPLY LTD., 238 Cross Ave., Oakville, Ontario. 845-0411. "Hillview" and "Vigoro".

HILLVIEW FARMS LIMITED, R.R. 4, Woodstock, Ont. (519) 537-7942. Toronto office: (416) 231-0589. Producers of "Hillview" Brand Cattle and Sheep Manures. Potting Soils, Wild Bird Seed mixtures and other horticultural products. Exclusive Distributors of GRAND PRIZE GYPSUM.

NATIONAL GARDEN SUPPLY OF CANADA LTD., 150 Duke Street, Bowmanville, Ont. (416) 623-3345 or 366-2566. Best source of quality supplies.

GLEN D. OGILVIE LIMITED, Box 329, Caledonia, Ontario. "Redwood" Decorative Bark, Southern Pine Decorative Bark, Cattle and Sheep Manure, "WeedFree" Top Soil and Peat Humus, Genuine Ontario Marble Chips.

PREMIER BRANDS INC., PREMIER PEAT MOSS CORPORATION—Marketing, 25 West 45th Street, New York, N.Y. 10036, U.S.A. Phone: (212) 757-7606.

VIGORO, 1400 The Queensway, Toronto, Ontario. "Vigoro" Lawn and Garden Products — Made in Canada — Available coast to coast in every province through wholesale distributors.

WEN-HAL LIMITED, 729 Plains Road East, Burlington, Ontario. (416) 632-2411. Distributors for Premier and Hillview, Premier Decorative Bark and Mystic White Stone.

MULCH

CANADIAN INDUSTRIES LIMITED, Lawn and Garden Products Dept., P.O. Box 5201, London, Ontario N6A 4L6. Hydro Mulch.

PREMIER BRANDS INC., PREMIER PEAT MOSS CORPORATION—Marketing, 25 West 45th St., New York, N.Y. 10036. Phone: (212) 757-7606.

— La moisson.

Moissonneuse lieuse. — 1. Faux à râteau. — 2. Faucille.

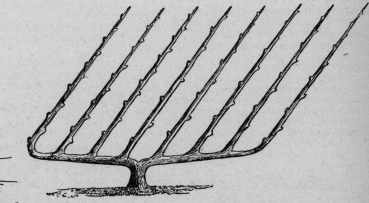

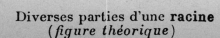

Diverses parties d'une **racine**
(*figure théorique*)

NURSERY STOCK

ALBERTA NURSERIES & SEEDS LTD., Bowden, Alberta. Wholesale Growers—Cotoneaster, Hedging. Phone 224-3362 Collect, Mr. Jim Anderson, Superintendent—Wholesale Division.

ASSAGI NURSERIES, P.O. Box 204, Schomberg, Ont. L0G 1T0. "Growers and Suppliers of Quality Specimen Sized Nursery Stock".

J. C. BAKKER & SONS LTD., St. Catharines, Ont. Ornamental trees and shrubs, Evergreens—B & B and Liners, Roses, Tree Roses, Rose Understock. "All home-grown quality stock".

BARRON'S FLOWERS, Highway 20, Box 250, Fonthill, Ont. Clematis Specialists.

BLUE MOUNTAIN NURSERIES & ORCHARDS LTD., Clarksburg, Ont. Phone Thornbury 599-3735. Specializing in virus-tested fruit trees, apple rootstocks and virus free raspberry plants in Georgian Bay apple region.

BROOKDALE-KINGSWAY LTD., 150 Duke Street, Bowmanville, Ont. (416) 623-3345 or 366-2566. Top quality Shade Trees, Deciduous shrubs, Hedging, Fruit Trees and Shade Tree Whips.

DACCORD NURSERIES LTD., P.O. Box 180, St-Polycarpe, P.Q. "Specimen Trees."

DOWNHAM GARDEN SALES & SUPPLIES, LTD., 626 Victoria St., Strathroy, Ont. N7G 3C1. Growers of a complete line of Evergreens, Bare Root and Packaged Nursery Stock.

DUTCH LANDSCAPING & NURSERIES INC., R.R. 2, Norval, Ont. L0P 1K0. (416) 457-4410. Shade and Ornamental Trees—Evergreens B & B, Container Grown or Potted.

FLAMBOROUGH NURSERIES & LANDSCAPING LIMITED, Box 33, Millgrove, Ont. Tel. (416) 689-6701. Healthy Evergreens, flowering shrubs. Large shade trees. Annuals and potted plants.

GREENWAY PLANT FARM, Fraser Rd., Leamington, Ontario — Earl Sergeant. Container grown evergreens.

GROEN'S NURSERY, R.R. 4, Dundas, Ont. Tel. 659-7072. "Understock and liners" of Mazzard Cherry, American Plum, Sand Cherry, Mahaleb Cherry, Myrobalan Plum, Tomentosa Cherry, Apple Seedling, Bartlett Pear, Green Ash, Silver Maple, Honey Locust, Nanking Cherry Shrubs.

D. HILL NURSERY CO., P.O. Box 8, Dundee, Illinois 60118. Phone (312) 426-3451. Complete line of liners, B & B and container grown plants.

KELOWNA NURSERIES LIMITED, Box 178, 1035 Sutherland Ave., Kelowna, B.C. (304) 762-3384. Growers of Fruit Trees and container grown shrubs and evergreens.

HENK KOBES NURSERY, R.R. 1, Bowmanville, Ontario. Phone 263-8814. Evergreens, Shrubs, Shade Trees, Landscape Material.

V. KRAUS NURSERIES LTD., Carlisle, Ontario. (416) 689-4022. Roses, Shade Trees and Fruit Trees.

MAPLE LEAF NURSERIES, R.R. 3, St. Catharines, Ont. (416) 934-1697. Evergreens, B & B and Liners, Ornamental trees and shrubs.

MASSOT NURSERIES LTD., 1606 Westminster Hwy., Richmond, B.C. Tel. (604) 273-3704. Growers and Wholesalers of fine quality Nursery Stock for the Landscape Trade and Garden Centres. Full line of Container and B & B grown plants from Ground Covers in 2¼" peat pots to 10" caliber trees. Descriptive catalogue on request.

THE McCONNELL NURSERY CO. LTD., Port Burwell, Ontario. (519) 874-4405. Growers of Roses, Trees, Shrubs, Evergreens, Vines, Perennials, Bulbs, Fruit Trees and Bushes, and Hedges.

OLIVER NURSERIES, R.R. 1, Oliver, B.C.

W. H. PERRON & CO. LTD., 515 Boul. Labelle, Chomedey (Laval), P.Q.

REDLEAF NURSERIES LTD., Lower Base Line at Trafalgar Rd., Oakville, Ontario. Specializing in trees for over 20 years.

SARCOXIE NURSERIES, INC., Sarcoxie, Mo. 64862. "Iris", "Hemerocallis", "Peonies", "Euonymus Sarcoxie". Write for lists.

SHERIDAN NURSERIES LTD., Head Office: 700 Evans Ave., Etobicoke, Ontario. Shipping Office: 1116 Winston Churchill Blvd., Oakville, Ont. L6J 4Z2. (416) 822-4841. Montreal Office: 650 Montée de Liesse, Montreal, Que. H4T 1N8. (514) 341-3604. Growers of hardy evergreens, trees, shrubs, vines, hedges, roses, ground covers and perennials.

LESLIE L. SOLTY & SONS LTD., 3850 Kingston Rd., Scarborough, Ont. Phone (416) 267-8294. Growers of Specimen Trees, Shrubs and Evergreens.

STEVENSON'S EVERGREEN NURSERY, Morris, Manitoba. F. B. Stevenson, Manager. Evergreens, Ornamental Trees and Shrubs, Seedling Evergreens a specialty.

WALTER VAN VLOTEN NURSERIES LTD., 11765 - 176th St., Pitt Meadows, B.C. "Arctic Brand" Nursery Stock.

JIM VLAAR NURSERIES, Lakeshore Rd., R.R. 3, St. Catharines, Ontario. Evergreens, Shrubs, Hedges, Flowering and Shade Trees.

WARREN COUNTY NURSERY, INC., Rt. 2, McMinnville, Tn. 37110. Phone (615) 668-8941 or 668-8004. Wholesaler on general line of Nursery Stock. Write for our Wholesale Price List.

Arboriculture. Abris divers.

A. Plantation d'un arbre. — B. Taille. — C. Ratissage. — D, E, F. Arbres taillés. G. Bâche. — H. Cloche. — I. Châssis et paillasson. — J. Serre.

GREENHOUSES & GREENHOUSE SUPPLIES

ATLAS ASBESTOS COMPANY, 5600 Hochelaga Street, Montreal H1N 1W1. (514) 259-2531. Offices: Montreal, Toronto, Vancouver. Distributors coast to coast. "Clearlite" Translucent Fiberglass and Nylon reinforced Greenhouse panels.

CANADIAN GREENHOUSES INC., P.O. Box 5000, Durham Road, Beamsville, Ontario L0R 1B0. Suppliers of "Canadiana" Glass and Aluminum Glasshouses, "Vary" Quonset Style Fiberglass or Double Poly Greenhouses, Free-standing or Gutter Connected, Vary Ventilation Systems, Dutch Garden Tools, Watering Systems.

CANADIAN INDUSTRIES LIMITED, Lawn and Garden Products Dept., P.O. Box 5201, London, Ont. N6A 4L6. Broad line of soluble fertilizers.

C. FRENSCH LTD., 168 Main Street East, Grimsby, Ontario L3M 1T4. (416) 945-3817.

GTE SYLVANIA CANADA LTD., 8750 Cote de Liesse Road, Montreal, Que. H4T 1H3. Manufacturers of complete range of lighting products, including lamps for Commercial Greenhouses and Hobbyists—GRO LUX and WIDE SPECTRUM Fluorescent lamps and High Intensity Discharge lamps.

ICKES-BRAUN GLASSHOUSES OF CANADA LIMITED, P.O. Box 2000, 90 Bartlett Rd., Beamsville, Ontario L0R 1B0. Suppliers of the following types of greenhouses: 'ARCH II"—Galv. steel frame with fibreglass glazing, "GLASSACRE" — Galv. steel frame with glass/fibreglass glazing. Greenhouse construction supplies.

IRRIGATION ST. THOMAS INC., St. Thomas, Cte. Joliette, P.Q. Manufacturer of Greenhouse Frames, Gothic type, cedar and galvanized frames. Fiberglass and Polyethylene Covers, Exhaust and Circulating Fans — Watering Systems — Greenhouse Accessories — Swimming Pool Covers.

JOSEPH LABONTE & FILS INC., 250 Chemin Chambly, Longueuil, Que. Lawn Seeds; Clay, Peat and Plastic pots; Garden and Greenhouse supplies.

LORD & BURNHAM CO. LIMITED, 325 Welland Ave., St. Catharines, Ont. Tel. (416) 685-6573. Canada's finest greenhouse designers, manufacturers, erectors since 1856. Complete greenhouse supplies and accessories. Please write for free catalogue No. 12C Handy Hand Book.

NURSERY SPECIALTY PRODUCTS, 410 Greenwich Ave., Greenwich, Connecticut 06830. "WILT-PRUF NCF" Anti-desiccant sprays.

GLEN D. OGILVIE LIMITED, Box 329, Caledonia, Ontario. Canadian made Jaco-Lite Cedar Home Greenhouses.

OUTLAND-HAFCO LTD., 55 Glen Cameron Rd., Thornhill, Ont. (416) 889-3190. Supplying Filclair Long-life Poly and P.V.C. Greenhouses and Accessories.

W. H. PERRON & CO. LTD., 515 Boul. Labelle, Chomedey (Laval), Que.

PLANT PRODUCTS CO. LTD., 314 Orenda Road, Bramalea, Ontario.

JACK VAN KLAVEREN LTD., P.O. Box 910, (R.R. 3, 7th Street), St. Catharines, Ont. L2R 6Z4. Phone (416) 684-1103.

PEAT POTS

PREMIER BRANDS INC., PREMIER PEAT MOSS CORPORATION—Marketing. 25 West 45th St., New York, N.Y. 10036. Phone: (212) 757-7606.

PET SUPPLIES

PREMIER BRANDS INC., PREMIER PEAT MOSS CORPORATION—Marketing. 25 West 45th St., New York, N.Y. 10036. Phone: (212) 757-7606.

POOL SUPPLIES

PREMIER BRANDS INC., PREMIER PEAT MOSS CORPORATION—Marketing. 25 West 45th St., New York, N.Y. 10036. Phone: (212) 757-7606.

POTTING SOIL

PREMIER BRANDS INC., PREMIER PEAT MOSS CORPORATION—Marketing. 25 West 45th St., New York, N.Y. 10036. Phone: (212) 757-7606.

ROSES

CARL PALLEK & SON NURSERIES, Box 137, Virgil, Ontario. "Rose Bushes", first quality Canadian grown. Wholesale price list on request.

CO-OPERATIVE ROSE GROWERS INC., P.O. Box 4400, Tyler, Texas 75701. Phone (214) 593-0234. Joe J. Burks, Manager. Rose bushes only — Car and Truck lot and contract growing.

SNOW REMOVAL EQUIPMENT

McKEE BROS. LIMITED, Industrial Drive, Elmira, Ontario. Phone (519) 669-5115. Manufacturers of Snolander—Rotary Snow Plows to fit tractors 18 h.p. and up—rear or front mount.

SOD

BLUEGRASS TURF FARMS LTD., P.O. Cedar Valley, Ontario. Phone Toronto 920-5511. The Right Sod for Every Situation.

FAIRLAWN SOD NURSERY LTD., R.R. 2, Lynden, Ontario; R.R. 5, Tilbury, Ontario; Coteau Station, P.Q.

MANDERLEY TURF FARMS LTD., North Gower, Ontario (serving Ottawa); Alfred, Ontario (serving Montreal); Napierville, Quebec (serving Quebec & The Maritimes). Quality sod grown on peat and mineral soil.

LESLIE L. SOLTY & SONS LTD., 3850 Kingston Road, Scarborough, Ontario. (416) 267-8294. Growers of the finest quality Nursery Sod.

ZANDER SOD CO. LTD., 23 North Park Drive, Toronto, Ont. M6L 1K1. Suppliers of all Bluegrass varieties. Grown on Mineral or Peat Loam.

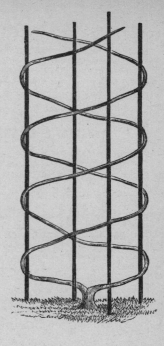

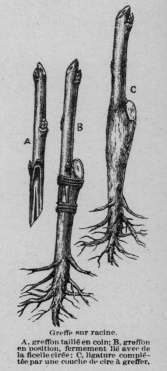

Upright Training.

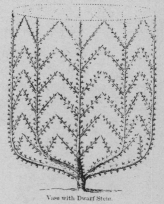

Greffe sur racine.

A, greffon taillé en coin; B, greffon en position, fermement lié avec de la ficelle cirée; C, ligature complétée par une couche de cire à greffer.

Travaux de vignoble.

Taille de la vigne.   Sulfatage de la vigne.   Vendange.

Peach Pruning.

FERTILIZERS

BROCKVILLE CHEMICAL INDUSTRIES LIMITED, 1232 Aerowood Drive, Mississauga, Ontario L4W 1B7. (416) 625-9030. "Nutrite" Plant Foods.

CANADIAN GYPSUM COMPANY LIMITED, 25 Clayson Road, Weston, Ontario. (416) 742-5334. Manufacturer of Grand Prize Lawn & Garden Gypsum (Calcium Sulphate) fertilizes by adding calcium and sulphur nutrients, conditions and loosens clay soils without changing acidity, and neutralizes winter salt damage. Ontario Distributor—Hillview Farms Limited.

CANADIAN HORTICULTURAL INDUSTRIES (Wholesale Distributors), 455 St. Peter Street, Montreal 125, Quebec. Milorganite, So-Green, Ortho, Needex, RX-15-20-30, Scent-Off, Ross Root Feeders, Atlas Patio Pots, String Balling Rope, Wheelbarrows, Garden Hoses, True Temper Tools, Niagara, Scott's Cure, Bracco, Vigoro, Black & Decker, Disston, Compitox, Seradix, Astro Turf, Melnor, Freunde Shears, Maytime Products, Green Thumb Gloves, Union Plastic Pots, Ridgecraft Planters, Ball-B-Q, Folding Fences, Moto-mowers . . . 84 gardening lines.

CANADIAN INDUSTRIES LIMITED, Lawn and Garden Products Department, P.O. Box 5201, London, Ontario N6A 4L6. Manufacturers of Golf Green, Lawn Doctor, and other premium quality lawn and garden fertilizers.

CHEVRON CHEMICAL (CANADA) LIMITED, Ortho Division, 1060 Industry Street, Oakville, Ontario. Write for free Ortho Booklets. "Community Action for Beauty" and "Trees for Better Neighborhoods".

D. & R. GARDEN SUPPLY LTD., 238 Cross St., Oakville, Ontario. 845-0411. "Nutrite", "Vigoro", "So-Green", "C.I.L.", "Ortho".

GREEN CROSS PRODUCTS, 1 Westside Drive, Etobicoke, Ontario. Phone: 622-0820, "Green Cross" brand lightweight lawn and garden fertilizers. "Lawn Green", "Weed 'N Feed with Killex".

SO-GREEN DIVISION, F. MANLEY CORPORATION, 25 Lesmill Road, Don Mills, Ontario M3B 2T3. (416) 445-7770. So-Green, Milorganite, Spreaders.

NATIONAL GARDEN SUPPLY OF CANADA LTD., 150 Duke Street, Bowmanville, Ontario. (416) 623-3345 or 366-2566. Best source of quality supplies.

GLEN D. OGILVIE LIMITED, Box 329, Caledonia, Ontario. "Aero Green" Lawn and Garden Fertilizers, ORGANIC Plantabbs, C-Food Liquid Fertilizer, Stern's Miracle-Gro Plant Food, Fertil-Gro Liquid Plant Food.

W. H. PERRON & CO. LTD., 515 Boul. Labelle, Chomedey (Laval), Que.

PLANT PRODUCTS CO. LTD., 314 Orenda Road, Bramalea, Ontario.

PREMIER BRANDS INC., PREMIER PEAT MOSS CORPORATION—Marketing, 25 West 45th Street, New York, N.Y. 10036. Phone: (212) 757-7606.

SIERRA CHEMICAL COMPANY, P.O. Box 275, Newark, California, U.S.A. 94560. "Osmocote" and "Agriform" Controlled Release Fertilizers.

LESLIE L. SOLTY & SONS LTD., 3850 Kingston Road, Scarborough, Ont. (416) 267-8294. C.I.L. Fertilizers.

UNITED CO-OPERATIVES OF ONTARIO, 2549 Weston Road, Weston, Ont. (416) 244-5604. Complete range of Horticultural Products—Fertilizers, Insecticides, Fungicides, Herbicides, Seed, Peat Moss, Hardware.

VIGORO, 1400 The Queensway, Toronto, Ontario. "Vigoro" Lawn and Garden Products — Made in Canada — Available coast to coast in every province through wholesale distributors.

WEN-HAL LIMITED, 729 Plains Road East, Burlington, Ontario. (416) 632-2411. Distributors for "C.I.L.", "Nutrite" and "Ortho" Fertilizers.

GRASS SEED

JOSEPH LABONTE & FILS INC., 250 Chemin Chambly. Longueuil, Que. Lawn Seeds; Clay, Peat and Plastic Pots; Garden & Greenhouse supplies.

SO-GREEN DIVISION, F. MANLEY CORPORATION, 25 Lesmill Road, Don Mills, Ont. M3B 2T3. (416) 445-7770. So-Green, Milorganite, Spreaders.

MAPLE LEAF MILLS LIMITED, P.O. Box 370, Station "A", Toronto, Ont. Suppliers of "Lion Brand" packaged lawn seed; Fylking Kentucky Bluegrass; all varieties of Bulk turf and forage seeds; Custom packaging. "SAT Turf and Garden Treatment" promotes rapid re-growth of grass, assists in control of Fairy Ring, Dollar Spot and Brown Patch.

OSECO LIMITED, Box 219, Brampton, Ontario. (416) 457-5080. Suppliers of packaged and bulk turf grass seeds and lawn grass mixtures. Premium quality HB-2, Campus Green, Cottage Green. Exclusive Canadian distributors for Baron Kentucky Bluegrass, Highlight Chewings Fescue, Emerald Creeping Bentgrass and Sydsport Kentucky Bluegrass. Complete seed cleaning, processing and packaging facilities at their Brampton plant.

W. H. PERRON & CO. LTD., 515 Boul. Labelle, Chomedey (Laval), Que.

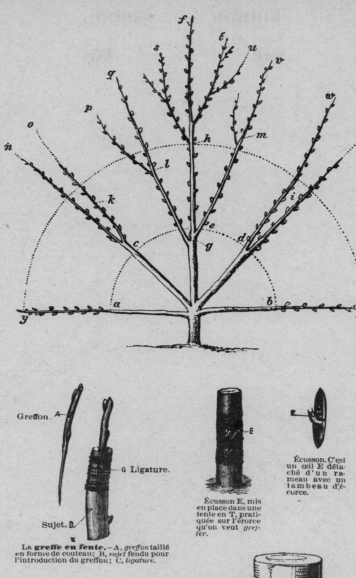

Greffon. A.

G Ligature.

Sujet. B.

La greffe en fente.—A, *greffon* taillé en forme de couteau; B, *sujet* fendu pour l'introduction du greffon; C, *ligature*.

Écusson E, mis en place dans une fente en T, pratiquée sur l'écorce qu'on veut *greffer*.

Écusson. C'est un œil E détaché d'un rameau avec un lambeau d'écorce.

Square Shield-budding

PACKAGING — BAGS

E. S. & A. ROBINSON (CANADA) LTD., 69 Laird Drive, Toronto, Ont. "Plant Fresh" plastic bags for Dry Root packing to extend seedling and plant life. Bags, printing, packaging materials, labels.

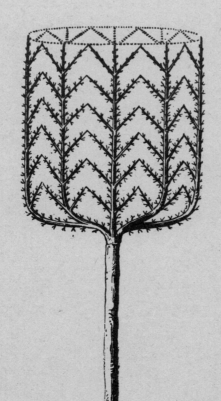

Vase with Tall Stem.

THE FIRST SHOOT FROM A BUD.

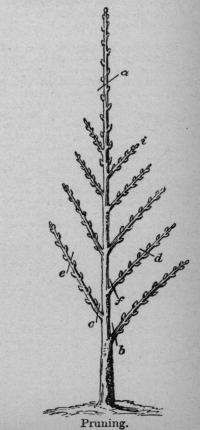

Pruning.

OTTO PICK & SONS SEEDS LTD., Box 126, Richmond Hill, Ontario L4C 4X9. Canada's Best Turf Varieties—Nugget Kentucky Bluegrass, Manhattan Perennial Ryegrass, Jamestown Chewings Fescue, and many more.

UNITED CO-OPERATIVES OF ONTARIO, 2549 Weston Road, Weston, Ont. (416) 244-5604. Complete range of Horticultural Products—Fertilizers, Insecticides, Fungicides, Herbicides, Seed, Peat Moss, Hardware.

WEN-HAL LIMITED, 729 Plains Road East, Burlington, Ontario. (416) 632-2411. Distributors for Tregunno Seeds.

CONTAINERS

ATLAS ASBESTOS COMPANY, 5600 Hochelaga Street, Montreal H1N 1W1. (514) 259-2531. Offices: Montreal, Toronto, Vancouver. Distributors coast to coast. "Premier" and "Rex" hand-moulded asbestos-cement Patio Pots. "Apex" hand-moulded asbestos-cement Planters.

KNECHT & BERCHTOLD LTD., 32 Rutherford Rd., Brampton, Ontario L6W 3J1. Telephone (416) 677-1030. "Alpha" planters for mobile gardens.

MAPLE LEAF NURSERIES, R.R. 3, St. Catharines, Ontario. (416) 934-1697. Green plastic nursery containers.

OAKVILLE WOOD SPECIALTIES LTD., Box 131, Oakville, Ontario. (416) 844-3296. Bushel and half-bushel hampers for shrubs, plant boxes, and labels.

GLEN D. OGILVIE LIMITED, Box 329, Caledonia, Ontario. "Fyba" Short and Long Life Containers.

PARIDON BULB CO. LTD., P.O. Box 1006, Coquitlam, B.C. Fertil pots, Paragon pots, etc.

W. H. PERRON & CO. LTD., 515 Boul Labelle, Chomedey (Laval), P.Q.

PLANT PRODUCTS CO. LTD., 314 Orenda Road, Bramalea, Ontario.

PREMIER BRANDS INC., PREMIER PEAT MOSS CORPORATION—Marketing, 25 West 45th Street, New York, N.Y. 10036. Phone: (212) 757-7606.

SHERIDAN NURSERIES LTD., Head Office: 700 Evans Ave., Etobicoke, Ontario. Shipping Office: 1116 Winston Churchill Blvd., Oakville, Ont. L6J 4Z2. (416) 822-4841. Montreal Office: 650 Montée de Liesse, Montreal, P.Q. H4T 1N8. (514) 341-3604. "Menne Pot", the plant pot Nurserymen prefer. Sheridan patio pots.

JACK VAN KLAVEREN LTD., P.O. Box 910 (R.R. 3, 7th Street), St. Catharines, Ont. L2R 6Z4. Phone (416) 684-1103.

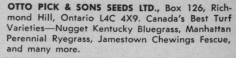

SOIL AMENDMENTS

CANADIAN INDUSTRIES LIMITED, Lawn and Garden Products Dept., P.O. Box 5201, London, Ont. N6A 4L6. Turface, Limestone.

MAPLE LEAF MILLS LIMITED, P.O. Box 370, Station "A", Toronto, Ont. "SAS Soil Treatment" conditions soil and stimulates plant growth.

PREMIER BRANDS INC., PREMIER PEAT MOSS CORPORATION—Marketing. 25 West 45th St., New York, N.Y. 10036. Phone. (212) 757-7606.

TREE ANCHORING SUPPLIES

C. FRENSCH LTD., 168 Main St. East, Grimsby, Ontario L3M 1T4. Phone (416) 945-3817. CF-Anchor Discs and Ideal and Spannfix wire tighteners.

MISCELLANEOUS

GTE SYLVANIA CANADA LTD., 8750 Cote de Liesse Rd., Montreal, Que. H4T 1H3. Manufacturers of complete range of lighting products and GRO-LUX PLANTERS, including GRO-LUX Fluorescent lamps for indoor gardeners and GRO-LUX WIDE SPECTRUM and HIGH INTENSITY DISCHARGE lamps for Commercial Greenhouse use.

HORICAN SALES COMPANY, P.O. Box 10, Station "Z", Toronto, Ont. M5N 2Z2J. Bamboo stakes, hand tools, Bonsai tools, containers, etc. (416) 486-9458.

JOHNSON NURSERIES (KINGSTON) LTD., Kingston, Ontario. Scent-Off Pet Repellents and Training Aids. Now in three long lasting forms. Twist-Ons, Pellets and Rub-Stik.

MAPLE LEAF MILLS LIMITED, P.O. Box 370, Station "A", Toronto, Ont. "SEPT-AID" odor control for septic tanks, campsites, poultry barns, etc.

GLEN D. OGILVIE LIMITED, Box 329, Caledonia, Ontario. Hollow-Log Bird Feeders and Bird Houses. Wilt-Pruf Anti-Desiccant.

PARIDON BULB CO. LTD., P.O. Box 1006, Coquitlam, B.C. Wholesale bulb growers and suppliers of all kinds of flower bulbs, tubers, perennials, miscellaneous supplies. Fertil pots, Paragon pots, etc.

WEN-HAL LIMITED, 729 Plains Road East, Burlington, Ont. (416) 632-2411. Distributor of True Temper Shear Magic, Little Giant, Redwood Planters, Edging, Fence, Sunset Books, Bamboo Stakes, etc.

PEAT MOSS

ATKINS & DURBROW LTD., Box 55, Port Colborne, Ontario. Sphagnum Peat Moss compressed in plastic bales. Shipped from A.&D. plants in Ontario and New Brunswick.

BROCKVILLE CHEMICAL INDUSTRIES LTD., 1232 Aerowood Drive, Mississauga, Ontario. (416) 625-9030. "Domtar Forest Compost".

D. & R. GARDEN SUPPLY LTD., 238 Cross Ave., Oakville, Ontario. 845-0411. "Fafard" and "Premier".

MAPLE LEAF MILLS LIMITED, P.O. Box 370, Station "A", Toronto, Ontario. (416) 362-1913. Atlantic Brand Peat Moss.

GLEN D. OGILVIE LIMITED, Box 329, Caledonia, Ontario. "Fafard" Peat Moss.

W. H. PERRON & CO. LTD., 515 Boul. Labelle, Chomedey (Laval), P.Q.

PREMIER BRANDS INC., PREMIER PEAT MOSS CORPORATION—Marketing. 25 West 45th St., New York, N.Y. 10036. Phone: (212) 757-7606.

LESLIE L. SOLTY & SONS LTD., 3850 Kingston Rd., Scarborough, Ontario. (416) 267-8294. Lambert Peat Moss in 2, 4, 6 cu. ft. bales.

UNITED CO-OPERATIVES OF ONTARIO, 2549 Weston Road, Weston, Ontario. (416) 244-5604. Complete range of Horticultural Products—Fertilizers, Insecticides, Fungicides, Herbicides, Seed, Peat Moss, Hardware.

WEN-HAL LIMITED, 729 Plains Road East, Burlington, Ontario. (416) 632-2411. Ontario Sales Agents for Premier Peat Moss.

WESTERN PEAT MOSS LTD., 10850 - 72 Ave., Delta, B.C. Suppliers of Peat Moss, Blue Whale brand Soil Conditioner, and Blue Whale brand Liquid Plant Food.

VIGORO, 1400 The Queensway, Toronto, Ontario. "Vigoro" Lawn and Garden Products — Made in Canada — Available coast to coast in every province through wholesale distributors.

WEN-HAL LIMITED, 729 Plains Road East, Burlington, Ont. (416) 632-2411. Distributors for Ortho, Niagara, Wilson and C.I.L. chemicals.

WILSON LABORATORIES (1973) LIMITED, Brock & Hatt Streets, Dundas, Ontario. Complete line of Insecticides, Fungicides and Herbicides for the home gardener.

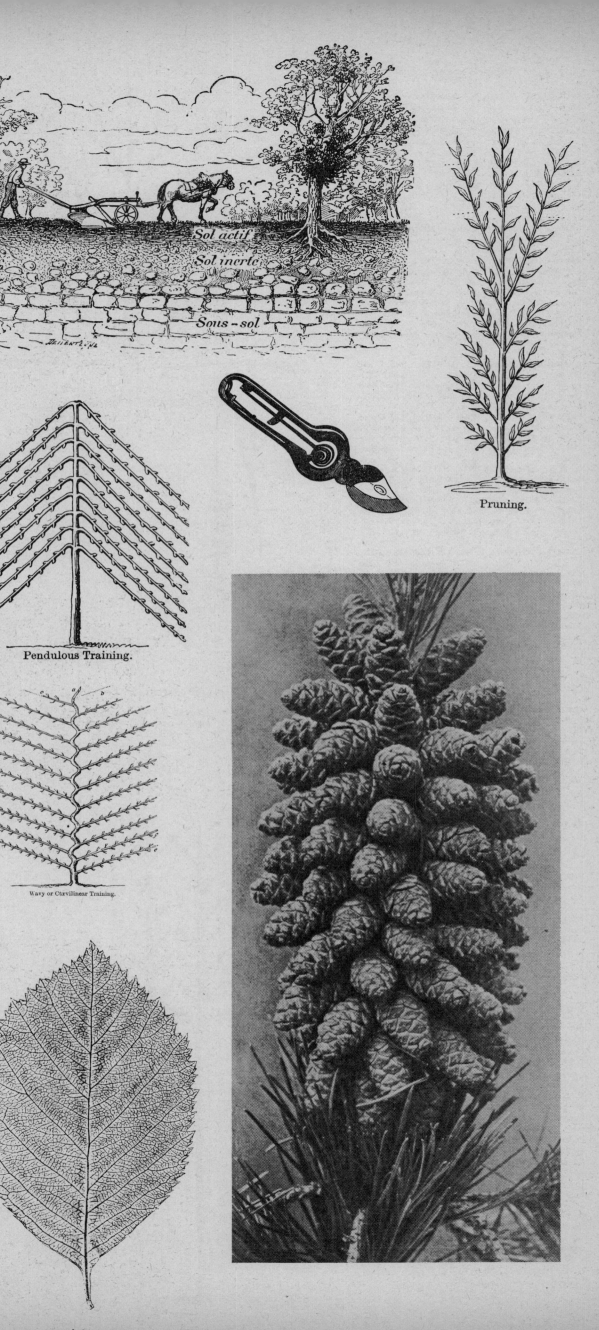

Sol actif

Sol inerte

Sous - sol

Pruning.

Pendulous Training.

Wavy or Curvilinear Training.

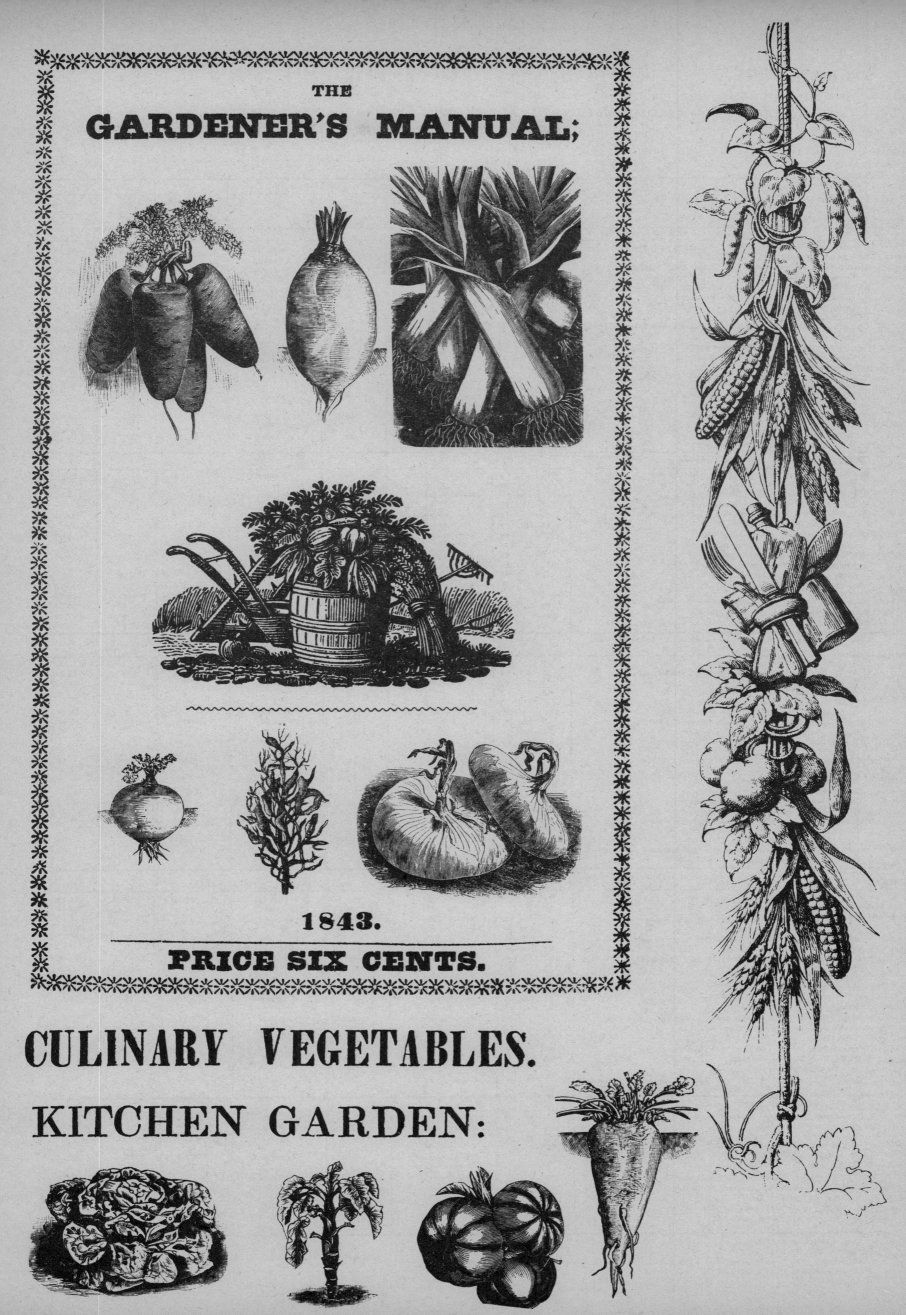

THE
GARDENER'S MANUAL;

1843.

PRICE SIX CENTS.

CULINARY VEGETABLES.

KITCHEN GARDEN:

Growing Vegetables

RECOMMENDED VARIETIES AND HOME GARDEN PLANTING CHART

Recommended Varieties (There are other good varieties for some areas.) KIND OF VEGETABLES · VARIETIES	Days to harvest	FOR FAMILY OF FIVE				PLANT SPACING	
		Average Planting Date	Feet of row	Seed or Plants	Planting depth (inches)	In Rows (inches)	Between Rows (inches)
GROUP A Hardy. Plant as soon as the soil dries out in the spring.							
ASPARAGUS – Mary Washington**, Waltham Washington**	Perennial	Mar. 15–May 1	100	50 plants	8	24	36-48
RHUBARB – Canada Red**, McDonald**	Perennial	Mar. 15–May 1	40	20 plants	4-6	24	36-48
BROCCOLI – Green Comet Hybrid, Spartan Early, Southern Comet	40 55 55	Mar. 15–July 15	50	25 plants	4	24	30-36
Green Mountain+**, Waltham 29***	60 74						
CABBAGE – Earliana, Golden Acre 84, Market Prize	60 62 76	Mar. 15–May 1	30	30 plants	4	12	18-24
Market Topper, Danish Ballhead*, Red Acre*	73 100 76						
Savoy King (mild flavor)*	86						
KOHLRABI – Early White Vienna	55	Mar. 15–May 1	25	1 ounce	¼-¾	1-2	14-18
ONIONS – Early – Ebenezer sets, Utah Yellow Sweet Spanish-transplants	80 90	Mar. 15–May 15	50	2 lbs. (300)	1¼-2	1-2	14-18
Seed – Evergreen White Bunching –							
green onions, Crystal White Wax-pickler	60 90	Mar. 15–May 1	25	1 packet	½-1	1-3	14-18
Utah Yellow Sweet Spanish – fall and storage*	110	Mar. 15–April 15	50	1 packet			
PEAS – Sparkle, Little Marvel**, Frosty**	59 62 64	Mar. 15–May 15	100	1½ pounds	1-1½	1-3	18-24
Green Arrow, Lincoln**, Wando (stands hot weather)	68 67 68						
Perfected Freezer 69**, Laxton Progress	60 60						
RADISH – Stop Lite, Cherry Belle, Sparkler	23 24 25	Mar. 15–Sept. 1	50	1 ounce	½-¾	½-1	14-18
Champion, Burpee White, Icicle	28 25 30						
SPINACH – Hybrid No. 7, Winter Bloomsdale	40 45	Mar. 15–May 1	60	1 ounce	½-¾	2-4	14-18
Viking, America	46 50						
TURNIP – Just Right, Tokyo Market	35 50	Mar. 15–May 1	25	1 ounce	½-¾	1-2	14-18
Purple Top White Globe*, Golden Ball*	57 60						
GROUP B Semi-hardy. Plant a week or two after "A" group.							
BEET – Tendersweet, Crosby Green Top, Ruby Queen	55 60 60	Mar. 20–July 15	50	1 ounce	¾-1¼	1-2	14-18
Detroit Dark Red*, Hi-Red*, Long Season*	63 69 80						
CARROT – Pioneer*, Nantes*, Short'n Sweet*	67 68 68	Mar. 20–June 15	100	1 ounce	½-¾	1-2	14-18
Golden Heart*, Gold Pack*, Spartan Bonus	70 73 77						
CAULIFLOWER – Snow King Hybrid, Super Snowball,	55 55 58	Mar. 20–July 1	30	20 plants	4	18	30-36
Snowball Imperial**	66 64 85						
ENDIVE – Salad King, Florida Deep Heart	75 85	Mar. 20–June 15	20	1 packet	½-¾	12	14-18
Green Curled, Full Heart Batavian	90 90						
LETTUCE – leaf – Oak Leaf, Salad Bowl	38 48	Mar. 20 – May 1	50	1 ounce	¼-½	6	14-18
Summer Bibb, Buttercrunch	62 64						
head – Slobolt, Great Lakes	48 78						
PARSLEY – Paramount, Deepgreen	70 85	Mar. 20 – July 1	10	1 packet	¼-½	12	14-18
PARSNIP – All-America*, Model*	105 120	Mar. 20–May 1	50	½ ounce	½-¾	2	14-18
POTATO – LaRouge, Red Pontiac	125 125	Mar. 20–May 1	1000	100 pounds	5-6	9	30-36
SALSIFY – Mammoth Sandwich Island*	140	Mar. 20–May 15	25	1 packet	½-¾	6	18
SWISS CHARD – Rhubarb+**, Lucullus+**, Fordhook Giant+**	60 60 60	Mar. 20–July 1	25	1 packet	¾-1¼	6	18-24
GROUP C Tender. Plant on the average date of the last spring frost, about when first apples bloom.							
DRY BEAN – Great Northern*, Pinto*	90 100	May 5–June 1	200	1 pound	1-1½	3	18-24
SNAP BEAN – Tendercrop**, Tenderette**, Tendergreen	53 53 54	May 5–June 10	300	2 pounds	1-1½	3	18-24
Executive**, Kinghorn Wax**, Goldwax	53 54 50						
Bush Blue Lake**, Pole Blue Lake**	58 63						18-24
CELERY – Utah*, Summer Pascal*							
(Hardy, but shoot to seed if planted too early).	125 115	May 5–June 15	50	100 plants	3	6	18-24
SWEET CORN – Seneca 60-11, Seneca Beauty, Golden Beauty	63 65 70	May 5–July 1	400	1½ pounds	1-1½	12	30-36
Northern Belle, Golden Earlipak, Tastyvee,	74 73 75						
Seneca Chief**, NK 199**, Illini Chief Super Sweet**	82 84 85						
Jubilee**	87						
CUCUMBER – Pickling – Ohio MR17, Wisconsin SMR18,	57 54	May 5–June 20	30	½ ounce	1-1½	24	48
(all female hybrids) Mariner, Pioneer	53 51						
Slicing – Tablegreen, Marketmore	70 67		25	1 packet			
Burpless 26, Ashley	60 62						
(all female hybrids) Gemini, Spartan Valor	61 65						
SPINACH – Summer, New Zealand**	65	May 5–June 20	20	1 packet	½-¾	12	36
SUMMER SQUASH – Yellow – Seneca Butterbar, Seneca Prolific	50 51	May 5–June 20	25	½ ounce	1-1½	18	36-48
Early Prolific Straightneck, Golden Zucchini	50 54						
Patty pan – St. Pat Scallop Hybrid							
Green – Zucchini Hybrid, Ambassador, Zucchini Elite	47 47 48						
Aristocrat, Hybrid Cocozelle	50 50						
GROUP D Very tender. Plant when the soil is warm, about two weeks after "C" group.							
LIMA BEAN – Fordhook 242**, Kingston**	75 65	May 20–June 10	100	1 pound	1-1½	4	18-24
SOY BEAN – Bansei**	90	May 20–June 10	100	½ pound	1-1½	2	18-24
CANTALOUPE – Burpee Hybrid, Harper Hybrid, Honey Rock	82 85 85	May 20–June 10	100	1 ounce	1-1½	24-48	48-60
Gold Star, Supermarket, Saticoy	87 88 90						
Hales Best, Powdery Mildew Res. No. 45, Hearts of Gold	88 88 92						
Iroquois	89						
RELATED MELONS – Golden Beauty, Casaba, Crenshaw**	110 110 106	May 20–June 1	100	1 ounce	1-1½	24-48	48-60
Honey Dew, Early Hybrid Crenshaw	110 90						
EGGPLANT – Early Beauty, Black Magic	62 73	May 20–June 1	30	20 plants	4	18	24-30
Classic, Black Beauty	76 80						
PEPPER – Canape, Bell Boy, Burpee's Tasty Hybrid	62 70 70	May 20–June 1	45	30 plants	4	18	24-30
Midway, Early Calwonder, Yolo Wonder	72 72 78						
WINTER SQUASH – Gold Nugget, Waltham Butternut*, Buttercup*	85 97 100	May 20–June 10	20	1 packet	1-1½	24	48
Golden Delicious*, Quality*, Banana*	103 103 110						
Sweet Meat	103						
TOMATO – Early Salad, Ball Extra Early, Moreton Hybrid	45 55 60	May 20–June 10	120	60 plants	4-6	24	36
DX-54, V. R. Moscow, Better Boy	70 75 70						
Tiny Tim (container or patio tomato)							
WATERMELON – Petite Sweet, Striped Klondike, Blue Ribbon Klondike	75 80 80	May 20–June 10	120	60 plants	4-6	24	36-48
Crimson Sweet, seedless – Triple Sweet, Tri X313	90 90 90						
GROUP E Special Plantings for fall harvest+							
BEETS – Detroit Dark Red*, Hi-Red*, Crosby's Egyptian*	63 69 60	July 1–Aug. 1	50	1 ounce	¾-1¼	2	14-18
CABBAGE – Fall-Market Prize, Red Acre	76 76	May 1–June 15	30	29 plants	4-6	18	24-30
Storage and Kraut – Glory of Enkhuizen*, Bonanza*, Danish Ball Head*	80 75 100						
Chinese – Michihli	75						
KALE – Vates, Dwarf Siberian (excellent greens for late fall and early spring harvest)	55 65	July 1–Aug. 15	40	1 packet	½-¾	13	18-24
LETTUCE – Head – Great Lakes, Over-wintering Great Lakes	80	June 1–Aug. 1	50	½ ounce	¼-½	12	14-18
ONIONS – Over-wintering – San Joaquin, Calred		Aug. 1–Aug. 10	50	1 packet	½-1	1-3	14-18
(bulb harvest next June 1)							
RUTABAGA – American Purple Top*, Macomber*	90 92	June 15–July 1	50	1 packet	½-¾	2-4	14-18
SPINACH – Viking, America	46 50	July 1–Aug. 15	60	1 ounce	½-¾	2-4	14-18
TURNIP – Purple Top White Globe*, Golden Ball*	57 60	July 1–Aug. 1	25	1 ounce	½-¾	1-3	14-18

*Suitable for common storage.
**Excellent for freezing.
+These may often be made as garden replantings (following harvest of early radishes, spinach, and peas, etc.)

Utah State University
Logan, Utah

AVERAGE ANNUAL PRECIPITATION (INCHES)

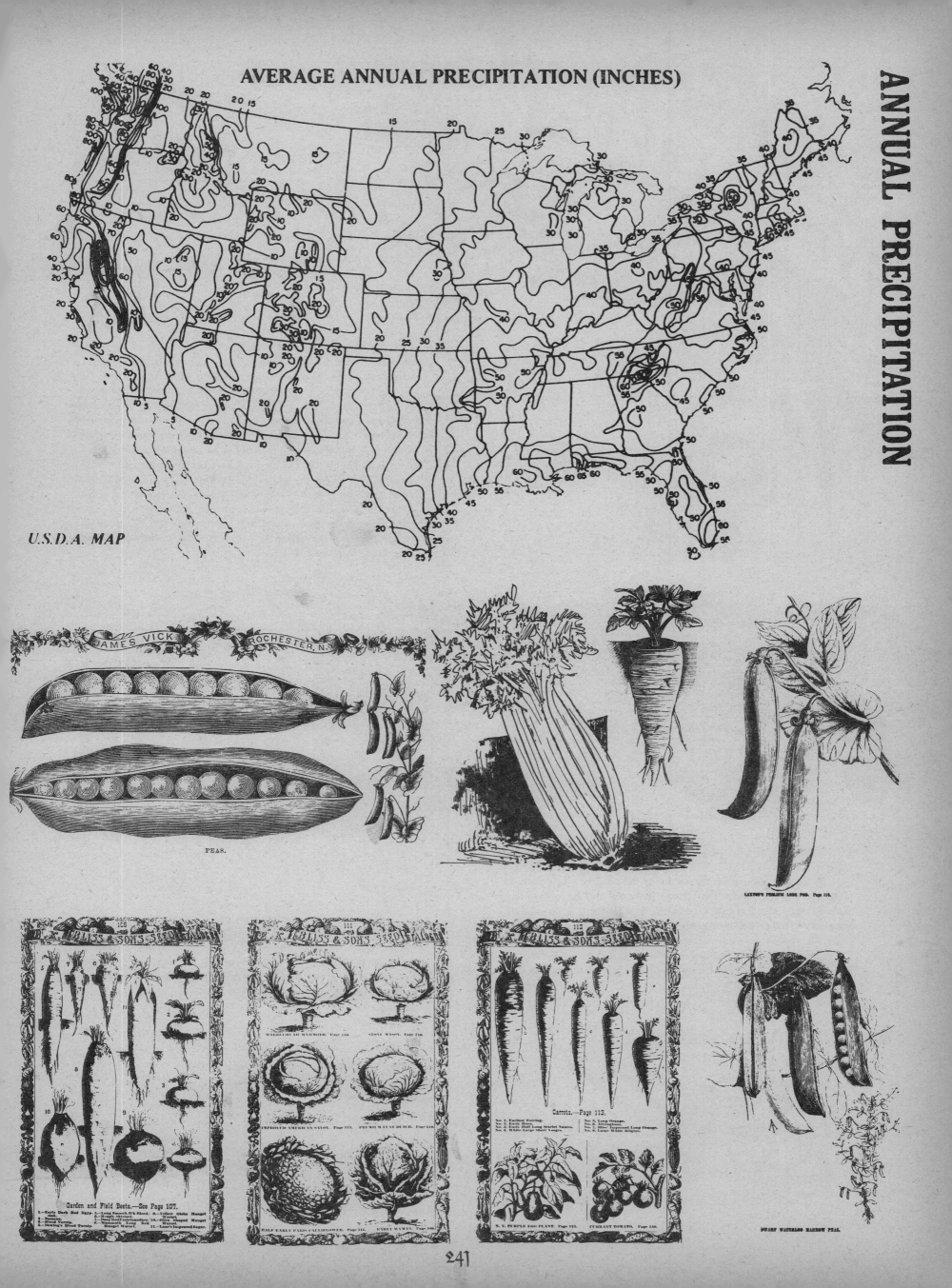

U.S.D.A. MAP

PEAS.

LAXTON'S PROLIFIC LONG POD. Page 115.

Garden and Field Beets.—See Page 107.

Carrots.—Page 113.

DWARF WATERLOO MARROW PEAS.

VEGETABLES.

COPYRIGHT 1884 BY JAMES VICK

PARSNIP

The Parsnip flourishes best, and gives the longest, largest, smoothest roots in a very deep, rich soil—one that has been made rich with manure the previous year. Manure, especially if fresh, makes the roots somewhat ill-shaped. Sow as early in the spring as the ground can be made ready, pretty thickly, in drills from twelve to eighteen inches apart and about an inch deep. Thin the plants to five or six inches apart. An ounce of seed will sow one hundred and fifty feet of drill very thickly. Six pounds of seed is the usual quantity sown on an acre. The part of the crop required for spring use can remain in the ground during the winter. If a portion is covered heavily with leaves, they can be dug at any time. A few can be stored in a pit or cellar. For feeding cattle, no root is superior to the Parsnip, and my opinion is that no root is equal to it for this country. There are several varieties, but they differ very little. Soil and culture are of more importance than varieties.

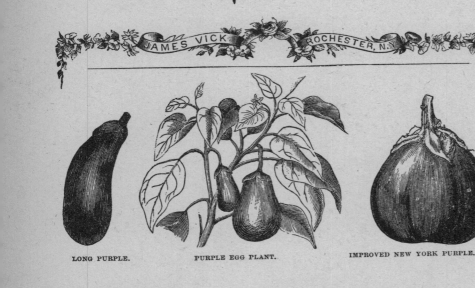

JAMES VICK   ROCHESTER, N.Y.

LONG PURPLE.   PURPLE EGG PLANT.   IMPROVED NEW YORK PURPLE.

EGG PLANT

A tender plant, requiring starting in the hot-bed pretty early to mature its fruit in the Northern States. The seed may be sown with Tomato seed; but more care is necessary at transplanting, to prevent the plants being chilled by the change, as they scarcely ever fully recover. Hand-glasses are useful for covering at the time of transplanting. Those who have no hot-bed can sow a few seeds in boxes in the house. There are various modes of cooking, but the most common is to cut in slices, parboil, and then fry in batter.

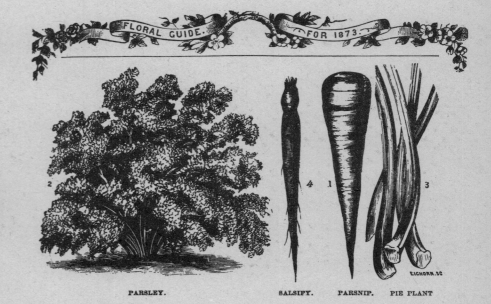

FLORAL GUIDE.   FOR 1873.

PARSLEY.   SALSIFY.   PARSNIP.   PIE PLANT.

PARSLEY

Parsley seed germinates very slowly; it should be started in a hot-bed, if possible. For out-door sowing always prepare the seed by placing it in quite hot water and allowing it to soak for twenty-four hours. When the plants are a few inches in height, set them in rows, three or four inches apart. Parsley makes a pretty edging for the walks of the vegetable garden, and is the most beautiful of all plants used for garnishing.

MATTHEWS' GARDEN SEED DRILL.

Hoe, Wheel Cultivator, and Wheel Plow.

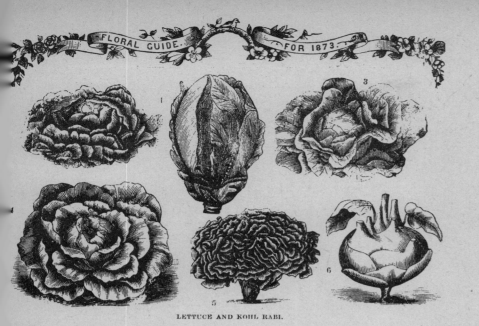

LETTUCE AND KOHL RABI.

KOHL RABI

Intermediate between the Cabbage and the Turnip we have this singular vegetable. The stem, just above the surface of the ground, swells into a bulb something like a Turnip, as shown in the engraving. Above this are the leaves, somewhat resembling those of the Ruta Baga. The bulbs are served like Turnips, and are very delicate and tender when young, possessing the flavor of both Turnip and Cabbage, to some extent. In Europe they are extensively grown for stock, and are thought to keep better than the Turnip, and impart no unpleasant taste to the milk. Seed should be sown, for a general crop, in May or June, like Turnip seed, in drills; or they may be transplanted like Cabbage. To raise a few for the table for winter use, it is not best to sow until the middle of June.

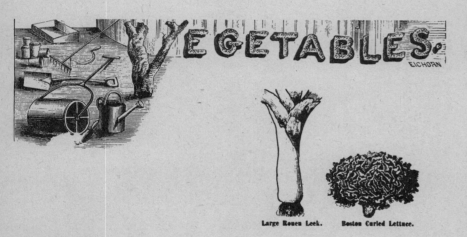

Large Rouen Leek.   Boston Curled Lettuce.

OKRA

Finely adapted to the South, where it is generally prized. The green seed-pods are used in soups, etc., to which they give a thick, jelly-like consistency, and a fine flavor. At the North the seed should be started in a hot-bed. Set the plants from two to three feet apart.

SORREL.

Sorrel—Sauerampfer-Oseille

LETTUCE

Lettuce is divided into two classes: the Cabbage, with round head and broad, spreading leaves; and the Cos with long head and upright, narrow leaves. The Cabbage varieties are the most tender and buttery, and the Cos the most crisp and refreshing. In Europe, the Cos varieties are used almost exclusively, and they deserve more attention here. The Curled varieties have the habit of the Cabbage, though not forming solid heads, and are very pretty for garnishing, but otherwise not equal to some of the plain sorts. Seed sown in the autumn will come in quite early in the spring, but not early enough to satisfy the universal relish for early salad. The hot-bed, therefore, must be started quite early. Give but little heat, and plenty of air and water on fine days. Sow a couple of rows thick, in front of the frame, to be used when young—say two inches in height. Let the plants in the rest of the bed be about three inches apart, and, as they become thick, remove every alternate one. Keep doing so, as required, and the last will be as large as Cabbages. Sow in the open ground as early as possible; or, if you have plants from fall sowing, transplant them. The soil must be very rich. For summer use, sow the seeds in a cool, moist place, as the north side of a fence. The large kinds of Lettuce should not be crowded— eight or ten inches is near enough.

MAMMOTH WHITE CORY.

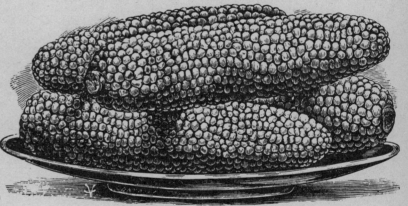

COUNTRY GENTLEMAN

CORN

The varities of Sweet Corn I offer are the finest grown, and great pains have been taken to secure entire purity. After years of trial, I am satisfied that the following list embraces all that can be desired, from the very earliest to the latest. Those who wish to plant largely for market, I can supply by the bushel.

Ruhlman's Wheel Hoe.

MELON

In this latitude we must give the Melon all the advantages we can command to secure early maturity. The most sheltered, sunny exposure, and the warmest soil must therefore be selected. The same course of treatment is recommended as for Cucumbers.

TOMATOES.

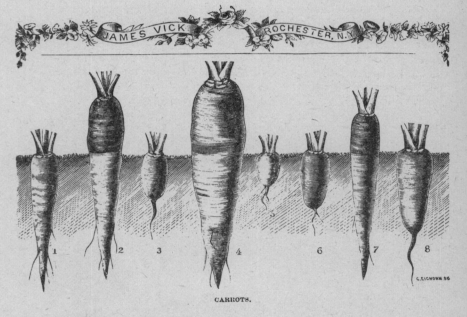

JAMES VICK ROCHESTER, N.Y.

CARROTS.

TOMATO

The Tomato is a long time in forming and ripening its fruit, and all lovers of this vegetable anxiously await the desired event. To obtain early varieties, therefore, is the great desire; and every year, almost, we have new kinds advertised from one week to five weeks earlier than anything known, and a great deal better. We have now so many good varieties that it must be a very excellent Tomato, indeed, to be worthy of being named and placed in the market. After trying every variety to be obtained, I am satisfied that Hubbard's Curled Leaf is the earliest Tomato grown. It is not, however, smooth, and its only merit is exceeding earliness. The Early Smooth Red, selected, as I offer it, is next in ripening, and Gen. Grant, a very good kind, ripens almost as early. Hathaway's Excelsior is about as early as either of the two last, of good size, smooth and solid. Having introduced it to the public, I have not liked to praise it as it really deserves. I sent it to several distinguished Horticulturists in Europe, last winter, and to the Botanist of the Royal Horticultural Society of England. The latter writes under date of October 8th: "Those who have seen Hathaway's Excelsior Tomato growing in the Society's Garden are altogether of opinion that it is the best Tomato that has as yet appeared." Pinching off a great portion of the side branches, and stopping others just beyond where the fruit is formed, hastens the ripening very much—certainly a week or ten days. To obtain plants early, sow seed in the hot-bed early in March. In about five weeks they should be transplanted to another hot-bed, setting them four or five inches apart. Here they should remain, having all the air possible, and becoming hardened, until about the middle of May, when they may be put out in the ground; that is, if there is little or no danger of frost. Very good plants can be grown in boxes in the house, starting them even in the kitchen. The soil for Early Tomatoes should not be too rich, and a warm, sheltered location selected, if possible. The Tomato may be made very pretty by training on a fence or trellis, like a Grape vine. No plant will better bear trimming.

CARROTS

The Carrot should always be furnished with a good, deep, rich soil, and as free from stones and lumps as possible. It is waste of time and labor to try to grow roots of any kind on a poor or unprepared soil. Seed should be got in early, so as to have the benefit of a portion of the spring rains. Sow in drills about an inch deep; the drills about a foot apart, and at thinning, the plants should be left at from four to five inches apart in the rows, according to kind. The Short Horn may be allowed to grow very thickly, almost in clusters. To keep the roots nice for table use, place them in sand in the cellar: but for feeding, they will keep well in a cellar, without covering, or buried in the ground. An ounce of seed will sow about one hundred feet of drill, and two pounds is the usual quantity per acre.

FLORAL GUIDE. FOR 1873.

TOMATOES.

CELERY

To obtain good Celery, it is necessary that the plants should be strong and well grown. Sow the seeds in a hot-bed, or cold-frame. When the plants are about three inches in height, transplant to a nicely prepared bed in the border, setting them about four or five inches apart. When some eight inches high, and good stocky plants, set them in the trenches—about the middle of July is early enough. Too many make trenches by digging out the top soil, and only putting a few inches of mold at the bottom, and never obtain good Celery. The trenches should contain at least eighteen inches of good soil and well rotted manure, in about equal portions. Take off all suckers and straggling leaves at the time of transplanting. Earth up a little during the summer, keeping the leaf-stalks close together, so that the soil cannot get between them; and during September and October, earth up well for blanching. Those who grow Celery for market extensively do not use trenches, but make the soil deep and rich, and plant in rows, earthing up with the plow. Take up the plants late in the fall, just before winter sets in. A little may be placed in the cellar, covered with stand or earth, for immediate use. The best of keeping is to dig a trench about a foot wide, deep enough to stand the stalks of Celery erect, leaving the tops a foot below the surface. Place them in this trench, without crowding; then cover with boards and plenty of leaves and straw. This can be opened at any time during the winter, commencing at one end, and removing enough to the cellar to last a week or ten days.

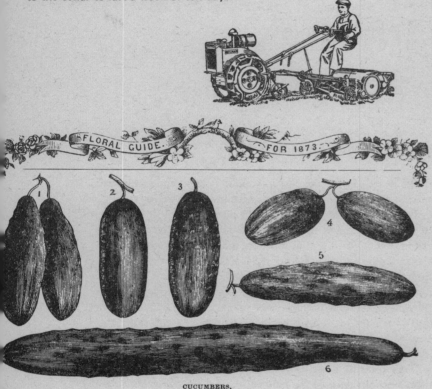

CUCUMBERS.

CUCUMBER

The hardiest varieties—in fact, all the American or common sorts—will produce a medium and late crop, if the seed is sown in the open ground in well prepared hills, as soon as the soil becomes sufficiently warm. In this latitude it is useless to plant in the open ground until nearly the first of June. Make rich hills of well rotted manure, two feet in diameter—a large shovelful of manure, at least, to each hill—and plant a dozen or more seeds, covering half an inch deep. When all danger from insects is over, pull up all but three or four of the strongest plants. The middle of June is early enough to plant for pickling. Make the hills about six feet apart. For early Cucumbers, the hot-bed is necessary; but the simplest and surest way to produce a tolerably early crop of the best kinds is, where it is designed to place a hill, dig a hole about eighteen inches deep and three feet across; into this put a barrow of fresh manure, and cover with six inches of earth; in the center of this plant the seed, and cover with a small box-like frame, on the top of which place a couple of lights of glass. When the plants grow, keep the earth drawn up to the stems. Water, and give air as needed; and if the sun appears too strong, give the glass a coat of whitewash. By the time the plants fill the frame, it will be warm enough to let them out, and the box can be removed; but if it should continue cold, raise the box by setting a block under each corner, and let the plants run under. The Fourth of July is the time we always remove the boxes or frames. Always pick the fruit as soon as large enough, as allowing any to remain to ripen injures the fruiting of the vine. One pound of seed is sufficient for an acre.

RADISH

The Radish must make a rapid growth to be fit for use; it will then be crisp and tender, and of mild flavor. If grown slowly, it will be hard, fibrous, and disagreeably pungent. For early use, seed should be sown in the hot-bed, in drills four or five inches apart and half an inch deep. Thin out the young plants so that they will stand two inches apart in the rows. Give plenty of light and air, or they will become drawn—that is, slender and worthless. For out-door beds, select a warm, sunny location, with a sandy soil. A little new earth from the woods, as a top-dressing, before the seeds are sown, will be of great service. A top-dressing of soot, or even coal ashes, will be of much benefit, as we have found by long experience. The great point is to get the plants to grow rapidly after the seed-leaf appears above ground, so as to be out of the way of the black beetle that proves so troublesome when they are young, puncturing every leaf. Sow soot, ashes, or dust, over them frequently, as the beetle dislikes gritty food. The Winter Radishes should be sown in July or August, about the time of Turnip sowing. Treatment the same. They may be kept in a cool cellar and covered with earth for winter use. Put them in cold water for an hour before using. An ounce of Radish seed will sow ten feet square; six or seven pounds are necessary for an acre.

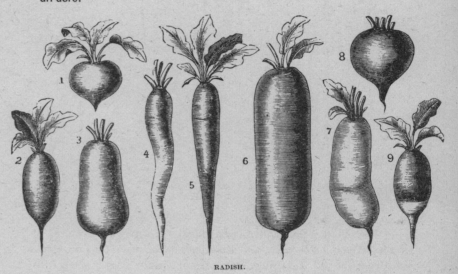

RADISH.

CAULIFLOWER

The most delicate and delicious of all the Cabbage family, and requiring the same culture and treatment; but, being more delicate, the good culture and richness of soil recommended for Cabbage are absolutely necessary for Cauliflower. Gardeners often sow seed in autumn for early Cauliflower, and keep the plants over in frames; but by sowing the early varieties in the spring, in a hot-bed or cold-frame, or even in an open border, they can be obtained in pretty good season. They require a deep, very rich soil, and the earth should be drawn well toward the stem, especially late in the season, when the flowers are about to form. For late Cauliflower, sow the seed in a cool, moist place, on the north side of a building or tight fence, and they will not be troubled with the little black beetle, so destructive to everything of the Cabbage tribe when young. The flower buds form a solid mass, of great beauty and delicacy, sometimes called the "curd," on account of its resemblance to the curd as prepared for cheese making. Its appearance we have attempted to show in the engraving. In the autumn, plants which have not formed the "flower," or "curd," may be taken up and placed in a light cellar, with earth at the roots, and they will generally form good heads for winter use. The best Cauliflower I saw in Europe were grown on mucky or swamp land, thrown up in wide ridges, wide enough for three or four rows, leaving a ditch of water between each, as shown in the engraving. Every evening the water was thrown upon the Cauliflower by means of a tin pan, like a small milk pan, fastened to a long handle. The ditches were occuped with Water Cress, and the two crops were said to be very profitable.

Herse à dents à ressorts.
Cette herse exige deux bons chevaux.

4, CAULIFLOWER.

AVERAGE DEPTH OF FROST PENETRATION (INCHES)

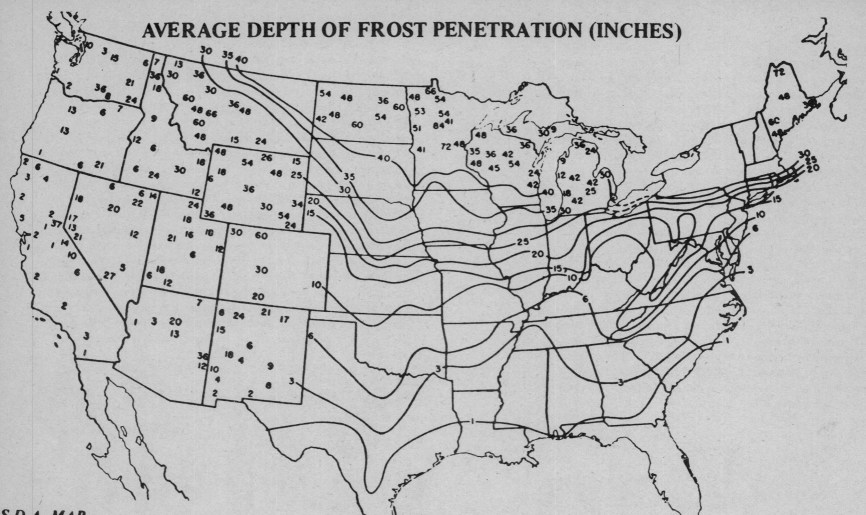

U.S.D.A. MAP

PEPPER

Capsicum or Pepper is cultivated mainly for pickles. It is used as seasoning in many ways, and sometimes medicinally. Sow the seed early in a hot-bed, if possible. If not, select a warm place in the garden for a seed-bed, and sow as soon as the soil is warm—in this latitude, about the middle of May. Transplant when three or four inches high.

CHOICE ENGLISH GARDEN PEAS

The Pea is very hardy, and will endure a great amount of cold, either in or above the ground; and as we all want "green peas" as early as possible in the season, they should be put in as early as the soil can be got ready—the sooner the better. If the Earliest sorts are planted about the first of April, in this latitude, they will be fit to gather in June, often quite early in the month. The Second will come in about the Fourth of July. By sowing two or three varieties of Early, and the same of Second and Late, as soon as practicable in the spring, a supply will be had from early in June to late in July, with only one sowing. After this Sweet Corn will be in demand. Sow in drills not less than four inches deep, pretty thickly—about a pint to forty feet. The drills should not be nearer than two feet, except for the lowest sorts. Those growing three feet high, or more, should not be nearer than three or four feet. As they are early off the ground, Cabbage can be planted between the rows, or the space can be used for Celery trenches. All varieties growing three feet or more in height should have brush for their support. The large, fine wrinkled varieties are not as hardy as the small sorts, and if planted very early, should have a dry soil, or they are liable to rot. Keep well hoed up and stick early. My Peas are mainly imported direct from the best growers of England, and will be found far superior to the varieties generally cultivated.

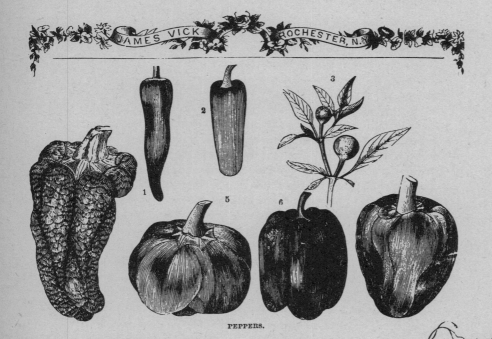

PEPPERS.

GARDEN PEAS.

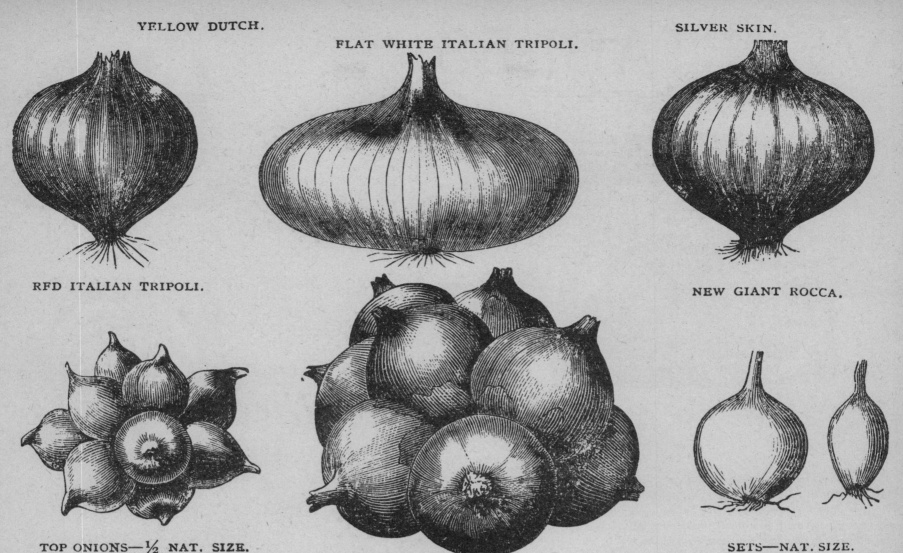

YELLOW DUTCH.

FLAT WHITE ITALIAN TRIPOLI.

SILVER SKIN.

RFD ITALIAN TRIPOLI.

NEW GIANT ROCCA.

TOP ONIONS—½ NAT. SIZE.

POTATO ONIONS—⅓ NAT. SIZE

SETS—NAT. SIZE.

ONION

The Onion must have a clean and very rich soil, or it will not do well enough to pay for the trouble. Use well rotted manure freely, and be sure to get the seed in as early as possible in the spring, no matter if it is every so cold and unpleasant; then thin out early, and keep the soil mellow and clear of weeds; and if your seed is good, you will have a large crop of Onions. On no other conditions can you hope for success. The Onion is very sensitive, and takes affront easily; it won't do to slight it in the least. Sow in drills not less than a foot apart. When the young Onions are three or four inches high, thin so that they will stand about two inches apart. Disturb the roots of Onions as little as possible, either in thinning or hoeing, and never hoe earth toward them to cover, or hill, as we do most other things. Four pounds of seed are sufficient for an acre.

NEW FOREIGN ONIONS

For several years past there has been a good deal of excitement among seedsmen and gardeners in Europe, respecting some new Italian Onions, of monstrous size, sometimes weighing as high as four pounds, and of very mild and superior flavor. We sent them out for trial two years since, and the report, particularly from the South, was generally favorable. After this report, and growing them in my own grounds, and seeing and eating them in various parts of Europe, I offered them to the American public in my Catalogue. They are monstrous in size, beautiful in appearance, and very mild and sweet in flavor, and excellent for autumn and early winter use, but not good keepers.

WETHERSFIELD RED.

EARLY RED.

VEGETABLES.

CABBAGES.

FILDERKRAUT, OR POMERANIAN.

CABBAGE

The cabbage requires a deep, rich soil and thorough working. If these requirements are met and good seed obtained, there is no difficulty in obtaining fine, soild heads. For early use, the plants should be started in a hot-bed or cold-frame; but seed for winter Cabbage should be sown in a seed-bed, early in the spring. Some varieties seem to do best if the seed is sown in the hills where they are to remain; and this is particularly the case with the Marblehead varieties. Sow two or three seeds where each plant is desired, and then pull up all but the strongest. The large varieties require to be planted about three feet apart; the small, early sorts, from a foot to eighteen inches. Always give Cabbage a deep, rich soil, and keep it mellow. For early winter use; store a few in a cool cellar. The main crop will be better kept out of doors, set in a trench closely, head down, and covered with straw, and a little earth over all. For very early summer Cabbage, it is well to sow seed in September, in a cold-frame, and the plants will be strong in November. Protect them by covering the frame during winter, giving plenty of air. Set out as early as possible in the spring.

"TRUE" JERSEY EARLY WAKEFIELD.

WHEELER'S IMPERIAL.

NEWARK EARLY FLAT DUTCH.

FOTTLER'S IMPROVED BRUNSWICK.

CURLED SAVOY CABBAGE.

LARGE FRENCH OXHEART.

MATTHEWS' COMBINED SEED DRILL AND CULTIVATOR,

MATTHEWS' HAND CULTIVATOR.

ASPARAGUS

This, now popular vegetable, is a native of the salt marshes of Europe and Asia. The seed may be sown either in the spring or autumn, in drills, about one inch deep, and the rows wide enough apart to admit of hoeing—about a foot. An ounce of seed is sufficient for a drill fifty feet in length. Keep the soil mellow and free from weeds during the summer, and in the fall or succeeding spring the plants may be set out in beds, about a foot apart each way. The beds should be narrow, so as to permit of cutting to the center without stepping upon them. The plants may be allowed to remain in the seed-bed until two years old. Before winter sets in, cover the beds with about four inches of manure. A good many varieties are advertised, with but little difference. Salt is an excellent manure for Asparagus, and an efficient assistant to the cultivator, keeping down the weeds with very little labor. When grown in large quantities, Asparagus may be planted one foot apart in the rows, and the rows three feet apart, for horse culture. Cut for use the second year after planting.

BEAN

Beans like a dry and rather light soil, though they will do well in any garden soil if not set out too early in the spring. Nothing is gained by planting until the ground is tolerably dry and warm. The Dwarf varieties grow from twelve to eighteen inches in height, need no support, and are planted either in drills or hills. The drills should not be less than a foot apart, two inches deep, and the seed set in the drills from two to three inches apart. The usual method in hills is to allow about four plants to a hill, and the hills two by three feet apart. Rows are best for the garden. A quart of ordinary sized Beans is about fifteen hundred, and will sow two hundred and fifty feet of rows, or one hundred and fifty hills. Hoe well, but only when dry. Running Beans are generally less hardy than the Dwarfs. The usual way of planting is in hills, about three feet apart, with the pole in the center of the hill. A very good way is to grow the running varieties in drills, using the tallest pea brush that can be secured conveniently. When the plants reach the top of the brush, pinch off the ends. The effect will be to cause greater fruitfulness below. In a stiff soil, especially, the Lima comes up better if planted carefully with the eye down, the hill a little elevated.

CAYENNE—LONG RED.

SPINACH

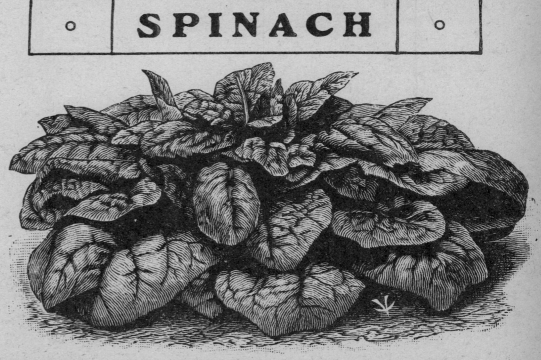

Vaughan's Norfolk Savoy Spinach

SPINACH

To grow Spinach in perfection, the soil must be rich. Sow in the autumn for spring use, in good drained soil, in drills a foot apart. As soon as the plants are well up, thin them to about six inches apart in the rows. Covering with a little straw or leaves before winter is useful but not necessary. For summer use, sow as early as possible in the spring.

CHICORY

This is the best substitute for Coffee. Should be planted in the spring, like Carrots, and receive the same culture. In the autumn the roots may be taken up, washed clean, cut up and well dried, and afterwards roasted and ground like Coffee. An ounce will sow about one hundred feet of drill; from two to three pounds to the acre. It is so hardy and so well adapted to our climate that it is very likely to become a weed.

SALSIFY, or OYSTER PLANT

A delicious vegetable. Cut into small pieces, it makes a fine soup, like that from Oysters. It is also par-boiled, grated fine, made into small balls, dipped into batter, and fried; also cooked whole as Parsnips. Culture and treatment same as for Parsnip.

Sweet Potato Vine in vase.

Long White, or Cow Horn Turnip.

CORN SALAD

A favorite salad plant in Europe, and very hardy. Sown in August and protected with a few leaves during the winter, it can be gathered in the spring very early. Sown in April, it is soon in use. The leaves are sometimes boiled and served as Spinach.

MUSTARD

Used as a salad early in spring, sometimes with Lettuce and Cress. Sow at intervals, in rows, quite thickly. Cut when about two inches high. For a crop of seed, sow in April, in drills a foot apart, and thin to about five inches apart in the rows.

MARTYNIA

A hardy annual plant of strong growth, with curious seed-pods very highly prized by many for pickling. They should be used when tender—about half grown.

Group of Squashes.

SQUASH

The Squashes are all quite tender, and therefore no progress can be made in starting them until the weather becomes somewhat warm and settled. The winter varieties should, however, be got in as early as possible, and a rapid growth encouraged. Treatment the same as for Melons and Cucumbers.

SHORT-LEAVED EARLY ERFURT KOHLRABI.

Connecticut Field Pumpkin.

PUMPKIN

The Pumpkin is now but little used, except for agricultural purposes, the finer varieties of Squashes having taken its place in the kitchen.

VEGETABLES.

TURNIPS.

BEETS.

BEETS.

MAMMOTH LONG RED MANGEL WURTZEL.

TURNIP

For early use, the Turnip should be sown as early as possible, so as to have the benefit of spring showers. The strap-leaved varieties and the Early Flat Dutch are the best for this purpose. For the main crop for fall and winter, sow during July and August, and just before rain, or during a showery time, if possible. Ruta Bagas should be sown about the first of June. The soil should be rich and mellow, and kept free from weeds. Sow in drills from twelve to eighteen inches apart and half an inch deep. Thin out the plants to five or six inches apart in the drills. Ruta Bagas should be ten inches apart. Two pounds of seed are sufficient for an acre.

The Beet is a favorite vegetable, and is exceedingly valuable, being in use almost from the time the seed-leaf appears above ground until we are looking for its appearance the next year. Treated like Spinach, the Beet is unequaled, and can be used in this way until the roots are large enough for cutting up. To preserve the roots in fine condition during the winter, take them up carefully before hard frosts, and pack them in a cool cellar, and cover them with earth. For spring use they may be pitted in the ground. The seed will germinate more surely and rapidly if put in warm water and allowed to soak for twenty-four hours. The soil should be rich, mellow and deep. Plant in drills, about two inches deep, and the rows about twelve or fifteen inches apart. The plants may be thinned out and used as needed from the time they are two inches in height, finally leaving the plants in the rows about six inches apart. Set the seeds in the drills about an inch apart. An ounce of seed will sow about seventy-five feet of drill, and five pounds are sufficient for an acre.

SWISS CHARD.   BRUSSELS SPROUTS.   BORECOLE.

BRUSSELS SPROUTS

A valuable member of the Cabbage family, giving a great number of little heads on the main stalk, as shown in the engraving. The stem sometimes grows more than four feet in height. These small heads are very tender and delicate in flavor late in the fall, or they can be kept in the cellar for winter use. Culture, same as for Cabbage.

BORECOLE, or KALE

The Kales are not very much grown in this country, though favorites in Europe, and every year are becoming better known here. In the neighborhood of New York and other large cities, some varieties, especially that known as German Greens, are grown somewhat largely for market.

A HOME GARDEN can provide a family with an abundant supply of high-quality vegetables, fruits, and herbs at low cost. Gardening is also an excellent form of relaxation and can give you the satisfaction of having grown your own produce.

To help ensure success and to derive maximum yields, the entire garden should be planned in detail before anything is planted. In planning you should consider the location of the garden, the crops and varieties of each to be grown, when and where each crop will be planted, and the amount of each crop to plant.

Ideally, the garden soil should be deep, granular or easily pulverized, well drained, high in organic matter such as compost and humus, and slightly acid. However, it is not always possible to have such a soil and it may be beneficial to improve your soil by adding fertilizer, lime, and organic matter.

The garden should receive direct sunlight all day. In addition, it should be far enough from trees so they don't compete with the crops for water.

If you have only a small site available for a garden, we suggest you grow crops that will yield the heaviest over the longest period of time. Vegetables suitable for a small garden include tomatoes, peppers, cucumbers, bush summer squash, bush lima and snap beans, and onions.

Vegetables that require much space and yield a small return include muskmelons, sweet corn, watermelons, winter squash, and pumpkins. These crops are adapted to a large garden.

Vegetables vary greatly in their response to temperature. Some make their best growth in the spring and fall, or winter in the South, when cool temperatures prevail. Other vegetables are very sensitive to cool temperatures and thrive only during warm weather. Temperature requirements of the common vegetables are given on page 132.

Although lettuce, spinach, collards, cabbage, mustard, kale, and turnips are cool-hardy plants, there are varieties of each that are more tolerant of warm temperatures than others. The heat-tolerant varieties are slower to bolt or produce a seed stalk.

Because of different climatic requirements and different maturity rates for various vegetables, it is wise to use successive cropping in the garden. This conserves space and enables you to grow a variety of crops.

Examples of successive cropping systems are: spinach, lettuce, green onions, or endive, followed by beans, tomatoes, peppers, or eggplant; cabbage, cauliflower, carrots, beets, or peas, followed by snap beans, cowpeas, or corn; beans followed by late cabbage, cauliflower, or corn; or corn followed by beans, beets, lettuce, turnips, carrots, or by spinach.

After deciding on the vegetables to be included in your garden, you must make the important decision of what varieties to grow. Vegetable varieties differ in their adaptation to different

Author ALLAN K. STONER is a Horticulturist in the Vegetables and Ornamentals Research Branch, Plant Science Research Division, Agricultural Research Service.

Coauthor HOWARD J. BROOKS is Chief of the division's Fruit and Nut Crops Research Branch.

Coauthor LLEWELYN WILLIAMS is a Botanist in the division's New Crops Research Branch.

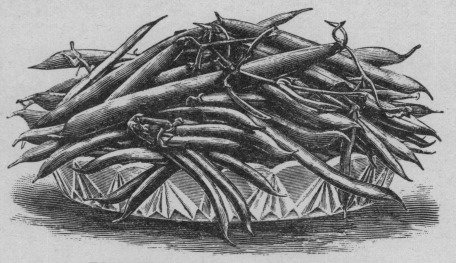

KENTUCKY WONDER OR OLD HOMESTEAD.

POLE BEANS.

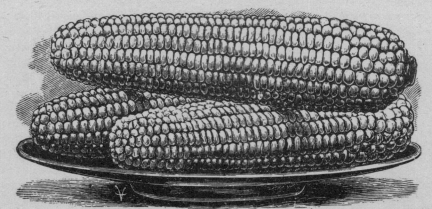

IMPROVED EARLY CHAMPION.

STOWELL'S EVERGREEN.

areas of the country and soil types; resistance to diseases and nematodes; quality for fresh use, canning, or for freezing; and days from planting to maturity.

Names of vegetable varieties adapted to your local area can be obtained from your State agricultural experiment station or county extension agent. Experienced local gardeners may also be good sources of information on the locally adapted varieties.

To insure a steady supply of crops such as sweet corn or snap beans, you can make successive plantings several days apart. Harvests can also be spread out by planting varieties that mature at different times. Ranges in maturity of different varieties of the common vegetables are given above.

Growing a variety resistant to diseases and nematodes often means the difference between obtaining a crop or having a total crop failure. This is especially true with plant diseases that cannot be controlled by spraying or dusting with chemicals. Examples of such diseases are fusarium and verticillium wilts of tomato, Stewart's wilt of sweet corn, tobacco mosaic virus of peppers, and cucumber mosaic virus of cucumbers and muskmelons.

Even though a disease can be controlled by chemicals, growing a resistant variety may eliminate the need for repeated applications of pesticides. Diseases that can be controlled by spraying, but to which resistant varieties are available, include downy and powdery mildew of cucumbers and muskmelons, and gray leaf spot and late blight of tomatoes.

It is not always necessary to grow resistant varieties since not all diseases occur in all areas of the country. For example, nematodes are most prevalent in warm climates, so it is not necessary to grow a nematode resistant tomato variety in the northern areas. Likewise, curly top virus is only a problem in certain western areas, so resistant beans and tomatoes are necessary only in these areas.

If vegetables are grown primarily for fresh consumption, we generally suggest you avoid growing varieties that have been bred for machine harvesting. Such varieties are developed to have their entire crop ripen at one time, whereas the home gardener usually prefers to spread the harvest over a long period of time. For canning or freezing, however, the machine harvest varieties may be desirable.

The quality (color, taste, texture, etc.) and the intended use (fresh, canning, or freezing) of the produce should be considered in the selection of varieties. Differences in quality include yellow vs. green podded beans, white vs. red radishes, and hot or pungent vs. mild-tasting onions. Some varieties are especially suited for fresh consumption, while others are suited for canning or freezing.

A partial list of vegetable varieties for home garden use begins on the next page. Additional information on varieties can be obtained from catalogs published annually by seed companies, newspaper gardening columns, and the garden or horticultural magazines.

Fruits take more space in the garden than vegetables but they can be equally rewarding. Once established, adapted varieties of fruits will bear year after year. Considerable care must be taken, however, to select those fruits and varieties most suited to each growing area. Like vegetables, fruits require full sunlight.

Here we will discuss strawberries, raspberries, blackberries, blueberries, grapes, cherries, peaches, plums, apples, and pears. These all require a well-drained soil. Blueberries require a soil pH of 4.5 to 5.0. Soil pH of other fruits should be between 5.5 to 6.5. (The pH of a soil is a measure of its acidity. Soil analyses can be arranged by the county agricultural extension agent.)

Since all fruits blossom early in the spring, frost pockets should be avoided. Even when your garden has good air drainage, the blossoms may have to be protected against cold. Temperatures of 30° F. will often kill blossoms and young developing fruit.

Apples, pears, and plums require cross-pollination. Thus, more than one variety of these fruits should be planted. Wild bees and other insects will pollinate the blossoms. Insecticides should not be applied in the garden during the period of blossoming and pollination.

The strawberry is probably the best fruit for use in the home garden. It takes but little space and fruits will be produced one year after planting. Strawberries are very productive. You can expect 1 quart of fruit for each foot of row. Plants should be set 1½ feet apart in the row with rows spaced 4 feet apart. Water strawberry plants frequently to develop good vigorous growth. The plants should be mulched with straw or hay in the late fall.

Only varieties resistant to the red stele fungus should be planted in most areas of the East and Central States. The following varieties are recommended: East—Midway, Surecrop, Raritan, Catskill, Guardian; West—Marshall, Northwest; South—Albritton, Florida 90, Dabreak, and Tioga.

Red raspberries grow best in regions where summers are cool and moist. Plants should be spaced 3 feet apart in the row with 5 feet between rows. The plants will bear fruit in the second year. Old fruiting canes should be removed each fall. In some areas, fruit canes may have to be covered to protect them during the winter months. Following are the varieties recommended: East—Latham, September, Taylor; West—Willamette, Meeker; South—Southland.

Black raspberries are less hardy than red raspberries. The Bristol and Black Hawk varieties are recommended in the East; Munger and Plum Farmer in the West.

Blackberries are generally less hardy than raspberries. They can, however, be grown over a large portion of the country. They should be planted at the same distance as raspberries. The plants will tolerate poor soil and drought conditions. Good soil moisture, however, is required for best growth and berry size. The Darrow, Raven, and Thornfree varieties are recommended for the East; the Boysen, Cascade, and Olallie for the West; and the Brazos, Raven, and Oklawaha for the South.

Blueberries require an acid soil and protection from birds. They will, however, provide an attractive bush and fruit to follow the strawberry season. Plants should not be planted closer than 5 feet. Blueberries have a very shallow root system. Mulch should be used around the plants to help retain moisture and suppress weeds.

The following highbush blueberry varieties are recommended: East—Bluetta, Blueray, Bluecrop, Berkeley, Darrow; South—Morrow and Croaton. Tifblue, Woodard, and Delite are rabbiteye blueberry varieties recommended for the South.

Grapes should also be considered for the home garden. The vines can be used effectively as a screen during summer months. One vine will cover 8 to 10 feet of the trellis each year. For good fruit production, however, vines must be pruned each winter.

The European grape can be grown in most of the sections of the United States. The Concord, Caco, and Niagara are recommended varieties. The Vinifera grape is grown mostly on the West Coast. Cardinal, Perlette, and Blackrose are suggested varieties.

Muscadine grapes are recommended for the South. The Magoon and Magnolia varieties are self-fertile and so do not require cross-pollination. The Scuppernong variety requires a second variety for pollination.

Sour cherries can be recommended for the home garden. They do not require cross-pollination and only one tree is required. Once established, the tree requires very little attention. The Montmorency, English Morello, and Early Richmond varieties are hardy over most of the United States. Because of the very serious problem with birds, sweet cherries cannot be recommended for the home garden.

The peach is an excellent fruit for the home garden. With the selection of early, midseason, and late varieties, the peach fruiting season can be extended to 6 or 8 weeks in most parts of the country. The tree will have to be pruned each winter. Developing fruit have to be hand thinned to about 5 inches apart. Peaches do not require cross-pollination and a single tree will bear fruit. You should plant trees no closer than 15 feet apart.

There are many peach varieties to choose from. Most varieties will grow satisfactorily in all regions. Freestone varieties are recommended for fresh fruit; clingstone varieties for canning. Nectarines are almost identical with the peach except that nectarines have no fuzz or hairiness on the fruit.

Plums also are excellent for the home garden. Care must be taken, however, to select only those varieties recommended for each growing area.

Japanese plums can be considered for most southeastern and western areas. Because of disease problems, however, they are not recommended for the Southeast. Trees and fruit buds will be injured in northern areas. Santa Rosa, Casselman, Laroda, and Beauty are recommended varieties for the West. Methley and Ozark Premier are suggested for eastern areas.

European type plums are more hardy and are suggested for northern areas. The Fellenburg, Stanley, and Shropshire varieties are recommended.

Plums require little pruning. Trees should not be planted closer than 15 feet apart.

Apricots are not recommended for the home garden. They bloom very early in the spring and their flowers are often killed by spring frosts.

Apples have to be sprayed for disease and insect control more than other fruits. If you are willing to go to this expense and trouble, you may wish to consider apples for the home garden.

Apples can be grown in all parts of the country. The standard tree grows well on all soils but it may grow too large for home gardens. Dwarfing rootstocks are used to reduce tree size but they are not adapted to poor soils. Different rootstocks cause different degrees of dwarfing. You must fertilize and water your trees if dwarfing rootstocks are used. Prune your trees each winter. All apples require cross-pollination.

The Red Delicious variety is the most common variety grown in this country. It is not a cooking apple. Golden Delicious, another popular variety, can be used both for fresh fruit and cooking. The Stayman and Jonathan varieties are also dual purpose varieties. The McIntosh variety is recommended for northern areas. McIntosh does not color well in the South.

Pears require less care than apples. Fire blight disease, however, is a serious problem in all parts of the country. This disease is most severe in the Central and Southeastern States where there are periods of warm moist conditions during the flowering period. Dwarfing rootstocks should not be used on poor soils.

The Bartlett pear is the most common variety. It is used for both eating out of hand and canning. It is, however, very susceptible to fire blight. Magness and Moonglow varieties have a degree of resistance. The Kieffer variety is quite resistant but lacks quality.

No matter what fruits are selected for the home garden, a fertilization program must be followed. Grass and

Vaughan's Magnum Dulce Pepper

EARLY CHANTENAY.

weeds should be removed from around all trees. When trees are watered, sufficient water should be applied to penetrate the top 5 inches of soil. Apply fertilizer in the early spring.

Fruit trees will have to be sprayed to control insects and diseases. Caution should be used in selecting and applying pesticides.

You must also anticipate that birds and squirrels will be major pests in the home fruit garden.

Many people include herbs along with vegetables and fruits in their garden. The word "herb" is applied to low plants, some of which emit a particular fragrance. Others possess medicinal virtues. A number of herbs are used to season, enrich, or otherwise to impart a flavor and aroma to certain foods, and thus make them more pleasing to the taste. Fragrant or savory leaves, seeds, buds, bark, and roots have been used for such purposes since ancient times, and many have long figured in folklore and tradition.

Many useful herbs, introduced and long cultivated in the United States, originated on the warm shores of the Mediterranean and the region eastward to India. In their natural environment they generally grow in sunny sites, or granular, or easily pulverized, alkaline soil. Under propagated conditions, the majority of herbs may be grown successfully under a wide range of soil conditions, but thrive best in a fertile, well-prepared soil, mixed with humus and fertilizer. Barnyard manure, compost, and wood ashes are especially beneficial.

Annuals, or herbs that have to be planted each year, are usually grown from seed and are sown directly in the garden in the early spring when the soil is sufficiently dry and there is no danger of frost. These annuals include: anise, sweet basil, borage, chervil, coriander, dill, fennel, marjoram or sweet marjoram, parsley, and savory.

Biennials or perennials may be purchased as seedlings, or started in a coldframe or window box from seeds or cuttings and the plants reset in the garden at the proper time. Among these

herbs (or mints) are: angelica, lemon balm, caraway, catnip, chives, geranium, lavender, lovage, peppermint and spearmint, wild marjoram, rosemary, sage, tarragon, lemon-verbena and thyme.

Consideration should be given to the location of the herbs in your garden. For example, sage, thyme, and rosemary are sensitive to moist conditions and require a well-drained, moderately humid situation. Chervil, parsley, and the mints, on the other hand, grow best on soils that retain moisture but have good drainage.

Such plants as sage, lemon balm, and rosemary may be propagated by stem cuttings. Stems from the latest growth or the upper part of the older stems make the best cuttings and root readily in the summer or fall. To start cuttings, use a shallow box with 4 or 5 inches of clean sand and fitted with a glass cover. This makes a good rooting bed. Insert the cuttings to a depth of one-half to two-thirds their length in moist sand, pack firmly, and saturate with water. The glass cover should have a ½- to 1-inch opening on one side to permit ventilation.

Place the box in a protected sunny place and keep moist, but not wet, at all times. To prevent wilting, protect the cuttings from direct sunlight during the first week or two by shading with paper or cheesecloth. On hot sunny days, increase the ventilation by raising the glass cover on one side. Roots should develop in about 2 weeks. In 4 to 6 weeks, the cuttings should be ready to pot or to set in a coldframe for protection during winter. The plants may be transplanted to a permanent site in early spring.

Some herbs—such as thyme, savory, and marjoram—can be easily propagated by layering. This method consists of covering the side branches with soil, and leaving the top exposed. When the covered branches have rooted, they are nipped from the parent and set out.

Other herbs, such as chives and tarragon, may be propagated by dividing the crown clumps, after 1 or 2 seasons of growth, into individual plants. These

subdivisions may be planted directly in permanent sites if removed in the early spring, or set in a coldframe for winter protection when removed in the fall.

Mints spread rapidly by means of runners that may grow several feet from the parent plant and usually at a depth of 1 to 2 inches beneath the surface. New plants spring up at the nodes of the runners during summer. These plants, with roots attached, can be removed and transplanted in the spring or early summer or the runners alone may be planted in rows and covered to a depth of 2 inches.

Whenever possible, herbs should be used when fresh, as some plants when dried lose their fragrance or flavor after about 1 year. They should be harvested on a clear morning, when the leaves are free of dew.

The leaves usually have the best flavor or fragrance when gathered immediately before the flowers open. Flowers or leaves should be cut with a sharp knife or scissors, leaving enough foliage for new growth.

Leaves should be washed, the excess water shaken off, and then dried on a wire or cheesecloth frame, or tied in bunches and hung up to dry in a dark place.

Seeds, also, should be thoroughly dried before storing to prevent mold and loss of viability. After curing for several days in an airy room, exposure to the sun for a day or two before storing will insure safe storage.

As soon as the leaves or seeds of herbs are dry they should be cleaned of stems and foreign matter. Then place them in airtight glass, metal, or cardboard containers, to preserve their delicate fragrance and flavor. Glass jars make satisfactory containers, but they should be painted black or stored in a dark room to prevent bleaching of the green leaves by light.

For further reading:
A Primer for Herb Growing, Herb Society of America, 300 Massachusetts Avenue, Boston, Mass. 02115, 35 cents.
U.S. Department of Agriculture, *Mini-gardens for Vegetables.* Home and Garden Bulletin 163, Washington, D.C. 20250, 1970.
—————, *Growing Tomatoes in the Home Garden.* Home and Garden Bulletin 180, Washington, D.C. 20250, 1970.

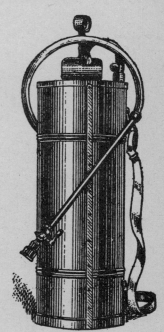

IMPROVED EARLIEST VALENTINE.

Beans planted at proper depth.

HONOR BRIGHT. (Best Selected Stock.)

Some Vegetable Varieties Suited for Home Gardens

Variety	Remarks
Asparagus	
Mary Washington	Widely adapted, tolerant to rust
Beans (bush)	
Topcrop	Widely adapted, resistant to bean mosaic
Contender	Resistant to bean mosaic and powdery mildew
Bush Blue Lake 274	Heavy yield, resistant to bean mosaic
Resistant Cherokee Wax	Yellow pods, resistant to bean mosaic
Resistant Kinghorn Wax	Yellow pods, resistant to bean mosaic
Beans (pole)	
Kentucky Wonder	Widely adapted, excellent for freezing
Dade	Adapted to South, resistant to rust, common and Southern bean mosaic
Romano	Widely adapted, good for freezing
Beans, lima	
Fordhook 242	Widely adapted
Henderson's Bush	"Baby" or small seeded
Jackson Wonder	Widely adapted
Beets	
Detroit Dark Red	Widely adapted
Ruby Queen	Widely adapted, good for canning
Broccoli	
Waltham 29	Widely adapted, good for freezing
Green Comet	Widely adapted
Brussels sprouts	
Jade Cross	Widely adapted
Long Island Improved	Heavy yield over extended period
Cabbage	
Golden Acre	Resistant to cabbage yellows
Early Jersey Wakefield	Slow bolting, resistant to cabbage yellows
Copenhagen Market	Widely adapted, early maturity
Red Acre	Red color
Chinese cabbage	
Michihli	Widely adapted
Carrots	
Danvers 126	Widely adapted, heavy yield of long tapered roots
Royal Chantenay	Widely adapted, broad-shouldered roots with little taper
Imperator Long Type	Widely adapted, long slender roots
Cauliflower	
Snowball Y	Widely adapted, produces over a long period
Early Snowball A	Early maturing
Celery	
Utah 52–70	Widely adapted, tolerant to celery mosaic, resistant to boron deficiency
Collards	
Vates	Slow bolting
Georgia	Widely adapted
Corn, sweet	
Iochief	Resistant to Stewart's wilt
Seneca Chief	Resistant to Stewart's wilt
Butter and Sugar	Mixture of white and yellow kernels, excellent quality
Golden Security	Resistant to Stewart's wilt
Cucumber (slicing)	
Ashley	Resistant to downy mildew
Saticoy Hybrid	Tolerant to downy mildew and mosaic
Marketer	Resistant to downy mildew
Cucumber (pickling)	
Pioneer	Tolerant to scab, mosaic, downy and powdery mildew, anthracnose, and angular leaf spot
Wisconsin SMR–18	Resistant to scab and mosaic
Eggplant	
Jersey King	Elongated fruit, widely adapted
Black Beauty	Oval globe fruit, widely adapted
Mission Bell	Early high yield
Kale	
Vates	Slow bolting
Siberian (sprouts)	Very vigorous
Kohlrabi	
Early White Vienna	Widely adapted
Lettuce (leaf)	
Salad Bowl	Slow bolting, high quality
Grand Rapids	Tip burn resistant
Lettuce (butterhead)	
Buttercrunch	Slow bolting, high quality
Lettuce (crisp head)	
Great Lakes	Slow bolting, widely adapted
Muskmelon	
Supermarket	Resistant to fusarium and downy mildew
Hales Best Jumbo	Large fruit
Saticoy Hybrid	Resistant to fusarium, tolerant to powdery mildew
Mustard	
Green Wave	Slow bolting
Southern Giant Curled	Slow bolting
Florida Broad Leaf	Slow bolting
Okra	
Dwarf Green Long Pod	Dwarf vine
Clemson Spineless	Spineless
Emerald	High quality
Onions	
Yellow Sweet Spanish	Large globe shape
Ebenezer	Yellow, quite pungent
Downing Yellow Globe	Good storage

—Properly cut seed potatoes. Each piece has two good eyes and is about the size of a hen's egg.

Variety	Remarks
Parsnips	
Hollow Crown	Widely adapted
Peas	
Alaska	Resistant to fusarium wilt
Little Marvel	Good quality, good for freezing
Progress No. 9	Large early peas
Peppers	
Calwonder	Sweet, widely adapted
Yolo Wonder	Sweet, resistant to tobacco mosaic virus
Keystone Resistant Giant	Sweet, resistant to tobacco mosaic virus
Hungarian Yellow Wax	Hot
Potato	
Irish Cobbler	Early, widely adapted
Sebago	Widely adapted
Kennebec	Widely adapted
Pumpkin	
Connecticut Field	Large smooth orange fruit
Cinderella	Bush vine, 10-inch fruit
Jack O'Lantern	Large uniform yellow fruit
Radish	
Cherry Belle	Red color
Champion	Red color
Icicle	White color
Southern Peas (cowpeas)	
California Blackeye No. 5	Good for freezing, large seed with black eye
Pink Eye Purple Hull	Elongated seed, light color
Mississippi Silver	Early maturing, large seed, light green to cream in color
Spinach	
Early Hybrid No. 7	Resistant to downy mildew and cucumber mosaic virus
Long Standing Bloomsdale	Widely adapted, slow bolting
Squash (summer)	
Zucchini	Bush plant, cylindrical
Early Prolific Straightneck	Bush plant, tapered cylindrical fruit
Yellow Summer Crookneck	Bush plant, fruit tapered cylinder with curved neck
Early White Bush Scallop	Bush plant, flat round fruit
Squash (winter)	
Waltham Butternut	High quality, elongated pear-shaped fruit
Table Queen	High quality, heart-shaped fruit
Hubbard	Large globular fruit tapered at ends
Golden Delicious	Large, somewhat oval-shaped fruit
Sweetpotato	
Centennial	Widely adapted
Puerto Rico	Widely adapted
Tomato	
Ace VF	Adapted to West, resistant to fusarium and verticillium
Fireball VF	Adapted to East and North, resistant to fusarium and verticillium
Manapal	Widely adapted, resistant to fusarium, gray leaf spot, and blossom end rot
H1350	Adapted East and Midwest, resistant to fusarium and verticillium
Better Boy	Resistant to fusarium, verticillium, and nematodes
Supersonic	Resistant to fusarium and verticillium
Small Fry	Small fruit, resistant to fusarium, verticillium, and nematodes
Turnips	
Purple Top White Globe	Widely adapted
Shogoin	Quick growing, primarily for greens
Watermelon	
Sugar Baby	Small round, early
Crimson Sweet	Blocky oval, resistant to fusarium and anthracnose
Charleston Gray	Oblong, resistant to fusarium and anthracnose

—Straight rows add to the beauty of the garden and are easier to cultivate. The simplest way to lay them off is to stretch a line between two stakes and mark row with a hoe, hoe handle or stick.

Approximate Number of Days From Planting to Harvest

Vegetable	Early variety	Late variety
Beans—green pod (bush)	45	65
Beans—green pod (pole)	56	72
Beans, lima	65	78
Beets	55	80
Broccoli [1]	70	150
Brussels sprouts [1]	90	100
Cabbage [1]	65	110
Chinese cabbage	70	80
Carrots	60	85
Cauliflower [1]	55	75
Celery	90	115
Collards	70	80
Corn, sweet	65	90
Cucumber	55	75
Eggplant [1]	70	85
Kale	55	70
Kohlrabi	55	62
Lettuce (head)	45	76
Lettuce (leaf)	45	50
Muskmelon	75	110
Okra	55	60
Onions	90	130
Parsnips	110	130
Peas	58	75
Peppers (bell or sweet) [1]	62	80
Potato	90	120
Pumpkin	100	115
Radish	23	30
Rutabaga	80	90
Southern peas (cowpeas)	65	105
Spinach	35	45
Squash (summer)	50	60
Squash (winter)	95	110
Sweetpotato	120	150
Tomato [1]	65	90
Turnips	42	55
Watermelon	80	95

[1] Days from transplanting. Additional time needed from seeding to transplanting.

—A tomato plant should be tied with a strip of cloth, at a height of ten inches, again at about 18 inches and again at about 26 inches. The plant here pictured is a good one from which to save seed.

TOMATO.

—A paper band folded into the form of a berry box, without bottom, is a good holder for indoor seed planting. The picture shows how these are placed side by side in a flat box.

—Lima bean vine on pole.

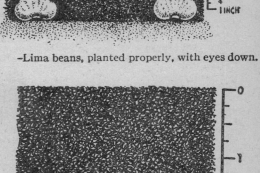

—Lima beans, planted properly, with eyes down.

—Corn, planted properly, at depth of 2 in

—Transplanting tomato plant from pot to garden.

Some Common Vegetables With Approximate Times They Can Be Planted and Their Relative Requirements for Cool and Warm Weather

Cold-hardy plants for early spring planting		Cold-tender or heat-hardy plants for late spring or early summer planting			Hardy plants for late summer or fall planting except in the North
Very hardy (plant 4 to 6 weeks before frost-free date)	Hardy (plant 2 to 4 weeks before frost-free date)	Not cold-hardy (plant on frost-free date)	Requiring hot weather (plant 1 week or more after frost-free date)	Medium heat-tolerant (good for summer planting)	(Plant 6 to 8 weeks before first fall freeze)
Broccoli	Beets	Beans, snap	Beans, lima	Beans, all	Beets
Cabbage	Carrots	Corn, sweet	Cucumber	Chard	Collards
Lettuce	Chard	Okra	Eggplant	Corn, sweet	Kale
Onions	Mustard	Squash	Melons	Soybeans	Lettuce
Peas	Parsnips	Tomato	Peppers	Squash	Mustard
Potato	Radish		Sweetpotato		Spinach
Spinach					Turnips
Turnips					

AS A GARDENER, you will compete with insects and mites, diseases, nematodes, and weeds for use of the plants you grow. The complex and competitive garden environment must be considered and efficiently managed to successfully grow productive food plants or plants of esthetic and ornamental value.

Entomologists say that more than 750,000 insect species have been identified. About 10,000 of these are known noxious pests. They cause losses estimated at more than $4 billion annually. In addition, 50,000 species of fungi cause 1,500 plant diseases; over 1,800 weed species annually cause serious economic losses; and about 15,000 species of nematodes attack crop plants with about 1,500 of them causing serious damage.

Don't be discouraged, though. As a home gardener, you will never be plagued with all of these pests. However, to understand the problems of pest control, it is important that you recognize and appreciate the competitive nature of the garden environment.

Insects and mite pests damage plants in different ways. There are insects that feed on leaves. There are insects that suck plant juices. These latter produce damaged and dead plant tissues. They also serve as disease vectors (carriers). There are insects that bore; they attack the woody parts of plants. Finally, there are insects that live in the soil and feed on roots and other plant parts.

Insects and mites only become garden pests when they do sufficient damage to result in loss. The insect population at the damage state reaches high enough levels to kill the plant or prevent its development. Many factors affect the ability of pests to develop large populations. The reproductive potential of most insects is tremendous.

Adult insects may lay several hundred eggs, increasing populations as much as five-fold or more in a generation. And a generation may be only 2 to 3 weeks. The numbers of insects present fluctuate greatly for many reasons. They are affected by seasonal and weather conditions, food supply, and natural enemies.

Assuming that an insect or mite species is adapted to an area, the most important factor regulating populations and preventing them from developing to damaging proportions is the presence of natural enemies (parasites, predators, and pathogens).

Less than 2 percent of the known insects are pests. Many others (parasites and predators) are vital factors regulating pest insect populations. These insects are among the best friends of the gardener. In addition, more than 1,100 viruses, bacteria, fungi, rickettsia, and nematodes attack insects in their environment.

These natural enemies of pest insects regulate the fluctuations of pest populations and keep them within bounds. In other words, they stabilize the pest population. Scientists call this the species equilibrium position.

When a species is stabilized at equilibrium where the numbers present are causing economic damage to the plant life in the garden, they are called pests; conversely if the equilibrium is established where the numbers present do not cause economic damage, they are of little concern and there is no need to further reduce their numbers.

Many of the insects that the home gardener sees are beneficial and destroy insects and mites injurious to the food crops or ornamental plants.

In home vegetable and ornamental gardens, very few pests will cause appreciable plant damage if parasites and predators are protected. The commonly observed aphid lion, assassin bug, lady beetle, praying mantis, and a variety of wasps are only a few of the beneficial insects which are continually working in the garden environment feeding on aphids, scale insects, mites, and a number of other pest species.

Spider mites, cabbage caterpillars, Colorado potato beetles, and aphids are common pests that attack vegetables in the home garden. If you find any of these, treat them promptly to reduce populations. Some pests of ornamental plants are spider mites, aphids, beetles, lacebugs, thrips, and scale insects.

Chemicals remain the number one weapon for immediate control of pest insects in the home garden. They probably will remain essential for the foreseeable future. However, chemicals used unwisely not only kill the target pest; they kill beneficial insects, too. Recognition of the pest-beneficial insect relationship is necessary if you are to take advantage of the best control features of both chemical and biological control.

Before selecting and applying any chemical, be sure you can accurately identify the insect. And don't apply chemicals unless they are absolutely necessary to prevent damage to your plants.

Author T. J. HENNEBERRY is Branch Chief, Vegetable, Ornamental, and Specialty Crops Insects Research Branch, Entomology Research Division, Agricultural Research Service (ARS).

Coauthor J. H. GRAHAM is Assistant Chief, Vegetables and Ornamentals Research Branch, Plant Science Research Division, ARS.

Coauthor L. L. DANIELSON is Leader, Weed Investigations—Horticultural Crops, Plant Science Research Division.

Coauthor J. M. GOOD is Leader, Nematology Investigations, Plant Science Research Division.

—Emphasizing the importance of spraying. On the left is a potato plant which was not sprayed. The ravages of the potato bug are plainly shown. On the right is a plant which was properly sprayed as a preventive measure.

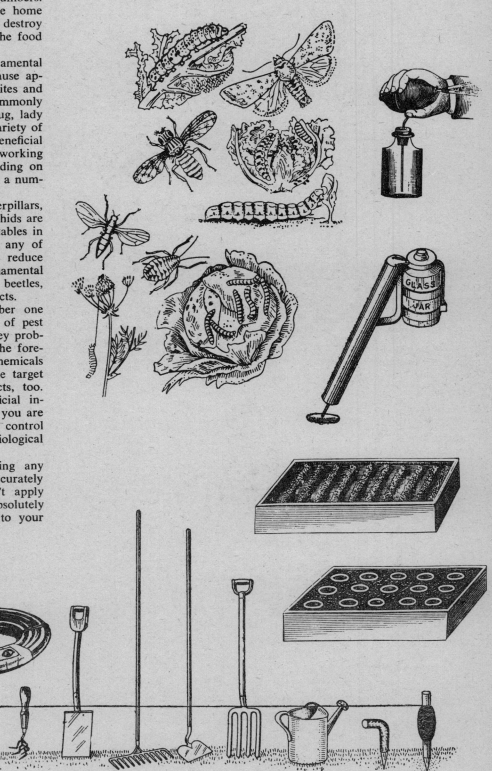

—Tools most commonly needed in a small garden. From left to right, between the balls of cord, they are: Trowel, weeder, spade, steel toothed rake, hoe, garden fork, watering pot and dibble.

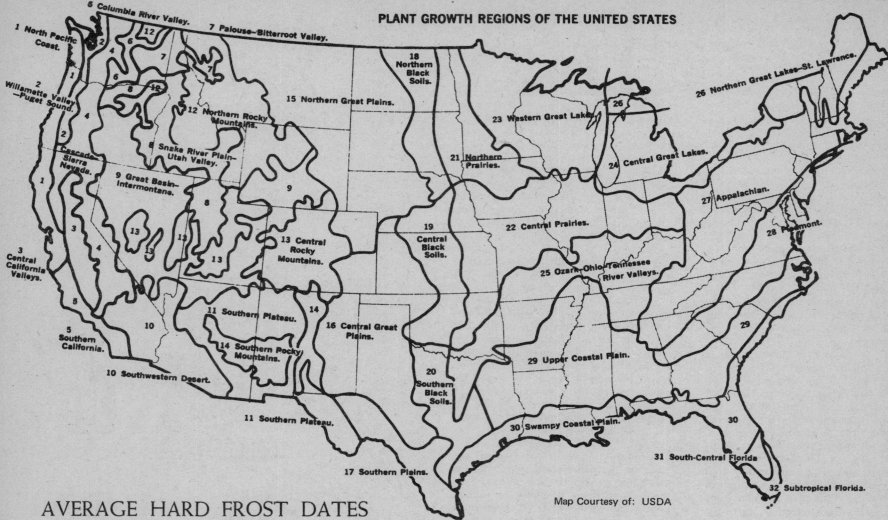

PLANT GROWTH REGIONS OF THE UNITED STATES

Map Courtesy of: USDA

AVERAGE HARD FROST DATES

Based on United States Department of Agriculture Weather Records.
Allow 10 to 15 days before or after the following dates to comply with seasonal weather fluctuations and your local climate.

STATE	Last spring frost		First frost in fall	
Alabama, N.W.	Mar.	25	Oct.	30
Alabama, S.E.	Mar.	8	Nov.	15
Arizona, North	Apr.	23	Oct.	19
Arizona, South	Mar.	1	Dec.	1
Arkansas, North	Apr.	7	Oct.	23
Arkansas, South	Mar.	25	Nov.	3
California				
Imperial valley	Jan.	25	Dec.	15
Interior valley	Mar.	1	Nov.	15
Southern coast	Jan.	15	Dec.	15
Central coast	Feb.	15	Dec.	1
Mountain sections	Apr.	25	Sept.	1
Colorado, West	May	25	Sept.	18
Colorado, N.E.	May	11	Sept.	27
Colorado, S.E.	May	1	Oct.	15
Connecticut	Apr.	25	Oct.	20
Delaware	Apr.	15	Oct.	25
District of Columbia	Apr.	11	Oct.	23
Florida, North	Feb.	25	Dec.	5
Florida, Central	Feb.	11	Dec.	28
Florida, South, almost frost free.				
Georgia, North	Apr.	1	Nov.	1
Georgia, South	Mar.	15	Nov.	15
Idaho	May	25	Sept.	22
Illinois, North	May	1	Oct.	8
Illinois, South	Apr.	15	Oct.	20
Indiana, North	May	1	Oct.	8
Indiana, South	Apr.	15	Oct.	20
Iowa, North	May	1	Oct.	2
Iowa, South	Apr.	15	Oct.	9
Kansas	Apr.	20	Oct.	15
Kentucky	Apr.	15	Oct.	20
Louisiana, North	Mar.	13	Nov.	10
Louisiana, South	Feb.	20	Nov.	20
Maine	May	25	Sept.	25
Maryland	Apr.	19	Oct.	20
Massachusetts	Apr.	25	Oct.	25
Michigan, Upper Pen.	May	25	Sept.	15
Michigan, North	May	17	Sept.	25
Michigan, South	May	10	Oct.	8
Minnesota, North	May	25	Sept.	15
Minnesota, South	May	11	Oct.	1
Mississippi, North	May	25	Oct.	30
Mississippi, South	Mar.	25	Oct.	30
Missouri	Apr.	20	Oct.	20
Montana	May	21	Sept.	22
Nebraska, West	May	11	Oct.	4
Nebraska, East	Apr.	15	Oct.	15
Nevada, West	May	19	Sept.	22
Nevada, East	June	1	Sept.	14
New Hampshire	May	23	Sept.	25
New Jersey	Apr.	20	Oct.	25
New Mexico, North	Apr.	23	Oct.	17
New Mexico, South	Apr.	1	Nov.	1
New York, West	May	10	Oct.	8
New York, East	May	1	Oct.	15
New York, North	May	15	Oct.	1
N. Carolina, West	Apr.	15	Oct.	25
N. Carolina, East	Apr.	8	Nov.	1
N. Dakota, West	May	21	Sept.	13
N. Dakota, East	May	16	Sept.	20
Ohio, North	May	6	Oct.	15
Ohio, South	Apr.	20	Oct.	20
Oklahoma	Apr.	2	Nov.	2
Oregon, West	Apr.	17	Oct.	25
Oregon, East	June	4	Sept.	22
Pennsylvania, West	Apr.	20	Oct.	10
Pennsylvania, Central	May	1	Oct.	15
Pennsylvania, East	Apr.	17	Oct.	15
Rhode Island	Apr.	25	Oct.	25
S. Carolina, N.W.	Apr.	1	Nov.	8
S. Carolina, S.E.	Mar.	15	Nov.	15
S. Dakota	May	15	Sept.	25
Tennessee	Apr.	10	Oct.	25
Texas, N.W.	Apr.	15	Nov.	1
Texas, N.E.	Mar.	21	Nov.	10
Texas, South	Feb.	10	Dec.	15
Utah	Apr.	26	Oct.	19
Vermont	May	23	Sept.	25
Virginia, North	Apr.	15	Oct.	25
Virginia, South	Apr.	10	Oct.	30
Washington, West	Apr.	10	Nov.	15
Washington, East	May	15	Oct.	1
W. Virginia, West	May	1	Oct.	15
W. Virginia, East	May	15	Oct.	1
Wisconsin, North	May	17	Sept.	25
Wisconsin, South	May	1	Oct.	10
Wyoming, West	June	20	Aug.	20
Wyoming, East	May	21	Sept.	20

Organic Gardening

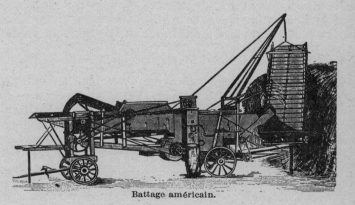

Battage américain.

Organic Gardening

Our Composting Program

Organic Gardening and Farming
Emmaus, Penna. 18049

OUR FIRST GARDEN PROJECT after moving from midtown Manhattan to midway out on Long Island was the construction of a good-sized, working compost pit. I chose six-foot lengths of 1-by-10 lumber, which gives us about 144 cubic feet of space, piling the 10-inch wood five boards high. Each section is removable as the level of the compost pile rises and falls with the advance of each season.

The system obviously has its disadvantages — the finished compost is always on the bottom, and a strain on the back when you want to get at it. So we added a second pit, this time of galvanized iron, which loads from the top, and discharges finished compost from the bottom when its redwood bars are shaken, just like emptying ashes from a coal stove. We use the two types of pit somewhat differently, and each serves its own purpose. Since the smaller pit has a tight lid, we refer to the pits as the open and the closed, to distinguish them.

Garbage Is Composted

We compost all wet garbage and all organic kitchen matter except meat scraps and fat which tend to putrefy and have a disagreeable odor. Even the meat scraps and fat are useful, however, because most of this material goes into our six fat-feeders which serve hordes of bird friends, who gobble it all up all year long before decomposition can cause a nuisance.

Paper, such as coffee filters, goes into the compost, as do the old paper sacks from our bagged fruit. We have not composted newsprint although there is no reason not to, if it is shredded. We do use newspaper in eight layers under mulch around trees and shrubs, where a grass- and weed-free area is desired.

Since the bulk of our compost is from leaves, grass and vegetable debris, we lack the bacterial elements which cause the pile to heat up and decompose rapidly. But because we use the compost only in spring and fall, our slower pace of production is no problem. We have tried the commercial bacteria additives and found them valueless. Earthworms abound in our compost and are added whenever we can catch one in the garden. We add a sprinkling of bone meal or lime to the pits at intervals.

Disagreeable odor and flies never have been noticeable, and our compost usually smells strongly of citrus from the many grapefruit and orange peels which we cut up in the garbage. This pleasant odor is noticeable even when compost is spread in the yard. We object to the back-breaking work of turning the pile, and do not do it. Each six months, when we want compost, only the thin top layer need be forked aside, and the remainder is usable.

In the big open pit we depend largely on whole leaves, ground leaves, grass cuttings and weeds. Twigs, branches and garden vines are added only after they have been ground, because otherwise they decompose so slowly that sieving the compost is necessary. With this grinding procedure, use of our chicken-wire sieve usually is not necessary. Originally, we put all wet garbage into the big open pit, but soon discovered that we got little profit from it. Blue jays took all the eggshells and many fruit or melon rinds; other birds took their share, and we attracted a steady nightly stream of opossums and raccoons with early-morning visits from squirrels and chipmunks. Now we put garbage into the open pit only if there are leaves or dirt for a covering layer. Enough moisture for the pile is furnished from rain and the frequent garden sprinkling.

All Ground Material Goes into Closed Pit

The closed pit measures 25-by-25-by-40 inches, holds about 15 cubic feet, and has been carefully set up so that all leaves are ground, and no coarse material is used. We fill the closed pit with alternate layers of wet garbage and ground leaves, with occasional sprinklings of lime and bone meal. Since the closed pit is not accessible to rainwater — the open pit is — we usually add an equal volume of water each time garbage is added, which keeps the pile sufficiently wet. When shaken out, this compost does not require sieving.

Our use of compost runs to about 70 bushels twice a year — spring and fall — but we use none in the garden where ground leaves, salt marsh hay and other mulch material take care of the soil. In the fall, we use the compost in October just before we empty the pit for ground leaves. In the spring, need for an empty pit before we grind the winter accumulation of leaves demands we use our compost in early April. The spreading program is the same, spring and fall, and is as follows:

1. *Orchard* — Each of the 22 fruit trees gets a bushel of compost within a radius of three feet around the trunk in the fall, covered later by salt marsh hay, but left uncovered after the spring application. Some of the heavier-bearing trees are given two bushels of compost. In addition to being great fertilizer, this material holds water very well. We put the compost mulch right up to the trunk and, although there are field mice around, they have not done any damage to the trees.

2. *Flower Beds* — Seven large flower beds get a fall sprinkling of compost, scattered but not in a solid layer. Since we have completely converted to perennial flowers, it is necessary to plan for their ability to push through a not-too-heavy layer. The water-holding capacity of the compost is readily apparent in comparison with non-composted areas which are dry a day after heavy sprinkling.

3. *Roses* — The 35 rose bushes get a half bushel of compost each, twice a year, covered by ground leaves. The application of ground leaves is carried all along the fence, in a two-foot-wide, four-inch-deep layer which holds moisture, and kills grass and weeds, making trimming or weeding rarely necessary.

4. *Trees* — We throw a bushel of compost under each of the 14 blue spruces. Around most of our large oaks and hickories, we have plantings of day lilies, cannas and various kinds of hostas to make mowing and trimming easier. Over these plantings we can spread compost because these strong perennials will push up. But around some trees we have a mulched area of pine bark planted with pachysandra, which does not die back, and which therefore cannot be composted easily.

5. *Shrubs and Vines* — The various specimen shrubs and vines lend themselves well to application of compost in proportion to their size. Although our compost is neutral in reaction, we add a little lime around such acid-haters as the lilacs.

All in all, our need for compost runs to about 70 bushels twice a year. By composting all available vegetable material and almost every scrap of organic kitchen waste, we meet our requirements and do our share in helping to avoid pollution of the environment.

Dr. and Mrs. Warner F. Bowers,
From THE BEST GARDENING IDEAS I KNOW,
Rodale Press Inc., Emmaus, Penna. 18049.

GENERAL SUPPLIERS OF ORGANIC SOIL CONDITIONERS

Anvil Mineral Products Corp., Bay Springs, Miss. 39422. Micro-Min, marcasite clay, rich in trace elements.
Badger Soil Serv., Inc., 3691 Fond du Lac Rd., Oshkosh, Wisc. 54901
Bedford Organic Fertilizer Co., Ltd., 2045 Bishop St., Montreal, Quebec, Can. Vitalite.
Benson-MacLean, Bridgeton, Ind. 47836
Blenders, Inc., 6964 Main St., Lithonia, Ga. 30058
Brookside Nurseries, Darien, Conn. 06820
Clapper Co., W. Newton, Mass. 02165
Deer Valley Farm, Guilford, N.Y. 13780
Degler, 51 Bethlehem Pike, Colmar, Pa. 18915
Dickinson Co., 9940 Roselawn, Detroit, Mich. 48204
Earp Laboratories, Inc., 20 West St., Red Bank, N.J. 07701
Eaton, Rte. 2, Wallingford, Conn. 06492
Fanning Soil Serv., 4951 S. Custer Rd., Monroe, Mich. 48161
Alvin Filsinger, Rte. 3, Ayton, Ontario, Can.
Garden Fare, 68 Newbury St., Hartford, Conn. 06106
Hallett, Woodhaven Rd., Orchard Pk., N.Y. 14127
Herzberg, Wells, Minn. 56097
Nat'l Soil Conservation, Inc., Medford, N.J. 08055
Natural Development Co., Perry Hall, Md. 21128
Carleton W. Neier, 6730 South Dr., Melbourne, Fla. 32901
Normal Soil, Inc., Box 162, Hinsdale, Ill. 60521. A man-made virgin soil, using nature's own raw materials.
North East Soil Serv., Wolfeboro, N.H. 03894

MANURE, DRIED COW

Maegeo Dehydrating Co., Lexington, N.C. 27292. Fertal-Gro.
Quaker Lane Products, Box 100, Pittstown, N.J. 08867
Wayside Gardens, 7 Mentor Ave., Mentor, Ohio 44060

MANURE, DRIED SHEEP

Consolidated Rendering Co., Springfield, Mass. 01100, and Boston, Mass. 02100
Hoffman, Landisville, Pa. 17538

COMPOST ACTIVATORS

Benson-MacLean, Bridgeton, Ind. 47836
Bio-Dynamic Compost Starter, Threefold Farm, Spring Valley, N.Y. 10977. Natural soil-building bacteria and enzymes.
Earp Laboratories, Inc., 20 West St., Red Bank, N.J. 07701
Schiff Agricultural Enzymes Division, S. Hackensack, N.J. 07610. Biorg.

MANURE, CATTLE

Organic Compost Corporation, Germantown, Wisc. 53022, Tampa, Fla. 33600, and Oxford, Pa. 19363. Fertrilife.

WHY COMPOSTED ORGANIC MATTER

Organic matter derived from plants of deep rooted growth are high in trace minerals and some major elements.

All organic matter is 5% nitrogen but most of this is locked up and unavailable. About 1/5 of this becomes available in any one year under organic practices. The organic elements are converted to inorganic elements as the bacteria and microbes feed on the organic matter. These nutrients are not available to the plants until the bacteria and microbes die and release them from within their bodies. The outer shell or covering of the bacteria becomes HUMUS which binds soil particles together to make sand hold more water, and clay hold less water. It loosens clay by joining fine clay particles together into larger units with air space between.

It is the regular life cycle of the soil life that releases inorganic nutrients and chelates. The chelates allow the plant to utilize these nutrients by covering the elements' molecule and causing them to be in a form available to the plants.

We believe the plants are capable of regulating the rate of nutrient release but at this time, we have no experimental work to prove the theory.

Plants convert inorganic elements back to organic forms which are better utilized by animals and man.

Nature has provided that the soil bacteria and other life of the soil need the same nutrients to live on as do plants, animals and man. Soils provide 5% to 15% of the nutrients required by a plant. Water and sunlight provide the remaining and major proportion by photosynthesis. This is why and how soil can rebuild itself over a period of years by lying fallow. This means returning the cover crop to the soil. This 85%+ gain is your plus from water and sunlight. Use it wisely and you will never lack for good production from your soil and you will at the same time maintain the soil fertility.

You may now be wondering why that chemical fertilizer has (according to the chemical industry), improved yields. Chemical fertilizer will provide more quantity for a period of time usually up to 3 years. At this time, you must increase the quantity per acre each year of the chemical fertilizer you use in order to maintain productivity. During the time of synthetic chemical feeding, the plant quality decreases because the chemical fertilizer destroys some of the soil life. The first two or three years this slaughter robs the soil of its latent pool of nutrients stored in the bodies of the live bacteria. New bacteria cannot be produced from dead bacteria and the soil life population decreases. You also lose the source of humus and chelates and you will end up with a hard soil, low in organic matter and poor soil structure. This type of soil produces unhealthy plants which attract insects. This is natures way of destroying poor specimens not fit for reproducing. If all the crop is weak, instead of only a few plants, as are found with organic practices, you will lose the unhealthy plants. This means you can lose a complete crop more easily with chemical fertilizers as your sole feeding program.

When insects invade a farmer's field that uses chemical fertilizers, he must continue the rape of the land by calling in the pesticide expert. He now has an unnatural situation and is hooked by agri-business. These crops can only produce poorly with the result of low quality food and seed. The quantity may be in excess of previous years but the total food value is not.

If the cultural practices of good soil nutrient profile are adhered to by organic methods, none of this soil rape need happen.

To return your soil to a healthy condition, you should start by using natural fertilizers or compost made from a variety of deep rooted plants, manures, or any matter that has once lived and is free of contamination.

Test your soil and add the nutrients it needs in the proper form.

Dr. Norman J. Curtis, R. D. No. 2, Worcester, New York, has a soil testing and soil feeding recommendation service. The fee is $2.50.

You should compost or return to the soil all unused matter from your garden. The nutrients you remove from your garden in the form of food can be replaced by organic materials and not destroy your soil by the killing of its bacteria and other soil life. This old proverb seems fitting for produce but not the soil.

Use it up—wear it out—make it do—or do without.

We have more than enough on this finite spaceship, Earth, if we but use it wisely.

INFORMATION PROVIDED BY NATURES OWN METHOD COMPANY
WATERTOWN, NEW YORK

Don't Waste Your GARDEN RUBBISH!

AVERAGE DATES OF LAST KILLING FROST IN SPRING

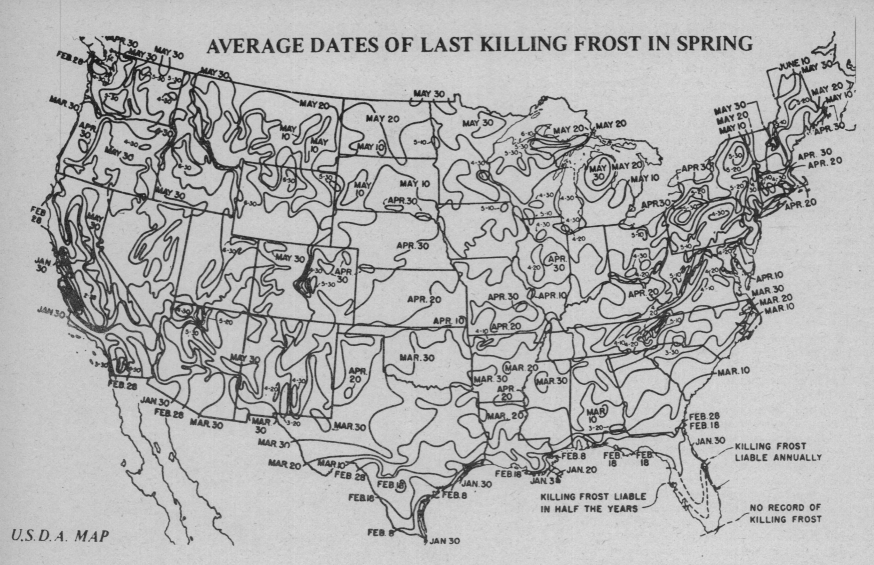

U.S.D.A. MAP

KILLING FROST
LIABLE ANNUALLY

KILLING FROST LIABLE
IN HALF THE YEARS

NO RECORD OF
KILLING FROST

Before Winter Sets In

From THE BEST GARDENING IDEAS I KNOW,
Rodale Press Inc., Emmaus, Penna. 18049.

RESTING ON YOUR LAURELS after this summer's harvest may be what you think you deserve — but that's a costly bit of indolence as far as your garden, and next season are concerned. Matter of fact, the things you do now can make a big difference in what happens come spring. Several steps that boost soil over the off season—actually part of getting your patch ready for winter — deliver more toward success the next time around than hurry-up measures when springtime arrives.

For one thing, there's more availability of valuable organic matter as autumn approaches. And there's really more time to do something about soil problems or about other garden needs.

Here in Colorado, for example, I used to frown at late-fall cleanup as thankless hard work because it doesn't lead to immediate results in blooming flowers and bearing vegetables. But then I found that nature comes along with the biggest soil-building bonus of the whole year, leaves that all by themselves can give us a rich start the following spring. It's a wonderful gift, goodness knows, but it must be taken care of immediately, or with the brisk fall winds, it is lost. And if, like me, you've developed a reputation for taking in all the leaves the rest of the town has to offer, the problem is compounded.

Well, my solution for that one is simple and very effective. I just stand up enclosures of metal fencing, a foot or so high, 20 feet long, the ends fastened together to form a ring. It isn't really necessary to peg each to the ground with long stakes pushed through the wires at intervals and driven into the soil, but I usually do it anyway. Three or four of these enclosures are enough to receive all the leaves I have any autumn. I stand them in alternate parts of the garden so that each section, at least once every four years, gets its fence-enclosed cover of leaves.

The leaves are tossed into the ring by myself or by neighbors who have contributions. Then when I have time I rake them out to a smooth three- or four-inch layer, put a thin covering of manure or a sprinkling of blood meal over them, a few wood ashes, a little compost and an inch or two of soil. Fall is the time of leftover dabs of this and that and my system is the best way I've found to use them. I then water down the whole layer and leave it ready to receive its next leaf layer. All this can be accomplished in minutes.

By the time the next layer is added, the first has packed down considerably so that when the last dumping of leaves, ashes, compost, manure and soil has been made and watered down, I have a rich source of plant food. In spring, it's ready to be raked over the garden, placed just where I can use it quickly and easily. No lugging wheelbarrows full from the back of the garden; it's right there with a bonus of wriggling, working earthworms. All I have to do is to pull out the fencing, roll it up, and put it away for next fall's leaf harvest, then start raking my compost over the garden. You can't help being happy with what you have to rake.

Here is an organic use for the grass that has crept into the garden and is threatening the perennials. Florists know about this and use it to provide themselves a source of rich organic soil without expense, hard labor or great expenditure of time. First, I dig up the grass with its roots and make "sandwiches" of the lumps, packing them into a

bottomless wooden box in an inconspicuous place in the yard, behind a lilac bush, under a low-branching tree or in the lee of a rock wall. I put the first layer in roots up, the second roots down, sprinkling every other layer with bone meal, dried blood or a little animal manure if I happen to have it. When I've used up all my sod, I cover the pile with soil and soak it well, to the point of water running off. Leave it like that if there is plenty of winter moisture in your locality. For my southwest dry winter region, however, I cover it with black plastic held solidly in place by rocks. In the spring this "waste grass" will have become a rich soil teeming with earthworms. Mixed half and half with garden soil, it provides a rich starter for my spring seedlings, as well as a gentle pickup for roses and other perennials.

I was surprised at an organic gardening club meeting recently when I mentioned preparing the bed for tomatoes, eggplant and peppers in the fall. No one else did it, or had even considered it as a possibility. Yet it's such an easy way to start the little plants off with a bang and saves time in spring when so much must be done all at once. I prepare a little bed for each of my tomatoes, eggplants and peppers before the ground freezes in the fall. I just dig out a hole about 18 inches deep three feet each way from the next. After that I put in some compost, a good layer of it plus whatever organic fertilizer I have on hand with a layer of leaves. Next, I put back most of the dug-out soil, watering it down well. Then I add a covering of hay to each. Often the soil under this protection doesn't freeze at all — even in zero weather — and earthworms and microorganisms go on working throughout the winter to give my little plants their quick start in spring.

Another fall cleanup device that rewards the gardener in spring is to start compost in the cold frame. The soil in there wears out with the constant replanting that goes on in a cold frame, and needs renewing for the next spring. Often I just pitchfork in some active compost from the pile, though it's sometimes easier to start fresh with manure, leaves, pulled-up tomato stalks, potato, eggplant and other dead plants. It speeds things up tremendously to put these through the shredder before adding them to the pile, but it isn't essential. The cover of the cold frame seals in the heat, and traps more from the sun, making compost long after it is impossible outside. Here is a good place, too, to dispose of the non-fat table trimmings and to empty the vacuum bag.

My neighbor down the road treats her cold frame the same way, except that she sows rye in it in July after removing the last seedling to the garden. Then when the rye crop is about as tall as it will grow, she pulls-it up, tosses it down into the frame, and builds her pile over it. Does this extra effort result in better compost? Candor forces me to admit that I have never seen more beautiful, larger-blooming or deeper-colored pansies than the ones she produces every spring, starting the seeds in February in the frame. First she scoops out a six-inch layer of compost which she uses for her indoor seedlings, and replaces it in the frame with four or five inches of soil.

Fall cleanup can destroy a great many villainous insects. This is such a good time to rid ourselves of many pests that overwinter in apple and pear drops, dead vegetable plants, or bits of organic debris — and at the same time add fuel to the compost furnace. All of these are tossed onto the pile, preferably just after it has been turned. Since they are havens for the plant enemies, they are destroyed before they get out of the dormant stage. That not only increases the amount of compost for the spring garden, but leaves it trim and neat over winter.

DOROTHY SCHROEDER

AVERAGE DATES OF FIRST KILLING FROST IN FALL

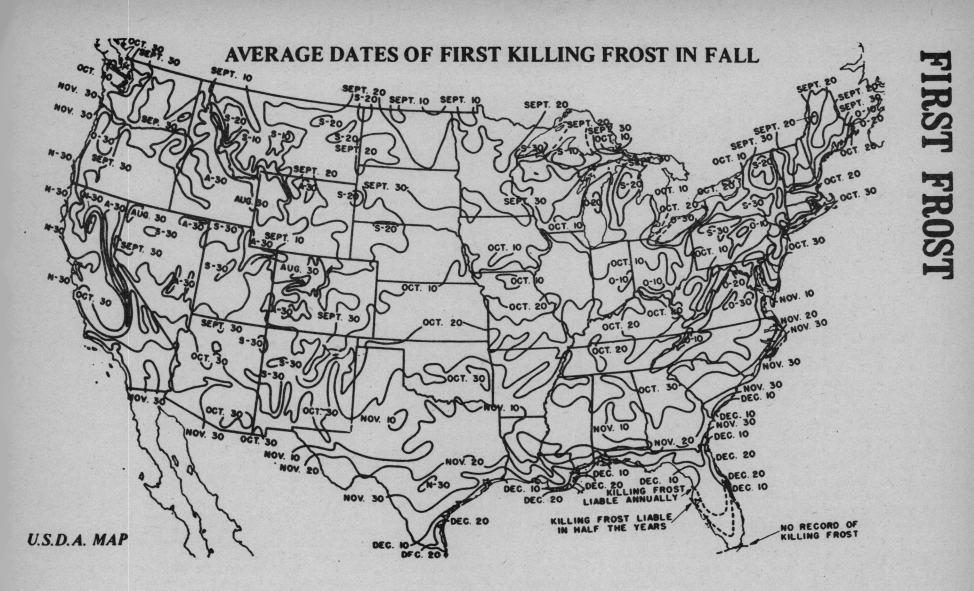

U.S.D.A. MAP

KILLING FROST LIABLE ANNUALLY

KILLING FROST LIABLE IN HALF THE YEARS

NO RECORD OF KILLING FROST

Root Cellars Are Great Harvest Holders

"THE OLD-TIMERS had the right idea when it came to storing their fruits and vegetables over the winter in a root cellar. Only thing is — there aren't enough old-timers left any more to tell us how to build one," says Howard Strenn of rural Greenleaf, Wisconsin.

A root cellar is a room built down into the ground to store fruits and vegetables. Strenn and his family make full use of this so-called old-fashioned method to store the harvests from their garden and orchard.

The labels on the apple boxes stacked on top of each other in the root cellar read like a litany of old-time favorites. There's home-grown NORTHERN SPY, MC INTOSH, WEALTHY, CORTLAND, GREENING, RUSSETS, TALMAN SWEET and JONATHAN — all available all winter long and all raised in the family orchard. While they sell some apples, the Strenns are mainly concerned with producing enough for their own use.

"We always had a problem keeping our potatoes and apples over winter," Howard recalls. "The basement in our home was just too warm. Then one day I happened to read a book called, 'The Have-More Plan,' written by a Connecticut couple who told how to survive on a small acreage. They wrote about raising garden fruits and vegetables and the proper storing in a root cellar. The idea sounded good, so we tried it."

The Strenn family built their first root cellar underground, but it was too damp. Next, they built a root cellar in a sidehill of their farm yard. The eight-by-ten-foot concrete block structure is banked on three sides with earth. The roof and west side are exposed.

"We had to learn by doing," Howard says. "Sometimes it was a little hit and miss. However, the results are satisfactory. We have apples stored in our cellar from early fall until late May. Our potatoes keep until the first ones are ready in the garden in early July."

The Strenn's root cellar is not an impressive building at first glance. However, it serves its purpose exceedingly well. The concrete block structure has a wood frame roof with asbestos shingles. The interior of the cellar is insulated with two-inch rigid foam, while the ceiling has an additional six inches of poured insulation. The wood frame doors con-

From THE BEST GARDENING IDEAS I KNOW,
Rodale Press Inc., Emmaus, Penna. 18049.

tain two-inch rigid insulation faced on each side with quarter-inch plywood. Divided into two rooms, the root cellar is wired for electricity.

The partition between the two rooms is insulated to keep the inner room from freezing in the coldest weather. "This gives us a compact inner room where we can store up to 30 bushels of produce," Howard explains. "With the partition and two doors, the inner room's temperature remains stable, even though the outdoor temperature varies. We use the outside room to hang our smoked hams, bacons and sausage."

Since temperature is extremely important in a root cellar, it is checked every day during the winter. "When the temperature gets down below minus 20, it sometimes freezes. Then we have to supply heat," Howard tells you. "On other days when it really gets cold, I don't open the door in order to keep the heat in.

"I've tried a small electric milk-house heater, but it produced too much heat. We now find a plain old-fashioned lantern is the best. The glass shade tends to get smoky, which is good because it keeps the light off the potatoes. Potatoes will sprout and turn green, even with a little light.

"They also tend to become sweet if we store them for several months at about 35 degrees, or the best temperature for storing apples. So we try to keep a happy medium with the heat.

"The sweet condition in potatoes can be corrected by holding them at about 70 degrees for a week or two before using."

The earthen floor of the root cellar is laced with concrete slats and wire mesh. Still they have a little trouble with rats and chipmunks trying to tunnel in. This makes it necessary to keep a sharp eye on the produce and a good supply of rodent poison on hand.

Howard stresses that ventilation is extremely important. "A good root cellar needs air intake and an outlet to allow an exchange of air," he explains. "We store everything in slatted apple boxes that are placed on concrete slats to keep them off the floor, and to allow good air circulation.

"Anyone can build a root cellar," Howard states. "But he must keep in mind it does need attention if it is going to work. I have to check this one every day during the winter. Each summer we empty the cellar out, and let it air good. We give it a thorough cleaning, fumigating it and all the containers we will be using. This kills any mold or fungus picked up in the past year.

"Each year we seal all cracks in the concrete blocks. The ground around the outside has to be filled in as it settles. And there are always some little repairs you think of during the year.

"If there is one bit of advice I can offer to anyone building his first root cellar, it is not to face the door to the west or to the prevailing winter winds." -

DARLENE KRONSCHNABEL

Organic Food Really is Better!

By simply trying to grow the purest food they know how, a small minority of farmers has incurred the wrath of the American agricultural establishment. They must be doing something right!

John Feltman

Thousands of americans are seeking out and buying organically-grown foods. They are looking for something extra, something they don't believe they can find in supermarket foods. Are they on the right track, or are they deceiving themselves?

Well, first and foremost, their own senses and awareness of what's happening haven't been misleading them. They *know* that organic vegetables, fruits, grains, meats, poultry, eggs, taste far better than the plasticized products of giant agribusiness. They *know* these foods, usually from within their own areas, are fresher, that they've been grown and marketed by people who care about the quality of what they're producing. And they *know* the organically-grown foods they seek are not drenched in pesticides when they're in the field or on the tree; that they're not carrying unwanted chemical residues, additives, preservatives, colorings, etc.; and that they haven't had their natural goodness processed out of them.

Is there a discernible difference in food values? For years, establishment nutritionists have maintained that organic foods are not nutritionally superior in any way. The fact is, all such assumptions either pro or con have been made in a scientific research vacuum. Asked whether organic agriculture produces measurably more nutritious food, Dr. Joan Gussow (herself a nutritionist at Columbia Teachers College replies, "At this point there is no *convincing* scientific evidence that it does — or does not." The long-term intergenerational feeding studies that would be required *have simply not been made*, she points out. In the meantime, she is willing to keep an open mind.

Actually at this point the issue of verifiable nutritional superiority is almost irrelevant to many consumers. In growing numbers, they're expressing a preference for organic foods because their heightened environmental and health awareness tells them such foods are better for many other reasons. As a result, some state governments are now officially recognizing a distinction between organic and regular foods. Oregon, for example, has set legal standards for organically-raised foods, defined as grown without synthetic pesticides, fertilizers or chemicals; in soil in which the humus and mineral content is increased only by natural means. Meat and poultry products are defined as "produced in an organic environment" if the animal is maintained with grasses, feeds and water free from intentional application of

synthetic pesticides or chemicals, and raised without artificial growth stimulants, hormones or antibiotics unless specifically prescribed by a veterinarian. New Hampshire and Massachusetts have already established similar standards.

Obviously, consumers do see a distinction between organic and commercially-raised foods, one that is important enough to justify legal standards and certification. They expect organic foods to be fresher, more flavorful and more wholesome, with less toxic residues. They expect the food to have been produced in a minerally-balanced soil, so that no trace elements are lacking. They expect the food to be grown in a manner that builds soil quality, wastes less energy and natural resources, avoids environmental pollution, and recycles animal and crop wastes. They expect the food to be produced on small family farms *by people who care*, rather than on large mechanized factory farms managed by absentee corporate landowners.

Let's take those factors one by one. To the extent that organically-grown foods are sold locally — either at roadside stands, farmers' markets, or regional natural food stores or other outlets — they are fresher. Commercially-grown produce, on the other hand, is often shipped thousands of miles, then stored and distributed from warehouses, and finally sold from supermarket shelves often weeks after harvest.

Commercial growers raise crops bred for yield, easy mechanical picking, etc., but not for flavor. Then food processors rely on artificial flavors and "flavor enhancers" like monosodium glutamate to give the food taste. The addition of artificial flavorings, colorings and other chemical additives to commercial foods is a source of concern to today's more health-conscious shopper. Such chemicals have recently been linked to behavior problems in hyperactive children, by Dr. Ben Feingold of the Kaiser-Permanente Medical Group in San Francisco ("Food Additives Make Problem Children," January, 1974 OGF).

Far from being a faddist, the organic food shopper is "motivated by a desire for a healthier and a simpler diet," says Professor Robert J. Wolff of the University of Hawaii's School of Public Health. Such a person is reacting against the commercial food industry which, he says, "increasingly considers food as an economic resource to be engineered and marketed rather than as the staff of life."

COTTON WASTES
Cotton Hull Ash
Brookside Nurseries, Darien, Conn. 06820
Consolidated Rendering Co., Springfield, Mass. 01100

Cottonseed Meal
Buckeye Cotton Oil, Div. Buckeye Cellulose Corp., Memphis, Tenn. 38101
Cocke and Co., 32 Peachtree St. N.W., Atlanta, Ga. 30303
Goldenrod Oil Meal Sales Co., Box 152, Memphis, Tenn. 38101
Humphreys Godwin Co., Box 3897, Memphis, Tenn. 38114
Nat'l Cottonseed Products Assoc., Dallas, Texas 75200

DIATOMACEOUS EARTH
Desert Herb Tea Co., 736 Darling St., Ogden, Utah 84400

EARTHWORMS
Bell's Worm Garden, Bells, Tenn. 38006
Carter Fish Worm Farm, Plains, Ga. 31780
Clark's Worm Hatchery, 49 Falmouth St., Attleboro, Mass. 02703
Copps Worm Farm, Box 77, South Barre, Mass. 01074
Gary Road Farms, Roselle, III. 60172
Georgia Worm Farms, Dawson, Ga. 31742
Hall Farm, Hilton, Ga. 31758
Hillaire, Northville, Mich. 48167
Lindsey, Alamance Worm Ranch, Haw River, N.C. 27258
Oakhaven, Cedar Hill, Texas 75104
Ontario Earthworm Farms, Rte. 3, Pickering, Ontario, Can.
Putnam, Sunrise Ave., Amherst, Mass. 01002
Red Box Earthworm Farm, Livingston, Cal. 95334
Shady Pine Hatchery, Spring Lake, N.C. 28390
South Worm Farm, 6417 E. 37th St., Kansas City, Mo. 64129

EARTHWORM CASTINGS
Carter Earthworm Farm, Plains, Ga. 31780
Excello, Kosciusko, Miss. 39090

ELECTRIC BEACONS
Franklin's Electric Service, 118 E. Main St., Calipatria, Cal. 92233. Revolving lights or beacons.
Trippe Manufacturing Co., 133 N. Jefferson St., Chicago, III. 60606. Tripp-Lite, revolving light beam.
Nixalite Co. of America, 2509 Fifth Ave., Rock Island, III. 61202

ESSENTIAL OILS: patchouli
Organic-Ville, 4207 W. 3rd St., Los Angeles, Cal. 90005

FEATHER TANKAGE
Brookside Nurseries, Darien, Conn. 06820

FISH SOURCES
Fish Emulsions
Acme Peat Products, Ltd., 687 No. 7 Rd., Rte. 2, Richmond, Br. Columbia, Can. Liquid whale plant food, bone, and baleen.
Standard Products Co., Inc., White Stone, Va. 22578. Stapco.

Dried Fish Meal
Brookside Nurseries, Darien, Conn. 06820

Fish and Mammal Paste
Brookside Nurseries, Darien, Conn. 06820

GEESE RENTED OR SOLD FOR WEEDING
Stahmann Farms, Inc., Las Cruces, New Mex. 88001

GENERAL INSECTICIDE
Barth's, Valley Stream, N.Y. 11580. Insect Killer, contains mineral oil, sesame oil, and pyrethrins.

GRANITE
Fletcher Co. Granite Quarry, W. Chelmsford, Mass. 01863. Super Granits.
Hocking Granite Industries, St. George, Maine 04857
Keystone Granite Quarry, Zionsville, Pa. 18092

GREEN LACEWINGS
Insect Pest Advisory Serv., 762 S. First St., Kerman, Cal. 93630

HAIR AND HIDE TANKAGE
Brookside Nurseries, Darien, Conn. 06820

INSECTS
Ted P. Bank, 608 Eleventh St., Pitcairn, Pa. 15140. Praying Mantis.
Fountain's Sierra Bug Co., P.O. Box 114, Rough & Ready, Ca. 95975.

KELP
Brookside Nurseries, Darien, Conn. 06820
Kel-Min Corp. of America, 301 Admiral Blvd., Kansas City, Mo. 64106. Kel-Min; dehydrated ocean kelp.
Norwegian Import-Export Co., Ltd., 6970 W. North Ave., Oak Park, III. 60300. Algit.

LADY BEETLES
Bio-Control Co., Rte. 2, Box 2397, Auburn, Cal. 95603
Insect Control Center, 2 First Ave. E., Norwalk, Conn. 06855
Insect Pest Advisory Serv., 762 S. First St., Kerman, Cal. 93630
H. A. Mantyla, Rte. 2, Box 2407, Auburn, Cal. 95603
Robert Robbins, 424 N. Courtland St., E. Stroudsburg, Pa. 18301

LEAF MOLD COMPOST
Brookside Nurseries, Darien, Conn. 06820

The American Association for the Advancement of Science's February symposium labeled organic foods a "myth." The media got the message and didn't question it.

Organic foods also offer the advantage of freedom from toxic pesticide contaminants. Although purists argue that no place on earth is now entirely untouched by chlorinated hydrocarbons like DDT and other lingering poisons, laboratory analyses have confirmed that organically-raised foods contain significantly less residue. The new organic regulations in Oregon set up a pesticide tolerance of just 10 percent of the residue allowed in other foods.

Chemical contamination is also a hazard in commercially-raised livestock. Fifty to 70 percent of beef livers are currently being condemned due to abscesses. But no such problems are reported by organic livestock raisers who let their cattle feed naturally on grass and hay, in a chemical-free environment. (See "The Secret Message of Beef Livers," in January, 1974 OGF.)

Trace element nutrition is another area where soil and fertilizer quality can make a difference in the final food product. In certain soils, corn raised with heavy applications of artificial phosphorus fertilizer is deficient in zinc, Dr. Rabindar N. Singh of the West Virginia University Agricultural Experiment Station has discovered. Such deficiency "could be detrimental to human health if not corrected by other foodstuffs," warns Dr. Singh. Zinc deficiency in man has been implicated in impaired wound-healing, stunted-growth, infertility, hardening of the arteries, skin disorders, and other diseases. And there is hard evidence that soils in at least 30 states have been seriously depleted of zinc in recent decades by intensive farming.

The West Virginia University studies further confirm a survey of 11 midwestern states which revealed that iron, copper and manganese contents of grain have also dropped in the past five years.

"The importance of trace elements in human nutrition is obvious and more research in this area should be carried out," Dr. Singh concludes. "Changes in the nutrient composition of plants could have far-reaching effects on the health of animals and men that consume them. Recent work at WVU by Dr. Robert L. Reid and others indicates that fertilization of pastures with high rates of nitrogen may produce changes in goat's milk

as revealed by feeding it to rats."

Organic fertilizer significantly increased the iron content of spinach in a study conducted at Kansas State University. Using feedlot manure as the sole nutrient source, W. S. Peavy and J. K. Griz found that the natural fertilizer produced a more iron-rich crop, compared to chemical fertilizers. "Our results likely came from decomposing organic fertilizer forming organic acids that caused iron to chelate into forms more readily absorbed by plants," the pair reported in the Journal of the American Society of Horticultural Science, 97(6), 718-723 (1972).

There is also some evidence that plants raised with chemical nitrogen fertilizers contain more of an antimetabolite that suppresses appetite. According to a National Academy of Sciences report entitled "Genetic Vulnerability of Major Crops," the substance (called gamma amino butyric acid) occurs naturally in small amounts in most vegetables, but levels are higher when artificial fertilizers are used.

But even without such health factors to consider, organic farming has tremendous appeal because it makes good sense environmentally. Garbage, sewage, animal manure and other troublesome wastes can be effectively recycled into the soil. Less energy is consumed in the form of manufactured pesticides and fertilizers. And pollution, in the form of persistent chemical sprays and water-fouling artificial fertilizer runoff, is avoided.

Best of all, organic agriculture offers hope for the small farmer who is being squeezed out of the farming picture by the giant conglomerates. As long as consumers are willing to seek out fresh, and high-quality foods grown with care, the small farmer will have a profitable market for what he raises. In effect, he will be able to compete with the giants.

A recent editorial in the Roanoke (Va.) World-News sums it all up: "Now, with the twists and turns of the energy crisis making heroes of nonconformists and devils of overzealous entrepreneurs, the organic farmer is getting his share of admiration, rather than derision."

Are organic foods better? You can see that there's more than one yardstick with which to measure, and for many reasons the answer is an emphatic "yes!"

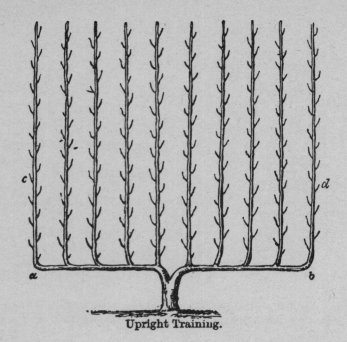

Upright Training.

Chandelier-training, with Branches Oblique.

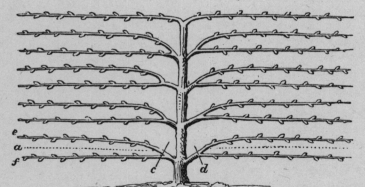

Modification of Horizontal Training.

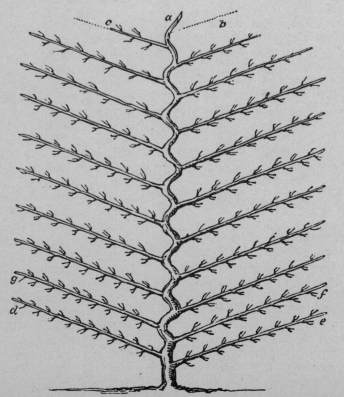

Wavy or Curvilinear Training.

LEATHER WASTES
Tyoga Products Co., Div. of Elkland Leather Co., Elkland, Pa.
16920. Elk-Organic. Tan Bark is waste material in leather-tanning process. It is made of wattle, mangrove, myrobolans, and valonia, and contains lignin, active part of humus.

LICORICE ROOT
MacAndrews & Forbes Co., Third St. & Jefferson Ave., Camden, N.J.

LIME
Brookside Nurseries, Darien, Conn. 06820. Limestone and gypsum rock; Aerosoil.
Kummer Limestone, Kendrick, Fla. 32655. Limestone, dolomite.
U.S. Gypsum, Falls Village, Conn. 06031. Ground limestone, also known as agricultural limestone.

LINSEED MEAL
Archer-Daniels Midland Co., 600 Roanoke Bldg., Minneapolis, Minn. 55440

LIVE ANIMAL TRAPS
Allcock Manufacturing Co., 148-A Water St., Ossining, N.Y. 10562. Havahart, small creatures.
Farmer Seed and Nursery Co., Faribault, Minn. 55021. Automatic mouse trap, does not kill, traps up to twenty mice at one setting.
Kness Manufacturing Company, Albia, Iowa. 52531. Ketch-all Mouse Trap; no bait necessary; trap is wound up with a key and will trap up to fifteen mice; mice are not harmed.

LIVE BIRD TRAPS
Allcock Manufacturing Co., 148-A Water St., Ossining, N.Y. 10562. Havahart, for small creatures and sparrows.
Animal Trap Co. of America, Lititz, Pa. 17543. Verbail, for hawks and owls.
Breck's, 250 Breck Bldg., Boston, Mass. 02110. English sparrow traps.
Russell S. Davis, Clayton, Ill. 62324. For small birds and pigeons.
Dodson Bird House Co., Box 551, Kankakee, Ill. 60901. Sparrow traps.
Johnson's, Waverly, Ky. 42462. Sparrow traps.
Ridgewood Box Mill, Detroit Lakes, Minn. 56501. Elevator-type traps for sparrows and starlings.
Charles Siegel & Son, 5535 N. Lynch Ave., Chicago, Ill. 60630. Pigeon bobs and pigeon trap entrances.

MARL: earthy deposits formed from snail shells and chara plants; takes lime out of water in which it grows
Alexander, Box 185, Penngrove, Cal. 94951. Marl-O.
Dickinson Co., 9940 Roselawn, Detroit, Mich. 48204. Greensand.
Kaylorite Corp., Dunkirk, Calvert County, Md. 20754. Glauconitic greensand, natural marine potash, and other glauconite minerals.

METAL PROJECTORS TO PREVENT BIRDS FROM ROOSTING
Nixalite Co. of America, 2509 Fifth Ave., Rock Island, Ill. 61202.

MINERAL OIL SPRAYS
Maw Manufacturing Co., 1326 Wilshire Blvd., Santa Monica, Cal. 90400. Maw Kienol.
G.B. Pratt Co., 204 Twenty-first Ave., Paterson, N.J. 07521. Scalecide.

MOLE TRAPS
Nash Mole Traps, Scotts, Mich. 49088

MUNICIPAL COMPOSTING RECLAIMED WASTES
Altoona Fam, Room 468, Altoona Trust Bld., Altoona, Pa. 16601
City of Schenectady, N.Y. 12300. Orgro, sludge.
Sears Roebuck, garden supply sections, organic sludge lawn food.
Sewerage Comm., Milwaukee, Wisc. 53201. Milorganite, sludge.
Wandel Machine Co., Inc., Pomeroy, Pa. 19367. Argomat, composter of garbage for home use; Somat, composter of garbage for commercial and industrial use.

NETTING FOR BERRY CROPS, FRUITS, AND VEGETABLES
Animal Repellents, Box 168, Griffin, Ga. 30223
Burgess Seed & Plant Co., Galesburg, Mich. 49053. Flying disks.
Chase Organics, Gibraltar House, Shepperton, Middlesex, Eng. Scaraweb, does not trap birds but frightens them; plastic; rots away after a few months; holes instantly repairable; forms a spider's web of rayon threads over seed beds, fruit trees, soft fruit bushes, vines.
Goodyear, Chemical Div., Akron, Ohio 44316. Pliolite Latex 480.
Joseph Hein, Eton Rd., Thornwood, N.Y. 10594. Cheesecloth.
Fred Howe, Box 267, Somerville, N.J. 08876. Zendel, plastic netting.
Visinet Mill, Div. Bemis Bros. Bag Co., 2400 S. Second St., St. Louis, Mo. 63104. Netting, variety of mesh sizes.

NEW JERSEY MOSQUITO LARVICIDE CONCENTRATE (contains pyrethrum)
Seacoast Laboratories, Inc., 156-158 Perry St., New York, N.Y. 10014

NICOTINE
Nicotine Sulfate

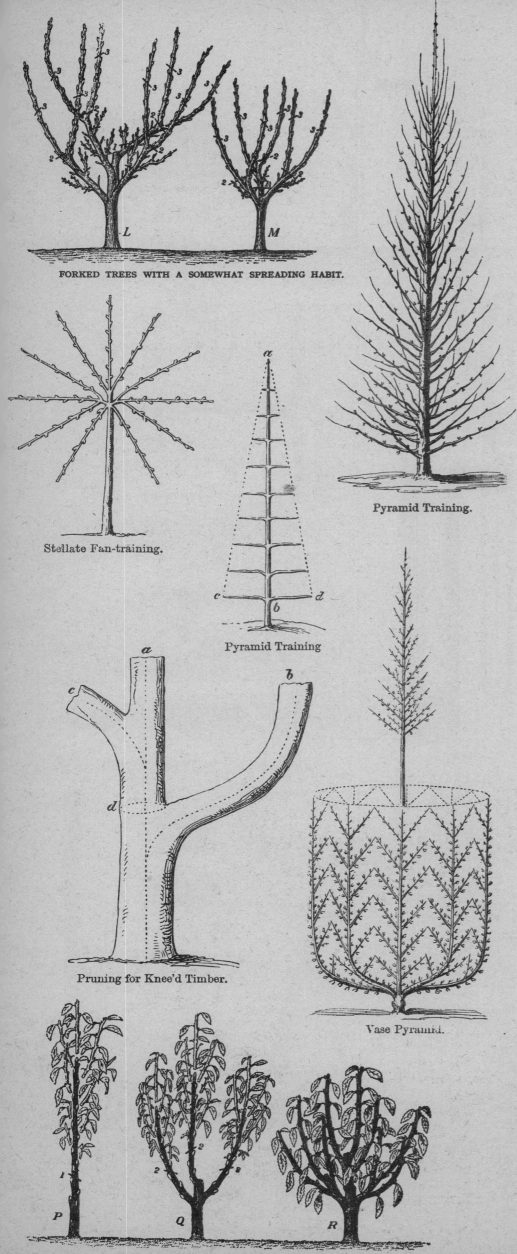

FORKED TREES WITH A SOMEWHAT SPREADING HABIT.

Stellate Fan-training.

Pyramid Training

Pyramid Training.

Pruning for Knee'd Timber.

Vase Pyramid.

LAYING THE FOUNDATION OF A FUTURE TREE.

NITRATE
Chilean Nitrate Co., 120 Broadway, New York, N.Y. 10005. Champion.

NONTOXIC SPRAYS
Old Herbaceous, Box 2086, Potomac Station, Alexandria, Va. 22300. Against greenflies, leafhoppers, slugs, mealybugs, thrips.

ORGANIC SOIL CONDITIONERS
Normal Soil, Inc., Box 162, Hinsdale, Ill. 60521.
William C. Rutherford, Oakham, Mass. 01068.
LaMotte Chemical Products Co., Chestertown, Md. 21620.
Breck's, 250 Breck Bldg., Boston, Mass. 02110. Owl effigy.

OTHER BOTANICAL INSECTICIDAL MATERIALS: aconite leaves, aloes, betony, henbane leaves, Irish moss, mandrake root, poke root, prickly ash berries and bark, etc.
Desert Herb Tea Co., 736 Darling St., Ogden, Utah 84400
Indiana Botanic Gardens, Box 5, Hammond, Ind. 46320

OWL AND HAWK EFFIGIES
Spencer Gifts, Spencer Bldg., Atlantic City, N.J. 08400. Owl effigy.
C. H. Symmes Co., Box 165, Winchester, Mass. 01890. Owl effigy.

PEANUT PRODUCTS
Peanut Meal
Humphreys Godwin Co., Box 3897, Memphis, Tenn. 38114

Peanut Shells
Tidewater Brokerage Co., Inc., Suffolk, Va. 23434

PEAT AND SPHAGNUM MOSS
Acme Peat Products, Ltd., Rte. 2, Richmond, Br. Columbia, Can. Blue Whale, whale solubles impregnated sphagnum moss, reinforced with baleen whalebone and marine marl.
Canadian Peat Producers, 114 Vancouver Block, Vancouver, Br. Columbia, Can.
Canadian Peat Sales, Ltd., New Westminster, Br. Columbia, Can.
Peat Moss and Sphagnum Center, Vicksburg, Mich. 49097

POWDERED ALOES AND CAYETTE PEPPER (capsicum)
Desert Herb Tea Co., 736 Darling St., Ogden, Utah 84400
Indiana Botanic Gardens, Box 5, Hammond, Ind. 46320

PRAYING MANTIS EGG CASES
Ted P. Bank, 608 Eleventh St., Pitcairn, Pa. 15140
Burnes, 109 Kohler St., Bloomfield, N.J. 07003
California Bug Co., Rte. 2, Box 2397, Auburn, Cal. 95603
H. P. Comeaux, Rte. 2, Box 259, Lafayette, La. 70501
Gothard, Inc., Box 370, Canutillo, Texas 79835
Insect Control Center, 2 First St. E., Norwalk, Conn. 06855
Lakeland Nurseries Sales, Insect Control Div., Hanover, Pa. 17331
Mantis Unlimited, Glenhardie Farm, 625 Richards Rd., Wayne, Pa. 19087

PYRETHRUM
George W. Parks Seed Co., Greenwood, S.C. 29646. Pyrethrum seeds for planting in home gardens to produce plants.
S. B. Penick & Co., 100 Church St., New York, N.Y. 10008
Pyrethrum Bureau, Inc. For names and addresses of nearest distributors, and general information:
    Pyrethrum Information Center, 744 Broad St., Newark, N.J. 07102
    215-217 Grand Bldg., Trafalgar Sq., London WC2, Eng.
    Box 420, Nakuru, Kenya
European Chemical Co., Inc., 124 East 40 St., New York, N.Y. 10016
Stauffer Chemical Co., 638 California St., San Francisco, Cal. 94108
California Spray Chemical Corp., Richmond, Cal. 94800
Fuller System, 226 Washington St., Woburn, Mass. 01801. Fulex Nicotine Fumigator.

READYMADE TREE BANDS (with adhesive)
Niagara Horticultural Products, St. Catharines, Ontario, Can.

ROCK PHOSPHATE
Grabar Mills, 802 Navarre S.W., Canton, Ohio 44700
Hocking Granite Industries, St. George, Maine 04857
McConnell, 200 S. Crawford Ave., New Castle, Pa. 16101

ROCK SILT: to make leafy or humus soil dense or heavier; material is in high colloidal state and holds nutrients from leaching.
Brookside Nurseries, Darien, Conn. 06820

ROTENONE AND CUBE
California Spray-Chemical Corp., Richmond, Cal. 94800. Ortho Rotenone Dust or Spray.
S. B. Penick & Co., 100 Church St., New York, N.Y. 10008

RYANIA (Ryania speciosa)
Hopkins Agricultural Chemical Co., Box 584, Madison, Wisc. 53701
S. B. Penick & Co., 100 Church St., New York, N.Y. 10008

SABADILLA SEEDS
Woolfolk Chemical Works, Ltd., Ft. Valley, Ga. 31030.

S. B. Penick & Co., 100 Church St., New York, N.Y. 10008. Activated concentrates.

SAND
Brookside Nurseries, Darien, Conn. 06820. Washed and screened bank sand to help heavy soils become porous.

SEAWEED
Atlantic & Pacific Research, Inc., Westerly, R.I. 02891. Sea Magic, liquefied seaweed.
Norwegian Import-Export Co., Ltd., 6970 W. North Ave., Oak Park, Ill. 60300. Norwegian seaweed.
Sea-Born, Box 465, Greenwich, Conn. 06830
Sidney Seaweed Products, 2543 Beacon Ave., Sidney, Br. Columbia, Can. Alginure.

SOIL-TESTING KIT
La Motte Chemical Products Co., Chestertown, Md. 21620
Sudbury Laboratory, Sudbury, Mass. 01776

SOYBEAN MEAL
American Soybean Assoc., Hudson, Iowa 50643
Archer-Daniels Midland Co., 600 Roanoke Bldg., Minneapolis, Minn. 55440
Buckeye Cotton Oil, Div. Buckeye Cellulose Corp., Memphis, Tenn. 38101
Humphreys Godwin Co., Box 3897, Memphis, Tenn. 38114

TOBACCO PRODUCTS
Tobacco Dust
Quaker Lane Products, Box 100, Pittstown, N.J. 08867

Tobacco Stem Meal
Brookside Nurseries, Darien, Conn. 06820

SQUIRREL AND CAT GUARD
Breck's, 250 Breck Bldg., Boston, Mass. 02110. Tree guard of flexible steel foils, rust-proof sections; fits any tree up to 24" around, yet allows tree to grow; prongs keep animals from passing.

TRICHOGRAMMA
Gothard, Inc., Box 370, Canutillo, Texas 79835. Trik-O.
Insect Pest Advisory Serv., 762 S. First St., Kerman Cal. 93630

VEDALIA
Insect Pest Advisory Serv., 762 S. First St., Kerman, Cal. 93630

WHIRLING, SPINNING, AND SHINY MATERIALS TO REPEL BIRDS
Comfort Specialty Co., 200 S. Seventh St., St. Louis, Mo. 63102

WHITE HELLEBORE (Veratrum album)
Desert Tea Co., 736 Darling St., Ogden, Utah 84400
Indiana Botanic Gardens, Box 5, Hammond, Ind. 46320
S. B. Penick & Co., 100 Church St., New York, N.Y. 10008

WINDMILL MOLE AND GOPHER CHASER
Walter Drake, 45 Drake Bldg., Colorado Springs, Col. 80900. Device makes drumming noise in ground, allegedly drives animals away; two devices enough for city lot.

WOOD WASTES
Bark Mulch
Nate Morrell, Box 112, Watertown, N.Y. 13601. Nomco.

Hardwood Bark Mulch
Box 455, Lancaster Rd., Chillicothe, Ohio. 45601. Paygro.

Sawdust
Brookside Nurseries, Darien, Conn. 06820

Wood Chips
Brown Paper Co., Berlin, N.H. 03570. Grobark.

QUASSIA
Desert Herb Tea Co., 736 Darling St., Ogden, Utah 84400
Indiana Botanic Gardens, Box 5, Hammond, Ind. 46320
George W. Parks Seed Co., Greenwood, S.C. 29646
Charles Siegel & Son, 5535 N. Lynch Ave., Chicago, Ill. 60630

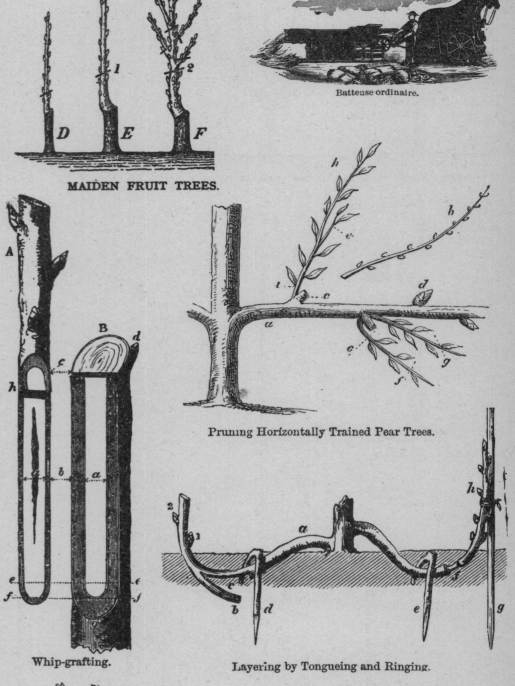

MAIDEN FRUIT TREES.

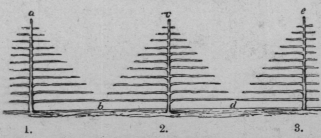

Batteuse ordinaire.

Pruning Horizontally Trained Pear Trees.

Whip-grafting.

Layering by Tongueing and Ringing.

Sylvan Inarching.

Pruning—Clean Stem.

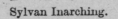

Horizontal Training.

PLANT SOCIETIES

AMERICAN BEGONIA SOCIETY
Secretary: Ms. Betty Burrell
14050 Ramona Dr.
Whittier, CA 90605
THE BEGONIAN (monthly)
Annual dues: $4.00. Seed fund.

AMERICAN BONSAI SOCIETY
Secretary: Herbert R. Brawner
229 North Shore Dr., Lake Waukomis
Parkville, MO 64151
THE BONSAI JOURNAL (quarterly)
Annual dues: $10.00.

AMERICAN BOXWOOD SOCIETY
Boyce, VA 22620
THE BOXWOOD BULLETIN (quarterly)
Annual dues: $5.00.

AMERICAN CAMELLIA SOCIETY
Box 212
Fort Valley, GA 31030
THE CAMELLIA JOURNAL (quarterly)
Annual dues: $7.50.

AMERICAN DAFFODIL SOCIETY
89 Chichester Rd.
New Canaan, CT 06840
DAFFODIL JOURNAL (quarterly)
Annual dues: $5.00.

AMERICAN DAHLIA SOCIETY
Treasurer: Lewis M. Culp
163 Grant St.
Dover, NJ 07801
Quarterly Bulletin and Annual
Classification Book
Annual dues: $6.00.

AMERICAN FERN SOCIETY
Dept. of Botany, Univ. of Rhode Island
Kingston, RI
AMERICAN FERN JOURNAL and
Newsletter (quarterly)
Annual dues: $5.00.

AMERICAN FUCHSIA SOCIETY
Secretary: Fred J. Clark
1600 Prospect St.
Belmont CA 94002
BULLETIN OF THE AMERICAN
FUCHSIA SOCIETY (monthly)
Annual dues: $4.00.

AMERICAN GESNERIAD SOCIETY
Secretary: Edmund O. Sherer
11983 Darlington Ave.
Los Angeles CA 90049
Magazine (bi-monthly)
Annual dues: $5.25. Seed fund.

AMERICAN GLOXINIA & GESNERIAD SOCIETY
Secretary: Mrs. J.W. Rowe
Box 174
New Milford, CT 06776
THE GLOXINIAN (bi-monthly)
Annual dues: $5.00. Seed fund.

AMERICAN GOURD SOCIETY
Secretary: John Stevens
Box 274
Mount Gilead OH 43338
THE GOURD (tri-annually)
Annual dues: $2.50. Seed fund.

AMERICAN HEMEROCALLIS SOCIETY
Secretary: Mrs. Arthur W. Parry
Signal Mountain TN 373777
THE HEMEROCALLIS JOURNAL (quarterly)
Annual dues: $5.00.

AMERICAN HIBISCUS SOCIETY
Secretary: James E. Monroe
Box 98
Eagle Lake FL 33839
THE SEED POD (quarterly)
Annual dues: $5.00. Seed fund.

AMERICAN HOSTA SOCIETY
Secretary: Mrs. Nancy Minks
114 The Fairway
Albert Lea, MN 56007
Annual Bulletin plus Newsletters
Annual dues: $3.00. Seed sales.

AMERICAN IRIS SOCIETY
Secretary: Clifford W. Benson
Missouri Botanical Garden
2315 Tower Grove Ave.
St. Louis, MO 63110
AIS BULLETIN (quarterly)
Annual dues: $7.50.

AMERICAN MAGNOLIA SOCIETY
Secretary: Philip J. Savage
2150 Woodward Ave.
Bloomfield Hills, MI 48013
Illustrated Newsletters
Annual dues: $5.00.

AMERICAN PENSTEMON SOCIETY
Secretary: Mrs. F.J. Schmeeckle
R, 2, Box 61
Cozad, NB 69130
Bulletin (annually)
Annual dues: $3.00. Seed fund.

AMERICAN PEONY SOCIETY
Secretary: Greta M. Kessenrich
250 Interlachen Rd.
Hopkins, MN 55343
HANDBOOK OF THE PEONY (quarterly)
Annual dues: $7.50.

**AMERICAN PLANT LIFE SOCIETY AND
THE AMERICAN AMARYLLIS SOCIETY GROUP**
Secretary: Dr. Thomas W. Whitaker
Box 150
La Jolla, CA 92038
PLANT LIFE; AMARYLLIS YEARBOOK
(combined publication annually)
Annual dues: $5.00.

AMERICAN POMOLOGICAL SOCIETY
Secretary: Dr. L.D. Tukey
103 Tyson Bldg.
University Park, PA 16802
FRUIT VARIETIES AND

AMERICAN POMOLOGICAL SOCIETY
Secretary: Dr. L. D. Tukey
103 Tyson Bldg.
University Park, PA 16802
FRUIT VARIETIES AND HORTICULTURAL
DIGEST (quarterly)

AMERICAN PRIMROSE SOCIETY
Treasurer: Mrs. Lawrence G. Tait
14015 84th Ave. N. E.
Bothell, WA 98011
Publication (quarterly)
Annual dues: $5.00.

AMERICAN ORCHID SOCIETY½
Botanical Museum of Harvard Univ.
Cambridge, MA 02138
AMERICAN ORCHID SOCIETY BULLETIN
(monthly)
Annual dues: $12.50.

AMERICAN RHODODENDRON SOCIETY
Secretary: Bernice J. Lamb
2232 N. E. 78th Ave.
Portland, OR 79213
Annual dues: $10.00

AMERICAN ROCK GARDEN SOCIETY
Secretary: Bernice J. Lamb
2232 N. E

AMERICAN ROCK GARDEN SOCIETY
Secretary: Milton S. Mulloy
99 Pierpont Rd
Waterbury, CT 06705
Bulletin (quarterly)
Annual dues: $5.00. Seed fund.

AMERICAN ROSE SOCIETY
4048 Roselea Pl.
Columbus, OH 43214
AMERICAN ROSE (monthly)
AMERICAN ROSE ANNUAL
Annual dues: $10.50.

ARIL SOCIETY INTERNATIONAL
Membership Chairman: Mrs. Richard A. Wilson
11500 Versailles Ave. N. E.
Albuquerque, N. M. 87111
Yearbook; Newsletters
Annual dues: $4.00. Seed fund.

BONSAI CLUBS INTERNATIONAL
2354 Lida Dr.
Mountain View, CA 94040
BONSAI (10 times annually)
Annual dues: $5.00. Seed fund.

BROMELAID SOCIETY
Membership Secretary
Box 3279
Santa Monica, CA 90403
JOURNAL (bi-monthly)
Annual dues: $7.50.

**CACTUS AND SUCCULENT SOCIETY OF
AMERICA**
Box 187
Reseda, CA 91335
THE CACTUS AND SUCCULENT
JOURNAL (bi-monthly)
Annual dues: $7.50.

DWARF FRUIT TREE ASSOCIATION
Secretary: Robert F. Carlson
303 Horticulture Dept.
Michigan State University
East Lansing, MI 48823
THE COMPACT FRUIT TREE (bi-monthly)
Annual dues: $3.00.

EPIPHYLLUM SOCIETY OF AMERICA
218 E: Greystone Ave.
Monrovia, CA 91016
EPIPYLLUM BULLETIN (7 times yearly)
Annual dues: $2.00.

HERB SOCIETY OF AMERICA
300 Massachusetts Ave.
Boston, MA 02115
THE HERBARIST (annually)
Annual dues: $12.50.

HOLLY SOCIETY OF AMERICA
Secretary: Bluett C. Green, Jr.
407 Fountain Green Rd.
Bel Air, MD 21014
HOLLY LETTER
Annual dues: $5.00.

**INDOOR LIGHT GARDEN SOCIETY
OF AMERICA**
Secretary: Mrs. James C. Martin
1316 Warren Rd.
Lakewood, OH 44107
LIGHT GARDEN (bi-monthly)
Annual dues: $5.00. Seed fund.

INTERNATIONAL GERANIUM SOCIETY
Secretary: C. W. Rager
2547 Blvd. Del Campo
San Luis Obispo, CA 93401
GERANIUMS AROUND THE WORLD
Annual dues: $4.00.

NATIONAL CHRYSANTHEMUM SOCIETY
Secretary: Mrs. Walter A. Christoffers
394 Central Ave.
Mountainside, NJ 07092
CHRYSANTHEMUM (quarterly)
Annual dues: $5.00.

NATIONAL OLEANDER SOCIETY
President: Mrs. Cortus T. Koehler
5127 Ave. O-1/2
Galveston, TX 77550
Annual dues: $5.00.

NORTH AMERICAN GLADIOLUS COUNCIL
Secretary: H. Edward Frederick
234 South St.
South Elgin, IL 60177
NAGC Bulletin (quarterly)
Annual dues: $5.00.

NORTH AMERICAN LILY SOCIETY
Secretary: Fred M. Abbey
North Ferrisburg, VT 05473
Annual dues: $7.50.

NORTHERN NUT GROWERS ASSOCIATION
Secretary: Spencer B. Chase
4518 Holston Hills Rd.
Knoxville, TN 37914
THE NUTSHELL (quarterly)
Annual dues: $6.00.

WHITE VIOLET.

BLUE VIOLET.

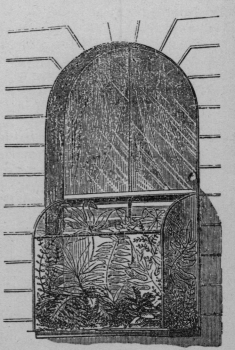

Have Fun With Herbs

The American Horticulturist Magazine
Mount Vernon, Virginia 22121

Mrs. Albert D. Farwell

To be able to grow the herbs, cut them when fresh, and use them for seasoning, is an experience everyone should have. Once having used herbs, without them that same food tastes flat and uninteresting. Caution must be taken in use of herbs for if too much is used, it is far worse than none at all. They should be used sparingly, sprinkled on as salt or pepper, just before serving, or cooked in the pan with the vegetables or meats for the last few minutes of the cooking period.

Before the days of ice boxes, meats were wiped with herbs to help keep the meat fresh and possibly to cover up taint. Herbs were used for flavorings and seasonings, to take the place of vegetables which were not a part of the bill of fare a few hundred years ago.

When you use herbs you are getting your vitamins in their natural form, and in the way in which they can easily be assimilated by the human body; not in synthetic doses as when taken in pill form. Parsley, for instance, has more vitamin A than cod liver oil, and more vitamin C than orange juice. During the first world war the children of England were given parsley tea to take the place of orange juice which was unobtainable. We have been accustomed to using parsley in this country merely as a garnish. Try using it with salt and pepper just as you do with radishes.

Herbs might be classified under three headings: medicinal, fragrant and culinary. It is with the latter that this article deals, how to grow and how to use them.

Every herb garden should have a definite design of some kind. It has been said a garden should look as well in the winter as it does in the summer. The theory of this being that if there is a good design the garden will always look well with or without plants. A wall, a hedge, or a fence for a background makes a good starter for a design. The design at the beginning of this article was taken from the Blair Kitchen Herb Garden in Williamsburg, Virginia. It was drawn by the late Mr. Milo Winter. A diamond is set in a rectangle encircled by paths. It is an interesting study of a well drawn design; no matter where you stand in this little garden, the lines are always good.

This diamond design can be applied to any size garden, using the diamond in the right proportion to the size of the bed. Refer to Sir Frank Crysp's book *Mediaeval Gardens* for designs of old gardens. Draw some designs for yourself during the winter months. It is a fascinating study and when you have drawn your own motif in the earth later, it is indeed a thrill.

Little dish gardens of herbs can be created in designs which are truly lovely. Fill a low dish with sand, moisten the sand, and place cuttings of *Teucreum chamaedrys*, gray santolina, box, or evergreens, just to mention a few. The cuttings will root and the little dish garden will keep fresh for many weeks in the house. Water with a spray. Later these cuttings can be potted up and make new plants.

The accompanying plan is very simple for a border planting of the culinary herbs. Place the high plants at the back if you are working against a background of a hedge or a fence, and if your bed is not a border but has paths all around it, place the high plants, lovage, French sorrel, and so on, in the center and the lower herbs in the front as shown on the plan.

Herbs should be grown in full sun and in a well drained soil. The earth should be friable, that is, able to be crumbled into small pieces when held in the hand. Little or no fertilizer is needed, as that has a tendency to make the plants large and luxuriant in appearance, but lacking in the volatile oils which are so necessary for the flavoring and fragrance of the leaves. Only one or two of each variety is needed in order to have sufficient flavoring for the small family. The fresh herbs

SAGE.

ROSEMARY.

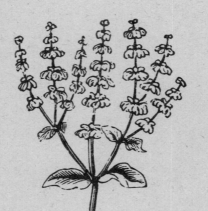

SWEET BASIL.

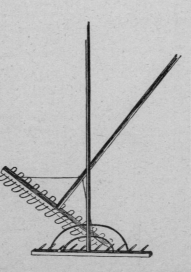

are always the best to use, but the dried ones are very satisfactory. To dry herbs, cut in midsummer just before the plants come into flower. Tie in bunches and hang in a dark, dry, airy place. At the end of two or three weeks, crumble, put through a sieve and bottle for use. Herbs probably are the easiest of all plants to grow. They are seldom attacked by pests, will stand drought; many will survive zero temperatures, and many can be taken indoors as house plants.

Plant your culinary herb garden as near the kitchen door as possible, so as to have your plants handy to take a snip of this or that for flavoring. If you do not have space for a garden, try growing the herbs in pots or boxes.

You will have to buy plants of tarragon as it does not set seed. If you are beginning a herb garden I would suggest that you buy all the perennial plants for a starter. The annuals: chervil, marjoram, sweet basil and summer savory, come up readily from seed.

See the following chart for uses of some of the herbs:

Chives *(Allium schoenoprasum)* perennial, no salad complete without this.

Chervil *(Anthriscus cerefolium)* annual, use in salads, soups, omelettes.

French Sorrel *(Rumex acetosa)* perennial, use the young leaves in salads, and for sorrel soup.

Garlic chives, *(Allium tuberosum)* perennial, has delicate flavor of garlic, use in salads.

Parsley *(Petroselinum hortense)* biennial, use as a food, not just as a garnish, sprinkle with onion salt.

Summer Savory *(Satureja hortensis)* annual, use in salads, a *must* for string beans.

Sweet Marjoram *(Majorana hortensis)* annual, used as a seasoning in creamed soups, meat and salads.

Sweet Basil *(Ocimum basilicum)* annual, use to season any tomato combination and any fish.

Thyme *(Thymus vulgaris)* perennial, for use in salads, soups, creamed soups and flavorings of all kinds.

Tarragon, French *(Artemisia dracunculus)* perennial, use in salads, meats, soups, vinegar. Do not cut until plant is well established. French Tarragon plants must be bought because they do not set seed, or cuttings may be taken from root of an old plant.

Rosemary *(Rosmarinus officinalis)* perennial, but not hardy in North. Use on meat before roasting, flavoring soups. Use leaves in deep fat when frying potatoes.

Lovage *(Levisticum officinale)* perennial, four feet high, has strong flavor of celery; use in salads, soups, vegetables, wherever a celery flavor is desired.

Be careful how you grow your seed. Plant to a depth of at least twice the diameter of the seed. Pour some of the seed from the packet into your left hand, and with your right hand take little pinches of the seed between your fingers and scatter them thinly along a row or over the area where you want your plants. Then press down firmly with the palm of your hand or the back of the hoe. If the seeds are large scatter a bit of earth over them before you press them down. If the soil is very dry sprinkle lightly with a watering can. When they show three or four tiny leaves, thin out to stand six to ten inches apart. Do not start your annual seeds until danger of frost is past.

After you have worked with the culinary herbs you will want to try a few of the fragrant herbs such as the sweet geraniums, heliotrope, lemon-verbena, sweet lavender or mignonette. "The fragrant geraniums are for enchantment only"; reason enough for having them in our gardens!

I hope I have whetted your appetites, stimulated your gastric juices and inspired you to grow your own herbs. You will find that you will be well rewarded. ◈

HERBS, GARDENING AND LORE

Knowledgeable herbalists have been respected and sought after throughout history for their expertise, whether it lies in the healing arts, the culinary arts, or, such crafts as dyeing, or bubbling a kettle full of mumbo jumbo and lizard parts.

Today, interest in herb lore grows apace with the movement towards natural lifestyles.

Young people hunt through dusty herbals seeking to master all but forgotten cottage crafts. They have been joined by medical researchers who scour the earth for valid herbal folk cures.

Of course, there are still mystics who seek magic powers reportedly hidden in herbs. But, most folks are just interested in cultivating herbs for their flavor and scent.

Most dictionaries define the word herb as: "a seed-bearing annual, biennial, or perennial that does not develop lasting woody tissues and dies down at the end of a growing season."

"But," you may say, "that eliminates plants like rosemary and thyme." So, we must expand the limited botanical definition to say that herbs are plants valued, in whole or in part, for their medicinal, craft, or savory and aromatic qualities.

In addition, some herbs are also used as pest controls when ground into powders or grown as companions to other plants.

Many herbs can be grown indoors on a window-sill, or under lights. But, indoors as well as in the garden, the same rules apply to herbs as most other plants. Some like lots of sun. Others require shade, and so on.

We are sure THE RODALE HERB BOOK, edited by William H. Hylton, will be informative to beginners and a treat for old time gardeners as well. It is available from the Rodale Press Book division, Emmaus, Pa. 18049.

Interested in old herbals? Sterling has reprinted CULPEPPERS COMPLETE HERBAL and excerpts from Gerard's Herbal have been published by Dover Publications under the title, LEAVES FROM GERARD'S HERBALL. However, if you intend to dose yourself with concoctions found in old herbals, remember that these books were written at a time when medical practices, such as bleeding and leaching were still widely used. While some prescriptions in old herbals may work, many are no more valid than those discredited practices.

But, whether you grow herbs to accent a sauce, scent your linens, dye wool, protect your plants from insects, or concoct love potions, we would like to hear from you. So, write and send pix.

May apples should be grown only in good rich woods' soil in shady or partially shady areas of the wild garden. They can be propagated by division of the rootstocks.

HERBS DESCRIBED

Asterisk (*) indicates varieties that are tender perennials. Must be grown indoors in winter. All others are hardy perennials except as noted.

ANGELICA (Angelica archangelica) family: Umbelliferae — 6'–10' in flower. Large growing biennial. CULTURE: Shade during heat of day and ample water. Propagate by seeds in fall. Seedlings develop around parent plants. Transplanting difficult except as seedlings. USES: Candied angelica, cooking with rhubarb, flavoring wines. Medicinal.

ARTEMISIA SILVER KING (Artemisia albula) family: Compositae — 3'. Lacy grey foliage. CULTURE: Easiest, fast spreader. Propagate by divisions. Benefits from frequent root pruning. USES: Arrangements fresh or dried.

ARTEMISIA SILVER MOUNT or ANGEL'S HAIR (A. schmidtiana nana) — 12". Soft silvery mounds useful in rock garden or as accent plants in border. CULTURE: rather poor soil in full sun. Propagate by divisions early spring.

BALM, LEMON (Melissa officinalis) family: Labiatae — 24". Lemon scented bright green leaves. CULTURE: Poor soil, half shade. Increase by divisions or cuttings, self sows. USES: Fruit cups and beverages, liqueurs. Also tea and furniture polish. Very attractive to bees.

BASIL, BUSH (Ocimum minimum) family: Labiatae — 12". Small leaved annual. Fine edging plant, nice compact habit. USES: Best variety for cooking. Especially in tomato and macaroni dishes; jelly; even ice cream.

BASIL, PURPLE BUSH (O. minimum purpureum). Ornamental annual unattractive to Japanese beetles. Best basil for vinegars.

BASIL, SWEET (O. basilicum) — 2'. Popular herb garden annual. In Mediterranean regions a pot kept on window sills to repel flies. CULTURE: Average soil, sun or partial shade. Sow seed in garden when soil warm, germinates quickly. USES: Seasoning tomatoes, salads, stews. Medicinal tea used as nerve tonic.

*BAY, SWEET (Laurus nobilis) family: Lauraceae — 3'–6'. Nice pot plant. CULTURE: As tub plant in cool room in winter; set outside in shade in summer. Prone to scales. USES: In soups, stews and fish stock. Has narcotic properties.

BEE BALM, BERGAMOT (Monarda didyma) family: Labiatae — 36". Aromatic foliage with showy blooms in Scarlet, Pink, White or Rosy Purple. CULTURE: Good soil, sun or partial shade. Fast spreader. Division in spring. USES: In fruit salads, wine cups, apple jelly, potpourri, Oswego tea. Attractive to hummingbirds.

BEE BALM, WILD BERGAMOT (M. fistulosa) — 36". Lavender flowered. Likes alkaline soil.

BETONY (Stachys officinalis) family: Labiatae — 18". Coarse green leaves, pink flowers. CULTURE: Average soil, sun. Increase by division. USES: Flower arrangements, in border.

BETONY—WOOLY (Lamb's Ears) (Stachys lanata) — 2'–3', purple flowers on woolly grey stalks. CULTURE: Sun or part shade. Good garden soil. Divided every 2 or 3 years as tends to die out. USES: For dried arrangements, dry stalks before blooms appear. Also self sows.

BURNET, SALAD (Sanguisorba minor) family: Rosaceae — 18"-24". Cucumber flavor, lacy leaves. CULTURE: Full sun, will tolerate dry soil. Propagate from seed. Sometimes short lived so have new plants coming along. USES: Young leaves in salads, vinegar. Has astringent properties; used in controlling hemorrhages.

*CARDAMON: GINGER PALM: GRAINS OF PARADISE (Amomum cardamon) family: Zingiberaceae. Ginger scented palm-like tender perennial. More house plant than herb garden. Commercial cardamon comes from flowers but only blooms in tropics.

CATNIP, CATMINT (Nepeta cataria) family: Labiatae — 24". Pungent downy leaves, lilac flowers. CULTURE: Sun or partial shade, good soil. Propagate by seeds, cuttings or divisions. "If you sow it, cats don't know it; if you set it, cats will get it." USES: Tea soothing to the nerves. Stimulant for cats.

*CHAENOSTOMA fastigiatum (AFRICAN BABY'S BREATH) family: Scrophulariaceae — 8". Fragrant foliage, numerous small white starry flowers. CULTURE: Full sun. Increase by cuttings. Good as border plant, having effect of Sweet Alyssum. As pot plant does well under fluorescent lights.

CHAMOMILLE, ROMAN (Anthemis nobilis) family: Compositae. Creeping perennial 1" with finely cut foliage. In bloom white daisy flowers 12". Apple scented. CULTURE: Sun to partial shade. Self sows readily. USES: Dried flower heads brewed for sedative tea.

CHIVES (Allium schoenoprasum) family: Liliaceae — 12". Mild onion flavor, lavender flowers. CULTURE: Good soil in full sun. Increase by seeds or divisions. USES: Omelets, cheese spreads, mashed potatoes, salads.

CHIVES, GARLIC (A. tuberosum) — 20". Fragrant white flower heads. CULTURE: Needs dividing every third year as it is heavy feeder. USES: Salads, cold and cooked dishes.

CICELY, SWEET (Myrrhis odorata) family: Umbelliferae — 24"— 36". Fragrant, fern-like downy foliage. Seeds have licorice taste. CULTURE: Shady, moist soil. Propagation by seed is slow (8—9 months) and they should be sown as soon as ripe in the fall. If sown in flats seeds should be pre-frozen; or plant outdoors and let freeze over winter. Otherwise propagate by division of long thick taproot in fall. USES: Decorative plant in border. Root boiled eaten as vegetable; leaves chopped with seafood.

*CINNAMOMUM camphora; CAMPHOR TREE family: Lauraceae. Small tree with cinnamon or camphor scented leaves. CULTURE: Shade. Tender perennial grown indoors as pot plant in north. In Florida and California used for ornamental and shade purposes.

COSTMARY; BIBLE LEAF (Chrysanthemum balsamita) family: Compositae — 48". Sweet scented leaf often used as book markers. CULTURE: Well drained soil, full sun. Propagation by root division. USES: Mint flavored leaves used in tea and iced drinks. Old name of ALECOST tells us used to flavor ale. Medicinal infusion used for catarrh.

*DITTANY OF CRETE (Origanum dictamnus) — 12". Gray woolly leaves, pinkish flowers. CULTURE: Rather poor soil on dry side. Keep trimmed. USES: Nice pot plant. Blooms good for dried arrangements and also made into tea. The oil used on cotton for toothache.

ELECAMPANE, HORSESEAL (Inula helenium) Family: Compositoe — 5'—10'. Very large leaves, small orange flower disks. CULTURE: Light moist soil. Propagate by seeds or root divisions. USES: Root in flavoring candy, pudding, vermouth. Also in cough medicines; treatment of asthma and skin diseases; veterinary medicine.

FENNEL, SWEET (Foeniculum vulgare) Family: Umbelliferae — 24". Aromatic finely divided leaf. CULTURE: Average soil, full sun. Sow seeds where they are to grow when soil is warm. USES: Leaves used in salads and seafoods; seeds in hot breads, spiced beets and saur kraut. Medically used in eye lotions and as corrective for unpleasant medicines.

GERMANDER (Teucrium chamaedrys) Family: Labiatae — 12". Dark green glossy leaves with pine fragrance, pink blooms. CULTURE: Sun, well drained, moist soil. Propagate by cuttings or layering. Cover with hay in winter to keep green. USES: Good edging plant, ornamental in rock garden. Medical use to combat scurvy and in fevers.

*GERMANDER (T. fruticans) — 30". Small shrub with silvery grey foliage and blue flower spikes. Tender greenhouse plant.

GOOD KING HENRY (Chenopodium bonus-henricus) Family: Chenopodiaceae — 18". Arrow shaped leaves. CULTURE: Full sun or part shade, good soil. Propagate by division or root cuttings in spring. Also from seed but slow. USES: Cooked as vegetable but better combined with spinach or sorrel. Medicinally used as a cooling infusion and laxative.

*HELIOTROPE, FRAGRANT (Heliotropium arborescens) Family: Boroginaceae — 2'-4'. Tender fragrant perennial with Blue, Light Blue, White, Dark Purple flowers. CULTURE: Full sun, good soil. Propagate from cuttings in greenhouse or sow seeds indoors in February for summer garden. USES: Greenhouse plant or summer garden.

HELIOTROPE, GARDEN (Valerina officinalis) Family: Valerianaceae — 2'-3'. Old-time hardy garden favorite. Cut leaves, pinkish-lavender flowers heads. CULTURE: Moist rich soil in sun or shade. Propagate by seeds or offshoots. USES: Root used to promote sleep, calm nerves, treat epilepsy and heart palpitations. The scent of the root very attractive to cats and dogs and is used as a rat bait.

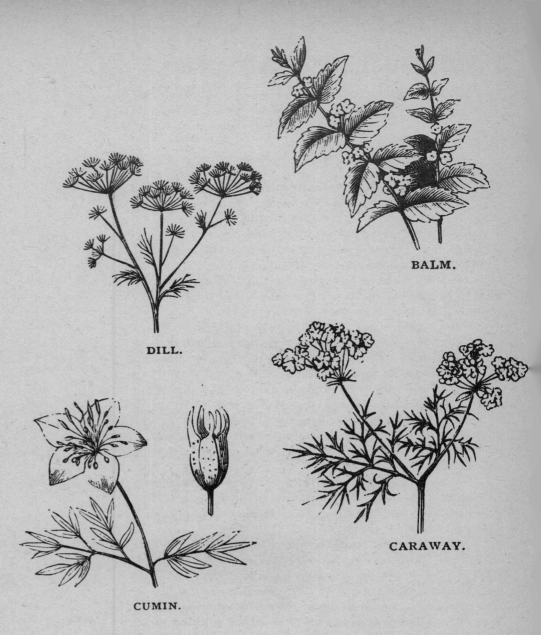

BALM.

DILL.

CUMIN.

CARAWAY.

The Planet Jr Single Wheel Hoe, Wheel Cultivator, and Wheel Plow Combined.

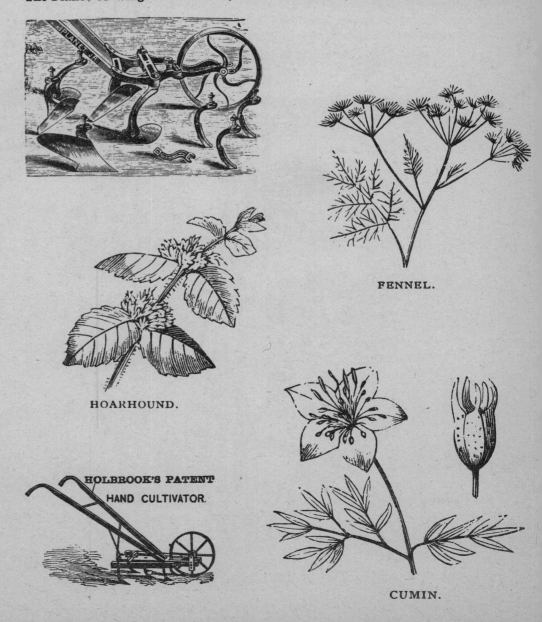

FENNEL.

HOARHOUND.

HOLBROOK'S PATENT HAND CULTIVATOR.

CUMIN.

*HOREHOUND (Marrubium vulgare) Family: Labiatae — 18".
Crinkled woolly leaves, white flowers. CULTURE: Full sun,
dry soil. Best propagated by seed. Treat as biennial and start
new plants each year. USES: Flavoring horehound candy. As
a tea and syrup to treat colds and coughs.

LADY'S MANTLE (Alchemilla vulgaris) Family: Rosaceae — 18".
Ornamental pleated, soft rounded leaves. Yellow baby breath-
like blooms, June and July. CULTURE: Full sun or partial
shade, average soil. Propagate by division or self sows freely.
USES: Decorative, good to use with cut flowers and dried bouquets.

LAVENDER, ENGLISH (Lavandula officinalis) Family: Labiatae —
18". True lavender. CULTURE: Sunny, well drained alkaline
soil. Propagate from heel cuttings or seed. USES: Dried leaves
and flowers in potpourri. Flowers in dried arrangements. Oil
of lavender in soaps and perfumes.

*LAVENDER, FERN LEAF (L. multifida) — 24". Fragrant foliage,
everblooming purple. USES: Pot plant, garden in summer.

*LAVENDER, FRENCH (L. stoechas) — 18". Lacy foliage, free
blooming dark blue or purple.

*LAVENDER, FRINGED (L. dentata) — 24". Fragrant, fern-like
foliage, everblooming purple flowers.

LEEKS (Allium porrum) Family: Liliaceae. Distinctive mild onion
flavor. White flowers late summer. CULTURE: Sun, average
soil. Propagate by seed or division. USES: Decorative garden
plant. Can be used instead of chives.

*LICORICE PLANT (Helichrysum petiolatum) Family: Compositae
— 20"–30". Trailing silver-grey foliage. CULTURE: Sun, average soil. Propagate by cuttings. Grows fast and rank so keep
trimmed. USES: Grey foliage plant in border or pot plant in
greenhouse. Useful filler in bouquets. Scented foliage.

LOVAGE (Levisticum officinale) Family: Umbelliferae — 72".
Celery flavored leaves, yellow umbels. CULTURE: Good soil,
moist, partial shade. Propagate by seed or division. USES: One
of our oldest salad herbs, also in soups, stews, sauces. Hardy
vigorous subject for background of garden or vegetable patch.

*MARJORAM, SWEET (Majorana hortensis) Family: Labiatae —
10". Aromatic grey-green leaves. Also called Knotted Marjoram due to curious knotty buds. CULTURE: Full sun light,
well drained soil. Seeds require careful treatment, very prone
to damping-off. Can also be propagated by root division. USES:
In egg dishes, salads, meats, soups. Decorative garden subject.

MARJORAM, SHOWY (Origanum pulchellum) Family: Labiatae —
18". Long blooming showy pink flowers. CULTURE: Full
sun. Propagate from seeds, cuttings or root divisions. Needs
dividing every few years. USES: For pizza and other Italian
dishes. Also decorative garden plant.

MARJORAM, WILD (Origanum vulgare) Family: Labiatae — 24".
Aromatic hairy leaves, pink blooms. CULTURE: Sun, average soil. Propagate by cuttings or division. Good soil-retaining
plant. USES: Leaves used in spaghetti sauce, salads, on tomatoes, herb mixtures. Tops were used as dye in Colonial times.
Decorative garden plant.

MINT, APPLE or WOOLLY (Mentha rotundifolia) Family: Labiatae — 30". Woolly leaf, apple scented. CULTURE: Can endure dry soil better than any other mints. USES: Best for
iced tea.

*MINT, CORSICAN: CREME DE MENTHE (M. requieni) — 1".
Tiny mossy trailer with lavender blooms. CULTURE: Moist,
well drained soil, shade or sun. Not very hardy so protect in
winter by covering of sand or salt hay. Propagate by division.
USES: Very fragrant, decorative around rocks.

MINT, CURLY (M. crispa) — 18". Crinkly leaves, spearmint flavor.
CULTURE: Full sun or partial shade, good soil, moist. Needs
resetting frequently. Can be root pruned to keep localized.
Propagate by division or cuttings. USES: In jellies, tea and
cold drinks. Good in arrangements and excellent ground cover.

MINT, ORANGE: BERGAMOT MINT (M. citrata) — 18".
Smooth dull green leaves with purple edges, strong scented.
CULTURE: Needs plenty of moisture and yearly pruning.
Should be reset every few years. USES: In fruit drinks and
iced tea. Use fresh or dry leaves in canned vegetables to give
fresh garden flavor.

MINT, PEPPER (M. piperita) — 24". Strong peppermint scent.
CULTURE: Same as Curly Mint. Location should be changed
every second or third year as tends to die out if remains in
same place. USES: Excellent tea without addition of any
other leaves. English Black Peppermint has the best flavor.
USES: Commercially used in chewing gum and confection-
ery; the oil used in dental preparations, soaps, liqueurs.

MINT, PINEAPPLE (M. rotundifolia variegata) — 18". Green and
white leaf. CULTURE: Not as hardy as other mints. USES:
Good substitute for spearmint in cold drinks. Pretty garnish
for fruit cup salads, cold drinks. Best for pot culture.

MINT, SILVER — Silvery foliage but not much scent. CULTURE:
Same as Curly. USES: Nice for arrangements.

MINT, SPEAR (M. spicata) — 18". Most common garden mint.
CULTURE: Same as Curly Mint. Keep cut back so fresh leaves
always available. USES: In jellies, iced tea, juleps, candy, salads, peas, garnishes.

MINT, STONE: MARYLAND DITTANY (Cunila origanoides)
Family: Labiatae — 16". Pink flowers. CULTURE: Sun,
average soil. Old plants may die out but self sows readily.
Propagate by seed or division. USES: Decorative, will grow
in dry areas.

MUGWORT, SWEET (Artemisia lactiflora) Family: Compositae —
4'. Fragrant white flowers. CULTURE: Average soil, full or
partial sun. Propagation by seed, root division or cuttings.
USES: Arrangements and moth preventative.

*OREGANO (Origanum onites) Family: Labiatae — 24". Aromatic
foliage. CULTURE: Sun and average soil. Propagate by cuttings. USES: In spaghetti sauce, pizza and other Italian dishes.
Sparingly on tomatoes, in salads and herb seasoning mixtures.

PARSLEY, CURLY (Petroselium crispum) Family: Umbelliferae.
Biennial. CULTURE: Average soil in partial shade. Sow seed
in moist location in autumn or start indoors late winter. USES:
Popular garnish and seasoning. Contains vitamins A and C.
The root is a mild laxative.

*PENNYROYAL, ENGLISH (Mentha pulegium) Family: Labiatae.
Mint scented creeper. CULTURE: Sun or shade, moist soil.
Propagate by division. Not dependably hardy so cover with
soil, pine needles or hay; or take into greenhouse. USES:
Ground cover. Lavender spikes of bloom in midsummer. The
citronella scent wards off fleas and mosquitoes.

ARNICA.

Leaf of
Mentha aquatica.

Lower leaf of
Lycopus americanus

Leaf of M. arvensis.

ANISE.

Wild Mint.   Mentha arvensis var. Canadensis.

*ROSEMARY (Rosmarinus officinalis) Family: Labiatae — 6'
where hardy. Spicy pungent odor. CULTURE: Warm, limey
soil in full sun. Propagation slow by seeds but cuttings root
easily. When treated as house plant or wintered indoors protect from drying. USES: Roast chicken, roast lamb, pork,
eggplant, pickles, biscuits. Medicinal tea for nervous headaches
and smoked for asthma. Traditionally used at weddings and
funerals. Blue flowers.

*ROSEMARY, WHITE (R. officinalis alba) White flowered variety.

*ROSEMARY, PROSTRATE (R. officinalis prostratus) Low grow-
ing variety. Blooms freely all winter. Used extensively for
landscaping in California. As pot plant for Bonsai.

RUE (Ruta graveolens) Family: Rutaceae — 24". Blue-green lacy
leaves, yellow flowers. CULTURE: Sun to partial shade,
gravelly soil. Propagate from seeds. USES: Mix with cream
cheese for a roquefort cheese flavor, in vegetable cocktail,
salads, stews. May cause a contact rash, wash immediately with
yellow soap after handling.

SAGE, CLARY (Salvia sclarea) Family: Labiatae — 4'. Large
leaved biennial with intensely fragrant showy spikes of blue
and light pink flowers. CULTURE: Good drainage and full
sun. Comes easily from seed. USES: Industrial in perfumes
and wines. Name comes from "clear-eye" as large gelatinous
seeds were used to pick up foreign bodies in the eye.

SAGE, GARDEN (S. officinalis) — 2½'. Grey-green leaves, blue
flowers. CULTURE: Well drained soil in full sun. Increase
by seed in early spring or cuttings, layers, root divisions.
Should be renewed every 3—4 years. USES: Poultry stuffing,
sausage, pork. Also very popular tea for colds, rheumatism
and fevers. It is suitable as low hedge and attracts bees and
hummingbirds.

SAGE, DWARF GARDEN (S. officinalis nana) — 6"—8". Low
compact variety.

*SAGE, GOLDEN (S. officinalis aurea) — 12". Variegated grey,
green, gold.

*SAGE, PINEAPPLE (S. rutilans) — 24". Fragrant foliage, red
blooms late fall. CULTURE: Roots easily in water, propagated by cuttings. Makes good house plant and can be grown
under fluorescent lights. USES: Dry leaf loses its pineapple
flavor so use as fresh garnish in fruit cups, cold drinks.

*SAGE, TRICOLOR (S. officinalis tricolor) — 12". Grey-green,
white and pink leaves. More difficult than regular Sage. Makes
good pot plant.

SANTOLINA, GRAY: LAVENDER COTTON (Santolina chamaecyparissus) Family: Compositae — 18". Small grey leaves resembling grey coral, yellow flowers. CULTURE: Average soil and
water, good drainage, sun. Attains its best growth and bloom
near the seacoast. Propagation by cutting or layering. Do not
trim in fall or spring as leaves come from old wood. Must be
protected from snow settling into center. USES: For border
and rock garden. Medical use of flower as general vermifuge
while stem used as moth preventative.

SANTOLINA, GREEN (S. virens) — 24". Feathery green persistent
foliage.

SAVORY, WINTER (Satureja montana) Family: Labiatae — 12".
Shrub-like growth, white flowers. CULTURE: Sun, not too
rich soil, well drained. Propagation by layering, cuttings. USES:
Good edging plant but must be kept clipped. (Summer Savory
is S. hortensis.)

SENNA (Cassis marilandica) Family: Leguninosae — 5'-6'. Yellow
flowers with locust-like leaves which close at night. CULTURE:
Sandy soil in full sun. Self-sows freely, otherwise increase by
root division. USES: Medicinal use as cathartic and vermifuge.

SKIRRET (Sium sisarum) Family: Umbelliferae — 36". Edible root,
decorative foliage and white umbels. CULTURE: Rich, alkaline, well drained soil. Increase by root division in spring.
USES: Root boiled and eaten with butter and salt. Medicinal
use ditto for chest diseases.

SORREL, FRENCH (Rumex scutatus) Family: Polygonaceae —
36". CULTURE: Full sun, heavy soil. Self-sows freely or by
root division. Divide every second year. USES: Popular herb
for soups and salads. Also used in diet for scurvy.

SOUTHERNWOOD (Artemisia abrotanum) Family: Compositae —
36". Shrub with fragrant grey-green foliage. CULTURE:
Average soil, full sun and lifting every three years. Increase
by cuttings or division. USES: Leaves hung in closets to discourage moths. If burned in fireplace banishes odors.

STRAWBERRY, RUNNERLESS (Baron von Solemaker) Family:
Rosaceae. Ever-bearing. Propagate by seed or division.

TANSY, COMMON (Tanacetum vulgare) Family: Compositae —
4'-5'. Fernlike foliage, yellow flowers. CULTURE: Good
garden soil, dry. Self-sows readily or can be divided. USES:
Keeps ants and flies away and rubbed on meat as preservative. Considered dangerous if taken as an infusion so dried
herb cannot be sold in drug store or by mail.

TANSY, FERN LEAF (T. vulgare crispum) — 24". Decorative
border plant with wider more curled foliage and larger
flowers than species.

TARRAGON (Artemisia dracunculus) Family: Compositae —
24". Anise flavor and fragrance. CULTURE: Sun and well
drained soil. Propagate by cuttings or root division. Transplant every three years. USES: Steaks, fish and in salads;
also vinegar. Medicinal use for scurvy.

THYME, CARAWAY (Thymus herba-barona) Family: Labiatae
— 6". Caraway scent, rosy-pink blooms. A carpeting Thyme
not too winter hardy or vigorous but excellent ground cover
for sandy banks. Name originated from English custom of
rubbing leaves on huge roasts of beef for banquets. Still delicious. Propagate divisions or cuttings.

THYME, CREEPING: MOTHER-OF-THYME (T. serphyllum) —
3". Used for terraces and between flagstones. Pink, White,
or Crimson flowers. Pink variety most vigorous. CULTURE:
All creeping Thymes require gritty soil or stone chips to provide dry soil surface for leaves and cool root run. They do best
in alkaline soil. Propagate by division.

THYME, CREEPING GOLDEN — clear gold leaf.

THYME, ENGLISH (T. vulgaris) — 8". Common cooking Thyme.
CULTURE: Sun and good drainage. Propagation by division
or cuttings. USES: In fish, soups, stews, pork dishes. Combine
with other herbs in meat and poultry dishes. Tea used as sedative and cough medicine. For drying leaves gather just before
flowering.

THYME, FRENCH — Narrower leaf than English form, small white
blooms. CULTURE: Protect with pine boughs or salt hay.
Easily grown from seed. USES: Widely used cooking herb.

THYME, GOLDEN LEMON (T. vulgaris aureus) — 6". Green and
gold leaf. Not as winter hardy. Propagate by cuttings and
division of large clumps in spring.

THYME, LEMON (T. vulgaris citriodorus) — 6"-8". Plain green
leaf. CULTURE: Not as hardy as English Thyme but equally
as good for culinary use and preferred by many. Also used in
teas and jellies. Propagate by cuttings or division of large
clumps in spring.

USEFUL HERBS.

A few Pot Herbs, or Sweet Herbs, as they are usually
called, should have a place in every vegetable garden.
Every cook and every good housekeeper knows the
value of the little patch of herbs upon which she makes
daily drafts in the summer, and which furnishes such a
nice collection of dried herbs for winter seasoning, without which the Thanksgiving turkey would be scarcely
worth the having; while as domestic medicines several
kinds are held in high repute. A very small space in
the garden will give all the herbs needed in any family.
The culture is very simple, and the best way is to make
a little seed-bed in the early spring, and set the plants
out in a bed as soon as large enough. As a general rule
it is best to cut herbs when in flower, tie them up in
small bunches and hang in the shade to dry. We give
a list of the herbs generally cultivated and prized, with
engravings showing their appearance when in condition
for cutting. All kinds are *five cents a paper*, except
Tarragon, which is 20 cents a paper. This seed is always very high. As Sage is grown quite extensively
we sell this seed for $1.50 per lb., 15 cts. per oz., and this
is the only kind that will be likely to be needed in quantities. Of some kinds we furnish roots, as will be seen below.

Anise,	Lavender,
Arnica,	Marjoram, Sweet,
Balm,	Rosemary,
Basil, Sweet,	Rue,
Bene,	Saffron,
Borage,	Sage,
Caraway,	Savory, Summer,
Catnep,	Savory, Winter,
Coriander,	Tansy,
Cumin,	Thyme, Broad-Leaved
Dandelion,	English,
Dill,	Thyme, Summer,
Fennel, Large Sweet,	Thyme, Winter,
Hoarhound,	Wormwood,
Hyssop,	Tarragon, ... 20

Sage, roots, by mail, per dozen $2.00; each, ... 25
Lavender, roots, by mail, per dozen $2.00; each, 25
Tarragon, roots, by mail, per dozen, $2.50; each, 25
Shallots, per quart, ... 50

MARJORAM.   FENNEL.   LAVENDER.

274

THYME, SILVER LEMON (T. vulgaris argenteus) — Variegated green and silver. Excellent cooking Thyme and for flavoring tea. Not as winter hardy. Propagate by cuttings, layering.

THYME, WOOLLY (T. serphyllum lanuginosus) — 3". Gray form of creeping Thyme. Pink blooms. Propagate — division. Does not tolerate dampness.

THYME, HALL'S WOOLLY — Less woolly, free flowering pink. Hardier than species. Propagate division.

THYME, WOOLLY STEMMED (T. lanicaulis) — trailing, hairy leaves, rose-pink flowers. Rapid spreader. Propagate by layering or cuttings.

*VERBENA, LEMON (Lippia citrodora) Family: Verbenaceae — to 6' bushy growth. Deciduous. CULTURE: Light well drained soil, full sun. Cut back and winter indoors. Never allow to dry out. Susceptible to red spider. Propagate by cuttings. USES: Tea, potpourri, finger bowls.

WOODRUFF, SWEET (Asperula odorata) Family: Rubiaceae — 8". Fragrant ground cover with delicate white star-like flowers. CULTURE: Woodland area or rich moist half shade. Easily propagated from cuttings or divisions. USES: Makes a delightful tea, used in potpourri and traditionally sprigs are placed in German Maiwein. Regarded as a spring tonic and contains the blood thinner coumarin.

WORMWOOD, COMMON (Artemisia absinthium) Family: Compositae — 48". Gray lacy foliage. CULTURE: Full sun, well drained poor soil. Excellent seashore plant. Propagation by seed. USES: Source of absinthe and oil used in "Absorbine Jr."

WORMWOOD, ROMAN (A. pontica) — 18". Feathery gray foliage. CULTURE: Propagate by runners. Tends to be invasive. USES: Good border plant and in flower arrangements. Prunings can be used as moth preventative. Medicinally it was an old vermifuge.

Iron Age Horse Cultivator, Hoe, Coverer, &c.

WORMWOOD.

SAGE.

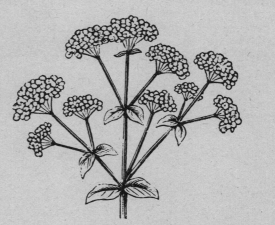

MARJORAM

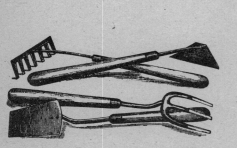

LAVENDER.

HOARHOUND.

DILL.

PLANTS THAT REPEL PESTS

BORAGE (Borage officinalis), Annual, plant seed.
Repels tomato worms.

BASIL (Ocimum basilicum), Annual, plant seed.
Repels mosquitoes and flies. Potted, it can be placed near outdoor sitting areas.

ALLIUMS (Perennials), plant bulblets or sets. Garlic (Allium sativum), Onion (Allium cepa), Chive (Allium schoenoprasum), Leek (Allium porrum).
Garlic and onions repel mice and moles and also deter Japanese beetles, aphids. Leeks and chives deter the carrot fly and improve the general health of plants.

GERANIUM (Pelargonium), perennial, but not hardy in cold climates. Overwinter indoors or propagate from cuttings.
Geranium (white is most effective) attracts Japanese beetles away from other plants; stuns the beetles which can then be picked up and destroyed. Plant near rose beds.

PYRETHRUM, the painted daisy (Chrysanthemum cocineum), perennial.
A source of insecticides, repels aphids.

MARIGOLD (Tagetes) Annual, seed. The old-fashioned "smelly" varieties provide better control.
Repels nematodes and other garden pests. Use spent plants as mulch around chrysanthemums and clematics. Also repels bean-beetles and Japanese beetles.

MINT (Mentha spicata, and other species), hardy perennial. Once established, spreads.
Deters ants from dwellings and patios, and also deters cabbage moth from laying eggs.

ROSEMARY (Rosemarinum officinalis), tender perennial. Can be potted and taken inside for winter.
Deters Mexican bean beetle and cabbage moth from chewing foliage.

TANSY (Tanecetum vulgare), perennial.
Repels Japanese beetles, ants and mosquitoes.

THYME (Thymus vulgaris and other species), perennial. It will spread when established.
Deters cabbage worm.

ROSEMARY.

CORIANDER (*Coriandrum sativum*, L., Fig. 157—Pentandria Digynia, L.; Umbelliferæ,

PARSLEY (*Petroselinum sativum*, Hoffm.; Pentandria Digynia, L.; Umbelliferæ, D. C.;

HERBAL OUTLETS

Aphrodisia
28 Carmine Street
New York, New York 10014
Unusual botanicals.
Catalog twenty-five cents.

Black Forest Botanicals
Route 1, Box 34
Yuba, Wisconsin 54672
Catalog ten cents.

Borchelt Herb Gardens
474 Carriage Shop Road
East Falmouth, Mass. 02536
Catalog ten cents.

W. Atlee Burpee Company
P.O. Box 6929
Philadelphia, Penna. 19132
Seeds and plants.

Casa Yerba
Star Toute 2, Box 21
Day's Creek, Ore. 97429
Seeds and plants

Caswell-Massey Co., Ltd.
320 W. Thirteenth St.
New York, N.Y. 10014
Catalog free.

Cedarbrook Herb Farm
Route 1, Box 1047
Sequim, Wash. 98382
Brochure twenty cents.

China Herb Company
428 Soledad
Salinas, Calif. 93901

Gardens of the Blue Ridge
Ashford, North Carolina 28603
Native live herbs.

Greene Herb Gardens
Greene, Rhode Island 02872
Herbs, herb plants, seeds.

Hahn and Hahn
Homeopathic Pharmacy
324 West Saratoga St.
Baltimore, Maryland 21201

Haussmann's Pharmacy
534-536 W. Girard Ave.
Philadelphia, Penna. 19123
Unusual botanicals.
Catalog available.

Heise's Wausau Farms
Route 3
Wausau, Wisc. 54401
Growers and dealers in American ginseng.

Herbarium, Inc.
Route 2, Box 620
Kenosha, Wisc. 53140
Botanical drugs and spices.

TANSY.

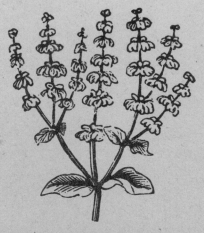

SWEET BASIL.

HYSSOP

Hickory Hollow
Route 1, Box 52
Peterstown, W. Vir. 24963
Herbal products.

Hilltop Herb Farm
Box 866
Cleveland, Texas 77327
Herbs, herb plants, seeds,
unusual botanicals.
Catalog thirty cents.

Indiana Botanic Gardens, Inc.
P.O. Box 5
Hammond, Indiana 46325
Wide variety of botanicals
and herbal products.
Catalog twenty-five cents.

Joseph J. Kern Rose Nursery
Box 33
Mentor, Ohio 44060
Old varieties of roses.

Kiel Pharmacy, Inc.
109 Third Ave.
New York, N.Y. 10003
No catalog.

Meadowbrook Herb Garden
Wyoming, Rhode Island 02898
Seeds, plants, herbal products.
Catalog fifty cents.

Dr. Michael's Herb Center
1223 North Milwaukee Ave.
Chicago, Ill. 60622
Complete line of herbal
medicinal preparations.

Nature's Herb Company
281 Ellis St.
San Francisco, Calif. 94102
Unusual botanicals.
Catalog twenty-five cents.

Nichols Garden Nursery
Pacific North
Albany, Oregon 97321
Herbs, vegetables, flowers
and other plants, seeds, botan-
ical products.
Catalog fifteen cents.

George W. Park Seed Co.
P.O. Box 31
Greenwood, S. Car. 29646
Catalog.

Penn Herb Co.
603 North Second St.
Philadelphia, Penna. 19123
Dried herbs, seeds, and
herb products.

Pine Hills Herb Farms
P.O. Box 144
Roswell, Georgia 30075

Snow-Line Farm
11846 Fremont
Yucaipa, Calif. 92399

Snug Valley Farm
Route 3, Box 394
Kutztown, Penna. 19530
Wool, mordants, dried dye
plants, and dye starter kit.

Straw Into Gold
5550-H College Ave.
Oakland, Calif. 94610
Mordants, natural dyes.

Tillotson's Roses
802 Brown's Valley Road
Watsonville, Calif. 95076
Catalog of old roses, $1.

Well Sweep Herb Farm
451 Mount Bethel Road
Port Murray, N.J. 07865
Price list available for
seeds, plants, and products.

The Woolgatherer
47 State St.
Brooklyn Heights, N.Y. 11201
Yarns and dyes.

CARAWAY (*Carum Carui*, L., Fig. 155—
Pentandria Digynia, L.; Umbelliferæ, D.C.;

LENTIL (*Ervum Lens*, L.—Diadelphia De-
candria, L.; Leguminosæ, D. C.; Fabaceæ,
Lind.)—The lentil (Fig. 158) is an annual

Fig. 158.

ANISE.

Proliferous Daisy

ARNICA.

BENE.

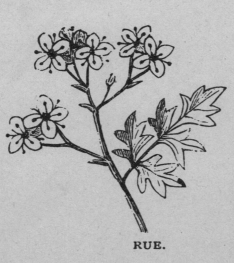

RUE.

277

OLD USES FOR MEDICINAL HERBS

Information excerpted from
THE DISPENSATORY OF THE UNITED STATES
Wood & Bache, Philadelphia 1845

Farmers' Museum
Cooperstown, N.Y. 13326

APPLE MINT — Aromatic stimulant; used for upset stomach or nausea.

ASPARAGUS — Roots used in France to purify the blood. Considered to be very wholesome.

BEE BALM — Melissa, Oswego tea. A pleasant tea.

BLACKBERRY — Roots used for astringent. Home remedy for bowel affections and diarrhea.

BONESET (Thoroughwort) — Tonic, also used for intermittent fever and inflammatory rheumatism. Flowers and leaves brewed as tea for body aches.

BORAGE — Leaves and flowers with honey or syrup for catarrhal affections, rheumatism and skin disorders.

BURDOCK — Root considered aperient and diaphoretic, used for gouty and rheumatic affections.

BUTTERCUP (Crowfoot) — Never used internally, inflames and vesicates the skin. May be dangerous.

CALENDULA OFFICINALIS (Marigold) — Leaves and flowers used as tea for low grade fevers and scrofula. Also used for cancerous and ulcer conditions.

CARAWAY — Sometimes used for flatulent colic and as adjuvant of other medicines to stimulate the digestive organs.

CARAWAY THYME — Used in baths, fomentations and poultices with other aromatic herbs. Used most commonly in cooking.

CATNEP — Tonic similar to most mints. Also used to relieve toothache.

CAMOMILE — Mild tonic or, in larger doses, used as an emetic. Also used to stimulate the appetite.

COMFREY — Roots used in cough syrup and for chronic catarrhs and consumption.

COSTMARY — Used as infusion for catarrh.

CURLY MINT — Tonic and flavoring for other medicines.

DANDELION — Slightly tonic, diuretic and aperient and thought to act on the liver and digestive organs. Considered good for obstructions of the abdominal system.

DOCK — Roots used as astringent and mild tonic. Externally used for skin eruptions and ulcerations. Powered root used as dentrifice.

DOCK — YELLOW — OBTUSIFOLIUS — Used as common dock.

EUROPEAN PENNYROYAL — Used as other mints.

FEVER FEW — Tonic. Seldom used in the United States.

FOX GLOVE (Digitalis) — Narcotic, sedative. Used in treatment of dropsy and heart ailments.

GARLIC — Acts as stimulant, quickens the circulation and excites the nerves.

GOLDEN ROD — Aromatic and moderately stimulant. Used to relieve pain due to flatulence and nausea. Dried flowers used as substitute for tea.

HERB ROBERT (Geranium) — Used internally for intermittent fever, consumption, hemorrhages and as a gargle for affections of the throat.

HOLLYHOCK — Roots used for irritations of the Mucous membranes. Sometimes used as a poultice.

HOPS — A tonic, and mildly narcotic. Used for diseases associated with nervous derangement. May induce sleep and relieve nervous tension.

Aspidium Filix Mass, or Male Fern.

(THE ROOT.)

This plant grows in shady pine forests from New Jersey to Virginia; it is likewise a native of Europe, Asia and North of Africa. It is used as a remedy against tape worm. Dose of the powdered root from one to two teaspoonfuls, given with powdered white sugar, white of egg, beat up, or the thick juice or water of slippery elm; this dose to be repeated night and morning for two days; then give a brisk purgative of castor oil, and should that not operate in three hours, give a dose of Epsom or Rochelle salts.

This is a valuable popular remedy, and a mild sudorific (causing sweating) acting safely, without producing any stimulating effect upon the body. Its action is specifically upon the lungs, to assist suppressed expectoration, and to relieve the difficult breathing of patients laboring under pleurisy. It relieves difficulty of breathing and pains in the chest. It sometimes acts as a mild purgative, and is suitable to the complaints of children. In low stages of typhus fever, and other diseases of a like nature, it has been known to excite perspiration when other medicines have failed.

From twenty grains to a drachm of the root, in powder, may be given several times a day; but as a diaphoretic (to produce sweating), it is best given in decoction or infusion (tea), made in the proportion of an ounce to the quart of water, and given in the dose of a teacupful every two or three hours till it operates.

Asclepias Tuberosa, or Pleurisy Root.

(THE ROOT.)

HOREHOUND — Tonic and laxative in large doses. Also used for sore throat.

HORSE-RADISH — Stimulant, also used for palsy and chronic rheumatism.

HYSSOP — Gentle stimulant, seldom used in the United States.

LAMB'S EAR — WOOD BETONY — Roots considered emetic and purgative. Seldom used in the United States by 1850.

LAVENDER (Lavendula Officinalis) — Aromatic stimulant and tonic for nervous debility; also used to flavor other ingredients.

LEMON BALM — Pleasant flavor; tends to promote effects of other ingredients.

LETTUCE (Lactuca) — Used in place of opium as it does not have side effects. It is a sedative.

LILAC — Used mostly in France as a tonic for intermittent fever.

LILY OF THE VALLEY — Taken internally as emetic and cathartic. Seldom used in the United States.

MANDRAKE (May apple) — Poisonous narcotic, similar to belladonna. Seldom used in the United States.

MENTHA — Orange mint (Piperita) — Aromatic stimulant.

MONKSHOOD — wolfsbane (Aconite) — Whole plant is poisonous if used in excess, causing headache, nausea and weakness in the joints. Used as remedy for rheumatism, neuralgia and cancer.

MULLEIN — Leaves used in ointment as an anodyne; demulcent and emollient, useful in pectoral complaints.

PARSLEY — Roots said to be aperient and diuretic. Sometimes used for nephritic and dropsical affections with more active medicines.

PLANTAIN (Plantago Major) — Demulcent and emollient and may be used internally or externally in the same manner as flax seed, which they resemble in medical properties.

POKE BERRY — Emetic, purgative and somewhat narcotic, causing drowsiness, vertigo and dimness of vision. Used in treatment of chronic rheumatism.

POPPY — Similar properties to opium, but strength too small for medical use. Lettuce used later for same purpose.

PRIMROSE — Cowslip (Primula) — May produce on some people dermatitis similar to poison ivy. There is a toxic principle contained in the glandular hairs.

QUINCE — Liquid made from seeds, used to treat looseness of the bowels.

RHUBARB — Cathartic with astringent power. Also used as a tonic.

ROMAN WORMWOOD (Arboratum) — Highly tonic and probably enters the circulation. Remedy for digestive problems and intermittent fever. Seldom used in U.S.

ROSE GERANIUM — Used as a tea for sedative.

RUE — Stimulant when used in small doses. Large doses act as narcotic poison.

SAGE (wild) — Tonic and astringent — for reducing fever and as a throat gargle. More commonly used as a condiment.

SAGE (Salvia officinalis) — Slightly tonic and astringent. Mostly used as a gargle for throat inflammation.

SOUTHERN WOOD — Antidote for deadly poisons.

TANSY (common) — Seldom used in U.S.

TANSY (curl) — Similar properties to aromatic bitters. Less active than common tansy.

THYME (Thymus Vulgaris) — Used as a flavoring like sage and lavender. Mostly used in cooking.

TOUCH-ME-NOT (Jewel Weed, Balsam Weed) — Acts as emetic, cathartic and diuretic, but seldom used because of danger of poisoning.

THORNAPPLE (Datura Stramonium) — A strong narcotic. Seeds are most powerful. Roots and dried leaves are used. Considered good for rheumatic affections, sores and asthma.

TREE PRIMROSE (Enothera Biennis) — Used as a vulnerary. Considered beneficial in reuptive complaints, especially tetter.

VERONICA — Considered to be a tonic. Not commonly used in this country.

VIOLET — The herbaceous parts of the plant were considered to be emollient and slightly laxative. Leaves contain vitams A and C.

WILD GERANIUM — Roots used as a styptic for wounds and as a gargle for sore throat.

WINTER SAVORY (Satureja Montana) — Used as a gentle stimulant. After 1850 used only for flavoring.

WORM WOOD — Tonic may cause headache or affect the nervous system.

YELLOW MINT — Used as a stimulant like other mints.

HORSE MINT (Monarda) — Stimulant and carminative but seldom used. Sometimes used as a family remedy for colic and stomach disorders.

Polypodium Vulgare, or Common Polypody.

(THE ROOT AND TOPS.)

This is found in mountains, on rocks, throughout the United States and Canada; the root has a sweet, mucilaginous taste. This plant is good for colds, coughs, influenza, and worms. Some of the plant stewed in syrup and a tablespoonful given every hour or two, is an excellent thing in colds or chronic cough. United with an equal quantity of liverwort, and made into a syrup, it makes an excellent remedy in diseases of the lung and throat; to be taken freely every two hours. The root powdered, and mixed with powdered rhubarb, in equal parts, and the same quantity of syrup, given once or twice a day; from ten to twenty grains at a dose, to children, will expel worms after many other remedies fail. It may be used also as a tea, in colds, etc.

This shrub blossoms in April and May; the berries ripen in June. The whole shrub, even the root, is acid or sour; the bark is yellow and bitter. The berries contain a red and very sour juice, that is beneficial in chronic dysentry, or diarrhoea; also, as a cooling drink mixed with water, sugar, and orange peel, or cinnamon bark; it is useful in fevers for abating heat and quenching thirst. A syrup may also be made from the berries or bark; or a tea may be made of the bark, mixing cinnamon or allspice to suit the taste, and give a wine glass, cold, every three hours. The bark or berries added to hard cider, and used freely three times a day, are recommended in diseases of the liver.

Berberis Vulgaris, or *Barberry*.

(THE BUSH.)

279

HERB DISCLAIMER

Please be warned that these, as many other herbal remedies, were published long ago and may or may not be valid.

We are not trying to suggest that herbs have no healing virtues at all. Many herbal cures are well documented.

But, for the ignorant and uninitiated, to prescribe these herbal remedies for themselves would be as foolish as taking potent modern drugs from unlabelled bottles.

If you wish to follow the healing lore of herbs, we suggest you seek the advise of a well informed M.D. or a competent shaman.

Asclepias Syriaca; or Common Silk Weed. (The Root.) This plant, growing plentifully throughout the United States, along roadsides and sandy grounds, is a powerful diuretic (operating on the kidneys), and is useful in dropsy. Boil eight ounces of the root in six quarts of rain water down to three quarts; strain before using. For dropsy, take a gill of this decoction four times a day, increasing the dose, or otherwise, according to the symptoms. It is used the same way for suppression of urine. It may be taken in powder, twenty to thirty grains three times a day.

(THE ROOT.)

Sanguinaria Canadensis, or Blood Root.

This is an emetic (producing vomiting), narcotic (reducing the pulse and quieting the nerves), expectorant (for cough), etc. It must be used with care, to avoid taking an over dose. It is recommended in rheumatism, diseases of the liver, typhoid—pneumonia, coughs, colds, etc. Dose, from one to five grains of the root powdered, and given in the form of a pill, every three or four hours, according to the symptoms, disease, etc.

(THE PLANT.)

Scutillaria Laterifolia, or Scull Cap.

This is found in all parts of the United States, in meadows, woods, near water, etc., flowering in the summer. It is highly recommended for St. Vitus' Dance, given in the form of tea, (cold,) a wine glass full, or more, three times a day on an empty stomach. Given in the same way, it is highly recommended also for worms, to be followed the third day by a purge of castor oil.

The plant or leaves may also be powdered, and given in doses of from ten to fifteen grains three times a day.

Asclepias Syriaca, or Common Silk Weed.

Arislotochia Serpentania; or, Virginia Snake Root. (The Root.) This was first introduced as a remedy against snake bites, from which it derives its name, and was used by the Indians for that purpose. It possesses powerful and lasting stimulant virtues; but besides this general action, it acts also on the skin, producing perspiration. It is very useful in all cases where there is not active inflammation, in promoting perspiration, especially in typhoid fevers, etc. Dose of the powder, ten to twenty grains, in syrup or flaxseed-tea; or it may be used as an infusion (or tea), which is preferable, putting half an ounce to a pint of boiling water; of which four or five tablespoonfuls may be given every three or four hours.

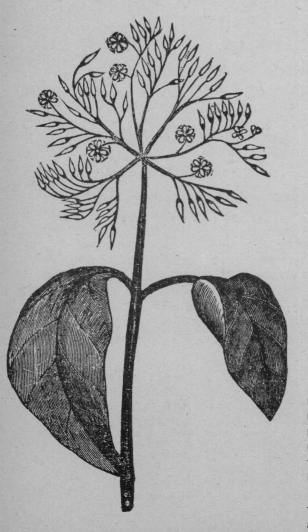

This grows near brooks, along the banks of rivers, and on upland meadows; it is known throughout the United States by the name of red rose-willow, which distinguishes it from the black willow, or the puss willow, which grows in swamps, and along the sides of moist meadows. It is a powerful astringent and tonic—preferred by some to the Peruvian bark or Columbo Root, and is much employed in the Northern States, in substance or otherwise, in diarrhoea and dyspepsia. In vomiting, this is an excellent remedy, given in the form of an infusion; in the vomiting particularly arising from pregnancy. This is a valuable article. It is mostly administered in the form of infusion, or tea, given cold.

Cornus Sericea, or Rose Willow

Arislotochia Serpentaria, or Virginia Snake Root.

FRUITS AND SMALL FRUITS

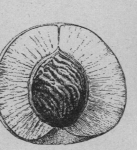

FIG. 170. — Peach. Longitudinal Section of Fruit.

BUBACH STRAWBERRY.

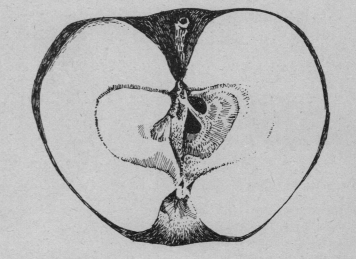

How to Plant Strawberries

1. A STRAWBERRY PLANT SET TOO DEEP
2. SET AT JUST THE RIGHT DEPTH
3. PLANTING WHICH IS TOO HIGH
4. THE POINT AT WHICH THE ROOTS SHOULD BE PRUNED

Hill System:
12 to 18 inches apart in rows 2 to 3 feet apart. Keep all runners nipped off.

Matted Row:
Rows 4 to 5 feet apart, plants set 24 inches apart in row. Allow runners to fill to 24 inches wide.

Plow or spade land deeply before planting. Plant by pushing spade into ground to its full depth in spot where plant is to be. Press it to one side, insert roots and spread them out in fan shape and hanging down to their full length. Set plant with crown at surface or a little below it. (See illustration.) Remove spade and press dirt against roots.

Extremely long roots may be cut back for convenience in planting. Carry plants in pail of water. Water each plant after planting.

Bush Fruits

Currants and Gooseberries

Set 2 or 3 inches deeper than in nursery. Cut off half the tops. Plant 4 or 5 feet apart. Most currant or gooseberry pests can be controlled by dusting or spraying with Rotenone. Always cut out infested canes.

Red & Black Raspberries and Blackberries

Plant in good garden soil 3 to 5 feet apart in rows 6 feet apart. Set Red Raspberry plants 1 to 2 inches deeper than they were in the nursery and Black Raspberries 1 inch deeper. Firm soil over roots, and water. Cut back all plants to about 6 inches in height. Don't let any fruit set first year. Allow new shoots to make rows 6 to 8 inches wide.

After fruiting each year, cut out old canes and burn, leaving a few vigorous new ones to grow for fruiting the following year. These fruiting canes should be cut back to about 2½' early in the spring to encourage fruiting laterals. Mulching always pays. In the spring, spray raspberries and blackberries just before the buds open, with lime sulphur or Bordeaux mixture.

FIG. 274. — Red Raspberry Bush, in Fork of a Maple.

Grapes

Dig the hole broad and deep. Cut back the top to 2 or 3 strong buds. Plant deep to prevent roots drying out. Fill the hole with compost or rich soil. Plant firmly, water well and mulch top. The first year tie most vigorous shoot to stake to form trunk of vine and frequently remove all other shoots and suckers.

PLANT JUST ABOVE SECOND BUD

—I, Strawberry ; II, Raspberry ; III, Mulberry.

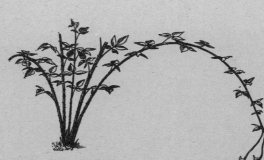

Plant of a Black Raspberry, showing One Branch (Stolon) with Several Tips rooting.

WHERE ARE THE APPLES OF YESTERYEAR?

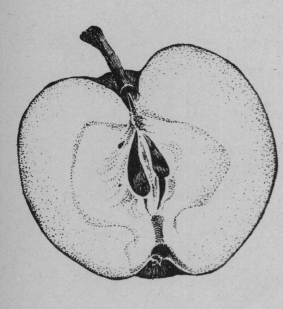

On all the roadside stands that dot the countryside, and in all the fruitmarkets of our cities, we doubt that you will be able to find more than ten varieties of apples. Yet, in 1872, when FRUITS AND FRUIT TREES OF AMERICA was published, about one thousand apple trees of American origin were listed.

Our interest here is not merely historical, nor just related to apples, though.

All of us remember backyard orchards filled with apples we can no longer find. We can still conjure the tastes of fruits we can no longer buy. For, many more varieties of almost every fruit you can think of existed years ago. Now, most are unavailable to us.

Where can you get a "banana apple," these days? Does anyone still grow strawberry apples? What was the name of that apple that tasted of roses when you bit into it? And, where can you find it today?

We suppose insects and disease took their toll. But, for the most part, fruit varieties disappeared as pomologists and commercial growers moved towards easier to grow, more profitable varieties. While it is difficult to attack scientists employed by businessmen for seeking greater profits for their bosses, we must wonder whether picking and packing requirements should be considered before the flavor and aroma of a food product.

This is just one more area where commercial standardization has cost consumers, in terms of the richness and variety in their lives. And, we doubt very seriously that commercial growers will return to the culture of almost forgotten fruits, anymore than General Motors will retool to bring back the 1952 Pontiac.

But, gardeners who want to grow antiquarian fruit varieties, should find it easier to fulfill their desire, than a lover of four-wheeled anachronisms.

Though seeds and culture of old fruit varieties are no longer available commercially, many are kept by independent pomologists and the United States Department of Agriculture.

For information about well known fruit, as well as old varieties, queries should be addressed to The Small Fruits Division of the USDA at Beltsville, Maryland and The American Pomological Society Magazine, Fruit Varieties Journal, 114 Horticulture Field Laboratory, University of Illinois, Urbana, Illinois, 61801. Keep in mind that the USDA will supply information most easily understood by novices. APS material requires a good understanding of the subject.

Both groups, though, are made up mostly of scientists, who are plugged directly into the horticultural industry. Let them know what you want and the word will reach their patrons.

Let them know that though we may never see old varieties in commercial cultivation again, they would make extremely interesting and personal additions to any backyard orchard.

Sure, there's a search involved, perhaps even a romantic quest. But we suspect there is treasure to be found and great rewards to be gained.

Whatever your results may be, keep us informed.

TRAINED FRUIT TREE

Sweet Bough
Tetofsky
Transcendent (Crab)
Twenty Ounce
Victoria
Wealthy
Williams
Wolf River
Workaroe
Yellow Transparent

Admirable
Alexander
Arctic
Benoni
Bismarck
Blenheim
Cabashea
Champlain
Chenango
Collamer
Constantine
Cox Orange
Cranberry Pippin
Detroit Red
Dudley
Early Harvest
Early Harvest
Early Joe
Early Ripe
Early Strawberry
Excelsior (Crab)
Fall Orange
Fall Pippin
Fameuse
Fanny
Fishkill
Gladstone
Golden Sweet
Gravenstein
Haas
Hawley
Hoadley
Hook
Hyslop (Crab)
Jefferis
Jersey Sweet
Judson
Keswick
Landsberg
Large Red Siberian (Crab)
Late Strawberry
Lee Sweet (Section)
Lee Sweet (whole fruit)
Longfield
Lowell
Magog
Maiden Blush
Martha (Crab)
McIntosh
McLellan (Section)
McLellan (whole fruit)
McMahon
Montreal Beauty (Crab)
Mother
Munson
Ohio Pippin
Oldenburg
Patten
Parry White
Pease
Pomona
Porter
Primate
Pumpkin Russet
Pumpkin Sweet
Red Astrachan
Red June
Red Siberian (Crab)
Ribston
Sharp
Shiawassee
Sops of Wine
Sour Bough
Stump

Pollination Requirements for Fruits and Nuts

Published by Oklahoma State University

Glenn Taylor
Extension Horticulturist, Pecans and Tree Fruits

Apples, apricots, blackberries, cherries, figs, grapes, muscadines, peaches, pears, persimmons, plums, strawberries, pecans and walnuts are found growing in many areas of Oklahoma.

Fruit set must be secured before a crop can be produced. Many factors influence pollination: general health and nutrition, insects and diseases, late frost or winter injury, and too much rain at blossoming time. The chief cause, however, in most instances is that of poor pollination. The flavor or color of fruit is not affected by cross-pollination.

Fruits do not cross-pollinate outside of their own species. For example, stone fruits (peaches, plums, apples, and apricots) do not pollinate one another.

Most fruits are insect pollinated. Two or more varieties of each kind of fruit should be used in all fruit plantings unless it is positively known that the variety is self-fruitful. Following is a brief discussion of selecting varieties to improve fruit set.

Selecting Apple Varieties

The flowers of the apple are true hermaphrodites. The blossom has five stigmas. If each one is fertilized, better apples will be produced. The June drop of apples in many orchards is a direct result of poor pollination. Unless three or more seeds are developing, the young apples will not reach true size and will no doubt drop immature sometime before harvest time. Most apple varieties require cross-pollination. Those not requiring it usually produce more and better fruit when crossing occurs. In normal blossoming years, from 5% to 10% of the blossoms, if properly pollinized, will usually result in a satisfactory fruit set for the tree. It should be remembered that about 90% of the fruit set of apples is the result of insect activity during the period the tree is in full bloom.

The pollinizer trees should make up from one-fourth to one-tenth of the total number of trees in the planting. It is possible to have the pollinizer trees of a variety equally as productive and valuable as the principal variety. They should bloom at the same time and have plenty of mature pollen. They should be self-fertile or receive pollen from the principle variety.

It is difficult to classify the varieties because they do not behave in the same manner in different producing areas. The following general classification should be helpful:

Self-fruitful: Yellow Transparent and Grimes Golden.

Partly self-fruitful: Ben Davis, Black Ben, Gano, Summer Champion, Lodi, and Rome Beauty. (These varieties need cross-pollination. Yellow Transparent blooms at the right time and is considered a good pollinizer for this group.)

Partly self-fruitful: Jonathan, Blackjon, and Jonared. (They need to be cross-pollinated. Golden Delicious, Starking, or York Imperial are good pollinizers for this group.)

Self-unfruitful: Delicious, Starking, Arkansas Black, and Red June. (Jonathan and Golden Delicious are good pollinizers for this group.)

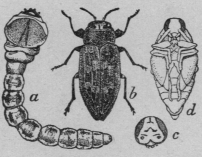

—FLAT-HEADED APPLE-BORER.

Self-unfruitful and pollen sterile: Winesap, Turley, Stayman Winesap, and its sports. (Jonathan and Golden Delicious are good Pollinizers for this group.)

Where pollination problems occur in existing plantings, an application of nitrogen fertilizer applied three weeks before blooming could help solve the problem.

Add some bee colonies to the orchard. Bouquets of flowers of suitable varieties can be attached to the trees. Graft or add new pollinizer trees.

Apricots, Bramble Fruits and Cherries

Most of the bramble fruits produced in Oklahoma are considered self-fruitful. The recommended varieties are self-fruitful. The Dallas variety of blackberries requires cross-pollination.

Apricots are generally considered self-fruitful.

Sour cherries are self-fruitful. It is better to have two varieties (Early Richmond and Montmorency). Sweet cherries are self-unfruitful.

Figs and Grapes

Figs generally need cross-pollination.

Grapes are mostly wind-pollinized. Most of the varieties are self-fruitful and cross-compatible. The exceptions are America, Enda, Last Rose and Brighton. They require cross-pollination by other varieties. Grapes bloom late in the season and seldom are the blossoms injured by late spring frost; however, winter injury will sometimes kill buds that would otherwise produce fruiting wood during the summer.

CORDON and ORDINARY ESPALIER TRAINERS

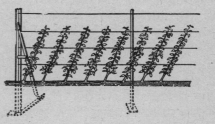

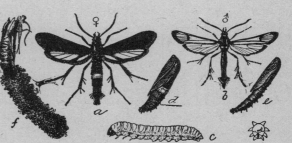

—PEACH-BORER.

Pecans and Walnuts

Pecan trees are monoecious (having both male and female flowers on the same tree). The male flowers are three-branched catkins produced on last year's wood. The pollen is carried by the wind to the female flowers, borne in clusters on the current season's growth.

Most varieties are considered self-fruitful; however, better production is obtained when more than one variety is planted.

Wet weather during the pollination period may reduce dissemination of pollen. A good plan is to leave a few native pecan trees in the vicinity of the pecan grove to furnish additional pollen. Some native trees bear their pollen early and some late. Pollination is usually completed most years during the last days of May. The tip ends of the nutlets turn brown and harden immediately after they are pollinized or their receptive period has passed. If the female flower fails to receive pollen, it usually turns yellow and falls to the ground within a week or so. According to Dr. G. W. Adriance, Head of the Horticulture Department of Texas A&M College, 75% of the small nut drop that usually occurs in June or about six weeks after the pollination period is a result of the female flowers not becoming fertilized.

There is no evidence of cross-incompatibility in varieties tested. The problem develops because the male and female flowers do not mature at the same time. Moore, Texas Prolific, and San Saba have pollen available in time to pollinate the earliest flowers of any variety. Moneymaker and Success usually depend upon other varieties for pollination. Stuart, Burkett, Schley, and Delmas sometimes require pollen from other varieties.

No pollination difficulties have been experienced in Oklahoma among the native or improved varieties of walnuts. The male and female flowers of the walnut occur in a similar manner as found in pecans. Two or more varieties of walnuts are recommended for a planting. (Some difficulty may be experienced with the Carpathian varieties.) Some of the young trees produce female flowers for two or three years before they develop catkins to furnish the pollen.

Persimmons, Plums and Strawberries

Japanese or Kaki persimmon (also referred to as Oriental) is dioecious. Some plants produce male (staminate) flowers and some produce female (pistillate) flowers. Some produce both and are self-fruitful. Some persimmons bear male flowers only when the tree is young, later change to the production of female flowers only, and in some cases, produce both male and female flowers.

The persimmon tree is usually a male or female. American and Japanese trees are not inter-fruitful.

Most of the Japanese plum varieties are self-unfruitful. Varieties like Bruce, Hanska, Gold, America, and a dwarf variety, Sapa, are considered self-fruitful and cross-compatible. It is a good plan, however, to plant two or more varieties.

The recommended varieties of strawberries are self-fruitful. Pollination problems, however, do occur in some of the everbearing varieties, but in most cases it is the result of high temperatures.

Material prepared by E.L. Whitehead, former Extension Horticulturist.

Muscadines, Peaches and Pears

Most varieties of muscadines are self-sterile. Pollen is carried by the wind from the male plant to the female plant. About one-fourth of the planting should be made up of male vines. Where only a few vines are planted, the male vines may be located nearby on the fence row or edge of the field.

The Wallace and Willard (white) varieties have perfect flowers, are self-fruitful, and can produce the pollen for the female vines in the planting, thus eliminating the need of the male vines.

Most varieties of peaches are considered self-fruitful. The exception is J. H. Hale. It produces abortive pollen but can be pollinated by most any variety.

Most varieties of pears are partly self-fruitful. Usually two or more varieties will result in a better pear crop. Bartlett and Seckel are cross-incompatible. Bartlett and Kieffer are considered self-incompatible. Garber is a good pollinizer for Kieffer. Maxine, Magness, and Moonglow are three new varieties believed to be blight resistant. Magness is pollen-sterile, thus requiring a pollinator.

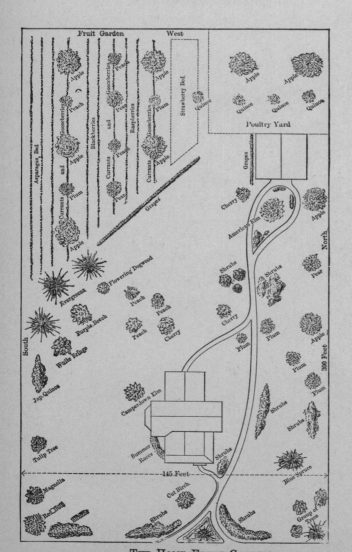

—THE HOME FRUIT GARDEN.

FRUIT VARIETIES JOURNAL

A Publication of the American Pomological Society

(Formerly Fruit Varieties and Horticultural Digest)

Volume 28   January 1974   Number 1

Published by
THE AMERICAN POMOLOGICAL SOCIETY

Fruit Varieties Journal is published by the American Pomological Society as an annual volume of 4 issues, in January, April, July and October. Membership ($8.00 per year) in the Society includes a volume of the Journal. Most back issues are available at various rates. Library and institutional subscriptions are $8.00 per year for 4 issues. Paid renewals not received in the office of the Business Manager by January 1 will be temporarily suspended until payment is received.

Editorial Office: Manuscripts and correspondence concerning editorial matters should be addressed to the Editor: Roy K. Simons, 114 Horticulture Field Laboratory, University of Illinois, Urbana, Illinois 61801. Phone: (217) 333-1527.

Publishing Office: American Pomological Society, 103 Tyson Building, University Park, PA 16802. Second class postage paid at State College, PA 16801.

Business Office: Correspondence regarding subscriptions, advertising, back issues, and Society membership should be addressed to the Business Manager: L. D. Tukey, 103 Tyson Building, University Park, PA 16802. Phone: (814) 865-2572.

Page Charges: A charge of $16.00 per page ($8.00 per half page) plus cost of cuts will be made to authors for those articles constituting publication of research.

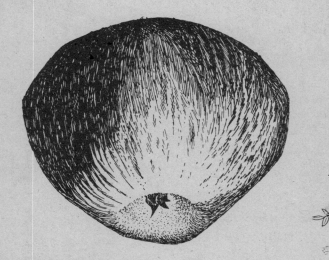

FRUIT TREES. With branched fruit trees as Peach, Cherry, Plum, Apple and Pear Trees, select three to five side branches on different sides of the trunk and 6 to 8 inches apart and cut back one-third their length. Select

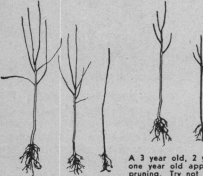

A 3 year old, 2 year old and 1 year old apple tree before pruning.

A 3 year old, 2 year old and one year old apple tree after pruning. Try not to leave two branches nearly opposite, they will form a bad crotch when the tree is older.

one of the top upright branches and cut it back in proportion to the side branches. Cut off all other branches close to the trunk. (See illustration above.)

With Fruit Tree Whips having no side branches, simply cut off the top just above a bud 2 to 2½ feet from the ground. (See illustration above.)

Protect young fruit tree trunks from rodent and rabbit damage with collars of hardware cloth 6"-8" in diameter and 2' high.

Prune for the plant's sake, not for pruning's sake.

DWARF FRUIT TREES. Plant with bud union at least 4 inches above the ground. Trunks should be tied to permanent stakes.

To plant follow same procedure as given on page 7.

Fruit trees should always be protected against bark girdling by mice and rabbits. Two foot lengths of a galvanized wire screen (hardware cloth) formed into an 8" circle about the young trunks is a reliable protection.

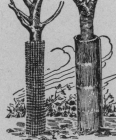

Wire or other rabbit guards must be fastened loosely to permit expansion

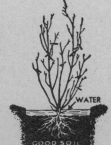

How to Plant Blueberries
Highbush Blueberries are a worthwhile addition to the home fruit garden — IF soil requirements are right. Soil should be moist, light textured, contain a high proportion of organic matter, test acidity from pH 4.0 to 4.5. Set bushes 6 feet each way. Mulch each year with 3 to 4 inches of sawdust or peat. Cultivate shallowly because of shallow root system. Plant in sun for good yields.

NORTH AMERICAN APPLES: Varieties, Rootstocks, Outlook.
W. H. Upshall, Editor
Sponsored by the American Pomological Society
Michigan State University Press. 197 pages. 1970. $8.50

The American Pomological Society is proud to announce the publication of this fine book on apples, which it is sponsoring. In it, a number of outstanding pomologists and a freelance writer have succeeded, through their joint efforts, in bringing together many interesting and pertinent facts about the leading apple varieties of North America, their bud sports, certain of the minor and discarded varieties, and the important rootstocks.

In a chapter entitled "Varieties of Yesteryear", A. P. French gives a brief history and description of a number of old American varieties which have fallen by the wayside or are no longer important.

Emery Wilcox provides significant facts and figures, skillfully tracing apple variety trends in the United States and Canada during the past 27 years.

The major portion of the book consists of a series of chapters dealing with the seven leading North American apple varieties: Delicious, McIntosh, Golden Delicious, Rome Beauty, Jonathan, Winesap, and·York Imperial; and the minor variety, Northern Spy. Each chapter reflects the careful research of each author, namely, Virginia Maas (the freelance writer), R. P. Larsen, W. H. Upshall, J. B. Mowry, and E. S. Degman. Fascinating episodes connected with the origin of each variety are revealed. Valuable lists of strains and new varieties bred from the original varieties are presented by most of the authors. It is unfortunate that such tables were not prepared for Delicious and Golden Delicious, as well.

The chapter on rootstocks by R. F. Carlson is a very important part of the book, since the performance of a scion variety is strongly affected by the rootstock to which it is grafted. What is more, one can hardly deny that clonal rootstocks are themselves varieties in every way. The mechanisms by which rootstocks control size, and cause flowering and fruiting effects in the scion variety are discussed. The important clonal rootstocks are described, and their strengths and weaknesses pointed out.

"North American Apples" is concluded very appropriately and effectively with a chapter entitled "Apple Orchards of Tomorrow", by H. A. Rollins. He sees the commercial apple orchard of the future as more deliberately planned for a specific harvesting technique; as largely either on size-controling rootstocks, or spur-types on seedling rootstocks; more intensely trained trees; and more generally irrigated and protected from frost than they are now.

This book is a "must" for the apple grower—commercial, amateur, teacher and student. Order it now, directly from Michigan State University Press, Box 550, East Lansing, Michigan, 48823.

George M. Kessler, Editor
Fruit Varieties & Horticultural Digest
Department of Horticulture
Michigan State University

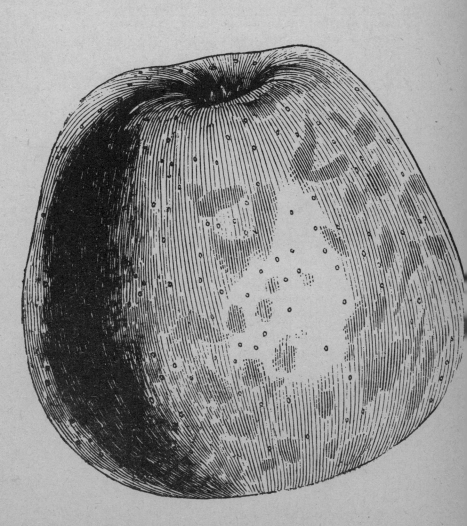

Propagating Peaches by "T"-Budding

OSU Extension Facts

Published by Oklahoma State University   Distributed Through County Extension Offices   No. 6227

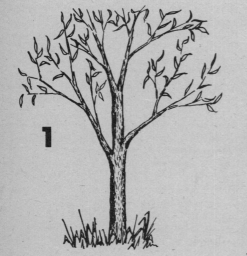

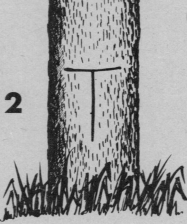

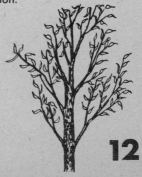

1. PREPARING STOCK
A young seedling as large in diameter as a pencil or larger is preferable. In preparing the stock for budding, remove all the growth on the lower 6 to 10 inches of the tree.

2. MAKING FIRST CUT
The first cut is made lengthwise of the stem near the ground line, preferably on the north side of the stock. Next, make the cross cut by a rolling movement of the knife, which lifts the corners of the bark where the two cuts cross each other.

3. OPEN THE MATRIX
The same area with the matrix opened out to receive the bud.

4. CUTTING THE BUD
Cut the bud from the stick by making the cut upwards just underneath the bud. This cut should be from ¾ to 1 inch in length, extending below and above the bud.

5. REMOVE THE BUD
Remove the bud from the bud stick by making a cut across the top through the bark and peel the bark and bud from the stick, leaving the wood attached to the stock. The bud may be held on the blade of the knife with the thumb on the leaf stub while it is being inserted in the stock. If the bark does not slip, leave the wood attached to the bark.

6. INSERT UNDER BARK
Insert the bud in the matrix under the bark and push it down until it is firmly in place. If a part of the tissue extends above the top of the "T" cut, it should be removed.

Glenn Taylor
Extension Horticulturist, Pecans and Tree Fruits

The "T" or shield-bud method of propagation may be used on many kinds of plants; apples, pears, peaches, and a large number of ornamentals. The "T" bud is considered the easiest method of plant propagation.

Peaches are usually propagated during the seedling stage of growth when they are at least as large in diameter as a pencil. If this size is attained in June, they may be budded and forced into growth in a short time. When seedling development is delayed, budding is usually performed in August and early September and the buds are not forced into growth until the next spring.

Bud wood is secured from desirable varieties at the time the budding is done. Select strong, vigorous, new-shoot growths. Bud wood is big enough to use when a reddish color develops on the twig and the buds show brown-colored spots.

Immediately remove the leaves from the bud stick. Use a knife or hand shears to clip off the leaves, leaving a short stub of the petiole of the leaf (on the stock) ¼ to ⅜ inch long.

This stub can serve to protect the bud adjacent to it and also serve as a handle to hold the bud while it is being cut from the stick and being inserted into the seedling.

The immature wood at the terminal end of the shoot should be removed. Ordinarily, bud sticks would be from around 10 to 15 inches in length. Keep the bud sticks wrapped in moist burlap sacks or suitable material to prevent drying out.

Material prepared by E.L. Whitehead, former Extension Horticulturist.

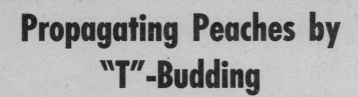

7. WRAPPING THE BUD
Secure the bud to the stock by wrapping with ⅛ inch rubber budding strips, making at least two wraps below the bud and two above. The band maintains constant pressure, but expands with the growth of the tree.

8. FORCING BUDS
When June budding, to force the bud, break the top over about one-half the distance from the ground to the top of the seedling, leaving it attached to shade the row of seedling trees. When "T" budding is performed during late August or early September, the buds should callus well during the remainder of the growing season and be forced into growth the following spring.

9. NEW GROWTH STARTS
Shows the new growth from the inserted bud.

10. REMOVE THE TOP
When the forced bud starts to grow, remove the top of the seedling just above the new shoot.

11. REMOVE NEW GROWTH
Keep the new growth removed from the base of the seedling below the bud. Some of the shoots on the new top growth may be removed near the base to force more length of growth into the new tree. In June budding, the old top should be removed as soon as the bud starts to grow. Keep the surplus growth removed in order to produce a larger tree during the growing season.

12. THE TREE IS READY
The converted tree, the new variety, after a season's growth. The tree is ready for transplanting to its permanent location.

EXTENSION SERVICES

BOULTON AND PAUL,
HORTICULTURAL BUILDERS,
NORWICH.

WALL FRUIT TREE PROTECTORS.

Standard Fig Tree (From a specimen grown under glass).

BANANA PLANT.
(MUSA ENSETE.)

Branch of Fruiting Fig (showing the mode of fruiting in the axils of the leaves).

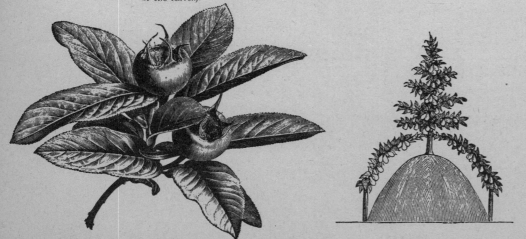

Fruiting Branch of the Medlar.

287

U.S. DEPARTMENT OF HEALTH, EDUCATION AND WELFARE

FUTURE FARMERS OF AMERICA IS A NATIONAL ORGANI-ZATION OF STUDENTS OF VOCATIONAL AGRICULTURE AND AGRIBUSINESS. FOR ADDITIONAL INFORMATION ADDRESS:

> U.S. Office of Education
> Division of Vocational and Technical Education
> U.S. Department of Health, Education and Welfare
> Washington, D.C. 20202
> Mr. H. N. Hunsicker, National Advisor
> Ph: 202—245-9824

U.S. DEPARTMENT OF AGRICULTURE

Agricultural Extension Service

The Agricultural Extension Service is the most extensive and readily available source of information on agricultural subjects including horticulture in the United States. This service is a joint effort of the county government, the state college or university responsible for agriculture, and the United States Department of Agriculture. Local agricultural extension agents may be found in most counties and many major municipalities of each state. The telephone number and address for your Extension Agent will usually be found under the county government listing in the phone book as Agricultural Agent or Extension Service. Horti-cultural knowledge of each individual agent does vary, often depending on the importance of commercial horticulture in the county. If a local agent does not have personal knowledge to answer an inquiry, he is supported by the resources of the ag-ricultural college and the U.S.D.A. Answers to some of the most frequently asked questions are available in printed form —fact sheets, circulars and bulletins. This literature, including a list of all the titles available, may be obtained from the De-partment of Agricultural Information (or similar title) of the state university. Addresses for these offices are shown.

The Agricultural Extension Service also sponsors the na-tional 4-H programs, the largest youth programs in agriculture, horticulture and home economics. For additional information contact:

> 4-H Program
> Extension Service
> U.S. Department of Agriculture
> Washington, D.C. 20250
> NATIONAL 4-H NEWS (monthly)
> Dr. E. Dean Vaughan, National Director
> Ph: 202—447-6144

AGRICULTURAL EXPERIMENT STATIONS, RESEARCH CENTERS, AND PLANT INTRODUCTION STATIONS

Agricultural Experiment Stations were created to do scientific research in the broad field of agriculture. This includes finding the how and why of animal and plant growth, developing new cultivars, learning how to control diseases, insects and weeds, and information in many other fields. The results of this research provide the basis for the fact sheets, circulars and bulletins issued by the Extension Service. Bulletins on technical subjects are issued by the experiment station but are usually available from the same office as the Exten-sion bulletins.

It was found in most states that research only at the state uni-versity did not provide answers to the many unique agricultural situations found in different parts of each state. To overcome this problem, specialized branch experiment stations were created. The stations may be state, federal or jointly supported. Experiments and plantings at some of these stations should be of interest to persons traveling around the country.

ALASKA

Alaska Agricultural Experiment Station
University of Alaska
College, AK 99701

Alaska Agricultural Experiment Station
Box AE
Palmer, AK 99645

ALABAMA

Alabama Agricultural Experiment Station
Auburn University
Auburn, AL 36830

Chilton Area
Horticulture Substation
Clanton, AL 35045

Gulf Coast Substation
Auburn University
Fairhope, AL 36532

N. Alabama Hort. Substation
Alabama Agricultural Exper. Station System
Route 7 Box 508
Cullman, AL 35055

Ornamental Horticulture Field Station
Box 8276
Spring Hill Station
Mobile, AL 36608

EXTENSION SERVICE LISTS

HORTICULTURAL SCHOOLS

Piedmont Substation
Auburn University
Camp Hill, AL 36850

Sand Mountain Substation
Crossville, AL 35962

Tennessee Valley Substation
Belle Mina, AL 35615

Wiregrass Substation
Headland, AL 36345

ARKANSAS

Arkansas Agricultural Experiment Station
University of Arkansas
Fayetteville, AR 72701

Cotton Branch Experiment Station
University of Arkansas
P.O. Box 522
Marianna, AR 72360

Fruit Substation
University of Arkansas
Clarksville, AR 72830

Peach Substation
University of Arkansas
Nashville, AR 71852

Southwest Branch Experiment Station
University of Arkansas
Route 3, Box 218
Hope, AR 71801

Strawberry Substation
University of Arkansas
Box 543
Bald Knob, AR 72010

Vegetable Substation
University of Arkansas
Box 358
Van Buren, AR 72956

ARIZONA

Arizona Agricultural Experiment Station
University of Arizona
Tucson, AZ 85721

Citrus Branch Experiment Station
University of Arizona
Route 1, Box 715
Tempe, AZ 85281

Mesa Branch Station
University of Arizona
Mesa, AZ 85202

Safford Experiment Station
University of Arizona
Box 1015
Safford, AZ 85546

Yuma Branch Station
University of Arizona
Route 1, Box 587
Yuma, AZ 85364

CALIFORNIA

California Agricultural Experiment Station
University of California at Davis
Davis, CA 95616

California Agricultural Experiment Station
University of California at Los Angeles
Los Angeles, CA 90024

California Agricultural Experiment Station
University of California at Riverside
Riverside, CA 92502

Deciduous Fruit Field Station
University of California
125 North Winchester Blvd.
San Jose, CA 95128

Imperial Valley Field Station
University of California
1004 East Holton Road
El Centro, CA 92243

Lindcove Field Station
University of California
22963 Carson Avenue
Exeter, CA 93221

South Coast Field Station
University of California
7601 Irvine Boulevard
Santa Ana, CA 92705

Tulelake Agricultural Field Station
University of California
Tulelake, CA 96134

U.S. Plant Introduction Station
Box 1040
Chico, CA 95927

U.S. Date and Citrus Station
ARS-USDA
40-455 Clinton Street
Indio, CA 92201

USDA Horticultural Station
Plant Science Research Division
2021 South Peach Avenue
Fresno, CA 93727

USDA-ARS
Plant Science Res. Division
1636 East Alisal Street
P.O. Box 5098
Salinas, CA 93901

West Side Field Station
University of California
Box 158
Five Points, CA 93624

Western Region, ARS, USDA
2850 Telegraph Avenue
Berkeley, CA 94705
H. Rex Thomas, Deputy Admin.
415-841-3431

COLORADO

Arkansas Valley Branch Station
Colorado State University
Rocky Ford, CO 81067

Colorado Agricultural Experiment Station
Colorado State University
Fort Collins, CO 80521

National Seed Storage Laboratory
Colorado State University Campus
Fort Collins, CO 80521

San Luis Valley Station
Colorado State University
Route 2
Center, CO 81125

Western Slope Branch Sta.
Colorado State Univ.
3168B 1/2 Road
Grand Junction, CO 81501

CONNECTICUT

Connecticut Agricultural Experiment Station
University of Connecticut
Storrs, CT 06268

Connecticut Agricultural Experiment Station
Valley Laboratory
Box 248
Windsor, CT 06095

Connecticut Agricultural Experiment Station
123 Huntington Street
Box 1106
New Haven, CT 06504

DELAWARE

Delaware Agricultural Experiment Station
University of Delaware
Newark, DE 19711

DISTRICT OF COLUMBIA

ARS-Information Division
Office of the Director
Washington, D.C. 20250
Robert Rathbone, Director
202-447-4433

Chesapeake & Potomac Area
U.S. National Arboretum
28th & M Streets, Northeast
Washington, D.C. 20002
John L. Creech, Agri. Admr.
202-399-5400

4-H Program
Extension Service
U.S. Dept. of Agriculture
Washington, D.C. 20250
Dr. E. Dean Vaughan, Natl. Dir.
202-447-6144

NATIONAL 4-H NEWS

National Program Staff
Plant & Entom. Sciences
ARS-USDA-Administration Bldg.
Washington, D.C. 20250
M. Cleveland, Hugo O. Graumann, Staff Scientists
202-477-4465

Office of Administrator
ARS-Administration Bldg.
Washington, D.C. 20250
T.W. Edminster
202-447-3656

Program Analysis and Coordination Staff
USDA-ARS
Washington, D.C. 20250
Ernest Corley, Jr., Director
202-447-6961

FLORIDA

Agricultural Research Center
Monticello
Box 539
Monticello, FL 32344

ARS, Southern Region
U.S.D.A. Hortic. Res. Lab.
2120 Camden Road
Orlando, FL 32803
Wm. Cooper, Location Leader
904-377-2240

Big Bend Horticultural Laboratory
University of Florida
Box 539
Monticello, FL 32344

Citrus Experiment Station
University of Florida
Lake Alfred, FL 33850

Everglades Experiment Station
University of Florida
Belle Glade, FL 33430

Florida Agricultural Experiment Station
University of Florida
Gainesville, FL 32601

Florida Agricultural Exp. Sta.
University of Florida
Watermelon and Grape Investigation Laboratory
Leesburg, FL 32748

Gulf Coast Experiment Station
IFAS, University of Florida
5007 60th Street, East
P.O. Box 2125
Brandenton, FL 33505

Potato Investigation Laboratory
Box 728
Hastings, FL 32045

Ridge Ornamental Horticultural Laboratory
Route 1, Box 980
Apopka, FL 37203

Sub-Tropical Experiment Station
IFAS, University of Florida
18905 S.W. 280th Street
Homestead, FL 33030

Subtropical Horticulture Research Station
13601 Old Cutler Road
Miami, FL 33158
Dr. R. J. Knight, Jr.
305-235-2533

U.S. Horticultural Field Laboratory
2120 Camden Road
Orlando, FL 32803

U.S. Plant Introduction Station
13601 Old Cutler Road
Miami, FL 33158

University of Florida Agricultural Experiment Sta.
Plantation Field Laboratory
3205 S.W. 70th Avenue
Fort Lauderdale, FL 33134

GEORGIA

Americus Plant Materials Center
University of Georgeia
Box 688
Americus, GA 31709

Georgia Agricultural Experiment Station
University of Georgia
Athens, GA 30601

Georgia Agricultural Experiment Station
University of Georgia
Experiment, GA 30212

Georgia Coastal Plain Experiment Station
University of Georgia
Tifton, GA 31794

Georgia Mountain Branch Experiment Station
University of Georgia
Blairsville, GA 30512

Southwest Georgia Branch Experiment Station
University of Georgia
Plains, GA 31780

U.S. Plant Introduction Station
Route 4, Box 433
Savannah, GA 31405

HAWAII

Hawaii Agricultural Experiment Station
College of Tropical Agric.
University of Hawaii
Honolulu, HI 96822

Hawaii Branch Station
HAES-University of Hawaii
Hilo, HI 96720

Kauai Branch Station
HAES-University of Hawaii
Kapaa, Kauai, HI 96746

Kona Branch Station
HAES-University of Hawaii
Kealakekua, Kona, HI 96750

Maui Branch Station
HAES-University of Hawaii
Kula, Maui, HI 96790

IOWA

Agricultural Experiment Station
Iowa State University
Plant Materials Investigations
Ames, IA 50010

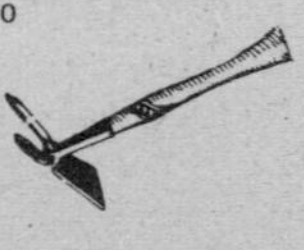

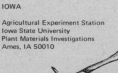

Iowa Agricultural Experiment Station
Iowa State University
Department of Horticulture
Ames, IA 50010

IDAHO

Idaho Agricultural Experiment Station
University of Idaho
Moscow, ID 83843

Idaho Branch Experiment Station
University of Idaho
Parma, ID 83660

Idaho Branch Experiment Station
University of Idaho
Aberdeen, ID 83210

ILLINOIS

Illinois Agricultural Experiment Station
University of Illinois
Urbana, IL 61801

Small Fruit and Grape Investigations
Southern Illinois University
Plant Industries Department
Carbondale, IL 62903

U.S.D.A.-ARS
North Central Region
2000 West Pioneer Parkway
Peoria, IL 61614
Earl Glover, Deputy Admin.
309-673-9577

INDIANA

Agric. Research Service, USDA
Location Leader
2336 Northwestern Avenue
West Lafayette, IN 47906
Paul Fitzgerald
317-463-4413

Feldun Purdue Agricultural Center
Purdue University
RR2
Bedford, IN 47421

Purdue University Agricultural Experiment Station
Purdue University
Lafayette, IN 47907

KANSAS

Garden City Experiment Station
Kansas State University
Box L
Garden City, KS 67846

Kansas Agricultural Experiment Station
Kansas State University
Manhattan, KS 66502

Northeast Kansas Experimental Fields
Kansas State University
Wathena, KS 66090

Southeast Kansas Branch Experiment Station
Kansas State University
Mound Valley, KS 67354

Southeast Kansas Exp. Field
Dept. of Hort. and Forestry
Kansas State University
Box 245
Chetopa, KS 67336

Tribune Branch Experiment Station
Kansas State University
P.O. Box 307
Tribune, KS 67869

KENTUCKY

Kentucky Agricultural Experiment Station
University of Kentucky
Lexington, KY 40506

Robinson Substation
University of Kentucky
Quicksand, KY 41363

Univ. of Kentucky Research and Extension Center
Princeton, KY 42445

LOUISIANA

ARS Southern Regional Office
701 Loyola Avenue
P.O. Box 53326
New Orleans, LA 70153
Arthur Cooper, Deputy Admin.
504-527-6753

Fruit and Truck Experiment Station
Louisiana State University
Route 2, Box 71
Hammond, LA 70401

Louisiana Agricultural Experiment Station
Louisiana State University
Baton Rouge, LA 70803

North Louisiana Experiment Station
Louisiana State University
Calhoun, LA 71225

Plaquemines Parish Experiment Station
Louisiana State University
Route 1, Box 437
Port Sulphur, LA 70083

U.S. Field Laboratory for Tung Investigation
Bogalusa, LA 70427

U.S. Pecan Field Laboratory
Route 1, Box 223
Shreveport, LA 71105

MASSACHUSETTS

Cranberry Station
University of Massachusetts
East Wareham, MA 02538

Massachusetts Agricultural Experiment Station
University of Massachusetts
Amherst, MA 01002

Waltham Field Station
University of Massachusetts
240 Beaver Street
Waltham, MA 02154

MARYLAND

Agricultural Environmental Quality Institue-Chmn.
Beltsville Agr. Res. Ctr.
Beltsville, MD 20705
Loran Danielson, Plant Physiol.
301-344-3030

ARS/IPD
Federal Center Bldg. 1
Hyattsville, MD 20782
Martin Weiss, Acting Director
301-436-8307

ARS/IPD
Federal Center Bldg. 1
Hyattsville, MD 20782

ARS Plant Science Research Div.
U.S. Plant Introduction Sta.
Box 88
Glenn Dale, MD 20769

Director's Office
Beltsville Area
Beltsville Research Center
Beltsville, MD 20705
Angus Hanson, Dir. Belts., MD Res.
301-344-3078

Chesapeake & Potomac Area
Office of Director
6505 Belcrest Road
Hyattsville, MD 20782
Raymond Hoecker, Agrl. Admr.
301-436-8615

Deputy Administrator Office
Northeast Region Area
Beltsville Agr. Res. Ctr.
Beltsville, MD 20705
Steven King, Dep. Adm. NE Reg.
301-344-3418

Fruit Laboratory
P.G.G.I. Inst.-USDA-ARS
Beltsville Research Center
Beltsville, MD 20705
Miklos Faust, Plant Physiol.
301-344-3567

Germplasm Resources Laboratory
P.G.G.I. Inst.-USDA-ARS
Beltsville Research Center
Beltsville, MD 20705
George White, Res. Agron.
301-344-3637

Maryland Agricultural Experiment Station
University of Maryland
College Park, MD 20742

Medicinal Plant Resources
P.G.G.I. Inst.-USDA-ARS
Beltsville Research Center
Beltsville, MD 20705
Robert Perdue, Jr., Botanist
301-344-2532

National Program Staff
Plant & Entom. Sciences
USDA-ARC-West, North Bldg.
Beltsville, MD 20705
Quentin Jones, Staff Scientist
301-344-3930

National Program Staff
Plant & Entom. Sciences
USDA-ARC-West, North Bldg.
Beltsville, MD 20705
August Kehr, Staff Scientist
301-344-3903
Warren Shaw, Staff Scientist
301-344-3301
Howard Brooks, Staff Scientist
301-344-3912

Ornamentals Laboratory-USDA
P.G.G.I. Inst.-ARS
Beltsville Research Center
Beltsville, MD 20705
Henry Cathey, Res. Hort.
301-344-3570

Plant and Entomology Sciences
USDA-ARC-West, North Bldg.
Beltsville, MD 20705
William Ennis, Jr.

Plant Genetics and Germplasm Inst.-USDA
Office of Chairman-ARS
Beltsville Research Center
Beltsville, MD 20705
John Moseman, Res. Plant Path.
301-344-3235

Plant Physiol. Inst. USDA
Plant Physiol. Chairman
Beltsville Research Center
Beltsville, MD 20705
Harry Carns, Plant Physiol. Chr.
301-344-3036

Plant Protection Inst.
Office of Chairman
Beltsville Research Center
Beltsville, MD 20705
Jack Meiners, Chairman
301-344-3660

Plant Taxonomy Laboratory-USDA
P.G.G.I. Inst.-ARS
Beltsville Research Center
Beltsville, MD 20705
James Duke, Supvry. Btnst.
301-344-3319

Turfgrass Laboratory-USDA
P.G.G.I. Inst.-ARS
Beltsville Research Center
Beltsville, MD 20705
Dayton Klingman, Res. Agron.
301-344-3642

USDA Plant Industry Station
Plant Science Research Div.
Beltsville, MD 20705

Vegetable Laboratory-USDA
P.G.G.I. Inst.-ARS
Beltsville Research Center
Beltsville, MD 20705
Raymon Webb, Res. Plant Path.
301-344-3380

Vegetable Research Farm
University of Maryland
Route 5
Salisbury, MD 20861

MAINE

Blueberry Hill Exper. Farm
Maine Agricultural Exper. Sta.
Addison, ME 04606

Maine Agricultural Experiment Station
Highmoor Farm
Monmouth, ME 04259

Maine Agricultural Experiment Station
University of Maine
Orono, ME 04473

Maine Agricultural Experiment Station
Aroostook Experimental Farm
Presque Isle, ME 04769

MICHIGAN

Graham Horticultural Experiment Station
2989 Lake Michigan Drive, N.W.
Grand Rapids, MI 49501

Michigan Agricultural Experiment Station
Michigan State University
East Lansing, MI 48823

South Haven Horticultural Experiment Station
South Haven, MI 49090

Upper Peninsula Experiment Station
Michigan State University
Chatham, MI 49816

W.K. Kellogg Forest
Michigan State University
Route 1
Augusta, MI 49012

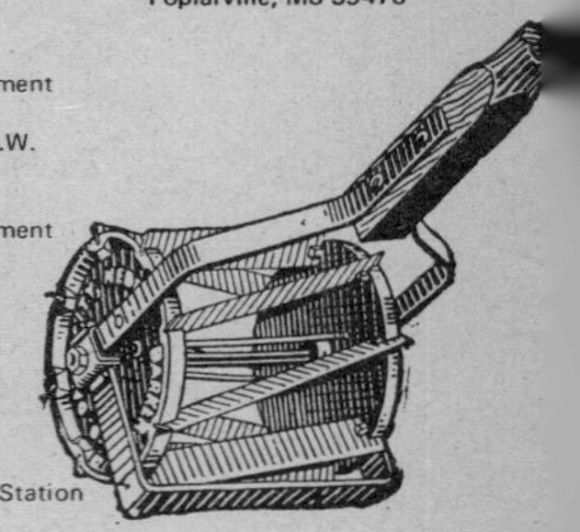

MINNESOTA

Minnesota Agricultural Experiment Station
University of Minnesota
St. Paul, MN 55101

Northwest Experiment Station
University of Michigan
Crookston, MN 56716

Northwest Experiment Station
University of Michigan
Crookston, MN 56716

Soil Science Building
University of Minnesota
St. Paul, MN 55101
C. Van Doren, Area Director
612-725-2974

West Central Experiment Station
University of Minnesota
Morris, MN 56267

MISSOURI

Agric. Research Service, USDA
Area Director
800 North Providence Road
Columbia, MO 65201
Loyd A. Tatum
314-442-3256

Missouri Agricultural Experiment Station
University of Missouri
Columbia, MO 65201

MISSISSIPPI

Coastal Plain Branch Station
Mississippi State University
Newton, MS 39345

Delta Branch Station
Mississippi State University
Stoneville, MS 38776

Mississippi Agricultural Experiment Station
Mississippi State University
State College, MS 39762

North Mississippi Branch Experiment Station
Mississippi State University
Holly Springs, MS 38635

Pontotoc Ridge-Flatwoods Branch Experiment Station
Mississippi State University
Pontotoc, MS 38863

South Mississippi Branch Station
Mississippi State University
Poplarville, MS 39470

Truck Crops Branch Station
Mississippi State Univ.
Crystal Springs, MS 39059

USDA Tung Research Laboratory
Box 287
Poplarville, MS 39470

MEN'S GARDEN CLUBS OF AMERICA

MONTANA

Central Montana Branch Station
Montana State University
Moccasin, MT 59462

Eastern Montana Station
Montana State University
Sidney, MT 59270

Huntley Branch Station
Montana State University
Huntley, MT 59037

Montana Agricultural Experiment
Station
Montana State University
Bozeman, MT 59715

North Montana Branch Station
Montana State University
Havre, MT 59501

Northwestern Montana
Branch Station
Montana State University
Kalispell, MT 59901

Western Montana Branch
Station
Montana State University
Corvallis, MT 59828

NEBRASKA

Nebraska Agricultural Experiment
Station
University of Nebraska
Lincoln, NE 68503

North Central Region
Kansas-Nebraska Area
P.O. Box 166
Clay Center, NE 68933
Dr. Keith E. Gregory, Area Dir.
402-762-3241

North Platte Station
University of Nebraska
Route 4
North Platte, NE 69101

Scottsbluff Station
University of Nebraska
Mitchell, NE 69357

NEW HAMPSHIRE

New Hampshire Agricultural
Experiment Station
University of New Hampshire
Durham, NH 03824

NEW JERSEY

Cranberry and Blueberry
Research Laboratory
Rutgers-The State University
New Lisbon, NJ 08064

New Jersey Agricultural Experiment
Station
Rutgers-The State University
New Brunswick, NJ 08903

NEW MEXICO

Middle Rio Grande Branch Station
New Mexico State University
Route 1, Box 28
Los Lunas, NM 87031

New Mexico Agricultural Experiment
Station
New Mexico State University
Las Cruces, NM 88001

San Juan Branch Station
New Mexico State University
Box 1018
Farmington, NM 87401

NEVADA

Nevada Agricultural Experiment
Station
University of Nevada
Reno, NV 89507

Southern Nevada Field Laboratory
University of Nevada
Logandale, NV 89021

NEW YORK

Agricultural Experiment Sta. of
Cornell University
Cornell University
Ithaca, NY 14850

Cornell Ornamentals Research
Laboratory
Melville Road
Farmingdale, NY 11735

Cornell University
Tower Road
Plant Soil & Nutrition Lab.
Ithaca, NY 14850
John T. Holstun, Jr., Agr. Admr.
607-272-5585

Cornell University Branch
Experiment Station
Riverhead, NY 11901

Grape Research Laboratory
New York State Agricultural
Experiment Station
Fredonia, NY 14063

New York State Agricultural
Experiment Station
USDA New Crops Research Br.
Plant Materials Investigation
Geneva, NY 14456

New York State Agricultural
Experiment Station
Geneva, NY 14456

New York State Agricultural
Experiment Station
Hudson Valley Laboratory
Highland, NY 12528

NORTH CAROLINA

Coastal Plain Vegetable
Research Station
Route 5, Box 43
Clinton, NC 28238

Horticulture Crops Research
Station
P.O. Box 397
Castle Hayne, NC 28429

Mountain Horticulture Crops
Research Station
RFD 2, Box 250
Fletcher, NC 28732

North Carolina Agricultural
Experiment Station
North Carolina State Univ.
Raleigh, NC 27607

Piedmont Research Station
Route 6, Box 420
Salisbury, NC 28144

Sandhills Research Station
Route 1
Jackson Springs, NC 27281

Tidewater Research Station
Route 2, Box 106
Plymouth, NC 27962

NORTH DAKOTA

ARS-USDA-Area Office
P.O. Box 5033
State University Station
Fargo, ND 58102
Claude H. Schmidt, Area Dir.
701-237-5351

Carrington Irrigation Station
Box 95
Carrington, ND 58421

North Dakota Agricultural Experiment
Station
North Dakota State Univ.
Fargo, ND 58102

OHIO

Agricultural Research and
Development Center
Ohio State University
Northwestern Branch RD 1
Custar, OH 43511

Muck Crops Branch Station
Ohio State University
Willard, OH 44890

Ohio Agricultural Experiment Station
Ohio State University
Columbus, OH 43210

Ohio Agricultural Research and
Development Center
Southern Branch
RD 1, Box 101
Ripley, OH 45167

Ohio Agricultural Research and
Development Center
Wooster, OH 44691

Shade Tree and Ornamental
Plants Laboratory
USDA-ARS Plant Science Research
Division
Box 365
Delaware, OH 43015

PUERTO RICO

Adjuntas Substation
University of Puerto Rico
Agricultural Experiment Sta.
Box 61
Castaner, PR 00631

Agricultural Experiment Station
University of Puerto Rico
Mayaguez Campus
Box H
Rio Piedras, PR 00928

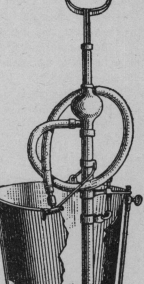

Vegetable Crops Branch Station
Ohio State University
Marietta, OH 45750

OKLAHOMA

Eastern Oklahoma Field Station
Route 2
Westville, OK 74965

Pecan Research Station
Oklahoma State University
Sparks, OK 74869

Vegetable Research Station
Oklahoma State University
Bixby, OK 74008

OREGON

Malheur Experiment Station
Oregon State University
Route 1, Box 302
Ontario, OR 97914

Mid-Columbia Experiment Station
Oregon State University
Route 4, Box 176
Hood River, OR 97031

North Willamette Experiment Station
Oregon State University
Aurora, OR 97002

Oregon Agricultural Experiment
Station
Oregon State University
Corvallis, OR 97331

Oregon State University
Cordley Hall
Corvallis, OR 97331

Oregon State University
Cordley Hall
Corvallis, OR 97720
Dr. R. Converse, Res. Leader
503-754-1507

Pacific Bulb Growers Research and
Development Station
Oregon State University Cooperating
Harbor, OR 97415

Pendleton Experiment Station
Oregon State University
Pendleton, OR 97801

Southern Oregon Experiment Station
Oregon State University
569 Hanley Road
Medford, OR 97501

PENNSYLVANIA

Agricultural Experiment Station
Fruit Research Laboratory
Pennsylvania State University
Arendtsville, PA 17303

Agricultural Experiment Station
Erie County Field Res. Lab.
Pennsylvania State University
Cemetery Road
North East, PA 16428

Eastern Reg. Research Center
Office of Director-USDA
Philadelphia, PA 19118
Ivan A. Wolff, Director
215-247-5242

Pennsylvania Agricultural Experiment
Station
Pennsylvania State University
University Park, PA 16802

Middle Tennessee Experiment
Station
University of Tennessee
Box 160
Spring Hill, TN 37174

Plateau Experiment Station
University of Tennessee
Route 9
Crossville, TN 38555

Tennessee Agricultural Experiment
Station
University of Tennessee
Knoxville, TN 37901

UT-AEC Agricultural Research
Laboratory
1299 Bethel Valley Road
Oak Ridge, TN 37830

West Tennessee Experiment
Station
University of Tennessee
605 Airways Boulevard
Jackson, TN 38301

TEXAS

Agricultural Research and
Extension Center
Texas A&M University
RFD 3
Lubbock, TX 79401

Lajas Substation
University of Puerto Rico
Agricultural Experiment Sta.
Lajas, PR 00667

RHODE ISLAND

Rhode Island Agricultural
Experiment Station
University of Rhode Island
Kingston, RI 02881

SOUTH CAROLINA

Edisto Experiment Station
P.O. Box C 247
Blackville, SC 29817

Pee Dee Experiment Station
Clemson University
Box 271
Florence, SC 29501

Sandhill Experiment Station
Box 1771
Columbia, SC 29202

South Carolina Agricultural
Experiment Station
Clemson University
Clemson, SC 29631

Truck Experiment Station
Clemson University
Box 3158, St. Andrews
Charleston, SC 29407

U.S. Vegetable Breeding Lab.
USDA-ARS Plant Science
Research Div.
Box 3348
Charleston, SC 29407

SOUTH DAKOTA

South Dakota Agricultural
Experiment Station
South Dakota State University
Brookings, SD 57006

TENNESSEE

Ames Plantation
University of Tennessee
Grand Junction, TN 38039

Highland Rim Experiment Station
University of Tennessee
R.R. 6
Springfield, TN 37172

Fruit Research-Demonstration
Station
Texas A&M University
Montague, TX 76251

Rio Grande Soil and Water
Research Center
Box 267
Weslaco, TX 78596

Texas Agricultural Experiment
Station
Texas A&M University
College Station, TX 77843

U.S. Pecan Field Station
USDA-ARS
Box 579
Brownwood, TX 76801

UTAH

Brigham Young University
Provo, UT 84601

Farmington Field Station
Utah State University
1817 North Main
Farmington, UT 84025

University of Utah
Department of Botany
Salt Lake City, UT 84112

Utah Agricultural Experiment
Station
Utah State University
Logan, UT 84321

Utah Experiment Station
Howell Field Station
530 West Elberta Drive
Ogden, UT 84404

VIRGINIA

Piedmont Research Laboratory
Virginia Polytechnic Inst.
Charlottesville, VA 22903

Virginia Agricultural Experiment
Station
Virginia Polytechnic Inst.
Blacksburg, VA 24061

Virginia Truck and Ornamentals
Research Station
Virginia Polytechnic Institute
P.O. Box 2160
Norfolk, VA 23501

VERMONT

Vermont Agricultural Experiment
Station
University of Vermont
Burlington, VT 05401

WASHINGTON

Coastal Washington Research and
Extension Unit
Washington State University
Route 1, Box 570
Long Beach, WA 98631

Irrigated Agriculture Research and
Extension Center
Washington State University
Prosser, WA 99350

Northwestern Washington
Research & Extension Unit
Washington State University
1468 Memorial Highway
Mt. Vernon, WA 98273

Plant Materials Investigations
Agricultural Experiment Station
Washington State Univ. Campus
Pullman, WA 99163

Southwestern Washington
Research Unit
Washington State Univ.
Vancouver, WA 98665

Tree Fruit Research Center
Washington State Univ.
1100 North Western Ave.
Wenatchee, WA 98801

USDA-ARS
Yakima & Mission Streets
Wenatchee, WA 98801
Max Williams, Research Leader
509-663-8317

Hancock Experimental Farm
College of Agricultural and
Life Sciences
University of Wisconsin
Hancock, WI 54943

Peninsular Branch Experiment
Station
University of Wisconsin
Sturgeon Bay, WI 54235

University of Wisconsin Experiment
Station
Rural Route 2
Marshfield, WI 54449

University of Wisconsin Experimental
Farm
Ashland, WI 54806

University of Wisconsin Experimental
Farm
RFD 1, Box 81
Lancaster, WI 53813

Wisconsin Agricultural Experiment
Station
University of Wisconsin
Madison, WI 53813

WEST VIRGINIA

Ohio Valley Experiment Station
West Virginia University
Route 1, Box 113
Pt. Pleasant, WV 25550

West Virginia Agricultural
Experiment Station
West Virginia University
Morgantown, WV 26506

West Virginia University
Experiment Farm
State Route 9
Kearneysville, WV 25430

WYOMING

Cheyenne Hort. Field Station
USDA-ARS Plant Science
Research Division
Box 1087
Cheyenne, WY 82001

Wyoming Agricultural Experiment
Station
University of Wyoming
Laramie, WY 82070

CANADA

Alberta Horticultural Research
Center
Alberta Department of Agric.
Brooks, Alberta, Canada

Washington Agricultural Experiment
Station
Washington State University
Pullman, WA 99163
2 4 5 6

Western Washington Research
and Extension Center
West Pioneer
Puyallup, WA 98371

WISCONSIN

Emmons Blaine Jr. Experimental Farm
RFD 1
Lake Mills, WI 53551

VICTORY DRYING, 1918

HOME DRYING MANUAL

Drying vegetables and fruits for winter use is one of the vital national needs. As a national need it becomes a patriotic duty. As a patriotic duty it should be done in every family.

Failure to prepare vegetables and fruits for winter use by drying is one of the worst examples of American extravagance. During the summer nature provides an over-abundance. This year, with the planting of 5,285,000 home food gardens, stimulated by the National War Garden Commission and the United States Department of Agriculture, this abundance will be especially large. The excess supply is not meant to go to waste. The over-abundance of the summer should be made the normal supply of the winter. The individual family should conduct Drying on a liberal scale. In no other way can there be assurance that America's food supply will meet our own needs. In no other way, surely, can we answer the enormous demands made upon us for furnishing food for our European Allies.

Fig. 1. Carrots cut lengthwise.

IMPORTANCE OF FOOD THRIFT

Winter buying of vegetables and fruits is costly. It means that you pay transportation, cold-storage and commission merchants' charges and profits. Summer is the time of lowest prices. Summer, therefore, is the time to buy for winter use.

Every pound of food products grown this year will be needed to combat Food Famine. The loss that can be prevented, the money saving that can be effected and the transportation relief that can be brought about make it essential that every American household should make vegetable and fruit Drying a part of its program of Food Thrift. The results can be gained in no other way.

Vegetable and fruit Drying have been little practiced for a generation or more. Its revival on a general scale is the purpose of this Manual. There is no desire to detract from the importance of canning operations. Drying must not be regarded as taking the place of the preservation of vegetables and fruits in tins and glass jars. It must be viewed as an important adjunct thereto. Drying is important and economical in every home, whether on the farm, in the village, in the town, or in the city. For city dwellers it has the special advantage that little storage space is required for the dried product. One hundred pounds of some fresh vegetables will reduce to 10 pounds in drying without loss of food value or much of the flavor.

This year's need for vegetable and fruit Drying is given added emphasis by the shortage of tin for the manufacture of cans. This condition has created an unusual demand for glass jars. For this year, therefore, Drying is of more than normal importance. Dried products can be stored in receptacles that could not be used for canning. This is excellent conservation.

DRYING IS SIMPLE

A strong point in connection with vegetable and fruit Drying is the ease with which it may be done. The process is simple. The cost is slight. In every home the necessary outfit, in its simplest form, is already at hand. Effective Drying may be done on plates or dishes placed in the oven, with the over door partially open. It may be done on the back of the kitchen stove, with these same utensils, while the oven is being used for baking. It may also be done on sheets of paper or lengths of muslin spread in the sun and protected from insects and dust.

Apparatus for home Drying on a larger scale may be made at home or bought at small cost. Still larger equipment may be bought for community drying operations in which a group of families combine for cooperative work, at a school or other convenient center. This latter is especially recommended as giving the use of the most improved outfits at slight cost to the individual family.

Best results are obtained by rapid drying, but care must be taken not to let the temperature rise above the limit specified in the directions and table.

One of the chief essentials in Drying is free circulation of air, in order that the moist air may escape and dry air take its place.

Fig. 2. Potatoes prepared by use of meat chopper.

METHODS OF DRYING

For home Drying satisfactory results are obtained by any one of three principal methods. These are:

1. Sun Drying.
2. Drying by Artificial Heat.
3. Drying by Air-blast. (With an electric or other motor fan.)

These methods may be combined to good advantage.

SUN DRYING

Sun Drying has the double advantage of requiring no expense for fuel and of freedom from danger of overheating. For sun Drying of vegetables and fruits the simplest form is to spread the slices or pieces on sheets of plain paper or lengths of muslin nailed to strips of wood and expose them to the sun. Muslin is to be preferred if there is danger of sticking. Trays should be used for large quantities. Sun Drying requires bright, hot days and a breeze. Once or twice a day the product should be turned or stirred and the dry pieces taken out. The drying product should be covered with cheesecloth tacked to a frame for protection from rain, dew and moths. During rains and just before sunset the products should be taken indoors for protection.

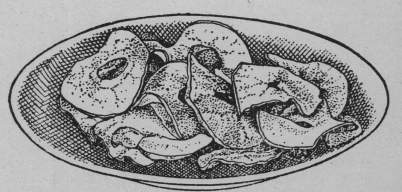

Fig. 3. Apples peeled and sliced for drying.

TRAYS FOR SUN DRYING

To make a tray cheaply for use in sun drying, take strips of lumber three-quarters of an inch thick and 2 inches wide for the sides and ends. To form the bottom, laths should be nailed to these strips, with spaces of one-eighth of an inch between laths to permit air circulation. A length of 4 feet, corresponding to the standard lengths of laths, is economical. Nail 3 strips across the bottom in the opposite direction from the laths to prevent warping and to allow space when the trays are stacked. The trays should be of uniform size in order

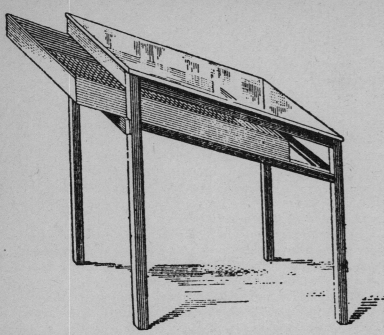

FIG. 4. Small outdoor drier, easily made at home. It has glass top, sloping for exposure to sun. Tray is shown partly projecting, to indicate construction.

that they may be stacked together for convenience in handling. Never put trays directly on the ground. They should rest on supports a few feet above the ground and should face the south or southwest so as to receive the sun's rays the longest possible time.

A small homemade Sun Drier, easily constructed (Fig. 4), is made of light strips of wood, a sheet of glass, a small amount of galvanized wire screen and some cheesecloth. A convenient size for the glass top is 18 by 24 inches. To hold the glass make a light wooden frame of strips of wood ½ inch thick and 1 inch wide. This frame should have legs of material 1 by 1½ inches, with a length of 12 inches for the front legs and 18 inches for those in the rear. This will cause the top to slope, which aids in circulation of air and gives direct exposure to the rays of the sun. As a tray support, nail a strip of wood to the legs on each of the four sides, about 4 inches below the top framework and sloping parallel with the top. The tray is made of thin strips of wood about 2 inches wide and has a galvanized wire screen bottom. There will be a space of about 2 inches between the top edges of the tray and the glass top of the Drier, to allow for circulation. Protect both sides, the bottom and the front end of the Drier with cheesecloth tacked on securely and snugly, to exclude insects and dust without interfering with circulation. At the rear end place a cheesecloth curtain tacked at the top but swinging free below, to allow the tray to be moved in and out. Brace the bottom of this curtain with a thin strip of wood, as is done in window shades. This curtain is to be fastened to the legs by buttons when the tray is in place.

DRYING BY ARTIFICIAL HEAT

Drying by artificial heat is done in the oven or on top of a cook-stove or range, in trays suspended over the stove or in a specially constructed drier built at home or purchased.

When drying with artificial heat a thermometer must be used. This should be placed in the drier and frequently observed.

OVEN DRYING

The simplest form of Oven Drying is to place small quantities of foodstuffs on plates in a slow oven. In this way leftovers and other bits of food may be saved for winter use with slight trouble and dried while the top of the stove is being used. This is especially effective for sweet corn. A few sweet potatoes, apples or peas, or even a single turnip, may be dried and saved. To keep the heat from being too great leave the oven door partially open. For oven use a simple tray may be made of galvanized wire screen of convenient size, with the edges bent up for an inch or two on each side. At each corner this tray should have a leg an inch or two in length, to hold it up from the bottom of the oven and permit circulation of air around the product.

An oven drier which can be bought at a low price is shown in Fig. 5.

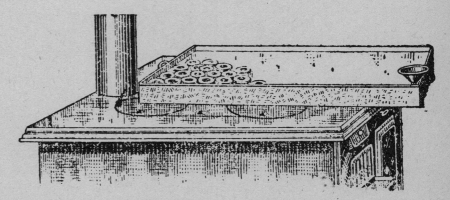

FIG. 6. Commercial drier which may be placed on top of cookstove or suspended over a lamp.

DRYING ON TOP OF OR OVER STOVE

An effective Drier for use over a stove or range may be made easily at home. Such a Drier is shown in Fig. 9. For the frame use strips of wood ½-inch thick and 2 inches wide. The trays or shelves are made of galvanized wire screen of small mesh tacked to the supports; or separate trays, sliding on strips attached to the framework, are desirable. This Drier may be suspended from the ceiling over the kitchen stove or range, or over an oil, gasoline, or gas stove, and it may be used while cooking is being done. If an oil stove is used there must be a tin or galvanized iron bottom 4 inches below the lowest tray, to prevent the fumes of the oil from reaching and passing through the material which is to be dried, and to distribute the heat. A bottom of this kind may be easily attached to any Drier, either

FIG. 5. Commercial drier for use in oven.

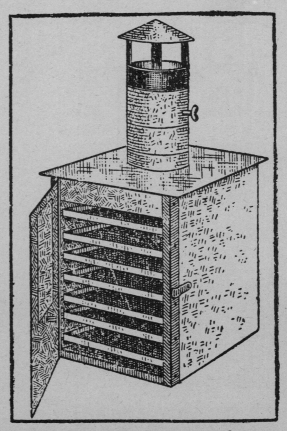

FIG. 7. Commercial drier for use on stove.

FIG. 8. Home-made drier of galvanized iron, for use on stove.

home-made or commercial. A framework crane as shown in Fig. 9 makes it possible for this Drier to be swung aside when not in use.

In Fig. 8 is shown another form of Home-made Cookstove Drier, more pretentious than that shown in Fig. 9, but still easily and cheaply made. A good size for this is: base, 16 by 24 inches; height, 36 inches. The lower part or supporting framework, 6 inches high, is made of galvanized sheet iron, slightly flaring toward the bottom, and with two ventilating holes in each of the four sides. The frame, which rests on this base, is made of strips of wood 1 or 1½ inches wide. Wooden strips, 1¼ inches wide, and 3 inches apart, serve to brace the sides and furnish supports for the trays.

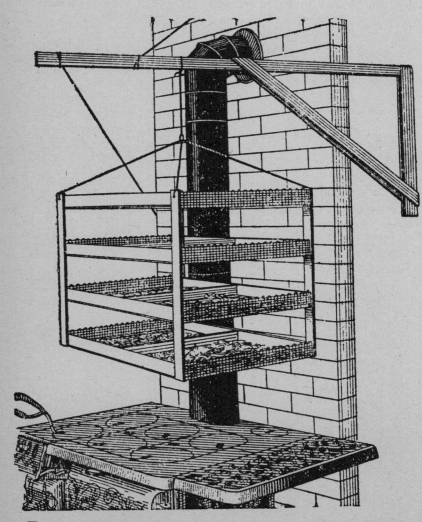

FIG. 9. Home-made drier with swinging crane.

In a Drier of the dimensions given there is room for eight trays. The sides, top and back are of galvanized iron or tin sheets, tacked to the framework, although thin strips of wood may be used instead of metal. Small hinges and thumb-latch are provided for the door. Galvanized sheet iron, with numerous small holes in it, is used for making the bottom of the Drier. To prevent direct heat from coming in contact with the product, and also to distribute the heat by radiation, a piece of galvanized sheet iron is placed 2 inches above the bottom. This piece is 3 inches shorter and 3 inches narrower than the bottom and rests on two wires fastened to the sides.

The trays are made of wooden frames of 1-inch strips, to which is tacked galvanized wire screen. Each tray should be 3 inches shorter than the Drier and enough narrower to allow it to slide easily on the supports in being put in or taken out.

In placing the trays in the Drier push the lower one back as far as it will go, leaving a 3-inch space in front. Place the next tray even with the front, leaving the space at the back. Alternate all the trays in this way, to facilitate the circulation of the heated air. It is well to have a ventilating opening, 6 by 2 inches, in the top of the Drier to discharge moisture. The trays should be shifted during the drying process, to procure uniformity of drying.

One of the simplest forms of homemade Drier is a tray with bottom of galvanized wire screen, suspended over stove or range, as shown in Fig. 12.

FIG. 10. Commercial drier.

COMMERCIAL DRIERS

Cookstove Driers are in the market in several types. One of these, shown in Fig. 7, has a series of trays in a framework, forming a compartment. This is placed on top of the stove. A similar drier is shown in Fig. 10. Another, shown in Fig. 6, is a shallow metal box to be filled with water, and so constructed that one end may rest on the back of the stove and the other on a prop reaching to the floor, or it may be suspended over a lamp.

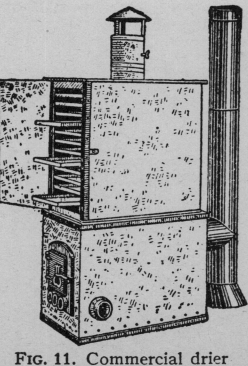

FIG. 11. Commercial drier with furnace.

Commercial Driers having their own furnaces may be bought at prices ranging from $24 to $120. This type is pictured in Fig. 11. Some of these, in the smaller sizes, may be bought without furnaces, and used on the top of the kitchen stove, as Fig. 7. The cost is from $16 upwards.

AIR-BLAST—ELECTRIC FAN

The use of an electric fan is an effective means of Drying. Fig. 15 shows how this household article is used. A motor fan run by kerosene or alcohol serves the same purpose. Sliced vegetables or fruits are placed on trays and the fan placed close to one end of the box holding the trays, with the current directed along the trays, lengthwise. Insects must be kept out by the use of cheesecloth or similar material. Drying by this process may be done in twenty-four hours or less. With sliced string beans and shredded sweet potatoes a few hours are sufficient, if the air is dry. Rearrange the trays after a few hours, as the drying will be more rapid nearest the fan.

As artificial heat is not used in fan drying it is important to blanch or steam the vegetables for the full specified time. It is also necessary that all fan-dried products be heated in an oven to 180 degrees F. for 10 or 15 minutes before storing.

FIG. 14. Motor-fan, run by kerosene or alcohol.

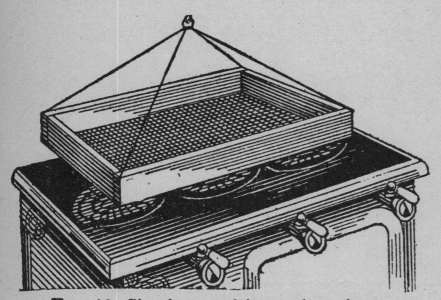

FIG. 12. Simple tray drier made at home.

DETAILS OF DRYING

As a general rule vegetables or fruits, for Drying, must be cut into slices or shreds, with the skin removed. In using artificial heat be careful to start at a comparatively low temperature and gradually increase. To be able to gauge the heat accurately a thermometer must be used. An oven thermometer may be bought at slight cost. If the thermometer is placed in a glass of salad oil the true temperature of the oven may be obtained.

The actual time required for Drying cannot be given, and the person in charge must exercise judgment on this point. A little experience will make it easy to determine when products are sufficiently dried. When first taken from the Drier vegetables should be rather brittle, and fruits rather leathery and pliable. One method of determining whether fruit is dry enough is to squeeze a handful, if the fruit separates when the hand is opened, it is dry enough. Another way is to press a single piece; if no moisture comes to the surface the piece is sufficiently dry. Berries are dry enough if they stick to the hand but do not crush when squeezed.

PREPARING MATERIAL FOR DRYING

A sharp kitchen knife will serve every purpose in slicing and cutting vegetables and fruits for Drying if no other device is at hand. The thickness of the slices should be from an eighth to a quarter of an inch. Whether sliced or cut into strips the pieces should be small so as to dry quickly. They should not, however, be so small as to make them hard to handle or to keep them from being used to advantage in preparing dishes for the table such as would be prepared from fresh products.

Food choppers, crout slicers or rotary slicers may be used to prepare food for drying.

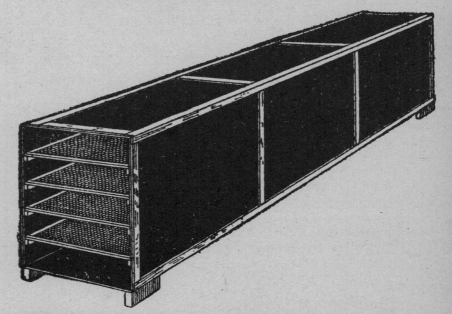

FIG. 15. Series of trays enclosed in wall-board box, for use with electric fan.

Vegetables and fruits for Drying should be fresh, mature and in prime condition for eating. As a general rule vegetables will dry better if cut into small pieces with the skins removed. Berries are dried whole. Apples, quinces, peaches and pears dry better if cut into rings or quarters. Cleanliness is imperative. Knives and slicing devices must be carefully cleansed before and after use. A knife that is not bright and clean will discolor the product on which it is used and this should be avoided.

FIG. 13. Electric range, useful for drying.

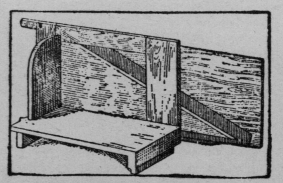

FIG. 16. Crout slicer.

BLANCHING

Blanching is desirable for successful vegetable Drying. Blanching gives more thorough cleansing, removes objectionable odors and flavors, kills protoplasm and softens and loosens the fiber, allowing quicker and more uniform evaporation of the moisture, stops destructive chemical changes, and gives better color. It is done by placing the vegetables in a piece of cheesecloth, a wire basket or other porous container and plunging them into boiling water. A more desirable way is to blanch in steam. For small quantities a pail or deep kettle is serviceable. A false bottom raised an inch or more is necessary. Upon this rests a wire basket or cheesecloth filled with the prepared vegetables. The water should be just below the false bottom and be boiling vigorously when the products are put in. Cover with a tight-fitting cover. Keep the water boiling during the blanching period. For larger quantities a wash-boiler partially filled with water is convenient. Bricks set on end or a wooden frame raised a few inches above the water make good supports for the containers.

After blanching, drain to remove moisture and arrange on trays.

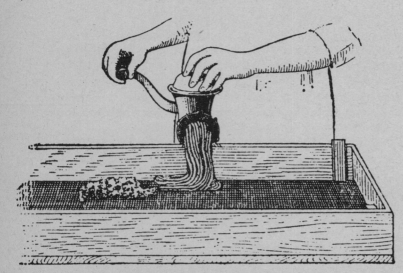

FIG. 17. Meat chopper for preparing vegetables.

DANGER FROM INSECTS

In addition to exercising great care to protect vegetables and fruits from insects during the Drying process, precautions should be taken with the finished product to prevent the hatching of eggs that may have been deposited. One measure that is useful is to subject the dried material to a heat of 180 degrees F. for from 5 to 10 minutes. By the application of this heat the eggs will be killed. Be careful not to apply heat long enough to damage the product. Store as soon as removed from the oven.

"CONDITION" BEFORE STORING

The word "conditioning" as used in connection with drying vegetables and fruits simply means "thorough drying." It indicates the after treatment of products on their removal from the drying trays.

Put the dried products in bins, boxes, or, if the quantity is small, in bowls. Once a day for a period of ten days to two weeks, stir thoroughly or pour from one box to another. The containers should be in a clean, dry room, and protected from light and insects. Shutters and screens at the window are desirable. Otherwise protect the dried food by spreading clean cloths over it. If any part of the material is found to be moist, after this process, return it to the drier for a short time. When for several days no change in the moisture content has been noticed, and therefore no extra drying has been necessary, the products are ready to be stored.

Properly conditioned products can be stored without danger of spoiling, because spores and fungi cannot begin growth if there is uniform freedom from moisture on the surface.

Practically all dried products should be conditioned.

STORAGE FOR DRIED PRODUCTS

Of importance equal to proper Drying is the proper packing and storage of the finished product. With the scarcity of tins and the high prices of glass jars it is recommended that other containers be used. Those easily available are baking-powder cans and similar covered tins, pasteboard boxes having tight-fitting covers, strong paper bags, and patented paraffin paper boxes, which may be bought in quantities at comparatively low cost.

A paraffin container of the type used by oyster dealers for the delivery of oysters will be found inexpensive and easily handled. If using this, or a baking-powder can or similar container, after filling adjust the cover closely. For storage on a larger scale use closely built wooden boxes with well-fitted lids. Line each box with paraffin paper in several layers. The paper should cover the top of the contents.

It is essential that the container should exclude light and insects but it should not be air-tight. Products stored in air-tight containers suffer damage through moisture which escapes from the product and condenses in the package.

If a paper bag is used, the top should be twisted, doubled over and tied with a string. Another good precaution is to store bags within an ordinary lard pail or can or other tin vessel having a fairly close-fitting cover.

The products should be stored in a warm, dry place, well ventilated and protected from rats, mice and insects. An attic or upstairs-room which is warmed by pipes or flues passing through makes a very satisfactory place. Shelves near a furnace also make a suitable storage place.

In sections where the air is very moist, special care must be used. The containers should be opened occasionally and if any moisture has been taken up the contents should be placed in the oven until dry.

It is good practice to use small containers so that it may not be necessary to leave the contents exposed long after opening before use.

For convenience label all packages.

Before storing products prepared by sun drying, artificial heat must be applied to destroy possible insect eggs. To do this place the products in the oven, spread in thin layers, and allow them to remain until the temperature reaches 180 degrees F. as indicated by a thermometer inside partially open oven.

FIG. 18. Vegetable and fruit slicer.

FIG. 19. Slicing corn.

WINTER USE OF PRODUCTS

In preparing dried vegetables and fruits for use the first process is to restore the water which has been dried out of them. All dried foods require soaking. After soaking the dried products will have a better flavor if cooked in a covered utensil at a low temperature for a long time. Dried products should be prepared and served as fresh products are prepared and served. They should be cooked in the water in which they have been soaked, as this utilizes all of the mineral salts, which would otherwise be wasted.

There can be no definite rule for the amount of water required for soaking dried products when they are to be used, as the quantity of water evaporated in the drying process varies with different vegetables and fruits. As a general rule from 3 to 4 cups of water will be required for 1 cup of dried material.

In preparing for use, peas, beans, spinach and like vegetables should be boiled in water to which there has been added soda in the proportion of 1/8 teaspoonful of soda to 1 quart of water. This im-

DIRECTIONS FOR VEGETABLE DRYING

Potatoes

Wash well, and pare very thinly. If a rotary peeler is used, the potatoes should be graded for size, and those of similar size pared in groups. The eyes will have to be removed by hand. Cut into slices 3/16 to 1/4 inch thick. Blanch in steam 1 to 3 minutes; or in boiling water 2 to 3 minutes. The water should boil vigorously enough to keep the pieces separated and in motion. Drain and place on drying trays in one-inch layers, then dry at once. The blanching should be just long enough to prevent darkening while the potatoes are drying. Start drying at a temperature of 125 degrees F. and raise gradually to 145 degrees to 150 degrees F. toward the end of the drying period. When dry enough, the pieces of potato will be free from opaque, spongy white places, and will rattle when stirred. Remove from drier, condition and store.

Beets, Carrots and Parsnips

Wash well, scrape off skin, and cut into slices of a uniform thickness—3/16 to 1/4 inch. Blanch 2 minutes in steam or boiling water. Drain well, spread on drying trays, and dry at an initial temperature of 120 degrees F. and not exceeding 145 degrees F. during the entire drying period. These products are sufficiently dry when the pieces break if an effort is made to bend them, and when no moisture shows if they are pressed between the fingers.

Cabbage

Take heads which are well developed. Remove all loose outside leaves and central stalk. Shred or cut into strips a few inches long. Blanch in steam 3 minutes, or in boiling water 4 minutes. Use a wire basket, fill not more than 6 to 8 inches deep; and stir well during the process. When drying, spread in layers not over 1 inch deep, and stir frequently until the product is dry enough not to stick together in close masses. Begin drying at 115 degrees to 125 degrees F. and when the cabbage is nearly dry, raise the temperature not to exceed 135 degrees F. Remove from drier when no moisture can be squeezed out of thicker pieces by strong pressure between the fingers.

Cauliflower

After cleaning, divide into small pieces. The head may be cut by a vegetable slicer, if preferred. Blanch 6 minutes in steam or 4 minutes in boiling water. Spread in thin layers on drying trays. Start at a temperature of 120 degrees F. and gradually increase to 130 degrees F. Although turning dark while drying, cauliflower will regain part of original color in soaking and cooking. The drying is complete when strong pressure between the fingers does not squeeze out moisture from the thicker pieces.

Celery

After washing, carefully cut into even-length pieces—3/4 inch or 1 inch is a good measure. Blanch 3 minutes in steam or 2 minutes in boiling water. Drain well, and spread on drying trays in 1/2 inch layers. Dry at 135 degrees F., stirring occasionally.

Garden Peas

If the pods are dusty, wash well before shelling. Garden peas with non-edible pod are taken when of size suitable for table use. Blanch 3 to 5 minutes according to size, then drain and spread on drying trays. A depth of 3/4 to 1 inch is practicable, but single layers will dry quicker. Start the drying at a temperature of 115 degrees to 120 degrees F., raising it gradually to 140 degrees F. Stir occasionally. When sufficiently dry, peas will show no moisture near the center when split open.

For use in soups or puree, shell mature peas, pass them through a meat grinder, spread the pulp on trays and dry.

Spinach

Select plants which are well grown. Remove roots and wash well. Steam 2 minutes. Spread on tray and dry at a constant temperature of 130 degrees F. Remove from drier before the leaves break when handled.

Green String Beans

Select only such beans as are in perfect condition for table use. Wash carefully and string. If full grown they should be slit lengthwise or cut—not snapped—into pieces 1/4 to 1 inch long. Blanch 5 to 8 minutes according to age. To set the color of nearly grown beans add 2 level tablespoonfuls of baking soda to every gallon of boiling water. Drain well after blanching and spread in thin layers on drying trays. Begin the drying at a temperature of 130 degrees F. and gradually raise it to 140 degrees or 145 degrees F. Drying is complete when no moisture can be pressed from freshly broken pieces.

Lima Beans

Choose mature beans. Shell and blanch 3 minutes in boiling water, keeping the beans well stirred by the motion of the rapidly bubbling water. Drain to remove surface moisture. Spread in thin layers on drying trays, and stir occasionally during the drying process. Start drying at 120 degrees to 130 degrees F. and raise this temperature gradually to 150 degrees F.

Okra

After washing, blanch young tender pods 2 to 3 minutes in boiling water or steam. Allow 2 minutes for older pods, which should be cut into halves or quarters. Dry the younger pods whole. Spread on trays in single layers and start drying at a temperature of 115 degrees F. to 120 degrees F. Gradually raise this to 135 degrees F.

Okra may also be dried by being strung on a string and hung over the stove. This should not be done except with young and tender pods. Heat in oven before storing.

Onions

Peel and cut into 1/8 to 1/4 inch slices. A rotary slicer is convenient for this. Blanching is not needed. Spread in thin layers, on drying trays and dry at a uniform temperature of 140 degrees F. Stir occasionally when the process is three-fourths done to prevent pieces scorching. Remove promptly from drier when pieces break on bending.

Pumpkin and Squash (Summer and Winter)

Pare, remove seeds and spongy portions. Cut into 1/2 inch pieces. Blanch 3 to 6 minutes, or until the pieces are semi-transparent. Spread on trays. Start drying at a temperature of 135 degrees F. and raise this slowly to 160 degrees F. These products will be pliable and leathery when dried enough, and show no moisture when cut.

The strips may be hung on strings and dried in the kitchen above the stove.

Shell Beans and Peas

Beans of different kinds, after maturing and drying on the vines, and being shelled, should be heated to 165 degrees to 180 degrees F. for 10 to 15 minutes to destroy any insect eggs which may be in them. This may be done in an oven. These heated beans cannot be used for planting, because they are devitalized and will not grow. Store in a dry place in bags.

Mature lima beans need only to be shelled and stored in bags. Cow peas or any field pea can be treated in the same way.

Sweet Potatoes

Wash, pare and slice, blanch 6 to 8 minutes and spread on drying trays. Dry until brittle, starting at a temperature of 145 degrees to 150 degrees F. and gradually raising it to 155 degrees to 165 degrees F., when the drying is nearly done. Remove from drier when pieces are brittle and break under pressure.

Tomatoes

Select fruit which is firm and well ripened. Blanch 1 or 2 minutes, or long enough to loosen the skins. When cool enough to handle, peel, and cut into slices 3/8 to 1/2 inch thick. Spread in single layers on drying trays, placing cheesecloth or other thin open-mesh fabric over the tray bottoms if made of wire. Start drying at a temperature of 120 degrees F. and raise it gradually to 140 degrees F. When dry enough the tomatoes will break when bent, on conditioning they will become somewhat pliable.

Turnips

Turnips for drying should be in prime condition and free from pithiness. Prepare as directed for potatoes. Blanch 1 to 2 minutes, drain and spread on drying trays. The drying temperature is 135 degrees to 140 degrees F. at the beginning, gradually raised to 160 degrees to 165 degrees F. When dry enough the pieces will rattle when stirred.

Wax Beans

These are dried in the same manner as lima beans.

Soup Mixtures

Vegetables for soup mixtures are prepared and dried separately. These are mixed as desired.

Sweet Corn

Select ears that are at the milk stage, prime for table use and freshly gathered. Blanch on cob in boiling water for 8 to 12 minutes to set milk. Drain thoroughly, and with a sharp knife cut off in layers or cut off half the kernel and scrape off the remainder, taking care not to include the chaff. Start at temperature of 130 degrees F. and raise gradually to 140 degrees, stirring frequently.

Corn is dry when it is hard and semi-transparent.

FIG. 20. Arranging vegetables or fruits on trays.

FIG. 21. Preparing dried products for storing.

proves the color.

In preparing to serve dried vegetables season them carefully. For this purpose celery, mustard, onion, cheese and nutmeg give desirable flavoring, according to taste.

From 3 to 4 quarts of vegetable soup may be made from 4 oz. of dried soup vegetables.

BOTANICAL GARDENS AND ARBORITAE

UNIVERSITY OF ALBERTA BOTANIC GARDEN
Department of Botany
Edmonton, Alberta, CANADA

ARNOLD ARBORETUM
Jamaica Plain, MA 02130

BARNES ARBORETUM
300 N. Latches Lane
Merion Station, PA 19066

BARNWELL MEMORIAL GARDEN AND ART
CENTER
501 Clyde E. Fant Memorial Parkway
Shreveport, LA 71101

BARTLETT ARBORETUM
University of Connecticut
151 Brookdale Road
Stanford, CT 06905

BARTLETT TREE EXPERTS
Box 3067
Ridgeway Station
Stamford, CT 06905

BAYOU BEND GARDENS
16 Westlane
Houston, TX 77019

BERKSHIRE GARDEN CENTER, INC.
Stockbridge, MA 01262

BICKELHAUPT ARBORETUM
340 South 14th Street
Clinton, IA 52732

BIRMINGHAM BOTANICAL GARDEN
2612 Lane Park Road
Birmingham, AL 35223

BLANDY EXPERIMENTAL FARM
Orland E. White Arboretum
University of Virginia
Boyce, VA 22620

BOWMAN'S HILL STATE WILDFLOWER
PRESERVE
Washington State Park
Washington Crossing, PA 18977

BOTANICAL GARDEN
University of British Columbia
Vancouver 8, B.C., CANADA

BOTANICAL GARDEN
University of Helsinki
Unioninkatu 44
SF-00170 Helsinki 17, FINLAND

BOYCE THOMPSON SOUTHWESTERN
ARBORETUM
University of Arizona
P.O. Box AB
Superior, AZ 85273

BROOKGREEN GARDENS
Murrells Inlet, SC 29576

BROOKLYN BOTANIC GARDEN
1000 Washington Ave.
Brooklyn, NY 11225

BUCKS COUNTY COMMUNITY COLLEGE
Swamp Road
Newton, PA 18940

UNIVERSITY OF CALIFORNIA ARBORETUM
University of California
Davis, CA 95616

UNIVERSITY OF CALIFORNIA BOTANICAL
GARDENS
405 Hilgard
Los Angeles, CA 90024

UNIVERSITY OF CALIFORNIA
Bio-Agr. Library, Serials Dept.
Riverside, CA 92502

IDA CASON CALLAWAY GARDENS
Pine Mountain, GA 31822

CHICAGO BOTANIC GARDEN
775 Dundee Rd.
P.O. Box 90
Glencoe, IL 60022

CORNELL PLANTATIONS
100 Judd Falls, Rd.
Ithaca, NY 14850

DENVER BOTANIC GARDENS
909 York St.
Denver, CO 30206

DUKE GARDENS
Duke University
Durham, NC 27706

FAIRCHILD TROPICAL GARDEN
10901 Old Cutler Rd.
Miami, FL 33156

FLORIDA INSTITUTE OF TECHNOLOGY
P.O. Box 1150
Melbourne, FL 32901

FRELINGHUYSEN ARBORETUM
Morris County Park Commission
P.O. Box 1295 R
Morristown, NJ 07960

HAVERFORD COLLEGE ARBORETUM
Hidden Valley Lane
Newtown, PA 18940

HAYES REGIONAL ARBORETUM
801 Elks Rd.
Richmond, IN 47374

HELLMAN PARK-DUNSMUIR HOUSE, INC.
2960 Peralta Oaks Ct.
Oakland, CA 94605

HENRY FOUNDATION FOR BOTANICAL
RESEARCH
801 Stony Lane
Gladwyne, PA 19035

HERITAGE PLANTATION
Box 566
Sandwich, MA 02563

HOLDEN ARBORETUM
Sperry Road
Mentor, OH 44060

HOLMDEL ARBORETUM
Monmouth Co. Shade Tree Comm.
20 Court St.
Freehold, NJ 07728

HUNTINGTON LIBRARY & ART GALLERY
Preparations Dept.
San Marino, CA 91108

HYSLOP FOUNDATION, INC.
5820 Third Ave.
Kenosha, WI 53141

KANSAS LANDSCAPE ARBORETUM
c/o W.A. Flynn
Route 5
Abilene, KS 67410

KINGWOOD CENTER
P.O. Box 966
Mansfield, OH 44901

LOCKERLY ARBORETUM
Irwinton Road
P.O. Box 534
Milledgeville, GA 31061

LONGUE VUE GARDENS
7 Bamboo Rd.
New Orleans, LA 70124

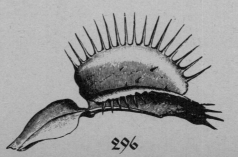

LONGWOOD GARDENS
Kennett Square, PA 19348

LOS ANGELES STATE & COUNTY
ARBORETUM, LIBRARY
Box 688
Arcadia, CA 91006

LONGWOOD PROGRAMS
University of Delaware
Newark, DE 19711

LYON ARBORETUM
3860 Manoa Rd.
Honolulu, HI 96822

MEMPHIS BOTANIC GARDEN
750 Cherry Rd.
Memphis, TN 38117

McARTHUR
Billings, 40 Lake Drive
Winter Park, FL 32789

UNIVERSITY OF MINNESOTA
LANDSCAPE ARBORETUM
Rt. 1, Box 132-1
Chaska, MN 55318

MISSOURI BOTANICAL GARDEN
2315 Tower Grove Ave.
St. Louis, MO 63110

MONTREAL BOTANICAL GARDEN
4101 est, rue Sherbrooke
Montreal 36, P.Q., CANADA

MORRIS ARBORETUM
University of Pennsylvania
9414 Meadowbrooke Ave.
Philadelphia, PA 19118

MORTON ARBORETUM
Library
Lisle, IL 60532

NEW YORK BOTANICAL GARDEN
Bronx, N.Y.

PACIFIC TROPICAL BOTANICAL
GARDEN
P.O. Box 340
Lawai, Hauai, HI 96765

PAINE ART CENTER & ARBORETUM
Box 1097
Oshkosh, WI 54901

PENN STATE UNIVERSITY
c/o Dr. R.W. Hepler-Horticulturist
101 Tyson Building
University Park, PA 16802

PENNSYLVANIA HORTICULTURAL SOCIETY
325 Walnut St.
Philadelphia, PA 19106

PLANTING FIELDS ARBORETUM
St. of NY Planting Fields
Oyster Bay, NY 11771

PLANT RESEARCH LIBRARY
Biosystematics Res. Inst.
Res. Bra. Agr. Canada No. 49
Ottawa KIA 006, CANADA

PRINCETON UNIVERSITY
Physical Plant Department
Princeton, NJ 08540

RANCHO SANTA ANA BOTANIC GARDEN
1500 N. College Ave.
Claremont, CA 91711

REFLECTION RIDING, INC.
c/o Pioneer Bank
801 Broad St.
Chattanooga, TN 37401

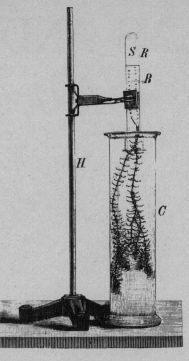

ROYAL BOTANICAL GARDENS
Box 399
Hamilton, Ont. CANADA L8N 3H8

SAN DIEGO BOTANICAL GARDEN
FOUNDATION
Casa del Prado
Balboa Park
San Diego, CA 92101

SAN DIEGO ZOOLOGICAL GARDENS
c/o Horticulturist
P.O. Box 551
San Diego, CA 92112

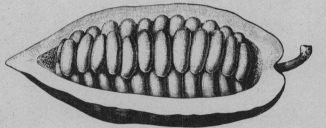

STANLEY M. ROWE ARBORETUM
4500 Muchmore Rd.
Cincinnati, OH 45243

STRYBING ARBORETUM SOCIETY OF GOLDEN
GATE PARK
Hall of Flowers
9th Ave. & Lincoln Way
San Francisco, CA 94122

TENNESSEE BOTANICAL GARDENS
Cheekwood, Cheek Road
Nashville, TN 37205

UNIVERSITY OF TENNESSEE BOTANICAL
GARDEN AND ARBORETA
Martin, TN 38237

TEXAS STATE TECHNICAL INSTITUTE
The Library
Waco, TX 76705

UNITARIAN CHURCH OF SOUTHERN NEW
JERSEY ARBORETUM
401 N. Kings Highway
Cherry Hill, NJ 08034

VANCOUVER BOTANICAL GARDENS
ASSOCIATION
1200-900 W. Hastings St.
Vancouver 2, B.C., CANADA

SANTA BARBARA BOTANIC GARDEN, INC.
1212 Mission Canyon Rd.
Santa Barbara, CA 93105

SCOTT HORT. FOUNDATION
Swarthmore College
Swarthmore, PA 19081

ST. GEORGE VILLAGE BOTANICAL GARDEN
OF ST. CROIX, INC.
Box 1576 Christian St.
St. Croix, U.S. V.I. 00820

SELBY BOTANICAL GARDENS
Palmer First Natl. Bank & Trust Co.
P.O. Box 2018
Sarasota, FL 33578

SHERMAN FOUNDATION GARDEN
2647 E. Coast Highway
Corona del Mar, CA 92625

WAIMEA ARBORETUM
59-364 Kamehameha Highway
Haleiwa, HI 96712

UNIVERSITY OF WISCONSIN ARBORETUM
1207 Seminole Highway
Madison, WI 53711

WATER ISLE BOTANICAL GARDEN
Box 570
St. Thomas, V.I. 00801

WOODWARD BIOMEDICAL LIBRARY
University of British Columbia
Vancouver 8, B.C., CANADA

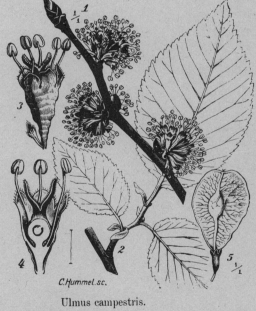

Ulmus campestris.

MAGAZINES

The Avant Gardener,
P. O. Box 489,
New York, N.Y. 10028

Flower and Garden,
4251 Pennsylvania,
Kansas City, Mo. 64111

Horticulture,
300 Massachusetts Ave.,
Boston, Mass. 02115

Organic Gardening and Farming,
Emmaus, Penna. 18099

Plants Alive,
2100 N. 45th,
Seattle, Wash. 98102

Under Glass,
Lord & Burnham,
P.O. Box 114,
Irvington, N.Y. 10533

Collecting Wild Plants

Perennial Wildflowers by Color

White
American bugbane
Bearberry
Bishop's-cap
Black cohosh
Bloodroot
Boneset
Bowman's root
Bunchberry
Canada anemone
Canada mayflower
Canada violet
Common yarrow
Confederate violet
Creeping snowberry
Culver's root
Dutchman's-breeches
Dwarf ginseng
Early white snakeroot
False spikenard
Flat-topped aster
Frostflower aster
Galax
Ginseng
Golden seal
Goldthread
Grass of Parnassus
Hairy alumroot
Hepatica
Large white trillium
Mayapple
Mountain lady's-slipper
Musk mallow
Nodding mandarin
Nodding trillium
Ox-eye daisy
Ozark trillium
Painted trillium
Partridgeberry
Purple loosestrife
Pussytoes
Red baneberry
Rock geranium
Rue anemone
Seneca snakeroot
Shinleaf
Shooting star
Showy lady's-slipper
Small white lady's-slipper
Snow trillium
Spikenard
Spring beauty
Squirrel corn
Starflower
Star-flowered false Solomon's seal
Star-of-Bethlehem
Sweet white violet
Tall meadow rue
Trailing arbutus
Twinflower
Twinleaf
Two-leaved toothwort
White baneberry
White mertensia
White phlox
White turtlehead
Wild calla
Wintergreen
Wood anemone
Woodland strawberry

Yellow
Barren strawberry
Blue cohosh
Bluebead lily
Canada goldenrod
Canada lily
Celandine poppy
Common cinquefoil
Common tansy
Cypress spurge
Downy yellow violet
Ginseng
Golden ragwort
Grass-leaved goldenrod
Hoary puccoon
Indian cucumber
Lady's mantle
Lakeside daisy
Large-yellow lady's slipper
Marsh marigold
Merrybells
Moneywort
Nodding mandarin
Ox-eye
Prairie goldenrod
Silverweed
Smooth yellow violet
Solomon's seal
Stoneroot
Swamp candles
Trout lily
Wild oats
Wild senna
Yellow stargrass
Yellow trillium

Orange
Blackberry lily
Butterfly flower
Canada lily
Michigan lily
Tiger lily
Turk's-cap lily
Wild columbine
Wood lily

Pink to Red
Bearberry
Blazing star
Bowman's root
Cardinal flower
Common milkweed
False dragonhead
Fringed polygala
Jessie's red violet
Joe-pye
Kansas gayfeather
Mountain phlox
Musk mallow
Nodding wild onion
Oswego tea
Partridgeberry
Pink bleeding heart
Pink lady's-slipper
Pink skullcap
Prairie phlox
Prairie smoke
Prairie trillium
Purple corydalis
Purple trillium
Queen of the Prairie
Red turtlehead
Rose Mandarin
Rose trillium
Rose verbena
Rue anemone
Shooting star
Spotted cranesbill
Spring beauty
Swamp milkweed
Toadshade
Trailing arbutus
Twinflower
Two-leaved toothwort
Western bleeding heart
Wild ginger
Wine cups

Wake Robin.
Trillium erectum.

Berry of T. undulatum

Painted Trillium.
Trillium undulatum.

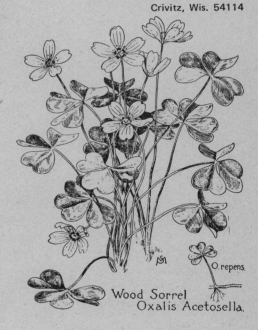

Melanthium virginicum.

YELLOW ASPHODEL.
(ASPHODELUS LUTEUS.)

Potentilla recta.

NOBLE FUMITORY.

NEW YORK IRON-WEED.
(VERNONIA NOVEBORACENSIS.)

FESTUCA GLAUCA.

O. repens

Wood Sorrel
Oxalis Acetosella.

Wild Garlic.
Allium Canadense.

Wild Leek.
Allium tricoccum.

Ragged Fringed Orchis.
Habenaria lacera.

Habenaria leucophaea.

Deptford Pink.
Dianthus Armeria.

Maiden Pink.
Dianthus deltoides.

Swamp Buttercup. Ranunculus septentrionalis.

Leaf of Ranunculus fascicularis.

Early Meadow Parsnip. Zizia aurea.

Berula erecta.

Sium cicutaefolium

Fruit twice size.

Hedge Bindweed. Convolvulus sepium.

Common Dodder. Cuscuta Gronovii.

4

Lady's Slipper

SELECTED REFERENCES FOR WILDFLOWER OBSERVATIONS AND CULTIVATION

Hoover, Helen
THE LONGSHADOWED FORREST
Crowell, New York 1963

House, Homer Doliver
WILDFLOWERS
Macmillan, New York 1934

Hull, Helen S.
WILD FLOWERS FOR YOUR GARDEN
Barrows, New York 1952

Hulme, F. Edward
WILD FLOWERS IN THEIR SEASON
Cassell, London 1909

Lounsberry, Alice
A GUIDE TO THE WILDFLOWERS
Stokes, Philadelphia 1899

Matthews, F. Schuyler
FAMILIAR FEATURES OF THE
ROADSIDE
Appleton, New York 1897

McCurdy, Robert M.
GARDEN FLOWERS
Doubleday, Garden City 1926

Miles, Bebe
BLUEBELLS AND BITTERSWEET:
GARDENING WITH NATIVE AMERICAN PLANTS
Von Nostrand Reinhold, New York 1970

Pellet, Frank C.
FLOWERS OF THE WILD
DeLaMare, New York 1931

Preece, W.H.A.
NORTH AMERICAN ROCK PLANTS
Macmillan, New York 1937

Quinn, Vernon
LEAVES, THEIR PLACE IN LIFE AND LEGEND
Stokes, New York 1937

Rickett, Herald W.
THE NEW FIELD BOOK OF AMERICAN
WILDFLOWERS
Putnam, New York 1963

Rickett, Herald W.
THE ODYSSEY BOOK OF AMERICAN
WILDFLOWERS
Odyssey, New York 1964

Rickett, Herald W.
WILDFLOWERS OF AMERICA
Crown, New York 1953

Rickett, Herald W.
WILDFLOWERS OF THE UNITED STATES
McGraw Hill, New York 1966

Roberts, Eda Dr. and Rehmann, Elsa
AMERICAN PLANTS FOR AMERICAN GARDENS
Macmillan 1929

Rowntree, Leslie
HARDY CALIFORNIANS
Macmillan, New York 1936

Saunders, Charles F.
WITH THE FLOWERS AND TREES IN
CALIFORNIA
McBride, Nast & Co., New York 1914

Schulz, Ellen D.
TEXAS WILD FLOWERS
Laidlaw Bros., Chicago 1928

Stack, Frederick Williams
WILDFLOWERS EVERY CHILD SHOULD
KNOW
Doubleday, New York

Steffek, Edwin F.
WILDFLOWERS AND HOW TO GROW THEM
Crown, New York 1954

Taylor, Kathryn S.
A TRAVELLER'S GUIDE TO THE ROADSIDE
WILDFLOWERS, SHRUBS AND TREES OF
THE UNITED STATES
Farrar Straus, New York 1949

Taylor, Kathryn and Hamblin, Stephen
HANDBOOK OF WILD FLOWER CULTIVATION
Macmillan 1963

Monkshood

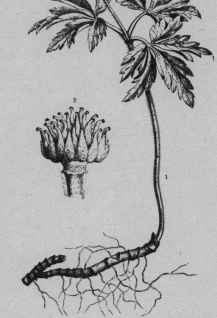

Fig. 250.—Wood Anemone (*Anemone nemorosa*).
¹ Complete plant; natural size. ² The collection of carpels
from the centre of the flower; magnified.

Dutchman's breeches

Aralia
nudicaulis.

Ginseng
Panax quinquefolium.

Panax
trifolium.

New York Ironweed.   Vernonia Noveboracensis

Water Pennywort.   Hydrocotyle Americana.

A Leaf of Red Clover.
At the left, leaf by day ; at the right, the same
leaf asleep at night.

PURPLE FLOWERING RASPBERRY.
(RUBUS ODORATUS.)

Aiken, George D.
PIONEERING WITH WILD FLOWERS
Genessee Press, Rochester 1933

AMERICAN WILDFLOWERS
Hastings House, New York 1946

Barton, J.G.
WILDFLOWERS
Spring Books, London 1963

Beecroft, W.
WHO'S WHO AMONG THE WILDFLOWERS
AND FERNS
F.P. Barton, New Haven 1917

Blanchan, Neltje
NATURE'S GARDEN
Doubleday, New York 1915

Birdseye, Clarence and Eleanor G.
GROWING WOODLAND PLANTS
Oxford, New York 1951

Bonker, Frances
THE SAGE OF THE DESERT AND
OTHER CACTI
Stratford, Boston 1930

THE BOOK OF WILDFLOWERS
National Geographic Society
Washington 1924

BULLETIN OF POPULAR INFORMATION
Morton Arboretum
Leslie, Illinois
Various issues

Clements, Edith S.
WILD FLOWERS OF THE WEST
National Geographic, May 1927

Daly, T.A.
THE WISSAHICKON
The Garden Club of Philadelphia 1922

Dana, Mrs. William Starr
HOW TO KNOW THE WILDFLOWERS
Scribner, New York 1903

Durand, Herbert
MY WILD FLOWER GARDEN
Putnam, New York 1927

GARDENING WITH NATIVE PLANTS
Brooklyn Botanical Garden 1962

Gottscho, Samuel H.
WILDFLOWERS, HOW TO KNOW AND
ENJOY THEM
Dodd, New York 1951

Gress, Ernest M.
COMMON WILDFLOWERS OF PENNSYLVANIA
The Times Tribune Co.
Altoona 1928

Haskin, Leslie L.
WILDFLOWER OF THE PACIFIC COAST
Dinfords and Mort
Portland, Ore. 1934

Henshaw, Julia W.
MOUNTAIN WILDFLOWERS OF AMERICA
Ginn, Boston 1906

Chickweed.
Stellaria media.

Mountain Sandwort.
Arenaria Grœnlandica

Long-leaved
Stitchwort.
Stellaria
longifolia.

Spines of Rosa lucida.

Smooth Rose.   Rosa blanda

ACHILLEA PTARMICA.

SEA LAVENDER.
(STATICE LATIFOLIA.

TURK'S-CAP LILY.
(LILIUM SUPERBUM.)

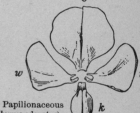

FIG. 21. Pulse Family. Papilionaceous
corolla of sweet pea (*Lathyrus odoratus*)

A, side view. *B*, front view: *s*, standard;
w, w, wings; *k*, keel

Walton, George
PRACTICAL GUIDE TO WILD FLOWERS AND FRUITS
Lippincott, Philadelphia 1909

Wherry, Edgar T.
WILD FLOWER GUIDE
Doubleday, New York 1948

Wright, Mabel Osgood
FLOWERS AND FERNS IN THEIR HAUNTS
Macmillan, New York 1901

Indian Cucumber.   Medeola Virginica.

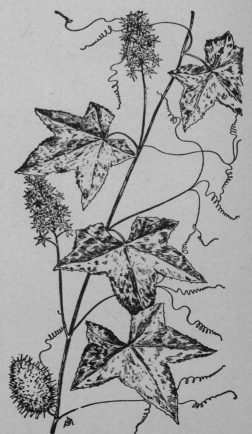

Climbing Wild Cucumber. Echinocystis lobata.

PLANTING TO ATTRACT BIRDS

Choice of plant materials is sufficiently great so that interesting and well-designed plantings can be made on home grounds, vacation spots or public areas and still provide food, shelter and nesting sites for birds. The same plantings that screen out undesirable sights or frame good views can be homes for birds. Conifers that make interesting skylines also can be roosts for Siskins or homes for Owls. The thorny and brilliant-fruited crab provide interesting textures and make shelters, perches and food for Bluebirds. The low to tall height plantings that give depth and perspective to a garden view also make varied height nestings sites. A check of mail order nurseries or the local garden center will locate many of the suggested kinds.

FOR HUMMINGBIRDS
Bearded-tongues
Beebalm
Cardinal flower
Columbines
Coral bells
Flowering-tobacco
Gladiolus
Larkspur
Lupine
Petunia
Red-hot-poker
Scarlet-sage
Trumpet-creeper
Weigela

CARDINAL FLOWER.
(LOBELIA CARDINALIS.)

ANNUAL SEEDHEADS FOR BIRDS
Bachelor's-button
Black-eyed-susan
Coreopsis
Cosmos
Gaillardia
Grains
Marigold
Millet
Portulaca
Scabiosa
Sunflowers
Thistle
Verbena
Zinnia

ERIANTHUS RAVENNÆ.

FRUIT, SHELTER, ROOSTS, NESTING SITES
Arborvitae
Apple
Autumn-olive
Bayberry
Beautyberry
Birches
Blackberry
Buckthorn
Buffaloberry
Cedars
Cherries
Chokeberry
Cotoneasters
Crabapples
Dogwoods
Elderberries
Evodia
Golden-rain-tree
Grapes
Hackberry
Hawthorns
Hemlock
Holly
Honeysuckles
Inkberry
Junipers
Mountain-ash
Mulberry
Oaks
Pines
Poke
Privets
Pyracantha
Roses
Shadbush
Spicebush
Sumac
Viburnums
Virginia-creeper
Wahoo
Winterberry
Yews

Great Tobacco

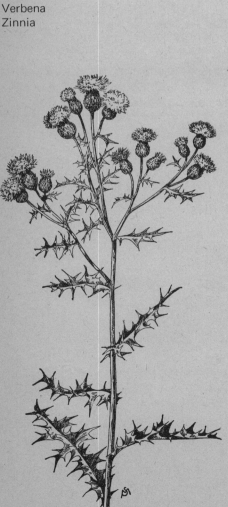

Canada Thistle.   Cirsium arvense.

Ten-petaled Sunflower.
Helianthus decapetalus.

Wild Virginia Strawberry.
Fragaria virginiana.

American Wood Strawberry.
Fragaria vesca var americana.

303

FRIENDS OF THE GARDEN

Transference of pollen to the bodies of insects by means of explosive apparatus.

Reptiles and Amphibians

The reptiles and amphibians are residents of the garden you may or may not encounter. Many of them are nocturnal and forage only when they cannot be observed. Amphibians require a moist or wet habitat, reptiles do not.

Snakes, toads, frogs, turtles, and salamanders all share the ecosystem; each plays a significant role in filling an ecologic niche. The garden provides a variety of habitats.

Below are listed some common species in the garden. A field guide to the reptiles and amphibians will help you with identification of these and others we have not yet discovered.

Snakes are reptiles which live exclusively on animal food and are known to eat meals that comprise 50% of their body weight. With the exception of the water snake, the snakes of the garden are usually found around the edges of the pond, on ledges and under old logs and stumps.

Eastern garter snake, *Thamnophis sirtalis sirtalis*
Northern black racer, *Coluber constrictor constrictor*
Common water snake, *Natrix sipedon sipedon*

One is most likely to find the shelled reptiles, as well as the snakes described above, in the spring and fall, for they retire in the heat of mid-summer sun and hibernate in the winter. The box turtle lives on land and the painted turtle and snapper are prone to bask and can often be seen in the shallows of the pond.

Common snapping turtle, *Chelydra serpentina*
Eastern painted turtle, *Chrysems picta picta*
Eastern box turtle, *Terrapene carolina carolina*

The salamanders, often confused with lizards, are amphibians which require a moist habitat and hibernate in the winter. Unlike other amphibians, the salamanders have a tail throughout their lifetime. They are most readily seen in the spring and fall in damp places under rocks, leaves, and rotting wood. In the spring the salamanders and their eggs may be found in shallow water.

Northern two-lined salamander, *Eurycea Bislineata bislineata*
Red-backed salamander, *Plethodon cinereus cinereus*
Common newt (red eft), *Diemictylus viridescens viridescens*

The American toad lives on land but breeds and lays its eggs in the water of the pond. The toad has warty skin and helps to control the garden insects. The frogs, like the toad, depend on water for reproduction but they also live in or near water all year. Both frogs and toads can be seen and heard in the springtime when the males are calling the females to the breeding pools. The bull frog is the only frog to exceed four inches in length and lives in permanent bodies of water. Most frogs are nocturnal and can be seen by shining a flashlight into a quiet stream at night.

American toad, *Bufo americanus*
Green frog, *Rana clamitans melanota*
Bull frog, *Rana catesbeiana*
Leopard frog, *Rana pipiens pipiens*
Pickerel frog, *Rana palustris*
Spring peeper, *Hyla crucifer crucifer*
Wood frog, *Rana sylvatica*

Birds

The raucous chatter of a kingfisher or the enticing song of the cardinal may be the first bird sound the garden visitor hears; this is only an advertisement of the variety of bird life in the Wildflower Garden. Sharp eyes, listening ears and patience are all that are required for one to be rewarded with the sight or the sound of these feathered garden inhabitants.

Cardinal

Screech Owl

Early morning and late afternoon are the best times to look for birds, for it is at these times that many birds do most of their feeding. Some of the more common species such as the cardinal and the friendly chickadee may be seen throughout the day.

Just as the plant life of the garden changes with the seasons, so does the bird population. Its numbers are swelled in the spring with the arrival of transitory migrants and the summer residents. In the fall, the migrants pass through once again and are joined by the summer residents on their way southward. By the time the leaves have fallen, only the hardy species remain. Occasionally a summer resident such as the robin spends the entire year in the garden.

The following birds have been seen during the year in the garden. It is not a complete list and unfortunately we haven't the space to describe each bird. Use a good field guide and you should be able to add to our interesting collection. The order follows that in *Peterson's Field Guide to The Birds*; S= summer, W=winter, P=permanent, M=migratory.

Bird	Scientific name	
Wood duck	*Aix sponsa*	S
Black duck	*Anas rubripes*	S
Mallard	*Anas platyrhynchos platyrhynchos*	M
Sparrow hawk	*Falco sparverius*	P
Screech owl	*Otus asio*	P
Mourning dove	*Zenaidura macroura*	P
Pileated woodpecker	*Hylatomus pileatus*	P
Flicker	*Colaptes auratus*	P
Hairy woodpecker	*Dendrocopus villosus*	P
Downy woodpecker	*Dendrocopus pubescens*	P
Eastern kingbird	*Tyranus tyranus*	S
Black capped chickadee	*Parus atricapillus*	P
Brown creeper	*Certhia familiaris*	W
White breasted nuthatch	*Sitta carolinensis*	P
Robin	*Turdus migratorius*	S
Cedar waxwing	*Bombycilla cedrorum*	M
Myrtle warbler	*Dendroica coronata coronata*	M
Yellow throat	*Geothlypis trichas*	S
Purple Grackle	*Quiscalus quiscula*	S
Red-wing blackbird	*Agelaius phoeniceus*	S
Wood thrush	*Hylocichla mustelina*	S
Cowbird	*Molothrus ater ater*	S
Starling	*Sturnus vulgaris vulgaris*	P
Kingfisher	*Megaceryle alcyon alcyon*	P
Blue jay	*Cyanocitta cristata*	P
Crow	*Corvus brachyrhynchos*	P
Baltimore oriole	*Icterus galbula*	S
Phoebe	*Sayornis phoebe*	S
Catbird	*Dumetella carolinensis*	S
Bank swallow	*Riparia riparia riparia*	S
Veery	*Hylocichla fuscescens*	M
Purple finch	*Carpodacus purpureus purpureus*	W
Cardinal	*Richmondena cardinalis*	P
Evening grosbeak	*Hesperiphona vespertina*	M
American goldfinch	*Spinus tristis tristis*	S
Rose breasted grosbeak	*Pheucticus ludovicianus*	S
Slate colored junco	*Junco hyemalis*	W
Towhee	*Pipilo erythrophthalmus*	S
Fox sparrow	*Passerella iliaca iliaca*	M
Tree sparrow	*Spizella arborea arborea*	P
Song sparrow	*Melospiza melodia*	P
White throated sparrow	*Zonotrichia albicollis*	M

Mammals

Mammals of the Wildflower Garden are much more common than is readily apparent to the visitor. Many of the small mammals are active only at night and some of the large ones are also nocturnal. A person who knows where and how to look, will notice signs such as scats (droppings), clipped vegetation, nut shells, tracks, or burrows and holes. The common mammals of the garden are listed in this section. For a complete description of these mammals, Collins' *A Field Guide to American Wildlife* is a good source.

Opossum, *Didelphis marsupialis*
Eastern cottontail, *Sylvilagus floridanus*
Red squirrel, *Tamiasciurus hudsonicus*
Gray squirrel, *Sciurus carolinensis*
White-footed mouse, *Perymyscus leucopus*
Meadow mouse, *Microtus pennsylvanicus*
Short-tailed shrew, *Blarina brevicauda*
Woodchuck, *Marmota monax*
Eastern mole, *Scalopus aquaticus*
Muskrat, *Ondatra zibethicus*
Raccoon, *Procyon lotor*
Chipmunk, *Tamias striatus*
Little brown bat, *Myotis lucifugus*
Skunk, *Mephitis mephitis*

Raccoon

meadow mouse

CONSERVATION PLANTINGS

Dutch Mountain Nursery,
R. 1, 7984 N. 48th St.,
Augusta, Mich. 49012

Miles W. Fry & Sons Nursery,
R. 3,
Ephrata, Penna. 17522

Game Food Nurseries,
Box 371,
Oshkosh, Wisc. 54901

Pellett Gardens,
Atlantic, Iowa 50022

FOR BIRD LOVERS

Antiques, Inc.,
Box 1887,
Muskogee, Okla. 74401

Audubon Workshop,
44 Park Dr.,
Glenview, Ill. 66025

Conservation Enterprises,
2929 Country Club Rd.,
Winston-Salem, N.C. 27104

The Dilley Mfg. Co.,
17805 Euclid Ave.
Cleveland, Ohio 44112

Duncraft,
25 S. Main St.,
Penacook, N.H. 03301

Feather Hill Industries,
Box 41,
Zenda, Wisc. 53195

Conclusion

Much work has been done in the Wildflower Garden and much more remains to be done. Green islands play an important role in our quality of life and will continue to do so as population pressures increase. Within the limitations of Cornell Plantations staff and budget, this natural area will remain the beautiful area it is. With public support, cooperation, and constructive criticism, the Wildflower Garden will continue to be an asset to Ithaca and Central New York.

R. Stephen Shauger

FLOWER GARDEN PLANTS

Larkspur	Young plant, Seeds	Digestive upset, nervous excitement, depression, May be fatal.
Monkshood	Fleshy roots	Digestive upset and nervous excitement.
Autumn crocus, Star-of-Bethlehem	Bulbs	Vomiting and nervous excitement.
Lily-of-the-valley	Leaves, Flowers	Irregular heart beat and pulse, usually accompanied by digestive upset and mental confusion.
Iris	Underground stems	Severe, but not usually serious, digestive upset.
Foxglove	Leaves	One of the sources of the drug digitalis, used to stimulate the heart. In large amounts, the active principles cause dangerously irregular heartbeat and pulse, usually digestive upset and mental confusion. May be fatal.
Bleeding heart (Dutchman's breeches)	Foliage, Roots	May be poisonous in large amounts. Has proved fatal to cattle.

VEGETABLE GARDEN PLANTS

Rhubarb	Leaf blade	Fatal. Large amounts of raw or cooked leaves can cause convulsions, coma followed rapidly by death.

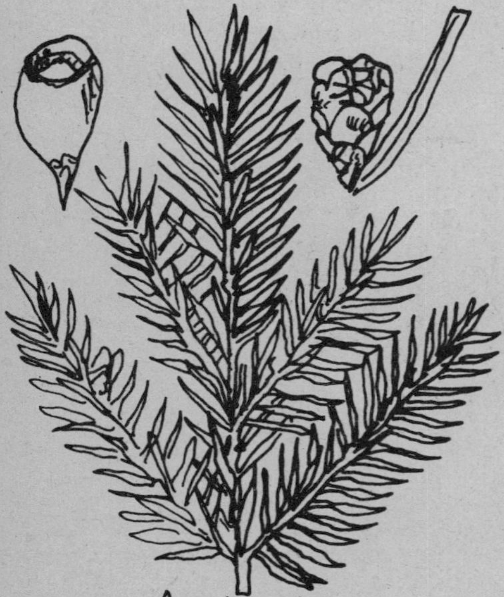

American Yew

Jimsonweed

NARCISSUS.

TYPE OF HOOP-PETTICOAT NARCISSUS.

White baneberry

Dutchman's breeches

PLANTS THAT POISON

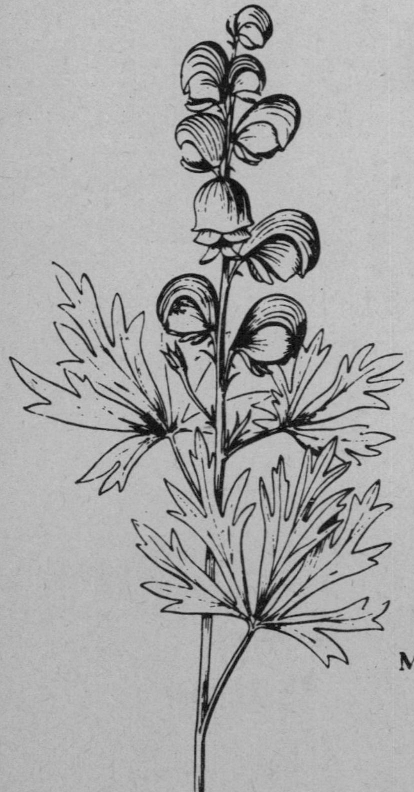

Monkshood

blade

stalk

Rhubarb

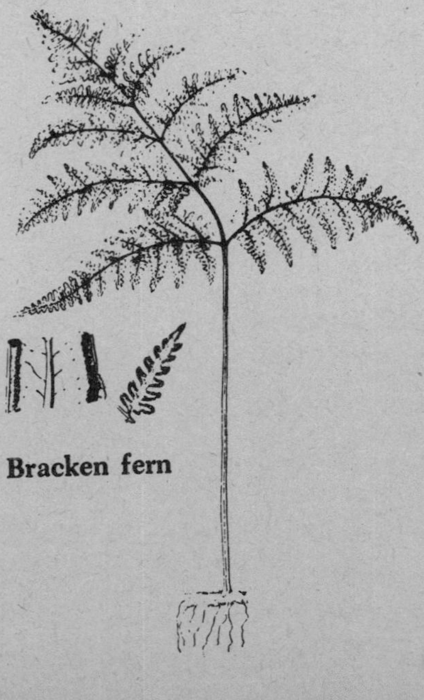

Bracken fern

Top: Lily-of-the-valley

Bottom: Star-of-Bethlehem

COMMON POISON HOUSE AND GARDEN PLANTS

Anyone can understand the attraction that brightly colored berries and foliage have for children and pets. So, a guide to poison plants should be a standard reference in every home where plants, pets, and children live together.

Statistically, there is little danger from poisonous plants. Yet, each year an estimated 12,000 children manage to ingest some dangerous plant. The peril increases as the green-plant boom brings an ever growing variety of new material to the market.

A recent study showed that ten out of 100 child poisoning cases observed involved kids who had eaten toxic plants. In six out of the ten, their parents did not know their plants were dangerous.

If a plant is attractive and has commercial value, there is a good chance it will find its way into your home or garden. If it is poisonous, there is a chance it may kill or discomfort someone you love.

It is best to keep all plant material beyond the reach of children and pets. "Look, but please don't touch," should be the rule. Also, it is wise to know the botanical names of plants, the common names often change from place to place.

Poisoning by plants is difficult to diagnose—it may be confused as poisoning by some other agents, like paint, insecticides or contaminated water. So, catalogue the potentially dangerous materials your child or pet is likely to get hold of. Know the symptoms these materials will manifest. There are few antidotes for plant poisoning. Treatment should be undertaken only by a physician, veterinarian or knowledgeable first-aid practitioner.

Each year, hospitals report more cases checking in after ingesting psychotropic mushrooms, seeds, roots and berries. We recommend that anyone contemplating this path, seek the services of a competent shaman. Many of these plants are deadly.

Jimson weed is a common psychotropic plant, often found in backyards and waste lands. It is reponsible for more poisonings than any other plant.

Diffenbachia is a common house plant. Did you know its stalk contains needle like crystals of calcium oxalate? These can become embedded in the tongue and tender tissues of the mouth, causing swelling and strangulation. The leaves of the Oleander bush contain a heart stimulant that can kill a child. Cherry twigs release cyanide when ingested. Peach leaves contain hydrocyanic acid, one of the five most dangerous poisons known.

Even the common potato and tomato plants contain alkaloid poisons in their foliage and vines that can create nervous and stomach disorders.

We have listed here the most common of poison plants. Hundreds more are listed in John M. Kingsbury's book, DEADLY HARVEST, a Holt, Rinehart & Winston publication.

Play it safe. Inform yourself and your kids. Write to us about the dangerous plants in your area. And we'll try to spread the word.

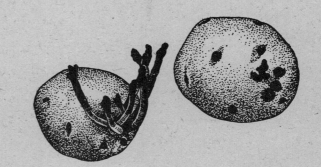

TREES AND SHRUBS

Wild and cultivated cherries	Twigs, Foliage	Fatal. Contains a compound that releases cyanide when eaten. Gasping, excitement, and prostration are common symptoms that often appear within minutes.
Oaks	Foliage, Acorns	Affects kidneys gradually. Symptoms appear only after several days or weeks. Takes a large amount for poisoning. Children should not be allowed to chew on acorns.
Elderberry	Shoots, Leaves, Bark	Children have been poisoned by using pieces of the pithy stems for blowguns. Nausea and digestive upset.
Black locust	Bark, Sprouts, Foliage	Children have suffered nausea, weakness and depression after chewing the bark and seeds.

Black locust

Celandine poppy

Horsetail

HOUSE PLANTS

Plant	Toxic Part	Symptoms
Hyacinth, Narcissus, Daffodil	Bulbs	Nausea, vomiting, diarrhea. May be fatal.
Oleander	Leaves, Branches	Extremely poisonous. Affects the heart, produces severe digestive upset and has caused death.
Dieffenbachia (Dumb cane) Elephant ear	All parts	Intense burning and irritation of the mouth and tongue. Death can occur if base of the tongue swells enough to block the air passage of the throat.
Rosary pea, Castor bean	Seeds	Fatal. A single rosary pea seed has caused death. One or two castor bean seeds are near the lethal dose for adults.
Poinsettia	Leaves	Fatal. One leaf can kill a child.
Mistletoe	Berries	Fatal. Both children and adults have died from eating the berries.

Mt. Azalea

Rhododendron

American Mistletoe

Indian tobacco

Privet

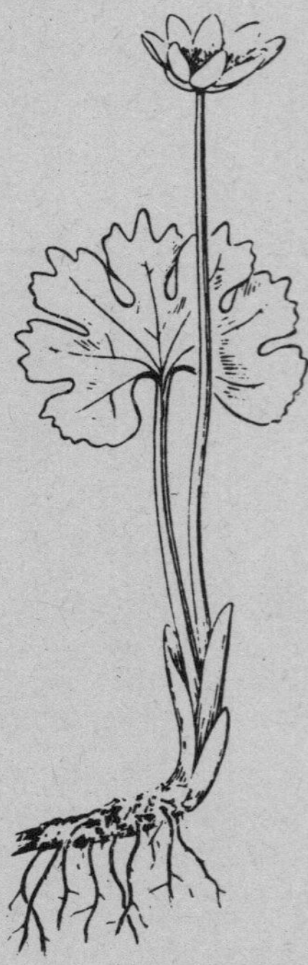

Bloodroot

Box

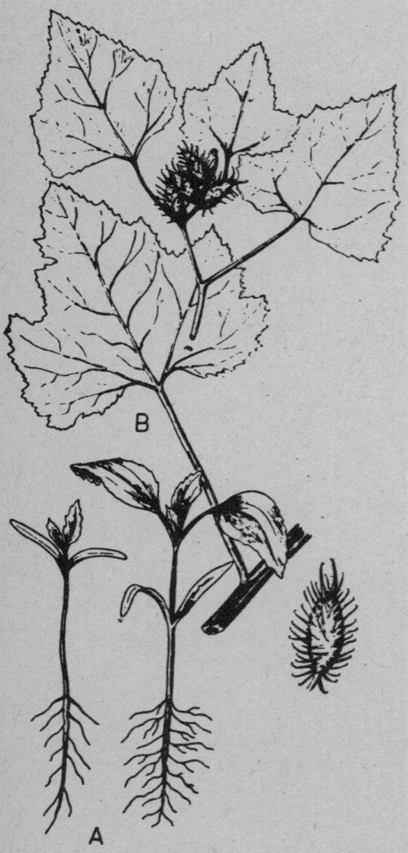

Cocklebur

Daphne

St. Johnswort

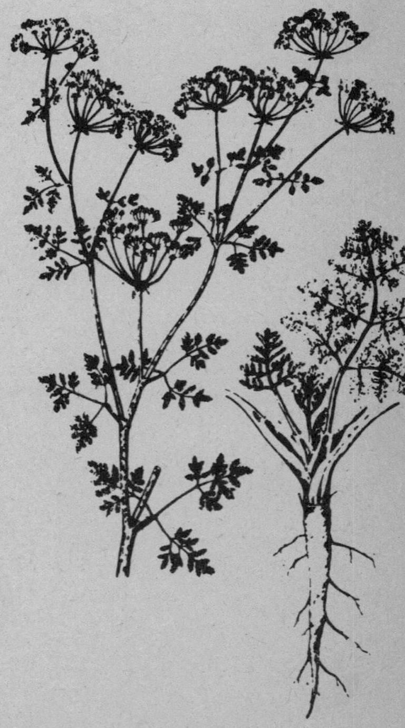

Poison hemlock

ORNAMENTAL PLANTS

Daphne	Berries	Fatal. A few berries can kill a child.
Wisteria	Seeds, Pods	Mild to severe digestive upset. Many children are poisoned by this plant.
Golden chain	Bean-like capsules in which the seeds are suspended	Severe poisoning. Excitement, staggering, convulsions and coma. May be fatal.
Laurels, Rhododendron, Azaleas	All parts	Fatal. Produces nausea and vomiting, depression, difficult breathing, prostration and coma.
Jessamine	Berries	Fatal. Digestive disturbance and nervous symptoms.
Lantana camara (red sage)	Green berries	Fatal. Affects lungs, kidneys, heart and nervous system. Grows in the southern U.S. and in moderate climates.

Water hemlock	All parts	Fatal. Violent and painful convulsions. A number of people have died from hemlock.

PLANTS IN FIELDS

Buttercups	All parts	Irritant juices may severely injure the digestive system.
Nightshade	All parts, especially the unripe berry	Fatal. Intense digestive disturbances and nervous symptoms.
Poison hemlock	All parts	Fatal. Resembles a large wild carrot. Used in ancient Greece to kill condemned prisoners.
Jimson weed (thorn apple)	All parts	Abnormal thirst, distorted sight, delirium, incoherence and coma. Common cause of poisoning. Has proved fatal.

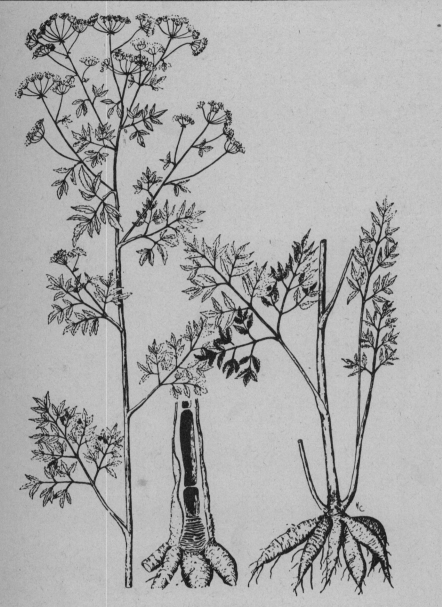

Water hemlock

Black nightshade A to C; Buffalo bur D and E; Horse nettle F and G; and European bittersweet H to K

PLANTS IN WOODED AREAS

Jack-in-the-pulpit	All parts, especially roots	Like dumb cane, contains small needle-like crystals of calcium oxalate that cause intense irritation and burning of the mouth and tongue.
Moonseed	Berries	Blue, purple color, resembling wild grapes. Contains a single seed. (True wild grapes contain several small seeds.) May be fatal.
Mayapple	Apple, Foliage, Roots	Contains at least 16 active toxic principles, primarily in the roots. Children often eat the apple with no ill effects, but several apples may cause diarrhea.

POISON IVY

POISON SUMAC

POISON OAK

ECOLOGY
Ecology is everybody's baby...

It's not just the concern of the fellow with the big smoke stack or the one polluting the stream, but everybody's job, to keep America beautiful.

For most of us it means recognizing and preserving the beauty of our own environment. It means giving our plants and shade trees, which like so many things these days are becoming more and more dependent on scientific research for survival, the opportunity to develop their full potential.

As a company with a long history of effort on behalf of the environment, we are continuing to spend substantial amounts of time, talent and money in research to provide the means of preserving the shade trees of tomorrow. But we are more than just a laboratory. We have the people with the ability and experience to help you improve the health and beauty of your trees. Call your local Bartlett representative today—together there is so much that we can do.

BARTLETT TREE EXPERTS

Home Office, 2770 Summer Street, Stamford, Conn.

Research Laboratories and Experimental Grounds, Pineville, N.C.

Local Offices from Maine to Florida and west to Illinois and Alabama.

CONSERVATION ORGANIZATIONS

All those organizations listed are national in scope and influence and welcome participation by unspecialized individuals. Their principle publications are listed.

COUNCIL ON ENVIRONMENTAL QUALITY
722 Jackson Place, N.W.
Washington, D.C. 20006

FRIENDS OF THE EARTH
529 Commercial Street
San Francisco, CA 94111
415-391-4270
NOT MAN APART (monthly)

NATIONAL AUDUBON SOCIETY
950 Third Avenue
New York, NY 10022
R. Boardman, Public Info.
212-832-3200
AUDUBON MAGAZINE

NATIONAL COUNCIL OF CONSERVATION DISTRICTS
Box 855
League City, TX 77573

NATIONAL ONION ASSN.
201-1/2 East Grand River Ave.
East Lansing, MI 48823
Roger N. Foerch, Exec. Sec.

NATIONAL PARKS AND CONSERVATION ASSN.
1701 18th Street, Northwest
Washington, D.C. 20009
O. J. Neslage, General Manager
202-265-2717
NATIONAL PARKS AND CONSERVATION
MAGAZINE: THE ENVIRONMENTAL JOURNAL
(monthly)

SIERRA CLUB
1050 Mills Tower
San Francisco, CA 94104
Michael McCloskey, Exec. Dir.
415-981-8634
SIERRA CLUB BULLETIN (10 issues/year)
NATIONAL NEWS REPORT (48 issues/year)

THE AMERICAN FORESTRY ASSOCIATION
1319 18th Street, Northwest
Washington, D.C. 20036
William E. Towell, Exec. V.P.
202-467-5810
AMERICAN FORESTS (monthly)

THE IZAAK WALTON LEAGUE OF AMERICA
1326 Waukegan Rd.
Glenview, IL 60025
OUTDOOR AMERICA

THE NATIONAL WILDLIFE FEDERATION
1412 16th Street, Northwest
Washington, D.C. 20036
CONSERVATION NEWS
RANGER RICK'S NATURE MAGAZINE

THE NATURE CONSERVANCY
Suite 800
1800 North Kent Street
Arlington, VA 22209
703-524-3151

THE WILDERNESS SOCIETY
1901 Pennsylvania Avenue, N.W.
Washington, D.C. 20006
Educational Services Dept.
202-293-2732
THE LIVING WILDERNESS

THE WILDERNESS WON'T LAST FOREVER

So little of the shrinking American wilderness remains that it is becoming increasingly difficult to discover a lonely spot, uncontaminated by noise and the refuse of civilization.

Not too long ago, giant basswoods grew along what once was the beautiful Oswego river in upstate New York. Now they are gone. Our generation has also watched the stately American elm die in our fields and parks. The California redwood, the oak, and the birch are disappearing at an alarming rate.

But then, what can we expect? We permit lumbermen to raze stands of native ash and hickory to make baseball bats and bowling pins.

We allow strip miners to level mountains searching for concealed minerals. We stand quietly by, while the Atomic Energy people quarantine as much as 250 square miles at a crack because they've had a little accident.

THE WILDERNESS WON'T LAST FOREVER

Keep this in mind when you wander the wild, unspoiled retreats of nature searching for exciting new plants for your garden.

Your first rule should be: Leave the shovels at home. Just imagine how long it would take to turn a forest or pasture into a desert if everyone felt compelled to dig up specimens for their own backyard.

We understand the very human compulsion to collect and own beautiful things. But, the bloom in a photograph will outlast the one in a vase. So, take a camera instead of a shovel. The act of shooting wild plants will bring you so close, you cannot help observing the minutest, most fantastic detail of their structure.

If you want to grow a plant you've admired in its native state, take cuttings from healthy, full grown specimens. Or, gather seeds after they have bloomed.

If the only way to bring it back alive is to dig it up, just thin out patches where the plants are plentiful. Always leave enough healthy specimens to propagate and maintain an ecological balance. In every case, before you dig, check the local laws. Many species are protected by conservation laws with large fines attached.

Also, remember, wild woodland pests may stow away on your specimens ready to infest your garden. The best way we know of to avoid this and assure that sensitive micro-ecologies (which we are just beginning to understand) are not tampered with, is to order rare plants and wild flowers you have admired in your ramblings from dealers who grow or collect their seed under controlled conditions.

Please, let's all try to leave some native woods and fields for our children. Let's work actively to restrain commercial pillagers and restrain ourselves as well.

—JAPANESE PLUME-GRASS (*Eulalia zebrina*).

THE AIR IN OUR CITIES that smarts our eyes and chokes our lungs also damages—and sometimes kills—our shrubs and trees. Runoff of salt spread on streets to melt snow and ice in winter harms lawns and other growing things. Plants are needed that will survive, even thrive, amid smoke, grime, fumes, chemicals.

Plants absorb carbon dioxide and supply us with oxygen in the process of photosynthesis. At the same time, they reduce pollutants in water and soil. They also remove significant amounts of gaseous pollutants and particles from the air. The microscopic plants in soil also reduce air pollutants and degrade many toxic chemicals that enter the soil.

Plants hold topsoil in place. Thus, they reduce sediment and excess nutrients which pollute water. Plants also make effective sound barriers, and so reduce noise pollution.

In the United States, ozone is the major pollutant that affects vegetation.

Other air pollutants of concern to plant scientists are peroxyacetyl nitrate (PAN), sulfur dioxide, and fluorides. Nitrogen dioxide and ethylene are not as likely to cause acute injury, but they may stunt the growth of plants and cause their premature old age.

Ozone and PAN are photochemical oxidants formed by sunlight acting on products of fuel combustion, particularly the nitrogen dioxide and hydrocarbons that come from motor vehicle exhausts.

Ethylene is also a product of fuel combustion, and to a very minor extent it is produced by vegetation.

Sulfur dioxide results from smelting ores and from burning fuels containing sulfur—such as coal and crude oil.

Fluorides are emitted in the production of aluminum, steel, ceramics, and phosphorus fertilizers.

Some of the injuries caused by air pollutants are given on the next page.

Ozone causes many small irregular lesions, called fleck or stipple, on the upper leaf surface of broad-leaved plants. Injury can develop on both leaf surfaces on upright growing species like grain or grass. Veins of the leaves tend to remain green unless general yellowing (chlorosis) occurs. Chlorotic lesions occur also on pine needles, along with tip dieback. Injury occurs primarily on lower leaves of plants.

Peroxyacetyl nitrate (PAN) causes collapse of tissue and silvering, glazing, or bronzing usually of the lower leaf surface. The injury may appear as transverse bands. PAN affects younger leaves than are affected by ozone.

Sulfur dioxide causes irregular blotches between the veins of leaves. These blotches show on both leaf surfaces. Injured tissue is white, gray, or ivory with larger veins remaining green. On grasses and similar plants with parallel veins, injury appears as streaks and general blight on leaf tips.

Nitrogen dioxide suppresses plant growth without marking the leaves when concentrations are low. High concentrations may produce leaf markings resembling sulfur dioxide injury.

Fluoride causes necrosis (death) of leaf margins and tips. On some plants—for example, citrus, poplar, and corn—chlorotic patterns on the leaves may be the principal symptoms.

Ethylene causes wilting of blossoms and drooping of the younger leaves, followed by premature yellowing and defoliation.

Pollution in towns and cities is seldom from a single pollutant. Usually there are many pollutants and their total effect is often much greater than you would expect, knowing their individual effects. There are also symptoms that mimic air pollution injury. They may be caused by insects and diseases or by poor nutrition, soil compaction, drought, cold, and high salt content in soil. Injury from air pollutants may make plants more susceptible to injury from some diseases and insects.

Premature aging of leaves caused by air pollutants is often confused with natural aging. The best way to know the full effects of photochemical oxidant air pollutants on plants is to grow the same plants in greenhouses in both unfiltered air and clean filtered air. Scientists have done this, with remarkable results.

GROUND-NUT

For example, studies near Los Angeles with citrus showed that yields of fruit were only about half as much in unfiltered air as in carbon-filtered air, even though the leaves were almost free of injury in the unfiltered air. Ozone was considered the primary cause of the reduced yield. It and other oxidants are effectively removed by activated carbon filters. Special filters are required to remove pollutants such as fluoride and ethylene.

Other studies, at Beltsville, Md., have shown that many plants benefit from air filtered through carbon to remove oxidants. Certain varieties of potato, onion, radish, and beans almost doubled their growth in greenhouses with carbon-filtered air. And they were free of the injuries observed in unfiltered air.

Sycamore seedlings in the carbon-filtered air were 25 percent taller than those in unfiltered air.

FIRE-WEED

Levels of the photochemical oxidants at Beltsville and along the East Coast are only about a third of those in the Los Angeles basin. But plants grown in the East, with its higher soil and air moisture content, are much more sensitive to pollutants than plants grown in the arid West.

Losses from air pollutants can be serious or minor, depending on the variety of crop planted. One variety of potato, Norland, showed severe leaf injury and marked reduction in yield of tubers in unfiltered air, whereas another variety, Kennebec, did not.

Eventually, there will be increased demand from the public for plants that tolerate air pollution. The greatest need will be for plants tolerating photochemical oxidants. Levels of these pollutants are increasing, and their distribution is widespread.

Scientists know that genetic variation in resistance to pollutants occurs in many species of plants. One plant survives; another does not. So, they identify and save seed from the one that does on the theory that the plant has a natural tolerance to air pollution. The widespread use of tolerant varieties will do much to reduce losses.

Losses from air pollutants may be further reduced by breeding plants to increase tolerance. This has been done successfully for cigar-wrapper tobacco in the Connecticut Valley.

To some extent, the breeders of crop and horticultural plants unknowingly have developed pollution-tolerant plants when selecting plants most free of the leaf injury. For example, the alfalfa variety Team developed at Beltsville has greater tolerance to ozone than varieties developed in other parts of the country with less air pollution. The cotton variety Acala SJ–1, developed and used in California, has more tolerance to ozone than varieties from the Southeastern United States, where levels of these pollutants are much lower.

Plants are good air pollution detectives, and their use for this purpose will increase. West Germany requires planting of forest species around certain industries as a check on emission of

—THE DUNKELD LARCHES, AS THEY APPEARED IN 1876.

Trees and pollution could almost make a separate chapter. Although trees generally live a long time, air pollution can kill them.

For more than 95 years the sulfur dioxide spewed out by smelters in the United States and Europe has been killing trees, mostly the conifers, like pines, spruces, and firs. Extreme damage to conifers by sulfur dioxide was found in timbered areas around smelters, but losses also occurred in urban industrial centers where sulfur dioxide was the major pollutant.

In 1924, after a long struggle with conifer culture, the Royal Botanic Gardens decided to concentrate its future conifer plantings in rural Kent rather than at Kew, near London.

Ozone and sulfur dioxide cause chlorotic dwarf disease and other ailments of white pine in the Eastern United States. Some of the affected white pines are in rural areas far removed from industry and urban centers. However, during periods of air stagnation the blanket of polluted air may cover a whole region from Maryland to Massachusetts.

But these are trees of the forest. In the East or the West, or anywhere in between, we might plant a Douglas-fir, a ponderosa pine, or an eastern white pine as an ornamental to grace our home grounds or to landscape a factory site, but they are not the usual trees of urban areas. What about the shade trees—elms, oaks, maples, planes; what about our ornamental trees—cherries, magnolias, flowering crabapples? We do not know the extent that these trees, which make life so much more livable, are suffering because of a polluted environment. Both acute and chronic injury are known to occur on some of these species because of pollutants.

Especially in our cities, trees are of inestimable value as they reduce noise, produce shade, filter out dust particles, and perhaps most importantly, provide an esthetic link between urban man and his wilderness heritage.

Reducing air pollution at the source will help to maintain the trees, but pollution probably cannot be eliminated.

NETTLE

POPPY

toxicants. Sensitive plants may show visible effects of pollution long before their effects can be observed on animals or materials.

Plants are cheaper than specialized instrumentation as pollution detectives. They respond to several pollutants—effects can be additive—and they indicate whether pollutants of biological significance are present.

Of course, we also need instrumentation including, for some pollutants such as photochemical oxidants, a national grid of devices with the information summarized by computers and made available immediately to the public. The monitoring is primarily needed from June through September when oxidant levels are highest and vegetation is making most of its growth. In the Los Angeles basin the need is almost year round.

When plants are injured by pollutants we know they are, at the same time, removing some pollutants. In the case of fluoride pollution, leaves of tolerant species may contain several hundred parts per million of fluoride without visible injury. Leaves also remove pollutants, such as ozone and dust particles, just by contact with leaf surfaces. But more of the gaseous pollutants are removed when stomata or microscopic pores are open. There are several thousand of these pores on each square inch of leaf surface. Normally they are open in the day and closed at night.

Lower forms of plant life also remove pollutants in air, soil, and water. For example, some of the micro-organisms in soil remove carbon monoxide and hydrocarbons, such as ethylene, when the air above the soil surface mixes with air in the soil. Other micro-organisms degrade toxic chemicals so residues do not build up.

Chemical reactions seem to be primarily involved in soil removal of other pollutants such as sulfur dioxide and nitrogen dioxide.

Maintaining an abundance of vegetation is essential for pollution control. Top soil should be kept in place, and we need to propagate more plants than we destroy by our activities.

Therefore, we must find ways for man and trees to live better under urban conditions.

Any reduction in vitality of a tree makes it a more likely host for insect and disease attack and lowers its resistance to other environmental stresses such as drought. What can be done to improve the resistance of trees to pollution?

As with horticultural and crop plants, trees must be found that are sufficiently tolerant of pollutants so as to be free of acute injury. Also, they must maintain satisfactory vigor when exposed to existing pollution levels. Even if pollution is reduced significantly at the source, tolerant trees will still be needed to thrive at the reduced pollution levels.

How can we select pollution-resistant trees? One obvious technique is to survey urban trees to determine which species have endured on our city streets over the years.

Two species immediately come to mind. These are the ginkgo and the Chinese tree-of-heaven (Ailanthus), the tree that grows even in Brooklyn. The ginkgo is an acceptable shade tree, especially the male trees that do not produce the characteristic odoriferous fruit. Ailanthus, however, cannot be considered at all desirable, except perhaps in the most desperate situations.

Reports of "natural" resistance vary from one region to another, and a tree species deemed resistant in Houston may be quite susceptible in Buffalo.

But town and city streets are not an ideal laboratory. Growing conditions vary tremendously, even from one side of a street to the other, and may influence a tree's response to gaseous air pollutants. Furthermore, since urban air pollution—especially photochemical smog—is a rather recent manifestation of civilization, there has not been sufficient time for any significant degree of natural selection for pollution tolerance to have taken place.

We can select for resistance by subjecting young tree seedlings or detached plant parts to measured amounts of pollutant gases under controlled conditions. Special fumigation chambers are being used to study the effects of various gases, alone or in combination, on trees as well as other plants. Even with the limited facilities available at the present, some progress is being made.

What has been found? Certain relationships between species have been established. For instance, European linden is more tolerant of ozone than is white ash. On the other hand, linden is more susceptible to salt in the soil. But the most important finding of the fumigation studies, exceeding even the differences between species, is the significant differences in resistance among *individual* plants within a species.

Urban tree culture is rapidly turning from dependence on particular species to the use of selected clones. All the members of a clone are propagated vegetatively from an individual tree (by grafting, budding, or rooted cuttings) and have the same genetic constitution, like identical twins.

It is in individual selection that our greatest hope lies. The selection of pollution-tolerant trees, and the combination of air pollution resistance with other desirable characteristics such as disease resistance and tolerance to drought and salts, is possible by selective breeding. Trees could be developed also for efficiency in removing pollutants from the atmosphere.

Trees live a long time; tree breeding takes a long time. But the improved trees resulting from today's research will last a long time—to enhance our towns, suburbs, and cities for the good of the people.

Salt Pollution

Salts occur naturally in soils and waters and may be considered pollutants only when man introduces extraneous salts. This obviously occurs when salt is used to de-ice city streets and highways.

Salts supply plants with mineral nutrients essential for their growth. When present in excess, however, salts are injurious.

In humid regions, rain readily leaches salts out of the soil, and salinity is not normally a problem. In subhumid and arid regions, plants must be watered, and salts present in irrigation waters are the main source of salt accumulation in the soil. Many irrigated areas in modern as well as in ancient times have been "salted out" or severely damaged as a result of salt accumulation.

When you water your plants they absorb water, but leave behind in the soil most of the salts that were in the water. The only way to remove these salts is to use more water than that which evaporates and is used by the plants. If the excess water can drain away below the roots, it will carry with it the excess, unwanted salts. This is called leaching.

Leaching with a 6-inch depth of water, for example, will reduce the salinity of the top foot of soil by 50 percent, and a 12-inch depth of water will reduce it by 80 percent. Chemical amendments, such as gypsum, are needed to reclaim sodium-affected soils. Subsoil drainage must be provided if it is not naturally adequate.

What are the symptoms of salt injury? As the level of salinity increases, leaves, stems, flowers, and fruits are generally smaller. Stunting and, in extreme cases, death of plants are usually the only observable effects on most *nonwoody* plants. *Woody* plants—that is, trees, shrubs, and vines—are damaged by accumulations of sodium or chloride in the leaves. Characteristic tip or marginal leaf burns develop. Burned leaves often drop off the plants, and this may be followed by dieback of stems and eventual death of the plants.

Plant species exhibit a wide range of salt tolerance. The most tolerant economic species, such as Bermudagrass, are able to tolerate salt concentrations about 10 times as great as those tolerated by the most sensitive species—African-violet, rose, and strawberry for example.

Some idea of the salt levels tolerated by plants can be given in terms of the total salt concentration in soil water bathing the roots. Sensitive species are affected when the soil water contains more than 0.2 percent total salts in solution. Moderately tolerant plants are affected above 0.5 percent, and tolerant plants above 1 percent. For comparison, sea water has a salt content of 3.5 percent, and saturated brine a concentration of 35 percent.

Most nonwoody flower crops are moderately salt tolerant. Shrubs vary widely in salt tolerance. Natal plum, bougainvillea, oleander, dodonea, bottle brush, and the ground cover, rosemary, are quite salt tolerant. Most shrubs are moderately tolerant. The most sensitive shrub species include Algerian ivy (a groundcover), Burford holly, pineapple guava, and rose.

Trees from normally saline habitats, like the tamarisks and mangroves, are highly tolerant. Other tolerant species include the black locust and honey locust. Coniferous trees, such as the blue spruce, white pine, and Douglas-fir, are relatively sensitive, but ponderosa pine and eastern red cedar are moderately tolerant as are also white oak, red oak, spreading juniper and arborvitae.

Plants normally absorb salts through their roots, but many will take up salts directly through their leaves if the foliage is wetted by sprinkling. Fruit trees, such as plum and other stone fruits, and citrus absorb salts so readily through their leaves that sprinkler systems usually must be designed to avoid wetting the foliage of these trees. Uptake of salt by the leaves of shrubs has not been studied, but salt-spray damage has been observed in coastal areas of Florida and Australia where sea spray wets the foliage. Leaf damage from salt-water spray has also been noted for trees and shrubs planted along highways that were de-iced with salt.

The extensive salt damage to trees, shrubs, and grass along streets and highways de-iced by salt is harder to control by plant selection. Salt concentrations in water draining off the highway can be so high that no plant adapted to northern conditions may be able to survive. Further, the loss of magnificent roadside trees may not be acceptable, even if some humble salt-tolerant replacement species is available.

It would be better to install drains to carry the brine solutions away from the highway without damaging roadside trees. Design of new highways and roadside plantings should take into account the effects of de-icing by salt.

Land will be increasingly used for the disposal of liquid and solid wastes to reduce contamination of our waterways and to take advantage of the exceptional capacity of soil to remove and decompose many waste materials. Tolerance of plants to salinity, as well as other pollutants, will have to be taken into account.

Salinity, like air pollution, cannot be completely eliminated. However, if adequately salt tolerant plant species are readily available, the salinity may not be damaging.

—CATALPA SPECIOSA.

Author H. E. HEGGESTAD is Leader in Charge of the Plant Air Pollution Laboratory, Plant Science Research Division, Agricultural Research Service (ARS).

Coauthor F. S. SANTAMOUR, JR., is a Research Geneticist, U.S. National Arboretum, Plant Science Research Division.

Coauthor LEON BERNSTEIN is a Plant Physiologist, Soil and Water Conservation Research Division, ARS.

Green is the color of hope

Henry M. Cathey*

By tradition, the horticulturist has planted seed, taken cuttings, and grown and protected plants for food, utility and beauty.

Today, his job is bigger than the tradition. The environmental crisis is growing more threatening every day. The horticulturist can help meet that crisis. He can put greater horticultural knowledge and experience into man's efforts to improve the world he lives in. The world needs all of his techniques and skills to develop plants to survive in a changing environment, plants to meet changing life styles, and plants to fit the shrinking limits of available time and space.

What the world needs now is smog-resistant trees and shrubs, including plants for compact and often hostile areas.

Today's horticulturists are prepared for this role with their special knowledge of plant genetics, physiology, and pathology. Already they have made great advances. They have increased productivity, and bred pest and disease resistance into many horticultural lines. They have given us new ornamentals. They have learned how to induce plants to bloom on schedule so that florists can offer spring-flowering plants with the popular poinsettia at Christmas time and chrysanthemums the year round.

They have accommodated their work to new developments in other fields. For instance, they have adapted the fragile tomato, as well as other fruits and vegetables, to mechanical harvesters. They grow orchids in Hawaii and carnations in Colorado to take advantage of favorable growing conditions; then they use improved storage and transpor-

*Henry M. Cathey, Acting Leader Ornamental Laboratory, Plant Genetics and Germplasm Institute, National Agricultural Research Center, Beltsville, Maryland.

tation to get their products to market quickly.

To accomplish so much, horticulturists have had to overcome incompatability of seed plants; eliminate disease reservoirs of stock plants, utilize artificial soil mixes and fertilizers; and become manipulators of plant growth through the use of light, temperature and special growth substances.

While the horticulturist is seeking to improve our fruits, vegetables, and ornamentals, the rest of us are indirectly working against him. The public is taking out of production some of the best land for horticultural use. We are saturating our surroundings with machines, concrete, buildings, and with a rapidly developing excess of people.

Our planet contains a number of limited consumables. The major limiting consumable may be readily available carbon dioxide. To maintain the present level of photosynthesis on earth, we must recycle all of the CO_2 every 250 years. But this rate is being accelerated. Increased population and increased mechanization have caused our global society to tie up oxygen and to release CO_2 faster than in any previous generation. We are slowly changing the balance of life on earth. Furthermore, at this point in history, we do not know the long-term effects—on a global scale—of increased CO_2 levels, increased growth rates of plants, changes in temperatures in our urban areas, and the shift in the balance of nature.

We do know this: Photosynthesis is essential to life. And we know that:

1. Almost three-fourths of all photosynthesis occurs in water—in algae—so that most of our oxygen supply comes from tropical oceans.

2. Cultivated plants probably contribute less than ten per cent of the total photosynthesis.

3. Photosynthesis occurs only at a specific range of temperature, relative humidity, mineral nutrition, and so on.

4. Plant release of O_2 occurs

only in sunlight. Thus, during part of each day (night), and part of each year (winter), plants do not add O_2 but actually remove it from the atmosphere.

5. The level of photosynthesis depends on light intensity and the CO_2 level. CO_2 is usually a limiting growth factor.

On the average day our environment contains 0.03 per cent CO_2. There are many intervals, during the daylight hours, when the level of CO_2 falls greatly, depending on the kind of plants and on other environmental factors.

Nevertheless, plants have a unique function in the recycling process. They recycle CO_2 and O_2, complementing the cycling of animal metabolism. However, plants contribute to the recycling system *only* when they are in active growth, with all of their green leaves carrying on photosynthesis.

The plot of grass in one's garden is not related to any specific group of people, as implied by the claim that fifty square feet of grass liberates enough oxygen to serve a family of four. Such claims are based on classic information from textbooks plus a slide-rule expansion to 365 days a year. Most plants grow in marginal circumstances. Since they give off O_2 only under the specific conditions described above they are efficient in the range of 3, 5, or 7 per cent of the classic ideal; routine slide-rule expansion is misleading.

Although plants cultivated by man contribute only a small percentage of the total photosynthesis on earth, these green plants are important to us because they live where we live. These green plants surround man, and help him and his habitat create the landscapes of earth.

The ability of plants to play their role in photosynthesis depends on the kind of plant and on light. Plants vary greatly in the minimum-maximum range of light levels they require to support their growth. For instance, beans need a minimum of 100-foot candles. Oaks can live in a range from 300- to 1,500-foot can-

SWEET-SCENTED SHRUB.
(CALYCANTHUS FLORIDUS.)

NEW SINGLE TULIPS.

ENGLISH HAWTHORN.
(CRATÆGUS OXYACANTHA.)

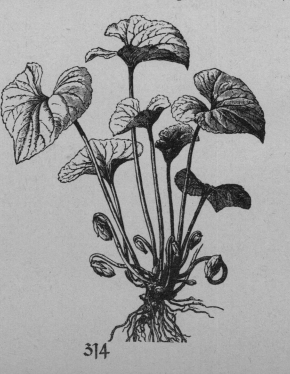

dles, pines from 300-to 9,000, and philodendron from a minimum of 25- to a maximum of only 500-foot candles.

Scattered remains of rubbish, floating in our air, filter out some light and retard the recycling of CO_2 and O_2. We are told that plants in our urban environment today are receiving sixteen per cent less light than they did a generation ago. This means that the efficiency of city plants is reduced, since they may be growing at a minimum or lower than the maximum light levels.

In the interest of improving our environment with plants, some mistakes have emanated from well-meaning but misguided assumptions and slogans. Let us consider a few, and also the positive approach that can be made.

"We should plant a tree." This is good advice in the right place. Ask the men and women who know—the horticulturists. Look to them and get involved in sensible gardening and sensible planting. There are organizations to suit all tastes; work with the ones that best suit you.

"Plants purify the air." This in itself is an oversimplification and can be misleading. Plants suffer in polluted air filled with chemicals that attack the life-support system of plants. These chemicals are by-products—wastes—of man's machines. Some may even be created in space by photochemistry. During the daylight hours, plants have their mouths, or stomates, wide open. They take up ozone, sulfur dioxide, peroxylacetyl nitrate (PAN), carbon monoxide, ethylene, and other harmful substances. Plants may not be fully effective in ridding the environment of these, but they trap and remove from the air much that is a threat and even potentially lethal.

Plants also help to recycle water. Man rejects water that is not palatable. Plants are just as demanding of good quality in water. Some of the materials dispersed and dissolved in water reduce its availability to plants, and thus limit plant growth.

The amount of water required by even one annual plant is enormous. For example, in one growing season a single tomato plant requires thirty-four gallons, one corn plant fifty-four gallons, and one sunflower plant as much as 130 gallons.

Of the total water required for each plant, less than five per cent is used directly to maintain its life processes. Plants lose water to the atmosphere as part of the recycling of the earth's "consumables." The remaining ninety-five per cent of the required water cools the surrounding areas and sets up the recycling—from contaminated to aerated rain water.

Plants can serve man in a other area of "pollution"—noise. Man and his machines generate a steadily rising din. Over the years, noise levels have increased to the point where they are producing both psychological and physiological problems for us. Green plants can be used in strips, buffers, and screens to deflect, absorb, break up, and muffle many of the sounds that make community living unpleasant and uncomfortable.

Light upsets nature's balance. Man's need to see—to see movement of other men and machines after dark—has brought "moonlight" during the night hours over most of our urban environment. Ordinary mercury vapor lamps have been the standard urban lighting for many years. Although they have only slight effect on the growth and development of our green plants, the blue light emitted from them attracts night flying insects from surrounding areas. The insects consume decorative plants, lay eggs for future generations, and disfigure the landscape.

To prevent this kind of pollution, many of our cities now are substituting so-called "color-improved" lamps for the blue ones. These are not the answer, either. They emit enough red light to cause the green leaves of many kinds of plants to hold on and delay the necessary onset of dormancy. Yellow lights generally are better because the red is at such a low level as to have little or no effect on plant growth. Night lighting with the wrong kind of lamps can greatly decrease the survival potential of some of our most desired trees and shrubs.

"Man will continue to find ways to adapt himself and his plants." This is an optimistic view. Man may be able to do some things to adapt himself, his plants, and his environment, to survive. Many plants are extinct today because they were not able to survive. Others such as the magnolia, dogwood, and the ginkgo, have survived many environmental changes and still are beautiful and widely used.

In this adaptation process Man can call upon all of his resources. But he must still look to the horticulturist to propagate, to grow, and to protect our plants.

The horticulturist will be pressed to select tolerant plants for even a scrubbed environment. The pressures will be so great that he will be impatient to wait for years to find out whether a seedling possesses desired color, form, resistance, sound baffling, and fragrance, as well as tolerance to polluted air, soil, and water. He will have to learn more about relating the early stages of plant growth to the desired performance of mature plants. He will have to develop plants that use inherent resources and characteristics to ward off pests and diseases. He must continue to look for plants for the consumer to plant EVERYTHING.

Green is the color of hope. In the green of our plants is the hope of survival. It begins in the hands of the skilled horticulturist but ultimately it moves through the hands of horticulturists to the hands of all people who grow plants—fruit, vegetables, ornamentals.

The decisions are in our hands, in our propagation beds, in our fields. In the seeds that we planted last week or the cuttings we shall make next week lies our hope for survival. ✥

RED-HOT POKER.
(TRITOMA UVARIA.)

WISTARIA SINENSIS.

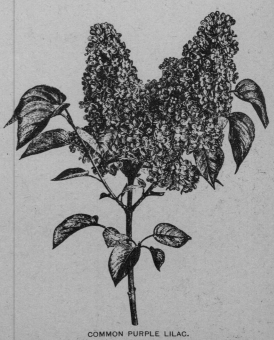

COMMON PURPLE LILAC.
(SYRINGA VULGARIS.)

IT'S TOO LATE TO HIDE

When we began to compile THE GARDENER'S CATALOGUE, we carefully took stock of our own attitudes concerning every one of the subjects in the table of contents. All of us, we discovered, were strongly prejudiced against the use of chemical fertilizers and pesticides. Each of us, having researched the issues, had already determined that we would not use these chemicals in our own gardens.

Yet, we felt that since THE GARDENER'S CATALOGUE was our gift to all gardeners, whether they grow organically or with chemicals, we were duty bound to explore both sides of this question as fully as possible. That way, not only could we let ourselves off the hook on this sensitive issue, but more importantly, our readers could decide for themselves what they would do in their own gardens.

That was our original intention. So, we canvassed the garden chemical industry. We spoke to representatives of the ecology movement—the most persistent having already earned the appellation "Eco-Jerks" in press circles. And, we contacted the government, in particular, the U.S. Department of Agriculture.

That way we hoped to come up with a balanced presentation of both sides of the issue. Then, the question could be answered intelligently by our readers. You see, one of our other collective prejudices is, that you ought to be able to cultivate your own garden in whatever manner you feel is right for you.

POISONS IN OUR GARDENS
YES OR NO?

In answer to our queries, we were bombarded with books and broadsides from the ecology people. That was to be expected. Crusaders will talk to anyone who listens. The government, that is, the extension services and the USDA, also returned an overwhelming amount of material. It's their job. But, from the garden chemical industry, we heard not one word.

So, we tried the telephone. In one case, we were told that the director of publicity was on vacation and would be on vacation until some time after our deadline. Nothing could be released for publication without his permission. Another company wanted to see our copy before releasing their material. That was unacceptable to us.

If we are to be the conscience of the industry, we cannot allow the industry to edit our copy.

And, so it went with all the manufacturers and suppliers of garden chemicals. All our inquiries were greeted with suspicion and evasion.

They all pointed to increasing population pressures and raised the specter of mass starvation if chemical fertilizers and pesticides would be made unavailable.

Now, nobody wants that. But, both "The New York Times" and "Organic Gardening Magazine" have recently featured articles that claim high yields have been achieved by commercial growers who conscientiously avoid using chemicals. Not only is their production competitive, but they report higher unit prices for their produce when compared to the market prices of chemically grown fruit, vegetables and grains.

Our feeling grew that the fert/pest/chem industry had something to hide. But, let us digress for a moment to see just what their products are and how they affect THIS GARDEN EARTH.

Pesticides is the general name for chemical pest killers. Some specific pesticide products on the market under various brand names are 2-4-D, DDT, chlordane, malathion, toxaphene, aldrin, endrin, dursban, DDVP, DDD, TDE and heptachlor.

For the chemical content of these and thousands more, we refer you to the Pesticide Handbook, compiled annually by Dr. E. E. H. Frear. It is available by writing to College Science Publishers, State College, Penn. or The Entomological Society of America, 4603 Calvert Road, Box AJ, College Park, Maryland 20740.

However, these pest killers, once heralded as boons to mankind, have a fatal flaw, the Eco-Groups say. They work too well.

Sure, they kill aphids, mealy bugs, borers and so on. But, they also kill honey bees, lady bugs and almost every one of the other 800,000 species of insects known to inhabit THIS GARDEN EARTH.

Keep in mind that only 3,000 species of insects are known to be harmful to man. The birds, fish, small mammals and occasional humans that are killed by these chemicals, were not harmful at all. In fact many birds, reptiles and insects play a vital part in the natural control of garden and field pests.

We are just beginning to understand the subtle ties that bind all the life on this planet together. But, one thing is rapidly becoming clear. We already suffer from blind, large-scale tampering with micro-ecologies that have had disastrous effects upon the macro-ecology. This certainly is unacceptable, ecologists cry out.

Wrong, says the chemical industry, raising the specter of the hungry horseman, again. If you want to eat, we must spray and fertilize, because the land will no longer yield up its bounty to outdated methods.

Unfortunately, in some areas this is true, the ecology people agree. The nitrogen cycle in the Napa valley, for example, has become inoperative, they say. Constant application of phosphates and pesticides have killed the bacteria and other tiny organisms that make the natural revitalization of the soil possible. The soil of this once-fertile valley is now sterile. Without chemicals, it would become a desert.

What's more frightening, though, is the fact that many of these deadly chemicals are dispersed by wind and water. They are absorbed by micro-organisms, which are eaten by macro-organisms, which, in turn, are eaten by little fish, that are eaten by bigger fish, and so on, until a whole food chain is infected by poisons. The chemicals become more concentrated with each step up the food chain. A very important fact, when you remember that humans sit at the top of the chain. And, no mother's milk is free of DDT today. We certainly can't let it get any worse.

Well, the industry spokesmen remind us, we must be rid of the insects and use chemical fertilizers if we are to eat. So, we must tolerate a certain percentage of these poisons in our bodies.

But, ecologists point out that insects are among the most adaptive creatures in THIS GARDEN EARTH. Pesticides weed out the weak, but, the survivors breed resistant strains.

So, we must escalate the war and resort to other insecticides, the industry says. But another resistant strain of insects will evolve, ecologists answer. Then we must escalate again, says the industry. And so on, and so on. . .

Well, isn't that what you'd say if you were selling the stuff? the ecology people warn. Beware of self-serving industry propaganda. These are the same companies that brought you the "Gas Crisis" and air pollution. As an example, the ecologists remind us that the well-known Ortho garden chemical company is owned by Chevron; also, Agrico used to be owned by Continental Oil.

So, which are we to believe—the ecologists or an industry that seems to be hiding something? The problem was solved for us when we read the USDA Guidelines For Handling Pesticides, which we reprint from the 1973 Yearbook of Agriculture.

USDA GUIDELINES FOR HANDLING PESTICIDES

"Pesticides are toxic chemicals used to control or repel insects, plant diseases, rodents, weeds, nematodes, and other pests. They are available in a number of different forms and concentrations such as liquids, solids, gases, powders, dusts, and granules. Insecticides are for control of insects, fungicides for plant diseases, herbicides for weeds, and rodenticides for rodents.

"Safe use of pesticides is the responsibility of every purchaser. Your responsibility begins when you buy a pesticide and ends only when all the material has been used and the empty containers disposed of safely. Some pesticides retain their potency long after they have been applied. They should be stored, handled, and applied with respect for their dangerous nature.

"The label of the pesticide container, by law, clearly lists the precautions needed for safe use. Before buying a pesticide, read the label to be sure the precautions are understood and they can be followed. Many pesticides used on food crops have limitations on the time intervals required between last application and harvest.

"Store all pesticides where they cannot possibly be contacted accidentally by children or pets. A sturdy locked cabinet in a toolshed which is isolated from the house is an ideal place to store them. Remember to keep them locked at all times except when in use.

"Observe the following precautions in using pesticides:

—Read the label carefully and completely and be sure you understand it fully. Follow it explicitly.

—Never stir any chemical solution with your hands. Be sure to wash clothing and equipment thoroughly after each use.

—Do not eat, drink, or smoke while mixing or applying pesticides. Wash hands and face immediately after working with pesticides.

—Rinse and drain all empty pesticide containers with water or other dilutents being used in your spray operations. Each container should be rinsed three times and the residue poured back into your spray tank before you dispose of it.

—Crush empty pesticide containers and bury them 18 inches deep in soil where they will not contaminate water supplies. If you burn the containers, stay out of the smoke. Do not burn containers for volatile substances such as 2,4-D. Never burn aerosol containers.

—If you live in an apartment, wrap empty rinsed containers in several layers of newspaper, crush, and/or puncture the container (except aerosols) and place them in your garbage container.

—Mix only the quantity of pesticide you need for a specific job. Avoid storage if possible. Protect labels so they won't become lost or illegible. Never use unlabeled pesticides.

—Avoid applying pesticides that might contaminate wells, ponds, streams, and water supplies.

—Dispose of leftover spray materials in a safe manner. The best way to do this is to use up the material for its purpose.

—Store chemicals in a separate locked storage area. Keep all chemicals out of reach of children, pets, and irresponsible persons. Label the storage area and never allow small children to play in or around a mixing, storage, or disposal area.

—Apply pesticides only on quiet days when the wind is at a minimum and blowing away from susceptible plants.

—Buy only as much pesticide as you need for a single season.

—If you store them under your kitchen sink or in cabinets where they can be reached by small children, you are asking for trouble. Inventory the materials that are accessible to small children whether you have any kids or not, for the simple reason that your grandchildren or other children who might be visiting you could get into them and be poisoned accidentally. Cans and bottles seem to attract small children, and those containing toxic materials contribute significantly to the total number of cases of accidental poisonings and deaths."[1]

Remember that the men who wrote this document are government employees, working in a department controlled by political appointees. Their bosses, therefore, are susceptible to political pressure. So we must not be too surprised when they throw the burden of responsibility on the consumers' shoulders. After all, the oil and chemical industries have always demonstrated that they have muscle in Washington. Once again, it's the old story of: "Let the buyer beware."

However, many of the men at the USDA are scientists who know the dilemma we all face. In good conscience, they could not ignore it.

But, they bury the key to this government document quoted above in the lines that advise, "AVOID APPLYING PESTICIDES THAT MIGHT CONTAMINATE WELLS, PONDS, STREAMS, AND WATER SUPPLIES." (emphasis supplied)

AS FAR AS WE ARE CONCERNED, THIS INCLUDES ALMOST EVERY CHEMICAL PESTICIDE AND CHEMICAL FERTILIZER ON THE MARKET.

WHETHER THEY ARE SPRAYED OR SPREAD, THEY ALL EVENTUALLY END UP DISSOLVED IN OUR WATER SUPPLY OR SITTING IN THE OOZE AT THE BOTTOM OF OUR FOOD CHAIN.

WE DEFY THE INDUSTRY TO PROVE OTHERWISE.

WE URGE THE GOVERNMENT TO RESIST THE PRESSURES OF INDUSTRIES THAT COULD TURN THIS GARDEN EARTH INTO A DESERT.

[1] Authors of the above-quoted material are: L. C. Gibbs, Program Leader, Pesticide-Chemicals, Extension Service; and Ovid Bay, Program Leader for Information, Agriculture and Natural Resources, Extension Service.

We started out trying to be objective about the garden chemical industry. But, after seeing the mass of data concerning this subject, we determined that the only objective position on the subject of chemical garden poisons, whether they are called pesticides or fertilizers, is total outrage.

We, the American people, have been sold hard on the idea that chemicals are necessary if our gardens and fields are to survive. Now, we're beginning to hear crys of alarm from rapidly growing numbers of reputable scientists and just plain gardeners. They believe that a sterile globe is the inheritance we will leave our children if we do not stop poisons from being introduced into our environment.

The oil and chemical industries are very powerful, and it was perhaps understandable that the USDA threw the bulk of the responsibility for control back to the citizen consumer.

We must realize that none of these companies will pull a successful product off the market without a fight. So, fight.

Our advice is: "If you don't need it, don't buy it." There is no reason, that we can see, to use chemical fertilizers and pesticides in your garden. There are plenty of natural controls that work very well on a small scale. As we have shown, even prize-winning roses can be grown without chemicals. Of course, not every plant will be perfect. But, we suggest that pure drinking water is more important than a few more perfect roses.

The same is true of food gardening. Here too, much of the spraying is done for cosmetic purposes. We are not concerned merely with the dangerous practices of adding dyes and preservatives to the produce in the packing houses, though, but with practices like field-spraying apples to prevent scab.

Scab in no way affects the flavor or food value of apples. In this case, they just spray to make the fruit look pretty. And we wonder if pretty looking fruit is worth the price our children will have to pay.

Unless farmers and gardeners have spoiled their land beyond redemption, there's no reason to use chemicals at all. There are many large commercial growers who have beaten the market producing without chemicals. We wonder if increased profit is not enough of a temptation to induce any farmer trying to hold onto his land, to take part of his acreage out of cultivation each year for detoxification and revitalization. The government could help here by backing farmers willing to go it without poisons.

In view of the world food crisis, we hesitate recommending that all chemicals be banned. In areas like the Napa Valley, farmers are doomed to use them forever unless the soil scientists develop methods of saving sterile soils. Unfortunately, we cannot afford to let this land lay until nature takes its course. We need the food too badly. However, we must make certain that until a breakthrough is made, only necessary chemicals are used and only in the minimum quantities required.

What happens next is up to all of us. As individuals we must do what we can. Each of us is responsible for his or her piece of THIS GARDEN EARTH.

But, there are more people gardening than those engaged in any other hobby. There are more gardeners, for example, than there are members of the politically important National Riflemans Association. If we act together, we can save the gardens we hold in trust for our children. Otherwise, they are doomed to spend their lives living and working in glass caves, subsisting on algae and yeast processed to look like pizza and beer.

What are you going to do? Write and let us know.

Germinating Seeds and Seedlings.

THE CIVILIZATION THAT GARDENING BUILT

Primitive men lived by gathering wild fruit and grains. They grubbed up tubers and ate insects until they learned to hunt and bring down larger game.

It was in their wandering search for food that our antedeluvian ancestors learned to discriminate between plants that were nourishing and those that brought illness and death. One wrong root or seed in a primitive stew could wipe out a small pocket of evolving humanity. The lessons were harsh, but survivors were able to communicate vital information from one generation to the next.

The first gardens probably were sown by accident. Perhaps one of our more prudent or greedy antecedents hid an over abundance of seeds underground but was forced to flee by wild animals, enemy hunters or angry spirits. Imagine the surprise and joy the first sower of seed experienced when returning in another season. The seeds had disappeared, leaving instead new plants bearing an abundance of grain.

It was thought that bad spirits lived in poison plants and good spirits inhabited nourishing and healthful ones. In an effort to transfer the positive influence of spirit friends, some primitive wanderers probably transplanted specimens at their campsites and accidentally discovered it was possible to propagate new plants from cuttings.

As it slowly dawned on our ancestors that a plentiful supply of food could be insured by sowing seed and transplanting selected food and other useful plants in a cultivated area—they stopped their wandering. Civilization was born.

Though it may be difficult to realize, the way we live and think today began to take shape around primitive garden plots.

Scholars speculate that the men of the tribe continued to hunt while the women gardened. The huntsmen followed the gods of the chase, excluding women from their rites. The women gardeners cultivated fertility mysteries forbidden to the men. Traces of these ancient cults can still be seen in modern world religions. And this early division of labor and cult is probably one of the things most responsible for the legendary war between the sexes, which is now labeled sexism.

While our ancestors lived as nomads in a world uncrossed by fences, investing no work in the soil, they could with little difficulty pack up quickly and move if they were threatened or attacked. But in time they came to think of these earliest of gardens as their own. Thorny border hedges became walls and fortifications. The boundaries which kept outsiders out, also kept insiders in, and eventually developed into the nation-states we all live in today.

The new concept of land holding also led to rigid laws of inheritance and marriage, resulting in the gradual accumulation of wealth and power in the hands of an ever-decreasing number of landlords. This in turn probably led to the institution of slavery, as hungry and landless families first bartered their time and then their bodies for food and a place to settle.

To defend the civilization that gardeners were building, the harvester's scythe was developed into limb-severing scimitars. But in the meantime gardening cultures produced the abundance of food which allowed leisure for gentler arts and scients to also develop. And eventually prophets dreamed of a time when swords would be beaten into plowshares, and spears into pruning hooks.

The fences that kept enemies and predators out allowed the peace of the garden to develop within. It is this feeling of serenity and well being that gardeners in every epoch share, wherever they live, whatever their differences.

LISTS

TOO LATE TO HIDE

Our ancestors were frail creatures who survived by learning to live in an environment that threatened to overwhelm them. From the huge amount of evidence we have seen, it is clear that now it is we who threaten to overwhelm our environment. The abundance that generations upon generations have worked to increase is threatened. The air, soil, and water of THIS GARDEN EARTH are being made unfit to support the plants that have fed and delighted us since the dawn of time. Even the amount of life-giving sunlight which plants require is being reduced by an ever-thickening haze of pollutants.

The horticultural industry today is going under glass as much to escape the destructive effects of pollution as to gain better control of plant growth. Plant scientists everywhere are beginning research to develop plants that will thrive in a poisoned environment and perhaps act as filters to remove pollutants.

The science-fiction potential of the situation is almost too awesome to consider. Imagine man with all his plants and animals forced to live in giant air-conditioned glass or plastic caves, with the caves pumping wastes outside into ever-darkening clouds of pollution.

It is time we pause and reflect. And that is one of the reasons we included so much material from the past.

Whether THE GARDENER'S CATALOGUE remains a pleasant ramble through patches of THIS GARDEN EARTH or becomes a nostalgic goodbye to gardening as we know it, is up to you.

The choices that will shape our future must be made soon.

Good Words From The Past . . .
Pictures From Forgotten Gardens

Most of the work which we do in our gardens has changed very little with time. Of course there have been advances in instrumentation, technique, and the basic understanding of how things work, but it is now clear that many advanced techniques involve unacceptable side effects.

It is not our wish, however, to encourage a blind retreat into a less-painful past despite the antique images we offer in The Catalogue. We just want to pass on some good words from the past and a few pictures from forgotten gardens.

While some of the old material has lost its scientific value much of it remains remarkably up-to-date and botanically correct.

A number of our flowering herbaceous plant cuts, for example, were retrieved from a collection entitled "Eden," or a "Compleat Body of Gardening," published in 1757. When you come across "The Hundred Leav'd Rose" or any other questionable antique material, we suggest you consider what Dr. Samuel Johnson said about the man who compiled the Eden collection. "John Hill," he said, "was an ingenious man, but had no veracity. Had he been contented to tell the world no more than he knew, he might have been a considerable man." Since Hill also wrote plays, another waggish tongue added, "For physic and farces his equal there scarce is/ His farces are physic, his physic a farce is."

Just the same, in many ways Hill was ahead of his contemporaries—in suggesting, for example, that there was a relationship between insects and pollination a decade before Koelreuther made the idea acceptable.

The VICKS FLORAL GUIDE OF 1873 is another gardening treasure we uncovered. Issued as a catalogue by a fastidious, rather opinionated commercial seedsman, it includes some of the most beautiful and instructive material we have come across in producing this book.

The material we title VICTORY GARDENING, 1918, could also become very useful in view of soaring food prices and threatened shortages. Though it may have a slightly hysterical tone its basic premise is sound. Small home victory gardens will insure cheap fresh food for your family and beat the cost of out-of-season fruit and vegetables.

References to the century-old Vicks catalogue and Victory gardening during World War One, provide as good a point as any to mention a problem we've had in reproducing old material in this book. Bringing back old illustrations, old engravings, can usually be done most successfully, as any fading or fuzziness that time has put into the originals may even add to their charm. But photographing old print, especially from the sometimes cheap paper of ancient pamphlets or magazines, can be quite another thing. Faded or fuzzy print is not charming—it's simply hard to read. So it has been necessary in some cases for us to present new type for the text that goes with our photographic copies of old pictures. But what kind of type? Well, we decided that any attempt to use old-fashioned type faces would give a misleading if not actually dishonest impression. So in every case where resetting has been necessary, we have used an ultra-modern, sans-serif type similar or identical to the one in which these particular lines are set. As for style, we have not monkeyed at all with the way the original material is phrased or emphasized or capitalized. If it says Lawn Mower in the old copy, that's the way you'll find it in our new reprint.

Illustrations